ISBN 978-0-259-02031-8
PIBN 10244340

1 MONTH OF
FREE
READING

at
www.ForgottenBooks.com

By purchasing this book you are
eligible for one month membership to
ForgottenBooks.com, giving you
unlimited access to our entire
collection of over 700,000 titles via
our web site and mobile apps.

To claim your free month visit:
www.forgottenbooks.com/free244340

THE

NEWCHURCHMAN—EXTRA.

Nos. IV.—XVI.

CONTAINING

A REPORT ON THE TRINE

TO

THE CENTRAL CONVENTION,

AND OTHER

DOCUMENTS

FOR

NEW-CHURCH HISTORY:

EMBRACING

AN HISTORICAL SKETCH

OF THE

RISE, PROGRESS, AND PRESENT STATE, OF THE TRINE

IN

THE NEW-CHURCH MINISTRY

OF

ENGLAND AND AMERICA;

TOGETHER WITH

ARGUMENTS FOR A MINISTERIAL TRINE

FROM

SCRIPTURE, THE WRITINGS OF SWEDENBORG, AND STILL EXISTING
REPRESENTATIVES,

AUTHORITIES FOR THE TRINAL ORDER,

A

FORM OF THE TRINE

FOR THE

NEW CHURCH AND HER MINISTRY IN THE UNITED STATES,

SOME REMARKS

ON WILKS'S REPORT AND MASON'S LETTER,

AND AN

APPENDIX OF DOCUMENTARY MATTER.

BALTIMORE:
PRINTED AND PUBLISHED FOR THE CENTRAL CONVENTION.
J. H. JONES, PRINTER, 34 CARTER'S ALLEY,
PHILADELPHIA:
1848.

PREFACE.

Let not the size of this book frighten any one from its perusal. It is by no means necessary that all of it should be read. Each one of its sections is sufficiently independent to be read by itself. The report here presented is a very different thing from what it would have been, if, as was intended, it had been laid before the seventh annual meeting of the Central Convention, or had been published in connection with Journal No. IX. It has swelled greatly in size, and presents a much greater diversity of matter. There is a great deal which may be judged not strictly pertinent to the subject of the trine; and there is, indeed, a large portion which need not be read for information or satisfaction on that subject.

The report opens with a brief introduction, which states, among other things, the reason for its being written. After which comes a short chapter on the necessity of order; which is followed by another on the way in which order is to be induced. Then there is a long chapter, which gives a pretty full historical sketch of the rise, progress and present state of the question of trinal order in the new church in England. Next is a still longer chapter—taking up nearly one-third of the volume—with an historical sketch of the same thing in the new church in America. Indeed, this section of the work contains a somewhat extended history of the rise of the new church in this country, with an account of ordinations in the ministry up to the time when the question of a trine began to be agitated, and an extended review of the proceedings of the General Convention, in reference to the origin of tendencies to an episcopal form of government in that body, and the peculiar effects upon its polity of the principles, influences and measures of its eastern leaders. Those who wish to find the pith of the report, however, had better pass over both of these chapters, that is, Sections III. and IV., and read the able scriptural argument for a trine of N. F. Cabell, Esq. This will well repay an attentive perusal.

Especial attention is also bespoken for the plain but cogent argument for a trine, from mainly two passages of the Universal Theology, with which the Rev. David Powell has obliged the church. The excellent common sense views of this chapter, or section, cannot fail to be appreciated. And if his confirmatory reasoning, for the true order of the church from the trinal order of the heavens, can be fairly refuted, it will be a matter of no little astonishment.

Section VII., although deemed important by the writer, may
prove too long and tedious to the reader. It argues for a ministerial trine, and for its nature, from the fact that true or internal
representatives are not done away in the christian church. After
an extended statement of the argument in general, the section
proceeds to the discussion of the following eight topics: I. The
Lord, in his advent to the christian church, and abrogation of the
jewish ritual, did not do away representatives in themselves considered, but only abolished representative *worship*—II. The Lord,
in abrogating the jewish ritual, merely took off an excrescence, or
peeled off an external rind, of the Word, which made no part of
its *true* representative form, that may furnish the true representatives appropriate to the christian as an internal dispensation—III.
Even parts of the jewish ritual were not wholly abrogated in the
christian church—IV. The Lord's humanity has fulfilled all the
representatives of the churches that preceded the christian, by
coming wholly and fully into them; and has for ever established
them, by becoming itself wholly and fully representative of the
same things which they represented—V. But not only has the
Lord fulfilled all representatives as the rituals of external worship,
he has also fulfilled them as a celestial man in the body of common society—VI. Representatives in themselves considered can
never be done away without the total subversion of the divine
economy—VII. The New Jerusalem is to be the celestial church
restored, and, in retracing the footsteps of the church in her
decadency, will, in at least one of the stages of her upward progress, be a true representative church, as the ancient church
was—VIII. The New Jerusalem is to be a celestial church in
form as well as in *essence*—hence is to have an external, representative, ritual worship even as a celestial church, and this
because she, unlike the most ancient church, is never to fall away.
This syllabus of the seventh section will sufficiently indicate its
probable dryness, and yet afford enough to the detester of big
books to take with him to the following section. Let him, then,
pàss on to Section VIII., which furnishes our authorities for the
trinal order in the new church and her ministry. This is, or ought
to be, the back bone and marrow of the report. There is a lively
hope that its contents will be duly examined, and lead to strong
convictions. It cannot easily be imagined how much reluctance
there was to making any thing like a show of learning in the
examination of Coronis 17 in the original; for no one can be more
sensible than the writer was, of his having no right to any pretensions on that score. But he will be glad if his blunders shall
provoke the truer expositions of more competent scholars.

Section IX. presumes to offer what is imagined to be a proper
form of the trine in the new church and her ministry in the United
States. The views here presented will doubtless be scoffed by

many. Some will deem them utopian. Others may think them chimerical. Nevertheless, all are intreated to scan them candidly, consider them deeply, and better that in them which they disapprove.

The report concludes with some rather stringent remarks on the report of the Rev. Thomas Wilks and the letter of the Rev. William Mason. No very strong desire is felt that these should be read; by any body. It must afford as little pleasure to read them as it did to write them. Still it is hoped that they may do some good; and they certainly cannot hurt any one who kindly cons them.

There can be no doubt that the Appendix contains important documents. The reports of Messrs. Noble, Howarth and Weeks are invaluable. The document on the origin of the new-church ministry is most interesting. Those illustrating the early history of our church in Baltimore are at least curious. And all the rest will go down the stream of time freighted with rich monition to posterity.

In the course of this report intimations are given of further publications in the continuation or completion of this work. But since this volume has been finished and read over carefully, it has been concluded to take the advice of judicious friends and let the work end here. A good deal is written or digested in continuation of the Strictures on Wilkins's Letters. But so much time has elapsed since No. III., containing the First Section of those Strictures, was published, and the church has developed itself so fully in the West, that there does not appear to be any use in saying any thing more on that subject now. Besides, enough is said in answer to those letters in the present publication. As to the rest, involving as it does so much personal matter, the editor of this work has resolved to say no more *in his own defence.* While there was a prospect that secret detraction might be effective in undermining his reputation, and destroying his usefulness, in the more particular and circumscribed sphere of his official action, it seemed incumbent on him to defend himself from the General Convention's official condemnation of him. But since the efforts of its presiding officer to discountenance and prevent the employment of him in the capacity of a missionary and stationed pastor have of late most signally failed; and since the caluminous charges of *falsehood,* of *malversation* of *official duty,* and of *revolt* under the influence of the *worst sort of spirits,* blazoned to the world, and echoed from across the Atlantic, by the General Convention's publication with its Journal of its presiding officer's correspondence setting forth such untried, unproved and unjust imputations, are likely to find their more effectual confutation in the silent record of both private and official conduct, which will *live down* calumny; nothing more shall be *said* on this subject, if repeated charges or taunts do not make it necessary. But it is confidently hoped that controversy will now cease. All need for it seems to be ending. And the editor of this work indulges the pleasing expectation, that he will now be allowed to retire from that painfully conspicuous position in the eyes of the general church,—into which he was most reluctantly dragged,—to those shades of silence and obscurity, which are not less congenial to his own feelings, than suitable to his very slender capacities.

As there is still some space left requiring to be filled, a word or two shall now be said about much smaller matters. Besides the far too many other errors, for which we have had to apologize elsewhere, something may be here said respecting certain typographical peculiarities. The question is asked, Why do you make the title of your work one word, *Newchurchman*, while it is so commonly written *New Churchman?* For the same reason that we say Newfoundland and not New Foundland or New-found Land. Besides, the latter term does not express the character of our work, or involves a very different idea. In common ecclesiastical parlance, a Churchman is the advocate of high church principles among Episcopalians. It would be a very great error to imply by the term *New* Churchman, that our work was devoted to any thing like the advocacy of *such* principles in the New Jerusalem! We regard the compound word *new-church* as an adjective qualifying the substantive *man ;* and, by a very usual tendency in our language, unite these in one word to imply the one substantive idea of a work which is a representative image of those theological and religious principles which present in form the man of the new church. It was, perhaps, presumptuous in us to give so high a title to our periodical ; but we can only say, that we used the term to express, not what our work *is*, but what we *wish it to be*, and what we would have been very glad to make it, if we could.

It is hardly necessary to state here that *The Newchurchman— Extra* was designed to be a repository of such controversial matter as pertains to the private and personal history of our church in this country, and was, therefore, unsuitable for insertion in the Newchurchman as a work of general circulation. As such a repository, we expect that this work will be read by only the members of long standing in our church ; and, therefore, there is not only much matter of a private nature inserted in it, but it is withheld from the usual channels of publication, and will be sent, by the editor alone, to those only who subscribe for it, or gratis to some of the principal societies of the church in this country and in England.

Philadelphia, Nov. 21, 1848.

CONTENTS.

NOTICE TO THE READER.

As some of the numerous errors that will be found in the following pages materially affect the sense, the reader, before he begins the perusal of this report, is requested to mark with a pencil the following

ERRATA.

In the eighteenth line from the top of page 2, the word "opinion" should be italicised. For it is quoted to show that the order, when adopted, would seem to rest on the *opinion* of the ordained ministers; and hence it was underscored in the manuscript.

Page 6, line 26 from the top, for *External* read *internal.*

" 11, " 8 " " for *brother* read *father.*

" 16, note, line 15 from the bottom, for *Dunkards'* read *Dunkers'.*

" 21, " " 8 " " for *John* read *Thomas.*

" 53, line 7 from the top, for *Woodville* read *Woodman.*

" 74, " 11 from the bottom, for *one year* read *three years.*

" 81, " 25 " " for *a year* read *two years.*

" 90, " 4 " " after *performance* insert *or non-performance.*

" 93, " 24 " " for *Signers* read *fingers.*

" 99, " 16 " top for *twenty-two* read *thirty-four.*

" 118, " 21 " " the words "In April, 1818," should begin a paragraph.

" 162, " 17 " " for *man's* read *men's.*

" 192, " 16 " " after *church* insert a comma.

" " " 18 " " instead of the semicolon after *members* put a comma.

" 196, " 3 " " for *condemnible* read *condemnable.*

" 204, " 5 " " before *know* insert *to.*

" 212, " 25 " " for *teacher* read *teachers.*

" 226, " 16 " " for *our* read *one.*

" 228, " 4 " bottom, for ὸς read ὸι.

" 240, " 13 " top for *principles* read *principle.*

" 252, " 20 " " for *are* read *were.*

" 263, " 8 " bottom for *inductive* read *vindictive.*

" " " 6 " " for *conclusion* read *conclusions.*

" " " 4 " " for *putrifying* read *putrefying.*

" 272, " 16 " " for *indiscretely* read *indiscreetly.*

" 275, " 6 " top, after "It will be found that," insert "with some few exceptions,"

" 335, " 16 " bottom, for τῳ read τον.

" 394, " 26 " " instead of the comma after *writing* put an *s.*

" 400, " 8 " top, for *a crown* read *an appendix.*

" 402, " 26 " " for *effect* read *affect.*

" 403, " 15 " " for *Fifth Lemma* read *Sect. V. of Lemma I.*

" 406, " 27 " " for *truths* read *truth.*

" 463, " 23 " " for *judiac* read *judaic.*

" 474, " 7 " bottom, for *these* read *there.*

" 478, " 2 " top, for *derived* read *derive.*

" 479, " 18 " " between *same* and *order* insert *relative.*

" 487, " 10 " bottom, after *the same* insert *by.*

" 506, " 5 " top, between *pulse of* and *heart* insert *the.*

" 519, " 25 " " after *true* insert quotation marks thus (").

" 529, " 7 " " for *church* read *state.*

DOCUMENTS FOR NEW-CHURCH HISTORY.

NO. XLIV.

REPORT ON THE TRINE TO THE CENTRAL CONVENTION.

The undersigned deem it their duty to present to the members of the
Central Convention this

REPORT

ON THE SUBJECT OF A TRINE IN THE MINISTRY.

By the constitution of the Central Convention, the principle of a trine in the ministry is acknowledged; and it is made the duty of its ecclesiastical council to determine this trine from the doctrine of the Word, as set forth in the writings of Swedenborg.

In the original draft of the constitution, there was an article defining the ministerial trine. But this article was expunged, because it was known that such a definition, without any reasons for it drawn from the teachings of the Word and the writings of the church, would be regarded and resisted, by many worthy members of the convention, as the arbitrary prescription of mere ecclesiastical authority. It was not that the ministers then present in the convention had any doubts about the principle of a trine in the ministry, or any serious objections to the ministerial trine as so defined; but it was their wish to harmonize all the members of the convention in a clear understanding of the principle, and a rational adoption of the mode of applying it in their body, by such a display of the church's authorities on the subject as it was confidently believed could not fail to satisfy every sincere seeker of truth.

In the proceedings of another convention, a different course was pursued. There the duty of devising rules of ecclesiastical order was assigned to the committee of ordaining ministers. That committee was especially requested "to take into consideration the subject of degrees in the ministry, to endeavor to define and settle with greater distinctness, the limits of each degree, and the appropriate duties of each, the name by which each degree shall be designated, the qualifications requisite for entering upon it, together with the circumstances and the mode of initiation into each degree," and to report on these matters to the next convention. (Journal of Eighteenth Gen. Con. p. 368, §39.) Here the principle seemed to be involved, that the *determining* and *settling* of the ecclesiastical order were vested in the ordaining ministers alone, *whose opinions* were to guide and govern the

1

convention. For at the next convention (the nineteenth) this committee of ordaining ministers, in making their report, say—" *We propose* that the three degrees in the priesthood or ministry should be designated" so and so : " *We esteem* it to be the office and duty of those who are in the first or lowest degree" to do so and so ; " *We conceive* that the bishop should also have authority and power" to do so and so. And throughout the report it is " *We think*" this, or " *We propose*" that—without reference to a single passage of the Word of God, or the quotation of a single line from the writings of our church, to show that the order proposed was drawn from those sources. The same view was strengthened by witnessing, in the following convention, the twentieth, in which the Rules of Order were adopted, the " Report of the Ordaining Ministers on Baptism into the New Church." (Journal for 1838, p. 382.) For in that report the whole matter is settled in three lines, thus—" Upon this question [namely, " whether those who are said to have been baptized in the old church, should be baptized when they are received into the new church,"] the committee [of ordaining ministers] would express their opinion, that all such persons *should* be baptized by a regularly authorized minister of the new church." A question about the mode of administering the holy supper was settled in the same summary way. It is true that a more elaborate report on the subject of baptism was made to the convention in 1839 ; but this was called for by a revision of the Rules of Order, with a view to their alteration in the very next year after their adoption, and was manifestly owing to some dissatisfaction at the prescriptive and authoritative way in which the ecclesiastical order of the visible church had been determined.

Now it was in consequence of the ministers of the Central Convention having discerned the reaction, opposition and resistance produced among the lay members of the church by this mode of proceeding in the Eastern Convention, that they, in adopting a fundamental law for their body, only acknowledged the general principle of a trine in the ministry, and assigned to its ecclesiastical council the duty of determining that trine " as taught in the Word, and from thence in the writings of Swedenborg." The principle here involved is, that the ecclesiastical order of the church is to be drawn, like all her doctrine, from the Word—that is from the Lord, who is the Word ; and in the New Jerusalem from the Lord by Swedenborg as his expressly commissioned servant. And the ordaining and other ministers of the visible church are not deemed or expected to draw this order as doctrine from the Word, in the light of *their own* immediate illumination from the Lord, but to determine it as the preachers in heaven are said to preach, " according to doctrines" already taught by the Lord himself through Swedenborg. For as " all the preachers are appointed by the Lord, and *derive the gift of preaching from their divine appointment*," so it is conceived that Swedenborg was appointed by the Lord to be the instrument of his second advent in the spiritual sense of his Word,—" which is doctrine itself," or " the genuine doctrine of the church," (A. C. 9086, 9380, 9430, 10.400,)—thus that Swedenborg is the especial agent of the Lord to teach " the true doctrine of the church, which is also the internal of the Word," (A. C. 9410,)—that he derived the gift of teaching it "from his divine appointment," and that no other should be allowed to teach it as from the Lord immediately, but that all other ministers of the church on earth should teach and determine the church's external order "according to doctrines" taught through him. Hence the article in the original draft of our constitution, which determined the trine in our ministry, was expunged, simply because its order seemed to be *prescribed* as the *devisings* of our ecclesiastical functionaries; and it was made the duty of those functionaries to determine that trine as the teaching of the Lord in his Word and by the doctrines of his church. Thus our order was to rest on the Lord's authority, and not on the authority of the ordaining ministers. And it was designed that the members of the convention, in adopting the order, when thus determined, should do so in regard to the truths and reasons which their ministers might present from the Word and the writings, and not in any regard to them, or their authority, as the head ministers of the church. It was to be adopted by the members of the convention because they saw it, in the light of their own minds, to be true; and their ecclesiastical council were to be regarded as their ministers only so far as they helped them to see it in that way. For so only could they make it their own, and act efficiently under it, as a law of their will; because "nothing can be appropriated to any one which is not acknowledged from his own proper intuition, that is, which he does not know from himself, not from another, to be so." (A. C. 5376.) Thus it was hoped and expected that the ecclesiastical order of our convention, when adopted by its lay members on the Lord's authority—on the authority of its truth and rationality, would harmonize them in efficient co-operation for the advancement of our heavenly cause on earth, instead of dividing them, and distracting their efforts, by reactions upon what they might deem the assumptions of arbitrary ecclesiastical authority.

But the undersigned have been convinced by subsequent events, that the postponing of the determination of the ecclesiastical order of our convention was an error. Such determination should have been made as a part of its fundamental law. For the fundamental or organic law, should involve all the principles of our body's future development as a seed involves all the principles of a plant, or the human soul, of the human body. Hence the convention ought not to have been constituted until that matter was settled by all the authorities which could be brought to bear upon it from the Word and the doctrines of the church at first. That, with every other matter which was likely to involve doubt or disputation, ought to have been settled *before* the convention was constituted, because the discussion of such matters *afterwards*, would divide its members in contentions for principles, when they ought to be *united* in *action* from principles previously agreed upon and clearly understood. And, therefore, the putting the settlement of this matter off "to a more convenient season," was but "sowing the wind" to "reap the whirlwind."

However, the error was discovered only when it was too late for cor-

rection; and efforts were made by the ecclesiastical council to perform
the task which the constitution had assigned them. In a division of
labor, a certain portion of the theological works of Swedenborg was
given to each member, so that all those works might be thoroughly
examined anew for the authorities bearing on the trine in the ministry—which were to be transmitted to a certain member of the council to work up in a report on this subject. But for reasons which it
is needless now to recite, if it were possible to ascertain, the members of our ecclesiastical council never could be made to do the duty
assigned them in this division of their labors. Notwithstanding they
were urged by the repeated monitions and injunctions of the convention, in its annual meetings, to bring out their report, the person
appointed to draw it up was never able to do so, because the other
members either could not or would not aid him by the performance
of their tasks: and he was not willing to bring in a report which should
set forth merely his own views, while it was his duty to draw up and
present one which comprised the views of the whole council.

Thus the matter stood, when, in the last annual meeting of our convention, circumstances made it imperatively necessary that a temporary
platform of ecclesiastical order should be raised for the ordination of ministers; and, for this purpose, a hasty report had to be drawn up on the
subject of a trine in the ministry so as to justify the adoption under the
constitution of the laws of order which were then felt to be indispensable. And an implied duty was left incumbent on the ecclesiastical
council, then recruited by two new members, to engage in a more
thorough discharge of their constitutional obligations. Accordingly, the
members of the council again had the labor of examining the writings
of the church divided among them. But although fifteen months have
now elapsed since the adjournment of the last annual meeting, the
member whose duty it still is to draw up the report on the trine in
the ministry, has to complain that only one of his co-laborers in the
work has sent him the results of his examinations: and he is left to the
disagreeable alternative of neglecting this part of their duty, as often
heretofore, or of presenting another crude and partial report, in which
mainly his own views and examinations of the subject are alone set
forth. Still he is aided and encouraged by the co-operation of the
brother whose name is signed with his below. And he feels that he
cannot be justified in putting off the discharge of his part of their duty
any longer. Instead, therefore, of a report from the whole ecclesiastical council, which ought to have been given, the undersigned must
beg leave to report, only for themselves—

I. AS TO THE NECESSITY OF ORDER.

In the report to the last annual meeting, the necessity of order was
cursorily shown. The convention could not have the Lord's power
to ordain unless he were present in it; and the Lord can be present
in his church only in and by his own divine order: because he "is
order itself." It was shown that divine order in form "appears as a
man." There should be, therefore, both external and internal order;

because man is both internal and external. And external order should be developed first in time,—although internal order is first in end and lies latent in it,—because the body of man is developed before his soul. Further, good and truth flowing in from the Lord is according to reception with every one, and " reception must be altogether in the natural principle ; for unless the natural principle gives aid, it is impossible for any birth of interior truth to exist." Wherefore, " during man's regeneration, the natural principle is first prepared to receive, and so far as this principle is made receptible, so far interior truths and goods can be brought forth and multiplied. (Ap. Ex. 441, A. C. 2536, 4588.) Thus it was demonstrated that both external and internal order is necessary in the church ; for what is here shown of *good* and *truth* is so in respect to *order*, because good is order in essence, and truth is order in form. (A. C. 1728.) Thus good is internal order and truth is external order : and as truth is first in time, while good is first in end, so the church's external order is to be formed at first, as means whereby her internal order is to be developed at last.

The whole question, then, in respect to the trine in the ministry, or any subject, or form, or law of order whatever, resolves itself into the simple consideration, *whether the thing is true.* For if it be *true*, it must be good for the church to be conformed to it. And the church, in seeing a certain order,—as that of a trine in the ministry, for instance,—to be true, may not, after she has once acknowledged it, deny, reject or contravene it, without the most fearful peril. But before we come to consider this particular principle of order, and as introductory to it, we desire to make some more extended observations on the necessity of order in general.

" Let *all things* be done decently and *in order*," was an apostolic injunction to the first christian church, which ought not to be disregarded by the second. For the enlightened revelator of the new christian church has declared, that, " where order is not, neither is the Lord present there ;" but " where the Lord is present, then, from his presence, all things are arranged into order—the Lord being order itself; so that where he is present, there is order, and where order is, there he is present." (A. C. 5703.) Can there be a stronger argument for the necessity of order in the new church ? For is she not the bride, the Lamb's wife ; and can she be conjoined with her Divine Spouse, if she be not made ready in all the adornment of that true order in which alone he can be present with her ?

Yes, order is indispensably necessary in the church. For without it the church can never be secure. Since " the security of a large, as well as a small, society, depends on order." (C. L. 283.) Indeed " on order depends the consistence of all things." For " what would be the case with man, unless all and every single part of his body were arranged in a most distinct and orderly manner, having a general dependence upon one heart and lungs ? What would the whole be but a heap of confusion ? For how else could the stomach, the liver and the pancreas, the mesentery, and mesocolon, the kidneys and the intestines, perform each their respective offices ? It is by the order reigning in and amongst those several organs that they appear to man, all and each of them, as one. Without distinct order, again, in man's mind or spirit, and without a general dependence on the will and the understanding, what would it be but a confused and undigested chaos? Without such order, how could a man think and will any more than his portrait or statue which ornaments his house? What, again, would man be without a most orderly arranged influx from heaven, and the reception thereof? and what would this influx be without that most universal one from God, on which the government of the whole and of all its parts depends, and unless all things had their being, lived and moved in him?" . . . "For instance, what is an empire or kingdom without order, but a troop of robbers, several of whom, collected together, would slay their thousands; and, at last, a few of this band would slay the rest? So, again, what would become of a city, or even a house, without order? and what would become of a kingdom, city, or house, unless there were in each some supreme head and director?" (U. T. 679.)

Nothing can be more conclusive for the necessity of order than are these authorities. The consistence of all things depends upon it. The security of all society, and therefore of the church, depends upon it. And the church cannot be conjoined with the Lord as a wife with her husband, without that true order in which alone he can be present with her for her existence, preservation and blessing.

Such is the doctrine of the church in respect to the necessity of order in general. And our argument for the priority of external order in time, is simply this. The external church is the earth, in respect to the external church as heaven. And the Lord God, in reforming and regenerating the souls of men, as in creating the material universe and their bodies, invariably acts from first principles by last. Hence he creates the earth first as a ground-work for heaven. And this being a universal law, which applies as well to the spiritual as to the material world, therefore the external order of the church must be formed first in time, as a fundament, laboratory and continent of its internal order, which at all times lies within it as first in end and means. It is true that the heavens exist as a medium through which the earth is created as an ultimate. But the heavens do not exist and subsist in form until they close in that ultimate as a basis and continent—just as the will cannot exist and subsist in form until it flows through the understanding into acts. Hence there can be no sight without the eye, no hearing without the ear, no smelling without the nose, and no touch without an ultimate organization of the skin. And as the eye is formed before there is any sight, or the ear before there is any hearing, and thus before the will and understanding, which are as heavens through which they are formed as an earth, can come into form and activity, so must the external church be first formed in time before any internal church can exist and subsist in its form and activity. And this is our answer to the argument, from A. C. 4223, that uses are prior to the mediums or personal agents of use. For although it is true that ministerial uses are prior in end and means to their personal agents, yet no ministerial use can exist in form and efficiency before or without its personal agent, just as the use of sight cannot exist in form and efficiency before or without the eye. Hence, if there is a trine of uses, there *must* be a trine of personal agents before those uses can possibly exist and subsist *as a trine*. And it is a great error to imagine that a trine of ministerial uses can exist in *form* and *efficiency* in *one* person. For the priesthood is a *complex* and not a *simple* personal unity. The *one* priesthood is made up of a trine of priests, just as the *one* skin is composed of a trine of skins in the body. Undoubtedly every one priest has a trine in himself, just as the Levites, who sustained the lowest grade in the jewish priesthood, had a trine among themselves in the three families of Gershon, Kohath and Merari —to whom peculiar and distinct duties were assigned in the time of David, (1 Chron. xxiii. 2—6:) and as the trine in the one grade of the Levites did not make unnecessary a trine of discrete grades in the jewish priesthood, so the trine in the individual priest or minister does not make unnecessary a trine of ministers in the christian ministry. And this is proved by the Lord's example. For if the christian priesthood ever could have existed in one person, it must have been in the person of the Lord when on earth: but the Lord when on earth, ordained twelve apostles to be with him, and seventy disciples to go before him to those places whither he himself should subsequently come. Thus we find, in the christian priesthood, as established by the Lord himself, a trine of personal agents, to effect his priestly uses in establishing and extending his church on earth. So that *then* the one priesthood was a complex of a trine of priests; and the personal agent or medium of the priestly use existed first in time as the indispensable means of its development. And so we argue it *must* be, now and at all times, in *just* order.

II. AS TO THE WAY IN WHICH ORDER IS TO BE INDUCED.

To the report of last year serious exception has been taken, because there was an effort in it to determine the external order of the church in a *factitious* or *artificial* way. It is imagined that external order is to be a *spontaneous* growth in the new church. We are not to resort to any of the science or means of *spiritual agriculture* for its production. We are not to concern ourselves at all about it; because the external order of the new church is always to correspond to its internal state, and when the internal state is right, the external order will flow from it as a matter of course, and without any effort, or even consciousness, on our part. Only concerning ourselves with the work of internal purification, we shall, when this work is properly done, lie down to sleep, and, waking up some morning, find that all our external order is nicely fixed for us without any labor or exertion whatever of our own.

But, in the view of the undersigned, this is another of the instances which we have witnessed in the establishment of the new church, of attempting prematurely to make the order of heaven the order of earth. It is indeed true, that, in the heavens, external order flows spontaneously from the internal states of the angels. Therefore we are taught that heaven consists in the mutual love of one towards another —*whence comes order in heaven*," (A. C. 5718): and further, that, "as soon as angels or spirits are assembled together, they are instantly arranged into order, as from themselves." (A. C. 6338.) But the external order of earth must be different, because the circumstances of earth differ greatly from those of heaven. In heaven it is not allowed that there shall be any disagreement whatever between the external and the internal of the angels; so that every thing there corresponds directly and fully to their internal states. Hence even the food and clothing of the angels so correspond—both being given to them gratis by the Lord, and without any efforts of their own to procure them. Hence the whole external order of the church in heaven is correspondent to the states of the angels as they now exist. But on earth the external circumstances of men may not only not correspond to their internal states, but be directly opposite to them. Thus an evil soul may have a handsome body. The wicked may enjoy external prosperity, may wear fine clothes and dwell in sumptuous houses. The churchman may be the hypocrite. Ambition and love of gain may seek their ends by the most perfect external order. And even the abomination of desolation may stand in the holy place. On earth, men must *appear* to attain their ends by their own prudence. Human prudence always comes face foremost: the Divine Providence is only seen on the back. Here men must labor for food, raiment and habitation; and it is a melancholy fact that great success in the attainment of these things too often waits on the strenuous and unremitted efforts of selfish and worldly men, while the godly and heavenly minded are permitted to pine in penury and want. Thus the external circumstances of men on earth do not correspond to their internal states. And this is permitted in the economy of the divine mercy that evil internal states may be reformed. For if, when men were inwardly evil, their external circumstances invariably corresponded to their internal states, they would be wholly condemned in their evil by the full influx into them of reprobate spirits from hell. In short, entire and permanent correspondence between the external and the internal states of men is not produced by life in the natural world, but is the effect of judgment in the world of spirits. The life on earth is now and ever will be probationary; and to produce or allow the correspondence here spoken of would be to effect judgment before the time, and so preclude the entire fulfilment of the probationary state, which would be a virtual preclusion of the salvation of men. Hence, in order that men may be at all saved, there must be an external order entirely different from their internal states. That is, there must be external *representatives*, as shadows of good things to come, by which heaven may inflow and be brought into external connection with them for their preservation. Hence, in the church on earth, the external order is not to be correspondent to the states of the men, who are its professing members, as *they now exist*, but is to be representative of higher and better states into which *they are to come in future*. Thus baptism is not a sign that a man *is* a christian, but that he *may become* one, if its uses are effectuated in him. So the holy supper is a strictly

representative rite—is a gate through which the worthy participant
may pass up into heaven, but does not signify that a man is in heaven
when he is only in the *gate* that leads to it. In fact, the external
order of the church on earth should be representative of the Lord's
internal state, and not of man's; to the end that, by affording a connecting link of heaven with earth, it may be the means of reforming
and regenerating men's internal states into the image and likeness of
the Lord's.

Therefore the idea of the earthly church's external order flowing
spontaneously from the internal states of its professing members, is
absurd. This might be, if mutual love prevailed on earth as it does in
heaven. This might be, if man's natural will were not destroyed.
This might be, if it were not needful now that a new will should be
formed, out of, distinct from, and entirely above the old one, in the
intellectual plane of the mind. The Lord does indeed, now as at all
times and in all states, arrange all things of the external church into
order from himself as good. But in the church on earth as in the
church in the first or ultimate heaven, good from the Lord is only
obedience to *truth*, as a *law* of order. It is only in the spiritual and
celestial heavens, that the Lord can arrange things in external order
from himself as the good of charity and the good of love. Thus it is
only in the spiritual and celestial heavens that there can be any
spontaneous external order from the love of truth or the love of good
for its own sake. Here on earth, the only principle of good which
can arrange the external church in order is the good of constrained
obedience to truth as a law in the intellectual plane of the mind.
And this, as we have said, is owing to the old natural will having
been destroyed, which causes the need of the formation of a new
will by means of truth in a reformed intellect. The need of this
makes all true and good external order a most painfully laborious and
persevering *agriculture* of the soul. What is true order in externals
must first be determined by the rational thought of truth, and a will
to the good of this truth must be formed by a forced obedience of the
natural man to its external form. And there is no other possible way,
by which the internal or spiritual man can be formed or developed in
his internal order, than this. Grace, politeness, elegance of manners
and propriety of external deportment all correspond to love in heaven
and charity in the church. And when men can talk well, walk well,
dance well, or conduct themselves with ease and elegance in the
various relations of polite life, without constrained obedience to the
rules of science in childhood and youth, or when they come into
these external proprieties *spontaneously* from nature, then we may
expect a perfect external order in the church to gush spontaneously
from its internal principles. But until then, the external of the
church must be first formed to order, just as the external of common,
civil, or social life is. For " reception must" ever be " *altogether* in
the natural principle ;" and " unless the natural principle gives aid, it
is *impossible* for *any* birth of interior truth to exist." Wherefore, in
" man's regeneration, the natural principle" must " *first*" be " *prepared* to receive,"—thus external order must first be induced upon

the obedience of the natural man, and of course must first be scientifically, rationally and intellectually ascertained and determined,—before any internal order can be brought forth; "and only so far as the natural principle is thus made receptible, *can* interior truths and goods be brought forth and multiplied."

It is true that, in all cases, the external is formed *through* the internal. Thus the earth was formed through the heavens as concentric spheres or radiant belts of the spiritual sun, in which was the Lord. And in the present case the internal *through* which external order is formed, as above stated, is the *intellectual* plane of the mind. This intellectual plane is, indeed, first formed, and through it, as a heaven, the external is formed as an earth, just as the new church is formed through the new heaven. But still this intellectual plane makes no part of the *visible* church. The visible church is first seen in the formations of its external order. And so its external order is first in time, like the earth in creation. Besides, the church is good. The internal church is good from which truth flows as light from flame. The external church is the good of conduct which is formed by truth. Now the truth by which external good is formed, though it is the interior of this good, is itself the external of the church that consists in internal good; and as this truth is first formed in the intellectual plane, as a means of forming a new will, and thus of *developing* or *bringing forth* internal good in outward conduct, therefore the existence of truth in the intellectual plane of the mind is still the *external of the church, formed first in time.*

In answer then to those who object to our inducing external order upon the church in a factitious way, we reply this is the way expressly indicated by Swedenborg. That is, laws of order for the church on earth are not to flow spontaneously from the internal states of her members, as they acknowledgedly do from the internal states of the members of the church in heaven; but they are to be learned, as are the principles of any other science; and then are to be applied to life like any other doctrines of truth. They are to be deduced from the proper authorities by the exercise of the intellectual and rational faculties of the mind; and then the will is to be conformed to them as intellectual principles. The knowledge of them is even to be acquired like scholastic learning—which is first a matter of memory before it is a matter of use. Hence laws of order, when determined by intellectual and rational investigation, are to be stored in the memory, and brought out thence for use in the ordering of the external church, just as the documents of any other science are in inducing order upon the concerns of business, or upon legislative, executive, military and naval affairs. And to show that this view is founded on the teachings of Swedenborg, we quote only one passage (from A. C. 9048)—"*The laws of order* [in the other life] are not *learned from books,* and thence stored up in the memory, *as with men in the world,* but are inscribed on hearts—the laws of evil on the hearts of the evil and the laws of good on the hearts of the good."

This passage of Swedenborg's writings is express and conclusive. It shows, without any doubt, that the circumstances of heaven and earth are totally different in respect to the production of external order. It shows that, while external order does indeed flow spontaneously from the hearts of the inhabitants of heaven, it must be, in the field of the church on earth, the work of cultivation. And in the express intimation that the laws of order are to be learned from books, and stored in the memory, by men in the world, we have most clearly pointed out the way in which order is to be induced on the external church. And in what books are the external laws of order of the New Jerusalem to be learned, if not in the Word of God, and those theological works which the Lord himself has caused to be written for its right interpretation? Therefore the Central Convention directs its ecclesiastical council to determine the trine in its ministry, and all its ecclesiastical order, by learning what those books teach to be true on the subject. And whoever may think this way of inducing external order upon our church is *factitious*, it is the only *right* way.

III. AS TO THE PARTICULAR ORDER OF A TRINE IN THE MINISTRY.

Under this head, we design to give an historical sketch of the rise, progress and present state of this question in our church. We will present and consider the authorities for it under another head. Here, as a general premise, we will only say, the argument for a trine in the ministry is, that there is a trinity in God, and in all things that are created by him and bear his image and likeness. Hence a trine is a universal principle, which pervades all things; and, therefore, must be in the ministry, because the ministry is the Lord's representative in the church on earth. Why, then, has this principle ever been called in question in the new church? First, because the principles of the new church are modified by the forms into which they flow; and because the states of men vary their perceptions of truth. Hence some receivers of new-church doctrines, who have been brought up in those sectaries of the old christian church, that are opposed to the doctrine of degrees in the ministry, because they imagine it to be a popish corruption of christian simplicity, and hence have early and long contracted a prejudice against a ministerial trine, receive the doctrinal views of the new church only in such a way as to perceive a perfect equality of ministers. This, as a preconceived notion, fills their minds; and whatever they read contrary to it in the writings of Swedenborg, they do not see to be contrary, or bend so as to make it conform to, and confirm, their previous view. Hence they not only deny a trine in the ministry, but confirm their denial by the authority of Swedenborg himself. Secondly, many professed members of the new church are very little versed in theology, and have very imperfect knowledge of what the new church teaches on this subject; and, being impelled by strong wills, and led by vivid imaginations, run tilt against phantoms, which they mistake for realities in the shades of obscure understandings. And thirdly, because particular, partial and wrong applications of the

universal trinal principle have, in respect to the ministry, been confounded with the principle itself.

For instance, in the english translation of the passage from the
Coronis to the Universal Theology, in which this principle is
expressly applied to the ministry, the terms are so rendered as to
make it seem that Swedenborg intended to apply and confine the
principle to the existent hierarchy of his day. Hence all opponents
of a hierarchy in the present day are opposed to a trine in the ministry of any sort, because it is supposed that this principle necessarily
involves a hierarchy in its most odious form. But the undersigned
humbly conceive that this is a mistake. They believe that Swedenborg taught only the universal principle and not the particular application. This may and must vary according to states, times and
circumstances; while that is immutable. Hence the undersigned
believe that Swedenborg, in Coronis, n. 17, did not allude to any
existent ecclesiastical order—that he only intended to illustrate the
principle in its application to the ministry in a general or universal
form; and that a trine may and must exist in every ministry or
priesthood, whatever may be its character, if it is properly representative of the Lord, or is correspondent to divine and heavenly
order, or at all suited to secure the stability and prosperity of the
church.

Another instance of confounding a particular application of the
principle of a trine in the ministry with the universal principle of a
trine itself, may be seen in Wilkins's Letters. An object of the
writer of those Letters is, to show that the tendency to the *episcopal*
form of government in the new church in this country did not arise
in New England, but in these middle states. And to do this, he very
adroitly or cunningly confounds *episcopacy* with "*different grades* in
the clergy" and the mere "use of a *liturgy.*" Thus a trine in the
ministry is made necessarily to involve an *episcopal form* of government and *worship.* Hence the opponents of an episcopacy in the
new church in this country are of course opposed to a trine in the
ministry. Whereas a trine of ministers—grades and ranks among
the officers of an ecclesiastical polity—may and must exist wherever
there is true or heavenly order in either the genuine or the perverted
church on earth, whatever may be its form of government or forms
of worship—whether it use a liturgy or extemporaneous worship—
whether its form of government be congregational, presbyterian,
episcopal or papal. And the undersigned think that a trine, either
in the bud or full blown form, may be traced in every form of church
government which has ever existed. Hence, in their view, the
acknowledgment of the principle of a trine in the ministry has not
committed, and does not commit, the Central Convention to a romish
hierarchy, an english episcopacy, or to any other specific form of
church government. It leaves her free to adopt whatever specific
form of the trine may be suited to the genius of the civil government, the church and the people of this country; and only commits
her to that subordination of ranks in her clergy, which is just as necessary to the consistence, stability and prosperity of the church, as sub-

ordination of ranks in the offices of our civil government, or its army and navy, is indispensable to the existence, subsistence and well being of our commonwealth. And, in our humble opinion, the advocates of a republican or democratic form of government in our civil polity, might just as well object to a trine of officers in the navy, army or state, because a *trine of such officers* is kingly or monarchical, as the advocates of the most democratic form of church government in our convention, object to a trine of grades in our clergy, because a *trine in the ministry* is episcopal or hierarchical.

The truth is, a trine *must* exist in every thing that is in *just* order. And this is that universal principle of order, on which "depends the consistence of all things." Hence such an order in both the constitution and arrangement of the ministry, has, from the earliest time, if not from the very first, been deemed needful to the existence, efficiency and prosperity of the visible bodies of the new church. At least, this question was agitated at an early time, has been forced upon the consideration of the church in this country by opposition to regular ordinations and even to the existence of a regular ministry at all, and cannot now be got rid of, without a clear determination of its truth or falsity, and a formal adoption or rejection of it accordingly.

The need of a ministry in the new church, and of a trinal order in it, may be seen from the fact that one was instituted in the very beginning of the church's visible existence, and from the fact that a trine was soon acknowledged to be its true order. A cursory glance at the history of the rise and progress of the church in England and in this country, will show this.

· In the establishment of the visible new church a clergy was in fact first formed. This was done from the Lord's example in establishing the first christian church. This proceeding was also founded on the doctrines taught in U. T. 146 and 784—namely, that the clergy are the special medium of that divine virtue and operation of the holy spirit which consists in illustration and instruction, and that the clergy are the internal of the church's visible body, so that in this as in other things, the external can be formed only through the internal as a medium. Hence a clergy must be formed and brought into orderly arrangement and subordination simultaneously with the very existence of the church's visible body; for if there is disorder in the constitution, arrangement and action of the ministry, there will be a disorderly reception of the divine influx of the holy spirit into it, and in consequence a necessary confusion and destruction in the visible body of the church. Consequently, the history of the rise and progress of the new church shows that, in her very beginning, the subject of a ministry first engaged the attention of the receivers of her doctrines. There were, indeed, lay receivers of these doctrines from the writings of Swedenborg before there were any regular preachers of them, or administrators of the church's external ordinances; for the earth had in this case to be formed first in time, that the priesthood as a representative man might be placed upon it. But the church as an *ecclesiastical* polity could not exist without a priesthood and external sacraments, and before these were in being, the church could not be said to have a *visible* body. Hence her very inception as a visible body was the constitution of a ministry distinct from that of the old christian church. In this, the authority of Acts i. 22—26 was observed, and an appeal was made to the Lord by lot to designate the first ordaining minister of the New Jerusalem. The lot fell on Robert Hindmarsh, a printer of London, who ordained his brother James and another person, named Samuel Smith, both then ministers in the methodist denomination of the old church. From this root all the clergy of the new church in England have sprung. And it is remarkable, that Mr. Robert Hindmarsh preached and performed all the duties of a minister by the common consent of the church in England for many years afterwards, without ordination by the imposition of hands, which he never would receive, because he believed himself to have been ordained directly by the Lord, in his designation of him, by lot, as the ordainer of other ministers.

It does not appear that any questions about the particular order of the ministry were entertained and determined in its first formation. Only two ministers were at first ordained by the providentially designated ordainer: and thus there were but two grades in the inceptive ministry—the one ordaining minister and the two ordained ministers. The same was true in the formation of the ministry of the first christian church: the Lord first ordained the twelve. Then he was the ordaining minister, and they the ordained ministers. Thus there were at first but two grades. The third grade was ordained afterwards in the seventy. Likewise in the jewish church: Moses first ordained Aaron and his sons. Here Moses was the ordaining priest and they the ordained priests. The third grade was ordained afterwards in the giving of the Levites to minister under Aaron and his sons. That Moses, as well as Aaron was a priest of the Lord in the jewish dispensation, appears from Psalm xcix. 6, "Moses and Aaron among his priests, and Samuel among them that call upon his name." Therefore when the ministry of the visible new church was first formed, we should not have expected to see more than two grades. It could not be expected that the question of subordination of ranks would arise so soon among so few. This order could only arise in the external church's greater enlargement and fuller development. Therefore the time for the question of the *trine* in the ministry was not yet. But that time was not far distant, as the sequel will show.

The first establishment of the new church as an external polity distinct from the old, took place in London in the spring of 1789. A conference, called for that purpose by a circular issued in the December previous, was held on the 13th of April of that year, and continued during the four following days. The circular had set forth certain propositions for the consideration of the conference; and as those propositions embodied only general principles pertaining to the question of separation in external form from the old christian church, and the establishment of a new external church distinct from the old, therefore the proceedings of the first conference consisted chiefly in the adoption of resolutions by which the principles of those propositions, and others, were affirmed. But these general propositions involved the necessity, and implied the formation, of a priesthood or clergy distinct and separate from that of the old church. And, as above intimated, it is a matter of new-church history that such a clergy had in fact been formed. Hence this first conference, by not taking any action on that matter, either implied that it was already done, or deferred the doing it in a more general and formal way to some future period. Hence having recommended "all the readers and lovers of the theological works of Emanuel Swedenborg," both in England and in other countries, "to form themselves into societies distinct from the old church, and to meet together, as often as convenient, to read and converse on the said writings, and to open a general correspondence for the mutual assistance of each other," this conference resolved unanimously that another general conference should be held in London in the following year, for "the serious consideration of such further matters respecting the establishment of the new church distinct from the old as might at that time appear necessary."

Such was the first attempt to establish a general church in a visible form; and this led to the formation of the present English General Conference. But previously a particular society of the new church had existed in London. It was first formed in the year 1783, which was eleven years after the demise of Swedenborg, who died in London in 1772. Its members at first met at each other's houses, or in hired rooms, on Sabbath-day evenings, until 1788. On the 27th of January, 1788, this first society of the visible new church opened the first "chapel for the public worship of the Lord Jesus Christ as the only God of heaven and earth." The chapel was located in Great East Cheap, near London Bridge, and not far from the site of the Boar's Head Inn, of shaksperian notoriety. It was also in the neighborhood of the London Stone—"supposed to have been the Milliarium of the Romans, from which they commenced the measure of distances to their several stations throughout Britain." It was the society meeting in this most remarkable *central place* of Ancient and Modern Britain, which called the forementioned first "general conference of the members of the new church signified by the New Jerusalem in the Revelation." The circular which called that conference was signed by the seventy-seven male and female members of that society. Among the signatures to that circular, are the names of Robert Hindmarsh, James Hindmarsh and Samuel Smith,—the first three ministers of the new church, of whom we have above spoken,—which shows that the persons who called the first general conference were the same who had previously formed the first ministry of the new church. There are also the names of Ralph Mather, Manoah Sibly, John Hawkins, and others, who, it is believed, were among the first ministers of the new church both in England and America. Mr. Mather, it is known, opened a place of worship for the new church in Liverpool, Eng., on Sunday, the 16th of October, 1791—preaching on that occasion from Rev. xxi. 2; and it is still better known that the same person, assisted by the Rev. John Hargrove, was the first regular preacher of the new church in the United States of America, in a chapel, hired of the people called Dunkers, in the city of Baltimore, some time in the year 1798.* And by ordination from these, the whole new-church clergy in America has sprung.

Now, of the first society in the world, which, we have said, opened the first place of worship in Great East Cheap, London, early in 1788, and which, by a circular, signed by its seventy-seven male and female members, and issued in the close of that year, called the first general conference, it is further said—"the leading members, having been Methodists, were desirous of having a variety of preachers. They accordingly set apart one evening a week for persons to preach probationary sermons, before the society only; upon which the members afterwards gave their opinion in a spirit of kindness and brotherly love, pointing out the imperfections to be avoided, and the kind of improvement to be attempted. Mr. Sibly was one of the early probationers; and, after two or three private discourses, preached his first public sermon on Good Friday, March 21, 1788, and his first Sunday sermon in the following May. Although, by this means, they, in a short time, *had eight preachers who regularly officiated*, yet, in consequence of several of them removing from London, and other circumstances, there was every appearance that they would be obliged to close the doors for want of a minister. In this exigency they solicited Mr. Sibly to undertake the charge." From diffidence and fear of the responsibility, Mr. Sibly at first declined the invitation. But, influenced by a remarkable dream, in which he thought he received a direct call from the Lord to the ministry, he at last complied with the wishes of the other members of the society to which he belonged, "and was ordained into the ministry of the Lord's new church, April 7, 1790, by the Rev. James Hindmarsh and Samuel Smith."

These facts show that the very first organization of the visible new church in London, as a society which called the first general conference, had been chiefly engaged in forming a ministry in its beginning, and had held meetings for public worship distinct and separate

---

* We are aware that the Rev. James Wilmer opened what was called a church, in the city of Baltimore, by preaching, in the court house, on the first of April, 1792, that the same minister preached on the following Sunday in the Dunkards' meeting house; and that a society, formed around him, took, afterwards, "the old theatre for one quarter of a year, until they could procure some better accommodation, or raise a temple;" but Mr. Wilmer was a minister of the church of England, and never was ordained, or otherwise inducted, into a separate or distinctive new-church ministry. On the contrary, Mr. Mather,—never, we believe, a minister of the old church,—received a sort of authority to preach from the first society of the new church, which was formed in London; and, for this reason, we have called him "the first *regular* preacher of the new church in the United States of America." Both he and Mr. Hargrove were ordained into the ministry, by what was then supposed to be the whole church in the United States. The church, as a collective body, set them apart, by the imposition of hands, on the 8th of July, 1798. And other ordinations in the United States have flowed from this beginning, as the influx from a seed into the expanding plant: for influx is "what proceeds in order from a seed and twig, and makes a tree." (C. L. 313.)

from that of the old christian church for at least a year previous to the meeting of the first conference. It is also stated, in contemporaneous documents, that the same society "had framed a liturgy agreeably to their perceptions of the new christian church." It is clear, therefore, that the very·first thing, in establishing the visible new church, was the determination of her ecclesiastical order. The proceedings of the first general conference were not, indeed, employed in this matter; but this was only because it had been previously attended to, or was supposed to be involved in the general principles, which were affirmed by that conference, and which were to be developed in the proceedings of subsequent ones.

Accordingly, in the next conference, we find it stated that hymns for the use of the new church had been prepared by one of the ministers; and having "agreed to have a liturgy" by the revision of "the services of the church then in use," the conference "sanctioned the ordinations" of two more ministers. This shows that the first acts of the general church as an organized visible body, were employed in matters concerning a ministry.

The thing most disputed then was the propriety of any external or formal separation from the old church. The first two conferences were composed of all receivers of the doctrines of the New Jerusalem, whatever might be their opinions on this point. But the third conference "restricted its members to readers 'friendly to the establishment of the new church distinct from the old;' and though all other readers were permitted to be present, they were restricted from speaking." This conference did nothing more than adopt the order of a committee of fourteen, "to represent the whole body of the new church until the next annual meeting;" and give directions "for drawing up rules for the government of the church, to be recommended to societies." Consequently further proof is here furnished that the general representative body of the church was at first employed in determining its ecclesiastical order. ·

The fourth and fifth conferences, held in April of the years 1792 and 1793, "agreed to various forms for the public services of the church," and "*determined upon the ecclesiastical government of the church.*" And having thus furnished the church with *the means of proceeding in an orderly mode of worship*, the conferences were discontinued for some years, having, probably, been deemed no longer necessary for common deliberation; for, although that of 1793 had adjourned to the 21st of April, 1794, it did not then meet.

The conferences were, however, revived after a lapse of fourteen years. And the reason assigned for their revival was "the want felt by the three societies then in London, of a general intercourse and communion among the societies of the new church throughout the kingdom [of Great Britain,] and of some general regulations, *particularly as to the mode of admission into the ministry.*" The assembling of the sixth general conference, on the 6th of May, 1807, in the city of London, in fact "arose out of some meetings previously held by the ministers and delegates of the three societies then in London . .

· 2

. . for the purpose of making some regulations relative to the forms of public worship as administered in those societies."

These historical facts prove, beyond a doubt, that the subject of *order in the ministry*—involving, most probably, subordination of functions, ranks and powers among the administrators of its sacred offices —led to the revival of general conferences of the new church in England. Hence the visible new church on earth, both in its inceptive form at first, and in its revived form in subsequent years, was employed in forming its ministry and in determining its ministerial order. Therefore the primary and fundamental importance of *this order* in the church, is clearly shown by experience.

The proceedings of the sixth conference are thus summed up :— " various regulations were adopted respecting the discharge of the ministerial duties. Besides which, the conference revised the ordination service; recognized, as duly ordained, those ministers who had been admitted into the office under the form previously agreed upon; revised and agreed to the order for consecrating a place of worship ; with some other forms contained in a small publication intitled ' The Rites and Ceremonies of the New Church,' &c. The conference also considered the duty of external worship, and the necessity of performing it according to the doctrines of genuine truth ; and inserted in the minutes various extracts from the writings of Emanuel Swedenborg, proving these points," &c. &c. &c. Thus we see that the sixth conference was chiefly engaged in regulating *the order of the ministry*, and such matters as pertain to the functions of ministers—whose province it clearly is to teach, lead, and administer, or govern, in those ecclesiastical concerns that pertain to the exposition of the divine law, and worship according to it. And it should be well observed, that these doings of the English General Conference, which determined the duty of external worship, and of course the order of the ministry for the administration of its ordinances, were founded upon, and confirmed by, " *extracts from the writings of Emanuel Swedenborg.*" Was this a spontaneous sprouting of external order from the internal states of the new church in England? Or was it not something of that *factitious* way of inducing order on the external church, which those standing in high places have, in the spirit of uncourteous rebuke —not in that of brotherly counsel—recently charged opprobriously on the Central Convention ? But it does not yet appear that we have any authority in the history of the new church in England for the particular order of a *trine* in the ministry. Where then did the *first* suggestion of this order come from ? We shall see.

The seventh conference, which was held in June of the next year, 1808, at Birmingham, " recognized various persons ordained under the regulations of former conferences ; and again enforced the duty of public worship. A number of propositions, containing the rudiments of several measures that have since been adopted, relating to the ministry, and to the good government of societies, were agreed to be submitted to the further consideration of the church at large." And in these measures consisted the larger part of the proceedings of this conference. So that the determination or regulation of the order of the ministry was still the chief work of the general church in England.

After this conference there was another suspension. For "although the seventh general conference appointed another to be held the ensuing year at Manchester, it did not, in fact, assemble till after an interval of seven years; the church being then not sufficiently advanced, either as to numbers or pecuniary means, to be able to keep up the regular annual meetings." "This revival of the conference again took place at the instance of the three societies in London; which, to supply, as far as could be done among themselves, the want of a general conference, at this time held quarterly meetings, by their ministers and representatives, under the denomination of "The London Conference; for the purpose of consulting on such measures as might be suggested for the general well-being of the new church. Some things having thus been presented which it appeared desirable to have brought before the church at large, they communicated with other societies on the propriety of again convening the general conference. Accordingly, as stated in the minutes, this conference was 'convened with the approbation and consent of the several societies in London, Birmingham, Manchester, and elsewhere.'" It was held in Manchester on the 14th of August, 1815. What "the measures for the general well-being of the church," for the consideration of which this conference was convened, were, appears from its being said, "the conference determined *that the ministry should consist of* THREE DEGREES, and framed various resolutions thereon"—declaring, at the same time, who were "the ministers of the second degree, since denominated ordaining ministers," in England. And further, that "the establishment of Sunday schools was recommended, and a 'missionary ministry' was determined to be commenced."

Thus we come to the important fact, that the object in a second time reviving the general conferences in England, was still to determine and regulate the order of the ministry, and that here, for the first time in the history of the new church, the particular order for the new-church ministry is determined to be a TRINE of *degrees.*— And let it be remarked, that *this order was determined by the general body of the new church in England in 1815—two years before the assembling of the first convention of the new church in America.*

From this time the English General Conference became a permanent ecclesiastical polity, and has at length assumed the form of a legally constituted and established body. The order of a trine in its ministry has not yet been fully carried out. There are as yet but two degrees. But this subject has been repeatedly discussed, so as more fully to confirm the position that there is, or ought to be, a trine of degrees in the ministry. And hence if that order has not been carried out in the english new church, this must be owing to some peculiar circumstances which make its practical operation not feasible or prudent now, rather than to any question of its abstract truth and propriety.

In the ninth conference nothing appears from the minutes to have been done with especial reference to the ministry. That subject was, probably, noticed or acted upon only informally. But in the tenth, "some resolutions, intended for the improvement of the ministry of

the new church, were passed; with several others, tending to conso-
lidate the general conference, and improve the order of its proceedings." "A large portion of the business" of the eleventh conference,
like that of the two preceding, "consisted in regulating the affairs of
the missionary institution." "But the mode of admission into the ministry was further defined" by this conference. The attention of the
twelfth conference was occupied with "the subjects of uniformity in
worship, and the establishment of sunday schools, besides the usual
business of the missionary institution." The thirteenth conference
seems not to have occupied itself at all with the subject of the ministry; and the only thing relating to the church's external order, was
the appointment of a committee "to prepare a draft of a liturgy for
the consideration of the next conference."

In short, although "the subject of the ordering or regulating of the
ministry had, for some years, engaged a portion of the time of each
conference" of the new church in England, yet no attempts to carry
out the order of a trine occurred, until "the possibility of forming a
third order in the ministry occupied considerable attention" in the
twenty-third conference, which was held in Salford, in 1830. On
this occasion, the subject was "very fully entered into, and some of
the difficulties which had previously been felt to attend it, appeared
to be partially surmounted."

In the twenty-third conference, or that of 1830, the subject of the
ordering or regulating of the ministry was brought up by considering
the condition of certain societies, which, being without ordained
ministers, had "long felt the inconvenience of being deprived of the
privilege of having the sacraments of baptism and the holy supper
administered to them, except in a way which had not been considered
strictly within the laws of order." At the conference of 1829, a
committee had been appointed to devise means by which this might
be remedied. The report of this committee to the conference of 1830
involved necessarily the order of the ministry, but declined determining this matter, and led the conference to refer it to another committee, with instructions to report thereon to the next conference, to
the end that it might then "be finally arranged." In fact the question
of administering the ordinances of the church without a regular
ministry *forced* the consideration of ministerial order upon this conference in England, as the same question had upon the conventions
in this country. It appeared "from various communications made to
the conference, that many persons consider the conference to have
power, by a mere vote of theirs, to *authorize the administration of
the sacraments by unordained persons.*" This therefore would have
been the *disorder* in the ministry, which would have flowed *spontaneously* from the internal states, and external wants, of the professing
members of the new church in England at that time. But "the conference entered upon the consideration of the question; when, after
again perusing the report of the committee appointed by the last
conference, and the observations on the subject in a letter from Mr.
Knight, and after having read a paper by the Rev. Mr. Noble on
these three questions—First, Whether the existence of a ministry, as

a distinct order, is to be established in the new church? second, What are their functions? and third, How are they to be admitted?—it was resolved unanimously That this conference is fully convinced that the law of divine order on the subject, *as deducible from the Word and the writings of Emanuel Swedenborg*, particularly in the last chapter of the work on the Heavenly Doctrines, and in n. 386 of the treatise on Conjugial Love, is, that the administration of the sacraments belongs properly to persons invested with an ecclesiastical character, and that such character can only be imparted by prayer and the imposition of hands."

Thus it is established as an historical fact, that the general body of the new church in England formally declared a ministry, ordained by prayer and the imposition of hands, for the administration of the sacraments of the church, to be according to the law of divine order on the subject—that this order was deduced "from the Word and the writings of Swedenborg"—and that the conference was led to the declaration and deduction of this order by its having been called in question by professing members or societies of the new church in that country. It is important that this historical fact should be known and noticed by those who have objected to the agitation of this subject in the institution of the Central Convention, or to the way in which it has been sought to settle it by the constitutional provisions of our general body. For, as we shall show by and by, the same or similar circumstances forced the consideration of this subject upon the general bodies of the church in this country, just as they had done in that.

The paper read by the Rev. Mr. Noble, above alluded to, is appended to the Minutes of the Twenty-Third General Conference, together with some remarks on the same subject by the Rev. Mr. Howarth. Both present a very lucid and cogent argument for a trine of distinct degrees in the ministry; and with other reports, made by the same gentlemen, to the Twenty-Sixth Conference, will be republished in the Newchurchman–Extra, for permanent record and reference in the new church in this country.* Mr. Knight, a legal gentleman of profound erudition and deep piety, had stated the matter

* When this was written, it was expected that this report would have been submitted to the late annual meeting of the Central Convention, which met in Philadelphia, in October, 1847. But, for the reason given on page 23 of Ap. II. to the Journal (No IX.) of that meeting, it was not so submitted. Afterwards, in consequence of minute n. 31 of the Journal of its proceedings, (Jour. No. IX., p. 4,) and *so soon as it was called for* by the chairman of the publishing committee, more than fifty pages of this report in manuscript—all that were then written—were sent to the printer of that Journal. But the publishing committee imperatively charged him not to insert any thing in the Journal, or its appendices, which did not come to him through their hands. The publishing committee,—thus stickling for a mere formality which the annual meeting itself had utterly disregarded, in receiving, adopting and publishing the Rev. John Wilks's report on the trine, which he had no constitutional or other authority to make, without its passing through the constitutional organ, the ecclesiastical council,—interdicted the publication of this report in the Journal of the Seventh Annual Meeting of the Central Convention, although that meeting had expressly resolved that it should be so published, if furnished within a reasonable time. Therefore, this report appears now in only the present work, and the reports here referred to will be found in the Appendix, Nos. XLVIII., XLIX., and L.

thus:—"Firstly, the ministry of every church, if formed after a heavenly pattern, ought to form a trine, or, in other words, consist of three classes of persons : secondly, persons filling the higher degrees should perform some duties not common to the lower: thirdly, the persons admitted into such degrees should be solemnly inaugurated; and fourthly, persons in each degree of the ministry should officiate in a different dress." He further adds, "Persons in the first degree, may *read* and *expound the Word* and *administer the ordinance of baptism;* persons in the second degree may perform the duty of the first, *and administer the ordinance of the Lord's supper, and the consecration of nuptials;* and persons in the third degree may perform the duties of the first and second degrees, *and ordain others.*" And " of the remarks of the Rev. S. Noble and of the Rev. D. Howarth appended to the minutes of the twenty-third conference," he says, they "appear confirmatory of this view of the subject; and it is impossible to read them without profit, as they throw much light upon the important subject." Undoubtedly they do; and we shall be very much mistaken if intelligent and reflecting members of the new church in America do not think so too, when they come to read them more generally. And then it will be seen whether this country alone is obnoxious to the charge of having broached the uncharitable and bad-spirited principle of "separating what God had joined together," by dividing the sacraments of baptism and the holy supper in assigning one to a lower and the other to a higher grade of the ministerial trine; as well as that most heinous sin of regarding marriage as a holy thing of the church, which is to be consecrated by a priest of a higher order than he who administers baptism.

But a great many professing members of the new church in England did not accord with this view of the subject, as appears from the proceedings of subsequent conferences. In the minutes of the twenty-fourth there are strong indications of dissent, which, in following ones, came out more manifestly: But, nevertheless, that conference passed the following strong resolutions :

"*Resolved unanimously,* That the conference is of opinion, that, agreeably to the statement of Emanuel Swedenborg, the most perfect arrangement of the ministry is that of a trine or three-fold order.

"*Resolved unanimously,* That the grounds on which the conference concludes that the ministry should form a trine, is the satisfactory evidence offered in the writings of Emanuel Swedenborg, that there is an immutable analogy or relationship between spiritual things and natural, by and through which the former are most fitly and fully manifested and preserved in order in the latter: and that the necessary subordination of duties in the ministry will thus ultimately create a three-fold order therein; but in order to guard against its being misunderstood, the conference considers, that spiritual benefits can only result to the church from forms founded in rational use."

This conference also declared its conviction, " that the law of divine order requires, that the administration of the sacraments belongs properly to persons invested with an ecclesiastical character; and that they can find no authority, either in the Word or in the writings of

Emanuel Swedenborg, for any other mode of investing persons with such character than by prayer and the imposition of hands." From this we learn that there were then in England, as there are now, strenuous opponents of "man-made priests" by "finger-ordination."[*] Otherwise it would not have been necessary for the general body of the church in that country to make such a declaration as the above. It will be well to observe this for the sake of comparison of the state of the new church in this country and in that.. With respect to the question of other persons than ordained ministers administering the sacraments, it appeared, in this conference, "that the general feeling in the societies without ordained ministers as to the administration of the sacraments by other persons, *was not that it was actually in order*, but only that *necessity required it*." The conference, however, did not seem to think that any necessity could ever require things to be done in the true church in a *disorderly* way; and set to work in devising the outlines of a plan for relieving the wants of such societies, which plan was submitted to the maturing labors of a very able committee, to report thereon to the next conference.

In the twenty-fifth conference the plan above mentioned, which did not come up to view in the minutes of the last, appears now more distinctly. It seems to have been a proposition to make a sort of extemporaneous ordinations, or inductions into office, of certain persons other than regular ministers, "to administer the sacraments, and perform the usual duties of public worship, more particularly in the society to which they belong." Thus it was a sort of *substitute* for regular ministers in societies which had not, and could not procure the services of, such ministers; probably a kind of mongrel priesthood, or half lay, half clerical ministers, not strictly in order, but made necessary by circumstances, and having their irregular ecclesiastical character cloaked by their being introduced "*in an orderly manner*" into *an office* not *strictly* in *order*—as if a disorderly thing could be made orderly by merely passing it through the external formularies of order. After debating this plan at great length, it was first proposed to postpone the subject till the next conference; which proposition was negatived by a majority of eight. Then it was proposed to approve the plan except as to the administration of the holy supper; which was negatived by a majority of two. At last it was proposed to agree to the whole plan; upon which the conference being equally divided, it was negatived by the casting vote of the president. And so this conference was prevented from proceeding further with the plan which had been proposed to it, to admit, by some solemn service, persons not regular ministers to administer the sacraments; and submitted to two special committees, with instruc-

---

[*] See "The True Priesthood of the Holy Jerusalem Vindicated, and the False Shepherds Exposed, in a Letter to a Friend. Dunfermline, J. Miller & Son, 1846." This is a pamphlet of about forty pages, written by a Scotchman, in the bitterest and most biting spirit of "the most straitest sect of the religion" prevalent in Scotland; and is of pretty much the same stamp as the John S. Williams and William Elder publications in this country. This pamphlet was sent, by some anonymous friend in England, to the writer of this report, and was received by him shortly before he penned the above sentence.

tions to report to the following conference, the question "whether it is in accordance with the laws of divine order to admit persons, by some solemn service, to administer the sacrament of baptism *only*, and not that of the holy supper." The secretary of conference was also directed, by circular, to obtain the views of the ministers and leaders of the several societies throughout the kingdom on this question, and convey them to the committees intrusted with its consideration. Thus was the subject of a trine of distinct offices and distinct duties in the ministry, involved as it necessarily was in the determination of this question, kept up in the very axis of the visible church's eye, and the duty of determining it made more obvious and imperative by the indispensable necessity of ecclesiastical order which every year's experience was evincing.

To the twenty-sixth conference, held in Bath in the year 1833, the two committees above referred to, made exceedingly able and conclusive reports. To enable them the more easily to collect the views of all the ministers, leaders and societies of the new church throughout the whole kingdom, one of these committees was appointed in Manchester and the other in London. The report made by the former was signed by David Howarth, chairman, and Samuel E. Cottam, secretary, and the report made by the latter, by Samuel Noble, chairman, and John Newbery, secretary. The question for their consideration was, "Whether it is in accordance with divine order to admit persons, by some solemn service, to administer the sacrament of baptism only, and not that of the holy supper?" As we have said, this question, of course, involved that of discrete or subordinate grades in the ministry, with distinct duties, scopes of administration, and badges of office, assigned to each grade. For without such distinctions and subordinations there can be no arrangement in order whatever. (See U. T. 680.) And so the committees in fact considered the question submitted to them. To give an idea of the sentiments upon this question which were entertained generally in Great Britain, we here quote the observations of the London committee on the communications which had brought those sentiments to light.

The London committee say—"To assist their judgment in coming to the consideration of this question, the committee have carefully examined the answers from various societies and individuals to the circular issued by the secretary requesting opinions upon the subject; and also to a circular issued by the Manchester committee to the societies in the northern part of the kingdom. The communications which have thus come before them amount in number to about twenty-six. They regret to observe, that the object of the question does not, in general, appear to have been well understood, and that comparatively few of the letters throw any direct light upon the subject. Most, also, mix the question with other topics; and most treat it more upon the ground of *expediency at the present time*, than of *principle*. Several seem to suppose, that the conclusion, that it is lawful to ordain persons to the administration of the sacrament of baptism without giving them authority to administer the Lord's supper, would be an exclusion of many societies from the Lord's supper entirely; which, certainly, the conference never could contemplate. A few of the letters enter into the question of the propriety of there being any distinction whatever of order or degree in the ministry, and urge arguments against it. And one or two propound the opinion, hitherto quite unheard of in the new church, that every society is competent, not only to determine whom they will accept to be their minister,— a right which, in the new church, has never been disputed,—but actually to confer upon the object of their choice the ministerial capacity, and *ordain* him to the office."

This shows how similar to the opposition in this country has been that in England to the introduction of true ecclesiastical order into the external church.

The London committee, after deprecating the undue warmth of expression, and intolerance of feeling towards the sentiments of others, which were manifested in some of the communications, proceed to consider the question submitted to them, and come to the conclusion, that while a numerical majority of the suffrages expressed in the various letters is against it, yet the weight of argument decidedly preponderates in its favor. They however take a wider scope than the mere question submitted to their consideration, and show—

I. That there is to be an institution of ministers as a distinct order of persons, who are "to administer those things which belong to the divine law and worship," thus "the things belonging to the priesthood appertaining to the Lord," "and thus those relating to benediction and blessing;" and that there is a necessity of their ordination, or solemn inauguration into the "ecclesiastical order," by prayer and the imposition of hands.

II. That although a true church might exist admitting no distinction of order or of functions among its ministers, yet true order calls for a trine of distinct degrees. This point is argued at length, and the latter clause very clearly and ably proved by quotations from the Holy Word and the writings of its new-church expositor.

III. That "as the most perfect arrangement of the ministry is that which admits a distinction of degrees, and that the number of degrees is properly three," therefore there should be distinct duties or functions assigned to the ministers of the several degrees, and that the administration of baptism might be assigned to a lower degree of the ministry, while the administration of the holy supper was assigned to a higher.

IV. That the first or lowest degree is but an initiatory one of the ecclesiastical order, and that it is agreeable to divine order that the distinguishing feature of such initiatory degree should be the power to administer the first of the sacraments but not the second.

The committee observe that the order of a trine of degrees in the ministry exists in the established church of England and of most other nations of christendom—"in which the ministers of the lowest degree have the power of administering baptism, but not the holy supper; those of the second degree have power to administer the holy supper, and perform all the functions required in a congregation, but not to ordain other ministers—this belonging to the third order alone:" and they argue, from this, that the order which they think ought to prevail in the new church cannot be condemned on the ground of novelty. They had also shown, very conclusively, from ecclesiastical history, that the order which admits of three distinct degrees prevailed in the first christian church in the first three centuries, having been established throughout its whole extent very soon after the time of the apostles; and as we have the authority of Swedenborg that the first christian church existed as a pure church till the council of Nice in the year 325, they argue that the order of a trine in the ministry must be the true order because it was that of the first christian church while in its purity. Whereas the order of but one class of ministers, having been broached and adopted by Calvin and his followers in the sixteenth century, when the first christian church was corrupted, it must therefore be presumed that this is not true order, because it was the order of a false, and not of a true, church.

In concluding their report the committee however state, that, while they give a qualified affirmative answer to the abstract question which was submitted to their consideration, they are of opinion that it will not be advisable to act upon it in the present state of the church. As there is a strong feeling against a trine, they think it ought not to be established, lest separation from the general body of the church should be resorted to by some. Even should the calvinistic plan of a ministry without any difference of degrees prevail, this committee is prepared to acquiesce, because they think a true church might still exist under that constitution. But they nevertheless think "that the most perfect order of the ministry is that which is arranged in three degrees—that, with its ministry so arranged, the church would be in a form into which the heavenly influx would flow more interiorly and copiously than would be possible under a lower and more external species of constitution—and that the final prevalence of the calvinistic plan could only be, because it was most in correspondence with the present low and external state of the human mind, out of which, even the profession of the heavenly doctrines of the new church does not raise men at once." But the committee hope that the calvinistic plan will not, from any such cause, prevail finally in the new church. They think the apparent bias to it arises out of the present political condition of their country; and that "the clouds which have thence, in some degree, overcast the vision of even some of the members of the new church, will have but a temporary prevalence;" so that "the clear light of heaven will again ere long burst forth, and will lead the church to do what is most agreeable to genuine order, and what will most tend to keep her under the Lord's auspices, and in unreserved obedience to him for evermore."

Thus we see that the clearest and strongest minds of the new church in England demonstrated, in 1833, from the Holy Word and the writings of Swedenborg, a trine of distinct degrees in the ministry to be the true order of our church. And we cannot close our notice of the report of the London committee without calling the attention of the members of the Central Convention, to this further quotation from it—"They were much surprised," say this committee, "to find the Lord's words, 'What God hath joined together, let not man put asun-

der,' cited, in several of the letters, as a conclusive argument for the
negative, [of the question, whether the sacraments of baptism and the
holy supper should be administered by ministers of distinct grades,]
when it appears so obvious that *that divine saying can have nothing
to do with the subject.*" The Manchester committee take the same
view. And we only allude to it here, that the members of the Central Convention may see from whence the recent uncalled for and
petulant rebuke of *their* proceedings came ; while they discern, at the
same time, that those members of their common faith in England
whose intelligence and force of character entitle their opinions alone
to any weight in our estimation, were by no means fairly represented
in the administration of that rebuke.

It is only necessary to state, further, that the twenty-sixth conference, to which the able reports above referred to were made, "*Resolved*,
This conference concurs in the opinions expressed in these reports
relative to the sacraments, and the administration of them; but the
conference deems it inexpedient to legislate -upon the subject at
present, from the conviction that the time to do so, with permanent
advantage to the church, has not yet arrived."

Of these reports we have spoken in high commendation. Truth
demands, however, that we should say this is -not without some qualification. We must dissent from the position, that the first or lowest
degree is *but* an *initiatory* one of *the ecclesiastical order.* This militates
against the truth that there are *three degrees in the order itself*, and
admits of baptism, as a representative sacrament of the church, being
performed by a person who is not yet *in* the ecclesiastical order, but
only coming into it. We humbly conceive that this is not sustained by
the express teaching of Swedenborg. It is true that the first or lowest
degree of the ministerial trine is *preparatory* to the second, and so
initiatory to *that ;* but this is no more true of the first in respect to
the second, than it is of the second in respect to the third; for the
second is *preparatory*, and so *initiatory*, to the third. The truth in
this matter is very clearly indicated to our minds by Swedenborg, in
U. T. 106, where, in illustrating the two states of reformation and
regeneration, through which every man must pass, who from natural
becomes spiritual, by those " various circumstances and effects in the
universe" which represent them, "because they are according to
divine order," which " fills all and every thing in the universe, even
to the most minute particulars," expressly specifies the case "of every
student, who is preparing for the ministry, before he becomes a priest,
and of every priest before he becomes a pastor, and of every pastor
before he is a primate." Here we see that Swedenborg in exempli-
fying that "*divine order*" which " fills all and every thing in the universe, even to the most minute particulars," so applies it specifically
to the ecclesiastical order as to call for *three degrees in the order itself*,
and distinctly points to. the state " of *every student who is preparing
for the ministry*" as that "first or lowest" step which, properly, " is
but an initiatory one of the ecclesiastical order." On this groundwork, the Central Convention has built its order of a licentiateship as
introductory to her ministry.

Again, we cannot agree with the report in admitting that a true church might exist under the calvinistic constitution of a *one-* or a *no-graded* ministry. And to our view the report is painfully inconsistent in making such an admission, while it expressly states "that the most perfect order of the ministry is that which is arranged in three degrees"; for this admission involves the idea that a *true* church, by correspondence, *may exist* in the external order which the report itself argues in another part has existed by correspondence from a *false* one. In respect to the New Jerusalem especially, which, as it is to descend from the Lord out of heaven, must be a most perfect church, it can, by *correspondence*, flow only into that external arrangement which "divine order" effects "in the universe." Although in its very first existence it may not come into what we have called a *full-blown* trine; yet it must at first come into a trine in a rudimental form, just as the human soul does into the infant human form, which, although it may not have all its parts fully *developed*, yet *has* them in a *bud*-like state. So the New Jerusalem as a visible church on earth must, in its infantile body, have a rudimental trine of ministers, which is to be more and more fully developed in a series of various trines, as its body shall enlarge, its uses become more complicated, and the machinery, so to speak, of its external order become more involved. In short it can come *only* into that "most perfect order of the ministry" "which is arranged in THREE degrees." And to admit or assert the contrary, is to maintain that the *most perfect* church may by correspondence exist in an *imperfect* external order. But this, we humbly conceive, is not according to the divine economy. For we do not see such a manifestation in any church which has clearly existed by divine appointment on earth. Show it to us in the most ancient, the ancient, the jewish or the first christian churches. To show it to us in any *corrupted* form of the first christian church, will not do. Show it to us any where among those "various circumstances and effects in the universe" which "are according to divine order." Show it to us in the anatomy of the human body, which is the material type of all true order. Show us a single instance in which the principles of the soul or mind, do not flow into a *trine* in the very lowest or corporeal plane. Show us a single unity in the ultimates of even the human body which does not consist of a trine—as a skin, for instance, which consists of only *one* cuticular membrane, and not of *three*. Show us a single instance which indicates that a true church, flowing according to "that divine order which fills *all* and *every thing* in the *universe* even to the *most minute particulars*," will come into such an arrangement of its ministry, or such a constitution of its external ecclesiastical order, as admits of but *one* grade, and we give up the point! But until this one instance is shown, we must say, the assertion that the *New Jerusalem*, or any *true* church, *can* exist under such a *calvinistic* constitution, is a solecism. The calvinistic or solifidian church is a dire corruption of the first christian church as established by the Lord and his apostles; and in our opinion no external order, which *originated* in it, can ever be the proper form of the New Jerusalem. Or the calvinistic form can only be proper for the New Jerusalem so far as it bears the image and likeness (though defaced) of God's universal order.

All heaven and all earth, being more or less in the human form, is most distinctly *jointed*. The earth is the Lord's footstool; heaven and the church are his body. The external church may, in one aspect, be regarded as the legs by which he stands on the earth. And to imagine that a church, coming down to earth from him out of heaven, would be arranged in only one grade of its ministry, would be to suppose that his legs would be as one stiff member *without any joints*, instead of a flexible one with *three*. And if, in another aspect, we suppose the external church to be only the Lord's *foot*,* then the trinal order is still more manifest in its *articulations*. For there is a two-fold trine in the arrangement of the pedal bones. Thus there are the tarsal bones, the metatarsal bones, and the bones of the toes—forming the first trine; and there is besides a trine of bones in the toes themselves. And thus it is a curious fact, that the trinal articulation becomes most distinctly marked in the most ultimate degree of the very foot. For in the thigh—extending from the hip to the knee joint—there is but *one* bone; in the leg—extending from the knee to the ankle joint (not including the knee pan, which is common to the thigh and shin bones)—there are *two* bones; while in the foot there are *twenty-six!* The same observation holds true of the arm. What will the advocates of *but one grade* in the *natural* plane, say to this? Let this law of order in the human body, be borne in mind; for we may have to refer to it hereafter. Here we will only ask, does it not most strikingly show the *necessity* of a *trine* on *earth?* Nay, so universal and pervading is the law of correspondence between natural and spiritual things, that every thing which exists on earth does in fact figure forth the trinity which is in God. And so imperatively does the law of a trine in the ministry call for' obedience, that no ministry ever does or can exist without something like it. It may be in some cases less developed, less distinctly formed, or less acknowledged, but in all there is at least a shadow of it. Hence even in the calvinistic constitution, as it is now seen to exist around us, we see the distinct arrangement of licensed preachers, ordained ministers, and doctors of divinity; and, in one form of the calvinistic church in this country, there are ministers who are now openly called " bishops."†. Let it be observed, too,

---

* "The church on earth is that to the angelic heaven, which a foundation is to a house that rests upon it, or *as the feet upon which a man stands*, and by which he walks." (Ap. Rev. 645.) If, therefore, the angelic heaven is the Lord's *body*, the church on earth is the Lord's *foot*.

† In a Baltimore newspaper just come to hand, we find the following marriage notice :—"On the 17th instant, by [the] Rev. Dr. Musgrave, Bishop of the Third Presbyterian Church, R. EWING ANTHONY to Miss ELLEN GAULT, all of this city." This shows that a D. D. of the presbyterian church has the title of *bishop :* but it is evident that the term is used in a very limited sense, as designating merely a pastor or overseer of a particular society or church, and does not imply any thing like an adoption of the *episcopal* grade as it exists in the romish or english churches. It does, however, indicate *something like* gradation in the ministry. And who, that knows any thing about it, will undertake to say, that the D. D.s of the presbyterian church, as to all'those powers of mental influence and control which master spirits exert over their fellow-men,

that there is here also the preparatory stage of the theological student. It is true that licensed preachers are not supposed to be in the ministry before they are ordained as pastors over particular churches; and there may not be any acknowledged discrete gradation between the ordained minister and the doctor of divinity, who is constituted such only by an academic decree: but there is here seen to be a sort of struggle of the internal world to produce a trine in external order, where a hard, unyielding material presents peculiar obstructions. And it will be well for us to consider whether the Calvinist, in his anxiety to get rid of what he regards as the flummery, or mere cookery, of the "mother of harlots," has not striven to throw away some of the esculent substance of that "divine order" which "fills all and every thing in the universe," without being able wholly to do without it.

From this time the subject of the trine in the ministry seems to have slept in England for some years. Whether the action of the English Conference upon this report was such a settlement of the matter as was likely to secure entirely the future quiet of the church, we must leave for those who are more expert than we are in discerning the signs of the times since, to decide. Some may think, that the report, in the admission to which we have objected, went too much on the temporizing policy of deferring matters of *principle* to matters of *expediency*. And if "by influx is meant 'all that which precedes, and composes what is subsequent, and by things subsequent in order composes what is last," (C. L. 313;) and if what was first in the establishment of the English Conference, was, by things subsequent in order, to flow into and qualify the state of the church in it at any future time; may it not be conjectured that this general body of the church has not evinced its usual wisdom in *postponing so long* all action correspondent to the principles which it at this time acknowledged to be true? Has any experience shown, that errors,—incorporated into the constitution of a body, from the prudential consideration that at some future time its members would be in a better state to see, acknowledge and renounce them,—were ever worked out without convulsions? In short, can it be truly expedient, on the ground of mutual concession, to concede any thing to error or injustice, in establishing any organic law? Supposing slavery to be inimical to the fundamental political law that all men are born free and equal, was it wise to incorporate *that* into the constitution of the United States upon

do not exercise as great an authority over a presbyterian synod, or assembly, and presbyterian clergy, as an episcopal bishop ever does over his diocese. If so, then the presbyterian church has the essence of episcopacy without its form. Now, in the very constitution of human nature, in the very nature of things, in the very order of influx and arrangement in the divine economy, this controlling influence of superior minds, superior men, or superior functionaries, is right and indispensable. It is the order of heaven, as well as the order of hell. It is only wrong in the visible church, when it is the control of imperiousness—of those who desire to rule from love of dominion—as in hell. It is right when it is the control of superior love, or superior wisdom, or superior intelligence, or even of the *representative* of these virtues in the Lord's divine humanity, and if it results from the *voluntary subordinations* of other members of the church and ministry to it, as in heaven. (See A. C. 7773.)

the assumption that the individual states would of themselves, in due time, renounce it as an evil? And has experience shown that the whole United States, as one man, are now, after the lapse of more than seventy years of their independent national existence, any nearer a peaceable, quiet, *constitutional* acknowledgment that human beings are *not property*, entitling the holders of them as slaves to a certain weight in the legislative councils that are to determine the law, which should be the justice, of the land? And is the English Conference, now, after a lapse of about fifteen years, any nearer the time when all its members can see eye to eye in carrying out into correspondent action the trine in the ministry, which, from 1815 to 1843, had been decreed true order, but which "it was deemed inexpedient to legislate upon, from the conviction that the time to do so, with permanent advantage to the church, had not yet arrived"? The Lord says, "Work, while ye have the day"—"while ye have the light, walk in the light." And under these injunctions, is it not imperative on the collective bodies of the Lord's church, whenever they see, and formally declare, any principle of order to be true, to bring themselves into external conformity to it instantly? And if they put off to a more convenient season entire conformity to what they have light enough now to see and know to be true order, is it impossible that they may find themselves at last in that "night" in which "no man can work"? At least, will they not subject themselves to the necessity of putting off their temporary expedients by convulsions, and greater difficulties than would have attended the constituting themselves on the principles of true order at first? The future history of the New Jerusalem on earth can alone, perhaps, answer these questions satisfactorily.

The Twenty-Sixth General Conference, having thus settled the questions which had grown out of the order of a trine in the ministry, by decreeing it to be the true order. and yet postponing indefinitely all action in carrying that order fully out, no notice was taken of this subject for about nine years: except that the Twenty-Seventh General Conference adopted and published a supplemental paper on this subject by the Rev. Mr. Noble. (See Ap. No. L.) The Thirty-Fifth General Conference had its attention called to it by the communication from what is styled the General Convention of Societies in the United States. That communication solicited information or opinions from the General Conference, from a committee of it, or from any individuals of which it was composed, upon the following topics—"*First*, as to the order of the ministry, as consisting of a trine in just order; *secondly*, as to the order of the church, as consisting of a trine in just order; *thirdly*, as to the relation of an orderly ministry and an orderly church to each other." This conference resolved, "with regard to the question specifically proposed for its opinion, that its consideration be submitted to the consideration of the ministers whose names follow : viz. David Howarth, William Mason, and John Henry Smithson; and that they report thereon to the next conference." But this committee made as good as no report to the next conference. Probably the members of it could not agree in the views which they should present. Subsequent events have rendered it likely that they, in 1842, were divided, two to one, on the principles as set forth in the reports rendered in 1830 and 1833. In short, there was a prolongation of the original differences of opinion, which had prevented the settlement of this question, and correspondent action upon it, from the first, in England. Be that as it may, this committee only reported to the next conference that they had not been able "to arrive at any solid and satisfactory conclusion on a subject so weighty and important as that which was committed to their charge"; and recommended "the appointment of another committee for that purpose, should the conference of the present year be of opinion that it is still desirable to carry out the object," which the previous conference had in view in appointing the former committee. The Thirty-Sixth General Conference did resolve, "that a committee be again appointed to consider the said subject," and "that John Henry Smithson, David Howarth and James Bradley, ministers, be such committee; that John Henry Smithson, minister, do act as secretary; and that such committee do apply to any person they may conceive likely to afford useful information on the subject." The conference, also, invited "all the members of the church to communicate their views on this subject to the committee above named." It will be observed that James Bradley is substituted in the second committee for William Mason in the first. This indicates whom subsequent events have shown to be most probably the one, who, from disagreement with the views of the reports of 1833, in all likelihood, prevented agreement in a report to the conference of 1843. It is not a little remarkable, too, in this connection, that, in this same conference of 1843, the old question was again brought up, "whether it be in agreement with the laws of divine order for other preachers than ordained ministers, to baptize and administer the Lord's supper"? In reply, the conference "*Resolved*, That this subject, having been frequently under the consideration of conference, and its opinion thereon fully expressed, the conference deems it inexpedient to enter upon it now; but recommends that the former minutes of conference be consulted thereon, together with the reports appended thereto." The reports here referred to are those of which we have taken such extended notice, and of which we now intend to give reprints in an appendix to this report. (See Ap. Nos. XLVIII. and XLIX.) Thus it appears that the English General Conference again, in 1843, sets its seal of confirmation upon the trine in the ministry, which it had declared to be true order in 1815 and in 1833.

The Thirty-Seventh General Conference met in London in August, 1844. To this conference, the second committee, mentioned above as having been appointed by the thirty-sixth conference, made an extended report, on the trine in the ministry, in answer to the American General Convention's solicitation of its views on this subject. In respect to this report, the minutes of the thirty-seventh conference say—"Before proceeding to read the addresses arising out of the interchange of communications with the new-church conventions in America, the report of the committee appointed by . . . the last conference, on the subject of the existence of a trine in the ministry, was again read; and it was *resolved*, that such report be received. *Resolved*, That the conference, fully concurring in the view of the subject presented in this report, trusts that it will prove satisfactory to the members of the General Convention, by whom the subject was proposed for consideration; and conducive to the well-being of the new church generally in the United States. *Resolved*, That this report, so clearly defining the opinions of the church in this country, on the subject to which it relates, be printed in the Appendix to the Minutes of the present conference."

This report on the trine, more fully confirming the principles of previous reports on this subject, and reiterating the declaration of the English General Conference, almost from its very beginning, that a trine is the true order of the new-church ministry, was officially communicated to the Central, as well as to the General, Convention of the New Church in this country. We say this report was officially communicated to the Central Convention, because the person appointed, by the conference which received and approved it, to address our general body, expressly referred us to it in the address which he sent. These are his words, (see Address, from the English General Conference, to the Central Convention, by the Rev. Thomas Goyder, published in Appendix IV. to Journal No. VII. of Cent. Con. p. 47):—
"The members, generally, of the church here, as with you in America, seem to have a constitutional acknowledgment of the principle of a TRINE in the ministry; and the english church has for years generally acted, and still continues to act, in agreement with such acknowledgment. The views held upon this subject by our General Conference are expressed in the report of its committee appointed to consider the subject of a trine in the ministry, to which I beg to refer, as printed in the minutes of the Thirty-Seventh General Conference, (page 55,) copies of which are herewith sent." When this express reference of the Central Convention to the report as printed in the appendix to the minutes, is viewed in connection with the "trust," which the conference expresses, in the minutes themselves, as quoted in the second of the above cited resolutions, namely, "that it will prove conducive to the well-being of the new church generally in the United States" as well as "satisfactory to the members of the General Convention," it must be evident that the General Conference designed to communicate it officially to the Central Convention also. So viewing it, it was published in connection with our Journal, "for a permanent record in immediate connection with the paper which refers to it," and "for future reference in the proceedings of our convention." Hence we refer to it now as a document for history appended to this report. (See Journal No. VII. Ap. IV. p. 53.) It is also proper to say, that the ecclesiastical council of the Central Convention, in its hasty report to the sixth annual meeting, (see Journal No. VIII.—Ap. I. Reps. Nos. VIII. and IX. pp. 28—44,) drew its authorities mainly from this and other reports made to the English Conference; and that our present report is mainly founded upon the same authorities. This is done because the members of the Central Convention's ecclesiastical council have failed themselves to

3

draw the authorities from the Word and the writings of Swedenborg directly. The authorities are drawn *mainly* from those sources, but not wholly : for there has been some, nay, not a little, original investigation—though that investigation may have been spread through some fifteen or twenty years of reading and study, without express reference to the proceedings of the Central Convention, and, indeed, for the most part, before its existence. This statement is made here, that the strenuous opposers of the principles of our former report, both in this country and in England, but especially in England, may see that we found the groundwork of those principles in the formal declarations of the english church, as officially communicated to our convention. For it will be observed that this last report to the english conference, expressly says, "it is scarcely necessary to do more than to refer to the results of the labors of former committees, as reported in the Appendix to the Minutes of the 23d, 26th and 27th General Conferences." These former reports, therefore, being thus referred to, are in fact included in this last report. Consequently, the authorities of those are the authorities of this. And hence we now print, in an appendix to our present report, those reports which are above cited, that they may be documents of reference for the church in this country, together with the one which is printed in an appendix to Journal No. VII., and as furnishing, with that, many of the authorities upon which the principles of our own reports to the Central Convention are founded. (See Ap. Nos. XLVIII. XLIX. and L.)

Mr. Goyder says the members of the church in England have *generally* held to a trine in the ministry. This implies, what we have fully seen, that there were *particular* exceptions to this assertion. And among these were the Rev. William Mason. We mention him here by name, because, in his official capacity of president of the English General Conference, he has undertaken to administer a severe rebuke to the Central Convention for its "forced construction and misapplication of passages in the writings of Swedenborg, cited in the journal [No. VIII.] in support of the superstitious conclusions [respecting the trine in the ministry] sought to be established thereby." He felt it to be right, and to be his duty, as the presiding officer of the body which represents the whole new church in England, to send copies of his communication to our convention to the General and Western Conventions also, "in order that the sentiments generally entertained in that country by members of the new church might not be unknown throughout the United States." Knowing, as he did, that those conventions had drawn the same conclusions, in regard to the trine in the ministry, which we had, from the writings of Swedenborg, he probably designed, in sending to them, his communication to us, to administer to them also their share of our castigation. They, especially the General Convention, must, undoubtedly, have felt under great obligations to the president of the Thirty-Ninth General Conference for communicating to them the *information*, that, according to "the sentiments generally entertained in England," the trine in the ministry, which *they* had deduced and carried out for years in this country, was deemed to be founded on only "*superstitious* conclusions," drawn from the "*forced construction* and *misapplication* of passages in the writings of Swedenborg"—more particularly "the *unwarranted* construction of Coronis, 17." To have judged from the *official proceedings* of the English General Conference, as set forth in the Minutes of that body, all the conventions, and all the members of the new church, "throughout the United States," might have *supposed* that directly contrary sentiments were "generally entertained in that country by members of the new church;" and it was certainly charitable in Mr. Mason, if the reverse were in fact the case, to strive to have this fact known by the whole new church in this country. But we apprehend that it will be hard for Mr. Mason to make it appear that he is a truer representative of what sentiments are generally entertained in England than the General Conference.

We shall feel it our duty to publish and review the communication made by the Rev. Mr. Mason, in the name of the English General Conference, to the Central Convention. We shall do so in immediate connection with this report. And with unfeigned sorrow do we feel compelled to say we think it must appear, from what is here shown, that Mr. Mason has most unwarrantably availed himself of his temporary station of president of the General Conference, to give currency in the United States to the views of *himself* or of his *party* in England, by clothing them with the official sanction of that highly respected body of the general church. The Minutes of that body, and the Rev. Mr. Goyder, in its name, both declare, that the members of the church in England have generally held to a trine in the ministry as we do. It may be that very many members of the new church in that country hold views different from ours and similar to Mr. Mason's. It is certain that the suffrages, in twenty-six communications "from various societies and individuals," were in favor of his views about the time of the twenty-sixth conference; although the weight of argument—which means the force of truth—and the decisions of that conference, were against them. Still Mr. Mason ought not to have said, *as president of the conference*, that his views were generally prevalent in England, when his assertion is against all its previous official declarations. He might have said, that his views, and those of others in England, differed from the previous official declarations of the body over which he was then presiding, as they had been previously communicated to the church in this country; and thus he would have made known officially to the new church in this country an historical fact, which is here, perhaps, first elicited. For we have seen that Mr. Mason could not agree with the first committee, appointed by the thirty-fifth conference, in a report on the trine, which should affirm and extend the principles of the reports of former committees of the conference. Those who read those reports as now reprinted in our appendix, will see that his views were then the same as they are seen now to be in his communication to our convention; and they will also see how conclusively they were then confuted.

We may here observe, that Mr. Mason was very highly respected in this country, and especially by the members of the Central Convention. He had gained this respect by his published works, and by his letter to our body sent in the name of the english conference in 1843. It may be, because the response of our body to this letter was so highly commendatory of it, that Mr. Mason felt called on to communicate his individual views in dissent from, and even in reprehension of, those of the General Conference, of which he is a member, as made known to us in the report now under consideration. Seeing that he was a man of great intellectual and moral authority among us, he may have felt himself bound in conscience to exert his influence in saving us from its errors. He was certainly entitled to express his individual opinions to the General Convention; for that body had invited an expression of opinion upon the subject, not only from the conference, but also "from a committee of it, or from *any individuals* of which it is composed." · And he probably intended to communicate his views to that body, and the whole church in the United States, through ours. Hence he communicated to our corresponding secretary the "Remarks on the Questions propounded in Minute 85 of the Conference of 1843," which he had "furnished to the committee appointed by Minute 86," in answer to the request of that conference "that all the members of the church" in England would "communicate their views on" the trine to said committee. These Remarks were written by Mr. Mason in July, 1844; and, subsequently seeing that the report differed widely from his views, he, in February, 1845, adds a postscript to his communication to our convention, in which he charges the committee of conference with being "*too superstitious*" in "drawing conclusions from Swedenborg's writings which were never intended to be drawn." This communication and its postscript are printed in Ap. IV. to Journal No. VII. pp. 58—64, immediately after the report above referred to.

From this it appears that Mr. Mason's charge against us of *superstition* in founding our views of a trine in the ministry upon the forced construction and misapplication of passages in the writings of Swedenborg, is only a repetition of a charge made by him against the thirty-seventh conference; for that conference "fully concurred in the view of the subject presented in this report" to it in 1844; and it was as much "too superstitious" in the conference, as in the writers of it, to draw the conclusions from Swedenborg's writings which the report did. Or it may be considered as nothing more nor less in fact than Mr. Mason's assuming that his particular understanding, (or that of those who agreed with him,) of what conclusions Swedenborg *intended* should be drawn from his writings, was the only true one; and that whoever had a different understanding must of course view them through a superstitious medium. Now, however little respect many, both in America and in England, may think due to the Central Convention—and certainly it has no just claims to any very great acumen in discerning *Swedenborg's intentions*—might not some deference have been paid, even by Mr. Mason, to the declared understanding and conviction of the English General Conference; and was it, to say the least, *courteous* in him, who has since evinced so much sensibility of our want of courtesy to that highly respectable general body of the church, to virtually charge it with being "too *superstitious*" in adopting and sending to the new church in America, as the views of the new church in England, these conclusions in respect to the trine in the ministry, drawn from the writings of Swedenborg by a committee of its appointment?

Still Mr. Mason does not deny the doctrine of a trine in the ministry, but limits it to a trine of uses, and specifies the trines as he supposes they should exist both in the ministry and in the church. He seems opposed, as many are in this country, to the instituting of an english episcopacy, or a romish hierarchy, in the New Jerusalem. Yet, he does not clearly appear to be opposed to a personal trine; for his trine of ministerial uses seems to require a trine of ministers for their performance; but the use of superintending the ministry he thinks "may be carried on by the ministry alone, *or in conjunction with the laity.*" This, according to former reports to the english conference, would be subordinating the centre to the circumference. But Mr. Mason may think that any interpretation of Swedenborg's writings which are so strict as to lead to such a forced conclusion, is superstition.

These views of the Rev. Mr. Mason have been referred to here, not simply because they are opposed to ours, or because we ourselves are opposed to him, (for we know not how nearly we may be found to agree with him,) but because the truth of history requires that we should show how the question of a trine in the ministry was viewed in England by a minority of the english conference at the time when the report before us expressed the views generally prevailing in that country on this subject.

The report on the trine which the thirty-seventh conference sent to America as expressive of the views prevailing in England on that subject, brings up the history of this question in that country to the present time. For in the thirty-eighth and thirty-ninth conferences the question was no further agitated. The only proceeding, having any reference to the ministry, in these two conferences, was a resolution, "that the rules and regulations relating to the ministry be submitted to a committee of four members for the purpose of ascertaining whether any alterations can be made therein that will render such rules more efficient." But it does not appear that this led to any modification in the conference's views of a trine, or any further carrying out of the views previously expressed. We may therefore conclude, that the new church in England has, from virtually first to last, declared a trine in the ministry to be the true order of our church. The report before us shows, that this is a trine of persons in the external ministry, and not merely a trine of uses to be performed by only one rank or grade of ministers. Mr. Mason and others in England do indeed affirm that the external order of the new church may admit of the latter; but it must be observed, that the conference which adopted this report was composed of ten ministers and twenty-three representatives from thirteen societies, being, with the ministers not present and known to be in favor of the trine as thus set forth, a large majority of the official representers of the whole church in England.

In conclusion of the historical sketch of the question of the trine in England, then, let us recapitulate these doings and declarations of the General Conference, as expressive of the views now entertained on this subject by the church in that country. In 1842, the conference appoints a committee to report to the church in America the views generally prevailing in England in respect to the trine. That committee cannot or does not agree in a report, and another committee is appointed by the conference in 1843. In 1844 this second committee reports:—1st. that there is great diversity of opinion in England as to the propriety of discussing this subject now—some assuming that the state of the church is not such as to warrant the statement of any principles that can be reduced to practice, and others alleging that no practical good, but only controversy, can arise from such discussion; so that the committee think the minds of the members of the new church, as it is to be eminently an internal one, are to be directed to internals, as the only secure way of promoting and establishing its real interests; for unless heavenly order is established within, all external order will be merely factitious and hollow:—2d. that any principles of uniformity, either as to the order of the ministry, or as to the order of church government, can never be established in respect to the Lord's new church; that such an establishment, if it could be made, is not desirable; that all externals in relation to these matters, will ever be accommodated to the peculiar genius and customs of nations, and even of the same people inhabiting different provinces of the same country; and, in proof of this, that Swedenborg never contemplated any changes in the external ecclesiastical order of the different churches which existed in his day:—3d. that, notwithstanding, there is, from divine order, a trine in all uses, corresponding to end, cause, and effect; that this order exists in the distinguished uses of the ministry; that this trine was represented by the jewish priesthood; and, although a mere representative priesthood itself is not continued from the jewish into the christian church, yet still the order of the trine, which that priesthood represented, being the universal divine order by which uses flow and are performed, that therefore the ministerial uses of the christian church must necessarily, as that church advances, be developed as a trine in its ministry. Having laid down these principles, the report of the committee proceeds at length to deduce the authorities from Swedenborg for both an essential and a formal trine in the ministry and in the church. From its authorities it concludes, "that there cannot be a full formation in any ministry, until it exists in a trine." As to the church, it concludes that there is an essential trine of those who are in love, those who are in wisdom, and those who are in use. In this trine the minister is included with the other members of the church as a spiritual brotherhood. From this essential trine in the church as a spiritual body there is deduced a formal trine of " offices, uses or duties, and thereby a trine of persons who are to fill the offices and perform the uses," in the church as an ecclesiastical polity. In the church the priesthood is "the first order;" for the performance of "primary uses." But besides these there are "secondary and last uses," which are uses partly clerical and partly laical, and peculiarly laical. The persons who are to perform the secondary uses possess a mixed character like the uses themselves, and are called deacons or wardens. And the purely laical or last uses are to be performed by mere laymen. Thus in a church in just order there is an internal or essential trine constituting internal order and use, and also an external, formal or visible trine, corresponding to that for the purposes of external order and use. The report then shows how a trine may exist in the collective bodies of the church, and their respective functionaries, as well as in the individual member or single society of it. And it shows that the ministry and the church are not two distinct things, but distinct parts of the same thing; and that the relation between them is two-fold, internal and external—the relation of brothers to brethren—of brethren connected in a spiritual relationship of mutual love, charity and use, and therefore of brethren in the first order of uses to brethren in the secondary and last orders. And as in all things there is a trine, thus a trine in each grade of use, as well in the primary as in the secondary and the last, therefore "there is obviously a trine of *primary* uses as well as of the two other kinds; hence it is according to order, that, so far as the state of the church and its uses require, *there should be a trine in the ministry alone.*"

Such is the final conclusion of this report, namely, that in the priesthood or ministry of the New Jerusalem, considered distinctively from the laity of this church, there should be *a formal, visible* or *personal trine of ministers*, as the "first order of the church," to fill the most sacred offices, discharge the most solemn duties, and perform the primary uses, pertaining to the Lord's church and kingdom on earth.

It is to be observed, however, that this last report to the english conference seems to differ from the former reports to which it refers, in not admitting so explicitly that christian ministers are still priests representative of the Lord—though not a *mere* representative priesthood as the jewish was. Hence the external or visible trine of officers in the church are deemed to correspond to the internal or essential trine of celestial, spiritual and natural uses in it as an internal or spiritual body. Consequently, there cannot be, according to this view, the higher grades of the trine in the ministry, until there are celestial and spiritual men in the church, or until the celestial and spiritual degrees of the church are opened on earth, for the ministers of those grades to correspond to. Of course, there cannot be a trine of ministers while the church is only in the natural degree. And all this flows from the assumption, in the beginning of the report, that internal order must be established first, and external order flow from it. So that if any external order is induced without, before heavenly order is established within, it "will be merely factitious and hollow." This is the view of Mr. Mason, and those whom he stands up for in England; and the writer of this last report seems to have wished to conciliate them in this part of it. The same view is entertained by

many in this country; and was expressed by the president of the
Central Convention in the communication which he wrote to the
English Conference in 1843—to which the letter of Mr. Mason,
written in the name of the conference next year, was a reply. It is
also the view of the report "concerning the ministry and ordinations,"
which was made to the last Western Convention; which body has radically changed its ecclesiastical order, and remodelled it after the
pattern sent by Mr. Mason. But this is not the view of the writers*
of the present paper, and never was. And, with all deference to wiser
men, they must say it is perfectly manifest to them that this view cannot be true, because the end and.object of instituting a christian priesthood on earth is to disseminate those *knowledges* of truth by which
alone conjunction of man with God can be effected. (See A. C. 1616.)
The very end and object of instituting a christian priesthood, is,
through it as a medium, to form the church in a laity. (See U. T. 784.)
The christian priesthood is instituted to be an especial medium of
those virtues of the Lord's holy spirit which consist in illustration
and instruction from his Word—this is called "the mission of the
holy spirit." (See U. T. 146.) Hence a christian priesthood must
exist in true external form and order in the very institution of the
church, or shortly after its beginning as a visible polity, to the end

---

* Mr. De Charms *knows*, from six years' intercourse with him in the West, as well
as from repeated intercourse and correspondence with him of late, that Mr. Powell agrees
with him in his view of the trine, and of the strictly representative character of the christian priesthood; although he may not be able to subscribe to all that will be set forth in
this report, especially in respect to what should be the particular manifestation of the trine
in this country. As the part of the report which will have this respect, is not yet written,
and Mr. Powell has been consulted in only a very general way about it, it remains to be
seen whether he will concur in it or not. Mr. De Charms has also reason to believe that
Mr Burnham agrees substantially with him in his view of a trine. And he well knows that
there was at last the utmost harmony of views on this subject between him and his most
beloved friend and brother the late Rev. C. J. Doughty. Dr. Beers never was a member of the Central Convention, although he took part in the meetings which formed its
constitution, and sanctioned its proceedings by administering the holy supper to it; but
he never signed its constitution. Hence Mr. Doughty was opposed to the placing of his
name on the list of its ministers; and Dr. Beers, in a letter to Mr. De Charms, has said
that Mr. Doughty was right, and that his name ought not to have been placed there. It,
however, was so placed, because Mr. De Charms understood Dr. Beers to say that he
meant to sign the constitution of the Central Convention, when he had taken a friendly
leave of the Eastern or "old" Convention, as he called it, to which he considered himself as then belonging; and therefore a blank space was left, that his name might
appear signed first, as the head member of our general body. But subsequent developments and events caused him to feel dissatisfied with our body, or with some of its leading members, and he has formally signified his wish to remain in the Eastern as the
General Convention. Therefore his views on the trine are not noticed here, although
they were communicated by him to the ecclesiastical council of our convention. As so
communicated, he holds to a ministerial trine in one person, or to but one ordination by
the imposition of hands. In other terms, he holds to the induction of a person into the
three degrees of the ministry by one ordination, with power to perform all the functions
of those degrees himself, and to delegate his powers in the two lower degrees to other
persons by appointment. At least, so we have understood his views. He also holds
that the christian *priest* must be himself a *celestial* man, and not merely the *representative* of the Lord as one. (See Jour. No. IV., Ap. II., p. 27.)

that the internal church *may* be developed, ever or at all, in its internal order, purity and perfection. In short, in our view, a christian priesthood is instituted, at first and at last, to *represent* the Lord to his church, and not at any time to *correspond* to "the advancement of the individuals, who compose it, in the love of the Lord and the neighbor," or to any "heavenly order" which may be "established within" them.

Nay the trine, or any order, in the christian priesthood is not to *correspond* to any heavenly order which may be established within even the *priests*: for Swedenborg expressly speaks (A. C. 3670) of "all priests" as among "the representatives which exist even at this day,"—the day in which Swedenborg fulfilled his mission of ushering the Lord's second advent, therefore the day in which the first christian church came to its end, and the new and true christian church, called the New Jerusalem, began,—and says of them that they so represent the Lord in his holy priestly office, that the Word preached by them, or baptism, the holy supper, and the like, administered by them, are holy, whatever may be their personal quality. Therefore it is clear that christian priests, and all the external order by which their functions, duties and uses may be performed, must, in the christian church, represent the Lord, and the internal order which exists in him, and not correspond to any establishment of heavenly order, either within themselves or within the church individually or collectively considered. And the idea that the celestial or spiritual degree of the priesthood must only exist in form or external order, when there is a spiritual or celestial man regenerated to these degrees to fill the office; or when the spiritual and celestial degrees are opened in the church, so that these offices may flow by the correspondence of an external priesthood with those internal states of the church; is not only dangerous, because leading to the old-church conceit that the minister is and must be, by virtue of his office, better or more holy than any other man, but, as it appears to us, is altogether inadmissible: because, if an external priesthood is not first instituted to represent the Lord in his work of salvation in the spiritual and celestial degrees, and to administer those sacraments which also represent him in the same work, so that the heavens may have in those representatives the only plane which they can have for consociation with men on earth, (see Ap. Ex. Vol. III. n. 475, p. 193, and Vol. IV., n. 724, p. 407—Eng. Edit. of 1811–15,) and thus become mediums of the Lord's influences to men in their natural states, for their salvation in spiritual and celestial states—*the spiritual and celestial planes of the mind never could be opened in men of the church on earth!** Or if

---

* By this it is not meant that some persons, here and there, who are so circumstanced that they cannot avail themselves of the ordinances of an external church, may not be saved by internal worship alone: for this, we know, would be to make internal worship external. (A. C. 1175.) But we mean that no internal church can exist and subsist without an external one (A. C. 6587)—hence that mankind cannot be saved without a church on earth (A. C. 637, 4288)—that such a church cannot exist without its ritual ordinances and sacraments, (A. C. 1083,) which are representatives in the letter of the Word, (Ap. Ex. 475, 724,) because the church and worship must have both

men had become celestial and spiritual, so that there were no longer any need of their becoming so from natural, there would be no need of a church—no need of a doctrine of truth—no need of preachers of that doctrine—no need of sacraments representative of spiritual and celestial truth and good yet to be developed in the church; and thus no need of any visible priesthood whatever. Therefore, if there is any need of a priesthood at all, it is a representative one—a priesthood having a trine of ministers, not *corresponding* to the essential trine in the church, but *representing* the essential trine both in the Lord and in the church by regeneration from him, or representing the Lord's work of saving men in the three discrete degrees of their being, and thus forming a representative *image* of his humanity in the natural world, as we are told the three heavens do in the spiritual world. And this, we believe, is at least implied in the reports made to the English Conference in 1830, 1833 and 1834, which are referred to in this report made in 1844.

But whether the opinion that external order in the ministry should precede internal order in the church is generally prevalent in England or not, it is certain that, according to the view which does prevail in that country, the priesthood of the new church, whenever it comes into true order, will consist of a trine of ministers of discrete or distinct grades, in which the lower will be subordinate to the higher. We are persuaded that this is the view of a majority of the strongest and most enlightened minds of the new church in England. And it is most clearly set forth in the authorities which are quoted from Swedenborg in this last and the former reports to the english conference. Therefore we take it to be the view generally prevalent in the english church. For "the conference fully concurred in the view of the subject presented in this [last] report," which includes those of former years; and declares that it "clearly defines the opinion of the church in England on the subject to which it relates"

Therefore the history of the question of the trine in England, may be summed up in these words of the Rev. Thomas Goyder, already quoted from a communication of the General Conference to the Cen-

---

an internal and an external, as the Word, upon which they are founded, has (A. C. 10.603)—that such an external church must exist first in time as the means of developing an internal church, and subsist at all times, as the basis, continent and firmament of its internal principles (A. C. 3857, Ap. Rev. 533, A. C. 9216)—and that, when such a church is established, and acts as a heart and lungs to the body of mankind, (A. C. 2054,) then persons who do not, because they cannot, partake of its external ordinances, may be saved by internal worship from common influx without it—as the good among the heathen are—because they who are out of the church, and yet live well, "are in communion with those who are in it," (A. C. 10.765.) But if there were no church on earth, having the Word in its letter and sacraments from its letter—thus if there were no external church on earth—no flesh could be saved, (A. C. 4423, 9276, 10 500.) And this is so because the external or natural man is opened first, and the internal or spiritual man is opened afterwards (Ap. Ex. 150)—because this external principle is a foundation, without which the internal principle of the church would perish (A. C. 6299)—and because correspondence between the internal and the external, by which alone man is saved, must take place on earth, or not at all, (A. C. 3993.)

tral Convention—"the members, generally, of the church here, as with you in America, seem to have a constitutional acknowledgment of the principle of a TRINE in the ministry; and the english church has for years past generally acted, and still continues to act, in agreement with such acknowledgment." Nevertheless, it is a fact, that the English General Conference has as yet but two grades in its ministry, namely, ordaining ministers and ordained ministers. This sketch has shown that attempts were made to institute a third grade in or about 1833, and so to carry out fully the order of a trine in the ministry; but, although this order was then declared to be true, yet it was deemed inexpedient to legislate in carrying it out then; and as it has not been carried out since, a question will very naturally arise, how it can be said that the english church has for years past generally acted, and still continues to act, in agreement with its constitutional acknowledgment of the principle of a trine in the ministry? All that past history can say is, that the english church has generally acknowledged such to be the true order: and it remains for future history to record the fact that such order has been carried out fully.*

In this historical sketch, we have said, (p. 19,) that " the particular order for the new-church ministry is determined to be a *trine* of degrees" " for the first time" in the Eighth General Conference, held in Manchester on the 14th of August, 1815. But it should be stated that the subject of the ministry of the new church had been discussed at length in the London Conference, composed of the ministers and delegates of the three new-church societies in that city. And it was this London Conference which led the way in reviving the General Conference, which had been suspended, at one time for fourteen, and now again for seven years. The reason assigned for reviving the General Conference was, that, in the London Conference " some things had been presented which it appeared desirable to have brought before the church at large;" and " they communicated with other societies on the propriety of again convening the general conference," " for the purpose of consulting on such measures as might be suggested for the general well-being of the new church." Now what were the measures thus presented, and here proposed to be brought before the church at large, by the London Conference? The answer to this question determines more truly, or specifically, where the suggestion of the order of a trine in the ministry first came from.

---

* The materials for this sketch have been taken mostly from the Intellectual Repository. We have in our possession the minutes of the First General Conference, together with the " Reasons for Separating from the Old Church," which set forth the principles that engaged its deliberations. And we made every effort to procure a complete set of the Minutes of the General Conference, that we might learn its history from them. But all our efforts were in vain. We have, however, received, through the kindness of its present secretary, some more of them than we before possessed. These came to hand after thus much of our report on the trine was in type. And as we find among them the Minutes of the London Conference, (*vide supra*, p. 19,) which afford us a more particular insight into the origin of the idea of a trine in the ministry of the new church in England, we insert some things as additional matter here, which would have filled the second interregnum of the General Conference in the body of our historical sketch of it, if these materials had been sooner in our hands.

The London Conference sprung out of a "desire in the societies of
the Lord's new church in London to enter into a closer conjunction
with each other," from "the sentiment being general, that in consequence of such conjunction, many useful suggestions might arise,
calculated to be of advantage in promoting the welfare of the church
in general." It was in continuance about two years. At first there
were three societies, represented by their three ministers and twelve
delegates—four from each. Afterwards two of the societies were
joined in one, because one of the ministers had removed from London
to Birmingham. This being the case, it was determined that the
delegates from each of these two societies to the conference should
consist of six members besides the ministers : so that, at last, the conference was composed of two ministers and twelve delegates. It held
in all fifteen meetings. The first was held March 15, 1813, the last
January 23, 1815. In these meetings the whole business transacted
pertained to the determination of ecclesiastical order. In this, the
chief thing was the maturing of ordinances for the regulation of the
ministry. In the tenth meeting it was resolved, "that a copy of the
ordinances respecting the ministry be transmitted to the meeting at
Hawkestone Park for their consideration." The meeting at Hawkestone Park "declined giving any decided opinion respecting the
subject." Therefore, the London Conference, whose object, in regulating the ministry, was "the welfare of the church in general,"
resolved to bring the subject before a general conference, to be called
for its consideration. In the minutes of its twelfth meeting, we find
the following resolution—"that this conference having, in agreement
with the testimony of the Holy Word, and of the new-church writings,
thought it necessary that there should be three orders of ministers in
the church, this meeting is of opinion that it will be expedient, as
speedily as possible, to establish these three orders, in conformity with
the ordinances already agreed on, so far as the same shall obtain the
concurrence of the church at large." This tenth meeting was held
September 26, 1814.

The subject of order in the ministry was brought before the London Conference by a communication "containing some observations
respecting ordination"—read in its fourth meeting, which was held
August 9, 1813. This communication was referred for consideration
at the next meeting; at which its general principle was approved,
and a committee appointed to digest the subject for further action in
a subsequent meeting.

The conference had been called upon to consecrate places of worship at St. Osyth and Brightlingsea, and ordain "Mr. Munson a priest
and minister of the Lord's new church," to officiate in them. This
made necessary a determination of the order of the ministry; and we
see that the order then deduced from the testimony of the Holy Word,
and of the new-church writings, made "it necessary that there should
be *three orders* of ministers in the church." It was also deemed
"expedient, *as speedily as possible, to establish these three orders.*"
And thus we learn that the particular order of a *trine* in the ministry
was first suggested by the three societies and ministers of the new

church in London in the years 1813 and 1814: for it was first suggested to the London Conference by a communication to it in the former year, and by this conference to the church at large in the latter year. And it was adopted and proclaimed as the true order of the new church by the Eighth General Conference in the year 1815. Such is the precise and true history of the rise of the question of a ministerial trine in the new church of England.

Some may be curious to know who were the ministers of the new church that first suggested this order. It is not stated by whom the communication, to the fourth meeting of the London Conference, on the subject of ordination into the ministry of the new church, was written. Therefore, we are unable to say who—whether clergyman or layman—was the first person that made this suggestion. But the three ministers of that conference, when it approved the general principle of this communication, were the Rev. Joseph Proud, the Rev. Manoah Sibly, and the Rev. Dr. T. F. Churchill. And Mr. Samuel Noble—so much distinguished for his learning and ability as a minister of the new church since—was the secretary of the London conference for the first year. Mr. Noble was one of the delegates to the conference during its whole existence. And it is not unlikely that his strong hand was at work in the very origination of this order in the new-church ministry, as it has been in maintaining the same by his very able reports to the English General Conference in subsequent years. Thus it is presumable that the strongest men of the new church in England were employed in determining the trine to be the true order of her ministry at first. And that they proceeded deliberately, cautiously and prudently in their work, and did not hastily embrace this as a crude idea, must, we think, appear clear to every one who examines the minutes of their proceedings.

We have seen that the communication which brought this subject up was read at the fourth meeting of the conference, August 9, 1813, and "referred for consideration at the next meeting." The next, or the fifth meeting, was held September 13, 1813. At this the general principle of the communication was approved, and a committee appointed "to digest the subject, and report to the next meeting of this conference." At the sixth meeting, December 12, 1813, "the committee appointed to consider the subject of the ministry, presented a plan, which was minutely discussed and amended, and again referred to the same committee to incorporate the amendments." At the seventh meeting, March 14, 1814, "the amended ordinances for the regulation of the ministry, were maturely considered and unanimously agreed to; and a committee appointed to modify the form of ordination agreeably to these ordinances." At the eighth meeting, June 13, 1814, "some further improvements on the ordinances respecting the ministry being proposed, a long conversation ensued; after which, it was resolved to meet again, on Monday evening of the next week, "to reconsider the ordinances respecting the ministry, and to adapt the forms of ordination to them;" and the secretary was "directed to write to each of the absent members of this conference, particularly requesting his attendance on that evening." At the ninth meeting,

June 27, 1814, the ordinances were again approved, but referred for
still further modifications. At the tenth meeting, July 4, 1814, it
was resolved that a copy of them should be transmitted to the meeting
at Hawkestone Park for its consideration. At the eleventh meeting
nothing was done in respect to the subject of ministerial order. At
the twelfth, the resolution was passed which we have before quoted.
At the thirteenth, December 12, 1814, the minutes of the conference
from its fourth to its present meeting were ordered to be printed,
" together with the ordinances respecting the ministry," " that they
might be submitted to the consideration of the church at large." At
the fourteenth meeting, January 9, 1815, " some additions to the
ordinances respecting the ministry being suggested, it was thought
proper to call a special meeting of the conference, for the purpose of
determining these points before sending to the press." This special
meeting, which was the fifteenth and last of the London Conference,
was held January 23, 1815, and finally adopted "the ordinances for
the regulation of the ministry of the new church, in their amended
state"—directed " 250 copies to be printed and distributed among the
societies"—and "resolved, that a letter signed by the secretary be
printed, and addressed to all the known ministers and leaders of the
new-church societies in the united kingdom, accompanied with copies
of the ordinances."

Thus we see that the order of the ministry was first discussed and
elaborated for near two years by the new church in London, before
it was brought before a general conference of the whole church in
England. It is well for us to know these facts, for they not only show
us that this important subject was not hastily brought forward, and
impulsively adopted, in a crude form, by the english new church, but
they also show us, that it came up in a due time after the first establishment of the external church—that the circumstances of the church in

" *necessary*"—that it was cautiously, intelligently and wisely canvassed, by some of the strongest and clearest minds then in the
church ; and; therefore, that the Eighth General Conference, in determining " that the ministry should consist of three degrees," and in
framing " various resolutions thereon," acted understandingly, and
truly expressed the views generally prevailing on this subject at that
time in England.

order which she has adopted in later years was that which was approved
and adopted by the new church in London at so early a period, we
here reprint the "*Ordinances for the Regulation of the Ministry in
the New Church*," which were submitted to the Eighth General Conference, and acted upon with implied approval by that body.

PREAMBLE.

The new church, called the New Jerusalem, which the Lord is now
establishing in the world, having considerably increased since the last regulations respecting the ministry were formed, and is now widely spreading
her heavenly influences ; it becomes expedient that a system of ordinances
should be adopted, more calculated for her advancement into order ; since it

is from order alone, that the church can obtain a permanent establishment among us; and nothing can be more conducive to the effecting the divine end, than that the ministry be constituted according to this primary law of heaven, from whence the whole body of the church will be more easily disposed into angelic form.

To contribute towards this most desirable object, the London Conference have agreed to adopt, and recommend to other societies, the adoption of the following ordinances; subject, however, to the revision of a general conference of the new church, to be called as speedily as possible.

FORMATION AND FUNCTIONS.

First, That the degrees of persons officiating in holy things, in the Lord's new church, be formed into a trine, according to the instruction afforded in the writings of Emanuel Swedenborg.

Secondly, That, in order to adapt this trine as much as possible to the growing state of the new church, it be constituted as follows,

A third or senior degree, formed of such as may be invested with the full powers of the priesthood.

A second or middle degree, who, as appointed ministers of a society, shall be empowered to exercise all the functions of priesthood, except the ordination of ministers, and the consecration of new places of divine worship

A first or initiatory degree, including readers and assistants to a fixed minister, or to a society, who may, on emergency, perform all the duties of the second degree, except the administration of the holy supper, and the celebration of nuptials.

QUALIFICATIONS.

Thirdly, That no persons receive ordination into any one of these three degrees, except he be of exemplary life, and previously have made full acknowledgment of the faith and life of the new church, in having undergone the initiating rite of baptism, and put his seal thereto, in partaking of the holy supper with some one of her societies.

Fourthly, Ministers of the first degree, not to be under twenty-one years of age; to be well acquainted with the Holy Word, and with the heavenly doctrines of the New Jerusalem church, as revealed from the Lord in the writings of Emanuel Swedenborg; and to possess sufficient voice and judgment, to enable them to read the Scriptures and other parts of the service, with propriety and effect. But persons entering this degree, professedly with the view of exercising themselves regularly in the ministry, otherwise than as readers, shall be twenty-four years of age, and shall be required to give proof of ability for the work, by preaching at least three probationary sermons, prior to ordination to this first degree.

Fifthly, Ministers of the second or middle degree, to have been in the first degree, for one year at least; and in addition to the qualifications before mentioned, to possess a competent knowledge of one of the three languages, Latin, Greek or Hebrew; and, as soon as the state of the church shall afford a sufficient supply of ministers so qualified, a knowledge of all the three shall be required. They shall also have preached seven probationary sermons, and at least one before the ordaining minister or ministers.

Sixthly, Ministers of the third degree, to be not under forty-five years of age, and to have been in the second degree at least seven years.

Seventhly, It shall be the province of the ordaining minister, to examine into the qualifications of candidates; but should it be inconvenient for him to attend the examination, he may appoint any well-qualified person to act for him.

MODE OF ORDINATION.

Eighthly, That in the present infant state of the church, six senior priests will be sufficient, and whenever a vacancy may occur, the surviving seniors shall nominate the person whom they judge best qualified for the office, and present him to a general conference of the new church, for acceptance or rejection; before which conference the formal ordination shall take place.

Ninthly, That the ordination to the second or middle degree of ministers, have the concurrence of two ordaining ministers, although one shall be competent to perform the ceremony; as thereby some check may be put upon improper persons obtruding themselves into the priesthood.

Tenthly, That the approbation of one ordaining minister, shall be sufficient for the ordination of a minister to the first degree.

Eleventhly, That any minister of the established church, or of any denomination of dissenters, who shall recede therefrom, and be desirous of entering into the ministry, and of performing services in the new church; or any unordained teacher of a new-church society, shall be eligible for the second degree, if he has been an affectionate recipient and promoter of the heavenly doctrines of the New Jerusalem for two years: and if he has received and promoted them for seven years, he shall, after remaining one year in the second degree, be eligible to the third; and if he has professed the doctrines of the new church for fourteen years, he shall at once be eligible to the third degree, provided he is in other respects qualified according to the foregoing ordinances.

Twelfthly, That these ordinances are not intended to have any retrospective operation, by interfering with the ordinations which have already taken place in the new church, but to be considered binding in all future cases.

The Eighth General Conference, which was convened to consider these ordinances, met in Manchester in August, 1815. Not having the Minutes of that conference, we cannot say in what precise form these ordinances were acted upon. From the minutes of the next conference, however, we infer that the code was not adopted exactly as here set forth. It was determined that the ministry should consist of three degrees, and it was declared who were the ministers of the second degree, since denominated ordaining ministers. Of course, this designation of the second degree determined who were those of the first, namely, such as had not ordaining powers. And it seems to have been indicated, at least, that the third degree should be "a minister-superintendant." For in the Minutes of the Ninth General Conference, which was held in London from Tuesday the 16th, to Thursday the 18th of July, 1816, we find the following: "The conference then proceeded to take into consideration the Minutes of the last General Conference; when it was *Resolved*, unanimously, That the said Minutes be confirmed, subject to the amendment contained in the next resolution, and with the exception of those resolutions which have reference to a minister-superintendant; and that the consideration of those resolutions be adjourned till the next General Conference." The amendment here referred to, as contained in the next resolution, respected merely the qualifications of a candidate for the ministry when about to be admitted by ordination into the first degree. It required the insertion, after the words " in consideration thereof," of the words " and of his general good character;" so that the part, when amended, should read thus—" That no candidate for the ministry shall be admitted by ordination into the first degree, without the express recommendation of at least one regularly ordained minister, nor without having exercised his talents as a teacher or leader in some society or societies of the new church a sufficient time to enable them to judge of his public usefulness, and in consideration thereof, and of his general good character, to recommend him as a proper person to receive ordination." This clearly indicates that the ordinances for the regulation of the ministry were not adopted by the Eighth General Conference precisely as they had been elaborated, and were submitted, by the London Conference. And it is sufficiently, clear that the General Conference proposed to have one " minister-superintendant" as the third degree of the ministry for the whole new church in England, instead of the " six senior priests," with which the London Conference proposed to fill that degree " in the [then] present infant state of the church." Thus we see there was at first a tendency to a sort of episcopacy in the new church in England. But this measure was postponed from time to time, or put off from conference to conference, until it was wholly lost sight of, and has never been even attempted to be carried out.

In the body of our sketch of the history of the question of the trine in England, we glided from the thirteenth to the twenty-third conference, without particularly noticing such measures of the intervening conferences as bore upon this question. We will, therefore, just say here, that, in the fifteenth conference, or that of 1822, somewhat extended "regulations of the office of the ministry" were adopted. In the sixteenth conference, "the best mode of ordering the ministry" was again considered; and it was " *Resolved,* That this conference considers it to be agreeable to divine order, that the persons officiating in holy things be arranged in three degrees, such being the order that obtains in the heavens, which consists of three—a third, a middle and a first ; and in man, who consists of three constituent parts—the head, the body and the feet ; in each of which, also, there are three degrees of life : but that, nevertheless, the conference does not regard it practicable to establish this order at present ; it is, therefore, recommended to the consideration of future conferences." This conference also determined " that WHITE is the proper color for the dress which ministers of the new church should wear in their sacred ministrations." In the seventeenth conference, "the subject of the ordering of the ministry was entered upon," having been " pressed upon the attention of conference in a letter from Haslingden," as well as brought up by the consideration of matters left unfinished by the preceding conference : but nothing more was done than to refer the subject to a committee, consisting of the Rev. Messrs. Sibly, Hindmarsh, Noble and T. Goyder, to " sketch a plan," which was to be sent to the ministers of the church at Manchester, namely, the Rev. Messrs. Jones, Howarth and Pownall, who were appointed a committee to revise it—both committees being directed to communicate with each other thereon as often as they should find necessary. " Two forms of ordination drawn up by Mr. Hindmarsh were presented for consideration" to this conference, and " referred to the committee appointed to consider of the best mode for ordering the ministry." We learn from the letters to this conference, that a proposition came from Glasgow and Paisley, " that leaders of societies recognized by conference should be authorized to

4

administer both the sacraments, viz. baptism and the holy supper;" and that "the administration of the ordinance of baptism by unordained persons [which seems from this to have taken place thereabouts] is mentioned in the letters from those cities, as being extremely irregular." This shows why the conference was again and again called on ·and constrained to apply itself to the consideration of "the best mode of ordering the ministry."

We have not seen the Minutes of the Eighteenth General Conference. But in those of the nineteenth, we find the following: "The subject of the ordering of the ministry, which had engaged the attention of the last two conferences, at each of which committees of the ministers had been appointed to consider that subject and to report thereon, being resumed; but no report being presented by the last committee; the Rev. S. Noble stated that he had with him the minutes of the several meetings of such committees; which being read," the subject was referred, for further consideration, to the same committees, of London and Manchester, which had previously had it in charge; with additional authority given to each committee " to add to its number any other minister of the new church;" and an injunction to " present a report, containing the result of their deliberations, to the next conference." In the twentieth conference no report was made or received, and the subject was referred in precisely the same way—the resolutions to this effect being almost verbatim the same as in the previous two conferences, with the exception that the Rev. Mr. Sibly was made chairman of the London committee by the seventeenth, and the Rev. Mr. Hindmarsh chairman by the nineteenth and twentieth. And so probably the subject continued to be brought up and referred through the twenty-first and twenty-second conferences, until the Rev. Mr. Noble's able inquiry into it was submitted to, and acted upon, by the twenty-third, in 1830. From this time our sketch has been sufficiently minute and full.

And now we again see, that such men as Hindmarsh, Jones, Noble, Sibly, those " bright particular stars," among others of lesser magnitude, which, in the Lord's kind providence, were permitted first to shine out upon the new church in England, all deemed a trine of distinct and subordinate degrees in the ministry to be the true order of the New Jerusalem on earth. And it was not until certain later, still lesser, and, as we must think, fatuous lights arose in our external and visible church, that this order began to be called in question.

But the English General Conference has not deemed it expedient to carry this order out. The constitution of that body was suffered to begin with a defective fundamental organism of its ministry. Though the trine was acknowledged to be the true order, a ministry was formed without a trinal determination—as if an architect had begun to build a house without a plan, trusting to hap-hazard arrangements according to future circumstances, for both the laying of his foundation and the rearing of his superstructure,—because, " as there was a strong feeling against a trine, they thought it ought not to be established, lest separation from the general body of the church should be resorted to." Thus the external new church in England, while blossoming, had, from prudential considerations, a canker germ of ministerial disorder deposited in its seed vessels, which has grown with the growth, and strengthened with the strength of the expanding and enlarging plant, until now at last, in the necessary subsequent reactions of incoherent principles and parts at first blended in attempts to produce mere external harmonies and agreements, the sickly fruit seems ready prematurely to drop. For we see, by the Minutes of the Fortieth General Conference, just received, that that body, now in the fifty-eighth year since the first general conference was held in England, and in the thirty-third since the trine was formally declared to be the true order of its ministry, is called upon to determine "the distinction between ordaining and ordained ministers"—the only two quasi grades which *necessity* caused at first to be acknowledged— because it had never been determined before. Thus do we learn the momentous historical fact, that the assembled intelligence and wisdom of the whole new church in England, almost from the first, decrees a trine to be the true order of her ministry; yet deems it not advisable to act upon that order at the time when it is seen and declared to be the true one; but seems to establish and acknowledge two grades in her ministry, without so defining their functions and limiting their provinces, that it is necessary, *thirty-three years afterwards*, to inquire and determine what ought to be the distinction between them, because "it appears that the principles on which a distinction has heretofore been drawn between the ordaining minister and the other ministers, has never yet been declared"! And we now at length perceive, as the issue of temporizing policies, that systematic efforts are set on foot to bring about in the English General Conference, what has taken place in one of the conventions of this country, a *repudiation of the trine* as the true external order of the new church. Will the English General Conference falsify all its previous record, by such a repudiation? We shall await with much solicitude the answer which time alone can give to this question. At present it is surely not wrong for us to inquire, how it is that such opposite issues should now be likely to be brought about in that body. Nay, this is demanded by our object of giving an historical sketch of "the *present state*," as well as of "the rise and progress," of the question of the trine in England.

When this report, with its accompanying documents, is published and read, it will be seen that the Rev. William Mason, could not agree with his brethren on a committee of the thirty-fifth conference in reporting to the church in this country the opinion, as generally prevailing in England, that the trine is the true order of the new-church ministry. Whatever his views of the trine might then have been, and may now be, he could not endorse the views of the Rev. Messrs. Noble and Howarth as reported to the conference in 1830 and 1833. And when the Rev. Messrs. Smithson, Howarth and Bradley report substantially the same views as generally prevailing in England in 1844, in answer to the application of the General Convention of the new church in this country for information on that subject, he takes it upon himself to charge that committee with superstition in deducing the conclusions they had from the writings of Swedenborg; and communicates his own views to the Central Convention of the new church in America.

In 1846, Mr. Mason becomes president of the Thirty-Ninth General Conference, in which capacity he is appointed to address a letter to the General Convention, and to countersign, so as to give the full sanction and authority of the body over which he was presiding, to two other letters directed to be sent to the Central and Western Conventions, in this country. In former letters to our body, (Jour. No. VI., Ap. II., p. 19; and Jour No. VII., Ap. IV., p. 58,) he had been supposed to condemn, indirectly, the principles, order or proceedings of the General or Eastern* Convention; and in this letter to that body itself, he now seems desirous to make amends, by personal adulations as undignified as his former implied reprehensions had been severe. True, these reprehensions were only implied, and were directed as much against the english conference as the american convention. But the reprehensions were as, nay more, truly applicable to that body, than to the General Conference, or the Central Convention, because it had established the trine in a more obnoxious form—at least in a form which was supposed to involve very obnoxious principles; besides establishing it in, to us, a most obnoxious way. Yet although the Eastern Convention had established the trinal order of its ministry on, to say the least, *quite as* superstitious a basis as the Central Convention, and in certainly a more factitious or artificial way, no mention of this in the Journals of that body is deemed by Mr. Mason as a justifiable cause why the usual expressions of charity, courtesy, and good fellow-feeling should not be conveyed to it in the name of the General Conference, *without qualifications*. Nay, Mr. Mason may have seen in the Journal of the Seventeenth General Convention, (p. 6,) in a report to that body, which was *adopted, acted upon*, and embodied in the very record of its proceedings, as well as received, quite as real, though not so express, a slur upon his favorite child, the Conference Hymn Book, as he discovered in the report to only the *acting committee* of our convention, in Appendix I. to Journal No. VIII. (p. 22,) and only printed there, without being adopted or acted upon by the convention itself; yet he did not now, nor did the president of the General Conference, when that Journal of the General Convention was received in England, deem its contents so *uncourteous* as to justify his withholding the unqualified official sanction of the conference to a letter breathing sentiments of brotherly love and kindness to that convention in the following year. Yet Mr. Mason, for both these reasons, cannot countersign the excellent and most affectionate address to our convention by the Rev. Woodville Woodman, "but with the qualification set forth in the accompanying letter

* We use this latter appellative for the sake of distinction and not in disrespect. See Proceedings of Sixth An. Meet. of West. Con., Precursor, Vol. I., No. 13, p. 214—where it will be seen that the Rev. Thomas Worcester says he "was appointed by the Eastern Convention of 1837, to attend the Western Convention of 1838, and to confer with it on the subject of forming a general convention."

of the same date." This accompanying letter,* (see Ap. No. LII.,) couched, as our readers will see, in the most uncourteous, disrespectful and magisterial terms, reads a lecture to the Central Convention upon certain heinous departures from right states of mind, that are indicated in the recent Journal of its Proceedings, or its accompanying Reports—intimates that, as this Journal came to hand after the late conference had authorized Mr. Woodville to address our body in its name, the conference had not then had an opportunity of 'expressing its disapprobation of its contents, so that he felt called on to do so in its name now, and then sends us some resolutions, which he (God willing,) intends to submit to the next conference for the purpose of expressly arraigning and condemning the proceedings and principles of our convention, in its sixth annual meeting, before that general body of the church, in a land *foreign* to ours. ' Nor was Mr. Mason satisfied with sending this epistle to our convention. He endeavored to increase his *charitable* correction of us, by sending copies of it to the two other conventions in our country, where, in the painful antagonistic relations in which we ·have been obliged to stand to one of them, he probably imagined his castigation of us would afford pleasure. We will not stop here to stigmatize this letter of Mr. Mason to our body as it deserves. We will only say, it was uncalled for; because the Central Convention had not asked Mr. Mason for his opinions as the Eastern Convention had. It was unbecoming, because the General Conference has no supervisory control over the new church in America, and therefore its presiding officer should not, in its name, have taken the curule chair and brandished its rod over us. It was impertinent; because 'the church in America, or its divisions, not being subordinate to the church in England by any sort of ecclesiastical arrangement, Mr.,Mason, as its presiding officer, had no business to arraign any of the proceedings of our convention before the bar of the general body to which he belonged. And it was exceedingly indiscreet, to pick out a random passage from one of our reports, and magnify the individual sentiment of its writer into the studied intention of the whole convention, to throw contempt upon a work of the General Conference, when no such intention was entertained by even

* We pray the reader of this letter to the Central Convention, to compare its tone and spirit with the address of Mr. Mason to the Eastern Convention, and with his article in the Intellectual Repository for February, 1848, p. 58. How striking an illustration of the puritanic spirit of the commonwealth time in England, when men BUTCHERED their *fellow-countrymen* all the while they were *singing psalms to the Prince of Peace!* It is said by Cooper, in his Naval History of this country, that the·pirates who once infested our West India seas, were accustomed to engage in prayer to God before they, took a prize and massacred its crew. And what atrocities were not committed in the religious wars of Europe, with lip professions of exalted christian perfections. Alas! how true is it that the mere *science* of the celestial state, and the mere *intellectual* perception of what character that state requires in the church, are very different things from the *celestial state itself,* and the *perceptions* of its *simplicity!* Alas! alas! how easy it is for professed Newchurchmen to stab their brother under the fifth rib, at the very time they are saluting him with a kiss, and subtilely to assail the vital principles of their faith under the garb of extra pretensions to the simplicity of its love and the kindness of its peace making spirit!

the writer of the report himself, and much less by the body of which
he was a member. Had Mr. Mason been in any degree of that *celestial simplicity*, about which he discourses so eloquently in his late
address to the General Convention ; or had he been at all free from
those " coveted redundancies over and above the simple perceptions
of celestial love," of which he therein speaks ; he would have passed
by unnoticed this want of *courtesy*, so grievously complained of, as the
peccadillo of a spiritual youngling, which so venerable and venerated
a general body of the church as the General Conference might well
afford to overlook.

But we cannot—we ought not to—shut our eyes to what we
believe to be the truth. It was not the Central Convention, or its
errors, which were aimed at. Our body was indeed the target : but
we cannot resist the conviction that there was something behind,
which the shot was designed to hit, after we had been pierced. It
was *the order of the trine*, as established by the Eastern Convention,
and decreed to be true by the General Conference, which was to be
assailed through us as it had been for years in the conference itself.
Thus both the Eastern Convention and the General Conference were
to be flogged over our shoulders, if not shot through our body. Hence
neither the Eastern nor the Western Convention took any notice of
Mr. Mason's letter. They could not notice it without a most glaring
and unkind want of respect to us ; they could not publish it without
an equally glaring disrespect to themselves. . And we now see that
the General Conference too did not act upon the resolutions condemnatory of us, which Mr. Mason threatened, " *God willing*," to lay
before it. It has not published his letter to us, nor any part of his
report, as its last president, by which his rebuke of us was laid before
it. Thus it has not assumed his action, in the capacity of its president, as its own ; and we are left free to treat it with the respect
and affection which we have always felt for it, and to continue our
communications with it, as if no insults had been offered to us in its
high and venerable name.

We say the order of the trine was assailed through us. For proof of
this look at the resolutions, which Mr. Mason, in his letter to our body,
says he intends to lay before the Fortieth General Conference, and
compare their contents with what may easily be discerned to be his
sentiments on the same subjects, in the communications to the
Twenty-Sixth General Conference, which called forth the able
reports to that body in 1833. What those sentiments were, may be
gleaned from those reports (which see, Ap. Nos. XLVIII. and XLIX.);
and it cannot but be seen, in the comparison we suggest, that Mr.
Mason, by his letter, sent to all three of our conventions, to make
known " throughout the United States," "the sentiments generally
entertained in" England, purposely designed to mingle in our meal
the same leaven which had fermented the new church in his country,
and, by submitting his proposed resolutions to the conference of which
he was the presiding officer, with equal directness of purpose, designed
to agitate again in that body the question of the trine, with the end
of undoing what had been so often previously done in the way of its

settlement. The leaven has worked here, and the Western Convention, under the lead of certain *noves homines,* has repudiated the trinal order of its ministry. The same leaven is working in the Central Convention, under similar leadings. We shall not be surprised, if we discern, by and by, its workings in the Eastern Convention too. But now a faithful historical sketch of the present state of this question in the new church of England requires us to look at the Minutes of its last conference. Here we find Mr. Mason following up his purpose. In his capacity of late president, he reports the letter which he had written to our body, and of course submits to the body over which he had presided his resolutions, in which he tries to make it resolve, "that this conference, having reference to minute 49 of the Journal No. VIII. of the Central Convention, not received at the last conference, is of opinion," that said Central Convention has, for certain reasons, been guilty of a bad spirit and a great want of proper courtesy to this conference; and that the order of the trine, as this conference had previously deduced and determined it from the writings of Swedenborg, especially Coronis 17, is founded only on "superstitious conclusions sought to be established thereby." This, we say, is *virtually* the purport of Mr. Mason's resolutions; and we say he submitted* them to the fortieth conference—although the fact

* Our authority for this assertion is derived from an article, over Mr. Mason's initials, in No. 98 of the Intellectual Repository, or the number for February last, p. 49. In this article Mr. Mason lays before the church at large, what he had intended to lay before the General Conference in its last meeting, *his* views on the "trine in the church:" and in express allusion to this, the 129th minute of that meeting, he says, "The conference has requested the opinion of the societies on this proposition, and it seems perfectly fitting that *the originator of that proposition* should place the *general view which he takes* of the subject before the societies in the Magazine for their consideration, seeing that it so far found favor with the conference as to be intermediately entertained." This, surely, is clear enough in showing who the originator of the above proposition was.

We may also observe, in this article, unmistakeable proofs of the drift which we ascribe to this proposition: Mr. Mason not only reiterates, *as his,* the arguments which we have seen formerly advanced against the trine as declared to be the true order in England, but he expressly recommends for adoption by the General Conference, in its next meeting, that "new arrangement of the ministry on the most simple plan" by which the Western Convention in this country has decreed that "there is from henceforth to be *only one class* or *order* of *ministers* in its connection." We, in this country, who know who it was that led the Western Convention in this "new arrangement," this "*radical* and highly important change in its form," (see Jour. of 15th West. Con. p. 6,) can have no difficulty in seeing that this is but an echo of Mr. Mason's views, as set forth in his letter to us, across the Atlantic. Therefore, Mr. Mason, in endorsing this proceeding of the Western Convention, is but *seconding his own motion* in the General Conference. He is, in fact, seeking to bring about in *that* body too, such a new arrangement of its ministry as shall, in form as well as essence, *reject the trinal principle,* and substitute in its place "the *most simple* plan" of "*only one* class or order of ministers." This, probably, is deemed one form of that "celestial *simplicity*" —lost to us in the fall—which is to be restored in the "yea, yea, nay, nay," of the New Jerusalem, that is "intended to be a church of celestial genius." And probably Mr. Mason thinks the millenium is already come, when this *simplicity* or *oneness* in the arrangement of the new-church ministry is not to be seen in the light of *rational* investigation of what Swedenborg teaches from the Lord in the Word (although *Swedenborg says* this is the only way in which even spiritual truth—the spiritual sense of

that he did so does not appear on its minutes—because we presume
he could not have violated his virtual *oath* to that effect, Of course
the General Conference could not˙ pass those resolutions without
inscribing *false* on all its decisions respecting their subject matter, so ˙
the Word—can be seen by man or the church in a natural state)—is not to be seen by
"the talented and lengthened argumentation," which necessarily comes " of *evil*," (as,
for instance, Noble and Howarth's argumentation for the new-church
ministry repeatedly referred to here; but not, of course, Mr. Mason's own " variety and
ingenuity of subtle reasoning," on the materiality of the Lord's risen body, in his *high*
if not *ill* tempered answer to Mr. Noble on that subject)—is not to be seen in any such
lumen as this " legacy of the fall;" but is to be discerned in " the simple perceptions
of celestial love," " the brighter light of the wisdom of love," which, when it sheds " its
mild and safe glory upon the delighted vision of our *pliant* and *teachable* minds," will
enable us to assent to this "*most simple* plan" of "*only one* order" in our ministry,
without asking any *questions* of those " more active minds that take the lead among"
us, and give " tone and tendency to the proceedings" of the " general assemblies of the
Lord's church." But, for our part, as we have not by any means come through regeneration into this celestial state of simple perception, we need, we ask for, we demand
from Mr. Mason, and the other more active minds which are taking the lead in the
General Conference of England, a clearer *rational* demonstration than ·he· or any of
them have yet given us, from the Word and the writings of Swedenborg, that celestial
simplicity, in the external order of the New Jerusalem, will produce an arrangement of
her ministers in *only one* order instead of a *trine* of distinct grades or discrete degrees.
For our part, we think the new church does, in this respect, most clearly and expressly
teach *multiplicity* in *unity*, and not *simplicity* in *unity*. This latter is too *unitarian*
for us. We take our stand upon the universal law—" in God, infinite things are dis-
tinctly one." And on this ground assume that every *unity* must be a complex of
distinct constituents. We therefore hold to a *trinity* in the *unity* of the new-church
ministry, and not to any "*most simple* plan" of "*only one* order" in it. And until
Mr. Mason demonstrates to our rational mind from Swedenborg, that " *no good* reason
can be given" "for distinguishing and continuing the distinction, between ordaining or
other ministers," or between the *three* grades of a proper and suitable new christian
ministry, we shall declare and contend that he, in seeking to " obliterate˙ the distinction,"
in the General Conference, " as a *purely imaginary* one, as the Western Convention
has done," is aiming a blow at the essential order, and so at the very vitals, of the new
church as a visible body on earth!
And seeing that this is Mr. Mason's drift in the proposition above quoted. we cannot
but express our surprise, that the editor of the Intellectual Repository should append, to
his article just referred to, remarks, without any limitation, in " *confirmation* and *illustration* of the view taken of this subject in the above paper." The editor doubtless
intended to confirm and illustrate only what seemed to be Mr. Mason's argument, from
Coronis 17, that Swedenborg did not intend, in that passage, to sanction in the New
Jerusalem the episcopal order of the trine, as it has existed in the catholic church, and
in the protestant churches which have sprung from it. And here it gives us pleasure
to say, that, in this argument, we most fully agree with the editor in these remarks,
and so far with Mr. Mason. But we cannot agree with Mr. Mason in his argument for
a trine from Coronis 17, when it leads him to the implied conclusion that there is no
"good and practical reason for *distinguishing* between ordaining or other ministers,"
so that " the purely *imaginary*" distinction which has hitherto been established, may be
obliterated in the arrangement of new-church ministers, and a more simple arrangement
of them be made into " only *one* order," in which there shall be virtually *no distinction*
between them : for, in continuous degrees, as of more to less light, there is no *visible
limit*, as the " signs or tokens" of the degree of official function, scope of administration, and grade of subordination, by which alone ministers of a church can be arranged
in *trinal* order. (U. T. 680.) And it was to us a matter of inexpressible astonishment,
that a man of Mr. Mason's reputed intelligence, should *think* that he is arguing for a

far as they pertained to the question of the trine, for thirty-three years. Therefore those resolutions do not appear on the minutes as having been presented and acted upon. The conference gives them the silent go by: and "the correspondence, having been read, which the late president (in the exercise of the discretion committed to him during the time the conference is not sitting) entered into with the American Conventions; *resolved*, That it is not expedient specially to notice it further in the Minutes." Would that the late president, in the exercise of the discretion committed to him, had acted a little more discreetly! Would that he had waited until he had first submitted his resolutions to the General Conference, and permitted that body *to express for itself* the sentiments of the church in England in condemnation of our Journal and its contents! Would that he, "in the exercise of the discretion committed to him during the time the conference was not sitting," had, "from a regard to that *pacific policy*," which he had reason to believe the conference itself would have acted on, kept his resolutions to himself, and not suffered them to "pass" to this country, with their insulting, fermenting and disorganizing tendencies! But that would not have effected Mr. Mason's purpose of assailing the principle of a ministerial trine in the church in his own country, as well as in ours. From which purpose, he is not to be diverted by the failure of the conference to notice his resolutions, or his condemnation of us. Hence we find him submitting, or causing to be submitted, the following proposition, "which was included in the notices of motion in the secretary's circular," and which we extract from number 129 of the Minutes of the Fortieth General Conference:

trine, when he comes to such a conclusion! But our astonishment ceases when we see him *still* contending, that to assign to a lower grade of the clergy the administration of the rite of baptism, while a higher grade administers the rite of the holy supper—an order most clearly indicated in the Word, by the Lord's assigning baptism to his disciples, while he himself, though he baptized not, administered in instituting the supper— is a violation of the divine injunction not to put asunder what "God hath joined together." For, to our minds, it is an evidence of *very low intelligence* in the things of the Word and of the church, when a minister of more than twenty years' standing in our church cannot see, not only, (with Mr. Noble,) "that *that divine saying can have nothing to do with the subject*," but also that the Lord, who is God, *did himself*, when on earth, *actually separate these ordinances, instead of joining them together!*

In fine, we think that Mr. Mason, under the appearance of arguing for a trine of ecclesiastical uses, is really seeking to establish a simple unity or parity of ecclesiastical functionaries for their performance in the arrangement of ministers which is to constitute the external "ecclesiastical order" of our church. This, we are confident, is the drift of the proposition which he has moved in the General Conference. And we are not less sorry, than surprised, that the editor of the Intellectual Repository did not point this out, in a qualification of the remarks which he has made "to confirm and illustrate the view taken of this subject" in Mr. Mason's article on "The Trine in the Church." Surely every attentive reader of that article in this connexion must see that we have been justified by it in saying, Mr. Mason has *designed*, by his letter to us, and by his submission of this proposition to the General Conference, to agitate again in that body the question of the trine, with the expectation of bringing about at last a repudiation of the trinal arrangement of the new church ministry in that country as well as in this. And thus do we prove that the order of the trine was assailed through us.

The notice of motion was as follows:—

That it appears that the principle on which a distinction has heretofore been drawn between the ordaining ministers and the other ministers, has never yet been declared.

That the principle which ought to regulate the distinction between the two classes of ministers is this,—that the ordaining ministers on whom devolves the duty of carrying out the votes of the conference (that is, of the churches assembled by their ministers and representatives in the General Conference) consenting to new ordinations, ought to be persons of great experience in the pastoral office, and thence best able to advise the individuals whom they ordain, concerning the various points of duty and demeanor connected with the pastoral office.

That every minister shall become an ordaining minister after having officiated during twenty years from the date of his ordination; but that no period during which he shall not have been actively employed, shall be counted as part of the twenty years.

That the application for the removal of the name of a minister, to the list of ordaining ministers, shall be made by the society of which he is the minister, or to which he last ministered, and that a statement shall accompany such application under the minister's hand, declaring that he has officiated during the prescribed period, and specifying the societies to which he has officiated, and the respective periods during which he has officiated to each society.

That it be optional to any minister, on the removal of his name to the list of ordaining ministers, to apply to an ordaining minister with a view to the celebration of such removal, by the performance of the service in the Liturgy, called the "Consecration Service," according to his individual view of the utility or propriety of such celebration.

That [as no one can pretend for a moment, that the performance or non-performance of the "Consecration Service," can increase or diminish the suitability of an ordaining minister for the discharge of his peculiar duty,] the non-performance of that service, shall not be deemed any bar to an ordaining minister discharging the duty of ordaining any person whom he may be called to ordain, under the authority of the conference, and according to the conference regulations on that head.

Nobody can mistake the drift of this proposition. No one can fail to see whence it comes and whither it tends. That it involves principles against the trine as previously determined to be the true order of the ministry by the General Conference, no one can be so blind as not to see. There is certainly *natural* perception enough to see this, however little there may of that *celestial* perception, which Mr. Mason thinks ought to exist in the general bodies of our church, and which he probably requires to see that the distinction, between the ordaining and ordained ministers, on which he founds his proposed order, is drawn from "the testimony of the Holy Word and of the new-church writings." But he, doubtless, thinks that his observation to the General Convention, in his late address to that body,—"when general assemblies of the Lord's church take place, the tone and tendency of their proceedings must mainly and essentially depend upon the tone and tendency of the more active minds that take the lead amongst them,"—must apply to the conference of which he is a member, as well as to any other general assembly of the church. Hence he must regard the decisions of the General Conference hitherto upon the questions of the trine in the ministry, as nothing more than effects brought about by certain more active minds that happened to have the lead in it when those decisions were made. And he probably imagines that now, when certain other active minds are taking the lead in that body, with different views of the trine, it will be quite as easy to lead that general assembly of the Lord's church to essentially, if not formally, opposite decisions of this question.

The fortieth conference did not act upon the motion, of which it had been thus notified : but " *Resolved*, That the consideration of this subject be postponed till the next conference, and that the opinions of the various societies be requested thereon." We shall, therefore, wait for the Minutes of the Forty-First General Conference. We expect then to see, whether that body, as the representative of the whole church in England, can "blow hot and blow cold" on this important subject—whether it is indeed true, that the members of this body, for thirty-three years, have had no rational convictions in their own minds of the truth of its decisions, but have been only *led* to their conclusions by the more active minds which happened to "take the lead amongst them"—and thus whether they can be brought to decide in their next assembling, that they were wrong in all their previous decisions of the question of the trine, by those certain other more active minds which are now the influential leaders of their councils. Whatever may be their decisions, we beseech them to allow us to hope, that they will not consummate the rejection of a trinal order of the ministry, without the most thorough investigation, and the most satisfactory demonstration, of what the Word and the writings of the church teach on this subject ; so that whatever they do, may be done understandingly and after the fullest consideration. Constituted as we are to act in *freedom* according to *reason*, we implore that the decisions of this vexed question which the church in England may now make, shall be seen to rest on a clear and stable *rational* basis. May the Lord guard his church, now in still her beginning, from any more conceits of *celestial perception*, in determining what is the proper *relation* of her ministers to her people or to one another ! Knowing that "that is first which is natural, and afterwards that which is spiritual;" hence that "the unerring judgment of 'yea, yea; nay, nay,'" which belongs to the celestial state, must be yet very, very far from the visible bodies of our church in this *natural* world; and that even in the spiritual world, the Lord takes especial care lest "truth should instantaneously be so confirmed as to leave no doubt concerning it," so that "it is according to the laws of order" even there, "to think and consider whether a thing be so, and *to collect reasons*, and thereby to bring that truth *rationally* into the mind" (A. C. 7298)—we do most sincerely deprecate any settlement of this question now by any other decision than the stroke of the *rod of iron*, which, in the hand of the man-child, born of the woman in the wilderness, is to *rule* our *nations*, and to dissipate our fallacies as the vessels of a potter are broken to shivers ! In short, we implore our english brethren, when they shall next settle this question in their general conference, that they will commend them-

selves to us as *wise* men, and so found their building of external order
on "the *rock*," that our church may no longer be shaken, as it has
been, by the tempests, which can only beat dangerously upon those
structures that rest upon the *sand!*

We have now faithfully, we believe, traced the question of a ministerial trine from its rise, through its progress, to its present state in
England. And in final review of all that has been here shown and
seen, we have but a few concluding observations to make. It does not
appear, from the history of the new church in England, that "*before*
any idea was agitated about a trine in the ministry, such a trine did
exist." It does not appear that *after* that idea has been agitated in
that country for more than thirty years, such a trine exists now. It
does appear that this idea, as a spiritual conception of the clearest,
strongest and best minds of the new church in that country, has been
struggling in gestation and agonizing in birth, against the most
strenuous, persevering and even obstinate oppositions to its being
brought into corresponding ultimate form and order. And so far is
it from being true, in either the early or late exemplification of the
external order of the english church, that a trine "had actually come
into *spontaneous* existence without any external contrivance;" we in
fact see it has been from the first uniformly declared to be inexpedient to carry this order out in the english ministry, because the time
had not come for it yet; and even now there are but *two* instead of
three grades acknowledged; and it is found necessary to determine
what is the *distinction* between these *two*, because that distinction has
never heretofore been declared. Indeed so far has a trine of *ministers*
—*regular* ministers—been from coming into *spontaneous* existence in
the new church in England, the whole history of it shows, that the
spontaneous efforts of professing members of the new church there
have tended to an administration of the most holy sacraments of our
church *without them:* and the attempt to bring about this *disorder* by
"external contrivance," has all along *forced* the general bodies of
the church to agitate the idea of a trine, with the end of settling it
by deductions from the Word and the writings of the church. Even
now, in this comparatively late and advanced period of the church,
so far are we from discerning that "such a trine" does now spontaneously exist; we, on the contrary, behold, with pain, systematic
efforts set on foot to break up even the imperfect approaches to a
trinal arrangement of ministers which the english church has been
struggling for thirty-three years to make. What was the order of the
english new church from 1788, when Mr. Hindmarsh, the first minister, was ordained, to 1813, when the idea of a trine seems first to
have been agitated in it, we have had no documents to show: but we
conclude that the ministry in that period had not come spontaneously
into a trine, or there would have been no necessity of suggesting that
order subsequently, and of expressly providing in its ordination, that
it was "not intended to have any retrospective operation, by interfering with the ordinations which had already taken place in the new
church, but to be considered binding in all *future* cases." And why
should it have been deemed "expedient," in 1814, "as speedily as

possible to *establish* these *three* orders," if "such a trine" "had actually come into spontaneous existence" before, and "without any external contrivance?" In this country, the case, in this respect, was somewhat different, as we shall presently see. But we have as yet no historical evidence to show that a trine has ever come into full and clearly defined existence, either spontaneously or factitiously, in England.

IV. AS TO A TRINE IN THE MINISTRY OF THE NEW CHURCH IN AMERICA.

We at first supposed that all we had to write on the history of the question of the trine in the ministry of the new church, might be embraced in one topic. But the sketch of that question as agitated and determined in England, has so extended itself, that it seems best to put the history of its rise, progress and present state in the new church of America, under a distinct head.

In America, as in England, the question of a trine was not agitated when the new-church ministry was first instituted. Indeed there was no original institution of a general ministry in this country as in that. There was, indeed, somewhat of an original institution of an *american* new-church ministry. But there seems to have been an acknowledgment that a general new-church ministry had originated in England, so as to have its root and stock there; and the ministry here has been deemed the sprouting of a bud inoculated from that stock. Still there was not a regular and formal translation of ecclesiastical power or authority from that country to this. Circumstances would not admit of such a translation. The new church was so small and feeble in her beginnings in this country, that only measures for the support of public worship in a single and very small society could at first be carried out. Hence the institution of a ministry in only a lower and simpler degree could be made at first. A minister to conduct the forms and ceremonies of public worship in a single society was all that was first thought of. And of course the idea of originating a general ministry for the gradual establishment and unlimited extension of the church in this and all lands, could not be at all entertained. A ministry of a more general character, and having higher degrees of rank, or wider scopes of administration, even in this country, could only arise gradually, as the receivers of the church's doctrines became more numerous, and the growth of her visible body increased. At first, all that could be done, and all that was aimed at, was to obtain, or provide, the administration of the holy sacraments, and other ordinances of an external church, for those few persons who first received the doctrines, and found themselves in sufficient numbers to be "of one accord together in one place" in the discharge of the duties, or in the fruition of the enjoyments, of public worship according to the principles of the new faith. In the providence of the Lord the circumstances for forming a regular ministry first occurred in the city of Baltimore and state of Maryland. And it would seem as if the first society was formed here in consequence of influences vibrated from the general conference of the new church in England. But let us take a brief survey of the rise and first establishment of the new church in this country.

We have seen that the First General Conference, which was held in London in 1789, recommended, "to all the readers and lovers of the theological works of Emanuel Swedenborg, both in England and other countries, to form themselves into societies distinct from the old church, and to meet together as often as convenient, to read and converse on the said writings, and to open a general correspondence for the mutual assistance of each other." This was the thirtieth of the thirty-two resolutions passed unanimously by that conference. The first echo to these recommendations from this side of the Atlantic, was heard from Halifax, in Nova Scotia, then, as now, a British possession. It is found in a letter dated November 19, 1791, signed by Joseph Russell, and printed in "The New Jerusalem Journal," edited and published by Robert Hindmarsh in London in 1792. Mr. Russell says—"Agreeable to your thirtieth Resolve of Conference held in Great East-Cheap 1789, we have separated ourselves from the old church, by fully embracing the doctrines of the New Jerusalem Church, as now first organized by you. We therefore, though small in number, wish to hold a correspondence with your society, as it will serve to strengthen and excite us to pursue, with more order, those pure revealed truths contained in the writings of the Honourable Emanuel Swedenborg. We know it will afford you pleasure to hear what progress the church is making in any part of the world, and we therefore shall now inform you, that we have for more than six years met together for the sake of reading, and conversing on the subjects unfolded in the important writings of Emanuel Swedenborg; and since the publication of your Liturgy for the New Church, we have in every respect conformed thereto in public worship, and read some part or other of the Theology, forenoon and afternoon every sabbath-day. We likewise meet every Friday evening, for the further improving ourselves in the knowledge of the said truths, with psalmody and christian conversation. Also, agreeable to the twenty-second Resolve, we have formed ourselves by baptism into a church, and have since baptized our children, and thus hope to increase by degrees. We shall be very glad to receive any further instructions, which you may think necessary and useful for us."

We thus learn that the first meetings for social worship according to the doctrines of the New Jerusalem upon the american continent, were held in Halifax, Nova Scotia. In fact we learn that the receivers of those doctrines had met together for the sake of reading and conversing upon the subjects unfolded in the writings of Swedenborg for more than six years prior to November, 1791, that is, for about four years before the first general conference of the new church was held in London. Probably early receivers of our doctrines in · England, migrating to this continent, had, like birds of passage, brought the seeds of truth to this country, before the church had assumed any organized form in that. And so soon as a general conference in the mother country had projected a form of external order, its recommendations were immediately conformed to by receivers in her colonies, because they were only remote nerves of feeling and action whose nervous centre was still in England. We also learn that these receivers in Nova Scotia formed themselves into a church by baptism, and afterwards baptized their children. And it seems they did this without a regular minister—which they could hardly have at so early a time, and in so remote a place, where they were so " small in number." Probably they thought and acted as some of their brethren in England did at even a later period, and supposed that a church could exist without a minister, or could ordain a minister for itself, or could authorize its leader to perform the sacraments of baptism and the supper, as well as to preach and teach, without his having any direct or formal commission from the Lord, by the sign of the translation of his holy spirit. In short, they probably acted on the supposition that lay baptism was of equal authority and validity with clerical baptism. And hence they virtually concluded that a church could be formed and exist without a clergy. If so, they widely differed in opinion on this subject from the first instituters of our church in the United States. And it is, perhaps, a striking proof of the error of the one opinion, and of the truth of the other, that the new church has made so little, if any, advance in the British Possessions of North America, in the more than fifty years which have elapsed since this beginning of it there, while, during the same period, it has, comparatively, grown so much, and extended so widely, in our portion of the continent.

The brethren in Halifax say they formed themselves into a church by baptism, and afterwards baptized their children, " agreeable to the twenty-second resolve" of the First General Conference. This makes it important that we should know what were the terms of that resolve, and whether it set forth a recommendation to receivers in distant countries to form themselves into churches by baptism without a clergy. The twenty-second resolution of the first conference is in these words :—" Resolved unanimously, That it is the Opinion of this Conference, that as Baptism in the Old Church is a Baptism into the Faith of Three Gods, between which Faith and Heaven there can be no Conjunction; so Baptism in the New Church, being a Baptism into a Faith of One God, between which Faith and Heaven there is Conjunction, is highly necessary, inasmuch as the Person baptized thereby takes upon him the Badge and Profession of genuine Christianity, and is at the same time inserted among Christians even in the Spiritual World. —— It is therefore recommended to all who desire to become Members of the New Jerusalem Church, to be baptized, both themselves and their Children, in the Faith of that Church; and in case they have already been baptized in the Faith of the Old Church, to be re-baptized in the Faith of the New." In this we observe nothing like a recommendation to receivers of the doctrines in distant countries to form a church by baptism without a new-church clergy regularly instituted distinctly from that of the old church. The recommendation to them " to form themselves into Societies distinct from the Old Church," is set forth in the thirtieth resolution before quoted, and only specifies the purposes of meeting for reading and conversing on the writings, and corresponding for mutual assistance. And the General Conference could not have recommended any to form a church without a clergy, because the doctrines and canons of the New Jerusalem do most distinctly and expressly teach, that the Lord's holy spirit, by which alone the church can be formed on earth, "passes by men to men, and in the church,'especially by the clergy to the laity"—"proceeds from the Lord by the clergy·to the laity by preaching, according to the reception of the doctrine of truth thence, and also by the sacrament of the holy supper, according to the repentance exercised before receiving it"—is received by the clergy in their inauguration with the sign or representation of its transfer—and operates in and by them "the divine virtues of illustration, perception, disposition and instruction." Therefore this attempt to begin the formation of the new church in the British Possessions of North America, by baptism, before a clergy was formed distinctively from that of the old church to administer this and the other sacrament, was irregular; and there was no right to expect that the new church would grow, spread, or "increase by degrees" in this country from such a beginning as this. But it was otherwise in the United States of América.

Among the receivers of the new-church doctrines residing or sojourning in London about the time when the questions of establishing the New Jerusalem in a visible form distinct from the old christian church, and of instituting a ministry for that purpose, were agitated there, was one James Glen. This gentleman became a resident of Demarara in South America, whither he migrated, as others did to North America. From thence, he, "at his own expense, made two voyages to Europe, in order to purchase as many of the writings as he could possibly obtain in England, Germany and Holland, which he dispersed through various parts of North and South America." (N. J. Mag., Lond., April, 1790, No. IV., p. 175.) We have no records to show when Mr. Glen left the eastern for this western continent: nor can we tell whether his personal intercourse with the new church in London was prior to emigration from Europe, or during one of his two voyages thither from Demarara. Of the fact of such personal intercourse we have proof in his own words. For we find him addressing the new church in London, in a letter under the date of February 14, 1787, and saying, "I beg leave again to say, that I never said any thing to the New Church in London, which I do not more and more see the *truth* of." Afterwards, in another letter, dated June 1, 1788,—the very day on which the first ordination of Mr. Robert Hindmarsh, as a minister of the new church, "by the Lord's auspices," took place in the first place of worship opened ·in Great East-Cheap, London,—he says, "The Apocalypsis Explicata confirms more and more whatever I said to the Society concerning the necessity of divine truth, and also the necessity of embracing divine truth unadulterated, that is, altogether distinct, separated and removed from the Old Church." And he closes this letter with—"I heartily wish the Society may increase and multiply, and that speedily :

every member will please accept my kindest affections, and I remain
its willing servant, and its meanest member." We are aware that
these sentences do not prove Mr. Glen's *personal* intercourse with the
new church in London, because he might have *said* what he formerly
did to his brethren there by letters from Demerara, as he makes these
more recent communications; but, taken in connection with the facts,
that he went from England, and returned thither for books, they lead
fairly to the presumption that those former communications were
made in person. The probability is, that Mr. Glen was among the
first receivers of the doctrines in England, that he resided in London
and became a member of the society for the propagation of those
doctrines which was instituted there in the year 1783, and that he
afterwards came to this continent as a sort of volunteer missionary
for their propagation here. The society which he here addresses as
the " New Church in London," and of which he signs himself the
" meanest member," was unquestionably the one above specified,
which was instituted in 1783, and styled " *The London Universal
Society for Promotion of the New Church.*" Other members of this
society were avowed propagandists of the principles of the new
church in foreign lands. To the members of that society, in conjunction with certain receivers of the doctrines in Sweden, confessedly
belong the singular honor of having originated the idea of a society
or colony in Africa for the suppression of the slave trade. And we
have it on record that one of them, a Mr. Robert Jackson, " went out
from England in the month of October, 1790, with the firm and
laudable resolution to introduce the doctrine of truth among the
Negroes in the West Indies." He went to the Island of Jamaica,
one of the dependencies of England; and in a letter, dated Kingston,
27th of January, 1791, he gives an account of the slaves in these
words :—" As to the slaves, upon every inquiry, I find that they are
as quiet as ever they were previous to the attempts made for their
emancipation; and I am convinced that any sudden alteration, would
prove more injurious than beneficial to them. A member of the New
Church knows that an immediate removal of *evil* and *false* is not
possible; that to attempt it would be destructive of the individual.
It holds good in every respect as to nations and people. As far as
lays in my power, with the blessing of our Lord, I will endeavor to
introduce among them the *True Christian Religion.*"* Now it is

* To this the editors of the " New Jerusalem Magazine," published in London in
1790–91, by " several members" of the forenamed society, and from which the above
has been extracted, append the following note : " It may be expedient to observe here,
that the *Emancipation from Slavery* is quite different from the *Abolition of the Slave
Trade.* which may take place independent of the former, which requires a previous
preparation with respect to the improvement of the intellectual faculties of the negroes,
before it can take place." It has seemed to us right to state these things here, that the
early members of our church in England may not be judged obnoxious to the charge of
having been *Abolitionists*, in any thing like the, as we think, justly odious sense of this
appellative. The immediate abolition of the *slave trade*, and the immediate abolition
of *slavery*—without regard to the previous intellectual, moral and spiritual preparation
of the slaves for the right use and lasting enjoyment of freedom—are two very different
things !

5

probable that Mr. James Glen was some such a new-church propagandist as this Mr. Robert Jackson. He was a man of learning, known to have been versed in the Hebrew and Latin, and probably in other ancient languages. We do not know that he was by profession a clergyman. But he was a theologian, and devoted himself to the propagation of the doctrines of the new church by public lecturing. It is quite probable that the first receivers of our doctrines in England, who had sufficient learning and ability, all considered themselves, before any regular ministry was instituted, a sort of volunteer or militia clergy. Hence the first society of the new church in London tried all its members as to their preaching abilities, and actually " had eight preachers who regularly officiated " for it at or about the same time. This was in the early part of 1788. But Mr. Glen had left England in 1784. And it is quite likely that, when he was in England, the first receivers of the new-church doctrines had the custom of administering or taking the sacraments among themselves, as well as—such of them as were able—preaching or lecturing in public. Hence the course of the brethren in Nova Scotia was probably nothing more than a continuance of a custom which they had previously observed in England. And hence we find Mr. Glen, in another letter to the new church in London, dated February 4, 1789, conveying the following information : " I have seen Mr. Blatchy and Mr. Mosson. They both continue steady in the truths of the New Church. Sunday, August 3, 1788, Mr. Blatchy, Mr. Lincoln Rogers, Mr. Andrew Shanks, and I, met in Mr. Blatchy's house, where, after Messrs. Rogers and Shanks were baptized into the New Church, we four received the Holy Supper together, which was all done after the form made use of in London on July 31, 1787."

The facts here stated are not a little important in an historical point of view. By Doc. No. LI., in our Appendix, it may be seen that the ordination of ministers in the new church first took place in London in 1788. It was on Sunday, the first of June in that year. But Mr. Glen informs us, above, that a form for the administration of the holy supper was "made use of in London on July 31, 1787"—ten months before. This, therefore, establishes the fact, that the sacraments were administered, according to a form of the new-church faith in England, prior to the first ordination of ministers there, " by the divine auspices of the Lord." Of course, the presumption is, that the first receivers of the doctrines, such of them as were qualified for it, took upon themselves the discharge of the duties of the ministerial office, or performed those duties for themselves in a mere lay capacity. Probably the great exigencies of a merely incipient state of the church made this irregular proceeding permissible from necessity. But we cannot think that there could then, or can ever, be any necessity for *beginning* a church *wrongly*. The only possible just plea, which is conceivable to us, for this beginning of a church by this administration of its sacraments without a ministry to represent the Lord in them, is the imagination that the taking of such external representative sacraments is *needful to salvation*. This, we know, is the conceit of the Romanists and other Old-church Christians. But,

as the new church now teaches us that a man may be saved by internal
worship alone, whenever he is placed in such circumstances as make
it impracticable for him to engage in the corresponding external worship, (see A. C. 1175,) we cannot see that there was any necessity
for the first receivers of our doctrines to form·a church by instituting
baptism and a supper, or an external worship, without a regularly
ordained, or consecrated, or commissioned priesthood or ministry of
the Lord for its orderly administration—although the writings of our
church do also, in the above cited and other places, most expressly
and strenuously insist upon the importance and necessity of an external church.   We believe that the Lord's example should have been
followed in this: and as he, in establishing the first christian church,
appointed apostles, that is ministers or servants *sent* by him from
himself for this purpose, and "through whom," as Swedenborg expressly says, he in fact effected it; and as he, in establishing the New
Jerusalem on high, as the means of its descent from him out of heaven
to earth, again called and commissioned the same apostles to preach
his "everlasting gospel" anew throughout the spiritual world; therefore, we think the very first thing to have been done in establishing
the New Jerusalem on earth, was to appoint, ordain or consecrate a
ministry, to preach that same gospel anew throughout this natural
world, as well as to administer her holy sacraments.   For the sole
end and object of establishing a church on earth is to effect thereby
the *conjunction* of men with angels, and, through them, with the
Lord; and this " cannot otherwise be given," (Ap. Ex. 475,) than by
baptism, and the holy supper, and the written Word, and ministers
of them and preachers of it, as *representative* mediums of the Lord's
holy spirit to men.   And that it is impossible for this *conjunction*
with God, and therefore man's salvation,—for Swedenborg expressly
says, " salvation is that very conjunction,"—to be given through the old
christian church or its faith, and therefore through its sacraments
which involve that faith, or its clergy who preach it, must, we feel
sure, be manifest to every one who reads and receives as authority the
tenth and last chapter of Swedenborg's " Canons of the New Church."
Consequently, we cannot think that it was right, or admissible, for the
first receivers of our doctrines to begin the new church, either in
England, or in America, or any where else, by instituting its preachings, its sacraments, or any of its external worship, without a regularly
appointed priesthood or ministry.   Still the fact stares us in the face,
and we must record it.

   For aught we now know to the contrary, Mr. James Glen, a native
of Scotland, a resident of England, and subsequently of Demerara in
South America, was the first to usher the New Jerusalem, as an
external church, upon this western continent.   And we have advanced
the above details to show that he did so in the virtual capacity of a
preacher or minister of her faith.   He baptized and virtually administered the holy supper, in Demerara, in August 1788.   This was
before the First General Conference was held in London, namely, in
April 1789.   Therefore, it was not in consequence of the recommendation of that conference, as the procedure in Halifax was.   And, in

fact, the doctrines of the new church were proclaimed in America by Mr. Glen about four years before the first conference was held, and about three years before the first ordination of ministers took place in England.

If the reader will turn to Newchurchman, Vol. I., p. 70, he will there see our first Document for New-church History. There, in the note on that page,—ascertained from the original records in the Library of the Philadelphia Athenæum, by the writer of this report, then editor of the Newchurchman,—the fact will be found recorded, "that the Doctrines of the New Jerusalem were promulgated by public lecturing in America first in Philadelphia, on Saturday Evening, the fifth day of June, in the year of our Lord's first advent 1784." Miss Bailey's Letter will there show, also, that the first person who thus promulgated those doctrines was Mr. James Glen. It will be further learned that he was probably a native of Scotland,—the name, indeed, indicates this,—"though he had resided many years in England." And thus it will be seen that Mr. Glen, in the next year after the institution of "the London Universal Society for Promotion of the New Church," of which we have heard him acknowledge himself a member, was proclaiming the doctrines of the new church in Philadelphia. And this was four years before we hear of him in Demerara, and about five years before he tells us he baptized and administered the holy supper there. The conclusion is, that he first came to America from England with the purpose of propagating the new-church doctrines here—that he came to North, before he went to South, America—and that it was subsequent to his delivering a course of lectures in Philadelphia in June 1784, that he made his two voyages to purchase books for distribution on this side of the Atlantic. Probably his first trip this way, made part of his first voyage.

A further reference to Miss Bailey's Letter shows us, that the first permanent receivers of our doctrines in America, were those in Philadelphia, who received them from books brought in a box consigned to a Mr. Bell for Mr. Glen. These arrived after Mr. Glen's departure from Philadelphia; and as they were never called for by him, and as his consignee died shortly after, they were sold at the public sale of the consignee's effects. At this sale Mr. Francis Bailey purchased all the english editions of Swedenborg's books; and, as is well known, became the first and most active man in promulgating in this country the doctrines which they contained. Between the years 1787 and 1796, he published the works entitled The Universal Theology and Conjugial Love; and there is hardly a receiver of any years in this part of our country now, who cannot trace his reception of the doctrines to the perusal of one or other of those two works, or to some smaller ones printed and published by the same person.

Those who first received the doctrines in this country, either from Mr. Glen's lectures or his books, met at Mr. Francis Bailey's house, in Philadelphia, for conversation on the doctrines. This occurred in 1784. And this, therefore, is the time and place to which we might have traced the beginning of social new-church worship in America, if this had appeared to be any thing more than merely a friendly and informal meeting of persons of congenial minds, to converse on theological matters, without assuming any thing like the organized form of a church society. The receivers in Halifax had held similar meetings about the same time, that is in 1785; but they made what they supposed and intended to be the formal organization of a church in 1791, which was prior to any similar organization any where else, because Mr. Glen's procedure, in Demerara, in 1788, was evidently a transient thing, and not done for the purpose of forming a permanent church, which was expected " to increase by degrees" as this in Halifax was. Hence we have said the first meetings for social *worship*, according to the doctrines of the New Jerusalem, upon the american continent, were held in Halifax, Nova Scotia.

About 1793–4 " the little society in Philadelphia" " began to gather some strength, and assume a form," when " Mr. Ralph Mather and family came to reside in this country." He, as we have seen, was among the first preachers of the new church that were appointed by the first society which was formed in London. Dr. Duché, an episcopal clergyman, officiating in Philadelphia before. the revolution, and flying to England during that struggle, returned to this country about the same time that Mr. Mather came. Dr. Duché was known to be a receiver of the new-church doctrines, though he never openly preached them. His daughter married the Rev. William Hill, who came to America in the year 1795, and, by preaching in old-church pulpits, as well as distributing the works of Swedenborg, was eminently instrumental in disseminating the doctrines of the new church in this country. He placed a latin copy of the Arcana Cœlestia in the library of Harvard University, at Cambridge, near Boston. And from this, as a seed for a while hidden beneath the cold clods of winter, has at last sprung those prosperous growths of our church which we now behold in Massachusetts and other parts of New England.

But some time before this, the luminous point of new-church light which was first lit up in Philadelphia, soon shot its rays to Maryland and Virginia. The vehicles of its conveyance were the publications of Mr. Francis Bailey, or the books and pamphlets which he and others now began to import from England. In this way the Minutes and other printed documents of the first general conferences were brought to Baltimore. And by these the first impulses were given to the regular formation of an external church and ministry in this country.

In " The Maryland Journal and Baltimore Advertiser," printed by W. Goddard and James Angell, and published April 17, 1792, there is a communication, dated " Baltimore, April 3, 1792," with the signature " A. B.", which states the following facts. On the Saturday previous a hand-bill was circulated announcing that, on the next day, a gentleman would preach, at the court house, on the *doctrine of the New Jerusalem Church*. Novelty and curiosity induced a good many to attend the meeting thus announced. , The Rev. Mr. Wilmer read a form of prayer and worship to Jesus Christ as God, and delivered a discourse from the eighth and ninth verses of the second chapter of St. Paul's Epistle to the Colossians. As the doctrines preached by Mr. Wilmer seemed, to some that heard him, to contradict the fundamental tenants of Christians for above seventeen hundred years, they were astonished, and applied to such of their neighbors as were competent to give it, for more particular information respecting the doctrines of the New Jerusalem. A summary of the doctrines of this new church was put into the hands of one of those inquirers, who sent it to the printers of the above named newspaper, "to publish for the consideration of the inhabitants of this town." The printers of said newspaper accordingly published a fair statement of the creed or articles of faith of the new church. And thus did the New Jerusalem seem to *begin* her descent in Baltimore.

An account of this beginning was communicated to the brethren in England by Mr. Christian Kramer, in a letter addressed to Mr. Robert Hindmarsh, and dated "North America, Baltimore Town, April 10, 1792." From this letter we learn that Mr. John Cooper, residing on Fell's Point, and a Mr. Boyer, were, probably, the first receivers of the new-church doctrines in or about Baltimore. From the former Mr. Kramer borrowed a copy of Mr. Hindmarsh's edition of the True Christian Religion. And these three, stigmatized as "*Swedenborgers*," began the work of propagation. At first they were violently opposed; but, notwithstanding, they increased in numbers, till, in 1792, they were encouraged to open a correspondence with their brethren of the same faith in England, with the avowed object of procuring aid "in building a church." It appears that their acquaintance with the brethren in England was brought about by magazines received through Mr. Francis Bailey of Philadelphia. There is no doubt that the books which first conveyed the doctrines to Baltimore, were some of those belonging to Mr. Glen, which Mr. Bailey bought at the sale of his consignee's effects. And we see it distinctly stated, that the Baltimoreans were stimulated in their efforts to establish the church by reading the Minutes of the Third General Conference, held in London in 1791. We therefore presume that the new church took its rise in Baltimore from impulses transmitted from England through Mr. Glen's operations in Philadelphia.

We further learn, from Mr. Kramer's letter, that those professing the doctrines of the New Jerusalem Church who formed themselves into a society under the lead of Mr. James Wilmer, were twenty-two in number. He says, "Mr. James Wilmer, a clergyman of the episcopal church, has received the doctrines, and opened the church the first day of April, in the court house of this town, to a large concourse of people." This fixes the precise day when the new church first appeared in a visible form in these United States, and states the number of persons who formed the first society. We also learn that the first minister was a clergyman of the episcopal church, and that the form used by him in opening the church was the liturgy, with the hymn book composed by the Rev. Joseph Proud, a copy of which had been furnished by Mr. Robert Carter, "living at Nomony

Hall, Westmoreland County, Virginia," and was subsequently reprinted in Baltimore. It is further stated that the "Life and Death of Swedenborg, with the Nine Queries, was reprinted there by Samuel and John Adams—the latter of whom was a member of the new church."

The facts stated by Mr. Kramer in his individual capacity, were officially communicated to the new church in England, with more precision and fulness, by the following documents:

I.

Extract of a Letter from the Rev. Mr. J. Wilmer, of Baltimore in Maryland, to R. Hindmarsh.

State of Maryland, Baltimore, April 23, 1792.

DEAR SIR,

As preacher in the New Jerusalem Church, the first formed within the United States of America, I take the liberty to address you and the society through you. We have had vast trials, but the Kingdom of our God being stronger than the power of darkness, we trust, through the *divine humanity*, and doubt not but we shall prevail. I was some time at Christ Church College, Oxford, though an American born; and for years past have been not satisfied with the old church. In a most wonderful manner the doctrines of the Honorable E. Swedenborg falling into my hands, I very soon became a sincere and zealous convert to the heavenly doctrines, and, by permission, opened them in the court house of this town the first Sunday in the present month, from Coloss. ii. 8, 9, to a very crowded and learned audience; and my proceedings were announced in the next paper published in this town, with every degree of satisfaction, considering it at once striking at the errors that had been so long established. My next discourse was the Sabbath following, to an uncommon audience, from 1 John, iv. 16. The third was from Gen. xviii. 21 : this and the first will be shortly published by particular desire. The body of the church rests here with four worthy and respectable characters, now a standing committee for three months to come, and all your *official* information will be pleased to be directed to them, to the care of Mr. Henry Didier, or Mr. Robert Mickle, merchants, Baltimore, Maryland.

I forgot to mention that I was a regular ordained clergyman by the late Dr Terrick, bishop of London, and have now cast my everlasting all in the Heavenly Jerusalem. Our numbers at present are but small, and few of us rich. But all things are possible with the Lord; and as the heavenly seed, we believe, has taken deep root in this soil, we trust ere long to see a glorious temple reared to the alone God, the Lord Jehovah.

A Mr. Carter from Virginia lately sent me the Psalms by E. S.; also a form of prayer done in London. Every edition or recent sermons will oblige your faithful friend and servant in the Lord Jesus Christ. We have rented a building in this town for three months.

With every good wish I have the honour to be, respectfully, Sir, your affectionate servant,

J. WILMER.

II.

Extract of a Letter from the Society at Baltimore to the Society in London.

Baltimore, April 25, 1792.26.

DEARLY BELOVED BRETHREN,

Finding by your conference of April 1791-35, held in Great Eastcheap, London, a committee appointed for the purpose of settling all business of correspondence as well as other matters concerning the church; likewise having an invitation from Mr. Ralph Mather of Liverpool, to open a correspondence with you, now that we have formed ourselves into a society; we address you as a body, though small, yet we hope, by the grace of Jehovah, in whose cause we are associated, to increase and multiply; and that the grain of mustard seed, which is cast into our garden, will grow up, and shortly become a great tree, so that our citizens may come and lodge in its branches. We have great encouragement to hope for the event, as we have an enlightened community; yet at present we encounter many difficulties from our want of books to circulate the doctrines, and a settled place to preach them in.

The Rev. Mr. Wilmer, formerly of the church of England, has been raised up to preach the doctrines unto us, in which office he is indefatigable; and divides his time, by sometimes reading, out of what books we have, such parts as are best suited to the reception of those that are unacquainted with the doctrines; which answers the purpose of raising a curiosity and consequently a desire to read the writings, and which we find ourselves at a great loss to supply them with, as we have but very few books at present, and we are convinced, if they were more general, they would answer an excellent purpose to propagate the divine truths.

Our worst enemies here are the Methodists, who are a large body of people, and take much pains to prevent any communications between us, as by ordering the members of their society not to read any of the books. But we pray for the enlargement of their minds for the reception of truth and for the destruction of bigotry, which has so long held the world in darkness; but light now begins to prevail, and stupid bigotry vanishes before its splendor.

Since the first beaming of the true light in this place, the wars and rumors of wars spoken of in the Revelations, begin to make their appearance, dissensions in various societies of the old church having lately taken place.

We are persuaded that numbers begin to feel a want, and we would invite them to come and lodge in the branches of this heavenly dispensation; but as every rational and enlightened mind would wish to taste of our fruit before they swallow it, to know its excellence, as a more certain source of knowledge, (as we are all but young in the doctrine and not fully able to answer the numberless questions that are asked us by sticklers for doctrinal profession,) we would wish to have more of the books, as we find them of infinitely more service, even with those characters, than our answers to their questions, which naturally beget an argument.

Our church was opened the first instant in our court house, where Mr. Wilmer delivered an enlightened discourse to a very respectable audience from the second chapter of Colossians, eighth and ninth verses; and on the Sunday following in the Dunkers' meeting house, from the first Epistle of John, fourth chapter and sixteenth verse. But as these were only temporary indulgences, we have now taken the old theatre for one quarter of a year, until we can procure some better accommodation, or raise a temple, which, in our present infant state, we are not able to accomplish. Yet we hope to surmount these difficulties, and mean soon to put a subscription on foot for the purpose of raising some money, and flatter ourselves those of other societies will assist us. In the mean time we would beg your assistance and support, to forward our work.

The society have formed themselves after the manner of yours, as seen by your conference. We would therefore wish you to consider all letters sent prior to this as from private persons, and not from the society as a body.

May the grace of our Lord and Saviour Jesus Christ attend us all, and forward us in his great work. We remain your obedient humble servants in Him.

HENRY DIDIER, JOHN BOYER,
JOHN COOPER, JOHN MICKLE.

N. B. Please to direct your letters to Mr. Henry Didier, merchant, Market Street, Baltimore. Please to send us the plan of your temple in London, and the temple in *Birmingham*.

[*New Jerusalem Journal, London*, 1792, *pp.* 335–340.]

The above documents afford an official account of the opening of what professed to be the first church or society of the New Jerusalem in the United States of America. Therefore we have reprinted them entire here, that they may appear on permanent record in this country. Their historical value is great. We learn from them several facts which it is well to recapitulate. The professed preacher of the first society of the new church in the United States was a clergyman of the church of England. The society was formed after the manner of the first society in England, that of London ; and this was done from the influence of the Third General Conference, or that of April, 1791. But the General Conference had acknowledged a distinct new-church ministry instituted in London on the first of June, 1788. Yet the first society in Baltimore acknowledged a clergyman of the old-church ministry, and he styled himself, " as preacher of the New Jerusalem Church." Thus the New Jerusalem was not regarded as a new and true christian church, totally distinct from the first christian church, so far as concerned the ministry. The Rev. J. Wilmer, though educated at Oxford in England, and ordained by the Bishop of London, was "an American born." The facts stated by the correspondent of the " Maryland Journal and Baltimore Advertiser," and by Mr. Christian Kramer, are confirmed, although it is intimated that the latter were communicated by only a private letter. It is seen that Mr. Ralph Mather of Liverpool had an influence in inducing this first American Society to open a correspondence with the new church in England. The new church here was at first most violently opposed by the Methodists, yet it was not to be long before her most efficient minister was to come in from that denomination. After opening in the court house, which then stood about where the battle monument now stands, in the very centre of the city, and worshiping the next Sunday in the Dunkers' meeting house, in South Paca Street, west side, near the corner of Lombard Street, the society rented " the old theatre for one quarter of a year." This building stood somewhere in what is now East Baltimore Street. But even at this time a subscription was projected for the purpose of raising money to build a temple, and the plans of the temples in London and Birmingham were asked for—doubtless as patterns for the one to be built here.

The facts thus displayed conclusively show, that, in beginning the New Jerusalem, as a visible church, in these United States, there was no thought, at first, of forming a ministry for the new church distinct

from that of the old. Nor was there, at first, a manifest acknowledgment of the new-church clergy that had been formed in England. It
seems to have been assumed that the Lord would send down the New
Jerusalem from himself out of heaven through the clergy of the old
and consummated christian church. The same idea had had many
advocates in England, and seemed to be proved true by the fact that
such eminent clergymen of the old church as the Rev. John Clowes
were instrumental in advocating, defending and promulgating the
new-church doctrines. This question agitated and divided the receivers of these doctrines in England for years. It is not wholly
abandoned there even yet. And that it prevailed more or less here,
is evident from the fact that several who were early members of the
Baltimore society, reunited themselves with some one or other of the
denominations of the old church. This idea, however, did not prevail
here wholly, or long; and has never prevailed extensively any where
in the United States. In fact, some of us have not regarded this
opening of a church in the court house by the Rev. Mr. Wilmer, as
the beginning of the New Jerusalem in this country, because he could
not by his own act constitute himself a minister of the New Jerusalem,
or rather transform himself from an old-church minister into a new-
church minister by his own volition. Believing that the jewish
church began with the jewish priesthood, and the first christian
church with the Lord's apostles, we believe that the New Jerusalem,
if she be indeed the new and true christian church, as Swedenborg
declares, must begin with a new and distinct ministry of her own.
And, therefore, we date her beginning as a visible church in this
country at the time when her first minister was ordained here.

The Rev. Mr. Wilmer preached for the society during the time for
which it rented the old theatre. Shortly after the society was formed,
Mr. Robert Carter, who had favored its formation, removed from
Virginia to Baltimore, to enjoy the spiritual advantage of new-church
association. He was a native of England; a man of wealth, who, on
embracing the doctrines of the New Jerusalem, had manumitted his
slaves—about one hundred in number. He purchased a house in that
part of Baltimore called Old Town; removed his family to it; and
when the society gave up the old theatre as its place of worship, and
was about to be scattered, he rallied its members for worship in his
own house. He took Mr. Wilmer and his family in, and gave them a
home and support. Mr. Wilmer continued to officiate as the minister
of the society for about one year after it was first formed. Being a
man of considerable pretensions to learning, priding himself on his
clerical standing, and expecting more success and support in the new-
church ministry than he gained, he became dissatisfied, and reunited
himself with the episcopal church. When the Rev. Mr. Hargrove,
incidentally meeting him, some years afterwards, in Baltimore, asked
him how he came to leave the new church, he assured him that it
was not owing to any want of belief in the truth of its doctrines, but
he found mankind were not in a state to receive them, and he felt
there could be no use in his preaching them any longer. When Mr.
Wilmer left the society, Mr. Carter still kept up its meetings at his

house—leading the worship and preaching himself. He also administered the sacrament of baptism, to any who were willing to receive it at his hands; and when he was not present, he authorized other members of the society to do it. And we are informed that a Mr. Starr, who was baptized by Mr. Carter, did actually baptize others. However, Mr. Starr afterwards felt it to be right to be baptized again by Mr. Hargrove; and, notwithstanding, finally followed the lead of Mr. Wilmer, out of the new church, back again into the old.

Mr. Carter did not claim to be a minister, but led in worship, preached, and baptized, in his lay capacity. In this he but carried out the views of the early receivers of the doctrines in England, of whom he was one. And he kept up the society until a new one was formed on a different principle, under the Rev. Mr. Hargrove's influence, in 1798, which he took no part in, and never joined. Mr. Ralph Mather, who had come to this country some time between 1793 and 1795, and had held meetings for preaching in Philadelphia, at first visiting Baltimore, and at last making it his residence, preached occasionally for the society meeting in Mr. Carter's house.

In 1793, General Washington, being then president of the United States, made a tour through the country. Many, if not all, of the religious denominations presented him with respectful and patriotic addresses. And among the rest, the members of the new church at Baltimore addressed him. The address of the new church and General Washington's reply were published in No. II. of "The Aurora," a new-church periodical published in London in 1799. And as these are curious documents, which must be of permanent interest in this country, we cannot refrain from reprinting them in our Appendix. (See Ap. No. LIII.)

While the Rev. Mr. Wilmer was preaching in Baltimore, he made occasional excursions to proclaim the new-church doctrines in surrounding parts. On one of these occasions, he preached in Harford County, where the Rev. John Hargrove, then connected with the methodist denomination, was residing. Mr. Hargrove heard him; was startled by his doctrine; took an opportunity to confront him in argument, and thought he confuted him. In this way Mr. Hargrove's attention was first drawn to the new church. He began to read some of Swedenborg's smaller works, and followed up what he thought the advantage he had gained over Mr. Wilmer by written communications to the newspapers. But he continued reading, and subsequently became acquainted with the Rev. Adam Fonerden, of Baltimore, also a minister of the methodist church, who had been for some time a reader of Swedenborg's writings, and a receiver of the truths they contain. Mr. Fonerden aided Mr. Hargrove much in his ultimate reception of those truths. In February 1797, Mr. Hargrove became a teacher in the Baltimore Academy, a methodist institution. This brought him to Baltimore to reside. Mr. Ralph Mather, then living in Philadelphia, visited Baltimore, and preached in the house of Mr. George Higson. Mr. Hargrove heard him. He still felt inclined to combat the doctrines thus preached, and battled them in private argument; but to be able to expose and confute them fully, he felt bound to become still better acquainted with them, and in his investigation of, them he found their truth too strong for him. He became a receiver of the doctrines in the spring of 1798. And in the summer of that year, he and Mr. Fonerden had become so fully imbued with the principles of the New Jerusalem, and had, in consequence, undergone so radical and total a change of their previous faith, that they could no longer remain in the methodist connection. They withdrew from it together, by "a valedictory address to the people called Methodists," on the 5th of June, 1798. This address was published in the first number of "The Aurora," and may be seen reprinted in our Appendix No. LIV. Mr. Hargrove became a very zealous minister of the new church; and, through much trial and varied opposition, continued such to a late period of a great old age. But Mr. Fonerden never, we believe, became a proclaimer of the new-church doctrines in public, and soon went back to the Methodists, without wholly renouncing the truths of the new dispensation. Indeed, it required men made of very stern stuff to withstand the opposition and obloquy which Newchurchmen had to encounter then in Baltimore!

Mr. Mather, we have said, came to reside in Baltimore. This was, probably, some time in 1797. He lived here till 1800, when he returned to his native country. From thence he visited France, taking an active part with a small society of the new church in Paris. In 1802 he returned to America, settled at Norfolk, Virginia, and died in 1803. He was a resident of Baltimore about three years, was instrumental in introducing Mr. Hargrove into the new church, and was associated with him in forming what we regard as strictly the first society of the New Jerusalem in this country, of which he and Mr. Hargrove were the first ministers. The society, or church, opened by the Rev. Mr. Wilmer in 1792, being in fact the work of an old-church minister in a new-church garb, soon went to seed in his relapsing to the old church from which he only seemingly came out, and in the lay preaching and baptizing of Mr. Robert Carter and his converts. The Rev. Mr. Hargrove did not join that society, and only paid a few visits to Mr. Carter, to borrow books from him. Nor did Mr. Mather, although he preached for it, as he did for any meeting of new-church worshipers. The ground on which Mr. Hargrove stood and acted was, that the New Jerusalem is a totally distinct church from the first christian dispensation, and therefore should have an entirely distinct ministry. He believed her doctrines should be preached, and her sacraments administered, only by a clergy regularly ordained, consecrated, and set apart for those sacred uses. He did not think that a man's having been a clergyman of the first or old christian church entitled him, of course, to style himself a minister of the New Jerusalem, merely because he had embraced the doctrines of this church as true. Hence, although he had been ordained, at one of the methodist conferences, in the autumn of 1795, by Bishop Asbury, a deacon, which is the first grade in the trine of the methodist ministry, he did not *therefore* believe himself entitled to set himself up, or go forth, as a preacher of the new-church doctrines, or an administrator of the new-church sacraments, without a new ordination. Not did he think that even Mr. Mather's officiating in that capacity was altogether regular, because he had not been ordained by the imposition of hands. .He believed that there was a new arrangement of christians in the spiritual world consequent on the last judgment, and that the influx of the Lord's holy spirit for the establishment of an entirely new and really true christian church, to be called the New Jerusalem, on earth, was to be effected by influx through this new arrangement. And he was convinced that the translation of this holy spirit to a clergy for the establishment and extension of this new church, could only be effected by a *new sign*, that is, a new imposition of hands, or a new ordination. Therefore, although he was, undoubtedly, as much entitled to preach the doctrines of the new church as Mr. Wilmer, and probably did, at last, infuse those doctrines into his sermons from the methodist pulpit, yet he could not feel justified in doing this openly and distinctly from the methodist church, with the assumed title and authority of a minister of the New Jerusalem church, much less could he sanction a mere layman's right to do this, by becoming a frequenter and supporter of Mr. Robert Carter's meetings for new-church worship in his private dwelling. He could not regard those meetings as the new christian church, or a society of it, in an incipient form. He believed the receivers of the new-church doctrines should be constituted a new christian church -by a distinct ministry and a distinct baptism. Therefore, on this ground, those who were composing the church opened by Mr. Wilmer and continued by Mr. Carter, formed a new society, or came into a new social organization, on the 27th of June, 1798. In this formation,—although he, in his absence, was chosen an officer of it,—Mr. Robert Carter, the self-constituted leader of the former society, would take no active part.

However, the society, formed as above mentioned, did not at first take the shape of a church, or a meeting for public worship on the Lord's Day. Like the first society in London, it was an association of the receivers in Baltimore for the purpose of " promoting the doctrines of the New Jerusalem Church." Its first meeting for business was held, on the day above stated, at No. 3 North Gay Street, and its first business was to promote the doctrines by the press. John Hargrove was chosen president, and Joseph Starr secretary. A committee was appointed to print 1000 copies of a tract of two sheets. The president then read Swedenborg's account of himself given in a letter to Dr. Hartley, together with an article from the London New Jerusalem Magazine, stating and explaining the doctrine of the trinity. After which Mr. Mather gave a suitable exhortation; and " the president concluded the meeting by singing the doxology and extempore prayer." It was unanimously agreed, before breaking up, that the meetings should be renewed every Wednesday evening, at 6½ o'clock, at the same place, until altered by a majority. But it does not appear, from the records, that any more Wednesday evening meetings for business were held. It seems to have been determined to institute at once a church on the principle which we have stated above. And a special meeting was called for this purpose on the second Sunday of the following month, that is, on the 8th of July.

This brings us to the point where the ministry of the new church took its rise in America. For, in this second meeting of the Baltimore society, Mr. Ralph Mather was ordained the first pastor of a society of the New Jerusalem in the United States; and Mr. Hargrove was also ordained as his assistant, after having been baptized by Mr. Mather. It is evident from the record, that the "select meeting," as it is called, was held for the specific purpose of ordaining a minister and having the sacrament of baptism administered. And, therefore, it appears that the society had determined to change its character, from that of one meeting for the business of promoting the doctrines of the new church by the press, for this of a visible church or an ecclesiastical polity.

The records do not show that the church thus formed began now to hold regular meetings on every Sunday for public worship. It does not follow, however, that such meetings were not held, because they are not noted in the Book of Records. They might have been, and probably were held first at the houses of some of the members, and afterwards in a large room, or meeting house, hired for the purpose. The second meeting of the society, according to the record, was held on a Sunday at the school-room of one of its members; and the next, or the third meeting, was not held till six weeks afterwards, that is on Sunday, the 19th of August. This was held "at Mr. Kerr's house;" and "the holy supper was administered in private by Mr. Mather and Mr. Hargrove." And the record says—"The communicants were, viz. the Rev. Mr. Ralph Mather, the Rev. Mr. John Hargrove, Dr. Joseph Brevett, Mr. John Calef, Mr. Wm. Ensor." Thus the third meeting was held for the purpose of having the sacrament of the holy supper administered.

"On Sunday the 9th of September, it was resolved by the members to address the citizens at large, and solicit their assistance in building a house of public worship." Accordingly an address was drawn up by Mr. Hargrove to that effect and published in all the newspapers once a week for six times.

On the twenty-third of November, "it was resolved to take a lot of ground on annual rent by perpetual lease to build a house of worship on." A lot was so taken up on the southwest corner of York (now East Baltimore) and Exeter Streets. It was also resolved, "that the society let Mr. Mather have one half the aforesaid lot, viz. forty feet front and eighty back; and that they only should retain the other half for the purpose of building the said church." The corner of the lot was reserved by the society for the place of worship, and the other half was "leased in trust to five or seven members of said church for the use of the preachers of said church." During the autumn of 1798 and the spring and summer of 1799 active measures were taken in raising funds and building the temple which now occupies the corner of the lot. For a part, if not the whole of the time, that that temple was in building, the society rented, and met for worship in, the Dunkers' meeting house, in South Paca Street, near Lombard Street, and adjoining the lot on which the Medical College of the University of Maryland now stands. The money to build the temple was procured by subscriptions from the members, donations from the citizens at large, and contributions from friends of the church in distant parts. The temple was finished and opened for worship on the first Sunday of the present century. A parsonage or preacher's house was subsequently erected on the other half of the lot: and in respect to it, we find, in the First Book of Records, this memorandum in Mr. Hargrove's hand writing—" Memo. 2d June, [1802,] Mr. Steward began to lay the foundation of the preachers' house on the church lot."

We have said this society was a new one, formed distinctly and separately from the church which the Rev. Mr. Wilmer had opened, and Mr. Robert Carter had continued. The following minute of the proceedings of the meeting of Nov. 23, 1798, shows this :—" It was further resolved on, that all such members of the New J. Church as had formerly signed their names as members of the New J. Church *directed by Mr. Carter*, [underscored in the original record,] should (if they had no objection) first wait on Mr. Carter and request their names to be taken of [off] his society paper—in order, that they might proceed to subscribe a fresh society paper, under the pastoral or ministerial care of the Rev. Mr. Mather and the Rev. Mr. Hargrove, who now offer their services as the ministers of said church, and whose services are accepted."

At a meeting held for consultation on the 25th December, 1798, and continued by adjournment from time to time until the 6th of January, 1799, a constitution was adopted, vesting the spiritual and civil powers and functions of the society in " the priesthood and an acting committee." The priesthood consisted of the two ministers, and the acting committee of " either three, five or seven male baptized members," to be chosen quarterly by ballot. The number of the committee actually chosen was five. In the quarterly meeting of April 7, 1799, John Hargrove was duly elected, by ballot, president of said committee of five members, other than himself. This constitution was subscribed by thirty-three male members. There were probably thirty-four names, as a corner of the leaf of the Book of Records, on which they were subscribed, has been cut off with a penknife, taking away the largest part of one name, and probably the whole of another.

The seventh article of this constitution is to be remarked. It provides for the future appointment of a minister of the society; and is in these words—" The existing committee aforesaid, shall appoint an approved minister of the new church to examine into the qualifications of the candidate, and if a majority of the committee approve of the report of the examining minister, they shall request him to ordain the candidate." This is important; because it shows that the ordaining power was not believed to reside in the society as such : for, in this case, the society might have ordained a minister for itself at any time, as Messrs. Mather and Hargrove were ordained at first. The principle involved in that first ordination, we shall notice presently.

. Mr. Mather did not long remain the pastor of this society with Mr. Hargrove as his assistant. In conversation with an original member of this society, Mr. George Higson, twenty-one years ago, on the subject of the first formation of the new church in Baltimore, we learned that the arrangement of a society with two ministers did not prove harmonious. Jealousies and contentions soon arose between the ministers. The first incidental disagreement was a slight but very significant affair. There was a platform on which the officiating pastor stood; and Mr. Hargrove complained that he, as the assistant minister, was assigned a seat in a chair on the floor below that platform. Undoubtedly Mr. Hargrove was the leading mind and controlling spirit of the first new-church society in Baltimore. He was chosen president of the society in its first meeting: and " Mr. Mather, then, (*after leave obtained of the president*,) gave a suitable exhortation." And after the society was organized under its constitution, Mr. Hargrove was superadded to the acting committee as its president. There can be no doubt that this society was formed distinctly from the church meetings at Mr. Carter's house through Mr. Hargrove's leading influence. And there can be as little question, in our minds, that Mr. Hargrove was the first choice of a majority of its members for the pastorship. He probably felt and knew this; and therefore he did not rest easy in a seat on a plane below that on which Mr. Mather stood—he did not like to act only an assistant or secondary part in a society when he felt himself to be the first man. Why then did the society choose Mr. Mather as the pastor with Mr. Hargrove as only his assistant? There was in this an implied acknowledgment that the first formation of a new-church ministry had taken place in England, and the evident design of receiving a translation of ministerial authority from thence. This was supposed to be received through Mr. Mather, who had been a member of the London society, the first formed in the world, had, as such, participated in the original formation of the new-church ministry in England, was himself one of the eight ministers chosen by that society to officiate for it before the first ordination, namely, of Mr. R. Hindmarsh, and had, in his capacity of a licensed preacher, opened a place of worship in Liverpool and preached there, as well as elsewhere, both in England and America. But Mr. Mather was not a minister ordained by Mr. Hindmarsh; and therefore could not fully transmit or propagate that first ordination. Hence a repetition of Mr. Hindmarsh's ordination was necessary here. For it was not possible for the new church in this country, in its then very feeble infancy, to send to London some person to receive ordination by the imposition of hands there. Otherwise the new church would have been propagated in this country from England as the methodist church was,—Bishop Asbury having received ordaining powers in England. The writer of this report, who was once an assistant of Mr. Hargrove, received this impression from Mr. Hargrove himself. The exigencies of the *disjecta membra* of the unformed new church here, called for the preaching of the doctrines and the administering of the sacraments of a church to themselves. They therefore did the most and best they could under the circumstances. They crystalized around the nucleus which the Lord in his providence had brought them from England. They made Mr. Mather their first pastor, *because he had been a minister of the new church in England.* But they wanted Mr. Hargrove as their minister, and therefore they ordained him as Mr. Mather's assistant. Now if they had regarded the ordination of Mr. Mather as an *original* one, there was no necessity of their ordaining two. They might have ordained Mr. Hargrove at once. But Mr. Mather was ordained first, to receive Mr. Hargrove by *baptism*, that gate by which alone there is an entrance into the church. And when Mr. Hargrove was thus made a member of the church, he was ordained a minister of it. He was, indeed, ordained in the same way as Mr. Mather: but this, in our opinion, was irregular. As an *assistant* minister, he ought to have been ordained, as well as baptized, by Mr. Mather. But so it was. Mr. Hargrove, as the assistant, was ordained on the same plane as the pastor, whom he was to assist. And when Mr. Mather, the pastor, afterwards assigned to Mr. Hargrove, his assistant minister, a seat off of the platform on which he officiated in discharging the functions of the pastoral office, Mr. Hargrove felt as if he was degraded. And in feelings engendered by a collision of spirits consequent on this state of things, disagreements arose, which, however externally suppressed for the sake of order and quietness, caused Mr. Mather tacitly to resign his office and return to England, after officiating for the society about a year, and never to resume it, although he came again to this country. When Mr. Mather left, Mr. Hargrove stepped into his place without any formality, and became the active and efficient pastor of the society until greatly advanced age compelled him to relinquish the more active duties of his office—although he retained the parsonage, and administered occasionally the sacraments of the church, for about nine years after he resigned the pastorship. "He resigned his pastoral charge on the 17th of April, 1830, in the 80th year of his age, and the thirty-second of his ministry in the new church. On this occasion, the society tendered to him, as a testimony of their regard for his long services, the use of the parsonage-house adjoining the temple, as a residence during the remainder of his natural life."[*] The records show that he baptized five persons, children from thirteen to three years of age, on the 8th of June, 1839. And he departed this life, near six months afterwards, on the 6th of December, 1839, in the ninetieth year of his age. Some have said, and many have thought, that Mr. Hargrove was the first minister ordained in this country; but we have seen that Mr. Mather was. However, all the ordinations in this country have flowed from Mr. Hargrove. And esteemed for his early and self-sacrificing espousal and defence of our cause against the most appalling opposition, respected for his talents and long services, venerated for his age, he has gone down to the grave regarded and honored as the Patriarch of the American Church.

[*] See article signed " J. F." in N. J. Mag., Boston, Vol. XIV. p. 491.

6

This somewhat extended survey of the rise and first establishment of the New Jerusalem as a visible church in America, has been deemed a needful introduction to a full examination of the question of a trine in the ministry of this country. We will now return to the first ordination of ministers in the Baltimore society, and from that as a starting point trace the line of ministerial progress, so far as it runs into the agitation and settlement of a trine of orders, grades or degrees in the ministry.

It is to be observed that the point where the ministry of the new church took its rise in America, was the second meeting of the Baltimore society held for the special purpose of instituting such a ministry. It took place, as we have seen, on the second Sunday, being the 8th day of July, 1798. And as the proceedings of that meeting are of paramount importance in the history of our church in this country, we deem it our duty to insert them here entire, and accompany them with some remarks. We copy them from the First Book of Records of the Baltimore society, to wit :—

Sunday, 8 *July*, 1798–42.

The members of the New J. Church held a select meeting in Mr. Carr's [Kerr's] School-room.

After Mr. Mather had opened the meeting with prayer, the following question was proposed, for resolution, to the members.

Quest. 1. Is a reappointment and reordination necessary in the case of Mr. Mather, who (though licensed by the magistracy of England, and also by the members of the new church there) has not as yet been formally appointed or ordained in these United States?

Ans. Unanimously in the affirmative.

Mr. Mather was therefore ordained according to the form of the New Church, viz., by prayer and laying on of the hands of the elders or representatives of said church in Baltimore, being ten in number exclusive of himself.

Immediately after this, three adult males were baptized into the faith of the New Church, viz. Mr. John Calef, Dr. Joseph Brevett and Mr. John Hargrove

Mr. Mather then proposed Mr. John Hargrove (late a minister of the Methodist E. Church) for ordination in the New J. Church as an assistant to Mr. Mather; which proposal was accepted by the members unanimously.

Upon which the elders and representatives present, being ten in number, (exclusive of Mr. Hargrove,) proceeded to ordain him according to the mode or ceremony aforesaid, as assistant minister of the said church.

The meeting then was concluded with prayer, and broke up.

The writer of this report may be allowed to state that he, at first, did not regard this beginning of ordinations in this country as valid or orderly. He thought that ordinations here should have flowed regularly from the Rev. Robert Hindmarsh, who was providentially designated as the ordainer of ministers in the visible new church " by the Lord's auspices," (see Ap. LI.,) in the city of London, on the first of June, 1788. Therefore, when he was about to be introduced into the new-church ministry—had in fact entered the first grade as a licentiate, and was expecting to become the minister of the Baltimore society when Mr. Hargrove should be in Providence removed, he felt reluctant to receive ordination in this country. He went to England, resided in London two years, pursued the study of theology there during that time, and his principal aim was, that he might receive ordination there. As the pastor-elect of the Baltimore society, a formal application was made, by that society, for his ordination in England, in the year 1831—Mr. Hargrove having resigned the pastorship of that society in 1830. He presented that application to the Rev. Samuel Noble, in the year 1832. But Mr. Noble deemed a compliance with the request injudicious, and advised him to receive ordination in his own country. He bowed in deference to the decision of wise men, whom he profoundly respected and deeply loved. He took their advice, received ordination in his own country, and thus has acknowledged its validity.

The principle upon which this validity rests is, that the New Jerusalem is a *universal* church, which will embrace as many *general* churches as there are general or grand divisions of countries and nations on the surface of the globe. In this respect the New Jerusalem is to resemble the ancient church, which was spread throughout Asia, and had general divisions according to the countries through which it was extended. The New Jerusalem will differ from the ancient church, in this respect, only in being *more* universal. Hence it is conjectured, that, as the new church springs up more widely, and comes into visible form among distinct nations, whose people have different vernacular tongues, it will appear as so many general churches, having each a ministry or priesthood of its own, originating in itself. Thus, as the new church spreads throughout Europe, there will be the church of France, the church of Germany, the church of Russia, and so forth, as well as the church of England. And either of those european churches will not derive its ministerial power and authority by translation from the church in England, but will have a new appointment or ordination of ministers of its own. Therefore, as the continent of America is one of the largest divisions of the earth, separated from the continent of Europe by a vast ocean, much more must the New Jerusalem in the United States of America, now a great nation, be a general church, not deriving its ministry from the new church of England, but having an ordination and ministry of its own. This, or something like it, we believe, was the view of our brethren in England, and we submitted to their judgment. Hence, according to this view, the church in Baltimore was right, when it determined that Mr. Mather, although licensed by the magistracy of England, and also by the members of the new church there, ought to be formally reappointed or reordained in these United States.

We have no doubt that the ordination of Mr. Mather in this case was right, because he had not been ordained in England. We do not believe that a license to preach introduces him that receives it into " the ecclesiastical order." We believe that the imposition of hands is necessary for this; and that, as there are discrete powers communicated by inauguration into discrete planes, there must be a distinct ordination for each of the three degrees of the ministry. Hence, in our view, Mr. Mather's ordination was also right, because he was ordained into a discrete degree. By this ordination he was raised from the grade of a licentiate (which was, for some time, though we think improperly, regarded as the first grade of our ministry) to the grade of a pastor; and the imparting of discrete powers requires a new ordination. But had Mr. Mather been ordained into the higher discrete degree in England by the imposition of the hands of the english church, we cannot think that it would have been right or *necessary* to reordain him here on the ground that the american church should have an ordination of its own. Suppose that Mr. Hindmarsh himself had come to this country, either to reside here as Mr. Mather did, or as an apostle of the english church, sent to propagate the new church on this continent. He might have been reordained in England, for this special mission, as Saul was, when he was sent to preach the Gospel to the Gentiles, after he had preached it fruitlessly to the Jews: but would it have been necessary or proper for him to have been formally reappointed or reordained in these United States? If so, why was not the Rev. James Robinson re-ordained into our american ministry when he came to this country? Why was he admitted into our ministry without being formally re-appointed? (See Journal of 12th Gen. Con., 1830, p. 6, n. 31.) No, although we believe that the New Jerusalem is to be a universal church, and that each nation of the earth may have a general new church as a subdivision of it, yet we believe that it, like light, and every thing else which flows in order, *must be propagated or extended from one great centre*. And as, in the arrangement of Christians in the world of spirits, some one christian nation is central to the rest, we cannot see why that nation may not be central to all other nations in the arrangement of New-church Christians in this world of men. And as the ordination of ministers in the first christian church began from the Lord through his apostles at Jerusalem and radiated from thence as a centre throughout all christendom then; we cannot see why true order does not require a radiation of new-church ordination from a similar centre throughout all christendom now. Or, if we take our type of order from the human form—the truest and perfectest form of it—should we not expect the ordination of ministers of the New Jerusalem to begin in some one nation of Christians, as a central organ or viscus of the grand man of the church on earth, and flow from thence to all other parts or nations of christendom, just as the pulmonic motions flow from the lungs, the blood from the heart, and the animal spirit from the brain, to all other parts of the human body? Now, as the whole church on earth appears before the Lord as one man—as the arrangement of Christians in the world of men must correspond to the arrangement of them in the world of spirits—as "the Reformed in the world of spirits constitute the inmost part thereof or centre," and "the English occupy the middle in that central part," so that "the better sort amongst the English are in the centre of all Christians" in the world of spirits; why should not the centre of new-church ordination here on earth be in England? And when a beginning of that ordination has actually taken place in London, very manifestly "by the Lord's auspices," why should not the ordination of ministers for the new christian church now, in the Lord's second advent, radiate from London as a centre, just as the ordination of ministers for the old christian church radiated from Jerusalem as a centre in the Lord's first advent? We think it should. And therefore we must still think that this first ordination of ministers in America was not strictly in order any farther than it was a derivation from the first new-church ordination in London. But we submit, with profound deference, to the judgment of our superiors. Still, while we so submit, we must be allowed the privilege of remarking certain facts, which go to show that, in these United States especially, the new church must needs have been propagated from England, and ordination derived from thence.

In the time of the last judgment these United States were colonies of Great Britain. We are not mentioned by Swedenborg as a distinct nation. A large part of those who give character to the United States as a nation now, have english blood in their veins. Not only have we sprung from the same stock, but we still have the same common law, speak the same language, have the same literature, and have substantially the same constitution of government. If ever, therefore, a child should be expected to have the same propensities as the parent by hereditary transmission, we should have been expected to have received the new church and its ordination by propagation from England. And we have seen that the new church was in fact so propagated. Therefore it seems to us that new-church ordination should have flowed from the same source. And we think we see that it was in fact so derived, in as far as circumstances would permit.

Let us, in proof of this, remark, that in the first ordination of ministers by the church at Baltimore there were *two* ordained—a pastor and an assistant—for a society of *ten male members!* Why ordain two for so small a society? The use of an assistant is to aid a pastor, when his society is so large that he cannot discharge his pastoral duties to it himself. If there had been an ordination of apostles, to go forth and preach the gospel to nations,—as in Acts, xiii. 2,—it would have been in order to ordain two of the same grade: but for the use of ministration to a single and very small society in one place, there was no propriety in ordaining more than one. There must, therefore, have been another reason for ordaining Mr. Mather as pastor, and Mr. Hargrove as his assistant, in this case. And we think we have good reason for saying that the design of this was to procure regular ordination of Mr. Hargrove from England through Mr. Mather. And we believe that he, in the divine providence of the Lord, was brought over from England for this purpose. And therefore we believe that, in fact, new-church ordination was derived to this country from England. It was, we say, propagated by a *bud*—an incipient form of vegetation—a propagative form of vegetation in its *first degree*. This bud, with the scion of the vine from which it was cut, planted in american soil, was to propagate the same vine in a new form here. It sprouted and grew when Mr. Mather from a licentiate became a pastor. Had he been made a pastor in England, we should have taken from thence our vine in a more advanced degree of propagation—a layer which had been allowed to strike root while it was still drawing sap from the parent vine. But he was taken as a *bud*, and not as a rooted *layer*.

Therefore we remark, secondly, that this institution of a ministry in these United States by the Baltimore society, in its second meeting, was not an *original* ordination. It was merely a reordination, such as is proper when a minister is inducted into, or receives the powers of, a higher discrete degree. That this had to be performed by the church itself, instead of by the church through its ordaining minister, was in this case a matter of necessity. It would have been better, or more orderly, if this reordination could have been received through the imposition of the hands of the english ordaining ministry: but, as this was not practicable, it was needful to have recourse to ordination " according to the form of the new church, viz. by prayer and laying on of the hands of the elders or *representatives* of said church in Baltimore." The only difference was in the *representatives* of the church. If Mr. Mather had been ordained by the imposition of the hand of one or more ordaining ministers in England, he would have been ordained by the representatives of the church in England ; but as it was he was ordained by the representatives of the church in Baltimore, which was then the *whole visible* church in the United States.

Hence we remark, thirdly, that the principle involved in this first american ordination is, that ordination comes from the Lord through the church as a whole, by its representatives, or the representatives of him in it. We do not know what were the views of Mr. Mather, Mr. Hargrove, or the church in Baltimore on this point; we can only say this is our view. It seems to us that this principle was intended to be involved in that ordination. We imagine that Acts, xiii. 1—3, was the authority for it, and the type of it. Mr. Mather had been appointed a minister of the first grade in England—he had been licensed to preach there. He was now to be advanced to a higher grade in the United States. So Saul had been called by the Lord in person, and had been ordained by the imposition of the hands of Ananias, to be an apostle, Acts, ix. 6, 7. In the strength and power of that first ordination he " preached Christ in the synagogues," to "the Jews that dwelt at Damascus." For Paul knew " it was necessary that the Word of God should first have been spoken to the Jews :" but when " they put it from them, and judged themselves unworthy of eternal life," he " turned to the Gentiles." (Acts, xiii. 46.) This was his chief and highest mission : for his mission to the Jews was particular or general ; but his mission to the Gentiles was general or universal. The two were separated by a discrete degree. To fit him, therefore, for his second office, he had to receive the powers and influences of the Lord's holy spirit in a discrete degree. He needed a *new* or a *re*-ordination. He was re-ordained by the imposition of the hands of the church at Antioch. And by the holy spirit given unto Saul and Barnabas in this ordination, they received power to go unto the Gentiles when they were utterly rejected by the Jews. So Mr. Mather was re-ordained by the church at Baltimore to perform the functions of the ministry in a higher degree than those which he had been performing as a mere licensed preacher. His ordination in this case was that " he might receive his sight and be filled with the holy ghost"—that he might receive the powers of illustration and instruction from the Lord's holy spirit. This invariably flows through the whole into its parts, and not vice versa. The whole church is the body of which the Lord is the soul: and the Lord is from the whole in each part, and flows through the whole by each part just as the soul is in and flows through its body by its particular members. The soul is not in the pineal gland or in any other one part, and through that in the whole, but it is in the whole, and flows through the whole into each part, as a vast machine turns on its pivot. And just so it is in respect to the Lord's influx by his holy · spirit through his body, the church. The Lord does not act upon any one part of his church, which he sees "as a single man," .(U. T. 412,) separately from the rest, and through that upon the whole, "but upon *all together*" (D. P. 124.) Therefore the Lord being the sole ordainer of his ministers, and the Lord being actually in the whole church, the Lord's ordaining power lies in the whole church; and in his twelve apostles, because they represent his whole church ; and in one or more ordaining ministers, because they are the whole church's representatives; and in the elders, or any other minister chosen for this purpose, for the same reason. And the Lord's holy spirit is determined through the heavens into any one on earth by the imposition of the church's hands, that is by the hands of the representative or representatives of the whole church, because heaven is consociated with men, or the Lord through heaven is conjoined with them, by correspondences, significatives or representatives. Such conjunction, we are taught, (Ap. Ex. 475,) can be effected in no other way. Hence the holy spirit can be communicated to a clergyman in no other way than by imposition of the hands of some one or more persons who represent the Lord; because this imposition of hands is a *representative sign*, perceived in heaven, so as to effect consociation of heaven with the person who receives it, and thus to determine into him, from the Lord through heaven, the *powers* of the Lord's holy spirit in man's conjunction with the Lord. The hand is that by which the body exerts its power. Hence the hand signifies power. And the imposition of the hand denotes the communication of what the hand signifies. Hence the imposition of the hand denotes, signifies, or represents the communication of power. And the imposition of the hands of the Lord's representative, represents the communication of his power, which is the power that men receive by the influx of his holy spirit into them through heaven and the church. Whether this representative takes place by the imposition of the hands of one man, two men, three men, five men, seven men, ten men, twelve men, or by the whole church of any number of men, it is the same thing— it is the imposition of the hands of the representative of the Lord. It is in either case the imposition of one man's hands, that is, it is the imposition of the hands of either an individual or a collective man,

which last is seen by the Lord and angels as one. For Swedenborg
says, (U. T. 412,) "a society is a single man, and the individuals that
compose it form, as it were, one body, and are distinguished one from
another like the members in one body. *The Lord*, and *from him the
angels*, when they look down upon the earth, *see a whole society of
men under no other view than as a single man.*" Consequently, when
any number of men, as the representative of the Lord in the church
as his body, place their hands upon a person, there is, in fact, the
imposition of the hands of a whole church "as a single man;" and
the Lord's power, as the power of the spirit or soul of that body, is
imparted to that person by those hands, just as the whole power of an
electrical battery is communicated by a person in connection with it
when he lays his hands upon some person next to him.   And in the
former case, just as in the latter, the effect is the same, namely, the
full communication of the divine spirit, (as of the electric fluid,) according to the form and state of the recipient subject, whether the
medium of its communication be one man or an entire circle of any
number of men. All that is wanted is the point of contact. Without
this, no possible communication can be effected in an ordinate, quiet
and peaceful way.   If communication takes place without a proper
medium, and without suitable preparation on the part of the subject
to receive it, it effects only violent concussions, rendings or dissipa-
tions, as in the phenomena of lightning and thunder.   Now, in the
divine economy, the medium for communicating the Lord's holy spirit
to the clergy, and by the clergy to the laity, is *the imposition* of *hands ;*
because this is a sign, perceived in heaven, of the translation of power,
which sign, as a *representative* on earth, is a means of so consociating
heaven with the person who receives it as actually to determine into
him the influx of the Lord's spirit through heaven, and thus actually
to impart to him the Lord's power. Men may sneer at this,—as
some are found to do even in the professing new church,—as a *superstitious* notion.* But, they may with equal propriety sneer at the

---

* It will be our duty in another part of this report to show that *true* representatives
are not wholly done away in the new and true christian church because the *mere* representatives of the jewish ritual worship were abrogated in the Lord's advent. There is
a great difference between a true representative church, such as the ancient church was,
and the mere representative of a church, such as the jewish church was. And it will
not be difficult to show that when the Lord abrogated the mere representative worship
of the Jews, he did not abrogate all true representative worship among Christians.   Nor
could the Lord abrogate the eternal law of order by which the spiritual world flows into
and is re-presented correspondentially in the natural world, and by which the heavens
are conjoined with the earths.   In the perceptions and intelligences of the operations of
this law, the wisdom of the most ancient and the ancient churches consisted.   And in
the operations of the same law the forms and ceremonies of even civil society have
taken their rise and have their present power.   Much more must the sacred forms and
ceremonies of the church have the same derivation and force.   Swedenborg expressly
says, (A. C. 6292,) "The circumstance of putting the hand on the head when blessing
was given, was derived from a ritual received from the ancients.   .   .   .   From that
ancient time, the same ritual remains even at this day, and *is in use in inaugurations.*"   And, in another place, (D. L. & W. 220,) where he shows the reason of
inauguration by the imposition of hands, he says, "I have often wondered that the
angels have such knowledge from the mere action of the body by the hands; but never-

idea that an infant is consociated with heaven by the sign received in baptism; or that the Lord is actually present with his divine humanity, and flows in with his whole redemption, in and by the *representatives* of his body and his blood in the most holy sacrament of his

theless it has been occasionally made manifest by lively experience, and it has been told me that *this is the reason why inauguration into the ministry is performed by imposition of hands,* and why touching signifies communicating" This shows that *this* representative of the imposition of hands is not done away in the present day : and we see that the ground of its power is in the fact that angels perceive and flow into its correspondence. But the grand reason of the present and perpetual power of representatives on earth is, that the Lord's power, which is *a all* power in heaven and on earth," consists in his acting from first principles by ultimates; and " representatives and significatives are in ultimate things." This was the reason that he took humanity on earth to get power to redeem and save mankind ; and this is the reason why " whatsoever the Lord did in the world was representative, and whatsoever he spake was significative." (Ap. Ex. 31.) This is the reason that the Word was written by such things in the natural world as correspond to and represent the things which are in the spiritual world, because thus divine truth comes into ultimates and so is in its sanctity and its power. This also is the reason why the Lord collated all representatives of heaven and the church into baptism and the holy supper, because hereby the *celestial* things of heaven and the church are brought down to ultimates and so into power. Hence these sacraments are the especial powers, and may be called the two grand pillars of the church on earth. Hence it is clear that the power of representatives lies in their being the ultimates of divine order ; " for with representatives the case is this ; those things which appear in nature, in her threefold kingdom, are the ultimates of divine order ; for all things of heaven, which are called spiritual and celestial, terminate in them." (A. C. 10.728.) Consequently, it must be evident that true representatives are not and cannot be done away, because this would be to undermine the foundations of heaven and the church; and without the church the human race would perish. (A. C. 10.500.) In short, representatives cannot be done away, because the salvation of men and the very existence of the universe depend upon conjunction with God through consociation with heaven; and neither of these can be effected without representatives, or without the Word which is written according to them; for " angelic discourse, which is incomprehensible to man, as being spiritual and celestial, when it is conveyed down to man, who is in a natural sphere, falls into representatives and significatives such as exist in the Word : and hence it is that the Word is a holy code or volume; for what is divine *cannot be presented or exhibited otherwise before the natural man,* so as that a full correspondence may exist." (A. C. 3419.) Thus it is impossible that correspondence of man with God can be effected without representatives. And so it is impossible for the Lord's spirit to be communicated to his clergy as the medium of it to the laity of his church on earth, without this *representative sign* of the imposition of hands. And that mankind are now disposed to ridicule this as a superstitious notion, is owing to their ignorance of the law by which the conjunction of the spiritual and natural worlds is effected. The same reason accounts for the present *radical* contempt for, and opposition to, certain civil ceremonies which have been handed down from time immemorial, and are now deemed senseless mummeries because men of the present day have lost the knowledge of their origin and no longer see their groundwork in the representatives and significatives of both nature and the ancient church. In illustration of this, and in confirmation of the fact that representatives may still have power in the church when known and thought of by the Christian, we commend to the reader's attentive perusal the following extract from A. C. 4581 :—" That such things are signified by oil and drink offering, cannot indeed be seen except from the internal sense; but still it may be seen by every one, that holy things were represented thereby : for unless this had been the case, *what would the offering of a drink offering and the pouring oil upon a statue be but mere ludicrous and idolatrous ceremonies ?* In like manner as, in the creation of a king, to set a crown upon his supper. It is sufficient for us to know that the Lord reveals this truth in his Word, and teaches it to us in his new church by his servant Swedenborg. And when we see the Lord calling the apostle, Paul, to a high and holy mission, and sending him to Ananias " to be filled with the holy ghost" by the imposition of his hands ; or again causing him to be " separated to the work whereunto he had called him" by the laying on of the hands of the church at Antioch; we most religiously believe that there is an imparting of the divine powers of the Lord's holy spirit by this representative sign of its translation, which cannot possibly be effected in any other way : and we feel the more strongly that Swedenborg teaches the truth when he says, (U. T. 146,) "*inauguration into the ministry brings with it [inauguratio in*

head, to anoint him with oil out of a horn on the forehead and wrists, to put a sceptre into his hand, and moreover a sword and keys, to clothe him with a purple robe, and then to set him on a silver seat, and next to set him on horseback in his royal trappings, and also afterwards to have him waited upon at table by the great men of his court— unless these ceremonies represented holy things, and *were themselves holy by correspondence with the things of heaven, and the church derived from heaven,* they would be nothing else but plays, like those of little children, but in a greater form, or like plays on the stage. Howbeit all those rituals derived their origin from the most ancient times, when rituals were holy in consequence of their representing holy things, and corresponding with the holy things which are in heaven and thence in the church. At this day, also, they are accounted holy, not in consequence of its being known what they represent, or to what they correspond, but by interpretation as of emblems which are in use. But if it was known what a crown, oil, horn, a sceptre, a sword, keys, riding on a white horse, being waited on at table by the great ones of the court, represented; and to what holy things they each corresponded; mankind would think of them much more holily. But this is not known ; and, what is wonderful, mankind are not willing to know it—*to such a degree are the representatives and significatives, which are contained in such things and in the Word throughout, destroyed at this day in men's minds.*"

The reasoning of the above passage, is so clear and conclusive for the present use and power of representatives, even in the ceremonies of civil society, as well as for showing why mankind are now so prone to ridicule and dispense with them, that we are sure our new-church readers must feel its force in showing the present use and power of representatives in all the sacred ceremonies of our church. They will now see, more clearly, why the Lord, through Swedenborg, has opened the representative and significative import of the sacraments of baptism and the supper, and thereby rescued them from the obloquy of being unmeaning or superstitious ceremonies in the christian church. And they will surely see that a representative and significative inauguration of new-church clergymen into any and every degree of their sacred office, must be attended with the communication of peculiar divine powers : so that, if the consecration service, by which ordaining ministers are inaugurated into their office in the new church of England, is at all truly representative and significative in its character, it must be to them a matter of consummate surprise that a minister of twenty years' standing in that church should now be heard seriously and publicly proclaiming to the world in its general conference—" no one can pretend for a moment that the performance or non performance of the ' consecration service' can increase or diminish the suitability of an ordaining minister for the discharge of his peculiar duty"!!! Must they not imagine that he too was among those peculiar political partizans of his country whom we have heard, in their newspapers, ridiculing and throwing contempt upon those ceremonies by which their queen was not long ago inaugurated into her regal office? For can any one pretend for a moment that the performance of the " consecration service," and the other solemn coronation ceremonies, by which she was inducted into her office,—which is among those that are representative at the present day, (A. C. 3670,)—could increase or diminish her suitability for the discharge of her peculiar duty ?

ministerium illas secum portat] that divine virtue and operation of the holy spirit which consists in illustration and instruction;" and (Canons, ch. iv. 7) "that the clergyman, because he is to teach from the Word by doctrine concerning the Lord, and concerning redemption and salvation by him, is to be inaugurated by the promise of the holy spirit, and *by the* REPRESENTATION *of its translation.*" We repeat, then, that the ordination of Mr. Ralph Mather by the imposition of the hands of the representatives of the church at Baltimore, involves the principle that ordination comes from the Lord through the church as a whole—that Mr. Mather by this ordination was raised to a higher grade of the ministry than that on which he had previously stood and ministered—that it was a *re*-ordination of him to what then might have been regarded as the second grade of the ministry, and that in and by this imposition of hands he *did* receive an increased suitability for the discharge of his peculiar duty. We will also take occasion to state here our conviction that Mr. Robert Hindmarsh was ordained by the Lord, although he was not inaugurated by the imposition of the hands of *representatives* of the church. In our view he was ordained by the imposition of the Lord's hand. For since the Lord left the world as to his personal appearance, and went up on high, that is went into the inmost of all things, his hands and feet are the ultimates of his divine order and providence. Hence when he, in his providence, caused the *lot* to fall on Robert Hindmarsh, that *ultimate* operation of his providence *was his hand* placed on that person and divinely designating him as the ordainer of ministers in his new church on earth. And, in our humble opinion, *this* is the orderly and true way in which every *apostle*, as the highest representative of the Lord in his priestly office on earth, should be ordained of the Lord now. We think he should be one—of two candidates chosen by the whole church—thus *designated* by the Lord, and afterwards *ordained* by the imposition of the hands of the whole church through some member or members of it, chosen to represent it in that ceremony. This would be a full ordination, similar to the calling of Paul by the Lord immediately, together with his ordination of him mediately through the imposition of the hands of Ananias and of the church at Antioch. Or it would be full because it would represent the ordination of him from the Lord by both the *immediate* and the *mediate* influx of his holy spirit.

We now remark, lastly, that there was, in this institution, or first formation, of a new-church ministry in America, a *trine* of the church—although there was no acknowledgment, and probably no thought, of it at the time. For the trine of essentials in the church is God, charity and faith; or in man there is the trine of mind, will and understanding, as to his internal, and the trine of the body, the heart and the lungs, as to his external (U. T. 712); and as at Jerusalem there was the trine of the church, the apostles and elders, (Acts, xv. 4); or at Antioch, the trine of the church, the prophets and teachers, (Acts, xiii. 1); so here in Baltimore, there was the trine of the *church*, the *pastor* and his *assistant*. And as in the former of

these trines, "God," "the mind," "the body," and "the church,"
are correlatively the highest terms, and each of the last three holds
to its respective trine the same relation which the first one does to
its trine, so that each may represent "God," or the highest term in
the trine of essentials, to the other two terms in its respective trine
of formals, so "the church," here in the Baltimore trine, as a whole,
or a complex man, represented the Lord in this institution of a
ministry. Such was the tendency of influx from the spiritual world.
That influx tended to an arrangement in this trinal order. But
the order was not seen or not acknowledged. Mr. Hargrove was
ordained on the same plane with the pastor; which was an error,
into which the members or ministers of the church would not have
fallen if they had then known, or considered, the trine to be the true
order. Hence we have said the question of a trine was not agitated
when the new-church ministry was first instituted in America. Still
the trine was there in an embryo form. It was not seen, because it
was not yet brought forth or born into the clear light of day. The
time for seeing it in rational light had not yet come. The new
church in America had to grow into the more matured form of a
general body, before this question could arise or be agitated. And
we will now proceed to trace the advancement of the ministerial
formation until this question did arise. It will be seen that the
ministry gradually assumed a trinal arrangement; so that when the
question of a trine was agitated, and this was shown, by a report of a
committee, to be the true order, the General Convention of the New
Church in this country declared that such an order was found to be
actually in existence.

Since the above was in type, we have had the sight of a short
manuscript, and a letter, written by Mr. Hargrove, in 1836, when
he was severely afflicted with the asthma and borne down with the
weight of eighty-seven years. In the manuscript, he gives an account
of his early reception of the doctrines, which squares very nearly with
ours. But as there is some variation in dates, and he states some
things more minutely, we deem it right to let the church hear him
speak. He also makes some specific statements respecting Mr.
Mather, and his own ordination, which it is important should be
given in his own words.

Describing the way in which the new-church doctrines were first
brought to his notice, Mr. Hargrove says:—"About the year 1795,
the report of a new sect having obtained in Harford county, where I
then resided, induced me to go, on a certain Sunday, to the Protestant
Episcopal Church, to hear the Rev. James Wilmer (the Episcopal
clergyman who had embraced the New Jerusalem doctrines) at a
Protestant church in Bush Neck; and as a Methodist preacher I
openly opposed him there, after he had done preaching. And, in
order to be better prepared to oppose him the next Sabbath, I borrowed some of the smaller works of E. Swedenborg; and actually
published some unfriendly strictures on them in the newspapers then
published in Baltimore. But, after reading some more of the *writings*,
I was struck with the luminous view of the Object of Divine Wor-

ship in the first volume of the Universal Theology; and having removed to Baltimore in 1796, I fell in with the Rev. Adam Fonerden, of the Methodist Episcopal Church—a very sensible and esteemed minister, who had partially received the Swedenborgian System, and by him was more and more prepared to receive the N. J. Doctrine, yet without the least intention of receding from the Methodist E. Church—in which I had preached for near twenty years, and in which I obtained ordination, several years before, at the hands of their then only ruling Bishop, Francis Asbury." The rest of his account agrees with ours.

In giving an account of his ordination "in conjunction with Mr. Mather," Mr. Hargrove says—" Mr. Mather had a *license* to preach from the government of England, and indeed had publicly preached these doctrines in England in conjunction with a Mr. Salmon. The form of ordination was similar to that previously used in England at the ordination of Mr. Sibly and some others—with *prayer* and the imposition of hands of all the male members (ten in number:) for it was thought proper to relinquish all claim to the ministry originating from the old church, and own our ministerial authority to be derived from another and a higher source, or more immediately from the Lord." This shows very clearly the principle that governed this ordination. It was to derive ministerial authority, not through the old church or its clergy, but more immediately from the Lord through the whole new church then visible in this country. For the *ten* were in fact *all* of the male members of the church then present, and might have been supposed to represent the power of the whole church in the United States at that time as the power of the whole body is represented by its ten Signers. Thus was Mr. Mather ordained, and through him Mr. Hargrove.

In the course of his manuscript, Mr. Hargrove states the striking fact, that "not less than between thirty-seven and forty heads of families openly joined" them "in about one year after" they began preaching in their temple.

The letter referred to, contains the following interesting statement: "Mr. Mather appeared in Baltimore (living then in Philadelphia); and about the spring of 1798, was, with Thomas Higson, of *Wigan* in England, then on a visit here, chiefly instrumental in erecting the first N. J. temple, or church of worship that ever was built in North America: which was opened by Mr. Mather in the morning of the first Sabbath of the present century. In the afternoon of the same day, I preached, in the same place, from the words, ' *Worship God.*' The sermon was delivered from notes, and is printed."

In answer to the question "When and by whom was I ordained?" he gives the following importantly minute statement: "I answer, first, by Bishop Asbury in the year 1769; and again in June, 1798,[*]

---

[*] Mr. Hargrove's memory evidently fails him here. The original record, which we have seen and extracted in the foregoing pages, proves that the *first* meeting of the society, which was for business, was held *June* 27, 1798; but the ordination took place in its *second* meeting, which was held on the 8th of *July*. He is, therefore, wrong in saying he was ordained "in June, 1799." It is quite likely Mr. Hargrove's memory may have failed in his statement of other dates; but we have thought it our duty to give

by a deputation of all the professing male members of the N. J. Doctrine—with the Rev. Mr. Ralph Mather as their chairman and consecrator: on which occasion they all imposed their hands on my head,
under the influence of an appropriate prayer."

This statement is important, because it corrects an error, into which
we were led by following an article already cited from the N. J.
Magazine, (p. 81, note,) respecting the time of Mr. Hargrove's ordination by Bishop Asbury, namely "at one of the Methodist Conferences, in the autumn of 1795." But the specific statement of the
mode of his ordination by the deputation of all the male members of
the church at Baltimore with "the Rev. Mr. Ralph Mather as their
chairman and *consecrator*," is peculiarly important, because it shows
that Mr. Hargrove was in fact ordained by *Mr. Mather with the concurrence* of the church at Baltimore. This we are aware was the
design of raising Mr. Mather to the pastorate—namely, to ordain
through him Mr. Hargrove, and so to derive an ordination from the
new church in England. We received this impression from personal
intercouse, in former years, with some of the old members of the
church at Baltimore.

When, therefore, we say above, that, in the first institution of the
new church both in London and Baltimore, there was a *trine*, we
must not be understood to speak in reference to the priesthood distinctively. In London there were at first but two grades of priests—
the one ordainer and the two ordained. There were indeed licensed
or other preachers, eight of whom, appointed by the London Society,
were employed in preaching to it before the ordinations of June 1,
1788: but if inaugurations *into the ministry* are to be made by the
promise of the holy spirit and by the representation of its translation," (Canon iv. 7,) then a mere license to preach does not introduce
into the ministry, and consequently the licentiateship is not a grade of
it. Therefore we say there were at first but two grades in London.
So in Baltimore, there were at first but two—the pastor and his assistant. And these were not acknowledged as distinct grades. For
Mr. Hargrove was considered equal to Mr. Mather, and took his pastoral office without any additional formal inauguration into it. So
the Rev. Messrs. James Hindmarsh and Samuel Smith, were ordained
on the same plane with their ordainer, and immediately took his
office out of his hands, by ordaining Messrs. Wright and Sibly, the
next candidates for the ministry.* It is believed that Mr. Robert

his statements in his own words, and leave the church to judge of them. Our statements have been made, either from our own knowledge, or from documents before us,
or from the information of the older members of the church here with whom we have
conversed.

* The Rev. Mr. Mason contends, "that in the new church, *before* any idea was
agitated about a trine in the ministry, such a trine did exist; it had actually come into
spontaneous existence without any external contrivance; it needed no thought, no effort,
to bring about this result, because it is one of the things that 'must be' in the very
nature of things, and therefore a matter in which man has no choice." (Int. Rep. for
Feb. 1848, p. 50.) To this we reply, Is not a man a *rational* free-agent, and co-
operator with the Lord, in establishing the external order of his church? Are men to
be led by *instinct* in this as animals are in the order of their creation—bees, for instance,

Hindmarsh, the first ordainer, was not at first regarded as a minister for any other purpose. At length, however, he became a regular preacher, and administrator of the sacraments, without any other ordination than that of the lot, by which the Lord ordained him. And the General Conference has for years acknowledged him as standing at the fountain head of the new-church ordinations. Still it is clear, that neither in England, nor in America, was there any distinct idea of the order of a trine of ministers in the new-church priesthood, when the first ministers were ordained. This remark will now be seen to be especially true in respect to the new church in America.

The Rev. Messrs. Mather and Hargrove, the first new-church mi-

in the government of their hive, and the constitution of a new queen bee, when the old one dies or is killed? Must not the order of the church be first the knowledge of truth formed in the intellectual plane of the mind. and this order be brought out as a new will thereby produced, in the conformity of the natural man to the spiritual man in ultimates? Undoubtedly, there was in England, there was here in America, and there will be every where, a *tendency* to a trine in the first institution of the church : for this is according to the universal flux of the divine order. But this trine must be indistinctly marked at first ; and can only come into more distinct and perfect form as the rational mind of the collective church is more fully formed. And the doctrine of the trine, no more than any other doctrine of the church, comes into spontaneous existence as " a matter in which man has no choice;" because the divine order flowing into the church must always be modified by man's form, as a being made to act in freedom according to reason. But if, in fact, the trine had actually come into spontaneous existence, as a matter in which man has no choice, and we may add, no consciousness, knowledge or acknowledgment, where was the trine existing here when Mr. Sibly was ordained by Messrs. James Hindmarsh and Samuel Smith, instead of Mr. Robert Hindmarsh? How does Mr. Mason see, and define, the first, second and third grades of the trine, as having come into actual spontaneous existence in the new church of England at this time ? Mr. Sibly was made an ordaining minister at once, without inauguration into any lower grades ; and not long after his ordination, he had an assistant, who read the prayers and otherwise led the worship of the congregation, while he preached. The having of such an assistant, is, we believe, a general custom in England now. But is this assistant regarded as holding the office of the ministry in its first or lowest grade ? Was it so when the assistant was first employed? Listen to what Mr. Sibly's first assistant says of himself. Mr. Jonathan Pratt, in a letter addressed to the Rev. John Hargrove, of Baltimore, and dated London, February 28, 1803, says—" With regard to myself, *I am no minister.* I only read prayers to our little society, of which Mr Sibly is minister. I am now in my sixty-fourth year : and so long as the Lord sees fit, I am desirous of being useful. But we are volunteers, as neither Mr. Sibly or myself have any thing for what we do; and never will have—only the best of all rewards, a consciousness, in our own breasts, that, to the best of our abilities, we are doing the Lord's work." Mr. Sibly was ordained in 1790 ; and in 1803, thirteen years afterwards, Mr. Pratt, his assistant, says of himself, "I am no minister." Where, then, was the trine in the ministry, as an acknowledged order of the new church in England at this time ? There was, indeed, the licentiate receiving his authority to preach from the magistracy of England, and appointed to preach by the London Society ; such as Mr. Mather, Mr. Salmon, and others. And we have supposed that this was the first grade in the english new-church ministry. But was it so regarded and acknowledged at the time in England ? And if this were, how could there be a trine acknowledged, when Mr. Robert Hindmarsh was not acknowledged as standing in a grade above those whom he ordained ? Are we not justified in saying there was no distinct idea of the order of a trine of ministers in the new-church priesthood, when the first ministers were ordained in England ?

nisters in America, were ordained July 8, 1798. From this time, we
have no record of any ordination having been performed for twelve
years. The first that appears was that of the Rev. Hugh White, who
is mentioned as a minister of the new church, residing in Virginia,
and as the author of a learned pamphlet entitled "Cosmogenia,"
which was commended, and, we believe, reprinted, in England. He
was a native of Scotland, and a deeply learned, though, as some thought,
an eccentric man. A memorandum on the manuscript of Mr. Hargrove
above mentioned, makes the date of his ordination 1810. Mr. Hargrove says—"The Rev. Hugh White, a Scotch Presbyterian, living
near Monticello in Virginia, received our doctrines, and made a journey to Baltimore to obtain ordination in the New Jerusalem Church—
having brought sufficient vouchers of his moral character, and standing as a highly graduated linguist and mathematician, from the first
characters in his place of residence."

From this ordination we can learn nothing in regard to a trine. It
does not appear that Mr. Hargrove had yet any notion of grades in
the ministry. He does not say with what powers he ordained Mr.
White. Although there was a trine in the methodist church, from
which he had come, of bishops, elders and deacons, it is probable he,
as yet, thought only of one grade and one ordination in the new
church. Therefore, it is quite probable, that he ordained Mr. White,
as Mr. Mather and himself had been, merely a pastor of a church or
congregation, without saying any thing about specific powers and
specific limitations. The question of trinal order had not yet risen
in his mind, as it was not agitated in England, when the form of
ordination, used in the case of Mr. Sibly and others, and adopted
here, was devised there. We have no evidence that this form was
drawn professedly from the writings of Swedenborg, where alone the
order of the trine is *distinctly* taught. Our english brethren did not
begin to do this till the year 1813, when, as we have seen, the circumstance of the ordination of a minister and the consecration of a
temple made the consideration of this question *necessary* in the London Conference. Then the propriety of looking to the authoritative
teachings of our church in the theological writings of Swedenborg
for *what is true order* in this matter, seems first to have been thought
of. And we have seen that the elaboration of this question in the
London Conference led to the formal declaration of the trine as the
true order of our ministry by the English General Conference in
1815. Now we have evidence that Mr. Hargrove had his mind
turned to the consideration, and brought to the affirmation, of this
order by the Minutes of that Conference, before he performed his
next ordination, in 1816. In the "Minutes of a General Conference," held in London, "from Tuesday the 16th to Thursday the
18th of July, 1816–60," p. 11, we find the following—"Besides the
letters addressed to the Conference, the Rev. M. Sibly read a letter
which he had lately received from the Rev. J. Hargrove, of Baltimore, in America, in which that gentleman *states his approbation of
the plan for arranging the ministry, as agreed to at the last Conference,* and communicates the intelligence of the welfare and gradual

increase of the Society of the New Church in that city." The plan of arranging the ministry here alluded to, was that of the trine, declared to be the true order by the Conference of 1815. And thus we see that Mr. Hargrove had thought of and approved that plan at or about the beginning of 1816.

The third minister, then, ordained in the new church of America, was the Rev. Hugh White. The fourth was the Rev. Adam Hurdus, who had formed around him a society of the new church in Cincinnati, Ohio. Mr. Hurdus was born, not far from Manchester, England, April 16th, 1760, and resided in that town for twenty-one years before coming to America. He was born and brought up in the established church of England, but joined the Methodists early in 1783. His attention was first drawn to the new church by the Rev. J. Wesley's thoughts on the writings of Baron Swedenborg published in the Armenian Magazine. In this way he was led to read those writings, and became favorably impressed by them, until the refutation of Mr. Wesley's thoughts, which he read in the New Jerusalem Magazine, published in London in 1790, more fully convinced him of the divine mission of Swedenborg. He was among the first who established a society of the new christian church, separate from the old, in Manchester. This society was formed in 1793, and erected the first temple for new-church worship in England, situated in Peter Street. In this society, Mr. Hurdus continued an active member till April, 1804, when he emigrated to the United States. He stopped first in Philadelphia; then crossed the Alleghany Mountains to Pittsburg; and at last settled in Cincinnati. Here, in 1808, with eight children, and with the view of preserving them from the falsities of the consummated church, he performed worship according to the new faith in his own house. Being a man of mechanical genius, and having made a small chamber organ, he used it as an accompaniment to his singing in worship, and was at first both minister and organist. His organ was the first in Cincinnati. The novelty of it, with singing, attracted many to the service, which was conducted according to a liturgy altered from that of the church of England for the use of the first society of the new church in that country. Similarity to the episcopal forms induced many of the Episcopalians to think that Mr. Hurdus was one of them; and led them to attend regularly on his worship, for that reason. The few books of the new church which he had were loaned freely, and their truths received by some; so that in 1811, seventeen or eighteen persons signed their names in a book, provided for that purpose, as believing in the Lord's second advent. This was the origin of the Cincinnati society, which has flourished so much since. Meetings were held regularly every Lord's Day, and continued to be well attended. And several who met with this society at different periods, leaving it to cultivate new lands or settle in new towns, propagated the seeds of the new faith throughout the western states. "In the summer of 1816," says Mr. Hurdus himself, "in a mercantile trip to Philadelphia, Adam Hurdus called and staid some days with the Rev. J. Hargrove, Baltimore—at whose request he was baptized and ordained. The certificate of the same bears date July 29, 1816."

7.

Not having seen Mr. Hurdus's certificate of ordination, we do not know with what powers he was ordained. It seems that he was ordained by Mr. Hargrove alone, and *at Mr. Hargrove's request*, without any formal concurrence of the churches at Baltimore or at Cincinnati. This was certainly a rather loose way of doing this sacred business. · But it must be borne in mind, that the notions of ecclesiastical order, that prevailed at first in this country, respecting the admission of persons into the new-church ministry, were extremely indefinite and lax; and there is nothing, perhaps, which we have had more cause to regret, than the extreme readiness and great haste which those who first assumed ordaining powers evinced in conferring ministerial powers upon any body and every body who asked for them, as well as pressing them upon some who did not ask for them, without previously determining from the Word and the writings of the church what should be the true order of the ministry and the right source of its ordinations. In England we have seen, they proceeded more cautiously. And it was not long before the sad effects of a contrary course produced more caution in this country. At first, there seemed to exist something like a disposition to offer a sort of *premium* to candidates for our ministry, by making admission into it as easy as possible, and by conferring its highest powers upon whomsoever should first ask for them. The idea seemed to prevail that the only thing needed to make a minister of the New Jerusalem was a society to preach to, a temple to preach in, and a *formal* ordination. A *divine call* and *suitable preparation*, seem not to have been at all looked for. We suppose that a person is divinely called to the new-church ministry, by that vein of his love which leads him from affection to the pursuit of theological studies, and by that mental aptitude for the performance of clerical functions, which a man receives by influx from the Lord through the spiritual world in his very conception. For such influx is tacit divine speech. And whatever use to mankind a man, by influx from the Lord through the spiritual world into him in his conception and birth, is designed and fitted to perform, to that use as his office, he is called by the Lord in a voice that is spiritually audible to the moral and mental perceptions of his fellow-men. In this way we believe men are divinely called to the various civil, military, naval, judicial, and executive offices of state, as well as to the leading offices of science, and the skilful handicrafts of art. And there is no difference in kind, whatever there may be in degree, between a divine call to these offices and that to the ministry of the church. Such is the Lord's *essential* call. There may be, when the Lord in his wisdom deems it proper, a *formal* call also. Such was the case with Swedenborg. No reflecting man of the new church can now doubt that he was called by the Lord, in his conception, gestation, birth, and education to mature manhood, to the high and holy office which he filled. Who can doubt that it was the concentrate influx through the spiritual world, in its preparation for the last judgment, into the soul of Swedenborg at its conception, as a focal point of that influx, which fitted and enabled him to see, in the spiritual world within himself, that judgment, as it

actually took place, and reveal the knowledge of its facts for the
use of the new church which was to be subsequently formed on
earth? For, in this case, the seeing or perceiving of the judgment
was but the unfolding of what was subsiding in him at his conception, comparatively as the expanding of a plant from a seed is but the
unfolding of what had subsided from the spiritual world. in the production of that seed from its plant. During his childhood, such were
the indications of his peculiar genius, that his parents were wont to
think angels were. speaking through him. He himself says that his
first thoughts were upon religious matters, and that at a very early
age, he was prone to reason with theologians about their tenet of
salvation by faith alone—saying that he was kept by the Lord from
imbibing such parts of the dogmatic theology of the day as would
have interfered with his full reception and clear transmission of the
theology of the new heaven and the new church. And he expressly
says that he was prepared by twenty-two years of study of the natural
sciences for the spiritual office to which he had been called. . Thus
it is manifest that Swedenborg had the *essential* divine call and *preparation* of which we speak. But in his case there was need of a
formal call too; and he assures us that the Lord did appear to him
in person for that purpose. (U. T. 779, 851.) And as to ministers
for the new church, we have quoted, in a former report, his assurance
that they would come from the universities or institutions of general
learning. For here, such as the Lord has called by their love, and
its latent vein leading them to the performance of clerical uses,
receive that *preparation*, as of " every student who is preparing for
the ministry before he becomes a priest," (U. T. 106,) without which
they never can effectively perform the functions of the clerical office.
And we have always thought that the ostensible new church in
America greatly erred in beginning the institution of a ministry by
giving merely the formal sign of the translation of the holy spirit,
and the conferring of only its formal powers, without first looking
for this essential divine call, and this suitable providential preparation
for the right and effective discharge of its duties. The consequence
of this error has been seen in the almost total failure to establish and
extend the church by the labors of her first ministers. The societies
which ordained them, could hardly stand up to do it, and very soon
reclined on sick couches to die of marasmus after their work was
done. Or they rose up to more efficiency only when the Lord, in
his providence, had sent more effective laborers into his vineyard.
Such is the general rule to which we suppose there may be exceptions. The Lord's calling illiterate *fishermen* in his first advent was
for the sake of the representation and signification: for " whatever the
Lord did *in the world* was representative, and whatsoever he spake
was significative." (Ap. Ex. 31.) But after he left the world he
called Paul, who was a man skilled in the theology of that day. And
now, in his second advent, the ministers to propagate the doctrines of
his church must have a preparation similar to that of the servant
whom he raised up to teach them. Still, even now, there may be
exceptions to this general rule. For men may possess· the learning

and talents requisite for the effective preaching of our doctrines without having graduated at the literary or theological institutions; and to certain classes of society in the very beginning of the church, preachers not learned in classic lore, but possessing strong native powers of mind, with good common sense, acute common perceptions, and the requisite acquaintance with our author's doctrinal expositions, are the best adapted mediums. Such a man was Mr. Hurdus : to some minds he was admirably suited as a teacher of new-church truths; and there can be no question that his thorough acquaintance with the theological writings of Swedenborg, combined with not a little general information, and his stern integrity in adhering to the true principles of our faith, more than once saved the little barque he was steering from being swamped in the storms which we all know it has so often encountered. And to our minds it is morally certain that recent radical changes would not have taken place in the Western Convention, if Mr. Hurdus were now on earth. In one of the documents of our appendix, (No. LV.,) we shall see him standing alone, for the true order of our church, against an otherwise unanimous vote of his society. And, therefore, we do not suppose that, because he was not a classical scholar, he ought not to have been ordained. The same remark may be made of others who have been, and are, very efficient ministers of our faith. But we contend that they would have been much more efficient, if to their other excellent qualifications, had been added the preparation for their office which Swedenborg had for his.* And we confidently assert, as a general rule, that, until this preparation is looked to, and required of all who now come into our ministry, we shall in vain endeavor to establish the New Jerusalem as a growing and prospering visible body in our land. And we repeat, that too great laxity in admitting persons into our ministry at first without it, was one chief cause of many of those societies which were first formed in this country having become defunct. Let any intelligent Newchurchman seriously inquire, what would have been the condition of our visible church now, in these middle states, if the money which was expended in building or purchasing the first three temples, had been laid out in establishing and endowing a seminary for the instruction of the children of newchurch parents upon the principles of their faith. Could not the incipient churches have continued to perform all the uses of public worship, and gradually gained the strength of numbers, by meeting in hired rooms suited to their infantile state ? And if they had laid out their chief strength in establishing a seminary for their children, may we not presume that some of these children, born from and to the ecclesiastical province of the *maximus homo*, would have been borne, on this stream of the Divine Providence, in all requisite preparation for it, to the clerical office? Then, for every minister so called and ordained of the Lord, should we not now have had a firmly

---

* Swedenborg, (U. T. 418,) asks, "who loves a prelate, a minister of the church, or any canonical person, except for his *learning*, integrity of life, and zeal for the salvation of souls?" Does not this imply that learning is a first and necessary qualification for a minister of the church ?

established and prospering society of the church, worshiping in a temple *permanently* its own property? But alas! how sad a reverse to this picture, does reality now present! Let us drop the curtain over what cannot be helped, and profit in future by the experience of the past. We have reason to believe, that, though there was an idea of grades in the new-church ministry when Mr. Hurdus was ordained by Mr. Hargrove, yet that idea was very imperfectly carried out in his ordination. He was probably ordained as a priest and teaching minister, with full powers, except the ordaining of other ministers. For he exercised all the powers except this last, until it was asked for him of, and granted to him by, the General Convention of 1828. (See Journal of 10th Gen. Con. p. 2.)

, The next ordination was that of the Rev. M. M. Carll, in Philadelphia, December 31, 1816. This brings us to a brief consideration of the charge that the tendency to the *episcopal* form of *government*, which has, in later years, been detected in the General Convention, took its rise in the Philadelphia society. The consideration of this matter comes up in the way of tracing out the first agitation of the question of a trine in the new-church ministry of this country. For we must see that this question did not arise in the Philadelphia society, nor was it first agitated by any of its leading members, but *was first broached by a leading New England minister.* The charge is, that grades in the ministry, and the use of a liturgy, adopted from the episcopal church as a model, were a tendency to episcopacy in the Philadelphia society, and from thence in the General Convention, before the eastern brethren took any part in the proceedings of that body. It is even asserted by Mr. Carll, who ought to have known better, that "so far as the First New Jerusalem Society Philadelphia is concerned, in her first public services and ministrations, the episcopal church was regarded as the model: a liturgy, now extant, was used, ceremonials, such as rising up and kneeling in certain parts of the service, the dress of the minister, reading the services in one place and delivering the sermon in another, the rule requiring written sermons, *as well as grades in the ministerial office, were all adopted* and FULLY RECOGNIZED *by the above society*, and were not objected to by the convention." (See Precursor, Vol. III., p. 22.) The reason assigned by Mr. Carll for the adoption of this order, is, at least, curious. "This choice arose," says he, "not from any strong attachment to external forms, but because it was thought by our leading members to be *at least as orderly* and *respectable* as *any;* and from a strong desire that the first public ministrations of the New Church should, by their propriety and decorum, *silence opposition* and *ridicule.*" A very cogent reason indeed why "*grades* in the *ministerial office*" were "adopted and *fully recognized* by the above society"! But we think it was a *great mistake* to assert that grades in the ministerial office were *adopted* and *fully recognized* by the First Philadelphia Society; and we think we shall be able to show that the adoption of something resembling the episcopal form of *worship*, sprung from a very different cause than the intention or the desire to adopt the episcopal form of *government*. Still the assertion is made by one who was the first minister of the Philadelphia society, and the fifth that was ordained in the new church of America, that grades in the ministerial office *were* adopted and fully recognized by that society, "and were not objected to by the convention." Thus it is asserted by high authority that the question of the trine was first agitated and fully recognized by the Philadelphia society before it was agitated in, and recognized by, the General Convention. This is certainly a very important historical fact, *if it be true.* And, therefore, in our historical sketch of this question in America, we are bound to examine its truth now when we are to portray the institution of the First Philadelphia Society and the ordination of its minister.

The charge which we are now considering, was made in reply to one of the reasons that were assigned for constituting the Central Convention, namely, "that we do not think the episcopal form of *government*, which the Eastern Convention is evidently seeking to induce upon the entire church in this country, is advisable at present." It is attempted to invalidate this reason by charging that there was a tendency to this form of *government* in the Philadelphia society, and from that in the General Convention, because that society adopted the episcopal form of *worship*—adopted and fully acknowledged grades in the ministerial office, before the eastern brethren took any part in the proceedings of the General Convention. Before we look at the origin of the Philadelphia society, we take leave to say a word in answer to this charge, and in explanation of what our objection to the Eastern Convention really was.

We state distinctly that we did not allude to grades in the ministry, or to the episcopal form of *worship*, when we objected to the Eastern Convention that it was seeking to induce upon the entire church in this country the episcopal form of *government*. For, in our view, there should be a trine in the ministry of every church, whatever its form of government may be; and the episcopal form of government exists in churches which have not the form of worship of the church of England. Thus the Methodists have both a trine in their ministry and an episcopal government, although they do not use the episcopal form of worship—although they have not a liturgy after the model of the church of England, nor "ceremonials, such as rising up and kneeling in certain parts of the service," nor "the dress of the minister," nor "reading the service in one place and delivering the sermon in another," nor "the rule requiring written sermons." Moreover, in objecting to the episcopal form of government in the Eastern Convention, we did not object to a trine in the church, because the presbyterian form of government has a trine. Thus there are, in the government of the presbyterian church, presbyteries, synods and general assemblies. And the general assembly is a supreme judicatory, having such a control over the lower bodies as a court of appeals has over inferior courts—having, for instance, the right to inspect the *records* of the proceedings of the lower bodies, and the power to annul, alter, or condemn them.

What then *did* we object to in the Eastern Convention? We

objected to the tendency to place supreme ecclesiastical power, influence or control in the ordaining ministers as bishops of the general church. And we more especially objected to the vesting such power, influence or control in *one man* as the head bishop. This, whatever might be its propriety as a principle of abstract order, we did not think applicable to the present condition of our church in this country, and especially in these middle states. We thought the form of government for our church in this country should be assimilated as near as possible to the form of civil government. Hence we would have had the supreme power vested in the whole church as a general body, in which the clergy should have been an ecclesiastical council, for the administration of such things as relate to the divine law and worship. The clergy were to be arranged in a trine of subordinate grades for *their own* government, and not for the government of the church. Those were to hold the highest grades who performed the most general functions. 'And the *representative* ecclesiastical head was to be the presiding officer of the council for the time being. This officer was not to be permanently but annually elected; and the office, like that of the president of the United States, was to be held by any one man for only a limited time. The great thing to which we objected was the vesting supreme and *lasting* power in any one man. This we regarded as a tendency to papacy in *essence* if not in *form*. The general body of the church was only to have a general government for the performance of general uses; and was to have no more control over particular churches than the general government of the United States has over the particular states. These, for all local uses, were to be independent of the general body. Hence the president of the general body, or any ordaining minister, was to exercise no episcopal authority—was not, in other words, "to institute societies" or "to watch over" the minister of any particular society. And a tendency to vest in the president of the General Convention a supervisory authority over the ministers and particular societies in its connection,—so that a society in its connection would have no right to employ a minister not belonging to that body, without first consulting its president as to the propriety of its doing so,—is something more than an *episcopal* form of government in our church in this country, to which we have all along objected and to which we do still most strenuously object. The pastor or teacher of a society was, in our view, to be subordinate to the officer of the higher grade in the general government of the church; but by virtue of this the general officer would no more have a right to inspect and control the order and doings of a particular society, than the pastor or teacher has a right to inspect and control the domestic order and private doings of any one of the families which compose his society. Thus we would have had the ecclesiastical order of our church resemble the civil order of our country.

Well, then, the question is, where did this tendency to episcopal *government* begin? And supposing that this form of government is necessarily involved in the order of a trine of discrete grades in the ministry, where, and when, and by whom was the question of this

order first agitated in the General Convention? Did it arise in the
First Philadelphia Society? Were the leading men in that society
originally Episcopalians, so that they were prone to induce an episcopal form of *government* on the society itself in its original formation, and, through it, to create such a form in the General Convention
that was first called by it? It matters not, that a clerical robe was
adopted for the priest, or a liturgy for the use of the people; for
these, we will show, sprung from a very different root than a banker-
ing for an episcopal government. And it matters not that a trine of
grades gradually and imperceptibly came into being in the ministry
during the early conventions; for this was a natural consequence of
the new church being propagated in this country from England,
where the order of the trine had been decreed to be the true order for
our ministry before the first convention in this country took place,
and before the First Philadelphia Society was constituted a church.
But where did the tendency to vest supreme ecclesiastical · control
and influence, or even ordaining power, in the highest grade of the
clergy, or in the clergy alone, arise? This is what we call a tendency
to episcopacy; and this was not propagated in this country from
England. Did it begin in the Philadelphia society? Nay, did the
adoption and *full recognition* of grades in the ministerial office first
take place in that society, and flow from it into the convention called
by it?

If the reader will turn to Newchurchman, Vol. I., p. 162, he will
see our Second Document for New-church History. In that, Condy
Raguet, Esq., who was secretary of the First New Jerusalem Society
of Philadelphia when it was constituted a church, brings down the
history of that society from 1810 to 1817, when the First General
Convention was called. And we now state the following facts, as
historical events of some importance in their bearings on the question before us.

First, "The American Society for disseminating the Doctrines of
the New Jerusalem Church" was instituted at Philadelphia on the
25th of· December, 1815. This was a general society, like that
instituted in London in 1783, for the dissemination of our doctrines,
but nothing in the nature of a church, or ecclesiastical polity, for the
appointment, ordination, or consecration of *ministers* to publish the
glad tidings of salvation to the world. We have seen that the Baltimore society, instituted June 27, 1798, was also of this character in
its first meeting. But as this, in its second meeting, about two weeks
afterwards, became a church for the ordination of ministers; and as
the London society had, for the same purpose, five years after its
first institution; so this society, instituted in Philadelphia, became a
church for the ordination of ministers about one year after it first
came into existence. Before this time it had been merely a meeting
of congenial minds,—for a while exclusively males,—to read and converse on theological subjects. But about the time this general society
was instituted, the members of it in Philadelphia held meetings of
both male and female receivers of the new-church doctrines, for
social worship, with a leader and appropriate external forms.

Second, The receivers of the doctrines of the New Jerusalem in thé city of Philadelphia, first instituted a church there, with the title of ".The First New Jerusalem Church in the City of Philadelphia," . on the 24th of December, 1816.

Third, The Rev. Maskell M. Carll was ordained the minister of that church, Dec. 31, 1816.

, Fourth, the Temple which that church erected was consecrated on Wednesday, the first of January, 1817.

Fifth, at a meeting of a number of members of the new church, from different parts of the United States, held in Philadelphia, on Wednesday, the first of January, 1817, the Rev. Mr. Hargrove in the chair, it was resolved to hold a convention of the receivers of the doctrines of the New Jerusalem throughout the United States, at the temple in Philadelphia, on the 15th of May, 1817—that being ascension day.

Thus we learn that the institution of a church in Philadelphia, the ordination of its minister, the consecration.of its temple, and the calling of the First General Convention of the New Church in the United States, were simultaneous events. And the First General Convention was actually held in Philadelphia only four and a half months afterwards. Therefore, as the beginning and formation of the Philadelphia society, was almost the same thing as the beginning of the General Convention, it is an event of leading importance in tracing out what was the ecclesiastical order that most probably gave form to that body in its inception. Now we think it demonstrably clear, that the plastic influences, in Philadelphia, or through the church there, which gave form to the General Convention, in its inception, were *congregational* and not *episcopal*. This was the form of *government* which the influence of the leading men, or the forming minds, in Philadelphia, tended to produce in the General Convention at first. There was no idea of a *trine* of *ministers*, in the highest grade of whom ordaining powers were exclusively to reside; and there was no tendency to produce this order, either in the principle on which the church was instituted, or in the institution of the church on that principle, or in the ordination of its minister, or in the relation in which he stood to it after he was ordained. The leading man and forming mind was not an Episcopalian, by birth, education, or propensity; and, therefore, there was not, on this ground, a tendency to the episcopal form of government in-the society which was formed through him. The ruling principle which seems to have prevailed in and pervaded the beginnings of the new church in Philadelphia, was this—to institute a church which should possess and exercise ordaining powers as well as control the minister ordained by it, as *a congregate* or *collective man*. And the tendency of this principle, as it should flow into the formation of a general body of the church, was from *minus* through *major* to *maximus homo*. The tendency was from individuals to make *a church* in a particular form, which, as to its own order and local government, was to be independent of all others; and then to. form the general body as *the churches* in an aggregate, and not as *a church* in a general form. In other words, the tendency was from a small, through a larger, to the largest *congrega-tion.* And the largest congregation was not to be an assemblage of legislators for *government,* but a meeting of members of the church on the largest plane, for common sympathy, or common support in embracing the faith and common effort in disseminating it. *The churches* were to combine for common ends or general uses; and might have a general government, with general officers—officers of, the highest grade—to effect such ends or perform such uses. But the general government was not to control or govern the churches in any thing relating to their local government or domestic economy. How this differs from what the General Convention was tending to become, under the leading influence of our eastern brethren, will clearly appear as we proceed in this historical sketch of the rise, progress and present state of the question of the trine in this country. Here we will only observe, that this differs from that as the *union* in our government differs from a kingdom, a monarchy, or an empire as a *unit.* For if the General Convention were to become *one church* as a kingdom, monarchy, empire or the roman catholic church is one, then it should have *one visible personal head.* But if the general church were but a union of particular churches, then it might have for its visible head a *council,*—as the first christian church had in the twelve apostles and other ministers at Jerusalem,—the president of which might *for the time being*—for "that year"—*represent* the Lord as *pontifex maximus.** Thus a sort of states general of the New

* Swedenborg, in a letter addressed to the universities of Upsal, Lund, and Abo, says—" I have been informed by two gentlemen in the senatorial department of justice, that the senators are *pontifex maximus,* to which I then gave no answer ; but, in case I should hear such assertions from them, I shall answer, that they are not at all *pontifex maximus,* but *vicarius vicarii pontificis maximi ;* because Christ our Saviour is the only *pontifex maximus ;* the states of the kingdom are his *vicarius ;* wherefore they are answerable to him; and the senators are the *vicarius,* for the states; because they are appointed ; and that hence they are *vicarius vicarii pontificis maximi.* That the. pope of Rome called himself *pontificem maximum,* is of pride, because he has taken and assumed to himself all the power of Christ our Saviour, and placed himself on his throne, making the people believe that he is Christ on earth. Every inferior *pontifex* or *vicarius pontificis maximi* ought to have their consistory. The states of the king-dom have their consistory in the ecclesiastical division of the states, and the senators have their consistory, particularly at the universities."

It is remarkable here that Swedenborg makes the Lord's vicar on earth a *collective body.*—" the states of the kingdom,"—and not any individual man. That the senate is but the vicar of that vicar. And that the Lord alone is *pontifex maximus*—the pope of Rome having claimed that title arrogantly. It is therefore clear that there ought not to be any visible personal head of the church on earth. And we say above, the president of the council may *represent the Lord* as pontifex maximus—not be pon-tifex maximus himself; just as the president of the United States represents the Lord as the common good. Are not *the churches* the spiritual states of the Lord's kingdom on earth? May not the general clergy, that is, clergy of the highest grade, with repre-sentatives from all the local clergy of these churches, form an ecclesiastical senate, for consultation, advice and recommendation on matters pertaining to the whole as a com-mon body? The general government of the church should be that of superior love and wisdom ; and these would be best represented in and by the congregate intelligence and wisdom of such a senate. Then the churches of *his* kingdom would be the Lord's vicar, and the senate would be the vicar of this vicar. And the president, for the time

Jerusalem in our country would be supreme, and not any one man as pontifex maximus. And so we should have a congregational government on the largest scale in our general church, and not an episcopacy or a papacy. The office being held only one year, by the same man, or for a short term of years,—as in the case of the president of the United States,—would tend to show that the power was in the *office*, and so to divest *that* of mere personal influences. And thus would the church be guarded against the abuse of power by personal ambition. We will observe further, that, as to the trine in the ministry, the tendency of the principles active in instituting and forming the Philadelphia church was to develop the trine first in its lower degrees, and in its higher degrees afterwards, or in its highest degree last. Hence ordaining powers were first assumed by, or vested in, a particular church, and in the pastor or teacher of this church in connection with it—not in the pastor, or teacher, or other minister alone. Next these powers were vested in two or more particular churches, with their particular ministers, acting concurrently. And then in the General Convention of all these particular churches as a whole, or aggregate of them, represented by the pastors of those particular churches in whom ordaining powers had been from the first vested. This, we say, is true of the Philadelphia church. It is not so true of the church at Baltimore. For we have shown that ordaining powers were not at first supposed to rest in the Baltimore society; and we have shown that Mr. Hargrove ordained Mr. White and Mr. Hurdus on his own responsibility, and without any manifest or declared concurrence of the Baltimore church. But we shall show, that, when the Philadelphia church was instituted, ordaining powers were supposed to rest in the society, and only in the minister as a member of it. Thus, from first to last, it has been supposed that ordaining powers were vested in the church as a *whole man*, and not in the minister or ministers of any grade as either the individual or collective *head* of that man. The head ministers merely *represent* the whole man, or the Lord, who is the soul, and therefore the sole head of his church. And the general organ of the collective church was to have only *recommendatory* and not *legislative* control over the churches. Consequently the form of government was first and last *congregational*. For the General Convention was but a congregation in a larger form; and its government extended only to itself.—But to the proof in the institution and formation of the church in Philadelphia.

While we inspect the character of the Philadelphia church in its origin, we must not fail to call to mind the law which determines

being, might *represent* the Lord as the high *priest*, or chief *good*, because he would represent the churches, and their interest, as a whole, or a greatest man. In this case, the laity should have their house of representatives, with jurisdiction concurrent with that of the senate, and forming with the senate a sort of ecclesiastical *congress* of the whole new church in the United States. And the reason why our ecclesiastical senate and its president should be in the relative position of the civil and political president with his cabinet and other general officers, is, because ours is a general ecclesiastical government only—for the *general* regulation of those matters that pertain to " the administration of the *divine law* and *worship*."

the form and regulates the constitution of societies of the church. A society of the church "is a single man, and the individuals that compose it form, as it were, one body, and are distinguished one from another like the members in a body." (U. T. 412.) This is the law. Hence in every society of the church there must be those who hold the province of the head, with its internal and external organs: those who hold the province of the breast, with its organs and members; and those who hold the province of the abdomen, with its viscera and extremities. And hence, in both the formation and subsequent action of every religious society, there are those who give determination to its will, distinct thought to its understanding, and rational guidance to its common action, just as the brains, heart and lungs influence, direct and maintain the action of all the other members of the body. This law is universal in its application to all society. Hence, even in our democratic country, the action of political parties, conventions, or other meetings, is always determined by a comparatively few leading men. And, therefore, it could not have been otherwise in the First New Jerusalem Church in Philadelphia, when that was instituted. Who now was the head man and forming mind of this? What are the facts? The following is the account of the institution of this church which we find in its book of records.

Philadelphia, December 24, 1816.

A number of gentlemen, receivers of the doctrines of the New Jerusalem Church, composing part of the religious society which has, since the commencement of the present year, held its meetings for worship at the school room of Mr. Maskell M. Carll, and for whose accommodation the temple, just completed at the corner of Twelfth and George Streets, was erected, assembled on the evening of the twenty-fourth day of December, in the year of our Lord one thousand eight hundred and sixteen.

Present—Maskell M. Carll, Daniel Thunn, Jonathan W. Condy, William Schlatter, Johnson Taylor, Condy Raguet, John Stirling.

An instrument of writing was presented to the meeting by Mr. Condy, which, having been unanimously adopted as the articles of an association, and signed by the gentlemen present, it was,

On motion, *Resolved,* That the same be presented for signature to those gentlemen who have evinced a disposition to co-operate with us in the management of the concerns of the church, and who are full receivers of the doctrines.

Condy Raguet was then appointed secretary of the society, and the meeting was adjourned to meet on Wednesday, the 25th of December, at 10 o'clock, A. M.

The following is the Instrument of Association:

WE WHOSE NAMES ARE UNDERWRITTEN, Readers and Receivers of the Doctrines of the New Jerusalem Dispensation set forth in the writings of Emanuel Swedenborg, Messenger of the Lord, being desirous of becoming a church under the said dispensation, do hereby agree to unite ourselves into a Religious Society or Congregation for the worship of our Lord Jesus Christ, in his Divine Humanity, as the Only God of Heaven and Earth, according to the said doctrines, under the name of

"*The First New Jerusalem Church in the City of Philadelphia:*"

with power to form rules and regulations for the good government of such our Religious Society or Congregation, and for the admission of new

, members, and the conduct of divine worship therein; and to take the necessary measures for obtaining a charter of incorporation, when it shall be deemed expedient to apply for the same.

The society shall meet on the morning of to-morrow, being Christmas Day, at 10 o'clock, at the New Jerusalem Temple, with power to adjourn to such time and place as may then be determined upon.

Done at the City of Philadelphia this twenty-fourth day of December, in the year of our Lord's First Advent MDCCCXVI.

ORIGINAL MEMBERS.

Francis Bailey,	*J. H. Brinton,*	*Wm. Kneass,*
Daniel Lammot,	*, Jno. K. Graham,*	*Wm. Schlatter,*
Daniel Thuun,	*Maskell M. Carll,*	*Tho. Smith,*
J. W. Condy,	*John Stirling,*	*John Parr,*
Johnson Taylor,	*Condy Raguet,*	*Frederick Eckstein.*

Thus was the First Philadelphia Church instituted. At the meeting next day, nothing more was done than to authorize the secretary to let the pews in the temple for one year, with the restriction that the privilege of holding a pew should "give no right of membership, or of voting in any of the concerns of the church."

. At a meeting held December 27, 1816, "the following resolutions . were severally proposed by Mr. Condy and unanimously adopted."

Resolved, That Maskell M. Carll be ordained a Priest and Minister of "The First New Jerusalem Church of the City of Philadelphia," with power under the authority and at the request of the society, and in the manner and under such restrictions as they may prescribe, to ordain other Priests and Ministers of the New Jerusalem Church, with power also to conduct public worship, to celebrate the sacrament of the Lord's supper, marriages, baptisms and funerals, and generally to perform all holy rites and divine ordinances of the church.

Resolved, That the office of the ordination be celebrated on Tuesday, the 31st inst., at 9 o'clock, A. M., and that the Rev. John Hargrove, minister of the New Jerusalem Church in Baltimore, be requested to perform the same accordingly; and that, previous to such ordination, this and the preceding resolution be publicly and openly read.

Resolved, That the doctrines taught in the church shall be in agreement with the doctrines of the New Jerusalem as set forth in the writings of Emanuel Swedenborg, Messenger of the Lord.

Resolved, That worship in the Church be according to the Liturgy lately printed in Philadelphia, and the hymn to be sung, be selected from the book now publishing for the church. No other shall be sung, but with the assent of the vestry when appointed.

Resolved, That a vestry consisting of seven members be chosen, who shall, until otherwise ordered, have the superintendence of the church, subject to the revision of the society. They shall at least once a month report their proceedings.

Resolved, That, in reading the Word, and in addressing the Lord in prayer, the minister be habited in a black gown, as correspondent to the state of deep humiliation and self-abasement into which it is incumbent on the people to enter in those sacred offices of worship; and that, whilst preaching and teaching the doctrines of the church, he be clothed with a white gown, as corresponding with the divine truth from which flow all the truths of the church: and that Mr. Condy and Mr. Carll be a committee to procure the said garments.

The next meeting of the society was held on the 30th of December, 1816. This was merely for the purpose of making preparation for the ordination of Mr. Carll next day. There were seven members present. And it was

Resolved, That the hour of ordination be changed from nine until half-past eleven o'clock to-morrow morning; that it be performed in the new temple, and that timely notice thereof be given to all the members of the church.

Resolved, That Messrs. Condy and Schlatter be a committee to present Mr. Carll to the officiating minister at the time of ordination.

On the following day, December 31, 1816, Mr. Carll was ordained according to the tenor of the foregoing proceedings; and the follow- ing intelligence of this ordination was published in the first number, p. 65, of " The New Jerusalem Church Repository," issued in Janu- ary 1817, and edited by Mr. Condy.

On Tuesday, the 31st of December last, agreeably to the unanimous invi- tation of the members of " The First New Jerusalem Church in the city of Philadelphia," Mr. Maskell M. Carll was " ordained a priest and minister of said church, with power, under the authority and at the request of the society, and in the manner and under such restrictions as they may pre- scribe, to ordain other priests and ministers of the New Jerusalem Church; with power also to conduct public worship, to celebrate the sacrament of the Lord's supper, marriages, baptisms and funerals, and generally to per- form all holy rites and divine ordinances of the church." The ceremony of ordination, which was performed by the Rev. Mr. Hargrove, of Baltimore, will be given at full length, in the second number of the Repository.

The Rev. Mr. Carll, thus ordained by the Rev. Mr. Hargrove, assisted that clergyman in consecrating " the New Jerusalem Temple, in the city of Philadelphia, situate at the corner of George and Twelfth Streets," the next day, that is, " on Wednesday, the 1st of January, 1817, in the presence of a large assembly; of whom there were some members of the New Church from different states." And at a meeting, held in this temple, on the same day, the first conven- tion of the new church in this country was called.

We here see the origin of the First Philadelphia Church in clear light. And it is conspicuously discerned, that the head man and forming mind in the institution and constitution of this church was *Jonathan W. Condy*. Who was he? By his *fruits* we must know him. Was he an Episcopalian? Does his work here show that he was? No. We happen to have known him well. He was the chief means of bringing the writer of this report into the new church, and into its ministry. Well, who was Jonathan W. Condy? He was a descendant of the Huguenots, and was thought to have had some remote relationship with the Great Condé. From a graduate of the Pennsylvania University, he became a man of general learn- ing and distinguished ability in various callings. He was clerk of the House of Representatives in Congress, when that body assem- bled in Philadelphia. And at the time now alluded to, he was a lawyer of high eminence at the Philadelphia bar. But he was also a classical scholar, an oriental linguist, and a theologian of the highest order. He had a critical knowledge of the hebrew, as well as of the greek and latin languages—was well versed in general theology, and profoundly read in the theological writings of Swedenborg. And, in our humble opinion, a more powerful, brilliant, or commanding intellect, never served or honored the visible body of our church in this country, and perhaps in any other.

Now Mr. Condy was originally a Presbyterian; and he himself says, (N. J. C. Repository, p. 155,) "in Philadelphia, there are more from the Presbyterian Church than any other." Francis Bailey, one of the first receivers of the doctrines in Philadelphia, and perhaps in the United States, and Mr. Carll himself, with Johnson Taylor, and other leading members, were also Presbyterians. Thus the leading and forming influences in the First Philadelphia Society were presbyterian; and, as we clearly see, from the documents just presented, gave it a *congregational* constitution. There was certainly no tendency to an *episcopal* form of *government* here. There was no clergyman, who, having been first commissioned and sent forth to preach, as the apostles were, by the Lord, or no Titus sent by him, and appointed, to "set in order the things that were wanting and ordain elders" in this city. There was nothing like a bishop to "institute this society" or to "order this church." There was nothing like a bishop ordained over it. The minister was in fact a very secondary man, and made to hold quite a secondary office. He was, indeed, endued with ordaining power, but he was to exercise it only "*under* the *authority* and at the *request* of the *society*, and *in the manner* and under such *restrictions* as *they* may *prescribe*." Thus, in fact, the ordaining power was in the society, and it was only exercised by the minister as the member or organ of the society. Was this any thing like *episcopal* government? Observe, too, that the mode of worship is prescribed by the society, and even the hymns that were to be sung, were to be selected "but with the assent of a vestry when appointed." The "vestry consisting of seven members" were to "have the superintendence of the church, subject to the revision of the *society*"—mark, not of the *minister*. Quite episcopalian, truly!

And now we come to the *liturgy* and the *clerical robes*, those irrefragable proofs of a tendency to an episcopal form of *government* in the Philadelphia society! Here they are, prescribed in the fifth and last resolution quoted above. In the adoption of these, Mr. Carll says the episcopal church was taken "as a *model*." If this was so, then all we have to say is, the modellers were very poor artists. The liturgy was formed mainly by Mr. Condy; and his model, if he had any, was a distinctively new-church liturgy, made some years before, by the Rev. Robert Hindmarsh of England. The leading principle of this was to take the formularies of worship wholly from the Word in the letter. Mr. Condy did not adhere to this principle strictly, except in the afternoon service, which consists almost altogether of passages taken from the Word. Was this an episcopal form? And as to the black and white gowns, we see that the order was entirely reversed. For in the episcopal church the minister prays in the white gown and preaches in the black one. The first new-church minister that we ever heard preach in Boston was Mr. Samuel Worcester, then a licentiate. We heard him preach, if we recollect rightly, in the winter of 1820–21, in, we think, Boylston Hall, and we very distinctly recollect that he wore in the desk a sort of clerical *black* silk robe, something in the shape of a morning gown. Was this an *episcopal* tendency in Boston? Oh no; this was the habit of the unitarian clergy there. Why then should Mr. Carll's preaching in a *white* linen robe, be an episcopal tendency in Philadelphia? No: the true reason for adopting a clerical robe, and the kind of one, was, that there might be a spiritual *correspondence* between the form and the function of the minister.

But the forms of worship of the church of England were, in some measure, adopted. Why? Mr. Carll foreshadows the reason—"This choice arose, not from any strong attachment to external forms, but because it was thought to be at least as orderly and respectable as any, and from a strong desire that the first public ministrations of the new church should, by their propriety and decorum, silence opposition and ridicule." Yes, that was it—not to appear *ridiculous* in the eyes of those who should attend the worship. Hence those forms were adopted, not from any episcopalian predilections in the members—not because episcopal forms, either of worship or government, were deemed the only proper ones for the new church—not because they were thought to be abstractly right, or in the only true order, but simply from a desire to make a favorable impression on the surrounding community. But why was not the presbyterian form of extemporaneous prayer and preaching adopted? Was not this equally respectable? Would it not, if ably filled, have made as good an impression upon promiscuous audiences? Undoubtedly; and we have reason to believe that this form might have been adopted, if it could have been. When Mr. John Burtt lectured on the new-church doctrines in the commissioners' hall of the Northern Liberties, he prayed extemporaneously; because he had that gift. But the minister of the First Philadelphia Society had a liturgy prepared for him, because he had not that gift; and would have made himself ridiculous if he had attempted to exercise it. Besides, without a gift, and much preparation, extemporaneous efforts in the pulpit would expose a novice to the influx of enthusiastic spirits, as well as subject him to disparaging observations. The same reason may be assigned for "the rule requiring written sermons." Some of us will never forget the signal failures of the minister of the Philadelphia society when he had the temerity to attempt extemporaneous preaching without the slightest qualification for it!. In short, we well know, that, in the view of the leading mind and forming spirit, whose plastic hand moulded the First Philadelphia Society into ecclesiastical shape, any and every external form of worship and of government was admissible in the New Jerusalem, according to the circumstances of that church, or the peculiar genius of its professing members. And nothing could have been farther from his desire, or his notions of propriety, than the idea of inducing and fastening any one form—whether episcopalian, presbyterian or congregational—upon the whole new church in either her particular or general formations. He was just as far from this, as he would have been from the wish or effort to make all the kingdoms or monarchies of Europe democracies.

As to the order of a trine in the ministry, we have no evidence that Mr. Condy, or any of the members of the Philadelphia society, had distinct ideas on this subject. There is no evidence that this had been a subject of mature thought and deliberate investigation with them. And nothing can be clearer, or more certain, than that " grades in the ministerial office were" *not* "adopted and *fully recognized*" by their society, either in its beginning, or in its progress to the formation of a general convention. There was, indeed, a wish, at first, to have two ministers conjointly in the pastoral office of this society, as well as in that of Baltimore; and so there might have been an embryo trine in this society as there was in that: but this wish was not gratified. And there is not a vestige of testimony in the whole proceedings of the Philadelphia society that the question of a trine was ever agitated in it, as we have seen it was, for two years, in the London Conference, or that there was any attempt to deduce this order from the Word and the writings of Swedenborg, with a view of bringing it before the General Convention, for its deliberative action or adoption.

The fact that the Philadelphia society did at first desire two of its members to take the pastoral office conjointly in its connection, is an interesting one, and deserves to be fully displayed here. As the society needed the gratuitous services of a minister, they had to look for some person who could support himself by some other calling while he discharged the duties of the ministerial office in their connection. We are persuaded that the attempt to do this was an error ; and that all efforts to establish and build up the new church in this way, will prove abortive. The only way is to develop ministerial abilities in those youths who are called to the ministry by the Lord ; and then to support them as properly qualified men in an exclusive devotion of all their powers to the duties of their sacred office. Such ministers will, in the Lord's divine providence, never want a temporal support. And the church must flourish under their ministrations. But societies, like individuals, can gain wisdom only by experience. So the Philadelphia society had to learn. And as they wanted a man to do the duties of the ministerial office gratuitously, they thought of dividing the duties between two, so as to make a supply of their wants more practicable. They offered the office of pastor to their former leader, Mr. Carll, in conjunction with Mr. Condy. The latter was a lawyer with a lucrative practice, the former was the principal of a female seminary in high repute and profitable success. Mr. Carll had been the leader of the society's worship in its meetings both in Norris's Alley and in his own school room back of his residence in Arch Street. For this office he was well qualified by an excellent voice, much skill in reading the prayers and leading the singing, and also by a certain grave and devout manner, which squared with what people generally thought becoming in a minister. But he was not a man of classical education. He was not a theologian. And he was greatly deficient in that mental or persuasive force, and leading influence, which are indispensable in the leader and former of a religious society. In short, he had neither the original genius nor the

8

acquired ability, to lead or teach the master men who helped to make
up the society of which he was the formal pastor. All these qualifications Mr. Condy possessed in a high degree. If, therefore, the two
could have been induced to act in the office conjointly—if they could
have had Mr. Carll to lead the worship, and Mr. Condy to write and
preach the sermons—they would have been completely made up.
This idea being conceived and entertained, brought about the following correspondence:

Letter of the First Society of the New Jerusalem in Philadelphia.

We, whose names are hereunto signed, residing in the city of Philadelphia, receivers and readers of the doctrines of the New Jerusalem Church,
as revealed to the world in the writings of Emanuel Swedenborg, servant
of the Lord Jesus Christ, being desirous that divine worship in the temple
now preparing for our use, should be conducted by clergyman, called to the
high and responsible office of pastors in a manner conformable to received
order; and reposing the most implicit confidence in the uprightness, piety
and qualifications of our beloved brethren in the Lord, Jonathan William
Condy and Maskell M. Carll; do hereby express and make known our
unanimous and solemn wish, that those brethren would consent to receive,
at an early period, the holy rites of ordination, and to take upon themselves
conjointly the ministry of the new dispensation in the first temple consecrated in Philadelphia to the sole worship of our Lord God and Saviour
Jesus Christ.

Philadelphia, Dec. 1st, 1816–60.

Daniel Thuun,	*Ann Parr,*	*Frederick Eckstein,*
Charlotte Thuun,	*Wm. Kneass,*	*Jane Eckstein,*
Condy Raguet,	*Mary Kneass,*	*Louisa Adilesterren,*
Catharine Raguet,	*Wm. Strickland,*	*Frances Bailey,*
John H. Brinton,	*Thos. Smith,*	*Eleanor Bailey,*
George Garth,	*E. and Sarah Smith,*	*Margaret Bailey,*
William Schlatter,	*daughters,*	*Lydia Bailey,*
C. N. Schlatter,	*John K. Graham,*	*Abby Bailey,*
John Stirling,	*Michael Baker,*	*Elizabeth Harper,*
John Hunt,	*Johnson Taylor,*	*Anna Raguet,*
Christian N. Hunt,	*Daniel Groves,*	*E. Duche Hill,*
Daniel Lammot,	*John Keemle,*	*Rebecca Keemle,*
Susan V. Lammot,	*Robert Gill,*	*Anna Keemle,*
John Parr,	*John Eckstein,*	*Elizabeth Lammot.*

ANSWERS TO THE FOREGOING LETTER.

I. *From J. W. Condy, Esq.*

Baltimore, Dec. 6, 1816.

DEAR SIR,
    Your letter of the second instant, reached me on the fourth, inclosing the
very unexpected testimonial of affection and respect on the part of the receivers of the N. J. verities in the city of Philadelphia, by which they expressed their wishes that Mr. Carll and myself would take upon us the holy
rites of ordination in the ministry of the new dispensation, for the purpose
of receiving the pastoral charge of the church in Philadelphia. This high
mark of their confidence I felt to be as painful as it was to me honorable.
For whilst, on the one hand, I experienced an ardent desire that the Lord
would qualify me for a use so noble and exalted in his church, on the other
hand, in searching the state of my own mind, I could find no freedom to

take upon myself so sacred and responsible a charge. I had previously also received, from my two very worthy friends, Mr. Schlatter and Mr. Taylor respectively, letters urging the same request, and leading me to anticipate your communication. I had no hesitation with myself in perceiving that, at present, I was not at liberty to comply with so urgent, affectionate and flattering a request. Yet it appeared that an answer by return of mail would manifest a precipitancy ill comporting with that respectful disposition which I felt for my kind friends of the new church, and which they so justly merited, and a precipitancy which the importance of the occasion imperiously forbade. The answer was therefore deferred until next morning, when the mail brought me letters from Mr. Thuun and Mr. Stirling, expressed in such terms, and breathing such an affection, and so urgent a spirit of friendship, as could not have been resisted, had I not been satisfied, that, at least for the present, it was not my duty to comply. The last communication deserved the delay of another mail. Thus has my answer been procrastinated until the present moment. My worthy friends of the New Church will, I am sure, appreciate justly the feelings I must necessarily experience in finding myself under the necessity of declining to comply with so flattering an invitation. At the same time I feel free to declare that, if my judgment should at any time be clearly convinced that it is my duty to take upon me the sacred office of the ministry in the N. J., no worldly consideration will restrain me.

Whilst I make this declaration with respect to myself, it gives me great pleasure to declare my perfect concurrence in your call to Mr. Carll, and in the measure of requesting him to come without delay to Baltimore for ordination; and that he be accompanied by at least two of the members. * *

J. W. CONDY.

C. Raguet, Esq.

II. *From Mr. Maskell M. Carll.*

Philadelphia, Dec. 15, 1816.

MY DEAR BROTHER IN THE LORD,

I had the honor to receive a communication from you, signed by our brethren and sisters, professing the heavenly doctrines of the New Church; expressing a wish that Mr. J. W. Condy and myself would take upon us conjointly the pastoral charge of the first congregation, professing the above doctrines, in the city of Philadelphia. Knowing the result of the application to our beloved brother, I hasten to lay before you, without further delay, my own views and determination.

The present is not a proper time for me to express my sincere regret at the declination of Mr. C.: let it suffice to say, that no one would have more sincerely rejoiced than myself, if the acceptance of the call, could have been compatible with his present views and feelings. Yet "we will not sorrow even as others who have no *hope*;" but will submit to the Divine Providence.

With regard to myself, I feel truly grateful for the high honor you have conferred upon me, in inviting me thus unanimously to become the pastor of the First New J. Temple in Philadelphia, to be dedicated exclusively to the One Only Living and True God, our Lord Jesus Christ. At the same time I regret that I am not better qualified for the high and honorable office, with regard to human learning, but more especially with respect to that *holy oil* of love, which should perfume the garments of every son of Aaron.

I hold that it is the *duty* of every man, and I sincerely hope it will be the uniform practice of the members of the Lord's New Church, to be as useful in their particular sphere as they possibly can; and that no notions of self-interest merely should deter a man from performing what he sincerely believes to be his duty. To make an application of the above principle to myself, I would say, that the probable effect my present decision may have upon my constitution from the additional duties that will necessarily devolve upon me; or upon my present connection with my employers; should not influence me, because it would betray a want of trust and confidence in that Divine Providence who " numbers the very hairs of our head," and " feeds the ravens when they cry." I *therefore*, decidedly and without the smallest hesitation, accept your kind 'invitation; and for the following reasons:

1. Because I have for several years had the honor to conduct the worship of our society, and naturally, of course, feel a greater freedom and liberty than any person among us can be supposed to possess without any previous preparation.

2. Because it will extend my sphere of usefulness.

3. Because the present state of our infant church requires that the service to which I am called should be performed gratuitously.

4. Because I hope to improve my own spiritual state, and acquire, by the Lord's assistance, an imperishable crown of glory.

As to the time and mode of ordination, I submit to the rule of a majority of the society, intimating my wish that it would emanate from them.

With sentiments of love and respect, I remain yours, &c.

MASKELL M. CARLL.

These letters are very expressive, and speak for themselves in testimony of the characters and caliber of the two men. Viewing them in the hues which distance gives, and with the calmness of an historic eye, we cannot discern, in the four reasons assigned above, a single one which would have been adequate to give us " freedom to take upon" ourselves " so sacred and responsible a charge." There is not a word of an inward conviction of a call from the Lord to the sacred ministry with a single eye *to the salvation of souls*. There is previously a confession of a want of the requisite learning, and " more especially" of that holy unction of love for the use, which we suppose to constitute the Lord's essential call to the priesthood, and the mainspring of all of man's external efficiency in it. Merely leading or conducting the external worship of an incipient society of the church for several years, must, surely, be deemed a very small part of that *preparation* for the ministry which is indispensable to admission into it. It should be observed, however, that mention is made of " the pastoral charge of the first *congregation*, professing the new-church doctrines, in the city of Philadelphia"— of an invitation " to become the *pastor* of. the First N. J. *Temple* in Philadelphia," and of a wish that either the ordination itself or the time and mode of administering it, " would emanate from them," or that it might be submitted " to the rule of a majority of the society." Recollecting from what sect of the old church Mr. Carll came out, we need to make this observation, in order that we may see how much of a tendency to *episcopal government* he, probably, brought with him into the First Philadelphia Society, on becoming its pastor.

As to Mr. Condy, we recollect that he was subjected to some unkind imputations. He was believed by some to be a haughty, overbearing man, and *ambitious* of *clerical distinction* and *rule*. Those who knew him well, as did the friends whom he mentions in his letter, were very far from holding him in any such estimation. But there were those, either in the gateways or avenues to the new church, who did not hesitate to speak thus of him. And we are persuaded that the knowledge of this was one thing which made Mr. Condy hesitate to take upon him "the sacred office of the ministry in the New Jerusalem," "at least for the present." Moreover, he had a most profound reverence for the holy office of the priesthood. This we know. And this made him stand abashed before the invitation "to take upon himself so sacred and responsible a charge." He declined the office; and yet he was not exempt from the surmise, on the other hand, that notions of regard to worldly interests had influenced him in doing so. On these points, as we happen to know something about them, from having been conversant with the Philadelphia society ever since the autumn of 1816, we also will show forth our opinion.

There can be no question that the only person in this society fitted by genius, education and ability to fill the pastoral office in its connection, was Mr. Condy. All eyes, therefore, were upon him, and all hearts yearned towards him, as the fitting candidate. But as all truly great men are inherently modest men, Mr. Condy was the only one who did not think himself qualified for this sacred office. Certainly his reverence for the holy office was so great that he did not think himself *good* enough for it. It was not every man who could appreciate Mr. Condy. He was a remarkable instance of one in whom *diffidence* could be mistaken for *pride*. The great strength of his intellect, and the herculean manner with which he laid his arms about him in argument, made him seem to shallow men hard and overbearing: but we have seen him weep like a child in his study, while contemplating the transcendant glories of the New Jerusalem, and the worse than egyptian darkness which was spread like a pall over the minds of men and prevented their seeing and embracing them for their eternal good. His affections, therefore, were tender, and his spirit modest and diffident of its own powers. And without what he would have regarded as a direct call from the Lord to the sacred ministry, it was impossible to get him to enter it. This was the true reason why he declined the office when tendered to him by the society. Some thought that, as he had a lucrative practice at the bar, which afforded him ample means of supporting his family, he could not, in justice to them, engage in a calling which would divide his mind and impair his efficiency as a lawyer. For he was not the man to do any thing by halves. And if he had gone into the ministry, he would have so put his whole soul into it, as to have been a burning and a shining light in it; and he could not have done this without dimming the lustre of his legal fame. There are some secular callings more compatible with the sacred office of the ministry than others. Such is the teaching of children and youth. But the practice of the law, as now conducted in our courts, is, perhaps, of all others, least homogeneous to it. Doubtless Mr. Condy felt this. He must, therefore, have confined himself to one or the other; and if he had come into the ministry he must needs have given up the practice of the law altogether. The society was in no condition to support a minister in an exclusive devotion to his clerical calling; and therefore Mr.

Condy could not be expected to give up his legal profession for this purpose. This, some supposed, was the reason why he declined complying with the society's solicitation. But we do not believe it. And we are sure, that if he had felt the Lord calling him as he called Matthew, he would have left all and followed the Lord in the ministry as Matthew did. But not feeling it to be his *duty* to come into the ministry, he did not. He was not, however, a drone in the new-church hive. As editor of the New Jerusalem Church Repository, he proved himself a valiant champion of our heavenly cause. His pamphlet, by which he silenced and demolished the battery which the Rev. Jackson Kemper, of the episcopal church, had raised against the New Jerusalem, proved him a most efficient soldier of our church militant. And in the society, he was still the leading mind during all its prosperous growth. Mr. Carll, the pastor, being weak in bodily health, as well as borne down by the weight of his secular engagements, could not devote that time and labor to the writing of sermons, and to his other pastoral duties, which full efficiency in them demanded. He had to be aided. And Mr. Condy, as one of a committee to select, alter, arrange and write sermons for him, was allowed to devote some portion of the energies of his powerful mind to the uses of the pastoral office also. In April, 1818, Mr. Carll had to address a letter to the society, stating "that his secular employment, added to the bad state of his health, would compel him to relax in the performance of his ministerial duties, and suggesting to the society the advisableness of looking out for a suitable person to share with him in the labors." This letter was referred to a committee that reported at the next meeting the plan of raising by voluntary contribution a salary of $500 per annum, which, it was thought, would enable Mr. Carll to give up his afternoon school, and so to find more time for his clerical duties. Whether this plan was successfully carried out, the records do not show. It is probable that it could not be effected. The temple had been erected solely by the means of Mr. William Schlatter, who, intending to give it to the society, failed in business before his generous purpose could be consummated. It thus remained his property; and as the ground rent and interest on the money invested were a heavy annual expense which his straitened affairs made it inconvenient for him to pay, the society resolved that the pew rents should be assigned to him for this purpose. Thus was the proper resource for the minister's support diverted from its right channel. And Mr. Carll's health so sunk at last under the weight of his accumulated burdens, that his new-church friends were compelled to furnish him funds for a voyage to Europe, as the only means of its restoration. But, before this, an attempt was made to lighten his labors by the appointment of lay readers. A resolution to this effect was passed at a stated meeting of the society held at the temple, October 2, 1819, in these words—"Resolved, That lay readers be appointed to read the service of the church, as occasion may require; and that, in that case, they perform that duty in the chancel of the church." Under this resolution three lay readers were appointed at the meeting of December 24, 1819. They were persons who were looking to the ministry of the new church, and were preparing for it by studies under the direction of Mr. Condy. One of them was a graduate of Brown University, at Providence, R. I. They read the service and delivered sermons selected for them by the committee above mentioned, whenever sickness prevented Mr. Carll's officiating. For several years Mr. Carll thus liberally and generously gave his services to the church. The number of its members increased largely. It became a body corporate in law in January, 1822, and held its first meeting under its charter on Tuesday, the 19th of February, in that year. And it continued to prosper until all of its leading members became prostrated in their worldly circumstances by the inscrutable dispensations of Divine Providence. Mr. Carll, at length, felt that he could not any longer serve the church in the pastoral office gratuitously: for he, too, had suffered the almost total loss of his property by the reverses of the times. He was induced to withdraw from the temple and open his school room again for worship. The temple which, on the settlement of Mr. Schlatter's affairs, had been purchased, subject to a heavy ground rent, for one thousand dollars, now passed out of the hands of the new church, and became the museum of the Academy of Natural Sciences. This it remained till the year 1841, when it was razed to the ground to make way for a private residence. The southeast corner of the wall of the temple was not removed, but remains as part of the foundation of the residence, so that the corner stone, which was laid with religious ceremonies, "in the name, and to the honor, of our ever-blessed and ever-adorable Lord and Saviour JESUS CHRIST," on the 6th of June, 1816, (See N. J. C. Rep., p. 20,) is still there. But "the First New Jerusalem Temple built at Philadelphia" is gone, and the society which worshiped in it is extinct— the remnant of it having united with a part of the Southwark Society in forming the present First Philadelphia Society, which is now flourishing under the pastoral care of the Rev. William H. Benade. "*So passes the glory of the world.*"

We have deemed this glance at the history of the first new church instituted in Philadelphia, as a useful illustration of the results that have flowed from a beginning with the ordination of ministers not properly called to their office, nor suitably prepared for it, nor exclusively devoted to its duties. Similar results in Baltimore, and in New York, illustrate with equal clearness the futility of all attempts to establish and permanently extend the new church, by building temples and forming societies to worship in them, without first looking for ministers to "the universities, whence they are to come," and then consecrating them, setting them apart, and sustaining them in an exclusive devotion to the duties of the clerical office. We return now to the subject of ordinations into the new-church ministry, so far as it leads us to see where, and when, and by whom, the question of a trine in it was first broached in the General Convention.

We have seen that the Rev. M. M. Carll was ordained December 31, 1816, by the Rev. John Hargrove, of Baltimore. The record has shown that he was ordained with full powers as the pastor of a *congregation* of the new church. And we have seen that he could exercise his powers only *under* the *authority* and at the *request* of the *society*, and in the manner and with such *restrictions* as they might *prescribe*. It is evident, therefore, that no idea of a trine of ministers, having for its highest grade a *bishop*, was entertained in this ordination. And it is quite as evident that there was an idea of but one grade and one ordination, as in the parity of the presbyterian and congregational churches. Something of Mr. Condy's views of new-church ordination, may be partially gathered from his articles on that subject in the N. J. C. Repository. But, much to the regret of the whole church, he was prevented completing those articles by the discontinuance of his work. We have no reason to believe that he entertained, or had made up his mind fully on, the doctrine of the trine, before it was broached in the General Convention by a distinguished new-church clergyman of New England. The report of that clergyman to the convention, we know, was approved by Mr. Condy, and through his influence and persevering efforts was published when there seemed to be a disposition in certain quarters to suppress it. And we are satisfied that Mr. Condy, until the time when that report was made, did not contemplate, in the least degree, the order of a trine in any of the ordinations to which he was instrumental in giving shape. We believe he was first fully convinced of the truth of that order by the report alluded to. We confess that we ourselves never heard of the order of a trine in the ministry until it was brought to our notice in that report; and we frankly declare that it was that which first convinced us of its truth. This was the case with some others that we know. As to the Rev. Mr. Hargrove, we have shown that he knew of, and assented to, the plan of arranging the ministers of the new church in a trinal order, as early as the close of 1815. But the address which he delivered on the occasion of Mr. Carll's ordination, proves that this principle had no episcopal tendencies in his mind then. That address may be seen in the N. J. C. Rep., p. 337. He opens it with a declaration of the grand design of the Great Head of the Church in the appointment and ordination of a gospel minstry. Then he asserts that the uninterrupted succession of that ministry is involved in the design of its appointment. And says—

It does not follow, however, that the power of transmitting this succession *should be confined to a few of the clergy only :* nor can we find that Jesus Christ or any of his apostles, ever intended that it should, to the exclusion of other pious and useful ministers, *who had either no friends, or no ambition, to obtain* " the chief seats in the synagogue."

This is pretty explicitly against episcopal ordination any how! What did Mr. Hargrove allude to, in the second clause which we have underscored above? Could he have imagined that any one thought of objecting to his exercising ordaining powers in the new church because he had been only a *deacon* in the methodist church?

Mr. Hargrove then proceeds to admit that the Lord in establishing the first christian church instituted grades in its ministry—giving "some apostles, some prophets, some evangelists, some pastors and teachers; for the perfecting of the saints, for the work of the ministry, for the edifying of the body of Christ." But he argues—

* * * * that, as the three first classes of ecclesiastical officers, to wit, the *apostles*, the *prophets*, and the *evangelists*, were of an extraordinary and distinct order from the *pastors* and *teachers*, and from all christian ministers of the present day, they were only designed to be continued during the peculiar state and trials to which the church was subject during its infant state.

Hence the Scriptures no where intimate an intended perpetuity of those *extraordinary* officers; and as ecclesiastical history (we mean that which may be depended on) is also silent on this point, it is more than probable that these extraordinary officers in the christian church, became very soon extinct; while the ordinary and standing ministry of the pastors and teachers alone remained, as fully sufficient to feed the flock of Christ.

Next Mr. Hargrove answers the argument for bishops from the fact of their being mentioned in the apostolic writings. He contends that the bare mention of *bishops* does not prove that they were a distinct grade. He thinks they were only senior or presiding *pastors*, in particular churches, or congregations, where several of this grade resided and alternately officiated. And as deacons were ordained an inferior grade; he leaves us to infer that the trine in the ministry of the apostolic church, consisted of pastors, teachers and deacons. All of these might officiate in a particular church as a congregation. And therefore we see that Mr. Hargrove, when he ordained Mr. Carll, held to the congregational form of government in the new church; and, if he held to a trine, it was only one of ministers in that form. But the probability is, that he had not yet formed to himself any distinct idea of what should be the trine in the new-church ministry; or believed that the time was not yet come to attempt to carry out this principle in this country.

Dr. Lewis Beers, of Danby, Tioga County, N. Y., was ordained into our ministry in this country next after Mr. Carll, and very nearly about the same time. Less than three weeks was the interval between the ordinations. And the powers given to him were precisely those given to Mr. Carll. Dr. Beers was invited to the ministry by the Incorporated New Jerusalem Society of the county aforesaid. His application for ordination was laid before the church at Philadelphia in a meeting of January 17, 1817. The church, in this meeting, being fully satisfied, by his credentials and by personal intercourse with him, of his competency, and of his religious and moral character, formally authorized his ordination, requested Mr. Carll, its minister, to ordain him, and appointed a committee of two of its members to present him in its name to the officiating minister for that purpose. And on the 19th of January, 1817, being the following Sunday, in the temple, in the city of Philadelphia, Dr. Lewis Beers was "ordained a priest and teaching minister, in the Lord's church of the New Jerusalem, with power, under the authority, and at the request of the said New Jerusalem Society of the County of Tioga, in the State of New York, and in the manner and under such restrictions as they may prescribe, to ordain other priests and ministers of the New Jerusalem Church, and with power, also, to conduct public worship, to celebrate the Lord's supper, marriages, baptism, and funerals; and, generally, to perform all holy rites and divine ordinances of the church." (N. J. C. Rep., p. 127.)

This was the common formulary of the Philadelphia church, according to which Mr. Carll was ordained, and according to which that church seemed disposed to ordain all who sought its authority. Thus the full powers of the ministry were transferred at once from the Philadelphia *church* to *other churches*. Hence there was as yet no idea of grades in the ministry, and the vesting of ordaining powers in the highest grade. It is to be observed, too, that Messrs. Mather, Hargrove, White, Hurdus and Carll, were all ordained before a general convention of the new church in this country had come into existence. Therefore, there was not yet any thing like an organized general church, in which, as a congregate man, ordaining powers could be supposed to reside. The idea seemed to prevail in some minds, that such a body ought to exist, and that all things pertaining to the regulation of the ministry properly belonged to it. A general conference had early been formed in England for this purpose, and that example led to the formation of a similar body here. The General Conference of the New Church in England having been twice suspended, was the second time revived by a call from the London Conference for the express purpose of ordering the ministry. But no such avowed object was projected in calling the First General Convention. This was called simply "for the purpose of consulting on the general concerns of the church."

The first annual convention of the receivers of the doctrines of the New Jerusalem was held in Philadelphia from Thursday the 15th until Saturday the 17th of May, 1817. This was assembled in compliance with the call that had been made on the first of January preceding. We find only two things in the minutes of this convention that are pertinent to the subject before us. Application was made by the Steubenville society for the ordination of Mr. David Powell. Upon this application, the convention made the following minute—

> The convention took the same into consideration, but conceiving that the great importance of regulating the ministry would require more ample deliberation than it would be in their power to bestow at the present meeting, and considering that the New Jerusalem Churches of Baltimore and Philadelphia have hitherto, with great discretion, exercised the power of ordaining ministers,
> *It was ordered,* That the said application be referred to the Rev. Messrs. Hargrove and Carll, with a request that they will favor it with their early attention.

Three facts are to be noted here. First, the convention assumes the province of "regulating the ordination of ministers." This, therefore, was a chief general concern of the church, upon which this body felt itself called to consult. Undoubtedly, such is the appropriate province of general bodies of the church; and its assumption by any particular church, or congregation, could have been proper only in the church's incipiency. Second, this general convention did not attend to this matter, because its importance required more de-liberation than could be bestowed upon it in the present meeting, and referred the immediate action called for by the present application to the Baltimore and Philadelphia Churches. Consequently, the duty was only deferred, not surrendered. Third, there is a formal declaration, of what we have shown, that the *churches* of Baltimore and Philadelphia *exercised the power of ordaining ministers*. Therefore, ordaining power was supposed to be vested in the *churches*, including their ministers, and not in their ministers alone. Consequently, such was the principle of order and government that was infused into this general body in its beginning, so far as it was affected by the influence of those churches. For the inference from this would necessarily be, that ordaining power would rest in the General Convention, as a church in a larger form, and not in its ordaining ministers, except as its representative and organ. Hence the tendency was not to episcopal government, but to congregational government on a larger scale.

The other thing pertinent to our present subject, in the proceedings of this first convention, is this resolution—

Resolved, That a committee of clergy and laity be appointed, to inquire whether it be expedient to establish any, and, if any, what general regulations for the ordination of ministers in the new church, and that they make report to the next convention. This committee was made to consist of the Rev. Lewis Beers and Nathaniel Holley, of New York—Rev. Maskell M. Carll and Jonathan W. Condy, Esqr., of Pennsylvania—Rev. John Hargrove and George Smith, of Maryland—Rev. Hugh White and Richard H. Goe, of Virginia—Rev. Adam Hurdus and David Powell, of Ohio.

The union of clergy and laity in this committee still wears the hue of congregational government. The resolution was required by the principle that it was the province and duty of the General Convention to regulate the ordination of ministers, or, as they have it in England, "to order the ministry." The doctrine of the church on which rests the principles that a general body should have the making of general regulations for the ministry, is thus taught—"There must needs be a general, in order that there may be any particular thing; and what is particular can in no wise exist and subsist without what is general—indeed, it subsists in what is general; and every thing particular is circumstanced according to the quality, and according to the state, of what is general:" (A. C. 4325:) and thus confirmed—"There must needs be a general sphere in order that there may be particular spheres, which cannot exist but in a general one; for all particulars relate to generals, which direct particulars, and at length reduce them into that order in which generals are: otherwise, they must of necessity be expelled from the general sphere." (Diary, 210.)

The application to this convention for the ordination of Mr. David Powell, which was referred to the Rev. Messrs. Hargrove and Carll, for the action of their churches, led to the ordination of both Mr. Powell and Mr. Goe, according to the following proceedings of the Philadelphia church, which, as they afford a sufficiently minute historical detail of the matter, we present here entire.

Extract from the Proceedings of a Meeting of "The First New Jerusalem Church in the City of Philadelphia," held, at the temple, on Sunday afternoon, May 18, 1817, and continued by adjournment in the evening of the same day.

Mr. Carll reported, that, at the late convention held in this city from the 15th to the 17th instant inclusive, an application, signed by a number of the members of the New Church composing "The Society of Steubenville, Jefferson County, in the State of Ohio," stating their confidence in their "beloved brother, David Powell," who, it is declared, had, "for some years, administered the Word" to them "as a faithful and worthy servant," and earnestly·desiring that he might be ordained a preacher of the New Jerusalem Church—was presented to the same; and that the said convention, not feeling itself at this time prepared to take up the subject of ordination, and expressing a confidence in the discretion which had hitherto been exercised by the churches of Baltimore and Philadelphia upon that subject, had resolved to refer the same to the Rev. Mr. Hargrove and himself. Mr. Carll further reported that Mr. Powell had been examined by Mr. Hargrove and himself, and that the results had been so satisfactory to both, that they had no hesitation in recommending him to the church for limited ordination. Whereupon, a number of the members present, who had known the candidate personally, by correspondence, and by reputation, having expressed themselves fully satisfied as to his moral and religious character, and as to his capacity and usefulness as a public preacher, it was

Resolved, That the Rev. Mr. Carll, as minister of this church, do, at 12 o'clock, M., on Tuesday the twentieth instant, ordain the said David Powell as a priest and teaching minister of the New Jerusalem Church, with power to conduct public worship, celebrate the sacrament of the Lord's supper, marriages, baptisms and funerals, and generally to perform all holy rites and divine ordinances of the church, excepting that of ordaining other priests and ministers.

A letter was then laid before the society, addressed by the Rev. Robert Ayres, of Brownsville, Fayette County, Pennsylvania, to "the clergy and laity attending the convention of the New Church at Philadelphia," recommending for ordination Richard H. Goe, of the vicinity of Wheeling, in the western part of Virginia, and now attending the convention in this city. A recommendation was also presented to the society signed by David Powell and others, members of the convention, testifying to the moral and religious character of Mr. Goe, and his capacity for great usefulness in teaching the doctrines of the New Jerusalem in the western country; and the members of this society, from their personal intercourse with Mr. Goe, having had many opportunities of ascertaining his qualifications and attainments in the truths of the New Church; and it appearing to the society that, in the present infant state of the church, the labors of a missionary in disseminating a knowledge of the heavenly doctrines of the New Jerusalem throughout the western parts of the United States, would be highly useful; and Mr. Goe having signified his intention to devote his talents to that object; it was

Resolved, That the Rev. M. M. Carll, as minister of this church, do, at 12 o'clock, M., on Tuesday the 20th inst., ordain the said Richard H. Goe, as a priest and teaching minister of the New Jerusalem Church, with power to conduct public worship, celebrate the sacrament of the Lord's supper, marriages, baptisms and funerals, and generally to perform all holy rites and divine ordinances of the church, excepting that of ordaining other priests and ministers.

At this meeting of the Philadelphia church, there were twelve members present, including J. W. Condy, Esq., the president, Condy

Raguet, Esq., the secretary, and the Rev. Mr. Carll, the minister. And in its proceedings here presented, we have to remark two things. First, although the General Convention had referred the application for the ordination of Mr. Powell to the Rev. Messrs. Hargrove and Carll, yet they conclude "to recommend him to the church" for ordination: and the church resolves that Mr. Carll "as minister of this church," shall ordain him. If any thing were wanting to prove our position, that ordaining power was then supposed to be in the church, and not in the officiating minister alone, full evidence is furnished here. We hope that a pin will be stuck, or a leaf turned, at this place, for we shall have to refer to it hereafter. The thing to be remarked is, that the *ministers recommend* to the church for ordination, and *the church ordains*. Second, here is the first time that ordination with limited powers is mentioned. Why this distinction was made in the case of these two ministers, we are not informed. Mr. Powell had a society or a church in Steubenville, in which, for aught we know, ordaining power might as well have been vested as in that of Danby. Therefore, it could not have been said of him, as it might of Mr. Goe, that he was to be a missionary, without connection with a particular church, under the authority, at the request, and by the restrictions and prescriptions of which he should ordain other priests and ministers. Did this distinction arise from the idea of both or either of the ministers that there should be grades in the new-church ministry? The probability is, that it did not. It is most probable that the suggestion was made by Mr. Hargrove; and his reason for it was probably the same as that which induced him to give a limited ordination to Mr. Hurdus. What this reason was may, perhaps, be gathered from a letter of his which we shall have to adduce in respect to some subsequent ordinations. It will not appear from that, that any idea of distinct grades in the ministry produced the distinctions now for the first time made in this "limited ordination."

At a stated meeting of the Philadelphia church, held at the temple, June 6, 1817, "the Rev. Mr. Carll reported, That, agreeably to the resolutions adopted by the society on the 18th of May, he ordained, on the 20th of the same month, David Powell and Richard H. Goe, with the powers authorized by said resolutions."

From what has now been shown, it appears, that, of the eight ministers who were ordained in this country from July 8, 1798 to May 20, 1817—a period of about nineteen years—five of them were inducted into the ministry within a space of ten months' time before and after the institution of the First Philadelphia Church and the meeting of the First General Convention.

In further tracing the ordination of ministers in this country, we now come to the proceedings of the Second General Convention, which was "held on Thursday, the 30th day of April, being Ascension Day, and continued until Saturday, the 2d day of May, A. D. 1818–62, at the New Jerusalem Temple, in the city of Baltimore." The following extracts from the report of the committee on business are pertinent—

As the committee, appointed at the convention held in 1817, "to inquire whether it be expedient to establish any, and, if any, what, general regulations for the ordination of ministers in the New Church," is not yet prepared to report, it is recommended to the convention to continue the said committee, with instructions to report at the next general convention. In the mean time, however, in order to guard, as far as possible, against the introduction into the ministry of persons who do not possess sufficient qualifications to render the sacred office of the priesthood respected, it is strongly recommended to the convention to express it as their desire, that, until some other regulations shall be established upon the subject, no person shall be ordained to the ministry, under the sanction of the Church at Baltimore, or at Philadelphia, without the concurrence and approbation of the ministers of both those churches. This subject necessarily leads your committee to another, upon which they feel it incumbent on them to express an opinion. In the present infant state of the church in America, it cannot be expected that the same orderly system in the ministration of the Word, and the sacred ordinances of the church, will obtain, as at a more advanced period. In places distant from an established ministry, laymen will frequently be called upon to officiate as leaders of societies; and it were very much to be desired, that, as far as possible, they would confine their labors to the reading of the Word, the Lord's prayer, the writings of the herald of the new dispensation, and such prayers, sermons and hymns as are known to contain the orthodox sentiments of the church. The influx which produces illumination and illustration in the minds of the clergy is not received in the same measure, or with the same power, into the minds of the laity, as will be evident from a reference to U. T. 146 and to A. C. 6822, in which the following passage occurs: "None ought to teach truths but ministers appointed to teach; for, if otherwise, then the church is disturbed with heresies, and rent asunder." Whilst your committee thus suggest a caution against the delusive tendency of extempore preaching by the laity, they think it their duty to protest against the practice, which they have heard somewhere to have existed, of the administration of the holy sacraments of baptism and the Lord's supper by laymen. They conceive this to be a dangerous precedent, which is fraught with more injury to the cause than may readily be imagined; and they trust that the good sense of the members of the church, wherever they may be dispersed, will lead them to discountenance this deviation from order, whenever it may be introduced.

    *   *   *   *   *   *   *   *

A second paper referred to your committee, was a letter dated Frankfort, Kentucky, March 25, 1818, from Thomas H. Roberts to the Rev. Mr. Hargrove, announcing that there are five families in that vicinity who are receivers of the doctrines; and that a system of worship has lately been established, at which many strangers attend, who are desirous of inquiring into the truths of the new dispensation. Mr. Roberts himself performed the service, *according to the printed Liturgy of Mr. Proud, and reads the sermons of some of the most approved new-church ministers.* Such a proceeding your committee highly applaud; and cannot but express the wish that the labors of Mr. Roberts, as a reader of the New Jerusalem Church, may be crowned with success, and that his example may be followed, wherever opportunities are presented to gentlemen qualified for the undertaking.

    *   *   *   *   *   *   *   *

This report was read, amended and approved; and two resolutions were passed—the one appointing a committee of Messrs. Hargrove, Carll and Beers to prepare a catechism, and the other a committee to select from the journal of the convention such parts as they might deem proper to publish in the Repository. And there being no further business, the convention, next day, adjourned to meet the next year in Philadelphia.

From the proceedings of this second convention we learn that another step was taken in vesting ordaining power in the concurrent action of the two churches of Baltimore and Philadelphia, instead of each of them. This was proceeding towards the vesting of that power in the General Convention as the representative of the whole church in the United States. In our opinion, an orderly progress. We learn, too, that more caution began to be used in respect to admitting persons into the ministry, who did not possess " sufficient qualifications to render the sacred office of the priesthood respected." Without doubt this was a salutary and needed prudence. In this country, as in England, we find there was a tendency, not only to lay preaching, but to " the administration of the holy sacraments of baptism and the Lord's supper by laymen." Hence, here as there, there was a *necessity* for the determination of the true order of the ministry by a general body of the church. This was made necessary by proceedings among the lay receivers of our doctrines which tended to undermine the priestly office in the new church, and negate the right or propriety of formal ordination into it. How the same thing led to the agitation of the question of the trine in this country, will be seen presently. This convention approves of lay readers who shall read the sermons of approved ministers of the new church and lead worship according to prescribed and approved forms—instead of " *extempore* preaching by the laity." Most assuredly the convention exercised a sound discretion in this approval—for the obvious reasons, that such lay readers stood in the place of the regular ministers whose sermons they read, and that extempore preaching by the laity was a rank field for the influx of enthusiastic spirits. Extempore preaching in a regular minister is only admissible in the case of those who have been a long time in the office, have had much previous exercise of their faculties in writing, and have, with all, a certain natural tact, *quid nascitur non fit.* Therefore the convention did right in discountenancing extempore lay preaching, and especially in protesting against the practice of administering baptism and the supper by laymen. But the office of lay reader is a good one in the beginning of a church, as a preparatory stage for the ministry. There is intrinsic evidence that the report above quoted from, was written by Mr. Condy of the Philadelphia church; and we have seen that three lay readers had been appointed in that church, as a means of exercising young men who were preparing for the office of regular preachers. We shall soon see that Mr. Roberts, mentioned above, shortly afterwards applied for ordination in the new church ministry and received it.

The first action of the two churches of Philadelphia and Baltimore upon the principle established by the Second General Convention, as above detailed, was the ordination of Charles John Doughty, Esq., of the city of New York. Who Mr. Doughty was, and what was his character, the members of the Central Convention need not to be informed. Others, who know not, and wish to know, may read Newchurchman, Vov. II., pp. 651—665 and 673—719. Mr. Doughty was ordained on the 9th day of August, 1818, with precisely the same powers, and with the same relation to his society, as Messrs. Carll and Beers were to theirs. "The ceremony of ordination was performed in the city of New York, by the Rev. M. M. Carll—the approbation of the Rev. John Hargrove, of Baltimore, having been previously obtained, as recommended by the convention, at the second annual meeting." (N. J. C. Rep., p. 539.)

The second action of those two churches, in accordance with the principle of the Second General Convention, is found in the minutes of a special meeting of the Philadelphia church, held August 31, 1818; as follows—

A letter addressed to the Rev. Maskell M. Carll, and others, members of this church, dated the fourth instant, signed by Joseph Canby, and others, members of the New Jerusalem Society in the vicinity of Lebanon, in the state of Ohio, was presented, stating that the Rev. David Powell intended to visit that section of the country in the ensuing month, and requesting that he might be invested with the power to ordain their beloved brother Thomas Newport to be their pastor, and also, in consideration of their great distance, and of the circumstance that several persons in that section of the country are qualified for the ministry, suggesting the expediency of investing Mr. Newport with power to ordain other ministers with the consent of the said society in the vicinity of Lebanon, and of the church in Philadelphia.

The said letter was read, and considered; whereupon it was

Resolved, That, if the Rev. John Hargrove of the New Jerusalem church in the city of Baltimore, shall testify his concurrence herein, the said Rev. David Powell be authorized and empowered to ordain the said Thomas Newport, as a priest, &c., [*according to the usual formulary,*] and with power also, with the consent and approbation of the said society in the vicinity of Lebanon, and of the Rev. John Hargrove, of the New Jerusalem Church in the city of Baltimore, or of the First New Jerusalem Church in the city of Philadelphia, to ordain other priests and teaching ministers with the same powers, *except that of ordaining others*—[underscored in the original record.]

Resolved, also, That the Rev. Maskell M. Carll be requested to affix his signature to a copy of these minutes, and that the secretary, having affixed his attestation, forthwith transmit the same to the Rev. John Hargrove, of Baltimore, for his consideration; who, if he concur in the same, is requested to transmit it, with a certificate of concurrence subjoined, to Dr. Joseph Canby, Lebanon, Warren County, Ohio.

No one can fail to observe how distinctly the *church* in Philadelphia is engaged in giving authority for this ordination. The Rev. Mr. Carll is requested " to affix his signature to a copy of these minutes"—that is all. And these words should not be overlooked—" if *the Rev. J. Hargrove*, of the N. J. C. in the city of Baltimore, or of the New Jerusalem Church of the city of Philadelphia." Why was not *the Rev. M. M. Carll* named in the same connection with the church in Philadelphia, as the Rev. John Hargrove is with that in Baltimore? The legal precision and accuracy of the men who drafted these forms forbid us to suppose that these expressions were used inadvertently.

A copy of the proceedings of this meeting having been transmitted to Mr. Hargrove, by the Secretary, a letter from him was received and laid before the Philadelphia church at a stated meeting of October 3, 1818. This is the letter to which we have before alluded, as affording the probable reason of Mr. Hargrove's being in favor of limited ordinations, and of recommending them in the cases of Messrs. Powell and Goe. In this letter Mr. Hargrove states that his assent to the ordination of Mr. Thomas Newport had been given in the words following, viz :

City of Baltimore to wit

The undersigned hereby consents to all the preceding resolves of the New Jerusalem Church in Philadelphia, *except* that of conferring upon any of the brethren referred to, the power of ordaining other priests or ministers, previous to consent thereto being first obtained from any two of the N. J.. Churches already established in the three cities of Baltimore, Philadelphia and New York, expressed under the signature of the respective ministers of the said churches for the time being. Witness my hand, this 2d day of Sept., 1818.

    (Signed)   JOHN HARGROVE,
                Minister of the N. J. Church in Baltimore.

[This having been laid before the Philadelphia church] it was, on motion, *Resolved*, That the society do concur in the amendment made by Mr. Hargrove.

The reason which weighed in Mr. Hargrove's mind and induced him to limit the ordination in the above case, will be shown by the following extract from his letter. The sentence in italic, is underscored by us.

I have just received your favor of the 31st ult., inclosing your Church Resolves, and shall this day forward the Resolves, with my provisional concurrence, to our friend in Lebanon, by post. For the satisfaction of yourself and the church in Philadelphia, I will here transcribe a full and true copy of what I wrote at the bottom of your Resolves; and hope it may please you all. *Indeed, I could not consent upon any other terms, lest our ordination should run wild through the western wilderness, and ultimately discredit us and give us an incurable pain.*

This, we think, is sufficient proof, that the distinction between ordaining ministers, and ministers without ordaining powers, first arose in this country from prudential considerations, and not from an idea that there should be a trine of discrete grades in the priesthood. For the having ordaining powers or not, is not of itself enough to make the third grade discrete from the second. The ordaining of ministers is but a function of the office, and the third or highest ecclesiastical office must itself be made distinct from the second or middle office by a discretely superior degree of use. It must be made distinct by a discrete extension of province or jurisdiction. Hence the mere limiting of the function of the office by taking away the power to ordain, did not constitute a discrete degree of it in the exercise of the remaining powers. And there was, evidently, no reason in the nature of the office, why Mr. Newport with the Lebanon society, or rather, the Lebanon society with Mr. Newport, should not have had ordaining powers as well as the Philadelphia church with Mr. Carll. The same observation is

9

true of the Steubenville church with Mr. Powell, or the Cincinnati church with Mr. Hurdus. But there might have been a very solid objection to the vesting ordaining powers in those churches for the reason above assigned by Mr. Hargrove. The fact is, that the church in this country, as the church in England had before it, began to feel the need of caution, lest they might fatally disregard the wise apostolic injunction—" lay hands *suddenly* on *no* man." The ordination of seven (four of them *ordaining*) ministers in about two years, was found to be going too fast in the beginning; and more heed to the adage of " slow and sure," was felt to be necessary.

" Thomas Newport, of the vicinity of Lebanon, in Warren county, state of Ohio, was, in the afternoon of the Lord's Day, the 27th of September, 1818, at the request of the New Jerusalem Society of that vicinity, ordained as a priest and teaching minister of the Lord's Church of the New Jerusalem," with the powers as above authorized. " The ceremony of ordination was performed by the Rev. David Powell, of Steubenville, Ohio, who was to this purpose specially empowered by order of the First New Jerusalem Church of the city of Philadelphia, concurred in and approved by the Rev. John Hargrove of Baltimore." (N. J. C. Rep., p. 540.)

The next event in our history, is the granting of a *license* to Mr. Samuel Worcester, late of Boston, but, at the time the license is given, a resident of Natchez. This, it is believed, was the first license granted in the new church of America. It is of some moment, therefore, to discern, whether there was a deliberate design of instituting hereby a first or lowest grade in the ministry of this country.

Among the communications to the first General Convention, held in May, 1817, there was one from Boston, saying, a small society had been lately formed in that city and its vicinity. And in a letter from Mr. Samuel Worcester, dated " Newton, May 27, 1817," to Condy Raguet, Esq., then secretary of the Philadelphia church, there is the following more particular information—

You have been informed that the readers of the writings of Swedenborg in Boston and its vicinity have established social meetings for the purpose of becoming more acquainted with each other—aiding each other in the acquirement and use of divine truth, and uniting their efforts to disseminate the doctrines of the New Jerusalem. At our last meeting, May 24th, it was resolved to commence a correspondence with the society at Philadelphia, that we may obtain from them such advice and instruction as shall the better enable us to effect the purposes of our association, and that we may have the most regular means for communicating to all the societies of the New Church any information which will gladden their hearts and strengthen their hands. For this purpose a secretary was appointed and directed to inform you of our present state, and our desire for a correspondence.

At our first meeting there were but nine present—eleven at our second, and the same number at the last. However, this is not our whole number. We have about twenty in this vicinity, who may be considered receivers, and many more, who are reading, with a great degree of interest and some satisfaction.

We live too remote from each other, to assemble often; and most of us are so situated in life, that we find it difficult either to furnish a suitable place for our meetings, or to devote much time to them. We think, however, it may safely be said, that those who have met, feel considerable zeal in the important cause we have espoused, and that we shall not readily abandon it.

The progress of the church will probably be slow in this vicinity. The errors which prevail among us, involve so much scepticism, that they do not easily give place to the sevenfold light of the New Jerusalem. We, therefore, think it best at present to be rather silent in our operations; although we shall not shrink from a full avowal of our sentiments, when it will effect any use—being well aware that the members of the New Church have the least reason of all in the world, to deny the Lord before men.

* * * * * * * *

P. S. It is not to be understood that we are a regularly organized society; and, therefore, you will regard us only as corresponding brethren. It is the request of our members that all communications from your society should be directed to me at "Newton, to be left at the Post Office at Brighton."

This minute account of the beginning of the new church in Boston and Massachusetts, where it has since flourished so much, must prove highly interesting. The new church assumed this provisional form there early in 1817—four or five months after the instituting a church and opening a temple in Philadelphia. When the Rev. Mr. Carll visited New York in the summer of 1818, to ordain Mr. Doughty, the receivers in Boston were ready to assume the form of an organized church. They applied to Mr. Carll to extend his visit to Boston to help them to do it. He went, and a most interesting account of his proceedings there is published in the N. J. C. Repository, pp. 521–527. The following shows the formal action that was taken for this purpose—

At a meeting of the members of the New Jerusalem Church Society of Boston and its vicinity,

I. *Resolved*, That this society deem it not only expedient, but important to their spiritual improvement, and the interest of the Lord's New Church, to become organized as a church, and to hold public religious meetings regularly on the Sabbath.

II. *Resolved*, That Dr. James Mann, Mr. Samuel Worcester, and Mr. Thomas Worcester, be a committee to make the necessary preparations for these meetings.

III. *Resolved*, That the secretary of this society request the Rev. Mr. Carll, minister of the New Jerusalem Church in Philadelphia, to visit us, as soon as to him may be convenient, for the purpose of organizing us as a church, and administering to us its ordinances.

Boston, July 31, 1818.

A true copy, attest

SAMUEL WORCESTER, *Secretary*.

The Boston society was organized as a church on Saturday, August 15, 1818, at the house of Dr. James Mann. The ceremony of organization was preceded by the baptism of nine adults. The articles of faith of the new church as contained in the Philadelphia Liturgy were then distinctly read and signed by all present: the whole concluded with a prayer that the Lord would bless what had been thus auspiciously begun. The next day, Sunday, there was preaching in Boylston Hall, a spacious room, elegantly and conveniently furnished, and calculated to contain about a thousand people. The room was filled and the worship was conducted according to the form used in the temple at Philadelphia. The service of the morning was concluded by the celebration of the Lord's supper, of which twenty-six of the members of the new church partook, besides *two or three others of different churches.** Thus was the Boston church organized, under Mr. Samuel Worcester as its first leader; who was soon to give place to his brother Thomas, around whom as licentiate and pastor, it has gradually increased and flourished so much in later years, till it has now become the largest and most respectable society in the world. And thus we see who were the leading men and forming minds that have given ecclesiastical shape to the church at Boston. Mr. Samuel Worcester was a graduate of Yale College, New Haven, Ct., and Mr. Thomas Worcester, of Harvard University, Cambridge, Mass. And by their abilities and success in building up our church in this country, have helped to verify Swedenborg's prediction that ministers for the new church were to come from the universities.

In about three months after the church was organized in Boston, Mr. Samuel Worcester was induced to go to Natchez, to take charge of a school there, and with a prospect of being useful as a new-church preacher, too, in a parish which was there vacant. He had a brother-in-law there who gave him a home. He at first purposed to take Philadelphia in his route, and receive ordination before he went. But he probably concluded to go by sea from Boston or New York; and it became necessary for him to make application for a license by letter from Natchez. The following extract from the records of the Philadelphia church places this subject in clear light—

A special meeting of the society was held at the temple on Thursday, January 21, 1819. Present Messrs. Carll, Condy, Schlatter, Mecke, Thuun, Graham, Hemple, Smith, Parr and Kneass.

The object of the present meeting was stated to be for the purpose of taking into consideration the propriety of granting a license to Mr. Samuel Worcester of Natchez, in the State of Mississippi. Whereupon, it was, on motion,

Resolved, That, in consequence of Mr. Worcester's not having it in his power, from the great distance of his residence, to present himself for ordination to any ordained minister of the New Church, he be licensed under the authority of this church, for the term of seven years, to celebrate the rites of public worship, the sacrament of the Lord's supper, baptisms and funerals.

Resolved, That the following be the form of the license, which the secretary is requested to transmit to him as early as convenient.

LICENSE.

To All to whom these Presents shall come, The First New Jerusalem Church of the City of Philadelphia, greeting:

WHEREAS the said Church have full confidence in the piety, knowledge and zeal of their beloved brother, Samuel Worcester, lately of the town of

---

* Our eastern brethren were then too *young* in the church to be so much horrified at this exceeding great *disorder*, as they were at the irregularity which occurred in Providence, R. I., some twenty-two years afterwards, when the *wife* of the leader of the society very recently instituted there, communed without having been re-baptised or having formally embraced the new-church faith.

Boston, in the state of Massachusetts, now, of Natchez, in the state of Mississippi, and are desirous that he should, as soon as possible, take upon himself the sacred office of a priest and teaching minister in the Lord's New Church of the New Jerusalem, and present himself for ordination to the same, but from the remoteness of his present residence, their desire cannot be gratified at the present; and whereas it appeareth, that, according to due order under the necessity of the case, their said brother may, in the mean time, be licensed to celebrate the rites of public worship, the sacrament of the Lord's supper, baptisms and funerals; Now KNOW YE, that the said First New Jerusalem Church of the City of Philadelphia, have, and do hereby, for the period of seven years from the date hereof, license and empower their said beloved brother, Samuel Worcester, to celebrate public worship, the sacrament of the Lord's supper, baptisms and funerals, according to the doctrines of the Lord's Church of the New Jerusalem, as revealed in the writings of Emanuel Swedenborg, messenger of the Lord; hereby recommending their said brother, as soon as conveniently may be, to take upon him, by due ordination, the sacred office of priest and teaching minister of the same.

IN WITNESS WHEREOF, Maskell M. Carll, priest and minister of the said First New Jerusalem Church of the City of Philadelphia, hath hereunto affixed his hand and seal, this twenty-first day of January, in the year of our Lord, eighteen hundred and nineteen, and of his second advent the sixty-third.

(Signed)   MASKELL M. CARLL,
Minister of the First N. J. Church
of the City of Philadelphia.
Attest: CONDY RAGUET, *Secretary.*

It has been necessary to exhibit this license, with the proceedings in regard to it, in full, that its nature may be seen. And from *prima facie* evidence, nothing can be plainer, than that there was no design to institute a first or lowest grade in the ministry by this giving of a license. The same appears from the resolution which precedes it. For in the distinction of grades, there must be circumscriptions of province, subordinations of office, and limitations of function. And this license was granted merely to impart authority to perform the functions of the only one grade then acknowledged, until such time as the minister could receive a regular or formal ordination. All the powers usually granted—except that of ordaining other ministers, which limitation, we have seen, was not made with any express reference to the trine—are conferred upon Mr. Worcester by this license. And the reason for conferring a license instead of ordination is, that Mr. Worcester is so far away as to make it impossible for him to "take upon himself the sacred office of a priest and teaching minister," and "due order under the *necessity* of the case" makes it admissible for him to take *that office* by license to discharge its functions for a term of years, or until he should be in circumstances to avail himself of regular inauguration into it—which the license itself expressly recommends him to do. Does not this show that *it was not intended to confer by license* the powers of another office, discretely or distinctly lower than that of a priest and teaching minister? It is therefore clear, that the members of the Philadelphia church, in granting this license to Mr. Samuel Worcester, had no distinct idea of the order of a trine of ministers in their minds. Consequently, there is here no evidence that this question was as yet agitated in the new church of America. There is, on the contrary, full evidence that the church in Philadelphia had very general and even loose ideas of the distinction between the powers which a license and an ordination should respectively confer. And that the church in Boston had begun to form more distinct ideas on this subject, if not to agitate the very question of the trine, will appear from the following extract from one of Mr. Samuel Worcester's letters. It will be observed that the license to him was granted in January, and in a letter dated " Natchez May 9th, 1819," between three and four months afterwards; he says—

One of my Boston friends questions whether authority can be given me to administer the sacraments, without the imposition of hands. I have some doubts on the subject of ordination, and the just method of giving the different degrees of authority: but if we are to go back to the apostles and primitive christians for our forms, it is, I believe, equally unjustifiable to authorize me to preach, as to administer the sacraments, without the imposition of hands. The subject is of great importance in the present state of the church, and I am very sorry and much disappointed, that we are to lose Mr. Condy's dissertations. I expected they would have led to a candid discussion, by which the question would have been completely settled. I am now very earnest to have some mode adopted for having all the churches in the United States understand and agree upon some order. Before this can be done, the subject must be discussed between individuals of the different churches; and then, *perhaps*, proposed in a convention. The great object appears to me to be, to have all the churches act in unity. My opinion on the whole subject is easily expressed. It proposes one law— "*Act in unity, and as the case requires.*" No one should have any authority given him but by consent of at least one church; and that authority should be given in the way that the case seemed to require. I mean much by this principle, but have time to say little. I have not yet baptized any; but have no doubt that many will be offered. I wait for the opinions of the Boston members, that I may injure the feelings of none. Some decision of the churches must be made, or we shall be in danger of serious difficulties.

We look upon this as a document of exceedingly great interest in the history of the question before us. The Philadelphia church, it would seem, had assumed to itself ordaining powers, and had proceeded to confer those powers on other churches, without first determining from the Word of God, and the writings of the new church, what should be the true order of the church in this respect. To have provided for its own worship in this way, might have been admissible in the extreme infancy of the church. Thus did the Baltimore society, and the London society before that. But when the functions of a general church were to be discharged, a general conference was called in England; and among these functions, the ordering of the ministry stood foremost. When, too, the need of determining how the different degrees of authority were to be given, the London Conference, after determining its order, in this respect, from the Word and the writings, called the General Conference, and submitted the matter to that body, because it was deemed the manifest function of a general body to settle it. And whether the Philadelphia church ought not to have proceeded in this way too—that is, have waited until the proper order was determined, and generally agreed upon, before it

proceeded to exercise the function of a general church; or, at least,
ought not to have clearly ascertained what was the right order, as the
London Conference had done, before taking action upon it; may well
be questioned now. The need of such a proceeding is very clearly
indicated by these words of Mr. Worcester—"I am very earnest to
have some mode adopted for having all the churches in the United
States understand and agree upon some order."—"Some decision of
the churches must be made, or we shall be in danger of serious difficulties." As it was, that church conferred almost the entire powers
of the ministry upon Mr. Samuel Worcester by a license, which was
even then deemed a very questionable way. So that Mr. Worcester
hesitates to baptize under his license, because a friend of his in Boston
questions whether authority *could* be given to him to administer the
sacraments without the imposition of hands. And now we learn that
he too had "some doubts on the subject of ordination, and the just
method of giving the *different degrees of authority.*" Here, for the
first time, is the *shadow* of degrees in the ministry, as it were of an
April cloud, cast upon the field of the church in this country. For
this *necessarily* involves the question of ministerial grades; and therefore the consideration of the just method of giving the different degrees
of ministerial authority was no other than cogitations about the order
of *grades* in the ministry. And as Mr. Samuel Worcester was a
Boston man,—though now residing temporarily in Natchez,—and
mentions his having had doubts on this subject in connection with his
statement of certain questions in the minds of his Boston friends,
whether he could exercise the authorities given to him by the Philadelphia church without the imposition of hands, we may conclude
that this matter had been, or was then, a subject of discussion in the
church at Boston. Mr. Worcester regrets, too, the loss of Mr. Condy's
dissertations, as if he had expected that this subject of degrees of
ministerial authority would have been discussed in them; and from
the intimation that other views might have been elicited by that discussion, from other churches than the one at Philadelphia, leads us to
infer that Mr. Condy's views were more in favor of *one continuous*
degree than of *three discrete* degrees of such authority. We are satisfied, in our own minds, that this was at first the case with Mr. Condy;
and if he had been permitted to finish his dissertations, we believe
that his presbyterian and congregational predilections, or preconceived
ideas, would have been seen to have had a modifying influence on
the light of the new church as it flowed into his mind, so as to have
made his dissertations a confirmation of that form of order which had
been impressed by him upon the Philadelphia church. He might
have, and probably had, heard of the decisions of the English General
Conference of 1815, respecting the trine as the true order of the
new-church ministry; but we feel sure that he had not so made up
his mind on the subject as to have come to a clear and full adoption
of the trinal principle himself. As we shall show hereafter, we think
he did not begin to make up his mind on this subject till about the
year 1824. At the time now referred to, we think he was in favor
of new-church congregationalism, verging to new-church presbyte-

rianism. But his dissertations were not finished; and subsequently his views were changed, by that lucid exposition of what is true order in this respect, which we well know changed more views than his. We may say, then, that the question of *grades* in the ministry, if not the *trine*—the question of *church authority* as involved in that—was first agitated in this country at Boston, or by New England men.

Mr. Samuel Worcester's opinion, as expressed in this letter, seems to have a congregational turn. This was to have been expected from the prevalence of congregationalism in New England, where he was born and educated. At least, the one law, which he lays down, seems to drift to a justification of *his use* of the authority to administer the sacraments, which the Philadelphia church had conferred upon him, as his Boston friend thought, in a wrong way. His law was—"*Act in unity, and as the case requires.*" We cannot say we like this law. For action in unity may be good or bad, according as the principles of action previously determined upon are true or false; and "acting as the case requires" is too temporizing. Nothing is so easy as to imagine that a case very urgently requires us to do what we love to do. And equally easy is it for us to believe that to be true which we wish to be true. But the great thing is, in faith to determine *rationally*, before hand, what is true in God's Word, and then to *will* it and *do* it, *because it is right* : and to lay it down as a principle never to be swerved from, that no case can ever require us to deviate from the road, when the Word of God says, " This is the way, walk ye in it." We much prefer a more homely adage, and would give it a wider application than its author did—would put it in the place of Mr. Worcester's law here—"*Be sure you're right*, THEN *go ahead.*" But this adage was not born when Mr. Worcester wrote this letter; or we are not certain that he would not have adopted it himself. We can hardly think he would have had all the churches act in unity *before* they had ascertained and were sure that their mode of action was right. Still he thought " No one should have any authority given him but by consent of at least *one church*, and that authority should be given him *in the way that the case seemed to require.*" And he could not possibly have framed an opinion better suited to meet and justify his own case. The authority to administer the sacraments had been given to him by the one church at Philadelphia, and that church had judged it *necessary* in his case to confer that authority *by license.* But he hesitated to exercise the authority to baptize, until he learned whether the opinion of "one of his Boston friends," that such authority could not be given him " without the imposition of hands," were that of "the Boston members" generally—lest he "might injure the feelings" of any. He was anxious that "all the churches in the U. S. should understand and agree upon some order." But he thought that, "before this could be done, the subject needed to be discussed between the individuals of the different churches, and then, *perhaps*, [underscored by himself,] proposed in a convention." This implies the congregational order as existing, and that there were differences of view among the members of the particular churches, both as to what was the just method of giving " the different degrees of ecclesiastical authority," and as to whether the questions, growing out of this subject, should be settled by the churches in their particular form, or be proposed for settlement in a convention. The conclusion is, that Mr. Condy then held to but one ordination, and to the vesting of the power of this in the particular churches; and that the church at Boston began to think of grades in the ministry, and of the vesting of ordaining powers in the ministers of some one or all of those grades, acting in convention. The probability, at least, of this latter conclusion, will appear as we go on.

The Third General Convention was to have met in Philadelphia, on the 22d of October, 1819; but why it did not, the following minute, of a meeting of the Philadelphia church, held on the second of October in that year, will show—

Resolved, That, owing to the existence of pestilential diseases in Baltimore, New York and Boston, and other unfavorable circumstances, which, from information received, we have reason to believe, will prevent a general attendance of our distant brethren, it be recommended, to those who shall attend at the convention, to be held on the 22d instant, to adjourn the same until ascension day in the year 1820, and that a copy of this resolution be transmitted to as many as conveniently may be notified.

At a meeting of the Philadelphia church, held March 28, 1820, the Rev. Mr. Carll submitted a letter received by him from the Rev. John Hargrove, bearing date the 25th of the same month, and enclosing one to him from Thomas H. Roberts, of Frankfort, Ky., bearing date the 2d instant; whereupon the following preamble and resolution were passed—

Whereas, Thomas H. Roberts, of Frankfort, in the state of Kentucky, at the instance and by the request of a number of receivers of the doctrines of the New Jerusalem Church in that vicinity, hath offered himself for ordination in the ministry, and hath been also recommended to us for such ordination by the Rev. John Hargrove, of Baltimore, by whom he was baptized; and whereas, from the great distance of Mr. Roberts's place of residence, it is not practicable for him to come to Philadelphia or Baltimore, and it is suggested that it will be convenient for him to meet the Rev. Thomas Newport, of Lebanon, in the state of Ohio, at some suitable place in the country; therefore

Resolved, That the said Rev. Thomas Newport be, and he is hereby authorized and empowered, with the approbation and concurrence of the New Jerusalem Church in Baltimore, in due manner, according to the order heretofore used, to ordain the said Thomas H. Roberts as a priest and teaching minister of the Lord's Church of the New Jerusalem, with power, &c. [according to the usual formulary;] expressly excepting, however, the authority to ordain other priests and ministers; and that a copy of this resolution be signed by the Rev. M. M. Carll, and attested by the secretary; and that the same be transmitted to the Rev. John Hargrove, of Baltimore, for the concurrence and approbation of the New Jerusalem Church there, if they see fit.

The only thing to be observed here is, that the Baltimore *church* is mentioned as concurring in the granting of authority for this ordination, instead of Mr. Hargrove alone, as in the case of vesting power in Mr. Powell to ordain Mr. Newport. So that the church at Baltimore is now supposed to " exercise the power of an ordaining minister,"

as well as the church at Philadelphia. There is still no evidence
that any idea was entertained of an arrangement of ministers in trinal
order.

At a special meeting of the Philadelphia church, on the 15th of
May, 1820, Mr. Carll read a letter which he had received from Mr.
Adam Klingle, " expressing his desire to be ordained to the ministry
of the New Church; whereupon it was, on motion, *Resolved*, That
the said letter be referred to the vestry of the church." It does not
appear that Mr. Klingle was ever ordained. But, although the
record says nothing about it, it is a fact that he was subsequently
licensed. The above, too, shows that ordaining power was not supposed to reside in Mr. Carll as the minister alone, but in the church,
and to be exercised through him. Hence it may be considered as
fully established, that this was the view of the Philadelphia church
until after the meeting of the Third General Convention in 1820.

The Third General Convention assembled and sat in Philadelphia
from the 11th to the 13th of May, 1820. In this the fact, which
we have noticed, that three lay readers had been appointed by the
Philadelphia church, is thus formally stated by the committee on
communications—

It may not be amiss here also to mention, that the church in Philadelphia
has appointed, as *lay readers*, three young gentlemen, who are studying with
a view to prepare for the ministry, with authority to read the established
service and approved sermons, in aid of the pastor, or during his absence—
a measure which, if pursued by other churches, with discretion and a strict
regard to qualification, may be highly instrumental in educating laborers for
the Lord's vineyard.

This informs us what end was proposed in appointing those lay
readers, namely, the education of candidates for the ministry. While
they pursued their studies, they were authorized to aid the pastor by
reading the service when he was present, and, in addition to this, by
reading approved sermons when he was absent. Thus, although their
office was like that of the present assistant of the pastors of the new-
church societies in London, it was not intended here to be any grade
of the ministry. It was the office of " every student who is preparing for the ministry, before he becomes a priest," as mentioned in U.
T. 106, and was the same as the present licentiateship of the Central
Convention. Of the three young gentlemen, above alluded to, one,
Mr. Elias Fiske, a graduate of Brown University, died in Philadelphia while pursuing his studies for our ministry :—another, Mr. John
Burtt, a Scotchman, from the neighborhood of Burns—a poet too—
impressed on board a British man-of-war, and kept there for five years
without ever touching land, but, availing himself of the first opportunity to escape while his ship was off the coast of New Jersey in 1817,
was teaching a country school in that state, and, having our doctrines
presented to him by Mr. William Schlatter, who was rusticating with
his family at the house where he boarded, in the summer of 1818,
received them in the most promising way, as any one may see who
will read the articles, written by him, headed " Progress of the Recep-

tion of Truth," and published in the N. J. C. Rep., pp. 358-367 and
508-511 ; this Mr. Burtt, having received the doctrines of the new
church, came to Philadelphia to teach a school, procured for him by
his new-church brethren, and study for our ministry; proving a man
of much ability, he not only acted as lay reader in assisting Mr. Carll,
but also delivered lectures on the doctrines, written by himself, to
large audiences in the Commissioners' Hall of the Northern Liberties;
this Mr. John Burtt, the second of the lay readers above alluded to,
proved a renegade before he came into our ministry, studied theology
under Dr. Neal of the Scotch Presbyterian church of Philadelphia;
was ordained into the ministry of that church, became the pastor of
a church of that denomination in Salem, N. J., afterwards went to
Cincinnati, as editor of an old-school presbyterian periodical there,—
also enacting the secret detractor and scurrilous persecutor of the new
church in that city,—and, after some years, returned to his former
charge in Salem, where, if he is yet alive, he probably is now :—and
the third of those lay readers, after pursuing his studies for our ministry with Mr. Condy for about a year, then prepared for, entered
and graduated at Yale College, pursued, after that, the study of our
theology, under most embarrassed circumstances, for some years more,
was at length licensed to preach by the Rev. Messrs. Doughty, Roche.
and Carll, then ordained into the second degree by the Rev. Adam
Hurdus, then into the third degree by the same, has, by divine mercy
and aid, continued in our ministry, under the most unexampled opposition, until the present time, and is now the writer of this report.

In the report of this same committee to this convention, we are
informed—

* * * that, in one of the universities of our country, there are *five*
resident graduates studying theology, *who openly profess the doctrines of the
New Jerusalem.* There are in the same institution, two under-graduates,
who are receivers; as also, in the same vicinity, two graduates, who are
studying theology with private clergymen, and a third, in an academy.

In Massachusetts, a minister of the old church, who is represented as a
man of excellent talents and good character, has heartily embraced the doctrines, and zealously preaches them to his congregation.

Experience in the knowledge of events then future, but now past,
affords us much food for practical reflection upon the two things above
stated. The first is, that nine graduates of Harvard University embraced our doctrines, from the works of Swedenborg, especially his
Arcana Cœlestia in the original latin, deposited in the library of that
institution by the Rev. William Hill. These graduates, or a majority
of them, became the nucleus of the new church in its form distinctive from the old church, as it has since flourished so greatly in Massachusetts and the surrounding New England States. The reflection
upon this fact is, that the New Jerusalem, as a new and true christian
church, is to be established by the Lord, through a separate ministry,
now in his second advent, as an external visible body, entirely distinct
from the old and consummated christian church, which was established
by the Lord, through his apostles, in his first advent—that the ministers for this new church are to come from the universities, and that

we are not to expect that its doctrines will be generally received and taught by the clergy of the old dispensation.

The second thing is, that a clergyman of the old church, in Massachusetts, a man of excellent talents and good character, had heartily embraced our doctrines and was zealously preaching them to his old-church congregation.—We might mention similar instances in this quarter; as the cases of Dr. Allison of Burlington, and the Rev. Mr. Boswell of Trenton, N. J.—The inference from this would have been the reverse of the above, namely, that the new church was to come forward in the old christian church, and not in any distinct, visible or external form—that our doctrines were to be received and preached by the old-church clergy, and, therefore, that the idea of separation from the old church which was begun in England and continued in this country was an error, while the non-separatists, as they were called, were, under the lead of the Rev. John Clowes, in the right. But the reflection upon this second thing as here stated, which subsequent events have enabled us to make, is, that this latter inference would have been altogether erroneous. If we mistake not, the clergyman in Massachusetts alluded to above, was a somewhat distinguished pastor in Boston, who did not at all succeed in bringing the sheep of his old-church congregation into the external fold of the New Jerusalem. And whatever may be said of Mr. Clowes's efficiency in establishing the New Jerusalem in a separate external form by his published writings, or by his conversational meetings, it is certain that his effort to introduce the doctrines into the parish of St. John's, Manchester, of which he was rector for about sixty years, by preaching them from the pulpit, was an almost total failure. The sermons which he preached in the morning, were for a time preached against by his curate in the afternoon. And after his decease, his place was supplied by a rector of the most thorough old-church stamp—which could hardly have been the case, if his parish had been in any considerable degree imbued with the doctrines or principles of the new church by his preaching. We are, then, rationally led to the conclusion, that the new church is not to come forward in the old by the means of the old-church clergy receiving and preaching her doctrines; that the New Jerusalem, as Swedenborg says, is to exist and remain for centuries distinct from the first christian church, as the first christian has from the jewish church; and that the New Jerusalem is to be established in a distinctly visible or external form by means of a new ministry entirely distinct and separate from that of the old church. This conclusion is the more important now, when certain distinguished clergymen of the old church, having embraced our doctrines, essay to expound and preach them, without distinct baptism into our faith, or without coming into our ministry, and even with the charge of a breach of *charity* on our part, because we object to their acting as formal preachers or teaching ministers without inauguration into our priesthood as an entirely new, distinctive and separate one. We must, therefore, be indulged in some remarks on this subject here.

We are not disposed to find fault with those ministers of the old

church, who embrace our doctrines and feel it to be right for them
to remain and preach them in their former connections. If the professing members of the various sects of the old christian church will
allow their ministers to embrace and preach to them new-church
doctrines, we say, with all our hearts, so be it. If they, in fact, are
found to cast out devils in the name of the Lord, we shall not think
of forbidding them, because they follow not with us. (Luke, ix. 49.)
Especially in England, Sweden, and other parts of Europe, where the
church is a political establishment, there may be strong reasons why
a minister of the established church should not dissolve his connection
with it and receive ordination in a distinctive new-church ministry.
But in this country, where there is no connection of church and state,
and every one is guaranteed the most perfect freedom to worship
God according to the dictates of his own conscience, there is not the
same reason why ministers should remain and preach new-church
doctrines in the old church; and there are, to our mind, the strongest
possible reasons why the New Jerusalem should assume a distinct
external form, with a ministry wholly distinct and separate from that
of the old christian church. And when this ministry has been
formed, and acknowledged for years, by those who have embraced
the new-church doctrines, and come into the organizations of general
bodies of an external church for their orderly propagation, we cannot
see any good reason why ministers of the old church should assume
to preach the doctrines of the new church, *in this connection*, without
regular introduction into its ministry, or without being regularly
clothed with the authority and sanction of its peculiar and distinctive
priesthood. There may be reasons for this course which seem good
to them and to others; we only say *we* have not yet seen, and cannot
yet see, them.

In England, we have seen that the first receivers of the new-church
doctrines were greatly divided on this subject. That eminent minister, and truly excellent man, the Rev. John Clowes, of Manchester,
was the chief leader of those who were called the non-separatists,
and the Rev. Robert Hindmarsh the leader of the separatists. The
controversy between these parties assumed, at times, considerable acri-
mony, and led, at length, to an attack upon the Rev. Mr. Clowes by
the Rev. Joseph Proud. This, in a letter, from a leading member of
the new church in London, dated June 12, 1818, to the corresponding secretary of the " American Society for disseminating the Doctrines of the New Jerusalem Church," is thus noticed:—

Since I had the pleasure of hearing from you, the question of the expediency of separation from communion with the Established Church has
once more, after many years of repose, been roused in a late Publication
from Mr. Proud; in which, arising from a mistaken view of *what constitutes
the church,* he is not sparing of unseemly epithets on those, who, with Mr.
Clowes, view it as an interior dispensation, as much disconnected from
forms and ordinances, as a man is from his dress. This has produced a
reply of justification from the charges of hypocrisy and prevarication in a
Letter well worthy the expansive and interior mind of the Rector of St.
John's. Such discussions, if a spirit of party be suffered to infuse itself,
are worse than useless; they destroy the beauty of that *human form,* into

which, interiorly, the good of the community is collated, and introduce the *only real* Old Church, with all its deformity, and exclusive spirit.

From this we see the ground of action of the non-separatists; namely, that the New Jerusalem is " an interior dispensation, *as much disconnected from forms and ordinances as a man is from his dress.*" In fact, the New Jerusalem, in their view, was either to be a *naked church*, or to have *old-church clothes on*. It was, then, nothing more nor less than the original type of that new-church *transcendentalism*, which has been vamped up in certain recent publications in this country—in which all the organizations of an external new church here, with its distinctive ministry, have been branded as sectarian and exclusive misconceptions of "what truly constitutes the church," and as contraventions of that all expanding new-church *charity*, which is, with undiscriminating and meretricious ardor, to give the *fraternal hug* to any thing and every thing under the sun! We hardly need say that we are not the advocates, or tolerators, of any *such* views of the New Jerusalem as a *universal, transcendental, "interior dispensation,"* which is to be developed on any other ground than a *perpetual* renunciation of evil as sin against God—which is to appear in a *regeneration* without previous *reformation*. We reject and abhor such a heresy! And we hold to the *impossibility* of having the New Jerusalem established as an interior dispensation, or an internal church, without a correspondential external one. We hold, too, that there can be no external church without its external rites, ceremonies, ordinances, sacraments and " priestly offices." And when these offices have been instituted according to a certain order, with its " distinctions," " proofs" and " signs or tokens by which its qualities may be known and ascertained," (U. T. 680,) we cannot think that true new-church charity requires us to award the right to any to do battle against the enemies of our faith in the army of our church militant, until they have taken upon themselves those badges, " signs, or *distinguishing* marks," by which they shall be known as the sub-ordinate or co-ordinate members of our " one body." In short, we cannot believe that *that* charity which produces the *most distinct* arrangement of the new from the old christian heaven in general, and between the societies of each of these heavens in particular, can confound all distinctions between the New Jerusalem and the old christian church on earth. And we hesitate not to say, that the charity which would do this, is a coin of spurious gold, which ought to be nailed to the counter as counterfeit!

But we have no idea that the Rev. Mr. Clowes—whose memory we revere with the profoundest love!—was an *opponent* of the manifestation of the New Jerusalem as a distinctive external church. He did not think it was *his* duty to give up *his* connection with the established church of England and come into such an external new-church organization. And we have never doubted that he was right in this. When he embraced the doctrines of the new church and began to proclaim them, the time had not yet fully come for the institution of an external new church. Certainly he might have thought so. He might also have thought that the beginnings which were in fact made were not of the right sort, or did not manifest the right spirit. He might have thought they *were* too sectarian and external in their tendency. He was entitled to his opinion in this matter, and ought not to have been condemned for acting according to his opinion conscientiously formed. And we do believe that it was a violation of new-church charity to charge him with hypocrisy and prevarication in his course. We say we have never doubted that the course which he took was the right one for him. It was his duty to preach the Gospel at Jerusalem, while it was the duty of Hindmarsh and others to preach it to "*gentile* christendom." In our view—to use a geological simile—he was a sort of *transition* rock, between, and serving to connect, the old and new formations. And it must not be forgot that, although Mr. Clowes did not throw off the badge of the old-church ministry, yet he was more than any other man instrumental in planting, or maturing, the germs of those social formations which have, in later years, expanded into the most important and most flourishing distinctive new-church societies in England. A remarkable proof of Mr. Clowes's very early engagement in this work has just come to our hands, in turning over certain old documents in our possession. It will be recollected that the first society for propagating the doctrines of the new church in the world was formed in London in 1783. Of this Mr. James Glen was a member; and, as a sort of apostle of it, first proclaimed those doctrines in America by a series of lectures which he began to deliver in Philadelphia on the 5th of June, 1784. From this Mr. Glen went to Demerara, perhaps sooner than he intended, so that some books came to him from London after he had left Philadelphia, which, being sold, not long after their arrival, at public sale, were the means of permanently propagating the doctrines of our church in this country.* Now we have in our hands a letter from Mr. John Augustus Tulk, dated "Esher, Surry, 7 February, 1785"—with postscripts of the 12th and 22d of that month—addressed to Mr. James Glen, at Philadelphia, stating that a certain box of books had been sent to him there, and, among other things, giving a detailed account of what had transpired in the London society after he had left it. This letter undoubtedly arrived about the time the books did, and therefore after Mr. Glen had left Philadelphia; so that he never received it. Hence it has come into our possession among other papers kept in the archives of the First Philadelphia Society. In this letter, after giving an account of certain alternations in the London society, from day to night, or from a summer to a winter state, in which it was almost frozen to death, Mr. Tulk cheers up with the following recital—

To restore and awaken us from our nocturnal state, on the 3d of October, I received a letter from Mr. Wright, announcing the arrival from Man-

* In a letter from the widow of the Rev. Dr. Hodson to a friend in Philadelphia, dated London, June 20, 1815, we see it stated that, on the day previous, (19th of June,) "the anniversary of our Lord's sending his disciples forth to preach the new doctrines of the spiritual world was kept" by the London society, "who dined together to the number of fifty;" and that "a letter from Mrs. Scott, of Demerara, was read by Mr. Charles Tulk, announcing the death of Mr Glen of that place." From this we may infer that Mr. Glen died in Demerara, either in the end of 1814, or in the beginning of 1815.

chester of our Rev. Friend and Brother Mr. Clowes, the Editor and Translator of the Arcana; who has been instrumental in establishing a church in Manchester and the adjacent parts, consisting of near fifteen hundred persons, some of whom, by visions, voices and spiritual communications, have borne oral evidence to the Truth of the Doctrine. This Gentleman came purposely to visit the state of the Society, which included a more important end than the Visit at first portended; inasmuch as it is evident the Society increased most rapidly during the stay of our Rev. Friend—meeting, shortly after his departure, six and twenty in number, women included. Many conversations tending to illustrate important points of Doctrine passed with that Gentleman, whom the Society met every evening during his stay in London. Being absent, I can give but little account thereof; but, on the Thursday following, when I arrived in Town, I had the pleasure of paying my respects to him, and received much illustration and entertainment from a Discourse which he made in order the more clearly to define the nature of the three Minds, the Natural, the Rational and the Spiritual, which he very properly elucidated and demonstrated by the quality and nature of the things received; concerning which I forbear enlarging here, inasmuch as the substance of his discourse was derived from, and is contained in, the second volume of the Arcana Cœlestia.

Mr. Tulk then goes on to relate what was the subject of Mr. Clowes's second night's conversation, which he heard, namely, the origin of evil; and at last says—

To conclude. He manifested himself a pious, learned, and sensible man, full of that brotherly affection which prompted him, for the good of others, to make himself a profitable and useful servant in the hands of Providence.

Thus we learn that Mr. Clowes, so early as 1785, in the second or third year after the London society was first instituted, was instrumental in reviving and strengthening it, by a visit to it for that purpose. And we learn, that, before that time, he " had been instrumental in establishing a church, in Manchester and the adjacent parts, consisting of near fifteen hundred persons." How manifest, then, is his agency in establishing the new church in a distinct and separate form!

But we have a letter from Mr. Clowes himself, to Mr. Hargrove, which expresses so clearly his opinion that they who became separatists were not in the *wrong*, that we cannot refrain from giving to the church an extract of it here. It seems that Mr. Hargrove had, like Mr. Proud, and others, objected to Mr. Clowes's remaining in the old church to preach there the doctrines of the new. Mr. Clowes, in a letter dated " Manchester, Dec. 29th, 1802," thus replies:—

Your name was not strange to me, nor is it less dear, because we differ in sentiment about *external* things; for the question about *true spiritual union of minds* has little or nothing to do with *opinions*, especially where those opinions do not relate to the essentials of Christian Life and Worship. If the Lord Jesus Christ be acknowledged as the only God in Heart and in Life, true christian Charity must needs prevail in that Mind, and where true Christian Charity is, there is the very Cement of all spiritual conjunction; and in such case, whatsoever variety there may be in points of *outward speculation*, (as Varieties there will be,) it will only be like the variety in the shapes, and forms, and uses of the bodily members and organs, which, so far from destroying Unity, tend rather to establish and perfect it.

If I have judged it right to continue in the Ministry of the *Old Church*, I
trust it has been solely from a conviction in my own mind, that a sudden departure from, and violent opposition to, the *Externals* of that church, would
have tended to excite unnecessary prejudices in the minds of many against
the New Doctrines, and that therefore the Wisdom of heavenly Love required
rather a *temporary toleration* of some Abuses and Corruptions, than such a
hasty rejection, as might have given Birth to an Idea, that the New Church
was intent more on *outward* than *inward* Reformation, and that she was
besides *sectarian* in her practices, and *intolerant* in her *principles*. On the
other hand, if you, Sir, have thought it right to pursue a different line of
conduct, I am ready and willing to indulge the same Hope, that you also
have acted in agreement with the Conviction of your own mind, and from
the best Intention of promoting the prosperity of those Doctrines which
your Understanding approved. It is *possible*, therefore, (and I humbly trust,
probable,) that we may both have acted right, and in a manner the best calculated, in our respective Stations, to recommend and disseminate the Truths
which we each of us most ardently loved. The Divine Providence of the
Lord, we know, has, in all ages, permitted the Children of Wisdom to be
influenced by a *Variety* and even *Diversity* of Sentiment, and has even rendered that Variety and Diversity subservient to its own blessed purposes of
making known to mankind the Counsels of its own Mercy. And who can
say but that some procedure of this kind has been in operation under the
New Dispensation, and that the Descent of the *New Jerusalem* has been
accomplished by those very means which, (to judge only from human appearances,) seemed likely to retard it? At all events, I am persuaded you
will agree with me in Opinion, that the *surest* and most effectual method of
recommending and establishing the Truths of the Lord's New Kingdom is
first to form them well in our own Lives, so that we may be enabled to
press them upon others, not so much from *intellectual Light*, as from *voluntary Life*, and may thus convince mankind, that, in making them converts
to the New Jerusalem verities, we are not eager to change their *persuasions*
only, but their *principles*, by calling them out of all *disorderly Love*, to
become happy and undefiled in the Love of God and their Neighbour. Is
not this what is meant by *casting the net on the right side of the Ship?*

Undoubtedly, in *establishing* a church through a ministry, as the
Lord established the first christian church through his apostles, all
teaching should be the doctrine of *life*. But this supposes that a
ministry is first ordained, and an external church first instituted as a
plane for the development in life of the church's internal principles.
Hence Swedenborg intimates, in Ap. Ex. 403, that "the new church
will, in its beginning, be external." But we agree with Mr. Clowes
that the sole end in first instituting a "teaching ministry" for "the
insinuation of *truth*," should be the implantation of *good;* and that
all efforts to establish the church will be ineffective until "*good* is
insinuated by every one in the country." (A. C. 6822.) Finally, we
cheerfully accord to Mr. Clowes, what he grants to us, that he was
right in his course; and are heartily willing to tolerate, in the present
day, all who, with his conscientious convictions of duty, follow in *his*
footsteps.

In the proceedings of the Third General Convention we find the
following:

The committee appointed at the First General Convention, to take into
consideration the subject of the ordination of ministers of the new church,

10

not being ready to report, begged leave to be continued—which was agreed to. And it was *Resolved*, That it be recommended to the churches at Baltimore, Philadelphia and New York, respectively, to ordain no person to the ministry, without the concurrence and approbation of the ministers of the other two churches, until some regulation shall be established on the subject.

Thus it appears that the regulation of ordinations in the ministry was again postponed by the General Convention, and the power of ordaining was vested in *three* instead of *two* churches as before. The truth is, that the receivers of our doctrines throughout the United States were so few in number and sparse in residence, that there was not yet the material to form a general church; and the attempt to make general regulations for the whole church in a country like this, was felt to be premature. Therefore there was, and could be, as yet, no agitation of the question of a trine in the ministry in the General Convention. Consequently, so far as episcopacy may be supposed to be involved in this, or identical with it, there is the fullest evidence that no tendency whatever to the episcopal form of *government* had, up to this time, become manifest in either the Philadelphia church, or in the General Convention by influence from that. How was it with New England, or with our eastern brethren?

It has been shown that Mr. Samuel Worcester, a Boston man, in Natchez, was the first to throw out hints about "the *different degrees of authority*" in our church. This was in May, 1819. And we came to the conclusion that it was probable this subject had been canvassed by the church at Boston. This probability we thought would appear as we proceeded. And we think it will, if we now turn our steps to that quarter.

For some reason, which does not now appear, Mr. Samuel Worcester did not remain long in Natchez. A letter of Mr. Hargrove's now in our hands, contains a proposition to him to come to Baltimore, where a school would be provided for him, and a way opened for him into the ministry of the new church. This proposition he did not accept: but he preferred yielding to the solicitation of his Boston friends to come and take charge of a school in that city or its vicinity. There we find him as leader and preacher of the society in the beginning of 1820. He probably returned thither some time in the middle of the preceding year, so as to avoid the sickly season of a southern climate. But in Newchurchman-Extra, No. I., p. 31, is an extract of a letter from him to Mr. Condy, dated Boston, June 30, 1820. This was just after the meeting of the Third General Convention, and therefore now comes up to our notice in the order of time. A perusal of that document, No. XV., in connection with the two, Nos. XIII. and XIV., which precede it, will show how strong a tendency—even in the estimation of people there—there was to *strong* and "*arbitrary government*" in the Boston society then. The tendency to exercise rigid *discipline* for violations of "the *rule*" of the church, is clearly seen. And in the greater freedom in externals which Mr. Condy shows to have prevailed in Philadelphia, we think it is made clear that there was a much stronger tendency then to church discipline and episcopal government in New England than in this quarter. But what is pertinent to the subject now before us is, that Mr. Worcester distinctly repudiates Mr. Condy's idea of our eastern brethren's notions of church order and government being derived from the congregational system then prevalent in New England; and expressly avows that they were looking to a "general ecclesiastical establishment" in "the United States," and only until then had been *constrained* to adopt "the congregational system." And that the notion of this "general ecclesiastical *establishment*" did; in the minds of our eastern brethren, at that time, involve the idea of subordinate grades in the ministry, must appear plain to every one from these words of Mr. Samuel Worcester's letter above referred to—"Do we not want *some officers* of *rank subordinate* to our priests? I have not been informed whether deacons or any officers of similar order exist in your church." Here is the first clear and distinct suggestion of the question of subordinate ranks or grades in our ministry, which we find made in the new church of America. And mark, *it is made by a Boston man in Boston*.

And now, too, what was called the "Boston heresy," was broached. This letter from Mr. Samuel Worcester speaks of it. But it is formally propounded by its author, Mr. Thomas Worcester, in the following document, No. XVI., p. 37. Let that document be inspected, for *there* undoubtedly is the *spring*, from whence has gushed all episcopal and papal tendencies in the church in this country. For in the conjugial relation the husband is the *head* of the wife, so that the church is formed in the wife *through* the husband as a medium between her and the Lord. And when the clergy are placed in this relation to the laity, the pastor becomes the *head* of his society; and this leads inevitably to a similar head of the church in every larger form. How, then, could it possibly have been otherwise than that the originator of this notion, when it became his duty to frame rules of order for the whole church in the United States, should have devised both the office and the name of "*bishop*" in the new church of America? In our opinion, Swedenborg's doctrine of the trine by no means coincides with or favors this notion; but it was very easy for those who wished to establish this order, to lay hold of that doctrine, and use it, so far as they could make it suit their purpose. And now the great difficulty which we have to encounter is, the so disentangling Swedenborg's doctrine of the trine from the weavings of their web, as to cause it to be seen in its true form and adopted in its proper use.

Thus have we traced the first tendency to episcopal *government*— to the exercise of church *discipline* and *strong* government—to Boston. There, too, we find the first agitation of the question of subordinate ranks in the ministry. And that the first distinct presentation of the order of a *trine* of such ranks was first made to the General Convention by one of our eastern brethren, a member of the Boston society, will in due time appear.

The next person ordained into the new-church ministry in this country, was the Rev. Holland Weeks. This gentleman had been a distinguished minister, for many years, of the so-called orthodox persuasion in New England. For a series of years he officiated as the pastor of a congregation in Abington, Massachusetts. While there he embraced the doctrines of the New Jerusalem, and quietly infused them into his sermons. His congregation, at first, expressed much delight at the original and striking views which he gave forth—until he felt it his duty to declare that he drew them from the writings of Emanuel Swedenborg. Now the scene was quickly shifted, and the same actors came on the stage in different dresses to enact new parts. Every tongue was vociferous in condemning the very doctrines which had been previously so much approved. Persecution and proscription followed. Their pastor was arraigned, tried, condemned and deprived of his living. But the circumstances attending his dismissal, and the conspicuous position which he had held in the eye of the New England church in general, drew crowds to his trial, and the result was a more searching inquiry into the principles of the new church, followed by the embracing of its doctrines by quite a number in the town of Abington, and its very remarkable extension throughout the county of Plymouth.

Mr. Weeks, thus expelled from his former connection, became a member of the Boston society of the New Jerusalem. And the following proceedings of the Philadelphia church in regard to him and Mr. Samuel Worcester, are of too much importance not to be given entire.

A special meeting of the society was held at the temple on the 9th of August, 1820.

Mr. Raguet stated that the meeting had been called in consequence of a letter received by Mr. Condy from Mr. Carll, in which the latter stated his intention of visiting Boston, and the object of the meeting would be seen in the resolutions he was about to submit. They are as follows:

Whereas, the Rev. Mr. Carll, who is now upon a missionary visit at the city of New York, has intimated, by letter, his intention of proceeding to the town of Boston, in company with the Rev. Mr. Doughty, of the former place; and whereas, Mr. Samuel Worcester, formerly of Natchez, in the state of Mississippi, and who derived from this church, on the 21st January, 1819, license, "for the term of seven years, to celebrate the rites of public worship, the sacraments of the Lord's supper, baptisms and funerals," is now resident at Boston and leader of the society there, and may wish to avail himself of the opportunity now afforded of being ordained to the ministry of the Lord's church of the New Jerusalem; therefore be it

Resolved, That the Rev. Mr. Carll be authorized, if application be made for the purpose, to ordain our well-beloved brother Samuel Worcester, of Boston, a priest and minister of the Lord's church of the New Jerusalem, with power, under the authority and at the request of the church in Boston, and in the manner and under such restrictions as they may prescribe, to ordain other priests and ministers of the New Jerusalem church; with power also to conduct public worship, to celebrate the sacrament of the Lord's supper, marriages, baptisms and funerals, and generally to perform all the holy rites and divine ordinances of the church.

And whereas it is probable that the Reverend Holland Weeks, of Abington, in the state of Massachusetts, formerly a minister of the calvinistic persuasion, but who has lately been dismissed from his pastoral charge in consequence of having embraced the doctrines of the New Jerusalem church, may wish to be ordained, as a priest and minister in that church; therefore be it

Resolved, That, should the church at Boston deem it expedient to confer ordination upon the said Mr. Weeks, either with full or limited powers, the entire concurrence of this church to the said act is hereby granted, and the Rev. Mr. Carll, if present at the time, is authorized to assist at the ceremony: *Provided,* That, if Mr. Weeks apply for ordination before Mr. Worcester shall be invested with authority to grant the same, the Rev. Mr. Carll be, and he is hereby empowered to confer it upon him, with all the powers expressed in the preceding resolution, except that of ordaining other priests and ministers.

Resolved, That, agreeably to the recommendation of the last General Convention, the concurrence of the churches of Baltimore and New York be solicited to the foregoing measures.

As the writer of this was then a member of the Philadelphia church, and was present in the meeting which passed the above resolutions, he may be allowed to condemn this proceeding now. Certainly very great changes have taken place in his mind upon the subject of ecclesiastical law, order and authority in twenty-eight years. There were present in this meeting but seven members. Mr. Condy was not present, and Mr. Carll was in New York. Only two persons of leading minds and force of character were there—Mr. Raguet and Mr. Burtt. And most assuredly, the others were any thing but a conclave of intelligent and wise theologians, with age and experience suited to pass on matters of such grave moment to the church as those set forth in the above resolutions. They were passed, of course, *nemine contradiscente.* And they certainly show that there was as yet no jealousy or mistrust of the church at Boston, on account of its notion of a conjugial pastoral relation, on the part of the church at Philadelphia. How short a time sufficed, in the turmoils which that matter produced, to justify the exclamation—*tantæne animis cœlestibus iræ!* it is needless now to say. We can only now express our astonishment, that a church so small in numbers, and so deficient in all the requisites to give shape and tone to the ecclesiastical order of the New Jerusalem in this country by the exercise of ordaining and other powers, should have been in such a *hurry* to transfer *all* those powers *at once* to persons whom they as yet had never seen or heard preach, so soon after reception of our doctrines, unless, from a feeling sense of incompetency, great anxiety had been felt, *to shift on to other shoulders the great responsibility of this weighty concern as soon as possible.* And to effect this, Mr. Carll was wafted on as a southern cloud, *full* charged, to pour, in one vivid flash and loud report, on the cooler, more cautious and discrete heads of our northern brethren, *all* of our electricity at once. It matters not that Mr. Weeks, as well as Mr. Worcester, subsequently proved himself altogether worthy to have received these plenary powers; the churches at Philadelphia, Baltimore and New York had had no opportunity of *proving* this *before* they proceeded to lay hands *so suddenly* upon him. And that our Boston brethren *very properly* used more prudence, and therefore showed themselves more fit " to exercise with great discretion the power of ordaining ministers," we think the following will show.

Friday, September 22d, 1820.

A special meeting of the society was held at the temple.   Nine members present—among them Messrs. Carll, Condy, Raguet, Thuun, and Fiske.

Mr. Carll stated to the meeting that, during his late visit at Boston, he had received a copy of the resolutions adopted on the 9th of August, as also the concurrence of the churches of Baltimore and New York in the measures therein authorized, *but that he had not been called upon to act under the same,* [underscored by us.]

Mr. Carll then laid before the meeting a communication which had been addressed to him, in the following words; viz:

Boston, August 7, 1820.

REVEREND SIR AND BROTHER,

At a regular meeting of the New Jerusalem Church in Boston, holden on Lord's Day, Aug. 6, 1820,

On request of Brother Holland Weeks that this church should approve of his sending to the Rev. Mr. Carll, of Philadelphia, Rev. Mr. Hargrove, of Baltimore, and Rev. Mr. Doughty, of New York, for a license to preach the Gospel according to the order of the New Jerusalem church.

Resolved, That this church cordially grant the above request.

Attest,   JAMES MANN, *Moderator,*
                                 SAMUEL WORCESTER, *Secretary.*

Agreeably to a subsequent resolution of this church, *We hereby certify* to the church of the New Jerusalem in Philadelphia, our approbation of Mr. Weeks's design. The excellent character sustained by him, his attainments in spiritual knowledge, and the prudence and firmness with which he has conducted under persecution, give him high claims to our confidence and love.

On the 6th instant he was admitted into our church as a brother in regular standing.

We recommend, that, on his application for a license, it be granted to him. This recommendation, with the resolution given above, will be communicated to the churches in Baltimore and New York, with the additional request, that they will certify to you their concurrence.   In this case it will be expected of you to send the license to Mr. Weeks.

With much respect and affection, we are, Reverend Sir, your brethren in the Lord,

JAMES MANN,
SAMUEL WORCESTER.

Whereupon, it was, on motion,

Resolved, That a license be granted by the church to Mr. Weeks, agreeably to his request, and that, after the same be prepared and signed, it be transmitted to the churches of Baltimore and New York, for the purpose of obtaining their approbation on the same.

As an ardent lover of order, for its own sake, and for the sake of its great uses, we confess the perusal of the above proceeding of the Boston church has swelled our bosom with the most pleasing emotion. It is an orderly thing done in an orderly way.   By comparing dates, it will be seen that two days before the church at Philadelphia was providing for the ordination of Mr. Samuel Worcester with full powers, so that the church at Boston might, through him, if it "should deem it expedient," "confer ordination upon the said Mr. Weeks, *either with full or limited* powers," the Boston church had recommended Mr. Weeks to the southern churches "for a *license* to *preach*" merely.   Let us not fail to observe, too, that this was done "on *request* of *Brother Holland Weeks.*"   It was all *he* asked at first. And does it not imply that he even then thought, that a minister, on coming from the old into the new-church ministry, should first pass through a *preparatory* and *initiatory* plane, before receiving its unlimited powers? It may have been that he was influenced by the Boston church in making this request, and that his mind was first turned to the order of the trine there. Subsequent events make this probable. At any rates, here is the first indication of a license as affording a lower or preparatory grade in our ministry. And it is asked for by Holland Weeks, who afterwards became the instrument of the Divine Providence in so clearly illustrating and enforcing the doctrine of a ministerial trine for the first time in our connection.

After Mr. Weeks was licensed, or rather after authority was given to license him, he received an invitation to come southward on ·a missionary tour. Fifty dollars had been given to the Philadelphia church, for a missionary fund, by a Mrs. Simmons, of Charleston, S. C. The New York Society, "had subscribed fifteen dollars to defray so much of the expenses of a contemplated visit of the Rev. Holland Weeks." And the Baltimore society "had proposed to raise their proportion of Mr. Weeks's expenses on his journey." Therefore, the Philadelphia church, in a special meeting, held January 6, 1821, resolved—

That our brother Holland Weeks be invited to visit New York, Philadelphia and Baltimore, and that the expenses of the journey be chargeable on the missionary fund.

That the Rev. Mr. Carll be, and he is hereby requested to invite the Rev. Mr. Weeks, and at the same time to transmit to him the sum of thirty dollars, out of the missionary fund, on account of his travelling expenses.

Mr. Weeks accordingly visited Philadelphia, and "on the 15th of April, 1821, was re-baptized into the faith of the New Church, at the Temple, by the Rev. Mr. Carll. On the succeeding Lord's Day, April 22d, he was ordained a priest and teaching minister in the New Jerusalem. The ordination service, on this occasion, was performed, and the charge delivered, by the Rev. Mr. Carll, after which a sermon was preached by the newly ordained minister to a numerous congregation." (Jour. 4th Gen. Con., p. 1.) From Philadelphia Mr. Weeks proceeded, on a missionary tour, through Maryland and Virginia, and, with a firm step and strong hand, sowed broad-cast there the seeds of truth.

Though a plain man, we have perhaps never had a stronger and more intensely intellectual one in the new church than the Rev. Holland Weeks. He had been a leading minister in the Hopkinsian faith, and as such, was well known and much respected throughout New England. He was well versed in the learned languages, armed cap-a-pie in dogmatic theology, and thoroughly grounded in the letter of the Word. There was "a river of his own, and he had made it." He had a name, in which he might have boasted, if he had been so disposed. Assuredly, he had as good a right to preach our doctrines on the broad ground of *charity*, without taking upon himself any distinctive badge of the New Jerusalem, as any who ever preceded or succeeded him in our ranks. Certainly he had as good a right as an

to *ask* for ordination into our ministry with full powers at once.
But he chose to enter as a child, rather than a full grown man. He
only asked for a license; and availed himself of the very first opportunity to receive *baptism*, as the distinctive sign of the new-church
faith.

Mr. Weeks asked a *license* to preach, and the church at Boston, of
which he was a member, recommended him to the Philadelphia
church for one, with a request that the New York and Baltimore
churches would give *certificates* of their concurrence. Why did they
not withdraw this application for a license when they found that Mr.
Carll had *authority enough in his pocket* to enable the Boston church
themselves to *ordain* Mr. Weeks with *full* or limited powers if they
should think it expedient? Probably the Boston church were not
willing to have Mr. Samuel Worcester ordained over them as their
priest and teaching minister. Probably they wished to have some
other man in that office, and therefore preferred not to ask Mr. Carll
to exercise the ordaining power of the Philadelphia church just then.
But why did they not allow Mr. Carll to ordain Mr. Weeks with the
limited powers prescribed by the Philadelphia church, in the contingency of the Boston church's not receiving power to ordain him with
full or limited power according to their discretion? Does not this
indicate that the Boston church thought Mr. Weeks ought first to
receive a license to preach, and to act under that, *before* he was ordained even with a limited ordination? It seems so to us. And,
therefore, we think we see here, for the first time, a tendency to a
formal institution of the licentiateship as the *first grade* of our ministry. For it must not be forgotten that Mr. Samuel Worcester, who
was the leader and secretary of the Boston church at this time, asks,
"do we not want some officers of rank subordinate to our priests?"
And is it not clear that the licentiate was to be regarded by him and
them as an officer in a rank so subordinate? The following confirms
this view.

A special meeting of the Philadelphia church was held, Lord's Day
morning, March 11, 1821, after divine service. Fourteen members present.

The Rev. Mr. Carll presented a letter from Mr. Thomas Worcester, of
Boston, requesting to be licensed " to preach and administer the ordinance
of baptism according to the doctrines of the New Jerusalem." A letter
from the Rev. Samuel Worcester was also presented and read, in which it
was requested that the license be granted. Whereupon, it was unanimously
Resolved, That the following license be granted to our Brother Thomas
Worcester.

[Here follows a License in due form, authorizing " the said Thomas Worcester to administer the holy ordinance of baptism, and to preach and
  teach the doctrines of the said church as set forth and declared in the
  writings of Emanuel Swedenborg, Messenger of the Lord."]

Here Mr. Thomas Worcester asks for a *license* to preach and baptize; and his brother Samuel, then leader of the Boston church,
seconds his request, which is granted. There can be no question that
the Philadelphia church would just as readily have granted ordination
with unlimited powers to Mr. *Thomas* as to Mr. *Samuel* Worcester,

in connection with the church at Boston. All that was wanting was the request. Bùt these powers were not accepted for Mr. Samuel Worcester, although repeatedly tendered, and even pressed upon him; and now Mr. Thomas Worcester, and the Boston church through its leader, ask for a license, with only power to preach and to administer the sacrament of baptism. Could this have been, if the Boston church had not *intended* to establish the precedent of the appointment by license of a subordinate or first grade of ministers with the still more limited powers of preaching and baptizing only? We see, then, that it was the Boston church which first *practically* defined, what was afterwards formally acknowledged to be, the first grade of the trine in the ministry of the american new church. Previously, there had been the third grade of priest and teaching minister, with the full powers of administering both sacraments and ordaining others; and the second grade of priest and teaching minister with the limited powers of administering both of the sacraments, without ordaining others; and now we see the first grade of licentiate, with the still more limited power of administering only one of the sacraments. Thus do we trace the virtual definition of our ministerial trine to Boston. Or, as the Rev. Wm. Mason would say, "before any idea was agitated about a trine in the ministry, such a trine did exist" in this country. We cannot, however, say that "it had actually come into spontaneous existence without *any* external contrivance"; or that "it needed no thought, no effort, to bring about this result." For we think it must be manifest that this result was brought about here by the thought, the effort and the contrivance of our eastern brethren. They did not, indeed, make the distinction between the two higher grades,—which *we* think have never yet been properly discreted,— but assuming the quasi distinction which had grown up in practice, as we have shown, without any regard to the trine, they made the trine visible by the determining of this first grade. Or, in our opinion, if *this were* a *spontaneous* growth of the ministerial trine in the new church of America, it was like the growth of a wild tree in a forest, or a wild flower in an untilled field—the flux of the divine order through the heavens was made to come into irregular and imperfect forms by the wilderness state of the visible church in her beginning. And it was not until the Lord, as a *rational* husbandman, had transplanted the wild olive tree, or had set out in cultivated soil, as well as pruned, the wild vine, of his new church's external order, that it was to grow into proper form, blossom in true beauty, and produce the fruits of genuine order.

When Mr. Weeks arrived in Philadelphia, he then asked for ordination. To this, he was probably prompted by the southern churches. For when the application was made for him by Mr. Daniel Lammot, whose guest he was in Philadelphia, the very next day after his arrival in that city, the record says, "the Rev. Mr. Carll then stated that the churches of Baltimore and New York had communicated to him their approbation of the ordination of Mr. Weeks as a minister of the New Church." Hence we conclude that the ordination of Mr. Weeks was concerted between the three churches of Philadelphia,

New York and Baltimore, before he came south. And that Mr.
Weeks consented to apply for ordination on his arriving at Philadelphia, makes it more probable that he first asked for a mere license at
the suggestion of the Boston church, of which he was then a member,
and of which, according to the custom of its members, he would ask
the opinion, and receive the advice, before taking so important a step.
(See Extra No. I., p. 31.)   Upon the application being made as above
stated, it was resolved—

> That our brother the Rev. Holland Weeks be ordained a priest and
> teaching minister, &c. [according to the usual formulary;] and with power
> also, under the authority and at the request of either of the churches of
> Baltimore, New York or Philadelphia, and in the manner and under such
> restrictions as they may prescribe, to ordain other priests and ministers of
> the New Jerusalem Church.

Thus Mr. Weeks was ordained with full powers in connection with
the southern churches.   And this shows that these churches had not
yet adopted the principle of a trine of discrete grades.   Otherwise,
they would have ordained him with limited powers first; and left
the conferring of full powers upon him to some future period, when
he might be the settled pastor of a particular church.   For when
"grades in the ministerial office" are "adopted and fully recognized
by" the church, it then becomes highly improper to disregard the
regular gradation in causing a man to rise to the third grade by taking
either two or three steps at once.   In the List of Ordaining Ministers
printed in the Journals of the General Convention, of late, it is said,
in a note, "most of them were introduced into two or more grades at
the same time:" but, with the exception of the Rev. Thomas Worcester, it is hardly correct to say so, because, at the time of their ordination, the order of a trine was not acknowledged, and a minister
could not be introduced into grades which were not defined.   There
is not a single instance of a licentiate having been raised by any
formal inauguration to the office of a minister ordained with limited
powers, or of a minister ordained with limited powers, having been
raised to the office of a minister with full powers, as distinct or discrete
grades, *before the order of a trine was formally acknowledged in the
General Convention in Baltimore in* 1827; and this proves that, prior
to that time, there were not supposed to be three distinct grades; and
how could a minister be introduced into two or more of them when
they were not supposed to exist?   The introduction of the Rev.
Thomas Worcester into two grades at once *after* a trine of distinct
grades was acknowledged by the General Convention, has ever since
appeared to us a culpable violation of true order.   And the more
recent act of Dr. Beers, of introducing Dr. S. Brown at once into the
highest grade, *without the previous sanction of any general body of
the church*, at a period when the order of the trine was so much more
fully acknowledged and carried out, was certainly a much more culpable violation of it.   But the General Convention has tacitly sanctioned this procedure, although *it was a violation of their own order*.
What concessions will not men make, when they want power!   And

what flimsy bonds are laws of order on paper, when they come athwart arbitrary or ambitious men in effecting their purposes!*

The ordination of Mr. Weeks was performed by the Rev. Mr. Carll, in the temple at Philadelphia, on the Lord's Day, in the morning, April 22, 1821; and of this Mr. Carll was directed by the church of which he was minister to issue a certificate under his hand and seal; which was done, in all due form, on the 14th of the ensuing May. Mr. Weeks, after completing his missionary tour to the south, returned to New England. From thence he applied, by a communication to the Rev. Mr. Carll, for authority to act as the missionary of the Philadelphia church in the State of Vermont. This communication was laid before that church in a meeting held January 30, 1822; and a formal certificate of such authority was directed to be issued and forwarded to Mr. Weeks. This was the last formal act of the Philadelphia church in licensing or ordaining ministers, or in clothing with its authority and sending forth general missionaries, which appears on its Book of Records. There might have been others that were not recorded. We know of a license, which we shall notice hereafter. And we surely need not now say, that there is not a scintilla of evidence of the truth of the assertion that "grades in the ministerial office were adopted and fully recognized by the above society, and were not objected to by the Convention."

In the early Journals of the General Convention, from the first to the seventh inclusive, there is no mention of the receivers of our doctrines present from the distant parts of the United States. We cannot, therefore, tell exactly when our eastern brethren were present and began to take part in the conventional proceedings. From Mr. Condy's letter on p. 30 of Newchurchman Extra, No. I., we learn that one of the brethren from New England—"a most excellent friend, originally of Connecticut—a zealous receiver, and very amiable and intelligent—showing great liberality in his views and evincing great discretion and freedom from local prejudice"—appears to have been in attendance on the Third General Convention, held in Philadelphia in May, 1820. But we think we have shown that a tendency to strong church government began to manifest itself in Boston in the spring of that year. We have also traced to the same source, the first suggestion, in the same year, respecting subordinate ranks in the ministry. In the autumn of the same year, we find our Boston brethren establishing by precedent the licentiateship as the first grade in the trine of our ministry. And, above all, we have seen that the notion of a conjugial pastoral relation originated there in the same year, which, we conceive, contained the rankest root of all episcopal and papal tendencies. Now when did any influence first begin to be

* Witness the treatment of the Rev. C. J. Doughty, by the Rev. Thomas Worcester, when he was to be punished for having " signed *that pamphlet*"—Reasons and Principles. (See Ap. No. LIX.) This correspondence shows how readily men can violate their own order, when it would tie up their hands in the castigation of those whom they deem their enemies. It illustrates, moreover, the nature of the charge brought against those who moved in the establishment of the Central Convention, of a *breach of charity* in having broken away from the General Convention.

exerted by the Boston church upon the General Convention? We answer, the very next year after the above developments.

The Fourth General Convention assembled in New York on the 2d of July, 1821. To that convention the church in Boston sent a communication, which with those from other churches, was referred to a committee,—consisting of the Rev. Messrs. Doughty, Beers and Carll, with Messrs. Higson, Schlatter and Woodworth, to consider and report on their subjects-matter. This committee, in their report, say, "The subject which excited the most attention and interest, and which elicited from your committee the most liberal expressions of opinion, was a communication signed by the corresponding secretary of the New Jerusalem Society in Boston." Unfortunately, this communication was not published with the Journal, so that we cannot judge now of the nature of the influence it was likely to exert on the body to which it was sent. We can judge of that only by the notice which the committee of that convention take of "the various subjects expressed and hinted at in this important document;" which, it is said, "were very freely and deliberately discussed," and met with the adoption of a unanimous opinion of the committee against them.

The first subject, in which the committee of the convention disagreed with their Boston brethren, was the principle laid down by the Boston church, that a minister should be set apart and supported in an exclusive devotion to the duties of his clerical calling. Against this the committee argue at length, and, as we have ever thought, most inconclusively. We have no doubt that the Boston church were right in that principle. And if any thing were wanted to prove it, it has been furnished by all experience in the fact that every society which began with the Boston principle has flourished, while almost every one which went upon the opposite principle has failed. If any society acting on the Boston principle has failed, it was because a suitable person was not chosen for the minister.

The second subject upon which the committee animadvert is thus noticed—

2dly. With respect to *church discipline*, it is the unanimous opinion of your committee, that every distinct society of the new church ought to be left *perfectly free* to adopt such rules, regulations and laws of government, as a majority of such society may deem most congenial to its state and circumstances. If the "truth hath made us *free*," let us be "*free indeed.*"

Here it is manifest that the very first influence of the Boston society upon the General Convention, was a tendency to *church discipline* in that body, which involved the making of rules, regulations and *laws* of *government* by the *general body* for the *particular societies* of the church. And in the view which this committee of the Fourth General Convention took of that subject, *we most heartily concur!*

·Let now the calm and dispassionate scrutinizer of the events which transpired in the doings of the General Convention from this time until the pastor of the Boston society reported the "Rules of Order," drawn up by him, to the Nineteenth Convention, in 1837, in which both the title and functions of "*bishops*" are assigned to the ordaining ministers—deliberately determine, and truthfully declare, whether the influence of our eastern brethren, from first to last, did not tend, directly and constantly, to induce an *episcopal form of* GOVERNMENT upon the whole new church in this country. That they have, since they were opposed on this ground, " drawn in their horns," made the most inconsistent modifications of their order, and yielded even abject *concessions* to popular demands, (without, be it observed, having altered a particle of the *spirit* of their " Rules of Order" as *recommendations*,) does not in the least militate against the conclusion that they were previously seeking episcopacy in form and have not even yet abandoned it in essence. Now, whatever may be said of episcopacy in the abstract,—and we are not against it, but admit it to be an orderly form of ecclesiastical government for the new church wherever and whenever her members rationally choose it as best adapted to their genius and their wants, just as we admit that kingly government is an orderly one to those who choose it, and to whom it is best suited,— yet we still hold that it is not the form of church government suited to these middle states, and, therefore, whatever may have been, individually, our hereditary inclinations or our early predilections, we are opposed to the inducing or establishing such a form of ecclesiastical government here. But we do not think that the order of a trine in the ministry necessarily requires episcopacy ; and as we think a trine is the essential order of any ministry, while we most religiously believe that it is taught to be the true order by Swedenborg, we *are* in favor of *that*, and must do all we can to establish it in the new church.

The Fifth General Convention was held in the city of Philadelphia from Monday the 3d to Wednesday the 5th of June, 1822. There were in attendance on this convention " delegates and receivers from Baltimore, New York, Boston, Greensburg, Brownsville, Bucks County, Hulmeville, Frankford and the City of Philadelphia." For the first time Boston is represented by delegates or receivers in attendance. At this convention Mr. Thomas Worcester was baptized ; and it was expected would have applied for ordination. But he did not, because it was ascertained that there were strong objections to his ordination on account of his notion of a conjugial pastoral relation. The harmony of the social intercourse of the members of this general meeting was much disturbed by reasonings and disputes between the Boston members and those of the south, especially of Philadelphia.

In the proceedings of the Fifth General Convention, we find the following relating to the ordering of the ministry.

The importance of guarding against the admission into the ministry of persons unqualified from a want of sufficient knowledge of the doctrines of the church, or from disqualifications as to life, is so evident as to be universally acknowledged ; therefore the adoption of the following resolutions is recommended. *Resolved*,

I. That, in the opinion of this convention, no person ought to be licensed as a teacher of the New Jerusalem Church without the written recommendation of at least seven male members, who shall unequivocally acknowledge its doctrines as contained in the theological writings of Emanuel Swedenborg.

II. That, in the opinion of this convention, no person should in future be ordained as a priest and teaching minister without the recommendation of at least twelve male members, who shall be full receivers of the doctrines of the New Church, and well acquainted with the moral and religious character of the person proposed to be ordained.

III. That the said licenses and ordinations ought to be considered as virtually at an end, when any such licensed teacher or priest and teaching minister shall call in question any of the doctrines of the New Church, contained in the theological writings of Emanuel Swedenborg, or when their lives shall evidently not be conformable to the divine commandments.

IV. That this convention recommend to the ministers of the churches established at Baltimore, Philadelphia and New York, upon the examination of candidates for the ministry, to request the attendance of the male members of their respective congregations, and, after the examination shall be concluded, to require of the said candidates to deliver one or more discourses before the congregation, on some text from the Holy Word, previous to their receiving license or ordination, as the case may be.

These resolutions were severally considered and adopted.

This proceeding is a quiet but severe rebuke of the course of the Philadelphia church, which had licensed and ordained men, without seeing them, hearing them preach, or knowing any thing about them except by common fame. But now, when a certain candidate for the ministry, who had been licensed by that church to preach and baptize without any hesitation, comes to this convention with a very general understanding that he intends to apply for ordination, he does not apply, because it is ascertained that he will not get it if he does ask for it; or it is, at least, so supposed; and now it is resolved to lay down for the first time, certain stringent rules respecting the licensing and ordaining of candidates for the ministry. All this does not appear on the face of the printed Journal: but we know that the journals are so prepared for the press as sometimes to present only an outline of all the doings of a convention, and seldom take any notice of the under currents of action in the social or other meetings usual in such assemblages. Yet a true history of the church requires that these should sometimes be known. And the facts here stated are from our own knowledge, or documents in our possession.

The fact is, that the foregoing resolutions were introduced to prevent the ordination of the originator of the notion of a conjugial pastoral relation, until evidence should be given that that heresy was renounced. We learned this fact from the Hon. John Young, of Greensburg, by whom, we believe, the above resolutions were introduced. Judge Young was one of the first receivers of the new-church doctrines in this country. He was a native of Scotland—served his time as a lawyer's clerk in the office of Sir Walter Scott's father, and was residing in Philadelphia, a clerk in the office of the celebrated Mr. Duponceau, when Mr. James Glen delivered his lectures on the principles of the new church in 1784. He heard his lectures, purchased some of his books, and received the doctrines at the same time that Mr. Francis Bailey did. He aided Mr. Bailey in getting out the first edition of the Universal Theology in this country. "In 1788," says the Judge, (Jour. 10th, Gen. Con., p. 9,) "the Universal Theology, was received by me from London, and presented to Mr. Bailey for the purpose of being reprinted as soon as a sufficient number of subscribers could be procured. For want of encouragement (the work being large) this was delayed some years." But not for any lack of Judge Young's efforts to procure them. He made personal application to the most influential men in the community, and succeeded in getting the subscriptions of Dr. Benjamin Franklin and Robert Morris, Esqr. And throughout a long life he was the staunch friend of the new church, the zealous promoter of her every interest, and the uncompromising advocate of true and strict order in her ministry. He it was who introduced the foregoing resolutions, or, certainly, strongly urged their passage, in the Fifth General Convention. We well remember to have heard complaints of him, in and about Philadelphia, on account of his strict notions of order, and his warmth in advocating them, in that convention. And he himself informed us, that the object in introducing them was as we have stated. This may not have been publicly or generally bruited at the time; but we have not the slightest doubt that it was in the minds and in the private councils of the leading men of that body in that meeting.

A document in our appendix (No. LVIII.) will show that Judge Young was a warm advocate of the order of a trine in our ministry, after the idea of it had been broached. But we cannot see that he had any distinct idea of that order in his mind in this convention. The resolutions indeed show a distinction between the licentiate and the priest and teaching minister. But we have shown that that was a Boston precedent. And they do not allude to any distinction between a second and a third grade. Moreover, the last clause of the fourth resolution,—"previous to receiving license or ordination, as the case may be,"—implies that either might be conferred at first; which could not be, if the idea of regular steps, the lower of which should at first be taken as preparatory to the higher, had been prevailing. So that we may say the question of a ministerial trine is not yet agitated in the General Convention.

The committee appointed to select from the communications to this convention such parts as it might be deemed useful to publish, make the following, among other statements—"In the town of Abingdon, in the southwesternmost part of Virginia, between fifty and sixty persons were baptized into the New Church last year; and lately, in the same place, Mr. Nathaniel Holley has been called, settled, and *licensed* as a public teacher of the doctrines, with authority *to administer the rite of baptism, and attend upon funerals.* From the spirit and temper which are manifested in Mr. Holley's correspondence, and the strength and respectability of the society, great hopes are entertained that the New Church will be established in Abingdon upon an extensive foundation." The statement here made, upon what was supposed to be good authority, that Mr. Holley was only a *licentiate* with power merely to baptize and officiate at funerals, led to some misapprehension at a subsequent time. Both he and the Rev. Mr. Wills, ordained by him, were ranked lower than it now appears

they ought to have been.   Of this we shall take some notice when
we come to the proceedings of the Ninth General Convention.   Here
we may only further remark, that, in the first number of "The New
Jerusalem Missionary," edited by Mr. Samuel Woodworth, and published in the city of New York in May, 1823, after quoting what we
have done respecting the church at Abingdon, and Mr. Holley's
having been *licensed*, adds, " Mr. H. has since been regularly ordained,
to administer all the ordinances of the church."   This implied that
Mr. Holley was first licensed to preach and baptize, and *afterwards*
was ordained with the additional powers of administering the holy
supper and solemnizing marriage.   There seems never to have been
any official report to the convention of his ordination, and of the
extent of the powers conferred by it.   Hence, as he was supposed to
have been inducted into the first grade by a license, and to have
been advanced from that to only the second grade by ordination ; and
as it was conjectured that he had only licensed Mr. Wills at first, as he
himself and others about this time had been ; therefore his name was
placed in the list of ministers of the second grade, and Mr. Wills's
in that of those of the first, by the convention of 1827.

The Rev. Nathaniel Holley was a graduate of Yale College, afterwards a school-teacher in the city of New York, and, when the New
York society was first organized, he was associated with Mr. Samuel
Woodworth in the lead of it.   It was through his instrumentality
that the Rev. C. J. Doughty was brought into the new church.   In
the summer of 1822, a highly intelligent and most respectable society
of receivers of our doctrines, in Abingdon, Va., brought into form and
activity by the missionary labors of the Rev. Holland Weeks, were
desirous of having the services of a settled minister.   Their attention
was turned to Mr. Holley.   And a written request was made for his
ordination.   He removed from New York, with his family, to Virginia.
On his way, he received the concurrence of the Rev. Mr. Carll in his
ordination, and was ordained by the Rev. Mr. Hargrove, in Baltimore,
on the 27th of October, 1822.   It now appears that he did not receive
a mere license to preach and baptize, nor ordination into only the
second degree, but that his ordination was in the formulary of the Philadelphia church, that is, with all the usual powers of the ministry, and,
under the authority, request, restriction and prescription of the Abingdon society, to ordain other ministers.   Mr. Holley's ministrations in
Abingdon were not crowned with much success ; and after remaining
about two years, he removed from thence to Cincinnati, Ohio.   Here
he preached occasionally for a short time ; then edited the Herald of
Truth for one year ; at last ceased from all active discharge of the
duties of the ministerial office, and resumed his occupation of schoolmaster, in which, if living, he is still engaged.   Before leaving Abingdon, Mr. Holley ordained Mr. Samuel H. Wills with even more extended ordaining powers than he himself possessed : for he gave him
" authority, at the request, or with the approbation, of ANY *regularly
organized society of the New Jerusalem*, to license or ordain other
priests and ministers into the said church."   Thus Mr. Holley gave
to Mr. Wills more powers than he himself possessed : for Mr. H. had

power to ordain only under the authority of the church at Abingdon; but he vested this authority in Mr. Wills himself, to be exercised by him merely "at the *request*" or "with the *approbation*" of some or any society of the New Jerusalem; and this is the first instance which we have, in the history of the new church in America, of *authority* to ordain being vested in the *minister* instead of the *church.* And let it be well observed, that *Mr. Holley was a New England man.* But in this act, the Rev. Mr. Hargrove, who ordained Mr. Holley, himself decided, that he had transcended his legitimate powers, so that his ordination of Mr. Wills with unlimited powers was null.—But more of this hereafter.—The Rev. S. H. Wills was ordained by the Rev. N. Holley on the 28th day of August, 1824. But under his minis-trations also the Abingdon society did not flourish. Thinned by removals and deaths, it continued to dwindle, till Mr. Wills, embar-rassed in his business concerns, was obliged to follow in the footsteps of his ordainer, and migrate to the West. That society is now reviv-ing; and by the erection of a new and handsome house of worship, is giving evidence of recuperative energies, which, if directed by a well selected and properly sustained minister, may spring into vigor-ous, progressive, and lasting spiritual life.

We have now before us a memorial, dated Mansfield, Ohio, October 1, 1822, signed by thirty-three professed receivers of our doctrines, and addressed to the New Jerusalem Society, Philadelphia, asking for one Silas Ensign "the authority to preach the Gospel, and perform all the duties of a preacher in the New Jerusalem church." To this is appended a concurrent recommendation—dated October 21, 1822, from four male and three female "members and receivers of the heavenly doctrines of the Lord's New Church near Wooster, Wayne county, state of Ohio"—of said Silas Ensign, to the Philadelphia church, with the request that he might be "ordained a priest or teaching minister in the Lord's New Church, under such restrictions as they in their judgment might think best." This Mr. Silas Ensign probably received a license to preach and baptize from the church at Philadelphia, as did Mr. Adam Klingle and Mr. John Lister, who are not mentioned, as having been licensed, on its Book of Records. Mr. Ensign proved a sort of wolf in sheep's clothing. Not finding the eclat in the new-church ministry which he expected, he offered him-self to the Methodists as an itinerant minister in their connection, engaging, if they employed him, to bring a certain number of con-verts in a given time. He received a temporary commission, and handed over as many of his new-church society as he could get to follow him; but failed to procure promotion in the methodist ranks, because the bishop, or presiding officer, at one of their conferences, had heard from whence he came, and would not receive into perma-nent connection a deserter from the new-church ranks. And, at last, his name was stricken from the list of our ministers, by the Fifteenth General Convention, at the request, made through the Western Con-vention, of some of the very receivers who had originally asked for his ordination. Thus did experience prove the need of more caution, or less haste, in admitting persons into our ministry. And as a con-

11

clusion of our remarks on this subject here, and as a confirmation of
what we have said on the same subject before, we cannot do better
than quote these words of the Rev. Mr. Hargrove, in the charge
which he delivered at the ordination of the Rev. Mr. Roche. After
saying that the minister of the new church should have "a thorough
knowledge of the Holy Scriptures," not only " written on his memory
but deeply graven on his heart;" and should have besides " an acquaintance with philosophy, with history, and the sciences in general ;" and having pictured in colors sufficiently glowing the " awful
responsibility" of " assuming this sacred office" without suitable preparation and with sordid motives; yet observing there can be little
danger *as yet* of men's coming into the new-church ministry from the
lust of filthy lucre ; he thus proceeds—" There may be danger, however, from another quarter; from *laying hands* too suddenly upon
candidates for the ministry, before they have acquired even a *tolerable*
fitness for the arduous duties of the office; and, certainly, it is at
man's infinite hazard to *rush* into it before they have in their own
souls some rational and pleasing evidences of a divine call to the
work, and before they have made some progress in the regenerate
life, so as not to be easily shaken by every wind of doctrine, or
moved by *reproach* or *persecution* in the course of their ministry."
We will only add, that we had not read these words of Mr. Hargrove
when we penned the preceding pages of this report, and that, in our
opinion, he had very good reason to utter them, in view of the early
course of the new church in this country.

The proceedings of the Sixth General Convention are remarkable
in one or two respects. That body assembled in the city of Baltimore in June, 1823. The first thing to be remarked in its proceedings is the fact, that the committee on business, in reporting upon
the unfinished business of previous conventions, say not a word upon
the subject of " general regulations for the ordination of ministers in
the new church," to report upon which a committee had been appointed in the first convention, was recommended to be continued
" with instructions to report at the next general convention" in the
second, and " begged leave to be continued" in the third. Perhaps,
as this subject had not come up in the fourth convention, and resolutions regulating, in some measure, the admission of persons into the
ministry, had been passed in the fifth, it might now have been supposed to be settled. But as it was a subject of too much importance
to be settled in so summary a way, without any report, from the
committee appointed to consider it, of the principles which should
govern ordinations into our ministry, the inference is, that there was
a disposition to drop it by tacit consent, on the ground that the new
church in this country was not yet ripe enough for either its discussion or its settlement. There was a disposition to put it off to " a
more convenient season." We hope that this will be noted, for it
is a good ground on which to bring into bolder relief the *necessity*
that soon arose for the agitation and discussion of the question of a
ministerial trine in America.

The next thing worthy of remark in the proceedings of the Sixth

General Convention is, "that a committee of three persons, in the city of Philadelphia," was appointed "to draw up some general RULES OF ORDER for the regulation of the future conventions of the New Jerusalem Church." The resolution to this effect was introduced by the Rev. Manning B. Roche, who had recently embraced our faith from the episcopal church; and the committee was made to consist of Messrs. Roche, Condy and Lammot.

We remark, thirdly, that it was this sixth convention, too, which adopted the famous resolution "recommending that, at all future conventions of the New Church, each Society shall be represented by a number of Delegates *not exceeding three.*" The why and the wherefore of this, on which hangs a good deal pertinent to another matter, shall be briefly noticed presently.

We remark, lastly, that, although Mr. Roche was ordained, yet no application for his ordination was made to the convention, and the convention took no action upon that matter. This is a very remarkable fact, which we are unable to explain satisfactorily to ourselves. We find in the Journal the following:

After the morning service had been·read by the Rev. John Hargrove, of Baltimore, and an appropriate sermon by the Rev. M. M. Carll, of Philadelphia, the initiatory rite of Baptism was performed on the Rev. M. B. Roche, who had lately separated from the Episcopal Church, in consequence of receiving the Heavenly Doctrines of the New Jerusalem.

The convention assembled on Thursday the 5th and adjourned on Saturday, the 7th of June. Mr. Thomas Worcester was present, and the Rev. C. J. Doughty, also, who was now strongly bound to him in the fellowship, advocacy and defence of his peculiar notions. No application was made for his ordination, and he was not ordained. He most probably did not expect to be. He could not be, according to the order established, without the concurrence of the three churches of Baltimore, Philadelphia, and New York, and without preaching before the assembled male members of one of them. The concurrence of two of those churches it was known he could not get; and it was equally well known that, *at that time*, there would have been a wide and strong difference of opinion between a majority of the male members and the minister of the third in regard to ordaining him. This very convention was violently·agitated by opposition to him on account of his sentiments. Therefore, it was probably felt that the convention was not in a state to act with that calmness, deliberation and seriousness which became so important a matter as the ordination of ministers, and this matter was left in the hands of the three churches. But we do not perceive that there was any formal concurrence of these in Mr. Roche's ordination. Yet Messrs. Carll and Doughty, ministers of the churches at Philadelphia and New York, were present, and concurred by taking part in it. And Mr. Roche, having left the episcopal church on the 15th of December previous, had preached to overwhelming audiences in the Commissioners' Hall in Southwark and Carpenters' Hall in Philadelphia, with marked efficiency and ·great approval. His new-church brethren in Philadelphia, therefore, had had ample opportunity to judge of his fitness for our ministry; and they, without doubt, tacitly concurred in his ordination. And *he was* ordained, according to the following notice—

The Sixth General Convention closed its session on Saturday, June 7th, 1823–67; and, on the following day, after morning service, the Rev. M. B. Roche was solemnly ordained by the Rev. John Hargrove, assisted by the Rev. Messrs. Carll and Doughty. The charge pronounced by Mr. Hargrove, on this occasion, was truly solemn and impressive; and will appear in the third number of the " *New Jerusalem Missionary and Intellectual Repository*," published in the city of New York, by Brother Samuel Woodworth. The *Ordination* was followed by the Communion Service, in which all the members of the Convention participated, together with their Brethren and Sisters of the Baltimore Society.

Mr. Roche received at once the same unlimited ordination as Messrs. Carll, Beers, Doughty, Weeks and Holley—the propriety of which, under the existing circumstances of the church, was then questioned, and is still very questionable. The limited ordination of Messrs. Hurdus and Powell, who were unquestionably as well fitted to exercise ordaining powers in the West, where there was no ordaining minister, as Messrs. Holley and Roche were to exercise them in the middle and eastern states, where there were five; was a precedent for Mr. Roche's having received a limited, before he received a full, ordination. Moreover, the precedent of license to preach and baptize first, given to Mr. Thomas Worcester, was as safe and as necessary a one for Mr. Roche as for him. And the inducting of both Mr. Holley and Mr. Roche into the highest grade of the ministry at once, while others equally worthy were made to take lower steps first, savored too much of caprice or favoritism. But in all this we only see evidence that " grades in the ministerial office" were not yet distinctly thought of, and acknowledged, in the general conventions of the new church of this country; nor were they as yet " adopted and *fully* recognized" by either of the churches at Philadelphia, Baltimore, or New York. It is certain from this, at least, that Mr. Hargrove's reason for limiting ordinations in the case of the western ministers, was not the purpose of thereby making a third discrete degree in the ministry of this country: for had he purposed this, he could not, with any show of consistency, have done otherwise than give Mr. Roche a limited ordination at first. From this, and the fact that he invested Mr. Roche himself with ordaining power, and not a church, of which he was the minister, and likewise the fact that he did this without the formal concurrence of the three churches of Philadelphia, New York and Baltimore, which, according to the established law of the General Convention, he ought to have had, all these facts, we think, conclusively prove, that Mr. Hargrove had no very strict notions either of trinal order in the ministry, or of ministerial order in the new church.

It may be thought that the appointment of a committee to draw up general *rules of order* for the regulation of the future conventions was a tendency to episcopal government in this convention. It is true this measure was introduced by Mr. Roche, who had been an

Episcopalian, and, as an episcopal clergyman, might have been supposed to have a predisposition to episcopacy. And he was the chairman of the committee to draw up these rules. But his associates on that committee were never remarkable for a disposition to strong ecclesiastical discipline or government in the convention or any where else. And whatever might have been Mr. Roche's project, design or wish in introducing this resolution for rules of order, it is certain that no episcopal or other stringent governmental regulations ever could be devised or enacted in the General Convention under his influence. As to the test of the use of a *liturgy*, there is some evidence that Mr. Roche was not very strongly grounded in this as an episcopal principle. In his valedictory to the vestry, communicants and members of Trinity Church, Philadelphia, we find this stated among his altered sentiments—"That no forms and ceremonies are prescribed in the Gospel, and that men may worship God acceptably, with or without a set form; though a liturgy appears more consistent with order, and that used by the Episcopal Church would be highly proper, if some slight alterations were made." This certainly shows a preference for a liturgy, but does not indicate a disposition to press it as an episcopal form in the new church. This and other parts of his valedictory are evidently thrown out as a lure to the members of Trinity Church to follow him and form a society around him as a new-church preacher. To use the simile of Mr. Weeks, in one of his communications to this convention, many of them not only nibbled "at the fisherman's hook," but "took a full bite," and were "drawn out of their waters:" for, in fact, a good many of the members of that church did follow Mr. Roche and form a society around him, which at first met for worship in the Commissioners' Hall, Southwark, and afterwards erected the temple in Fourth just below German Street, which now belongs to the Southwark or Second Philadelphia Society. That most of these were governed more by personal regard to their preacher, than by spiritual regard to the principles of the new church, is proved by the dwindling of the society when Mr. Roche left it. A good many, however, were led by him into the New Jerusalem, and still remain burning and shining lights in our connection. Undoubtedly Mr. Roche was a minister of fine talents and great promise in our church, as well as a most popular one in the church which he left. That he should have risen and glared upon us like a bright meteor, to sink so low in darkness, is a cause of profound grief. It will be well, however, if his case leads all of us to heed the apostolic monition, "Let him that thinketh he standeth, take heed lest he fall." (1 Cor. x. 12.) As to the tendency to episcopacy of Mr. Roche's measures in the General Convention, it is certain that they did not in fact lead to any thing like episcopal government until that body was controlled by our eastern brethren, and he was completely under their influence. Next to Mr. Doughty, he was the most efficient minister in propagating the conjugial theory in the middle states. And all the measures of a distinctive Boston, or New England type—especially the Rules of Order as first reported and now adopted—which have given form and character to the General Convention, were favored and strenuously advocated by him.

In the proceedings of the Seventh General Convention, held in Philadelphia, from the 3d to the 5th of June, 1824, there is the following—

The following report was received from the committee appointed by the last convention to prepare rules of order, and was accepted.

The committee appointed by a resolution of the "Sixth General Convention of the Receivers of the Doctrines of the New Jerusalem," to prepare rules of order for the regulation of future conventions, have attentively considered the subject, and concluded, that, until it be deemed advisable to change the nature and character of this assembly, it will be unnecessary to form a special code of laws—They therefore submit the following Resolve:

Resolved, That the rules and regulations, which obtain in deliberative assemblies generally, be, for the present, adopted by this body.

This shows very clearly that the General Convention up to this time had been regarded as merely a general congregation of members of the same faith throughout our common country. It was not yet regarded as a body of ecclesiastics, needing ecclesiastical rules for its own regulation, or exercising legislative powers for the enactment of laws which were to govern the churches in their particular form. It was merely an assemblage for deliberation, counsel, advice and recommendation upon those matters which pertained to the general interests of the church. And if the motion by Mr. Roche to introduce rules of order had an episcopal tendency,—and indeed, from the tenor of the above report, it may be supposed that the members of that committee thought it had,—yet it is clear that this tendency was here nipped in the bud, by the determination that a special code of such rules or laws was not necessary until it was "deemed advisable to *change the nature and character of this assembly.*" Can there possibly be stronger proof than this affords, that the General Convention, up to this time, was not in the estimation, drift, or purpose of the First Philadelphia Church, an assembly having any thing of the "nature" or "character" of an episcopal polity, or involving any thing of a tendency that way? So far, therefore, as the First Philadelphia Church, or the influence of its leading members is concerned, it is perfectly clear, that nothing like a tendency to episcopal government had, up to this time, been engendered in the General Convention. Nor can we believe that Mr. Roche had, at this time, any other idea than the regulation of the convention as a deliberative body for common purposes of use in disseminatin the principles of the new faith. The Rev. Mr. Hargrove, as president of the preceding convention, addressed a hortatory epistle to the ministers and lay delegates that were about to assemble in the seventh. In this, he foreshows the purposes of the convention thus—

Agreeably to a resolve of our *last* General Convention, our *next* is to be held in Philadelphia, in the first week of June next, for the laudable and important purposes of promoting the *heavenly doctrines,* and the general interests of the church—renewing correspondence with our distant brethren; forming such rules as may be calculated to guard against dangerous innovations in doctrine or worship; settling any divisions that may have arisen; circulating the writings of our illuminated Scribe; and adopting every measure necessary to preserve the *life, peace, spirituality* and good order of the church.

Here he very clearly states, that general uses are the objects of the General Convention. And then he proceeds to recommend the formation of district conventions, because the members of the church spread over so widely extended a country as this, could not attend, or be fairly represented in, one general convention. On this subject he says—

District conventions, therefore, may be expected ere long to obtain, from which *delegates* may be appointed to attend our GENERAL conventions. These district conventions, therefore, should rather be encouraged and sanctioned, than otherwise:—Moreover, while it would be found that their chief aim and design would only be to prepare materials for the consideration and adoption of the *General* Convention, in which last body alone, every rule and resolve that would obtain the sanction of a majority of the members there assembled, should be considered as the act and deed of the whole united new church of the Lord in these United States; inasmuch as every distinct society would there be represented, and have equal rights, and would hence feel themselves bound, as one compact body, to abide by all such rules and resolves as were made and confirmed by their own consent and approbation.

Here the purposes or objects of the General Convention, and of the formation of rules of order for the government of that body, are distinctly stated. And it must be obvious to every reflecting mind, that an *episcopal* form of *government* for the whole church in the United States was not an end distinctly proposed to the mind of Mr. Hargrove at this time. His idea of district conventions, in which certain quarters of the country would be fully and fairly represented by the attendance of receivers in those quarters; then the representation of these district conventions by delegates from them in the general convention, which should act only on materials prepared in the district bodies for its consideration and adoption; so that nothing should be considered as a rule binding on the whole church which had not been first suggested and acted upon in the districts, and then considered and sanctioned by a majority of delegates from them in the general body; and the reason assigned for this, namely, that each and all of the societies being thus fairly represented, so as to "have equal rights," "would hence feel themselves bound, as one compact body, to abide by all such rules and resolves as were made and confirmed by their own consent and approbation"; these views of Mr. Hargrove, we say, most distinctly show us something very different from that tendency to an episcopal form of government which we have thought our eastern brethren were seeking to induce upon our whole church in this country. Does any intelligent Newchurchman now believe, that if the plan here suggested by Mr. Hargrove, had been carried out, and rules of order for the whole church had been devised in a general convention so constituted, and recommended to the particular churches, they would not have been adopted without any difficulty, or that they would have been resisted as the present rules of order of the General Convention have been, with the divisions, dissensions and disorders which the arbitrary enactment and enforcement of them have produced? We shall by and by point out one or two of the episcopal tendencies in the measures of our eastern brethren in the conventions, which we think it may be useful to contrast with these suggestions of Mr. Hargrove. At present we will only observe, that nothing in this plan indicates that the Sixth General Convention, in passing a resolution to devise rules of order for the future regulation of the conventions, looked to the inducing of episcopacy upon the whole church in America. And if it did, the report of the committee, on devising such rules, to the Seventh General Convention, put an effectual stopper upon the tendency, until the character of the general body should change. In other words, if the regulation of ordinations in the ministry required the establishment of an episcopacy, the church at Philadelphia was disposed to stave it off as long as it could.

But the time for change was nigh at hand. A communication to this, the seventh convention, made the consideration and determination of the whole subject of ordinations in the ministry and government in the church indispensably necessary. And now we come to the time when the question of a trine in the ministry was about to be first agitated in the new church of America. It was to this seventh convention, that the notorious *Daniel Roe Letter* was sent from Cincinnati. Thus we find it noticed and acted upon—

A communication was then received and read from the First New Jerusalem Society in Cincinnati.

On motion, *Resolved*, That the communication from the Society at Cincinnati, be referred to a committee of seven persons, in different parts of the United States, three of whom shall be ordained ministers, and the remaining four laymen; who shall make report to the next Convention, and transmit to the Society of Cincinnati, a notification of their appointment.

The Convention then went into an election:—Whereupon, the Rev. M. M. Carll, Rev. Lewis Beers and Rev. Holland Weeks, of the clergy, and Jonathan W. Condy, Esqr., Mr. Daniel Lammot, Hon. John Young and Mr. Samuel Woodworth, of the laity, were duly chosen the committee.

This communication from the Cincinnati society brought up before the General Convention the entire subject of ecclesiastical order and government. It denied the right of ordination, undermined "the ecclesiastical order," and levelled the holy sacraments of the church to matters of ordinary social arrangement and governance. And it so presented these subjects that the convention could not avoid considering and acting upon them. Now, therefore, the matter of church order and government became a topic of general study and discussion. And from this time, we have no doubt that thoughts of episcopacy did begin to prevail in some minds. And we think it not unlikely that Mr. Roche and others in Philadelphia did now look to that form of government in our church. But we are sure they were not *before* our Boston brethren in this. As to the First Philadelphia Church, its glory and its strength had now passed from it. It had ceased to exercise any longer the functions of an ordaining minister. Its pastor had for a considerable time been absent in England on account of his health. During a greater part of this time, its temple was closed, and was only opened for an occasional sermon from Mr. Roche. But Mr. Carll had returned and was present in this seventh convention, or that of 1824. Soon after, however, the temple, in consequence of the pecuniary embarrassments of most of its efficient members, passed out of its hands. This was because Mr. Carll declined officiating any longer gratuitously; and it was_not possible for the society to pay its very heavy ground rent and support a minister too. This happened in 1825. Mr. Carll commenced preaching in his school room, whither some of the First Society followed him, and rallied round him: but most of its intelligent and influential members left him, and joined the Southwark Society under Mr. Roche. The First Philadelphia Church, as a body corporate in law, ceased to exist when its temple was alienated, because its charter called for certain stated meetings in its temple; and therefore when its temple was gone, its charter was gone too. But those of its members who followed Mr. Carll, retained, we believe, by special law, corporate capacity enough to hold for several years, and at length to sell, a small burying ground which belonged to it. This kept a few together for years after Mr. Carll had left Philadelphia and gone to discharge the duties of the ministerial office in other parts. And it was this remnant, which we have spoken of, as reuniting with those from the first who had joined the second society, and uniting with others, original members of said second society, who had withdrawn from it—to form the society which now bears the title of the First Society of the New Jerusalem in Philadelphia. Therefore the original society of the new church in Philadelphia had no longer any power to determine the order or the government of the General Convention after the year 1824. We mean, it had lost this power *as a church*. Still Mr. Condy, and others, who had been leading and influential members of that church, could and did exert considerable influence in the two conventions that were subsequent to the seventh, that is, in the conventions of 1826 and 1827. And although, as we have said, there is no evidence that Mr. Condy had at first, and for some time after the institution of the Philadelphia church, entertained distinct ideas of the trinal order of the ministry, yet now, when the subject of ministerial order was, as it were, forced upon the consideration of the General Convention, it is not to be supposed that a man of his reading and intelligence would fail to make himself acquainted with all that had been said and written on this subject, if he were not thoroughly acquainted with it before. Most probably he had never been ignorant of the question of the trine as it had been agitated in England; as he would have been hardly less likely than Mr. Hargrove to have his attention called to that subject by the Minutes of the General Conferences. We do not think, however, that he had made up his mind on this subject prior to the convention of 1824. We do not believe, that, before this time, he deliberately introduced this order into the ordinations of the Philadelphia church, whatever may have been his knowledge respecting its approval in England. But after this time, we do believe that he looked into this matter, and was at last convinced of the truth of this order by the authorities for it from Swedenborg advanced by Mr. Weeks's report. We know that he approved that report; and, as we have said, moved its publication in connection with the Journal of the Ninth General Convention. But we also know,—for we were intimately associated with him in his action at this time,—that he was opposed to carrying out in this country the principle of the trine, so far as it was supposed to involve episcopacy. He did not deny that the trinal order might involve episcopacy, and that it might in time develop the episcopal form of government. But he did not think that this form was suited to the new church in our country at the present time, and he was not in favor of giving to the General Convention this shape. Respecting him almost to veneration as we did, we confess that he, as our instructor, formed our views on this subject. And as a member of the original Philadelphia church, we do know, that, at no time, from its first institution up to the period of its virtual extinction, or till the question of the ministerial trine was agitated by Mr. Weeks's report, were any considerable number of its leading members in favor of episcopacy in the new church. And we also know, that a large number of the members of that church, were, when it was first broached, and have ever since been, *opposed to the principle of a trine in our ministry in any form.* The present agitation of this question in the Central Convention, and the probable repudiation of this principle in the near approaching annual meeting of that body, are both owing to a reaction upon it from those in the original Philadelphia church who were opposed to it from the first, and fought against it tooth and nail in the very constitution of our body. We, therefore, feel sure that we are right when we record it as an historical truth, that at no time did the First Philadelphia Church produce any thing like a tendency to episcopacy in the general body of the new church in America. As to a trine in the ministry, *that* is another matter. Mr. Condy and other influential members of the Philadelphia church—though, very probably, a minority of it—*were* in favor of a trine, and *did* exert all their influence to bring about an acknowledgment of this principle in the General Convention. But they, and we believe Mr. Weeks himself,* did not

---

* In a communication to the Ninth General Convention from Henderson, N. Y., Mr. Weeks says—'' So far as I have been able to learn, the receivers in this quarter are of opinion that ecclesiastical, as well as civil power, is in the hands of the people; that government should be representative; and that, in the priesthood, as our Swedenborg says, ' There is the state of every student, who is preparing for the ministry before he becometh a priest, and of every priest before he becometh a pastor, and of every pastor before he becometh a primate, the reason of which is, because they are according to divine order, and divine order filleth all and every thing in the universe, even to the most minute particulars.' (U. T. 106) By the state of a priest before he becometh a pastor, we understand the same as a candidate, or licentiate, before he is ordained the pastor of a particular church or society; by a particular ordained pastor, we understand one who has been ordained to the care and oversight of a particular church or society; and by a primate, we understand one who has been ordained to the care of a district, which consists of several pastors and churches. We understand, therefore, that the ministry is a trine; and may be denominated licentiates, particular pastors, and general pastors. This we conceive to be, as Swedenborg says, ' according to divine order.' ''— It is impossible for us to conceive, how those who held that all ecclesiastical power is in the people, and that ecclesiastical government should be representative, could hold that a trinal arrangement of ministers of the church into licentiates, particular pastors and general pastors, necessarily involved episcopacy.

think that the trinal order necessarily involved episcopacy. And thus we think we have fully vindicated the First Philadelphia Church from the charge brought against it.

We have now sketched an historical view of ordinations into the new-church ministry of America from the first until the question of the trine began to be agitated, and until ordaining powers were clearly vested in the General Convention. This is all we proposed to do. What was remote, obscure and difficult of distinct discernment in this matter, we have brought so near, into such clear light, and into such directness of vision, that it will not be difficult for some one who may come after us to give a full and entire history of new-church ordinations in this country. The Journals of the Conventions from the year 1826 are full of details and numerously circulated throughout our land. From these, with such biographical sketches of the ministers, as present knowledge may afford, such a history might now be written, and might, perhaps, prove a work not wholly uninteresting or useless to the church in coming years. Let those whose duty it may be, attend to this. It is ours now to trace the question of a ministerial trine, and ecclesiastical order and government as involved in that, in the church of our country, from its first agitation in the General Convention, during the years 1824—1827, until the present time.

What first made the agitation of the question of a ministerial trine in America necessary? The same thing that made it necessary in England—a calling in question of *ordinations* in the new church. The right or propriety of ordination by the imposition of hands was denied. It was denied that this could rest on apostolic precept or usage in the first christian dispensation. It was contended that it was founded solely in roman-catholic corruption. And it was proposed to do away with formal ordinations in the new-church; to make the ordination of a minister consist in simply an official notification of his appointment by the society to which he was to officiate; and to arrange and govern the administration of the holy sacraments in so loose a way as to deprive them of much, if not all, of their representative power and sanctity. As we have seen, this agitation was produced by a communication from the Cincinnati society, written in its name by Mr. Daniel Roe, its secretary and licensed preacher,* and sent to the Seventh General Convention in 1824. Why was this communication never published? Those into whose hands it was put, have taken especial care to keep it out of sight. For years

---

* We say Mr. Roe was a *licensed* preacher; because we presume he would not have been allowed to preach without some of the usual official sanctions; but we have no evidence that he was licensed by Mr. Hurdus, or any other minister of the church; his name is not recorded on the General Convention's list of ministers as a licentiate; and, therefore, it is possible that his sole authority to preach was the certificate of the clerk of the Cincinnati society that said society had made a preacher of him. That society, in time, discarded him: when he renounced the faith of the new church, turned its most sacred things into ridicule, and became a confirmed and open atheist. But at last, after he was made to shudder at the effects of atheism on his son, he returned to something more of respect for the New Jerusalem, and died with some degree of penitence for his railings against her.

we strained every nerve to get the original or procure a copy of it.
All hope was gone, when we providentially succeeded. We have
found, among some old papers in the West, a copy in the hand-writing
of Judge Young, one of the committee of the seventh convention to
report upon it.   And we esteem it our great privilege now to record
this famous communication for the use of history. (See Ap. No. LVI.)
Let no one fail to read it.   No one who does not read it, and the
documents we shall publish in connection with it, can at all understand the reasons why it has been *necessary* to agitate the subject of
order in the ministry so much, or why it was necessary to introduce
the question of a ministerial trine into the General Convention.   And
without the perusal of these documents, no one can discern the causes
of certain recent changes in the Western Convention, by which that
body has now emphatically *gone down.*

The signal refutation which Mr. Roe's letter found in Mr. Weeks's
able report in answer to it, made the Cincinnati society subsequently
ashamed of it.   And the idea was given out that this letter did not
fairly express the sentiments of the society, in whose name, and by
whose officer, it was sent ; but rather the individual sentiments of its
writer.   Therefore, it became a matter of some importance to ascertain this fact—to ascertain whether the Cincinnati society had, or
had not, by any of its formal acts, adopted or sanctioned the sentiments of its leader, Mr. Roe.   Now it was our *hard lot* to be called
to Cincinnati to carry out, in pastoral connection with the society
there, the principles of order set forth in Mr. Weeks's report.   This
was the express understanding between ourselves and those who were
instrumental in getting us there.   And we do know, better than any
body else can possibly know,—by the reactions upon our ministry
there,—that Daniel Roe's letter *did* express the sentiments of the
Cincinnati society at, and for some time previous to, the time it was
written.   But that society is remarkable for nothing more than this—
a camelion like quality of taking its hue from those men of intellectual force who happen to be leading it.   Hence, as its leaders have
changed, the hue of its sentiments has altered.   And what is more,
as it has been, from time to time, under the influence of a great
variety of leaders, its sentiments have been fluctuating and its courses
inconsistent.   Hence, at one time, it was dead against order in the
ministry ; at another time, it was hot for it : at one time, as the central
force of the Western Convention, it was in favor of the ministerial
trine ; at another, it repudiated it : at one time, it was in favor of a
convention as a general society of receivers ; at another, it was for a
convention of delegates from societies : at one time, it was for a general
convention in the West, on the ground that there should not be but
one such body in the United States, because the West could not be
properly represented in it; and then, in one short year, when some
twelve or eighteen delegates of societies came together to adopt and
act under a new constitution, these few delegates, without any instruction to this effect from their constituents, did, under the lead
of a new man imported freshly for the purpose, set aside their newly
framed organization, and by a sort of clerical legerdemain, turn them-

selves into an Ohio Association of the General Convention, *in a whiff* —wherein what was last year the Western Convention is to be represented this year *by one delegate!* And let it not be said that this last was not the act of the Cincinnati society. It is just as much the act of that society as the shaking of an animal's tail is the act of its brain and spinal marrow. For is the Ohio Association any less a *Cincinnati convention* now than when it had the *false name* of the Western Convention one year ago? It has no more ceased to be the Cincinnati convention, than what is called the General Convention has ceased to be the *Eastern Convention,*—when all three of its general officers are Boston men; the chairman of every one of its standing committees and boards is a New England man, or *young* son of one; and *five* out of *eight* of the ministers and *thirty-one* out of *thirty-nine* of the delegates in convention are New England men!—merely because three associate bodies in the West, *all governed or led by New England men*, have *verbally* acknowledged it as such without any thing like a fair representation in it. Need we wonder, then, that this Cincinnati society should send a communication to the Seventh General Convention, through Mr. Daniel Roe, opposing all ordinations in the ministry; then another to the Tenth General Convention, through Mr. Luman Watson, complaining that its sentiments had been misrepresented by the former, and avowing a concurrence in a resolution by which "a threefold principle" is recognized as existing in the ministry; and now a third to the Thirtieth General Convention, through the Rev. B. F. Barrett, complaining that it *cannot see* the need or use of such a threefold principle, and asking to be embosomed in that general body *with a rejection and violation of its fundamental law and trinal constitution!* What can be more astounding than the fact that the General Convention, so called, should have admitted into association with itself a body which violates its fundamental law! Is not this concession with a vengeance! Swedenborg says—"each society is an image of the whole; for *what is unanimous is composed of so many images of itself.*" (A. C. 4625.) How then can the Ohio Association help to *compose* the General Convention of the whole church in the United States, if it is not such an image of it as has the trinal order of its ministry? The law of variety urged by Mr. Barrett does not apply here, where the *fundamental law* or *constitution* of a general body is concerned. There may be *varieties* of the *trine* in the components of a general body which has a trinal constitution; but there cannot be the *rejection* of the *trinal principle* in any component part without making that part *heterogeneous* to the whole. This may be illustrated thus. The general body is in the human form —in which, by the by, the trine of head, thorax and abdomen with their extremities, is essential—which is its *constitutional* order. Now every association of this general body must be in the human form too. Yet there may be every variety of this form in the associations; and the greater this variety, the more perfect will be the form of the general body. But to introduce the form of a horse, an eagle, a fish, or a serpent, into an association, would, although there might be a *sort* of a *trine* in the form of this association—make the general body as incongruous as a centaur or a griffin. This would be a variety in its parts that would destroy harmonious unity in the general body. And the General Convention, with its present trinal constitution, can no more take the Ohio Association into itself, without its being in the image of a similar trinal constitution, than these United States, as a general government, or a nation, could take into their union a state with a monarchical instead of a republican form of government. But the General Convention was *afraid* to tell the late Western Convention the truth. There was a fear that the West might fly off, set up for itself again, and not " come into the brotherhood of churches." *Charity* required that they should *humor* the West, lest they should lose the power of *leading* and *governing it for its good.* Hence they had to talk gently to it, and open their arms to receive it. But the instinct of self-preservation made them *tie its hands,* lest, from its heterogeneous nature, it might by and by get excited and hurt them! Well, the General Convention has swallowed the Ohio Association; let us see how they will digest their food. And, on the other hand, let us see whether what was once the Western Convention, a co-ordinate body, will rest content as an Ohio Association, subordinate to the Eastern Convention, with a representation of *one* or *two delegates,* who shall have *no right to vote in that body upon the regulation of its ministry, or the form of its ecclesiastical government !!!* Will not the West be then FAIRLY *represented in* ONE GRAND NATIONAL CONVENTION ? especially when they have it *meeting in Cincinnati* for the purpose of *undoing the trinal arrangement of its ministry?*

We have felt it our duty to furnish ourselves with documents to show where Daniel Roe's letter really came from. And it is most important now to see that the Cincinnati society, under the lead of said Daniel Roe, was, at one time, almost unanimously in favor of his sentiments. In our Appendix, No. LV., the reader will find some things that occurred in the Cincinnati society by some extracts from its records. A true history of the new church in the West imperatively demands the publication of this document. For it is impossible to explain certain events which have transpired there, without a knowledge of the facts which it sets forth.

Now these Extracts from the Records of the Cincinnati Society will show that the sentiments of Mr. Daniel Roe on ordination were *unanimously* adopted by that society in the autumn of 1822—with the exception of *one vote,* which was cast by the excellent and venerable Father Hurdus. We beseech the reader not to fail to read attentively the proceedings of the meeting of Sept. 13, 1822, and to compare them with some things that we have shown, in a previous part of this report, as having occurred in the new church of England. Certainly he will not fail to see how similar were the circumstances of our church in the two countries, as calling loudly and imperatively for the action of a general body in determining what was to be the true order of our ministry. These extracts will also show that the said society, in the spring of 1823, did also pass sundry enactments calculated to degrade the most holy sacraments of our church; and that these were passed unanimously, too, with the most honorable exception of the same one vote. But in August, 1824, when the report of the explosion which Daniel Roe's letter made in the seventh convention had been heard in the West, these proceedings of the Cincinnati society were repealed, under the manifest influence of the Rev. Mr. Hurdus, for the purpose of "harmonizing in charity with the rest of their brethren." Thus, by reading No. LVI. in connection with No. LV. of our Appendix, we shall see that Daniel Roe's letter was truely the communication of the Cincinnati society; and that it ceased to express the sentiments of that society, only when it was known that those sentiments were severely, though tacitly, reprehended by the General Convention. And we shall see more. We shall see that the Roe sentiments of the Cincinnati society were not crushed, but were only kept down by the external pressure put upon them; so that now, when altered circumstances have taken that pressure off, they, by the resilience of elastic substances, have sprung up again in the repudiation and flagrant violation of the trinal order of the ministry by the late Western Convention.

The reader will see that the Cincinnati society, in 1829, adopted the trinal principle, so as to have all three of the grades of ministers in itself at one time. The object of this was to settle differences among its members that were generated by its having more ministers than one. It had three ministers, and each had its party of partial admirers and supporters; and disputes arose between the ministers as to who had a right to the pulpit at certain times. To settle these disputes, a factitious and irrational application of the trine was made, so that one society was to have a pastor, a minister and a teacher; and it will be seen that, in the assigning of the duties to these grades, there was, in fact, no discreteness between that of the pastor and that of the minister. In short, it was only a contrivance by which the friends of rival pastors might be satisfied with temporizing concessions and compromises. There was in fact an effort to have a society with three heads; and the monstrosity could not enjoy harmonious or vigorous life. So that it was not long before another committee had to be appointed to settle *differences between* the *ministers*. True, it was professed to carry out the order of the General Convention by the adoption of this trine; but it was a perversion of that order by applying it to the justification of a system which had obtained in the Cincinnati society in Daniel Roe's time; and it was against it, because that order called for one pastor to one society, to whom all other ministers in that society should be strictly subordinate. How this was violated in the above mentioned case, any one can see. Mr. Hurdus was to be the nominal pastor, to administer the sacraments and *preach occasionally*. But Dr. Atlee was to be the real pastor, because he was to preach, and so feed the flock, regularly, and administer the sacraments when Mr. Hurdus was sick or out of the way. So Mr. Hurdus was to *preach in the morning*,—the point of precedence contended for,—only when Dr. Atlee was missionating. And any one might know, that Mr. Kinmont was not going to act in a capacity subordinate to Dr. Atlee! What was the consequence, therefore, of this attempt at *ar*-rangement? Why, *de*-rangement. The collisions were made stronger, and the differences increased.

Knowing that such must, in the nature of things, be the inevitable consequence of that arrangement; knowing that where there were more ministers than one, of the same or similar grade, in the same society, there would inevitably be parties in it, one favoring one minister, and another, another; so that, if an honest and faithful minister were, in the discharge of his duty, to offend the self-love or worldly love of any of its members, they would fly off directly and array themselves against him in an opposing party; and thus the society's growth in spiritual life would be retarded or destroyed: knowing these things,—without knowing that any such difficulties had in fact occurred in the society of Cincinnati, before we went there,—we made it a *sine qua non*, in the negotiation for our removal thither in the capacity of minister, that neither Mr. Hurdus nor Mr. Kinmont, nor any other man, was to be associated with us in the pastoral office in connection with that society. This was the understanding which we had of the order of the trine at that time. And, moreover, that order was held to require that a pastor should be exclusively devoted to the duties of his office—be set apart from all secular callings for that purpose, and be supported by the free-will offerings of the society in return for this performance of his peculiar use. This order we were *called* expressly to carry out, and there was an express stipulation made with us that we should be sustained in carrying it out. Mr. Hurdus, who had never been supported in an exclusive devotion to the ministerial office, retired to make way for our coming on this ground. Some of the society would have preferred Mr. Kinmont as their pastor. They desired his services in that capacity. There were some who liked the novelty of a new man, and would have preferred our services. A committee was appointed to confer with, and procure the services of, both. Mr. Kinmont decidedly declined accepting the office on this ground. We, for the reasons stated above, would not accept it in connection with him or any other man; and consented to accept it only on the stipulation above stated. We proved to be a minister peculiarly obnoxious to certain strong characters in Cincinnati. *This stipulation was deliberately and grossly violated,* for the purpose of getting us away and getting a more able and desirable minister in our place. This was the true reason of our expulsion from the West. This was the planning and working of certain *leaders* there. That a majority of the people would not come into their plans after we had been put out of the way, was not the fault of the leaders or their instruments. The enginery to work with, was the secret insinuation of certain charges—among others, that we were a catholic priest in disguise, who would forbid the people to read the Word unless they had a priest to expound it; and that we were striving covertly, not only to introduce catholic forms of worship, but to propagate the *conjugial theory,* or *Boston heresy.* These charges were mere pretexts to be used as levers in breaking the stipulation. The first charge was too foolish to be noticed. But the last, and the necessity of vindicating ourselves from it, led to that revival of this matter in recent years, of which some have so much complained; and must afford our apology for having been so conspicuously and so painfully prominent in the exposure and refutation of this error.

Thus we see that there was a time when the Cincinnati society *could see* the need and use of the trinal order in the ministry which the General Convention adopted, and, through our instrumentality, propagated in the Western Convention; for our going to Cincinnati was nearly simultaneous with the institution of that body. Therefore, if that society does not *now see* the need and use of that order, as, by the recent communication of its present pastor to the General Convention, it says it does not; then it must be because it has been of late years wearing other spectacles; or because, as we suppose, the sentiments which it entertained in former years were never really changed, but have shot up again from old roots, in the late opening of a spring season congenial to their growth.

Wherefore, it is of great importance in the history of the question before us, to know and show the fact, that its first agitation in our General Convention was brought about by certain disorganizing tendencies from the professing new church in the West, especially in Cincinnati. For this alone can explain the present reaction from the West upon the trinal order, both in the Eastern and in the Central Convention. The present agitation of this question in the Central Convention, making necessary the present defence of the trinal order in that body, is the direct effect of the innoculation of opposition to it from the West, by means of a member of the Cincinnati society, who was a friend and adherent of Daniel Roe in his palmy days. The virus of this opposition, acting upon similar matter from the First Philadelphia Society in the core of our convention, has produced the present eruption on its surface, by which our trinal constitution is to be destroyed. Whether the disease will conquer the constitution, or the constitution have power to throw off the influences which are tending to destroy it, remains to be seen. We can only point to the source of the disease, by referring our readers to Documents No. LV. and LVI. of our Appendix. And the conclusion to which we now come, is, that the trinal order is that of heaven and the spiritual church: so that the difficulties which we meet with in carrying this order out in our external church, all flow from the inherent opposition of the natural to the spiritual man.

The Seventh General Convention, which met in Philadelphia in June, 1824, adjourned for *two* years, to meet in New York "on the first Thursday of June, 1826." The reason for this unusual interval does not appear. It may have arisen, in some way, out of the decay of the First Philadelphia Church. The journal of the seventh convention was not published, until it was printed as an appendix to that of the eighth, in 1826. The reason of this was, that it had been the custom to print and publish the journal at the expense of the society where the convention was held; and the pecuniary embarrassments of the Philadelphia society had made the publication of the journal of the seventh convention impracticable there. May not the unpropitious circumstances of the churches in both Philadelphia and New York have made an increased interval between the seventh and eighth conventions advisable? Thus the committee of the seventh convention, to whom Daniel Roe's Letter was referred, had two whole years

12

to read and write upon it.   It became, in that time, the subject of a
good deal of discussion, and subjected the West to the imputation of
being led by disorderly and disorganizing spirits.   The duty of drawing up a report upon it, was assigned to the Rev. Holland Weeks,
who, as we have seen, was a member of the Boston society, and had,
most probably, imbibed from thence some notions of a trinal order of
the ministry.   The intelligent men of Boston, as well as those of
Baltimore and Philadelphia, must have had their thoughts turned into
this channel, by the Minutes of the Eighth General Conference in
England, which had decreed the trine to be the true order of our
ministry, in 1815.   Perhaps their own original investigations of the
writings of Swedenborg, might have discovered this order.   And receiving his clue from them, Mr. Weeks too might have found it,
where they did, by his investigation of the same writings.   Certain
it is that he *found* it there, and by an elaborate, and, as we think,
very able, report upon the communication of the Cincinnati society,
brought it clearly and distinctly to view in the Eighth General Convention.   Here, then, in the year 1826, was the question of a trine
in our ministry first agitated in the new church of America.   And
thus do we prove, *that the trinal ministerial order was first brought
forward in this country by a New England man, and a member of the
Boston society.*   Of course, so far as a trine in the ministry is identical with episcopacy, this tendency to an episcopal form of ecclesiastical government was induced upon the whole church in this
country by an influence from our eastern brethren.   Yet we admit
that this order was *adopted* or *declared* by the General Convention of
1827, in which there was only one eastern delegate.   But we do not
believe that a trine in the ministry and episcopacy are identical; and,
so far as they were supposed to be so, we have shown that the action
on it, in that convention, of the Philadelphia members, was designed
to fend off all that was episcopal in its tendency.
    At this eighth convention, too, the Philadelphia church began to
sink, and our eastern brethren began to rise, in exerting an influence
on the general bodies of our church in this country.   Mr. Carll is
the only representative present from the First Philadelphia Society.
Mr. Thomas Worcester is there; and it is on his motion, that Mr.
Weeks's report on the trine is ordered to be printed.   This was the
convention's formal sanction of it, and was equivalent to Mr. Worcester's endorsement of it.   Thus have we shown, that this subject of
ministerial grades was first broached by members of the Boston
society; and now that the order of a *trine* of such grades was first
brought forward by members of that society in the General Convention.
    Mr. Thomas Worcester is present in the eighth convention with
two delegates from Boston, and another minister and two more delegates from New England.   Now any one who knows how much
Mr. Worcester's influence worked in favor of his cause, when only
sustained by Mr. Doughty, against a most violent opposition, in the
convention at Baltimore in 1823, may very easily calculate how
much stronger his influence would be in this convention at New York

in 1826, where, besides Mr. Doughty, he had another minister and
four delegates from New England to back him.   Moreover, Mr. Roche,
of Philadelphia, (and we believe Dr. Belding, of Leraysville, Pa.,
was tainted with it,) was subsequently a full receiver and strong
advocate of Mr. Worcester's conjugial theory, and, therefore, was,
in all probability, strongly under his influence in this convention.
Hence he could prevail in setting aside all inquiry into his peculiar
notions.   The Steubenville society, through its delegate Judge Young,
had made a communication to the seventh convention on this subject.
The documents thus communicated, were referred to the same committee which had charge of the Cincinnati communication.   In the
eighth convention, that committee reported verbally, respecting those
documents, that their subject matter, on deliberation, was not deemed
of sufficient importance to engage the attention of the convention,
therefore, they had not prepared a written report upon it, and requested to be discharged.   Whereupon, on motion of Mr. Thomas
Worcester, it was voted that said committee be discharged.   Thus
was the famous Boston heresy whitewashed, and set aside, by the
General Convention, although the originator of it had not acknowledged it was an error, and put it away as sin.   It was not a subject
of sufficient importance to engage the attention of the convention!
Yet the Rev. Charles J. Doughty, who then voted to sanction this
decision, has since solemnly declared, in the face of the whole church,
" *I believe it to be a dangerous and destructive heresy*": and on the
verge of the grave, has been heard to say—" When I look back, I
cannot conceive how it was possible I could have been so hoodwinked
by those Boston principles: and I do verily now believe, *they were
from hell!*" , These solemn declarations were made between 1842–44.
Why, then, was the subject deemed of such little importance by the
eighth convention in 1826 ?   Mr. Worcester had sufficient influence
to make it appear so then, all the while that it was of sufficient importance to be propagated by the most sedulous persuasive efforts.
The holders of that notion in Boston, had then determined to talk no
more about it openly, but did not fail by secret influence to spread it
widely.   And whatever may be said to the contrary, we *know*, from
the best opportunities of knowing, and confidently assert, on the
authority of an unimpeached and unimpeachable veracity, that this
conjugial theory *was* embraced by some of the leading ministers of
the General Convention, *did* exert an influence on its councils, and
had a very considerable prevalence in the eastern and the middle states up to the year 1840.   And he who asserts the contrary,
must be destitute of proper information, or not an honest man.   The
sacredness of historic truth demanded that this matter should be placed
in clear light.   It has been so placed in No. I. of The Newchurchman—Extra.   Before that was issued, it was boldly asserted that this
theory was an obsolete idea.   At the time of its preparation we were
said to be fighting with *shadows.*   It was intimated that it never had
been a matter of much moment or of general interest even in Boston.
All *respectable* paternity was denied to it even there.   It was expressly said, by one of its reputed originator's veriest instruments,

"Indeed, all the literature of the whole matter seems to have consisted of *a few private letters*, and *the tonguey expositions of a few old women*." And yet the editor of the above named work, was, *in terrorem*, threatened with the *deepest infamy* for his exposure of those few private letters in which the whole literature of the matter seemed to have consisted. The exposure was made; and not half, perhaps three-fifths, of the private letters which could have been published, and which needed to be, to show the true *spirit* of the principle in its *actual workings*, were given. And lo, and behold, there was so much literature exhibited *in the way of official teaching from the pulpit*, and in the way of *formal communications to the church here and in England*, as well as in other documents *intended* for an influence upon *societies of the church*, that the originator of the theory is constrained to come out publicly before the whole church, acknowledge its paternity, apologize for his offspring, and give the reason why he now disowns it. Duty requires that we should publish his present renunciation of the theory in the series of our documents for new-church history. We shall cheerfully place it there, and accompany it with some comments to show what is the present state of that theory in this country. Here we take the author of it at his word, and say, *the theory is now entirely abandoned as false*. At the same time we declare that we are most sincerely glad of it. But the truth of this historical sketch requires that we should state that this theory was once held, and did exert an influence in or upon our conventions. And we are not to refuse to hear the still reverberated thunder, although the lightning's flash has ceased to glare. It was held and acted upon by Messrs. Worcester and Doughty, and determined an important measure in the convention of 1823, as we shall show in another place. It was held by Messrs. Worcester and Doughty certainly, and probably began to be, by Messrs. Roche and Belding, in this eighth convention, or that of 1826. It was afterwards embraced by other ministers in this quarter, as it had been by the Rev. Samuel Worcester at first, and, we believe, by a majority of the New England ministers in after time. There can be no doubt, too, that the leading lay members in Boston, and other parts of New England, embraced it; and that it entered into and qualified all the measures of the General Convention leading to the establishment of ecclesiastical order from 1826 to 1839, is now beyond all reasonable question. We have heard the confession of the Rev. C. J. Doughty— than whom an honester or more truthful man never breathed the atmosphere of this earth—that, so far as he was concerned in devising them, this conjugial theory, entered into and wholly qualified the Rules of Order which were adopted by the General Convention in 1838. And, when we were residing in Philadelphia, we were informed, by a person to whom he said it, that the Rev. Mr. Roche made a similar declaration. If our memory does not fail us, we can point to a sermon in the New Jerusalem Magazine, in which this theory is incidentally but plainly taught; and we can put our finger on articles in that work teaching the relation of ministers to the people, as the *only mediums of truth*, in such a way, as to make us

sure that the writer was a conjugialist, even if we did not know him
well, and know him to have been even a *rabid* advocate of the conjugial theory in our borders. And could the editors of that work—
Boston men, the brotherhood, if not the spiritual progeny, of the
originator of this theory—have admitted those articles, if they too
were not conjugialists at the time of their publication? And is it to
be believed, that this theory should have been held as a " *new* principle," " deeply rooted"—as " a most penetrating and soul-searching
principle," by our eastern brethren, and by so many leading ministers
and lay members of our church under their influence here in the
south, and yet not have entered into and qualified all the order and
all the measures which flowed from them into the General Convention? Believe it who can—we cannot! Nay, we think we see that
principle still pervading the Rules of Order as even *now* modified and
finally adopted by the General Convention—as we shall presently
show. Then let men be honest. Let them confess that they did
once hold this principle and carry it out; but having been made sensible that it was erroneous, they have now renounced it. Then,
when they have obliterated every seeming vestige of it from the
Rules of Order, as the only proper practical evidence of their having
sincerely renounced it, we can take them by the hand, and honor and
love them as brethren in the church. But let them not, in the mean
time, falsify the truth of history by denying that this principle was
ever held and operative in our conventions.

These observations are not irrelevant to the subject before us.
They show that we are bound to advert to the conjugial theory and
its prevalence at the time when the events were transpiring of which
we are now treating, although we admit it may be at the present time
given up. We most religiously believe that this theory, or the desire
of rule and pride of intellect in which it originated, was at the very
root of all those tendencies to strong and arbitrary ecclesiastical government in our church in this country to which we have objected.
And as it has laid hold of, or flowed into, and qualified, the trinal
order of our ministry as actually adopted in the General Convention,
we could not possibly sketch truly the history of this question as agitated here, without noticing it in this connection.

We have shown, that, in the conventions of 1821, 1822 and 1823,
there was a disposition to drop the subject of regulating the ordination
of ministers by the General Convention, and to leave this matter in
the hands of certain particular churches; but that the communication
from the Cincinnati society to the convention of 1824, brought up
the whole subject of ecclesiastical order and government, and made
it necessary for the General Convention to take this matter in hands,
so as to determine more accurately its own organization, and to devise
some form of ecclesiastical government for the several churches and
the church at large. In short, that the time for a change in the character of the General Convention was come, and that this could be
no longer postponed. Hence in this eighth convention it was—

Voted, On motion of [the] Rev. Mr. Roche, that a committee be appointed
to take into consideration the subject of organizing this Convention, and

also the several Churches and Societies of the New Jerusalem in this country, into some form of Ecclesiastical Government.

Said committee was made to consist of five clergymen and eight laymen, who, on the second day of the convention, brought about the following measure—

The Committee instructed to report on the expediency of organizing this Convention and the Churches in this country into some form of Ecclesiastical Government, reported, recommending the two following resolutions; which were adopted by the Convention, and the Committe discharged.

Resolved, That a candidate for ordination present himself before the Convention and Delegates, with the requisite recommendations already prescribed, and there receive ordination:—unless it should be the particular desire of his own Society to have him ordained in their presence; in which latter case, the candidate shall present a certificate of approbation from the Convention, to any two ministers possessing ordaining powers, and then receive ordination at their hands.

Resolved, That this Convention is sensible that some more definite order and mode of Ecclesiastical Government than does at present exist, should be adopted by the General Convention of the New Jerusalem churches in the United States; and that the several societies be requested by this Convention to send in, by their Delegates or otherwise, to the next General Convention, their sentiments upon the mode of Ecclesiastical Government to be adopted.

It should have been stated that Mr. Weeks's report in answer to the communication from the Cincinnati society, and in favor of a ministerial trine, was read to the convention on the second day of its session, and then laid on the table. There can be no doubt, therefore, that the order adopted in the above resolutions was founded on the principles of that report. We have no objections to this order. We could only object to the summary way in which it is established—without any statement of the grounds on which it is founded. Certainly it is most objectionable in a general representative body, to *prescribe* laws of order to the churches, without seeking to convince them rationally of their truth and fitness by the authorities of the Word and the church's writings. But it was probably thought that the principles on which this order was founded would be fully displayed in Mr. Weeks's report. If so, this was a strong reason why that report should be published; and this convention did right, therefore, in directing its publication.

We think the order adopted by the Eighth General Convention was right. It vested the *exercise* of ordaining powers in the *convention* of ministers and delegates as the *representative* of the *whole* church. Here, we believe, is where such exercise ought only to be placed. For the whole church is the Lord's vicar on earth—not the ordaining ministers or ecclesiastical senate. They are the vicar of that vicar, who must have a convention as a consistory. In the weakness of the church's infancy, those powers were exercised by one particular church. Afterwards, and before the General Convention was full grown enough to act, they were confided to the concurrent action of two, and then of three, particular churches. Now the church is sufficiently advanced to come into a truer order. And there was no need of going beyond this. Such vesting of ordaining powers, not in the convention, but in the head ministers alone, was a tendency to episcopacy to which we object. The order, too, which called for the sentiments of the several societies upon the mode of ecclesiastical government to be adopted, so that, when adopted in convention, it should be a sort of common-sense sentiment of the whole body of the church, was likewise, in our view, true and good. On the contrary, that order which trusted the devising of rules and regulations for the government of the church to one man, or a few men, in the highest grade of the ministry,—which rules and regulations, when so devised and passed by nominal conventions as packed juries, were to be adopted by the churches, on the principle of unity by conformity, and on the penalty of exclusion from the congregation of churches,—was, in our estimation, a most reprehensible tendency to episcopacy in our church in this country. This was that *ex cathedra authority*, against which we protested and warned the church, in a voice from the West. (See Journal of 16th Gen. Con., p. 22.)

It being, then, a true and good order to vest the exercise of ordaining powers in the convention, and not in one or more particular churches; and this order having been now adopted by the Eighth General Convention; therefore, from and after this time it became disorderly and wrong for any particular churches to *exercise* those ordaining powers which had been previously vested in them. Those churches coming by their ministers and delegates into the General Convention, and acting in that, either in adopting this advanced order, or in subsequently carrying it out, surrendered their previously vested rights or powers, just as the states of the confederacy surrendered all of theirs that they did not reserve, when they came into the present union, by adopting the present constitution of the United States. At least the ordaining powers of those particular churches from henceforth became obsolete: and it was indiscrete, if not disorderly, to exercise them against, and in violation of, a more advanced order, for some time, and generally, adopted by the churches in their collective capacity. And hence, in our opinion, any ordination performed by a particular church in this country after the adoption of the present order by this eighth convention,—especially if it was performed by any church represented in, or by any minister present in, this convention,—was morally and spiritually null. We like exceedingly the recent saying of a minister in the West—" *While the present is the order, we should abide by it!*" It is worthy to be written in letters of light, as a standing new-church maxim, or aphorism of wisdom. If the present order is wrong, abrogate it; or alter it and make it right. But *while it is the order, abide by it.* Above all, do not violate it, by keeping out of sight or acting against its principles, in temporizing concessions to popular prejudices, for the purpose of gaining honor from the churches, or retaining or extending the power to influence and govern them as a brotherhood.

It need only be stated, that Dr. Lemuel C. Belding, and Mr. Eleazer Smith, were ordained into the second grade of our ministry, in the presence of the Eighth General Convention, and according to the order adopted by it as aforesaid.

The report by Mr. Weeks on the trine, which was read and laid on the table on the second day of the session of this convention, was taken up on the third day, when, on the motion of Mr. Worcester, it was—

Resolved, That the Rev. L. Beers and the Rev. M. M. Carll, members of the Committee appointed at the *last* to report at the *present* Convention, be a Committee, to whom shall be referred the report of the said Committee rendered yesterday, for the purpose of adapting it for publication with the Journal.

And the Rev. Mr. Doughty, and Mr. Hayward, the secretary, were added to said committee.

Thus the eighth convention did all that was required of it in the way of making known the reasons and principles on which the order adopted by it was founded. But the committee to whom the report on the trine was referred for publication with the Journal, assumed the responsibility of disregarding their instructions, and presumed to exercise a judgment, not committed to them, in regard to the expediency of publishing it. In fact, Mr. Weeks's report on the trine was not published with the Journal of the convention to which it was submitted, because the committee, to whom it was referred for that purpose, "had done nothing in the way of preparing it for the press, as they were unable to agree in the opinion that it was advisable to publish it"! Thus was the order adopted by the eighth convention to be induced upon the general church without giving any of the reasons for it. Thus were the several societies of the church throughout our country requested to send in to the next meeting their sentiments upon the mode of ecclesiastical government to be adopted by the General Convention, without having before them, in the intervening time, those documents of truth—those authorities of the Word and the church, by which their minds might be enlightened, and on which their judgments should be founded. And thus were all of the receivers of the doctrines, and members, of the new church in the United States, who did not happen to be present in the Eighth General Convention, to be kept from reading that able paper, which set forth the principles that had the most remarkable forming and determining effects upon the whole ecclesiastical order of our church in America.

Nevertheless, the strong hand which wrote that report, had made its indelible mark upon the convictions of most of our leading minds—as we shall now see, in reviewing the proceedings of the Ninth General Convention. The Ninth General Convention met in Baltimore, and sat for three days, the 7th, 8th and 9th of June, 1827. In that convention, we had to take a part as a sort of *locum tenens* of a Boston delegate. Elsewhere we have had to say something about the proceedings of this convention in reference to the general body coming under the control of our eastern brethren. But here we will confine our attention to the subject before us. From what has been said about the proceedings of the eighth convention, the subject of ecclesiastical government would of course be the first thing to come up in the ninth. Accordingly, so soon as the convention was organized and ready for business—

On motion of Mr. Hubbard, it was ordered, that the Rev. Dr. Beers, the Rev. M. B. Roche, Mr. Condy, Mr. Lammot and Mr. Cunningham be a committee to consider the propriety of establishing a more orderly form of ecclesiastical government; and particularly as relates to the ministry; and that they report thereon to this convention.

It so happened that, on our way to Baltimore from Philadelphia, we fell in company with Dr. Beers, the chairman of the above committee; and as we proceeded in the steamboat, we distinctly recollect conversing with him on the probable action of the convention, which we were going to attend, in the making of rules for the government of the church in this country. In stating to him our opinion, we well remember that we used this simile—our church is now in its infancy; and for us to make rules now to govern her in coming years, would be just as irrational as to make pantaloons for our boys and lay them up to be worn when they should be men. Dr. Beers concurred with us fully, in this opinion. And it is mentioned here merely to show what were likely to be the opinions of the First Philadelphia Church on the subject of establishing an orderly form of ecclesiastical government for our church then. We had not then read Mr. Weeks's report on the trine. Our ideas of church order and government were very crude. We were emphatically a novice, and most willing to sit at the feet of some Gamaliel. Twenty years of age and experience have materially changed our opinions on most subjects. And we are far from believing that we should have expressed the same opinion then, with the views which we have now. We erred in being too external. What was wanted then was a fundamental law or constitution of the church; and we erred in comparing this to outer *garments*, or the making of it to the making of clothes. It should have been compared to the conception and formation of the infant in the womb—where we know the being is organized, and all the principles of its life are formed for perpetual development in future years. But so it was. And we believe there were very few of the First Philadelphia Church who had any distincter ideas than we had of inducing an episcopal form of government on the whole new church in this country at that time. As to Mr. Condy, he had undoubtedly made up his mind upon the trine now; and had cast over in his mind the subject of episcopacy in the new church. He had certainly thought of episcopacy as a contingency. Here is the proof—

The Rev. Dr. Beers, from the committee appointed yesterday on the subject of ecclesiastical government, made the following report:

Your committee are aware of the great importance of the subject submitted, and of the general and anxious desire of their brethren to come into an orderly arrangement of ecclesiastical government. They fully agree in opinion, and believe it to be the prevailing sentiment of the receivers of the doctrines of the New Jerusalem, that a trine ought to exist in the ministry; and they cannot doubt but that the societies, in their more advanced state, will assume that principle, as the true order of the church.

The subject, your committee therefore conceive, is chiefly to be viewed in relation to what is practicable at present. Should an episcopal mode of government be established, the office of ordination can with propriety be performed only by a bishop. The distance of the various societies throughout the United States, would require from a bishop, for this purpose and that of visiting the different churches, a degree of labour in travelling to which no individual would be competent. The appointment of an adequate number of ministers to that office, is a measure for which we are not yet prepared.

Your committee therefore respectfully offer their opinion, that the time has not arrived for the establishment of such a mode of government, and recommend that each society be regulated by what may appear to be expedient, in conformity with existing rules, leaving for the future the adoption of such measures on the subject of church government as may become requisite for the general benefit and good order of the church.

This report was written by Mr. Condy. We have him now in our mind's eye as he sat writing it. It was written, with pencil, on a loose sheet of paper, held on his knee, as he sat apart, in a pew, in the south-west corner, under a south window of the temple in which the convention was taking a recess, or deliberating on other matters. And here we see that, whatever he might have thought of episcopacy in the abstract, he did not think it a practicable or suitable form of ecclesiastical government for the new church then. Hence he was for putting it off, and leaving *each society*, or *particular church*, to regulate itself as it saw proper. Thus we discern that he did not now swerve from the principle on which he had acted from the first. He expresses no opinion as to the abstract propriety of episcopacy. But argues—*if* that form of government *ought to be* established, it is not practicable now; the time for it is not yet; therefore, no measures towards its establishment are to be taken now, and the congregational system with which we began, is still to be retained. Thus there is even yet no tendency to episcopacy in the General Convention generated by the First Philadelphia Church or its leading members.

Of course we subscribed to this report at the time it was made—as we probably should have done to any opinion which Mr. Condy might have advanced. But now its reasoning seems to us inconclusive. The first question to have been determined was, What is the true order? For this, in the Lord's providence, *must* be practicable in the *beginning* or never. For such as the *seed* is, such will be the expanding plant. In the establishment of the order of the church, as in all other things, the immutable law is, As we *sow*, so shall we *reap*. The first question, then, to have been determined in the present case, was, Is episcopacy the right form of government for the new church or not? If it is, then it does not do to argue that it is not practicable now, because one bishop cannot travel all over the United States; for neither in the youth nor in the age of the church, can so vast an extent of country be the province of one bishop. If episcopacy is right, we must begin with it; and if we can have but one bishop, we must begin with one, and let him travel as far as he can. If he cannot travel to the extremities of the United States, then those who need ordination there can meet him half way or come to him as well as to a church of Philadelphia or a convention. As the church extends, another bishop may be sustained. Nay, this is the radical error—that there must be an external or visible society of the church professing the doctrines of the *faith*, before there can be a minister. There must be *charity* before there can be *faith;* there must be *good*, before there can be *truth*. Truth is indeed apparently first, because visibly so; but good is really first, although invisibly so. In the beginning of the new church, the good of the old church, or of the Gentiles, is the ground in which the seeds of its truth are to be sown. The berries on the outermost fruitful branches of the old and dieing olive trees are to be the very first germs of the new church. Through these, the good of the gentile world is impregnated. Hence the members of the new church who come from the old church must always be few, and those who are to form the great body of it *must* come from the Gentiles. For the old church, being in general vastated as to genuine charity and true faith in the time of its consummation, when a new one is to be raised up, and the interior contents of the Word are opened for that purpose, therefore, the doctrine which teaches or conveys to men those interior contents cannot be understood or received by any in the consummated church *" except the few,* who are in the *life* of *good,* and are called *the elect,* who now *may be instructed*, and amongst whom a new church is about to be established. But where these are, *the Lord alone knows*—[they constitute his *invisible* body *on earth.*] *There will be few within the* [old] *church*. The new churches in former times have been established among the Gentiles." (A. C. 3898 comp. with 2986.) Wherefore all who are in good, wheresoever they may be throughout the world, or howsoever scattered as to place of abode, constitute the Lord's universal or catholic church, which appears before the Lord as one man (*homo*.) See A. C. 6637—especially 3263 and 8152, where these words occur: " The church of the Lord is not here or there; but is every where, as well within those kingdoms where the [visible] church is, as without them,—where the life is formed according to the precepts of charity. Hence it is that the church of the Lord is spread throughout the whole earth, and yet that it is one." This is evidently the Lord's church as to good, which is *universal*. But the Lord's church, as to *truth*, which is *general*, is where the Word is, and the doctrines of a true church are taught from it. (A. C. 3857.) The one is the Lord's *invisible* church, the other is his *visible* church. Into the former, baptism introduces the *spirit* of a person, into the latter it introduces the *person* of a spirit. Or into the sphere of the former, baptism introduces the will and its affections, and into the sphere of the latter it introduces the understanding and its thoughts. And the Lord's universal, or invisible church, or church as to good, or his holy catholic church, however dispersed its members may be in space, is in the sight of the Lord one female man—one man as to *affection* of truth—and is the Lord's bride and wife. And this church is " Eve, the mother of all living," by whom the Lord forms societies, or visible churches, or churches as to truth. For a society, or a visible church, is formed just as a man is formed. It must, like him, have a concep-

tive, gestative and parturient process. And after birth, it must grow to
maturity. Now in the gestation of man, although all the parts are
together in embryo, yet the heart and head are at first the largest
parts; and through these, the other parts are gradually developed,
according to their more immediate or more remote use. The head, the
heart, and the lungs, and all other parts, are formed by the mother
from the Lord. The father is the Lord; the mother is the universal
church; the child is the society or the particular church; the priesthood is the superior organ corresponding to the highest use. And
through this organ, as an instrument, the mother gradually forms and
develops the body of her child. Thus the Lord, in preparing to establish
the christian church, first drew around him disciples from those
who were in good any way receptive of his truth. These in general
formed his body, as a spouse. In this body (1 Cor. xii. 28,) he placed
twelve apostles, then seventy, to preach, teach, and heal. The whole
of the Lord's operations, from his baptism by John till his resurrection,
and after that till the day of pentecost, was the divine conceptive,
gestative and parturient process by which the church was formed, in
the womb of good, as a visible body in time and space. The christian
church as an infant was born at pentecost. And thus, as Swedenborg
says, the Lord established the christian church "*through* the apostles,"
and reared it up by their ministration to the full stature of the image
and likeness of him its generator. So that there must be a ministry
from the Lord, by whom the members of the church may be formed
into visible societies. And *every minister* that is *called* and *sent by
the Lord*, will form a society of members of the church around him,
out of those who are principled in *good*. They who are principled
in good, will flock to his spiritual-rational instructions of truth as
"*doves* to their *windows*." (Isa. lx. 8.) Hence, if episcopacy is the
true order, there will be a church made by or through every bishop
that the Lord makes. Wherefore, Mr. Condy's other conclusion is
fallacious; for, if episcopacy be the right order, it does not do to say
the appointment of an adequate number of bishops is a measure for
which we are not yet prepared; inasmuch as, when the time comes
to establish the church, the Lord will *begin* its establishment by calling and sending an adequate number of ministers, *through whom alone*
its establishment *can* be effected. And if the Lord has not sent these
ministers, the time to *begin* is not yet. If Mr. Condy's argument
were sound, it would have been as true and forcible in the time of
the Lord's first advent as now. In short, his error here was, in trusting
more to *human prudence* than to the *divine providence*. And, in our
opinion, if there has been any error in establishing the new church,
both in England and in America, it is the not having begun to establish the new christian church as the Lord himself established the old
one, that is, *through his twelve apostles*, trusting to *him* to support
them by *his* providence.—But more of this in the sequel.—In fine,
the thing to be done was, to have ascertained what was true order,
and then to have set to work immediately in *making preparation* for
bringing it into effect; and not, because we were unprepared for it,
to begin with an order which was defective or untrue. The great

thing was, *to be sure we were right* in STARTING, and THEN *to go ahead*.

But we do not think that episcopacy or papacy *as it has obtained in the old christian church*, is the right or true order for the New Jerusalem in this country. Therefore we are neither disposed to *begin* with that order, nor to *aim at it*, in our form of the new church. Our law, like Mr. Samuel Worcester's, is a very simple one, and very easily enunciated—*To follow the Lord's example—do as he did, and as we believe he would do again if he were now on earth.* This way we are sure is right—would go ahead in it, and banish all *doubt as to the end*, as a temptation from the gates of hell trying to prevail against it.

But the most important thing in the report before us, and the most pertinent to the matter in hand, is the unanimous opinion of the committee, and their belief of its being the prevailing sentiment of the receivers of the doctrines of the New Jerusalem, that *a trine ought to exist in the ministry.* Thus this committee endorses the Rev. Holland Weeks's report to the preceding convention; and the present convention not only sanctions and adopts that report, but declares that its threefold principle has been recognized, and does in fact exist in the ministry, by the church's usage. This was the opinion of the Rev. Mr. Roche, expressed by him in his off-hand way, and adopted at once by the convention in a sort of acclamation. In our opinion, a more deliberate mode of determining and declaring this fact ought to have been adopted. A commission should have examined and reported upon this matter; and then the convention should have passed upon the facts and findings of the report. If this had been done, the errors which occurred in the gradation of the ministry in the list of them which was published in the journal of this convention, would have been avoided; what was effective in the trinal arrangement as it had flowed by common influx into usage, might have been pointed out; and the true discrimination of the three grades, with the proper demarcation of their provinces, subordinations and functions, might have been taught from the writings of the church. But any how, we here come to the important historical fact, that the Ninth General Convention, or that of 1827, did adopt the trinal principle as the true order for the ministry of the new church in America. The following is the proceeding to that effect—

The report of the committee on ecclesiastical government, which was yesterday laid on the table, was taken up and considered : whereupon it was

Resolved, That the convention are deeply impressed with the considerations involved in the subject presented by the report, and fully concur in the recommendation offered by the committee. They are disposed to be contented, for the present, with the order now subsisting in the church, inasmuch as, for all necessary purposes, a threefold principle has been recognized, and does in fact exist in the ministry, by the usage heretofore adopted in the church, in the establishment of the several ecclesiastical offices of licentiates, priests and ordaining ministers.

But, whilst the convention feel satisfied in making this declaration, it is their unanimous desire, that the members of the various societies throughout the United States should continue freely to offer their opinions on the sul-ject, for the serious consideration of their brethren at large, and the more deliberate investigation of the next convention.

Thus, while this convention adopts the trinal principle, it very properly leaves the question an open one. For it needed to be determined on rational grounds whether the trinal arrangement of ecclesiastical offices which usage had prescriptively established, was a true and orderly one according to the authorities of the church. For the mere *fact* of usage did not prove the *right.* We have already expressed the opinion that licentiates are not a grade of the ecclesiastical order, for reasons fully stated in former parts of the present report. The principal reason is, that *inauguration into the ministry* is to be effected by the *promise* of the *holy spirit*, and the *representation* of its *translation*—which are given with *prayer* and the *imposition of hands.* Now ordination by prayer and the imposition of hands is a *representative rite,* "received from the ancients" and remaining "even at this day," (A. C. 6292 :) and this can no more be given by license, than baptism, the supper or any other representative rite, can be administered by license. If, then, this reason be good, mere prescriptive usage in our church was not a valid ground for decreeing that "a threefold principle does in fact exist *in* the ministry." All that could be said in truth was, that common influx from the spiritual world had, by its usual tendencies, brought about such a form of the trine as the crude and amorphous state of the incipient church would allow. And the time was now come when the collective church, as a youth verging to manhood, should acquire the knowledges of truth, as a groundwork for its action "in freedom according to reason" when it should become a man.

It should not be unnoticed in this connection, that the Rev. Holland Weeks, in his communication to this ninth convention, suggests, as a proper trine for our ministry, "licentiates, particular pastors and general pastors." He undoubtedly brought his order from the calvinistic church, from which he had but recently come out ; in which, there is "a candidate or licentiate before he is ordained the pastor of a particular church ;" and did not take it from the apostolic church, in which deacons were ordained in the lowest grade, by the imposition of the hands of the apostles. Nor did he take it from the very passage of Swedenborg's writings (U. T. 106) which he quotes to support it. For Swedenborg observes *four* grades, the *three* higher a trine *in* the priesthood, and the *one* lower a step preparatory *to* it, on which the *candidate* is to stand *before* he is *ordained a priest* as the lowest grade of the *priest*-hood. It is plain that Mr. Weeks was only bringing Swedenborg's doctrine down to the state, and applying it to the prescriptive usage, of the church, instead of elevating the imperfectly formed church to a conformity with the more perfect standard of that doctrine. Or, perhaps, he intended his suggestion to serve merely as an illustration, of the argument for a trine in his report, drawn from what had providentially become the church's usage.

The ninth convention having thus decreed the trine to be the true order of our ministry on the ground that the church had in fact recognized and adopted the trinal principle by providential usage, next proceeded to demonstrate the fact by the record and publication of a list of the ministers who had actually come into three several ecclesiastical offices. The following is the minute of this proceeding:

On motion of the Rev. Mr. Roche, *Resolved*, That the following be placed on the minutes of this convention, as a list of the ordaining ministers; the priests and teaching ministers; and the licentiates of the New Church in the United States of America, so far as has come to the knowledge of the convention:

ORDAINING MINISTERS.

Rev. Messrs. John Hargrove, *Baltimore*; Maskell M. Carll, *Philadelphia*; Lewis Beers, M. D., *Danby, N. Y.*; Charles J. Doughty, *New York City*; Holland Weeks, *Henderson, N. Y.*; Manning B. Roche, *Southwark, Philadelphia.*

PRIESTS AND TEACHING MINISTERS.

Rev. Messrs. Adam Hurdus, *Cincinnati, O.*; Richard H. Goe, *Wheeling, Va.*; Isaac C. Worrell, *Frankfort, Pa.*; Nathaniel Holley, *Cincinnati, O.*; Thomas Newport, *Lebanon, O.*; Eleazer Smith, *Bridgewater, Ms.*: Lemuel C. Belding, M. D., *Pike, Pa.*

LICENTIATES.

Messrs. Thomas Worcester, *Boston, Ms.*; Samuel Worcester; Silas Ensign, *Worcester, O.*; Samuel H. Wills, *Abingdon, Va.*; John Lister, *Frankford, Pa.*; Edwin A. Atlee, M. D., *Philadelphia*; Adam Klingle, *Philadelphia*; Jonathan Horton, *Riverhead, L. I.*; William Pitts, *Danby, N. Y.*; Thomas Newport, Jr., *Lebanon, O.*; Benjamin Essex, *Lynchburg, Va.*

Several matters of grave moment come up here for consideration. Several references or allusions have been made to this place in the preceding pages. And we must now examine the substance of these matters, the shadows of which were cast upon us in our approach.

In the infancy of the new church in this country, the power to ordain ministers was assumed by a particular church, on the ground that the Lord's ordaining powers are vested by him in his whole church, just as the powers of the soul are vested in its body, or just as the powers of the Essential Divinity are vested in its Divine Humanity. "As thou hast sent me into the world, even so have I also sent them into the world. * * * That *they all may be one*, as thou, father, art in me, and I in thee; that they also may be one in us." (John, xvii. 18–21.) These words are spoken apparently of the twelve apostles, but really of all goods and truths in a complex, which flow from the Lord, and constitute charity and faith as the church in men. Hence the twelve apostles represented all the men in a complex, in whom the church thus is. And the Lord, by charity and faith, dwells in that complex as a soul in its body. Hence the whole church is the Lord's body, and the Lord is the church's soul. And thus the church and the Lord are one as body and soul are one.*

---

* "It is an acknowledged truth among Christians at this day, that the church constitutes the body of Christ, and that every particular person in whom the church is, is in some member or other of that body, according to what is said by Paul, Eph. i. 23; 1 Cor. xii. 27; Rom. xii. 4, 5." (U. T. 372.)

So that the Lord vests his ordaining powers in the church as the soul
vests its powers in the body. Now "the activity of man does not
proceed from his soul by his body, but out of his body from his soul."
(U. T. 188.) Therefore, the Lord's ordination does not proceed from
his soul by his body, but out of his body from his soul. Hence the
Lord does not ordain ministers *by* the church, but the church ordains
ministers *from* the Lord. Thus the Lord's ordaining powers are
vested in the church, as a whole. When the Lord ordained the
twelve, he as to his humanity in himself and his disciples, was representatively the whole church, or whole body of those divine goods
and truths that constitute the church. When the twelve became
ordaining ministers from the Lord, they were *representatively* the
whole church, and ordaining powers were vested in *all* of them, for
they all were one in the Lord and his father, as he and his father
were one. But as the church was established by or through the
apostles as the Lord's representatives, the whole church being an ex-
pansion of the twelve, as a plant is of its seed,* and therefore including the apostles as its members; became the Lord's actual body
on earth. Then the church, as a whole body, became the Lord's
vicar, and the apostles with all the clergy ordained *by* them, became
the vicar of that vicar.

Now the Lord *produces* the church,—as a soul produces its body,—
does not *consist* of it. For there is a *discrete* relation between the
soul and the body, and therefore a *reciprocal* conjunction between
them. But there is not a discrete relation between the body and its
organs or members; for the body does not produce its organs and
members, but consists of them. There may be a discrete relation
between certain members of the body and certain other members of
it, but there is not a discrete relation between the body as a whole
and its members as its parts. Hence there is no reciprocal conjunction between the members and their body, so as to form the same
relation between them that there is between the body and its soul.
Consequently, the members do not act *from* the body, as the body
does from the soul; but *the body acts* BY *its members* as instruments.
But *all men* who are reciprocally conjoined to the Lord by means of
charity and faith, (U. T. 372,) "are the body of Christ, and members
in particular. And God hath set some *in* the church—first *apostles*,
secondarily prophets, thirdly teachers," &c. (1 Cor. xii. 27, 28 and
Rom. xii. 3-5.) Hence ordaining powers were not vested in the
apostles, so that the apostles ordained from the Lord, or his body the
church; but ordaining powers were vested in the church as the
Lord's body, so that the church, as his body, ordained *from* the Lord
by the apostles as *its members*. Thus the apostles in ordaining were
not the Lord's vicar, but the vicar of his church, which alone, as the
Lord's vicar, has his ordaining powers vested in it, and ordains *from*
him. Wherefore, we conclude, that it is an eternal and immutable

* The twelve apostles were the kernel of the seed, and the other disciples, in their
order, were its husks or outer coverings.

law of divine order, that ordaining powers are vested inalienably in
the whole church as the Lord's body.*

But let not any deduce from this the insane conclusion, that the
Lord's ordaining powers are with the *laity* of the church, so that
ordination flows from the circumference to the centre; for the laity
are not the *whole body* of the church, but only *various members* of it;
and they are *not those* members *by* which the *body* exercises ordaining
powers *from* the Lord. Hence, when ten male members, as the
representatives of the whole church at Baltimore, ordained Messrs.
Mather and Hargrove as the first new-church ministers in this country,
it is not to be inferred from this that the appointing, nominating or
ordaining power is with the *laity*. The power to *choose* ministers is
indeed with the laity; because they have the power to choose or
reject the Lord, whom ministers represent; but they have no right or
power to *ordain* ministers, because the Lord alone has the right and
power to commission those that are to represent him. Hence the
appointing, nominating or ordaining of ministers on earth as in heaven
is solely with the Lord; but on earth these powers of the Lord are
vested in the whole church as his body, which exercises them from
him; and the laity, or members of the church considered distinctively
from the clergy, are not the *whole* church, and so the Lord's body,
but are only some component *parts* of it. This is an important distinction, an ignorance or disregard of which has caused certain weak
expounders of our church's ministerial order to put weapons in the
hands of its enemies for its destruction. So, on the other hand, the
clergy, considered distinctively from the laity, do not have *in themselves* the power to ordain other ministers, but they are merely the
organs *by* which the whole church, as the Lord's body, *exercises* his
ordaining powers *from* him. We repeat, then, that, in the infancy
of the new church in this country, the power to ordain ministers was
assumed by a particular church on the ground that *the Lord's ordaining powers are vested by him* IN HIS WHOLE CHURCH. In that case, this
particular church *represented* the whole.

---

* Any one can now see where the gist of the Boston heresy lies. It lies in the falsification of the truth above shown—that the minister, whether an apostle, a pastor or a
teacher, is *set in* the church as a member of it, and is not *joined to* it as a husband.
The Lord is *alone* the husband of his church, both in her smallest and her largest form :
because he alone is " *reciprocally conjoined* to her by means of charity and faith."
Therefore the heresy of the conjugial theory consists in its putting the minister in the
Lord's place, by making the relation to his society one of *conjunction* instead of one of
insition. In other words, the idea of the pastoral relation being a *conjugial* one,
involves the principle of a *reciprocal conjunction* between the pastor and his society.
Hence the minister had to be formed from the Lord as the truth of good, and the society
had to be formed from the Lord as the good of that truth, as conjugial partners are born
and brought up; and then these two, brought together in the providence of the Lord, had to
be joined together in one as a church, as the husband and wife together make a church.
Thus the great object of a newly made licentiate was to get a society, for whom as a virgin
he was to look out, and court for a wife. Therefore, " upon this principle, *candidates*
for the *ministry* must be the *only* missionaries." (I'. W.'s *Letter* to J. W. Condy,
Esqr , Extra I., p. 37.) How this principle flowed into the Rules of Order, we shall
show by and by.

In the early adolescence of the new church in this country, a progressive change took place. A general convention was called, which
was at first too few in numbers and too weak in organization to take
upon itself the discharge of the duties rightly assignable to it. However, the whole church, in and by it as its representative, advances
so much beyond its root or infancy, as to confide its ordaining powers
in the concurrent action of two or three particular churches. These,
as cotyledons, were to nourish the stock of the plant until it was
sufficiently formed and strong enough to stand and shoot forth
branches, with leaves, and flowers, and fruit.

And now, in advancing adolescence, our church, in the eighth
convention, undergoes an organic change. The powers of ordination,
which had previously been confided to certain particular churches,
were now assumed by, or vested in, the General Convention as the
consistory or representative of the whole church. As we have
shown, the law is, and ever was, that ordaining powers are vested
inalienably in the general body of the church, and are only *exercised
by* ordaining ministers as the members or organs of that body. This
law is most fundamental, and of incalculable importance in its application to the subject before us. Hence we have labored so hard to
bring it into view. Let it never be lost sight of. According to this
law, the General Convention rightly underwent that organic change
by which it took to itself the power to ordain ministers and regulate
their ordinations. While the church was in extreme childhood, or
feeble adolescence, when a general representative body of the whole
church could not exist or operate with efficiency, it was admissible
that its powers should be exercised by one or more particular
churches; for these could then be the only representatives of the
whole church. But whenever the General Convention could act, it
was its duty to exercise the powers legitimately belonging to it; and
when it had in fact assumed the exercise of these powers, it then
became wrong or disorderly, for the particular churches to exercise
them.

So now, in the ninth convention, there is a formal acknowledgment
"that a trine ought to exist in the ministry." This too is a fundamental law, which the General Convention, in its ninth meeting,
formally adopts as such. It furthermore makes a formal declaration
of the way in which the law has found an actual application in the
church's usage. It acknowledges this usage as a sort of *common law*
and enacts it into *statute law*. Or it *legalizes* mere usage. Hence it
now becomes a fundamental law of the whole new church in the United
States, that there *must* be a trine in its ministry; and a statute law
that this trine does and shall for the present exist in the three ascending grades of licensed minister, priest and teaching minister, and
ordaining minister.

Now, in determining the force and application of this law, so as to
discern its violations or infringements, four observations must here be
made. First, The law is a moral or spiritual one. It is a law of the
church, which has all its authority from the Lord's teaching. Hence
its enactment by the General Convention, is not like the enactment

of a civil law by a political legislature, but is like the conclusion of
an enlightened understanding, which is to form and guide the will of
the church as a shepherd does his flock.   Hence, as the understanding leads the will which it represents, so the General Convention was
to lead the brotherhood of churches which it represented.   Its laws,
therefore, were recommendations of principles found in the doctrines
of Him who alone teaches with authority and not as the Scribes.   We
presume, then, that this enactment of the church's usage into a spiritually statute law was nothing more than a formal declaration of
those conclusions which the wise and intelligent men of the church
had, in council, drawn from the Word and the writings of the church.
Consequently, every member of the church was bound by a moral
and spiritual obligation to observe this law as a divine means of the
church's coming into true external order, and not simply because the
General Convention had enacted or declared it.   All the General
Convention has to do, is, as a collective minister, to teach truth, and
by truth to lead to good.

Second, The new church teaches that the law is to be made by
those who are skilled in it, and at the same time in love and wisdom
from the Lord; and when the law is thus made, then all the officers
of government from the highest to the lowest are to be subject to the
law, as well as the people whom they are to govern by it.   Supposing, then, that Swedenborg was the Lord's servant to effect his
second advent in the spiritual sense of his Word; and to teach from
heaven, that is from that sense of the Word which is in heaven, the
true doctrines of the church, as the laws of spiritual life to men on
earth ; then he, of all others, must be the man most skilled in those
laws; so that he is the proper one to make the ecclesiastical law for
the external order of the New Jerusalem.   And if this law is laid
down any where in his writings, it must be especially in that work
in which he himself says there are " truths continuous from the Lord."
Now we suppose the General Convention's committee, whose duty it
was to ascertain the laws of order which were to settle the questions
brought in issue by the Cincinnati communication, selected the Rev.
Holland Weeks as the man most skilled in the law as laid down by
Swedenborg, and therefore made him the pivot of their action.   His
report does in fact draw the trinal order of the ministry from Swedenborg's Universal Theology.   The action of this ninth convention in
decreeing the trinal principle to be the true order, and declaring its
actual existence in our ministry, is founded wholly on Mr. Weeks's
report.   Therefore the enactment of this law by the Ninth General
Convention, the declaration of it as a general statute, and the recommending it to the adoption of the churches, is nothing more than
bringing to bear upon the church that ecclesiastical justice to which
all the ministers of the church of all grades are to be subject.   And
no minister of any grade or date of appointment, nor any particular
church, much less the General Convention, in any of its subsequent
meetings, should have contravened or violated this common law, now
it was made a statute, and was unrepealed.

Third, The apostolic church taught, that, before the law came,

the violation of it was not sinful; but after the law came, then sin
revived, and he whose conduct was obnoxious to the law died, that is,
became condemnible by it. The Lord also taught, "If ye were blind,
ye would not have sin; but now ye say, We see, your sin remaineth."
Hence, before the law of trinal order was declared in the new church,
violations of it were not culpable, but after it was declared, they
were.

Fourth, The law of trinal order, as taught by Swedenborg, and by
the report of Mr. Weeks, decrees that there are three discrete degrees
or grades in the ministry; that these are subordinate, the lower to
the higher; and that the lower are stages preparatory for induction
into the higher. Hence it is disorderly for a man to be introduced
into the higher, and especially the highest, at once, before he has
passed regularly through the lower grades. The great use of all such
laws of order is, to protect the church from injury; and nothing can
be more injurious to the church than the induction of men into offices
for which they are not fit; and no man can be fit for an office until
he has passed through the stages that are preparatory to it. The
importance of the trinal principle and the great danger of violating
it, both rest on its indispensableness to that preparation for office
without which the uses or functions of office cannot be performed or
discharged for the common good. In civil affairs, the operation of
this law is every where seen. In the Roman Republic especially,
the gradations of office were most distinctly marked, and the need
of passing through the lower to the higher grades most strenuously
insisted on. Sometimes young men of extraordinary talents were
soon or suddenly raised to the higher offices; but this, if not made
necessary by the exigencies of the state, was always a reproach. It
was the constant *boast* of Cicero, that he had regularly ascended by
all the steps of preparative office to the highest, the consular dignity.
It is said that men are sometimes appointed at once to the supreme
command of armies; but this is still a violation of order, which is
admissible only in extraordinary cases, and in respect to extraordinary
men, who must have acquired the requisite fitness in some other than
the ordinary way. No community can so outrage common sense as
to put a man at the head of an army, by taking him from the mass
without any preparation for the right discharge of the most responsible
duties of that high office: and although, in certain particular and
peculiar cases, a man may have acquired a sort of military skill by
something else than regular military education,—as by surveying wild
lands, hunting wild animals, or fighting Indians,—yet, in general, due
preparation for the office of commander of an army cannot be effected
in any other way than by ascending grades of subordinate office, by
which, as steps, men must rise to the highest. And he that climbs
up any other way, cannot be regarded as any other than a burglar,
who breaks into the house of order. Such is the general law as it
applies to ecclesiastical, as well as to military, affairs. The truth and
propriety of this general law are vindicated by the theory and practice of Napoleon, who took his marshals from the ranks, and led them
up by gradual steps, instead of making them jump from the base to

the pinnacle. No man is fit to command, who has not learned to obey; and no man can learn to obey, unless he begins in the lowest grade. The springing of Minerva from the brain of Jupiter, was a representative fiction of mythology, involving something very different from this award of common sense, which declares that no man is fit to command an army who has not passed regularly through the subordinate ranks and grades of office, by the discharge of the duties of which, a proper preparation for the exercise of such command can alone be secured. In the life of the famous Marshal Turenne, it is first said, his mother "sent him, when he was not yet thirteen years old, into the Low Countries, to learn the art of war under his uncle, Maurice of Nassau, who commanded the troops of Holland in the protracted struggle between that country and Spain. Maurice held that *there was no royal road to military skill*, and placed his young relation in the ranks, as a volunteer, where for some time he served, enduring all hardships to which the common soldiers were exposed." And it is afterwards said—"Four years a captain, four a colonel, three marechal de camp, five lieutenant-general, he had served in all stations from the ranks upwards, and distinguished himself in them, not only by military talent, but by strict honor and trustworthiness." At last "he was created Marshal-General of the French armies," with the probability that the monarch, who made him such, " meditated the revival [by his appointment to it] of the high dignity of Constable of France, which could not be held by a Protestant." This illustrates most forcibly the use of grades in the ministry, and of the need of passing to the highest, from the lowest, through the higher, as the only means of securing that *preparation* for the highest office, without which the church cannot be served, benefited or secured by the right discharge of its functions. Let it not be forgotten, that Swedenborg, in 106 U. T., on the authority of which passage the need of discrete, progressive, ascending or preparative grades in the ministry is founded, is treating of two states in the Lord's glorification and man's regeneration, the former of which had to be passed through as a *preparatory stage* for the latter. So that it is just as impossible, in true order, for a man to be made a minister of the highest grade at once, or to be advanced from the lowest to the highest grade without first passing discretely through the intermediate grade, as it was for the Lord to be fully glorified at once without having been previously exinanited, or as it is for man to be regenerated at once without being previously reformed, or as it would be for a butterfly to be made such at once without having first been a worm and then a chrysalis. For all these are illustrations of the law made by Swedenborg. Hence we contend, that, now this law has been established by the General Convention, the violation of it involves the greatest peril of the church. It involves just such disturbances of the whole body of the church, as softenings of the brain produce in the physical body— falling fits. He, therefore, cannot be the true friend of the church, who contemns or disregards those regular gradations of the trinal order, by which men are properly prepared for the right and efficient discharge of the duties of her highest ecclesiastical offices. And every one does so contemn or disregard them, who either seeks to be, or allows himself to be, raised into the higher, without passing through the lower, *after* they have been defined by the general organ of the church. Before the law was decreed, it might have been unwittingly broken without danger; but after its enactment, the most scrupulous observance of its order should have been observed, for the sake of the order and its great uses. For if a precedent is set, of disregarding the lower gradations, by those who may be deemed by others, or may deem themselves, fit at once for the higher, where will be the security against the fatal elevation of those who are unfit?

These remarks upon what we have previously shown in this historical sketch of ordinations into our ministry in this country, and these observations upon the law of trinal order which is here for the first time declared in the Ninth General Convention, have been necessarily made, to justify our condemnation of certain things, and in explanation of certain others, which have transpired in the course of those ordinations.

When the Journal of the Ninth General Convention was published, and this list of the three grades of ministers was thereby shown to the church at large, as the evidence that the new church in our country had actually come into the trinal arrangement which was deemed to be the true order, it called forth a letter from the Rev. S. H. Wills, of Abingdon, Va., to the Rev. John Hargrove, who had been president of that convention. Mr. Wills complained that the convention had degraded him; and, submitting his certificate, or other voucher, of his ordination with unlimited powers by the Rev. Mr. Holley, asked if wrong had not been done him. The president called into consultation the secretary of the ninth convention, who was then residing in Baltimore as a student for the ministry and his assistant preacher. It was at once decided, that the publication of the list in the journal of the ninth convention was merely a declaration of who were the ministers of the church in this country in three actual gradations "so far as had come to the knowledge of the convention." And as no information had been given to the convention, or to its officers, respecting the ordination of Mr. Wills, the placing of his name among the licentiates merely was an unintentional error. But where Mr. Holley's and Mr. Wills's names ought to have been placed, did not appear clear. After considering the matter maturely, the president came to a decision on the following grounds: 1. Ordaining power was vested in the *church* at Abingdon, and not in Mr. Holley separate from it. Therefore, Mr. Holley, having left the Abingdon church, and not being in connection with any other church, could not be regarded as an ordaining minister, unless the General Convention were expressly to acknowledge him as a minister of that grade in its connection. Consequently, as the General Convention had not done this, Mr. Holley was now nothing more than a priest and teaching minister, and his name was rightly placed among the ministers of the second grade. As to the Rev. Messrs. Carll, Beers, Doughty, Weeks and Roche, the convention had acknowledged them to be ordaining ministers by placing them on its list, after it had undergone the organic change of 1826. 2. The ordaining of ministers is a power vested inalienably in the whole or general body of the church; and therefore could not be transferred to any particular part of it. The General Convention might confide the *exercise* of *its* power temporarily to certain particular churches, while it was not in a state to exercise that power itself; and the convention had in fact confided such exercise to the concurrent action of the three churches of Philadelphia, Baltimore and New York. These having been specified, were in fact the only churches to which the exercise of general ordaining powers was then confided by the convention. And, therefore, to give the *unlimited* exercise of this power to the Abingdon church, *without the express vote* and *sanction of the General Convention*, was irregular and null. Nor was it the *intention* of Mr. Hargrove, when he ordained Mr. Holley, to confer upon him, or upon the church of Abingdon, such unlimited ordaining power. He intended that the Abingdon *church*, by Mr. Holley its minister, should have the power to make another priest and teaching minister, or to license preachers, in connection with itself, and under its authority. But he did not intend that it should make *an ordaining minister for the whole church in the United States.* This he believed the General Convention, as the representative of that whole church, could alone do. Wherefore, Mr. Holley, in giving Mr. Wills general ordaining powers, had imparted to him more than he himself possessed—had transcended the powers given to him under the authority of the Abingdon church, and therefore his ordination of Mr. Wills was in so far null. 3. But Mr. Holley, under the authority of the Abingdon church, was fully competent to ordain Mr. Wills a priest and teaching minister; and as he had ordained him into that grade, and the nullity extended only to the giving the additional power to ordain, therefore Mr. Wills ought to be regarded as a minister of the second grade, and his name ought to be placed among the ministers of that grade on the convention's list. 4. Even supposing unlimited ordaining power—the power to ordain ministers for the whole church—*had* been given to the Abingdon church, yet, when the General Convention had taken this its legitimate power to itself, or had expressly confided the exercise of it to three particular churches, the Abingdon church ought not to have exercised that power in such a way as to make Mr. Wills an ordaining minister of the whole church, without first consulting the General Convention, and getting its express authority to do so. 5. As appeal had been made to the General Convention, through its presiding officer, by Mr. Wills, to know in what grade of the ministry that body regarded him as standing, the placing of his name in any grade in the convention's list now, would be the *convention's* acknowledgment that he was in that grade, which would be tantamount to giving him the authority of it; and as it was not intended to give the Abingdon church the *convention's power* to do this act *for it*, and as Mr. Holley had transcended his powers in transferring to Mr. Wills more power than he himself possessed, therefore it would be wrong to do that, by placing Mr. Wills's name in the convention's list of ordaining ministers, which it was wrong in

Mr. Holley to do. Wherefore, on these several grounds, Mr. Hargrove decided, that both Mr. Holley's and Mr. Wills's names ought to be placed in the second grade of ministers on the convention's list; and substantially these views were communicated to Mr. Wills by letter.

But, as neither the president nor the secretary of the ninth, attended the two following conventions, this subject was not brought before the General Convention by them, and Mr. Holley remained a minister of the second grade, and Mr. Wills only a licentiate, on the convention's list, for two years more. To the twelfth convention, however, communications were made respecting both Mr. Holley's and Mr. Wills's grades. The Cincinnati society inquired about the proper rank of Mr. Holley; and Mr. Wills himself submitted his case to this convention as he had previously done to the president of the ninth. There were present in this twelfth convention a more than usually large number of ministers. Of the ordaining ministers there were present the Rev. Messrs. Hargrove, Carll, Beers, Roche and Worcester—five out of eight, the whole number. Of the second grade, there were the Rev. Messrs. Worrell, Robinson and Belding. And of the first grade, there were Messrs. Stebbins and De Charms. In all there were ten ministers—half of them of the highest grade. On the motion of the Rev. Thos. Worcester, Mr. Holley's case was submitted to a committee, consisting of the Rev. Mr. Hurdus, the Rev. Dr. Beers and the Rev. Mr. Carll. As Mr. Hurdus, the chairman of this committee, resided in Cincinnati, where Mr. Holley then was, and was not now present, a report from this committee could not be made to the twelfth convention. Mr. Wills's case was not submitted to a committee; as it had been so fully considered by the president and secretary of the ninth convention, who were now present and holding the same offices in the twelfth. Two years of time had not altered Mr. Hargrove's opinion, and his decision of Mr. Wills's case being approved by the common perception of those to whom it was stated, "it was, on motion of the Rev. Mr. Roche, voted that the Secretary do place the name of the Rev. Samuel H. Wills upon the list of priests and teaching ministers; and that the President notify Mr. Wills of his being recognized by this Convention as belonging to that grade of the ministry."

The thirteenth convention assembled in New York. Of this, too, Mr. Hargrove was first elected president. But declining the office on account of the infirmities of age, the Rev. C. J. Doughty was chosen president in his stead. Five of the ordaining ministers were present at this convention also—the Rev. Messrs. Hargrove, Carll, Doughty, Roche and Worcester. The Rev. Mr. Robinson of the second grade, and Messrs. Stebbins and Howard of the first, were present too—making eight ministers in all. And on p. 4 of the Journal of this convention, n. 20, we find the following minute:

The Rev. Mr. Carll, chairman of the committee on the case of the Rev. Mr. Holley, reported that it had been found that the certificate of Mr. Holley's ordination authorized him to exercise ordaining powers only with the consent of the society in Abingdon, Va., with which he was then connected ;

and the committee were of opinion that as that connection is now dissolved, "the above-mentioned certificate, so far as relates to the power of ordination, becomes void."

Voted, That this report be accepted and approved.

Thus both Mr. Hargrove who ordained Mr. Holley, and Mr. Carll, who concurred in his ordination, decided that he was no longer an ordaining minister of our church, and the General Convention approved the decision.

When the Central Convention came into existence, Mr. Wills forwarded his vouchers to that body also. They were laid before its ecclesiastical council, who, after mature deliberation, unanimously concurred in the decision of the General Convention; and the Central Convention itself re-declared that decision by a formal reiteration.

But the Western Convention, the year before its death, and with one foot in the grave,—without a single ordaining minister, to judge in the matter,—by young and inexperienced ministers of an inferior grade, who seem to have been without the knowledge of the facts above stated, determined that both Mr. Wills and Mr. Holley *are* ordaining ministers, against the decision of the Rev. Messrs. Hargrove and Carll, through whom they received whatever of ordaining power they might be supposed to possess.

There is no doubt that Mr. Wills's certificate of ordination bears on the face of it the gift of the authority of a general ordaining minister. There is quite as little doubt that the Abingdon church's ordination of him, by Mr. Holley, without the express sanction of the General Convention, is equally valid with the Danby church's ordination of Dr. Brown, with the same powers, by Dr. Beers, without the sanction of any general body of the church. And as the General Convention has now placed the names of both Mr. Wills and Dr. Brown among the ordaining ministers on its list, they are both, undoubtedly, thereby clothed with all the authority of that highest grade. And the name of Mr. Holley ought to be placed there too—unless he has gone to the world of spirits.

Nevertheless, for reasons hereinbefore stated, we enter our *solemn protest* against the elevation of Dr. Brown to the third grade, without his having passèd through the second, *without the authority of a general body of the church*, and *without the consent of other ministers of that grade*, as a most flagrant, and a most dangerous, violation of the established order of our church. We enter our protest against this case in particular, because it occurred at a later period; when the external order of our church was more clearly defined and more fully established: and because there was no such necessity as existed when Dr. Beers was ordained, who received power to ordain other ministers under the authority of the church at Danby, before the General Convention was in existence.

It has been urged by Dr. Beers, that this was a *"vested right,"* which could not be taken away. But there is no parity between vested rights, conferred by the civil law, and appointment to ecclesiastical office. This, Swedenborg expressly says, is not in the person, so that no honor or dignity enures to him when he is not in it—

which implies that he may cease to perform the functions of the office,
or that the office may be taken away from him. The rights vested in
certain persons by civil law, or charter, are privileges granted in the
way of *contract* between the community and them, on account of
certain benefits which they are supposed to render to the community
as a *quid pro quo*. These clearly ought not to be taken away by the
community without the consent of the other contracting party. But
appointment to either ecclesiastical or civil office confers *powers*, not
rights, upon the officer; or it only confers the right to exercise powers
in the name, and by the authority of, the community, whose good is
to be secured by the due performance of the uses of office; and, when
this good requires it, that right may be taken away from one officer
and transferred to another. Thus the king, who represents the Lord
in his kingly office, as he cannot be every where in his kingdom at
the same time, deputes his royal power, by appointing certain persons
to act for him—to act in his name and by his authority—where he
cannot be to act for himself. And can it be imagined that any
such appointment to office is a *right vested inalienably* in the officer?
can it be imagined that it is a *right* at all? The idea of a vested or
divine *right* in the king himself to rule, is exploded. How then can
there be a vested right in any of his officers to rule under him? No
more is ordaining power, given by the churches to a particular church,
to be exercised by its minister, either a *vested right*, or any thing in
the nature of one. We say, then, that the above was not a vested
right at all; it was a vested *power*. And we repeat that all power to
ordain ministers vested in particular churches before the General
Convention came into being, was virtually surrendered, when that
body was in existence, and after it had taken to itself the exercise of
that power which is of right vested in it solely, as the representative
of the whole church. From that time it became wrong for any particular church to *exercise* such power. And there can be no *vested
right* to *do wrong*.

The next thing which we need to notice in the proceedings of the
Ninth General Convention is its resolution recommending—

That Mr. Thomas Worcester be ordained a priest and teaching minister
in the Lord's church of the New Jerusalem, with power to conduct public
worship, to celebrate the sacrament of the Lord's supper, marriages, baptisms and funerals, and generally to perform all holy rights and divine
ordinances, *except that of ordaining other priests and ministers*; and that the
said ordination may be received at the hands of any *two* ministers possessing ordaining powers.

We have underscored the sentence and word above, to call particular attention to them. The convention having now formally
acknowledged and declared the trinal arrangement of ministers to be
the true order of our church in this country, could not with any consistency violate it, in its very first proceeding under that order.
Therefore this convention recommended that Mr. Worcester, from a
licentiate, which he already was, should be ordained into the second
grade only. And the convention recommended that he should be
ordained by *two* ministers possessing ordaining powers, not only

because this was according to the law established by the eighth convention, but because now the *trine* of grades was established, it was perceived that inauguration into the first grade should be effected by *one*, into the second by *two*, and into the third by *three* ordaining ministers.

Complaint might have been made that Mr. Roche had been quite recently ordained with full powers at once; and that Mr. Worcester was as well or better fitted than he to receive such powers; or that it was more admissible to let Mr. Worcester take *two* steps at once, than Mr. Roche *three*. Of this, we think, there can be very little doubt. But the grades were not formally acknowledged by the General Convention when Mr. Roche was ordained. Application for his ordination was not made to the convention. He was ordained by the authority of three ordaining ministers only, without any formal or expressed concurrence or *commission* of their *churches*, to whom the exercise of ordaining power had been confided by the General Convention—which, under the circumstances, was a serious irregularity. And although his ordination with all the powers of the highest ministerial grade at once could not then be deemed *irregular*, because the *rule* of arrangement in three grades was not then established, yet we know that the investing him at once with all the powers of our ministry, so soon after he had come, with considerable *enthusiasm*, from the old church into the new, was judged by several thinking men to be exceedingly injudicious. On the principle, "as with the people, so with the priest," (Isa. xxiv. 2,) or "like people, like priest," (Hos. iv. 9,) it was thought no minister,—if not made the minister of a convention as a general body,—should be ordained with full powers, except as a *head member* of a full and undoubted *new-church* society, so that he might, by its sphere of general affection for the truth, be kept from wandering into error. But ordaining power was given to Mr. Roche himself, and not to any church of which he was the minister; and the society which he was forming around him, consisted almost wholly of persons who had followed him from the old church, led by personal attachments. Under these circumstances, there were those who thought his sudden and full ordination very injudicious, imprudent and unwise. And when they saw Mr. Roche taking the stand with some female quaker preachers, and, by praying with them, sanctioning their ministration in the public hall which was the usual place of worship of his own society, they were made more sensible, than they had at first been, of the impropriety of so suddenly laying hands upon him to induct him into the full powers of our ministry at once. But, as we have said, this was not *irregular* at the time, because the three grades were not then formally acknowledged. And as they *were*, when authority was given to ordain Mr. Thos. Worcester, he could not be advanced from the first to the third grade, without an unjustifiable violation of the established order. The Ninth General Convention did right in tacitly saying—"*While it is the order, let us abide by it.*" And the Tenth General Convention would have commended itself to our respect, and its proceedings to our approval, if it had emulated the doings of the Ninth.

It is said that the recommendation to ordain Mr. Thomas Worcester was made in consequence of a desire expressed by Mr. Loring, of the Boston society, that he should be ordained. But the truth of history requires that this matter should be explained. We can explain it, because we happen know all about it. The truth is, that Mr. Loring, the only delegate* of the Boston society present, had no authority from his society to express any desire, or make any thing like an application, for Mr. Worcester's ordination. Having been foiled on a former occasion by the Philadelphia church, he was probably not disposed to ask that church again, or the convention, while it was supposed to be under its influence. But the members of the Philadelphia church present in this convention, were anxious to bury the hatchet and smoke the pipe of peace. They imagined that the queer notions of their Boston brethren were now given up.—It was, however, seen in time that they were only *covered* up.—But having ceased to say any thing about them, and evincing much that was commendable in their intelligence, order and efficiency in church affairs, their southern brethren were disposed to forgive and forget what was past, and to be good friends in future. In this spirit, the Philadelphians, especially Mr. Condy, urged Mr. Loring to give them an opportunity of showing their present kind feelings towards Mr. Worcester, who had, on former occasions, received pretty rough usage from them. Mr. Loring being a nervously conscientious man, and therefore not liking to express a desire which he did not feel, or make an application which his society had not authorized him to make, hesitated for a long time; but at length yielded to the eloquent importunity of Mr. Condy, and "having expressed a desire that Mr. Thomas Worcester, licentiate and pastor elect of the Boston Society, should be ordained into the ministry of the New Church," a resolution to that effect was, on motion of Mr. Condy, passed unanimously. How these overtures of the southern members were received—how this recommendation, made by them, in a large majority, for ordination into the *second* grade by *two* ordaining ministers was disregarded and set aside, and how the order of the trine was violated by the hoisting of Mr. Worcester, as it were, by a sort of running horse pulley, up at once from the first to the third grade, may be known by inspection of the Journal of the Tenth General Convention. We will only add here, that it was quite *natural* for Mr. Worcester to sanction, in Dr. Brown's case, what had been done by Dr. Beers's recommendation, with rather more of legitimate authority, in his own. But we felt it our duty to condemn the irregularity of the latter case, as a bad precedent in our church, in "Reasons and Principles," p. 17; and we have felt under the same and even a heavier obligation to protest against the irregularity of the former in this place.

---

* We have said that we held the place of a delegate from Boston in this convention; but by this we mean, that the money which would have defrayed the travelling expenses of Mr. Worcester, or some other person, as a delegate to the convention, was given to pay our expenses in travelling for another purpose. For we were then engaged in setting on foot, procuring subscribers for, and printing and publishing, "The New Jerusalem Magazine," for the Boston society.

The last thing which requires notice in the proceedings of the ninth convention is the following minute :

On motion of Mr. Condy, ordered, that the report of a committee of the last convention, which was referred to another "for the purpose of adapting it for publication with the journal," but which was not published, because this committee "had done nothing in the way of preparing it for the press, being unable to agree in the opinion that it was advisable to publish it"— be printed with this journal,

The report here alluded to was the Rev. Holland Weeks's justly celebrated report on the trine, which, as we have seen, first agitated that question in this country, and led to the declaration of the trinal order as the true one for our ministry, by the General Convention. Why the committee of the eighth convention could not agree that it was advisable to publish it, and yet could assume the unwarrantable responsibility of not publishing it against the instructions of the convention that appointed them—we have been utterly unable to divine. We know that this was the theme of much conversation, and the subject of not a little reprehension, in the coteries of members of the church. And we think the above order, introduced by Mr. Condy, implies a sub-censure of the committee of the eighth convention for a neglect of duty. It became our duty to see that Mr. Weeks's report was printed with the journal of the ninth convention. And it is right that we should here relate how much difficulty we met with in discharging that duty. We applied to Dr. Beers, Mr. Carll, Mr. Doughty, Mr. Hayward, Mr. Thomas Worcester, Judge Young, and every member of the former committee, and every other person, in whose hands we supposed the report as rendered to the convention might be: but in vain. It was no where forthcoming. That and Daniel Roe's Letter seemed both to have been consigned to the tomb of the Capulets. There seemed to be a deliberate design somewhere to suppress both. Why this should be so, we have never been able even to conjecture a reason—unless somebody, we know not who— somewhere, we know not where—dreaded the superior influence in the church which this able report might win for its author, or the dimming of dull lights by this far brighter one. Could it have been that the members, or some of the members, of the committee appointed to publish it, did not approve the doctrine of the trine in the ministry as set forth in it? Some things make this probable. The Rev. Dr. Beers recommended to the tenth convention the ordination of Mr. Thomas Worcester into the third grade without his passing through the second; and the Rev. Mr. Carll did not hesitate so to ordain him? Could they have done so, if they had not held loosely to the trinal principle? But discarding conjecture, and coming to fact, we could no where get a copy of the report that it might "be printed with this journal." Disappointed and chagrined, we had concluded to do the best we could under the circumstances, and had set up in type and worked off at the press, two long letters from Judge Young, to the ninth convention, which were supposed to embody the substance of Mr. Weeks's report, and therefore, as we imagined, might supply the place of it. While this was going on, the thought struck us, that, *possibly*, Mr. Weeks might have an original draft of his report, from which he had drawn off a fair copy for the committee of the convention, and from which he might draw off another fair copy for publication with our Journal. Vivid with hope, we instantly stopped the press, sat down, and forthwith wrote, by mail, to Mr. Weeks, then in Henderson, N. Y., not very far from Boston, where the Journal was then in press. In due time a letter came from Mr. Weeks, inclosing a copy of his report, and, in about half a dozen lines, expressing a strong injunction on us to carry its principles out in the church. This report was set up, the sheets containing Judge Young's letters were cancelled, at an expense out of our own pocket of some twenty dollars, to make room for it, and it *was* printed with the Journal of the Ninth General Convention, where, in the Appendix to that Journal, p. 10, it may now be found. But as it *is* not easy to meet with that Journal now,—few of the members of the church having been in the habit of preserving their loose copies of the Journals of Convention,—we are sure that we shall entitle ourselves to the thanks of the church at large by reprinting that report among the documents of our appendix. (See Ap., No. LVII.) Let it, by all means, be read and studied. It is a master piece. For terse style, conclusive argument, withering refutation of error, triumphant defence of truth, and the quality of *multum in parvo*, it has not its superior. We well recollect the effect of this report on our own mind, and attentively observed its effect on the minds of all we met. The force of its argument seemed to us like the blow of a sledge hammer in knocking down an ox—so effectually did it prostrate all opponents and silence all opposition. For years it was the rarest of all rare things to find a single man who had hardihood enough to stand up and openly deny the doctrine of a trine in the ministry. Even those who were previously in decided opposition to the trinal principle altogether, were now found *to hold to a trine in some modified form.* And can it be possible that the *young gentleman*, who wrote the flimsy report to the Fifteenth Annual Meeting of the Western Convention "concerning the ministry and ordinations," ever read this report of the Rev. Holland Weeks? He was *very young* when it was first published; so that he could not have read it then; and we cannot imagine that he has ever read it since, or he certainly would not have made that clerical *faux-pas*, and suffered his unkind friends to *put it in print*, as a permanent record of his weakness! But it seems now that Mr. Weeks, and those of us who were blindly led by him without investigating the subject for ourselves, were all mistaken. For "in regard to the institution of degrees or ranks in the ministry, there is no express authority for it to be found in the doctrines of the church"— " a mere *passing remark* in a *posthumus* work" is *all* that *can* be found to hang " a *mere inference*" upon, for the doctrine of a trine in the ministry! New lights have risen in the church, and by their superior discernment of what Swedenborg truly teaches in his writings are manifesting the ignorance of the old plodders and rectifying their mistakes. Well, ought we not to be thankful, that now the *latter day luminaries* have arisen, there is *so much clear light on all dark subjects*, notwithstanding the *little twinkling lights* of former times have been wholly put out in their superior effulgence! Nevertheless, we hope our younger and wiser brethren will pardon our fatuity,—inasmuch as old age is creeping upon us,—and allow us, like Old Mortality, to raise and set up again this fallen tablet, and retrace and freshen the words of truth which the strong and steady hand of a most intelligent and wise man of old did erst inscribe upon it!

In the tenth convention, held in Boston, in August, 1828, the committee on business say—

They find that several of the brethren are anxious to have some alterations made in the ecclesiastical government. Upon this subject a majority of your committee agree in thinking that nothing need be added to the report made by Dr. Beers to the last convention, and to the resolution of said convention adopted thereon.

The report on business to this convention was made by Mr. Thomas Worcester. And it was—

Voted, That this convention accord in the opinion, expressed, by the committee, in the third clause of their report, respecting ecclesiastical government.

There was no *manifest* disposition for rules, and regulations, and strong government, in Boston just yet. Oh no, the time was not yet come. The central control or influence was not yet sufficiently obtained or secured.

The proceeding in regard to the ordination of Mr. Thomas Worcester is too important to be omitted here.

The following petition, signed by a committee of the Boston Society, was presented by Caleb Reed, Esqr., their delegate.

To the General Convention.
The Boston Society of the New Jerusalem Church request of the Convention, that Mr. Thomas Worcester, who has officiated as their pastor-elect for more than seven years, may be ordained as pastor over said society, at the present convention.

Whereupon the following resolutions were unanimously adopted:
Resolved, That the above request of the Boston Society be complied with.
Resolved, as the sense of this convention, That the resolution of the last convention respecting the ordination of Mr. Worcester, was of temporary application, intended to apply to a case that might arise during the recess of the convention, and has become inoperative and null, since that body has again assembled.
Resolved, That the Rev. Mr. Carll, president of this convention, and the only person possessing ordaining powers now present, be authorized to ordain Mr. Thomas Worcester as pastor of the Boston Society, and into the class of ordaining ministers.

When we first read this proceeding of the tenth convention, it appeared so much in the light of a manœuvre of party men in a political meeting to effect their purposes, that we felt supreme disgust. Can it be possible that these were the doings of the New Jerusalem which was to come down from God out of heaven! And now, does any candid man wonder that we should cease to feel *any respect* for *that* convention?

It is believed that no society from the south but that of New York was represented in the tenth convention. Mr. Carll was there, but only a small portion of the first Philadelphia church, which was now broken up, had rallied around him; and, therefore, he represented next to nothing in this quarter. Mr. Beynroth from the West happened to be there; but was in no respect a delegate. In all, the southern members in that convention did not exceed five! There are reports from four *delegates* of societies in New England; which make it probable that they with the Boston society were the only ones actually represented in it. According to the reasoning of certain persons about the Middle and Western Conventions more recently, this, then, was nothing more than a *Boston Convention.* So that, after all, it was not the *General* but the *Boston* Convention which violated the trinal principle in Mr. Worcester's case. It is said, however, that "the convention was very numerously attended by receivers, both gentlemen and ladies, from all parts of New England." This, therefore, was a New England convention, and nothing more. It was, unquestionably, an *eastern,* and not a *general,* convention. From its extreme northern place of assembling, it could not, at that time, be otherwise. Hence our eastern brethren *had all the power in their hands,* and *did every thing in their own way.* What was there to make this convention identical with the preceding one but the *name?* It is said that all the particles of a human body pass out and are replaced by others in the course of seven years. But all the particles in the General Convention, except one, had passed out of it to be replaced by others in *one year!* In fact, it would not more puzzle the believer in the resurrection of the material body to prove the identity of the risen body with the one that was laid in the grave by showing that it had the same particles, than it would puzzle one who should believe that the Tenth and Ninth General Conventions were the same body, to prove *their* identity by showing them to have had the same component parts! Mr. Carll was the only member of the ninth who was present in the tenth convention; and facts have proved that he was only a southern cypher used to give value to New England digits by being placed on the right side of them. That office he has not failed to serve in other parts, and in later years.

It is not pleasant for us to dwell on this proceeding. If it had not led to violations of order in recent years, we should not have noticed it again. It is enough for us to observe that a more concentrate insult could not have been cast on the ninth convention than is couched in the second of the above resolutions. Who believes that the action of that body—in which *four* of the *six* ordaining ministers of the church were present—in respect to the ordination of Mr. Worcester into the second grade of the ministry, "was of *temporary* application," "*intended* to apply to a case that *might* arise during the recess of the convention"? Did any member of the ninth convention for an instant suppose, that its first action under the law of trinal order then for the first time declared in this country, would not be as lasting as time and co-extensive with the whole church? Did any one dream that the next or tenth convention would have the temerity or impertinence to set its solemn acts thus frivolously and insultingly aside? And how *could* that action "become *inoperative* and *null*" merely by that body's *having again assembled?* Did this talking *ecclesiastical nonsense* prove that *that same body* had assembled again?

In fine, it was not modest in our Boston brethren to act with this high hand against the Ninth General Convention. It would have been more becoming if they had humbly and meekly received the proffered ordination into the second grade, given as a rainbow on a retiring cloud of dissension, in token of approaching sunshine, calm and good fellow-feeling. In short, it would have been more modest, if they had received ordination for Mr. Worcester into the *second* grade from what was more truly the *General* Convention, instead of ordaining him themselves, as the *Boston* Convention, into the *third.* They would thereby have shown a most commendable respect for the then established order of the church—a respect made more marked and praiseworthy, by their voluntary yielding (of what was due to the acknowledged high qualifications of their pastor for any the highest office in the church) to the sanctity of the rule of order when established. There was no need of hurry. The cause of the church in New England would not have suffered by Mr. Worcester's being without ordaining powers for one year more. How long was it in fact before he did ordain any minister in New England? Did not years elapse before he did? And has not this fact proved that there was no need of ordaining him into the highest grade just then? Would it not then have been judicious to have ordained him into the second grade, by the irregularity of *one* ordaining minister, instead of *two?* Nay, would it not have been better even to have waited another year for ordination, out of respect to this law of order too? But this was not necessary. All that modesty and generous self-denial asked, was, to wait another year or two for regular ordination into the *third* grade; which, received from three ordaining ministers in the south, would not only have brought with it the representation of the translation of plenary powers, but would have afforded another opportunity for his southern brethren to have mingled their waters of life with his in peace. And above all, it would have established confidence in our eastern brethren here, instead of distrust. For we can assure them that from this very moment, a distrust *was* engendered by their action in this tenth convention; and a firm conviction sprung from it into the minds of many, that, *if they had power,* THEY WOULD ABUSE IT! Now we admit that it was not a good thing to have this distrust engendered, or this conviction induced; but we appeal to the calm decision of every candid mind, if this proceeding, upon which we are now animadverting, was not just such a one as could produce no other results. It would have been better, therefore, if our Boston brethren had not taken this course. It would have been far better if they had helped, at every personal sacrifice, to carry out the order which had been established instead of seeming to violate it. In short, it would have been far, far better if they had seemed to *receive* power instead of *taking* it. But Divine Providence knew

14

what was best. There was freedom needed to act out their real internal principles, that they themselves might see them in their true
nature and get rid of them, and that the church at large might see
and resist them for the general good. That freedom began now to
be given. And instantly that the outward pressure of opposition was
taken off, the force of the internal principles bounded. The avidity
with which the *reins* were clutched, only showed the strong disposition to *drive*. And under the guise of great moderation at first,
there gradually arose that disposition to vest supreme ecclesiastical
power in a few head officers, instead of the whole body of the church,
which we have regarded as a tendency to episcopacy; and with this
those tendencies to severe discipline, strong government and arbitrary
authority in the church, which have made so much of resistance necessary for their correction in recent times.

In the Tenth General Convention, "the following, offered by Mr.
Worcester, was unanimously adopted:"

Resolved, That the president of this convention be authorized to confer
upon the Rev. Adam Hurdus, of Cincinnati, by a written certificate, the
power of licensing and ordaining to the ministry.

This was the third violation or disregard of true order by the tenth
convention. The first was, the ordaining Mr. Worcester into the
third grade without his previous ordination into the second as a preparatory step. It matters not that Mr. Worcester might have been
fully prepared for the third grade without passing through the second;
the law of order required, *for its own sake*, a sanction in his case
above all others; and there was no exigency of the church in New
England which imperatively required the convention to violate the
law in its very first action under it there. The second was, the
ordaining him into the third grade by only *one* ordaining minister.
This may seem to some a trifling formality; but wise men do not
regard the *representative* forms in the solemn inauguration of the
ministry of a spiritual church as trifles; and there was no such *great
necessity* as made the dispensing with the forms of solemn inauguration in Mr. Worcester's case imperative. Besides, it was a violation
of a formal law of the Eighth General Convention; as any one may
see, by consulting its Journal, p. 3, n. 16. It cannot be that induction
into the third grade with full powers, made a less number of officiating
ordaining ministers in order. Nay, by having only one in this case,
the law of order was more violated. And the third was, this raising
of Mr. Hurdus into the third grade by a mere *written certificate*,
without any of the formalities of solemn inauguration at all. There
was no need for this too; as Mr. Hurdus could have come to the
convention for formal induction into this high office by the imposition
of hands or some other holy representative ceremony. The order of
our church, as established by the organic change which took place in
the Eighth General Convention, above referred to, required "that a
candidate for ordination should present himself before the convention
of ministers and delegates, . . . and *there* receive ordination."
This order was not now repealed; and in the twelfth convention it

was made to apply to the case of Dr. Atlee, whose ordination into the second grade was then asked for by the Cincinnati society. There is no reason why it should not have applied now to the case of Mr. Hurdus, if the third grade is separated from the second by a discrete degree, so as to need a distinct ordination for induction into it. And we see that Mr. Hurdus could have attended; because he in fact *did* attend the next convention, although it also was held in Boston. But it was now the time for the Bostonians to be liberal and easy in their views of order. And the Cincinnatians had been so severely scored by Mr. Weeks's report, that they needed this *concession* to *their* free and easy views, as a salve to heal their wounds. And Mr. Worcester, probably, did not hold now so strongly to the principle of trinal order in the ministry as he did subsequently, when he found it might be used as an engine in propagating his peculiar notions, or effecting his particular ends, in the church. Or if he did hold to the trine of discrete grades as his early proceedings in the Boston society have indicated, and as a proceeding of his in the Twelfth General Convention, Jour. p. 4, n. 21, would indicate, then was he more culpable in suffering that order to be violated in his own case.

From this period, *Boston* became the *core* of the visible new church in this country. For a time, men from this quarter were designedly put forward, that measures might seem to originate here; but these men were more characterized by *good* than by *truth*—more by weak subserviency to the views of stronger minds, than by strong intellects of their own and vigorous powers of independent thought. Such men as had this latter cast of character, have been looked at only out of the *corners of the eyes* of our eastern leaders. And whenever those who had formerly been under the lead and influence of eastern men in the General Convention—as the Rev. C. J. Doughty, for instance,—withdrew and thought and acted for themselves against that body or its leaders, they were proscribed and put down, as he most cruelly was. As for those more fractious animals who sooner broke away from their traces, or would not yield to their sway at all, a mark has been put upon them; and where the outbreaking of human infirmity has not manifested sufficient error and wrong doing to blast their reputation, destroy their influence, and cast them in the shade, secret detraction has not been wanting to do the work. Nor have pliant instruments for the doing of this work been *scarce* even here in the middle states. If there were none ready made out of southern stuff, they were manufactured and sent out from the north. How these tools have been worked with here and in the West, will be shown in another place. Now we beseech every dispassionate scrutinizer of past events in our church in this country, to divest himself of all prejudice, and of all foreign influence, so as to observe with a calm eye, and judge with a candid mind, what transpires in the Tenth and subsequent General Conventions. As to episcopal tendencies, strong rules of order, stringent discipline and arbitrary government, their most obvious beginning may be dated from this tenth convention in Boston in 1828. Not that any measures having such tendencies appear on the Journal of this convention; but now the great magician seats himself in the centre of his machinery, and though all unseen and unsuspected, pulls those wires that effect all those ecclesiastical slights-of-hand by which our visible church is BROUGHT *into order*. The more immediate machinery is the *Boston society*. The more remote, is the leading influence of *New England men*, either travelling through the mass of receivers of our doctrines and calling on them as they go along, or residing in official station or business occupation in distant places, or acting in or on associations either wholly composed of or wholly controlled by them. The former works within the latter, as a small wheel within larger.

An eastern apologist, in rebutting the charge of tendencies to an episcopal form of government induced upon the whole church by our eastern brethren, and in showing how great was the difference between what episcopacy *does not do* and our eastern brethren *have done*, says— " She does *not form societies*, in the new-church sense of the Word. . . . . . She does not expect any particular congregation to develope particular characteristics, or cultivate such a habit of understanding and living her doctrines, as shall entitle them *in any sense* to be considered a *church* as *distinct* from the *general body*." Perhaps not. But episcopacy, and papacy before her, have acted upon the same principle, or done the same thing in another way. For episcopacy or papacy has made the HEAD CLERGY "a church as *distinct* from the *general body*"—has vested in *them* supreme authority—has constituted *them* the authoritative expounders of the Word, [and teacher of the church's doctrine, so that their decision in council is final as to what the Word teaches, and as to how it is to be "*understood* and obeyed" by the laity or brethren of the church in all its general, particular and singular forms—has, in short, made *them* the *sole devisers* of the church's law and order. Episcopacy and papacy *have done this;* and *our eastern brethren have done it too!* And although it is conceded that the whole church *may* do this *by* all its clergy as a complex organ, as the whole body operates by its particular members, yet it was not the order of the apostolic church,— as any one may see who studies the Acts of the Apostles,—nor is it the order of the new and true christian church, to make the *head clergy* DISTINCT FROM the general body of the church, so as to place them *in the pastoral relation to it of a husband to his wife*, instead of *setting them* IN *the church as head* MEMBERS *or* SERVANTS *of it.* This our eastern brethren *have done*, in developing the *particular characteristics* of THE *particular congregation* called the Boston Society of the New Jerusalem. And papacy *has done this too*—in principle, if not in precisely the same way. The conjugial theory was, when first broached, vaunted as "a *new* principle"—"lately started" by "several of the most intelligent and influential members of our [the Boston] society." But in reference to this the saying of the Preacher of old may be applied, " Is there any thing whereof it may be said, See, this is new ? It hath been already of old time, which was before us." (Eccles. i. 10.) So the principle of a conjugial pastoral relation between the priest and the church is "no new thing under the sun." It is as old as the love of dominion from the love of self. And in our visible body of the new church in this country it was begotten of the *desire* to *rule*, by the *pride* of *intellect.* This is its pedigree in our country, which we have honestly and faithfully traced in another place.* But it is a child of papacy too. It is also a principle of the catholic church. For the plea for celibacy in the priest of that church is—The pope is in the Lord's place; and the priest "is a representative† of the Lord." The Lord was not married: the church was his bride and wife. Therefore, the priest must not marry; for the church is his wife. And in the natural degree, the husband is the *lord* and *rules* his wife: the wife is all *obedience.* The Indian makes his wife a beast of burden, and flogs her if she disobeys him. Hence that the priest may rule the church, the love of dominion generates a *distinction* between the apostles, pastors and teachers of the church and the church itself. They are taken *out* of the church, *in* which the Lord had set them; and instead of *members* of *her, by* which she is to act as her instruments, as a mother by her children, or a mistress by her servants, they are constituted a church distinct from her, and placed between her and the Lord as a *marital medium,* through whom the Lord is to form the church in her. Further, the head ministers, as the apostles, are separated from the clergy of the two lower grades—which "trine constitutes *one* thing," (Cor. 17)—and to them alone is confided forming and presiding powers. Thus is the true doctrine of the priest being a *representative* of the Lord, and so a *medium* of the illustration and instruction of his holy spirit, perverted and falsified by a desire to rule. So also is the grand truth of the Lord's being the bridegroom and husband of his church falsified, and its good adulterated. And in like manner is the true doctrine of a trine of grades in the ministry perverted, when the same desire of rule takes hold of it as a means of effecting its end. How this was done by our eastern brethren, will now very soon appear. At first, their desire to rule, or *to bring the whole church in this country* INTO TRUE ORDER *through the* BOSTON SOCIETY, had a form of innocence and harmlessness, like the young of savage animals. But it only needed to grow up, to show its ferocious propensities. All that is wanting is complete power in entire control of the whole church, to exercise their discipline upon unruly abnegators of their sway. And even now, when the errors of our brethren have been laid bare, and they themselves opposed in their efforts to get dominion over the whole church, observe the relentless severity with which they pursue to official destruction, any one who has been instrumental in impeding their progress, or causing them to meet with a temporary fall. In the very spirit of the Old Roman Form of the Love of Dominion, their motto is—*Carthago delenda est!*

Yes, "episcopacy does not *form societies* in the" *Boston* "newchurch sense of the word," "to develope *particular characteristics,* or *cultivate* the *habit* of *understanding* and living her doctrines," in a *particular* way, so as "to see *particular* truths in a *common* light

---

* See Newchurchman, Vol. I., pp. 489—521; and Extra I. *passim.*

† This is true; but that it affords no foundation for the theory of a conjugial pastoral relation, see Newchurchman, Vol. I., p. 498.

and to *do them as a body;*" or make this "the WORKING POINT of
their endeavors for a long time" in the general conventions of the
church. Nor did the visible new church ever dream of doing this
before it was thought of in Boston. And it is very important that
the whole church should now see what was the original drift, and
is the present operation, of this GREAT EFFORT to *form societies*, as
a *working point* in the general conventions of our church in this
country. In our solemn and firm conviction that drift and this operation was and is, *to* RULE *the* WHOLE CHURCH *by the* BOSTON SOCIETY!
And wo to the liberty, the integrity, the spirituality and the permanent prosperity of our visible church, if she does not now see and
forfend this!

Men, and especially religious men, and more especially young religious men, are often under the influence of sinister ends unconsciously
to themselves. And when, in such cases, they distinctly propose to
themselves their end, it always comes up in some form of *apparent
good* to themselves or others. In like manner, when they cast about
for means to attain their end, they always lay hold of either *real* or
apparent truths. Even the rogue feigns honesty of purpose, and
cheats by fair pretences. Saul thought he was doing God service,
when he persecuted the Christians. And the originators of all
heresies in the church have been remarkable for their *reputation* for
goodness, or piety, or zeal for the church's interests. Hence the lust
of dominion in seeking to *rule*, always professes to *serve* the church.
And the most arrogant of popes have been those who have risen from
the lowest stations and have worn their high and blushing honors
with most of seeming humility. Let it be especially observed, that
the desire to rule avails itself of *true* principles or *self-evident* postulates as the means of effecting its end. For by these it can most
effectually influence, control, or bring into its measures, the simply
good, who are the subjects of rule. We say that this end is often
proposed by even religious men unconsciously to themselves. And
all men, especially young men, on coming into the new church, or
on first embracing her doctrines, and seeking to propagate them, before
they themselves are reformed or regenerated by them, *must*, more or
less, be actuated by the ends or principles of the natural man. And
the only way in which they or the church can be convinced that
such is the fact, is by seeing the quality of the seed and its tree in
its fruit.

Now it has been seen that the great working point of our eastern
brethren in the general bodies of our church in this country had confessedly been "for a long time," to "*form societies* in the *new-church
sense* of the *word*." What is this *new-church sense?* So to form
societies as "to develope *particular characteristics* or *cultivate* the
habit of *understanding* and *living* the church's doctrines" in such a
way as to form a society which is "to be considered a church *distinct*
from the *general body*." The object is to make the society a church
distinct FROM the general church. Mark, every society would be a
particular church distinct from all others *in* the general church,—just
as each member is distinct from every other member in the human

body,—if it were formed as *the Lord forms societies*, that is, *in* and *through* the general or the universal church. For sustentation is continued creation; and "as there must needs be a general thing, in order that there *may be* any particular thing; and what is particular can, *in no wise exist* and *subsist* without what is general;" (A. C. 4325;) therefore every particular church or society of the church must be created and formed from the Lord *through the general church* and subsist *in* it. But the working point of our eastern brethren has been to form societies DISTINCT FROM the general body, and then by *uniting them* to FORM *a* GENERAL *body*, so that the general body may exist and subsist from this working point. Hence a whole chapter of a certain work is most industriously devoted to prove the necessity of forming societies as the means of sustaining the General Convention. Now the exceedingly important question here presents itself—Why should the Boston leaders, of our general conventions in their crude and unformed condition, have desired to form societies thus *distinct from* the general body, and to have made this a *working point?* Why, especially, should they have worked hard to make the *Boston society* a church thus distinct? Why, if not for the very same end which papacy and episcopacy had in view in forming the head clergy a church *distinct from* the whole church—to *rule* the general body? The end in papacy and episcopacy is to *preside over* and *rule* the whole church *from* the *head bishop* as the representative of the Lord, *by* a society as a church distinct from the general body. What that society is in the catholic church, we need not say. What it is in the visible new church of this country, *let past and present facts say.*

In all sincerity and candor of honest purpose to see only the truth and apply it to life for the good of all, let us look at this matter full in the face. What was to have been expected from the character of the Bostonians in this respect? They were young men; the leading ones sons of clergymen. They were born in the country and brought up on farms. *The* leading one, we have been informed, once made a horse shoe. But that business did not suit his genius. He was born to be a clergyman; and, *perhaps*, with a desire to rule other clergymen, and the church through them. They received liberal educations. The chief one graduated at Harvard—that alma mater who proudly sits the queen of learning in our country. Studied theology. Embraced the doctrines of the new church from the works of Swedenborg in the Library of Harvard University. Took part in the formation of the Boston society of the New Jerusalem. Both of the brothers led that society successively. The younger began his career with originating "a *new* principle"—the theory of a conjugial pastoral relation. The older, still the leader of the Boston society, embraced that theory as "a deeply rooted sentiment," and "a most soul-searching principle." The same was heard to declare, in substance, at one of the quarterly meetings of a church, "New England is the centre of the New Church, and influx from the spiritual world enters the natural world here." And all had a conceit that they were *celestial* men, who do not eat the flesh of animals—*perceive* truth, and

therefore do not *reason* about it.   Now as a matter of history, what
must have been the principles at work in, the ends proposed by, these
young men, and especially the younger of them, when he became
the leader of the Boston society, and, as such, the presiding influencer
of the General Convention?   What must have been the end and
object of forming societies as the working point of our eastern brethren in the general conventions for a long time?   What the object
of forming the Boston society, so as to develope its *particular characteristic*, and make it as a church *distinct from* the general body?
We do not say or suppose that that object was consciously an improper one in their minds. ` Supposing them sincerely to believe that
New England was the centre of the whole new church, and that
influx from the spiritual world did enter there; what must they
honestly have desired to do, and endeavored to do, in carrying that
belief out into effect?   Must they not have proposed it to themselves
as an end, and must they not have tried to effect it as an end—to form
the church in this whole country from New England as a centre, and
then to guide it, and direct it, and if it went wrong to correct it—to
bring it back to the right path, if it strayed into wrong ones—and thus
to *rule* and *govern* it?   We do not suppose they would think this
wrong, or propose it to themselves, as a bad end.   But would they
not think it right, and propose it to themselves as a good end?   We
pause for a reply.   No one answers, No.   Well, then, the end and
object in taking the lead in the Boston society, and so developing its
particular characteristics as to make it a church distinct from the
general body, was, and is, *to* FORM *the general church through it*, and
then to RULE *the general church by it*.
    This undoubtedly is the end of working by the formation of socie-
ties in the general conventions.   But these men are not any less
natural than any of the rest of us.   They are certainly not yet "those
angels whose province it is to rule evil and infernal spirits."   They
were as much under the influence of natural proprium as any of us,
even when they were imagining themselves celestial.   Now "the
desire to bear rule is somewhat of human proprium different from
what is received of the Lord." (A. C. 1755.)   And although the end
in this case may seem to those who propose it to themselves a good
one, it is, in our estimation, a bad one.   We believe it was born of
the DESIRE *to rule*, impregnated by the pride of intellect, originating
something new in the church.   What that new thing was, which was
to be developed as the *"particular characteristic"* of the Boston
society, may be learned from a member of that society's own account
of it`in the New Jerusalem Magazine, Vol. XI., p. 118.   Here it is
enough to repeat that its direct tendency was to rule the whole church
by the Boston society.   As a means to this end, the true doctrine of
the need of societies in heaven and the church was taken hold of and
falsified.   It was magnified unduly, and distorted by the refraction of
a false medium.   Great efforts were made to *bring* men into societies,
and to get them to *force themselves* to join societies, though "a hundred or a thousand miles off."   Nobody denies the need and importance
of forming societies in the new church.   Some indeed there are who

cannot form societies on earth; and the best of angels do not in heaven. But wherever receivers of the same faith live together or in close vicinity on earth, they should and will come into society here. There is no need to exert great effort to *make* them do it. They must do it in obedience to the laws of influx. The bad as well as the good must do it. Even robbers must associate to plunder. And hell is most distinctly arranged into congregations as well as heaven into societies.

As we shall show presently, when we come to speak of the institution of societies by an ordaining minister as a feature of episcopacy, this effort to form societies flowed from an error of the conjugial theory. It was man's effort to do by the medium of *truth*, what the Lord does by the medium of *good*. And the effect in this case was what it always is, when man lifts up his tool upon God's work—a marring of it. In short, the leaders of the convention, in and by the Boston society, availed themselves of this good thing as they did of every thing else, with a single eye to their end—superior influence, control and government in the church.

When the General Convention was one of receivers and not of delegates, Mr. Thomas Worcester availed himself of that order to effect his purpose in the convention of 1823. His purpose was, to put down and punish Samuel Woodworth, for having assailed his conjugial theory in "The New Jerusalem Missionary." The measure to be voted upon was the recommendation of that work by the General Convention. This measure was introduced by Mr. Hargrove, the president. A large majority of the whole church in these middle states was in favor of it, as the "Recommendation" of it on pp. 20, 21, 22 of the Journal of the Sixth General Convention, will show. But the receivers in Baltimore, characterized by *good affections* more than by *acute intellectual discernments*, were just such subjects as Mr. Worcester's powerful *persuasive sphere* could work upon. He and Mr. Doughty, the only conjugialists in that convention, go around among the Baltimore folks, and electioneer in a way peculiar to the New England people—bring them into the convention "when *a very unimportant* vote* is taken," and when the motion to recommend Mr. Woodworth's Missionary to the church in the United States is made, vote it down by the Baltimore receivers, who outnumber those from other places. The Philadelphians, not expecting such a manœuvre, were surprized and irritated by what they regarded a *Yankee trick*; and, while certain persons were chuckling at the triumph, one of the Philadelphia receivers, Mr. William Schlatter, rose and moved that "at all future conventions of the new church, each society shall be represented by a number of delegates *not exceeding three.*" Mr. Schlatter's object in this was—as he himself told us the next week after that convention—to prevent the eastern people from carrying their measures by such trickery in future. Vain imagination! He

---

* Unimportant to whom? Unimportant it might have been to the subtle minded Mr. Worcester, or the simple minded Baltimoreans: but surely not so to Mr. Woodworth, or the church at large, which had been greatly benefited by his Halcyon Luminary, and might again be by his Missionary.

did not know as we do, how *cute* the eastern folks are in carrying their measures by any forms of organization or procedure which they may find any where in actual existence. They take all such actual existences as capital to trade upon in their political and ecclesiastical operations. But if you will give them the making of the laws and rules of order for you, then, if they do not rule you, it is because their bodies are dead, and their spirits are risen to rule spirits in the other world.

In regard to this organic change, by which the General Convention was made one of delegates from societies instead of one of receivers only, an eastern man says, it " was made in 1823, on the motion of a Philadelphia member. He made it under the influence of the Philadelphia society, and it was sustained by the whole Philadelphia influence. . . . It is true that *the East did not oppose it. I do not say that we were not pleased with it.*" No, indeed! the East *did not* OPPOSE it! Certainly, the East *would* be pleased with it—if their end was what we have shown it to be. For is it not easier for one or a few leading men to influence and control three delegates in a convention, than their thirty, sixty or ninety constituents in a society? And when those few leading men have thirty of those delegates from ten societies under their influence, is it not easier to get them to pass measures by which the whole church shall be governed, than by any direct action upon their constituents in their primary social organizations? What other possible way is there for a few men in Boston or any where else, to direct the opinions, determine the judgments, and influence the actions, of ten or any number of societies scattered throughout our country, than by taking the hand, seeing the eye, or getting the ear, of three of their most intelligent or most influential leading men sent from each of them? If they can succeed in bringing these three men under their influence, will they not most effectually influence, *through them*, the societies to which they belong and which they represent? Is not this the sole ground of action of political parties in their conventions and clubs? What then are our eastern brethren doing else than availing themselves of an enginery to obtain rule over the church by this forming of societies who shall come up into the General Convention by their delegates? Who does not see that these delegates will be used as clay by the Boston potters? And who does not see that any clay which will not work, will be thrown aside? Is it any wonder then that the East did not oppose, but was rather pleased with, the change which was effected in the General Convention by the prevalence of Mr. Schlatter's motion in 1823?

Now look at the facts. If any thing is true, in this matter, it is, that a general body should be organized for the performance of general uses. And they who, in fact, do perform general uses, are the rulers of the general church. What then are the facts in this respect? The Boston society set on foot a periodical for the whole church, on the principle that the editor of it *should be a member of that society.* An effort was made in subsequent years by Mr. Henry A. Worcester, (a most excellently good and true man, humanly speaking,) to make that an organ of the whole church, by having it the property of the

General Convention, and edited by a committee of members of the church from various parts of the whole church. This was referred to a committee, of which a leading member of the Boston society was chairman, who reported a recommendation that *the matter should rest as it was:* and *the convention* LET IT! So the periodical, which should be the organ of the General Convention, is owned, edited and wholly controlled by the Boston society. And what is the consequence? Nothing is or has been admitted into it but what has been digested in the stomach of the Boston society, so that it feeds and fattens the whole church with nothing but Boston fish or Boston flesh. In vain have the editors invoked contributions from other parts of the church. It is not the organ of the general church in fact, and therefore the parts of the general church out of New England, and not under the direct influence of the Boston society, cannot, as such, send blood or nervous energy—nourishment or support—sympathy or co-operation to it. It is the organ of the Boston society, which essays by it to perform this general use for the whole church. Therefore, *quoad hoc,* the general body *is governed by the Boston society.*

While the General Convention was too feeble to perform this use, it might have been confided to the Boston society as a particular church, just as the general use of ordaining ministers was confided to the particular churches of Baltimore, Philadelphia and New York. But when the General Convention was fully organized, it should have been for the performance of just such uses as these; and then the Boston, and every other, particular church should have surrendered the performance of them up to it as the general body. And to retain the performance of these uses, which of right pertain solely to the general government of the church, is nothing less than to *rule* the general church.

Again, the translating, printing and publishing of Swedenborg's theological works, is a general use, which should be performed by a *general,* and not by a *particular,* society of the church in the development of its "particular characteristics." But the works of Swedenborg are translated and printed, in certainly *a most distinctive Boston way,* by the Boston society, or societies composed of its members: and if a printing society is got up in the West, or in the middle states, it is put down by the influence of the Boston society. If books are to be imported from Germany and sold for the encouragement of Dr. Tafel, it is done by a member of the Boston society; who has a pre-emption right, that makes it the duty of every other friend of Dr. Tafel in the United States to import his books only through him as a member of the Boston society. If works are to be imported from England, no one must do it so as to undersell the member of the Boston society, who has undertaken to perform that use for the whole church, and must be supported, as he only can be, by the patronage of the whole church, on the principle that "the laborer is worthy of his hire." If the formularies of worship are to be provided for the general church in a book for that purpose, the Boston society takes the lead and makes one for itself, and this, though covered all over

with the *developed peculiar characteristics* of that society, is forged
and riveted upon the whole church, to the exclusion of hymns, and
other prayers than the Lord's prayer, as the peculiarities of some
other societies, with contempt.   If again the mode of teaching children in sunday or day schools is to be induced upon the whole church,
a resolution is passed in convention requesting *all* the societies to
communicate to the general body an account of their mode of doing
this thing, when it is known that few of them are doing it at all,
and it is supposed that not any of them are doing it perfectly.   Then
the Boston society communicates its mode of doing the thing in what
is deemed *the* right way.   Presently we see all the societies copying
from the Boston mode.   But we do not begin to see the Boston society
deriving any benefit from the suggestions of her sister societies.   So,
when the Boston society has found out the right way of taking the
holy supper in the new church, then, in the same way, the whole
church is to be made to take the communion in *private.*   Next, the
Boston society finds out that *tything* is the true financial principle for
the new church; soon other societies in New England follow the
example, and all try to pull the General Convention along, *nolens
volens,* in the same track.   Lastly, when the Rules of Order have
been devised by the pastor of the Boston society, and are to be put
upon the whole church by the General Convention, the Boston
society makes a communication of its view of what ought to be done,
and the General Convention is made, by hook or by crook, to adopt
its recommendations.   Thus has the Boston society, by making a
distinct form for itself, and then by inducing that form on the
whole church, so as to produce a unity of the whole in that form,
sought to rule the general body.   And by the means of societies
and associated bodies, got up and led by eastern men, or by means
of the resources of eastern men in sustaining ministers and missionaries throughout the whole country, by the instrumentality of the
General Convention as acknowledged by such bodies,' where have
not the *leaders,* in and by the *Boston society,* been seeking to RULE
the whole church in our country?   In short, where, and in what, and
by whom as a leading man every where, does not the Boston society
exercise such an influence or control, as virtually or in fact *to govern
the whole church in the United States even now?*
    But let us proceed to show that all the laws of order and forms of
organization, by which the whole church in this country, has been,
is, and is to be, ruled and governed, have flowed from the Boston
leaders through or by the Boston society from the time when that
society became, as we have said, the core of the General Convention.
These, as indisputable facts, will prove, beyond controversy, as the
fruit proves the quality of the tree, that, in the beginning, there was,
in the leading minds in Boston, from the *desire* to rule, the *fixed purpose* to form and govern the whole church in this country.   To this
conclusion our mind was brought by all of our personal intercourse
with them; but more especially by observing the nature of their
influence, and the influence of their conjugial theory, on our own
mind.   To this conclusion we had come when we warned the general

church against the establishment of *ex cathedra authority* in it, in a communication to the General Convention of 1834. From the same conviction, we opposed the rules of order, and helped to form the Central Convention as the only means of preserving the freedom of the church in these middle states. And now, when the Western Convention, under the lead of the Rev. B. F. Barrett, has become an Ohio Association of the General Convention, and when, by his advice and effort, a New York Association shall next be formed, all that will remain "will be for the Central Convention (consisting of only three or four societies, and these quite small,) to follow their example," according to his kind advice or friendly suggestion; and then a General Conference of all the societies and associated bodies in the United States will be a consummation of what was begun in the Tenth General Convention of Boston in 1828. The seed was then sown which is now whitening to harvest throughout the whole extent of our vast country.

But let Mr. Barrett know, that we do not think his advice or suggestion good. Let him know that there are devout knees humbly bent, and honest hearts most fervently going forth in supplication, to the True, the Great, and the Only, Head of his Church, beseeching him to ward off this great impending peril to our freedom. And most sincerely do they hope, that the little, insignificant Central Convention, may remain firmly fixed on its principles, so that our Great Haman may still find a Mordecai sitting at the King's gate! But if that Collective Mordecai, as a true Jew of the New Jerusalem, shall prove faithless to his people, and, in their destruction, endanger the life of even the Queen, the wife of the King, by bowing his head and neck to the Haman of the present day; there will still be prayers offered up in secret for the true freedom and integrity of our church, and many a single, isolated Daniel, who will not bow down to the golden image which Nebuchadnezzar, the king of Babylon, has set up!

But let us not be misunderstood. We do not deny that there should be a local centre for the visible church in time and space. There must be a heart and lungs to the collective man of the church on earth. But we believe, for reasons before stated in this report, that the centre for the new church in this world is England—Old England. It is there because that country corresponds to the central arrangement of Christians in the spiritual world. Hence, by influx, the new church in fact takes its beginning there, and is propagated, as we have shown, from thence to this country. And sustentation being continued creation—as it has been, so it will be. As the celestial man is not conscious of, and does not reflect upon, his celestial perfections, so the English, who are in fact central, and performing central and universal uses, are not conscious of the fact, do not reflect upon it, *did not talk about it in the beginning*, and have not proposed to themselves contrivances, the development of "particular characteristics," for the ruling of the universal church as an end. That this was done in New England, "was of pride."

Again, we are not opposed to the having of laws and rules of order

in the new church. Nor do we object to the government of the
church by them. But we are decidedly opposed to the *way* in which
our eastern brethren have made, or would make, laws; and above all
to *their* government of the church by them. We believe that their
way is not true, and their government is not good. We believe that
"the security of a large as well as a small society depends on order."
(C. L. 283.) And there can be no order without laws and obedience
to them. And there can be no salutary obedience, if there be not
government according to the laws which are justice. This, we are
certain, is true of ecclesiastical as well as of civil affairs. And,
therefore, we are for governors in things ecclesiastic. The only
thing in controversy between us and our eastern brethren is, the *form*
of government, and the *way* of inducing it on the church. Let them
not, then, say we are striving " to pull down," rather " than to build
up"—merely because we would demolish their peculiar brick-work,
which is put up with untempered mortar. We are opposed to episcopacy in *this country*, because it is not congenial to our clime; and
we are opposed to all sorts of even seeming *arbitrary* government,
because it is repugnant to the spirit of the New Jerusalem.

Before we proceed now to point out the episcopal and arbitrary
tendencies of the measures of our eastern brethren in the General
Convention, one word more about *laws* and the *maker* of them for the
new church. We believe there is a parity between the New and
the Old Jerusalem in this respect. Moses was the lawgiver to the
jewish church. He represented to that church the Word in its internal sense. He as well as his brother Aaron was a priest and teaching
minister. (Ps. xcix. 6, Exod. xviii. 20.) He taught the members of
the jewish church " ordinances and laws"—showed " them the way
wherein they must walk, and the work that they must do." Aaron
and his sons, as the priesthood, were a mouth to Moses, who was slow
of speech. The laws which Moses made were brought to bear upon
the people by doctrine from the letter of the Word. It was the
province and duty of the priesthood to teach this doctrine and so to
·declare the law. Just so in the New Jerusalem, we have Swedenborg, as our divinely appointed lawgiver. He reveals the spiritual
sense of the Word to us from the Lord This is embodied in the
doctrine of the church, which, under immediate illumination from the
Lord, he has drawn from the Word in its letter. In his theological
works, therefore, is all of our *ecclesiastical law* made for us by an
expressly commissioned servant of the Lord our God. Consequently,
we have no need of a council of bishops, as an ecclesiastical legislature, to make laws for the church. Hence we are opposed to such
councils. All we need is a teacher, minister, or apostle of the law—
to study it, expound it, or declare it from the statute books in which
it is enacted. Thus we need a priesthood, as an Aaron or brother of
our Moses, who shall be a mouth to him—a doctrine which shall
involve and convey to our understandings and our reason the principles of the internal sense of the Word as the laws of our wills in
bringing the church within us and without us into order. Such then
is the province of the new-church clergy. It is to *teach* the law

from the Lord, or the Word, by Swedenborg—not to *make* it from
the Word immediately. When they teach the law from those parts
of the Word which Swedenborg has not explained, they must do it
by the principles revealed in those parts which he has explained.
And in all that the clergy thus teach, the church must exercise the
right of private and public, or particular and general, judgment—just
as the Béréans judged of what the apostles taught in the Lord's first
advent. Hence, in the declaration of our ecclesiastical law, by either
the clergy in council, or the delegates of the whole church in convention, there must be nothing like dictation, prescription, or the
arbitrary enforcement of enactments based on any thing like the *ex
cathedra* authority of the ministers of the church. The sole thing is
for the church as a body to be brought into order and governed by
the Lord as her soul. *In* this body, the clergy, in their several
grades, are set by him as members,—superior and inferior indeed,—
but nothing more than *members*, through or by whom the whole body
itself, compact together in the Lord as its head, freely and rationally
comes into the order which *he* immediately by good induces on it—
and is not *brought* into that order by them as a medium of truth
acting as an agent standing *out* of it and *intermediate* between him
and it. Thus we do not hold, in any sense, or in any degree, to a
bishop, as standing *between* the Lord and the church, and presiding
over it, and so *ruling* it from him. We hold, indeed, to the minister's
being a *representative* of the Lord. But, before the Lord's assumption
and glorification of humanity, he had to be represented by an angel
or a man *to* the church. Now, when he is ever present with her in
his humanity, he is to be represented *in* the church. The jewish
church especially was not a true church at all. It was only the
representative of one. There were none of the principles of a true
church *in* it. Therefore the *representative* of the Lord as those principles could not be *in* it; but had to be *to* it, and *over* it. Consequently, what was *over* the church then, cannot be *over* the church
now. Let us now see whether the measures of our eastern brethren
in the General Convention were for or against this order.

A striking fact is now to be observed. Four out of six of the conventions, from the tenth in 1828 to the fifteenth in 1833, were held
in Boston. This was the forming time. The substance was tender
and impressible. The plaster-of-paris was fluid, and ready to take
the mould which should be made for it. In the tenth, the moulding
power was assumed at Boston; and in the very next convention, the
eleventh, the eastern leaders show their hands, with sleeves rolled
up, as ready for the work. In this convention,—held at Boston too,—
certain resolutions were offered by T. Parsons, Esqr., who, we all
know, was only a hand stretched out by an arm and a shoulder behind it. These resolutions proposed "that the convention should
resign to the ORDAINING MINISTERS the *power* of *licensing* and *ordaining* to the *ministry*." It would not have done for the ordaining
ministers to bring forward this proposition themselves; therefore a
layman did it. This is what we regard as the first and chief tendency
to episcopacy in our church in this country; and it confessedly arose

in Boston from Boston men.   This was, in ecclesiastical theory and
practice, putting the soul in the pineal gland.

Now look and see who were the ordaining ministers at that time.
The Rev. Messrs. Hargrove, Carll, Beers, Doughty, Weeks, Roche,
Hurdus and Thomas Worcester.   Here are eight men to whom *all*
power of licensing and ordaining was to be resigned.   Were these
men *remarkable* for their " *learning,* integrity of life, and zeal for the
salvation of souls" above all others in the church at that time?   Were
they appointed to this highest ecclesiastical office, *because* they were
so judged by the general body of the church? · Heaven forbid that
we should wish or seek to disparage these excellent men!   But *Truth*
is the *God* we worship; and we must bow in reverence to him, and
not respect any *persons* of men.   Take Messrs. Weeks, Doughty and
Worcester out, and there was no man there with any pretensions to
learning—even theological erudition.   Mr. Doughty was not a theologian by profession, nor much by study.   And Mr. Doughty was
then wholly under Mr. Worcester's influence.   Mr. Weeks was undoubtedly a sterling man: but he,—as his report on the trine was
sought to be,—was put out of the way.   Though a good, strong, serviceable ship, he was laid up in ordinary at Henderson—a sort of
American Gallilee of the Gentiles.   Mr. Hargrove, though naturally
a strong-minded man, was not an educated one, and was as easily led
as any of us by flattery, or some other appliance to his natural loves;
and was, besides, verging then to superannuation.   Mr. Roche was
as much under Mr. Worcester's influence as Mr. Doughty.   Mr.
Hurdus was too far off in the West to take any active part, and if he
had been near, would have been as easily influenced as any other
man of the eight.   As for the other two, no men could be fitter
subjects for persuasive influence.   What, then, was this proposition
to resign all licensing and ordaining power into the hands of the
ordaining ministers more or less than the giving chief forming and
moulding power in our ministry into the hands of the Rev. Thomas
Worcester of Boston?   We beseech the intelligent members of
our church throughout our land, to look at this matter dispas-
sionately.   Let them not fail to see, that, although this proposition
did not prevail at this time, yet it did, in some measure, prevail afterwards, and that *it in fact led to the Rev. Thomas Worcester's making
the law of ecclesiastical order for the whole visible church in this
country, and now at last to his actually ruling our whole church by that
law through the Boston society !*   Could this power be now seen to
spread itself, as it does, like a green bay tree, overshading our whole
land, if the seed of it had not been sown, or its germ planted, at the
time of which we are now treating?

Well, this is undoubtedly an eastern measure.   The convention
was held in Boston, and there was a great preponderance of eastern ·
men in its composition.   The proposition was brought forward by a
Boston man; and it was referred to a committee of three clergymen
and twelve laymen—*all of whom were New England men, except one!*
The chairman, Dr. Beers, was a New England man.   There were but
two delegates from the south, those of the New York society, Messrs.

Chesterman and Goddard. Of these, Mr. Goddard was a New England man—at one time a strong advocate of the conjugial theory, and then, probably, strongly imbued with it. Mr. Chesterman was an Old England man—a very sensible one, well read in the writings of our church, and never, we believe, a conjugialist. With the exception of him, all the members of this committee, for aught we know, were eastern men. They rendered a report, recommending "that this convention propose for the consideration of the next convention, the propriety of relinquishing to the ministers who possess ordaining powers, the authority hitherto exercised by the convention, in regard to licensing and ordaining teachers and ministers of the New Jerusalem; the *said authority to be exercised in such manner and under such rules as the said ministers may jointly determine.*" This was certainly putting the reins, and the whip too, into the hands of the ordaining ministers! And that it was a radical and total change of that form of ecclesiastical government which had been induced upon the General Convention by the church in Philadelphia and others in this quarter, is manifest on the face of it. But Dr. Beers, who had been familiar with the churches in this quarter from the first, well knew that such episcopacy would not go down here; and, with the prudence which has often characterized his rare goodness, he moved, "that the consideration of the subject be indefinitely postponed;" and his motion was passed. Still Dr. Beers averred that the general principle of this proposition was held to be correct with great unanimity; and that time only was wanting for the New Jerusalem to acquire the maturity of growth in intelligence and wisdom, or charity and faith, in which "*the laity could confide to the ministry that* POWER *of which* THEY *are the* PROPER MEDIUM, and the ministry could exercise that power only under the influence of the new heaven." Thus *the principle was acknowledged to be true;* and there was only a postponement of the time for carrying it out. Hence there was just as much of an establishment of this order by the eleventh convention, as there was of the trinal order by the ninth. In both cases the order was merely *declared* to be true; which is all that a convention ought to do; and from the moment that this was done, it became morally and spiritually binding upon the consciences of its members. Consequently, there was in fact an effort to carry the order out from this instant, although the formal consideration and enactment of it was indefinitely postponed. We here, too, learn the *principle* which ruled in Dr. Beers's mind; and discern, in this, the mainspring of that recent action of his, against which we have protested. We think, then, it is conclusively shown, that *the episcopal tendencies to which we have objected* BEGAN *in New England,* and *were infused into the General Convention from Boston.*

Among the members of the committee above mentioned, was Mr. Hoskins, of Gardiner, Me. We mention him here to bring into view, in this connection, a communication of his to the Twentieth General Convention, in 1838. We antedate the notice of this communication, because it shows the nature of the principle involved in the above proposition as an effect shows its cause. It also enables us, in con-

15

nection with the consideration of the above principle of order and government, to contrast it with that suggested by the Rev. Mr. Hargrove, in his hortatory letter to the General Convention of 1824, which we have hereinbefore quoted.

The Rules of Order were proposed at the nineteenth convention, in 1837. There seemed to have been an expectation that they would have been adopted by that convention as a matter of course. There was certainly a very deliberate purpose to carry them through by the Boston society, whose pastor had made them. But there happened to be, very unexpectedly, in that convention, a messenger from the West, whose unruly and disorganizing spirit felt restive under the bands or chains with which he thought the church was about to be bound or shackled. He objected to the making of a constitution for the whole church by what was only a legislative body under a previous constitution: and which was, in fact, nothing more than the instrument of our society. He held, that the General Convention, as then constituted, could no more make a fundamental law for the whole church, such as these Rules of Order were, than congress could make a constitution for the United States. It was only right for the convention to make rules for its own government as a deliberative body; but here were rules for the regulation of societies of the church, by which the church at large was .to be governed; and involving principles of order and government, which, when carried out, must produce the most radical and important organic changes in the whole body of the church. And it was contended, that such a constitution of the church as these rules involved, ought not to be passed by any thing in the nature of a legislative assemblage, but by a convention called expressly for the purpose, and composed of representatives of the whole church in some fair ratio. It was contended, too, that, when a constitution was made by such a body, it should not be finally passed by it, but be submitted to the members of the church in their primary associations; and that then it should be regarded as the fundamental law of the visible church, and binding on the individual or other members of it, only so far as it was freely and rationally adopted in those primary associations. To pass these Rules of Order now, it was contended, when the West was not at all represented in the General Convention while it was making them, would seem so much like arbitrary prescription and enforcement, that the West could not but resist them. And it was urged upon the Boston leaders of the convention, with all the pathos of the deepest good feeling, not to drive the West off by such a proceeding. In reply it was urged, that the West was, and had been from the first, in a disorderly state—that the General Convention had been striving to *regenerate itself* for years—that now it was about to effect its purpose—that *it had now the power in its own hands*—would exercise that power in making an order for itself to come into—and if the West saw fit to come into it, it might—if not, it might stay out. To this it was rejoined, that the West contained a large number of highly intelligent and worthy members of the church, who ought not to be thus superciliously cast off. Admitting, for argument's sake, that they were, or had been, disorderly, they were undoubtedly good and well-meaning men, whom true charity would desire to keep within the sphere of the church for *their* good. And supposing the General Convention was the church, or fairly represented it, and was now coming into true order for the reformation of the external or visible body of the church, this was the strongest possible reason why the general body should throw the mantle of charity over the remote extremities of the West, that by keeping them warm, and in healthful connection with the body, its life-blood might extend to them and vivify them with its order and efficiency. This argument could not be resisted. A committee, of which the messenger from the West was the chairman, was appointed to consider what should be done with the Rules of Order now submitted. That committee reported, that one thousand copies of these rules should be printed in a separate form, and sent to all of the known receivers of our doctrines in the United States—that then a convention should be called *de novo* to deliberate upon these rules as a constitution for the whole church in this country, and either adopt them, modify them, or make an entirely new constitution—that this convention should be constituted by representatives, in a fair ratio of representation, of all the known receivers in the United States; who should meet at a proper time and at a suitably central place; and when they had elaborated a constitution it should be submitted, as the constitution of the United States was, to the receivers in their primary assemblies, for adoption or rejection; and should only be deemed the fundamental law of the whole church, so far as it was freely and rationally adopted by a previously designated and fair majority of the whole. Such was, in substance, the report of the committee to whom the rules of order were referred in the nineteenth convention. And we now confidently appeal to the good sense of the whole church to decide, whether, if this course had been pursued, depending on the Lord in faith and charity, there would not have been such an harmonious organization of the whole church in this country as would have led to its most consentaneous and efficient co-operation in doing heavenly uses on earth? And was it generous, was it just, was it faithful, was it charitable, to strive to brand the suggester and advocate of this course as a fractious and unruly disorganizer in the church? The Lord and heaven know and will testify how ardently he has desired only the church's true peace and prosperity. And now he declares his solemn conviction, that this peace and prosperity never can be secured until the course recommended in the Nineteenth General Convention is taken. For there are those who never will be bound by laws enacted by a body in which their own understandings have not been fairly represented,[*] and which have not received the free adoption of their own rational volitions.

Our doctrine is, that the whole church in this country is a *congre-*

[*] "Nothing can be appropriated to any one which is not acknowledged from his own proper intuition, that is, which he does not know, from himself, not from another, to be so." (A. C. 5376) How then can an individual member, or a society of the church, receive and obey rules of order which are prescribed by the ordaining ministers, and are not the exponents of his or their own understanding of truth.

gate man—that into this man the Lord flows as *his whole body*, so that he does not act upon any part separately from the rest, and through that part upon the whole, (according to the conjugial theory,) but that he acts upon all together, and that then the whole body from him as its soul, acts *by* its parts, as its members, according to their several uses and functions.   Hence, in our view, there must be a common will, a common affection, a common understanding, a common thought, a common perception, a common sense and a common action.   And we believe that each of these common things is full and perfect in the degree that it contains within it the particular and singular things that are homogeneous to it, in the particular churches, and the singular members, of the general church.   For instance, the common will or understanding of the church is full and perfect only in the degree that it is a congregate of the particular and singular wills and understandings of the whole church, which must be perceived or seen to enter into it and form it *distinctly* one.   There must be no blending, confounding, or obscuring, of the particular and singular elements; or there would be that *consolidation* to which we so strenuously objected on a former occasion.   Nor ought there to be any sort of substitutes of a particular or singular will or understanding for the common one ; for then there would be that prescription, arbitrary enactment, or tyrannical enforcement, which has in fact flowed from the effort to make rules of order for the whole church, and then to govern the whole church by them through *the Boston society*—to which *we have ever been opposed,* and which *we will never cease to resist,* SO HELP US THE LORD!   Consequently, we believe that the whole body of the church has a *common voice ;* and as this is the speech that flows from the influx of its divine soul into it and action upon its parts "all together," therefore we believe that there is truth in the adage—*vox populi,*[*] *vox Dei*.   The great thing is to *ascertain* this voice ; and all the evil, all the tyranny and oppression, which has ever existed in either civil or ecclesiastical governments, has resulted from the substitution, in some way or other, of the *voice of man* for this *voice of God*.   And here, we take it, lies the whole difference between our principle of church government, as displayed in Mr. Hargrove's plan of district conventions *echoing* the voice of God from *ultimates,* where alone he speaks *audibly,* to the General Convention as a central organ of the whole body; and our eastern brethren's principle of church government as displayed in Mr. Hoskins's letter to the twentieth convention as above quoted—in which societies of the church are to have no particular voice, but to turn their eyes reverentially upwards to the General Convention, with her committees—"as the eyes of a maiden unto the hands of her mistress," and implicitly receive and obey her *nod*.

---

[*] By *the people* we mean *the whole body* of a nation, comprising all classes as a whole human body comprises its members.   The idea of democratic politicians, that the people are the poor as distinguished from the rich, or the working men as distinguished from the gentry, or the commonalty as distinguished from the aristocracy, or the ὶς πολλοὶ as distinguished from the select few, or any general and comprehensive part of the body politic as distinguished from any other comprehensive part of it, is not our principle. We do not hold to democracy in this sense—to the *power* of *this* people.

The report above mentioned was set aside by the Boston leaders. The chairman of the committee who made it, met two of them on the corner of two streets hard by the temple where the convention had been assembled, but was now adjourned to meet again next morning to receive the report of its committee. Those two leaders were the secretary of the convention and the editor of the New Jerusalem Magazine. The messenger from the West, now chairman of the committee to report what disposition was to be made of the ordaining ministers' report on the rules of order, accosted them, repeated to them his appeal to the convention for a kind consideration of the many excellent members of the church in the West, and implored them not to throw them off. The secretary, who is a truly excellent and kind-hearted man, seemed disposed to regard with favor the proposition for a convention *de novo*, in which the West might be fairly represented in making the fundamental law; and even the editor, who is a man of much sterner and harder stuff, shaped by the more angular and sharper forms of bare intellect, condescended to say, " We know it is the duty of the *strong* to defer to the *weak*;" and parted saying, " We will see what can be done." These two sentences are impressed so indelibly on our memory—warm, heated and softened as were the substances of our mind by the strong emotions of the ardent affections which were then active in it—that they can never be forgotten. We are sure, therefore, that they are now in substance stated correctly. Well, the next morning the committee made its report, in the form of resolutions embodying the propositions above stated. This report was then laid on the table; and in the afternoon session was taken up and suddenly dispatched as the last business before the convention. When the resolutions of this report were read again, the editor immediately got up and offered a series of resolutions as a substitute for them. No one said a word. The messenger from the West felt that his saying any thing would be utterly useless. He felt how entirely alone he had been in the debate of the previous day. His spirit knew that it had not a single hand to hold it up, or a single heart to cheer it, in that convention! All was seen and felt to be completely under the control of the Boston leaders. The way in which poor Mr. Carll was put down—may we not say *knocked* down—by the editor, when he had essayed to warn the eastern people against their efforts to induce episcopacy by making "*bishops*" in the new church, was a great caution. The Western messenger, therefore, took warning and held his peace. And the western measure fell like lead, and the eastern measure went up like a downy feather, without a word being said in favor of the one or against the other. There seemed a temporary surprise that the animated debate of the previous day was not renewed now. But it was the afternoon session of Saturday, the last day of the convention, when lagging business was to be spurred on in haste. And it was deemed utterly useless, besides, to contend any longer against an almost unanimous sphere of favor for whatever was done by the Boston society and proposed by Boston men. All the action of that convention was seen to be nothing more than the fluttering of a charmed bird. The Boston

leaders had had a whole night to sleep on it, with a whole half day
to ascertain *how much* they thought the *strong* ought to defer to the
weak in this case. All the deference they could make was to postpone the adoption of the Rules of Order for one year. The whole
matter was dispatched by the following—

Resolved, That the Report rendered yesterday by the committee of Ordaining Ministers be recommitted to the same committee, with instructions to
report to the next convention; and that said Report be printed with the
Journal.

The Rev. Thomas Worcester was sent as a messenger to the Western Convention to feel the pulse of the Great West, and prescribe for
its diseases. And the General Convention took care to provide, that, if
its next meeting in June, 1838, should occur too soon for Mr. Worcester to be present in it on his return, said meeting should be put off
to a later time. For how could the body act in coming into its order
when its head was off? Mr. Worcester found that episcopacy would
not go down in the West. No sort of gilding could get them to
swallow the pill there. And he, in conjunction with Mr. Doughty,
then entirely his subject spirit, with some others perhaps, affected so
to modify the Rules of Order, by striking out the name of *bishops*,
and so forth, as to expunge their episcopal *form* without touching their
episcopal *essence.*

Thus we see that the Boston leaders were *manifestly* inducing an
episcopal form of government upon the whole church in this country,
by the Rules of Order, which their head man had devised, and they
were trying to pass in the Nineteenth General Convention. For if
the episcopal form had not been in those rules when first submitted
by the committee of ordaining ministers in the convention of 1837,
how could it have been expunged by that committee when they submitted them again to the convention of 1838? And hence, when
we endeavored to prevent this by our resolutions for a convention *de
novo*, the instincts of the ruling love of the Boston leaders at once
perceived, that the passage of those resolutions would be death to
their plan of forming and governing the whole church by the Boston
society. For it would take out of their hands the instrument of
the General Convention as then constituted, which was then wholly
under their control, and has ever since been. It would give the
opponents of their plans—even though a minority—a large field of
opposition, in which their order might be defeated. If one *weak*
man from the West had done so much to impede their progress in
the nineteenth convention, where they had all the power in their
hands, what might not *many strong* men from the West do in entirely
stopping them in a convention where all the parts of the church in
our country should be fairly represented? It was, therefore, conced-
ing too much to the *weak* by the *strong*, to suffer those resolutions to
pass. And see—mark it well, brethren of the new church—how
those resolutions were treated. They were not only suffered to fall
in silent death as in apoplectic fit in the convention; but no requiem
was sung to their memory—no notice was taken of them or of their

death—*no record was made of their name, their character or their drift, in the Journal of the Convention.* They were buried in the dark, without even the glare of torch light. And why was it that no notice was taken of them; so that a Boston chronicler of these times, in speaking of the report of the committee that submitted them, could say, "I do not remember, nor does the Journal state, *what their report was*"! Why, we ask, did not the Journal state that? Does any intelligent Newchurchman hesitate *now* to answer why? Goethe, in dying, called for "more light:" but the Boston leaders, lest they or their plans might die, called for "more darkness." In short, it was seen and felt that the plan of a general convention called expressly to form a constitution for the whole church in the United States, and fairly representing all the parts of that whole, would have been death to the plan of forming and ruling the whole church through the Boston society. Therefore, all light in relation to it was to be put out. What was thought to be the congregational, republican, or democratic form of church government, *which comes from hell*, was to be strangled in the new church of this country. Hence the motto was—

"Put out the light, and then—put out the light!"

Therefore our report and its resolutions were like a candle turned up, and extinguished in darkness. The Boston leaders, knowing that they had the power in their hands, were not disposed to part with it; and concluded to act according to the boast made for them in the convention, that they would exercise their power in bringing the General Convention into order—leaving the Western free to come into it or not, as they might choose.

But the Rules of Order were printed with the Journal of the Nineteenth General Convention; and, although nothing was said to that effect in the Journal or its appendix, there was an impression generally spread abroad, that the particular societies of the church would be expected to communicate their views of them to the twentieth convention. Of course no society in the West made any communication on this subject to that body. But several did from the eastern and middle states. Among these was the one from Mr. H. B. Hoskins, in the name of the Gardiner society. And as this is the antipode of Mr. Hargrove's hortatory letter, and sets forth the principles of that episcopacy in the General Convention, to which we have been all along opposed, let us briefly examine it.

The society in Gardiner, Maine, could not send delegates to the convention of 1838; and Mr. Hoskins makes, in its name, a communication, from which we extract the following—

It has been intimated to us, that it would be desirable for every society to express its opinion on the Report of the Ordaining Ministers upon the degrees in the Ministry, presented to the last convention. Did we suppose that the expression of our views upon this subject would in the least enable the convention to attain a more correct perception of it, we should not hesitate, though with distrust of ourselves, to give it. But this mode of getting at principles of order, which have relation to the government of the whole church, seems to us to be improper; and would rather tend to promote confusion in that body, which, we think, alone has jurisdiction upon the subject. We suppose that individual societies hold the same relation to the convention, that the different members do to the whole body; and as no one part can act but from a common influx, so neither, do we suppose, that societies can act in their separate capacities upon matters of order relating to the whole church.

The " Committee on matters of Finance" seem to have fallen into what appears to us to be a like error, in a circular issued by them some time past. They solicit of the societies comprising the convention, *their views* relating to contributions to the convention, when we in fact think they ought to *direct us* to some principles to govern us in the matter. We desire to look *upwards* for instruction, and to get rid of the prevalent notion, that the components of a body possess more power as such, than they do in the aggregate. Until such is the case, *we shall have distrust of the true, efficient mediums of instruction and government,** and be constantly looking upon the perversions, instead of the blessings of every complex form, in which reside the true elements of efficient power and government—thus our eyes will be directed to hell instead of towards heaven.

This document is one of rare value in showing the tendencies to episcopacy in the minds of our eastern brethren. It is evidently written by a well-meaning man, who has not, or does not wish to use, any art in concealing his real sentiments. But it affords a singular instance of how truth is turned upside down as it flows into some minds. We have not time to point out all its fallacies. Observe that the writer was in favor of resigning the convention's power of licensing and ordaining ministers into the hands of the ordaining ministers in 1828. In 1838, ten years afterwards, all that power has, at least virtually, been resigned to them, and to them has been assigned the duty of making the fundamental law, or rules of order, for the government of the whole church. Hence, as the powers of the general body were all vested in the ordaining or head ministers, therefore the particular societies of the church in looking "*upwards*" to "that body which alone has jurisdiction upon the subject" of " principles of order, which have relation to the government of the whole church," were in fact turning their eyes solely to those head ministers. And these were deemed those " true, efficient *mediums* of *instruction* and *government*," to whom it was thought, in Dr. Beers's report to the eleventh convention, "the laity" might, in time, " confide *that power* of which *they* are the *proper medium*." And it was very probably judged that the time was now full come when " the ministry might exercise that power only under the influence of the new heaven, and for the greatest good of the church." Here, then, we see, in Mr. Hoskins's communication ten years afterwards, a commentary on that general principle which was involved in the proposition, made to the eleventh convention, to resign into the hands of the ordaining ministers alone the licensing and ordaining power which had been previously assumed and exercised by the General

---

* We underscore this sentence as a very striking practical application of the conjugial theory in the mind of Mr. Hoskins, and the Gardiner society. There can be no question that this theory thus pervaded the whole of New England at one time. The pastor in the society, and the ordaining ministers in the convention, were " the true and efficient mediums of instruction and *government*." Mark that.

Convention. Mark, that general principle involved this postulate—that the ordaining ministers *alone* were "the true and efficient *mediums* of *instruction* and *government*" to the whole church. All that was needed to carry this principle out, was the confidence of the laity, that the ministry would exercise only under the influence of the new heaven, and therefore without abuse, the power which they might confide to them as the proper mediums of it. Now is not this episcopacy of the rankest sort? And how easy was it for a man of strong persuasive sphere to bring the laity *very soon* to that degree of manufactured confidence, which would render the carrying of this order out in the visible church practicable, long before either the laity or the clergy were so reformed and regenerated by the Lord, as to secure the church from abuse of power by *natural* clergymen in the garb of *spiritual* and *celestial* pretensions? At any rate, is it not clear that the Gardiner society at least was made ripe for the admission of that general principle of order by which its pastor was to govern the whole church by the Boston society? And does it require any very great discernment to see, that the adoption of the Rules of Order, devised by the pastor of that society, which recommend the formation of societies, and then their formation into Associations, each presided over by an ordaining minister, all of whom shall report to said pastor of the Boston society as the president of the General Convention, as well as come up under his influence in that assemblage—where he shall have and exercise the appointing power of all the standing committees, and official boards, throughout the length and breadth of our land—in the exercise of which power he does in fact appoint either New England men, or such as he knows to be wholly under his influence and control—does it require, we say, any very great discernment to see that *the whole new church in these United States is in fact* GOVERNED *by* ONE MAN *through the Boston society?* Thus, by putting the first end and last end together, we have shown the *circle* in which our eastern brethren have moved in seeking to induce an episcopal form of government upon the whole church in our country. The *name* of head bishop, or episcopacy, or prelacy, is nothing—the *thing* is there. And need we imagine that he who likes and wants the thing is any the less pleased with it because he enjoys it under another name? "Would not the rose, with any other name, smell as sweet?"

There are two fallacies in Mr. Hoskins's communication, which we must point out. He says, "that *individual societies* hold the same relation to the *convention* that the different members do to the whole [human] body; and as no part can act but from a common influx, so neither can societies act in their separate capacities upon matters of order relating to the whole church." Here is truth, as we say, turned upside down in Mr. Hoskins's mind. He has the truth as to the order of the human body, in which the particular parts or members act only from a common influx of the Lord through the whole: but he inverts, perverts or falsifies this truth by his application of it: and the fallacy which leads him to the false application, is that common one which ever reigns in the minds of our eastern

brethren, when they put the convention in the place of the whole
church, or the ordaining ministers in the place of the convention.
The fact is, that the General Convention is only the *representative* of
the whole or general church, just as the ordaining ministers are the
representative of the General Convention. The whole body of the
church is alone the Lord's vicar on earth. The General Convention
is the vicar of that body. And the ordaining or head ministers are
the General Convention's vicar. Nothing is clearer from Swedenborg
than that the general church is composed of particular forms or
recipients of charity and faith, which, "howsoever they may be
separated as to place of abode," appear before the Lord and his angels
"as a single man." Nations, too, as well as general churches, are, as
Swedenborg says, made to assume this form so far as it can be effected
in freedom; for it is the very tendency of the divine truth, which
has this form in itself, to produce this form in all those bodies of
men into which it flows and operates. (See A. C. 6637, and 7396.)
" The Lord, also, wheresoever this can be done, so conjoins societies
[on earth as in heaven]; for the very divine truth, which proceeds
from the Lord, introduces that order wheresoever it is received. . . .
Those scattered societies are collected by the Lord, that *they also
may represent one man* as the societies in heaven." Now if this be
so, then " *individual societies* hold the same relation" to this *collective*
or *congregate man* of *societies,* " that the different members do to the
whole body ;" and do not hold that relation " to the *convention,*" as
Mr. Hoskins says. The convention is a body meeting only occasionally in space, and is composed of *delegates* from societies, and not of
societies themselves. If this convention is composed of delegates
from all the societies, which make up the congregate man of societies, in a fair proportion, then these delegates in the convention may
hold the same relation to the whole convention, which the different
members do to the whole human body, and which the particular societies from which they are sent as delegates, do to the congregate social
man which they compose. But to say that the societies themselves,
instead of their delegates, hold that relation to the convention, is a
fallacy which perverts the whole truth in relation to the subject now
before us.

Again, Mr. Hoskins holds that when the General Convention in
this country, as the General Conference does in England, asks societies to send up by their delegates in convention their views on the
" principles of order which have relation to the government of the
whole church," that there is a looking downwards to hell, instead of
upwards to heaven, for the light and voice of truth in these matters.
But surely Mr. Hoskins thinks and speaks here most inconsiderately.
Does not Mr. Hoskins know, that since the Lord assumed and glorified
humanity on earth, he pervades all common forms of that humanity
on earth still; so that he is immediately and fully, infinitely and
omnipotently, present with every particular and singular part of it,
just as the whole soul is as much in any one part of the body as in
the whole of it ? Well, then, the Lord speaks and acts from himself
in intimates by himself in ultimates, in every common form of huma-

nity on earth, just as the soul from the brain speaks by the mouth in the human body. Where then are we to look for the Lord's working and speaking but in the *ultimates* of *humanity*? And are not the particular societies which make up the congregate man, the ultimate members of that man by which its common voice is uttered, or its common sense is felt? Is not the sense of touch in the skin and other ultimates solely, so that the heart, the lungs, the brains, and other internal viscera, have none of that sense? Where then is the General Convention, as a central organ of the whole body of the church, to look for the church's common sense, on any subject of order or of government, but to those *ultimates* in which that sense resides? But Mr. Hoskins says he will not look thus *below;* he will look *up* to the ordaining ministers, and other committees, in convention? Why, we ask, will he not look below, and listen to the voice that comes from thence, *if the* LORD *be there, and from thence utters* HIS VOICE? Even in the conjugial theory—in which the husband is always interior to the wife and is the medium of forming the church in her—still, must not the husband look to the wife as the sole medium of conjugial love to him from the Lord? But when the Lord girded himself with a towel, and, taking a basin of water, washed his disciples' feet, and from his feet spoke to Peter, was Peter looking down to hell when he looked below to the Lord there? And was the Lord's voice from Peter's feet a voice from hell to his hands and his head? "The Lord's divine operation to save men is from first principles through ultimates: . . . . . the ultimates through which the Lord operates, are upon earth, and indeed with men; on this account, in order that the Lord himself might be in ultimates, as he is in first principles, he came into the world and put on the humanity. Every divine operation of the Lord is from his first principles through ultimates—thus from himself in first principles AND *from himself in ultimates.*" (Ap. Rev. 798.) "A spirit hath not flesh and bones as he hath"—he, in his divine natural form and substance, is more ultimate than spirits. His divine humanity, as a sphere of good, not only pervades all men in their collective or individual forms, but goes beyond them, and envelops them as by an atmosphere, which holds their spiritual bodies in consistency; so that "*in* him we live, and move, and have our being." As then the whole church is the Lord's body, which acts from him as its soul; and as he invariably acts and speaks from himself in first principles, and from himself in ultimates; and as this must be true of his body the church, as well as of his divine humanity; therefore *we must look to the* ULTIMATES *of that body*, when we wish to see his operation or hear his voice. It is only in its *reverberation* by the arches of heaven, or by the skies, the atmospheres, or the rocks of the earth, that his voice can be heard. It is as *echoed* from thence, that we can alone hear the *sound* of his spirit. And we can only pity the fallacy of the man, who imagines that he looks to hell, when he thus looks below, and vainly conceits that he turns his eyes "*upwards*" to *heaven*, and the *Lord*, when he looks to *the ordaining ministers*, or any other *committee*, of the *General Convention!*

Observe then, we say, that the ordaining ministers were regarded as "the true and efficient mediums of instruction and *government*" from the Lord to the whole church, in 1828. Observe that how, in 1838, the making of the rules of order, by which the whole church was to be governed, had been assigned to the ordaining ministers, and that one of them in Boston had devised them. Then see that the particular societies, when called upon by the General Convention to express their views of the rules of order which have been thus devised, reply that they have nothing to do or say in respect to matters of order relating to the whole church—that it is the duty of particular societies of the church to look upwards to the committees of the convention to "*direct them* to *principles* to *govern them* in the matter." What then is to be done by the societies but to take the rules of order as devised by one man and obey them as the *directions* of the true and efficient medium of instruction and government to the whole church? Truly, this is episcopal government with a vengeance! What becomes of the delegate and representative system here? If there is a parliament, is it not wholly under the dictation of a Cromwell or a Charles? Suppose these views were applied to civil as well as to ecclesiastical government; are they not as good an argument for the rule of kings as for that of bishops? And as to the fiscal power, which is the sinew of all governments, how does the matter stand? The Gardiner society thinks the convention's committee of finance ought to *direct* the societies to some principles to *govern* them in this matter. They are to look upwards to the finance committee of the General Convention to instruct and govern them in making their pecuniary contributions for the support of the general church. Well, if this is a true principle in ecclesiastical government, it is also in civil. But what is there of the *delegate* and *representative* system here? Is it not plain that, on this principle, the colonies should have looked up to the mother country to direct them how they were to contribute for the support of government; and when the parliament of the mother country assumed the right to tax the colonies without their representation in colonial legislatures for the imposition of those taxes and the appropriation of the proceeds of them in promoting the general interests of the colonies themselves; ought not the colonies to have submitted and obediently paid the parliamentary imposts? And was it right, in this case, to *resist* the tax on tea? For our part, we cannot see but that this conclusion is inevitable from those premises. Therefore we conclude, that the measures of our eastern brethren in the General Conventions have *tended* to the establishment of an *episcopal* form of *government* in our whole church in this country, and thus to the *subversion of that representative system of church government* which *we* think *ought* to obtain in it.

The twelfth convention was held in Philadelphia. At the eleventh, a committee, consisting of the Rev. Messrs. Beers, Carll, Weeks and Stebbins, had been appointed to define "the respective duties of the three orders of the clergy, to report to the next convention." In the duties of this committee, Dr. Beers was not likely to take any part, because he thought the time for action in this matter, was not come yet. To judge from Mr. Weeks's communication to the twelfth convention, it would seem that he had not been consulted on the subject, because he says nothing about it. Mr. Carll was not competent to the task. Mr. Stebbins was left alone to do that or nothing. He, too, felt incompetent, and his report was an apology for doing nothing. It was written during the sitting of the convention. We know when and where he wrote it; and we know that he expresses in it the views of southern members of the church, and not those of the eastern. This was the last time that the churches in this quarter even *went through the motions* of making rules or laws of order for the government of the new church in this country. From this time, this work was taken in hands, begun, continued and finished by our eastern brethren, and especially by the Boston society or its leading members.

In the twelfth convention, the Rev. Thomas Worcester submitted resolutions, requiring a candidate for a license to be twenty-five years of age—to be a member of a society, and to possess, in addition to qualifications for church membership, ability "to teach the doctrines of the church in a clear and intelligible manner:" also, that every candidate for ordination should be thirty years of age—*should have acted under a license for at least one year*, and should be invited by some society to become its pastor. These were excellent rules, and distinctly set forth the principle of passage. through a lower grade as a necessary preparation for induction into a higher. These resolutions were not acted upon by this convention. And this fact shows that the conventions held in the middle states, and composed principally of delegates from societies in this quarter, were not disposed to act in "defining the respective duties of the three orders of the clergy," or to make stringent ecclesiastical laws for the government of the whole church. Therefore the fact that motions were made by Mr. Roche, and others, in this quarter, having episcopal predilections, which seemed to call for laws of order of an episcopal nature or tendency, was no evidence that the First Philadelphia Church, to which he or they did not belong, and of which he was not a leading member, had exerted an influence in bringing about the enactment of such laws in the General Convention. The *acts* of the delegates of that society, the sentiments of its leading members, as expressed in reports written by them, must be taken as the evidence of what its influence was in the conventions. And these we have seen and shown were uniformly and consistently against any such change in the nature of the General Convention, as might make it an *Ecclesiastical Council*, in the usual acceptation of the term, with power to make stringent laws of order or of government, and to govern the church by them when made. On the contrary, we have seen that the subject of subordinate grades in the ministry was first suggested in Boston—that there, too, tendencies to strong discipline and arbitrary government in the church first arose, that from thence the precedent of the licentiateship as the first distinct grade in the ministry first came into the General Convention; and now we show that although a motion for the appointment of a committee to define the respective duties of the several ministers in

the three grades of the ministry was made by Mr. Carll, who had been
the minister of the First Philadelphia Church, yet he made that
motion in a convention which was held in Boston and wholly under
Boston influence, and did not take any active part in doing the duty
assigned to the committee appointed on his motion, but left it in the
hands of Mr. Stebbins, an eastern man, who recommended the doing
of nothing, because the General Convention had not acquired that
fullness of growth which could alone give it the intelligence and
strength needed to do the work properly or efficiently. On the other
hand, the Rev. Thomas Worcester, who was not appointed on that
committee, brings forward resolutions in this twelfth convention,
which were a practical defining, in some degree, of the two lower
grades in the ministry; and which are laid on the table, and not acted
upon by this convention, because they were evidently in the face of
Mr. Stebbins's report, which it was prepared to accept and adopt.
It is therefore clear, that, so far as defining the duties of the ministers
in the trinal order goes, and consequently, so far as respects the carrying of the trinal order out in this way in the General Convention, the
work was thus far chiefly done by our eastern brethren.

But the thing most worthy of observation and remark is a statement
in the communication from the Bath society to the twelfth convention. Five males and five females, having all, except three, been
recently excommunicated from the societies of the old church in that
town, on account of their withdrawal from those bodies—

Signified a desire to be duly organized as a society of the New Jerusalem
Church, in a communication made to the Rev. Thomas Worcester, of Boston, and the society of the New Jerusalem under his ministry; and on the
20th of October Mr. Worcester, accompanied with a delegation from his
society, met the receivers in Bath for that purpose.

After having administered baptism to four of the receivers and one infant,
Mr. Worcester proceeded with the business of the occasion in the manner
noticed in the New Jerusalem Magazine, No. 2 of Vol. III.—after which,
the ten associated brethren and sisters were pronounced "a regularly instituted society of the New Church—as possessing all the rights and privileges of a distinct society, and commended to the fellowship of the other
societies of the New Jerusalem."

In the number of the New Jerusalem Magazine referred to as giving
an account of this formation of a society in Bath, Me., it is said,
"Not having seen any particular account of a *similar transaction*, we
have thought that it might not be uninteresting or useless to detail the
proceedings on this occasion." "Application having been made by
the receivers in Bath, to the Boston society to be present and take
part in the services, that society appointed delegates for the purpose,
who, at the set time, met the receivers at Bath. Then, first, the
application of the receivers in Bath was read by a delegate from the
Boston society, and the proceedings of the Boston society were read
by one of the Bath receivers. Secondly, those from among the candidates who desired to be baptized received that ordinance. Thirdly,
a summary of the doctrines of the New Jerusalem was read, and the
candidates were asked, whether they believed in those doctrines;

whether they wished to live according to them; and whether they now formed themselves into a society for that purpose. And fourthly, when these questions had been answered in the affirmative, *the* DELEGATES *from the* BOSTON SOCIETY ACKNOWLEDGED *them as a* REGULARLY INSTITUTED *society of the new church,—as possessing all the rights and privileges of a distinct society,*—and *commending them to the fellowship of the other societies of the New Jerusalem.*"

This is in fact an *ordination* of societies into the new church. We have ever regarded it as a *peculiarity* of our eastern brethren. There is no question in our minds that it flows directly from the conjugial theory, whether the originator of that theory and the deviser of this order thought so or not. It is the formation of a particular social virgin, who is to become a wife, when a suitable conjugial partner, distinctly formed, in the providence of the Lord, as the truth of her good, is found for her. The ordination of this partner, when found, as her pastor, to watch over her, provide spiritually for her, and form the church in her from the Lord, would " correspond to the marriage ceremony." (See Extra I. p. 37.) And if, for any good reason, this pastor should be subsequently dismissed from her by the powers which ordained him over her, this " dismission would correspond to divorce." We see the society is formed *without* a pastor or minister, acknowledged to be one regularly *instituted*, that is regularly *set* or *placed in* the church, declared to possess all the *rights* and *privileges* of a *distinct society*, and commended to the *fellowship* of *the other societies* of the New Jerusalem. Of course there is a *full* formation of a church society. And this formation, or this institution, is effected by another society, or delegates from it nominally, but really, as the Bath communication asserts, by the Rev. Thomas Worcester,—to whom, in Boston, application had been made by the Bath receivers for this purpose,— " accompanied with a delegation from his society." Of course, the institution is the work of an ordaining minister of the church, and is a function of his ordaining power. Hence we here see the forecast shadow of that substance which was to appear in the Rules of Order, that were devised by Mr. Worcester, as the forming and governing laws of the whole church in this country. It was, then, a form of order conceived in his mind when he became the leader of the Boston society, and through that was seeking to form and govern the whole church in this country. We have supposed that he took the seat of power in the tenth convention, and then began the construction of the machinery around him by which his end was to be effected. His more immediate engine was the Boston society. And with this, we now see him beginning his work, after the tenth and before the eleventh convention. The first piece of work done was this institution of the Bath society, according to those very principles of order which we subsequently see entering into and qualifying the *rules* of that order to which the whole visible church in our country has now at last become subjected. This work of instituting the Bath society must, of course, be reported to the next, or eleventh, convention. Because all the societies of the church represented in that are to be brought into order by this good example. The New Jerusalem

Magazine too,—an organ of the Boston society, as we have seen, established indeed for the use of the whole church, but to be edited by a member of that society, owned and controlled by its members solely, and in fact first edited by the Rev. Thomas Worcester,—was to be an important and efficient lever in this enginery. Hence this first work of instituting the Bath society is heralded to the whole church by that. It has seen *so similar* transaction, and details the proceedings of it as not uninteresting and useless. This is supposed to be the first of the kind, and is published as a precedent for other societies of the church, in their being *brought into order* by a *regular* institution.

But the New Jerusalem Magazine forgot that there had been one *somewhat* similar transaction before. It could not be altogether similar, because the time for carrying out the principles was not yet so fully come. But the same principle was in it; and, therefore, in this respect it was similar. The transaction to which we allude, was the institution of the Boston society, an account of which we have detailed, and in which we have seen the presence of an ordaining minister of the church was needed, asked, received, to do the work. Here, therefore, in the institution of the Boston society, the principle first came into form and into sight. A similar transaction in first forming a society of the new church, in England or in this country, had never, we believe, occurred before. It took its rise with those who originated the theory of a conjugial relation between a pastor and his society. It germinated and sprung up in the same soil, and almost simultaneously with the first sprout of that theory which we saw. We have not the least doubt that it was a sucker from that theory as a bulb or root. And we, therefore, aver, that the existence of this principle in the Rules of Order of the General Convention *now*, is *proof* that the conjugial theory is *still* carried out and existing in the constitution of that body—all the *verbal* renunciations of that theory by the originator of it himself, and all the *official* disclaimers of its existence or operation in the convention, which may have been made by his minions, to the contrary notwithstanding.

This is an *episcopal* tendency in the measures of our eastern brethren to which we decidedly object. If we have ever conformed to it in our capacity of an ordaining minister of the General Convention, we have done so on the principle, that episcopacy is not in itself wrong for a natural church, or the natural man, that this feature is not *essentially* or *fatally* wrong, and "while it is the order, let us abide by it." But even in this case, where our opinion as to the propriety has been asked, we have advised non-conformity—in one case, to serious offence, and the sundering of our official connection with that society. But when a general body was formed, as the Central Convention, and its ecclesiastical order was so developed, that we, as a general minister, could represent it as a general body, we did not go through the formalities of instituting any more societies in connection with this convention.

We say this is a feature of episcopacy. But it is a form of that *peculiar* new-church episcopacy which arose among our eastern brethren, in their efforts to form societies as a "working point," and especially in "developing the particular characteristic" of the Boston society, "as a church *distinct from* the general body," but as an engine to form, rule, and govern it. Now we have seen that it calls for the ordination of a society by an ordaining minister. The society is formed and instituted as such without a minister of its own, so that the society is acknowledged to exist as a component part of the general church, declared to possess *all* the rights and privileges of such, and commended to the fellowship of other societies composing the general body of the church, *while it has no minister.* Consequently, this institution of a society is based on the theory that a church may exist and be formed distinctly from a minister, as the peculiar good of his peculiar truth, so that, when he, as the peculiar truth of that good, as a male, is, in the providence of the Lord, brought to her, as the peculiar good of his truth, as a female, they may be united in one by the marriage ceremony of his ordination over her as her pastor, so that they *two* may become spiritually *one flesh* in the Lord, and so become a church in a more perfect form. Hence the formation or institution of a society of the church in this way, is the work of a minister of *truth.* The society is *brought* into order by a minister of truth as "the *true*, efficient *medium* of *instruction* and *government*" —*directing* a society of the church, receiving it into order, acknowledging it to be in order, and officially declaring, *as by the authority given unto him,* that it has a right and title to the possession of all the privileges of a society of the church. This, in *principle*, is, unquestionably, the institution, formation, or ordering of a church by a *bishop*, who is the Lord's agent, or internuncio, standing between him and his church, and bringing that ̇church into order, or sanctioning its existence as a distinct church, *from* him as a *medium.* This, there-fore, *is* EPISCOPACY!

Now our first objection to the exercise of this episcopal power by an ordaining or head minister in our church is, that said minister has no more power nor right to give to any receivers of the doctrines of the New Jerusalem, either the *formal acknowledgment* that *they are* a society of that church, or the *official declaration* that they *do possess* all the rights and privileges of such—than a certain distinguished personage had to offer the Lord all the kingdoms of this world, if he would fall down and worship him!

Our second and more serious objection to this *order* for the institution of societies is, that it is *devised* by the Rev. Thomas Worcester. He, in making it as a rule ̇of order, is our law *maker;* and he, in giving it to us as a means of our coming into order *regularly*, is our law *giver.* Whereas we have shown that, under the Lord, Swedenborg is the only legitimate law-maker and law-giver for the New Jerusalem. Mr. Worcester does not pretend to show us where this order is taught in the writings of Swedenborg. He does not teach it to us from the Word. He does not show us the type of it in that order of heaven, and of heavenly societies, which is displayed in those revelations from the spiritual world that the Lord has made, in these latter days, for the use of his new church which is to be called the New Jerusalem on earth. Speaking in the name of

16

the ordaining ministers he says, *we* "would *propose* the following mode of instituting societies and *receiving them into the church*"— "they should apply to the *bishop*"—"the *bishop* should visit them" . . . . . "the bishop" should say, "*By the authority committed unto* ME, *I* receive you all as one into the new church. *I pronounce you to be* a regularly instituted society; and *commend* you to the *fellowship of all other* societies of the New Jerusalem"! It is ostensibly the ordaining ministers who *propose* this: but really it is *the* ordaining minister, the Rev. Thomas Worcester, who *proposes* it. He had suggested and acted upon it long before. He had already received the Bath society into the church in this, as the truly orderly and regular way. Thus he had prescriptively *proposed* it to the church in his former usage. And now he does not *say* that Swedenborg teaches it. He does not *say* that the Word teaches it. He does not refer to a passage of the Word or of Swedenborg's writings in which we ourselves may see that it is taught us by the Lord. We have not a single instance given in the revealed order of heaven, by which we might know that the New Jerusalem coming down from God out of heaven, would, by correspondence, come into this order of instituting and receiving societies in the church. There is not a single illustration brought forth from the treasure house of natural knowledge, by which we may see this to be true order in the representatives of heavenly things which this natural universe, as a theatre of the Lord's operations, displays. He only virtually says, *I propose* this order for the adoption of the new church. Therefore we *object* to this order, because it is only *proposed* to us by the *Rev. Thomas Worcester*, in *Boston*, and is not *taught* to us, by *Swedenborg*, from the *Lord* in *heaven*.

Our third and most serious objection to this order for the institution of societies in the new church is, that it is contrary to the Lord's way of forming societies in the church. What we regard as this way, we have already stated in a previous part of this report. We believe the Lord, as a husband, begets formal societies of the church as truth, of Eve, the mother of all living, the essential and universal church as good. The principle of good is the womb of that mother. It is the "womb of the morning," from which the Lord's "people are made willing in the day of his power." They are here conceived from him "in the beauties of his holiness"—formed from his good by his truth. And in this formation of societies of his church, so that they are made visible to men in his order, the minister is set in the society as a member, just as the society is set in the whole visible body of the church as a member. In its incipient state, the body of the society is formed through the minister as a head member, just as the inferior parts of the foetus are formed in the womb. Hence the first christian church was formed by the Lord through the apostles. And, in like manner, we must have now a clergy, a priesthood, as internal members of the body of the church, who shall be formed with that body existing simultaneously around them. So that the notion of forming or instituting a society of the church without a minister, and then procuring a minister for a society so instituted, is as if the Lord were to conceive and bring forth a body in one womb, and a head for it in another, and then, putting this head upon that body, by a sort of marriage, make it a perfect church. But the Lord does not in truth do so. And it is not orderly for men to attempt to do so for him. The Lord is the only Bridegroom and Husband of his invisible church, and the societies of the visible church, are the children which she brings forth from the Lord. They are, in short, the *truth* forming itself in associations of men, from the influx of *good*. In other words, societies of the church on earth are formed by influx from the Lord out of heaven as a principle and sphere of *good*— which, entering into the hearts of men, and being shed abroad there, causes them to *associate themselves together* by the laws of spiritual affinity, which produce the attraction of moral cohesion in all the collective organizations of human beings. Societies of the church on earth are, *in principle*, formed or instituted just as societies of angels are in heaven; and this is precisely the way in which crystalline forms are produced in matter on earth. All that is needed here is, to break up the substance from those amorphous forms which hold *it* chained in prison-houses of its disorder, and then to put it *in some* solvent, where, in quietness, it may be free to obey the laws of spi-. ritual-natural affinity, which, like the Lord, are ever standing at the door and knocking for entrance. Then the parts of this substance begin to obey the laws of their attraction, and freely arrange themselves around and among one another, in the order of their nature; and thus produce those pure, transparent crystalline forms which are the earthly types, or representatives, of the heavenly associations of the New Jerusalem. And that this is the way in which societies of the angels in heaven are formed, may be clearly seen by any one who reads A. C. 6338—"As soon as angels or spirits are assembled together, they are instantly arranged into order *as from themselves*, and thereby constitute a heavenly society, which is an image of heaven." This is what *Swedenborg teaches*. This is what the *Lord proposes*. Here is no archangel commissioned by the Lord, as a "true, efficient *medium* of *instruction* and *government*," from him, and sent to these angels and spirits to bring them into order, or to institute them as societies, and receive them into heaven. The Lord, by the sphere of his love, and the spirit of his wisdom, arranges them in a sort of divine or heavenly crystallization, in which THEY "*as from themselves* are instantly arranged into order, and *thereby* constitute a heavenly society." And this we contend, is the way in which the Lord *constitutes*, and therefore *institutes,—sets in the church,—* societies of men on earth. The truth must make them "free indeed." The truth must separate between the joints and the marrow of all their mere natural associations from natural affections. The truth must reform them. In the doctrine and life of truth as a solvent, they must crystallize from the *good*, the *end* of use to others, that is flowing into them from the Lord out of the spiritual world. Obeying this law of spiritual affinity, they *will*, necessarily, and "*as from themselves*," *come* into social arrangements, and thereby constitute a church society. They will not do this *instantly* as the angels and spirits do, because they crystallize in a denser and more obstructive medium. On first leaving their natural associations, and while in the state of transition from natural to spiritual principles of action, they may, while tacking, stand with their sails flapping in the wind, and for a time "cease the assembling of themselves together, as the manner of some is": but so soon as they have fairly taken their new course, and the wind strikes them fully, they will come into good and true new-church association "as from themselves." And even in doing this, they will have sometimes to struggle with obstacles. They will have often to encounter the resistance of some viscid medium, and to assume irregular shapes from the neighborhood of heterogeneous substances. But, in *principle*, the way is the same. Hence they do not need a minister of truth to ordain, to institute, or to bring them into order from without. There is just as much need of ordaining ministers to institute flocks of birds or herds of cattle. They have one Master—one Great Ordaining Minister—who acts upon them from within. And he ordains them into societies of the church by causing them, acting "in freedom according to reason," to come "as from themselves" into order. Hence there is no need to *preach* this *duty* up to them *so much*. There is no necessity for making the *getting* them to come into societies of the church so much of a "*working* point in the conventions for a long time." The danger is, that they will TRY *too hard—force themselves* to come into societies *too fast—run* and *wrestle* from the *natural* man, *bringing* them by the *efforts* of *others* into *factitious* forms of order, that flow by artificial work and so mechanically from men on earth, instead of fighting against their inbred corruptions, so as to be made free in the *truth* to *come as from themselves*, and therefore with the free and rational efforts of the *spiritual* man, into the celestial- and spiritual-*natural* forms of order, which freely flow from the Lord out of heaven. And the great danger of these running and wrestling efforts is, that the mere natural professing members of our church may run into, or fall entangled in, "the *snare* of the *fowler*"!

There is little in the proceedings of the thirteenth convention, held in New York, in 1831, requiring our notice. The Rev. Mr. Carll's report respecting the grade of the Rev. Mr. Holley, has been noticed before. A committee, of the Rev. Mr. Doughty and two New York lay members, was appointed "to prepare rules and orders for the future government of conventions." These were to be simply rules for the regulation of the conventions in their meetings; and, manifestly, were not expected to be any thing in the nature of the constitution of a general church. Mr. Doughty, the chairman of this committee, was now so completely under the influence of the Boston leaders, and so completely "hoodwinked"—to use his own word—by their principles, that he was virtually an eastern man. Another committee was appointed "to consider the subject of a more perfect organization of the General Convention." The aim of this clearly seems to have been a constitutional change of formation. The chairman of this committee was Caleb Reed, Esqr., a lawyer of Boston, and a Boston leader in the convention. His legal qualifications were undoubtedly those looked to in his appointment. There were associated with him, the Rev. Messrs. Robinson, Roche and Doughty. There can be no question that this committee was eastern, three to one. The committee of business for this convention consisted of the Rev. Messrs. Carll and Thos. Worcester, with Mr. Charles Sellers. By the medium of this committee's report, Mr. Worcester introduces into the General Convention his mode for the "formation of societies and the admission of members." That mode conveys substantially the principles involved in the institution of the Bath society. The report is "accepted, adopted and printed with the journal."

In August, 1832, the fourteenth convention assembled in very small numbers at Boston. That was the year of the cholera in the United States. In consequence, there was not a single delegate or representative from the church in the middle states in that convention. Eleven societies in New England were represented by four clerical men and twenty-two lay delegates. That convention, therefore, was a pretty strong one, though exclusively an eastern one. Mr. C. Reed very properly declined making any report on the subject of "a more perfect organization of the General Convention." The committee of which he was chairman was continued, with a request to report at the next convention. But, in answer to a request made by the society in Henderson, N. Y., through the Rev. Mr. Weeks, for a license to be granted to Mr. Luther Bishop, it was, on motion of Mr. C. Reed—

Resolved, That this Convention do not deem it necessay to take any step in the case, as licenses have heretofore been usually granted by any ordained minister, on a recommendation agreeable to standing rule No. 7.*

Rule VII. gives no authority to an ordained minister to grant licenses. No other rule of the convention does. The proposition made to the eleventh convention to resign "the authority previously exercised by the convention in regard to licensing and ordaining ministers" to the ordaining ministers, proved that that authority was in the convention, and therefore ought to be granted by it. The Rev. Mr. Weeks, and the society at Henderson, were "of opinion that ecclesiastical, as well as civil power, is in the hands of the people; that government should be representative;" and therefore, that the authority to license ought to be given by their clerical representatives in convention. Consequently, they now ask the Fourteenth General Convention to grant a license to Mr. Bishop. Wherefore, the above proceeding was, in fact, a carrying out, or adoption, of the proposition, made to the eleventh convention, to resign the convention's authority to license ministers to the ordaining or ordained ministers. This was one step to the entire adoption of that proposition. It was a moving onward to episcopacy by our eastern brethren.—Mr. Thos. Worcester reports to this convention the institution of a society in Portland, Maine—a transaction similar to that in Bath in 1829.

* As follows: "VII. No person should be licensed as a teacher of the New Jerusalem Church, without the written recommendation of at least seven male members who shall unequivocally acknowledge its doctrines as contained in the theological writings of Emanuel Swedenborg."

The fourteenth convention sat only one day, and adjourned to meet again at Boston, in June of the next year. It is only further remarkable, that this convention received a "Circular" from the West, apprizing them of their western brethren's intention to hold a western convention—deprecating the taking of a wrong step in that—asking counsel from their eastern brethren on the occasion, and respectfully requesting them to send a delegation to their meeting. As this eastern convention had met on Thursday, and sat only one day, the western circular was not received till after its adjournment. No action, therefore, was taken on this circular in the convention, and it was simply "published for the information of the church at large," in connection with their journal—without one word of comment, without one breathing of sympathy, without the slightest indication of approval! So that we in the West always felt as if there had been turned to us, at this time, "the *cold* shoulder." But it was not the only *unspoken* evidence that our eastern brethren never felt any cordial concurrence in the western movement. And we were made to experience in several ways how effectually some people can "damn by *faint* praise."

In the fifteenth convention, held in Boston in 1833, although there was a majority of eastern ministers and delegates, the middle states were fairly represented. The two committees appointed in 1831, on the making of rules for the convention and a more perfect organization of it, reported now. Mr. Reed reported truly the defects of the previous organization, and recommended sundry amendments which were just and called for. Mr. Doughty reported, that it would be injudicious to propose any extensive alterations in the existing rules of the convention until it was determined what changes might take place in its organization as the result of the labors of the other committee ; but recommended some modifications and additions to the existing rules, which were adopted. On the whole, nothing appeared in the spirit of this convention, or was seen in its proceedings, to which reasonable objection could be made. Our eastern brethren did indeed advance somewhat their peculiarities in respect to society making : but all they did was apparently in a liberal and cordial spirit, in kind concession to the views of their distant brethren, and with a very strong seeming wish to do that, and nothing more than that, which the wants and exigencies of the growing convention really required. It affords us great pleasure to say this. There was certainly no manifest advances towards episcopacy in this convention.

In the convention of 1831, a proposition for a general missionary and tract board had been brought forward by the Rev. James Robinson. It will be recollected that he was a new-church minister who had migrated to this country from England. He brought with him a fondness for the measures of the English General Conference, to which he belonged, and in which he had taken a conspicuous part. The getting up a missionary and tract board in the General Convention in this country, was an imitation of the doings of the General Conference in that. A committee, of Messrs. Carll, Roche and Robinson, were appointed by the convention of 1831, to draft a con-

stitution for such a board. That committee now report to this convention of 1833. A constitution is reported and passed in an amended
form. The board goes into operation, and for two years is remarkably
efficient. Then, like a steam engine, it becomes inoperative, because
the fire goes out. To the duties of this board, there was subsequently
superadded, on the motion of Mr. Zina Hyde, a very worthy eastern
member of our church, that most excellent and most laudable use of
supplying the universities, colleges and principal literary institutions
throughout the country with the theological works of Swedenborg.
Although it was an error to blend two such important uses in one
committee, and to make them both draw life from the too slender
resources of one,—so that we can only imagine that the object of
engrafting the one was to do, what in fact occurred, exhaust the sap
of the other,—yet we mention these things here, because they are the
dawnings in the General Convention of that *attention to the performance of general uses*, which we believe to be the legitimate object of
a general representative body of the church ; and because, amid the
too frequent and most unpleasant fault-findings which duty imposes
on us, we love even to go out of our way to find some things which
we can, and do, with all our heart, commend!

To this convention the Rev. Mr. Carll made a communication in
writing on the subject of sectional conventions, which was referred
to the committee on organization, and ordered to be printed with the
journal. We have ever believed that the principle of that communication, in regard to three sectional conventions, held annually,
with a more general convention to embrace them and make them one
common body, was true and right. It accords with the views of Mr.
Hargrove, previously expressed. The same was recommended to the
General Convention by the committee of the Western Convention in
1834. It was even a feature of the Rules of Order, as they were
first reported in the Nineteenth General Convention. But above all,
it is accordant with that trinal order of the *human* form, which has
the head, with its extreme parts, as a nervous centre—the thorax, and
its extremities, as a sanguiferous centre—the abdomen, and its extremities, as a nutricious centre, and those common parts of the organism
which unite these three discrete parts into one. This order exists in
the heavens, which are as one man before the Lord. And, in our
opinion, it ought to exist in the churches, which should also be one
man in every distinct nation of the earth. For it is the *trine* in just
order which " constitutes *one* thing." (Coronis, 17.) In small countries, there need not be a trine of general bodies. In such, especially
where the people are homogeneous, all can be fairly represented in
one. But in a country of such vast extent as this, fair representation
in one body is most inconvenient, if not impossible. Besides, there
is not sufficient homogeneity in the mass of receivers of our doctrines
spread over the whole surface of our land. There are men of distinct genius in certain distinct parts of this country. And by three
distinct general churches united in one more general one, the freedom of the whole church in this country can be preserved ; but not
without.

To the sixteenth convention, assembled in Philadelphia, in 1834, the Western Convention made a communication of its "views in relation to sectional conventions and a general convention of the whole church in the United States." The committee of the General Convention of 1831, on the more perfect organization of that body, which reported to the convention of 1833, was continued and recharged with the same subject for a further report. To this committee was referred Mr. Carll's communication respecting sectional conventions, which was directed to be published with the journal—as if the propositions of that communication were to be passed upon by the committee on organization, and the church at large was to express its views upon them. Under these circumstances, the West felt called upon to express its views. Those views were fairly collected, by a committee of the Western Convention appointed for that purpose, in a pretty extensive conference with the leading men of the West, and honestly expressed. The General Convention, now in our estimation the Eastern, takes umbrage at what was felt to be imputations of a desire to assume and exercise *ex cathedra* authority. It was not intended to charge that design on the convention. From a sincere desire for the church's good, there was an honest warning given, lest the principles and measures of our eastern brethren, in their honest efforts to produce " a more perfect organization" of the general body, might lead to that vesting of power in a few, and that consolidation of the mass, which were felt to be great impending dangers, and were greatly deprecated in the West. The truth of this suggestion, the need of this warning, was what gave it its sting. The eastern leaders of the General Convention feel themselves touched, and read a homily to the West upon the sin of indulging in "jealousies, unkindness, misconstruction and hard judgments," while they cover up their own *particular* sin in a sort of *general* confession of *all* evil. It is intended that the West shall feel herself rebuked. As is common with good but weak men, the leaders in the West resolve to hang down their hands, to let things take their course, and not to act in doing what they conscientiously believe to be right, *lest wrong motives may be imputed to them.* A committee is appointed by the Eastern Convention to confer with a similar committee of the Western, and " to enter into any arrangements concerning a convention of societies and members of the New Jerusalem in the United States." But, for the very weak and insufficient reason above stated, this action met with no reaction in the West. And the East, too, ceased for a while its vigorous and formal action in bringing the whole church into order. In the next, or seventeenth convention, " the committee on organization made a verbal report, and requested to be discharged; which was voted :"—" and the same committee requested to be discharged from the further consideration of the subject of sectional conventions; which was agreed to." But the blow from the West only knocked off the sprout that appeared above ground; the root beneath was not hurt : and it was not long before it shot forth new sprouts. The New Jerusalem Magazine uttered its voice. The oracle in the east was frequent in its prophetic responses. We receive instructions

about the "*Authority of the Church*," as a kind of prophetic enunciation of what the new church in this country, whenever it is in a state
to come into true order, will acknowledge. Great light is thrown
upon the subject of *government* too. Much is said about *bad* government, *good* government, and what is *no government at all.* The
American idea of *self* government is exploded. The idea that we
create or *can* create a government over ourselves—and, what is
worse, the wish to have it so—must be got rid of. Governors and
government *must be made for us.* We are to have no *particular* voice
in the matter. We have nothing to do but *obey.* There are certain "true, efficient *mediums* of government," which we must see,
acknowledge and submit to as legitimate rulers; and the having a law
within ourselves, the governing ourselves, the making our own governors, or the entering into compacts, or making constitutional forms,
as a machinery of civil order and arrangement, for the submission of
our wills to the laws of true order, and our conduct to the restraints
of executors of those laws of our own appointment, is begetting a
bastard polity, full of false and inefficient mediums of government.
In short, we are left to infer,—what has been openly stated in private,—that regal and episcopal government is more in the order of
heaven, than representative republicanism; in which, the looking
below, to the ultimates of a civil humanity, for the voice and work
of God, is looking to hell. And when the church at large is
thus duly enlightened by "the true, efficient mediums of *instruction*," the work of making "true, efficient mediums of *government*"
begins again to be carried on. Step by step, slowly and cautiously
taken, our eastern brethren move to their end. Their Rules of
Order are conceived, gestated, and at last brought forth. When
first ushered to the light, they meet with an unexpected opposition.
They are thrown back into the hands of their makers, and the
enacting of them into laws is postponed for one year. With
altered *names* the same *things* are then presented again to a convention in which the chief opponents of them are not represented.
There had been a tacit agreement every where to let our eastern
brethren have their way, that they and all might see where it would
lead to. It was believed that they were aiming at arbitrary authority in the church. A warning was given to that effect. They
indignantly disavowed any such unholy desire or design! They
began to think, and expressed the opinion, that the church was not
ready for its true order. But they went ahead in modifying their
rules so as to make them take, and again brought them forward, for
all that. And without the most distant intention or idea ever having
been entertained of establishing ANY THING LIKE *ex cathedra authority*
in the church, and with a holy horror of even *imagining* that their
convention had, *could* have, or should have, any *right* to *coerce any*
members of the new church in *any way whatever,* they—in the very
convention that adopts their rules of order—just as that assemblage is
breaking up—*when nobody expected it*—the *recommendation of the
Boston society*, that all who do not conform to those rules in so far
as to adopt "the *working* point" of forming societies in their way,

ought not to regard themselves or be regarded as belonging to the
General Convention, being *some how or other, no body knows how,
incidentally brought up*—PASS THAT RECOMMENDATION, *with
an allowance of only* HALF *of the recommended time for societies to do it
in!* In fact, *they enact their rules into laws, and attach a penalty of virtual exclusion from the communion of the church for their non-observ-
ance!* And then the Boston, and other eastern societies, who *did not
think the church was prepared for this order yet*, WERE ASTONISHED AT
THE UNANIMITY WITH WHICH THEIR RULES WERE ADOPTED BY THAT CON-
VENTION!!! Did not these proceedings of 1838 prove that the warning
against the establishment of arbitrary authority in our church in this
country, which was given in 1834, had been just?

Although formal action in perfecting its organization was suspended
by the seventeenth convention, at New York, in 1835, yet we find
this upon its minutes—

The following resolutions, offered by Mr. S. Reed, were adopted:
Whereas the power of determining fit subjects of receiving ordination, as
well as that of conferring it, belongs primarily to the ministry; therefore,
Resolved, That all applications on this subject be hereafter made directly to
the Ordaining Ministers in convention assembled; and, if granted, that their
decision thereon be made known to the convention for its approbation previous to ordination.

Resolved, That the Ordaining Ministers be requested to determine what
qualifications shall be deemed essential for receiving a license, and also for
receiving ordination, in the New Church, and make known the same to the
next convention.

Resolved, That the first part of the 19th Standing Rule be amended to read
as follows; viz., "A candidate for ordination is to present himself before the
Ordaining Ministers at the General Convention, with the requisite recommendations already prescribed, and there receive ordination," &c.

This is not merely another *step*, but a *stride* to episcopacy! The
mover of the above resolutions was another hand of the Boston arm
and shoulder. There is, therefore, another instance here of our eastern brethren's holding up their hands for an episcopal form of government in the General Convention., We have seen that ordaining
power was given to the church at Abingdon, Va., to be exercised by
the Rev. N. Holley in its connection; and that Mr. Holley vested
that power in the Rev. S. H. Wills himself, for him to exercise "at
the *request*, or with the *approbation*, of any regularly organized
society of the New Jerusalem:" and we have seen that this was the
first instance, in which such power was overtly vested in the *minister*
instead of the *church*, in our country. Now the same is done in
regard to the General Convention. The ordaining power of the
general church is here vested in the ordaining ministers, to be exercised by them with only the *approbation* of the General Convention.
The ecclesiastical parliament is simply to record and approve the acts
of the chief magistrates. The power is in the *king*, not in the *whole
body* of the people. Instead of *authorizing* the ordaining ministers to
act, the convention is now to *request* them. Before, the ordaining
ministers were in the body as members of it, *by* or *through* which, as
chief instruments, *the body* acted from the Lord as its soul. Now

they are taken out of the body, and set over it; and power is given them to *grant requests* to it, as something subordinate to them, which *they* are to *act from* the Lord in serving. All applications for ordination are now to be made *directly* to the ordaining ministers in convention assembled; and, if *granted*, THEIR *decision thereon* is to be made known to the convention for its *approbation* previous to ordination." " Without a joke,"—as Mr. Wilkins would say,—is this not making the General Convention play second fiddle to the ordaining ministers? Nor is this all. Not only the power of *conferring ordination* is made to *belong* to the ordaining ministers, but also the power of *determining who are the fit subjects of receiving it*. If this is not giving *all* power, both above and below, in the church, to the ordaining ministers, what is it? Why did not the ordaining ministers *shudder* at the *very thought* of such powers being given to them! The Lord has taught them to pray, " Lead us not into temptation." Could, *could* they receive such power, and offer up that prayer in sincerity and truth? Could the convention give them the power and sincerely and truly make that prayer? Was it spiritually or charitably kind to subject any men in the present day to such temptation? Or if, with singular blindness, they both could, and did, utter that prayer, while they received and gave such power, what other answer could be heard in heaven, than—" Father, forgive them; for they know not what they do"?

" When the number of the disciples was multiplied" around the Lord's apostles in establishing the first christian church, and the twelve were no longer able to discharge all the duties which pertained to the ministerial office in their connection, they " called the multitude of the disciples unto them and said. It is not reason that we should leave the Word of God, and serve tables. Wherefore, BRETHREN, *look ye out among you* seven men of honest report, full of the holy ghost and wisdom, whom *we may appoint* over this business. . . . And the saying pleased the *whole multitude:* and *they chose* Stephen," and so forth: " whom they set before the apostles," who ordained them with prayer and the imposition of hands. (Acts, vi. 1–6.) Who were the ordaining ministers here? To whom did *they* think the power of determining fit subjects of receiving *this* ordination primarily belonged? Did our eastern brethren draw their principles of order from this authority? No! this is *old-church authority*, with which the *New* Jerusalem has nothing to do! Where *did* they find the authority for their principle? Was it a " new principle"—" deeply rooted" as a " sentiment" in their own minds— " considerably thought of by some in their society, and esteemed highly important"? Was it the principle that pastors are the sole mediums of truth to their societies, and, therefore, the ordaining ministers as pastors of the whole church should be the only " true, efficient *mediums* of instruction and government" to the whole body of the church? At any rates, *it is episcopacy to the core!* It is introduced into the General Convention by a Boston man, and unquestionably carried by the influence of eastern men. *They* were wide awake, as they most generally are when such measures as this are brought forward in convention, and the other members of the convention were most probably asleep, so as not to have heard rightly what was said when the motion was made and carried. There were some men attending that convention who must have been out at the time, or asleep if in, or they never would have suffered this motion to pass *without any dissent.* But the measure *was* passed, in the Seventeenth General Convention, in 1835, and was an informal preinduction of principles which were afterwards formally advanced in the Rules of Order.

The Eighteenth General Convention was held in Boston in June, 1836. This is most unequivocally eastern in every respect. Nine New England societies represented by six ministers and twenty-three delegates, besides the Rev. H. Weeks from Henderson, making the seventh New England minister, to six societies in New York and Pennsylvania, represented by four ministers and six delegates, is the large proportion in favor of eastern influence and control. Besides, Mr. Doughty and the two delegates from New York are all strong conjugialists. Mr. Roche too is a strong one now, and very many of the leading men of his society are with him in this sentiment. Dr. Belding is believed to be favorably inclined. We are informed by the best authority, that Mr. Weeks, who had so strenuously and ably opposed it at first, was favorably inclined to this notion now—although this has since been denied by those more nearly related to Mr. Weeks, and therefore supposed to be better informed as to what were his real sentiments. Dr. Beers did not oppose it—perhaps was not aware of its existence, so much had the holders of it ceased to talk about it, or to propagate it by argument. But there is not the slightest doubt or question in our mind that there was an almost unanimous tacit sphere in favor of that notion in this convention. Hence, as there were no large rocks at the bottom of its stream, its surface flowed smooth and unrippled by a single counter wave or eddy. The Bostonians were clearly in the ascendant, and there was nothing to oppose them. Therefore "all matters of a business nature were very harmoniously disposed of:" and there seemed "a growing disposition to leave mere speculations and theories of a general and abstract nature, and to come down into more simple and practical views." Principles inwardly held, were now to be secretly infused, and fully carried out, without any body's suspecting it, and therefore without any opposition, or with all apparent harmony. It was in this convention, that, in seeming contempt of all previous theories, a committee of laymen was appointed to "make arrangements for the religious services of the convention;" and "the ordaining ministers a committee on business." In the following, or nineteenth convention, the order in this respect was precisely reversed. There must have been, then, some reason why the ordaining ministers were this year made the committee on business. What other reason could there have been, than the desire of bringing forward in the convention, as its business matters, the peculiar views of order and of government which some leading ordaining ministers entertained and wished to have adopted?

The Western Convention had engaged in the getting up of a printing press: now, therefore, strenuous efforts are made so to put forward the Boston printing society as to crush the western press. The work is done—the western press is crushed. Of course, they did not intend any such thing in Boston. The Western Convention was a frail barque—all sail and no ballast—which could not live out of sight of land. It could not perform uses, because it was a general society of receivers all over the western country, who could only contribute money to a central organ of use, and was not a meeting of delegates from societies for four days somewhere in space. Hence it had of necessity to fall to pieces, because it could not limit the central influence. But the General Convention was in no such danger, *because it had no such central influence to limit!* In short, kind *words* were given to the Western Convention—as plentifully as the *good advice* of a miser who will not give a cent of his *money* to help his friend in distress. A large and respectable committee were appointed to answer the friendly communication of the Western Convention—but *they never did it:* and made the matter worse by a most lame and impotent apology for the *manifest slight.* But they still utter their *words* of favor, and even authorize the sending of a messenger to the Western Convention. So they subsequently did to the Central Convention—*charity* required this—all the while that the central forces in Boston were secretly opposing, undermining and prostrating the uses of both of the bodies—and then dryly exclaiming, We do not see what great use there is in having these bodies! We do not see *any uses that they are performing!!*

The committee of ordaining ministers, through their chairman, Mr. Doughty, reported some rules on the subject of licenses and ordination, which were adopted, and were altogether unexceptionable—were excellent. They embraced and extended the rules in the Rev. Thos. Worcester's resolutions offered to the twelfth convention in 1830. "The committee to revise the standing rules, reported a constitution and organization for the convention," which, "after considerable discussion," was "referred to the committee of ordaining ministers, to report to the next convention." The ordaining ministers, as the business committee of this convention, had briefly reported, merely suggesting six items of business. The third was the *opinion* of the committee, "that some provision should be made for the case of the transfer of the services of a pastor from one society to another, so that his connection with the second society may be *orderly* and *legal.*" It is manifest from whence this suggestion came, and what was its drift. It smacks of social marriage and divorce. But there was a disposition to come down from mere speculations and theories of a general and abstract nature into more simple and practical views. And now we see *what* business is brought before the convention—the *opinions* of the ordaining ministers of what was to be done in matters of ecclesiastical order and government—it does not appear so incongruous that those ministers should have been made the committee on business. The sixth item of business brought before the convention by that committee was a *suggestion* of the *propriety* of con-

sidering the *subject of recommending some uniform mode as to the
admission of members into new-church societies"*: a strictly ecclesiastical matter—pertaining to the original drift of forming and governing the whole church through the influence, example and agency of
the Boston society. The other four items of business were properly
such as would have been brought up by any committee which
examined the last or previous journals and brought forward from
them business projected or unfinished in former meetings. But these
two, the third and sixth, are original suggestions of matters pertaining
to ecclesiastical order and government, which it is evidently designed
the convention shall not act upon *now*, but shall merely direct to the
hopper, to be ground out by " the true, efficient *mediums* of instruction
and government." Precisely in the same way, or for the same purpose, did the committee on standing rules bring forward a constitution
and organization for the convention. This grain, too, is directed to
the regular hopper. In short, it is voted, that the third and sixth
articles in the report on business, " be referred to the committee of
ordaining ministers." In connection with " the report on licenses
and ordination," which, having been called up, was, as we have
already said, " accepted, and the articles therein contained adopted,"
it was—

Resolved, That the committee of ordaining ministers be requested to take
into consideration *the subject of degrees in the ministry*—to endeavor to define
and settle, with greater distinctness, the limits of each degree, and the
appropriate duties and offices of each, the name by which each degree shall
be designated, the qualifications requisite for entering upon it, together with
the circumstances and the mode of the initiation into each degree; and that
they report at the next convention.

The particularities of the journal of this convention do not, as
usual, enlighten us by informing us on whose influence and responsibility these proceedings rest. It does not state on whose motions
these votes and resolutions were passed. It is a pity that we are not
informed. But these proceedings are so like those of political meetings, in which the drafting of resolutions is assigned to certain men,
who are to *express the sentiments* of the community by *making them
before hand*, that we need not be in any doubt about who were the
movers of these proceedings in the eighteenth convention.

Some motions, however, are expressly ascribed to their movers.
One of these, made by a delegate from the New York society, it is
important that we should notice here. In the previous convention,
the seventeenth, that of 1835, a member of the Boston society, with
a view " to the promotion of *uniformity* and *order*," brought forward
a resolution which was adopted, requesting " the several societies, in
their annual communications to the next convention, to state what is
the form of admission of members into the church ; what is the creed
which is used ; how often and *at what times the Lord's supper is
administered*, and *whether in* PUBLIC *or* PRIVATE, and any other facts
in relation to this subject, which may be deemed interesting to the
convention." That same member once informed us that the Boston
society had been thinking a good deal on the subject, and had not

then determined how the holy supper ought to be taken in the new church. Now we suppose that matter is settled. And as the whole church is to be brought to uniformity by coming into this the true order, the example of the Boston society is in charity to be furnished as a model for the whole church. Therefore, every society is requested to communicate to the convention its mode. Of course, the Boston society, cannot but comply with the general request. Therefore, in the communications to the eighteenth convention, we are favored with a long statement of its modes and usages. And now for the first time the Boston and New England usage of administering the holy supper, in *private*, to only "the members of the society, and such members of regularly instituted societies as may be in town at the time, and express a wish to the pastor to be present and partake," is made known to the church at large. We are not aware that the mode of taking the holy supper in private, was ever before adopted by a single society of the new church any where else. It was certainly never in vogue in England or in this country in any former time. "The reason why the invitation is not extended to others, is not because they are esteemed less worthy receivers of the heavenly doctrines;* but because the laws of order seem to require that the sacrament of the holy supper, which is the holiest act of worship, should have *all the protection* which can be derived from the *social institution*† of societies, *as well as* the truths of the Word and doctrines of the church, that it may be saved from profanation and attended by the divine blessing." This has always seemed to us a sort of new-church *mysticism* that we never could fathom. The reason that the supper might be protected from profanation by the mere mode in which a society administers it *in addition to* the truths of the Word and the doctrines of the church, has always appeared to us so silly a one, that we have felt compelled to conclude, that the acute men of Boston were only hiding the true reason under a feigned one. We supposed that the holy supper was fatally profaned by men's coming to it and partaking of it unworthily—and that their unworthiness consists in *secret* sins—*inner* evils. Hence the strong injunction to self-examination and sincere repentance as preparatory to eating the holy supper worthily. Swedenborg, in Can. ch. iv. 9, says—The holy spirit "proceeds from the Lord to the laity by the sacrament of the holy supper, *according to repentance before it.*" Now how "the *social* institution of *societies*" can give *any* protection to the holy supper against profanation by those men who have not repented of inner evils *before* they come to it with outside fair professions of faith and semblances of sanctity, is what we have never been able to divine. The Lord protects an infant by the sphere of its innocence. Why should he not protect the holy supper by the sphere of its holiness?—

* The reader must bear in mind that in *charity*, a man regards and loves a woman in the comparative degree of her excellence—the *more* that she is *better* than other women; but, in *conjugiality*, a man regards or loves a woman in the positive degree of her fitness or adaptedness to him—in the degree that she is the peculiar good of his peculiar truth

† We confess we do not know what this means.

by the sphere of *his* innocence transfusing it? Certain it is to our minds that if *this sphere* does not keep an inwardly selfish, worldly, sordid, and impure man off, no social institution of societies ever will. But this has been given up of late in the Boston and New England societies: therefore, it was never held there.

The above was the exoteric ground for private communion in the Boston society. There was also an esoteric doctrine on this subject, which none but the initiated were allowed to know. We have been credibly informed, that the true reason for it was grounded in the conjugial pastoral relation—that the "celebrating it rather in *the privacy of the room* than in *the publicity of the temple*," grew, in some way, out of the notion that a pastor's administering this holy sacrament to his particular society corresponded to a husband's cohabitation with his wife. It is certain that a leading minister of New England did state this as his view. It is equally certain that another minister of New England, (or we have been credibly informed so,) acknowledged that his view of the matter was undoubtedly true, although he did not altogether approve his mode of expressing it. We *know* that, in Mr. Doughty's mind, the mode of private communion was grounded solely in his idea that the relation of a pastor to his society was a conjugial one. He preached a series of sermons to his society to prove the conjugiality of that relation. And on the strength of this, he removed the communion from the publicity of the temple to the privacy of a room in his own house—to the dividing, and at length to the breaking up, of his society, and at last to his expulsion from it.

Well, then, this mode of private communion flowed from the conjugial theory in at least the New York society. And one of the delegates of that society in this eighteenth convention, a conjugialist rampant, brings in a preamble and resolution, which are adopted, as follows:

Whereas it appears desirable that, as far as practicable, the external administration of the divine ordinances of the church should correspond with their internal signification, and that, to further this object, the views of *the church itself* be made manifest; therefore,
Resolved, That it be referred *to the committee of ordaining ministers,* to report, at the next convention, on the question, whether the ordinance of the Lord's supper was not of a private nature, so far as regards its celebration; and whether the object of its institution would not be more effectually promoted, and the effects of its administration more efficiently developed, by a conformity with the example of the Lord, in celebrating it rather in the privacy of the room than in the publicity of the temple.

We have underscored the two clauses above, to call particular attention to them in reference to the report of the ordaining ministers on this subject to a following convention. Are we to infer that the views of the ordaining ministers are "the views of the church itself"? Observe, this subject is referred to the committee of ordaining ministers to report, that the views of the church itself may be made manifest. What are the views of *the church itself?* In "the Universal Theology of the New Heaven and the New Church," there is a whole chapter on the subject of the holy supper. Are not the views of the church itself on that subject made manifest here, if any where? Is there a word here about the supper's being celebrated in the privacy of the room rather than the publicity of the temple? Is there a passage, line, or word in Swedenborg's explications of the Word, which teaches that the Lord's example of eating "his pass-over" with his disciples indicates or teaches that Christians should now eat his holy supper in remembrance of him in any private room *rather* than the most holy place of the temple of divine worship? If there is, show it to us. That is authority to which we will bow. But did the ordaining ministers do this? At the next convention, they were not prepared to report; and they were requested to report to the still next convention. Then they reported, through their chairman, the Rev. C. J. Doughty, in *eight lines*, thus,—after stating that they "were requested to report on the question, whether the holy supper should be administered in public or in private,"—

The committee would therefore report, that, on account of the manner in which the holy supper was instituted, and on account of the spiritual sig-nification and uses of the ordinance, they are of *opinion* that it *should* be administered in a room where no others are present but the members of the church.

Will it be believed that this is *all* that the committee of ordaining ministers—those "true, efficient *mediums* of *instruction* and govern-ment" to the whole church in the United States, "*upwards*" to whom the particular societies all over the country are to look as to *heaven*—*all* that *they* advanced to make manifest "the *views of the church itself*" upon this most important subject, the right mode of adminis-tering this most holy act of all worship!!! Not one word of *instruc-tion* as to what "the spiritual signification and uses of the ordinance" are! Not a syllable of a word to prove the internal and true doc-trinal meaning of the Lord's mode of instituting this most holy sacra-ment with his disciples—in which "all he did and all he said was *representative*"! "Tell it not in Gath, publish it not in the streets of Askelon: lest the daughters of the Philistines rejoice, lest the daugh-ters of the uncircumcised triumph"! In fewer words than the reso-lution requesting their instruction, and in a singular echoing of almost the very words of it,—as if the same voice had answered the resolu-tion which uttered it, "the views of the church itself" are made manifest by the simple declaration of the *opinion* of the ordaining ministers that it *should be so!* But we know that it was neither the opinion nor the practice of some of the ordaining ministers; and if the sifting could be accurately made, it is apprehended that a most fearful narrowing down of the number would be found.

But thus we see how the measures of the Boston society were gra-dually brought forward in the General Convention, and efforts were made to insinuate them into the whole body of the church. For why, was not the Boston society content to enjoy its peculiar modes and usages itself? Why did it seek to propagate them in other societies, and thus to obtrude them upon the General Convention? Does any one believe that because a New York delegate makes this motion, the

17

wire was not pulled in Boston which made this puppet move? And
to such a pass had the visible body of the church in this country now
come, that it was willing to give up its voice, its reason, its authority,
and its power all into the hands of some six or eight men ostensibly,
but, as we have shown, really into the hands of *one man*! In calmly
reflecting on this matter now, after some twelve years have elapsed,
we are utterly confounded at this thing, which to us is wholly inexplicable on the supposition that the receivers of our doctrines in this
country were any thing of spiritually minded men—men who loved
truth because it was truth, and had *spiritual* truth as the forming and
vital principle of their *lives*! But again, we look around and ask
ourselves is this any more confounding than the fact which we *now*
see, that the whole visible church *is* almost wholly formed, influenced
and governed by the Boston society, or one man in it, and yet all,
even reputedly the most intelligent men every where, seem *perfectly
willing that it should be so*! But the time is fast approaching when
a remarkable change will come over the face of the church.

In the eighteenth convention, then, the subject of a constitution
and organization for the convention, that of a transfer of a minister
from one society to another, that of a uniform mode of admission of
members into new-church societies, the question whether the communion in the new church should be administered in private or in
public, and especially the subject of *degrees in the ministry*, were all
referred to the ordaining ministers. The complete determining of
the ecclesiastical order of the church was wholly placed in their
hands. The time had now full come when the laity could, in charity
and faith, confide in them as "the proper medium of this power;"
and the convention wholly resigned it to them. They did not tremble, nor hesitate, nor seek to be excused from so weighty and responsible a task as forming a fundamental law or constitution for the
whole new church in the United States. And in the next convention, the nineteenth, that of June, 1837, in Philadelphia, the far
known and much celebrated Rules of Order were brought forth.
"The committee of ordaining ministers rendered their report on all
the subjects committed to them the last year, in one connected
report—except the subject of the administration of the holy supper."
What transpired in the nineteenth and twentieth conventions in regard
to these rules has already been detailed. They were substantially
adopted, and in form somewhat modified, but unaltered in essence,
have become the form of order and government for a large majority
of the whole new church in this country. Here, therefore, we come
in sight of the goal of our inquiry as to what is the present state of
the question of the trine in this country, so far as the General Convention is concerned. In and by that body, a modified and covert
form of episcopacy has been induced on well nigh the whole church
in this country; or this is the end which is proposed. The following
cursory observations on the Rules of Order, and on some of the General Convention's transactions since their adoption, will substantiate
this position.

We will state again here, that we were present in the nineteenth convention, when the Rules of Order were first reported. And it has been said that we then "spoke of the *principles* upon which they were based *in the highest terms.*" It is very easy to show the absurdity of this assertion. We will confess, in all frankness, that we were not opposed to the principles of the Rules of Order when reported in that convention; for, having only heard the report read once by the reporter, and dwelling in thought upon some parts while the reader was going on with the enunciation of the rest, we only heard a small part that was read, and really did not, and could not, *know what those principles were.* And we now declare, that we had not the most distant idea of the principles, which we now see to be involved in those Rules of Order, for three or four years after they were first reported. As to the doctrine of a trine in the ministry, we were rationally and fully convinced of the truth of that by Mr. Weeks's report, as we have before said. And hence the trinal principle in the Rules of Order we certainly did approve. But it was only the principle in general that we saw. Yes, there was one general application of it, which we heartily approved—the recommendation of *three* district or sectional conventions, one for the eastern states, another for the middle states, and a third for the western states; and the uniting these into one body by a common organization. But the *episcopal* mode of governing these bodies, we did not approve. Nor could any thing we said in debate be fairly construed into an approval of the episcopal feature of the Rules of Order in general. The Rev. Mr. Carll as well as ourselves openly spoke against this feature, on the ground that the church was not prepared for it; and we have already hinted at the way in which Mr. Carll was knocked down for what he said on that subject. Our views on that subject then, were the same as they are now; and what they are now, this report will show. We well recollect—we never can forget—our end in speaking, and the train of our thought by which we endeavored to attain that end. Our end was to prevent the adoption of those rules hastily. We deprecated the formation and adoption of a constitutional law in any other way than that in which it could secure the rational choice of the common will and understanding of the whole church, so that when adopted, as the fundamental law, it would prove a bond of union, harmony and efficient co-operation of the whole church in this country *acting as one man in promoting the cause of heaven on earth.* This our conscience now clearly testifies was our end, object or purpose in speaking. And we argued from the *vast importance* of the matters brought forward in the report, for the need of great deliberation, caution and prudence in adopting the order proposed. The stress that we laid on this, may have been construed into high commendation of the *principles* of the report; but all we can now say is, that if we did speak in such commendation, we were not then conscious of it ourselves. It is however right to say that we were pleased with the general show of order. A love of order is ingrained in the very warp and woof of our mental constitution—we love it as a duck does water! And we liked the seemingly orderly way in which ministers were to be inducted into office; and hence it was at our request that the mode of the rules was recommended in our own ordination. We likewise saw the need, and rejoiced in the prospect, of our having such a form of ecclesiastical government as would both define and secure the rights of clergy and laity, preventing the encroachments of either upon the just prerogatives of the other, and saving the interests, the characters and the reputations of both from that injury which has too frequently resulted from official caprice or popular injustice in disagreements between ministers and their people. But as to the principles of the Rules of Order, we say again, we did not then know what they were, and had not then the most distant idea that those principles were in them which we now see and oppose.

But what are the principles that you oppose in the Rules of Order? and why do you oppose them? We have written to very little purpose in this report, if this has not been seen already. The main principle that we object to is, the vesting of power and authority in *one man* as the head of the church. This principle is founded in our eastern brethren's understanding of our church's doctrine of the trine in Coronis, 17. It calls for *one, chief bishop* as a personal or visible head of the whole new church in this country. This is not the *form;* but this is the *essence;* and is now—we grieve to say it—the *virtual fact.* For we have, in fact, a constitution, or fundamental law, by which the whole church is first to be brought into order, and then governed, *by the devisings of* ONE MAN. And that one is now regarded as the visible head of the whole church in this country, by many who look up to him as such, and allow themselves to be influenced and governed in their opinions and practices by him as such. And although the Rules of Order do not enact this by so many words, it is, in our full conviction, the spirit of them. To this principle we are, with all our heart, and mind, and strength, *opposed!* Nor do we oppose it merely because we believe " the establishment of such an order in the church at the present day is utterly impracticable." We believe it is not the true order for the new church as taught by Swedenborg. Although permissible in the Divine Providence, and therefore admissible in certain states of human society and the church, we believe it is, in the light of the New Jerusalem, essentially untrue, and wrong in itself; and that it can prove only evil in its consequences to our church. This is strong language, we know; but it is not half so strong as our feelings of opposition to, and our rational convictions against, that form of order and government which shall put for its head any thing like a "pontiff." Yet this *principle* is involved in the Rules of Order; and is believed, by our eastern brethren, to be taught by Swedenborg as the true order of our church, which she is sooner or later to come into. They say, " If the inquiry is first made, whether there is a ' man in whom the church generally could be united, *to whom to bow as its* PONTIFF,' the answer would, in all probability, be in the negative. But we object to the inference drawn from this *against the order itself* [that is, the order of *one man* to whom *the church generally is to bow as its pontiff ;*] and what is in our view of much more serious importance, we object to this whole manner of putting the case and drawing the argument. The man does not exist before the place he is to fill is prepared, and it is not reasonable to suppose that the church can accept the *primus,* while it denies, or does not acknowledge the *office."* Is it not clear from this that our eastern brethren think the *primus* is the *pontiff?* Again, "If we see that the office is one which order requires," &c. Must we not infer that *they* see that the *pontifical* office *is* one which order *does* require? We agree that it is wrong to argue against the order itself from the fact there may not be the man whom we know or could acknowledge to be fit to fill the office which it calls for. The first and only question is, Is the order itself true and good? If it be, then it is our duty to acknowledge and adopt the order, in faith, and hope, and trust that the Lord will raise up men for all its offices. But is the order true? That is the question. And what do our eastern brethren hold? Is it not the direct inference from what is quoted above, that they hold the affirmative? Is it not clear that *they do* acknowledge the *office,* and are ready to *accept* the *primus?* And, in the present connection, is not this *primus* to be with them a *pontiff,* to whom the church generally is to bow? Most assuredly this is the true inference; and to this conclusion we had come in our own minds long ago. And if this is not aiming at new-church papacy, then white is not white, and black is not black. It was the Rev. C. J. Doughty's clear perception of this which led his honest mind to humble itself under the severe mortification of an open avowal that he himself had been in error; and at last to repudiate those Boston principles by which he then found he had been so long hoodwinked. And now it is perfectly clear, conclusive beyond a doubt, that our eastern brethren understand and acknowledge Swedenborg to teach in Coronis 17, that the New Jerusalem, as a whole church or body of the Lord, will have a *primus infulatus* as a pontiff. And episcopacy in this form—that is episcopacy tending to papacy—is most clearly discernible in the Rules of Order as first submitted by the Rev. Thomas Worcester to the nineteenth convention. It is to *this,* that we are now, and ever have been, so decidedly opposed. When we come to remark upon the above cited passage from the Coronis, we trust we shall be able to show, from other passages of Swedenborg's writings, that he does not teach the doctrine which our eastern brethren have drawn from it. But now, if the reader will take up the Journal of the Nineteenth General Convention, and open at page 370, we will show him where this episcopacy tending to papacy may be seen.

A glance at a sentence here and there will do. There is episcopacy in the very first word—"*We propose,*" &c. Here the order is devised by one man, as the ecclesiastical law-maker and law-giver. The order rests on the authority of the ordaining minister's proposition. The Word of God is not shown or made to speak. The doctrine of the church is not quoted or referred to. The simple declaration of the view of the ordaining minister "makes manifest the view of the church itself." This is episcopacy. Nay, it is worse than episcopacy as we find it in the Protestant Episcopal Church of Eng-

land and of this country. For there they have the representative
system, with some check upon the bishop. But here, there is a
looking up to the bishop as to heaven—as to the *only* " true, efficient
medium of instruction and *government.*" To this we are opposed.
And we are opposed to it because it is not according to the doctrine
of the New Jerusalem, and is inimical to her spirit. The order should
have been drawn from the doctrine of the church, which *the Lord*
has taught by Swedenborg. This doctrine is in those theological works
which have been written by a man, to whom the Lord manifested
himself in person, expressly commanding, and most providentially
qualifying, him to write them from his immediate illumination, so
that they contain truths continuous from him. And these works are
in the hands of nearly, if not quite, all receivers of the doctrine. Unquestionably, the clergy are the official medium of that illustration
and instruction which is the power of the Lord's holy spirit in opening the light of this doctrine in the minds of the members of his
church. And to them, as a complex organ or member of the general
body, belongs the province of teaching and expounding this doctrine
in the form of ecclesiastical law for the church's external order. But
in forming the *constitution* of the church as a visible body, in
declaring from the Word and the writings of the church those general
principles which are to form its fundamental law, *all the parts* of
that body should exercise a consentaneous judgment; and in adopting
that law, when declared, should exercise a concurrent action. Therefore, every intelligent and competent member of the church, who has
the proper authorities in his possession, should look into them, and
from them form his judgment. Then all these, fairly represented in
a general convention, called for this purpose, and forming a *collective*
man in effecting it, should present the conclusions of a *general understanding* as to what is the true form of order and of government for
the general church. These representatives of the whole church,
chosen on account of their being skilled in the law and principled in
love to God and charity to man, should devise the fundamental law
of organization for the body, by which its offices are created, their
functions defined, and their jurisdictions limited. Among these representatives, sent up into convention by the whole body, undoubtedly
ministers of all the grades would come. These, in committee, as a
complex man—not simply the highest grade of them alone—these, as
a trine constituting a one, might form an organ of the convention to
produce the authorities from the Word and the writings on which
any of its organic measures might be, or ought to be, founded. Then
the convention, as a whole man, with the ecclesiastical committee as
a member set in it, should deliberate, and determine, by a common
understanding, the law, the order, the organism, or the office. When
these as a constitution are thus formed in the intellectual principle
of the whole church as a body, then the will of the body is to be
determined to it by the rational adoption of it by the churches in their
particular form. And then the officer is to be chosen for the office
from those men best fitted to discharge its duties for the common
good. Officers are indeed appointed by the Lord. But he sets them

in his church, and his church, as his body, acts from him in appointing them—just as his humanity acts from his divinity. And he does not appoint them immediately from himself, so as to set them *over* his body, as a divinity acting *by* its humanity. The whole body of the church is his humanity in a lower form; and hence the church's *choice* is the Lord's *appointment.* This is the ordination of *good,* or of the *will.* And this is properly called *choice.* But there are *two* witnesses necessary to confirm this matter. The ordination of *truth,* or of the *understanding,* is also required. This is properly called *appointment.* And this is the church's appointment *from* the Lord *by* the head ministers as its members and instruments. Consequently, when the fundamental law is made and the office constituted by the representatives of the whole as the church's common understanding; and when this constitution is adopted by the church's common will, in some appropriate form of its free and rational exercise; then the higher and highest officers are chosen by the body in the exercise of its free will as enlightened by a rational understanding, and solemnly inaugurated into office by some sacred ceremony, which represents the Lord, in his work of redeeming and saving men, and of governing the hells for that end. And this exercise of the church's will is its action *from* the Lord, as the soul of which it is the body. Consequently, it is the Lord's appointment of the officer to his office. Whether we say the Lord, or an *end* to the *common good,* from him, in *all* of the members of his church, acted upon by him, "together," it is the same thing. Or whether we say the Lord or charity and faith from him, it is the same. An end to the common good, or charity and faith, from the Lord in the whole church, is the Lord as the *soul* of that church as his body. And when the whole church, from a common will of good and a common understanding of truth, chooses a head officer of its government, it does so by a sort of celestial- or spiritual-natural crystallization; or as a hive of bees choose their queen; or as a flock of birds choose their leader; or as a herd of horses theirs. The only difference is, that there is a rational free agency in the one case; and a non-rational instinct in the other. In all cases, it is appointment to office by the *Vox Populi—Vox Dei.**—But in the case before us, *the man who is to fill the office, makes it. The man makes the law, who is to govern by the law when made.* Is this right? Is this orderly? Is it suited to secure the church's freedom in con-

---

* When the church is consummated, the voice of God is falsified. When the whole jewish people cried out—"Crucify him! crucify him!" "Let his blood be upon us, and upon our children"—this was the voice of God as spoken by a wholly diseased body. God so spoke by this people, as to cause "the wrath of man to praise him." It was needful that "Christ should suffer these things," that he might "enter into his glory." And the permissive providence of Jehovah God turned the inductive passions of the Jews into, and guided them in, such a channel as would effect the glorification of his humanity. So, in all other cases, the conclusion and decisions of any whole people, are so ordained in the Lord's divine providence as to tend to the universal good—although that people, diseased from head to foot with "wounds and bruises and putrifying sores," is hastening to its own destruction. Even the hells, when reduced to order by the Lord's influences, do, in an outward and complex form, speak the will and utter the voice of God.

forming to the law, or her good in obeying it? We think not. We are sure that this is nothing but the egg of a cockatrice, which can hatch into only arbitrary authority on the one hand and servile obedience on the other. We, therefore, object to the Rules of Order, because they are based upon the *ex cathedra authority* of the ordaining ministers, or one of them.

The above, by showing what episcopacy is not, the more clearly demonstrates what episcopacy is, in the Rules of Order. It is "the office and duty of those who are in the second degree of the ministry to officiate in *receiving members into the societies* where they are settled," and "to *watch over the members.*" This is episcopacy indeed; and to us a most obnoxious feature of it. In our opinion, the good uses of a society do not require it. *Charity* is the cement of all social order in the church. By this, many members in particular are made one body. Charity "is the performance of use." And members of a church society are but particular organs for the performance of some specific use in the common social good. Hence the reception of members into a church society must be an act of its *will ;* that is, an act of its whole body. And the principle of reception is *spiritual affinity,* which draws what is homogeneous, and repels what is heterogeneous. The body will, indeed, act by its appropriate member in receiving or taking by the hand those who are introduced into it, as well as by its understanding in judging of their fitness for membership: but this should always be an express act of the whole body in each case. So that, when a member is proposed, he should be voted for by the whole, and thus appropriated by the will; and then the society may direct his admission by whatever form, or by whatever member, it chooses. This is the business of each society, with which the General Convention has nothing to do, and which may vary in different societies according to their genius. And as for the oversight of the members, this too is a function of the whole body. It is a matter of *sympathy.* It is the *feeling* of the *will ;* and not the *seeing* of the *understanding.* And if a member is not kept in the order of a society by its common opinion, its common sense, its common feeling or its common honesty, but must have a minister to *watch* over him, he is nothing but an *eye-servant,* instead of the Lord's freeman and friend. There is but one other feature in the episcopacy of our eastern brethren as it gradually manifested itself, which was more detestable than this. We want ministers to stand as watchmen on our walls, and *look out for our enemies ;* not with eyes turned in upon our own camp "to watch over the members" of it. And *who is to watch over the* MINISTER? Nay, *who is to watch over the* BISHOP? Does not the minister or the bishop need to be watched over? What have we seen? The man who is now the virtual bishop of the whole church in this country,—who would have been the formal one if the order which he himself devised had been adopted by the church as he devised it,—originated the theory of a conjugial pastoral relation, which has unquestionably qualified, in some degree, the whole of the present ecclesiastical order of the church; and he himself now confesses that he did so—apologizes for having done so—and abandons his theory because it is not to be found "in the Scriptures, nor in the doctrines of the church;" and because, if he were to hold it still, "it would grieve some; it would irritate and enrage others; thus it would disturb the peace of the church and turn their minds away from things which are far more important"! It is a "fixed fact," then, that even bishops may make to themselves broken cisterns—dig covered pits— and walk in wrong ways. Who, then, is to watch over the bishop? The Lord, undoubtedly. And cannot the Lord just as effectually watch over the sheep that hear his voice, as over the "porters" who open the door for them to go in and out and find pasture? Away, then, with this office, duty, and function of any grade of the ministry which *sets* a minister "to *watch over* the members"! Even in form, it is brimstone in our nostrils! Let the members of a society watch over one another. Let them confess to one another, and not to the priest. And let charity and faith as the Lord in each one of their own breasts, alone bind or loose that on earth which is to be bound or loosened in heaven! (See Newchurchman, Vol. II., pp. 124 and 193.)

The ordaining ministers say, "We esteem it to be the office and duty of those who are in the third degree *to institute* and *receive societies into the New Church*"—to ordain subordinate ministers, "and to *watch over them.*" Here are episcopal functions; and we have already said enough to show why we are opposed to them. In one word, the New Jerusalem does not *need* such functions for its true order and its proper use; and it is unkind to any functionary to peril *him* by placing him on such a high and giddy height.

But it is added, "to *preside* at the *meetings of the convention.*" This is objectionable because it constitutes the convention a *mere ecclesiastical* body. But it is not on this account that we object to it. We object to it because it involves the principle of *one* head bishop for the whole church, as the *primus.* This will appear as we go on.

Then "*the* bishop should also have *authority* and *power* to call a meeting of the ministers for consultation, whenever, *in his opinion*, the good of the church requires it." Was not this episcopacy going to seed? The head bishop and his council.

How the forms of initiation into the several degrees of the ministry are episcopal, we have shown heretofore. "*By the authority committed unto me, I hereby introduce you*"—"*I authorize you*," &c. This form is too magisterial for the new church. We prefer the form of the English General Conference, which makes its ordaining agent, as the representative of the Lord, simply *repeat the Lord's words*, from the New Testament, as if the Lord himself was ordaining through his ministerial representative.

It is unnecessary to repeat, that while we heartily approve the order of a *trine* of sectional conventions, comprised in *one* common body, and so forming a *triune* general body, yet we object to the episcopal form, both of their institution by the head bishop, and of their government by bishops under him. We would apply to the new church in all its forms, the representative and congregate system, or the system of the *maximus homo*, as now fully explained in this report.

The order for the transfer of the services of a pastor from one
society to another, is utterly inexplicable on any other principle than
that of the conjugial theory. According to that theory, " ordination
corresponds to the marriage ceremony"—" dismission corresponds to
divorce." Look now at the order ; and compare it with these postulates. " Whenever it is proposed to dissolve the connection between
a pastor and a society, it should be made known to their bishop, and
he should dissolve the connection, if, *in his opinion*, there is sufficient
cause." Is not this ecclesiastical *divorce?* Suppose the bishop should
not be of the *opinion* that there *is* sufficient cause—suppose the pastor
is the brother of the bishop, and it is, therefore, hard for him to see
sufficient cause—yet the society and the pastor do not and cannot
possibly agree, so that whatever instruction the pastor gives, is received by the society as wholesome food into a sour stomach : what
then ? Let the history of the Rev. Samuel Worcester's connection
with the Bridgewater society answer. " Dismission corresponds to
divorce." Married parties that cannot get a divorce from the proper
authorities, must live together " for better or for worse until death do
them part." Parties will, however, manage to disregard the authorities in such cases as this.

" A person who has been dismissed, and who has not been guilty of
any misconduct, should have authority to perform the duties of the
first degree in the ministry." Is this according to any doctrine of
the new church taught by Swedenborg ? Who can have the hardihood to say so—to even hint it ? We have supposed that inauguration
into the second degree of the ministry, is an elevation to a discrete
plane of official function, as from the command of a regiment, to the
command of a brigade in the army. Now when a brigadier general
has no brigade to command, " should he have *authority* to perform the
duties of" a colonel, a major, a captain, or a corporal ? Yet, according
to this law of *order* in the new church, a pastor whose connection with
any particular society of the church has been dissolved is to be *degraded*
to a discretely lower plane of official duty ! Who ever heard of the
shaft of a column going into the pedestal when it was knocked down ?
Yet the three discrete parts of a column are mentioned by Swedenborg, to illustrate his doctrine of a trine ; and a displaced shaft being
made to do the duties of a pedestal, would be relatively the same as
making a displaced pastor do the duties of the first degree of the
ministry. Could this have been, unless it had flowed from the postulates that, " ordination corresponds to the marriage ceremony," and
" dismission to divorce" ?

But " If *another society should desire* him to become their pastor,
and *he should consent* to it, we think that he should *be ordained into
the second degree*" again. We feel sick at the heart ! Oh, that
men—of reputed good sense and intelligence—yet led by fanciful
analogies, and absurd theories, should make such a farce of the most
sacred and important representative rites of our church ! Does any
one now doubt, that the conjugial pastoral theory entered into the
new-church doctrine of a trine in the ministry as that doctrine was
applied to the Rules of Order when first reported to the General Con-

vention? That it has entered into them here, is self-evident. How it entered into their episcopacy, we have shown before.

It is needless for us to point out again the form of episcopacy in the order for the admission of members into societies, or of the institution of societies. But let us come to the Laws of Order "concerning the Standing Rules of Convention." It will be recollected that these had been for several years in the hands of a committee charged with "a more perfect organization of the convention." This committee, at the preceding or eighteenth convention, had "reported a constitution and organization for the convention," which, being laid on the table one day, and taken up and considerably discussed the next, was referred to the committee of ordaining ministers to report to this nineteenth convention. They now report eleven articles of a conventional constitution, twelve particular rules for the mode of proceeding at the meetings of the convention, and eight general rules for its government. By the articles of the constitution the officers of the convention are to be "a bishop, a secretary and a treasurer." It is "the duty of the bishop to institute and receive societies into the new church; to administer the holy supper to societies that have no pastors; to ordain ministers into the subordinate degrees, and to watch over them; to preside at the meetings of the convention, and to administer the holy supper on those occasions." Also, "to call a meeting of the ministers for consultation, whenever in his opinion the good of the church requires it; and to propose to the convention such measures as he shall think necessary for the protection and welfare of the church." The sixth article provides for the first choice of a bishop by the General Convention; and then the seventh prescribes that "*the bishop shall remain in office until his death, his resignation, or until a majority of all the ministers and societies which have a right to act in convention, shall wish to have him removed.*" The secretary is to be appointed by the bishop, and to continue in office during *his* pleasure. In fact, he is the secretary of the bishop rather than of the convention. And the bishop is in fact the convention brought to a focus. When the convention is thus constituted and met for business, the bishop calls it to order—the secretary does what the bishop tells him to do—he makes out and settles a list of the delegates and other members present—the bishop reads it from the chair, and then announces that the convention is organized and ready to proceed to business—the secretary then does something more, in the way of bringing up unfinished business from the journal of the preceding meeting, and the bishop brings forward these subjects in their series, and takes care that "they shall be considered and disposed of successively"—then the standing committees and boards are appointed, by the bishop, of course—and next the bishop "brings forward any subject or subjects *which he wishes to have considered;* and *they* SHALL BE *considered and disposed of in the order in which they are presented!*" After this the members of the convention are to bring forward any subjects which they wish to have considered, and these. too, are to be considered and disposed of in the order of presentation. By the general rules, all religious services at the meetings are placed under

the supreme direction of the bishop, and all committees are to be
nominated by him, unless otherwise ordered.

Such are the episcopal features in the constitution of the General
Convention as made by the one ordaining minister, who was himself
to be the *primus infulatus*. We have seen how all the powers of the
convention were resigned to the ordaining ministers—how every
thing pertaining to the ecclesiastical order and government was given
into the plastic hands of them as "the true, efficient mediums of
instruction and government," and as "the proper medium of this
power." And now what do we behold? A constitution made by
one ordaining minister which provides for the office of *one bishop* as
head over all the church for life, or until he chooses to resign, or the
body chooses to cut him off. We have no means—perhaps there are
none—of measuring precisely the power which the convention gave
to its ordaining ministers: but it does seem to us that this is one of
the most remarkable verifications we ever saw of the adage—" Give
an inch, and they will take an ell." It is certainly a very remarkable instance of a bird's feathering its own nest. And if the human
form would have been induced upon the General Convention by this
constitution of it, it must have been in only that early stage of it when
the microscope displays it as a *human spermatorion*.

Our task would now have been completed. For we have shown,
with the clearest possible demonstration, that the germ of episcopacy
was first planted in Boston, and that it has now gone fully to seed in
that determination of the trinal order of the ministry which has been
made for the General Convention by the pastor of the Boston society.
But it is contended that these episcopal features of the Rules of Order,
as first reported, have been changed. We admit that they have been
materially modified. The manner in which they were induced upon
the church could not but provoke opposition to them. And opposition has prevailed to change their form in some respects. But the
serpent has only been scotched, not killed. The *principle* is not
given up. Episcopacy is held to be the true order of the new
church—just such episcopacy as calls for a *pontiff* as the *primus*—
and every sort of influence has been, is, and will be, used to induce
this order upon the new church in this country at last. And let it
be distinctly understood, that if our eastern brethren think this to be
true order, we do not object in the least to their adopting it for themselves. It is no part of our past or present purpose to *oppose them in
that*. But when they essay to set themselves up as the *rulers over us*,
and to rule us by that form of government—we must really beg to be
excused. We cannot in conscience—we cannot in spirit or in truth—
acknowledge them, or *look up to them*, as "the true, efficient *mediums
of instruction* and *government*" to us. And much as we shall deplore
the necessity, yet, if there is no other alternative left us, we shall go
out of the connection of the visible new church, sooner than submit
to their domination !

From the time that the Nineteenth General Convention refused to
act upon the principle of forming a constitution or fundamental law
for the whole church by a convention called expressly for that pur-

pose and composed of delegates from the whole church in the United States in some fair ratio of representation, but, on the contrary, tauntingly declared that they had the power in their own hands, and, keeping it, would adopt that order which they believed to be right, and then others might come into it or stay out as they liked—from that moment, we became alienated from that body in spirit. And when the Twentieth General Convention passed the famous resolutions, before noticed, of virtual exclusion from the General Convention of all those societies that did not become instituted and organized according to its rules, we followed the lead of the Rev. M. M. Carll, and did all we could to reiterate the constitution of the Western Convention as a co-ordinate body. We also took an active and a leading part in constituting the Central Convention as another such. We have done this, not only because we think a trine of conventions is the true order, but because we are most deeply impressed with a conviction that this is the only order which can possibly secure the whole church's freedom from *New England episcopal rule.* We have no doubt that such a trinal order will be ultimately adopted; and we are satisfied, that, if a fair convention of representatives from all parts in the United States were assembled to speak it, the common voice of the church in this country would now pronounce for such a constitution. At any rates, we would submit to and sustain whatever general organization of our church such a convention should make—but no other. This, however, cannot take place before the eastern boil has come to a head and broken. The eastern leaders have most industriously labored, by persuasive influence, by all their modes of peculiar management, and especially by the concession of whatever appeared to be obnoxious in their Rules of Order, to maintain their power and extend it more widely. This is the true ground of all the modifications which they have made in their ecclesiastical laws, organization or government. They have not given up one whit of their principles, or abated one jot from their original and fixed purpose. In all their bowing and bending they have only "stooped to conquer." Besides, they had to begin immediately to alter their rules, because they would not work in practice. Indeed, the history of their convention for the ten years that have elapsed since their Rules of Order were adopted, would be little more than a detail of *alterations* which they have been incessantly making in them. And this is our strong argument against them; for this would not have been the case, if they had been true, and formed and adopted in the right way, at first. Like a kettle badly made of bad stuff, no sooner did the church go to work at preserving in them, than they had to be sent to the tinker, who made three holes for every one he tried to mend. At the convention held in Philadelphia in 1840, almost every member had a copy of the Rules of Order in his hand; and so constant was the reference to the Rules, to correct this motion, or rightly direct that, or keep the convention from flying the track in running its race of true order, that a very worthy clergyman, who does not live very far from the city where the convention was then held, observed, he really thought the members of the convention studied the Rules of

Order more than they did their Bibles; and if they would pay a little more attention to their Bibles, and a good deal less to their Rules, he was sure the business of the convention would go on far more harmoniously and efficiently! This illustrates the first working of the convention under its Rules. And if it be urged, that the present extension of the order of the Rules over the whole United States, is proof of their excellence in the constant alteration, and repeated modification of them; we ask why is it, that the trinal order has been repudiated by the Western Convention, is about to be by the Central Convention, and, is cast into the back ground by even the General Convention itself in order to maintain its ascendancy? Depend upon it, that the higher a building goes up on a defective foundation, the sooner it will totter to its fall!

Let us illustrate the nature of the General Convention's modifications of its laws by a single instance. In the twentieth convention, as we have before intimated, the following was passed:

Resolved, That it is the sense of this convention, that no one of the societies, now its members, which shall neglect to become organized according to the Rules of Order adopted by the Convention until after the meeting of the Convention in the year 1839, ought thereafter to regard itself, or to be regarded, as a member of Convention.

Here we come to the exercise of arbitrary authority by the General Convention. The Rules of Order had been enacted; they were now to be enforced. And now we see the spirit of those who were trying to induce them upon the whole church. This resolution was passed on the motion of a delegate from the society in Abington, Mass. Where it came from, any one will see on p. 390 of the Journal of the Twentieth Convention. It was a recommendation of the Boston society, which had devised the Rules of Order, and was seeking to govern the whole church by them. There was another resolution, passed at the same time, designed to have the same authoritative bearing upon the ministers, which this had upon the societies, of the church. It made it " the *duty* of all the ministers of all degrees, whose names are upon the list, and who do not attend the meetings of convention, to make a report to the convention annually, stating whether they are employed in the ministry or not, where they are employed, and for what portion of the-time."* The spirit and design

* There can be no doubt, that every general body should know its constituent parts; and that these parts should acknowledge the authority of the general body over them. In the present case, therefore, that the General Convention, as now constituted by its Rules of Order, should know who freely and rationally adopted those rules, and so signified the wish to come into and make component parts of the body as constituted by them, was perfectly right; if, therefore, the General Convention had stated this in so many words, respectfully requesting all the societies and ministers of the church who approved those rules and wished to come into the convention as constituted by them, to signify the same; and then had put on its lists of societies and ministers those only who had thus signified their wills and wishes; there could not have been the slightest objection to their course. But what we have said and shown in this sketch, most clearly demonstrates that such a course could in no possible way come into the plan of the Boston leaders of the General Convention. The plan was, to make the law for the *whole church*, and then to govern the whole church by it. Hence, they sought to retain the

of both of these resolutions could not be mistaken. All the ministers and societies in the West who had constituted the Western Convention as a co-ordinate body were on the Eastern Convention's list. And the design of these resolutions was to draw off from that body all who were neutral, so as to leave a few disaffected and revolting spirits standing alone. Then it would be an easy matter to crush their opposition by the obloquy of excommunication from the church. But the arbitrary spirit manifested in the above resolutions produced a violent reaction upon them. A majority of the ministers on the list would not report. In fact, of all those who were not present in the convention, only two of the third degree, including the president of the Massachusetts Association, who was also president of the convention, two of the second, and two of the first, formally reported to the next or twenty-first convention. Hence, at that convention, held in Boston, in which there were *twenty-eight* eastern ministers and delegates to *eight* from the middle states, they had to pass resolutions to the effect, " that the secretary be directed to address a notice to each society on the convention list, which has not made a report to this convention, and *inquire into the reason of the* NEGLECT"! And " that the secretary be directed to address a similar note of inquiry to all such ministers as have *neglected* to comply with the resolution of last convention." With regard to the latter of these resolutions, it is a very singular fact, that the secretary put off addressing the inquiry until near the time of the meeting of the twenty-second convention, (just previous to which, by the by, the Middle Convention had come into being,) and then, by a *very* remarkable providence, he could get answers from only *two* of the most obnoxious of the recusant ministers. These were so simple as to take any notice of the missives they had received. Four of the six, the whole number addressed, made no reply. The answer of one of the two, was not noticed, because it was addressed to the *Eastern Convention*—the president observing, with *appearance* of temper, that if it were left to him to say what should be done with it, *he would throw it under the table!* When the answer of the other of the two was read,—stating, as the reason why he had not reported to that convention, that he had been the minister of the Western Convention, and was then the minister of the Middle Convention,—the Rev. Samuel Worcester instantly jumped

authority of the whole church for this purpose. They retained on *their* list all the societies and ministers in the United States. In *their name* and by *their authority*, made the law; and then by the same name and authority *demanded* their obedience But when the West, by its delegate or messenger, protested against such a making of the fundamental law, and distinctly declared to the General Convention's messenger, and to the General Convention itself, that it would not be bound by any law made by a general body in which it was not fairly represented, (see Jour. 20th Gen Con., p 398,) and then, in prospect of the adoption of the Rules of Order by the Twentieth General Convention, did not in fact cause itself to be represented by a single delegate in that body, and this for the implied purpose of publicly testifying that it would not acknowledge the convention constituted by these Rules of Order to be *the* general convention of the whole church, in the United States—under these circumstances, to pass the above resolutions making it the *duty* of the ministers and societies in the West to report themselves to that body, and afterwards to catechise them for *neglect* of duty in not doing so, was arbitrary in the extreme !

up and moved, that his name be stricken from the list of ministers of the General Convention. But this motion fell to the ground for want of a second. What a pity! All would not do. A majority, as we have said, could not be *made* to report. A stigma was then attached to their names on the list. Still this would not bend nor break the refractory spirits; and the General Convention has never yet been able sufficiently to isolate its opponents, so that it can destroy them as its enemies, without driving off from it some whose favor and support it has wished to conciliate. There is an appearance in the last, or thirtieth convention, of their putting the screws upon poor Dr. Belding. He is judged, condemned and executed upon current *rumors* against his moral character; and then the Pennsylvania Association, to which Dr. Belding does not and never did belong, is charged with the duty of acting according to the boasted laws of charity in n. 48 of the Rules of Order. What a melancholy instance of making the first last, and the last first! All the disgrace, all the penalty of moral delinquency—public proclamation to the world, and the striking his name from the list of ministers—is visited upon his head, upon the ground of current rumor, without his having been heard in his defence! And then the laws of charity are to be exercised towards him to see whether the rumors are well founded or not! What can this be for, unless it be to punish him for not reporting to the convention, his failing to have done which is the true ground of omitting his name from the list of ministers? And it is very easy to see how little difficulty there will be, by and by, of striking some other name from the list, because he "has neither attended the convention, nor made a communication to the same, for several years." Give but the power and impunity, and then the church will see, and perhaps shudder at, the spirit which lurked in the two resolutions above quoted from the proceedings of the twentieth convention.

Well, the first of those resolutions was judged arbitrary and resisted accordingly; and so strong was the reaction upon our eastern brethren, even in their own convention, that they were obliged to lower their crest and draw in their head. An exceedingly lame and miserably poor apology was put forth. "It was *certainly* done hastily, *perhaps* indiscretely. But at the worst, it is not worthy of the importance attached to it;* and one is entirely at a loss to see how it could acquire such importance, insomuch as *it clearly required nothing which the most tender conscience might not do.* It is now, however, *repealed; and the evil, which has been attributed to it, we may hope, will cease.*"

"It is now repealed." Let us see. It was annulled by a resolution of the twenty-third convention, in New York, in July, 1841, and the following rule of order substituted for it—

It is recommended that all the societies belonging to this convention, and all that may propose to join it, should be organized in the manner above described: but if any societies or associated bodies, desiring to join it, find it inconvenient to adopt this form, *they may present their cases, and the convention will consider and decide upon them as they arise.*

---

* Certainly not. It was a very silly and trifling affair to make so much fuss about—just like the tax on tea, a mere bagatelle, which such discreet men as our anterevolutionary forefathers ought to have had more sense than to have taken any notice of.

How condescending! The two latter clauses retain all that was objectionable in the principle of the original resolution. So that the softening—"*it is recommended*"—does not reach far below the surface, and the hard and bitter substance is still there. There was gilding enough, however, to make many simple minds take it all as solid gold. And that was all that the manufacturers cared for. The thing objected to was, the convention's *prescribing* forms of *external* organization to societies or particular churches. In this the societies ought to have been left entirely free to adopt whatever organization might be suited to their varieties of genius. And the convention should have confined its province, jurisdiction, organization and operation to what was common to societies—to whatever pertained to their common good. The common body might indeed have required societies proposing to come into it to have constitutions homogenius to its own as to *essential* forms* and principles. It might have required that any society coming into its connection, should not deny the divinity of the Lord, the spirituality of his Word, the necessity of life according to his commandments, or call in question any of the doctrines of the New Jerusalem, either by the declaration of its faith, or by the form of its organization or the order of its government. But any express rule for this would be invidious—inasmuch as it would imply that some societies of receivers of those doctrines were likely to do this; and the convention, like a mother, should never preimpute evil to her children. It would have been better for the convention to have let this matter alone—to have attended only to its own organization—to have let *that* serve as a *tacit* sample to societies for a mode of *their* organization, and to have left to the good common sense of the societies themselves to adopt freely and unrestrictedly so much of the order so set forth, as was necessary to make them homogeneous components of the general church, on the principle that "what is unanimous is composed of so many images of itself." (A. C. 4625.) But action on this principle would undoubtedly have led to the segregation of receivers into at least three general bodies; and this was against the end of *forming* and *governing* the *whole church* in this country by the *model* of one society. Therefore, in seeking the attainment of their end by its legitimate means, our eastern brethren could not do otherwise than they did—make the order by one man, and enforce it by the authority of a few, which, in the new church, must needs be arbitrary authority. Reaction upon such authority has compelled them to modify the *form* of their rule by changing it from a *law* to a *recommendation ;* but the *essence* of the rule is untouched, because the assumed *authority* to *admit* a society into the body on *the condition of conformity to some mode of external organization*, is still there. This authority is *the* objectionable thing. The *right* of any one man, or a few men, whatever office he or they may hold, to make a form of external organization for particular churches, on the principle that he or they are the "true, efficient

* "There are rites which are merely formal, and there are others which at the same time are also essential." (C L. 306)

mediums of instruction and government" to them; and then to say
that they shall or shall not regard themselves, or be regarded, as
members of the general church, only so far as they adopt that form
on that principle; is *the very thing* to which we most strenuously
object—as did the most honorable and most honored forefathers of
our eastern brethren themselves, when, in good old Boston, they
objected to the *right* to tax, in putting a whole cargo of tea to *draw*
in salt water!—and this objectionable thing, this right, is retained in
the clauses of the rule of order which we have underscored. We do
not choose to be *admitted* or *permitted* to do right, by any body that
constitutes itself the whole church.

A similar modification of the authoritative law for the ministers,
was made by the same convention, (Journ. 23d Gen. Con., p. 408, n.
56,) whereby "*shall* be the *duty*" is converted into "it is *requested*."
But the sting is still there—the fang of arbitrary authority is still
undrawn. Our eastern brethren had better abrogate the whole of
these two rules. Nay, as they have torn their Rules of Order to
tatters by so often mending them,* they had better lay the whole of
the garment aside. No new cloth which they can put upon their
old, will ever do otherwise than make greater and worse rents in it.
They were wrong in the beginning; and *no going on in that same way
can ever bring them right!* Therefore they had better come back to
the good old way of making a constitution for their church as a constitution was made for their country. And if this ever should be
done, let no man who takes a part in making the constitution be
eligible for ten years to any office which the constitution makes. Let
this be the law for the lower offices; and let *no man* that makes the
law be *ever eligible to the highest office.* Their country made a constitution for herself under God, by men whom she, acting from him,
chose out of those of her citizens that she judged to be skilled in the
laws and principled in the fear and love of God, to act for her as her
members and instruments in making the fundamental law of her
government. These men made the law and its office before the officer
was found to fill it. *They did not themselves fill the office which they
had made.* The country designated the man who was to fill the office;
and *Washington*, the man who filled the office, *did not make it!*
Least of all, did the country, in the very convention which made the
fundamental law, pass a penal enactment to enforce its adoption by
her constituent parts! The course which our country took was the
way pointed out by the influx of the new heaven. And if this is
the way pointed out by Truth and Goodness, let our eastern brethren
listen to, and heed, *His* monitions—"This is the way, walk ye in it."
"If ye *know* these things, happy are ye if ye *do* them." "Go, and
do ye likewise"!†

* It is a very curious fact that every convention for ten years since the Rules of
Order were adopted, has made some alteration in them.

† We are well aware that it may be charged, that the men who formed the constitution of the Central Convention filled the offices which they made. But the members
of that convention were so few, that it could not be otherwise. And so far as the writer
of this report is concerned, his course in that convention has been as consistent with the

The above instance illustrates very well how the Rules of Order have been *modified*. And a comparison of those rules, as published in the Journal of the Thirtieth General Convention, or that of 1848, with them as first reported to the convention of 1837, will show that, in some of their most objectionable and obnoxious features, the modifications have been only superficial. It will be found that there is no radical change, but that the principle is only covered over or suppressed.

There is, however, one radical change which the General Convention has made in its laws of order and government; and, whatever our eastern brethren may think, it gives us sincere pleasure to notice and praise it. The change to which we allude was made by the following minute of the proceedings of the twenty-second convention, in 1840, (p. 409, n. 77 of its Journal,)—" Resolved, That instead of the committee of ordaining ministers, *all the ministers belonging to this convention* constitute a committee on ecclesiastical affairs for the

principle here laid down as it could be. Few know, and none but those few can know, how much difficulty the framers of the constitution of the Central Convention had to encounter; and how imperfectly formed it confessedly was, in consequence of the reactions upon it, in its forming process, from hard and unyielding obstructive forces Two preparatory conventions were held for the purpose of forming it; and it was then submitted for a whole year to the members of the body for their free and rational adoption or rejection of it in a third, which was designated the first annual meeting under its adoption. When the constitution was formed in the second preparatory meeting, the writer of this report immediately resigned the office of corresponding secretary, and only consented to take the office again at the urgent solicitation of the New York society, because they *imagined* there was no one in the convention's central organ who could fill the office so well as he. But immediately that a suitable person for the office was presented, he resigned it, does not now hold any leading or presiding constitutional office in the convention, and, so far as his purpose is concerned, never will. His present office of chairman of the ecclesiastical committee or council is but a temporary one; and is now a most laborious and thankless one.

The constitution of the Central Convention was drafted by the Rev. C. J. Doughty. The original draft was indeed very much altered, and perhaps more than half of the constitution as it now stands was engrafted on it by others; but Mr. Doughty's draft made the chief office; and when, in the first annual meeting, the constitution was formally adopted, and Mr Doughty was elected the first president under it, it was owing to the firm and solemn protest of the writer of this report against it, that he resigned that office, and it was given to another. This is not generally known; but it is a fact; and Mr. Doughty was assured, that, if he retained the office, we would instantly withdraw from the convention. Then, upon our motion, an office was made for Mr. Doughty, *the president of the ecclesiastical council;* to which he was then elected, which he held till his death, which has never since been given to another, and which never will be held by any minister who took part in forming the constitution of the Central Convention. Our action in resigning the office of corresponding secretary was misunderstood at the time, and gave rise to some unkind reflections. But our reason is now for the first time stated. and may be inferred from what is said above. The charges, which have been more insinuated than openly brought against us, of acting from disappointed ambition, &c., in our opposition to certain men and measures in the general bodies of the church in this country, it may be our duty to answer in another place: but *they will be answered in the judgment of the world of spirits;* and to that award we now most cheerfully submit them Previous to that judgment, it is not at all likely that we shall have been proved to have sought power by having come into the actual possession, and the arbitrary exercise, of it.

ensuing year." This is not, indeed, made a permanent rule at once—it is only "for the ensuing year": but we believe it has at last become a permanent rule; and we have no doubt that it involves a true principle. Without any question, there are certain things which the head ministers, or ministers of the highest grade, in a church, should alone do. Thus they alone should formally ordain other ministers; and, in general, they alone should do whatever pertains to them as representatives of the Lord in his highest priestly office. But the making and executing of the ecclesiastical law for a general body of the church, does not belong exclusively to their province. And as the ecclesiastical organ of the General Convention, as its teaching and leading general or collective minister, they ought not surely to be put *alone* in a committee. This organ or committee should be itself a full man, an image of the whole body. Hence it should be constituted a *triune* committee by all the ministers of all the grades, and not be made a head as it were cut off from its body. This, therefore, was a radical change in the order of the General Convention, which we think was right; and if it was not made a permanent rule, it ought to have been.

There has also been the appointment of a lay committee, to counsel and advise with the ordaining ministers in certain matters of a mixed nature, which pertain to lay as well as clerical men. This, too, is a radical change. But we doubt whether this is not the province of the convention itself, which ought not to be assumed by, or given to, a mere committee. However, the order is a good one, if the convention chooses so to assign away its province. And, in regard to duties which are to be performed in the intervals of the convention's meetings, and have a bearing upon the interests and prerogatives of laymen, it is needed. This too, therefore, is a good radical change. But it was a fatal vitiation of this committee to ordain "that *any three members* thereof, have the power of the committee." This is still the radical error of vesting power in the hands of a few.

Moreover, the constituting the General Convention a permanent body, that is, a body existing all the year, instead of only during the sessions of three, four, or five days, was a radical and good change.

There is, however, this radical error in all of these and the other alterations of the Rules of Order, that, so far as they were any thing more than rules merely for the regulation of the convention's own action, they are changes of the constitution, or of the fundamental law, made by a legislative body acting under the constitution which they alter: whereas the constitution should have been made originally, and all radical changes of it subsequently, by the action of the whole body of the church itself, either by its representatives chosen expressly for the purpose, or by such constitutional court as might have been appointed for this purpose in the original constitution. The principle that the constitutional law should not be made by those who are to exercise the powers granted by it, must be preserved inviolable—otherwise, there can be no security against ambitious men's making powers for themselves to exercise, and the arbitrary exercise of unwarranted powers.

There was one alteration of the Rules of Order by the twenty-third convention, (Journ., p. 413, n. 97,) which seems to us to have been fundamentally wrong. It was the assigning of the duties of the highest grade of the ministry, to ministers of a lower grade, merely because they were employed as missionaries under the direction of the committee on missions. True order required that the ordaining ministers should have been made the missionaries, wherever the performance of their peculiar duties was called for; but to confer on ministers of a discretely lower degree, authority to perform the duties of a discretely higher degree, instead of formally inaugurating them into that higher degree for their performance, was *a most culpable subversion of true order*. And we know not how to class it, unless we place it among those concessions to unreasonable prejudice, by which the General Convention has, in other instances, sought to retain its power by the compromising, giving up, or violating of its established principles. Of a piece with this were the several alterations made in the Rules of Order by the twenty-sixth convention, in 1844, (see Jour., p. 407, nn. 55–60,) expressly to meet the case of Mr. Field, the delegate from the Michigan and Northern Indiana Association. A very cursory inspection will discern that those alterations were *ex post facto* laws, by which formerly established principles were made to bend to circumstances, for the manifest purpose of securing a wider acknowledgment of the General Convention, and a consequently greater extension of its power. And the more recent proceedings in regard to the Ohio Association,—upon which we have already animadverted,—have capped this climax!

We doubt that the granting ordination to the ministers of the first degree *upon their own application,* is according to true order. The twelve did not apply to the Lord for ordination, nor the seventy. The deacons first ordained by the apostles did not first make application to them for ordination. And we do not know where to find any authority for it in the Word, nor elsewhere. The Jews insisted upon being a representative people; but that, Swedenborg tells us, was from their lust of pre-eminence. 1 Samuel, ii. 35, 36, can hardly be taken as authority for the order; nor Matthew, x. 35, 36, 37. We object to it because it is against our order of *social crystallization,* in which the members of a church society, in appearance, *arrange themselves* around their nuclei. And we think that ministers for the first degree should be chosen from licentiates or candidates for the ministry, and application for their ordination be made by those whom they are to serve in their office—even if they be only associations of receivers of the doctrines who have not all yet become communing members of the church.

In the twenty-first convention, the next after the Rules of Order were adopted, questions arose as to those parts of the rules which we have shown most manifestly to have involved the conjugial theory. The marriage and divorcement of a pastor and his society was not seen to apply to a minister of the third grade. The reason of this was, because the minister of both the second and the third grades had not yet, in the full carrying out of the order, found their appropriate conjugial partners. According to the true order, the pastor and particular society should have been in the first, instead of the second, grade. And when associations of societies were formed, then a pastor of the second grade would have his appropriate counterpart in such an association. Still further, it required a consociation of associations to make a church 'in the highest degree, for the counterpart of the pastor of the third grade. Then the *primus*, as the visible head of the whole church, might be ordained or inaugurated into the conjugial pastoral relation appropriate to his degree. For, according to the conjugial theory, the husband being the head of the wife as Christ is the head of the church, (Eph., v., 23,) and the church being formed in the wife through the husband, (C. L., 125,) the church in any of its forms would require a visible head, just as a kingdom requires a king, or an empire an emperor. So that, if there were a church in a still larger visible form than a consociation, or a convention, as a church formed by all the visible churches in all the countries of the globe, then there should be " a *primus* or a *head*" for this, as well as for the church in any of its lower, less general, or more particular forms. Hence, for the most general form of the visible church on earth there must be a *pontifex maximus*. There is no escaping from this conclusion, if the theory of the conjugial pastoral relation is embraced as a premise. At any rates, this is, in our view, the conjugial theory as it has flowed from our eastern brethren into their Rules of Order, and into *their* trinal order of our ministry. And when we show, presently, that this is their view of the ministerial trine, and that this is the order which they are aiming at, by the rules which they have devised for the ordering and governing of our whole church in this country, we shall do all that we intended to do in the way of demonstrating that the conjugial theory still lurks in and qualifies their Rules of Order.

But in the twenty-first convention, as we have said, the inconsistency just noticed was felt, and the subject was thus brought up in the report of the business committee:

The committee on preparing business for the Convention, to which were referred the reports from the several societies, would call the attention of the Convention to the following subjects, viz.:

1st. To the importance of having the respective duties of an *ordained* minister and of an *ordaining* minister more clearly defined and respected, which seems to render it necessary to have the relation of Pastor and Society more attentively examined and determined.

2d. To an amendment of the Rules of Order, by which, as they now stand, a *Pastor*, or minister of the second degree, whose connection with his society has been dissolved, retains authority to perform *only* the duties of the first degree, and loses his rank as minister of the second degree; while the connection of an *ordaining* minister with his Society may be dissolved, and he still retains the rank and powers of the third degree. This, as it now stands, gives him power to officiate in all the degrees, although for the best of reasons his connection with his Society may have been dissolved.

This acute discernment of the exceedingly absurd inconsistency of the rule would have shown the great want of sagacity in the deviser of it, if it were not manifest that he was hampered by the difficulty

of carrying his principle fully out in the imperfect degree of the
order which the state and circumstances of the church would then
only admit of. To have come out boldly in an honest declaration of
the principle, and a full and consistent ultimation of it, in the order
devised and recommended to the church, would so have shocked pre-
existing opinions, and so unsettled previous usages, as to have caused
the entire rejection of the system at once. Therefore, all that could
be done, was done, in applying the principle as far as practicable to
the existing usages. But now the inconsistency is so clearly pointed
out, and so glaringly seen, something must be done to mend the
defect. The ordaining ministers make a most vague and unsatisfac-
tory report on the first part, and put off the determination of the
second to a more convenient season. The chairman of the committee
on business is an avowed conjugialist, and an honest one. He believes
the conjugial theory true and good, and he is for having it declared
at least, that it may be carried out when the church is prepared for it.
He thinks that the respective duties of the two higher grades in the
ministry cannot be clearly defined and respected until "the relation
of pastor and society" is "more attentively examined and determined"; for, in his view, the one is founded on the other. It was
from our intercourse with the chairman of this committee,—whom
we intimately knew and very much loved,—together with other
honest men like him, that we learned how generally and almost universally the conjugial theory had been embraced in New England.
We call the attention of the church to this report as affording official
evidence that, in the views of those who formed and first adopted the
Rules of Order in New England, the respective duties of the two
higher degrees of the ministry could only be clearly defined on a true
view of the relation of a pastor to his society, which was there deemed
a conjugial one. And this we now advance as irrefragable proof,
that the conjugial theory has entered confessedly into the Rules of
Order.

In a second report, the business committee call more strenuously
for "a more full and satisfactory *exposition* of the *Rules of Order*
adopted by the Convention." The vague report of the ordaining
ministers does not satisfy them. They then go on to show that the
principle of the Rules is true, but the imperfect state of the church
will not admit of its being carried out, and therefore they think a
qualification of them is called for, in order to adapt them to the existing infant and imperfect state of the church. The committee distinctly avow that when the church is in true order, the society, the
association of societies, and the convention of associations, will each
"have its *pastoral head*." But as, in the infancy of the church,
neither societies nor associations could be formed so as to settle and
maintain pastors over them; and as all that could be done at first was
the formation of a General Convention by isolated receivers; the first
thing required would have been, when these isolated receivers had
met together as a church once a year, "to have acknowledged and
elected a pastoral head." Thus *a* pastoral *head* for the General Convention was called for by this order at the very first. We like this;

because it is honest. "Then, after these receivers had multiplied, so as to form separate individual societies, these societies should have acknowledged and settled their own pastors, who should stand in the relation of ministers of the next lower degree to ministers of the General Convention"—which would then become a convention of societies. At last, these societies might form associations in' the several states with their several pastoral heads. And thus the character of the General Convention being perfected by its becoming a consociation of these associations, pastors of particular societies would go down relatively to the third grade, pastors of associations take the second grade, and *the one pastor* of the General Convention rise to the third grade. Then the principle of ordination and dismissal, as marriage and divorce, could be consistently applied to pastors in all three of the grades. For then a *primus* would be degraded to a pastor of an association, when divorced from the convention—an association's pastor to the pastor of a society, when divorced from an association—and the divorced pastor of a society to an expectant of a second marriage, as a candidate for the ministry in connection with some other society, and performing the office of a missionary or itinerant preacher until he found one.—Beautiful order!—very!

One fact is worth a thousand arguments. And there is a fact in reference to this subject, which ought not to be overlooked. After the Rules of Order were adopted, we have seen that the convention imperatively required the societies belonging to it to become organized according to them. The Leraysville society, under the pastoral care of the Rev. L. C. Belding, obeyed the mandate. Dr. Belding, it will be recollected, was ordained by, and in the presence of, the Eighth General Convention. He was ordained in what was afterwards 'deemed the second grade of the ministry. So that he had the General Convention's authority to act as the pastor of any particular society of the church which might choose him for its minister. But now the Rules of Order are adopted and to be carried out, what does Dr. Belding and his society do? Listen to the report of the Leraysville society, as read to the twenty-second convention :

In compliance with the REQUISITION *of Convention, and that we might be in order,* and members of that body, we sent a request to the Rev. Lewis Beers last February, who visited us, *organized our church,* and ORDAINED *Rev. L. C. Belding pastor* OVER *us*"!

Was not that sweet incense to the leaders and rulers of the General Convention? Suppose that every society in the United States had done the same; would there have been any renunciation of the conjugial theory then? Is there any man of sense and discernment who cannot see the image of that principle perfectly reflected from this proceeding of the Leraysville society as a mirror? Who, then, will say that the conjugial theory has not entered into the Rules of Order, and does not now qualify them? The rules, in this respect, have indeed been repeatedly and variously modified. For instance, it has been required that a pastor, when separated from one society, instead of being *ordained* again into the second degree, on becoming the pastor of another society, shall be "*installed*" in the pastoral office in its connection. It was a very learned man and acute philologist who proposed this alteration. But they were acuter men who adopted it. In short, this change of *words* only concealed the principle, did not extract it. It will be exceedingly hard to get the conjugial theory out of the Rules of Order without their entire abrogation. You might just as well try to get the *wool* out of woollen cloth, by sewing patches of *cotton* cloth upon it. The conjugial theory is still there—especially in the article on the transfer of the services of a pastor from one society to another. The principle that ordination corresponds to marriage and dismissal to divorce is involved in three things. First, the *judgment* and *decision*, of an ordaining minister, with his council, that there is sufficient cause for the dissolution of the pastoral connection. There is no authority for this principle in the express teachings of Swedenborg, either as to the order of societies in the heavens, or as to that of societies of the churches on earth. It is a *fiction* of the law-maker who devised the Rules of Order. And it could not but flow from what he regarded as the true relation of a pastor to his society. Second, the *degradation* of a pastor to the performance of "those ministerial duties *which do not result from his being a pastor of a society.*" This modification of the original rule, is another instance of the subtle expression of the same thing by other words. It means nothing more nor less than that a divorced pastor shall perform only the duties of a candidate for the pastorship—the duties of "a priest before he becomes a pastor"—which, in his case, is the grade or state of a *clerical widower*. Third, the requiring that "he shall be *installed* as the pastor" of another society, "by an ordaining minister." To install is "to *advance to any rank* or *office*, by placing in the seat or stall proper to that condition." In common ecclesiastical usage it is a ceremony of induction into the highest episcopal office. It is in all cases an original advancement "to any rank" or official grade. Of course, it is, in the present case, just the same as ordination; and, by an ordaining minister who was a conjugialist, would be so regarded. It is plain, then, that the ceremony of installation required by this rule of order is as much in the nature of a second marriage as a second ordination would be. Consequently, these three things in this article of the Rules of Order prove that the conjugial theory is still there.

Now we say again, while these rules are the order of the General Convention, *let the members of that body abide by them, or abrogate them*. Until they are abrogated, let them faithfully stick to them, and be honestly consistent in their practical application. Until they do this, we cannot record their names on the page of history as honest men. Let them not, we repeat, openly and shamefully violate the *principles* of their rules, in truckling subserviency to current prejudice, for the sake of leading station and controlling power.

When the Rev. Messrs. B. F. Barrett and S. F. Dike were to be ordained, in the convention of 1840, into the first degree of the ministry, the Rules of Order had this requisition—"*All* applications for ordination into the first degree shall be made to the ordaining ministers, *any three of whom may grant the same.*" But in this case there were but two ordaining ministers in the convention, the Rev. Messrs. Worcester and Roche. The Rev. C. J. Doughty was also present, a strong and confirmed conjugialist still, who, seeing the requisition of the Rules of Order, offered to act with the other two in granting the application for the ordination of those two ministers. The generosity of this offer in Mr. Doughty can only be appreciated by those who know the peculiarly delicate relations which had existed between him and Mr. Barrett in New York. But his offer was refused by the president of the General Convention, with the view of *punishing* him. for having taken part in constituting the Middle Convention. As illustrative of the *spirit* of the eastern leaders in their *government* of the church, we have given the correspondence, which passed between Messrs. Doughty and Worcester on this subject, as a document in our appendix. (See No. LIX.) It will be well for the church if that document is generally read. True history demands the reading of it. It shows that the Rules of Order were glaringly violated ,by the Twenty-second General Convention, in concurring with only two instead of three ordaining ministers in granting the application of Messrs. Barrett and Dike for ordination into the first degree. And it shows that this was done in the exercise of ecclesiastical *discipline* by its presiding officer. Thus we see how a spirit of *arbitrary* rule, if not of *vindictive* justice, could enter into the celestial rulers of a celestial church.

Again, the Rules of Order require, that a society of the General Convention should be " a body of *baptized* receivers"—baptized into the distinctive faith of the New Jerusalem, if they had not been before, at the time when they are instituted and received into the church by an ordaining minister; and they require, that " a candidate for the first grade *must* be a good and orderly member of some *regularly instituted* society of the new church ;" of course, must be a receiver of the new church doctrines, that has been *baptized* into the distinctive faith of the New Jerusalem. There can be no question about this being the requisition of the Rules of Order. But the Rev. B. F. Barrett, bound by all the solemn obligations of a member of the General Convention, to observe scrupulously its fundamental law, , violated this requisition by the ordination of the Rev. A. E. Ford into the first degree without his being a "baptized receiver." And the fact is now well known, that the Rev. Mr. Barrett came on to Darby from New York, to ordain Mr. Ford into the second degree also, and, actually would have ordained him, *without the consent of two other ordaining ministers*, if the Darby society would have consented to it. This violation of the Rules of Order was committed in *will;* and therefore has the guilt of sin in the internal man.

Further, the Rules of Order require, as we have shown, that, when the services of a pastor are to be transferred from one society to another, and his connection with the former has been regularly dissolved by an ordaining minister and his council, he should be installed as pastor of the latter by an ordaining minister. But the Rev. B. F. Barrett, having had his pastoral connection with his society in New

York regularly dissolved, was not regularly installed as the pastor of
the Cincinnati society. So that in this instance, too, the Rules of
Order have been violated.

Now we commend to the General Convention, and both its clerical
and lay members, the excellent advice of that honest and worthy man
in the West—" *While the present is the order*, WE SHOULD ABIDE BY
IT"! His advice would have been better, if instead of saying, " But
surely it may be improved to suit the expanding state of the church,"
he had said, Let the expanding church, acting in freedom according to
reason—*make a better and more suitable order for herself.* Let the
whole church do˜this as one full-grown 'free man, acting in his own
right ; and not as a minor child, an indentured apprentice, or a mere
natural man, who is in the degree of simple obedience—suffer certain
" true efficient *mediums* of *instruction* and *government*" to *make an
order for her.* At any rates, it is hard to *improve* a garment for the
church which was badly made and did not fit at first. And that the
Rules of Order were made *too tight* at first—*much* too tight—is proved˜
by the tailors' having had *to let them out* every year for ten years
since the suit was first put on! *Surely*, if the *expanding* church continues to wear this dress much longer, she will *burst* it. She had
better, therefore, take it off and lay it aside—discharge the *regular*
mantuamakers, and make a new dress for herself, by workmen in her
own house and under her own eye !

Lastly, since the Rules of Order enact, that " when any licensed
or ordained person *shall call in question* ANY *of the doctrines of the
new church contained in the theological writings of Emanuel Swedenborg* . . . . . he shall be suspended from the ministerial
functions . . . "—and since there is no doctrine more fully
contained, or more expressly taught, in Swedenborg's theological
writings than *that of the* TRINAL ORDER *of the ministry*—we most
respectfully adjure the General Convention not to suffer any of its
members or component parts to call in question *this doctrine* with
impunity !

In every government, one of the most important things is its *financial* concernment. In the episcopal form of government, therefore,
this is a prominent and striking feature. A single passage of the Acts
of the Apostles enables us to see, at a glance, what were the pecuniary
resources of the first christian church in its early establishment. The
early converts to christianity had all things in common, (Acts iv. 32.)
Provision for the temporal wants of the members of the church, and
especially for the sustenance of the poor, the widows and the orphans,
was the chief concern of the governors of the church at that time.
Hence it was among the ecclesiastical duties of the apostles to attend
to this concern ; and when the church grew too large for the apostles
to attend to this and to their other duties too, this, as a lower function of their office, was assigned to ministers of a lower degree. How
the apostles got their pecuniary means, is thus shown : " As many as
were possessors of lands or houses, sold them, and brought the prices
of the things that were sold, and laid them down at the apostles' feet :
and distribution was made unto every man according as he had need."

This distribution was a ministerial function in the apostolic church. And ecclesiastical history informs us, that provision for the support of the clergy, as well as for the poor, the widows and the orphans, which was still distributed to them by the clergy out of what was given for their own support, continued to be made, in the first centuries of the christian dispensation, by oblations, gifts, or offerings, in worship, on the Lord's day. At a later period, the giving of first fruits and tythes, was enjoined from the ritual of the jewish church. And, in modern times, *tythes* have been, and still are, one chief source of episcopal revenue. Now it was the singular conceit of some members of the Boston society, that they had discovered a "new principle," in supplying the fiscal wants of their church, by reviving this tything system. Soon it spread from that society to others in New England. Elaborate articles were written upon it for the Magazine. Reports upon it were made to the General Convention. And every thing was done to make this *the* system to supply money for the government and extension of the church throughout our whole country. This was an *episcopal* feature in the form of ecclesiastical government which our eastern brethren were seeking to induce upon our church here. And how the church was disturbed by it, let the Providence and Bridgewater societies of New England say. Now when we reflect how *odious* and *detestable* this feature of episcopacy has become in Ireland, England, and other european countries, is it not passing strange that our eastern brethren should have endeavored to introduce it into the new church of America! If they had sought to conjure up the most hideous and destructive demon from the deepest pit of the lower regions to fright the church and harass her with the most rending distractions, we cannot conceive how they could have more effectually attained their end than by raising up the *payment of tythes!* They were, however, innocent in this. Their ends were undoubtedly good; and they sought to attain them, as they thought, by orderly and right means. But they, in this, only afforded another instance of how easy it is for well-meaning men, even when they have the reputation of high intelligence, to be led into error by fanciful theory. The literal payment of tythes is the order of the mere natural man, and therefore of the merely natural church. It can never be the true order of the New Jerusalem, which is to be celestial in essence and spiritual-natural in form. The member of the New Jerusalem must do *what the tythe represents.*

There is one other feature of episcopal government, to which duty requires us to allude. The exercise of *discipline* upon the lay members by the clergy of a church. A tendency to this in the form of ecclesiastical government which our eastern brethren were seeking to induce upon our church in this country, was that to which we most strenuously objected. We admit that, when men are in a merely natural state, regal, imperial and even despotic government, (as that in Russia and Turkey,) becomes necessary, and therefore orderly, in the Lord's permissive providence. We are certain that the pure republican (not democratic, in the common acceptation of the term, for that we do not at all hold to,) system of government is celestial. But it is the government of only free and rational men. It cannot exist, much less flourish, in the soil manured and stimulated by the natural passions of the human heart. In the spiritual man, where truth is reforming the will, regal government may prevail as an orderly form. It is the somewhat strict and forcible government of the understanding, where the degenerate will must be broken by military and other similar power. But where there is a common *will* to *good* that *chooses* the government of its own *understanding* of *truth*, and where men are of this genius in their *natural* form, there is the country of free representative republicanism. So in respect to ecclesiastical government: while men are natural, and the church is natural because consisting of such men, we can readily admit that an episcopal, and even a papal form of government, becomes necessary, and therefore orderly in the Lord's permissive providence. Experience in this country may have compelled a good many of us to admit, that, while a certain class of persons are ignorant as well as merely natural, the only security of common society lies in the restraining influences of the catholic confessional. But, in our humble opinion, the government of neither papal nor episcopal *discipline* is congenial to the spirit of the New Jerusalem. Any man who has had his rational mind sufficiently opened to see by a light within itself *her* doctrines, and has a will at all subjected to *them*, needs not the *government* of a bishop. And any body of such men organized in the form of a society of any grade, *must be a law unto themselves*. Each one of them will have to exercise the discipline of the spiritual man upon his own natural man in himself; and the whole body of them, *as one man*, will exercise the same discipline upon its own members. Each society, as a society, must exercise a salutary discipline upon its own component parts; and does not need an *overseer* to keep it in order. This is the government of *slavery*, not of *freedom*. There are bishops in heaven; but, we opine, it is a spiritual or spiritual-natural heaven, or heaven in the spiritual or spiritual-natural degree. And there may be bishops on earth, in societies that correspond to that heaven. But in the New Jerusalem of *republican* America, we do not want bishops; nor her societies *their discipline*. Our societies should correspond to *those* in heaven, wherein " none is desirous to act all from himself; still less to *preside over the rest*, and *lead the choir ;* for whosoever does this, is of himself dissociated instantly ; but they *suffer themselves to be led mutually by each other*—thus *all* in *particular* AND in GENERAL to be led by the Lord." (A. C. 3350.) Still our societies are not to be without government and discipline, although they be not those of a bishop or overseer. They are not to be without governors and the subordination of lower to higher, as well as the co-ordination of both in their respective grades. But in our republican social crystallization of free will according to reason, the lower parts will *subordinate themselves* to the higher, or the exterior to the interior parts of our congregate man. Those who feel themselves to be less intelligent or less wise will subordinate themselves to those who are seen or perceived by themselves to be more intelligent or more wise, and this will take place by *the body's electing* them to their offices. Thus *all*

mutually led by each other will be led by the Lord to a free and
rational arrangement of themselves around central personifications, or
human organs, of superior love and wisdom—who, by exhortation,
advice and reproof, in charity, shall correct what is wrong, and direct
what is right, in the conduct of the lower members; and the whole
body, as a body, by its common sympathy, by its common attraction
of cohesion, or its common exhalation of repulsion, will bind to itself
and sustain what is homogeneous in its component parts, and will
evacuate whatever is heterogeneous and no longer conducive to its
life.   This is our republican government and republican *discipline* for
the societies of the new church in America.

How has the episcopal discipline of our eastern brethren differed
from this?   It is the desire of our heart to point out this difference
in kind monition, and not in censorious reproof.   In this collection of
elementary matter for a history of our church in this country; we
are led to record one instance illustrative of this difference.   It is
brought up by the proceedings of the twenty-third convention, in
1841, in respect to the Bridgewater society.   Let the reader look at
Jour. of 23d Gen. Con., p. 434, for a " Communication from Receivers
in Bridgewater ;" then read numbers 49, 64 and 85 of that journal,
in connection with Report No. 7, on p. 423—also n. 65 of Jour. of
24th Gen. Con., p. 409, with the Report from the Society of Bridgewater on p. 441, for these words, " Eighteen have voluntarily separated themselves from it ; but *most of these had been virtually
separated for a long time.*"   Then let him take up Newchurchman,
Vol. I., and, turning to page 428, read that and the next page.   He
will thus see the difference between the Rev. Samuel Worcester and
the Bridgewater society, which grew out of his exercise of what we
regard as the discipline of new-church episcopacy in New England.

The Rev. Samuel Worcester was the person of whom we have
before spoken in this sketch as having received the first license which
was given in the new church of this country.   He was then residing
and teaching school in Natchez, Miss.   Soon he returned to Boston
and became the first preacher of the society there.   Being succeeded
in this office by his brother Thomas, we do not hear much of him in
the new-church ministry for a few years, till he is engaged in missionary labors in the state of Maine.   At last he becomes active in
building up a number of small societies of the church in somewhat
contiguous parts of Massachusetts and Rhode Island ; and is ordained
as the pastor of the society in Bridgewater, Ms., with sundry receivers
of the doctrines and members of the church in connection with it in
Raynham, Fall River, New Bedford, West Bridgewater, Pawtucket,
Leicester and Gloucester, Ms., and in Providence, North Providence,
Cranston and Warwick, R. I.   In this field of labor he was very
efficient.   A man of undoubted talents, of great energy and decision
of character, and a sermonizer of the first order, he could not be otherwise any where.   From the start he was a leading man in the new
church of New England.   Able, frank, bold and persevering, he made
the doctrines known and respected wherever he went.   He had a
blunt, out-spoken, honest, downright way, peculiar to himself, of

acknowledging a fault or confessing an error when convinced of one, which made us like him despite of a somewhat harsh and overbearing mien that was at times exceedingly repulsive. We speak from only the transient impressions of a slight acquaintance. In a word, he was a *strong* man. But, like all of us, he had his defects. And, as with all strong men, his defects were strong ones. The most serious, the mantle of charity covered while he was on earth, and now the grave covers them. They are now known only where their exposure can be for his own eternal good. Here the only defect we need to mention was a disposition to exercise what seemed to others arbitrary authority in the church. It was under his administration, that, in the second year after the first beginning of the Boston society, it was thought "there was a disposition to an arbitrary government already growing in the leaders of that society." And to him, perhaps, more than to any of our eastern brethren, may be traced the tendency to that strict government of stringent rules, with all its severe disciplinary measures, which we have so much objected to in the eastern leaders of the General Convention. It is this that we are now about to illustrate.

In New England, the laws of some of the states require every one to contribute to the support of public worship. This law the Puritans brought with them from Old England. While there was but one religious denomination, called the Orthodox, the requisitions of the law were not galling. But as different sects arose, there arose with them reactions upon the law. Perhaps there was, at all times, reaction upon it from those who had no religion. But these were at first, and for some time after the settlement of New England, an inconsiderable and unfelt minority. In some states, we believe, the law has been repealed, and the support of religion left to voluntary contribution. And in all it has been modified, so as to allow every one the liberty of choosing to what religious denomination he will pay his tax. This has produced the custom of some persons joining, and contributing money to the support of public worship in, a religious society, the faith of which they do not themselves hold. And this has led to the distinction of the *legal society* from *the church*—the latter consisting of the baptized and communing holders of the faith.

It was out of this distinction of the legal society and the church, that the Rev. Samuel Worcester's difficulty with the Bridgewater society arose. In that society there were some who contributed to the support of its public worship who were not yet full receivers of the new-church doctrines; others who, although receiving the doctrines, had not made up their minds to become baptized and communing members of the church. These were not only a majority of the society, but also, some of them, men of property and good standing in the general community. Chiefly by the means and influence of these, the society had erected a very eligible place of worship, and were gaining respectability in the eyes of the surrounding sectaries. Soon Mr. Worcester conceived the plan of obliterating the distinction between the legal society and the church, by getting all the members of the former to become members of the latter.

With his usual frankness, he first openly proposed the measure. But he had in his society men of strong rational minds, stern integrity, and great good common sense. These were not disposed to join the church for any such reason. But upon these especially Mr. Worcester endeavored to exercise his powers. First kind suggestion in the way of social intercourse; then arguments; then persuasion; (and no one can know what we mean by this word unless he has felt the *sphere* of the two Worcesters;) and at last a certain authoritative, dogmatic look and tone, which no word will express, which can only be known by being seen and heard. These appliances were brought to bear on those strong men of his society whom we have indicated. Now, if any man has been in New England, and has learned by actual observation what sort of stuff the leading members of religious societies in its towns and villages are made of, he will know, better than we can tell him, what effect the exercise of any thing like arbitrary ecclesiastical authority by a priest upon them would have. And perhaps all our readers, by looking around them upon the material that religious societies are made of every where in America—by only turning their eyes inward on their own bosoms—may now discern how the Rev. Samuel Worcester's difficulties with the Bridgewater society were engendered. In short, precisely the same spirit which prompted Mr. Benjamin Hobart,[*] of Abington, Ms., to move the arbitrary measure of the twentieth convention respecting the enforcement of the Rules of Order upon societies, or Caleb Reed, Esqr., of Boston, to move the equally arbitrary mandate to the recusant ministers to report themselves to the General Convention, by which so much and such strong reaction upon that general body was provoked, incited Mr. Worcester to that exercise of arbitrary pastoral authority which alienated from him the Bridgewater society.

But there was a certain other exercise of arbitrary pastoral authority by Mr. Worcester, in respect to a very respectable and estimable lady of his society, which poured commingled oil and spirit upon the flame of opposition to him previously kindled. This lady had lost her first husband, who, dying, left her with one or more children. Their union had been peaceful and happy. And in the condolence wont to be given to the widow about the time of the funeral, some of the female members of the church declared they heard her express the conviction that her spirit was united to that of her departed husband, because she believed he was her true conjugial partner; and

---

[*] See Wilkins's Letters, p. 38. Mr. Wilkins, although present in that convention, says he does not know "who called the attention of the convention to the subjects noticed in the communication from Boston," and therefore was the person on whose motion the obnoxious resolution, n. 59, p. 367, of its journal, was passed. We have the above named gentleman's own authority for giving him this unenviable notoriety. We shall be very much mistaken if he is the only one, who, either in this world or the next, is doomed to be ashamed of, or sorry for, their motions in the General Convention. It is on only our own conjecture, that the resolution, n. 61, p. 368, Jour. 20th Gen. Con., is ascribed to Mr. C. Reed. We conjecture that he was the mover of that resolution, because it sounds like his thunder, and because the after-claps in nn. 19 and 20 of Jour. of 21st Gen. Con. are officially recorded as his.

this was a source of comfort to her in her affliction. The lady herself denies that she ever made any thing like such a declaration. Time rolls on. A younger man by fourteen years becomes in providence a widower with one or two small children. Being engaged in some mechanical employment, and having no female relative to take charge of his family, it is broken up by the death of his wife. He is obliged to put out his children to board, and takes boarding himself. It so happens that his children are put to board with the widow lady above mentioned, whose circumstances are such as to require her to take such boarders for a livelihood. The children are remarkably well taken care of; for the widow is a woman of rare excellence. The father visits his children, occasionally at first, but more frequently at last. He perceives the excellent care that is taken of them, and at the same time the excellent matronly qualities of her who has charge of them. Both receivers of the doctrines of the new church, their acquaintance ripens into interior spiritual friendship. The *mind* of the man, looking at the *mind* of the woman, forgets the age of the body. And the wants of the widower with the needs of the widow suggest to both the propriety of their each contracting a second marriage of convenience, upon the principles taught by Swedenborg in Conjugial Love, 319, 321, 325. This goes on, as usual, without any body's knowing any thing about it but the parties concerned. When they have made up their minds, they cause their proposed marriage to be published according to the custom in New England. Mr. Worcester, the pastor of the church to which the lady belongs, takes exception to the marriage; requests her to call on him; and, as she does not do so immediately, addresses her a note, upbraiding her for doing such a thing secretly, and of her own accord, without consulting him, as her pastor, or her new-church friends, as to the propriety of her taking such a step; or for the purpose of giving them all the good reasons which she had for taking it before she took it; and then admonishes her of the great impropriety that there is in her getting married separately and distinctly from the church to which she belongs. The lady sends an exceedingly well written, but tart reply, expressing her astonishment that Mr. Worcester should presume to exercise such authority over her, and that he should have so little good sense as to meddle in a matter with which he clearly had no business. Stung by this, he refuses to perform the marriage ceremony, and gives his reasons, at length, in a letter addressed to both of the contracting parties. They proceed to North Bridgewater, and are married by the Rev. Mr. Carll, who was then stationed there. This produces a disagreement between Mr. Carll and Mr. Worcester, which it takes a long time to reconcile. The lady, after her marriage, finds her residence in South Bridgewater very uncomfortable, and asks, about a year or eighteen months afterwards, through Mr. Worcester, a dismission from his society, that she may be received as a member in good standing by that in North Bridgewater. Mr. Worcester and his church refuse to give her a certificate of such standing, until she comes before them and *proves* herself innocent of the charge of *falsehood* in having denied that she had said her former husband was her

19

conjugial partner. The lady cannot in conscience undertake to prove her innocence of such a false charge; and she is suffered to go forth with a brand of official disgrace upon her fair reputation. She is most respectably connected. The wealthiest and every way one of the best families of Mr. Worcester's church is related to her. The head of this family, formerly Mr. Worcester's staunchest friend, and firmest adherent, fired by all the good feelings of a true man, takes up her cause. Others of the church, as well as of the legal society, side with him. They remonstrate with Mr. Worcester, and endeavor to counteract his efforts to destroy the lady's reputation in the community. *For this*, Mr. Worcester *subjects them to the church's* DISCIPLINE, and SUSPENDS THEM FROM THE COMMUNION OF THE CHURCH !!! These members of his church, thus suspended, he reports to the Twenty-fourth General Convention as those who "had been virtually separated for a long time," when they had "voluntarily separated themselves from" the Bridgewater society.

Other things occurred, with regard to Mr. Worcester's habits of life, which tended to alienate from him, as the pastor of his society, the respect and affection of a majority of its best members. Hence, just seven months after the refusal to give the lady above mentioned a certificate of good standing in the society, eleven of its most substantial 'male members, address a note to the Rev. Samuel Worcester and the other members of the society, respectfully requesting that a separation may take place between "the present pastor and the society," and "that it may be effected in as quiet and peaceable a manner as possible." Mr. Worcester consents, and the separation takes place. The separation is between him and the legal society, which holds the place of worship, while Mr. Worcester's friends, as the church, hold separate meetings in the court house. The former leader of the worship, whom the order of New England required to be a member of the church, resigned his office, and withdrew with the rest. Thus the legal society was left without any church member to lead their worship. They, therefore, addressed a note to the church requesting them to appoint one of their number to act as their leader. The church declined. They then addressed a letter to the Rev. Thomas Worcester, of Boston, stating what had taken place, and what they had done, asking him to advise them what course to pursue; and, that he might do so more understandingly, to come and see them, and make himself acquainted with their condition. He cannot come; and some of the members of the legal society go to Boston, and consult him there. Their statement of their case, and his advice to them, in respect to it, are made and given in such a way that they misunderstand each other, and several notes pass between him and them for explanation. The upshot of the matter is, that Mr. T. Worcester advises "the eleven" members of the legal society who had asked the separation, to go to his brother, and, exercising charity towards him, become reconciled to him, so that he and the church reuniting with the legal society, they might find again in *him* the leader of their worship. This mode having been fully tried before the separation to no effect, is deemed useless after it.

During this time, a very sensible and a very worthy man, the leader of the opposition to Mr. S. Worcester, is induced, though not a member of the church, to act as the leader of the worship for the legal society. But as this was deemed by him and by all irregular and disorderly, they applied to the Providence society, to depute one of their church members. That society deputes a Mr. Ames, who acts in that capacity for some time.

All the while, trouble between the parties ferments. The legal society really seemed desirous to live in charity with their brethren of the church; and if there were another pastor, there seemed to be no obstacle in the way of their coming together again, and acting in harmony. But they were not disposed to succumb to Mr. Worcester; and without that, the separated church, wholly under his influence, could present to the other party only an austere countenance. The price of reunion was a complete subordination of the legal society to the church, so that the latter should hold and control the property with Mr. Worcester as their pastor. How impossible this was, the issue of coming events alone could show.

The Massachusetts Association had been invited to hold their next meeting at Bridgewater. It was hoped that the influence of this body would avail in settling the difficulty there. The legal society, learning this, promptly wrote to the Rev. Thos. Worcester, president of the association, tendering their temple to him, for its use in its approaching session. Mr. Worcester gave them to understand that he was not the proper person to tender it to. The church at Bridgewater had invited the association to meet there, and was expected to furnish a place for it to meet in. Taking this hint, the legal society immediately tendered their temple to the church for the use of the association. The church replied, in a surly tone, if the legal society were disposed to give them the control of their temple, they would come back and worship in it; but they were not inclined to accept the tender of it for any other use. That chopped the matter of reconciliation off pretty short.

Seeing no other way to sustain themselves against the powerful influences brought to bear, so as to constrain them to a reunion with the church under Mr. S. Worcester, the legal society at length determined to try and get themselves regularly instituted as a society of the church. Their view in this was to call another minister, and sustain him as a preacher in their temple. They apply to the Rev. Thos. Worcester, as an ordaining minister of the General Convention, and presiding minister of the Massachusetts Association, to institute them. He replies that the Rules of Order require him to visit them and see whether their state is such as to make it right for him to comply with their request. He appoints a day when he will meet them at his brother's. Something occurs to prevent a conference. He meets with an accident—is thrown from a chaise, and has his left foot dislocated. This prevents his coming to Bridgewater again for some time. When he gets there again, he learns the difficulties between the legal society and his brother, as we have detailed them, with a good deal besides that we have not related. He uses all his influence to produce a reconciliation in vain. He then feels unwilling to decide against his brother, and calls into consultation a committee of the Massachusetts Association, consisting of two lay members from each of the societies belonging to that body, with the exception of the Bridgewater society. This committee are unable to decide any thing, because they do not know any thing. They, however, in general decide, that the legal society ought not to be instituted unless they are in charity with the church, and wish to be admitted into it on the ground of charity. This is a pretty obvious matter, and the legal society express some surprise that the ordaining minister, or his lay counsellors, should for a moment imagine that they had thought of applying to be, or had expected to be, instituted on any other ground. Then Mr. Thomas Worcester has to inform the committee how the matter stands between the legal society and his brother, so that they may see that it is right to institute another church in Bridgewater when there is already one there with his brother as its pastor. In short, he has to tell them what he learned of his brother's delinquencies as the causes of the alienation of the members of the legal society from him. But as he is not willing to trust his memory in so serious an affair, he writes to the legal society requesting *them* to prefer their *charges* against his brother to the committee. They reply that, under their present circumstances, they are not going to prefer charges against any body. Then Mr. Worcester says he and the committee must wait until they can find something to determine their judgments in deciding upon their application for institution as a society of the church. They rejoin that they have nothing further to say on that subject, and call upon him categorically to decide upon their application. Well, if he must decide *now*, upon their case as it *now stands*, he decides that, *under present circumstances*, it is *not* his *duty* to form them into a society.

More than the legal society did to keep in with their brethren of the General Convention, so as to sustain that body and carry out its order, it was impossible for men to do! All their predilections, feelings, affections, thoughts were decidedly eastern. And to be compelled to turn to other quarters of the general church, and look for help, to sustain them in maintaining and securing their spiritual and rational freedom, was a cause of grief. But they had no other alternative. The same spirit of arbitrary authority which was seeking to *crush* them into a *charitable* conformity to the laws of order,—to *make* them promote the peace of Jerusalem by quiet acquiescence in prescribed duties according to external interpretations of the laws of charity,—had brought into existence the Central Convention. With this body they seemed to themselves to be driven to make common cause. The Boston leaders fearing that this would be the result of Mr. Worcester's refusal to institute them, wrote to them urging them to apply to the General Convention itself, and offering to use their influence in that body to bring about their institution by another ordaining minister. They catch at the suggestion with avidity, and send, by the Boston delegation, a submission of their case to the General Convention. In the mean time, tired out by delays, and mistrusting any better issue to their future, than had happened to their past, applications to their own house and kindred, they determined to take time by the forelock, and invited the Rev. C. J. Doughty, the leading minister of the Central Convention, to visit them, preach for them, become acquainted with their circumstances, and advise them what to do.

The Boston delegation redeem their promise, and lay the case of the eighteen Bridgewater receivers who had applied unsuccessfully to the Rev. Thos. Worcester for institution as a society, before the Twenty-third General Convention. The Rev. Samuel Worcester is in that convention. What influence he exerted upon the appointment of the committee, we know not. A committee is appointed to act in the Bridgewater case. But its members are so widely separated in space, that they cannot or do not act speedily. The Bridgewater people had expressed an " earnest desire" that the action of the convention should be " prompt." They were not disposed to brook any longer delay. Mr. Doughty's intercourse with them, if it had not inclined them to the Central Convention, had at least shown them where a remedy lay. Two months having elapsed after the committee of the General Convention was appointed without any action being taken in their case, although they had applied personally to a majority of that committee to know if any thing was going to be done for them—in short there being no prospect that the committee would act at all, and if it did, there being a strong prospect that Mr. S. Worcester's influence would prevail in it to defeat them still in the attainment of their ends, they withdrew their application to the General Convention, and applied to another ordaining minister of the Central Convention, to institute them as a society. This was a sore trouble to the eastern leaders, and they did all they could to prevent it. This is not the place to detail what their efforts in this respect were. The citation already made from the Newchurchman, Vol. I., p. 428, has informed the reader, who was sent for, who went on, and who actually instituted the legal society of Bridgewater a society of the new church. The question was raised, while he was there, whether that society should join the Central Convention. A good many of its members did. Others, from their strong predilections for neighboring connections, did not. Had not the Massachusetts Association invaded the province of the Central Convention, connived at the displacing of Mr. Doughty, and then taken his society under its charge, it would have been right in us to have advised the Bridgewater society to seek connection with that association. Had not the Eastern Convention done all it could to put down the Middle Convention in its very first efforts to rise up,—advising, and, by their emissaries, actually getting up a Pennsylvania Association for the purpose of rooting it out,—it would have been improper for us to have interfered in the concerns or arrangements of the New England Associations. But the cause of the Bridgewater society and that of the Central Convention were identical—the *freedom of the whole church.* And when we had helped them to attain or retain their freedom, it was as little as they could do, in return, to help us to maintain ours. But the persuasive

influences by which they are surrounded have proved too strong for
them. They were told "that there is no need of the Central Convention." They believed the insinuation; and have withdrawn, many
of them, from its connection. By reuniting with the former church
under another minister, they have given up their institution as a
society by the minister of the Central Convention; and have made it
necessary for us now to place on record the grounds of our action in
that institution. It is due to our vindication in the eyes of our posterity, that we should demonstrate the existence and prevalence of a
spirit of arbitrary ecclesiastical authority in the measures of our
eastern brethren, to justify alike the establishment of the Central
Convention, and the institution of the Bridgewater society by its
minister. And this could not be done without the foregoing historical
sketch of the difficulties which had arisen between that society and
its pastor, and the publication of those documents which were placed
in our hands to make us acquainted with the nature of those difficulties, in order that we might judge of the propriety of its institution as
a society of the New Jerusalem. We, therefore, publish those documents now in our appendix, and thus redeem the promise that we
gave the church some time ago. They will be found in No. LX.
And we trust that they will be read, not only to our justification, but
to the present and the lasting profit of our church now and in all
coming time. We also deem it right to publish in immediate connection with them, (see No. LXI.,) the letter which was written in
answer to the communication of J. F. Street, Esqr., of Pawtucket, to
the Sixth Annual Meeting of the Central Convention. (See Jour.
No. VIII., p. 7, nn. 17 and 62, in connection with Ap. II., p. 62.)
The treatment which the ministers of the Central Convention received
at the dedication of the temple in Providence, to which they had
been officially invited by the Providence society, will probably be
mentioned elsewhere. No transaction can so well illustrate the spirit
which has actuated our eastern brethren as that. But enough, quite
enough, is displayed in this account of the church discipline and authority which the Rev. Samuel Worcester tried to exercise in the
Bridgewater society, to show us by what sort of episcopacy we should
now be swayed, if our eastern brethren had had their full swing in
our church in this country. And we most devoutly pray, that this
exposure of a tendency to such a form of ecclesiastical government
here, may, in the Lord's merciful providence, be owned and blessed
by him as an humble means of preventing it now, henceforth, and
for ever!

But one more thing remains. We have to look into the present
state of the question of the ministerial trine in the General Convention. We have seen that our eastern brethren have made the order
for that body, and are now wholly controlling it. What is their view
of a trine in the ministry? Turning to Jour. of 24th Gen. Con. p.
412, n. 96, we find that the following resolution, offered by the Rev.
Mr. Dike, was adopted :—

   Resolved, That the Rules of Order be committed to a select committee,
to report such alterations as they may think required; with particular refe-

rence, *first*, to the order of the ministry as consisting of a trine in just order; *secondly*, to the order of the church as consisting of a trine in just order; *thirdly*, to the relation of an orderly ministry and an orderly church to each other.

From the fresh agitation of the question of a conjugial pastoral relation in the West in 1838 ; from its revival in the middle states, especially in the cities of New York and Philadelphia, from 1839 up to the summer of 1842 ; and especially from the open renunciation of the conjugial theory by the Rev. C. J. Doughty—who had been one of its most strenuous advocates and successful propagators—in April of the latter year ; it was thought, by many in this quarter, that the above resolution, passed in June, 1842, was designed to bring out from the strong men of the East a full and irresistible confirmation of that theory. The Rev. Thos. Worcester, president of the convention which passed the above resolution, was the one appointed that year to address the General Conference of England. In his letter he called the attention of that body to this resolution, and asked the views of our english brethren upon its subject. The conference appointed a committee to report upon it. And the able report of the Rev. J. H. Smithson was the issue. But as this report presumed to give a most decided, unqualified and unmeasured condemnation of the conjugial theory, it was not very well received in a certain quarter. It was received in sullen silence. It was rendered to the conference in 1844, was received in this country, and published by the Central Convention in 1845; but it was not published by the General Convention till 1846 ; and had first to be submitted to the pastoral committee of the convention to determine whether it ought to be published or not, or to express their opinion of it. A committee of five ordaining ministers, report to the twenty-eighth convention, that " they are not prepared at present to express an opinion upon the above-named report, but recommend that it be printed in the journal of this convention." Now was the time for the General Convention, in a frank and manly manner, to have denied the charge which was implied against it in the english report, of having held the principle of a conjugial pastoral relation. But not a word is spoken by the convention itself. Not a word is said to the convention by the ordaining ministers. The invidious task is left to its agent to deny the charge, in the letter sent in its name that year to the General Conference, *with covert implications of* FALSE TESTIMONY *on this subject having been borne to that body by those who were not the friends of the General Convention in this country.* Did not the writer of that letter know, that the most elaborate, and far the ablest, argument for the conjugial theory which has ever been written, was sent by the Rev. Samuel Worcester to Mr. Arbouin, the celebrated author of that excellent little work entitled " The Regenerate Life" ? It is a fact ; and he ought to have known it, if he did not. He ought to have known, too, that, when Mr. Samuel Worcester's letter arrived in England, Mr. Arbouin having gone into the world of spirits, it came into the hands of the Rev. Mr. Sibly, of London, and was very generally read by the leading men of our church in that country. And does he imagine that men of their penetration have not discerned the conjugial principle ramifying through all the order of the General Convention, despite of all the efforts of the holders of it, to conceal it? Does he, in short, imagine that they are as ignorant as himself of what principles *have been* held in this country by those who have stood at the fountain heads from whence all the General Convention's order and government, and some of its distinguishing measures, have flowed for years? And does he think that they have as little discernment as he, so as not to perceive that the streams have the same water as that which issues from the fountain? But the General Convention, and the devisers of its order, do not *say* that the relation of a pastor to a society is conjugial; and in the report, which the select committee appointed under the above cited resolution rendered to the General Convention, there is nothing like a declaration of this principle. What of that? Is it necessary that *every* painter should write under the images of those objects which he paints, *this is the* MAN, *and this is the* HORSE?

The report of that committee was made to the twenty-fifth convention, and is to be found in pages 423—430 of the journal for 1843. It consists mostly of a critique upon the noted passage of Coronis, n. 17. Some of the remarks upon this passage are very just, and we shall have occasion to quote them, when we come to consider it. But we think the conclusion that Swedenborg intended to teach what should be the specific form of the ministerial trine for the new church by the terms *primus infulatus, antistites parochi, et flamines sub illis*, is not well founded. Why we think so we will state in another place.

· The committee found their trinal order almost wholly upon this one passage. It is indeed sufficient, because most express and entirely conclusive as to *a* trine in the priesthood. But we have to object to this committee's views of what that trine should be in the new church, that they are based merely on *their interpretation* of Swedenborg's language. And not only are the distinct offices and officers in the trine determined by the explanation of the meaning of the precise terms used, but also "the duties of the three grades in the ministry, and the relation of these grades to each other, are *inferred from the explanation that is given of the terms* which Swedenborg employs to designate them." This surely is too weak a base for so large and heavy a structure. For, in the first place, the latin words used by Swedenborg in this passage are susceptible of a somewhat different interpretation from that which the committee have given them; and, in the next place, we do not believe that what Swedenborg meant to teach should be deduced from this clause, merely by drawing out the specific meaning of its latin terms with the aid of etymology and the lexicon; but that we ought to interpret the meaning of this sentence by the general drift of the passage in which it is found, and by what Swedenborg says specifically in other parts of his writings on the same subject.

However, all we want to know now is, what *is* the order which the committee deduce from this passage? In brief, " there must be in the church, a *consecrated, ordained* or *acknowledged first* or *head*,

superintendant district ministers, and *local ministers* under them."
" Those of the first grade . . . stand in' the relation of pastors to
each individual of their respective societies; and *they* together with
the lay members of their societies, constitute churches in larger form."
Let it be observed that this important conclusion that a minister of the
lowest grade *must* be a pastor of a society, rests wholly on the interpretation of the latin term *flamen,* which Swedenborg uses to designate
him.   It is because, in roman usage, "*flamen* was the title of a priest
appointed over the worship of a particular god in his own particular
temple," and although " subject to the direction of a higher order of
priests," yet " was regarded as holding a highly important, and, to a
certain degree, independent rank in the priesthood," therefore, when
Swedenborg says there must be in the church *antistites parochi et
flamines sub illis,* he certainly means that the lowest grade of the
new-church priesthood must be a pastor of a society himself, and not
the *assistant* of such a pastor. Is not this a sandy foundation for such
a house? Observe, too, the two terms in the constituents of churches
in larger form—THE PASTORS *together with* THEIR SOCIETIES. How
does this flow from the trine of *primus infulatus, antistites parochi
et flamines sub illis,* as constituting one thing? Is it not plain that
Swedenborg, in this sentence, implies, by the term *ec lesia,* simply the
priesthood ; and not the church as composed of clergy and laity in a
complex form ? When he speaks, in the preceding sentence, of the
kingdom as a complex form, the lower terms of the trine are not official
personages as they are here. Therefore, as all the terms of this trine
are official personages, it is purely an *official trine* constituting an
official unit, that is, *one priesthood.* Consequently, this committee in
superadding a trine of lay terms to Swedenborg's trine of official
terms, have produced a *fiction* of their own and not taught a doctrine of his. They err in this argument—" if there be such a trine
in the ministry," therefore " there must be a similar trine in the
church." This may be true; but it is not the way in which they
should conclude or teach *what* the *trine* in the *church* is. They should
find and produce those passages of Swedenborg's writings in which *he*
teaches what is the trine in the church; and on *these* found the
church's trinal order. But in the passage which teaches simply the
trine in the ministry they should found only the *ministry's* trinal order.
But here *their own theory* creeps in. And we see *it* making the pastor
(as the *head*) *and* the society (as the *body,* or *wife,*) *together* constitute the church in the lowest grade of the church's trine. Next
"*those* [plural] of the second grade" . . . "stand in *a similar
relation* to *each* of the *societies* or *churches* within their *district
regarded as a unit or church in a larger form,* as the *pastors stand in
to* the *several individuals* of their *societies.* They are in a sense the
pastors of these *larger individuals* or churches. Their duties are not
with the *particular* individuals of the societies, but with the societies
themselves." And "*the* minister [singular] of the third grade may
be regarded as *the pastor* of the several associations which unite together" so as to form " a consociation" or " church in a still larger form"
as a larger individual. Thus we have *one man* the *pastor* of a *society ;*

one man the *pastor* of *an association* of *societies ;* and *one man* the *pastor* of a *consociation* of *associations.* Now in all honesty, sincerity and love of truth for its own sake, where, under the heavens or over the heavens, beneath the sun or above it, can authority be found for this order in these *eleven* of Swedenborg's words—*similiter in ecclesia, primus infulatus, antistites parochi, et flamines sub illis !* What is there in these eleven words to *prove,* that a complex society *may not have* a *complex* pastor, but *must have* an *individual* pastor ? Does any one think that the chairman of the committee which wrote and presented this report ought to have written *this* is the *man,* or *this* is the *horse, here !* Need *we say* here is *the conjugial theory gone to seed ?* But

Such is the opinion which your committee, from a careful consideration of the subject referred to them, have been led to adopt respecting an orderly ministry and an orderly church, and *their relation* to EACH OTHER. They do not *feel confident* that the view which they have here presented is *the true view of the subject ;* they *only know* that it is the view under which *the subject has presented itself to* THEIR MINDS, and *which has appeared to them to be the true one.*

What solemn mockery ! Ought they not, as *the ministers* of the *truth,* to have been *more confident* that the view of the subject which they were presenting *was* the true one, before they thus presented it to the whole church ? What did the church want of them—what did the church ask of them as her ministers of truth ? To teach her how truth *appeared to them ?* Or to teach her how *the Lord has taught it* to them ? What would the church say to them, if, in teaching her the truth that the Lord himself is God alone, they were to say, " this is the view under which the subject has presented itself to *our minds"*—this " has appeared to *us* to be the true view" ! And cannot even the external order of our church be taught from the Lord by Swedenborg ? If not, let *our* ordaining ministers say nothing about it.

But the committee are unanimously of the opinion, that the time has not yet arrived for carrying the order here explained into full practical operation, *even admitting it to be the true order.* [Still doubt on this point.] There are many and obvious reasons why it could not and should not be adopted entire at present. The most *we can expect to do,* or should *endeavor to* AIM AT, is, *to make such approximation towards it, as the advancing state of the church will permit.*

Why has not the time arrived to carry *any* truth out, *when it is seen to be truth ?* Does the Lord give men light to *see* merely ? Does he give men day *merely to see the light of it ?* Or does he give them day to *work* while it *is* day ? Does he not give them *light,* that they may become *the children of it ?* And when is the time to *begin* the work— in the evening, the mid-day, or the *morning ?* Truly, if the ordaining ministers are *not confident* that *this is* the true order,—if they have *any* hesitation in " admitting it to be the true order,"—the time for carrying it out " *into full practical operation*" has most certainly not arrived ! And *so confident* are *we* of its *not* being the true order, that, from the inmost adytum of our souls, do we most devoutly pray the

Lord, in his infinite mercy to ordain, that the time for carrying it out *may* NEVER *arrive !*

Yet we presume it cannot have escaped the observation of every reader, that, although this view of order has only " presented itself to their minds" as " the true one"—and although they " are unanimously of opinion that the time has not yet arrived for carrying it into full practical operation"—still *they do expect to carry it out into* FULL *practical operation at some future time*, are *now* " *endeavoring to aim at" this as their end*, and, until such full time arrives, are *striving "to make such approximations towards it," as the existing states of the church will permit*. Therefore we conclude, that the theory of a con-jugial pastoral relation has been secretly insinuated into the General Convention's trinal order of her ministry—that it lies covertly as an un-developed germ in that order—that it is not yet seen to expand, blossom and fructify in its full form, because it is imagined that the time for this has not yet arrived—that it has only come out into such approxi-mation to its full blown state as the circumstances of the church will permit—but that the leaders of that convention are now looking to the carrying it out into full practical operation in some future time as an end. And this is the present state of the question of a trine in the new church ministry in America, so far as the General Convention is concerned.

We had intended to close this head of our report with a summa-tion of its contents. But the thread of our discourse has spun out to such an interminable length, that it is more than time to cut it short. A complete sketch of the history of the question of a ministerial trine in this country, requires a portraiture of its present state in the West-ern and Central Conventions. But as the present head has swelled to so vastly a disproportionate size, we must discuss these topics in another place. We propose to place them in a *Postscriptum* to this report, containing *Reviews*, first, of the last two Journals of the Western Convention, and, second, of the last Journal of the Central Conven-tion.

One word more, and we have done. An apology is due for the exceedingly loose style in which this report is thus far written, for its defective arrangement, and for its great want of condensation. The simple statement of the following facts is all the apology we can offer. It is rather more than fourteen months since we began to write this report. It has been written under the pressure of the most untoward circumstances. We have written amidst domestic trials, pecuniary embarrassments, official distractions, and various interruptions. Four-fifths of what is now written has been sent to the press after all but a few of the preceding manuscript pages have been worked off. So that we have been made aware of its defects only when it was too late to remedy them. Over, and over, have we wished that we could stop the work and consign what was done to the flames. But this being impossible, and duty requiring us to go on, *we have looked up, sought light from on high*, and *endeavored to walk in the straight though narrow pathway of duty*, which that light has pointed out. And now to HIM, who alone can overrule all our errors and defects for his glory in the universal good, thus much of our work is committed!

V. A SCRIPTURAL ARGUMENT FOR A TRINE IN THE MINISTRY—BY N. F. CABELL, ESQR.

Pains having been taken, as we thought, to impair the force of truth in this report by the insinuation that it set forth only the views of the chairman of the ecclesiastical committee, we felt solicitous to procure and embody in it the views of other members expressed in their own language. N. F. Cabell, Esqr., of Warminster, Nelson County, Virginia, who has entitled himself to the respect and gratitude of the whole church for his very able advocacy of her cause, and defence of her principles, in several productions of his pen, has been from the first associated with the members of the Central Convention's ecclesiastical council in their labors. The plan of the division of labor in searching the writings of the church for authorities upon the trine was his suggestion. To him, therefore, was assigned a portion of that labor. And when the idea occurred to us of also getting out the report on the trine upon the same principle of the division of labor, he was the first person to whom we applied to take a task. He chose the branch of the subject which comes under the present head. The church will see that it has been in able hands. We must, however, state, that we do not agree with Mr. Cabell in some of his views. But we are glad of it. For it affords us an opportunity of showing how readily we would have inserted in this report, *other views opposed to our own*, if an opportunity had been allowed us. At first, we felt some regret, that there should not be entire unanimity, or harmony of views, on the present subject in the ecclesiastical council of our convention. But as we have been permitted to see the Lord—after he has passed us, hid by his hand in a cleft of the rock, while he was passing—on the back, we have become rationally convinced, that the Divine Providence has purposely ordered such a presentation of various and diverse views of the subject before us, as would enable the Central Convention to come to a more satisfactory, final and stable conclusion of the whole matter.

We endeavored to get the Rev. Messrs. Burnham and Powell to take part in our labors also. The former has been prevented by the engagements of a secular calling, to which provision for the support of his family has compelled him to resort. The latter has kindly furnished us with what will make the next, or sixth, head of our report.

————

REV. SIR:

You ask me to commit to writing my thoughts on the order proper to the ministry of the New Church. My present conclusions on this subject were reached by independent inquiry, though I believe they agree substantially with your own. Some of the reasons therefor were stated publicly; others have been freely imparted to yourself and other individuals; but I have never attempted to embody them until now at your request. Had the clergy been unanimous in their views hereon, I should certainly have declined a task which has now become invidious, and would willingly have deferred to them in the

deduction from the proper authorities, and declaration of the qualifications, duties and rights,—the gradation if any,—of their own order,
so long as the rights of the laity were not menaced. But though
we all acknowledge the Sacred Scriptures as the rule of our faith and
practice, and the writings of Swedenborg—their expositor and our
teacher—as the ultimate tribunal from which there should be no
appeal with Newchurch-men,—certainly none in matters of positive
institution,—yet he has been generally thought to have spoken, if not
ambiguously, with less clearness on this head than on most others.
While the fact is acknowledged, I think it can be shown that there
were sufficient reasons for such caution at the time, and yet that he
has *intimated* his views in many places, and has furnished more than
one clue to his meaning, which, taken together with principles which
he has broadly laid down, lead inevitably to the conclusion we have
adopted.

Several years since, a suggestion was made to the Central Convention, at once natural and obvious, and which, if carried out, would
have proved its own utility. It was proposed that the works of Swedenborg be apportioned among the clergy, and such of the laity as might
be invited to join in the undertaking, with a view to each individual
making himself perfectly familiar with the contents of one or more
of the volumes. In that case, whenever questions, new or unsettled,
or on which farther light was desired—arose, reference to such parts
of the entire writings as tended to their elucidation, might be promptly
collected and transmitted to some one at the centre, who might lay
them before the whole church, which would thus have, with a great
saving of time and labor, all requisite materials for an intelligent
judgment. Had this been done either here or in England thirty years
since, I hardly think this would now be an open question. But as
neither this nor any equivalent method of thorough research has ever
been adopted, the result is a continued agitation of the subject both
here and abroad, without much additional light being thrown on it.
Of the feeling which, it is feared, has sometimes been permitted to
mingle in the discussion, I am not called to speak. While I have ever
striven to avoid its undue exhibition myself, I am certainly bound
to presume that those from whom I am compelled to differ are actuated
by as sincere a desire to attain correct conclusions as that by which I
feel myself to be prompted. Without doubt, valuable contributions
have been made to the stock of our information, in various reports
made to the public bodies of the church, and essays scattered through
her periodicals. Such of these as were accessible having been procured, soon after my introduction to the doctrine, I possessed myself
both of their argument and authorities; nor have I neglected any thing
of like kind which has since appeared in the same repositories.
While reviewing my opinions in consequence of proceedings in the
late convention, I was recently led to a source of argument, wholly
new to myself, and which certainly has not yet been exhausted. It
is principally with the hope of calling the attention of the church to
these considerations that I overcome my reluctance again to participate openly in this inquiry. Although they should fail to modify

existing opinions—they may yet be worthy of examination, and if they can be shown to be fallacious or irrelevant, they may thenceforth be dismissed as useless in the solution of this question. If this can be made to appear, the writer hereby pledges himself to their instant renunciation. To abridge the labor of the reader, the several statements of fact and steps of the argument, shall be accompanied with references to authority by which the former may be verified and the latter authenticated.

The church in general consists of all those who acknowledge the Lord, have the word, and obey its requisitions. (H. D. 242, 245.) In another sense it consists of various visible societies, more or less organized, which have a separate order of men appointed to impart religious instruction, both public and private, to the people, and to conduct their *worship*, which we are told should be external as well as internal. (A. C. 1175, 1618.) Such external worship and such an order of men for its conduct have existed on this planet from the time of the ancient church. It was retained in the Jewish system. Our Lord himself while on earth established such a ministry in the first Christian church. His servant, who was called to expound his Word, has declared that such an order should exist in the New Christian church.

Matters pertaining to religion, therefore, are usually and properly distributed and treated of under three principal heads:—1. Doctrine, which relates either to faith or life. 2. Worship or rituals. 3. *Government*, which includes the *constitution of the priesthood*, as well as the regulation of the laity in their rights of communion with each other, and the exercise of Discipline. Though the great object of Swedenborg in his writings, was to restore and enlarge the knowledge of the first, yet he has not, as we shall see, wholly omitted instruction concerning the two latter. The difference between the first two is obvious and is implied throughout his writings. And that the third was not identical with either or both, in his view, is sufficiently proved by the fact that he has a separate chapter on " Ecclesiastical and Civil *Government.*" (H. D. 311–325.) This is a distinction which should never be lost sight of; and yet it is by confounding the third with the second that many passages of his writings have been misunderstood, or wrested from their true meaning. The inquiry now is, whether our Lord established any particular constitution of the ministry? whether that constitution was continued in the apostolic church? and whether a similar constitution should be adopted in the New Church? These questions can only be determined by a resort to such written evidences as the books of Scripture, of Ecclesiastical History and the writings of Swedenborg. But here we are met at the threshold by the assertion that none but the books of plenary inspiration shall be allowed to testify on this subject; and the restriction is attempted to be justified by such passages from Swedenborg as declare that the *doctrine* of the church should be derived from the literal sense of the Word and confirmed by it; and from those books of the Word which contain the spiritual sense. (T. C. R. 225, A. E. 816.) I am not aware that this rule has ever been denied by·any intelligent New Churchman, but do not see its application here. It is believed that the principle for which we contend may be fairly, nay *clearly deduced from those books*, but we·are not limited to them in this inquiry. Nor is the meaning of the Rule such as has been suggested. Swedenborg indeed deduces all his doctrines from the literal sense of those books and confirms them thereby; but with the exception of the Arcana Cœlestia, which refers to no other, we believe every other work of his,—certainly all the larger ones,—*confirms* his statements by citations from one or more of the other books also. Such was his own practice. Nor has he omitted to declare the real character of those books. He says "they have not the internal sense," but he does not deny the truth of their statements. Of the Acts and Epistles, ·he says in a letter to Dr. Beyer, that "they are dogmatic writings, *having communication with heaven* but only mediate," that "nevertheless *they are very good books for the church*," and that "the reason why the apostles wrote in their peculiar style was that *the New Christian church was then to begin through them*, and that the style of the Word could not have been proper for such doctrinal tenets, which required plain and simple language, suited to the capacities of all readers."—Those who choose then, may confine their deductions and confirmations of *doctrine* to the books of plenary inspiration, though he has not. But if we would seek for the *order* which Christ established in his church, and if the passages in the Gospels which relate to this subject have been differently interpreted, (which is a fact, though to us they now seem very clear,) how are we to ascertain that order without referring to the *practice* of the apostles, particularly as "the church was then to begin (N. B.) *through them*," and the *rules* laid down by them, both of which are recorded in the Acts and Epistles and frequently referred to in other documents which have come down from the early ages of Christianity? This is very plain; but farther. Such passages as the following, T. C. R. 137, 159, 174–178, 183, 184, 486, 487, 503, Cor. 2–4, D. P. 254–274, A. R. 914,—and multitudes of others in his different works, but particularly those of his memorable relations which give an account of the state of individuals, sects and nations in the spiritual World, *imply some knowledge of Ecclesiastical History*. Much of the Spiritual Diary and nearly the whole account of the Last Judgment cannot be properly understood without such knowledge. The advocates of one order in the ministry sometimes cite in their behalf the opinions of modern partizan historians, while they are in general chary in referring to the extant remains of the Anti-Nicene Fathers and early church historians, though these are of course the only sources from which modern writers can draw their materials. We claim the like privilege— though we shall have little occasion to use it.

We learn from Swedenborg that there have been, without reckoning ·the subdivisions of each, four different churches on this earth. The most ancient church had *no externals* of worship, (A. C. 4493) and needed none, for divine truth was impressed on their hearts or was read in outward nature. In the ancient church, while as yet men lived in houses and families, every man was a priest in his own house, and the head of the tribe was probably also a superior priest. ,Such a priest was Heber. Afterwards, when on the rise of conquerors and heroes, tribes had been organized into nations with settled governments, the priesthood and royalty were united in the same person, as in the case of Melchizedek,—(A. C. 6148) who was thence called the *high-priest*. To him Abraham as the *priest* of his family paid tithes. (Gen. 14: 20.) It is clear then that there was a gradation in the priesthood at that day; and as there were always inferior ministers of the altar, we may suppose that the gradation was trinal.

What was the function of a priest in the patriarchal church? Sacrifices were not originally commanded, but charity and faith. Neither the most Ancient nor Ancient churches knew any thing of them until the time of Heber, though they were adopted by other nations afterwards and from him derived to the Jews. (A. C. 922, 1241, 2180.) What then remained but that he should 1. *intercede*,—as did Abraham for Sodom : (Gen. 18: 23–33;) 2. *bless*, as Melchizedek did Abraham : (Gen. 14: 19,) and 3. *instruct* the people in the three great branches of duty—by doctrine, precept and example—"to do justly, to love mercy, and to walk humbly with God." (Micah 6: 6–8.) And for these purposes the function will be needed until the race is regenerated. (Jer. 31: 34.)

The use of sacrifice spread Westward, but never far to the East. "The Jewish statutes, judgments and laws were known in the Ancient church." (A. C. 4449.) The same has been discovered by learned writers in the Old Church, as by Gale in his "Court of the Gentiles," Spencer on "the Laws of the Hebrews," Michaelis and others. The Jewish was then a selection from other codes and rituals, (in all of which, so far as we learn, there was a gradation of priests) but purified from the profane admixtures of these latter. For though the people themselves of those nations were better than the Jews, their worship had become idolatrous in most countries. Moses was "learned in all the wisdom of the Egyptians," (Acts 7: 22,) where the priestly was the ruling caste : and was permitted, after he became the leader of Israel, to adopt some of the wise suggestions of his father-in-law, Jethro, an Arabian priest and ruler, descended of Abraham. (Ex. 18: 13–26.)

The Jewish statutes and rituals were preceded by a solemn covenant : (Ex. 19: 3–8,) and prefaced by the ten commandments, the essence of all moral law, (Ex. 20:) which yet was known to other nations. (Doc. Life, 65.) If the Jews had adhered to that covenant and had understood the real purport of the laws *at first* given them, (from Ex. 20: to 31,) they would have had a more liberal polity and more spiritual worship than any of their neighbors. (Ezek. 20: 11, &c.) And here we wish it to be particularly noted that *before* Aaron had consented with the people in the Idolatry of the golden calf, both *he* and *his sons* were promised the perpetual priesthood of this ritual, thus preserving the gradation which was known in the Ancient Church. (Ex. 28: 1, 4, 43.) But as the people were not prepared for a system so pure and liberal, the heavier yoke of ceremonies afterwards so minutely detailed, was imposed and from which they were not to be freed until the advent of the Lord. (Ezek. 20 : 25; Acts 15: 10; Gal. 5 : 1.) The rituals,—"the dress" (T. C. R. 55) was made more cumbrous, but the *constitution* and the *gradation* of the priesthood remained unaltered. *Aaron* and *his sons* were still retained as the High Priest and *Priests ;* and the *Levites* were afterwards given for *servants* in lieu of the *first born of Israel* which had been before dedicated to that office. (Ex. 40: 12–15; Num. 3: 5–13.)

The *duties* of the Jewish priesthood were, 1. To *intercede* for the people ; (Joel 2 : 17)—the various *sacrifices* which employed so large a portion of their time constituted a great part of this branch of their duty. For, on the part of the people, they were but a significant mode of self-dedication,—and acknowledgment of Jehovah as the source of bounty,—on the part of the priest of intercession on their behalf. (Lev. passim.) Then to offer up their *prayers :* (Lev. 16 : 12, 13;) 2. To *bless* them: (Num. 6 : 22–27.) 3. To *instruct* the people in the law. (Lev. 10: 11; Deut. 33: 10; 2 Chr. 17: 8–10; 30: 22; Neh. 8 : 1–9; Ez. 44: 23, 24; Hos. 4 : 6; Mal. 2 : 6–8; Matt. 23 : 23; A. C. 9809, 9925; such was the signification of the pomegranates and bells in Aaron's robe, 9918, 9921.) The delivery of *oracles* by means of the *Urim*, (Ex. 28: 30; Num. 27: 21,) was one mode of divine instruction; and the *adjudging legal controversies*, (Deut. 17 : 9–10,) was a corollary from this part of their function, and incidental to their peculiar polity.

The Jewish priesthood was thus like that of the Ancient Church, but with the difference that, owing to the national *propensity to Idolatry and wars*, it was *separated from the royalty*. (A. C. 6148.) We have stated its duties : it had also its rights, which were rigidly protected from invasion, under the most fearful penalties. (Deut. 33: 11; Ps. 105: 15.) Witness the fate of Korah and his company, who, although priests themselves, would have trespassed on the peculiar province of Aaron; (Num. 16:) the punishment of Saul for usurping the priest's office by the forfeiture of the kingdom (1 Sam. 13: 8–14) of king Uzziah, who, though before a successful prince, for a more daring instance of the same offence, was instantly smitten and driven from the throne in disgrace. (2 Chr. 26: 16–21.) And they had their effect; for we read of no more such instances in their subsequent history. The seed of Aaron was kept pure. Each reforming prince restored the worship, and the priesthood to their duties. This was the first object after their return from captivity ; and the nation continued in the outward observance of the law until the first advent.

When the kingdom of Israel was established by rebellion, Jeroboam "*made* priests that were not *Levites*," " of the lowest of the people," and "offered incense *himself*" on his unauthorized altar. He also was punished, though not fatally, because he was an idolater in his heart. (2 Chr. 11 : 14; 1 Kings 12 : 31, 33; 3: 4, 6, 33; A. C. 878.) The ten tribes followed his example and that of the nations around them, in spite of the most pathetic remonstrance on record, (2 Chr. 13: 4–12,) until they were carried into hopeless captivity. (2 Kings 17: 23. See also Ez. 44 : 7–9.) And are these things nothing to us ?

20

Do they convey no salutary moral to both clergy and laity? Who were those that long after spoke evil of dignities, and despised dominion, but the same who also *"perished in the gainsaying of Core?"* (Jude, vs. 8, 11.)

Isaiah predicted that when the *Christian* church was established among the Gentiles, the Lord would "take of them for PRIESTS and *Levites.*" (66 : 21.) The first term may include both *high* and common priests. (Ps. 99 : 6.) He also says, "they shall be called and *named priests* and *ministers.*" (Isa. 61 : 6.) Peter calls the Christian ministry "a royal priesthood." (1 Pet. 2 : 9.) Paul does not say that the priesthood was abolished in the Christian church, but that it "was changed." (Heb. 7 : 12.) He often calls Jesus Christ the "High Priest" of our profession; (as in Heb. 3 : 1; 2 : 17; 4 : 14, 15;) but though in one sense after the order of Aaron, he was more,—i.e. after the order of Melchizedek, both High Priest and King of Kings. (7 : 11; 5 : 6, 10; 6 : 20; Com. Ps. 110 : 4.) During his own ministry and before his glorification, he interceded for his disciples, blessed and taught them. (John 17 : 6-26; Mat. 5 : 1-3, &c.) The duties of the Christian priesthood also remained the same in substance though the forms were changed from those of the Jewish. The oracles are now given forth from the Divine Word : the sacrifices and most of the rituals are abolished: Christian priests are no longer judges of legal controversies, and the people are now taught plainly by *precept* instead of symbolical rites and laws. They continued also without a figure, to intercede for, offer up the prayers of, and to bless the people as before. A prejudice has long existed among certain classes of Protestants against the term "priest" as applied to Christian ministers. But Swedenborg often gives them this title, as a prophet, and as two apostles had done before him, not in accommodation to popular usage, but as significant of their duties, and as being a generic term for the functionaries of *all* religions. (H. D. 315-319; Doc. Ch. 86, 101; C. L. 306, 308; T. C. R. 106; A. C. 3670, 6148, &c.) But if he had not, shall New Churchmen be afraid of a *name* when the *thing* is daily before them,—be that name "priest," "apostle," or "bishop?" In general it may be said, "Strip any subject of the *obscurity* which has been thrown around it, and in the same proportion you strip it of its terrors." We are no longer to be awed in this way, the spell for us being broken; for "now it is lawful to enter into the mysteries of faith." (T. C. R. 508.)

As the Jewish Church was the *Representative* of the Christian Church, we believe it was so in general and particular;—in the constitution, gradation and essential duties of the priesthood, as well as in the divine truth, of which it was the unconscious depository. We maintain, that the trine of High Priest, priest, and Levites found its counterpart in 1st. the Lord, 2d. the Twelve, 3d. the Seventy; that after his ascension, the gradation was continued in 1st. Apostles, 2d. Bishops or Elders, 3d. Deacons; that, at a still later period, the first title, as a token of respect, was limited to the original *twelve,* to Paul and a few others, though there were persons who succeeded to all their rights as superior ministers of the church ; but while the gradation and authority remained the same, the titles came, after the first generation had passed away, to be as follows, 1st. Bishop, 2d. Presbyter, Elder or Pastor, 3d. Deacon. This has been disputed by various parties, but,—dismissing the Quaker idea that there should be no separate order of priests—only three *simple* forms or theories of Church Government have ever been deduced from the New Testament, to which the following names may be given for convenience sake, 1st. Episcopacy, as above described, 2d. Presbyterianism, 3d. Independency. To meet the prejudice which a word is often sufficient to excite, I may say that while I accept the gradation which the first implies, I deny many of the assumptions of that order as it has existed in the Old Church, believing at the same time that the enjoyment of the just rights of *all* the laity and of *most of the clergy* themselves is *only compatible* with such an order properly limited with well-defined powers. And before I am done, this may appear not quite so paradoxical as now it sounds. All three of these theories assert the necessity of receiving the commission from those who have been themselves ordained;—viz. deny lay-ordination. But the second and the third maintain that since the decease of the twelve apostles there has been but *one* order of ministers; though the second would have the church to be *governed* by a gradation of *assemblies,* while the third allows to such bodies only an *advisory* influence, without a direct power over congregations or individuals. The idea of some *Congregationalists* that the people have a right to *make* and *commission* a priest for themselves, is refuted by the names of Steward, Pastor, Ambassador, Messenger, given to Christian ministers in the following texts which indicate the source of their authority. (Eph. 4 : 11 ; 1 Cor. 4 : 1 ; Rev. 2 : 1 ; 2 Cor. 5 : 20. Who appoints a steward? or shepherd?—The flock?—An Ambassador or Messenger?—From whom and to whom? But this does not deny the right of the people to *choose* for *their* minister one who has already received a general commission from the proper authority. (Acts 10 : 33 ; 16 : 9.)

The divine promises are all *conditional.* The commission of a Messenger or Ambassador is continued so long as he adheres to his instructions. The Jewish priesthood, having made the Word of God of none effect through their traditions, was substituted by the Christian priesthood. The latter in turn corrupted their message. Swedenborg sent his works to the church authorities throughout Protestant Europe,—thus virtually telling them of their defection and inviting them to learn and report it anew. His rémonstrance being treated with neglect or contempt, nothing remained but to appoint new messengers. This was done by a resort to *the lot,* for which the apostles had afforded a precedent in a similar case, (Acts 1 : 23–26,) and which is a virtual appeal to the Divine Providence. (D. P. 212; T. C. R. 696.) A new ministry was thus originated, but having been begun, and under an assemblage of solemn circumstances *such as can never again occur,* it is not proper to make a fresh appeal of the same sort without the most manifest necessity. Robert Hindmarsh, who ordained the first two ministers of the New Church, received no other ordination himself than that which was thus providentially bestowed, and yet he properly retained the title and authority of an ordaining minister until his death.   These two first ministers may have served as a sort of connecting link with the priesthood of the first Christian Church, of which they had been ministers, just as a great company of the Jewish priests became obedient to the Christian · faith. (Acts 6 : 7.)   Their priesthood was derived *through* Aaron *from* Moses, who received his priestly character from the sacerdotal caste in Egypt, where it had continued pure from the origin of the Ancient Church.   And thus it is that from the origin of the order to the present hour, and through successive churches, the electric chain of priestly influx has never been wholly broken.*   Most of the New Church ministers obtained their ordination from some point in this line of succession.   So that there is nothing in New Church principles or practice which implies a power in the laity to make a priest. The effect of Jeroboam and his successors " making priests of the lowest of the people who were not Levites," we have seen above. I hope I shall not be misunderstood in citing this text.   At this day, and especially in this country, poverty and humble position is no disqualification to one who is otherwise worthy.   But in *the " Repre-*

---

* We cannot agree with Mr. Cabell here. Moses, we believe, received his priestly office from the direct and original appointment of Jehovah. And the Lord, in establishing a new church, has uniformly instituted a priesthood *de novo*. The twelve, or the seventy, were not descended from the jewish priesthood. That " a great company of the jewish priests became obedient to the christian faith," does not prove that they became *christian priests ;* and if they did, their having been jewish priests was nothing in their favor for that. " The electric chain of priestly influx" was certainly broken in the establishment of the New Jerusalem. Swedenborg, the prime and great teacher of this church, was not of the previous ecclesiastical order. His having been so would have disqualified him for his office. Hence he was not only not a clergyman by profession, but he was carefully guarded against imbibing, in early life, the dogmatic theology of the old church. By influx, (C. L. 313,) all that which precedes with a theologian and composes his erudition, flows perpetually into the conclusions of his mind, and therefore disqualifies an old-church clergyman for a new-church minister. The influx from the world of spirits into his mind, also disqualifies him. And it is only so far as the falsities of the old faith are extirpated, and this chain of influx is thus broken that his mind can be receptive of the truths of the new faith (U. T., 784); and it is only so far as his spirit is consociated with the new arrangements of the new heaven by a new baptism, that he can become a suitable medium of the influences of that heaven, for the establishment of a correspondent new church on earth. Hence Swedenborg expressly says, " The universities in christendom are now first instructed, from whence will come ministers ; because *the new heaven has no influence over the old clergy*. . . ." (Smithson's Documents, p. 171. See also Let. III. to Dr. Beyer, Ibid. p. 167.) Thus the chain of influx from an old priesthood to a new one, should be broken ; and this is the reason why the Lord always breaks it when he institutes a new priesthood. Thus Swedenborg was called to his office, because he was a spiritual *fisherman*. Robert Hindmarsh was chosen by the Lord's auspices (See Ap. No. LI. p. xxiv.) the first *clergyman* of the new church, because he was thus made, by the Lord, ὁ κληρος, the *lot*, and he was not a priest of the first christian dispensation. The first minister, in this country, the Rev. Ralph Mather, had not previously been an old church clergyman. That the Rev. John Hargrove did not account his having been a minister of the methodist church any thing of a claim to the ministry of the new, may be seen on page 93 of this report. And, in our humble opinion, any man's having been a minister of the old church, is the least of all of his recommendations for the new-church ministry.—*Ed.*

sentative of a church" external "lowness" implied internal meanness; whereas the New Church minister should be "one of God's noblemen," in whatever position he may have been reared.

The Jewish Priest was, 1st. *called of God*, as we have seen; 2d. Commanded to be *holy*; they were *washed* before consecration : (Lev. 8 : 6; Num. 8 : 6, 7, 21 ;) 3d. Required to be knowing in the law. (Mal. 2 : 7.)

So 1st. The ministry of Christ was attested from heaven : (Heb. 5: 5; Mat. 3 : 17.) 2. He was *holy :* (Heb. 7 : 26.) 3. At twelve years of age he was versed in the law, and afterwards fulfilled—i.e. filled it *full* of meaning. (Mat. 5 : 17; Luke 2 : 46, 47.)

So also a Christian Minister must, 1st. be called and properly commissioned : (Heb. 5 : 4; John 20 : 21; Rom. 10 : 15 ;) 2d. holy and exemplary : (John 17 : 17; 1 Tim. 3 : 2; 1 : 19 ;) 3. he must be learned and apt to teach. (Mat. 28 : 20; 1 Tim. 3 : 2.)

Such were the *three* principal qualifications for office ;—they were required to be called—holy—learned. There was a difference in the case of the Jewish orders, in that they were confined to the family of Aaron. But this was more ostensible than real. *Moses* represented the Lord as to Divine *Truth*, Aaron—being the *brother* of *Moses*—as to Divine *Good*—" for these are brothers in the heavens." The *sons of Aaron—truth derived from good.* (A. C. 9806, 9807.) The Christian Ministry are also required to be hereditary in spirit, which is effected by *ordination* derived from the first ministers, and learning and teaching *kindred principles* of life and doctrine. And therefore it is that Paul calls Timothy and Titus " *his own sons* in the faith." (1 Tim. 1 : 2; Tit. 1 : 4.)

And how was this ordination bestowed? 1st. Moses, after investing and anointing Aaron and his sons, "*filled their hands*"—which denoted *inauguration* to represent the Lord as to Divine truth derived from divine good, and the *power* thence resulting. (Ex. 28 : 41; 29 : 24; Lev. 8 : 27; A. C. 10019.) Again, when the Levites were brought by Aaron before the Lord, and the Children of Israel "*put their hands upon the Levites*" and the Levites " laid their hands on the heads of the bullocks ;" by the first act was signified " the *translation* of the *power* of ministering for them and reception by the Levites, thus *separation ;*" by the second "a translation [or ascription] of that power to Jehovah." (Num. 8 : 10, 12; A. C. 10023—see also 9955, 10019, 10076, 10493.)—2d. The dove—a symbol of the Holy Spirit or divine *Power*, descended on our Lord at his baptism. 3d. When he *first* sent forth the *twelve*, and afterwards the *seventy*, he gave each of them "*power* to cast out unclean spirits and to heal diseases. (Mat. 10 : 1; Luke 10 : 19.) 4th. Timothy was ordained *by the laying on of Paul's hands, with* those of *the Presbytery.* (1 Tim. 4 : 14 ;) and he in turn is charged to " lay hands suddenly on no man." (1 Tim. 5 : 22.)

· The parallelism between the Jewish priesthood—that of our Lord —and again that of the Christian Church has been traced as to their *three* leading duties : their *three* great qualifications ; and also as to the mode or significance of ordination. We proceed to inquire whether similar requisitions are made of the ministers of the New Church.

And first, according to Swedenborg, the ministry are a "sacred order;" (T. C. R. 138.) "The *first* order in the church;" (A. E. 229;)—"the *governors* over those things amongst men which relate to heaven:" . . . "*appointed* to administer those things which relate to the divine *law* and *worship.*" (H. D. 314, 319.) "They *provide* for the existence of things divine:" (Doc. Ch. 70.) "They ought to *teach* men the way to heaven and also to *lead* them:" (H. D. 315.) If they have sought the office from proper motives and have an original aptness therefor, the Divine Providence will fit them for the service still farther by unknown ways: (D. P. 164)—and to qualify them the better to discharge this duty, the Lord by his spirit operates with them in a particular way; for "*inauguration into office* brings with it the several powers of *Illustration, Perception, Disposition, Instruction.*" (T. C. R. 146, 155.)—And when thus qualified, they ought not only to give private instruction, but to preach;" (Doc. Ch. 101.) And they *only* have a right to preach. "Good may be insinuated into another by every man in the country, but not truth, *except by those who áre teaching ministers;* for if others insinuate truth it gives birth to heresies and the church is disturbed and rent asunder." (H. H. 226, A. C. 6822.)—They are in the *internals* of church doctrine while the laity are in its externals;" (A. R. 594;) and because "*the centre should produce the expanse* and not the converse," a church should be regenerated *through* the priesthood as a medium. (T. C. R. 35.) They offer up the *prayers* of the people, (T. C. R. 751,) and bless them: (A. R. 357.) They administer the *sacraments* of baptism, (T. C. R. 685,) and the holy supper: (H. D. 210, 214; Com. 319; A. C. 3670; Canons 4: 9;) and they should *consecrate marriages.* (T. C. R. 748; C. L. 306, 308.)—2. "All priests represent the Lord as to divine good;" (A. C. 6148;) accordingly in a real church they should strive to be *holy.* "They should seek after the holy office *for no other end* than that they may more fully do uses to the souls of men; (C. L. 266)—for "the office of the ministry is *to serve.*" (T. C. R. 415.) They "should *shun evils as sins* and do the appointed work of their ministry *sincerely,* justly and faithfully, if they would become *charities* in form." (Doc. Ch. 86.)—3. *In proportion* as this is the case they are affected by *truths,* for truths are the *means* of *leading* souls to heaven." (Doc. Ch. 86; T C. R. 422.) 4. "The holy spirit flows *by men to men,* and in the church it flows *principally by the clergy to the laity.* The clergyman, because he is to teach truths out of the Word, should be *inaugurated* by the promise of the Holy Spirit and *by the representation of its translation,* (Canons 4: 7,) that is, as we are elsewhere told "by the imposition of hands. (A. C. 878; C. L. 396; D. L. W. 220.)

As a separate order of men having distinct and appropriate duties, they also have their rights; and on account of their office, dignity and honor are to be paid them, but not to their *persons,* (H. D. 317,) and they are to be honored in proportion to their service. (T. C. R. 415.) Priests *ought* to be holy men, as well as able to instruct; and too great care cannot be taken in their selection. But such qualifications alone do not make them priests. They must also be inaugurated. Will and consent must concur with ability. Nor will these support the Roman notion that "the priesthood is indelible," and the consequent maxim "once a priest always a priest,"—an idea both absurd and dangerous. For a lawfully constituted priest may be degraded for misconduct, or may resign his office with a pure conscience, in either case divesting himself of his function and its privileges, (and instances of both we believe have occurred in the New Church)—the Divine Providence being ever careful to protect the liberty of all. On the other hand, a priest may have sought the office from improper motives, and be internally a bad man. But so long as he is prudent and maintains an exterior becoming his profession, giving no occasion of public *scandal*, he may be useful in that capacity; nor does his personal character in such case vitiate his official acts. Balaam was a true prophet, but personally corrupt. The sons of Eli and other wicked Jewish priests were not ejected from office except by death. Judas was one of the twelve. And the same has ever been true of ministers of the Christian Church. (Num. ch. 22 to 24; and 31 : 8 : 2 Pet. 2 : 15; 1 Sam. 2 : 12; Matt. 7 : 15, 22, 23; 1 Cor. 9 : 27; 13 : 1, 2,—A. C. 3670, 4311, 5764, 10309; L. J. 59; D. L. W. 244.) Swedenborg himself, the teacher of the New Church, (T. C. R, 779,) declares that his knowledge of sacred truth was imparted to him, "not for any particular *merit of his*, but for the great concern of all Christians' salvation and happiness;" • (Let. to King of Sweden, Smith. Doc. p. 83;) and that its acquisition was attended by the elevation of his *understanding* and *not* of his *will part*. (Extracts from Swedenborg's MSS.—N. J. Jour., Lond., 1792, p. 239.)

These various declarations are very express; and to gather the inferences fairly deducible therefrom might determine many questions which have been agitated in various branches of the old church. We have seen that there was a gradation in the priesthood of the Ancient and Jewish churches, and that in the last it consisted of a personal *trine*. It remains for us to inquire whether we can trace in the Scriptures a similar gradation in the Christian Ministry. And for this purpose it is natural and proper to first look into the Gospels.

There are *three* degrees in the Lord—the Celestial, Spiritual, and Natural, or Love, Wisdom, and Power; three heavens; three discrete degrees in Nature; three discrete degrees in man; three degrees in the church; and three churches before the coming of the Lord, without reckoning the subdivisions of each which also severally assumed the form of a trine. The primal seat of each of these churches was the land of *Canaan*,—from whence they were propagated to surrounding nations. (A. C. 567, 1238, &c.) Rivers were its first and last boundaries. (4255.) All places in that land were representative according to distance, situation and boundaries. (1585.) Its very names were significant and were preserved from of old on account of the spiritual sense of the Word which was to be written. Jerusalem, its capital and centre, represented the church as to doctrine. Surrounding countries were also representative according to their situa-

312

NEWCHURCHMAN—EXTRA.

tion relative to Canaan. And within Canaan itself, at first the seats of the twelve tribes, and afterwards its different provinces, their boundaries, the rivers, mountains, cities and villages of each were representative according to their distance from Jerusalem. After the revolt of the ten tribes, which set up the kingdom of Israel, that province represented the *spiritual* church, while Judah continued to represent the celestial. When Israel was carried into captivity, Gentiles were sent to occupy their country, particularly the northern part,—which last was ultimately set off as a third province. So that in the time of our Lord the whole of Canaan was divided into the *three* provinces of Galilee, Samaria, and Judea; of which, the first denoted the church among the Gentiles, or Spiritual-natural Church; (A, E. 447;) the second, the Spiritual Church, which was particularly in the principle of faith; (A. C. 2702;) the third, the Celestial Church, or those who are in love to the Lord, (A. C. 3654, A. R. 350)—but all of which were now in a state of perversion.

Motion signifies change of state. (A. C. 3356.) Journeyings signify, according to circumstances, progressions or retrogradations in the regenerate life. (1457, 1463.) Thus "journeyings *from the East* to the Land of Shinar," denoted the decline of the Ancient Church. (Gen. 11 : 2; A. C. 1289-1293.) The highway from Egypt—through Assyria—to Israel, denotes the regeneration of the uncorrupted natural man in regular order, from Science, by Reason, to Intelligence. (Isa. 19: 23-25; A. C. 119.) The journeyings of the Israelites from Egypt, through the *Wilderness*, to Canaan, represents the call and formation of a new church out of one which had come to its end.

Our Lord, as a private individual, obeyed the Jewish law both in its letter and its spirit. His advance through the three stages of Regeneration was adumbrated by the history of Abraham, Isaac and Jacob, (A. C. 7193)—and represented by his return from Egypt through Philistia to Canaan. Moses, the judges and the kings of Israel represented him in his kingly character; Aaron and the prophets in his character as a priest and teacher.

Jesus was baptized "beyond Jordan," (John 1 : 28,) but *opposite* Judea, and thus became the first *member* of the Christian Church. (A. C. 4255.) He also became the first *minister* therein, and preparatory thereto underwent his temptation in the *wilderness*; where he successfully resisted the *three* great temptations which have ever assailed the clergy in the three corresponding grades; viz: 1st. Sordid selfishness—desire of subsistence or gain. 2d. Spiritual pride or presumption. 3d. Ambition—the lust of power. (Mat. 4 : 1—11; Luke 4 : 1—13.) Luke inverts the order of the two last temptations for a reason which will presently be given.

After his return victorious from the trial, he preached *first in Galilee;* (Mat. 4: 17-23; Mark 1 : 14, 21, 39; Luke 4 : 15, 18, 44;) and that this was not without significance see Mat. 4 : 12–16. He taught in *all* her cities and villages. And this general statement that he preached in their "synagogues," or "villages," or "cities and villages," is *thrice* given with a double mention of the first, probably to indicate that his teaching had reference to both truth and goodness. (1. Mat. 4: 17, 23; Mark 1: 14, 39; Luke 4: 15, 44,—2. Mat. 9: 35; Mark 6: 6; Luke 8: 1,—3. Mat. 11: 1.) At first he was collecting his twelve disciples with a view of instructing them before sending them forth; in the second instance, Luke records that "the twelve were with him." Shortly after this he gave them their first commission and sent them forth to preach *repentance*, (Mark 6: 12,) —the first step in regeneration—after which he went forth the third time *alone*. Meantime the fame of his preaching and miracles reached the Pharisees, who also, according to John, had encountered him in his periodical visits to Jerusalem. They therefore sent deputies to watch his proceedings and report on his pretensions. (Mat. 15: 1; Mark 7: 1.) Yet during this first period he did not preach publicly, or only occasionally in Judea; but regularly in Galilee. (Mat. 11: 1.) At length he came to Mount Tabor, where he was transfigured, (Mat. 17: 1–8; Mark 9: 2–8; Luke 9: 28–36.) He then returned to Capernaum, (Mat. 17: 24; Mark 9: 33,) his usual place of abode, where he remained awhile before leaving Galilee.

After this, as the time approached that he should be received up, he "steadfastly set his face to go to Jerusalem." (Luke 9: 51.) "He went through the cities and villages [of Samaria] teaching and journeying towards Jerusalem." (13: 22.) "And as he went towards Jerusalem he passed through *the midst of Samaria* and Galilee." (17: 11.) But before commencing his ministry regularly in Judea, he appears to have gone into "the coasts of Judea *beyond* Jordan," where he *abode for a time* and taught and healed those who resorted unto him. (Mat. 19: 1; Mark 10: 1; John 10: 40.) Thus it appears that at the close of the first and second period of his course, he made a pause before entering on the next.

On entering Judea, we hear of him at Jericho, (Luke 19: 1,) at Bethphage, Bethany, and the Mount of Olives, (ver. 29,) at length he came to Jerusalem itself, where he appeared daily for several days during the passover, returning to Bethany in the evening.

In these three stages of his ministry, we find him preaching by the sea-shore, in the villages and cities, on mountains and in private houses to his disciples, from the plain and highway to the people,— from a ship, in their synagogues, and at length in that very *temple* which was originally dedicated to himself, but on entering which he found his authority first questioned by the successors of those very ministers whom he had first appointed to that service.

Such is a rapid sketch of our Lord's ministry. We have seen above that Galilee, Samaria and Judea severally represented the spiritual-natural, the spiritual, and celestial churches Swedenborg tells us that the priesthood of the *Levites* represented the work of the salvation of those in natural good; that of the *sons of Aaron*—the salvation of those in spiritual good; that of *Aaron*—of those in Celestial good, (A. C. 10017,) and this in successive order. Our Lord, in his regular ministry, passed successively from Galilee, through Samaria, to Jerusalem. Add to this the remarkable fact, that *three several times* his ministry was attested by *a voice from heaven;* once at his baptism,

(Mat. 3: 17; Mark 1: 11; Luke 3: 22)—again when he was transfigured, (Mat. 17: 5; Mark 9: 7; Luke 9: 35,) and lastly, when before his final glorification, the same voice proclaimed "I have glorified my name and will glorify it again." (John 12: 28, 30—com. with 17: 4; 19: 30; and Mat. 28: 18.) This threefold commission (with the pauses observed before advancing from one to another,) conferred or exercised in or near those several provinces: their representation; and the significance of the direction and goal of his journeyings being thus plainly given, cannot be without a material bearing on this question. And to complete the parallel, he is called by Paul (Rom. 15: 8,) a minister [in the original, "deacon:"] by Peter "the Shepherd and Bishop of our souls:" (1 Pet. 2: 25;) and again by Paul "the Apostle and High Priest of our Profession." (Heb. 3: 1.)

It is very true that after the miracle of converting the water into wine—or filling the natural with spiritual truth—when "his *disciples* believed on him," (John 2: 11,) he went up to Jerusalem and endeavored to purify the temple worship of its corruptions, but his authority was set at nought by those who were then at the head of the church; though some of the laity accorded a superficial faith on account of his miracles, (ver. 13–25.) Even the better-disposed, though timid "Masters in Israel," could not receive his doctrine, (3: 1, 2, 10;) and though "he tarried awhile in Judea and baptized," (ver. 22,) at length "he left Judea and departed again into Galilee, but he must needs go *through* Samaria," (4: 3, 4,) where he met with some who were in the affection of truth and believed on him. (ver. 7, 29, 39.) But "after two days he departed thence and went into Galilee," and "*the Galileans received him,* for they also had gone up to Jerusalem to the feast." (ver. 43, 45.) A second time also, we read that he came up to a feast at Jerusalem; (5: 1;) and though he now healed the cripple at the pool of Bethesda, and visited the temple, (14,) we do not find him preaching publicly here, farther than that he responded to the cavils of the Jews; so he returned to Galilee and prosecuted his ministry there. (6: 1; 7: 1, 9.) A third time he went to the feast of Tabernacles and taught in the temple; (ver. 10, 14, 37, c. 8: 2, 20:) but with so little acceptance that the Pharisees would have stoned him had he not withdrawn himself. (ver. 59.) He healed the man who had been blind from his birth, which exasperated them still more. (9: 1, 29, 35.) Again he attended the feast of dedication and walked in the temple, but as his answers to their ensnaring questions provoked them to a second effort to take him, he went away beyond Jordan where John at first baptized, and there abode. (10: 22, 23, 39, 40.)

But these episodes in his history, which are given by John alone, do not disturb the regular progression of his ministry as related by the other evangelists. And the reason of his being the sole narrator here will be apparent when we consider the genius and design of the different writers, whose own names are also significant. The province of Galilee being subdivided, Matthew's Gospel is addressed more particularly to those in natural truth, or Galilee of the Gentiles; Mark's to those in natural good, or Lower Galilee; and if their narratives

contain both spiritual and celestial truths in the letter, it is because
'things prior and posterior are *together* in ultimates." Luke (light)
alone relates the progress through Samaria or the Spiritual Church, as
in his account of the temptation he naturally gave the desire of *power*
precedence of the desire of holiness; while John, as the representative of charity in act or the Celestial Church and being thence in the
interior meaning of the Gospel, more fully and properly records the
efforts to enlighten the *authorities* of the perverted church, before
commencing a new one with the Gentiles. He would also be more
minute in his account of occurrences and instructions during our
Lord's regular ministry in Judea, and such we find to be the case.
Something analogous to this took place in the Jewish Church when
Aaron was commanded to offer the *first* sacrifices for himself—the
next for his sons, and the third for the people. (Lev. 9 : 7, 8, 12, 15;
Heb. 5 : 3; 7 : 27; 9 : 7.) And thus also has it fared with the truth
of the New Church. It was . first offered to the authorities of the
Old Church. They rejected it generally, though some few favored
it secretly. (John 12 : 42, 43.) Some of the second order, who loved
truth for its own sake, embraced it, but the great body of the New
Church, thus far, has been composed of men who were first in Gentile
good.

But though our Lord united in his own person all the excellencies
of which the various patriarchs, kings, prophets and priests of the
Old Testament were severally representative, yet each of those persons at one and the same time represented but *one* quality. Hence
the necessity, while founding his own church, that he should first set
an example of all the various gradations and qualities required in
those who were to be his ministers and instruments for its perpetuation and extension. And as those ministers were to be in some sort
representative characters, not only were they to be numerous as to
persons and various as to character and qualification, but, as we shall
proceed to show, different in rank also.

Soon after entering on his ministry, at several times, he called to
him certain individuals who were to be of the number of his most
trusted disciples. Of these we have mention made in the following
passages of Peter and Andrew, James and John; (Mat. 4 : 18-22;
Mark 1 : 16, 19, 20; Luke 5 : 10, 11 :) though John mentions Philip
and Nathaniel instead of the two latter. (John 1 : 35, 37, 43, &c.)
After this Matthew is particularly spoken of. (Mat. 9 : 9; Mark 2 : 14;
Luke 5 : 27.) At a later date from the general body of his disciples,
he selected *twelve* as the special depositories of his instructions; as
the observers and assistants of his ministry: (Thus while attending
their master, they *baptized* his converts:) (John 3 : 22; 4 : 2 ;) and at
length as witnesses of his resurrection. Of their names when thus
first selected we have two catalogues in Mark 3 : 13-19; Luke 6 :
13-16.

Jesus, compassionating the multitudes who were " as sheep without
a shepherd," directed his disciples to " pray the Lord of the harvest
that he would send forth *more* laborers into the harvest." (Mat. 9 :
36-38.) It was shortly after this that he gave *the twelve* their *first*

commission when he sent them forth into the cities and villages of
Galilee. (Mat. 10: 1, 7, &c.; Mark 6: 7–13; Luke 9: 1–6.) At
length he was transfigured on Mount Tabor near *the border* of Samaria,
and after entering the latter province "he appointed and sent forth
other *seventy* also." (Luke 10: 1–20.) There was a resemblance
between the charges given to those and the former, but with this
marked difference, that whereas the twelve, who had been his more
intimate associates, were sent to gather up, in the first period of their
service, "the lost sheep of Israel" in Galilee, (Mat. 10: 5, 6;) the
seventy were "sent by two and two into every city and place *whither
he himself would come.*" (Luke 10: 1.) The resemblance between
their instructions in other respects was natural and proper, in that
the elementary principles of doctrine and the primary duties of the
service are the same with all ranks. The fact also remains and cannot be without significance that the seventy were appointed *after* the
twelve, on a service where less was entrusted to their discretion. Nor
do we read in the Gospels that they ever received any further authority, whereas the twelve received a *second*, and at length a *third* and
final commission. By the second, the power of *discipline* was conferred. (Mat. 18: 15–20.) The nature of this discipline—which,
as set forth in Scripture, was only such as is indispensable to the
purity and protection of any society whatever and altogether different from the abuses afterwards engrafted on it, and which rendered
the very name odious to Protestants—we shall afterwards explain.
After their entrance into Samaria, it also became necessary to appoint
a new set of officers, who should in this province discharge the same
functions which in Galilee had been performed by the twelve who
were now raised to a higher grade.

The twelve represented the same things with the twelve princes of
the tribes of Israel; the seventy—the same with the seventy elders.
The former represented *all* things of faith in one complex, and each
one of them respectively, some essential and primary principle of
faith; (A.C . 2089;)—and thence they signified *all* truths *and* goods
in the aggregate. (A. E. 223.) But by the seventy elders and by the
seventy disciples are signified " all the *goods which are from truths*,"
which is especially the good of the *Spiritual Church*, (A. C. 9404)—
which again was represented by Israel or Samaria, in which the
seventy were first appointed. They returned to him before he left
that province. (Luke 10: 17.) If they attended him while in Judea
they were not at all distinguished, whereas the twelve accompanied
him throughout: received his final instructions, and were clothed with
special authority to continue his church after he had left the world.

After his own commission had been finally attested by anticipation,
(John 12: 28, 30,) he said to the twelve in his last consolatory
address, " He that receiveth *whomsoever I send* receiveth *me;* and he
that receiveth me receiveth *him that sent me.*" And here it should
be noted that this was the *third* time of addressing them in these very
terms—the strongest perhaps which could be employed to signify
that they were his accredited ambassadors; (1. Mat. 10: 40,—2. Luke
9: 48,—3. John 13: 20;) whereas they were said to the seventy but

once. (Luke 10: 16.) To the twelve he farther says, "*Henceforth I call you not servants;* for the servant knoweth not what his lord doeth: but *I* have called you friends; for *all things that I have heard of my Father I have made known unto you. Ye have not chosen me,* [you are not volunteer, self-made, or man-made priests,] *but I have chosen you,* and *ordained* you that ye should go and bring forth fruit, and that your fruit should remain. . . . And ye also shall *bear witness,* because, ye have been with me from the beginning. (15: 15, 16, 27.)—And in his prayer before his betrayal, "And now *I am no more in the world* but *these* [the twelve] are in the world, and I come to thee." (17: 11.)—Was any such language as this addressed to the seventy? If so, it is not recorded. But after his resurrection—still addressing *the eleven,* he gives *them* this final commission, authority and pledge, "As the Father hath sent *me,* even so send I you." (20: 21.) "Go ye and teach *all nations,* baptizing them . . . and teaching them to observe all things whatsoever I have commanded *you:* and lo *I* am with you *always,* even *unto the consummation of the age.*" (Mat. 28: 20; see also Mark 16: 15, 16; Luke 24: 47, 48.) He also confirms to them the power of discipline which had been conferred in Samaria. (John 20: 23; com. Mat. 18: 15-20.)

How shall we understand this? The twelve as individuals could not accomplish all this work. They were not to survive until the consummation of the age. What could it mean but that they, when they had finished their work as individuals, *should transmit their commission to others* who would thence be clothed with similar authority and be sustained by the same promise and power? He was no longer in the world, but they were. He sent them forth as the Father had sent him. Whosoever received them, received him. *Their work was to remain.* (We shall see anon *how* they performed it.) It was to embrace all nations—through an entire age or dispensation. No one can transmit to another what he does not himself possess. "The Christian Church," says Swedenborg, "was now to begin THROUGH *the apostles;* and accordingly we find that their first official act after the ascension was to take measures to have the vacancy supplied in their mystic number of twelve, occasioned by the treason and death of Judas. (Acts, 1: 15-26.) Why was this, if there was to be thenceforth no difference of rank between them and the other ministers shortly to be appointed? particularly as there was a difference of rank and power while the Lord was in the world; and that gradation was a trine of 1st. the Lord; 2d. the Twelve; 3d. the Seventy.

There are other particulars recorded in the Evangelists, worthy of mention in connection with this threefold commission of the twelve. *Three* of them, viz: Peter, James and John, were selected as the special witnesses of *three* remarkable events in the history of their Lord, which occurred successively in or near Galilee, Samaria, and Judea: 1st. The raising the daughter of Jairus, at Capernaum. (Mark 5: 37; Luke 8: 51.) 2d. The transfiguration, on Mount Tabor. (Mat. 17: 1; Mark 9: 2; Luke 9: 28.) 3d. His agonies in Gethsemane. (Mat. 26: 37; Mark 14: 33.) Now these three disciples represented the *three* leading principles of the church, faith, charity, and the good of charity, from which all the others are derived. All of them are becoming in a priest, but each quality in the ascending series should especially characterise the minister of the corresponding grade.

Now " preaching" is the proper work of faith; " intercession," of charity," and "blessing" is truly a work of charity. And these being the three principal duties of the Christian Priesthood—may have been the reason of our Lord's selecting Peter, James and John—the representatives of these virtues—to be also the representatives of the ministers of his church.

Again: Peter in particular, as the representative of the other apostles, received *three* several commissions; but each time rather by way of promise which was confirmed shortly after. They are recorded as follows :—1st. " From henceforth thou *shalt* catch men." (Luke 5 : 10.) 2d. " I *will* give *thee* the keys of the kingdom of heaven," &c. (Mat 16 : 19, com. 18 : 18.) 3d. " I have prayed for thee that thy faith fail not : and *when thou art converted* strengthen the brethren." (Luke 22 : 32.) After the resurrection, they were all confirmed to him in the same interview: "Feed my *lambs.*—Feed my *sheep.*—Feed *my* sheep ;" (John 21 : 15, 16, 17 ;) for which threefold duty, he had before unconsciously asked a *threefold preparation* : "What I do, thou knowest not now but shalt know *hereafter.*" "Lord, wash not my *feet* only, but my *hands* and my *head.*" (John 13 : 7–9.)

Now Peter, as the representative of faith, denoted truth derived from good; not natural truth alone, as has been thought by some, but truth in its triple gradation. For Peter signifies the same with Reuben ; (A. E. 434 ;) and Reuben in a spiritual sense signifies Wisdom, Intelligence, Science. (A. R. 351.) "They who are principled in doctrine, grounded in love to the Lord are to instruct those who are of his church," . . . not that Peter alone was to instruct, but *all those* who are represented by Peter." (A. E. 820.) To become "a fisher of men" was to gather them to the church. (A. E. 513.) For, to fish, signifies to instruct *natural* men, and at that time, both *within* the church and out of it, there were natural men who as they received the Lord and truths from Him became *spiritual.*" (A. E. 820.) In Mat. 16 : 15–19, Peter signifies *Divine* Truth from the Lord. (A. E. 411.) To *essential faith in the Lord* belong the keys of the kingdom of heaven ; *that* shutteth heaven to prevent the entrance of evil and false principles, and that opens heaven for goods and truths. (A. C. Pref. to Gen. 22.) And this higher faith was Peter both to represent and to teach. To feed *lambs* is to instruct those who are in innocence or *natural* good. To feed *sheep*—those who are in truth derived from good, or *spiritual* men: to feed sheep—when again mentioned—those who are in good derived from truth, or celestial men. (A. C. 4169, com. this with 10017.) To wash the feet, hands, and head, is to purify, first the natural principle—then the interiors of the natural principle—then the spiritual. (A. C. 7442.)

But though faith is an essential principle of the church and the first in point of time, it is neither the sole nor the most important. For it is but a means to an end, as all truth is in order to goodness.

And though Peter represented those who preach, neither is preaching the sole duty of the Priesthood. The priest should be holy—should have a love of souls—must endeavor to become a charity in form, and lead his people to heaven by setting them an example in his own life. The *intercession* and *prayers* of such an one are much more likely to avail in calling down a *blessing* on them. (Jas. 5 : 16.) And though Peter particularly represented the principle of faith, it does not follow that the other disciples should be wholly wanting in that respect, or that he in turn should be destitute of the qualities which they denoted. A variety of gifts is required in the ministers of the Christian church, who have to lead the various characters of mankind in the way to heaven. Accordingly we find that James and John also had a significant title of honor bestowed on them when the Lord called them "sons of thunder," (Mark 3 : 17,) which we are told signified "truths grounded in *celestial good*." (A. E. 821.) And are these less important to the higher regeneration than what Peter primarily represented?

Peter, we know, *thrice* denied his master, in which case he represented faith separated from charity, "which yet can teach," (A. C. 10087,) because it takes pleasure in learning and contemplating truths, though it may not always apply them to their proper .use. Hence when the three witnessed the transfiguration and saw the glory of the Lord refulgent through a bright cloud—the spiritual sense shining through the letter of the Word—it was Peter alone who said "it is good for us to be here." (Luke 9 : 33.) "When Peter was young, he girded himself and walked whither he would, but when he became old, he stretched forth his hands, and another girded and carried him whither he would not." (John 21 : 18.) "The faith of the commencing church is grounded in charity in the good of innocence; it learns truths freely and lives according to them. Towards its close, it is separated from charity and becomes servile. Truth is then not clearly seen, and that is accepted as such which is dictated by another." (A. E. 820.) Again, "Peter *turning*, seeth the disciple whom Jesus loved following . . . and saith . . . Lord, what shall *this* man do?" "If I will that *he remain till I come*; what is that to thee? Follow thou me?" (verse 20–22.) Faith at length fails—"in the last time of the church turns away from the Lord," but the goods of charity never fail. They make heaven and the church. They shall follow the Lord and acknowledge him, even to the last time of the old church and the first of the new. And as the Lord loved John above the rest of the disciples, (A. E. 9,) so those who are principled in the goods of charity follow the Lord and are loved by him, neither do they recede ; whereas the others are indignant, as was Peter, at the preference shown to the higher principle. (A. C. 10087.)

Such are the errors and perversions of the principle of Faith ; but it should not be forgotten that charity and zeal are also liable to misdirection. For we learn that both James and John *thrice* and most seriously erred. 1. When they aspired to sit, the one on the right hand of the Lord in his kingdom, the other on his left : (Mark 10: 35.)

2. When they saw one casting out devils and forbade him because he
followed not them. (Luke 9: 49, 50.)   3. When they would have
called down fire from heaven on the inhospitable Samaritans. (vs.
51–56.) Even charity and zeal may seek for precedence under the
delusive pretence that their good intentions may better qualify them
for dominion than others, while ambition may be the lurking motive.
Or bigotry may lead them to condemn others who are successfully
engaged in the same cause, but operate in another mode than their
own. Or lastly their zeal may be without knowledge, and they may
be inflamed with unholy resentment against those whose present prejudices reject the truth, or forbid their seeing it in a just light. From
all which we should infer that the union of faith or knowledge, charity
and good works is quite as becoming in a priest as in a layman, though
he may possibly be useful if he abounds in the first while the other
two are possessed in a minor degree or only feigned.

It may also be remarked in this connexion, that the *miracles* and
other incidents, the *parables* and other discourses of our Lord were
appropriate to the representative character of the places where they
occurred or were uttered. In his journey through one province unto
completion, as well as from one to another, there was a spiritual as
well as natural progression. And while the former may be compared
to the advance through the degrees of latitude—or from less to more,—
the latter bore an analogy to the assent through the degrees of altitude,
or from lower to higher. There were, for example, miracles of both
classes—the same in kind but differing in degree. Of the former, we
may mention the healing of 1. The Centurion's servant ; 2. The
nobleman's son ; 3. The Syro-Phenician woman's daughter; all of
which occurred in Galilee and were wrought on *Gentiles*, without his
immediate presence. Of the latter, we may find instances in the
restoration to sight of—the two blind men—of blind Bartimeus—of
him who was blind from his birth ; and again, in raising the daughter
of Jairus—the widow's son of Nain—of Lazarus, who had been dead
four days. An attentive examination of the other miracles will show
a similar succession or gradation ; and so also of the parables and discourses ; and this will be the more apparent if we note the variety in
the narratives of the different Evangelists, as hinted above.

It is believed that authorities have now been adduced from the
Scriptures and the writings of their expositor, sufficient to justify the
conclusions : that from the rise of the Ancient Church to the Ascension of our Lord, a separate class of men, called priests, has been set
apart for the service of his church in all the phases under which it has
appeared : that they have been ordained to discharge particular functions, for the due performance of which special qualifications were
required : that these have ever been essentially the same : that for
these uses they have ever been inaugurated and commissioned, substantially in the same mode : that a trinal distinction has been observed
to run through both the attributes and duties of the general office ;
and that within the priesthood itself there has been a distinction of
persons in trinal subordination ; that every attempt to invade the rights
of this order in general, or those of the higher ranks by the lower,

was punished of old either immediately and severely, or led in the issue to corruption and disaster : that a certain preparation was required for entrance into the order and that a probationary service was necessary before passing from the lower to the higher ranks,— each step in the ascent being marked by distinct ceremonies and a new investiture of power.   If such was the original appointment of the Lord in the Constitution of that order, and if that constitution has never been repealed, we are led to the farther inference that it is still binding.

To this order, founded as we believe in the nature of things, we think there would never have been an objection, but that all would have acquiesced in its existence and would have yielded due respect to the office and obedience to its lawful instructions, if the priesthood had always been sought from a proper motive and those who filled its different ranks had discharged their appropriate duties without usurping authority which did not rightfully belong to them.

In the Most Ancient Church indeed, there were no externals of *worship;* but men needed to be regenerated then as well as now; and this could only be effected by passing from the natural through the Spiritual to the Celestial State.   And though there was no separate caste of priests, yet there were *houses, families, nations,* and persons more or less *wise ;** and at first the head of each house, and then the wiser men of the family and nation were probably the usual mediums for conveying the instruction necessary to this progressive elevation, so far as it was imparted from without. But the question is not now— What were the agencies best suited to this purpose among the early inhabitants of this earth, or the present denizens of Mars, or Jupiter, or some other Earth in the Universe? (E. U. 49, 85, 90.)   "They that be whole need not a physician, but the sick." What are the

---

* This implies that the ministry or priesthood of the most ancient church consisted of " *wise* persons" on earth, whether heads of houses, families or nations. But were not *angels* the ministers of the most ancient church; did they not instruct by *representatives* in dreams; and were not these the Word as it exists in the heavens ? Then the only difference between the most ancient and subsequent churches was, that the former, having *immediate revelation,* were instructed by an angelic priesthood, while the latter, having *mediate revelation,* that is, by a written Word, were instructed by a human priesthood.   We are informed that the same is true of the celestial church which exists now in the centre of Africa, namely, they are instructed by the Word as *ministered* to them by the immediate revelation of angels. Consequently, the order of the mere celestial church does not admit of every man's being his own priest, or of his being instructed immediately of the Lord, " by parents" as heads of houses or families, c or by masters, preachers, books, and especially by reading it." (D. P. 172.)   There is in heaven, or the greatest man, a priestly office, function or province.   To the discharge of the uses of this office, certain angels are assigned ; and no others are permitted to discharge them. And for a natural or external church on earth, there must be certain men appointed, and so connected with angels and spirits of that office by ordination. as to give to the Lord, through angels, those corresponding ultimates, by which his will may be done on earth as it is in heaven.   But while the church is merely celestial and so without any corresponding natural or external church, the angels who discharge the uses of the priestly office in heaven, discharge them also for celestial men on earth. And thus the mere celestial church has a priesthood of angels, while the celestial-natural church, such as the New Jerusalem is to be, must have a priesthood of men.—*Ed.*

instruments best adapted to this end *now* and *here?* Our race is not
simply natural and ignorant, though innocent and docile. The generations of men for ages past and at present are fallen and immersed in
evils and *falses.* They know not their true interest until informed of
it; and are prone to forget it if not impressed by line upon line;
they will not pursue it until they have precept on precept, enforced
by *divine* sanction. For the effectual performance of these uses the
casual instructions of parents or friends, or the most impressive warnings of the wise and experienced, if they come not clothed with sacred
authority will be utterly insufficient. To meet the exigency new
measures and new instruments must be employed. Infinite mercy *has*
raised up and qualified a separate order of men to be the depositories
and dispensers of his truth : assigned them their duties : vested them
with authority for their performance ; and enjoined obedience on the
hearers, so long as the former keep within the limits of their commission. " *Levi*"—said Moses, " shall teach Jacob thy judgments and
Israel thy law. . . . Bless, Lord, his substance and the work of
his hands; *smite through the loins* of them that rise up against him, and
of them that hate him, *that they rise not again.*" " Touch not mine
anointed and do my *prophets* no harm," said Jehovah. " He that
receiveth *whomsoever I send,* receiveth *me,*" saith the Lord.
" Remember them *which have the rule over you,* who have spoken to
you the word of God: whose *faith* follow. Obey them . . . and
submit yourselves, *for they watch for your souls* as they that must
give account.—Esteem them very highly in love for their works
sake," said Paul. " Priests are *governors* over those things amongst
men which relate to heaven," said Swedenborg. " They who teach
truths and thereby lead to the good of life, and so to the Lord, are the
good shepherds." Dignity and honor ought to be paid to priests on
account of the sanctity of their office. . . . The honor of any employment is not in the person but is adjoined to him according to the
dignity of the thing he administers." And do not all priests represent the Lord? (Deut. 33: 11; Ps. 105: 15 ; Heb. 13: 7, 17; 1 Thes.
5 : 13; H. D. 314, 315, 317.)

In the present state of human nature, then, there is too much
reason to fear that the clearest truths and the wisest councils would
pass unheeded or be questioned as doubtful, if they proceeded not
from those who were authorized to proclaim them abroad as the truth
of God and to denounce as from Him the consequences of neglect.
There are *three* principal varieties of human character or spiritual
states. As it is the Divine will that all should be regenerated, he has
provided instruction suited to those several states. As some men may
minister instruction to those in lower states who could not labor
successfully for those in a higher, he has made a wise distribution of
powers and duties, and provided functionaries to fill those several
stations.

Taking men as they are, every man cannot now, under God, be his
own priest; nor can the services of priesthood be now fully rendered
by any man to his fellows without clothing him with a certain degree
of power. But the same state of human nature also leaves that

power liable to abuse. All that Omniscience could do, consistent with the freedom of man, was to warn both priest and people of their duties and dangers, and to furnish either class with weapons to protect itself against the encroachments of the other. But if unhappily abuses should arise,—as in the first Christian Church we know they did,—every other means should *first* be employed for their correction, and none but the weightiest reasons should induce a departure from that order which He has established in his own house; and to that order the church should return as soon as the occasion of revolt has ceased. We think it can be shown that all those usurpations may be traced to sources other than the trinal gradation in the Christian Ministry; and that similar abuses never can arise in the New Church while it remains in possession of the writings of Swedenborg, or until her priesthood becomes wholly corrupt and traitorous, and all her people false to themselves and the cause —But of this hereafter.

At present we will only say that the first Christian church, both priests and people, were fully warned of the danger,—the slightest tendency to such encroachments having been reproved both by the example and repeated precepts of the Saviour, who, though he must have foreseen the future, yet did not disturb that constitution of the Priesthood which he had ordained of old. We have seen that while in the wilderness he resisted himself the three great temptations which assail those who aspire to the several grades of the ministerial office. But as the Twelve may not have been apprised of this until it was recorded by Inspiration, *three several times* did he denounce to them *all unholy ambition* in the officers of his kingdom. And as they, like the rest of their nation, had mistaken the nature of that kingdom, he both spoke and acted on various occasions so as gradually to correct their misapprehensions. Thus when those whom he had fed miraculously would have forcibly made him a temporal prince "he departed again into a *mountain* alone." (John 6 : 15.) He refused to dispense, as a judge, either distributive or penal justice. (Luke 12: 14; John 8 : 11, 15.) He paid tribute himself and enjoined the same on others. (Mat. 17 : 25–27; 22 : 21.) To the Pharisees, who *ought* to have understood him, he said, " The kingdom of God cometh not with observation. . . Behold . . . it is *within* you." (Luke 17: 20, 21.) And though, when he rode in seeming lowly state into Jerusalem he permitted " his disciples" to hail him as King of Zion, (19 : 37–40,) yet, to quiet the jealous fears of Pilate, he assured him that ' his kingdom was not of *this* world." (John 18 : 36.) *Three several times* moreover,—viz., before and after his transfiguration, and again as they were approaching Jerusalem—did he take his disciples apart by the way and predict to them the reception he should meet with from the authorities of the Jewish Church, his passion and resurrection,—which at first was not believed, nor properly understood, then soon forgotten—nor again remembered until it was recalled to them by an angel after its fulfilment. (1. Mat. 16 : 21–23; Mark 8 : 31–33; Luke 9: 22; 2. Mat. 17: 22–23; Mark 9 : 31, 32; 3. Mat. 20: 17–19; Mark 10 : 32–34; Luke 18 : 31–34; 24: 6, 7.) But we must notice the first series of warnings more particularly.

The instructions of our Lord to his disciples on any particular subject were not always given entire and at once, but gradually—
according to their states—and as they could bear them.   They had
also the appearance of arising naturally from circumstances or incidents
as they occurred; which were thus made the occasions of imparting
instruction useful not only to them, but to his church in all coming
time.   The first instance in which this mistaken ambition manifested
itself, is spoken of by three of the Evangelists.   (Mat. 18: 1–6;
Mark 9: 33–37; Luke 9: 46–49.)   Luke says that "there arose
a reasoning among the disciples."   Mark,—that "they disputed among
themselves by the way."   Matthew—that they came unto Jesus saying "who is the greatest in the kingdom of heaven?"   Now we are
told by Swedenborg that the disciples at that time, had no other idea
of his kingdom than the Jews at this day have of the kingdom of their
Messiah, viz: a temporal sovereignty of the world, over the provinces
of which they were to bear rule.   And if he had immediately corrected their mistake, they would have abandoned him forthwith and
returned to their former callings. (A. C. 3857, 10582.)   Accordingly
he took a little child and set him in the midst, and said " whosoever
shall *humble himself* as this little child, the same *is greatest* in the
kingdom of heaven."   But this mild reproof it seems was insufficient
to repress their ill-directed ambition.   Some time after this, as they
were approaching Jerusalem, but still in Samaria, the same disposition
was *again* manifested.   And this is noticed by two of the Evangelists,
but with a difference.   (Mat. 20: 20–28; Mark 10: 35–45.)   The
first represents the mother of James and John as asking precedence in
his kingdom for her sons.   Mark relates that they made the same
request for themselves; but they were again rebuked and more emphatically than at first.   But as if this were to be the besetting sin of *all
ranks* of the clergy in the first Christian Church, we find them a
third time falling into it—in the very presence of their Lord and
during the last and holy supper of which they were to partake with
him.   Luke, who only records it, says, " There was *a strife* among
them which should be greatest.   And he said unto them, the kings of
the Gentiles exercise *lordship* over them; and they that exercise
authority upon them are called benefactors.   But ye shall not be so:
but he that *is greatest* among you, let him be as the younger; and he
that *is chief*, as he that doth serve.   For whether *is greater*, he that
sitteth at meat, or he that serveth? *is not he* that sitteth at meat?
but I am among you as he that serveth." (Luke 22: 24–27.)
   The general instruction to be derived from this last passage is not
easily mistaken.   But as it, and another from Matthew, (23–4, 8–12,)
have ever been relied on by the advocates of the parity of the clergy
as their strongholds in this discussion, let us inquire if their conclusion
is warranted by the literal or spiritual sense of either.   Our Lord, in
Matthew says—" The Scribes and Pharisees . . . bind *heavy burdens*
and grievous to be borne, and lay them *on other men's shoulders;* but
they will not move them with one of their fingers. . . . They love
. . . to be called of men, Rabbi, Rabbi.   But be not ye called Rabbi:
for one is your master, even Christ, and all ye are brethren.   And

call no man your father upon the earth : for one is your Father which is in heaven. Neither be ye called masters, for one is your Master, even Christ. But he that *is greatest* among you shall be your *servant*. And whosoever shall *exalt himself* shall be abased; and he that humbleth himself shall be exalted."

A very common inference from these passages is, that in the Christian Church there should be no distinction of office—superior and inferior—among ministers or teachers; and that they should consider themselves as being all on the same plane ; the Lord only being over them, their teacher, their father, and their master. But surely this deduction is mistaken, even from the sense of the letter. They were addressed to *the Twelve*—after the appointment of the Seventy, whose commission was subordinate, as we have seen ; and were designed by Omniscience to stifle in their first buddings the germs of that *self-derived intelligence* and love of *arbitrary dominion* which afterwards developed themselves, first in the pride of *Bishops* and then in POPERY. There were to be distinctions in the Christian Ministry. It was impossible to avoid them, whatever appearances might be assumed. Some were to be " greater" than others, although they were brethren. Some were " to be exalted." But—be it observed—the higher offices in the Christian Ministry were not to be sought from selfish motives. Neither were they to be sinecures. They only imposed additional burdens, heavier responsibility ;—they exposed to greater dangers, and the reward of fidelity was to be that happiness which results from the disinterested love and performance of use.

Is this merely our own fond interpretation? Let us then hear Swedenborg. " These words of the Lord are to be *spiritually* understood : for *who may not be called Rabbi,* [or doctor] who *is* a Rabbi ; and who may not be called father, who is a father? but whereas by father is signified good, and by Father in Heavens the Divine Good, and whereas by doctor or rabbi is signified truth, and by the Doctor, Christ the Divine Truth, therefore on account of the spiritual sense in all things of the word, it is said that they should not so call them. *In a natural sense they may be called doctors* and fathers, but representatively, because the doctors of the world indeed teach truth, but not from themselves, but from the Lord, and because fathers of the world are indeed good, and lead their children to good, but not from themselves but from the Lord." (A. E. 746.) Again: " There is not any archangel in the heavens; there are indeed superior and inferior angels, also angels more or less wise, and likewise in the societies of the angels there are *moderators set over the rest,* but still they are not archangels, under whose obedience *grounded in arbitrary appointment* the rest stand, *such* government not being given in the heavens, for all in the heavens acknowledge in *heart* no other above them but the Lord alone, *which is meant* by the Lord's words in Mat. 23: 8–11." (A. E. 735.) Yet again : Those who *preside* in heaven . . . do not *domineer* and rule, but *minister* and *serve,* for to do good to others from the love of good is to serve, and to *provide for its being done* is to minister ; [Compare this with Doc. Ch. 70;] nor do such persons make themselves greater than others, *but lesser,* since they set the good of society and their neighbor in the first place, but their own good in a lower place, and what is in the first place is greater, and what is in a lower place is lesser. Nevertheless they have honor and glory, dwelling in the midst of the society, in a greater elevation than others, and likewise in magnificent palaces; they *accept also* this glory and that honor, yet not for the sake of themselves, but *for the sake of obedience;* for all in heaven know, that they derive that honor and that glory from the Lord, and on that account are to be obeyed. *These are the things* which are meant by the Lord's words to the Disciples, in Mat. 20 : 27, 28 ; and Luke 22 : 26, [the very texts under consideration and which have been claimed as teaching the very reverse.] (H. and H. 218.) "Those who seek *recompense* for the works they perform are never contented, but indignant if they are not rewarded more than others, and they mourn and find fault if they see others more blessed than themselves. . . . Recompense at the resurrection of the just, is internal happiness, resulting from doing good without remuneration which they receive from the Lord when they perform uses ; and they who love to serve without recompense, are given *to preside over more noble uses*, and actually become greater and more powerful than others in proportion as they have a love to serve." (A. C. 6393.) " By uses are meant goods, and hence by doing uses is meant to do goods; and by doing uses or goods, is meant to serve others and to minister to them ; persons of this character, *although they are in dignity* and opulence, still do not regard dignity and opulence any otherwise than as means to do uses, thus to serve and minister. *These are they* who are meant by the Lord's words, " whosoever would be great among you," &c. These also are they, to whom government in heaven is entrusted by the Lord, for government is to them a medium of doing uses or goods, thus of serving, and when uses or goods are ends or loves, *in this case they do not govern, but the Lord,* for all good is from him." (D. P. 215.) In accordance herewith, we read in a certain Memorable Relation which contrasts with the sad fate of tyrannical and usurping Popes, the happier lot of those who aspired to civil and *ecclesiastical dignities* from pure motives. " I saw two angels standing and talking together." After describing their *dress*, accosting them and inquiring why they were there, they answered, " We have let ourselves down from heaven at the command of the Lord, to speak with you concerning the blessed lot of those who wish to rule from a love of uses ; *we are worshippers of the Lord ;* I am *prince* of a society, the other is HIGH PRIEST there ; the latter said that he was minister of the Church there, because in serving them he ministered holy things for the uses of their souls. . . . The *dignities* in which we are, we have indeed sought after, but for no other end, than that we might be able more fully to do uses, and more widely to extend them ; and we are surrounded with *honor* and we *accept* it not for the sake of ourselves but for the good of society." (C. L. 266.)

It was not then the design of the Lord in these famous texts to denounce all distinctions in the ministry of his Church, but to warn against their abuse. For we read here of "*high*-priests" even in heaven.   And there have been worthy bishops among .ne Protestants in *Nati nal* Churches, and in the early Christian Church, whom, for the sake of orderly proceeding *in their own rank* and to facilitate uses, it was found expedient to appoint as Archbishops and Metropolitans, but who at the same time acknowledged themselves to be each only "primus inter pares" or *first among equals*. And is not this the theory of our own Republican institutions, where there is as regular a gradation of office as in a Constitutional Monarchy—while yet the officers themselves, from the highest to the lowest, are regarded as "the servants of the people"?

There is yet another abuse against which we must be on our guard; and by which the church in this age and particularly in this country is more liable to be imposed on than by open usurpation and tyranny. There is a pride that *apes* humility: an ambition that *stoops* to conquer: a flattery that fawns on whom it designs to betray. Witness the proud bishops who, as well as the most humble and sincere, are inaugurated with the protest " nolo episcopari ;" or the still more accursed hypocrisy of the Popes who affected the title of "Servant of the Servants of God."—And we are warned emphatically by our Author against this also.—" Heaven does not consist in desiring to be the least *with a view to be greatest,* for in this case there is an aspiration and desire to be greatest." (A. C. 452.)   They who do good works for the sake of recompense, say also, *because they have learnt it from the Word,* that they are willing to be least in heaven, but in this case they think by so saying to become great, *thus they have still the same end in view."* (A. C. 6393.)

Here then we are willing to rest our case so far as the testimony of the Gospel is concerned; and now proceed to that of the other parts of the New Testament. We have already established our right to such reference; but if we had not, we cannot see the consistency of those who deny their credibility, in appealing to early Ecclesiastical History where it is thought to sustain the theory of Parity. Trustworthy history cannot be written without the consultation of documents. The characters of authors being otherwise equal, relevant documents are credible sources of evidence in proportion to their nearness to the events and facts recorded; and most of all where they are written by those who were either witnesses of, or contemporaneous with the facts. The authors of the Acts and Epistles were such witnesses. Those books "have communication with heaven," and " are very good books for the church." Can more—or as much—be said in favor of any other writings of the Early Church?—" All things that I have heard of my Father I have made known unto you." " The Holy Spirit shall teach you all things, and shall bring all things to your remembrance that I have said unto you." "Go ye and teach all nations . . . to observe all things whatsoever I have commanded you." "I am no more in the world, but these [the Twelve] are in the world." "I have chosen and ordained you that ye should go and bring forth fruit and that your fruit should remain." "As the Father hath sent me, even so send I you." " He that receiveth whomsoever I send, receiveth me."—Such was the language of the Lord to and of the Twelve before his glorification. After his resurrection he gave *them* the Holy Spirit, (John 20: 22,) and was seen of the Apostles for forty days— speaking of the things pertaining to the kingdom of God. (Acts 1: 3.) As they had received such repeated and particular instructions concerning their work which was to remain, it is not to be presumed that they would immediately violate such solemn injunctions or omit to carry any of them into effect as occasion arose. We must therefore look to their recorded acts and instructions if we would know the order which Christ established in the Church.

A trinal ministry of—Himself—the Twelve—the Seventy, existed while He was on earth. Was a similar ministry continued by his authority, and after his Ascension? Were the Eleven from thenceforth degraded to the rank of the Seventy? were the Seventy elevated to the station of the Eleven? and do we hear no more of any distinction among the ministers of Christ? Far otherwise, we hear nothing more of the Seventy as such; but the first official act of the Eleven was the appointment of two who had accompanied them from the Baptism of John to the Ascension, of whom Matthias was chosen by lot to take the place of Judas. (Acts 1: 15–26.) After the day of Pentecost the Twelve ordained deacons, (6: 1–6,) of whom the only two specially mentioned, *preached*, and Philip baptized, (vs. 8, 10; 8: 5, 38,) Apostles ordained elders, (14: 23,) and Paul as an Apostle invested Timothy and Titus (both of whom, as we shall prove, are also called Apostles) with the power of ordaining inferior ministers in Ephesus and Crete. (1 Tim. 4: 14; 2 Tim. 1: 6; 2: 2; 1 Tim. 5: 22; Tit. 1: 5.)

For some time Jerusalem appears to have been the head-quarters of the Apostles, (Acts, 1: 12; 2: 1; 6: 2; 8: 1; Gal. 1: 17, 18, 22; 2: 1, 2; 1 Thes. 2: 14,) from whence some of their number as well as of the lower grades were sent forth on Missionary excursions. To them were made reports of their progress and of the state of the cause: applications for ministerial service: appeals in questions of difficulty; and from thence were their decisions issued. Thus, the *Apostles* and *brethren* that were in Judea, heard that the Gentiles had also received the word of God. (Acts 11: 1.) "It was determined that Paul and Barnabas . . . should go up to Jerusalem unto the *Apostles* and *Elders* about this question, [of Gentile converts observing the law of Moses]—And they were received of the Church and of the Apostles and Elders;—And the Apostles and Elders came together to consider of the matter.—Then it pleased the Apostles and Elders with the whole Church to send chosen men . . . to Antioch. . . . And they wrote letters by them after this manner. "The Apostles and Elders and brethren send greeting, &c. It seemed good unto *us*, being assembled with one accord, to send unto you chosen men, &c." (15: 2, 4, 6, 22, 23, 25.) "And as they went through the cities, they delivered them the decrees to keep, that were ordained of the Apostles and Elders which were at Jerusalem." (16: 4.) Here we have repeated mention of at least two orders of ministers. But again: the Epistle to the Philippians is addressed by

"Paul and Timotheus (both of whom were *Apostles*) . . . to all the *saints* in Christ Jesus which are at Philippi with the *bishops* and *deacons*." (Phil. 1: 1.) The term "bishops" here refers to the second rank and was employed for reasons which we will presently give.—"I supposed it necessary to send to you *Epaphroditus*, my brother and companion in labor . . . but your messenger," [in the original, your *Apostle*.] Here are the three grades for which we contend in the same church. The same three grades, as we shall see, are also recognized in the Epistles to Timothy and Titus.

Turn now for a moment to the 12th Chapter of 1st Corinthians.— Paul, here speaking of spiritual powers, (vs. 1,) having declared that there are diversities of *gifts*; of MINISTRIES, and of *operations*, enumerates various "gifts," and—after alluding to the different functions of several members of the human body, between which and the Church he traces an analogy—says expressly that "God hath set some in the Church, first *Apostles*, secondarily *prophets*, thirdly, *teachers*," (vs. 28,) and through the remainder of this and the two succeeding chapters descants on the proper "operation" or *manifestation* of these "powers" (and not "miracles" as δυναμεις has been improperly rendered) which are distributed by the Spirit among these different officers for the common benefit. (vs. 7, 11, 25, 26.) Here the trine is again distinctly set forth but with new titles for the two lower ranks, the reason of which we will also give when we recur to these chapters as we shall do before we close. Nor is there any contradiction between this enumeration and that in his Epistle to the Ephesians, (4: 11,) where he says, "And Christ gave some, Apostles; and some, prophets; and some, pastors and teachers,"—as we will show at the same time. It is clear then from these citations that there was a ministry of three grades in the days of the Apostles.

But perhaps some will say that the Apostles were extraordinary officers, with special endowments and commissions for a peculiar work, none of which were descendible; and that after their departure they could have no successors in their own rank, but the guardianship and propagation of the truth, under God, would thenceforth devolve on the one rank of Presbyters. Can any of these things be justly inferred from the books to which we have appealed? or does Ecclesiastical History sanction such an idea? What was the distinctive attribute of those Apostles to whom all concede the title and its rightful powers? Was it "seeing the Lord after his Resurrection"? This was one qualification, but not the only one,—nor was it peculiar to them. "He was seen of above five hundred brethren at once." (1 Cor. 15: 6.) Was it the power of *working miracles*? The Seventy were gifted with this power; (Luke, 10: 17,) the deacons Stephen and Philip wrought miracles: (Acts, 6: 8; 8: 6, 7,) it was promised to believers in general: (Mark, 16: 17, 18,) and if we may credit history, continued in the Church for several centuries.—Was it *Inspiration*? This is not an abiding but an occasional gift, imparted according to the exigencies of the Church or individuals. (Mat. 10: 19, 20; John 14: 26; Com. 3: 34.) Mark and Luke were inspired; and though there is reason to believe that both were ordained to the

Apostolical office, yet were they not called immediately by the Lord
as were the Twelve and Paul. The Resurrection of Christ having
been *established* as an accomplished fact by many credible witnesses,
it was neither necessary nor proper that they should be gifted with
an immortality on earth to attest to succeeding generations what was
sufficiently proved to the first. The gift of miracles which was useful
to the Church in its origin and early struggles naturally ceased when
their purpose was answered and the Church placed on a firm foundation. Extraordinary Inspiration was no longer required when all
needfuldi vine instruction had been committed to writing under divine
guidance.

Paul it is, who declares what was the special gift of the Apostles
which they were virtually commanded to transmit to properly qualified successors. "All things are of God who hath reconciled us to
himself, and hath committed to *us* [Apostles] the *ministry of reconciliation.* Now then we are *ambassadors* for Christ, as though God
did beseech you by us: we pray you in Christ's stead, be ye reconciled to God." (2 Cor. 5: 18, 20.) Christ is indeed our High Priest
in the Heavens, (Heb. 4: 14,) but he delegated a part of his power
to Apostles on earth. They were his "Ambassadors" to "all
nations," "always, even to the consummation of the age." The
Twelve did not and could not execute the whole of that commission,
and its very terms imply that it was to be handed down to others.
Each Apostle was an Ambassador, *sent* (as the name imports) to the
people of whatever nation he might visit, and the elders and deacons
ordained by him were, so to speak, subordinate attachés of his embassy. The power of *ordination* then,—of conferring ministerial
authority on equals and subordinates, was one and perhaps the chief
peculiarity of an Apostle.

But do we read in the New Testament of any other Apostles than the
Twelve?—From the fact that *Paul* was called to be the Apostle to
the Gentiles, (Acts, 9: 15,) we might have presumed that others
would in time be called to share in the Herculean work. And we
are told of others who co-operated with him, with the same title and
similar powers. Writing to the Corinthians of the Resurrection of
the Lord, he says: "He was seen of Cephas, then of *the Twelve:*—
After that, he was seen of James, then of *all* the Apostles." (1 Cor.
15: 5, 7.) Does not this imply that there were other Apostles than
the twelve?—Again: Referring to his first visit to Jerusalem after
his call, "But other of the *Apostles* saw I none, save *James* the Lord's
brother." (Gal. 1: 19.) In the roll of the disciples we read of
James the son of Zebedee, and James the son of Alpheus, but this
James was not of the Twelve. We should rather infer from Mark,
3: 21, 31–35, that his brethren did not believe on him when the
others were first called.—*Barnabas* is twice called an Apostle together
with Paul, and again by implication. (Acts, 14: 4, 14; Gal. 2: 9.)
"Salute *Andronicus* and *Junia* [Junias] . . . who are of note among
the Apostles." (Rom. 16: 7.) Some modern critics have pretended
to doubt the justice of our inference here, pretending that Junia was
a woman, but the terms in the original, nouns, pronouns and adjec-

tives, are all masculine.—"Paul, *Silvanus* [or Silas] and *Timotheus* unto the Church of the Thessalonians,— . . . Nor of men sought we glory . . . when *we* might have been burdensome, as the *Apostles* of Christ." (1 Thes. 1: 1; 2: 6.)—" Paul and Timotheus . . . to all the saints in Christ Jesus which are at Philippi with the bishops and deacons.—I supposed it necessary to send unto you *Epaphroditus*, my brother and *companion in labor* . . . but your *messenger*," [in the original " your *Apostle.*"] The letter was sent by Epaphroditus, and would naturally be read by him to the Church. Hence the propriety of that other phrase, " And I intreat *thee* also, true *yoke-fellow*, &c." (Phil. 1: 1; 2: 25; 4: 3.) Again: Speaking of *Titus*, Paul calls him his " brother," (2 Cor. 2: 13,) into whose heart God had put an earnest care for the Corinthians,—who was also forward of his own accord to go to them; and Paul sent with him " a brother " whose praise was *in the Gospel* throughout *all the churches*,—who was also *chosen of the churches* to travel with them *in. the grace which was administered by them*, (as Paul and Barnabas had been before chosen, *after they were apostles*, to go on a similar expedition. Acts, 13 : 1–3; 14: 4, 14,) which brother Paul " had often proved to be diligent in many things but now more so, on the great confidence which Paul had " in the Corinthians.—If any inquire concerning Titus—he is my *partner* and *fellow-helper* concerning you : and both these " brethren " were " the *Messengers* [original, APOSTLES] of Churches, and the *glory* of Christ." . . . " Wherefore show ye to *them* and before the churches, the *proof of your love* and of our boasting on your behalf." (8: 6, 16–19, 22–24.)—It is not certainly known who this brother was, but from internal evidence and such passages as Acts, 16: 10; 27: 1, 2; 28: 7–10; Col. 4: 14; 2 Tim. 4: 11; Philemon, 24, it is believed to have been *Luke.* But if he had been nothing more than " a messenger " of the churches, as some suppose, the strong language here employed would have been wholly inappropriate.—Still farther, " Did *Titus* make a gain of you? walked we not in the same spirit?— *in the same steps?*" (2 Cor. 12: 18.)

Here then is positive proof that besides the original Twelve, Matthias, Paul, Barnabas, Silas, Timothy, Epaphroditus, Titus, and another " brother," Andronicus and Junias are all called apostles;* and of

* To these we might have added the names of Sosthenes or Apollos—of one certainly—perhaps of both. Sosthenes, who was the Chief ruler of the Synagogue at Corinth and had suffered in behalf of the Gospel, (Acts, 18: 17,) was united with Paul in the 1st Ep. to the Cor. In the 2d chapter (vs. 6. 7, 10, 12, 13, 16,) powers peculiar to an Apostle are attributed to himself and another, and that other must have been either Sosthenes (1: 1) or Apollos (v. 12). In Chap. 3: 5–10; 4: 1, 6–13 (16: 12) he speaks of himself and Apollos as having an equal title to the regard of the Corinthians, and in v. 9, he appears to call him an Apostle. If the latter had been only an Elder would not the dispute for precedence have been settled by another method? He is prompt enough to claim his apostolic rights in another part of this very letter. (Cb. 9.) In v. 5 of this chapter he asks, " Have we not power to lead about a sister, a wife, as well as the other apostles, and *as the brethren of the Lord*, and Cephas?" Should we not infer from this when taken with what precedes, that the " brethren of the Lord " after the flesh, held the same rank with the Apostles? Their names are given in Mat. 13: 55; and they could not have been of the Twelve. For while the Lord was going about with the Twelve the people of Nazareth said " his brethren were *with them.*"

these Barnabas and Silas labored with Paul on a footing of equality.
If these ten or more were raised to the rank of the Twelve, is it not
evident that the office was designed to be perpetuated in the Church?

Our belief in the correctness of this interpretation is strengthened by
various allusions in the New Testament to "*false* apostles" who usurped
the name and authority of that class of ministers. Thus in the second
Epistle to the Corinthians Paul says of some who had endeavored to
supplant him in their regard, " But such are *false apostles*, deceitful
workers, transforming *themselves* into the Apostles of Christ. And
no marvel; for Satan himself is transformed into an angel of light.
Therefore it is no great thing if his ministers also be transformed as the
ministers of righteousness." 2 Cor. 11: 13–15.) And in the Revelations, "Unto the Angel of the Church of Ephesus, write: I know
thy works, &c. . . . and thou hast *tried* them which *say they are
Apostles and are not;* and hast found them liars." (Rev. 2: 2.) The
Twelve had doubted the sincerity and commission of Paul himself
until Barnabas informed them of his extraordinary call; (Acts, 9:
26–28,) but afterwards recognized his official character. (Gal. 2: 9.)
And yet from the frequency and strength of his protestations on this
subject, it would appear that it had also been questioned by others.
As, for example: " Paul, an apostle,—*not of men*, neither by man,
but by Jesus Christ;"—(Gal. 1: 1,) and again: "*Am not I an apostle?*
Am I not free? have I not seen Jesus Christ our Lord? . . . If I be
not an apostle to others, yet *doubtless I am to you.* Mine answer to
them that *examine me* is this, &c." (1 Cor. 9: 1–3.) "For I suppose I was not a whit behind the very chiefest of the Apostles." (2
Cor. 11: 5.) Now had the office been confined to the Twelve and
Paul, and this been an understood thing among Christians, it is not
probable that such pretenders would ever have arisen; or if they had,
that their assumptions could have escaped immediate exposure. But
as others were admitted to the rank—it would appear from what is
said of " examining," " trying," &c., that there were means of readily
detecting imposters.

While collecting the testimony of the Gospels on this head, we
have observed the successive labors of our Lord in Galilee, Samaria,
and Judea,—and the representative character of each of those provinces. In his final commission to the Twelve before his Ascensio ,
he commanded that "repentance and remission of sins should be
preached in his name among all nations, *beginning at Jerusalem.*
And behold I send the promise of the Father upon you: but tarry ye
in the *city of Jerusalem* until ye be endued with power from on
high." (Luke 24: 47, 49.) And in Acts: "Ye shall be witnesses
unto me, both *in Jerusalem* and in all Judea, and in Samaria, and unto
the uttermost parts of the earth. . . . He commanded them that they
should not *depart from Jerusalem.* . . . Then returned they *to Jeru-*
salem," &c. (Acts, 1: 4, 8, 12.) Accordingly the gospel was first
preached in Jerusalem; next in Samaria; (8: 1, 5, 14, 40;) then in
Galilee; (9: 31;) and finally to the Gentiles; (Ch. 10, &c.:) thus
reversing the order in which he had traversed those scenes himself.
Now as he had not only prepared them for their duty at first by his

example and general discourses throughout his own ministry, and then by his special instructions during forty days after his Resurrection concerning the things pertaining to his kingdom, we might infer from this that the proper order of his church would first be exemplified *at* Jerusalem, which would thenceforth serve as a model for its establishment when propagated elsewhere. Do we then hear of any one of the Apostles as having peculiar spiritual authority at Jerusalem? When Paul first visited Jerusalem after his call, "other of the Apostles saw he none, save *James*, the Lord's brother." (Gal. 1: 19.) James presided in the first Council of Jerusalem. "And after they [the other Apostles] had held their peace, *James* answered, saying, 'Men and brethren, hearken unto *me*, &c. . . . wherefore *my* sentence is,'" &c. (Acts, 15: 13, 19.)—"Before that certain came from *James*, Peter did eat with the Gentiles." (Gal. 2: 12.)—"And Peter said, (after his miraculous deliverance from prison,) go show these things unto *James* and to the brethren." (Acts, 12: 17.)—"And when we were come to Jerusalem, the brethren received us gladly. And the day following Paul went in with us unto *James ;* and *all the elders* were present." (21: 17, 18.) Now is there not a manifest precedence here given to James? and do not the incidents here recorded illustrate and confirm the united testimony of the early Ecclesiastical Historians and of all Christian Antiquity that James was the first *Bishop* of Jerusalem and its dependencies?

It was shown above and *is* conceded by all that the Apostles ordained. Does Scripture record an instance in which that power was exercised by ministers of a lower grade? The advocates of Parity have been often challenged to produce a case of Presbyterian ordination from the New Testament—and the *only two* which they have ever been able to present as bearing the slightest resemblance thereto are the transactions recorded in Acts, 13: 1-3, and 1 Tim. 4: 14. But it may be clearly shown that neither of these is such a case. In the first, Barnabas and Saul were merely set apart to a particular work without conferring any additional ministerial powers.* For Paul

---

* As we shall feel it our duty to dissent from the views of a report made to the Seventh Annual Meeting of the Central Convention, " on the trine in the ministry," by the Rev. Thomas Wilks, so we feel it imperatively incumbent on us to enter our dissent from Mr. Cabell's view here and elsewhere in the course of this paper. But we have not time, and cannot take space, to argue matters here at length. We must be content with the privilege of simply stating the points wherein we do not agree, with a reason or two for our disagreement.

We *do* believe that Acts, xiii , 1 3, sets forth a regular and full *ordination.* and that *discrete powers of the Lord's holy spirit* were imparted to them thereby. And we cannot conceive why the solemn *representative* formulary of the *translation* of that *holy spirit*, by prayer and the imposition of the hands of the *church* at Antioch, should have been given for "a *missionary tour*"—a *particular* work of a previous ordination or commission to the apostleship. For this was the translation of a vastly greater power than the work required ; and we cannot imagine why the holy spirit should grant more or greater means than the end demanded.

Mr. Cabell says, "Barnabas and Saul were merely *set apart* to a *particular* work, without conferring ANY ADDITIONAL *ministerial powers.*" Is this the testimony of the record ? "The holy ghost said, Separate me Barnabas, and Saul, for the *work whereunto I have called them.*" Was that only a *particular* work ? Take the case of

certainly, and Barnabas probably, was an Apostle long before. (Acts,
9 : 20-22, 27-29 ; 11 : 22-26 ; Gal. 1 : 1.) And this work—a missionary tour, an account of which is given in that and the succeeding
chapter, (Acts, 13 and 14,)—was the same in kind with what they

Saul, about which we have more express testimony. And here we must observe, that
Mr. Cabell does not, in this paper, make the distinction that we do, between the Lord's
calling of Saul and the *ordaining* of him. He seems to think that Saul was at once
ordained into the highest grade of the apostolic ministry by his miraculous conversion from
judaism to christianity as recorded in Acts, ix., 1-9. But, in our view, this was only
his *call* to the apostleship; and this and his *ordination* to that office, were two very
distinct things. The Lord calls men to the ministry by *immediate* influx. He ordains
them by *mediate* influx. The object of the call is a change. or determination of the
love. the will, and the consequent life The object of the ordination is such a communication of the powers of the holy spirit as gives to the understanding illustration, perception, disposition and instruction in the things of divine wisdom from the Word. The
one flows immediately from the Lord into the love or essence of the mind, the other
mediately in the wisdom or form of the mind. By the former Saul was enlightened
internally to see the truths of christianity, by the latter he was endued *externally* with
power from on high to teach them to others. All power is exerted by the Lord from
himself in first principles by ultimates. These ultimates " are upon earth, and indeed
with men." (Ap. Rev. 798) " Representatives and significatives are in ultimate
things." (Ap. Ex. 31.) The conjunction of heaven with men cannot otherwise be
effected than by man's being in such things as are in the world as to his natural man,
and in such things as are in heaven as to his spiritual man. (Ap. Ex. 475) Thus
such conjunction cannot be effected without " representative and significative rites "
Inauguration into the ministry by the imposition of hands, is among representative rites
handed down from ancient times and in vogue at the present day. (A. C. 6292.) The
imposition of hands represents the communication of *power*, and is a correspondential
act which, when done on earth, causes what it represents to avail in heaven: for " correspondences have all force, insomuch that what is done on earth according to correspondence avails in heaven ; for correspondences are from the Deity." (A. C. 8615.)
Thus the *power* of the Lord's holy spirit, that is, the power of the Lord's influx through
the arrangements of angels and spirits in the spiritual world, into the minds of men in
the natural world, cannot otherwise be imparted than by the representative rite of the
imposition of hands, which signifies the communication of that power, and is an " ultimate with men " " through which the Lord operates " in saving men " from himself in
first principles and from himself in ultimates." (Ap Rev. 798.) Thus the Lord's call
is a very distinct thing from his ordination. He calls by a voice immediately from himself. He ordains by the medium of some man on earth. And the record proves that
this was true in Paul's case, as any one will see who consults it. For that the call in
his case was a very distinct thing from the ordination, is manifest from its effects. It
struck Saul with blindness, and did not at all impart that " illustration and instruction "
which is the virtue that comes by the communication of the Lord's holy spirit. Whereas
his ordination by the imposition of the hands of Ananias took place, that he " might
receive his sight, and be *filled with the holy ghost.*" (Acts, ix., 17.)

Now what was the work whereunto the Lord called Saul ? " The Lord said unto
him, [Ananias,] Go thy way : for he [Saul] is a chosen vessel unto me, to bear my name
before the Gentiles, and kings, and the children of Israel." This was the apostleship
to which Saul was called by the Lord. And we must observe that there is a trine of
discrete degrees in it, as there is in every other divine work. It is not our purpose here
to point out and discriminate fully these three degrees of apostolic operation. It is
sufficient to observe that the establishment of the church amongst the Jews, or Israelites,
was the lowest grade and the establishment of the church amongst the Gentiles was the
highest. And the lowest degree was the first stage of the apostle's labors, the highest
the last. The Jews and Gentiles were in all countries, but the work of establishing
the church amongst the one and the other was a discrete operation of the holy spirit.

had before performed in Damascus and Antioch, only the Gentiles were now included as its objects.

The other alleged example is supposed to be indicated in these words of Paul to Timothy. " Neglect not the gift that is in thee, which was given thee *by* prophecy, *with* the laying of the *hands of the Presbytery.*"* (1 Tim. 4 : 14.) To this it has been replied that

That is, the influx for the establishment of the church amongst the Jews came from the Lord through an arrangement of Jewish Christians in the spiritual world ; and the influx for the establishment of the church amongst the Gentiles had to come through an arrangement of Gentile Christians in that world ; for no church can exist on earth before a heaven is formed for it to descend from. The first influx was determined into Saul by the ordination of Ananias. Hence Saul, immediately on receiving it, " preached Christ in the synagogues." And there was just as much need for another and distinct ordination by the imposition of hands of the church at Antioch, or by some other ultimate mode of spiritual communication, in order to determine into him the second influx, as there was need of baptism by the Lord's disciples to determine the influx of christian spirits into those who had been previously baptized by John, whose baptism consociated the spirits of men on earth with only the spirits of the better sort of Jews. And without the powers of the holy spirit received by this second ordination, it would have been impossible for Saul to preach the Gospel effectively to the Gentiles, which was the *general* or *universal* work " whereunto the Holy Ghost had called him." The *particular* work unto which he had been called, was to " preach Christ in the *synagogues* " to the children of Israel. For this he was specially " filled with the holy ghost " by the imposition of Ananias's hands. But for this *general* work—this apostleship on a wider or more extended plane—he needed and did receive " additional ministerial powers," that is, other, variant. and greater powers of the Lord's holy spirit, which he received in that ordination which " *separated* " him from the distinctively jewish influx and conjoined .him to the distinctively gentile influx. And this, in our view, was a discrete ordination, and not merely the assignment of a particular work in a previous one. Hence, although both Barnabas and Saul were " apostles long before," that is, apostles to the Jews, they were now again made apostles in another and higher or more extended degree—apostles to the Gentiles. That Paul was *called* to be such an apostle at first, matters not. He could not receive the *powers* of this apostleship any more than those of the previous one, without some ultimate " with men," in and by which the Lord could operate in so ordaining him from " himself in ultimates," (Ap. Rev. 798.) as to send him to the Gentiles distinctly or discretely from the Jews. Or this is our opinion. And these are our reasons for thinking differently from Mr. Cabell in the position which he above takes.—*Ed.*

* The meaning of this text is very plain to our mind, and does not at all justify the construction of Mr. Cabell—namely, that the presbytery only concurred in the act of a principal ordainer. Paul exhorts Timothy not to neglect the gift or grace ($\tau\sigma\nu$ $\chi\alpha\rho\iota\sigma\mu\alpha\tau\sigma\varsigma$) that is in him by *two means*—prophecy *together with* " the laying on of the hands of the presbytery." Prophecy means the preaching of the apostles, by which Timothy was instructed in that gospel which it was now his duty and office to preach. (See 2 Tim. 2 : 13.) Thus he received the gift of preaching by prophecy as an internal means. And the laying on of the hands of the presbytery was then, as now, an external sign, or representative ultimate, by which, as an external means, he received those powers of illustration and instruction in preaching which are the special virtues of the Lord's holy spirit with the clergy. Thus there is but one ordaining medium alluded to here, namely, the presbytery. But we incline to the opinion that this word means an assemblage of the apostles and other ministers, whose organ Paul was. So that his hands were those of the presbytery. And hence we believe that Paul alludes to the same ordination in 2 Tim. 2 · 6; for if he were the organ, or ordaining member, of the presbytery, so that the body ordained by him as its member, it is manifestly the same thing whether he says Timothy was ordained by the laying on of the hands of the presbytery or of his hands.—*Ed.*

the Presbytery here mentioned were not the sole or the principal
ordainers, as is proved by the use of the term "with," which merely
implies *concurrence* on their part; and also by another passage in 2
Tim. 1 : 6, which says, "Stir up the gift of God, which is in thee by
the putting on of *my* hands."—It was Paul then who ordained, and
his superiority to ordinary Presbyters is conceded by the friends of
Parity. This is sufficient to refute the claim; and therefore I pass
over another interpretation which though backed by high authority,
I regard as doubtful; viz: that the first text merely speaks of Timothy's admission to the Presbyterate, or office of a Presbyter;—and
still another which urges that these Presbyters may have been
Apostles, just as Peter and John, though Apostles, call themselves
"Elders," (1 Pet. 5 : 1; 2 John, 1 : 1,) on the principle that the
greater office includes the less. Another exposition has occurred
to me as being more in harmony with all the facts and exhortations ·
recorded in these epistles. If we bear in mind that the Priesthood was not abolished in the transition from the Jewish to the
Christian Church, but merely "changed;" and that there is still an
analogy in the constitution of the latter to the former; if we recollect
also that when the *Levites* were ordained, "*the Elders of Israel laid
their hands on them,*" by which was signified "the translation of the
power of ministering for them and reception by the Levites, thus
separation," (Num. 8 : 10; A. C. 10,023,)—the which was not done
in the case either of Aaron or his sons, both of whom were ordained
by Moses alone,—as was also the case with the successor of Aaron,
for when the latter died, his son Eleazar, who was but a common
priest before, was raised to the high-priesthood by Moses' investing
him with the garments of Aaron, which was the mode of ordination
in the Jewish Church: (Num. 20 : 26–28,)—if then we return to
these two texts which appear in two different Epistles and find that
the one speaks of a gift imparted "*with* the laying on of the hands of
the Presbytery" or Eldership*—the other, of something conferred by
the laying on of Paul's hands; is it a strained inference that they
refer to *two successive ordinations?*—the first to his admission to the
first rank, analogous to that of the Levites,†—the second, to his being
raised to a higher? And whether these Elders were "Elders of the
people," (such as are alluded to in Luke, 22 : 66; Acts, 22 : 5,) or
preaching elders, the effect would be the same, for a minister does
not cease to be a *member* of the Church, and his concurrence in the

---

\# The Greek word is *presbuterion*—"a council or an assembly of elders." *Presbus,* an adjective, in the positive degree, denoted an aged person—hence, one held in
honor, because, among the ancients, old age was honorable—and hence a distinguished
person sent on some embassy, because ambassadors were chosen from those advanced
in years. *Presbuteros,* from which *presbuterion* is derived, is the comparative degree
of *presbus,* and denoted those who were older, more noted for their wisdom, and therefore honorable in a higher degree. Hence *presbuterion,* in the present case, would
seem to denote a council of the older and more honorable of the apostolic ministry, that
is, the apostles themselves, who were emphatically *the Lord's ambassadors.—Ed.*

† An objection to this is, that it is against the primal usage of Acts, vi. 1–6, in which
deacons, or ministers of the first rank, were ordained by the laying on of the apostles'
hands.—*Ed.*

ordination would be given in his private capacity or as a representative of the laity. The priestly character being once imparted, the after elevation of the subject would depend on the judgment of the ordainer, guided by the best information he could obtain as to his fitness. This interpretation appears to be favored by such expressions as "*Neglect not* the [first] gift that is in thee," as an Apostle might be tempted to omit the duties of the lowest grade; "Do the work of an *Evangelist*." (2 Tim. 4: 5.) Now Philip the *Deacon* is called an "Evangelist," (Acts, 21: 8,) and this title is also given to ministers of the first degree in Eph. 4: 11, corresponding with that of "teacher" in 1 Cor. 12: 28.—But when referring to the higher office which implies deeper qualifications, the exhortation is "*Stir up* the gift of God which is in thee." In any aspect, then, the case of Timothy gives no countenance to the theory of ordination by Presbyters alone;* and as this is the second and *last* example adduced from Scripture for that purpose, the advocates of that mode must seek some other source of authority than the Bible for their justification.

Besides the absence of any Scriptural example of its exercise, the claim in question is farther weakened by another negative argument. The qualifications of Elders are set forth in 1 Tim. 1: 1–7; Tit. 2: 5–9. Their duties, which may in part be inferred from these passages and from the first and second commissions of the Twelve, (their spiritual sense at this day,) are expressly declared in Acts 20: 28–35, and 1 Pet. 5: 2; and some of them are incidentally mentioned elsewhere in the New Testament, particularly in the Acts and Epistles; but no where is any thing said of the importance of filling up their own rank with qualified associates, or of the duty of rejecting unfit applicants. Without doubt the Apostles ordained. There is no record that any others did. If the Apostles were only extraordinary officers, after whose death this prerogative would devolve on the Eldership, we may fairly presume that some notice of the transfer of power or of its exercise would have been preserved. None such appears. The fair inference is that the Apostolic office was continued with this prerogative unimpaired.

Authority to ordain was committed by Paul to Timothy. We have proved (by comparing 1 Thes. 1: 1, with 2: 6) that he is expressly called an Apostle. But since, if the Apostolic character and rank be conceded to him—this would virtually be a settlement of the question, ingenuity has been taxed to the utmost to evade the force of the declaration. Two assertions have been chiefly relied on for this purpose. The first is, that although Paul here uses the plural ("we") he does it in a singular sense, referring to himself alone. The other is, that Timothy is not called an Apostle in the official sense, but simply as a "messenger." Neither hypothesis is consistent with all

---

* We do not differ from Mr. Cabell in this conclusion. We believe the apostles were the sole ordainers, and that ordination is exclusively the function of the highest grade of the ministry at any time. Therefore we do not believe that the above was an "ordination by presbyters alone" as the *second* grade of ministers in the apostolic church. We suppose that the presbytery which ordained Timothy was the council or sanhedrim of the apostles, which ordained deacons or evangelists in Acts, vi. 6.—*Ed.*

the facts of the case.   Fourteen of the Epistles are ascribed to Paul;
and though he probably wrote them all, yet in eight of them—a
majority—one or more persons united with him.   Those to the
Romans, Ephesians, Timothy, Titus and Hebrews were sent in his
own name alone, though the first (and probably others) was written
by an amanuensis. (16 : 22.)   *Sosthenes* was joined with him in the
first Letter to the Corinthians : *Timothy*, in the second, and in those
to the Philippians, Colossians, and Philemon : *Timothy and Silas*, in
those to the Thessalonians : and "all the brethren who were with
him" (probably the *ministers*, such as Mark, Luke, Aristarchus, &c.,
who formed a part of the retinue that usually accompanied him, for
a distinction is taken between *such* "brethren" and the "saints" or
church generally in Phil. 4: 21,) unite in that to the Galatians.   In
the Epistles of the first class, he uniformly employs the first person
singular, except where something is predicated also of those whom he
is addressing.   In the others, the plural pronoun is as regularly applied
to the joint subscribers, except where he refers to himself alone,
when he always returns to the first person.   The truth of this may
be readily tested, especially in case of the Epistle in question, so we
will not stop to adduce proofs.

Now Timothy, though the son of a Greek, was descended of pious
Jews in the maternal line: knew the Scriptures from his childhood:
as probably converted by Paul when he first preached at Lystra
and afterwards taken as his companion and most confidential friend
and trained to assist in his labors, (Acts 16 : 1–3; 2 Tim. 1 : 5; 3 :
15,) particularly in visiting and performing ministerial service in other
churches which Paul could not attend to in person.   Thus we hear
of Timothy as coming to him from Macedonia to Corinth : (Acts 18 :
5,) as being sent again to Macedonia: (19 : 22;) and as again going
with Paul to Asia : (20 : 4;) and in several of the Epistles he promises to send him to the churches addressed.   Thus, to the Corinthians, " I have sent unto you Timothy, my beloved son and faithful
in the Lord, who shall bring you into remembrance of my ways which
be in Christ, as I teach every where in every church.   Now if Timothy
come, see that he may be with you without fear; for he worketh the
work of the Lord, as I also do.   Let no man therefore despise him.   I
beseech you, brethren, . . . that ye *submit* yourselves to *such* [as
he and Apollos] and to every one that *helpeth with us and* laboreth."
(1 Cor. 4 : 17 ; 16 : 10, 15, 16.)   To the Philippians, "I trust in the
Lord Jesus to send Timothy shortly unto you, that I also may be of
good comfort, when I know your state : For I have *no man like
minded* who will naturally care for you. . . . But ye know the proof
of him, that as a son with the father he has served with me in the
Gospel." (Phil. 2 : 19, 20, 22.)   To the Thessalonians, "We sent
Timothy our brother, and minister of God, and our fellow-laborer in
the Gospel of Christ to *establish* you, and to comfort you concerning
the faith." (1 Thes. 3 : 2.)   To the Romans he speaks of him as his
"workfellow;" (16 : 21;) to the Colossians, to Philemon, and to the
Hebrews, as his "brother." (Col. 1 : 1; Phil. 1 : 1; Heb. 13 : 23.) To
the Corinthians, as being like himself "an ambassador for Christ :"
(2 Cor. 1 : 1 ; 5 : 20.)

In the same Epistle, in proof of his claims which had been questioned, he speaks of "the signs of an Apostle" which had been wrought by him among them. (12: 12.) What were some of these, as gathered from this and other parts of the New Testament? One was, that the Apostles spoke in demonstration of the *Holy Spirit* and of *power.* (Acts 10 : 44; 11 : 15–17; Rom. 15 : 18, 19; 1 Cor. 2 :4 ; 4 : 19 ; 2 Cor. 10 : 4, 5; Eph. 3 : 7, 20; Col. 1 : 29; 1 Thes. 1 : 5 ; 2 Tim. 1 : 7; Tit. 3 : 6; Heb. 2 : 3, 4 ; 1 Pet. 1 : 12.) Another was that they spoke the *wisdom* of God in a *mystery.* (1 Cor. 2 : 6–16 ; Eph. 3 : 3–5, 9 ; 1 Pet. 1 : 12; Col. 1 : 26–28 ; 4 : 3 ; 1 Tim. 3 : 16.) It is true that the Gospel generally is spoken of as " a mystery,"— unknown to the old Prophets—unknown to the wise Gentiles,—and foolishness to some of their philosophers ;—but yet it was " the wisdom of God," which, though withheld from none who sought to be " perfect," could not be fully imparted to the novice or unworthy, for to such it would be unintelligible. Now while the Elder is called " the Steward of God," (Tit. 1 : 7,) and the ministry in general, according to their gifts, " stewards of the *manifold* grace of God," (1 Pet. 4: 10,) so, in a special sense, an Apostle was the " steward of the *mysteries* of God," (1 Cor. 4 : 2,)—in obvious reference to the words of our Lord in Luke 12 : 41–48, and Mat. 24 : 42–51, where he speaks of the power conferred on the *Twelve* and predicts its abuse BY THEIR SUCCESSORS in the decline of that dispensation. Again : they had the power of imparting spiritual gifts in aid of those who would advance in the divine life. And to this there is frequent allusion in those passages of Scripture which speak of " babes in Christ" or " novices," (1 Cor. 3: 1; 1 Pet. 2 : 2; 1 Tim. 3: 6,) who when they had received the Holy Spirit, (as in Acts 8: 17, 18; 19: 6; Heb. 6: 2,) would "grow in grace," proceed " from faith to faith," be " strengthened," " confirmed," " rooted," " established" in the faith,—and finally grow up into " perfect men in Christ Jesus." (Acts 14: 22; 15: 32, 41; 16: 5; 18 : 23; Rom. 1: 11 ; 16: 25; 1 Cor. 1: 8; 15: 58; Gal. 3: 3 ; 5: 1; Eph. 3: 16, 17; 4: 12, 13; Col. 2: 7; 1 Thes. 3: 2, 8, 13; 2 Thes. 2: 15, 17; Heb. 6: 2; 13: 9, 20, 21; 1 Pet. 5: 10; 2 Pet. 1: 12.) In accordance with this distinction it is known that in the Early Church three classes of Christians were recognized. 1. Novices or " Catechumens." 2. Advanced Christians or " Energumens:" and 3. The Illumined, who, when their knowledge had been applied to self-purification, were called (in a good sense) " Gnostics" or Perfect Christians. Now, though we are told that for us, under the New Dispensation, it is in a special sense " allowable to enter into the mysteries of faith," (T. C. R. 508,) yet we also must pass through a similar process, the goal not being at once attained. (A. C. 9256.) The same classes of Christians are recognised as of the New Church, (A. C. 10017 and elsewhere,) and he also declares that " the divine principle which is understood by the Holy Spirit, proceeds from the Lord *by the Clergy to the laity* by preachings *according to the doctrine of truth thence derived.*" (Canons 4: 8.) Of course the higher the truth, the higher the gift imparted.

Such then, are some of " the signs of an Apostle." Turn now to

2 Cor. 6: 1, 4–10, (Com. 1: 1,) in which Paul refers to the evidences which he *and Timothy* had given that "*in all things* they had approved themselves as the ministers of God,"—and among others he includes "purity," "*knowledge*," "the holy spirit," the word of truth, the *power of God*, their being poor yet making many *rich*, as having nothing yet *possessing all things*. (See also 1 Tim. 6: 12; 2 Tim. 3: 10, 11; Heb. 13: 23.) Now, if these and the like are not signs of an Apostle what are? Can it be that such a man, happily born, carefully nurtured, selected by an inspired Apostle as his most intimate companion, trained by him for future usefulness, entrusted with the most delicate missions, the conduct of all which was fully approved, tried in the school of the most varied and bitter experience, enduring all sorts of persecutions and sufferings in behalf of the Gospel, (which in that age was a special mark of an Apostle, (1 Cor. 4: 9–13; 2 Cor. 4: 5–12; 6: 4, 5; 11: 23–33,) uniting with his senior in Epistles instructive not only to the Churches addressed but to all succeeding Christians,—can it be that, after having received other and such titles of honor, when he is also called an *Apostle*, as were others before him, he is so termed only in virtue of his being a messenger! either of charity or of some special and *temporary* instructions to those to whom he is sent? Let Christian candor give the response.

But I have not done. There yet remain other proofs of Timothy's Apostleship, of more practical import to us at this day than any we have mentioned. I refer to the powers of ordination and *discipline*. Having already proved the first I proceed to the second. Paul certainly was not inferior in power to the rest of the Apostles. They could add nothing to his knowledge, and he labored more abundantly than they all. (2 Cor. 11: 5; 12: 11; [Gal. 2: 6; 1 Cor. 15: 10.) Nor did he intrude into the scene of their labors, (Rom. 15: 20; 2 Cor. 10: 13–16,) but founded many churches himself: giving each the same rules of proceeding: and exercised care and the higher jurisdiction over them and their elders either in person or by proxy. (2 Cor. 11: 28; 1 Cor. 4: 17; 7: 17; 11: 2; 2 Thes. 2: 15; 3: 6.) He founded the Church of Corinth and probably ordained elders therein. When he wrote the first Epistle to the Corinthians, serious disorders had appeared among them which required the use of discipline, of both the exercise and remission of which we read in that and the succeeding Epistle. (1 Cor. 4: 19–21; 5: 3–5; 2 Cor. 2: 6; 7: 12; 10: 8; 12: 19, 20; 13: 2, 10.) Now at this time there were Elders in Corinth as is proved by the following passages, (1 Cor. 3: 10; 4: 15; 9: 12,) and by the fact that the Lord's supper was celebrated there, (11: 20.) Nevertheless, though these Elders had the right of discipline in ordinary cases, yet here the Apostles, being appealed to, interfered, and as they themselves were blameable in part, his rebuke extended to them also, who, as far as we know, *had no power of correcting each other's aberrations*.

He also founded the Church at Ephesus. And that church had Elders *before* he wrote his first Epistle to Timothy; for when, on his voyage to Jerusalem, he sent for them to Miletus and gave them his impressive charge, (Acts 20:) he predicted that *among themselves* perverse teachers would arise and that disorders would result. At the time of the first letter such teachers and such disorders *had* arisen. (1 Tim. 1 : 4, 6, 19, 20 ; 6 : 3, 4.) And yet he "commits" to Timothy the same power of discipline which he had himself exercised. (1 Tim. 1 : 18, 20 ; 3 : 14, 15 ; 4 : 6 ; and 1 : 3; 5 : 19–21 ; 6 : 5.) And similar jurisdiction over the Churches and Elders in Crete is imparted to Titus. (1 : 5, 13 ; 2 : 15 ; 3 : 10.)

When Paul as the senior Apostle is addressing himself to Timothy his junior, who, though his son in the Gospel, and trained by him for the Christian Ministry, was raised through its different grades to an equality of rights with himself, his expressions are " I besought thee," " Exhort therefore," " I will therefore," " Consider what I say."—(1 Tim. 1: 3; 1: 1, 8; 2 Tim. 2: 7.) But when referring to the authority over the Elders of Ephesus with which he had invested him, and giving him the benefit of his experience " *that he might know how to behave himself in the house of God*," his language then is, " That thou mightest charge some that they teach no other doctrine." " These things *command* and teach. Against an *Elder* receive not an accusation, but before two or three witnesses. Them that sin rebuke before all. I charge thee that thou observe these things." " From such turn away." And to Titus whom he had " left in Crete to set in order the things that were wanting and ordain elders in every city"—" Rebuke them sharply." " Rebuke with all authority. Let no man despise thee." " A man that is a heretic . . . reject." And as if to guard against the idea that this authority was but occasional or temporary, " I charge thee [Timothy] in the sight of God, . . . keep this commandment . . . *until the appearing of our Lord Jesus Christ*." (1 Tim. 6 : 14.) In this first Epistle (2 : 7,) he had spoken of himself " a *Preacher*, an *Apostle* and a *teacher* of the Gentiles," thus in effect saying that his commission included those of the two lower grades, (see 1 Cor. 12 : 28,) (for " prophet" and " preacher" are here the same thing.) In 2 Tim. 1 : 11, after repeating this in the same language, he thus declares his confidence in Timothy : " I know whom I have trusted, and am persuaded that he is able to keep that which I have committed to him against *that day*. Hold fast the form of sound words—which thou hast heard of me, ... That *good thing* which was committed unto thee keep by the *power of the Holy Ghost* which dwelleth in us. . . . And the things which thou hast heard of me among many witnesses, the same commit thou to *faithful* men, who shall be able to teach others also ;" (2 Tim. 1 : 12, 13, 14 ; 2 : 2, 9,) thus providing for the continuation of the ministry with similar authority, and immediately thereafter congratulating himself that though *he* was " in bonds, the word of God was not bound."

There were then Elders at Ephesus at this time. Timothy is here vested with authority over them and the power of appointing others. According to the theory of Parity, they ought to have been competent to fill up their own ranks and to exercise discipline over each other. If their disorders had risen to such a height that this was impossible, the better disposed might have appealed to an Apostle for aid in the emergency and the others might have yielded to *his* authority. But if Timothy had been nothing more than an Elder, although the legate or agent of Paul, is it probable that they would have submitted to its *continued* operation, implied in his retaining it until the " coming of the Lord" and " committing it in turn to other and faithful men" ? or that other churches would have recognised it at all without a similar special commission having reference to them. Should we not rather have heard of reclamations, similar to those so common in these last ages, against his " lording it over God's heritage"? and might he not have expected such a salutation as greeted the sons of Sceva ? (Acts 19 : 13–16.) Some have affected to doubt whether Timothy was at Ephesus when the 2d Epistle was written. But besides much collateral proof which the other Epistles afford, this letter itself contains internal evidence that he was there ; for it designates the place to which the bearer was to carry it, and contains a salutation to " the house and household of Onesiphorus" who resided at Ephesus. (4 : 12, 19 ; 1 : 16–18.)

The question, " whether Timothy was at this time *the* Bishop of Ephesus?" has also given rise to interminable discussion, and to pleasant remarks on " the *non-residence* of Bishop Timothy in his *diocese*" as proved by his frequent journeyings with Paul and visits to other Churches. The journeys and visits referred to in Scripture took place *before* the date of these letters, except one— that in which he was requested by Paul to visit him a prisoner in Rome ; (2 Tim. 4 : 12, 21,) and he may have been permanently settled over the Church in Ephesus afterwards, as Ecc. Hist. tells us he was. But we do not esteem it important to ascertain the precise date of his residence. Certain it is that Paul's second letter to him gives him superintendance over the Elders there and power to ordain others. This is *Apostolical* authority and sufficient for our argument.

But it may be asked, why was the name " Apostle" dropped so soon after the first age, if the office was intended to be permanent ? The answer is ready, and a brief explanation will show the propriety of a change in the title, the function still remaining. At the first advent of our Lord, the Jewish and Ancient Churches having both come to an end ; the various provinces of Earth had come under the influence of the powers of *darkness*, personified as "the prince of this world," " satan," &c. (John 12 : 31; 16 : 11, 33 ; Luke 10: 18; Eph. 2 : 2.) Our *Redemption* was effected by the Lord's combat with this influence. Hence he is styled " the Captain of our Salvation" who " has spoiled principalities," " delivered us from the powers of darkness" and " translated us into the kingdom of light." (Heb. 2 : 10; Col. 2 : 15; 1 : 13.) The *salvation* of the individual Christian is also wrought out by contending with his spiritual foes. Hence he is exhorted, if he would hope for success, to put on the armor of light, which is particularly described. (Rom. 13 : 12 ; 2 Cor. 6 : 14; Eph. 6 : 11–18 ; 1 Thes. 5 : 5, 8.) The design of the Christian ministry is " to turn men from darkness to light," (Acts 26 : 18,) and this service in particular is characterized by Paul as " a warfare," (1 Cor. 9 : 7; 2 Cor. 10 : 4, 5 ; 1 Tim. 1 : 18; 6 : 12; 2 Tim. 2 : 3, 4,)

placed under the immediate conduct of Apostles who might thence
be regarded as the commanders of the Christian army; for, was ever
an army heard of, without officers of different grades? (T. C. R. 680.)
While the provinces of this world remained ostensibly under the power
of darkness, Christianity yet struggling for a position, the church is
called "militant" and the organization and duties of her officers may
be so far likened to those of an army, in that the leaders are required
to select those points of the enemy's country which are most open to
invasion, *and are liable to be called to different parts of the field
according to the emergencies of the campaign.*

Such was the State of the nations when Christianity was first proclaimed. The kingdoms of this world must be won to Christ. The
Apostles are "sent" (as their name would imply) on this service. No
one *then* questioned their rank, or refused to concede the powers
necessary to the proper discharge of their duties. At that time their
position was attended by neither worldly honor nor profit. They
were ever in the front of the battle, foremost in danger, conspicuous
marks for Jewish and Gentile hatred and persecution, and most of
them fell by violence in the conflict. As province after province
was wrested from the enemy, each was given in charge to a superin-
tendent, who confined his inspection and labors to a particular district,
and appropriating one of the titles which had previously been given
to a minister settled over a single congregation or "parish" were
thenceforth and fitly denominated "Bishop" or overseer of such district or "diocese." But for centuries, the Missionary Bishops who
were employed in extending the conquests of the Faith among the
heathen, were occasionally distinguished as "Apostles," though generally the name was confined by courtesy to those who had first
borne it.

These hints may serve to show why Paul's career was marked by
so frequent changes of place: why those of his company, who under
him were learning the art of spiritual warfare would convey and execute his orders at various points: and why, having first learned to
obey and thence become qualified to command, they were themselves
placed in stations of authority over different parts of the new conquest.
When the new order of things was to be set in full operation, the
Christians as yet being but imperfectly instructed, the Apostle was
denominated an "Angel" or Messenger, (Rev. 2 : 1,) a term of import
intermediate between that of Apostle and Bishop. And history
attests that what we have just shown to be natural and probable,
actually took place. Thus *Eusebius*, the first historian of the Church,
says, "Those very persons were called Apostles, whom by usage of
speech the Church now calls bishops!" And *Theodoret* another
learned Church historian speaks more particularly to the same purpose. "The same persons were anciently called bishops and presbyters promiscuously, whilst those who are *now called bishops* were
styled Apostles. But, in process of time, the *name of* Apostle was
appropriated to such only as were more strictly apostles, and then
the *name of bishop was given to those who succeeded them:* thus
Epaphroditus was the Apostle of the Philippians, Titus of the Cre-

tans, and Timothy of the Asiatics." (Comm. on 1 Tim. 3: 1.) The term "Apostle" (or angel) is thus confined in the New Testament, to those of the highest rank except when Peter and John use that of Elder by way of Christian courtesy when classing themselves with their inferiors; just as we might say of Washington that he was a great general—a great captain—a great soldier,—without derogating from his dignity in the two latter cases.

The Scripture names of the two lower orders of the ministry were also varied according to the state of the Church and the duties in which they were immediately engaged. When Paul is speaking of the *number* and *order* of grades in the abstract, he says, "And God hath *set* [ιθιτο, appointed, stationed,] some in the Church, *first*, Apostles; *secondly*, prophets; *thirdly*, teachers, (1 Cor. 12: 28,) but when he would intimate that for the last two other titles might be used, as indicative of the particular service in which they were employed, his words are, "And he gave some, apostles; and some, prophets; and some, evangelists; and some, pastors and teachers." (Eph. 4: 11.) The terms "prophet" and "evangelist" denote those who preach where the church is not yet established; while those of "pastor" and "teacher" clearly indicate a more settled order of things in which ministers of the corresponding grades build on the foundations laid by the others. A Prophet under the Jewish dispensation was generally a priest of the second order who preached at large. An Evangelist was one who taught the first principles of the Faith or *Gospel* to those who had never heard it. The first person who in Scripture takes the title, is Philip *the deacon* (Acts 21:8,) who had first carried the Gospel to Samaria. (8: 5–8.) Hence it is, we suppose, that Paul here gives it to the minister of the lowest grade, and afterwards exhorts Timothy, though an Apostle, to "do the work of an Evangelist," by way of giving "full proof of his ministry;" having previously intimated that this would be no degradation, for that he Paul regarded himself as "a preacher, an apostle, and a *teacher* of the Gentiles." (2 Tim. 4: 5; 1: 11.) But when "deacon became the fixed designation of that order in the older churches, that of Evangelist, according to Eusebius, was sometimes though not always given to Bishops appointed to lay the foundations of the Faith in barbarous nations, to constitute them pastors; and having committed to them the cultivating of those new plantations, to pass on to other countries and nations." A Teacher, in the definitive sense, as every body knows, is one who instructs in the elements of knowledge the young or ignorant, as distinguished from the Prophet or Pastor who also expounds truths of a higher order to those of mature minds.

An additional reason for the use of these terms by Paul may be suggested as probable. In the ancient Church, while as yet the priestly and civil power were united, sacred wisdom was enveloped in myths and symbols. The priest who interpreted these to the initiated was called a Hierophant, and was generally of the second order. After the rise of heroes and kings on the one hand, and the declaration of mental independence on the other by the revolt of philosophy,—the philosophers undertook their exposition in prose and the poet in verse : and each professed to add to the original stores of wisdom by fresh revelations from the sacred muse or from enlightened reason. Hence it was that Poet and Prophet in the classical languages were signified by the same term. The name of Prophet had been known in the Ancient Church from whence it was transferred to the Jewish. But a prophet under the Christian dispensation is not solely or generally, one who foretells future events, but one who teaches and utters divine truth so as to bring it down to the level of the understanding." (A. C. 7268.) Now Pastor, Elder or Bishop as the designation of the second grade,—and Evangelist or Deacon of the first, were more significant and intelligible to the Jewish convert, and are therefore used by Peter and John, generally by Luke, and by Paul himself when instructing Timothy and Titus who would understand them. But when addressing the Gentile Churches as their Apostle, he employs the terms " prophets and teachers" which would have been ambiguous to the Jew, but whose import was less liable to be mistaken by his Gentile readers, as being analogous to that of characters already known to them.

Another difficulty remains to be disposed of—the assertion of Parity, that the "deacons" of Scripture are not an order of clergy at all, but simply lay-officers who took care of the poor of the Church and administered its funds. That these were a part of their duties is conceded : that they were the whole is denied : we will give the principal arguments on both sides. Parity points to the record in Acts 6 : 1–6 as the occasion of their *first* appointment and which only speaks of such duties : to the instructions of Paul to Timothy, (1 Tim. 3 : 8–13,) which require that they should be " grave, sincere, sober, *not given to filthy lucre,* tried, ruling well their own families,"—all of which traits were suited to such a function : and to the testimony of the Fathers and Church History which they say sustains their view.

To this it has been replied that a close inspection of the narrative in Acts will show that this was *not* the first appointment of such officers. " In those days, when the number of disciples was *multiplied*, there arose a murmuring of the *Grecians* against the *Hebrews* because their widows were *neglected* in the daily ministration." The *office* of a deacon then, had been discharged before, and now that the disciples had increased to many thousands, it was a complaint of neglect by the foreign Jews which occasioned this *additional* appointment of " seven," a number utterly insufficient of themselves to bear such a burden. Most of them were foreigners, as is proved by their names, which shows that the object was to satisfy their clients of the justice of the distribution ; and their complaints being thus quieted, the Twelve could give themselves *continually* (as they had done before) to their appropriate duties of prayer and preaching.* *They had themselves*

---

* Is this view sustained by the record ?—" Then the *twelve* called the multitude of the disciples unto them, and said, It is not reason that *we* should leave the Word of God and serve tables. Wherefore, brethren, look ye out among you seven men," &c. ; compared with Acts, ii. 44–46, and iv. 34–37. For is it not clear that distribution of alms belonged to the office of the apostles, and that serving of tables, furnishing

discharged just such a duty in Galilee, while in the lowest grade of the ministry, when they distributed the loaves and fishes first to the 5000 and then to the 4000,—(1. Mat. 14: 16, 19; Mark 6: 41; Luke 9: 13, 16; John 6: 11. 2. Mat. 15: 36; Mark 8: 6, 7,)— but they had now attained the highest rank and greater responsibilities rested on them. If deacons were nothing more than laics, why ordain them at all? But as they were ordained, the presumption is that they were more, and that those whom they were now called to assist, had been also. This is not mere presumption. The Seventy were appointed with a commission similar to that the Twelve had at first, and should we not infer that it might include all the duties the

supplies and distributing them to the widows, would have belonged to their office too, if deacons had not been appointed? For, the apostles and their acts were still in some degree representative; and is not feeding the body the representative of feeding the soul? And, therefore, did not ordination to the one imply ordination to the other? So that it was just as much the office of the deacon to evangelize, or preach the gospel, as it was to serve tables? Hence those were chosen for the office who were "full of *faith* and the *holy ghost* ;" and when ordained they "did great wonders and miracles among the people ;" and they who *disputed* with them were not able to resist the *wisdom* and the *spirit* by which they *spake.*" Moreover, they went to distant cities to preach "the things concerning the kingdom of God," baptize "in the name of the Lord Jesus," and do "miracles." These qualifications were not needed, and these duties they could not have done, if their sole office were to serve tables; or if the serving of tables were not an external representative duty of those whose spiritual function it is to feed the soul with the bread of life—the "word that proceedeth out of the mouth of God." Hence, in our view, these *apostolic* deacons were *evangelists,* because they were *apostles* of a lower grade: for there may be a trine in each grade of the ministry as well as in the whole ministry itself. And hence Philip exerted the apostolic power of doing miracles, as well as preaching the gospel in Samaria, and from Azotus to Cæsarea. And it was of this trine of apostles that Paul speaks in Ephesians, iv. 11—"Apostles, prophets, and evangelists."—In the episcopal church of the present day, the trine in the highest grade of the clergy is—prelate, archbishops, and bishops under them.—These were all ministers of the highest grade, in relation to the two lower, "pastors and teachers." And hence Paul repeatedly speaks of the *three* apostolic offices which he himself sustained—"preacher, apostle, teacher of the Gentiles." That an evangelist and a teacher of the Gentiles were the same, is clear from what Philip did, Acts, viii. 26–35, and from what he was called, Acts. xxi. 8. And that the twelve apostles represented a series of *trines ;* that is, *four* trines, just as the twelve tribes of Israel did, must be obvious to every reflecting mind. Hence there certainly might have been one trine of apostles in general, to represent the Lord's priestly offices on earth, as Peter, James and John, represented Moses, the Lord, and Elias on the mount of transfiguration. There were doubtless four apostles in each of these apostolic grades, as there were four writers of the Gospels in the New Testament, and as truth has to be accommodated to the celestial, the spiritual, the celestial-natural and the spiritual-natural principles of the mind. And that there were grades of distinction and duty among the twelve even when with the Lord on earth, is evident from the fact that one reclined on his bosom at the supper, (John, xiii. 2, 3,) and Judas had the bag, (John, xiii. 29,)—this latter office being the same as the one for which deacons were appointed in Acts, vi. 1, 2. When the disciples had become so many in number, it would have taken all the time of the twelve to attend to this one lowest function of their office as apostolic governors of the church; and that they might not be wholly drawn away from their other and superior functions of ministering the Word, which they had at all times to attend to, (and the deacons also,) seven additional ministers were appointed for the especial discharge of that office which had been specifically assigned to Judas in the Lord's time.—*Ed.*

latter had performed? They "returned" to the Lord (Luke 10 : 17,) accompanied him into Judea, and were probably of the number of disciples who proclaimed him King of Zion on his entry into Jerusalem. (19 : 37.) There was no occasion for the exercise of this part of their office until the Church was organised after Pentecost. But as the Lord had delegated a part of his authority to the Twelve, it is believed that the Seventy accompanied *them* as these had their master: that they were of the five hundred witnesses of the Resurrection : (1 Cor. 15 : 6;) of the hundred and twenty assembled when an Apostle was appointed in lieu of Judas, and that Matthias was taken from their body. When the first converts sold their property and placed the money at the Apostles' feet for the common use of Christians, who attended to its proper distribution?* The Twelve were otherwise engaged. Why not "the younger" disciples who attended the Apostles : who bore Ananias and Sapphira to the tomb, and who we will show reason for believing *were* the Seventy?†—"But the Seventy were never styled 'deacons'."—*Neither were the seven.* That title is never used in our Translation but twice,—when Paul and Timothy salute "the bishops and deacons" at Philippi, (1 : 1,) and when he is instructing Timothy as to their qualifications. It is not names, but things, we are in search of. We infer their office from their acts. The only two of them who are again mentioned preached. Stephen was "full of faith and power :" spoke with "irresistible wisdom and spirit :" "ceased not" to argue that the Jewish ritual was superseded, and so successfully that he raised a tumult in which he fell the first martyr to the Christian cause. Were such gifts essential to a distributor of alms?—Philip had the honor of first preaching the Gospel beyond the limits of Judea, (though it was necessary that his labors should be followed up by those of Apostles, Acts 8: 5–17,) and therefore was he called an "Evangelist," though Stephen was not, because he fell in Judea. Before they were appointed, "Seek ye out" says Peter "seven men *full of* the *Holy Spirit* and of *wisdom.*" And Paul, having just said "If a man desire the office of a *bishop,* he desireth a *good* work," requires that "deacons should hold the *mystery of the faith in a pure conscience :*" that they should be "first *proved,*" and concludes that "they that have used the office of a deacon *well,* purchase to themselves *a good degree* and *great boldness in the faith,* (1 Tim. 3 : 1, 9, 10, 13,) that is, they have earned promotion to the "good work," or higher degree of a bishop or

---

* We have shown that this was a lower apostolic office, which a portion of the twelve might have attended to in those hours of the day when the ministration of the Word were necessarily suspended.—*Ed.*

† If the seventy had been ordained by the Lord into a grade of the ministry below the twelve, and were now present, why ordain seven into a first or lower grade in the apostolic church? Why not assign the duty to any of the seventy who might be now present, to be exercised by virtue of the office which they had held in the Lord's time? Or were those present of the seventy holding the apostolic office in the second degree? Or how many of the Seventy "went back, and walked no more with" the Lord, so as to cause him to put that pathetic inquiry to the twelve, "Will ye also go away?" (John, vi. 66 67)? Or was this before the Seventy were commissioned? These are questions which occur to our mind on reading the above.—*Ed.*

Elder. Is any other construction possible? or are such qualities special requisites for taking care of money and the poor, any farther than as they should mark every Christian? Paul does require of deacons that they should not be given to filthy lucre, but the same is demanded of Elders. (vs. 3.) He does say that the latter should "be apt to teach," but deacons, by using their office well acquire that aptness.

We have heard Peter once; let us hear him again. Having exhorted the "Elders" of the Dispersion "to feed the flock of God, willingly, freely, not as lords over God's heritage," &c., he immediately adds " Likewise, *ye younger*, submit yourselves to the Elder, . . . submit yourselves under the mighty hand of God, *that he may exalt you in due time*," [to the good degree of an elder or higher.] (1 Pet. 5: 1, 2, 3, 5, 6.) And the context proves not only that he is speaking of ministers, but that he had in his mind at the time the last memorable reproof of his master to the Twelve when he announced to them the law of precedence in *His* kingdom; "He that is greatest among you let him be as *the younger*." (Luke 22: 26.) When the Twelve were called, some—probably all of them were men of mature years, and appropriately styled Elders as compared with the Seventy, who, as they were of later appointment were also, it is likely, their juniors in age.* The corresponding passage in Matthew (20: 26,) has it, "let him be as your *minister* [in the original, "deacon."] And hence also it was, that as a perpetual admonition to humility even in her highest officers, the Christian Priesthood in general was called a "ministry," [in the original a "deaconship."] This then is the third time in which this term " younger" is used in such connexion; in two out of the three it clearly refers to ministers,—in all of them most probably to the Seventy or to ministers of the same rank. The early Christian writers do say that they took care of the funds and poor of the Church, but they also attest, I believe without exception, that they taught, and preached, and baptised by authority and permission of the bishop; and who shall gainsay their report when fortified by the authorities just cited from Scripture?

The qualifications and duties of both Elders and Deacons are acknowledged to be set forth in the New Testament. But it has been asked "If the Apostolic office were designed to be permanent, why do we find there no detailed statement of the gifts peculiarly suited to such a functionary, and no recorded instructions for their exercise?" And is it indeed so? The highest degree includes the powers and duties of the other two, and as I read the New Testament I also find there much that is specially applicable to such a grade. I might instance our Lord's

---

* When the Twelve were first sent forth, the warning of the Master was, " Behold I send you forth as *sheep* among wolves;" (Mat. 10: 16,)—that to the Seventy was, " Behold I send you forth as *lambs* among wolves." (Luke 10: 3.) This idea is farther strengthened by a passage in the Epistle of Barnabas, " When he chose his Apostles, which were afterwards to publish his Gospel, *he took men who had been very great sinners*." As " lambs" are the special symbols of innocence, which again is a more probable trait of the young, the Seventy may be inferred to have been the juniors of the former on that account also.

last address to the Twelve in John (chaps. 13 to 16) and his last prayer on their behalf, (chap. 17.) Their powers and duties were exemplified in their recorded "Acts;" are particularly dwelt on in the Epistles to Timothy and Titus; and occasionally referred to in others—more frequently perhaps than is generally supposed. For there is a peculiarity in the style of Paul,—unnoticed I believe by professed Biblical Critics, much as they have written on the *poetical* aspect of many parts of Scripture as proved by their metrical arrangement and the progressive march of the sense in varying though *graded parallels;* the which characteristics I do not deny, but believe they were stamped there by the Holy Spirit and not by the genius of the human writers. But this peculiarity may be detected by those who will search for it, and I suppose it has not escaped your observation. I refer to his frequent use of what, for want of a better term, I may venture to call *triads* from their resemblance to those in the remains of the Welsh Bards or Druids. They recur so often that they appear to be the result of a systematic habit of thought, and induce the belief that among "the abundant revelations" to which he lays claim (2 Cor. 12: 7,) he may have been vouchsafed a partial insight into the "doctrine of *degrees*" so much employed by Swedenborg, and fully expounded in the third part of "Divine Love and Wisdom." At one time he appears to have in view *discrete* at another *continuous* degrees,—noted now in the ascending and then in the descending scale. Again, he will seize the middle term of either, from whence he will rise or stoop so as to include both extremes in the trine, not unfrequently commencing or closing with an expression which embraces the meaning of the whole. Sometimes the urgent rapidity of his thoughts leads him to omit one or more terms of the continuous triad, as if he supposed they would be implied by the judicious reader; and all these are varied by traits of Goodness or Truth—or their opposites—properly to be referred to the Will or Understanding. I cannot here go at large into the proof of this. Of divers examples in the Letters to Timothy take the following : "Till I come, give attendance to *reading*—to *exhortation*—to *doctrine*," (1 Tim. 4 : 13,) in which I think I perceive a tacit reference to the triple function of Timothy as an Apostle.

But lest this should be thought fanciful, let us return as was promised to the 12th and 13th chapters of 1 Cor.—the sense of which I will present briefly and arranged somewhat differently from the original.—He is here treating of different powers or *Gifts*—distributed by the Holy Spirit to and manifested by different *Ministries*—in different *Operations*. The gifts are Wisdom—Knowledge—Faith,—operative or manifested in *healing*—in the *exertion of powers* (not "miracles")—in *prophecy* (which in them was attended with power.) Again, there are the powers of *discerning spirits*—of using *divers tongues*—of *interpreting* tongues. Here we have a trine of gifts manifested in two different modes traceable through a double trine, first to the Will and then to the Understanding. Now the Church is the *body* of the Lord; but as a body is not one member but many, each of which has its own position and office assigned by Him for the

common good, so the various gifts of the Church are distributed to
different members or *Ministries* therein. And surely God's method
of proceeding should be a permanent rule of order in the Church
until He chooses to repeal it. These Ministries are *three* in the order
of Apostles—Prophets—Teachers. Their *powers* (not " miracles ")
are [such as] gifts of healing—their *helps* or aids, [such as] *rules* or
ordinances (not "governments" as we have it) and diversities of
tongues. Parallel with the titles of the Ministers he again enumerates the gifts of healing—of tongues—of interpretation as if referable
to those officers in like order.—But there is a higher gift than all
these which they should earnestly covet and which he would show
them. Then follows that splendid eulogium on CHARITY which has
delighted and stimulated and strengthened thousands, who perhaps
never dreamed that the Apostle designed to impress its importance
not so much on the private Christian as on THE THREE CLASSES OF
MINISTERS of whom he had just spoken, in whom, if it were permitted to dwell, it would generate the virtues *proper to their several sta-*
tions and *which would be becoming in the Christian priesthood long*
after the extraordinary gifts which were necessary to their predecessors
in the incipient struggles of the Faith, had ceased.—" Though I speak
[in many languages—in *all*] the tongues of men—or use the very
dialect of heaven : though I should prophecy—understand all mysteries—and all *knowledge :* though I have [little faith—great faith]—
all faith so that I could remove mountains: though I [be generous]—
bestow *all* my goods to feed the poor—or give my body to be burned,
—and have not *charity*, I AM PROFITED NOTHING." Charity in an
APOSTLE (or Bishop) who is clothed with the chief ministerial authority and responsibility, " suffereth long, *vaunteth not, seeketh not her*
own, rejoiceth not in iniquity, believeth all things."—Charity in a
Prophet or Elder, who is a subordinate spiritual governor and more
immediate instructor of the people, " is kind, *not puffed up*, not easily
provoked, *rejoiceth in the truth*, hopeth all things." Charity in the
Teacher or Deacon, who though as yet in a lower station should be
willing to labor if thereby he may be useful, " *envieth not, behaveth*
not unseemly, thinketh no evil, beareth all things, *endureth* all things."
Prophecy—tongues—knowledge may fail—cease—be transient and
therefore defective, but Charity never faileth and is enthroned above
Faith and Hope themselves. Here are many trines without any
forced construction. So again I ask you to look at the original and
say if any other interpretation is possible? And is this the less true
because it has not been generally observed? It was the *Ministers*
of Corinth who under the influence of " false Apostles " had corrupted
the flock and led them astray. Them did he especially rebuke and
recall to duty, by showing them an example of Charity as well as of
extraordinary gifts in his own person—that of a true Apostle; and
intimating, as was his wont, the peculiar evils into which they had
fallen by the presentation of *the opposite virtues.* (Acts, 24: 25.)
And if Charity had dwelt in the hearts of Christian Ministers from
that hour, their lawful God-given powers would never have been
questioned, nor should we now be engaged in defending their cause.

A like exhortation to Ministers, if not so particular, may be found in Rom. 12: 3–8, which certainly implies an inequality of rank, though the gradation is less clearly marked than in the chapters which have just been the subject of comment. And in Eph. 4: 11–16 we have the same trine of *offices*—a similar trine of *objects* for which they were appointed—and a double trine of *results* flowing from their labors.

This part of our argument has already been protracted beyond my original intention, but I must ask your forbearance while I present from the same source one other and the crowning consideration in favor of the order I advocate. All previous dispensations of religion have undergone decline and decay. To this result the priesthood in every instance have largely contributed,—not only by direct agency but by failing to use their legitimate powers and influence for its aversion—so that it grew to be a proverb, "like people, like priest." (Hosea, 4: 9.) Moses warned the Israelites against "false prophets," (Deut. 13: 1–3,) and the historical and prophetical books of the Old Testament often speak of their appearance and denounce the fatal mischiefs engendered by their course. The *unity* of brethren had been commanded by the Patriarch of old, (Gen. 45: 24;) lauded by the Psalmist in those beautiful terms known to all, (Ps. 133: 1;) and foretold by Jeremiah as one of the peculiar blessings of Israel on their return from captivity. (Jer. 32: 39.) The former also calls on all to pray for "the *peace* of Jerusalem." (Ps. 122: 6–8.) The one great schism by which a kingdom was reft away, appears to have been discountenanced by the whole Levitical order. But there were numerous lesser defections to Idolatry and consequent national calamities, hastened by the delinquencies of the lawful shepherds, and flatteries of false prophets,—"prophets" said the Lord "*whom I have not sent.*" Thus are they ever characterized. (Jer. 14: 15; 23: 21; 27: 15; 28: 15; 29: 9, 31; Ez. 13: 6; Micah, 3: 5; Com. Rom. 10: 15.) Of the Shepherds it is said, that they had suffered the flock to wander on the mountains without a guide—a prey to wild beasts; (Ez. 34: 5–8;) and that as Priests they had "corrupted the *covenant* of Levi." (Mal. 2: 8.) But as judgment in its course begins at the Sanctuary—the *house* of God, the promise was, that at His advent, he would "*purify the sons of Levi,*" (3: 3,) viz: that he would raise up a true and spiritual priesthood in place of that which had betrayed its trust. And the terms of this prediction, (when taken in connection with Jer. 33: 18, 21, 22,) are another proof of the analogy between the orders of the Jewish and Christian Churches.

And they were purified for a time. But alas! such was the depth of ignorance and corruption to which the nations had been previously sunk that they could not at once be elevated to the innocence of wisdom. Without doubt the partial knowledge then vouchsafed was a great advance. But there must again be a falling away before they could regain a firm footing. Ages must yet elapse ere they would render themselves worthy of that fulness of light which alone could lead to lasting purity and peace. Our Lord had foretold that the first Christian Church would also be assailed by false prophets who

should deceive many. (Mat. 24: 24.) And astonishing to tell they
made their appearance in the very life-time of the Apostles; for
these venders of heresy and fomenters of strife are often alluded to
in their writings. (Acts, 15: 1, 24; 20: 30; Rom. 16: 18; 2 Cor.
2: 17; 4: 2; Gal. 1: 7; 2: 4; 4: 17; 6: 12; Eph. 4: 14; Phil.
1: 16; 3: 2; Col. 2: 4, 8; 1 Tim. 1: 4–7; 4: 1–3; 6: 3–5; 2
Tim. 2: 17–19; 3: 5–9; 4: 3, 4; Tit. 1: 10, 11; 2 Pet. 2: 1–3;
1 John, 2: 18; 4: 1; 2 John, 7–11; Jude, 4; Rev. 2: 2, 9.) It
was among the latest commands of the Master to the Twelve that
they should "love one another;" (John, 13: 34, 35;) his *peace* also
he left with them; (14: 27;) and of his latest prayers was one for
the unity of all his disciples. (17: 21–23.)   In pursuance of the
sacred injunction, the Apostles did not omit to inculcate not only that
unity which proceeds from a spirit of Charity, (Rom. 12: 10; Eph.
4: 3; Heb. 13: 1; 1 John, 3: 14–19; 2 John, 5,) but that Christians
should be "of one *mind*" and "*speak* the same thing;" (1 Cor. 1:
10; 2 Cor. 13: 11; Phil. 1: 27; 2: 2; 1 Pet. 3: 8;) that they
should cherish that peace which was one of the blessed fruits of such
a course; (2 Cor. 13: 11; Gal. 5: 22; 1 Thes. 5: 13; James, 3:
17, 18;) and that they should mark and avoid the teachers of *heresy*
contrary to what they had heard, who had thus caused strifes and
divisions among them. (Rom. 16: 17; 1 Cor. 1: 10; 3: 3; 11: 18,
19; 12: 25; Gal. 5: 20; Phil. 2: 14; 2 Pet. 2: 1–3; Jude, 19.)
The Epistles to the Corinthians were intended to correct the disorders
which had been thus occasioned.   Those to Timothy and Titus were
sent partly with the same view and also to guard against their recur-
rence.   The second of Peter, (1: 1, 15; 3: 1–3,) the first of John,
and that of Jude may be regarded as Apostolic Letters Circular or
Charges to all Christians, warning them against the numerous errors
of the time and furnishing them with principles which would test
both the character and the doctrine of future deceivers.

And here it will be to our purpose to note some of the traits by
which all these Apostles characterized such false teachers.   Paul to
Titus (1: 10) speaks of them as "unruly"; and to the Corinthian
Church which he had founded he was constrained to vindicate his
claims as an Apostle against their machinations.   Nay, it is not improbable that the party who said "they were of Cephas" excused
their revolt by the very pretext which has been revived in modern
times—that the Twelve were an extraordinary class of officers who
could have no successors, and that therefore in their absence all other
ministers were on a level and all equally worthy of credit. (1 Cor. 1:
12; 9: 1–7; 2 Cor. 11: 5.)   "They *despise government*" said Peter
—"are presumptuous—*self-willed*—not afraid to *speak evil of dignities*,—who, while they promised *liberty* to their dupes are themselves
the servants of corruption." (2 Pet. 2: 10, 19.)   And Jude following
in the track of Peter, says "they despise dominion and speak evil of
dignities,—of those things which they know not—*murmurers*, com-
plainers, walking after their own lusts . . . who *separate* themselves.
Wo unto them! for they have gone in the way of *Cain*, [have separated Charity from Faith] and ran greedily after the error of *Balaam*

for reward, and PERISHED IN THE GAINSAYING OF CORE," [Korah.] (Jude, 8, 16, 19, 11.) All this is plain enough; for, had there been but one order of ministers, where were the "dignities" to complain of? and to have committed the sin of Korah, were impossible.

And what was the remedy for these deplorable evils where they had appeared and the preventive where they had not? for without exception they advise the same. It was nothing more nor less than that they should adhere steadfastly to that Gospel which was first preached by *them;* in a word, that Christians should "build on the foundation of *the Apostles* and prophets, Jesus Christ himself being the chief corner-stone"; for they (the Apostles) had first received it from Him, as He had before from the Father. (Luke, 10 : 22; John, 18 : 37; 14 : 26; 15 : 15; 13 : 20; 20 : 21; Acts, 2 : 42; 20 : 20, 27, 35; 1 Cor. 14 : 37; 15 : 1-3; 2 Cor. 11 : 3, 4; Gal. 1 : 6, 8, 9, 11, 12; Eph. 2 : 20; Col. 1 : 23; 2 Tim. 3 : 14; 2 Pet. 1 : 16; 3 : 1, 2, 17, 18; 1 John, 2 : 19; 4 : 6; Jude, 3, 17.) Christians at first " continued in the *Apostles'* doctrine," do ye the same. "Though *we,*" said Paul, " or an *Angel from heaven* preach any other Gospel . . . let him be accursed. . . . For I neither received it of man, neither was I taught it, but by revelation of Jesus Christ."—" *We* [the Apostles] have not followed cunningly devised fables," said Peter. " We are of God," said John, " he that knoweth God, heareth us."—" Contend earnestly for the faith once delivered to the saints," said Jude.

The skirts of the Apostles then were clear. They had warned the Church against the innovators, and their protest was placed on permanent record. I know we are told that the Church in general, as opposed to the World, is the pillar and ground of the Truth, (1 Tim. 3: 15,) but it is very manifest from these oft-repeated admonitions that THEY SUPPOSED THAT PURITY OF DOCTRINE COULD BE PRESERVED IN NO OTHER WAY THAN BY COMMITTING IT TO THE SPECIAL CHARGE OF THE HIGHEST ORDER OF HER PRIESTHOOD. Nevertheless, the plague was not fully stayed, as the whole current of Ecclesiastical History will evince. *But it is a fact that the authors of all the worst heresies which disturbed that Church were Presbyters or of a rank yet lower.* Such were the *licentious* Gnostics, Montanus the Austere and his follower Tertullian, Origen the Universalist, and the arch-heretic Arius himself, who persisted in propagating his error against the remonstrance of his bishop. The latter was probably aware that the primitive Christians believed in simplicity that in Jesus dwelt all the fullness of the Godhead; that the time had not yet come when they could bear to be told plainly of the Father; and that such simple faith was sufficient until He chose to clear up the remaining obscurities of that subject. The standard of Orthodoxy was changed after the Council of Nice, but we have the authority of Swedenborg for saying that the Nicene Creed was far less objectionable than that of Arius. And to that standard—such as it was—the bishops with scarcely an exception, both Catholic and Protestant, continued to adhere. If they held a different faith in private, it was not openly avowed. Pelagius who ascribed to man a freedom independent of God, Godoschalcus the Predestinarian, Luther the Solifidian, Calvin, Knox, Socinus—all were

23

Presbyters. And wherever an ancient heresy has been revived and
furbished up for modern taste, a priest of the same rank has generally
been the willing instrument for the work. The Church of Geneva
where Presbytery was first established, lapsed into Arian and Universalist opinions. A majority of the Presbyterian Churches of
England and many in Ireland took the same road. If the churches
of Holland and Scotland have proved exceptions, it is because they
have been petrified, as it were, in the opposite errors of Calvin.
Similar defections or obstinacy are observable in the Religious History
of the Independents both in Old and New England. It has been
remarked that those who are reared under either of those forms of
Church Government seem to know no middle ground of doctrine, but
(if they change at all) oscillate from one extreme to another: that,
for want of an umpire whose equity and intelligence all parties could
respect, controversies among them,—not only on fundamentals but
often on the most trivial points—are more frequent and acrimonious;
that, when once begun, heart burnings certainly, and oft-times divisions are inevitable; and that these are rarely if ever healed.

And shall Newchurch-men flatter themselves with the hope of perpetual exemption from all such dangers? "Heresies are *ever* attendant
on the true Church and the ground of heresy is the being intent on some
particular article of faith, and giving that the precedence; for such
is the nature of man's thought that whilst he is attentive to some one
particular thing, he prefers it to another, especially when his imagination claims it as a discovery of his own, and when self-love and
the love of the world conspire to work upon the imagination; in this
case every thing tends to administer fresh proof and confirmation of
his opinions, so that he is ready to attest their truth in the most
solemn manner, when nevertheless they may be utterly false." (A. C.
362.) If the opinion I now oppose be an error, I fear it has proved
no exception to this statement, for many of its advocates can see in
Scripture none of the numerous testimonies we have brought therefrom in favor of a different order,—taking it for granted that their
own is contained therein; while for their hypothesis the most plausible supports are two passages of the Gospels, one in the Acts and
another in the Epistle to Timothy, (Mat. 23: 8–12; Luke, 22: 23–26;
Acts, 13: 1–3; 1 Tim. 4: 14,) all of which we have shown to be
misinterpreted. I frankly acknowledge that such was formerly
my own case, and I know of many persons in the Old Church who
are alike unconscious of their position. But there have already been
among us differences of opinion on matters more internal—such for
example as the various views of the nature and identity of the crucified and risen body of our Lord,—of which I will say in passing, that
as it appears to me, one fact recorded by John and one principle
clearly stated by Moses,—but both of which have been strangely left
out of the controversy—ought long since, if properly applied, to have
reconciled the disputants. And can we hope to escape similar and
more serious difficulties in future? or shall we wait until the enemy
has ravaged our territory before we place watchmen on the *towers* as
well as on the walls?

And is all peaceful without? Ours is emphatically a church *militant*, and must be so for a long time to come. When assailed hereafter, as assuredly we will be, by sagacious, well-disciplined and unscrupulous foes, shall we trust to Providence for a miraculous deliverance and reject that order which He established in his church, as most conducive to victory in war and to her safety in peace? How shall we account for the success of the Romanists in propagating their system, clogged as it is with the most amazing absurdities, if we leave the organization and perseverance of their clergy out of view? Can we hope for similar success, scattered as we are and feebly cooperating? Must there be no subordination among *our* governors? Shall we *openly appoint* generals to our growing army,—or shall we reluctantly follow the unacknowledged leaders whom for our neglect of duty God shall permit to rule over us? *for, it is an eternal truth, that to escape them is impossible, whether we recognize them or not.*

You will not, of course, understand me as intimating by any thing here stated, nor yet by what was said above of the Apostles and their successors as "stewards of the *mysteries* of God," that ordaining ministers in the New Church can be in possession of any thing in the nature of the "unwritten tradition" claimed by Catholics for the Bishop of Rome;—though I do believe—for reasons which cannot here be given—that the Apostles had clearer perceptions on certain points of doctrine, particularly that of the Trinity, which they did not communicate to the Church generally nor to all of the ministry— but which were transmitted to many of their successors until the Council of Nice whose ill-judged statements soon obliterated them from the minds of all. My meaning is simply this. Ordination to the ministry is by the laying on of hands of other ministers. This signifies the impartation both of authority and spiritual powers. For discharging the duties of the higher grades there must of course be additional power, conferred by a new imposition of hands. Inauguration into office confers among other things Illustration and Perception as means of Instruction. The higher the office then, the clearer ought to be those powers in the persons inaugurated, other things being equal. Swedenborg is the interpreter of Scripture and the Teacher of the New Church. But as questions may hereafter arise as to *his* meaning in various parts of his writings, the materials for a judgment on such questions having been collected and submitted to the umpirage of the ordaining ministers,* I suppose that these powers may hereafter qualify them for giving a true interpretation. Not that such decision will in any case be arbitrary, but that they will be enabled to give such reasons for their judgment as ought to be satisfactory to the Church.

I have thus drawn out to a length which some will think tedious the argument from Scripture in behalf of a three-fold order of the Christian ministry In so doing I have freely availed myself of the

* How we differ from Mr. Cabell here, may be seen by referring to page 276 of this report. We believe that the clerical organ of the church should consist of ministers of all the grades as a trine, constituting one full man, and not of the ordaining ministers alone.—*Ed.*

labors of certain writers in the Old Church who have industriously examined this subject. But I have used the materials collected by them on the principle stated by Mr. Hindmarsh in his "Essay on the Resurrection," (pp. 236–7,) who, (on the authority of A. C. 1097, 3058, 4431,) thinks that such critics bear the same relation to the New Church that the Gibeonites of old did to that of Israel. This is moreover in a great degree an external subject, resting mainly on *facts* which lie on the surface of Scripture, or such plain deductions therefrom as commend themselves to the reason of every man. It is therefore not so much beyond their depth as would be a question of doctrine. Those writers, however, though concurring in their conclusions, did not always agree in their interpretations. Never yet did a good cause have always judicious defenders, free, from error. They all, however, knew the historical fact that a ministry of three grades could be traced up to the age of the Apostles; and in attempting to ascend higher and to find its warrant in Scripture, while ignorant of its Spiritual Sense, they might naturally overlook or mistake some of the true foundations of the edifice. Their references to the New Testament have been verified by the original in every instance, and any Greek scholar may do the same; but I have reasoned on them in my own way. In searching the Scriptures I have also, under the guidance of certain hints from Swedenborg, found much of relevant matter which I have seen in no writer either of the Old Church or the New; enough indeed as I conceivé, to give a new aspect to this entire branch of the subject and to justify its being examined afresh and thoroughly by the best minds of the church;—enough also to warrant the inquiry, whether it is not a hasty concession " that nothing conclusive can be drawn from the Apostolic writings either for or against this species of order." (Mr. Noble's Report of 1833.)

Consider this array of evidence drawn from many parts of both Testaments: the various lines of argument all converging to the same point, and say whether a cause thus sustained is not something more than plausible. Is there as much or as clear proof from the same sources (apart from the interpretations of Swedenborg) in behalf of infant baptism, the observance of Sunday as the Christian Sabbath, and other doctrines which might be named, as we have collected for a trine of offices in the Christian Church? Now the Bible cannot really contradict itself. Its teachings are " truths continuous from the Lord;"—"are all so many mirrors of Him." " He is a God of order—is order itself." " His power and wisdom, as well in the Universe as in all and every part of it, proceed and operate according to the laws of order." And " man was created a form of Divine Order and is so far in power against the Evil and the False and in Wisdom concerning the Good and the True from the Divine power and wisdom as he lives according to divine order." (T. C. R. 508, 53, 56, 65, 68.) " Many and great absurdities" also says Swedenborg, " have crept into the minds of men and thence, through the heads of INNO-VATORS into *the church* in consequence of their not understanding the order in which God created the universe and all and every part of it." (Ib. 52.) " The laws of that order according to which the

church is established are *as many as there are truths in the Word.*"
(55.)   And " what is a law of divine order but *a perpetual commandment of God* ?"   (A. C. 2634.)   Now if what we have
adduced from the Word be correctly interpreted,—if we have not
wholly mistaken the meaning of the divine oracles,—we might here
leave the question with those who reverence them as the dictates of
infinite wisdom and are willing to make them the rule of their
conduct.

But there is another and a collateral source of information which
has been diligently explored in reference to this question and to
which we have a right to appeal for evidence in aid of our cause
Swedenborg, rarely content with stating a principle in the abstract or
giving a naked logical process, is remarkable for his copious illustrations drawn from the whole field of knowledge.   Many of these
cannot be understood without some familiarity with the leading results
or prominent facts of several sciences and of Civil History.   But
such passages of his works as T. C. R. 137, 159, 172, 174—178,
183, 184, 380, 486, 487, 489, 503 ; Coronis 2–4 ; D. P. 254—274,
A. R. 914, imply an acquaintance with Ecclesiastical History also.
The Memorable Relations generally which give an account of the
state of individuals or sects and nations in the Spiritual World :
nearly the whole treatise on the Last Judgment, and much of the
Spiritual Diary would be unintelligible without such knowledge.
And if it be true that " innovators" have weakened the power of the
church by changes in doctrine, it behoves us to inquire whether
they have not also disturbed the *order* established therein by Christ
and thereby increased the mischief.

In some of the paragraphs above referred to we find the following
statements.   " By the *Apostolic Church* is meant not only the church
which was in various places in the time of the Apostles, but also in
the two or three centuries after their times."   Having spoken of the
Council of Nice and its proceedings in opposition to Arius, he adds,
" *From that time* heaps of abominable heresies concerning God and
the person of Christ began to spring out of the earth and thus *to
destroy* the temple erected by the Lord *through the Apostles.* . . .
The Apostolic Church knew nothing at all concerning three divine
persons from eternity.   That Church was like a new star appearing
in the starry heaven ; but the church *after* the two Nicene Councils
became like the same star afterwards when it is darkened and disappears.   From *the faith* of every church is derived not only all its
worship, but also all its doctrine.   The faith of the present time . . .
has extinguished the light in the word and removed the Lord from
the Church and thus precipitated its morning into night.   This was
done by heretics before the Nicene Council, and afterwards by heretics of that Council and after it."   (T. C. R. 174, 175, 176, 177.)
In another place (378) he enumerates many of these doctrinal heresies by which the church was vexed and torn, before this Council as
well as afterwards, but gives no hint of innovations in its order and
leaves us to infer that the great body of Christians had continued

faithful before the rise of Arius. In still another (137) he speaks of
a council of clergy who had lived in various ages down to his own
time, as having convened in the world of spirits, and as being attended
by some from the blest abodes " who in the world were called
Apostolic Fathers and lived in the ages before the Nicene Council."
The doctrines of the N. C., then recently published—being under
discussion, one of these Fathers on behalf of the rest who " were
filled with indignation" at the Tritheistic dogmas avowed by some
present, rebukes them sharply; " but *our* faith" added he, " is, *was*,
and will be for ever, in the Lord God the Saviour, whose Human is
Divine and whose Divine is Human, &c." From all which we are
authorized to infer that Swedenborg regarded the Christian Church
before the year 325 as mainly a pure church. The Ante-Nicene
Fathers then were not chargeable with corrupting the integrity of
the Christian doctrine, for every heresy of belief was marked as soon
as it arose and the faithful put on their guard.

Now if there is one fact in Ecclesiastical History more clear and
undisputed than another, it is, that the *order* for which we contend,
at that time obtained throughout the entire Christian Church. The
Council itself was composed of *bishops* assembled from every part of
it—some from the remotest regions of the three continents to which
the Gospel had penetrated ; though numerous presbyters and deacons
were also present and assisting their superiors. The earlier bands of
heretics had well nigh disappeared, and the only three remaining
bodies who dissented from the general church, the Meletians, Nova-
tians, and Donatists had also their bishops, as distinguished from presbyters, in attendance, though it does not appear that those of the
Donatists formed a part of the Council. Abuses there may have
been of episcopal power, and minor irregularities, some of which last
were brought to the notice of the body. One of their canons, for
example, forbids the appointment of more than one *bishop* in a city
as being *contrary to primitive usage*. But no one then disputed the
antiquity, the precedence or just prerogatives of the office itself.

Is it reasonable then to believe, that the leaders of the Church,
who down to that period had proved themselves vigilant and faithful
sentinels where truth was concerned, would be wholly indifferent to
the *order* which Christ and his Apostles had established therein? Or
if the peculiar functions of the Twelve and of Paul ceased at their
death, thenceforth to devolve on the general body of presbyters, must
it not have been known to the latter? and could any of that rank
have usurped a portion of those powers, or others been stationed over
them on pretence of succeeding the Apostles, without the knowledge
and protest of those whose rights were invaded. The Constitution of
a hierachy,—the number of its grades—the duties of its different
functionaries if such there be—the exercise of their respective powers,
are all external matters which can be and usually are subjected to
ocular tests. Concerning dogmas there might have been a doubt, for
many of them had not been clearly defined : others were then
obscure as being undeveloped; and thence might the simple be led
astray by the designing. But here there could be no mistake. The

great majority both of the clergy and laity must have known what the former were and had been from the beginning, for they or their predecessors had been frequently if not constantly the subjects or the agents of their exercise, and this of course attended with some outward ceremony or formality which could not, like matters of opinion, escape their observation, had there been a disposition to conceal. All Christendom could not have been asleep over their rights during more than two centuries. No syren song could have lulled them to sleep; and in either case no *"paulatim process"* (to use a phrase current in other communions) could have been so imperceptible, no steps so stealthy, no encroachment so gradual, as not to have waked some one conscientious and intrepid champion who would soon have roused the rest. Professing Christians were not all sincere then any more than now. Of their body some had ever been prompt enough to raise parties on less plausible grounds; but during all this period, though we read of heretical teachers who were restive under the authority and rebukes of their ecclesiastical superiors, we hear of no attempt to suppress the bishops as a class of men who claimed a rank and power to which they were not entitled. Supposing the Episcopate to be an usurpation, how are we to account for this extraordinary forbearance of all parties—equivalent to a universal conspiracy against the rights of all except the few who were elevated to what was the post of honor, though often attended with danger. Or if we leave the laity out of view, what are we to think of the clergy, in that the purest age of the church,—set for the defence of its character and rights—proving without exception delinquent and permitting a revolution to take place simultaneously through all her borders, without remonstrance; without bequeathing to posterity a single plea in defence of their negligence or surrender, or even so much as a hint of the fact? Are we to suppose that men specially dedicated to the Gospel on account of their regard for the spiritual interests of their fellow-creatures,—laboring and toiling and braving every danger for its spread and defence,—whose highest honor and pleasure was in their success and who counted not their lives dear if they might rescue their fellows from the slavery of sin and transfer them to His service which was true freedom; is it credible that *they* should universally turn TRAITORS to the cause they had solemnly vowed to support? Or, after having been selected for their responsible station partly in consideration of their superior abilities or cultivation; having been disciplined in such a school—with the Word of Truth ever before their eyes or minds,—with the most varied experience, the fruit of constant observation and intercourse with human nature in all its phases,—must we believe that they had all and entirely become FOOLS as regarded an essential portion of their rights and yielded them without a struggle? I hesitate not to say that it was morally impossible. The few would not have essayed such an enterprise if within their reach. They could not have accomplished it if they had dared. The greater number, unless all history has been falsified, were neither so weak or so wicked as the supposition implies. And if by a combination of moral elements such as never before occurred in the history of human affairs, such a consummation could have been effected, the memory of the revolution could no more have been suppressed than could that of the rise or submersion of a continent, were either to take place before the eyes of assembled mankind.   Now the origin of nearly every important institution among civilized men has been traced to its source.   There have ever been historians or antiquarians who delighted in such a task.   But if Episcopacy did not originate with the Apostles no one has ever been able to fix its date.   Many have pretended to trace the monster to its birth or infancy, but their conjectures as to the period have been as various and as vagrant as the colors and shapes of evening clouds.   Centuries intervene between the epochs assigned by learned and diligent and anxious.inquirers, and after all their labors the hypothesis of each vanishes beneath the wand of truth.

When the Nicene Bishops convened, the church had been but recently established by Constantine. While unrecognised by the state, its leaders had neither motive nor power to oppress their brethren. Their successful labors and exalted character had contributed much to render christianity both respectable and formidable in the view of the civil authority.   A very few may have proved recreant under the fires of persecution; but the case of Paul of Samorata who more than fifty years before was deposed by *a council of his peers* from the See of Antioch on charges of heresy, and immorality and *oppression of his inferior clergy*, was the solitary recorded exception to that generally exemplary conduct of the order which had challenged the regard, as well of their brethren within the fold, as of the world without.   No, there was no necessity for a gigantic conspiracy on the part of themselves or predecessors to filch unlawful power. The only powers they claimed over their brethren were *given by God himself* when he promised the Eleven that he would be with them *always— even to the consummation of the age.   Their* commission had been regularly handed down to their successors—even to the generation of those who assembled at Nice.   The principal question before the council was one which required the most scrutinizing search into Scripture and the other writings and traditions of the Church.   That was a learned age as had been those preceding, up to the advent. Records and monuments and traditions must have been extant in abundance sufficient to show the primitive constitution of the ministry.   For not two centuries had elapsed between the early manhood of some present and the death of the Apostle John.   Had there then been evidence of such a fraudulent assumption on the part of those who condemned him, or of their predecessors, is it credible that Arius—*a Presbyter, and complaining of the tyranny of his bishop,* would have failed to use so formidable a weapon against his judges? Every other act of sophistry, eloquence, intrigue and address had been called to the aid of open and legitimate discussion in propagating his opinions ; but he was too wise to urge a claim which he knew could not be sustained and which would therefore prejudice his cause.   This method *was* tried at a later day by a secret member of his party—Ærius by name—who is believed to have originated the notion of the primitive equality of Christian ministers, but he was promptly put down as an innovator and disorganiser, by a universal storm of indignation and shortly afterward he openly avowed his Arian sentiments. The total absence of any allusion to such a change of Government from Contemporaneous documents, or even of the whisper of Tradition in aftertimes to that effect, ought, were there no other arguments, to settle the question finally and for ever.

But why resort to probability or conjecture? Records sufficient for our purpose are extant *now* and bring the chain of evidence down from the very days of the Apostles to the period in question, and prove beyond all reasonable doubt that the order for which we contend had continued in the Church throughout. Such indeed is the' number and credibility of witnesses and so direct and conclusive their testimony that in attempting to use it, we find ourselves " embarrassed by our riches " and must content ourselves with a slight modicum selected from the mass before us.

Antioch was the first city where the disciples were called Christians. Of this numerous and important church, Ignatius, a disciple of John the Apostle, was *the* bishop for forty years, the third in the line from Peter the Apostle, and flourished about the year 100, but at length suffered martyrdom at Rome. Of his seven remaining Epistles written from thence to various churches most or all contain matter to our purpose ; but we have space for only a sentence or two from that to the Magnesians. " By my fellow-servant, Sotis, the *deacon* in whom I rejoice, in as much as he is subject unto his *bishop* as unto the grace of God, and to the *presbyters* as to the law of Jesus Christ. Wherefore it will become you not to despise the youth of your *Bishop* but to yield all reverence to him, according to the power of God the Father, as also I perceive that your holy *presbyters* do."

To *Polycarp*, Bishop of Smyrna, who was also a disciple of John and who likewise suffered martyrdom, A. D. 167, was one of these letters addressed. In a letter of his own to the Philippians he sanctions all the statements in those of Ignatius.—*Ireneus*, ordained Bishop of Lyons by Polycarp and who flourished A. D. 178, says " Polycarp was not only taught by the Apostles, and had conversed with many who had seen Christ, but was also by the Apostles appointed bishop of the Church in Smyrna." " We can enumerate those, who were appointed by the apostles, bishops in the churches and their successors even to us. The Apostles wished them to be very irreproachable in all things whom they left their successors, *delivering* (to them) *their own place of government*." (Against Heresies, B. III., chap. 3.) *Tertullian* (died A. D. 220) in his book " Of Heretical Prescriptions," (chap. 32,) thus writes :—" Let the heretics produce the original of their churches, let them recount their bishops *one by one*, so descending by succession from the beginning, that he who was the first bishop, had one of the Apostles, or of the Apostolical men who was in full communion with the Apostles, for his author and predecessor. For in this manner the Apostolical Churches derive their succession." *Clement of Alexandria* A. D. 194, " In the Church, the orders of Bishops, Presbyters, and Deacons are, I think, imitations of the angelic glory." (Strom. B. VI.) *Origen*, A. D. 230, "Shall I not be subject to my Bishop, who is ordained of God to be my father? Shall I not be subject to the Presbyter, who, by the Divine conde-scension is placed over me?" (20th Homily on Mat.) *Cyprian* the Bishop of Carthage, who after filling the office in a most exemplary manner suffered martyrdom A. D. 258, wrote separate treatises " On the power of the Presbytery when the Bishop is absent;" and " On the order of Bishops and Presbyters,"—besides frequent allusions to their several powers and duties in his other writings. But from these we will present but the following :—" What danger ought we to fear from the displeasure of God when some *presbyters*, neither mindful of the Gospel nor of their own station in the Church—neither regarding the future judgment of God, nor the *bishop* who is set over them, (*which was never done under our predecessors*)—with contempt and neglect of the bishop, do arrogate all rule to themselves!" (Ep. XVI.) *Firmilian*, Bishop of Cesarea in Cappadocia, A. D. 250, "The power of remitting sins was given to the Apostles, and to the Churches which they founded, and to the Bishops who succeeded to the Apos-tles, and to the Churches which they founded, and to the Bishops who succeeded to the Apostles by a vicarious ordination." (Ep. to Cyprian, Bishop of Carthage.) *Eusebius*, A. D. 325, says, " In the sequel of this history, the succession of bishops, *from the Apostles*, shall be set down in their order." (Ecc. Hist. B. III., chap. 4.) Now Eusebius was the most learned of all the Ante-Nicene Fathers (Origen perhaps excepted) and in compiling his history of the Church had the use of the best documents extant, to which his position also gave him ready access. He was present at the Council of Nice, and accorded in opinion neither with Arius nor Athanasius; but his doctrine of the Lord, though obscurely expressed, was both more rational and scrip-tural than that of either; and had his counsel been heeded, the cor-ruptions generated by the extreme opinions of both might have been crushed in the germ. His History throughout implies the superiority of Bishops to Presbyters, and that the former were the successors of the Apostles, up to whom he traces the line of Christian bishops in several of the larger cities of the Roman Empire. His catalogue of the bishops of Rome does not precisely accord with that given by some other writers, and it is therefore pretended that the whole is unworthy of credit. But none of them say that there was more than one bishop there at one time, or that presbyters were his equals.*

---

* There are two authorities which might have been cited—"The Clementine Recognitions" and " The Apostolical Constitutions"—either of which, if admitted, would place this question beyond all possibility of doubt ; for the gradation and duties of the ministry are defined in each with all needful precision. But as the genuineness or authenticity of one or both has been questioned (as I think on insufficient grounds) I omit to bring them forward. The former is generally conceded to have been written in the latter part of the first, or early in the second, century. The notion now is, that the latter was compiled in the fourth, and it is asserted that both have been interpolated. Having examined the pretended proof of this, I see no reason to believe that either—particularly the latter—has ever been corrupted, so far as this subject is concerned. Indeed it could not be done without altering the texture of the whole work. At whatever

And this is but a specimen of the evidence furnished by these writers to the same effect and which might be spread over many pages. The Fathers may at times have proved indifferent reasoners, or mistaken interpreters of Scripture; but it is generally allowed that *they are competent witnesses of facts*, and *that we may learn from hem what was thought to be true or false doctrine in their day*. Those who affect to consider their testimony on this subject as suspicious, do not scruple to use it themselves while discussing kindred questions, such as those which relate to Immersion, Infant-Baptism, the Divinity of Christ, and the Canon of Scripture. If then there be no sufficient reason for discarding this evidence, so great in amount, so unbroken in succession, so clear and pointed and yet so uniform and harmonious in its character, how is its force to be evaded? Some of the favorers of Parity in the Old Church have certainly attempted this, and even to wrest a portion of it to the support of their own views. But I doubt whether the Records of Party-Politics, or the Practice of Advocates who are paid to make the worse appear the better reason, can furnish examples of balder sophistry or grosser instances of the *suppressio veri* than are to be found in their books. Take a specimen or two:—

We read in 1 Tim. 5: 17, 18, as follows: "Let the elders that rule *well* be counted worthy of double honor, especially they who *labor* in the word and doctrine. For the Scripture saith, Thou shalt not muzzle the ox that treadeth out the corn. And, the laborer is worthy of his hire." Now although the 5th verse of the 3d chapter of the same Epistle, 1 Thes. 5: 12, 13, and Heb. 13: 7, 17, 24, declare that ruling is a part of the function of Elders as well as preaching, and the obvious sense of these texts is confirmed by their practice as proved by the whole current of Church History, and although the next succeeding verse shows that this double honor consisted principally in a provision for the temporal wants of such of that order as exhibited a talent for government, or were diligent in discharging their duties of the other division,—yet this is the principal and almost the only text offered by Presbyterians as the Scripture warrant for the class of "*Ruling* Elders" as distinct from those who preach; though the office wherever set up is notoriously hono-

period compiled, there is both internal and collateral evidence of the antiquity and genuineness of the materials. There is a mistake concerning the Resurrection of the body, and a marvellous tale in each relative to the magical doings of Simon Magus, (both natural enough at that day,) and the power ascribed to church officers, though probably needed in the beginning of that dispensation of partial light, was greater than any one could desire to see conferred on those of the New Church. Besides these I know of no other serious blemish. The gradation and necessary prerogatives are all for which I contend; and concerning these there could be no mistake, unless each work was a forgery throughout. There is matter in each condemnatory of Catholic and Protestant, Tripersonalist and Unitarian, and therefore are they out of favor with all parties. They have been thought by some to favor the views of Arius; but this is a mistake, as any intelligent Newchurchman may see who reads them in the light of his own doctrine with which they are in full accordance. The "Clementine Recognitions," despite its romantic form, is, in some aspects, the most interesting, and to a Newchurchman the most valuable of all the works of the Ante-Nicene writers.

rary, its incumbents receiving no pecuniary compensation for their services. But having invented a class of officers unknown to the early Christian Church, whether recognized in the Synagogue or not, their patrons could then find them in various passages of Scripture where no one had ever dreamed of their being referred to before. Thus say they, When Paul and Barnabas "ordained elders in every church," (Acts, 14 : 23,) one was the Pastor and the rest his "*ruling elders*" to be sure!—and that James [although called an Apostle] was but the Pastor of the Church at Jerusalem and that the Elders who assisted at the first Council, (15 : 4, 6,) were the ruling elders of his congregation!—as were also a part of the Elders of Ephesus whom Paul sent for to Miletus!! (20 : 17, 28, 30.) And one expounder of Church History sees in Ignatius' repeated mention of bishop, presbyters, and deacons, nothing but churches organized after the Presbyterian Model!!!—the first being the Pastor of the Church—the second, the ruling elders—and the third the almoners of the same. To one who will read with unbiassed mind the entire Letters of Ignatius consecutively : and then in series, all the extracts from the Ante-Nicene Fathers which relate to the officers and government of the Church, it must be apparent that "the force of doubting (and of prejudice) can no farther go."*

Among those who maintain the primitive equality of the clergy, there have also not been wanting persons of competent learning and zeal to collect from the writings of the Fathers whatever could be

---

* I do not deny that there were in the early Church, certain of the lay members, distinguished for their age and influence, or gravity and wisdom, called "Elders of the People," who stood between them and the pastor, and who might be regarded as the representatives of the former. From their more intimate knowledge of, and frequent intercourse with, the private members, they could aid the pastor in the maintenance of discipline, by reproving or warning those who went astray, or by offering examples of Christian conduct and conversation in their own persons and families. They could suggest to the pastor measures for the good of the flock, or dissuade from such as might prove injurious, and by assisting to carry out the former would render the ministry more efficient. They might also co-operate more directly and conspicuously in preserving order in the public worshipping assemblies : and in all the more secular concerns of the church their aid or counsel would be indispensable. But I cannot find that they assisted in administering the communion : or that they ever gave a judicial vote in the punishment of heretics or other offenders ; or that they had any other *spiritual power* in the church than such as was merely *advisory*. From the whole mass of early Patristic Remains some dozen scraps have been culled by the writers on this subject, which are supposed to indicate such a distinct office as that of "Ruling Elder." But on examining them closely, I find that most of them refer to Preaching Elders, or the second grade of the ministry. and the rest to such "Elders of the people" as I have described and which are clearly alluded to in the following from *Ambrose* [Hilary] of the fourth century : "Among all nations old age is honorable. Hence it is that the Synagogue, and afterwards the church, had *Elders*, without whose *counsel* nothing was done in the church; which by what negligence it grew into disuse I know not, unless, perhaps, by the sloth, or rather by the pride of the *Teachers*, while they *alone* wished to appear something." No one from this could justly ascribe to them any other agency than that of "standing counsellors" of the Pastor. Such an employment is in reason and the nature of things affords ample scope for usefulness to the church ; and persons should be designated thereto under that or an equivalent title in every church whatever.

made to assume the appearance of sanctioning their views. Having taken some pains to ascertain the character and amount of this evidence, I believe I may say that *the whole of it*, when properly sifted, *may be reduced to the following solitary passage from Jerome*, a Latin writer who flourished from A. D. 331 to 420. " Before there were, by the devil's instigation, parties in religion, and it was said among the people, I am of Paul, I of Apollos, and I of Cephas, *the Churches were governed by the common council of the Presbyters.* But afterward, when every one thought that those whom he baptized were rather his than Christ's, it was determined *through the whole world* that *one* of the Presbyters should be set above the rest. . . . These things have I written to show that *among the ancients* Presbyters and Bishops were the same. But, *little by little* [paulation] *that all the seeds of dissension might be plucked up*, the whole care was devolved on one. As, therefore, the Presbyters know that by *the custom of the Church* they are subject to him who is their President, so let Bishops know that they are above Presbyters more by the custom of the Church than by the true dispensation of Christ." (Com. on Titus.) *What* ancients?—the terms Bishop and Presbyter *are* applied to the same office *in the New Testament;* and we have shown when and why that of " Apostle " was dropped by their successors who thenceforth took the more modest and appropriate designation of Bishops, which was yielded up to them by Presbyters. It is also granted that the Churches planted by the Apostles (who could not be every where at once) were at first governed by the common council of the Presbyters whom they ordained in those churches. (Acts, 14 : 23.) The question is, who originated that " custom " of which Jerome speaks, and when did it begin? for we also concede that it was not directly appointed by Christ who ascended to heaven before the Apostles had left Judea. Let Jerome himself answer. *"By little and little [paulatim*, the very word] in process of time, others were ordained *Apostles*, by *those whom our Lord had chosen*, as that speech to the Philippians affirms, saying, 'I supposed it necessary to send unto you Epaphroditus, your Apostle.'" (Com. on Galatians.) In the first passage there is an obvious reference to the parties which had arisen in the Corinthian Church, (1 Cor. 1 : 12,) whose example had probably proved contagious—for the correction of which evil the *Apostles themselves* had adopted the plan of setting one Presbyter over the rest, who at first was called the Apostle and-afterwards the Angel or Bishop of that church. *This " paulatim process" then, must have been completed in their day;* and any measure instituted by them for the government of the church, was either founded in necessity and the nature of things, or (as we may infer from Acts 1 : 3,) should be held as equivalent to a divine dictate, and to be preferred above any mere precedent of a later date. Thus disappears the last vestige of evidence from the Fathers in behalf of the equality of the clergy,—or if any thing more were necessary for its explosion, it is furnished by the self same Jerome. " That we may know," says he " that the apostolic traditions were taken from the Old Testament, *that which Aaron and his sons and the Levites were in the temple, let the bishops, presbyters, and deacons claim to themselves in the church.* . . . What does a bishop do, *ordination excepted,* which a presbyter may not do? . . . . It is the custom of the church for the bishop to go and invoke the Holy Spirit, by imposition of hands, on such as were baptized by presbyters and deacons, in villages and places remote from the mother church. Do you ask where this is written? in the Acts of the Apostles." (Ep. to Evag. See also, Acts 8 : 5, 12, 14–17 ; 19 : 1–7.) " The apostles were thy fathers, because they begat thee ; but now that they have left the world thou hast *in their stead* their sons, the bishops." (Ad. Eccl.) A writer ought surely to be permitted to interpret himself.

But an argument, plausible at first view, against the trinal order of the ministry, is drawn from *the great number* of bishops mentioned by some of the early writers as assembling in *council* from a single province.—And *Mosheim,* a learned Lutheran of the eighteenth century, who, though superior to the usual prejudices of his sect in matters of doctrine, was not the less a partisan on this subject, has written as follows in his " History of the Church."—" Let none confound the bishops of the primitive and golden period of the church, with those of whom we read in the following ages. For though they were both designated by the same name, yet they differed extremely in many respects. A bishop, during the first and second centuries, was a person who had the care of one Christian assembly ; which, at that time, was, *generally speaking,* SMALL ENOUGH TO BE CONTAINED IN A PRIVATE HOUSE! In this assembly, he acted not so much with the authority of a master, as with the zeal and diligence of a faithful servant. The churches also in those early times, were *entirely independent!* none of them subject to any foreign jurisdiction, but each governed by its own rulers and its own laws. Nothing is more evident than the perfect equality that reigned among the primitive churches, nor does there ever appear *in the first century,* the *smallest trace* of that association of provincial churches from which councils and metropolitans derive their origin !" (Mosh. Eccl. Hist. I, 105–107.)

Mosheim's history of the early church is trustworthy only so far as it accords with the documents from which alone it should have been compiled And these sources—not very voluminous—are now quite as accessible to others as they were to him. If he means to say that in those early ages there was no difference of rank between a bishop and a common presbyter:—or that the churches in any of the larger cities where the Gospel had been planted, continued for any length of time as small as he here describes :—or that there was usually more than one bishop in a city :—or that there was ever a settled bishop without his subordinate clergy ;—a more extraordinary assertion was never hazarded by any man who valued his literary reputation ; for he would thereby flatly contradict every early record, including the New Testament, and all the writers whom we have just quoted. It is not denied, however, that bishops at that day were more numerous in certain districts than they have ever been any where in modern times. But for this there were several reasons, a few of which will remove the apparent difficulty.

1st. The order of civil society in those ages was eminently munici-
pal;—that is, a majority of the people were collected in cities and
their dependent villages, among whom the territory adjacent to each
was apportioned and tributary; the rural population proper being
comparatively small. Such was the constitution of society throughout the Roman Empire, as distinguished from the Teutonic or Feudal
arrangement which had obtained in the more northern countries, and
long afterwards essentially modified without destroying the former.
This order was at once a cause and an effect of their superior civilization, though in part owing to the continual wars which drove the
people to places of natural strength or to walled towns for refuge or
defence. Such cities were numerous in Egypt, Syria, Asia Minor,
Greece and the Mediterranean Isles, in Southern Gaul, Spain, and
Northern Africa—in a word, in all the provinces around the Mediterranean, but less so in Italy, owing to the wasting effect of the civil
wars and the monopoly of landed estates by individuals of the privi-
leged classes. Many of these cities were also very populous as compared with modern standards. In them was the Gospel first preached,
churches gathered, and elders ordained with authority to rule and
teach. As their numbers increased, to heal or prevent the rise of
parties, and for their better government otherwise, a bishop was
placed over them,—who, together with his clergy, extended the
conquests of the faith into the surrounding villages and territory;—
the ecclesiastical boundaries being generally co-incident with the
territorial limits recognized by the civil law, and the mother church
being that over which the bishop immediately presided, and to which
the minor divisions of his flock successively repaired when the communion was to be administered. 2d. There were for a long time few
or no separate establishments for the education of the Christian clergy,
who were generally selected *from the body of the flock,* and trained to
the special duties of their office under the immediate inspection and
example of the bishop. And this primitive plan was continued the
longer, partly because the helps to obtaining the necessary preparatory learning, now so abundant, had then to be created; and the
times were unfavorable to such an enterprise. For the church was
persecuted,—the battle between her and Paganism being long doubtful to human ken,—and the pens of her few learned advocates were
otherwise employed than in the preparation of such works—and
Christians were called to learn and suffer rather than to write. The
apostles indeed, and some others, were miraculously gifted therewith
or had enjoyed the instructions of the Master himself,—but afterwards, such knowledge must be acquired in the ordinary way. Moreover, the new recruits, coming generally from the ranks of Idolatry,
had to unlearn their old errors, and to form themselves after a new
standard. To aid in this, a Christian atmosphere must be generated:
a Christian public opinion must be formed: the Christian doctrine
developed: questions of casuistry settled; and the divine precepts
applied to the thousand occasions and exigencies of their new state.
And all this must be done under the constant guidance of those whose
duty it was to maintain the purity both of doctrine and worship, to

instruct the ignorant, correct the erring, encourage the weak and to
set an example to all as well in troublous as in peaceful times.
Instruction too, for the most part was necessarily oral. As yet the
press was not. The mighty energies of steam had not yet been
applied to the abridgement of labor and the facilitation of intercourse.
Manuscripts were slowly multiplied, and not easily understood by the
simple without an interpreter. Governments were jealous of large
assemblies, and of any one man whose spiritual authority and jurisdiction embraced an extensive territory and numerous subaltern agents
of the same kind,—jealous of frequent meetings of such functionaries
on whatever pretence. Such then, being the constitution and spirit of
society, and such the condition of the church, in that its formative
state, ought we to be surprised at the then number of bishops, and
the infrequency of councils. In her season of strenuous warfare
more general officers would of course be required than after the victory had been won and herself " established in peace." The multiplication of bishops, which suited her then circumstances, would be the
height of folly now, when the whole aspect of society and the whole
character of public opinion has been changed, idolatry conquered,
numerous and successive generations having grown up with a knowledge of the precepts of Christianity (however they may have fallen
short of them in practice,) and however they may have mistaken its
doctrine. And now that the means of acquiring and diffusing correct
knowledge are multiplied a thousand fold, twenty-seven bishops
are found sufficient for all England: fourteen for Sweden: sixty for
France, and forty are probably as many as would ever be needed in the
United States of America. The modern arrangement is, therefore,
equally efficient, more economical, and less oppressive than the
ancient.

Mosheim errs just as widely if he intimates that churches were then
governed on the Congregational or Independent plan. The churches at
first were governed by the Apostles, who planted them. (1 Cor. 4 : 17;
7 : 17; 11 : 2; 2 Cor. 11 : 28; 2 Thes. 2 : 15; 3 : 14.) In Acts 15,
we read also of the first *general council* which passed authoritative
decrees on the question submitted to them. Afterwards the church
(or churches) in each city and its environs was governed by its own
bishop. Bishops were appointed only by those of their own order,—
among whom there was frequent consultation by correspondence or
otherwise; recourse being more frequently had in cases of difficulty
to those in the important churches of Alexandria, Antioch, Byzan-
tium, Rome, Carthage, &c.,—or else to some individual who by talents,
learning or piety, had attained a merited influence. Councils of
bishops were rarely held, for the reasons just given, though they did
convene occasionally, and in small numbers, (as those for judging the
early heresies, and that for the trial of Paul of Samosata ;)—and the
church always retained the inherent right of holding them when
better times should supervene. After her establishment they were
frequent—both provincial and general,—and though some of them
condemned real heresies and others enacted useful canons, or contributed in a degree to the reformation of the church,—yet the one

false step having been taken at Nice, their after progress was generally into wider and profounder depths of error.*

*It has been thought by some, that Swedenborg when he says, "But my friend *trust not* any council, but trust the Word of the Lord, which is *above* councils," (T. C. R. 489,) has expressed a decisive condemnation of all such bodies, called for any purpose whatever. But is not this a mistake? Look at the context, and at a preceding passage which asks "*What confidence* is to be placed in councils *who do not enter through the door of the sheepfold but climb up some other way?*" For example, what confidence ought we to place in the council which established the vicarship of the pope, &c.? (177.) But is this an entire veto on all such assemblies? Does it mean any thing more than that their decisions should not be placed *above* Scripture, or to be received where they contradict it? He tells of various councils which met in the Spiritual World—some for good, some for bad purposes; and relates at length, and with commendation, the proceedings of one which *deduced from the Word the true doctrine of the Trinity in all its branches.* (188.) And may not the united wisdom of the wisest heads of the church on earth, aid in shedding light on disputed questions, now that we have a perpetual check on their possible abuses of the Word of God as expounded by Swedenborg. Could they not also be of use in promoting something like uniformity in the policy and plans of the church in different countries? I can conceive of a time and of occasions when such convocations will not only be useful but much needed in the New Church.[1]

[1] We do not object to councils; for we are taught that "in the multitude of counsellors is safety," (Prov. xi. 14;) and there is just as good ground for councils in the church as there is for them in the state, the army, or science. But we object to the *authority* of councils in the church—such authority as would be given to them by the Address to Receivers issued by the General Convention in September 1840—an authority to *decide* how the precepts of the Lord and his divine truth are to be *understood*, and what they *require all the parts of the church to shun or do.* In short, we object to any authority in ecclesiastical councils to *determine* matters of faith and conscience—what the Word teaches, or what are to be believed as its truths, on penalty of exclusion from the church's pale. Councils of the most intelligent and wise ecclesiastics may and should *declare* what the Word teaches, and give their authorities and reasons for it. But *judgment* and *determination* in these matters are with the member of the church, who is to go with the doctrine thus taught to the Word itself, (A. C. 5402, 6047,) looking to the Lord alone, who gives light according to the love of truth for its own sake, and thereby enables the member of the church to see in his own mind what the Word really teaches on the subject. For "the confirmation of truths is effected by illustration from the Lord when man studies the Word with the end of knowing truths." (A. C. 7012.) And "nothing can be appropriated to any one which is not acknowledged from his own proper intuition, that is, which he does not know, from himself, not from another, to be so." (A. C. 5376.) "To ask the Lord is to consult the Word; for in the Word the Lord is present, it being the divine truth which is from him; and he is with the angels in his own divine truth, and also with the men of the church who receive him." (A. C. 10. 548.) And "whoever reads the Word to the end that he may grow wise, that is, may do what is good and understand what is true, he is instructed according to such end and the affection thereof: for the Lord flows in, whilst he knows not, and illuminates his mind, and wherein he hesitates *gives understanding from other passages.*" (A. C. 3436.) Thus we hold that the Lord alone teaches with *authority*, and not as the Scribes. He flows into the *ends* and *affections* of men while *they read the Word*, and gives them to see truth by *its own light* in the Word and from it. Hence—certainly in the new church—we do not need a council of head ecclesiastics to *decide* for us how the Word is to be *understood* and *what* it teaches us *to do or not to do.* And in this sense we do believe that Swedenborg condemns all councils, and exhorts us not to *trust* in *any* of them; but to "go to the God of the Word, and thus to the Word itself"—so that we may see "the errors of many others," the errors of councils, as well as our own; not "to *depend* on *any council of men,* but on *the Word of the Lord*, which *is above all* councils."—*Ed.*

24

I have dwelt the longer on the testimony of writers earlier than A. D. 325, because Swedenborg has distinguished two epochs in her history,—as preceding and following that date. (T. C. R. 760.) The faith of the General Church down to that period having been kept pure, we may fairly presume that an order recognized as existing at various intermediate dates up to the age of the Apostles, was also derived from them. But the fatal virus having then been introduced into her system, which obscured her vision, gradually weakened her strength, and ultimately reaching the vitals brought her to an untimely end, suspicion might attach to the order which then prevailed unless it could be traced to a higher antiquity. Yet this would be a hasty mode of judging; for though one form of government may be preferable to another, it will not of itself preserve either her doctrine or her spirit unimpaired. Swedenborg declares that all preceding churches had a tendency to decline, (762) or at best were but preparatory to the New; and we know that the Old Church under all its forms has erred, and *those which adopted the order of Parity not less than the others.*

Our argument from presumption then is not weakened, but strengthened by the fact which all allow that, (with the doubtful exception of the Waldenses) thenceforward to the Reformation the same three grades of clergy were continued throughout the Church. The dioceses indeed were enlarged, and besides its lawful powers, a degree of wealth and influence attached to the office of a bishop, which were unknown to their predecessors. This might be a reason for restraining it within proper limits—not for its destruction. The Churches of England, Ireland, Sweden, Denmark and Moravia retained it after they had severed the tie which bound them to Rome. It is also a fact that all the leading Reformers,—Zwingle excepted but—including Luther, Melancthon and Calvin, desired its preservation; for they took care to express their wishes in writing and the record remains to this day. At first they pleaded necessity for the adoption of a different model : no Catholic Bishop, from whom they might have obtained the succession, having joined their ranks until some definite plan was to be determined on, when Calvin borrowed certain features of the one which then prevailed among the Bohemian Waldenses and composed the system of government which has since gone by his name. The step once taken was of course persisted in and defended,— and at length imitated in other countries. The class of officers, however, known in the Lutheran Church as " Superintendants " bore a considerable analogy and fell heir to some of the powers of the bishops. Many of the leading and most learned Pastors of the French Reformed Church have acknowledged the existence of Episcopacy in the Primitive Church and wished it to be restored. Two English bishops who attended the Synod of Dort—after their doctrinal decrees were drawn up—made a strong appeal to the body on the same subject, urging their return to this as the original form, and inferred from the reply of their President on behalf of himself and co-delegates from Presbyterian Churches, that they earnestly desired such a government, but thought the blessing unattainable. Eminent individuals in all those churches have since expressed the same opinions. Nor should it be forgotten that some of the most distinguished ornaments of the Church of England were reared under the system of Parity, and after full trial or examination renounced her claims as untenable. Witness the great Bishop Butler;—and Leighton, the wondrous symmetry of whose mind and character proclaim him the brightest Christian of all the Protestant world, perhaps the most perfect who ever appeared in the Old Church. Yet if there ever was a man whose merely human feelings might have kindled a flaming and undying hostility to Episcopacy, that man was Leighton. Witness also Secker, one of the most judicious and moderate of all who have reached her highest seat. It might be suspected that these men were induced to change their opinions by the hope of advancement; but neither of them sought promotion. It sought them; and the second laid it down without a sigh for his own loss. The ancient order was never lost in the Greek, Syrian, Armenian, Coptic, Abyssinian and Ethiopian Churches, in all of which it has been handed down entire from the Apostles' days. The Nestorians carried it to Persia and to remote Eastern Asia. And not the least remarkable instance is that of a body of Christians in India, discovered in the 16th Century by the Portuguese and visited in the 18th by Dr. Buchanan, who found them also similarly organised and tracing their spiritual descent from Thomas one of the Twelve Apostles. Now, if equality had at first been established among the Clergy of all these different and distant regions, is it not passing strange that they should all have changed to the same model,—and yet more so, that history which has kept a record of all revolutions of opinion in the Church should have made no mention of one which was external and could not be disguised.

The question concerning the "Apostolical succession" as it is called,—in other words, whether there has been an unbroken succession of bishops from the days of the Apostles? and which has been so strenuously debated between certain branches of the Old Church, is one in which we as New Churchmen are not particularly interested. For with us a new ministry has been originated and we acknowledge no allegiance to that of the former dispensation. I will say, however, that I believe the *principle* asserted to be both correct and important. I will go farther and add that all presumption is in favor of its having been regularly preserved, and that the burden of proof should rest on those who deny it. The divine promise to the Twelve was that "he would be with them [and their successors of course] *until the consummation of the age.*" Now a fire kindled in many places may be extinguished in several, yet not in all; and before the enemy shall have gone his rounds—it might be relumed where he began. So "a rope of many strands" may have some of its threads broken without being wholly severed in twain. The Episcopate we know, was established throughout the civilized world. Mahomedan and Vandal and Saxon invasions uprooted it from many of its seats: many lines of succession were cut off but far more were preserved, and in some there has been a reunion. It was an Apostolic Canon "Let a bishop be ordained by two or three bishops; a presbyter, by one bishop, and so likewise a deacon." It is also alleged that they appointed a form of consecration which was used in the Ante-Nicene Church, and placed such other safeguards around the station that successful intrusion into the office was well nigh impossible. Other forms for the same purpose, observed for centuries in the Northern, Southern, Eastern and Western Churches, are also extant. Eusebius, as we have already said, has given catalogues of bishops in several churches down to his own day, in some of which and in yet others, the recorded succession has been preserved to the era of printing, after which it could not well be lost. In the former period good men had no motive to exercise the office without being duly authorised. Afterwards they could not if they would; for the place had then acquired such attractions, and its ministrations were thought to possess such a divine virtue that it was the interest of all to omit no essential observance in consecrations. The first bishops of Protestant England and Sweden had been Romish Bishops,—long a standing objection with their opponents of Parity who taunted them with the "impure channel" through which their orders had reached them,—when yet, strange to tell, they also claim a similar succession for Presbyters, *and through the same channel!* But Swedenborg has settled that the personal character of a regular priesthood does not nullify their official acts; and reason would tell us that the same vessel might receive either pure wine or muddy water,—the same casket contain precious stones or their counterfeits. The later consecrations both in England and America are all recorded and all regular. A very slight knowledge of Arithmetic would suffice to show that a total obstruction or corruption of the succession is the most improbable of suppositions. Why should its preservation be thought more unlikely than that of the Jewish High-Priesthood from Aaron to Caiaphas, or of any particular dynasty of kings, or line of doges or Republican Presidents?

What then, it may be asked, do I condemn the movement of the Reformers against the authority of Rome? and must the church continue for ever in passive obedience to her governors because they have been appointed in due form and regular succession? Shall the sound or well disposed part of the body be perpetually enslaved by the corrupt, lest in withdrawing they should commit the sin of Schism? Certainly not. The office of the ministry is to serve; and though servants may differ in rank among themselves, they should not therefore forget their position and fancy themselves masters. It is very true that they are "Stewards" and "Governors in things Ecclesiastical." (Luke 12: 42–48.) But theirs is a delegated and limited, not an arbitrary or undefined power: a government not of caprice but of laws—and those divine laws. Nor should its *ordinances* concerning things indifferent or changeable, established for the sake of harmony or convenience, contradict its laws. Within those limits our obedience is due and should be voluntary and cheerful. Their duty is to instruct us in the truth, and by truth to lead us to good. But if, "because the Lord of the Church delayeth his coming" they scrape to themselves other powers than he has conferred and which are not necessary to the discharge of their duties,—and then pervert them all :—if they debase the treasures committed to their charge for the general benefit, and no warning or remonstrance can induce them to retrace their steps,—there remains but the one alternative of separation and the sin of Schism rests with those who have compelled its adoption. For the command is clear, to " cease from the instruction which causeth to err " and to receive no other Gospel at variance with that committed to the Apostles.

Both prudence and duty would have dictated that where the apostolic organization had been substantially preserved it should not have been rashly overthrown, or so long as there was a hope of Reforming its abuses,—for which purpose every other method should have been essayed. But when one bishop demanded precedence of all other bishops and pretended to be the vicar of Christ on earth, national churches might reclaim their rights which had been inconsiderately yielded. Or should these last in turn become intolerably oppressive, or their doctrine hopelessly corrupt, the friends of Truth and Piety retain a *Revolutionary right* of withdrawing from their jurisdiction. And if their divinely-appointed leaders should all refuse to head the movement, its conduct of course devolves on those of the next grade who would. In such case Parity might be continued as a *Provisional government*, to which the allegiance of peaceable and orderly Christians would in the mean time be due. For though a trinal ministry may be essential to the *perfection* of a church, it is not necessary to its existence ; even as a family may live in a cottage of one story, though a house of three may be best suited to the orderly conduct of its affairs. Should the Parent Church persist in its claims and its heresies, such revolutions so headed may be in progress for ages. But Division is a sad alternative at best, and Democracy, whatever it may be in the State,—in the Church can only be a choice of evils and never safely adopted unless in a period of transition and as a stepping-stone to something better. When therefore the Church has recovered the truth and its ministry is pledged to teach and maintain it, the imperfect frame of government should be laid aside and the divine pattern " reverently restored " as soon as it can be obtained, and the people have consented to its re-adoption.

I have no expectation that this will ever be done by those branches of the Old Church which have adopted the plan of Parity. The tendency with them is to farther dissolution. While they retain so many of the falses of Romanism, (A. R. 751,) or inventions of their own quite as objectionable, Divine Providence may have permitted the erection and continuance of this barrier to re-union, which would give to error a strength and an aspect so imposing that her victims would be less conscious of their chains and therefore less disposed to welcome the Truth that would set them free. Such is even now the case with those who are reared under Episcopacy—who base their adhesion to it not so much on the assurance that it still possesses the primitive faith as on the conviction that theirs is the Apostolic order. In this country and in England their laity enjoy fully as much liberty of inquiry as any other class of Christians and exercise it on all other

subjects *except that of religious doctrine.* A very slight examination
satisfies them that their faith is quite as scriptural, if not more so, than
that offered by any school of Parity. They also suppose their own
piety to be as rational and sincere,—if not so pretentious,—their discipline less inquisitorial; and their ritual is so immeasurably superior
to what they observe elsewhere,—that there is really some apology
for their conservative feeling. Is it wonderful then that they should
shun what they regard as useless wrangles, and leave such matters to
their spiritual guides, so long as they do not suspect—which seems
generally the case among them—that there is a church which possesses the truth of God without alloy: a ritual as becoming and more
sublime than their own, and which is not incompatible with a just
subordination among its ministers. And Parity also has its ancestral
recollections, its martyrs to Religious Liberty, justly dear to them:
its venerated precedents and standards which the less informed cherish
with a pious zeal as if they were Truth embodied, and to which the
more intelligent conform as thinking it better to bear the ills they
have than fly to others that they know not of." And this indulgence
may have likewise been permitted by Providence as a check on the
more ancient pretensions of the others, having moreover, in His wisdom left the language of the sacred records such as ingenuity *can*
weave into a pretext plausible enough for those who will not survey
the entire field of inquiry, and who adhere the more pertinaciously
to their claims as being in their view allied to the cause of political
freedom. But New Churchmen have been elevated to a position from
whence they should be able to perceive that in the conduct of either
class there has been something to commend—much to censure:
that many of the opinions of each, where they happen to be right,
are but little better than respectable prejudices: that nevertheless the
proceedings of both conservatives and innovators have been overruled
for the good of the future—the former having rescued much which
should not have been lost, and the latter having secured a *principle*
and formed a habit of inquiry which will ultimately conduct their
posterity beyond the dark regions into which themselves had wandered.
Let others then carry on the process of destruction,—our task is to
rebuild. While seeking a model to guide us in the new erection, let
not modern precedent triumph over principle, but let our precedents
be divine or conform to principles engraven on the eternal Word,—
in matters indifferent not wantonly discarding what has had the sanction of experience however it may have been blended with error,—
so that we may be always ready to give a reason for our order as well
as for our faith.

The nature of this discussion requires that I should advert briefly
to another objection;—viz: that *a graded ministry tends to Popery!*
This will do very well as a party argument in the mouth of English
Protestant Dissenters: of the Church of Scotland,—and of their
several counterparts here; but to the member of the New Church
who considers the character of her faith and the position of her
ministry, such an idea has much the appearance of a bug bear. It
seems however, that there are those among us who after divesting

themselves of the prejudices of their former faith, have retained this
one pertaining to the subject of order. I may be excused for so
terming it, as I do not claim to have been always exempt from it myself; though now it appears both unjust and irrelevant, and I think
we can afford to be as impartial in judging a question of order, as one
of doctrine. If we are sincere in our acceptance of the teachings of
Swedenborg there can be little danger of our falling into such an
error, as he has expressly and repeatedly condemned it and the council
which established it as unworthy of confidence. (A. C. Pref. to Gen.
chap 22 : 8581; L. J. 75. T. C. R. 177 ; A. R. 768, 798, 799, 802.)
Thus he calls the notion of " the vicarship of the Pope " " that grand
heresy which the wild and infernal love of self and the world" has
deduced from a misinterpretation of Mat. 16 : 15–19 ; and his comment on the 17th and 18th chapters of the Apocalypse is wholly
devoted to the exposure of the evils and falses of the Roman religion.
(A. R. 717–808 ; A. E. 1029–1204). He has also distinguished
between the papacy and the episcopal order in the abstract, without
ever condemning the latter, though there were frequent opportunities
for so doing, if he believed it to be a novelty, or wrong in itself, or to
tend necessarily to tyrannical abuses. But history, when read aright,
gives no countenance to such an idea. The Episcopal churches now
established in Europe are based on a principle which, as we shall
presently show, compels them to be irreconcileably opposed to
Romanism : and the latter, knowing this right well, has ever regarded
the Church of England especially as her most dangerous foe, and has
exhausted much of her strength in efforts to divide her people and to
reconvert them to her faith. On the other hand, has not England,
with all her faults, been the standing bulwark of Protestantism, when
her star has elsewhere paled through treachery or supineness ? The
Reformation once established, she has steadfastly resisted every tendency to a retrograde movement : refused to be led by blandishment
or driven by persecution : has expelled a dynasty of kings who pursued this object, and ever after opposed their return. And did not
Episcopal Sweden under the conduct of Gustavus and Oxenstiern save
the cause of Continental Protestantism when it was apparently at its
last gasp ?

It would not be difficult to show, were this the proper occasion,
that the Lord alone is the head of his entire church or kingdom on
earth, and that he never designed any one of its several provinces to
include a greater territory than that embraced by the *nation* from
which it was gathered. The dream of his self-styled vicar was always
impossible to be realized in its whole extent. His partial success was
only attainable in ages of ignorance ; and were the nations to-morrow
to surrender their spiritual freedom to such a claim, the impossibility
of one man's fulfilling the duties growing out of the acceptance would
ere long compel its resumption. If we search the Scriptures for some
one individual from whom to suspend the alleged chain of succession,
the pretensions of James the brother of our Lord, or of John or of
Paul would be quite as plausible, if not more so, than those of Peter ;
and after all, the power of a general Council of bishops would ever

be superior to that of any one singly.   But all this would lead into too wide a field.

The truth is, that *Popery or something akin to it is one of the necessary issues of any church whose leading tenets are unintelligible mysteries*, and its *principle*[1] lurks and is operative in those very branches of the Old Church, which profess to have wholly discarded it.   For such a system will of course give rise to many questions.   Discussion, strife, parties, divisions successively follow.   At length the friends of order and charity desire a cessation of controversy, and are willing to purchase peace by referring the questions to some common tribunal. They are joined by such as always submit to the authority of the day, and who habitually subject their understanding to their faith.   But as some show of reason or Scripture must accompany its decisions, and as these are often at best but probable, sometimes hardly plausible, independent thinkers will not bow to its mandates; and hence on the other hand incurable schisms.   Now the bishop of Rome, from the wealth and importance of his See, was often appealed to as umpire in such questions, and his council sought in other cases of difficulty, until at length he began to claim the decision of all such matters as his prerogative.   A fortunate conjunction and succession of circumstances favored the extension of his authority throughout Western Europe; and he had before him a perfect model of Spiritual Despotism in the Rabbinical system which has obtained among the Jews since their national independence was destroyed.[*]

The religious domination once established, the claim of temporal power or influence was but the revival of a precedent, long dormant in Europe, but which has flourished in the East from remote ages. When an idea has once taken root in Asia, it is apt to become inveterate; and as Orientals are not given to change, no religious revolution has ever taken place among them without violence.   We have early seen that in the ancient church, the priesthood and royalty were united in the same person.   The priestly long continued to be the ruling caste in Egypt and Ethiopia, Arabia, Persia, India.   Their power was first lost in Persia, though they made a bold stroke for its recovery in the person of Smerdis the Magian, the detection of whose imposture, however, only completed their subjection.   It was maintained in Egypt, with some interruptions, until the establishment of

---

[*] The resemblance between Romanism and modern Judaism has been noticed by many writers, but the analogy has been traced through a number of particulars by Whitby in one of the Appendices to his " Comments on New Testament," to which the reader is referred.

---

1 We think that Mr. Cabell does not go deep enough here for the *principle* of popery. A principle is the inmost of a thing—the third or highest heaven of it: for principles are causes of causes. (A, C. 2991.)   The principle here referred to is in the intellectual or middle region—where there is judgment or determination of matters of doubt growing out of a system of unintelligible mysteries.   We believe the principle of popery is in the voluntary, or, in this case, the lowest region—is *the love of dominion from the love of self*.   Hence Swedenborg speaks of " that grand heresy, which the wild and infernal love of self and the world hath broached from the Lord's words to Peter " in Matt. xvi. 15-19.—*Ed.*

the Grecian dynasty. Shortly after, a similar revolution took place in Ethiopia. The Brahmins retained their political power still longer. In Thibet the policy was carried to the highest point of exaggeration; for to this day it is taught that the Grand Llama is the Incarnation of Deity himself, and that when his body dies the Divinity passes into that of his successor. Mahomet united the two functions in himself, but after his death, his followers became divided into two parties, whose differences can never be reconciled, because the adherents of Ali cherished as their secret doctrine that he also was an incarnation of Deity. When the order in all those countries were compelled to take a position less conspicuous, they were quick to conceive the idea of "a power behind the throne greater than the throne itself;" and were willing that another should hold the sceptre so long as they guided the hand. They also knew that property and power must ever be indissolubly allied,—hence the strenuous efforts of the caste every where and by all methods to possess themselves of riches as a means of securing their spiritual influence.

Now Oriental ideas have ever been travelling westward and operating to modify European Systems. The bishop of Rome may have been encouraged by the successful examples to which we have referred to attempt the like in the West. Nor were there wanting suggestive precedents nearer home. Odin, the founder of the Teutonic Religion, was both king and priest. The power of the Arch-Druid in Ancient Gaul and Britain was often greater that that of the civil ruler. In the more ancient history of both Greece and Italy the high-priesthood was an appendage of royalty, certain public sacrifices being offered by the king alone in that character. In neither of those countries, was the priest's office generally incompatible with secular functions. The Flamen Dialis or high priest of Jupiter sat in the Roman Senate, and many priests in both countries had also rendered civil and military services. On the other hand the place of Pontifex Maximus was eagerly sought by her leading statesmen and generals, and was ultimately added to the other titles and prerogatives of the Emperor. On the fall of the Western Empire, and when Christianity had become paganised, the title was conceded to the bishop of Rome. But he also wished it to imply something more than sacerdotal duties. The piety of early Christians had enriched the Church by their donations, to which was added the bounty of the state wherever Christianity was established. Not content with this, other expedients were used— such as the statutes of Mortmain which permitted the church to receive and retain bequests—by means of which at length a large part of the wealth of Europe was absorbed. At one time the grand conception of Hildebrand seemed not impossible to be realised; and it must be owned that for a season this spiritual power was useful as an antagonist to the ignorance, the barbarism and the violence of the Feudal ages. But as her continued supremacy would have been fatal to the farther progress of society, her pretensions began to be more systematically opposed; and the leading measures of his fraudulent policy have been vigorously retorted on the Pontiff. Thus the German Emperor as successor of the Cæsars claimed to be the head of Chris-

tendom, and challenged the title of Pontifex Maximus for himself.
When Britain threw off the yoke, Henry was declared the Supreme
Head of the Church of England, the Reformation being established
both there and among the Lutherans on the basis of what was afterwards called *Erastianism*,—which acknowledged the right of Government to prescribe the religion which should be taught the people and
to nominate its chief ministers. *These powers can never be yielded by
those governments to the pretensions of Rome, and of course their hostility is mutual and undying.* The church when reformed was made
to disgorge much of her iniquitous gains in Britain and Germany :
at subsequent periods was shorn of her splendor in France, Italy
and Spain,—and herself has been subject to Erastian influences in that
the successor of Peter has been often appointed by the intrigues of
Austria or France or Spain, and has been a puppet in the hands of the
political power for the time in the ascendant ; nor could the Jesuits
do more than retard the progress of decay. While I write, the strength
of Rome has been farther lessened by a rapid succession of blows
which must hasten the dissolution of that power once so formidable.
For however it may be delayed by her policy or the supineness of the
people, the final issue we know is inevitable.

But what have we, as New Churchmen, to do with either of those
parties which have been battling for centuries? It may have been
thought, in the beginning of the contest, that the overshadowing
tyranny of Rome could not be efficiently opposed unless it was met
by a power of equal strength. From this motive and partly because
of the unhappy divisions among Christians, the friends of truth and
freedom acquiesced in the assumption of spiritual authority by kings,
so long as it was wielded for that purpose ;—just as commonwealths
in their extreme emergencies have sometimes vested individuals with
the powers of a dictator. But, though permitted by Providence, this
also was but a " provisional " arrangement, however long-continued.
For the Church of Christ in its origin and design was neither papal
nor Erastian. The state,—which controls the physical force and the
most copious fountains of secular influence and patronage, of course
has it in its power to persecute, tolerate, countenance, or endow the
church ; but she did not originate and cannot destroy. Their spheres
and duties are separate and distinct, and need not come into collision.
If favors are proffered by the former, they should not be accepted by
the latter on any conditions which would trammel her in the discharge
of her duty, or compromise her rights, or interfere with her allegiance
to her *divine* head. Any protection which the state affords is more
than repaid by the services which Christianity renders to her citizens
in their civil and social relations. So that a connection between
them—where such a thing is possible—can only be justified when
formed on the basis of an *alliance* as between equals ; and should the
terms of the contract be violated by either party, the other may
resume its independent position.

Again : I do not find that Swedenborg has any where intimated (as
some have thought) that " the *perfection* of the church's government
has always kept pace with its internal corruptions." The reverse may

be concluded from numerous passages of his writings, of which it is only necessary to refer to the oft-repeated principle that " every internal should have an external" as its ultimate basis, or continent for its preservation and protection. I deny also that papacy *is* the most perfect form of Ecclesiastical Government. I dare not accord that character to any other form than such as was ordained by Christ, and which, as I hope I have proved, he designed to be perpetuated in the Church. Now Papacy is clearly an innovation, a predicted abuse, against which both Christ and his Apostles had repeatedly warned his followers. To pretend to improve on the divine pattern, is like an attempt to gild refined gold or to paint the lily. The symmetry of that model may be marred by superfluous additions as decidedly as by mutilation. Presbytery has denied the clerical rank to deacons and forbids the exercise of their original and most important functions : it has suppressed the order of bishops, usurped their prerogatives, and would cover the encroachment by sharing a part of their own rightful powers with the factitious class of " Ruling " Elders. This is mutilation. In the Papacy, one bishop has claimed precedence and superiority over all his peers; and in effecting that conquest he has likewise subdued all below them. The perfect trine of orders has been overshadowed by a fourth. It is as if a part of a pillar's capital had swelled beyond its due proportion and crushed the remainder together with shaft and pedestal to the earth. This oppressive despotism is an incubus,—a fungous excrescence—a sign of disease and not of health : an unnatural bump—a mark of deformity and not a trait of beauty. All government, moreover, was instituted for the benefit of the governed as well of the governors. The principle we oppose is true to a certain extent when predicated of civil arrangements. A *strong* government may be a more perfect machine than a liberal one for the *restraint* of a corrupt nation. But restraint is not the one object in the government of the Christian Church. Religion cannot be forced. The service we owe our master is a voluntary obedience to laws ordained for our good, which yet is not inconsistent with a due subordination among those who declare and execute those laws. In opposition to this, the Papacy pretends that " the church is one ;"—one, *not* because it consists of all throughout the earth who worship the Lord, acknowledge the sanctity of his Word, and obey his commands,—but because all Christians were handed over to the governance of one earthly head, who was also to be the guardian and interpreter of Scripture and supreme judge of controversies. But our doctrine was " revealed from heaven." When properly applied to Scripture it dissipates its obscurities. We seek also in the same scripture for the kind of government established by Christ and his Apostles, and do not find it to be a Roman or any other Papacy. It is not probable then that we shall ever apply to the bishop of Rome to clear up for us a point of faith, or ask his aid in governing ourselves, or request any other "Old Man of the Sea" to ferry us over such a strait; nor can I well conceive of any other ground on which he could proffer or we accept his services.*

* It gives us great pleasure to find that Mr. Cabell and we come together again ; and that we *most heartily agree with him here.—Ed.*

This assumption and abuse of power *has* been reduced to a more perfect system and more widely exercised by that bishop than was ever known elsewhere. What then? shall we therefore run to the opposite extreme and abolish the Episcopate entirely, hoping thereby to keep the clergy within proper bounds and all on a level? Do not the best things by corruption often become the worst? and is there no danger lest in our dread of tyranny we should forget the blessings of good government. We may suppress an obnoxious name, but is it as easy to get rid of the thing? Never was there a truer oracle than the annunciation, "God sends us bishops whether we will have them or not"? We may declare their seats vacant, but they will be filled nevertheless. We may forbid the exercise of their functions, but the church must and will be governed,—if not by the regular officers of God's appointment, by others self-constituted, or to whom the church will yield greater powers than are claimed by bishops. Is it not so? Has not Presbytery its Licentiate, Pastor, and Doctor of Divinity—a virtual trine in her ministry, despite her pretence of equality? Nay more, there are now, there ever have been Presbyters in such regime who wielded proportionally a greater power than any Protestant Bishop whatever. Not to speak of Calvin and Knox, does any one doubt that Alexander Henderson, Principal Robertson, or the late Dr. Chalmers held a greater sway in the Church of Scotland than did the contemporaneous Archbishops of Canterbury in that of England? It might not be proper to mention corresponding instances here both among Presbyterians and Congregationalists, but they do now and ever have existed. Presbyterians, like other associations of men, require a leader or leaders and will have them. Such a leader, at this day, is generally either a popular preacher, or a Professor of Theology, or, it may be, the irresponsible editor of a sectarian journal. But whoever he may be, his influence over the opinions of his people is wider and more potent than that of any of those "prelates" whose assumptions he is in the habit of denouncing.

It may be said that this is but the homage due to distinguished wisdom and piety, or a just return for services rendered. This may have been true of the three celebrated Scotchmen named above, but such unreserved confidence and submission is against the whole theory of their government and demonstrates that episcopacy or its equivalent is inevitable. Nor is it true that such ascendency has always been the reward of merit. It is a regular adjunct of their accidental position. Such leader may be a man of parts and learning, of comparative liberality, a friend to progress in sacred knowledge as in other things,—and, being also endowed with a spirit of command, he may have his greatness thrust upon him. Or, he may be a mere spiritual demagogue who has cultivated the arts of popular eloquence rather than solid attainments and has crawled up to his position by intrigue, or a forward zeal for what they call orthodoxy, viz: by flattering the mental indolence or sectarian prejudices of their followers; the which process consists simply in dressing up and *returning to the people their own opinions*, under the pretence of instructing them. But however the station may have been won, tolerable prudence and a little management will generally suffice for its maintenance to the end.

I have had opportunities of observing both systems in their operation, and the result of not very limited research and comparison is, that Episcopacy is intrinsically more favorable to purity of doctrine, because to the formation of public opinion by the *best* lights; more favorable to freedom of thought,—of inquiry (where the laity choose to exercise it),—to the open declaration of opinion,—to cautious procedure in general,—to stability of well-digested plans,—to harmonious co-operation and to regularly progressive improvement: more favorable to moderation of sentiment and expression,—to all the charities of life; and particularly is it more favorable to the selection of suitable incumbents for the pastoral office,—to the efficiency of its ministrations when addressed to minds docile and willing to concede the priesthood its rightful authority and no more, and to the preservation of the rights of all parties,—than is the opposite plan of Parity. This will sound to many like paradox, but it is not a hasty opinion and I honestly believe it to be true in every particular. Why should it not? Usurpations, interregnums, provisional governments are not wont to be less oppressive or exacting than those of a more regular character; neither is a Venetian aristocracy—to which Presbytery bears a much stronger resemblance than to the Constitution of our American Republic.

It is one of the axioms of free government that its legislative, judicial and executive departments should as far as possible be kept distinct; and that these should check and balance each other. In Presbytery they are necessarily blended. Corporations, we are told, have no souls: an unchecked Legislature no conscience. Where many *decide* individual responsibility is lost. We have also a homely maxim that " what is every body's business is no body's business." Or if somebody makes it his business, he has often to resort to intrigue and management for effecting a lawful and desirable end, lest he should encounter resistance and heartburnings, and the interest of the church may languish from neglect, while those who are willing to attend to it would also avoid the charge of presumption or officiousness. The objects of a church cannot be accomplished without the exercise of a certain amount of power. This would be dangerous, if accumulated either in a single man, or order, or body of men. But *power, properly distributed in several hands and duly recognized, is more conducive to the public service, and to individual liberty than when exercised solely by a corporate body, or by individuals who may be both unknown and irresponsible.* Again : "discerning of spirits" was one of the appropriate gifts of an Apostle. (1 Cor. 12 : 10.) How could this gift be more beneficially used by one who now exercises the same office than in judging the qualifications of aspirants to the several degrees of ministry ?—for which duty his own experience also should still farther fit him as he may be presumed to have passed through its corresponding degrees of spiritual preparation. (Com. A. C. 10017 with T. C. R. 146.)

Indeed, all presumption is in favor of a graduation of the clergy, and that a trinal graduation. For to whatever department of life we look,—whether civil, military or economical,—we may perceive the

same principle operating with more or less distinctness. Thus if we
regard our national territory as a whole—or as divided into states—
which again are subdivided into counties, or cities and towns,—we
also observe the powers of the government which embraces such territory, distributed among three departments,—the Legislative—the
Judiciary—and Executive. Again, in the legislative we see the House
of Representatives—the Senate—and the President with his power
of veto or approval of laws. In the Judiciary we have a judge of
appeals—a district judge—a justice of the peace. In the Executive,
in one aspect we note the President—the heads of departments, viz:
the Secretaries of state, war, the navy, the treasury—and under them
respectively, ambassadors to foreign states, commanders of the army,
and navy, and collectors of revenue. Another subordination is that
of the President—the Governors of states—the heads of corporations. A regiment, which is composed of battalions and companies,
has its colonel,—its major—its captains,—just as we read of captains
of thousands—of hundreds—of fifties—in the armies of old. In a
family there are parents—children—servants. In every art, or trade,
we have the apprentice—the fellows of the craft—the master-work-
man. Thus, to whatever quarter we turn our eyes, we observe
appearances which would indicate that society is constituted on the
principle that "he who would command must first learn to obey."
Do we therefore doubt that we are living under a free, republican
government? and should not he who asserts that in the church all
this is reversed, be prepared to demonstrate his position by the most
unequivocal proofs?

_____

I shall not invade your province by quoting from Swedenborg the
numerous passages I have noted as tending in a greater or less degree
to illustrate the view I have taken of this subject. I cannot however
complete or enforce what I have already written, without presenting
(and at the hazard of repeating things well known,) a few of those
which confirm it so directly, or lead to it by such inevitable inference
that I think nothing but strong prepossession or extraordinary ingenuity
can evade their force.

1. There are two things which ought to be in order amongst men, viz :
the things which are of heaven and the things which are of the world. . . .
Order cannot be maintained in the world without governors. . . . Who
should be persons skilled in the laws, wise ; and men who fear God. There
must also be order amongst the governors, lest any one, from *caprice* or *inadvertance,* should permit evils which are against order, and thereby destroy
it, *which is guarded against when there are superior and inferior governors,
amongst whom there is subordination.* . . . Governors over those things
amongst men which relate to heaven, or over ecclesiastical matters are called
priests, and their office is called the priesthood. (H. D. 311-314.)
2. Every one who traces effects to causes, may know that the consistence
of *all things* depends on order; and that there are *manifold* orders, general
and particular, and that there is *one* which is the most universal of all, and
on which the general and particular ones depend in a continued series; and
that the most universal one enters into all, as the essence itself into forms ;
and that thus, and *thus only* they make one : *this oneness is what causes the*

preservation of the whole which otherwise would fall to pieces, and not only relapse into the first chaos, but into nothing. . . . . These things may be illustrated to the natural man by innumerable things. . . . What would a kingdom, state, or house be without order, *unless some one in each should act as supreme ?* Besides, *what is order without* DISTINCTION *? and what is distinction without* INDICATIONS? *and what are indications without* SIGNS, *by which the qualities are known ? For without a knowledge of the qualities, order is not known as order.* The signs in empires and in kingdoms are TITLES of dignities and *rights* of administration *annexed to them ;* thence are *subordinations* by means of which all are arranged together as into one. . . . The case is similar in *very many other things.* (T. C. R. 679, 680.)

3. If the instruction, reformation, and salvation of souls be the principal end with a *priest,* whilst opulence and eminence are the means, then the man is spiritual ; whereas if these last are his principal end, he is natural. With a spiritual priest opulence and *eminence* are blessings, but with a natural they are curses. (Ath. Cr. 78.)

4. They who place worship solely in externals may perform vile offices in the church. . . . Such indeed are not servants in the Lord's Church on earth, for there are several of those who are in much pre-eminence, and who *preside over others,* who do nothing from charity and conscience, and yet observe the externals of the church very strictly, even to the condemning of those who do not observe them ; such, however, *inasmuch as they are not principled in charity and conscience, and place worship solely in externals without internals,* [N. B. *Not* because they are usurpers] are servants in the Lord's kingdom, that is in another life, for they are amongst the unhappy. (A. C. 1103.)

5. "And they that are with him are called, and chosen, and faithful." Rev. 17 : 14. They that are with him signifies all such as approach the Lord, for they are with him ; by the called, chosen, and faithful, are signified those who are in the externals, internals, and inmost principles of the church, who, because they are in the Lord, go to heaven. . . . For the Lord's *church* is distinguished, like heaven, *into three degrees ;* in the ultimate degree are they who are in its externals—and in the second—and third —the other two classes respectively. (A. R. 744.)

6. By "they shall have the priesthood." in Ex. 29 : 9, is meant the Lord's work of salvation in successive order. There are three things which succeed in order: the celestial principle,—the spiritual—the natural. . . . There are also three heavens, and in them goods in that order. . . . The work of the salvation of those who are in celestial good is represented by the priesthood of Aaron ;—of those in spiritual good—by that of the sons of Aaron ;—of those who are thence in natural good—by the priesthood of the Levites . . . who were given to Aaron and his sons that they might perform the ministry of the priesthood *under them.* (A. C. 10017.)

7. That good is the neighbor is evident from all experience. Who loves a person except from the quality of his will and understanding, that is, from what is good and just in him ? As, for example,—who loves a *primate,* a *minister,* or *canon* of the church. but for learning, integrity of life, and zeal for the salvation of souls ? (T. C. R. 418.)

8. The two states [of Reformation and Regeneration] are represented by various things in the universe, . . . *because they are according to divine order* . . . which fills all and every, the minutest thing in the universe. . . The first state is represented by the state of every student who is preparing for the ministry, before he becomes a *priest,* and of every priest before he becomes a *pastor ;* and then of every pastor before he becomes a *primate.* (Ibid. 106.)

9. It is well known, that in order to give perfection to *any thing,* there must be a TRINE in just order, one under another, and communication between them, and that such a trine constitutes one thing ; not unlike a pillar, over

which is the chapiter, under this the lengthened shaft, and under this again
the pedestal. Such a trine is *man*; his highest part being the head, his
middle part the body, and his lowest part the feet and soles of the feet.
Every *kingdom* in this respect emulates a man; in it there must be a king
as the head, also magistrates and officers as the body, and yeomanry with
servants as the feet and soles of the feet; in like manner in the *church*, there
will be a mitred *primate,** superintendant-*governors of parishes*, and *priests*
under them. (Cor. 17.)

Now, it does appear to me that these extracts, when read in series,
will hardly admit of more than one interpretation; for they mutually
illustrate each other, and their united force tends to the support of an
official trine in the ministry.   There must be order both in church
and state,—which is maintained by governors.   But among these there
must also be order, which again is secured by subordination among
themselves.   This general proposition is illustrated *here* by affairs of
state; but if the general tenor of the chapter and the relative position
of the statement do not prove it to be equally applicable to those of
the Church, this ought to be placed beyond a doubt by the universal
propositions which follow.   " What is order without distinction?
what is *distinction* without indications? and what are indications without *signs by which qualities are known?*"—And " with a spiritual
priest eminence is a blessing."   If there always have been, are now,
and ever will be three stages of regeneration, and three classes of
worshippers for whose salvation provision was made under former
dispensations by a similarly classified ministry, are we to suppose that
a like provision has been omitted under the New?   No!   Aaron—
his sons—and the Levites represented such a ministry in the Jewish
Church.   Such a ministry was "according to divine order" in the
first Christian Church.   And in the New Church " there will be
(erit) a mitred primate—superintendant—governors of parishes—and
priests under them."   " There will be," says our author, speaking by
authority, or from his foresight of the inevitable operation of causes
which are in the nature of things.   For in *every—perfect—one* thing
there must be *a trine* in just order, *one under another*, and communication between them.   And why should we not aim at perfection?
or as Paul has it " covet earnestly the *best* gifts?"   (1 Cor. 12 : 31.)
Such a trine is man.   The human form being made in the image of
God, is perfect order.   Every society when properly organized should
emulate that form.   This is true of the state.   This will be true of
the Church. And if a graded ministry were disorderly in itself, would
he have referred to it as an example of perfect order?   But lest I
should darken by an attempt to explain what is so clear in itself, and

---

* I have not seen the Coronis in the original, but Mr. Noble gives the passage in
Latin thus: " Similiter in ecclesia, primas infulatus, antistites parochi. et flamines sub
illis." From analogy I should take this to be the correct reading; for in the body of
the book (T. C. R. 16, 106, 381, 418, &c.,) he uses the word " primate " in similar
connexion as answering to one who is commonly called a *bishop*. And unless the term
" primus " refers here to an officer who is *the type of a class*, it would seem to favor
a papacy in the church, which would be inconsistent with the whole tenor of his writings.
I am prepared to defend the correctness of the translation in the text, but cannot enter
into verbal criticism here.

so entirely in accord with our previous deductions from the Scriptures and the History of the former Church, I leave the extracts to make their own impression.

Again: The *heavens* are especially the kingdom of the Lord, but the Church is his kingdom on earth. And the order of the Church on earth should as far and as fast as possible be a reflection of that in the heavens. Now, we not only read of high-priests in heaven, but Swedenborg has thrice repeated the remarkable statement, that in the year 1770 the Twelve Apostles were sent forth into the whole spiritual world to preach the truths of the New Church;—(T. C. R. 4, 108, 791,) —thus retaining their character, and performing for the New Church there, functions the same in kind with those which occupied them here. May we not then infer that there should be a corresponding office on earth?

Thus has Swedenborg written; what was his own practice? He was the son of a bishop; born and raised in an Episcopal Church. To it he ever conformed in life, *and to no other.* He submitted to a trial by its dignitaries for his alleged heresies, and received its last offices in death. Would he have done so, had he believed its constitution to be an usurping tyranny? and does his conduct in this regard throw no light on his opinions as to Church order?

To rebut these plain testimonies, we are told that Swedenborg has commented with severity on the tyrannical spirit and craft of the English hierarchy—(A. R. 341, 675, 716,)—while he has spoken more favorably of the state of the Scottish nation in the other life than of any other—(T. C. R. 812;)—and because the government of the Church of Scotland is Presbyterian, we must therefore believe that that form was most approved by him. It is true that in those Memorable Relations he has denounced the spirit and proceedings of certain English bishops *of that day when the Church had come to an end,* and has enumerated various arts by which they had strengthened their power. But so far from declaring their station to be an unlawful novelty, (for which there could not have been a more fitting occasion, had such been his belief,) *he suggested an expedient for the correction of such abuses without abolishing the hierarchy itself.* His character of the Scots is predicated only of *the laity* of that nation. The English and Scotch are both favorably reported, " but it was perceived that they had a two-fold theology, *and that from the doctrine of faith was held by those who are initiated into the priesthood,*" while the laity held the invincible doctrine of charity. This does not strike me as aiding the cause of Parity, for it was in spite and not in consequence of the perverse teachings of their priests that those people attained their spiritual elevation. Much too large an inference has also been drawn from the fact that Swedenborg sent some of his books to certain Professors in a Scottish University. For he sent them indiscriminately to the authorities of all the Protestant Churches, that they might all see how far they had deviated from the original standard; and though in his writings he labors most to correct their errors of doctrine, he might also have had in his eye the departures

25

from true order of which the "innovators" who had ruined the Church
—(T. C. R. 52,)—had also been guilty.

Other passages of the writings have been misconstrued to the same
end,—of which, however, I can notice but a few of the most important. In T. C. R. 55, we read thus:—"A kingdom . . . republic
. . . or family is established by laws which make the order, and thus
the form of its government. *In* each of them, . . . laws of *justice*
make the head, *political* laws the body, and *economical* laws the *dress*,
which last, like the dress may be changed. In the Church," he adds,
"*ceremonies* answer to the dress." From which we are desired to
infer that the *whole* external order of the Church may be changed
according to the supposed exigencies of its internal state. Now, I
have ever supposed that the question between a ministry of one or
three orders, went to the *constitution*, the organic or fundamental law,
and was *not* a mere ceremony, or matter of economy. The number,
gradation, and powers of officers in a state, define its civil constitution
or frame of government. Providence has sanctioned a variety of
these, and has permitted both them and the subordinate laws by which
they are set in operation, to be changed according to the character
and wants of nations. The constitution may be changed, the laws
remaining the same—as with the Jewish nation; or the former may
continue while the laws are altered, as in the alternations of a paternal
or tyrannical despotism. But the Church is *His* kingdom. He has
established its constitution. Its ceremonies, and rituals, and ordinances, are very different things from that, and however they may have
been changed, I think it has been shown that the order, the powers,
and duties of the priesthood have remained substantially the same
under all dispensations, and that "whatever is of *divine* order is a *perpetual* commandment of God." (A. C. 2634.) He may have permitted without approving the mutilation of that order at the Reformation; and yet the order established by Christ and his apostles may be
the best for the Church under all possible circumstances.

A like power of change has been inferred from another place where
he says, "Washings, *and many such like things* were enjoined on *the
sons of Israel*, as being a representative Church. . . . Of all *these*
things the Lord [at his advent when representatives were abolished]
retained only two—baptism and the holy supper, instead of washings and the feast of the passover." (T. C. R. 670.)—Here we see
a similar confusion of rites, to be observed by all Christians, with
the constitution of the priesthood, when not one word is said of the
latter.

There is as little pertinence in another passage which relates that
"because the ancient or typical Church [in process of time] converted
its representative correspondences into things magical or idolatrous,
Jehovah raised up the Israelitish Church, in which he restored the
primitive types which were celestial, (which is but a repetition of
what he had before given more briefly, that the Jewish Church was
the ancient Church resuscitated." A. C. 4835.) Among these types
were all things of the tabernacles, the feasts, sacrifices, *priesthoods*,
the garments of Aaron, &c., (Cor. 42.) Now, because types were

abolished at the advent, it is pretended that there should be in the Christian Church neither priesthood, nor gradation in the ministry. If the first point could be established, the other would remain to be proved. But, Swedenborg here only refers to the typical priesthood *which offered sacrifices* [as is shown in A. C. 9808] which was afterwards substituted by a *real* priesthood which should teach *compendiously by precepts* what those sacrifices signified. And we have abundantly proved from the Old Testament that there would be in the Christian Church both " priests and Levites," but that " the sons of Levi would be purified,"—or in the words of Paul, that the priesthood was " changed," and not abolished.*

Once more; Jehovah appeared as *three* men to Abraham : our Lord, as *one* man to John. Opposite inferences have been drawn from these facts as to the proper order of the Christian ministry! Will you pardon me for saying that I cannot see the relevancy of either to the question before us, or find that Swedenborg has used either fact for such a purpose ? Both Jews and Christians have fallen into serious errors concerning the Divine nature. The former believe in the simple unity of the Deity : most of the latter in his tri-personality. Omniscience foreseeing these things provided an antidote in his word. The fallacy of the Jews should have been prevented by the appearance to their progenitor : that of the Christians by the vision of John. Similar correctives of other evils were also provided, which was all that could be done consistently with man's freedom. Thus the Christian ministry degenerated either into the Papacy or a lordly hierarchy. Could this have happened, had they duly observed the injunction of the Master, " he that *is* greatest among you, let him be your SERVANT ?"

--

What now is the fair inference from the whole of the preceding argument ? It is that the programme of the Convention concerning the ministry, its gradation, powers and duties, as stated in her Constitution, (Articles 17 and 20,) and Declared Principles, (13, 15,) is substantially warranted by the Word and the writings of Swedenborg. The minister of the first grade should only preach and baptize:—of the second, may also celebrate the holy supper and marriage. To the third should be confined the power of ordination.

For the titles of the several functionaries I am not disposed to stickle. As an individual, I should prefer that of Minister or Deacon for the first grade :—that of Pastor or Elder for the second; and *Bishop* for the third,—as " Ordaining Minister " has the aspect of a timid or needless periphrasis, and I know of no reason why New-Church men should be afraid of a word. For an Apostle is but a bishop at large, or who is *sent :*—a bishop is but an *overseer,* or

---

* A priest (sacerdos) according to the derivation of the Latin term, " is one who offers up sacred gifts,"—that is, sacrifices. When the literal sacrifices ceased, this part of his duty was performed in offering up prayers, praises and thanks of the people. Swedenborg sometimes calls the Christian clergy " priests," and sometimes " teaching ministers," which would also go to show that he believed their office to embrace other duties besides that of teaching.

inspector of a part of the church and its ministry,—names, both of them significative of the office, and both modest enough in themselves. But if any single term could be found, expressive of the same functions and unclogged by ancient prejudice, it might be adopted as a substitute. And then as for that other terrible phrase "jure divino," I would simply ask my brethren whether they do not believe that our *doctrine* was "revealed *from heaven?*" and whether, in view of what we have cited above from A. C. 6822, *any* minister should presume to expound it publicly, except "by divine right," viz. by derivation from those who first received it providentially, or from some equivalent authority?

Rules of action command things either good, bad, or indifferent. The first are binding in their own nature, or by the command of God, —the second are not binding, although ordained by human authority. But the Church has a right to enact *ordinances* for the better government both of the people and clergy, or as "helps," (1 Cor. 12: 28,) for carrying out its general objects, provided these do in nothing contradict the commands or principles laid down in Scripture. Such rules or canons were ordained as general or convenient precedents, first by the Apostles, (1 Cor. 4: 17; 7: 17; 11: 2,)—afterwards by councils general or provincial; but in subordinate matters the bishops prescribed rules, each for his own diocese. In the New Church, for a long time to come, ordaining ministers cannot well have separate districts assigned them, to which their immediate jurisdiction will be limited; but, like the Apostles of old, must exercise their powers at large wherever Providence shall open a field for them. Yet I suppose that such canons as are here alluded to, would also be more properly suggested by them after consultation with the other clergy and representatives of the laity concerning the wants of the church, (though either of the latter are competent to propose them,) and the assent of the people, direct or implied, should be obtained before they become obligatory. The enactment of rules concerning matters purely ecclesiastical, or for the government of the clergy, may be safely confided to their own order, the rights of the laity being left entire. With these safeguards, no oppression can come to any; for liberty consists in obedience to wise and just laws and ordinances, to which we have given our assent; and if hindered by reluctance, "to *force one's-self* to do good and resist evil is freedom." (A. C. 1937.)

But farther: a church which professes to submit to the laws of Christ has a right to judge from outward indications of the sincerity or fitness of those who would join themselves to their society, and to censure or exclude from their communion, by the proper authorities, those who violate those laws. Less than this would expose any society whatever to corruption and ultimate ruin. More than this would transcend the proper limits of spiritual power. Accordingly we find the power of *discipline* given by the Scripture to the Church. Where one brother thinks himself injured by another, the rule of proceeding is laid down in Mat. 18: 15-17. If one brother is conscious of having injured another, the proper course is equally plain. (Mat.

5 : 23, 24.) Gross immorality,—heresy,—a factious, turbulent, divisive spirit, are occasions of interference by the officers of the Church. (Rom. 16: 17; 1 Cor. 5: 9–11; Gal. 5: 12; 2 Thes. 3: 6, 14; 1 Tim. 6: 5; 2 Tim. 3: 5; Tit. 3: 10; 2 John, 10, 11.) As each pastor is the leader and governor of his own society according to acknowledged rules,—the sacrament of the holy supper being also committed to him as the symbol of communion, to be withheld or imparted to each member according to his standing,—so each minister of the first and second grades should be willing to accept the guidance, where necessary, of him who ordained him, or of some other to whom it may be more convenient to transfer that relation. And as each pastor, when offences come under his own knowledge, or have been proved to the satisfaction of the church, should declare and apply the law to the case,—so, should any clergyman walk in a manner unworthy of his calling and to the injury of the cause, a like declarative and judicial power ought to belong to the ordaining minister, who in turn is amenable to those of his own grade. In harmony herewith are the declarations of Swedenborg. " Priests are *governors* over matters ecclesiastical,"—" appointed to *administer* those things which relate to the divine *law.*" " He who believes otherwise than the priest, and makes no disturbance, ought to be left in peace; *but he who makes disturbance ought to be separated ;* for this is agreeable to order, for the sake of which the priesthood is established." (H. D. 314, 319, 318.)

The ordaining minister should be chosen by the clergy and people directly or through their representatives, from the order of Pastors,—but he should be ordained by those of his own rank alone, and where convenient, three should unite in the ceremony. When thus elected and clothed with dignity and authority, honor and lawful obedience should be paid to the office, (H. D. 317,) and to the incumbent a reasonable maintenance in proportion to the ability of the people. (Mat. 10: 9, 10; 1 Cor. 9: 7, 11–14; 2 Thes. 3: 8. See also A. R. 799, which declares " the annual incomes and *stipends* of the clergy to be lawful, if the receivers be content with them.")

There is one other point which I would also suggest for the consideration of the Church. Does not Swedenborg in T. C. R. 685 recognise the propriety of " sponsors " in baptism? And does not the use of sponsors imply in the subjects of baptism the duty of being *confirmed* at an intelligent age? Such a rite existed in the early church, and the performance of it was one of the bishop's peculiar duties. It seems to be expressly referred to in Acts, 8 : 5, 12, 14–17; 19 : 1–7; Heb. 6 : 2; and by implication in Mat. 3 : 11; John, 3 : 5; Acts, 2 : 38; Tit. 3 : 5; 2 Cor. 1 : 22; Eph. 1 : 13; 4 : 30; and though it has fallen into disuse in some branches of the Protestant Church, it may be well to inquire whether it should not be restored in the New ?

Let us now, ere we close, look back and gather into one view some of the salient points on which we have touched.—This is a question, not of doctrine, or ritual, but of order and government, and as such is not to be confounded with the former. In our decision we should be guided by light drawn from the Scriptures of the Old and New Testaments, including in the latter the Acts and Epistles,—from Ecclesiastical History—the writings of Swedenborg—from Reason, and the experience of other churches. On this earth three churches preceded the advent of our Lord. In the first, although there was no formal priesthood, some of the duties of the office were performed by other persons, and among these there must have been a distinction of ranks. Since then the priesthood has ever existed as a separate class with its peculiar rights and duties. In the second Church there were grades in the office, and these must have been three; for besides that the two higher are expressly mentioned—we are told that the Jewish was a resuscitation of the Ancient Church which preceded it, and in that we know that there was a High-priest—priests—and Levites. Its ritual was changed shortly after the Exode, but the order of the priesthood remained the same. It was prophecied that in the Christian Church there should be a ministry with similar grades. Our Lord himself passed through those several degrees, as was adumbrated in his temptation :—proved by his commission thrice attested by a voice from heaven; and signified by his progressive labors in the three provinces of Canaan and his journeyings from Galilee, through Samaria, to Jerusalem. While himself acted as High-priest and Apostle, there were below him the subordinate ranks of the Twelve and the Seventy. The Twelve received three several commissions :—of their number, three were particularly distinguished ; and of these again, Peter was promised a three-fold commission, which was confirmed to him after his Resurrection. Before his Ascension, the power of ordination was delegated to the Twelve, who afterwards did ordain both Elders and Deacons as priests of the two lower ranks. That the Apostolic office was to be perpetual, is proved by the terms of their final commission : by the direct testimony of Paul; and by the fact that others were admitted to their rank during their lives, with the same title and rights, and with power to transmit the office, though the name was afterwards changed.   Under all these dispensations and changes a three-fold qualification was required for the priestly office, which also embraced a trine of duties, and to which the subjects were ever ordained, substantially in the same mode. Some would deduce the equality of Christian ministers from two passages in the Gospels, which, however, prove the very reverse, and have been otherwise misinterpreted. A passage in the Acts, and another in the Epistle to Timothy, which are offered to show that Presbyters ordained, equally fail of their purpose; and these are the sole pretended proofs of Parity from Scripture. We infer from various declarations of Swedenborg that the Anti-Nicene was a pure Church. The remains of an unbroken succession of writers extending from the Apostles' days to that Council attest the existence of a trinal ministry throughout the same period. Though much corrupted, the same order was preserved in the general Church until the Reformation. If Episcopacy was an usurpation, history preserves no record of its rise or of a time when it was not. And the passage from Jerome—the solitary

one from all the Fathers which is urged in proof of its being an innovation—again shows the very reverse. Thrice did our Lord declare
to the Twelve the spiritual nature of his kingdom; thrice did he
rebuke in them all unholy or worldly ambition, announcing at the
same time the indispensable condition of precedence among his servants. The government which he established, though admitting a
distinction among its officers, gives no encouragement to Popery—or
Erastianism—or arbitrary rule of any kind, but is alone compatible
with true liberty and the rights of all, and is the only one which
secures the peace, the purity, and the greatest efficiency of the church.
In the *fact* of Apostolic Succession we as New-Church men are but
little interested, seeing that a new ministry has been originated for us;
but the principle of preserving *a succession of ordainers from such
new origin* is both true and important, and if in practice we have
departed therefrom, we should return to the right path. *Factum valet;
fieri non debet.* From the writings and conduct of Swedenborg we
cannot but infer that he approved the same order. If then the principles and frame of the government established by Christ and his
Apostles in the Church may be clearly deduced from the Scripture:
if the same has never been repealed by his own or any delegated
authority: if, at the Reformation, any part of it was lost in certain
branches of the Old Church, by an apparent though regretted necessity; yet is it binding on us of the New,—should be preserved where
possessed—and restored where it has been laid aside.

When I sat down to write, Sir, I little thought that this letter
would have been drawn out to its present length. But my sense of
the importance of the subject and the number of considerations in
support of the view I have taken, have both so much increased on
me as I proceeded, that I find myself unable either to suppress or
abridge the exposition. I could not otherwise meet what I regard as
the mistakes of others, or give the reasons for my own opinion. That
opinion, as you know, was not my first opinion. My belief—inherited
and strengthened by the accidents of association—once was, that any
superiority of office claimed by Christian ministers must needs be an
usurpation. Accordingly I had vowed an unwavering resistance to
every species of ecclesiastical oppression, and to this among the rest.
When however I was constrained to surrender the doctrine of Faith
on which I then reposed, the obvious duty was also to revise my
every opinion relative to the Church, and to discard my most cherished
prejudices at the mandate of Truth. The reasons here embodied in
part have convinced me that the notion of the original parity of the
Christian clergy was a prejudice. If those reasons can be shown to
be either fallacious or insufficient, I shall be ready to resume my
former position. But viewing the subject as I now do, I should
tremble to invade or mutilate that constitution of the ministry which
was established by the Lord himself while in the flesh : which has an
indefinite previous antiquity in its favor; and without which I feel
assured that the virtue of the heaven-descended doctrine of the New
Jerusalem can never be fully applied for the healing of the nations.

I have not the presumption to think that any thing I could offer should claim attention as such, nor do I desire that it should carry a weight which is not derived from its own merit—if any it have. Neither am I a volunteer in this cause. At your instance have I written, but the truth was first sought with diligence, and I hope with impartiality. For being a layman, with nothing to hope personally from an increase of clerical power, it cannot be said that I am striving to magnify my own office; whereas the same arguments, if presented by an ordaining minister, might be thought to take their form or coloring from an unsanctified proprium as their source. Should such a suspicion bias inquirers, it would not be unlawful to suggest a similar caution to the advocates of another order. We learn from Swedenborg that the Protestants of his day were still greatly under the dominion of the Catholics, *because the former had retained so many of the false doctrines of the latter.* (A. R. 751.) Would it not be well then, (as Mr. Noble has intimated,) for the friends of Parity seriously to inquire whether themselves may not be under the spiritual influence of JOHN CALVIN, the real author of the fabric, which, while it has at times afforded a refuge for every heresy that has distracted the Church, at others, under the semblance of liberty, has sheltered a spiritual tyranny worse than could elsewhere be found in the whole Protestant world?.

I remain, Sir, very truly yours,

N. F. CABELL.*

NOTES TO THE LETTER ON THE TRINE IN THE MINISTRY.

("Paul was an Apostle long before." p. 32.) Since this was written, I have thought it expedient to subjoin some proof of the assertions in the text. Paul was converted A. D. 35. Of this event we have three narratives in the Acts:—one by Luke, (9: 3–22,) and two by himself, (22: 1–16; and 26: 12–20.) Luke relates only in part what the Lord said to him on that occasion, as also does Paul in his address to the Jews at Jerusalem; but in his defence before Agrippa he gives it as follows;—"I have appeared unto thee *for this purpose—to make thee* A MINISTER AND A WITNESS both of those things which thou hast seen AND of those things in the which I will appear unto thee, delivering thee from the people *and from the Gentiles,* unto whom NOW I SEND thee, to open their eyes," &c., (vs. 16–18.) Is not the meaning here very plain! What other terms could better convey the idea that Paul was then commissioned as an Apostle, directly by the Lord, who appeared to him for that purpose? Some have supposed that Ananias, to whom the Lord appeared shortly afterwards, was sent to ordain him because " he laid his hands " on Paul. (9: 17.) But Ananias was not

* Though we have presumed to differ from him in some immaterial respects, we very sincerely thank Mr. Cabell for this elaborate and most able argument of his side of the question; and we do not doubt that the church at large will feel the same sentiment. Brought up in the school of parity he has become the advocate of episcopacy; while we, brought up an episcopalian, have become decidedly opposed to episcopacy, although not in favor of parity. We do not believe that the trine necessarily involves episcopacy or is identical with it. And all our reading, both of the Word and of ecclesiastical history, in reference to this report, has convinced us, that episcopacy, as it exists in the present day, has no just foundation in the order of the apostolic church, and is nearly if not quite, as " clearly an innovation" on that order as papacy. But in Mr. Cabell's other conclusions generally we coincide, and with his able argument for the trinal order we heartily concur.—*Ed.*

a minister at all that we know of.* He is here called "a disciple," (v. 10,) and afterwards by Paul "a devout man according to the law and well reported of the Jews;" (22 : 12,)—most probably therefore, he was a layman and only secretly a Christian. The same narrative states (9 : 12, 17,) that he was sent "that Paul *might receive his sight* and be filled with the Holy Ghost"—gifts then often exercised by private Christians, through the laying of hands, as was promised by the Lord before his ascension. (Mark 16 : 17, 18.) His appearance to Ananias also answered another purpose. It enabled him to confirm Paul's testimony concerning himself. For when the other Apostles distrusted his pretensions in his new character, Barnabas, who may have received his information from Ananias, removed their suspicions. (Acts 9 : 26-28.) If the laying on of Ananias' hands was the *act* of ordination,—the words of the Lord being merely the previous appointment to the Apostleship—how are we to reconcile such an hypothesis with the word of Paul elsewhere, "Paul, an Apostle—not *of* men [not a false Apostle] —neither *by* man† [not called and ordained in the ordinary way]—*but by Jesus Christ?*" (Gal. 1 : 1.) By this I understand that Paul, unlike the Eleven who had passed through the lower grades,—unlike Matthias who was appointed by lot,—was called directly and audibly by the Lord himself from the ranks of the laity to the highest grade of the priesthood, just as Minerva was fabled to have sprung all-armed from the head of Jove, or as one in whom is the spirit of command, is sometimes taken from the class of citizens to head an army.‡

Now the occurrence related in Acts 13 : 1-3, took place A. D. 45, ten years after Paul was called to the Apostleship, during which interval he had preached to the Jews in various cities. If then this *was* an ordination, it was *the second* which Paul had received, and in that way refutes the claim of Parity. But it is not said to be an ordination in Scripture. The Holy Ghost said "*Separate* me Barnabas and Saul to *the work* whereunto I have called them,"—viz: a mission to the Gentiles. But Paul's commission as received ten years before embraced them prospectively as well as Jews, though this part of his work was not entered on until now. *God* makes Apostles and sets them in the church, as he makes and sets the hand, eye or tongue in a human body.§ (1 Cor. 12 : 28, 18.) But the Church, which is his body, according as it is enlightened by Him, may, as in this case, assign an Apostle his field of labor or particular work, just as, to use the words of Swedenborg, "the body assigns to each member its task and allowance."‖ Prayer and imposition of hands are used for other purposes besides those of ordination. A minister we know is helped by the prayers of his people or brethren; (Rom. 15: 30; 2 Cor. 1 : 11; Phil. 1 : 19; Philemon 22.) And in the laying on of

---

* He was made a minister for this purpose, as Robert Hindmarsh was.—*Ed.*

† In our opinion this refers to Paul's reception of the Gospel, and the command to teach it—not to his reception of the *powers* of the holy spirit by that ultimate representative and significative rite, without which in his external man there could not possibly be that consociation of angels and spirits with him, whereby illustration in teaching it could alone flow into him from the Lord. Timothy received the Gospel by prophecy, that is, by preaching of Paul and the other apostles; but Paul received it not "of man,"—that is not from man as its source, nor "by man," that is not through man as the medium of its communication, but from the Lord immediately.—*Ed.*

‡ We cannot think this, because there is to our mind no just reason why the Lord should establish an order in regard to the eleven, and violate it, or deviate from it, in regard to Paul.—*Ed.*

§ True; but in this ordination God acts *mediately* as well as immediately. He acts immediately in calling, and mediately in ordaining. He called Paul by immediate influx, and he mediately ordained him. And we have shown in a previous part of this report that the Lord does not ordain through heaven and the church as mere passive instruments of his divine operation; but that the church and heaven as his body ordain from him as its soul, as the humanity operates from the divinity in him. Ananias, and the church at Antioch, were but the hands of the christian heaven in the spiritual world, and the christian church in the natural world, as the Lord's body.—*Ed.*

‖ This is ordination, and nothing else.—*Ed.*

their hands—significative of *blessing*—spiritual strength or *power* may have been imparted to aid him in his novel enterprise. What was here done, is afterwards only spoken of as " *a recommendation of them to the grace of God* for the fulfilling their work." (Acts 14 : 26.) But the same expression is also used concerning Paul and Silas when the former, after his separation from Barnabas, had taken the latter for his companion. (15 . 40.)

2 "The Church of Christ in its origin was neither Popish nor Erastian." p. 73. Christ was crucified *between two thieves*. And his Church, while on her errand of mercy through the world, was waylaid successively by two bandits in the forms of Popery and Erastianism. In escaping from the first she fell into the power of the second ; and each from having been her protector became her oppressor in turn. The example of our own country and the signs of the times in Europe betoken her ultimate rescue from both. One of the thieves repented. If conjecture on such a subject were allowable, I should infer that it must have been he who was the type of the political bandit.

VI. A BRIEF ARGUMENT FOR THE TRINE FROM THE WRITINGS OF THE CHURCH. BY THE REV. DAVID POWELL.

Having been called upon to give my views of what the writings of the new church teach respecting this subject, I take the leave to submit the following observations on the trine in the ministry.

There has been so much said and written on the subject of a trine in the ministry of the new church, that it might seem unnecessary to have any thing more said. This may be the case. And certain it is, that had all the members of the ecclesiastical council belonging to the Central Convention examined the Word and the writing, of Swedenborg, as they once agreed among themselves to do, for the purpose of making a combined report to the church, the undersigned would not now take up his pen to offer any thing to his brethren on the subject. But this was not done. It is, therefore, on account of the course the investigation has taken in the Central Convention, that of individual reports, that he feels called upon to give a frank expression of the honest convictions of his own mind, formed as he sincerely trusts from the express teachings of the writings of the church.

It may be said in truth that he does not expect to offer any thing to the church which her members do not already possess, because *they too* have the Word and the writings of our illuminated author. The main design is, to express his concurrence in the view, *that there is a personal trine in an orderly arrangement of the formal ministry of the new church;* and at the same time to turn the attention of his brethren to some of the authorities, which have produced in his own mind this conviction.

In justice to himself, as well as to the subject, the remark is here made, that the duties of the ministerial office in which he is now actively engaged, are so onerous, that he has not sufficient time for a full investigation of this point of church order. But it is his duty, as a member of the ecclesiastical council of the Central Convention, to give to the church this plain and unvarnished expression of his views. And he respectfully asks attention to these few points to be made—these few authorities to be adduced, and their application to the subject before us.

It is scarcely necessary to say that the desire is sincerely felt by the undersigned to address the receivers of the heavenly doctrines of the New Jerusalem as brethren of the same common faith, who have, or ought to have, the same common end in view. This end should be the advancement of the Lord's kingdom in heaven and on earth, by spreading a knowledge of the truth, and inculcating a life according to that knowledge. So that, when we come to make an application of truth to the external or formal order of the church, it should be done for the sake of internal order. With such feeling, and such desire, does the writer address his brethren.

It might seem strange that any great difference of opinion should exist among the members of the new church on any point, at least such as could not be easily harmonized without the sacrifice of any vital principle; inasmuch as they claim to have the same qualified Teacher, one whom all acknowledge and profess to confide in as the highly illuminated and divinely commissioned servant of the Lord. Were we left without this guide, different indeed would be the case. Nothing better than the old church would be our condition. In fact it would not be *the* new church. Were this our situation, then might *individual opinions* be called for. But it is believed that the Lord has, in his mercy, provided a safe expounder of His Word in a well qualified teacher of the genuine doctrines of His Church. So that it is only left necessary for the professed receivers of these doctrines to learn them understandingly, and consistently reduce them to practice. This being the case, the mere *opinions* of men need no longer be sought for as guides in ecclesiastical matters. And it appears to the undersigned that so long as *men's opinions* are called for, however good, however well educated, or high in authority those men may be, just so long there is danger of man's self-derived intelligence being inflated. There is danger that its fire and infatuated light may fill the mind to the exclusion of the Lord's love and wisdom. With much and deep regret has the undersigned heard, at various times and in different ways, the members of the church invoked to give *their opinions* on *this* or *that* important subject, instead of meekly asking them, What do the doctrines of the church teach on such subjects? The learned, the wise, the good, should only be asked to impart what the Lord has given them by the teaching of the church. For when *opinions* are asked, the natural tendency, in such form of appeal, is to turn the mind to *proprium* for them, instead of having it turned at once to the only true source—the Lord, in His Word and the writings of His illuminated servant. May not the difficulty now existing among the members of the new church, of seeing the true nature of the trine in the ministry, and its true application to just order in the church, be caused, in some measure at least, by the *manner* of asking for the information needed. Such has been the present writer's views for some time; and hence he has made allusion to that form of expression in this place. Most that has been written on the subject of a *trine* in the ministry from time to time has been carefully read by him, and he is sorry to say that much of it appears to him to be mere assumption and bold declaration, the natural offspring of *mere opinion*.

There is certainly a great difference between mere assertion and argument, or between mere opinions and the express teachings of the church. To these truths he would kindly call the attention of his brethren, when they may hereafter be examining the productions of reports or other documents on this or other subjects, that they may make a proper discrimination and act wisely. Humility is a grace much needed, and it is much to be feared that the way *opinions* have many times been called for, has not had the tendency of cultivating that christian virtue.

The foregoing remarks have been made without intending any disrespect to his brethren who may differ from him. He felt a wish to call their attention to this view of the matter, to press it affectionately upon their minds, and ask their prayerful attention to it. All will admit that the difficulty is not *in the doctrines of the new church*, but that it is *in the imperfect understandings of men*, and the perversions to which they are prone. How much more need then have we to turn from our own mere opinions, and to seek in humility to be led by, and taught of, the Lord in his Word and in the writings of his church.

It may be said in truth that many dangers surround us in the investigation of this as well as other points of church order. Dangers to which every mind is more or less exposed, because "Heresies are ever attendant on the true church, and the ground of heresy is the being intent on some particular article of faith, and giving that the precedence; for such is the nature of man's thought, that whilst he is attentive to some one particular thing, he prefers it to another, *especially when his imagination claims it as a discovery of his own*, (I italicise,) and when self-love and the love of the world conspire to work upon the imagination; in this case every thing tends to administer fresh proof and confirmation of his opinions, so that he is ready to attest their truth in the most solemn manner, when nevertheless they may be utterly false." (A. C. 362.) And who, it might be asked, is entirely free from the influence of self-love and love of the world? Is there not therefore great need of humility in these examinations, lest *our opinions* should be permitted to take the place of the express teachings of the church? That an *opinion* can be confirmed, is no evidence of its truth, because men may be only in the appearances of truth, and may reason very plausibly and even cunningly from such appearances, so as to make the doctrinal tenet, once embraced, whatever be its quality, appear like truth. The first thing then, with a man who would act wisely, is to see truth to be true. For "nothing is less the part of a wise man, yea, nothing is less rational, than to be able to confirm falses; for it is the part of a wise man, and it is rational, to see first that a thing is true, and next to confirm it, inasmuch as to see what is true, is to see from the light of heaven, which is from the Lord, whereas to see what is false as true, is to see from a delusive lumen, which is from hell." (A. C. 4741.) From this passage may be learned the first step to be taken in the matter before us, which is, *that the point of order be seen to be true.* It becomes the duty of the Newchurchman, then, to see first whether the trine in the formal ministry of the new church, when in just order, is to be in one grade of persons only, or in three. Or in other words, whether there should be a person acting officially in each degree of the trine to represent such degree, and thus have three grades or classes of officiating ministers, or to have all the degrees or grades of the trine always represented in one and the same person at the same time. This is first to be seen, because it is admitted by all receivers of the doctrines that there is a trine some how or other existing in the priesthood of the new church.

The question then arises as to how this point of order is first to be seen to be true, before it receives confirmation. For, if there should be but one grade, or class of priests or ministers in the new church that a trine in just order may be formed therein, thus one person always and at the same time officially to represent the trine, then this fact, if fact it be, must first be seen to be true, before it is confirmed, if the church would act wisely. Just so, on the other hand, if there should be three grades or classes of priests or ministers in the new church that a trine in just order may be formed in her formal ministry, thus that there must be three persons at the same time to represent officially the trine in the ministry; then this fact, if fact it be, must first be seen to be true before it is confirmed, if the church would act wisely.

This the undersigned thinks a fair and impartial statement of the case to be decided. And it certainly is an important one—one in which the church should act with great caution.

And how is the truth of the case to be seen? Certainly not by invoking mere opinions originating in our propriums; for Swedenborg tells us that man's self-hood " is in utter darkness respecting all things which relate to heaven and the church." (U. T. 233.) It is not therefore innate in man, but must be learned. Where, then, can the new church learn this truth so as to see it to be true, but in the writings of Swedenborg, which the Lord in mercy has caused to be written for the instruction of His Church. It is not to be sought in the Word itself without doctrine, because " The Word without doctrine is unintelligible." Hence it is said, that " They who read the Word without doctrine are in the dark concerning every truth; and that their minds must be.wavering, and unsettled, prone to errors, and *easily betrayed into heresies which they will even embrace with eagerness, in case they are supported by the authority and favorable opinion of mankind, and that they may do it with a safe reputation.*" (U. T. 228.) According to this passage the only correct way of seeing the trinal order in the new-church ministry in the Word itself, is to see it according to the doctrinal teaching of the church. It must, therefore, first be ascertained *how* the trine in the ministry is, and *what* it is, from the writings of Swedenborg, which are believed to teach the true doctrines of the new and true christian church, and to reflect the light in which the Word may be understood.

What then are the express teachings of our author, in which, as true doctrine, a light is given forth, which may enable the church to make a wise decision? Has he expressly taught, in any part of his writings, that, in the external or formal ministry of the new church, there should be but one grade or class of priests, that a trine in just order may be formed? If he has so expressly taught, in any part of his writings, he will certainly not contradict it in any other part. It must, therefore, be regarded as unquestionably true; and, when so seen, it may be rationally confirmed, by any one acting wisely. But, with due respect to the feelings and opinions of his brethren, the undersigned begs leave to say that he has not found any such direct teaching in the writings of Swedenborg, while engaged in reading them; nor has he seen any such direct teaching adduced by any writer holding the opinion that there should be but one grade or class of ministers in the new church. He has, on this account, been at a loss to know how it could first be seen to be true, (and still not quoted,) before the attempt was made to confirm it. If Swedenborg has said any where in his writings, in plain terms, that there should be but one order, grade, or class of priests in the new church, the undersigned, for one, would be most thankful to have the place cited. He is well aware that the advocates of that order in the ministry of the new church often say that there should be but one; but he feels bound to discriminate between what they say and what Swedenborg says; and also between the reasonings which they use to confirm their own sayings, and the rational arguments which may be used to establish and confirm the truth of what Swedenborg clearly teaches. This discrimination is necessary, because there is a difference between assertion and argument.

We repeat, then, as the writings of Swedenborg are received in the new church as full authority on this subject, it certainly rests fairly upon those who hold that there is but one degree or grade of ministers in the true church, that a trine in just order may be formed therein, to show that Swedenborg has so taught, in terms clear, plain, and in harmony with all his doctrinal teachings. Until they can produce the book, page, or number, they cannot, with propriety, ask others to believe it. When this is done, then arguments in its defence may be listened to. And here we leave them to go in search of proof.

But on the other hand, has Swedenborg expressly taught, any where in his writings, that in the external, formal ministry of the new church, there should be more than one grade or class of ministers, so that a trine in just order may be formed therein? If he has so taught, he will assuredly not contradict it in any other part of his teachings. True, he may, in one place, explain the meaning of what he has said in another; but he will not contradict it by teaching the opposite. His system is coherent throughout. As it is important, then, to *start* right, the direct teaching of Swedenborg is first sought, and kindly offered to the reader. By turning to the Coronis or Appendix to the True Christian Religion, what he *has* distinctly taught on the subject may there be found. As many persons in the church, who may read and feel an interest in this matter, may not have that little work to refer to, the whole of No. 17 is here inserted, in which the distinct teaching may be seen.

It is a well known truth, that in order to give perfection to any thing, there must be a TRINE in just order, one under another, and that there must be communication between the members of the trine, and that such a trine constitutes one thing; not unlike a pillar, over which is the chapiter, under this the shaft, and under this again the pedestal. Such a trine is man; his supreme part is the head, his middle part the body, and his lower part the feet and soles of the feet. Every kingdom, in this respect, is like a man; in it there must be a king* as the head, also magistrates and officers as the body, and yeomanry with servants as the feet and soles of the feet; in like manner in the church, there must be a mitred prelate, parish priests, and curates under them. Nor does the world itself subsist, without three things following each other in order, namely, morning, noon, and evening; also every year, spring, summer, and autumn; the spring for sowing seeds, the summer for their growth, and the autumn for their bringing forth fruit: but night and winter do not contribute to the stability of the world. Now since every perfect thing must be a trine, in order to be a regular coherent unity, therefore both the spiritual and the natural world consists of, and subsists from, three atmospheres or elements; the first of which proximately encompasses the sun, and is the aura; the second is under it, and is the ether; and the third is under them both, and is the air. These three atmospheres in the natural world are natural, in themselves passive, because they proceed from a sun which is pure fire; but the three atmospheres corresponding to them in the spiritual world are spiritual, in themselves active, because they proceed from a sun which is pure love. The angels of the heavens dwell in the regions of these three atmospheres; the angels of the supreme heaven in the celestial aura, which proximately encompasses the sun, where the Lord is; the angels of the middle heaven in the spiritual ether, under them; and the angels of the lowest heaven in the spiritual-natural air, under them both. Thus all the heavens are co-established, from the first to this last, which is building by the Lord at this day. Hence it may be perceived, whence it is that by three in the Word is signified what is complete; see the Apoc. Rev. n. 505, 875.

From this number now, the reader may not only see that Swedenborg does distinctly teach three grades in the formal ministry of the new church in express terms, but it may also be seen that he illustrates it by things that exist.

The Latin passage of the author is, "Similiter in Ecclesia, Primus Infulatus, Antistites Parochi, et Flamines sub illis." Give now what translation you please to these words, the fact of there being distinctly the *three grades or classes of officers,* is not altered. The peculiarity of each, it is true, may not be very distinctly understood; but it should be remembered that inability on the part of any one to understand a fact, is no justification for its denial. It is the *fact* itself concerning which inquiry is now made. And the *fact* declared by Swedenborg is, that in like manner in *the church,*—yes, *in the new church signified by the New Jerusalem in the Revelations, because it is of this church that the author is positively speaking,*—there must be, or will be, (which you please,) the three classes or grades which he

* In the New Jerusalem and Its Heavenly Doctrines, Swedenborg says "where such a form of government prevails," which only explains his meaning; but one place does not conflict with the other. He is only referring to the highest office in a civil government, and the highest officer, who may be a king or may be designated by another name.

mentions. The first, or that which is the highest in orderly arrangement, is *the "Primus Infulatus."* Consequently, the next, which are the "*Antistites Parochi*," must be ministers of a secondary rank, but still who stand before others; because the next grade or class mentioned, "*Flamines*," are "*sub illis*," under these, that is under the "*Antistites Parochi*"

The argument now offered is—Swedenborg has written this passage, in a crown to that work, in which we are assured there are " truths continuous from the Lord."[*] This passage asserts a fact, namely, that there will or must be three grades of ministers in the church. Therefore this fact must be a truth from the Lord. Consequently, it is to be believed, as a matter of fact, by every receiver of the heavenly doctrines. And it is right that it should be received, as one of those doctrines. Assuming then, that this is a truth, distinctly, clearly, plainly taught as a doctrine of the new church, we conclude that Swedenborg cannot contradict this doctrine either plainly or by implication, in any other passage of his writings; and the argument, that we ought not to conclude this to be a doctrine of the church, because Swedenborg teaches it *in only* ONE *passage*, is fallacious. Equally, nay much more, fallacious would it be to argue, because Swedenborg *has taught in only one passage of a posthumous work*, that there will be a *trine of grades*, THEREFORE in all the passages of the works published by himself he must necessarily teach that there will be *but one grade* of ministers in the church. On the contrary, may we not argue conclusively, that as Swedenborg *does* here unequivocally teach that there will be a trine of priestly officers in the church, therefore this is a truth, which, seen to be true, may be confirmed by the light of all the truths which his writings teach? For do not his writings throughout most distinctly teach that there is a trine in *every thing*; and, therefore, there must be a trine in the priesthood, wherever and whenever one exists as *a thing*. And do not those writings expressly declare the universal existence of both discrete and continuous degrees; so that every thing which exists has both; and therefore the priesthood, wherever it exists as a distinct thing, must have both also. Here, then, the undersigned takes his stand and start. In the spiritual light of truths taught from the Lord by his servant Swedenborg he fully believes that he *sees* the passage to be true because it is true, and *that too*, before any effort is made to confirm it.

And now, most seriously, can any mere declaration of any man, in howsoever much of candor and honesty such declaration may be made, that the order of the ministry for the new christian church admits of no distinction of superior or inferior degrees among the clergy, be a sufficient offset against the clear and positive teaching of our illuminated author? This position of the case is now most distinctly shown to every reader, and all are most affectionately invited

---

[*] " The church is totally ignorant of its desolation and consummation, and cannot know any thing of it, *until the* DIVINE TRUTHS *revealed by the Lord* in the work entitled True Christian Religion, are seen in the light and acknowledged." (*Con. of Cor.* LV.)

to look at it humbly—in the true light of the church from the Lord. It would really seem that all that need be done by any one, would be to satisfy himself that Swedenborg actually used the language of this passage, in order to be convinced of three grades in the formal ministry of the new church, and to be able to decide at once between what *that* author *says*, and what *others say*, and *argue* from their own assumptions. Much turning, twisting, and attempts at explanation are resorted to, in order to get round and do away with the force of the clear and positive language here used by Swedenborg; but still it stands here a stubborn fact, in strict harmony with the whole system of doctrines in which it is found.

We have just hinted, that some of our brethren to get over this difficulty in their efforts to pull down the grades of the clergy, and so to make an easier access to natural inclination—some of our brethren, in order to do away with the force of this clear and express teaching of our author, have called it a "mere passing remark in a posthumous work." (See Journal of W. Conv. 1847, p. 28.) What now can be meant by this but a direct insinuation that either the work itself in which it is found is *not genuine*, or that Swedenborg would use "passing remarks" *in which* the church should not have confidence, or by the *light of which* they should not be guided? But is either position correct? Was using mere "passing remarks" indifferently, that author's habit? The undersigned must declare, that he has not so regarded him, neither does he so read him. And he is much mistaken if his brethren in general can so receive it, when they come to reflect upon the matter, and are led to see the dangerous precipice to which it inevitably conducts them. There is and can possibly be only one sense in which this is a *passing* remark—namely, that those who wish to get rid of it because it is against their systems, *pass* it in *their* remarks upon Swedenborg's *propositions*. For in his work it is no *remark* at all. It is a part of a continuous thread in a well woven argument to prove this proposition—"it is a well known *truth,* that in order to give perfection to *any thing*, there must be a TRINE in just order, *one under* another; and that there must be communication between the members of the trine; and that *such a trine constitutes* ONE THING." This is a *truth* as a *universal law*, which Swedenborg lays down and proposes to establish; and any thing which he says in the paragraph is the specification of a *particular known truth* for the proof, illustration or confirmation of this *general* or *universal one.* Hence to regard *this* particular sentence of the paragraph containing the argument on the above proposition as "a passing remark," which may be set aside as not expressly teaching a universal truth to the church, namely, that there must be in every thing a trine and therefore a trine of officers in the church, is just the same as contending that in architecture a pillar should consist of only one continuous shaft, and not of three discrete sub-ordinate parts, or that man should be as it were a huge *worm* instead of a body with three discrete parts, or that in a kingdom there should be officers in only one continuous grade, and not in three discrete grades; because, forsooth, although Swedenborg does indeed specify these instances to show how there

26

should be a trine in every thing, yet these are mere "passing remarks in a posthumous work," which do not prove authoritatively that there shall, will, or must be three discrete grades of constituent parts in the particular things which he specifies! To what fatal *passes*, then, may we not be brought by this theory of passing remarks by Swedenborg? Only reflect a moment—if that principle of construing or disposing of portions of Swedenborg's writings were once admitted to be correct, or introduced into the church, where then would the safety of the church be? Cannot every individual see the dangerous door that would be opened? Every portion of his heavenly teaching that might come in conflict with the favorite opinion of any one, previously formed in the mind from the prejudice of education, or grounded in the love of self or love of the world, would soon be disposed of by being made a mere "passing remark." If it can be admitted in any single case, why not in another; and then where would it end? Swedenborg would no longer be confided in as authority from the Lord. For one, the undersigned most solemnly protests against any such mode of disposing of what the illuminated servant of the Lord has written touching the interests of the church, which are the good of mankind.

It is a posthumous work! This is granted. It was printed and published after the author's demise. The only question, however, that need arise is, did Swedenborg write the little book? and did he write the little book *after* he wrote the big book? Who that receives his writings doubts this? Therefore, if *he wrote* it, how could the *mere time* of its *publication* effect its genuineness, or take one whit from its authoritativeness as an addendum to the Universal Theology of the New Heaven and the New Church? Nay, on the other hand, does not the fact of its having been written after his having so long enjoyed illumination and intromission into the spiritual world, rather add to its authority, if any thing, than detract from it? Shall the *Coronis* to the *True Christian Religion*, in which "THE LORD has revealed DIVINE TRUTHS," be deemed to have less wisdom than that to which it is a sort of cap-stone? Surely, the mere circumstance of its having been printed and published after Swedenborg's death, does not avail to stigmatize any of its contents, as the *mere passing remarks* of that consummately wise man, expressed before his death, when he was in the full corn in the ear of his fully ripened wisdom! Consequently, its being a posthumous work can be no objection to the work, nor argument against the authority of its teachings.

And now if these remarks should fall into their hands, as it is hoped they may, and be read by those giving utterance to the passage in question, that it is a "mere passing remark in a posthumous work," the writer most affectionately beseeches them, as brethren professing the faith of the new church, to reconsider the matter, and see whether they will not, upon sober reflection, be disposed to view it quite differently. Can they not see that the same objection could be urged against the Apocalypse Explained, as well as other of the author's writings. There can be no doubt but the work is genuine, and all its

doctrines sound.   Therefore, order requires that there should be a personal trine in the formal ministry of the new church, because Swedenborg says, in like manner in the church there must be, or will be, the
three degrees or grades which he there mentions.

Reader, please now look at the whole matter in a spirit of candor,
and from a desire of seeing the truth, and see whether the whole
does not strictly agree with the principles of truth which the author
is there teaching—yea, see if you do not discover that it constitutes
an essential part of that teaching, because the Coronis itself is "treating of the four churches on this earth since the creation of the world;
and of their periods and consummation; of the new church about to
succeed them, which will be truly christian, and the crown of the
preceding churches; of the advent of the Lord to that church, and of
his divine auspices therein to eternity," &c.   Look, and you will find
in the Fifth Lemma, in which is number seventeen, where the passage occurs as quoted above, and about which so much has been said,
that the author is speaking directly of the formation of the new
heaven and the new earth, which earth he tells us means a new church.
In number fifteen of this Lemma he says, " The Lord Jehovah, when
He founds a new heaven and a new church, introduces *order*, (I
italicise,) *that they may stand under His auspices, and under obedience to
Him, to eternity, because the angelic heaven and the church on earth
constitute together one body, whose soul and life is the Lord Jehovah,
who is our Lord and Saviour.*"   Is it not perfectly plain, from this,
that Swedenborg speaks in reference to introducing *order* into the new
heaven and the *new church*—is not such order and the great importance of it, the very object which he has in view in speaking—is he not
illustrating and showing its great necessity, to the end "that they
may stand under his auspices," &c.?   Such is the connection in which
this passage is written; and how then can it, with any show of fairness, be regarded as a "mere passing remark," or counteracted by
any mere *assertion* that "there should be but one order of priests in
the new church"?

Before any other order than the trine spoken of by Swedenborg in
the Coronis, which evidently requires three grades or priestly ranks,
can be justly and rightfully established in the new church, those
attempting to establish that other order, ought to show where Swedenborg himself has expressly explained away this passage in the
Coronis.   They ought, in all justice, to show the church where that
illuminated author has said that he does not mean in this passage what
his words imply to common minds in their ordinary acceptation.   In
a word, they ought to show that he does not here mean three grades
or degrees in the external or formal ministry of the new church, as an
exemplification of the TRINE which he advances and describes, by
bringing forward the passage or passages where he says, with equal
plainness and expressness, that there should be but one grade.   If he
does not intend to teach, that order requires the three grades, classes
or degrees contended for, they ought to adduce the passage or passages
where he so explains himself.   And they ought to point out the passage where he says in the church there should *not* be any " *Primus*

Infulatus," nor " *Antistites Parochi*," nor " *Flamines sub illis*." But has he so said? Is it *presumed* that he has? Until, then, such passage or passages as are called for are shown, the undersigned cannot but think that there is in this far too much *presumption!* While, for his part, he cannot see the subject in any other light than that true order requires there should be three grades, or degrees, in the formal ministry of the new church, as Swedenborg has here declared it expressly.

The reader's attention is called next to a passage to be found in True Christian Religion, 106. The subject of which the author is there speaking is the progress of unition between the divine and human natures in the Lord. In accomplishing this, two states were passed through, " called states of exinanition and glorification."

He says, " These two states are represented by various circumstances and effects in the universe; the reason of which is, because they are according to divine order, and divine order fills all and every thing in the universe, even to the most minute particulars." The author then illustrates this principle by the progressive condition of every man; the first state by his infancy and childhood, and the second by his manhood. Next by saying, " The first state is also represented by the state of a prince, or the son of a king, or of a duke, before he becomes a king or a duke ; also by the state of every citizen before he is advanced to the office of a magistrate ; of every subject before he holds any post in the government ; likewise of every *student who is preparing for the ministry, before he becomes a priest, of every priest before he becomes a pastor, and of every pastor before he becomes a primate.*" After this he goes on with other illustrations, noticing some in both the animal and vegetable kingdoms.

Attention is here called to the fact, that Swedenborg says " These two states are represented by *various circumstances* and *effects* in the universe," and assigns as the reason " because they are according to divine order, and divine order fills all and every thing in the universe, even to the most minute particulars." Now, here, two important points may be seen to be true; first, the subject itself, of which the author is speaking; and secondly, the *things* by which *the* subject is illustrated. 1st. That the unition of the divine and human natures in the Lord was effected according to the laws of divine order ; for it is said, " the reason why the Lord passed through these two states of exinanition and glorification was, because there is no other possible way of attaining unto union, since this is according to the divine order, which is unchangeable." (U. T. 105.) 2dly. That the " circumstances and effects in the universe " which are used to illustrate this union, are themselves in true order, " because they are according to divine order, and divine order fills all and every thing in the universe, even to the most minute particulars." One of these orderly things, then, *is*, because used for this illustration, the state of " every student who is preparing for the ministry before he becomes a priest, of every priest before he becomes a pastor, and of every pastor before he is a primate." This, now, is certainly true order to be observed in the church, or it would not appear in this connection.

This may be abused by men, but that will not be considered in this place. The fact is, however, that the abuse of a thing, which must result in evil, is no argument against its use. Its truth is what is to be regarded. And if the order be true, then its right application and use must result in good.

We are aware that some mighty wrestler may come forward to throw us in our argument here by the assertion that this is only a " passing remark " of Swedenborg's. He has not, however, the ground to stand upon—that this is one of Swedenborg's posthumous works. And as the doughty champion has not yet come in sight, we will not strain any of our nerves for the struggle now.

Here, then, *three* distinct steps, of which the preparatory is not one, are declared to be orderly in the ministry, because it is an orderly " circumstance " taken to illustrate a principle of divine order in the Lord. It is now asked candidly, would it be reasonable to sup-pose that Swedenborg had in this place introduced a matter in itself out of true order, without even giving the least intimation of it being so, for the purpose of illustrating and establishing a point of divine order in the Lord? Would not such a supposition be a manifest absurdity? In what other light can it be viewed rationally? He has, then, declared here, in express terms, the principles of true order in the ministry of the new church, because the Lord, in founding the new heaven and the new church, " introduces order that they may stand under His auspices to eternity." The principle here established is, that three distinct grades of officers in the ministry are required by a law of divine order—give to them whatever names you please. We do not stickle for the *names*, we want the *things ;* because divine order requires us to have them, and because we must have them so that our church on earth may correspond with the church in heaven. In the old christian church-divine order had flowed so as to make a trine of ecclesiastical officers called by the above names; and we contend that the same divine order flowing into the new christian church *must* make *a trine* of ecclesiastical officers, which need not necessarily be called by the same names, but may have any new names which are rightly expressive of their discrete functions or uses. Thus, while we maintain that there *must* be a trine in the new church, we admit that such trine may be various in the several generic parts into which the New Jerusalem on earth will very probably be distinguished.

Swedenborg thus incidentally introduces the three grades, or degrees of the ministry, as " an orderly circumstance in the universe," to illustrate a point of divine order; which order of three grades he after-wards expressly applies to the church, in an appendix to the same work, in which it is introduced for illustration. In doing this Swe-denborg not only fully agrees with himself, but most unequivocally establishes, as a point of true order in the ministry of the true church, what he introduced to illustrate a state of divine order in the Lord. And thus, by this passage in no. 106 of the T. C. R. compared with no. 17 of the Coronis, we make Swedenborg himself explain his meaning in the latter passage ; so that it is clearly evident that he, in

Coronis 17, intended to teach just that doctrine, and no other than that, which the plain meaning of his words imports.

Now are not these passages taken together, if there were no others, sufficient of themselves to settle the question before us on Swedenborg's authority? Are not these enough to guide the church in rationally determining, from the doctrine which the Lord has taught her by his chosen servant, what is to be the true order of her ministry—even if no other passage can be found in Swedenborg's writings expressly teaching that such order must be a trine of discrete degrees? At least may we not come legitimately to this conclusion, since the advocates of an opposite order of only one degree, grade, or class of persons in the formal ministry, *have not shown a single passage* of Swedenborg's writings, from which we may even *infer* that he does not mean that there should be the " Primus Infulatus, Antistites Parochi, et Flamines sub illis," in so many different persons in the new-church ministry? For we have shown that they are called upon to demonstrate by Swedenborg's own words, that, in the external or formal ministry of the new church, there should be *but one* grade, degree, or class of priests, that a *trine* in just order *may be* formed therein. And if this cannot be done, the undersigned is unable to see how any other order can be justly established in the ministry of the new church, upon the authority of her doctrine, than the one in three grades, degrees, or classes, as expressly declared by Swedenborg.

From this conclusion it may not seem necessary to extend these observations any further. For the strength of an argument does not depend upon the number of its postulates, but upon their manifest truths, howsoever few they may be. Hence one passage in which a truth is directly and expressly taught has more conclusive force than a hundred which only teach it indirectly and by implication. Hence I might here rest my argument on one passage explained by another, in which the truth of a trine is directly and unequivocally taught. I could bring forward more, but they would not add force to these. Still a few more things will be added, not indeed for the purpose of showing this to be the true order of our ministry by mere inferences, or twisty explanations of doubtful passages, for it is confidently believed that Swedenborg has here expressly taught it; but because the desire is felt to show, in some measure at least, the harmony of this doctrine with what he teaches elsewhere on other correlative subjects. I will instance what he teaches concerning the three heavens and their orderly ultimation : for this subject, it seems to me, affords the means by which the formal trine in the ministry may be illustrated and confirmed.

The reader is requested to observe, that our present line of argument rests on the principle previously laid down in these words— " for it is the part of a wise man, and it is rational, to see first that a thing is true, and next to confirm ; inasmuch as to see what is true, is to see from the light of heaven, which is from the Lord." (A. C. 4741.) And as it is believed that the order of three grades, degrees, or classes in the external or formal ministry, is true from the express teaching of Swedenborg, in the passages of his writings above cited, therefore all I purpose now to do, is rationally to illustrate and confirm this truth.

Our illuminated author teaches, that "there are two kingdoms into which all the heavens are divided, the spiritual kingdom and the celestial kingdom." (Ap. Rev. 647.) There are therefore both the spiritual and the celestial principles in each of the three heavens. And speaking of the christian heaven as being distinct from the ancient heavens, he says, " for the heavens are like expanses, one above another; it is the *same with each particular heaven;* for each heaven, by itself, is distinguished into three heavens, an inmost, a middle or second, and a lowest, or first ; and so it is with this new heaven. I have seen them and conversed with them." (Ap. Rev. 876.) There are degrees of good and truth for these heavens, and men born with capacities for their reception, and to dwell in those heavens. This follows from what Swedenborg says above—"I have seen and conversed with *them.*" For he could not converse with the heavens in any other way than by talking with the angels in them, who had once been men. Hence it is said, "For there are three degrees of love and wisdom, and thence three degrees of good and truth ; the first degree is called celestial, the second spiritual, and the third natural; these degrees exist by birth in every man, and they exist also in common in heaven and in the church ; which is the reason why there are three heavens, the supreme, the middle and the ultimate, or lowest, altogether distinct one from another, according to these degrees; *in like manner the Lord's church upon earth.*" (Ap. Rev. 774.) Thus it is plain that the same things must exist in some way in the church on earth that exist in the heavens; and this, too, because the church on earth furnishes the angels for each of the heavens. And now, although each angel in himself, and each man also, has all three of the distinct degrees, yet are there three distinct grades of these angels themselves, as persons, constituting corresponding heavens. Therefore, an individual having all the degrees in himself, does not in the least interfere with the orderly arrangement of individuals into discrete heavens according to discrete degrees of love and wisdom. Nay, unless each particular man, spirit, and angel possessed all three of the degrees individually, they could not be arranged into so many heavens, as they are. Just so in reference to the formal ministry of the new church.

Each individual minister, when brought properly into the ministry, may have all the degrees in himself, although they may not all be officially opened at once for corresponding influx, as all the degrees in man are not opened at once for receiving heavenly influx ; still this condition does not interfere with their orderly arrangement into official grades, or classes, of the formal ministry in the church. And the reason why it does not interfere with such classification is, because a man is not a priest from his mere *personal state,* or from *his own individual regeneration,* but from his official adaptation, qualification, and induction into office. This is evident from what Swedenborg says—"The honor of an employment is not in the person, but is adjoined to him according to the dignity of the thing which he administers; and what is adjoined does not belong to the person himself, and is also separated from him with the employment." (H. D. 317.) In another place he says—"but the reasons why the clergy are particularly gifted with the graces of illustration and instruction are, because those graces have particular relation to their ministerial office, and their ordination to the ministry conveys those graces." (U. T. 146.) There is, therefore, a great difference between an individual's personal state and quality, in reference to his own regeneration, and his official and representative character, as an officer of the church. The two should not be confounded. Bad men may be in office and represent holy things as well as good men. Consequently, men internally bad may have strong powers of official qualification, while men internally good may have no powers of official qualification whatever. An inwardly bad man may be a skilful physician, an acute lawyer, an exquisite singer, or a physically brave soldier, while an inwardly good man may be a very quack, a dull pleader, without any ear for music whatever, and the most arrant physical coward. So an internally bad man may be an eloquent preacher of the truth, and a most impressive administrator of the church's sacraments, while an internally good man cannot preach at all, and may not be at all able to administer the sacraments with becoming external propriety. There must be a natural aptitude and an acquired fitness for the clerical, as well as any other, office. And with this a man, whether inwardly bad or good, natural or spiritual, infernal or celestial, may *represent* the Lord in his holy priestly office. For Swedenborg says—"that it is a thing of indifference what be the quality of the man who represents, whether he be evil or good, and that evil men may alike represent, and did represent, the Lord's divine principle . . . . the same may appear from the representatives which exist also at this day; (Idem potest constare ex repraesentativis quae etiam hodie.) For all kings, whosoever they are and of whatsoever quality, by virtue of the principle of royalty appertaining to them, represent the Lord; in like manner all priests, whosoever or of whatsoever quality they are, by virtue of the priestly principle; the principle of royalty (regium) and the priestly principle (sacerdotale) is holy, whatsoever be the nature or quality of the person who ministers therein." (A. C. 3670.) The law here is, that the divine humanity of the Lord pervades common society, so far as to keep that in external order by immediate influx, and thus prevent the disturbances which would result if men's internal states were to come out in corresponding ultimates of the natural world. · Owing to this law the devils cannot now possess the bodies of men, unless men give them a place in their bodies by the overt evils of actual life. Hence, no matter how evil a man may be internally, while he observes the laws of divine order in his externals, he may truly represent the Lord in the most holy external functions, for which he is naturally fit. Thus a man or woman who has a natural aptitude and acquired ability to produce musical harmonies, may representatively sing the praises of the Lord in the public temple of his worship, no matter how internally evil he or she may be, provided their internal evils do not so come out into ultimate life as to give them moral or physical unfitness in externals. So with the minister of the church, or the preacher of truth. While he is in external order, he may represent the Lord truly, although he is internally evil; but this representation must cease whenever his internals so come out as to disturb external order in him. Hence Swedenborg adds—"when a priest *acts* contrary to what is just and equitable, and contrary to what is good and true, in the same proportion he puts off the representation of holy priesthood, and [does not cease to be a representative character, but] represents the opposite." (A. C. 3670.)

This shows that there is *a priestly principle;* and can there be any doubt but that it is three-fold in the Lord, and may therefore be officially represented in three men, whatsoever be their nature or quality as persons? True preachers may act from proprium, but this "is permitted of the Lord, since they also thus perform uses; for good men still receive the Word from them well, since the Word, from whatsoever mouth it comes forth, is received by man according to the quality of his good." (A. C. 10.309.) "For what is external affects every one according to his internal, because truth enters, from *whatever* mouth it be uttered, into the hearing of another, and is received by the mind according to its state and quality." (D. P. 14.) From this it does not follow that bad men are to be put into the holy office when they are *known to be wicked;* external moral and spiritual integrity is an indispensable requisite for the priestly office; and if internally bad men come into it, they have to feign this as they do honesty in ordinary business transactions. All that is implied is, that the office is distinct from the man—that the holiness of the office is a representative one, and therefore that his internal quality has nothing to do with it—provided internal evils do not come out into external form, and provided there are external sanctities appropriate to the representative functions.

According to the teachings of the foregoing passages, then, a man's individual state, if in the way of regeneration at all, as to the life of regeneration, might belong to the highest heaven, and yet without any detriment to such state, he might be acting officially only in the lowest degree, or belong to the lowest class of the formal ministry of the new church on earth. And so of the middle or highest grade. In like manner the highest degree, grade, or office in the formal priesthood, might be filled officially with a person whose regeneration had only advanced to the state of the lowest heaven, if at all, and this. without any detriment to his spiritual state, so as to retard his regeneration, or without his being less competent to discharge the duties of that degree. For if an inwardly bad man may represent the Lord as a priest of the highest order, so may an inwardly celestial man, while he is in this natural world, represent the Lord as a priest in the lowest degree. The reason of this is, that in such cases their ministrations would be from the Lord by influx through the spiritual world into their official rank, standing and qualifications, and not into their personal states. All that would be required of them would be to maintain an external correctness of deportment, and to perform faithfully the duties of their respective stations, with a natural and acquired fitness for their discharge. It is indeed true, that the higher and highest grades in the ministry require the development in successive order of the higher and highest discrete *official* capacities of the priesthood, before functionaries are ordained into these grades. But these may be developed just like a talent for music, without the individual regeneration of the officer. Thus it is supposed that Swedenborg was fully qualified for the discharge of the functions of his high office, by the elevation of his understanding into preternatural light, without, necessarily, the elevation of his will into corresponding heat.

But to see the application of this ministerial trine to heaven and the church, having first seen it to be true from express teaching, it is only necessary to connect principles of truth together and view it in their light. The new church is taught that in heaven "all the preachers are from the Lord's spiritual kingdom, and none from the celestial kingdom." (H. & H. 225.) And that "all preachers are appointed by the Lord, and hence they have the gift of preaching; nor is it allowed any one except them to teach in the temples." (Ibid, 226.) And it is also taught that "there are two kingdoms into which *all the heavens* are divided, the spiritual kingdom and the celestial kingdom." From this is it not plain that, as there are three heavens, there are also three classes of preachers for them, because the spiritual kingdom, of which all the preachers are, belongs to each of the heavens? Preachers for the highest heaven are from the spiritual kingdom of that heaven; and so of the middle and lowest heavens, the preachers for each are from the spiritual kingdom of each heaven. Hence must there not be preachers of a celestial grade in the celestial heaven—preachers of a spiritual grade in the spiritual heaven, and preachers of a natural grade in the natural heaven? Thus in the three heavens "constituting *one thing*", that is, one grand man, must there not be *three grades* of preachers; and why may there not be three grades of ministers in the church as a similar and corresponding grand man on earth? There surely must be three grades of preachers in the heavens—" Inasmuch as the interiors appertaining to the angels of the inmost heaven, are open in the third degree, therefore their perfection immensely exceeds the perfection of the angels in the middle heaven, whose interiors are open in the second degree; in like manner the perfection of the angels of the middle heaven exceeds the perfection of the angels of the ultimate heaven. In consequence of this difference an angel of one heaven cannot enter into the angels of another heaven; in other words, it is not possible for any one to ascend from an inferior heaven, nor to descend from a superior heaven. He who ascends from an inferior heaven is seized with anxiety even to pain, nor can he see those who are there, still less discourse with them; and he who descends from a superior heaven is deprived of his wisdom, stammers in his speech, and is in despair." (H. & H. 34, 35.) Can it be then, as some have supposed, that all preachers in the spiritual world are from the middle *heaven*, which such have confounded with the spiritual kingdom, because the spiritual principle prevails in that heaven? From this view of what Swedenborg teaches in reference to the heavens, then, the trine in the ministry as operating in the heavenly societies, cannot be confined to one man-angel, although each angel has the trine in himself. So, by correspondence, must it be on earth. And therefore no one person can have the three grades of the ministry in his official capacity at the same time. There must be three persons to represent the three grades; and when a minister of a higher grade performs the functions of a lower, he must, for the time being, come down to the lower plane for that purpose—which, in this natural world, he may do representatively.

Order requires it to be so in the heavens, because they are three, "and the external of *each* heaven is what is called the ultimate or first heaven." (A. C. 9741.) Therefore the trine in the ministry, as to its operation even in the heavens, requires three men-angels to constitute it, one for each of the three heavens in particular, which are in each of the three heavens in general. And therefore, we argue that the church on earth, to make one with heaven, must come under the same general law of order. Hence in the church, as Swedenborg has taught, there must be, or will be, the three, no doubt corresponding to the heavens, and, in their official operations, communicating with them by influx according to such correspondence. And both in heaven and the church is there true subordination according to such degrees. "For such is the form of regulation in another life, that good spirits are subordinate to angelic spirits, and angelic spirits to angels, so as to constitute one angelic society." (A. C. 1752.) Again, "Things internal and things external have the same relation to each other, and are alike circumstanced, *in the heavens as with man;* the angels who are in the first heaven are subordinate to the angels who are in the second heaven, and these to the angels in the third; but this subordination is not as of rule or authority, but it is as in man, an influx of things internal into things external; for there is an influx of life from the Lord, through the third heaven into the second, and through the second into the first, and this by order of succession, besides the Lord's immediate influx into all the heavens." (A. C. 1802, see the whole n.)

Now, being first acquainted with the truth of the formal trine in the ministry, as laid down by Swedenborg, is it not clearly seen to agree with this order of subordination and influx? Besides the Lord's immediate influx into the ministerial function in general, there is successive influx according to the degrees into which that function is divided. Hence the necessity of its formal recognition and adoption in the church. The fact that all ministers are living together on earth in the body or in externals, forms no objection to this order and arrangement; because it does not depend upon the personal state of men, but their official connection with the laws of order. For it is a law of order that internal things or principles are together in exteriors. "In general, the things which are inmost in those which follow successively, are in the midst or centre in those which, by derivation from them, are simultaneous; as is the case in the natural principle; thus, in most things or (principles,) arrange themselves in exteriors." (A. C. 5897.)

Again, "there is an inmost principle, there are interior principles, under the inmost, and there are exterior things in man; all these things are most exactly distinct among themselves. They succeed in order, thus from the inmost even to the outermost. According to the order in which they succeed, they flow in; hence it is, that life flows in through the inmost into the interior principles, and through the interior into the exterior, thus according to the order in which they succeed, and that it does not rest but in the ultimate of order, where it stops; and whereas interior principles flow in according to order even to the ultimates, and there stop, it is evident that interior principles are altogether in the ultimates. But in this order the inmost principles which flowed in keep the centre there, the interior principles, which are beneath the inmost, encompass the centre, and the exterior constitute the circumferences; and this not only in general, but also in singulars. The former order is called successive order, but the latter simultaneous; and the latter rises from the former; for every thing simultaneous has birth from what is successive, and when it is born, its existence is such." (A. C. 6451.) Please read in this connection, A. C. 8603. Nothing, it seems, could more clearly, distinctly, and forcibly illustrate and confirm the truth of three grades or degrees in the external or formal ministry of the new church than these passages. Both kinds of order are plainly stated and explained. And as they exist in the individual man, must they not exist individually in the aggregate man, when existing in society— that the whole may stand as one man before the Lord? The inmost principle, which answers to the highest degree of the ministry, comes into the ultimate, but occupies the centre on that plane. Therefore, in forming individuals into societies, a larger man out of individual men, individuals should occupy the place of distinct principles, and represent them in the whole. Thus the inmost principle coming into the ultimate plane is not continuously the same as the ultimate of the interior or the exterior on the same plane. They are not blended there without distinction. The inmost is discretely the centre in the ultimate; the interior discretely encompasses the centre in the ultimate; and the outmost forms the circumferences in the same plane. Thus it is that the three heavens subside in ultimates, and rest upon externals; but not without preserving in this way their discrete differences. Hence it may be seen, that, in accordance with this law of order, in the church even in externals, among men, why it is that, in the formal ministry of the new church, which is the true church, there are three degrees, or grades, to answer to this ultimation of heavenly order, and for a plane in externals upon which it may rest and be received by influx, that earth and heaven, in this respect, may be conjoined.

Again, " moreover it is to be noted, that all and singular things from the first or inmost (being or principle) proceed *successively* to their *ultimates*, and there rest; also, prior or interior things have connection with the ultimate in *successive* order; wherefore, if the ultimates be parted asunder, interior things are also dissipated; hence, likewise, there are three heavens, the inmost or third heaven flows in into the middle or second heaven, the middle or second heaven flows in into the first or ultimate heaven, this again flows in with man, hence the human race is the last in order, into which heaven closes, and in which it rests; wherefore, the Lord, from his divine principle, always provides that with the human race there may be a church, in which there may be revealed truth divine, which in our earth is the Word." (A. C. 9216.) To this must be added one more extract: "That in ultimates there is power, and also the preservation of things interior in their state, *may be understood by those who know how the case is with things successive and thence simultaneous in nature,· viz. that things successive at length form in ultimates what is simultaneous, in which they are collaterally in similar order;* wherefore, things simultaneous which are ultimate, serve things successive which are prior, for *corresponding supports on which they may lean,* and thus by which they may be preserved together." (A. C. 9836.) What now can be more clear and forcible than these passages in illustration and confirmation of the necessity and importance of a formal trine in the new-church ministry in so many grades of official persons—which may, by preserving ultimate order from proper ends, keep "interior things" from being "dissipated"—which may serve the prior successive heavenly influxes "for corresponding supports" to the ministerial teachings of the three heavens, in the ministerial function of the grand man of heaven, "on which they may lean" correspondently, and "be preserved together"? Without such arrangement, is not the true order of influx interrupted, suffocated or perverted?

And can the church be in a healthy and prosperous condition without observing this order, which Swedenborg evidently teaches? For where order is, there the Lord is present, (A. C. 5703;) and His presence is essential to healthful prosperity. This order is not contended for separate from internals, but that suitable externals may be formed for corresponding internals to flow into and act simultaneously therein. We want the *empty* water-pots of *stone* to be set *first,* that they may *afterwards* be filled with *water* to the *brim,* and, at last, have that *water* turned into *wine,* at the marriage of Cana in *Galilee.* How desirable then it becomes for members of the new church to view this matter soberly and rationally, and in freedom to receive the teachings of Swedenborg!

Now, from the passages which have been adduced, the principle may be clearly seen, that the distinct degrees are preserved in the ultimate plane. But to carry out this illustration, it may be remarked, that to speak of an individual man or angel, in him the degrees are full—both successive and simultaneous. He has the highest or inmost, the middle or interior, and the lowest or exterior; and at the same time these become in ultimates or the exterior man, the centre, that which encompasses the centre, and the circumferences. This is so in the individual or in one person. But when it comes to be applied to the formation of societies in order to preserve the human form in them; then individual angels or men are required to fill the different degrees in both kinds of order. There are angels to form the highest heaven in which there are inmost, middle, and outermost principles among themselves; there are angels to form the middle and lowest heavens in like manner. But when all are taken together, then the angels of the highest heaven are relatively and by influx inmost to the middle heaven, and the middle relatively and by influx interior to the exterior heaven; but in coming into the exterior, the degrees do not, in this society relation, become ultimated in one single angel of one class, but in three classes corresponding to the inmost, the interior, and the exterior. Because it is said, "That it may be yet better known how the case is with the heavens, it may be expedient to say a few words on the subject; the heavens are distinguished into two kingdoms, into the celestial kingdom, and into the spiritual kingdom; and in each kingdom there is an internal and external. . . . . The external of each heaven is what is called the ultimate or first heaven, and was represented by the court." (A. C. 9741.) So that "Those things or principles, which are in a superior degree, exhibit themselves in an image *in those* which are in an inferior degree." (A. C. 3691.) Also, "To the intent that anything may be perfect, it must be distinguished into three degrees; this is the case with heaven, and with goods and truths therein; that there are three heavens, is a known thing, consequently three degrees of goods and truths there; every heaven also is distinguished into three degrees, for *its inmost must communicate immediately with what is superior*, its external with what is inferior, and the middle thus, by means of the inmost and the external with both; hence is its perfection." (A. C. 9825.) See also the whole of 10.044, where it is shown and proven from the Word, "That all things are held together in connection and stand together from the first or supreme by (or through) the last or lowest."—"That interior things close and are at rest in ultimates, and are there together, and that ultimates hold together interior things in connection—that on this account strength and power is in ultimates," and "that on this account sanctity is in ultimates," (A. C. 9824;) but these must, to be so, be in order.

May it not now be said, in the light of these truths, that on this account, when an individual is spoken of, he may have all the degrees in himself in ultimates; so when an aggregation of individuals is spoken of, in being arranged according to order in the human form, there must be distinct individuals to form the respective parts; and consequently, in speaking of the ministry in the new church, in which there must be a trine as forming societies, there should be different persons to fill each distinct degree of that trine? For order must be in the true church to conjoin it with heaven. "As to what concerns man, man in ultimates is the church in the earth, man in first (principles) is the Lord, man in interiors is heaven, for the church and heaven before the Lord is as one man, on which account heaven is called the Grand Man. . . . . There is a continual connection, and influx according to connection, of all things from the Lord through the heavens to the church in the earth. By the heavens are meant the angels who are there, by the church men who are true men of the church." (A. C. 10.044.) Thus, as the same discrete order must exist in a collective man which exists in an individual man; and as in an individual man there are three discrete parts which together constitute him one man; therefore, in the clergy, considered as one ministry of the church, there must be three discrete grades of priests to constitute them one priesthood. And without *such* a priesthood on earth, it is clear the three discrete heavens would have no suitable ultimate basis. Thus it is clear, that, in order to a saving connection between heaven and earth, there must be in the earth as an ultimate plane, three discrete degrees for the three heavens to flow into correspondently. And hence the necessity of the three grades or degrees in the formal ministry of the new church on earth in ultimates, that there may be proper correspondence and connection with the heavens, so as to make way for orderly ministerial influx from the Lord through the heavens according to such correspondence and connection, for the formation and growth of the church among men.

A few words only will be said in reference to abuses which some bring up as objections to the formal trine in the ministry. True order may be abused. Priests may pervert and render infernal the exercise of these orderly principles, or functions, from a love of dominion grounded in the love of self and love of the world. Out of every grade there may come "evil shepherds." But he who abuses the office "is so far a spiritual thief, and brands himself with the mark and character of spiritual theft." (A. C. 3670.) They may "attribute honor to themselves on account of the sanctity of their office, and prefer honor and gain to the salvation of souls, which they ought to provide for." This has been done in the old church to a great extent, and may, in some cases, be done in the new by some unworthy priests wearing the garb of Newchurchmen; but still, from such abuse no argument can be justly drawn against true order itself. For if it could, upon that principle, every good and truth of the Holy Word could be argued against, because all its truths have been perverted and abused by men in the consummated church. This is so manifestly true, that it is deemed unnecessary to say any thing more in reference to such objections.

It may be said, however, in favor of the trine, notwithstanding abuses, that Swedenborg very fully pointed out the abuses of the Holy Word—spoke of the falsifications of the truths of the Word, by the love of dominion, or by the lust of honor and gain, in the clergy of the old church, but *never spoke a word against the external* or *formal order among them.*

But these observations have been extended to a greater length than was intended when commenced, and must therefore be brought to a close.

In conclusion, then, it appears clear to the undersigned, firstly, That Swedenborg has expressly taught, in both the True Christian Religion and the Coronis or Appendix to that work, that there will or must be in the formal ministry of the new and true church three grades or classes of priests to constitute a *trine* in just order. 2dly, That the undersigned is not aware that Swedenborg has, in any part of his writings, explained this away by showing that he meant any thing else: or that he has, in any place, said there should be but one grade or class of ministers in the new church. 3dly, That this principle of a *trine* in the formal ministry of the church, as a doctrine of

order, is seen to be in agreement with, to be applicable to, and to harmonize with, that author's teaching concerning the heavens and their
connection with the church on earth. 4thly, That the abuse of a
thing, or the perversion of the ministry according to true order, is no
objection to, or is no argument against, such order in itself, because
falsity itself is but truth falsified, and evil itself is but good adulterated;
while truth and good still remain truth and good in the Lord, in his
word, and in his true church. And, lastly, The undersigned is not aware
that, in all that Swedenborg has said against perversions and abuses
among the clergy of the old church, as to the doctrines of the Word
and life, he has ever condemned their external order, or said a single
word against the formal trine in the ministry in the old christian
church, as in itself contrary to true order; and therefore he cannot
see why the trine should not be the true order of the new christian
church, even if the old clergy *have* perverted and abused this order,
by making it subservient to their lusts of dominion and of gain.

In these observations no attempt has been made to define the duties of
the three degrees, but only to inquire, in the light of the doctrine of
the church, as to the fact itself, whether such degrees exist or not, and
whether they should be recognised in the church.

In view, then, of all that has been presented, the undersigned cannot now see it in any other light than as presented in the authorities
adduced in these observations, and therefore subscribes himself to
these convictions, that there are three degrees, grades or offices in the
external or formal ministry of the new church, which should be filled
by as many persons.

Respectfully submitted to the church.

D. POWELL.

Steubenville, O., June 28, 1848.

VII.—AN ARGUMENT FOR A MINISTERIAL TRINE, AND FOR ITS NATURE, FROM THE FACT THAT TRUE OR INTERNAL REPRESENTATIVES ARE NOT DONE AWAY IN THE CHRISTIAN CHURCH.

In a former report we contended that the priesthood is representative of the Lord; and as there is a trine in him, therefore there
should be a trine in the priesthood that represents him. The representative character of the priesthood is clearly set forth in A. C. 9809.
"'*That he may perform the office of the priesthood to me*.'—that hereby is signified a representative of the Lord, appears from the representation of the priesthood, as denoting in the supreme sense every
office which the Lord discharges as the saviour." "Inasmuch as
the priesthood was representative of the Lord as to all the work of
salvation derived from the divine love, therefore also all divine worship was of the office of the priest; which worship at that time
chiefly consisted in offering burnt offerings, sacrifices and meat offerings, and in arranging the bread on the table of faces, in kindling the
lamps every day, and burning incense, consequently, in expiating the
people and in remitting sins: moreover also in explaining the law

divine, and in teaching; on which occasion they were at the same time prophets." This shows that, in the internal meaning of the letter of the Word, the priesthood signifies "a representative of the Lord." Hence although the mere letter of the Old Testament should be rent before the christian church by the abrogation of the jewish ritual, still the internal sense of it would remain in some representative of the Lord—in a priest to "represent the Lord as to his work of salvation" and to represent "the work itself of salvation by his office." Such is the doctrine of the new church in regard to the Mosaic priesthood. And from this it follows that every priesthood, in all times, must be a representative of the Lord.

Observe, now, this argument. In explaining the internal sense of this sentence of the Word of God, that Aaron "may perform the office of the priesthood to me," Swedenborg says, "inasmuch as *the priesthood was representative of the Lord' as to all the work of salvation derived from the divine love,* THEREFORE, also, *all divine worship was the office of the priest.*" Here we see the universal law stated, why there should be a priest at any time in every church. It is, that worship is the office of a priest, because the priesthood represents the Lord as to all his work of salvation from the divine love. Hence, as there must always be a church as a means of the Lord's salvation of mankind; and as there must always be worship in that church, to represent and correspond to the activities of the divine love in them for their salvation; therefore, there must always be a priesthood in the church, to represent the Lord to it in that work, and to conduct that worship in it in an orderly way. And that such a representative priesthood should exist now and at all times in the christian church, and for the very same reason, is proved by this single passage of Swedenborg's writings: "As the ecclesiastical order on the earth minister those things which appertain to *the Lord's priestly character,* that is, *to his love,* and thus also to those which appertain to benediction, it is expedient that marriages be consecrated by his ministers." (C. L. 308.) A priest is not present at a marriage ceremony in heaven, because *the Lord is represented* there by the husband, and the giving of his benediction by other representatives; for instance, the words "may the divine blessing be upon you!" are pronounced "by a certain person sent from the prince [of the heavenly society in which the married pair reside] as his representative," and the "ante-chamber is filled with *an aromatic smoke* as a *token* of blessing from heaven." But "it is expedient that a priest be present and minister at the marriage ceremony on the earth," in order that he may represent the Lord in its consecration and in giving a benediction to its parties. (See C. L. 20, 21.) Therefore, it is clear that "all priests are among the representatives which exist even at this day." (A. C. 3670.) And we have argued that there should now be a trine of christian priests to represent the trine in the Lord, because the jewish priesthood, which represented the christian priesthood in the Lord's humanity, had a trine of jewish priests.

To this it has been replied, that representatives have been wholly
27

done away in the christian church, by the coming of the substance of
which those representatives were the types or shadows.   That among
these types were the priesthood or priestly offices of both the jewish
and the noahtic churches.   Hence "the jewish priesthood, with the
dispensation of which it was an essential part, and with which it was
in perfect agreement, was entirely and for ever abrogated." So that,
if christian priests are now in any sense or way representative of the
Lord,—and this cannot be, and is not, denied in the face of A. C. 3670,—
"it is not surely in the sense in which the priesthood of Aaron was
representative of him."   Christian priests must represent the Lord to
the christian church according to correspondence, and not otherwise.
To the father of the jewish church the Lord, by correspondence,
had to appear as three men—his own constituent principles necessarily seeming divided to a corrupt nation.   But to the new and true
christian church, which is all *one* in charity, the Lord, by correspondence, appears not in his trinity, but in his unity, as one man; and
therefore the christian ministry should represent him to the christian
church in one person.   So that there should be but one grade and one
ordination of christian ministers, among whom there should exist the
most perfect equality.

Again, it is contended, that the external order of the new and
true christian church should correspond to its internal state, and as
the internal state of the new church is essentially different from that
of the representative churches which preceded it, therefore the external form also of the new church should differ as widely from their
external form.   Consequently, no argument can be drawn from the
representative jewish priesthood for the external form of a trine of
discrete officers in the christian priesthood.

To this we may rejoin, in the first place, that the premise is false.
It is not true that the internal state of the christian church is *essentially* different from the representative churches.   And it is not true
that the external form of a corrupt church should correspond to its
internal state.   The external form of the church, even when its internal is most corrupt, represents the internal of the true church, as it
exists at all times in heaven, and as it is the continual tendency of
Divine Providence to cause it to exist on earth. ·

The internals of all the churches established by the Lord on earth
have been the same.   Their external forms have been greatly various;
but these too have been essentially the same.   They have all been
representative of heavenly and divine things as they were to exist in
a true church.   Even the external form of the jewish church, excepting the sacrifice of animals and other merciful accommodations
to an idolatrous state of mankind, were representatives of the celestial church, of which natural Judah was the perverted type.   Although
the jewish church had no internal to its heavenly representatives in
itself, yet there was an internal to them in heaven, from which, in
connection with the external of the Jews, there was spiritual vitality
imparted to human society on earth, as life is imparted to the body
through a heart and lungs.   Thus we are expressly taught, (A. C.
6877,) the posterity of Jacob "were incapable of receiving any thing

but the external of a church, thus that which only represented its internal;" but "the external also was established amongst them, to the intent that *what was represented thereby might be presented in heaven in the internal form,* and thus there might still be some conjunction of heaven with man." Hence the external form of every church, even the most corrupt, has been, like the poetry and literature of the nation, in advance of the state of its morals and life, for the purpose of developing among mankind a better internal state. In the establishment of the jewish, as in the case of every other church, there was a sort of charity or good, like the natural innocence of infancy. And to this the external forms of intelligence and wisdom are applied, as means of developing the spiritual innocence of wisdom in ripened age. But this good may be adulterated and destroyed, like remains, in the development of latent hereditary evils, which is the consummation of the church. But the perversion of this internal state in the consummation of the church, has never availed to the vitiation of the external form, so far as it was truly representative of heavenly and divine things. Thus, in the consummation of the jewish church, the Lord, in cleansing the leper, told him to show himself to the priest and offer the gift that Moses commanded as a testimony to them. (Matt. viii. 4.) On another occasion he enjoined it on both the multitude and his disciples, to observe and do whatsoever the Scribes and Pharisees bid them, because they sat in Moses's seat, (Matt. xxiii. 2, 3,) although their works were to be eschewed—thus showing them that the externals of the jewish church were still holy, notwithstanding the evil internal state of the priests who administered them. In like manner, in the consummation of the first christian church, "baptism, and the supper, and the like, are still holy," notwithstanding the evil internal state of the christian priests by whom they are administered.

Swedenborg says, "the internals of the ancient church were constituted by whatever had relation to charity, and faith grounded therein—thus all humiliation, all adoration of the Lord from a principle of charity—every good affection towards the neighbor, and other things of a like nature. The externals of that church consisted in sacrifices, libations and various other rites, all of which representatively referred to and regarded the Lord. Hence, with them, internals were in externals, forming together one church. *The internals of the christian church were precisely similar to those of the ancient church;* but other externals, as the sacraments, succeeded to their sacrifices, &c., and *had a like reference to the Lord,* [that is, referred to him "*representatively.*"] And thus again, internals and externals form together one church. *The ancient church* did not then DIFFER IN THE LEAST *from the christian church* INTERNALLY, *but* ONLY EXTERNALLY; for *the worship of the Lord from charity cannot alter,* whatever variation may exist as to outward observances. (A. C. 1083.) Thus the internals of the christian church and the ancient church were the same; and their externals were *essentially* the same, in that they were both *representatives* that referred to the Lord. And the changes in the external form of the church in all ages have been *variations* of the same form and not the substitution of a totally *diverse*

●

*form.** Thus the sacraments are the christian sacrifices; as the sacrifices were the ancient sacraments; both " only *representative* and *significative* rites," (Ap. Ex. 475 ;) and, therefore, alike requiring representative priestly offices and a representative priesthood for their administration. And that the representative character of the priesthood was not abrogated with the jewish ritual, and *its* priesthood in the christian church, is proved by Swedenborg's expressly calling them " representatives which exist even· at this day." (A. C. 3670.) The argument, then, that the new church must have a no-graded ministry, and thus a totally diverse external form for its priesthood from that of the ancient, which was a truly representative church, and, as such, had a *trine* of priestly offices in its priesthood, because the internal state of the new church is essentially different from that of the representative churches—is futile. A trine is essential to the constitution of any one thing, (Coronis, 17.:) hence a trine is essential to every priesthood, and must exist in the priesthood of every church for that reason. Hence a trine has existed in the priesthood of every external church that has ever been established on earth. And it is a great fallacy to argue that the trinal form has been induced upon the priesthoods of the noahtic, jewish, christian and especially the roman catholic churches, on the principle that " *the perfection of the external order was in proportion to the internal departure of the men of the church from the order of heaven*"! The strangest argument we ever heard of in our lives! On the same principle the external order of hell ought to be *more perfect* than that of heaven. The heavens *are* arranged in trinal order, both in general and in particular. This constitutes the *perfection* of their external form, and the *justness* of their external order. (Coronis, 16.) And, undoubtedly, when the hells are reduced to order, the *external* order of them as to their *trinal* arrangements, both in general and in particular, will be *the same*, as those of the heavens, because their exact opposites; but that they should be *more perfect*, is a *new* light indeed! The external order of the noahtic church was not a more perfect one than that of the adamic church, in proportion to its internal departure from the order of heaven; but it was the same external order, namely, the perceptions of what ultimate things represented, which the celestial church had, reduced to a ritual form by Cain and

---

* For the distinction which Swedenborg makes between *varieties* and *diversities*, see C. L. 324. " By varieties are meant the varieties between those things which are of one genus or of one species, also between the genera and the species; but by diversities are meant the diversities between those things which are in the opposite principle." In the angelic heaven there are " innumerable varieties." And diversities " are the opposites of those varieties which exist in hell." So in all the changes which have taken place in the external form of the Lord's church on earth, there have been only *varieties* of the same externals, and never the substitution of *diversities* of totally different externals. And it is certainly not taught by Swedenborg that the New Jerusalem is to afford an exception to this universal law. Hence, as there has been a ministerial or priestly trine in every external church that has ever existed on earth, there may be a *variety* of this form, and so a ministerial trine of some sort in the New Jerusalem, but there cannot possibly be the substitution of the totally *diverse* form of a no-graded ministry.

Enoch, and given to the spiritual church called Noah as a seed, for the preservation of the celestial principle in the winter of the world, for sprouting again in its spring, ripening in its summer, and garnering in its autumn.

Nor is it different in regard to the jewish and the papal churches. The representatives of the jewish church were *celestial* representatives revived, as we shall show before we have done with this subject. The priestly offices of the jewish ritual were those of the ancient church, as we shall also show; and therefore were not abrogated with that ritual in the christian church. Hence these offices as to all *essential* principles—among which is the trinal arrangement of their officers—were continued in the christian church, and flowed from the apostolic into the papal and reformed churches. The corruption of the christian church did not consist in *the adoption* of the *ministerial trine*, but in *the making this principle subservient to the lust of dominion*. There have indeed been idolatrous superadditions to apostolical simplicity by the catholic superstition; but the principle of trinal order is not one of them. This is the order of heaven. And the "unco gude" of the reformation have endeavored to reform the papal church by making its *external form* so *entirely* different from what it was, as to *destroy the form of heavenly order* that had been abused in it. With pious ardor, they have striven *to restore the tree of life*, by *plucking it up by the roots!* And how vain their labor has proved, any man may see, who observes how little the love of dominion from the love of self is diminished in those sects who have the most simple forms of external ecclesiastical order—the Shaking Quakers, for instance, whose external order is modelled after the most primitive apostolic simplicity. And will any man presume to say that there is *now* less of the love of dominion from the love of self in the calvinistic churches, than in the papal church; or that this abomination of desolation is detruded from the holy place in any church by the mere *circumstance* of its having only *one order* or *grade* of ministers!!! How it is in the *kirk* of Scotland, or the presbyterian, *baptist*, or other similar churches of America, we are not able to say, as we have never enjoyed the privilege of any experimental knowledge of its internal state or of its external form and quality. We can only say, that we know not how to express our present sense of the anxious strait in which we should be placed, if our only escape from the dominion and tyranny of the vatican were the conventicle!

In short, the internals of the true representative church and the true christian church are the same—charity, faith and good works. The priesthood of every church is but the representative form of those principles. The true external form of these is the *human*. This, as Swedenborg expressly asserts, (Coronis, 17,) is the *trine* of head, body and extremities. The ancient church had this external form, both in itself, and its priesthood, as a superior part of itself. The jewish church had this form. This was the form of the first christian church. Will the New Jerusalem, or the second christian church, either in respect to its own form, or the form of its priesthood, differ *widely* from the former churches *in this?* It certainly will, if it is to be only a sort of continuous body without any distinguishable trine of discrete parts—a kind of *long worm* in external form. And it may be well, in their own view, for the professed theologians of our faith to come to this conclusion; but, in ours, it is very ill, for them to say that *Swedenborg teaches it!*

In the second place, we rejoin, that the jewish representatives were not wholly *done away* in the christian church, but were *fulfilled*. "Think not," says the Lord, "that I am come to destroy the law or the prophets: I am not come to destroy, but to fulfil. For verily I say unto you, 'Till heaven and earth pass, one jot or one tittle shall in no wise pass from the law, till all be fulfilled." (Matt. v., 17, 18.) Thus all the representatives of the jewish ritual, and, of course, all the representatives of the jewish priesthood, were fulfilled by the Lord, both in his own humanity, and in the christian church as his body. Hence Swedenborg declares expressly— "As all the representatives of the israelitish and jewish churches respected the Lord, therefore, also, *he, in himself, represented* and *perfected them;* for *thus* he fulfilled all things of the law. Hence it was that the whole life of the Lord in the world *was representative*— even to all those things which are mentioned in the Evangelists concerning his passion, which things represented what was the quality of the church at that time in its opposition to the Divine Being, and to the goods and truths of heaven and the church." (Ap. Ex. 654.) Again, "Whatsoever the Lord did in the world was representative, and whatsoever he spake was significative. The reason why he was in representatives and significatives, when he was in the world, was; that he might be in the ultimates of heaven and of the church, and at the same time in their first principles; and thus might govern and arrange ultimate things from first principles, and all intermediate things from first principles by things ultimate. *Representatives and significatives are in ultimate things.*" (Ap. Ex. 31.) And "those things which appear in nature, in her three-fold kingdom, are the ultimates of divine order; for all things of heaven, which are called spiritual and celestial, terminate in them;" so that representatives are "truths in the ultimates of order." (A. C. 10.728.) Therefore, to do away representatives and significatives in the christian church, would be to abrogate "*ultimate things*" in it—to do away in it the ultimates of order: which the Lord could not do and did not do. That he abrogated the jewish ritual, was because it consisted of *mere* representatives, that is, idolatrous, false, miraculous, external and hollow representatives. But in abrogating these he merely uncovered true, real, internal and full representatives in the christian church. This is as true of priestly offices as of any thing else. These are "real things," (A. C. 1881,) which exist from and represent the Lord in the heavens, and therefore must be representatives and so "in ultimate things" on earth, in order that the Lord may have divine power to effect his will on earth as it is done in heaven by the *correspondence* of the one with the other; because "correspondences have all force, insomuch that what is done on earth according to correspondence, avails in heaven, for correspondences are from the Divinity." (A. C.

8615.) As, then, "there is a church in the heavens as well as on the earth; for there also is the Word; there are temples also, and sermons delivered in them, and *ministerial* AND PRIESTLY *offices*," (A. R. 533;). therefore there must be priestly offices on earth; and, consequently, the Lord could not have abrogated *these* offices in establishing the christian church. And as there was a trine of officers in the jewish priesthood, which was representative of him, and "he in himself represented and perfected" this representative as well as all the others of the jewish law; therefore he must have instituted a similar trine of priestly offices, as representatives, and so as "*ultimate things*," that is, persons, in the christian priesthood. Wherefore, we find that he did in fact ordain twelve apostles and seventy disciples, which were as truly representative of him in the christian church, as the twelve tribes, and the seventy elders, of Israel were representative of him in the jewish church. That these were priests as well as *preachers* and *teachers*, is evident from the fact that there are BOTH *ministerial* and *priestly* offices in heaven, (A. R. 533,) and therefore there must be priests as well as ministers to represent and correspond to them on earth; and it is further evident from the fact that they baptized when the Lord did not—that they fed the multitudes, arranged seated by fifties on the grass, thus in subordination to them under the Lord, with the bread and fishes which he had broken, blessed and given to them for that purpose, and that they cast out devils, cured diseases and healed the sick, as well as proclaimed the glad tidings of salvation. The Lord himself was thrice ordained of the father, and performed three priestly offices—1, he *taught* in the synagogues; 2, he *preached* the gospel in the cities and villages; 3, he *healed* all manner of diseases among the people. He, together with his twelve, and the seventy, formed a personal trine in the first christian priesthood. And he instituted a trine of "apostles, pastors and teachers" in the christian church which he established through them.

But how is it that such different views are entertained by those whom we ought to acknowledge as our superiors in the church? We confess that we are confounded by this fact. But having most diligently searched the Scriptures, and the writings of our church, on this subject, now for five years, as well as written upon it enough to make a large book, we must say, the only way in which we can account for this fact is, that those who hold the contrary view, look only at passages of one sort in Swedenborg's writings, and do not balance them with other passages of another sort with which they abound.

We were at first perplexed, and led to the deep investigation of this subject, by often meeting those in the professing new church who averred that the Lord, in establishing the first christian church, and abrogating the jewish ritual, entirely abolished *all* representative worship. They were understood to hold, that, in the New Jerusalem, as a restored celestial church, there was to be no merely external worship whatever. Hence that there are to be no external, sacramental, ceremonial and ritual forms which are of a strictly representative character. Such was the reason assigned by prominent lay members of the church, and even by the leaders of worship in societies, for not partaking of the holy supper as an external ordinance. There was, in their view, to be no christian sacrifice, and no christian purification, of a representative kind; and, consequently, no representative christian priest for the administration of such a rite or ceremony. And we have more recently seen it taught, as from the Word and the writings of Swedenborg, that the *only* office of the christian minister is to teach truth and lead by it to good. Therefore, the christian minister should be called merely a preacher, and not a priest. It is maintained that Swedenborg applies the term priest to him purely on account of the common usage of that term in the prevalent church. As we have read Swedenborg, this is never his custom. A more careful or precise writer in the choice or use of his terms there does not exist in any language. But we old plodders are deemed, by the far wiser students of him in recent years, not to understand him truly. Hence, although Swedenborg does indeed say, (H. D.) " Governors over those things amongst men are called priests, and their office is called the priesthood;" we are directed to *note well* that " he does not say they *are* priests, but that they are *called* priests." Well, does he mean to say that they are called what they are not? Oh, yes: for, representatives having been wholly done away in the christian church, and along with them both the essence and form of the jewish priesthood, therefore the christian priesthood is " altogether of a different character from the former;" and so the christian *preacher* is not a *priest* at all, although he may be *called* so, by a writer who is remarkably precise in the use of his terms! But Swedenborg says preachers are to be called *priests*, because they are to teach *good* as well as truth; and priests signify those who teach good. (Ap. Ex. 750—ex. of Lam. i. 11, 16, 19.) And teaching and leading are two distinct functions, instead of one and the same, it being the province of the priest to lead, and the prophet to teach—*teaching* being the province of *intelligence* and *leading* of *wisdom*; for in those passages of the Word where prophets and priests are mentioned together, " by priests are understood those who teach life and who lead to good, and by prophets those who teach truths whereby they are to be led." (Ap. Ex. 624.) Thus preachers are called priests in the Word of God, and therefore there is the best possible reason why they should be called priests in the church on earth, namely, the fact that this term expresses their leading function.

Now it does seem to us that these contrary views are founded upon certain passages of Swedenborg's writings read out of connection with other passages relating to the same subject, and against the whole tenor of those writings. For instance, from the postulate, which all concede, that the church on earth must correspond to that in heaven, it is argued: " All preachers are from the Lord's spiritual kingdom, and none from the celestial kingdom; because all preaching is from the truths of good in which those of the spiritual kingdom are principled, and because those of the celestial kingdom are principled in the good of love, so that they see and perceive truth, and therefore do not talk about it—consequently are not fitted to be preachers of it; and hence the teachers of truth are called preachers, and not priests, because the priesthood of heaven is the celestial kingdom,"—*therefore*, christian ministers *on earth* should not be called *priests*, and their office is *only* to teach and lead. The fallacy of this argument lies in making the order of heaven and the order of earth *the same*, instead of making the one *correspond* to the other. The conclusion is not a legitimate one from the premise. The order of the church on earth must *correspond* to that in heaven, and this requires the heavenly order to appear in a different fashion by being *re*-presented by the things which correspond to it in a lower degree. Hence there being no priests in the societies of heaven, is no reason why there should be no priests in the societies on earth, because these are in ultimates, which are representatives, so that here the Lord's celestial kingdom can exist only representatively, and he can be only representatively present in what pertains to that kingdom by priestly mediation. Thus, in the things belonging to the Lord's love, the ministries of which pertain to the priesthood, such as benediction, blessing and consecration, these things on earth can be administered only by a priest. And, hence, the above argument is just as inconclusive as if you were to argue, that, because priests do not officiate at the marriage ceremony in heaven, therefore they ought not to officiate at it on earth. In this instance, then, we must observe that Swedenborg, in this passage, speaks of the celestial or spiritual heaven in distinction from the natural heaven, in which latter there may be priestly offices, if not in the former. And the whole tenor of Swedenborg's writings shows that the external order of earth must be different from that of the heavens in this respect, just as the external forms of order vary in the societies of the heavens according to their various functions or provinces in the greatest man. For here, as we have said, are the ultimates of the spiritual and celestial things of the heavens; and those things when they come into their ultimates, both in the world of spirits and the world of men, come necessarily into their correspondent representative forms: so that the priesthood of Aaron, which, in the Lord, is salvation by good, and in heaven is the celestial kingdom of good, must come as necessarily into the representative form of *priests* on earth; as the Lord's salvation by truth, which is his spiritual kingdom, must come into the representative form of *preachers*, *teachers* or *pastors*. And this is a perpetual law of order, which could not have been done away in the abrogation of the jewish ritual, nor in the institution of the first christian or any other church. Hence *priests* are among "the representatives which exist even at this day."

Wherefore, *we* conclude, that there must be *priests* on earth, to represent the Lord in his work of saving men by *good;* as well as *preachers*, to represent him in saving men by *truth.* For on earth the Lord's celestial kingdom can only exist in the *representatives* that correspond to it. For it is only by and in representatives that angelic spirits and angels *can* be consociated with men on earth for the pre-

servati n of the world and its inhabitants. Hence the Word is given,
which, being written by correspondences, has those representatives
by which angels can be consociated with men and children. These
representatives, in the israelitish nation, or in the jewish church,
effected communication with heaven " *miraculously*," as Swedenborg
teaches; because the Jews were not a church, but only the representative of one—that is, were only the representative of the true
christian church which was to come, namely, the New Jerusalem.
But this christian church also, must be subjected to the same universal
law of a communication effected with heaven by representatives,
because such communication cannot possibly be effected by any other
means. The only difference is, that the communication is not effected
in the christian church *miraculously*, as it was in the jewish. In the
jewish, the representative had no internal correspondent quality;
whereas, in the christian, it has. Therefore the Lord, in abolishing
the *mere* representatives of the jewish ritual, instituted in their stead,
the *true* representatives of baptism and the holy supper. And that
these were substituted because the christian church could not exist
and subsist without its appropriate *representatives*, as the indispensable means of effecting its communication with heaven, may be seen
from the following passage in Ap. Ex. 475. " The reason why
washings were instituted in the ancient churches, and afterwards *baptisms in their place*, which, nevertheless, were *only representative* and
significative rites, was, in order that *heaven might be conjoined to mankind*, and *specifically with the man of the church;* for heaven is then
conjoined to man, when man is in ultimates, that is, *in such things as
are in the world as to his natural man*, and *in such things as are in
heaven as to his spiritual man*. *Conjunction cannot* OTHERWISE *be
given*. It was for this reason, [namely, that the conjunction of mankind generally and the man of the church specifically with heaven
cannot be given otherwise than by representatives,] *that baptism was
instituted*, and *also the holy supper*—likewise that the Word was
written by such things as are in the world, containing in it a spiritual
sense, in which are such things as are in heaven, or that the literal
sense of the Word is natural and a spiritual sense is contained within
it." This passage shows conclusively that baptism and the holy supper were instituted in the christian church as strictly representative
rites, because conjunction of mankind and the man of the church
with heaven could not possibly be effected in that church without
representatives. Therefore, it cannot with truth be asserted that
representatives are wholly done away in the christian church. For
there is seen to be the same reason for the instituting of these representative rites that there is for causing the Word itself to be written,
namely, " that heaven might be conjoined with mankind, and specifically with the man of the church;" which conjunction is only
then effected, " when man is in ultimates, that is, in such things as
are in the world as to his natural man, and in such things as are in
heaven as to his spiritual man." And, consequently, such representatives can no more be done away than the Word itself—of which, in
fact, they form a part.

"The holy supper was instituted by the Lord, that, by means of it, there may be conjunction of the church with heaven—thus with the Lord. It is, therefore, the most holy thing of worship." (A. C. 10.519.) "Besides, the holy supper includes and comprehends all the divine worship instituted in the israelitish church ; for the burnt offerings and sacrifices, in which the worship of that church principally consisted, were called, in a single word, *bread*. Hence, also, *the holy supper is the completion* [or fulness] *of that representative worship*." (H. D. 210–214.) "Even so it is with the Word as to its *spiritual* riches, and with the sacraments as to their *celestial* contents." "With those who receive the *bread* and *wine* holily, there is effected conjunction with heaven and with the Lord *thereby ;* and the goods of love and charity flow in through the angels, who, on this occasion, do not think of bread and wine but of love and charity." (A. C. 6789.) These passages show that the conjunction of man with heaven and the Lord is effected by *representatives* in the holy supper, and that the whole of the jewish representative worship was included and comprehended in it so as to make it the fulfilment of that worship. Wherefore baptism and the holy supper are precisely of the same nature as the jewish rites and ceremonies—they are those rites and ceremonies in an internal, but still a representative, form. The holy supper is instead of the jewish sacrifice ; and hence it is a semblance of the jewish sacrifice itself continued in the christian church after a christian model. Hence "the Lord said, when he instituted this supper *as a conclusion of the jewish and a beginning of the christian* PASSOVER, 'This do in remembrance of me.' Luke xxii. 19 ; 1 Cor. xi. 24, 25." (U. T. 704.) Consequently, as there is a christian passover, and thus a christian sacrifice, there must be a christian priest. And we see that not only representatives, but even the jewish representative worship, and a *similar* priesthood, were not *wholly* abrogated in the christian church.

Baptism and the supper are "the most holy [solemnities] of worship," (U. T. 667 ;) and there must be a priest to offer up the formal sacrifice of worship, as well as a teacher, preacher, or pastor, to teach truths from the Word. Hence Swedenborg says, (A. C. 9925,) "because *priests presided over worship* and *likewise* taught, therefore by their ministry was signified worship and evangelization," or preaching the gospel. Thus it is not the *sole* duty of christian ministers "to teach men the way to heaven and likewise to lead them therein," (H. D. 315 ;) but it is also their duty " to *administer* those things which belong to the divine law and *worship*"—which is a province of ecclesiastical *government*. Hence, Swedenborg says, "*governors* in things ecclesiastic, or in the things of heaven, appertaining to man, are called priests, and their office the priesthood." (A. C. 10.793.) And what can be more disingenuous than the following statement ? "'Priests ought to teach the people, and to lead them by means of truths to the good of life ; but still they ought to force no one ; since no one can be forced to believe contrary to what he thinks from his heart to be truth.' H. D. 318. *This is* ALL *that is said* in H. D. concerning the nature of the priestly or ecclesiastical *government*." We have had frequently to complain that the enemies of our church have presented garbled extracts from her writings, so as to make them teach either more, or less, or something else than what they really do teach, for her disparagement; but we grieve to see the preachers of our own connection emulating their example. Do they imagine that nobody will read, or has read, the work from which they quote, but themselves? And does not Swedenborg say further, in the very same passage—"he who makes disturbance *ought to be separated ;* for this also is agreeable to order, for the sake of which the priesthood is established"? And is not this something more that is said " concerning the nature of the *priestly or ecclesiastical government*"? The fact is, Swedenborg's doctrine in the above passage merely implies that the christian priest has no authority by virtue of his office of ecclesiastical governor to *force the conscience in matters of faith.* In those all are to be left free. But it does expressly teach that priests are to exercise those powers of government which consist in separating from the visible body of the church such of its professing members as create disturbance, as well by the insinuation of their heretical notions, as by the evils of their life. And who can read the whole of the chapter which contains that passage in its connection, or, what is almost verbatim the same, A. C. 10.789 to 10.806, without discerning that Swedenborg intends to teach a parity between ecclesiastical and civil governors in the matters therein set forth? So that it is just as expedient that there should be order among *ecclesiastical* as civil governors. For are they not just as liable through lust or inadvertance to allow evils against order and thereby destroy it? Are not ecclesiastics just as liable "to make disturbance" by the broaching of heretical notions in the church, as laics are to make disturbance in the civil magistracy; and must there be no power of ecclesiastical government by which they too, as well as lay members of the church, *may be separated*, so as to maintain that *order*, for the sake of which the priesthood is established? But can such order among the ecclesiastics be effected except " by an appointment of *governors* of *different degrees, higher* and *lower, amongst whom there shall be subordination*"? And why may there not be such government and subordination in the church as well as in the state, if there is such in heaven? And could any one assert that Swedenborg did not intend to teach this in H. D. 311 to 325 or A. C. 10.789 to 10.806, if he were to interpret these passages of his writings by the following, and others like them, in other parts of those writings? "There are governments in heaven; for order must be observed, and all things of order are to be kept inviolable" even there! (H. and H. 213.) Must there not, then, be governments in the church on earth, so that order may be observed, and all things of order be kept inviolable here too? " Matters of justice which relate to life" come into dispute in heavenly societies; and in these matters "the less wise interrogate the more wise," who "inquire of the Lord, and receive answers" from him. Thus there are higher and lower grades among the governors and in the governments of heaven: why should this not be so in the church on earth also? It is a great fallacy to assume that Swedenborg uses the term *government* only to express *imperious* sway—that there is no government but that of domination—no subordination but that of constraint, or external force—no *government* of *love, no subordination* of *will*, and therefore of *freedom*. Hence, it is a great mistake to infer that subordination can exist only in the more perfect external order of the papal church! It may and must exist in every form of church government, whether in heaven or in hell. (See H. and H. 213 to 220.) It is just as necessary to free as to arbitrary governments—just as necessary to keep order inviolable in heaven, as to keep infernals under restraint in hell. The only difference is, that, in heaven, the governors " do not domineer and command imperiously, but minister and serve," and are those who " are in love and wisdom more than others :" for " the spiritual angels are led by the Lord, but mediately; wherefore they have governors, *few* or *many*, according to the need of the society in which they are—they also have laws, according to which they live one amongst another—the governors administering all things according to the laws—understanding them because they are wise, and, in doubtful cases, being enlightened by the Lord." But in hell, " infernal government springs from self-love; for every one in hell *desires to rule over others*, and *to be the greatest*." And the governors in hell are those infernal spirits who are in self-love and its insanity more than others. These are the most efficient in restraining other infernals. " Wherefore, the most malignant are *set over* them as governors, and they are obeyed from fear." And so far as the love of dominion from the love of self has crept into the church on earth, and has perverted its spiritual powers by making them subservient to temporal ends, even the just subordinations of heaven have been made to assume the form of the unjust subordinations of hell. But this is no argument against the propriety of the former in both heaven and the church. Here an inferior or singular thing should be subordinate to a superior or general thing, (A. C. 5305 ;) and "the natural man ought to serve the rational, and this the spiritual, and the spiritual the celestial, and the celestial the Lord. Such is the order of subordination." (A. C. 2781.) If, then, there is the need of subordination in the governments of the heavens, where men are in the higher natural, and the spiritual planes, how much more must they be needed in the ecclesiastical governments of men in this lower natural and corporeal plane ?

The above may be confirmed by many other passages from Swedenborg's writings. Take this from A. C. 7773. " Amongst the evil, as well as amongst the good, or in hell as well as in heaven, there is the form of government, viz.: there are sovereignties, and there are subordinations, without which societies could not cohere together. But the subordinations in heaven are altogether different from the subordinations in hell. In heaven all are as equals; for one loves another as a brother a brother. Nevertheless, *one prefers another to himself as he excels in intelligence and wisdom :* the love itself of good and of truth produces this effect, that *every one subordinates himself* AS IT WERE OF HIMSELF, to those who are in the wisdom of good and in the intelligence of truth superior to himself. But the subordinations of hell are the subordinations of imperiousness, and hence of severity : for he who is imperious is severe towards those who are not constantly at his beck ; for every one holds another for an enemy, yet outwardly for a friend, for the sake of leaguing together against the violence of others. This leaguing together is like that of robbers. They who are subordinate continually aspire at dominion, and also break all bonds to attain it. In this case the state of hell is lamentable ; for then follow severities and cruelties. This happens by alternations. From these considerations it may be manifest how the case is with subordinations in the other life." And as to ranks or degrees among the governors in heaven, nothing can be more express than Swedenborg's teaching on this subject. " There are in the heavens, as on the earths, distinctions of dignity and preeminence, with abundance of the richest treasures, for there are governments and forms of government, and consequently a variety of ranks and orders, of greater and lesser power and authority." (C. L. 7.) And although there may not be priestly dignities in the societies of the celestial kingdom, there are such in the representative forms of the natural heaven and the world of spirits ;—as may be seen in C. L., 266;—and there should be such representative ultimates of the Lord in the church on earth; because the Lord must rule all things from first principles by ultimates; and "the ultimates by which the Lord operates, are upon earth, and indeed *with men.*" (Ap. Rev. 798.) Hence, as the whole of the Lord's operation is the work of redeeming and saving men, therefore this work of saving men must have its representatives in ultimates. This work, in its three discrete degrees, constitutes his priestly offices; and that he may effect this work on earth, *these offices* must have their *ultimates " with men."* Thus there must be on earth priests of three degrees. So, also, as this work takes place in successive order, there must always be a priesthood to represent it in its successive discrete degrees. Consequently, there must be a priest to represent it in the natural degree ; another to represent it in the spiritual degree; and a third to represent it in the celestial degree. And these representatives of the Lord in these several degrees must be subordinate to one another just as the natural man is to be subordinate to the spiritual man, and the spiritual man to the celestial. (A. C. 2781.) Thus, as representatives themselves, that is, true or internal representatives, can no more be abrogated in the New Jerusalem on earth, than in the world of spirits, and the heavens of angels, therefore there must be in this church a priesthood, which may represent the Lord in the three discrete degrees of his work of saving men. And, therefore, there must be in the New Jerusalem, a ministry arranged in trinal order.

Again, Swedenborg says, " a sacrament is nothing else but a binding," (A. C. 3046;) and baptism and the supper are sacraments, for they bind the spirit of man to heaven by affording him an external, corporeal and sensual representative in the ultimates of his natural man, that may correspond, in his spiritual man, to the truth and good of the Lord's divine humanity, which is the

bread of life that cometh down from heaven and giveth life to
the world. Hence these sacramental rites are representative of the
Lord's *celestial* kingdom. Therefore Swedenborg speaks of "the
spiritual riches of the Word, and the *celestial* contents of the
sacraments." And speaking of "*the representatives which exist
even at this day*," and expressly saying, "all priests represent the
Lord by virtue of the priestly office" in which they minister—whatever may be their internal character—because "the priestly office
itself is holy;" adds, "hence it is that the Word taught by a wicked
person is alike holy as when taught by a good person, and *also the
sacraments* of baptism and the holy supper, and the like." (A. C.
3670.) Thus he specifies the *priestly* function of administering the
sacraments, as well as preaching and teaching truths from the Word.
Wherefore there must be a priest on earth to minister the *celestial*
things of the sacraments, as well as a preacher to dispense the *spiritual*
riches of the Word. And herein, also, the priest must represent
the Lord saving by good, just as the preacher represents him saving
by truth. Consequently, there must be *both priests* and *preachers* to
represent the Lord on earth. And the argument that christian ministers should not be called priests on earth, because there are only
preachers in heaven, falls to the ground. It is evidently an error
resulting from inspecting only one class of passages in Swedenborg's
writings, without comparing them with others.

Further, christian ministers have to *bless* and *consecrate* in the
name of the Lord, as well as preach and teach truths from the Word.
This Swedenborg teaches unequivocally. Therefore, it is not true to
say, that "to lead to good by teaching, is the *only* duty, which,
according to Swedenborg, appertains to the christian ministry." Not to
mention again their duty of conducting worship and blessing worshiping assemblies in the name of the Lord, and also their duty of
ordaining and consecrating other ministers in his name, it is expressly
said, that it is their duty to *consecrate marriages* on earth. This is
something else which they have to do on earth, and it is something
which priests are not needed to do in heaven. And mark well that
they have to do this as representatives of the Lord's *priesthood;* hence
in their representative character of *priests.* For these are Swedenborg's words—"As the ecclesiastical order *administers on earth the
things belonging to the* PRIESTHOOD *of the Lord*, that is, *the things
belonging to his* LOVE, and thus those relating to *benediction* or *blessing*,
it *is needful that* MARRIAGES SHOULD BE CONSECRATED *by his ministers.*"
(C. L. 308.) And (Ibid. 21) it is said, "it is expedient that a *priest*
be present and minister at the marriage ceremony on earth, *but not
in the heavens*, by reason of the representation of the Lord himself
and the church. . . . . But even in heaven a *priest* ministers
in whatever relates to betrothings or marriage contracts, and hears,
receives, confirms and *consecrates* the consent of the parties." Thus
it is evident that there are some purposes for which a priest is needed
even in heaven; and a priest is not needed at a marriage ceremony in
heaven, because the Lord himself is there representatively in the
husband, and his blessing in the "aromatic smoke," "which was a

token of blessing from heaven." But on earth a priest is needed, because here the Lord is represented as to his priestly office, that is as to his salvation by good, which is the work of his love, by the priesthood, who are among " the representatives existing even at this day." Thus again do we see how men may run into fallacies, by founding doctrines on only partial views of Swedenborg's teachings.

Thus we plainly see how erroneous views in regard to representatives having been entirely done away in the christian church when the Lord abrogated those of the jewish ritual, are founded on certain passages of Swedenborg's writings taken from their connection with other passages relating to the same subject. And it is exceedingly easy to confirm those views by such isolation of the passages which seem to sustain them. Among the passages thus brought forward are U. T. 670, Ap. Ex. 700, and A. C. 1003. There are many other passages like these, but the last may be taken as a very good specimen of all of them. "After the coming of the Lord, however, *when external rites were abolished*, and *representatives consequently ceased*, these were no longer changed in heaven into corresponding representatives; for, as man becomes internal, and is instructed in internal things, then externals are as nothing to him; for he then knows what is sacred, as charity, and the faith grounded therein." This, probably, is the strongest passage that can be cited to prove that there are to be *no representatives whatever* in the christian church, because *all* representatives were abolished in the abrogation of the jewish ritual with its types and shadows. Yet, there are one or two other passages, as some may think, even stronger than this, which, when read alone, do, in their apparent sense, teach the doctrine ascribed to them. But it will be found that their whole force lies in being read out of connection with other parts of the passages in which they occur, or without comparison with other passages of the same import or similar relevancy. Any one will see this, who reads what follows the sentences quoted above in the passage cited. Thus—"From these internal principles, therefore, *his externals are now regarded* [how could the Christian have *any* externals, if " external rites were abolished" in the absolute sense?] for the purpose of ascertaining how much of charity and faith towards the Lord is in them. Wherefore, since the Lord's advent, man is no longer considered in heaven in reference to externals, but to internals; and *if any one be regarded as to his externals*, [how could he be if external rites were abrogated?] it is solely because he is in simplicity, and in this state has innocence and charity, which are introduced by the Lord into externals, or into his external worship, without his consciousness." Can any thing be clearer than this in showing that the external representative rite is not wholly done away? What was *merely* external in the rite has been abrogated. Or the external rite has been wholly abrogated only so far as it was a mere *external* connective of heaven with mankind. The law of order is wholly changed in this, that the consociation of heaven with mankind no longer takes place by the medium of the external rite alone. The consociation is effected now by the medium of the internal thing which it represents. The external rite is still in existence; but it is no longer regarded in heaven except "for the purpose of ascertaining how much of charity and of faith towards the Lord is in it"; and it is no longer rested in on earth as the sole medium of consociation. Yet an external representative rite must still exist on earth, because children and simply good people can have no other means for the receiving and containing of their innocence and charity.* Of course Swedenborg, in this passage of his writings, does not really teach that all external representative rites were wholly abrogated in the christian church; and he can be made to teach this doctrine here, only by separating a part of the passage from its connection, and reading it by itself.†

But it is our purpose, in the present argument, to show, by other passages of Swedenborg's writings, that it was only *jewish* representatives *as such* that were abrogated; and this because those representatives, being merely specific types of the Lord's humanity, were comprised, and so fulfilled, in that humanity, which itself became, in their stead, representative of his divinity to the christian church. But as every church must be external as well as internal, and as all external things are in the very nature of their creation *representatives* of the internal things to which they correspond in a lower discrete degree, therefore the christian church, as well as the jewish, had need of "ultimate things," which should be representative of its intimate things, and so form a plane for its external worship.

In the course of this argument we expect to demonstrate the above position fully. Here, as a preliminary specimen of our argumentation, we will contrast with one of the passages that seem to teach

---

* "*No* church *can exist* unless it is *both* internal and external—the former being as something indeterminate unless manifesting itself by appropriate external ordinances: for the generality of mankind being unacquainted with the internal man and his properties, *the nature of holiness would remain unknown unless there were* EXTERNAL WORSHIP. Those who are in charity, and whose conscience is derived therefrom, are in internal worship *whilst in external ;* for the Lord operates on their charity, and on their conscience, and causes *all* their worship to partake of what is internal" (A. C. 1083)— thus makes even their external worship internal. Thus it is to be with the New Jerusalem, when she becomes celestial. Her celestial principle from within, descending into her external worship, will make that too celestial: and so she will continue to have external rites and ceremonies when she is in her celestial degree, and not be without any external worship whatever when she has become celestial.

† In days of yore, the ladies of Philadelphia, among other extravagances of the fashion, were very generally wearing a peculiar head dress. It was a sort of towering turban, that ran up into a summit, which the wags called a *top knot.* The excess of this fashion became so great, and at length so ridiculous, that preachers felt it their duty to inveigh against it from the pulpit. And, on one occasion, the pastor of a baptist congregation, whose place of worship was in or near to North Second, not very far from Market Street, took for his text—"Let him that is on the house-top not come down to take any thing out of his house," (Matt. xxiv. 17;) and cutting four words out of the middle of this sacred sentence—"top not COME DOWN" !—made them the theme of a most violent tirade against the prevailing fashion. And this shows what *may be done* by professed Newchurchmen, in taking parts of passages from Swedenborg's writings, and arguing from their apparent sense when read out of their connection.

28

the entire abrogation of representatives, another which cannot but qualify its meaning. We range them in parallel columns, thus :

The Lord " abolished the representatives of the jewish nation, because the greatest part had respect to himself—for the image must vanish when the effigy itself appears. He established, therefore, a new church, which should not be led *as the former was* by representatives to things internal, but which should know them without representatives." (A. C. 4904.)

" Wherever there is a church, it *must of necessity* be *both* internal and external ; for man, who constitutes the church, is both. Previously to man's becoming a church, that is, before his regeneration, he is in externals ; and, whilst being regenerated, *he is led from externals*, yea, *by means of externals, into internals.* Subsequently, when he becomes regenerated, all that belongs to the internal man terminates in externals ; and thus *every* church *must* be *both* internal and external, as was the ancient church, and *as is the christian church at the present day.*" (A. C. 1083.)

Now any one must discern by bare inspection that the comparing them makes the first of the above passages appear in very different light. From the first we should, at first sight, have supposed that the Lord, in establishing the christian church, would make its members internal men by simply revealing to them internal things, so that they would become conformed to them without being in any way led to them " by means of externals" of any sort. Because we know that " representatives and significatives are in ultimate things," and "whatsoever any where appears in the universe is representative of the Lord's kingdom, . . . ; for all and singular things in nature are ultimate images of the celestial things of good and the spiritual things of truth, from which proceed natural things," (A. C. 3483 ;) so that there could be no external church and no external worship without representatives. Hence, if Christians were, in no respect, to be led by representatives to internal things, they were to be initiated into internal things without any externals whatever, that is, by " knowing them without representatives." But it should be observed that all Swedenborg teaches in the first passage is, that Christians were not to be led by representatives as the *former or jewish church was;* for that church was not led to internals at all by them. The Jew, no more than the Christian, could see the immortality of the soul in the letter of his Word. This had to be revealed. So, although the letter of the Word does indeed teach that there is a heaven and a hell, a life after death, a judgment in the world of spirits, and myriads of other internal or spiritual truths, yet the Christian, now no more than the Jew, could learn these truths from the letter without revelation. But when these things are barely *known*, man on earth is not led to them by the mere knowing of them. Heaven must be conjoined to earth in him, that his knowledge may so become life by the influences of the Lord through heaven as to bring his spirit into those internal things of heavenly wisdom which can be only spiritually discerned. Hence the Christian, as well as every other natural man, in the natural world, must needs be led " by *means of externals* into internals :" and these externals must be representatives. The Christian must not indeed be led by them *as the Jew was :* for, as will be seen presently, the Jew was led *miraculously;* whereas the Christian is to be led *ordinately.* In other words, the Jew was consociated with heaven by an external correspondent of heaven on earth without any corresponding internal of it in himself—the conjunction of heaven was *immediately* with the representative in his external : but with the Christian, heaven is conjoined with the representative in his external *mediately* by the correspondent to it in his internal man. This internal lies latent in the Christian before regeneration, as a seed lies in the field during winter ; but is developed in regeneration as the seed grows to maturity of full corn in the ear through spring, summer and autumn. In the Jew, there was no such seed ; for he was only a natural man, incapable of being made spiritual and celestial, and if saved at all, could only be in a natural heaven. But the Christian is capable of becoming spiritual or celestial, although he too, like the Jew, may have only the natural degree opened in him. Now that a man should be made spiritual or celestial *from natural,* that is, should have the former developed *in* the latter by an influx from the Lord into the latter through the former, is according to heavenly and divine order, and therefore may be called *ordinate :* but the connection of heaven with representatives in the external of the Jew, without any internal correspondent to it in himself, was an *inordinate* or *miraculous* accommodation of the divine mercy, to save the world, notwithstanding mankind's internal separation from heaven. In this case, men were saved by the *mere* representative—by the representative as it were *alone.* But, in the christian church, men were to be saved by the representative in conjunction with what it represented. Hence the Christian was *not to be* WITHOUT *the representative,* although that was not to be the *sole* or *mere* means of saving him. He was still to have the *scabbard,* although he held the sharp two-edged sword of truth drawn from it in his hand in the hour of his conflict with the enemies of his soul. This scabbard was needed to carry the sword by his side when going to battle, and for it to rest in after the battle was over. Hence the Lord, in instituting the christian church, gave, instead of the specific jewish representatives of his humanity, certain generic or complex representatives of it, suited to the christian dispensation. Consequently, the Lord, in instituting the christian church, did not *wholly do away,* but *wholly fulfilled,* all the representatives of the jewish dispensation. He indeed abrogated them as external, hollow, or *mere* representatives, and so he " abolished " them *as " the representatives of the jewish nation;"* in which the representative " did not conjoin the *person,"* the member of the church, but merely " the *thing,"*—the divine human ultimate office or function for the Lord's operation,—" with heaven ": for the Jew had only the ultimate from this world in his natural man, and not what corresponded to it from heaven in his spiritual man ; and we have seen that without *both* of these it was impossible for heaven and earth to be conjoined *in him.* But the world was to be saved by the Jew notwithstanding ; inasmuch as spirituality had every where receded from the interiors of humanity on earth, so as to leave nothing but a cuticular or capillary plane for the divine human operations of the Lord in preserving even the material universe and the natural world from annihilation. For "there must of necessity be communication of heaven with man, in order that mankind may exist, and this by the church; otherwise men would become as beasts, without internal and external bonds, and thus would rush headlong, without restraints, to the destruction of each other, and would mutually extinguish each other. And when there is no [real] church, as was the case in the time of the Israelites, it is provided of the Lord that communication of heaven with man should be *miraculously* effected by representatives." (A. C. 4545.) Hence the Lord, out of heaven, took hold of and held the Jew, as it were, by only the hair of his head, or the skin of his body. There was no conjunction of heaven with his internal man. The internal man was not at all opened in him; and therefore the Jew was not a church, but only the shadow or representative of one. But the Christian *is* to be a church—not a church without *any* representatives; for this, as we have shown, is impossible; but a church with *internal* representatives instead of *external* ones, that is, *true* instead of *mere* representatives—things of this world, or ultimates, in the natural man, *corresponding* to things of heaven, or intimates, in the spiritual man. Hence the Lord, instead of the washings and sacrifices of the Jews, has instituted baptism and the supper, as their complex, in the christian church. These are distinctively *christian* representatives. But the christian church is not led by these representatives to internal things, as the former church was by its representatives; but knows internal things without them: for the Lord has revealed to his new church even the internal things of *these* representative rites, so that the Christian may *know* what his representative rite signifies, so as to be able to think of and have an affection for the internal thing signified by it, while he is in its external observance; and thus, being in the internal sense of his rite as to his spiritual man, at the same time that he is in the ultimate or representative forms of it as to his natural man, he may enjoy conjunction of his spirit with heaven by the spiritual sense of the Word, instead of being consociated with heaven by its literal sense alone, as the Jew was. Thus the christian church has a completion of the *jewish* in its *christian* representatives; and so representatives are not wholly done away in the christian church, but fulfilled. Hence every representative. form which is contained in the letter of the Word, and which may represent the internals of the christian church, may be used in external christian worship, provided the Christian, at the time of its use, knows, thinks of, and regards in it, its spiritual meaning. The Christian may not indeed use again the jewish sacrifices, and the large mass of its ritual which prescribes the forms of them; for, as we shall show hereafter, these were idolatrous superadditions to the true letter of the Word, permitted as the only representatives of heavenly and divine things which could exist for the connection of heaven with the world in an utterly idolatrous state of mankind; and therefore can never make any part of the external worship of a true spiritual church, which may be a truly representative one. But the Christian may have scriptural forms, as the ancient church had,

pictured and sculptured to his eyes—aromatic odors, with the forms
of the flowers that produce them in nature, or the incense of their
burning extracts as products of art, for his nostrils—sweet sounds of
harmonious choral music for his ears, and the sacred representative
and correspondential appliances to every sense, as the means of Moses's
taking up in him, and making a staff of, the serpent, in the most holy
acts of divine worship. The only difference is, that, whereas heaven
was consociated with these things in the external of the Jew, it is
to be conjoined with them in the internal of the Christian: so that
the representative in the sensual plane of the Christian's mind is
lifted up to the spiritual plane. Thus the serpent is not to be destroyed
in the christian church, because it was venomous and destructive while
it crawled on the ground in the mere external church, but *is to be
lifted up*. Thus representatives are not to be done away, but, by
conjunction with their proper internal things, are to give to the new
and true christian church the vastly increased *powers* of the ultimate
principle of the mind, in developing, forming, perfecting and securing
all her internal principles. And among the representatives thus lifted
up will undoubtedly be *priestly offices, priestly functionaries*, and
priestly garments. And we contend that by these means alone can
the children of new-church parents, as well as simple-minded gentile
men, be kept in, drawn into, and saved in, the New Jerusalem.

Such is an outline of our argument for a priesthood, and a trine of
priests, from the fact that true or internal representatives are not done
away in the christian church. To expand this argument as we have
done in our notes and writings upon it for the use of this report,
would alone swell the number of our pages to several hundreds. But
so very much of our space has already been taken up by the discussion
of other topics, that we have little or no room here for the expanded
discussion of this. Still the subject is one of so much importance,
the views taken of it by us are so variant from those of many others
in our church, and a clearer view of it is so essential to a right discernment of the truth and need of the trinal order of our ministry, that
we should be greatly derelict in duty, were we to drop it here without
any further attempts to illustrate and enforce it. Indeed, so important
does this subject seem to us, so much do we imagine instruction
respecting it to be needed, that we intend, at some future day, if circumstances should favor us, to give an extended discussion of it in a
distinct publication. But now we have only room to present some of
the heads of the projected work, and a somewhat extended enlargement of one or two of the topics which are most pertinent to the
matter here in hand.

Representatives themselves, that is, true or internal representatives,
are not wholly abrogated in the New Jerusalem, as the true christian
church, because—

I. *The Lord, in his advent to the christian church, and abrogation
of the jewish ritual, did not do away representatives in themselves
considered, but only abolished representative* WORSHIP.

By representative worship is here meant worship in *mere* representatives, or worship in representatives *alone.* For there was connection

of heaven with mankind through the jewish ritual, in the sanctity of
the bare representative of the holy thing represented, without any
regard to the internal state of the jewish person who was engaged in
its worship; whereas, in the christian church, worship is to be
internal as well as external, and therefore the representative rites of
this church are only to be regarded from the internal states of the
Christian who observes them. Therefore the change wrought by the
Lord in his advent and institution of the christian church, was simply
a change of the *principle* of worship : and whereas worship before his
coming was in representatives *alone*, he changed this principle so far
as to make worship consist in what was represented *also*. Thus
instead of *mere* external worship, he instituted an internal worship
within that which was external. And hence the difference of principle between the worship of the two churches is radically this—that
the jewish worship is worship in externals only, and the christian,
worship in internals *as well as* externals. Consequently, external
representative rites are not to be wholly done away in the christian
church, so that its worship is to be internal alone ; but every external
rite and representative may be adopted from the letter of the Word,—
and even from the jewish ritual, so far as that is representative of, and
correspondential to, divine things in the Word,—provided they are
congruent with the christian, as an internal, church.

II. *The Lord, in abrogating the jewish ritual, merely took off an
excrescence, or peeled off an external rind, of the Word, which made
no part of its* TRUE *representative form, that may furnish the true
representatives appropriate to the christian as an internal dispensation.*

Upon this topic there is need to expatiate widely. But here we
can only state, that it rests on Ezekiel, xx. 25, " Wherefore, I gave
them also statutes that were not good, and judgments whereby they
should not live," as explained by A. C. 3479–80 : and Exodus, xxxii.,
15–20, as explained by A. C. 10.453, compared with A. C. 4293.
The incident here explained is, the making by Moses of two tablets of
stone, for the reinscription of the decalogue upon them by the finger
of Jehovah, instead of the two tablets which he had broken when he
descended from the mount and found that the Jews had returned to
idolatry during his absence. The first tablets, made and inscribed as
they were by Jehovah himself, denoted such an external or literal
sense of the Word as its internal goods and truths would have assumed,
if they had flowed down into such forms of heavenly representatives
as would prefigure them to the spiritual and celestial man. But as the
Jews, who were to represent those principles to mankind in an utterly
depraved and idolatrous state, and who, as fit mediums for such a
function, were themselves internal idolators of the most inveterate
sort, could not, of course, serve as *true* representatives of the Word's
holy internals; therefore the tablets, denoting such representatives,
were broken in signification of that fact ; and Moses was commanded
to hew out other tablets, which, being made by him as the representative of the jewish nation, would denote such an external representative form of the internals of the Word as that nation could furnish.
Hence, as the jewish nation was inwardly idolatrous, and consequently

a false and an evil nation, the tablets which Moses made must have denoted an external of the Word which was not its true external, and which, therefore, would be put off from the Word in a new testamentary bequeathment of it, by the Lord, to his true church. And if the internal goods and truths of the church are still covered up in the historical or verbal recital of those parts of the jewish ritual which are no longer needed for the ritual of the christian church,—as they are in the Old Testament,—it is because Christians have still the jewish principle in their external man, and because there will be at all times in the world external men, having jewish characteristics, and needing to have the internals of the Word presented to them, at least intellectually, or in the imaginative plane of their minds, in a jewish fashion. But still, as such external men become internal men, and so members of the christian, as an internal, church, they will put off all that is distinctively jewish in the letter of the Word as it is in their ideas of thought, and will come into those true representative forms which make the Word's true letter, and constituted those tablets of Jehovah's own making and inscribing—representatives as they exist in the natural heaven—which Moses, as the representer of the jewish nation, had to break. Hence, as some things were allowed to the Jews in their ultimation of the Word, which make no part of the true external of the Word itself, it must be sufficiently evident, that some part, nay, the largest part, of the jewish ritual, must needs have been abolished in the institution of the christian church, without the total abrogation of all representatives. And when the difference between *true* and *mere* representatives is considered, so that the distinction between *the representative of a church* and *a representative church* may be clearly seen, it will not be difficult to admit that there may be such a thing as true representative christian worship, and that the New Jerusalem may be a true representative church.

Idolatry consists in worshiping or loving external things alone, without any regard to internal things. External things alone are worshiped, when truths are believed and goods are done from solely selfish and worldly ends. Internal things are worshiped in things external, when external things are desired and attained from an end to what is good and true in itself considered, which is the same as a supreme regard to God and the neighbor. Hence idolatry in its essential form is confirmed selfishness and worldlimindedness. Therefore, the Jews were of all nations the most essentially idolatrous, because inwardly the most selfish and sordid. That such was and is the character of the Jews, the Word and the revelations now made from the spiritual world for the use of the new church, both testify. Why, then, did the Lord choose them as instruments in ultimating and preserving his Word? The reason for this was the same as that for which the Lord chose this earth as the one on which his Word should be written, and on which he himself, as the divine truth, should become incarnate. That his Word, or his divine truth with his divine good in it, as the light of the sun with its heat in it, might be brought to all in all earths, and "established for ever in heaven," it had to be brought to the lowest earth in the universe, and to the

vilest people on that earth. Therefore the Word was ultimated on
this earth and among the Jews; for this is the lowest earth and the
Jews were the vilest nation—that is, the nation most characterized by
the activity of selfish and worldly loves. Heaven had to be consociated with mankind when sunk to the lowest depths of perverted
humanity by a church amongst a nation in which the principles of
heaven were in the state of their utmost perversion. Such a nation
was the jewish, because this was descended from Judah, who was
the type of the perverted celestial principle. But such being the
character of the jewish nation, it is clear, that the divine truth of the
Word, in coming into representative forms as its ultimates, would
necessarily be involved in representatives which did not truly belong
to it, and which, therefore, would be cast off as a slough, whenever
the Word passed from the Jews to the true church of which their
dispensation was merely typical.

This may be illustrated by the growth of a plant from the sowing
of its seed to the reproduction of new seeds in its fruit. Figuratively,
the good and truth of the Word, enveloped in true representatives,
were the essential oil and spirituous matter of the fruit of a tree as
they are involved in their interior coverings. And in the degeneracy
of mankind, or the decadency of the church, the representatives of
the Word in the adamic and noahtic churches were enveloped in the
idolatrous representative rituals and the merely external holy worship
in the hebraic and judaic nations, so as to preserve them—for use in
a future and better state of the church—during an exceedingly and
utterly debased state of mankind, comparatively as the essential oil
and spirituous matter in the kernel, with its interior coverings, are
involved in the outer prickly or bitter coverings of the chestnut or the
walnut, until the time for gathering and garnering of the fruit has
come. If the interior parts of the fruit are deprived of their outer
coverings before the fruit is ripe, it is well known that it will never
come to maturity, but wholly decay. So, if the internals of the
Word and its true representatives had not been involved in false
representatives during an evil state of the world, or if those false representatives had been stripped off before the time for the establishment
of the true church had come, those internals would have been utterly
profaned, and the whole world would have perished in the utter
destruction of any thing like a semblance of the true church on earth.
But when the time for the institution of the christian as an internal
and true church had come, then such parts of the jewish ritual as
were only accommodations to a low and the lowest state of mankind,
and were not the true representatives of the interior truths and goods
of the Word, were put off, just as the burr of a chestnut, or the bitter
rind of a walnut, or the husk of corn, or the chaff of wheat, is put off,
when the harvest of the year has arrived.

This simile clearly illustrates the subject. For it shows what parts
of the jewish ritual were abrogated, and why they were abolished;
and it moreover shows that other parts of the jewish ritual could not
be abrogated, and why they were retained. Those parts of the jewish
ritual were abrogated in the christian church, which were mere

external coverings of the internals of the Word, designed for their preservation and defence from profanation, while the Word was brought down to mankind as a complex sensual and corporeal man: and they were abolished in the christian dispensation, because the christian church was to be an internal or spiritual man, with whom the Word does not need *such* external defences. But this by no means proves that the Word, in the christian church as a spiritual man, does not need to have external defences of some sort; and therefore does not prove that representatives are wholly done away in the christian dispensation; for those parts of the jewish ritual which contain true representatives of the internals of the Word could not be abolished in the christian church, because the internal or spiritual man requires such representatives for the preservation and defence of the Word's internals with him, just as the essential oils and spirituous or farinaceous substances of chestnuts, walnuts, corn and wheat need the interior coverings of those fruits for their preservation in granaries and storehouses until we want to eat them. Thus the outer coverings of fruits are comparatively the *mere* representatives of the jewish ritual, which were abrogated and abolished; but the interior coverings of fruits are comparatively the *true* representatives of that ritual, which were neither abrogated nor abolished in the christian church, and which cannot be put away except into the rational and vital appropriation, by the Christian's internal man, of the internal goods and truths of the Word which they must still and for ever represent in and to his external man.

Thus it is that representatives themselves are not done away in the christian church, which must always have an external as well as an internal man, and which can no more have an internal man perpetually subsisting in it without an appropriate external representative worship, than a man's body can have food kept preserved for its sustenance, by garnering and reproduction, when the fruits that contain its food are wholly stripped of their interior coverings. Let any one crack his nuts, and expose their kernels without their appropriate coverings, and he will soon see how short a time their essential oil, spirit, or farina will keep sweet and nutricious, or retain the vegetative soul alive. To use another simile—if he is taking eggs on a long sea voyage, he must smear them over with oil, embed them in lime, or cover them with such an external defence from the surrounding atmosphere, as will preserve their internal parts from decomposition and evaporation, or they will rot before he can use them. Just so must the Christian have interior and true representative forms for the internal goods and truths of the Word and of worship, before the time or state for the appropriation of those goods and truths by his internal man has arrived, or they will decay and become useless to him. Wherefore, *all* external, ritual, or representative worship was *not* abolished in the christian church, when the Lord abrogated the jewish ritual.

III. *Even parts of the jewish ritual were not wholly abrogated in the christian church.*

The Christian, unlike the Jew, is consociated with heaven and conjoined to the Lord internally as well as externally; but the Jew, unlike the Christian, was associated with heaven and adjoined to the Lord only externally. The Jew is a mere natural, that is, a merely sensual and corporeal man; but the Christian is the celestial or spiritual man brought correspondently into the natural degree. Hence the Jew could be saved only as to the natural man; but the Christian is to be saved as to the spiritual or celestial man, or as to the natural man in the spiritual-natural or the celestial-natural degree. Hence the heaven of the Jews is far to the sides of the christian heaven, which is in the centre of heavenly arrangement in the spiritual world. Consequently, the representatives which foreshadow to the Christian in his natural state what he is destined to be, must be the representatives appropriate to the spiritual or celestial man. Therefore all those parts of the jewish ritual worship which truly represent spiritual and celestial things to the spiritual or the celestial man, may be retained in christian ritual worship; while all those parts that were representative or continent of the divine truth as it comes to, and is defiled by, the merely sensual and corporeal man, is wholly abolished, and can be no longer binding in any way upon Christians.

Although rituals of the jewish church were prescribed by the Lord as *mere* representatives of heavenly things, and although the type has been abolished by the coming of the Prototype, yet it is only as an *obligatory* form, and as an *end* of worship, and as a *needful plane* for the *lowest ultimation*, of the *Word*, that *true* representatives, which are the correspondences of heavenly things, are abrogated in the christian church. These representatives still exist as correspondences in the natural heaven, and are still necessary to the natural man on earth. So that the christian church, although it is not obligatory on her, as it was on the jewish church, to have *all* the representatives, significatives and correspondences of the letter of the Word of the Old Testament as her ritual worship, for the purpose of bringing the whole Word into an ultimate and permanent form, yet must have *some* representatives from the Word as *a* ritual worship, for the presentation and preservation of her celestial and spiritual principles among such of her members as are only in the corporeal, sensual, or natural plane, and as a continent and basis of those principles in the minds of all of her members, however elevated and internal they may have become. (See the first note, or that with an asterisk, at the bottom of page 433.)

Hence, such parts of the jewish ritual as were the representatives of a spiritual or internal church, were in fact not abrogated amongst Christians. In proof of this we bring forward A. C. 9349, where Swedenborg quotes four chapters of Exodus, the twentieth to the twenty-third, as illustrative specimens of the whole Word, in these three respects—1, as to *the things therein which are altogether to be observed and done;* 2, *those things which may serve for use, if the church be disposed;* and 3, *those which are repealed as to use at this day where the church is.* Thus it is evident that some parts of the jewish ritual are by all means to be observed and done by the christian church. And, of course, representatives were not wholly done away by the Lord's abrogation of that ritual.

A single instance will show us that the things retained from the jewish ritual in the christian church, are of a strictly representative character. Among the things therein which are altogether to be observed and done, is the literal observance of that law of the decalogue which forbids any kind of work on the sabbath day. The ground of this observance in the christian church must be the same as in the jewish—namely, that the sabbath, having been typical of the Lord's glorification of his humanity, in which he rested from his labors of conflict with the hells in his complete victory over them, and being still typical of that rest from similar spiritual labors which the human soul enjoys in its advancing regeneration, is therefore one of the most holy *representatives* of the *church*. Nay, as man's regeneration is a work of eternal progress, so that throughout eternity there never will be the time or state in which he can be completely regenerated, the sabbath will ever remain one of the most holy *representatives* of *heaven*. And as such it is to be literally observed in heaven throughout eternity, as it is to be observed in the church throughout all time. Hence the observance of the sabbath, as a day of rest, is still enjoined in the christian church as a ritual which may by no means be dispensed with. Whether it is the first or seventh day of the week, it matters not, provided it is one day in seven, which is made representative and typical of rest from conflict between spiritual and natural life. Such a seventh day is still to be observed by Christians. And hence, in the citations of those parts of the jewish ritual contained in chapters twenty to twenty-three of Exodus, which " are altogether to be observed and done by Christians," verse eight of chapter twenty is included, while verses nine and ten are put in the category of indifferent matters. The eighth verse is, " Remember the sabbath day to keep it holy." This law of the decalogue, therefore, is to be retained in the christian church. But the two following verses, which enjoin the desisting from all work on the *seventh* day of the week, and the giving of the first six days to merely secular employments, may be retained or not as the christian church chooses. Hence it is clear that *a* day of rest must be observed by Christians; but whether that day is the first or the seventh of the week, is immaterial. That part of the jewish ritual which so strictly forbids any kind of work being done on the *seventh* day of the week, is not *obligatory* on the Christian. The Christian may observe this ritual or not, as he thinks proper. But it *is* obligatory on the Christian to observe the sabbath itself. And this is to be observed as a day of spiritual instruction and of cessation from purely secular employments, because the Christian, as well as the Jew, still needs a type and representative of that spiritual rest from conflicts with the evils and falsities of a corrupt hereditary nature which the true Christian must necessarily undergo in passing from death unto life—that is, in passing from mere natural life unto true spiritual life. And without this representative of a sabbath day, in and by which the heavens could be consociated with men on earth, so as to impart to them, from the Lord, spiritual motives in natural pursuits, it would be morally impossible for natural men to become spiritual here or hereafter. Therefore this is one instance to prove that a portion of the jewish ritual as true representative worship is by no means abrogated in the christian dispensation. Consequently, it is established, by the express teachings of the new church, that the strictly representative rites of washing, supping and resting from labors as specimens of all other similar rites which are truly representative of the internals of the Word to the spiritual or celestial man, are still to be observed in the christian church. And therefore representatives in themselves considered, and *true* representative worship, have not been done away amongst Christians. If, then, the sabbath and the holy sacraments of the church, are to be observed by Christians as strictly representative rites, is it not clear that there must be strictly representative priestly offices in the christian church for the due observance and administration of these external rites, and, of course, *a strictly representative christian priesthood?*

But we must not fail to remark, that, in our view, the whole jewish ritual—even the law of the decalogue—*has* been abrogated in the christian church as *jewish* rituals. The decalogue is still binding on Christians, but they are bound to observe and do it from a principle radically different from that which actuated the Jews in its observance. The Jew observed the decalogue as a law of natural life merely—obeyed it from natural ends, and with a view to natural rewards, or from fear of natural punishments. But the Christian is to observe the decalogue as a law of spiritual life, and obey it from spiritual ends merely. And so with regard to the whole jewish ritual: so far as it contains the representatives of true spiritual worship, and embodies the laws of spiritual life, it also may be observed by the Christian as typical of spiritual and eternal life which is to be ever prospectively developed in him. Thus, while we admit that *mere* representative worship, as it was instituted amongst the Jews, has been entirely done away amongst Christians, yet we maintain that *true* representative worship cannot be done away in the christian, or in any, church which has just claims to be the true one. The Jews regarded the external form itself of the ritual as holy ; and esteemed themselves holy in their persons, so as to be entitled to the promises of worldly wealth and earthly happiness merely because they strictly observed the ritual in its external form alone. The ritual of the Jew, as *such* a principle of worship, has indeed ceased to be the law of the Christian. No Christian is or can be now saved by *such deeds of the law*. The Christian is now saved by the law of faith in the spiritual things which were promised by the jewish ritual as "a shadow of good things to come." The Christian, even in any external observance of the rites that may be adopted from the representatives of the letter of the Word of the Old Testament, is saved by the life of the love and understanding of the internal holy things which those external rites represent. Though he *has* an external observance and practice of them, which he may by no means intermit, yet that external observance and practice makes no part of the principle of his worship, and forms no part of the ground of his salvation. His ritual from the letter of the Word may, like the letter of the Word in heaven, *appear* to be done away in the internal sense of it; but it is nevertheless still in existence, just as the letter of the Word still exists, even when the angels seem to see *only* its spiritual sense. The only thing is, that the Christian does not any longer *rest* in the mere ritual of worship, as the Jew did. The principle of his worship and the ground of his salvation are both *faith*, as an *obedience of his spirit* to the internal dictates of God's Word. The life of the commandments as spiritual truths—which is true faith, because all true faith is *doing* what one *believes to be true*—is the Christian's principle of worship, therefore, in even his observance of external rites, and use of representative externals of worship from the letter of the Word. And as these same representative rituals of worship were very different things in the Jew's observance and practice of them,—the Jew's observance of the sabbath, for instance,— consequently, they have ceased *as jewish rituals* with the Christian. And this is what Swedenborg means when he says, "external rites were abolished and representatives ceased" in consequence of the coming of the Lord. He could not have intended to teach that all external rites and representatives in the externals of worship were wholly abolished in the christian church by the Lord's coming and abrogation of the jewish ritual, any more than the letter of the Word is wholly abrogated when the Lord comes as its spiritual sense. Now, as before, the church " has nearly similar rituals, that is, similar statutes, laws and precepts; but its externals correspond with its internals so as to make one," (A. C. 4288 ;) " and thus again internals and externals *form together* one church." (A. C. 1083.) Wherefore, as certain parts of the jewish ritual were retained, so that the christian church " has nearly similar rituals," it is perfectly clear, that the abrogation of the jewish ritual worship in the Lord's advent did not avail to the entire abolition of *all* external rites and representative worship in the christian dispensation.

IV. *The Lord's humanity has fulfilled all the representatives of the churches that preceded the christian, by coming wholly and fully into them; and has for ever established them, by becoming itself wholly and fully representative of the same things which they represented.*

We regret that we cannot enlarge upon this topic here as much as its importance demands, and its clear elucidation requires. We must be content with a general statement of our argument, and a single elucidation of it. This is our argument in general. The Lord, in assuming and glorifying humanity for human redemption and salvation, fulfilled the Word in ultimates. But " in ultimate things are representatives and significatives." (Ap. Ex. 31.) Therefore, the Lord, in glorifying his humanity, did not wholly do away representatives—even those of the israelitish or jewish church—but " represented and perfected them in himself." (Ap. Ex. 654.) And as the Lord, that he " might govern and arrange ultimate things from first principles," so as to hold in subjection to himself, and in subserviency to his end of saving men and making them eternally happy, and thus

arrange and govern "all intermediate things from first principles by
things ultimate," (Ap. Rev. 798,) came into representatives and
significatives while in the world, so that " whatever he *did* in the world
was *representative*, and whatever he *said* was *significative*," (Ap. Ex.
31)—therefore, the Lord, in instituting the christian church, with its
sacraments, and the clerical administrators of them, must have
established christian representatives, and fulfilled them in that church
as his body, comparatively as he fulfilled them in the humanity which
he took from the virgin Mary as the representative of his church.
Wherefore, representatives, even those of the jewish ritual, cannot
be wholly done away in the christian church, but must be established
in a new form, suited to the genius of the christian dispensation.
And hence the christian church as a spiritual body of the Lord now
on earth, must fulfil in itself all the true representatives, and put off
all the false ones, of the jewish ritual, just as the Lord did in the
assumption and glorification of humanity.

Now in elucidation of our argument, we make the following observations. The Lord, in his advent by the christian dispensation, so
far from abolishing true representatives, fulfilled them to every jot
and tittle, so as to make his humanity their perpetual complex form.
For instance, both his divinity and his humanity are wholly present
in his supper—in its bread and its wine, and in the appropriation of
these strictly representative and correspondential elements by the
love and faith of his disciples. The eating of bread and drinking of
wine are strictly representative acts, and heaven is consociated, and
the Lord through heaven is conjoined, with men by these acts as
representatives on earth. The Lord is *actually present* in *these representatives* of *bread, wine, eating* and *drinking*. He *fills* the representatives *full* of his presence. Therefore the representatives of the
jewish sacrifices, all of which were called " *bread*," are not done
away, but established. And *all* representative sacrificial worship is
here collated into one divinely instituted complex of the supper, just
as *all* representative purificatory worship is collated into the one
divinely instituted complex of baptism. In the various ritual washings of the Jews, and in their passover and other sacrifices, the Lord's
humanity was only representatively present, and only representatively
redeeming and saving the souls of men; but baptism and the holy
supper are the Lord's humanity itself in a representative form on
earth, by which that humanity, with the whole of its redemption and
the whole of its salvation, is *actually* present to the souls of men on
earth, so as *actually* and not *representatively* to redeem and save them
from their sins. The representative rite itself is the ultimate, into
which the Lord has come, so that he may operate " from himself in
ultimates" as well as " from himself in first principles." (Ap. Rev.
798.) In short, when the Lord instituted baptism and the holy supper
as a part of his Word of the New Testament, he made them his
humanity itself as his Word is his humanity; and these rituals, with
his divinity in them, as in all the other representatives and significatives of the Word, constitute the church his representative body upon
earth. The rituals themselves, as being a part of the letter of his

Word, in which he is as to his divinity in his fulness and his power, are representative of his work of redemption and salvation. Baptism is representative of human reformation, which is individual redemption; and the supper is representative of human regeneration, which is individual salvation. The one represents man's purification from infernal principles by truth, which is "the washing of water by the Word," and constitutes man's redemption from the powers of hell; the other represents his confirmation in good, which is his salvation, or permanent state of spiritual health. And, truth and good thus induced upon man's soul as a new spiritual form and quality, constitute the Lord's divine humanity itself redeeming and saving men actually from their sins. Therefore baptism and the supper, as ultimate representative things involving this, are the Lord's divine humanity itself coming into and fulfilling representative worship in the christian church. And these representative rites do involve this, because the Lord, by and through his angels, does actually, that is, with the substance of his good and the form of his truth, flow into the souls of men in their very acts of holy eating, holy drinking, and holy washing, as divinely appointed ultimates on earth.

Thus the Lord's humanity has fulfilled *all* representatives by coming wholly and fully into them, and has for ever established them by becoming itself wholly and fully representative of the same things which they represented. The only difference is, that the representatives of former churches represented a redemption and salvation which *were to come*, and the Lord's humanity represents the redemption and salvation which *have come*. Representatives in former dispensations were shadows of a substance that was approaching, and representatives in the christian dispensation are shadows of that substance, not only as it has approached, but as it is actually in, and intimately present with, the christian church. The substance has not, in mercy, ceased to cast its shadow still, but it is now the shadow of a real and a vital presence cast on Christians from within; whereas, in the jewish dispensation, it was merely a cold and lifeless shadow cast on the Jews from without. Hence the representative presence of the Lord in the jewish mere representative worship did not necessarily save the Jews—it was not the shadow of a then present substance, but of a coming one—it was not indicative of his actual internal presence with them as a nation—it, therefore, did not redeem and save them individually, as souls were then to be, and are now, saved in a christian heaven—it was instituted among them as the worst of nations, that mankind might be kept from entire destruction in their lowest state of spiritual degradation, and that a pure spiritual worship might be preserved, as an embryo, for development in a purer and better subsequent state of the church. But when the time for that purer and better state of the church has arrived, and the Lord, that substance which was foreshadowed in former dispensations, has come, he does not come as a substance without *any* shadow—his coming is not a totally shadowless advent—his substance *has* a shadow now as formerly; but his shadow is now the evidence of his actual presence—is the vital sphere of his divine humanity, which humanity is the summation, signing and sealing of all his efforts for human redemption and salvation. And thus it is clear, that the Lord has not abolished, but fulfilled, true representative worship in the christian church.

Such is our argument for the Lord's having fulfilled the *rituals of worship* in the christian church. From which we deduce this conclusion. As the sacraments and other external ritual worship of the christian church, are in fact the Lord's humanity itself in a representative form on earth, and as this ritual worship requires priestly offices and functionaries for its administration, that must be alike representative of the Lord and his divine work of redeeming and saving men, therefore there must be christian priests, in a christian priesthood, who shall represent the Lord in all the successive and simultaneous degrees of that work. Thus there must be three discrete degrees of priests in the christian priesthood. For, without these degrees in the christian priesthood as a complex man, it could not be a full or perfect representative of the Lord's divine human form and activity in its discrete parts.

V. *But not only has the Lord fulfilled all representatives as the rituals of external worship in the church, he has also fulfilled them as a celestial man in the body of common society.*

This is the theme of several chapters in our projected work. It requires an extended explanation of the historical relation in the Word respecting Samson and the Philistines. The drift of our argument upon this topic can be only stated thus briefly here. The Lord has fulfilled the representative of Samson destroying the Philistines in their temple, by so coming as a principle of common humanity into the sensual and corporeal plane of human society as to subvert therein the fundamental principles of the solifidian church. This principle of common humanity in common society is the Lord's divine celestial and spiritual powers brought into the proper representative ultimates of a correspondent natural degree. And it is the especial privilege and duty of the Lord's new church, which is now descending from him out of heaven, to bring her celestial and spiritual principles also into corresponding ultimates and proper representative forms in the corporeal and sensual plane, where alone they can be in their fullness and their power. The church must do this in her *formal* as well as in her *essential* worship. She must do it in the common body of society as well as in her own more distinctive outward embodiment of an external church. This implies, not only that she should have true representatives of her internal virtues in the architecture of her temples and the formularies of her worship, but that she should avail herself of the powers of representatives and correspondences in painting, sculpture, poetry, literature, the drama, and every other engine of the sensual plane, whereby her heavenly principles can be transfused, as a saving or healing efficacy, throughout the whole body of common society. It implies, most especially, the true church's provision of those recreations of charity by which alone the young and simple of mankind can be brought and kept within her pale for their preservation amidst the allurements and blandishments of a degenerate world. And there is the same reason that the church, as well as the Lord, should thus come into a most ultimate representative form *on earth*. For both rest on that common divine law, that all interior principles are full and perfect in their ultimates, and are more full and more perfect in the ratio of the ultimity of their descent. It was on this law that Jehovah God took unto himself greater power in human redemption and salvation, so that the light of his countenance became seven-fold brighter as with the light of seven days, when he became incarnate in Jesus Christ. It was thus that he became a Samson—a divine celestial man in a divine natural degree. And the church, as his image and likeness, must exert his power in the same way. Hence she must bring her celestial and spiritual principles into true representative forms in the sensual and corporeal plane. For this plane is the most ultimate, and therefore celestial principles have in it their greatest power.

The obvious conclusion from this argument, in its relevancy to our present subject, is, that the New Jerusalem should not fly from Aaron's rod, because it has become a serpent in being cast upon the ground. But Moses, the internal of the Word in her, must take this serpent up, that it may become a staff in his hand. In other words, all those representatives, as ultimate things, which bring the internal principles of the new church out or down into the sensual plane, so as to represent them to children and simple-minded worshipers, must be used in her external worship. And the powers of this principle must not be left in the hands of the Catholics, or other sects of the old and consummated christian church, under mistaken notions of christian *simplicity*. For if a learned catholic or episcopal priesthood, with clerical robes and a trinal arrangement—if painting, sculpture, music, and other appliances to the sense of the worshiper, are so potent in spreading the false doctrines of a false faith, much more should they be the means of spreading the true doctrines of the true faith. There is just as much reason why the New Jerusalem should have these or such like representatives of a true external representative worship, as the ancient church had. And until the new church does have them, her internal principles will be like a man with a withered hand, whom the Lord finds in her temple, when he has passed through the corn fields with his disciples on the sabbath day.

VI. *Representatives in themselves considered can never be done away without the total subversion of the divine economy.*

To prove this, we have to show, by extended quotations from the writings of the new church, what representatives in their true nature are. When this is seen, it is at once discerned that they never can be done away. We cannot, of course, recite those passages here, inasmuch as this alone would require many pages. Nor can we even refer to all of them. Our argument is, that true representatives—representatives in themselves considered—were not done away in the first christian church, and can never be done away in the New Jerusalem, because representatives are in their very nature such things as cannot be abrogated without the destruction of divine order itself. Among other passages which go to show this, we here cite A. C.

29

-1632, 1881, 2987, 10.728, 2988, 2990, 2991, 3000, 3002, 3213, 3223-25, 3241, 3343, 3344, 3347, 3475, 3483. These are some of the passages which may be cited to show what representatives are in their true nature. And in relation to man, or the Word as a means of his salvation, this brief extract sufficiently shows what is their use : "Unless all and singular the things contained in the Word were representative, and unless all and singular the expressions by which those things are written were significative of divine things belonging to the Lord, the Word could not be divine : and as this is the case, it could not possibly be written in any other style; for by this style, and by no other, human things and expressions correspond with celestial things and ideas, as to the smallest jot and tittle. Hence it is, that if the Word be read only by an infant, the divine things which are therein are perceived by the angels." (A. C. 2899.) Thus angels can have communication with men in no other way than by the representatives of the Word. The externals of the Word and the externals of worship are the same ; because all true worship of the Lord is from the Word. Hence angels can have communication with men only by the representatives in the ritual of a church. And there must of necessity be communication of heaven with men by a church in order that mankind may exist. (A. C. 4545.) Thus the great use of representatives on earth is, to ultimate the Word, and consociate mankind with heaven for their salvation, when, without them, they would be totally lost.

Wherefore, from what these and other parallel passages of our church's writings teach, we conclusively argue, that representatives in themselves considered can never be done away, because—

Firstly, They are the foundations of the internals of the Word; and, therefore, cannot be abrogated without the destruction of the Word itself, in its applicability to man and his salvation.

Secondly, They are the groundwork of all human arts, society and life, both civil and religious; and cannot be abrogated without the destruction of man, both as a member of common society and as a member of the church.

Thirdly, They are needful to spirits in the world of spirits ; so that, if they were to be done away there, spirits would have no plane for angelic influx, and must perish for want of conjunction with the Lord through the medium of the heavens.

Fourthly, They exist in all three of the heavens, serving as connecting links between them ; and if they ceased to exist there, the light, life and joy of the heavens would perish.

Fifthly, They are "real things" flowing from the Lord through the heavens and producing all orderly existences throughout the universe; and hence, if they were abolished, there would be no theatre representative of the Lord's kingdom, and none representative of the Lord himself.

Sixthly, They are all those things which exist in the natural world by derivation from spiritual things in the spiritual world ; and, therefore, if they were done away, the natural world would cease to exist.

Seventhly, They are the means whereby all higher discrete planes of being flow into, produce effects in, and give life to, lower planes; and, consequently, if they were done away, the things of the mind could not be expressed adequately in the things of the body—the things of the spiritual world could not be adequately exhibited in the natural world—angels and spirits could have no speech for converse with one another, and no plane for consociation with men—the deep arcana of divine truth could never be conveyed to mortals for their salvation, and thus no church could exist on earth or subsist in heaven, and all mankind must for ever perish.

Therefore, we conclude, representatives are, in their very nature, things so synonymous with the divine order and its influx, that if they were done away, divine order itself would be destroyed. And, consequently, it is fully established, that representatives can never be abolished, but, coming from the Lord, and existing in all the heavens, in the world of spirits, and in the universe of nature, they must for ever continue to form the externals of the church and its worship, as they will for ever constitute the externals of the Word.

VII. *The New Jerusalem is to be the celestial church restored, and, in retracing the footsteps of the church in her decadency, will, in at least one of the stages of her upward progress, be a true representative church, as the ancient church was.*

In expanding this idea, we have, at considerable length, to trace again representatives to their origin, and then to show the distinction between the true representative church and the mere representative of one, which is seen by comparing the noahtic church with the jewish church. Hence, after considering the character of the jewish church and people, in contradistinction to the christian, so as to see why some part of the jewish representative worship was to be retained and the most part to be wholly done away in the christian dispensation, we then go on to trace representatives, through their several discrete grades of descent, back again to the celestial or most ancient church. And not stopping there, but going beyond that, we trace them through the world of spirits, and the natural, spiritual and celestial heavens to the Lord himself. Thus we discover the Lord to be the Alpha and the Omega of representatives: for we had previously seen that he came into and fulfilled all true representative forms by assuming and glorifying humanity in the veriest ultimates of existence, and we now see that representatives flow from him above the heavens. For "representatives in their highest source are modifications of light by shade :" and the new church now reveals to us, that "the light which proceeds from the Lord, when it flows into the inmost or the third heaven, is received there as good which is called charity, [and the forms of good are representatives there ;] and when it flows into the middle or the second heaven, mediately and immediately, it is received as the truth, which is from charity, [and the forms of that truth are representatives there;] but when this truth flows into the last or first heaven, mediately and immediately, it is received substantially, and appears there as a paradise, and in some places as a city, wherein are palaces. Thus correspondences succeed each other even to the external sight of the angels. In like manner in man, in his ultimate principle, which is the eye, that [light] is presented materially by the sight, the objects of which are the things belonging to the visible world."

Thus representatives originate in *good* and *truth* from the Lord, which, as *heat* and *light*, descend through the heavens into the earths, and, coming into forms that are visible to the external sight of angels and men, *represent* thereby the Lord's divine qualities to angelic and human minds. Thus representatives exist first above the heavens; descend thence and flow into the heavens; pass through the heavens and exist substantially in the world of spirits; flow from thence into the natural world, and, taking to themselves corresponding forms in matter, exist materially there, so that " whatsoever any where appears in the universe is representative of the Lord's kingdom, insomuch that there' is not any thing contained in the universal atmospheric region of the stars, or in the earth or its three kingdoms, but what, in, its manner and measure, is representative: for all and singular the things in nature are ultimate images, inasmuch as from the Deity proceed the celestial things appertaining to good, and from these celestial things the spiritual things appertaining to truth, and from both the former and the latter proceed natural things: . . . . Wherefore, as all and singular things subsist, that is, exist, from the Deity, and all and singular things thence derived must needs be representative of those things whereby they had existence, it follows, that the visible universe is nothing else but a theatre representative of the Lord's kingdom, and that the Lord's kingdom is a theatre representative of the Lord himself." (A. C. 3483.)

Now the church is the Lord's kingdom on earth. Therefore, the church, like his kingdom, is " a theatre representative of the Lord himself." Thus the church is at all times representative of the Lord. But, as the church degenerates, it comes more and more into representatives alone. That is, its internal principles become closed, and the connection of heaven with mankind by it is more and more effected by what is external without any corresponding internal principle. And as the church is reformed, regenerated, and so restored to its pristine integrity, it comes more and more into the inner representatives of the discrete spiritual degrees, through which it repasses. Thus representatives are not and cannot be done away in any stage of the church's upward progress. It merely throws off outer garments, as it ascends into purer and more genial spiritual regions, to which its inner garments are better suited.

Now by actually tracing the church from the Jews back through all its discrete degrees, we find representatives in all, even in the celestial or most ancient church; and we discover that from the most ancient church they have flowed down through all the intermediate churches to the jewish as the last and lowest. Hence the New Jerusalem, beginning in the natural plane, and going back through the spiritual to the celestial plane, will have representatives in all of them. But most certainly will this church have an external representative ritual worship when she becomes a true representative church as the noahtic church was. And this appears from considering the difference between the noahtic and the jewish church, which is the same as the difference between the representative church and the representative of a church. The distinction between these two is shown in A. C. 4288. And the following five characteristics of a representative church show very conclusively that the abrogation of the jewish ritual did not necessarily ordain that the New Jerusalem should not be a representative church :—

Firstly, It has nearly similar rituals, that is, similar statutes, laws and precepts; but its externals correspond with its internals so as to make one.

Secondly, In it celestial and spiritual love is principal—is its very internal itself, while corporeal and worldly love is altogether subordinate.

Thirdly, Its internal is in an appropriate external.

Fourthly, Its members have communication with heaven as to their interiors.

Fifthly, To their interiors, their external worship serves as a plane.

These are the five characteristics of a true representative church—of a real church which *has* representatives in its external worship without being *in* them merely. Now, in view of these characteristics, we conclude—

Firstly, That the New Jerusalem, which is to restore the church from its lowest depths to its greatest heights, and, therefore, in its upward progress, must retrace the steps of its downfall, may be, at least in her spiritual stage, a representative church.

Secondly, And now especially, when she is only setting out on this journey of her eternal life, the New Jerusalem may and must have sandals on her feet, a breast plate and other armor on her body, a helmet on her head, and all other appliances for her security and defence in the journeyings before her.

Thirdly, The New Jerusalem, in her natural degree, may and must have an external, representative, ritual worship, so significant of, and correspondent to, her internal principles, as to present and convey those principles to the minds of the young and simple.

From these conclusions, it must be perfectly manifest now, that the Lord, in abrogating the mere representative worship of the jewish ritual, did not wholly do away representatives in the christian church, and did not annul, or interdict, in the New Jerusalem, the true representatives of the noahtic or ancient church. The noahtic was an internal church in an appropriate external one; and it is expressly asserted that the christian church is the same, with the exception that "other externals, as the sacraments, succeeded to their sacrifices, &c.," which, like the former, "*representatively* referred to and regarded the Lord." (A. C. 1083.) In fact, the abrogation of the jewish ritual, with its "sacrifices, &c.," was but the taking away of idolatrous superadditions to true representatives, which had been allowed in merciful accommodation to the posterity of the first ancient church, in order to withdraw them from idolatries of the more heinous sort by the permission of those that were harmless. Hence the true representatives of the ancient church were left untouched as a cuticle, or as an under dress, when the jewish sacrificial worship was taken off as a covering garment. And hence the true representatives of the ancient church may all be retained in the christian church, if it is so disposed; and some of them *must* be retained as an indispensable envelope, continent and defence of its internal principles.

There have been four grand divisions of churches on this earth—the adamic, noahtic, judaic and christian. Each of these has had, or is to have, a trine of churches in itself. The adamic church is called the most ancient—was the first on this earth, and from its celestial genius was styled the golden age. In its three phases, it degenerated into the most awful idolatries, by the perversion of its celestial representatives. Among these was the Lord's prediction that he would come into the world to save mankind, by being born a child and offering himself a sacrifice for their sins. In the perversion of this representative prediction, by the remote posterity of the most ancient church, human sacrifices arose.

In the consummation of this first or celestial church, a new one of a different genius was instituted by the Lord. This was a spiritual church, and the period of its integrity was styled the silver age. Like the former, this too had three discrete phases. The first was called Noah. As we have seen, it was a true representative church, that is, an internal church with an external, ritual or representative worship which truly represented its own internal principles. This church, "spread far and wide over the face of the globe, particularly in Asia, in process of time, as is usual with all churches in all places, grew degenerate, and was adulterated by innovations, both as to its external and its internal worship. This was the case in various countries, and was owing especially to this circumstance, that all the *significatives* and *representatives* which the *ancient church received by oral tradition from the most ancient church*, all which had respect to the Lord and his kingdom, were turned into idolatrous rites, and with some nations into magical ceremonies. To prevent the destruction which hence threatened the whole church, it was permitted by the Lord that a significative and representative worship should be again restored in a particular country. This was effected by Heber; and this worship consisted principally in external things. The external things employed were high places, groves, statues, anointings, *besides the establishment of* PRIESTLY OFFICES, *and of whatever had relation to their functions;* together with various other things which are included in the name of statutes or ordinances. The internals of their worship were doctrinals derived from the Antediluvians, especially from those who were called Enoch, who collected the truths which the most ancient church saw by perception, and thence framed doctrinals; and these were their Word. From both these sources was derived the worship of this church, which was called Heber, but *with additions* and *alterations*, particularly in this circumstance, that, above all other rituals, sacrifices began to be preferred, which were unknown in the true ancient church, except with the posterity of Ham and Canaan, who, being idolators, were allowed this kind of worship, to prevent their sacrificing their sons and their daughters. Hence it appears what was the quality and character of this *second ancient* church, which was instituted by Heber, and was continued by his posterity." (A. C. 1241.)

We here see mention made of *two* of the *trine* of ancient churches. The first was named Noah, and the different kinds of worship prevailing in it were signified by Shem, Ham, Japheth and Canaan. The first ancient church was an internal one, which, in process of time, became idolatrous by subsiding in mere external worship without any regard to internal worship. And the hebrew church, so called from Heber its founder, was a sort of new ancient church, instituted for the purpose of saving mankind from destruction in the perversion of the old one. It was, therefore, accommodated to mankind in that state of the world, and, consequently, was an external church, having a worship consisting principally in external things, but having also doctrinals of truth derived from the Antediluvians as the internals of its worship: so that it was a sort of internal church still. Now it should be well observed, that the first ancient church derived *significatives* and *representatives*, as the externals of its worship, "by *oral tradition* from the *most ancient church.*" This proves that the most ancient church, as a celestial one, had significatives and representatives. And "from both these sources," that is, both from the *ante* and the *post-*diluvian churches, was derived the externals of worship of the church called Heber, "but *with additions* and *alterations*," particularly and especially of a ritual enjoining the sacrifice of animals, "which was unknown in the true ancient church." We thus learn that the hebrew church had external things of two kinds in its worship—firstly, true representatives, or, as Swedenborg elsewhere styles them, "*genuine* or *internal* representatives," such as "high places, groves, statues, anointings, *priestly offices* and *whatever had relation to their* [priestly] *functions;* and, secondly, certain *new kinds* of worship, which were *additions to*, and *alterations of*, true representatives, elsewhere styled by Swedenborg *mere* and *external* representatives. In short, in the hebrew, or second ancient, church, *sacrifices* began first to be allowed as a divinely permitted and prescribed ritual of the church. Hence this hebrew church had true representatives mixed in a certain degree with false or idolatrous representatives,—as a sort of excrescences formed upon the body of the church in its degeneracy,—so as to furnish a true representative worship in some degree to an idolatrous people—that is, so as to serve as a medium between heaven and mankind in an idolatrous state. And every thing which is to serve as a medium between two other things which are so discretely separated as to be unable to unite without it, must have something of both so combined in its constitution as to give it the quality of a connecting intermediate. For example, oil and water are so discrete as to have no affinity, and, therefore, cannot be permanently commingled. To unite them, there must be some substance which partakes both of the quality of oil and of water. Such a substance is salt or sugar. So that, when oil and water are triturated with salt or sugar, they unite and form an emulsion. Just so, in uniting heaven with mankind for their preservation in an idolatrous state, the church, as the connecting medium, must have something of heaven and something of idolatry.

Such, therefore, was the quality and character of the church here called Heber. By this church a plane was formed for saving mankind when they were sunk or sinking into an idolatrous state. Consequently, the hebrew church was a sort of true internal church substituted for the first ancient church as a corrupt internal one; and, therefore, was the ancient church itself in a renewed, or more external, form. Thus it was still a part of the second grand division of churches on this earth.

But according to the postulate, this second grand division must have had a third discrete phasis. And our church, in her explication of the eleventh chapter of Genesis, which speaks of Babel and the confusion of tongues there, teaches that a third ancient church, besides the second one called Heber, did in fact exist. These are her words, in explaining the phrase, "the whole earth was of one lip" [or language.] This "denotes the ancient church in its integrity, as having everywhere prevailing within its borders one doctrine in general." But in the following verse is described how that church began to be falsified and adulterated; and afterwards, as far as verse nine, how it was altogether perverted, so that there remained no longer any internal worship. "The subject soon after treated of is concerning a *second* church begun by Heber; and, lastly, concerning a *third*, which was the beginning of the jewish church: for *after the flood there were* THREE *churches in succession.*" (A. C. 1285.) Here we learn that there were three discrete churches in the ancient church as the second grand division, and that the third of these was the beginning of the jewish church. In other words, the last of the second grand division prepared the way for the first of the third grand division. Hence we shall find that true representatives, derived by oral tradition from the most ancient church to the first ancient church, were transmitted from this by the second ancient church, with the additions and alterations of the rituals of sacrificial worship, through the third ancient church, to the jewish, as the third grand division of churches on this earth.

Thus having traced representatives up to their origin in the most ancient or celestial church, we turn and see how they have gushed from their pure fountain, and, flowing down, like crystal rivulets, through distant tracts, have acquired impure additions, according to the qualities of the regions through which they have passed, until they have come into the gross and impure form in which they are found amongst the Jews. And we present this further proof of the fact that the external representatives of the jewish ritual were merely the accretions of idolatrous sacrificial worship which true representatives received in their passage through the hebraic dispensation of the noahtic church:—"The most ancient churches, which were before the flood, were altogether unacquainted with sacrifices, nor did it ever enter into their minds to worship the Lord by the slaying of animals. The ancient church,* which was after the flood, was likewise unac-

---

* In reference to the appearance of there having been sacrifices in the first ancient church, because it is said, in Gen. viii. 20, that *Noah offered burnt offerings to Jehovah*, our church says, " this, however, is not a real historical circumstance, but a statement

quainted with sacrifices: it was indeed principled in representatives, but sacrifices were instituted in the succeeding church, which was called the hebrew church; and thence this mode of worship was propagated amongst the Gentiles, and descended to Abraham, Isaac and Jacob, and thus to their posterity." (A. C. 2180.)

That human sacrifices originated in the representative prophetic enunciation of "the most ancient time, that the Lord was to come into the world, and that he was to suffer death," is clearly inferable from A. C. 2818. This originated "a custom amongst the Gentiles of sacrificing their children." And it is expressly said, "the sons of Jacob also inclined to this abomination, and so likewise did Abraham. That the sons of Jacob were so inclined, appears from the prophets; but *to prevent their* FALLING *into that abomination, it was permitted to institute burnt offerings and sacrifices.*" (A. C. 2818.)

Thus it is clear that the jewish sacrificial worship, which takes up far the largest part of the jewish ritual, was a mere idolatrous superaddition to true representatives in the ancient churches. Hence our church, in teaching that the letter of the Word would have been different from what it is, if the Word had been written amongst another people than the Jews, expressly declares, "that every *genuine* or *internal representative* of the church departed from them before they came into the land of Canaan, where an *external representative* of the church was begun amongst them in full form." (A. C. 4293.)

But the Jews were brought out of Egypt, had the law given to them from Mount Sinai, and were introduced into the land of Canaan, that they might preserve *true representatives* for a future church, without themselves profaning them. They were chosen for this use,

---

composed in an historical form, [an historical allegory or fiction;] because, by burnt offerings was signified the holy principle of worship, as may be there seen." (A. C. 1343) And the same doctrine shows us in what light the offerings of Abel, and similar ones, in the most ancient church, are to be regarded. As the first chapters of Genesis are not a literal history, but only contain an allegorical description of the things of the church and of heaven in the language of representatives or correspondences, and thus, as there were actually no such persons as Adam, Eve, Cain, or Abel on this earth, therefore what is related of those persons, cannot have been *natural facts;* but must have been statements of only such internal things as related to the charity, faith, or worship of churches called by their names. Hence this appearance of sacrificial worship having been offered up by them as persons, does not show that any such worship was in natural fact instituted in the most ancient church. These were celestial representatives of those times, which existed only in the minds of celestial men by the revelation of angels from heaven. But these, descending by oral tradition to the churches which succeeded, might, in the long lapse of ages, become actual rites amongst the idolatrous gentile nations into which those churches degenerated, just as the celestial representatives of the Lord's incarnation came into the sacrifice of children and other human sacrifices in the remote posterities of the most ancient churches. These celestial idolators were doubtless Gentiles in the consummation of the first ancient church; and, possibly, may have been the origin of the cannibals now existing on our earth; so that the posterity of Ham and Canaan, residing in more or less contiguity with these gentile nations, were in danger of adopting their sacrifices Hence, the Lord, in mercy, allowed the sacrifice of animals to be instituted in the hebrew church, to keep "the posterity of Ham and Canaan" from "sacrificing their sons and daughters." (A. C. 1241. See, also, A. C. 2818.)

because they had become more external, that is, more selfish, worldly, sensual and corporeal than all other nations. This had been permitted by Divine Providence in order that they might represent the holy internal things of the church without profanation, because they thus "could act as representative of a church, namely, represent holy things in an external form without any internal holy principle." The obstinacy of their selfish and worldly delusions and desires made them perseveringly importunate to be called and considered the Lord's church, or peculiarly holy people; for by this means their desires of pre-eminence and wealth could be gratified. And for retaining the objects of their desires when once possessed, they could conform most strictly to the most ascetic and apparently self-denying forms of external holiness, so as to "act above all other nations as the representative of a church." Thus they were, of all nations or people that ever existed, best suited to represent the holy internal things of the Word without *any* danger of profaning them. And thus they were exactly suited, and were therefore chosen by the Lord, to preserve the true representatives of the church in that state of the world when mankind had sunk to the lowest stage of spiritual degradation, so that not the least possibility of saving them by an internal conjunction with heaven remained, and, unless the true representatives of heaven had been given to the Jews, covered up as they were in the mere, factitious, external representatives of their idolatrous superadditions, mankind must have sunk into remediless perdition, and all possibility of kindling the flame of pure spiritual worship, from these coals of heavenly fire now covered up in jewish ashes, in some future and better state of the world, would have been cut off for ever.

Let us take one instance of how a true representative of worship was preserved by the Jews for the christian church. All true external worship must be a type of the Lord's redemption and salvation of mankind in the complete glorification of his humanity. In the completion of this glorification, or, what is the same thing in regard to men, in the completion of our regeneration, which is our salvation, or complete redemption, which is the holy marriage of good and truth, the Lord rests from his labors of conflict with infernal evils and falsities as the enemies of our souls. (A. C. 9086, 10.780.) Of this, as we have before shown, the sabbath is to be representative in all time. Now how was this representative to be preserved in the jewish state of the world? The Jews, as the perfect type of that state, were the most selfish and avaricious of all people. Hence the Jew, like all avaricious people, was exceedingly *timid*—afraid of death. And it was this characteristic to which the Lord appealed in securing the perpetuation of the true representative of the sabbath. Hence Swedenborg says—"The reason why it was so severely forbidden to do any work on the feasts and sabbaths was, that, on such occasions, they might be in a full representative state, that is, in such things as represented things celestial and spiritual; which state would have been disturbed, if they had done works that respected the world and the earth as an end; for the representatives of the church were instituted amongst the posterity of Jacob, to the intent that, by them, there might be a communication of heaven with man, which is the end for which the church is established. This communication would not have been obtained unless, *under the penalty of death*, it had been forbidden to do any work on the days of the feasts and sabbaths; for things worldly and terrestrial had gained a place in their minds, and they were men of such a quality that they immersed themselves in such things with their whole heart. Wherefore, if they had been at liberty to employ themselves at the same time in those things, the communication by representatives would have been altogether interrupted and annihilated." (A. C. 7893.) Thus the representative of rest from labors on the sabbath day was preserved, in a condition of the world when attention to secular concerns was all-engrossing, by the penalty of death; and the Jew was of all men most susceptible of restraint by this penalty, because, being most avaricious, he was most in the fear of death. And we have shown that this representative has not been done away in the christian church by the abrogation of the jewish ritual. The sabbath is still to be a representative in the christian church—only it is now an *internal, genuine,* or *true* representative. The sabbath is now to be observed as a day of rest "for the sake of heavenly life on the occasion; and for the sake of doctrine, that it may be learned what faith and charity are," (A. C. 7893:) and "the representative state" which signifies "the heavenly marriage which is the conjunction of good and truth from the Lord" in christian, as well as any other, men, and which "represents in the supreme sense the Lord's union of his humanity with the very divinity in himself," would be as much disturbed in the christian as in the jewish church, if the Christian, equally as the Jew, were to do "works that respected the world and the earth as an end" on that day. Thus we see how the Jews were chosen by the Lord to preserve true representatives for the use of the christian church. For this one instance illustrates how all the true representatives, derived by oral tradition from the most ancient to the ancient church, and by the hebrew church transmitted thence, in the rough casket, as it were, of idolatrous sacrificial worship, to the jewish church, were, by this latter church, preserved, in the same casket, for the use of Christians, to whom they were given, in the institution of the christian church, by the Lord, who took them out of their casket by the abrogation of the mere external, idolatrous ritual which had contained, preserved and conveyed them.

We say true representatives, that is, representatives and significatives derived from the most ancient or celestial church, were involved in and conveyed by the jewish ritual as the books of the Old Testament. And we show, from the writings of our church, that the most ancient church had not only the objects of universal nature as representatives of the Lord's kingdom (A. C. 2750)—nor only those representatives which were correspondences of their internal man in their external man (A. C. 1563, 1568)—but also "paradisiacal representatives, and many other things of a like nature," by the immediate revelation of dreams and visions from the spiritual world—also "the significative or enigmatical representations of terrestrial objects." (A. C. 920.) Wherefore it is clear that the men of the most ancient

church had representatives in a form suited to their genius. And
Swedenborg says expressly—"From them first arose representatives
and significatives, which continued long after their times; and, at
length, were held in such veneration, by reason of their antiquity,
that books were written by mere representatives, and the books which
were not so written, were held in no estimation, yea, and accounted
of no sanctity, if written within the church. Hence, and for other
mysterious reasons, the books of the Word also were so written."
(A. C. 2179.) Thus it is demonstrated that there were representatives, the same as exist now in the letter of the Word, in the most
ancient church; and that from that church they were derived to all
subsequent churches on this earth, and were turned into idolatrous
rites and ceremonies, which were in some degree allowed in the
hebraic and judaic churches as a vehicle for their conveyance to the
christian church. Consequently, the jewish church is the most
ancient church brought into its lowest possible form of a mere
shadow of its substance. For "the members of the most ancient
church, which was of a celestial character, regarded all things terrestrial and worldly, with such as are corporeal also—indeed, all objects
of the senses whatsoever, no otherwise than as things dead: but as
all things which exist in the world, both generally and particularly,
present some idea of the Lord's kingdom, consequently of things
celestial and spiritual, when they apprehended them by sight, or any
other of the senses, they did not think of *them*, but of the spiritual
and celestial things of which they were significative: deriving also
this perception, not from the sensible objects as origins, but by them
as means: thus dead things with them became alive. These things,
thus signified by the objects of sense, were collected by their posterity
from the mouth of their forefathers, and were framed by them into
doctrinals, which composed the Word of the ancient church after the
flood. These doctrinals formed the significatives of the ancient
church; for by them they acquired a knowledge of things internal,
and raised their thoughts from them to things spiritual and celestial.
But when that knowledge began to perish, so that the significations
were no longer known, and men began to account those terrestrial and
worldly things holy, and to worship them, without any thought concerning their signification; then the same were made representatives.
Hence came the representative church, which had its commencement
in Abram, and was afterwards established amongst the posterity of
Jacob. It thus appears, that representatives had their rise from the
significatives of the ancient church, and these from the celestial ideas
of the most ancient church." (A. C. 1409.)

This passage of Swedenborg's writings affords another instance of
how easy it is to draw erroneous views from them without a due
comparison of one part with others. From this we might at first be
led to suppose that the jewish church alone had representatives, and
that it only was "the representative church." And then it would
be very easy to conclude, that, in the abrogation of the jewish ritual,
all representatives were abolished. But the comparisons which we
have made in the course of this argument, have abundantly shown

that Swedenborg, in this passage, by representatives means *mere* or *external* representatives, in contradistinction to *genuine* or *internal* ones. For he expressly says, the Jews had put off the latter before they came into the land of Canaan, and put·on the former. He also calls the former "*pure* representatives" and "representatives *alone.*" (A. C. 1361.) And it has been shown also, by his own discrimination of a representative church from the representative of a church, that the ancient church was a representative one, and the jewish the mere representative of one. Hence it is clear that Swedenborg by "the representative church," in this passage, means the representative of a church. In short, he merely designates representatives by the plane of their reception in the several discrete churches of which he speaks. Thus in the celestial church, representatives, that is, things as they flow from and embody·the goods and truths of the Lord, exist as *ideas* of the mind. Therefore, in that church, he calls them "*celestial ideas* of the most ancient church." But in the spiritual church, they are things external to the mind, either as objects of sight or some other sense, in nature or the rituals of external worship, which *signify* to the mental perceptions of the worshiper in and by them the heavenly and divine things which they represent. Therefore, in the spiritual church, he calls them "the *significatives* of the ancient church." But in the jewish church they are *mere* representatives, that is, external things which represent heavenly and divine things to a people who have not the slightest idea of their signification; or representatives as they had become in the church "after all internal worship had perished." Therefore, in this ·church he calls them "representatives" by distinction. Wherefore he means that *mere* or *external* representatives in the jewish church had their rise from the *true* or *internal* representatives of the ancient church, and these from the *ideal representatives* of the most ancient church. And this is just what we hold, and in this report maintain. Hence "spiritual and celestial things are the interior things contained in the representatives" of the Jews. (A. C. 8588.) They "were all representative of the spiritual and celestial things of the Lord's kingdom." (A. C. 4311.) "The sons of Israel and their posterity, as well as they who were of the ancient churches, in singular things represented the Lord's spiritual and celestial kingdoms. The representatives themselves were also instituted—with the jewish nation *the representative of the celestial* kingdom, and with the israelitish people the representative of the spiritual kingdom. But with that generation nothing but a *mere* representative could be instituted, and not any thing [really or truly] of the church or kingdom of the Lord; for they were not willing to see or acknowledge any thing in representatives but what was external, and not any thing internal. Nevertheless, that a representative might exist, and by it some communication be given with heaven and through heaven with the Lord, they were kept in externals; and it was then provided, by the Lord, that communication should be given by *a mere external representative*, without an internal principle." (A. C. 6304.) How "communication with the angels in heaven by [such] representatives was effected," namely, by simple good spirits, and even while the Jew was surrounded by evil spirits, by good spirits without him flowing into the mere external principle of sanctity in which he was for the time being kept, may be seen in A. C. 8588, 4311. Thus the Jews were of such a quality as a nation that "they knew not, and were not willing to know, what the internal or spiritual man is; wherefore, neither was it revealed to them—for they believed that nothing but an external and natural principle appertained to any man—neither did they regard any other principle in all their worship, insomuch that divine worship with them was no other than idolatrous worship; for when external worship is separated from internal, it is merely idolatrous." Hence "the church which was instituted amongst them, was not [really] a church; and *it is in this sense that the jewish church is called a* REPRESENTATIVE CHURCH." (A. C. 4281.)

It is impossible for any thing to be more express than this. It shows that Swedenborg, in the passage before quoted, A. C. 1409, calls the church "which had its commencement in Abram, and was afterwards established among the posterity of Jacob," "the representative church" in only a representative sense. That is, he means to say the jewish is no church at all—it only represents one. And in its character of the representative of a church, it is a mere shell, a mere shadow, a mere outside, skin-deep semblance of the most ancient church, from which its representatives, with idolatrous superadditions, have been derived. So that it still has the representatives of the most ancient and the ancient churches involved within its outward coverings. For "the most ancient church, which was celestial, and before the flood, was in the land of Canaan, (A. C. 567;) and the ancient church, which was after the flood, was also in that land, (A. C. 1238, 2385;) hence it came to pass, that all the nations in that land, and likewise all the regions, and all the rivers thereof, became representative; for the most ancient people, who were celestial men, through all the objects which they saw, perceived such things as appertained to the Lord's kingdom (A. C. 920, 1409, 2896, 2897, 2995)—thus also through the regions and rivers of that land. These representatives after their times remained in the ancient church—thus also the representative of the places in that land." Hence "the Word in the ancient church, also, had representative names of places. Also the Word after their time, called Moses and the Prophets. And this being so, therefore Abraham was commanded to go to that land, and a promise was made him that his posterity should possess it; and this not by reason of their being better than other nations, for they were amongst the worst of all; but that by them a representative church might be instituted, in which no attention should be paid to person or to place, but to the things which should be represented; and thus also *the names* [and so the *representatives*] *of the most ancient and of the ancient church, might be retained.*" (A. C. 3686.) "Hence it is plain that the jewish church was not any new church, but that it was a resuscitation of the ancient church which had perished." (A. C. 4835.) And "the most ancient or celestial church was the foundation of the jewish; whence all the representatives of the latter church had reference to things celestial, and by these to the Lord." (A. C. 886.)

Thus we presume we have shown most conclusively that representatives existed in the most ancient as well as in the ancient church—that they were derived from the most ancient through the ancient to the jewish and israelitish church—that the very object of Abraham's return to the land of Canaan and the institution of the latter church by his posterity in that land, was that the celestial and spiritual churches might be restored in a mere representative form in the lowest condition of mankind, and so their genuine or internal representatives be preserved for the christian, as a spiritual and celestial, church, which was to be again raised up in the fulness of time. And we have shown that the jewish and israelitish church, as it had the representatives of celestial and spiritual things only on the outside, without the least particle of a spiritual or celestial quality in its members, was the mere representative of a church, and not itself a church at all: but, in itself considered, was, as to its ritual form that was abrogated, a mere shell with the true representatives of the ancient church as a kernel within it, and the ideal representatives of the most ancient as an oil within that kernel.

Wherefore, our conclusion is, that, when the Lord abrogated the jewish ritual, he merely abolished idolatrous representatives, thus removed the judiac and hebraic superadditions to genuine or internal representatives, or cracked the shell, so as to give these true representatives as the kernel to the christian church. And as "priestly offices and whatever had relation to their functions" were among the true representatives of the ancient church, therefore these were not abolished in the christian church by the abrogation of the jewish ritual. We might go on to show that representative "statues," or representative paintings, and true representatives in other forms, might be used in the christian church, so as to bring its internal principles down to the sensual plane of the mind, and thus give them the fulness, power and sanctity of ultimates. But this would not be at all pertinent to the purpose of this report. It is enough for us to have shown that the New Jerusalem, as a spiritual church, may and must be a true representative one, as the ancient church was; and that, as such, she must have a representative priesthood, to represent the Lord's work of saving men in the natural, the spiritual, and the celestial degrees, and therefore constituted by grades of priests in a triple order. This follows irresistibly from the fact that priestly offices and *whatever had relation to their functions* were representative in the ancient church, and must be similarly representative in the New Jerusalem.

VIII. *The New Jerusalem is to be a celestial church in* FORM *as well as in* ESSENCE—*hence is to have an external, representative, ritual worship even as a celestial church, and this because she, unlike the most ancient church, is never to fall away.*

This is the citadel of our argument. For it defends our position from the very plausible reasoning of our opponents—that the most ancient as a celestial church had "a divine worship which was *exclusively internal,* and *in no respect external,*" (A. C. 920:) hence the New Jerusalem, being a church of a celestial genius, is not to have an external *representative* worship at all. Of course, her priesthood will not be representative, because her external worship, in which her clergy are to minister, is not.

Now this is our argument. The most ancient church began celestial and declined through a spiritual to an utterly natural state. These were the three discrete phases of the most ancient or celestial church in its trine of churches. But the New Jerusalem begins natural, and through a spiritual stage becomes celestial. And in thus restoring the church from its lowest depths to its highest heights, like the soul in leaving the corporeal body and rising into the spiritual or celestial heavens, takes with her an external, representative, ritual worship, as an involucrum from the natural plane, for a continent and defence of her internal principles in her highest elevation. Thus, not only will the New Jerusalem, in her lower degrees, need such an external ritual worship to present and convey her internal principles to the minds of the young and simple, but she will also need it to place, in all minds, "upon *all her glory* a covering," and to afford to her in all the stages of even her highest upward progress, "a tabernacle for a shadow in the day time from the heat, and for a place of refuge, and for a covert, from storm and rain." (Isaiah, iv. 5, 6.) The chapter of the Word in which this passage is found, treats of the final restoration of all things, after the church, from celestial, shall have passed through all its downward stages, and come to the extremity of its most ultimate evil condition. In that condition, this chapter predicts, "there will be a *new principle of the church* from the Lord; and *providence against the church's ever falling away again* by any further perversion of the Word."

The Word is divine good and divine truth brought into a representative, significative and correspondential form. Hence, perversion of the Word is perversion of the good and truth which are contained in its representatives, significatives or correspondences. The same is true of the church. For the church is good and truth from the Word. These are those internal principles which constitute the church itself as they constitute the Word itself. And that these as internal principles may be preserved from perversion, both in the Word and in the church, when the church is finally restored, they are always to be covered and defended by appropriate external things, which represent, signify, and correspond to, them. These internal principles are the glory of the Word, and the glory of the church that is from it; and those representatives, significatives and correspondences are for their covering and defence. They are as a tabernacle, which shadows them from the scorching influences of self-love, as well as tempers to them the burning brilliancy of the unveiled divine love. They are as a refuge and covert for them from all worldly and infernal influences.

In the most ancient church, there was no external ritual worship. Or its ritual was only the writing of God's finger, tracing representative forms on the sky and earth in its three kingdoms, and from the spiritual world on the tablets of the mind. Hence that church could fall away by coming into "idolatrous rites and magical. ceremonies." It had no external covering and defence for its internal principles. Hence those principles were perverted, and the church itself consequently destroyed. The Word, in the most ancient church, had its ultimate and basis in only the imaginative plane of the mind of the member of that church;—it had not an ultimate and basis in the very matter of this natural world as it now has in its form of a printed book;—therefore it could fall away from the men of the church, and the celestial principles of the church could fall away with it. But, in the restoration of the celestial church, when all things shall be brought back again to their pristine state of integrity and purity, that church will have an external ritual worship, truly representative and significative of its internal principles;—and the Word will have an ultimate and basis in the natural world independent of the minds of men. This will then be "a new principle of the church from the Lord," by which there will be "providence against the church's ever falling away again." For it will not then be tempted to go out into any external ritual worship which is false and idolatrous. For when "the Lord shall have washed away the filth of the daughters of Zion,"—cleansed the affections of the celestial church,—and "shall have purged the blood of Jerusalem from the midst of her,"—removed every profane principle from the internals of the spiritual church,— "by the spirit of judgment and the spirit of burning,"—by the life of spiritual truth and the life of celestial truth, and their renunciations of evil,—then he "will create upon every dwelling-place of Mount Zion, and upon her assemblies, a *cloud* and *smoke* by day, and the shining of a flaming fire by night: for upon *all the glory* shall be *a covering.*"

Mount Zion is the celestial church, or the principle of inmost good in the Word. Her dwelling-places denote her voluntary principle, and her assemblies, her intellectual principle. They also denote the internal and external worship of the celestial church, or the internal and external senses of the Word. The cloud and smoke by day, which are to be upon her dwelling-places and assemblies, denote the representatives from the letter of the Word, which are to be in the celestial church's external worship, so as to accommodate her internal spiritual principles to minds in the corporeal, sensual, or natural plane: and the shining of the flaming fire by night, denotes the light of perception, flowing from a principle of good, which illustrates the mind of the man of celestial genius even in the obscurities of his natural states, and gives to his natural man, and to his views of the veriest letter of the Word, a guiding light of spiritual interpretation from its true spiritual sense. For, as the new church now teaches us, (A. C. 10.551,) he who is principled in good, and is in the actual life of good, which is the performance of use from heavenly ends, is inwardly in the spiritual sense of the Word, although he knows it not. And representatives from the letter of the Word will be "a covering, as a tabernacle for a shadow in the day-time from the heat, and for a place of refuge, and for a covert, from storm and rain," because, they are

30

now the divine humanity of the Lord itself in ultimates, spreading a more full and ultimate plane for angelic consociation with men in the last days than ever the celestial church had in the most ancient times. They are a plane into which angels can' flow, not only with simple-minded good adults, but even with infants and children, and store up remains in the innocence of their infancy, so as to secure them from selfish and worldly influx from hell ever afterwards.

Thus, by representatives as an external ritual of worship in and from the letter of the Word, the celestial church's internal principles can be for ever defended and preserved whenever the church shall have been again restored. For thus it is, that, by representatives as the letter of the Word, having the divine humanity of the Lord actually present in them, and the sphere of that humanity around them, keeping infernal influences away from the spirits of all who shall worship in them in sincerity and truth, the glory of the Word, and the internals of the church, will for ever have upon them "a defence, or covering."

Such is our argument. Perhaps it needs a good deal of illustration to make it clear and conclusive to other minds. But we have only space for the following, which is a kind of summing up of what has been previously advanced and shown.

We have shown that the New Jerusalem, at least in one of the stages of her upward progress, may and must be a representative church. We mean a true representative church, and not the mere representative of one. We mean a real church, that has true representatives of its own internal principles, and not the mere semblance of a church, that has only representatives of the internals of a church which is yet future. Thus we mean a church that *has* representatives without being *in* them.

A church is designated by that principle which characterizes it most. The church is a complex man. All men have the same common properties. But some men are principled more in certain properties of mind or body than in others. For instance, in respect to the body, one man will be principled in muscular force, another in nervous energy; another will be remarkable for his sight, another for his hearing, another for the acuteness of his smell; and so on. And, in respect to the mind, one man will be a man of memory, another a man of judgment, another a man of fancy; or, more generally, one will be a man of will, another a man of understanding, and another a man of action; one will be noted for his inventive faculty, another for his powers of execution; and so on. It is not that the man of memory has not any judgment and fancy; or the man of will any understanding; but memory or will is the distinguishing characteristic—the prominent, chief, or ruling property of the man; and he is called by that which so distinguishes him. So, in respect to churches—all have the same common properties; but one church is distinguishingly characterized by some one property, and another, by some other. Thus there is the natural church, the spiritual church, and the celestial church; or the church as to the mere obedience of truth, the church as to the understanding of truth, and the church as to the perception of truth. It is not that the natural church has nothing of a spiritual or celestial principle in it whatever; or that the spiritual church has no natural or celestial principle whatever; or the celestial church has not any spiritual or natural principle whatever: but it is that each is called by that principle which most characterizes it, and by which it is peculiarly distinguished from the others. So, in regard to representatives—all churches have them, but all are not peculiarly characterized or distinguished by them. Hence, it is not that the natural, the spiritual, or the celestial church, has or has not any representatives whatever, which causes it to be called a representative church or the representative of a church. A church that has mere representatives, or which has nothing else that pertains to the true church belonging to it but representatives, and thus is principled in representatives alone, is called the representative of a church. For such a church, having none of the internal principles of the church, is in reality no church at all, but only the outward semblance of one : and as its representative forms are the types and figures of internal things which are to be developed at some other time amongst some other people, it is therefore called the *representative of* a church. It is not that this church has *no* internal principles whatever; but its principles are evil and false ones—totally void of genuine charity and true faith, and having, therefore, nothing of the church itself in them. Hence it is called the representative of a church, because it is principled in mere representatives, because representatives alone are all of the church that belongs to it, and because it represents a true church elsewhere.

Again, a true representative church is a real church; and it is called representative because it is principled in true representatives—yet, so as, at the same time, to have within itself the internal things which are represented by them. This is the spiritual church.

Still further, the celestial church is not without representatives, as the man of will is not without understanding; but it is not principled in them. The celestial church, either in its essential or formal worship, does not think of, or rest in, representatives, although it has them. As we have fully shown, the most ancient church on this earth, which was a celestial church, had, for its representatives, the whole natural world. The members of that church had, indeed, no external worship like ours; for they were radically different from us even as to physical constitution. For instance, they respired in the atmosphere of the spiritual world, in which angels and spirits breathe. Hence they had no external respiration like ours. They did not breathe in the atmosphere of this material world, as we do. Hence they had no natural vocal sounds. Of course, they could have no such prayers, praises, or glorifications as ours. Their speech with one another was pantomimic; and their external worship, therefore, might have been something like what we call dumb show. Hence they could not have had any of the external rites, ceremonies, formularies, or temples that we have. Still there must have been some sort of external to their internal worship, as a body to a soul. And as the new church now teaches, that " that is external which represents, and that is internal which is represented," the members of the most ancient church must have had representatives in their externals. They worshiped beneath the canopy of the skies, and surrounded by the objects of outward nature, as a vast living tabernacle, instead of temples made by their own hands. It was revealed to them by angels, in dreams and otherwise, what each thing which they saw before their outward eyes, represented and signified. And in their perception of this signification and representation, their souls were consociated with angels, and through them conjoined to the Lord. The Word, as the representatives of things existing in the heavens, was in the same manner revealed to them; and the memory, thought, and affection of the representatives, significatives and correspondences of the Word so revealed, became then the plane of that consociation and conjunction.

The most ancient church must have been representative, or must have had representatives, for another reason. Like every other church which preceded the Lord's incarnation, the celestial church too could have him present with it only representatively. Therefore, the celestial church was a representative one, because the Lord, not having come into the ultimates of nature, could be present with even that church in only the representative form of some angel. Hence, as we have before intimated, the *ministers* of the Word to the celestial church were angels in heaven and not men on earth. But besides this, the divine things of the Lord, and the celestial and spiritual things of heaven, could no more then than now be communicated to men on earth by any other means than by those representative forms which exist from, and correspond to, them in outward nature. And as we have shown that representatives originate in modifications of light by shade *above* the celestial *heaven*, so that representatives exist in that heaven itself; therefore, much more must divine, celestial, and spiritual things be presented *representatively* to celestial men on earth. Hence the celestial church in the most ancient times must have had representatives, as well as all the churches in subsequent times, but was not principled in them. It was not at all characterized or distinguished by representatives, and therefore was not called a representative church. It was principled in good, and the perceptions of truth from good. Its intelligence was instinct and not science. Its members thought not of the mere outward forms of good and truth, which everywhere in nature represented those principles to their minds. That is, they did not learn what was good and true by their means, or let their thoughts at all rest on them, although they were necessary objects of thought in perceiving the internal things which were in them, and which they represented. They had no affection whatever for those forms as such merely. As Swedenborg says, they " indeed perceived the external objects relating to their bodies, but did not care for them." (A. C. 920.) Thus they saw them indeed with the outward eye; but looked through them, with the inward eye, to the internal things which they bodied forth, and so represented. On these internal things alone their affections were set: and thus in the affection of these things that celestial church was principled. Hence it was called an internal church. Still it was not so called because it had no sort of external worship whatever; and this it could not have without representatives as its vehicle. For the Lord, who was worshiped, could be only representatively present, and therefore the worship of him must needs have been a representative one.

We see, then, that the argument from the fact that the most ancient church had no external ritual and formal worship *like ours*, is shorn of its power in respect to the New Jerusalem. For that church had an external worship *of its own*, consisting in its observance of the natural things by which its members were surrounded, and by which, as representatives, the minds of its members were led upwards to spiritual, celestial and divine things, and by which, as objects of thought their minds were kept in the contemplation, love and practice of the things which they represented. And, as we have clearly and fully shown, there was no other possible way by which beings on this, or any other, earth, could have divine, celestial, or spiritual things presented and kept exhibited to them for their apprehension and appropriation. Hence we have expressly shown, that the members of the most ancient church had "the significative or enigmatical *representations* of terrestrial objects." (A. C. 920.) Thus they had representatives in *their* external worship, which was in the external of their minds, and therefore was wholly internal in comparison with ours. But still it was an external worship *in* them; for terrestrial objects are truths in the ultimates of order in which the spiritual and celestial things of heaven, and the divine things of the Lord, terminate, and by which those things are continually presented to the minds of men. So that in the external region, in the imaginative faculty, of the celestial members of the most ancient church, they formed a living *internal* ritual of ideas of thought. And that church had no external ritual worship, merely because the minds of its members did not at all rest in the objects of sense. The objects of sense, however, were present to their senses, and furnished, as we have shown above, the temple of their internal worship. Thus they were like the angels of heaven, who, having the exact corresponding effigies of what is in their minds always out of them, have, as is now known, temples for worship, as well as houses and palaces—but never let their minds rest in the things which are objects of sight in them.*

Now, thus we argue. The same would be the character of christian

---

* Moreover, the most ancient church had no external ritual worship like ours, because, as we have before shown, its members had no external respiration and speech like ours. Of course, they could have no such prayers, praises, or preachings as we have. And does it not devolve on those who maintain that the New Jerusalem, as a celestial church, is to have a divine worship "*exclusively internal*, and *in no respect external*," like that of the most ancient church—to prove that the members of the New Jerusalem, in her celestial stage, will also *have no external speech or respiration?* At any rates, we can very confidently maintain, that the New Jerusalem must have an external ritual worship *now*, while the physical constitution of her members is so different from that of the most ancient people. And we can quite as confidently argue, that she will at all times, even in her highest celestial stage, continue to have such an external worship, because she will perpetually differ from the most ancient church in this respect.

worship, if, whatever external forms and ceremonies were performed without them, Christians did not at all rest in those externals, but passed through to the perception, love and practice of the internal things which they signified. Hence the New Jerusalem will become. a celestial church, not by putting off entirely all external forms and representative ceremonies, but, as we have now so fully shown, by fulfilling them, that is, by infilling them with the spiritual and celestial things to which they correspond. In short, it will become celestial, when its chief characteristic is the celestial principle. Hence, as the only difference between the most ancient church and those that succeeded it, in regard to representatives, was, that in the latter representatives became more and more dead, while in the former they were vital, therefore the New Jerusalem will become the celestial church restored when she too makes dead representatives alive. In the most ancient church representatives were " real things" from the Lord, and the temple of their worship was the universe of nature. But, in succeeding churches, men came at last to the imitation of terrestrial objects in temples made by their own hands. This, however, does not alter the principle : for it matters not whether the man looks at the real thing in nature, or at the imitation of it in art ; it is in both cases the idea of his mind with which spirits and angels are consociated ; and thus it is the thought, perception, or affection of his mind in regarding that thing which determines the nature and quality of his worship. For all worship consists in the acknowledgment of the Divine Being, the prostration of self before him, and conjunction of man thereby with him and heaven. Hence, if a man, when he sees an object of nature, or of factitious formal worship, thinks not at all of. the object of sense, but regards in it only the Lord and what belongs to him and heaven, and proposes to himself no selfish end whatever, but only looks to the universal good, then his worship is not at all representative, is not at all external, is wholly internal ; because it is wholly characterized by what is internal, and worship is called by its chief characteristic.

We conclude, then, that even the celestial church must have an external representative form appropriate to its internal celestial essence. And, therefore, every church must have representatives as the external of its worship. Consequently the New Jerusalem, even when she becomes, in her most consummate advancement, a celestial church, must still have an external, celestial, representative worship. Much more must she have a true, spiritual, representative worship, before she becomes celestial, and when she is passing through her spiritual stage. And still more must she have an external representative ritual worship, when she is only in the sensual, scientific and natural degree.

And the New Jerusalem, as a celestial church, will always differ radically from the most ancient as a celestial one, in this—the most ancient people were born celestial, that is, with celestial instincts. Hence that church could fall by becoming merely natural. But the people of the New Jerusalem are born natural, that is, in total ignorance and impotence as to all spiritual things, and only with a capacity of becoming celestial. And hence, as the New Jerusalem rises from the lowest plane to the highest, by a free and rational putting off of the evils and fallacies of the one, and a free and rational putting on of the goods and truths of the other, she, as a celestial church, can never fall away by becoming merely natural again.* Hence, as the New Jerusalem will at all times have the whole of the three degrees opening in her, because she incessantly begins in the natural plane, and will always have infants, children, youth and adults amongst her members, she will at all times, throughout her unending existence and her ever advancing perfection on this earth, have constantly an external ritual worship, formed from true representatives in the letter of the Word. (See the first note, or that with an asterisk, at the bottom of page 433.) These representatives will be the means of introducing and developing internal principles in the minds of children, born still in ignorance, and of containing and securing them in the minds of intelligent manhood and wise old age. And her advancing stages will be marked by deeper and deeper insights into, and more and more interior apprehensions of, the infinite divine things which will have been lying stored up from the first in her external rituals. So that, as the internal principles of the Word, having now come down to the lowest plane, and, resting on that plane as a house on its foundation, is " for ever established in heaven" and in all worlds, so the church, which is founded, like the Word itself, upon representatives in its letter, is for ever established, and can never again be destroyed. The church at first was instituted in internals alone, and fell away by coming into externals alone ; but now the church is to be restored

---

* This subject may be illustrated by what Swedenborg says of angels deriving a power of subsistence from having been first born men, in the Tract on Divine Wisdom, VIII. If angels had been created such, that is, had been formed men in the spheres of the spiritual world, they could not have subsisted, because their bodies would have been, like all the subsistences there, perpetually changing in correspondence with the changes of the state of their affections. He says—" substances in the spiritual world appear as if they were material; but still they are not so ; and inasmuch as they are not material, therefore they are not constant, being correspondences of the affections of the angels, and being permanent with the affections of the angels, and disappearing with them. *Similar would have been the case with the angels, if they had been created there.*" Thus, as angels would not have subsisted, if they had been first created men in the celestial heaven ; so men on earth, who were created with celestial instincts, could not subsist in their celestial state, for the want of a suitable *celestial-natural* ultimate as a continent and defence of their intimate celestial principles ; so that the church in them inevitably became extinct, whenever they became natural. But " an angel and a spirit, in consequence of being first born a man in the world, derives subsistence ; for he derives from the inmost principles of nature a medium with himself between what is spiritual and what is natural, by which he is bounded to subsistence and permanence, having relation by the latter to those things which are in nature, and having also a principle corresponding to those things." And thus, as angels are bounded to subsistence and permanence by having a natural substratum for their internal substances and forms, and a perfect reciprocal correspondence between them, so the members of the New Jerusalem as a celestial church, will be bound to subsistence and permanence, in consequence of having been first born natural, and having become celestial by divine recreation or regeneration, so as to take with them, into the highest celestial elevation of their church, an external ritual worship, as a truly representative form, and a celestial-natural correspondent, of their internal celestial principles.

from externals alone, and, having " its externals correspond with its internals so as to make one," and so as to have " its external worship serve as a plane to its interiors," its internal or celestial essence is so to be encased in and defended by its celestial, spiritual and natural formularies, that it can never fall away again.

Thus, to recapitulate and conclude, the perfection of the New Jerusalem, over the most ancient celestial church, will consist in this— that the New Jerusalem will be as fully in externals as she is in internals; whereas the most ancient church was not in externals at all. Hence the most ancient church could fall away, by coming into externals and resting in them alone. But the New Jerusalem begins in externals and rises to internals, without putting the externals wholly off; but, on the contrary, retaining them as the continent of her internal principles. Hence she will never fall away again, after she has once become celestial; for she will never be tempted to go out into externals alone, inasmuch as she has been in them, come out of them as the principle of her worship, and still holds them as the safeguard and defence of her celestial powers and privileges. It is equally impossible for her to fall away from her celestial state, when once she has risen from the natural degree through the spiritual degree into it, as it is for the celestial angels to fall from their empyrean; for however high may be her elevation, she will still have an involucrum from the natural degree, which will cause her to be still representative in form, however celestial she may become in essence; and, there-fore, she will always be a true representative church, so far as to have her " internal in an appropriate external," and thus to have " upon all the glory a defence, or covering—a tabernacle for a shadow in the day time from the heat, and for a place of refuge, and for a covert, from storm and rain."

It is high time to bring this head of our report to a close. The great importance of the subject has seemed to us to demand thus much of our attention. But, although it is far from exhausted, enough is here advanced to show, most conclusively, that the New Jerusalem is to have representatives in an external ritual worship, and therefore must have representative priestly offices for its administration. Hence there must be in the New Jerusalem a priesthood strictly representative of the Lord in his work of redeeming and saving men. And as the Lord saves men in three discrete degrees, that is, in the natural, the spiritual, and the celestial heavens, consequently there must be three grades of priests to represent him in these three degrees of his divine operation. For, as he has now come fully into ultimates, so as to operate in saving men " from himself in first principles and from himself in ultimates;" and " the ultimates, through which the Lord operates, are upon earth, and indeed with men," (Ap. Rev. 798;) therefore there cannot be a trine of priestly uses alone, but there must also be a trine of priestly men, as ultimates by whom the Lord may operate in the performance of those uses; " because the love of the Lord is to perform uses to the community, and to each society in the community, and he performs these by means of men who are principled in love to him." (Ap. Rev. 353.) And such we confidently maintain is the true nature of the ministerial trine as it must exist in the New Jerusalem on earth.

VIII. AUTHORITIES FOR THE TRINAL ORDER IN THE NEW CHURCH AND HER MINISTRY.

It is not our purpose to give *all* the authorities for the trine which the Word and the writings of our church are supposed to contain. The ecclesiastical council of the Central Convention has not done its duty in making a thorough search for those authorities. All we propose to do, and all we can do, is to collate the chief of the authorities previously advanced, and to offer such as have occurred in our own reading, or have been presented to us by the members of the council, with such remarks upon the most prominent ones generally acknowledged, as the objects of this report may seem to require.

We are required "to determine the trine in the ministry as taught in the Word, and from thence in the writings of Swedenborg." This requisition presents two questions for consideration and determination—Is there a trine? and what should that trine be? The first comes under this head, the second will come under the next.

The duty enjoined on us indicates two sources to which we should go in search of our authorities—the Word, and the writings of Swedenborg. To the first source, Mr. Cabell has professedly gone; to the second, Mr. Powell. Under the present head, the design is to go to the Word as explained by Swedenborg, that is, to the Word as it is expounded in his writings. To this there may be some exceptions, in regard to authorities drawn from the New Testament; but it is the general law by which the matters under this head are to be governed.

First, as to the trine in the church. In proof that there is a trine in the church, we shall advance but one passage from Swedenborg's writings; because this is so express, clear and conclusive, that the presentation of any others is wholly unnecessary.

In explaining Rev. xvii. 14—particularly these words, "and they that are with him are *called*, and *chosen* and *faithful* "—Swedenborg says, "by the called, chosen and faithful are signified they who are in the externals, internals and inmost principles of the church": and adds, "The reason why it means those who are in the externals, internals and inmost principles of the church, is, because *the Lord's church is distinguished*, like heaven, *into* THREE DEGREES : in the ultimate degree are they who are in its externals, in the second degree are they who are in its internals, and in the third degree are they who are in its inmost principles." Further, "It is here said, 'They that are with him are called, and chosen and faithful,' because it was said before, that they shall fight with the Lamb, and the Lamb will overcome them, that they may know that such as the Lord overcomes, that is, convinces, by the Word, are with him in heaven— some in the ultimate heaven, some in the second, and some in the third, every one according to reception." (Ap. Rev. 744.) A thousand quotations from Swedenborg's writings, or passages from the Word, could not add a whit to the force or conclusiveness of this one, in proving that there is a *trine* of *persons* in the Lord's church on earth—that this is a trine of *discrete* "degrees," because they are "distinguished" from one another as the natural, spiritual and celestial heavens are, and as are the externals, the internals and the inmost principles of the church. Wherefore, it is fully established, that *there* IS *a* TRINE *in the church.*

Second, as to the trine in the ministry. That there should be "priestly offices" in the New Jerusalem; that these should be representative of the Lord's work of saving mankind in the three degrees into which heaven is distinguished; and that there should be priests to act in those offices, and so to represent the Lord in overcoming those who fight with him as the Lamb, that is, in "*convincing, by the Word*," the "*three degrees*" of persons into which his "church is distinguished;" thus, that there should be priests of three degrees in the New Jerusalem on earth—has, we presume, been now proved beyond further controversy by the argument under the preceding head of this report. But, in repeated proof of this, take Ap. Rev. 533:

1. "It is to be observed that there is a church in the heavens as well as on earth; for there is the Word; there are temples also, and sermons delivered in them, and *ministerial and priestly offices; for all angels there were once men,* and *their departure out of the world was only a continuance of their life;* therefore they are also perfected in love and wisdom, every one according to the *degree* of the affection of truth and good which *he took with him out of the world.*"[*] This proves, not only that there are ministerial and priestly offices in heaven, and a trine of them, because they are in the three heavens, but also on earth. For observe the argument. There is a church, there are temples, sermons in them, and ministerial and priestly offices in *the heavens* [plural], *because all angels there were once men,* and *their life on earth is continued in heaven,* so that their love and wisdom may be perfected in *that degree* in which they were opened on earth, thus in the natural, the spiritual or the celestial degree. Hence there must be a church with ministerial and priestly offices in the three heavens, (each of which, too, has three discrete and three continuous degrees,[†]) *because there is a church with those offices on earth,* and ministers and priests, acting in those offices, are needed to instruct and illustrate the minds of its members in its external, its internal and its inmost principles, and so to be mediums of the Lord's holy spirit in opening their mind in its natural, spiritual and celestial

---

[*] "I saw a new church in the heavens, because there is a church *there* as well as on the earths: for these, in like manner, is the Word, and *preaching,* and *divine worship similar to that on the earths;* yet with this difference, that all things there are in a more perfect state, because they are not in the natural, but in the spiritual, world." (L. J. 1. See, also, H. & H. 221-227.)

[†] "There are three heavens, and each heaven is distinguished into three degrees; and in like manner the angels who are in them. Wherefore, in each heaven there are superior, middle and inferior [angels.]" (Ap. Ex. 342.)

degrees. There is no mistaking this argument. There can be no life without its formularies, functions and functionaries, just as there can be no substance without form, and no form without the organized arrangement of distinct parts. Those who die in the Lord, that is, live the life of charity on earth, are blessed, because "they rest from their labors and *their works do follow with them*," that is, their life,—consisting of works of charity,—is continued in the other world. But the continuance of life, is the necessary continuance of its formularies, functions and functionaries, just as the continuance of an essence is necessarily the continuance of its form, or as there must be organs of charity to do its works. And "the divine principle called the holy spirit, proceeding from God by his humanity, passes through the angelic heaven into the world—thus through the angels to men": and "thence it passes through men to men, and *in the church especially through the* CLERGY *to the* LAITY." (Can. iii. and iv.) Hence there must be priestly offices and priests in the heavens, because such offices and officers necessarily exist on earth. And conversely, they must exist on earth, because they are in heaven. Nay, there is greater reason for the existence of priestly offices and officers on earth than there is for them in the heavens. For, if there must be such offices and officers to *perfect* men in love and wisdom in the heavens, there certainly must be *a fortiori* such offices and officers to *form* and *open* their life in the several degrees of that love and wisdom on earth. Consequently, there must be ministerial and priestly offices, and ministers and priests, on earth; and there must be *three discrete degrees* of them, to represent, and correspond to, those offices and those officers as they exist in the natural, spiritual and celestial heavens, in order that those heavens may have a base to rest and subsist on. For the church on earth is a lower plane in which the three heavens subside, and form three discrete degrees of influx in simultaneous order from the centre to the circumference. (A. C. 6451, 9836.) And without their corresponding ultimates on earth, the prior or intimate things which flow in from the heavens and produce those ultimates would perish; or the angels through whom the divine principle proceeding from the Lord flows down to men, would be deprived of them; because " he who is deprived of ultimate things, is deprived also of things prior; for prior things exist and subsist in things ultimate," (Ap. Ex. 66 :) and hence, "the church in the heavens cannot subsist, except there be also a church on earth," as an " internal in an external man,"·or "a house on its foundation." (Ap. Rev. 533, A. C. 9216.) Thus, if there were not priestly offices and priests on earth, they could not be in heaven, and the angels would be deprived of the prior things, or heavenly principles, to which they correspond on earth. Wherefore, it is most clear that there must be three discrete degrees of priestly offices and of priests on earth, that they may exist and subsist in the heavens.

2. "The representatives of the church with the israelitish nation were truths in the ultimate of order. . . . The representative church was instituted, and such things were commanded as in ultimates altogether represented heaven, with all the truths and goods

therein." (A. C. 10.728.) "The Word in the letter consists of such things as appear to the sight in heaven, by which are signified correspondent spiritual things," (Ap. Ex. 482;) for the things seen by John, as related in the Apocalypse, as well as those seen by the prophets, "were nothing else but representatives which continually exist in heaven," (A. C. 4529 ;) and "in heaven *all things which appear before the eyes are representative;* for they represent, under a natural appearance, the spiritual things which the angels think and with which they are affected; thus their thoughts and affections are presented before their eyes in forms such as are in the world, or in similar forms of natural things, and this by virtue of the correspondence which is established by the Lord between spiritual and natural things," (Ap. Ex. 482;) and "angelic ideas pass into representatives in the world of spirits." (A. C. 2039.) Farther, "every thing in the vegetable kingdom which is beautiful and ornamental derives its origin through heaven from the Lord; and when the celestial and spiritual things of the Lord flow into nature, such objects of beauty and ornament are actually exhibited. Hence comes the vegetable soul or life. Hence also come representatives." (A. C. 1632.) And "angelic discourse,—which is incomprehensible to man, as being spiritual and celestial,—when it is conveyed down to man, who is in a natural sphere, falls into representatives and significatives such as exist in the Word : and hence it is that the Word is a holy code or volume; for what is divine cannot be presented or exhibited otherwise before the natural man, so as that a full correspondence may exist." (A. C. 3419.) Hence "all the *expressions* in the Word are *significative* of heavenly things, and all the *things* are *representative* thereof, and these even to the least tittle." (A. C. 5147.) Consequently, even in respect to the sacrificial worship of the jewish ritual, which has been wholly abrogated in the christian church, "still they are the holy things of the Word, by reason of the divine things which are in them and which they represented." (A. C. 8972.) Hence, as "the Word even of the Old Testament is most holy," containing the representatives and significatives of heavenly order ; and as there are priestly offices and priests in heaven, so that, in the abrogation of the jewish ritual worship with its *mere* representative priesthood, such offices and officers could not be abolished in the christian church; and thus, as there must always be an external worship, with temples, formularies and priests or ministers to officiate in them in the New Jerusalem even in her celestial stage on earth, because such things will ever be in the natural degree of the celestial heaven ; hence *the true order of the new and true christian priesthood may be determined from the external ritual order of the jewish church as the letter of the Word of the Old Testament:* for " all the laws of the jewish church, inasmuch as they derived their origin from the spiritual world, correspond to the laws of order which are in heaven," (A. C. 5135:) and, therefore, the abrogation of the ritual did not abrogate the laws of order which are in heaven, and which should exist correspondently in the church. This conclusion is irresistible, and cannot possibly be shaken. Consequently, as that which was represented in the jewish priesthood is, as we have now fully and conclusively shown, also represented in the priesthood of the New Jerusalem, therefore *the representative order of the jewish priesthood is the true order of the priesthood of the new christian church.* We have shown that baptism and the holy supper, as "only representative and significative rites," (Ap. Ex. 475,) have been instituted in the christian church instead of the jewish representative purifications and sacrifices. They are representative of precisely the same internal things in the Lord, in heaven and in the christian church. Therefore, they must have a representative priesthood to administer them; and we have in fact proved that the priests who do administer them are among "the representatives which exist even at this day," (A. C. 3670;) consequently, true christian priests represent the same things that the jewish priesthood did, and are representative in precisely the same way. Wherefore, the representative *order* of the jewish priesthood is precisely the order of the priesthood of the New Jerusalem.

What then is this order? To show this order from the letter of the Old Testament is to determine the true ministerial order of the new church from the Word of God. Take this passage as among the most striking :—"'And they [Aaron and his sons]' shall have the priesthood'—that hereby is signified the Lord as to the work of salvation in successive order, appears from *the signification of the priesthood,* as being *a representative of the Lord as to the work of salvation.* The reason why it denotes in successive order is, because the priesthood of the sons of Aaron is ·here treated of, and by his sons are represented those things which proceed, thus those things which succeed in order. The case herein is this. The priesthood, which is represented by Aaron, is the work of the salvation of those who are in the Lord's celestial kingdom, which kingdom is properly meant in the Word by a kingdom of priests. But the priesthood, which is represented by the sons of Aaron, is the work of the salvation of those who are in the Lord's spiritual kingdom proximately proceeding from his celestial kingdom. Hence it is, that by the priesthood is here meant the Lord's work of salvation in successive order. But the priesthood, which is represented by the Levites, denotes the Lord's work of salvation again proceeding from the former. *There are* THREE *things which succeed in order.* There is the celestial principle, which is the good of love to the Lord; there is the spiritual principle, which is the good of charity towards the neighbor; and there is the natural principle thence derived, which is the good of faith. Inasmuch as those three things are what succeed in order, there are also three-heavens; and in them goods in that order. The work of the salvation of those who are in celestial good, is represented by the priesthood of Aaron; but the work of the salvation of those who are in spiritual good, is represented by the priesthood of the sons of Aaron; and the work of the salvation of those who are thence in natural good, is represented by the priesthood of the Levites. And since those things which succeed in order proceed from the good of love to the Lord, which is represented by Aaron and his priesthood, therefore it is said by the Levites, that they should be given to Aaron;

for those things which proceed are of that from which they proceed;
for the things proceeding are successive, hence derived their esse.
That the Levites were given to Aaron and his sons, that they might
perform the ministry of the priesthood under them, see Numb. iii. 1
to the end." (A. C. 10.017.) Here we are taught, with all the
authority of the very Word of God, that "the priesthood," in the
abstract or internal sense, is " a representative of the Lord as to the
work of salvation." Therefore, the order of that work is the true
order of any and every priesthood. And the order of this work is
three things *succeeding* in order, that is, the order of three discrete
degrees. Consequently, as mankind are for ever to be saved in this
order—and there must always be a church on earth, that heaven may
be conjoined with mankind for their preservation, (A. C. 10.500,) and
there must be a priesthood in every church, because there are priestly
offices and priests in heaven, and they could not subsist there if they
did not exist here, therefore the true order of any priesthood is
the same as the order of the Lord's work of salvation, which the
priesthood at all times represents. Since then the Word, in this passage, teaches us that the work of salvation is effected by *three discrete
degrees*, or by *three things* in *successive order*, therefore, there must be,
in every priesthood, *three discrete degrees of priests*, to represent the
successive order of man's salvation. For there are three such degrees
of the *priesthood*, and there must be *priests* of so many grades to discharge its discrete functions. Thus there must be priests to represent
the Lord in his work of saving men in the celestial degree—priests to
represent him in his work of saving men in the spiritual degree, and
priests to represent him in his work of saving them in the natural
degree. So that the true order of the christian, as well as of any and
every other, ministry, is a TRINE *of discrete degrees.* Such is the doctrine of the Word of God: and it may not be gainsaid, " for the
mouth of the Lord hath spoken it"!

3. The foregoing shows the true order of the priesthood to be a
trine of discrete degrees from the representative character of the
priests themselves: but the same appears from the representative order
and nature of their functions. That is, the true order of the priesthood is a trine, because their functions are in trinal order; and the
order is a trine of discrete and subordinate degrees, because the functions are discrete and subordinate. Priestly functions, like all other
things pertaining to the externals of the Word and of worship, are,
as well in heaven as on earth, *representatives* of heavenly and divine
principles. Now the external order of the jewish church as revealed
to Moses on the mount, was an earthly portraiture in natural imagery
of the true external order of heaven, which is " truth in the ultimate
of order," which is the divine order, that is " nothing but a perpetual
commandment of God ;" for " in proportion as a man lives according
to God's commands, and so in divine order, in the same proportion, all
things are disposed in him by the Lord according to the order which
prevails in the heavens from the Lord." (A. C. 2634.) Thus " the
order which prevails in the heavens" is the true order of an internal
church, which is discernible in the external order of the jewish

church as a representative mirror. And the general type of this order was the tabernacle. For "the form thereof was shown to Moses by the Lord upon Mount Sinai, and what was shown in form by the Lord must necessarily represent either heaven or the things appertaining to heaven." (Ap. Ex. 700.) Hence "all the laws of the jewish church, inasmuch as they derived their origin from the spiritual world, correspond to the laws of order which are in heaven," (A. C. 5135;) and "all the statutes which were commanded to the sons of Israel, were laws of order in the external form; but those things which they represented and signified were laws of order in the internal form." (A. C. 7995.) From this it follows, that all the laws and statutes of the jewish church relating to priestly offices, or to priests and their functions, were "laws of order in the external form" which represented and signified "those things that were laws of order in the internal form." Consequently, the order which is prescribed in those things that represent and signify the priestly functions of the jewish priesthood, is the true order for priests and the priesthood both for ever in heaven and at all times on earth : because the same order must prevail in the correspondent· things on earth, that prevails in those things in the heavens which they represent and signify.

Now these are the words of Swedenborg, in explaining Exod. xxviii. 2 : "Inasmuch as the priesthood was representative of the Lord as to all the work of salvation derived from the divine love, therefore also all divine worship was of the office of the priest, which worship at that time chiefly consisted in offering burnt-offerings, sacrifices and meat-offerings; and in arranging the bread upon the table of faces, in kindling the lamps every day, and in burning incense; consequently in expiating the people and in remitting sins— moreover, also, in explaining the law divine, and in teaching; on which occasion they were at the same time called prophets." (A. C. 9809.) Well what is the order which is seen to prevail in these representative functions of the jewish priesthood? Why, here is a trine of trines—

First, *offering of burnt-offerings, sacrifices,* and *meat-offerings.*

Second, *arranging bread on the table of faces, kindling the lamps every day,* and *burning incense.*

Third, *expiating the people and remitting their sins, explaining the law divine,* and *teaching.*

How clear is it, then, from these "laws of order in the external form," that the true order for a priesthood in heaven, or in an internal church on earth, is a trine of grades or degrees?

But all the jewish worship, which was the complex of all the functions of the jewish priesthood, was represented by the tabernacle and the temple. Therefore the order of arrangement in the tabernacle and the temple is the same as the order that prevailed in the functions of the worship. Now the order of arrangement in both the tabernacle and the temple was an almost indefinite series of trines. Let us observe only the most general arrangement. The tabernacle was divided into two parts by a veil. The inner part was called the holy of holies, or the most holy place. Here, as the receptacle of the

Word, were the *ark*, the *propitiatory*, and the *cherubs*—a trine. The
part of the sacred tent without the veil, was called the holy place.
Here were the *table* of show bread, the golden *altar* of incense, and
the golden *candlestick*—another trine. And, thirdly, the court of the
tabernacle. Here were the brazen *altar* for sacrifices, the brazen *laver*
for washing, and the *gate* of the court—still another trine. Thus we
find in this case, too, a trine of trines. Wherefore "the laws of order
in the external form" produce the trinal arrangement of all things:
and "as they correspond to the laws of order which are in heaven,"
so as to "represent and signify the laws of order in the internal form,"
therefore all things in heaven, and in the internal or spiritual church,
must be arranged in trinal order. This is that "disposition of all
things according to the order which prevails in the heavens from the
Lord," that constitutes "the divine order which is a perpetual commandment of God." Consequently, this could not be abolished when
the mere external representatives which shadowed them on earth were
abrogated. Divine order perpetually requires that the Word of God,
and heaven and the church, as constituted by the Word, should be
distinguished into "three degrees"—that all things which pertain to
the worship of the church, both internal and external, should be distinguished in a corresponding manner, and thus that priestly offices
and the priesthood, which pertain to that worship, should be similarly
distinguished.

As to the representation of these things, this is the doctrine of
Swedenborg:—" The three heavens were what were represented by
the tabernacle; and the Lord himself by the testimony in the ark, on
which was the propitiatory. . . From which it might appear, that
the rituals or representatives of the jewish church contained in them *all
the arcana of the christian church;* and likewise that they, to whom
the representatives and significatives of the Word of the Old Testament are opened, may know and perceive the arcana of the Lord's
church in the earths, whilst they live in the world, and the arcana of
arcana which are in the Lord's kingdom in the heavens, when they
come into another life." (A. C. 3478.) Thus we are taught that
" the laws of order in the internal form" for the christian church are
so contained in, and figured by, the rituals or representatives of the
jewish church, as "the laws of order in the external form," that the
former may be known by the latter. Nay, by the same means we
may know what is the order that prevails in the heavens. Hence it
conclusively appears, as the teaching of the Word of God on this
subject, that the functions of priestly offices, and of course, the priests
who minister those functions, are, in just order, to be arranged in
three degrees. For the tent or tabernacle, which "denoted in the
supreme sense the Lord, and also heaven and the church, and in the
respective sense, every holy thing of heaven and the church, hence
also the holy principle of worship and the holy principle of the
Word, for these are of the church, and are of the Lord, because from
him," (A. C. 10.545,)—hence denoted "all the arcana of the christian
church," thus all its internal order to which its external order should
correspond, and therefore the laws of its external order, by which

its priesthood and its priestly offices should be arranged and governed—was arranged in the most complete trinal order.

In further proof of this, take the following more specific teachings, which also show that the same was true of the temple afterwards built and dedicated by Solomon :—" The tent of assembly represented the three heavens. The court thereof represented the ultimate or first heaven ; the tent itself even to the veil, where were the tables for the breads, the altar of incense and the candlestick, represented the middle or second heaven ; and the ark which was within the veil, upon which was the propitiatory with the cherubs, represented the inmost or third heaven ; and the law itself, which was in the ark, represented the Lord as to divine truth or the Word: and that the tabernacle, *equally as the temple*, in the supreme sense signifies the Lord, in the respective sense heaven and the church, and thence the holy principle of worship. See A. C. 9457, 9481, 10.242, 10.245, 10.505, 10.545. . . . . The tabernacle, together with the altar, was in an especial manner the most holy representative of worship ; for worship was performed upon the altar by burnt offerings and sacrifices, and in the tabernacle by burning of incense—also by the lamps which were daily lighted up, and by the breads which were daily disposed in order upon the table : *all these things represented all worship in heaven and in the church*, and the tent itself with the ark the heavens themselves." . . . And " inasmuch as the ark in the tent of assembly represented the third heaven where the Lord is, and the tent itself without the veil the second heaven, and the court the first heaven—so likewise did the temple : for the temple with its courts represented also the three heavens. Wherefore, there was nothing in the temple, nor out of the temple within the courts, which did not represent somewhat of heaven. . . . . The same was represented by the temple as by the tent of assembly, with this difference, that the tent of assembly was a more holy representative of the Lord, of heaven, and of the church, than the temple." (Ap. Ex. 700.)

Here we see that the distinct arrangements of the tabernacle and the temple represented the three heavens. And às these are arranged in *successive* order, therefore they are arranged by *discrete* degrees ; for " things successive are not connected *continuously*, but *discretely*, that is, distinctly, according to degrees." (A. C. 10.099.) And as the " tabernacle itself, with the ark, represented the heavens themselves ;" and " was in an especial manner the most holy representative of worship ;" so that the various distinct parts of worship, which were performed in the distinct arrangements of the tabernacle and its court, and were the functions of the priestly offices, " represented *all worship* in *heaven* and in the *church ;*" therefore, these functions too were discriminated " distinctly according to degrees," that is, were distinguished into three discrete degrees, according to " those three things which succeed in order in the three heavens," which are " goods in that order.". Consequently, the priests, who minister in leading the worship of any church, should be distinguished in like manner. For the true order of the priesthood is "*three* things, which

31

succeed in order." Hence Aaron alone ministered in the most holy place once a year; the sons of Aaron ministered in the holy place; and the Levites ministered in the court of the tabernacle. Aaron and his sons might minister in the two lower degrees, because they were included in the higher; but the sons of Aaron did not minister in the highest, nor the Levites in the middle degree,—except as the assistants of Aaron and his sons,—because their respective functions were separated or distinguished by discrete degrees.

A like order is observable in the ecclesiastical encampment of the Israelites. (Numbers, iii.) Those that encamped on the east, "before the tabernacle of the congregation eastward, were Moses, Aaron, and his sons, keeping the charge of the sanctuary, for the charge of the children of Israel." (v. 38.) "By Moses, Aaron, and his sons, was represented the Lord as to divine good and divine truth proceeding from the divine love. Hence their camp was towards the east." (Ap. Ex. 422.) Thus, in the ministry of the celestial or spiritual church, there must be a trine in just order. On the other three sides of the tabernacle were encamped the Levites, by their three families, of Kohath, Gershon, and Merari. The families of Kohath encamped on the south, and, in journeying, served in carrying the ark, the table of shew bread, the candlestick, and the altar of incense. The families of Gershon, encamped on the west, and served in carrying the tabernacle and tent with their several coverings. The families of Merari encamped on the north, and served in carrying the boards, bars, pillars and sockets, which were relatively the *bones* of the tabernacle and its court. Thus there is a trine in the lowest or natural degree of heaven and the church. And, of course, the church on earth, with its ministry, which is as the feet of the church in the heavens, when arranged in true order, will be distinguished into a trine of degrees. For "there are three things which fully constitute and form every universal essential principle, namely, the good of love, the truth from that good, and the consequent good of life. . . . . Those three are as the pulse of the heart, the respiration of the lungs, and the action of the body," which make one as the final cause, the efficient cause, and the effect, and represent the good of love, truth from that good, and the good of life, in the Word, in heaven, and in the church. And "*three like principles are in* EVERY THING WHICH EXISTS; and *when the three exist together*, THERE IS A FULL FORMATION." (Ap. Ex. 435.) The only question is, then, Is there to be a ministry in the new and true christian church at all? If there is, it is to be "*a thing which exists*" in that church; and *must* have in it "*three like principles*," that is, the representers of the good of love, the truth from that good, and the good of life; and when these "three exist together, there will be a *full formation*" of a christian ministry, and not before.

The same order is observable in David's arrangement of the priests and Levites when he sent them to bring up the ark from Obed-edom to the place which he had prepared for it in Zion. (1 Chron. xv.) And in the daily ministry before the ark when put in its place, there was a trine of duties and a trine of priests. (1 Chron. xvi.) "And he appointed certain of the Levites to minister before the ark of the Lord, and to *record* and to *thank* and *praise* the Lord God of Israel." (Verse 4.) In this ministry there were chief priests to offer burnt offerings on the altar, intermediate priests to conduct the worship by singing, and priests, subordinate to these as porters or keepers of the gates, whose especial province it was to act as almoners, in taking charge of the treasure houses, and receiving and distributing provisions for the priesthood, as well as taking care of the sacred utensils, and attending to all the subordinate ministries of the congregation of worshipers. In short, there was a trine of grades and a trine in each grade. (1 Chron. xxiv., xxv., and xxvi.) And no one, can fail to observe a similar order in the temple erected by Solomon. (1 Chron. xxviii. 13, compared with 2 Chron. viii. 14.) For here, also, courses of priests were appointed to their especial service, which was the offering of sacrifices on the altar, " and the Levites to their charges, to praise and minister before the priests, as the duty of every day required: the porters also, by their courses, at every gate."

As, then, all these arrangements were according to those " laws of order in the external form," which represented the disposition of " all things according to the order which prevails in the heavens from the Lord," it conclusively follows, that the just order for the arrangement of ministers of religion in any and every church on earth, is *a trine of discrete degrees.*

That the ministers of a church, arranged in three degrees, should be subordinate, the lower to the higher, follows as a corollary from the above conclusion. For they are in the order of " the good of love, the truth from that good, and the good of life," in which the lower are manifestly subordinate to the higher. They are also in the order of " the pulse of the heart, the respiration of the lungs, and the action of the body," in which it is equally manifest that there is a like subordination. And they are in the order of the three heavens, which form a collective man, and so a complex representative of the Lord : and that these are subordinate, the lower to the higher, as things external to things internal in man, is a well-known doctrine of our church. For instance—" Such is the form of government in the other life, that good spirits are subordinate to angelic spirits, and angelic spirits to angels, so as to constitute an angelic society." (A. C. 1752.) Again, "The angels who are in the first heaven are subordinate to the angels who are in the second, and these to the angels in the third; but this subordination is not like that of rule and authority; but it is like the subordination of things external to internal things in man." (A. C. 1802.)

Now the priesthood is a representative of the Lord; and, therefore, there must be three things in the priesthood to represent the three principles that are in the Lord, just as the three heavens do; and these three things must be subordinate, the lower to the higher, just as the lower heavens are subordinate to the higher heavens, and as the lower principles are subordinate to the higher principles in him. "The three heavens are images of the Lord's external man." (A. C. 1590.) And " the universal heaven, together with the church in the world appears before the Lord as one man—the inmost heaven constitutes the *head*, the rest constitute the *breasts* and *legs*, and the church in the earths constitutes the *feet*." (Ap. Ex. 413.) Hence it was that Aaron alone, as the high priest, (A. C. 9809,) could represent the Lord as the Great High Priest. For his head represented the Lord's work of saving men in the celestial degree—his breasts represented his work of saving them in the spiritual degree, his legs represented his work of saving them in the natural degree, and his feet represented his work of establishing the true church on earth as a basis of man's salvation in the three heavens throughout all time. Hence, whether the Lord appeared to Abraham as *three men*, whom Abraham at times addressed as *one*, (Gen. xviii.,) or to John (Rev. i.) as *one man*, he alike showed forth a trine of discrete degrees in his ministry, by the trine of his *head*, his *body*, and his *feet*, which several distinct parts are described by John as he saw them, and exist as well in the Lord's person, as in the universal heaven, the universal church, and every other complex form that does or can represent him. Hence the Lord's appearance to John as one man, does not indicate that there shall be a ministry of only *one grade* in the New Jerusalem; for such a ministry could not represent the Lord as one *complete* and *complex* man, because every one man is constituted such by a *trine* of distinct parts. "Such a trine is man; his supreme part is the head, his middle part the body, and his lowest part the feet and soles of the feet." (Coronis, 17.) Therefore, such a trine was the Lord as he appeared to John in the Revelations—such a trine is "the universal heaven together with the church in the world," which "appears before the Lord as *one man*"—and such a trine is the priesthood of the New Jerusalem, and of every other true church of the Lord on earth. The priesthood of the New Jerusalem, when in just order, must be constituted *one complex man*, by a *trine of discrete degrees of men*, which degrees of men shall have the same relation to each other that the three distinct parts of the Lord's person, or the three heavens, have to each other. And that this is a relation of due subordination of lower things and principles to higher, is conclusively shown by the following:—"Order consists in celestial things bearing rule over spiritual, and by spiritual over natural, and lastly by natural over corporeal. If things corporeal and natural have rule over things spiritual and celestial, order is destroyed." (A. C. 911.) And that this applies to priests as officers of ecclesiastical government on earth, as well as to principles in the spiritual world, is thus taught—"There must also be order amongst the governors, lest any one, from caprice or inadvertence, should permit evils which are against order, and thereby destroy it: which is guarded against when there are superior and inferior governors, amongst whom there is subordination." (H. D. 313.) "It is grounded in order that an inferior thing should be subservient to a superior, and so far as it is subservient it is called a servant. . . . . The general principle is that to which singular things are to be subservient." (A. C. 5305.) Thus the officer in a particular or singular province of ecclesiastical administration, should be subordinate to an officer in a general province. "The natural man ought to serve the rational, and this the spiritual, and the spiritual the celestial, and the celestial the Lord. Such is the order of subordination." (A. C. 2781.) Such, therefore, is the true order of a three-fold christian ministry. And, consequently, we conclude that the just order for the ministry of the New Jerusalem, is *a trine of discrete and subordinate degrees.*·

4. The conclusion we have now reached rests on the *successive descending order* of the representative jewish priesthood and its priestly functions, which is the order of the regenerated man. But the same doctrine is taught by the *successive ascending order* of the priestly representatives and significatives in the Word of the Old Testament, which is the order of man's reformation, or the order of man in the process of being regenerated. This involves proof of the propriety and need of a trine of discrete degrees in the ministry of the church from the order of *development of higher degrees in lower preparative planes.* The type of this is seen in 2 Sam. vi. 1–17, where we find an account of the translation of the ark from the house of Abinadab, residing at Baal of Judah, in Gibeah, and from the house of Obed-edom, in Gath, to the city of David. "The translation of the ark signified the progression of the church with man from its ultimates to its inmost, and this because those progressions are effected by divine truth, which was signified by the ark : for the man of the church advances from the natural principle to the spiritual, and through this to the celestial, and this continually from the Lord by his divine truth. The natural principle is the good of life, the spiritual is the good of charity towards our neighbor, and the celestial is the good of love to the Lord. In a similar progression are the goods of the three heavens. Wherefore, the ascent through them in their order was also represented." (Ap. Ex. 700.) The ark here, as before, signifies the Lord, and heaven, and holy worship. It was in three regions. First, in Gibeah, where Baal of Judah and Abinadab were. Second, in Gath, where Obed-edom was. Third, in Zion, where David dwelt. Gibeah, or Baal of Judah, where Abinadab was, "signified the ultimate of the church, which is called its natural principle." "Gath, where Obed-edom was, signified the spiritual principle of the church." "But Zion, where David dwelt, signified what is inmost of the church, which is called its celestial principle." Thus we have reformation by truths leading to goods in the upward progressions of the three heavens, represented by this historical account of the translation of the ark from Gibeah, through Gath, to Zion, the city of David. Of course, we have here a representation of the Lord's work of salvation in its three discrete degrees ascending. There is also a representation of the glorification of the Lord's humanity in its natural, spiritual, and celestial degrees. This makes one with his reformation and regeneration of mankind in the same degrees. And of this the priesthood in any church is representative.

By this part of the Word, therefore, we are taught, in the first place, that an external ministerial order, truly and perfectly representative of the Lord as to its external form, must be instituted in time before the internal principles which it represents are developed in the church. For men are now degenerate, and the church is instituted in external forms, as a means of reforming and regenerating them. Hence, as "the man of the church advances from the natural principle to the spiritual, and through this to the celestial, and this continually from the Lord by his divine truth," therefore, the ministers of this truth in their true order must stand and work first on the natural plane. But, in the second place, this part of the Word teaches us, that there should be in the priesthood of the christian church priests of three degrees. For there was Abinadab who ministered to the ark in Baal of Judah, or Gibeah; there was Obed-edom who ministered to it in Gath; and there was David who ministered to it in Zion. (1 Chron. xv. 27.) Hence, in the christian ministry, there should be a priest to represent the reformation and regeneration of men in the natural degree, or a priest for "the ultimate of the church which is called its natural principle;" a priest to represent their reformation and regeneration in the spiritual degree, or a priest for "the spiritual principle of the church;" and a priest to represent their reformation and regeneration in the celestial degree, or a priest for "what is the inmost of the church, which is called its celestial principle." And in the formation of this priesthood, the lower planes or discrete degrees must first be passed through in rising to the higher planes or degrees. In other words, the lower planes must first exist as preparative stages for the orderly development of the capacities for discharging the functions of the higher degrees of the priesthood. Otherwise, "things corporeal and natural would have rule over things spiritual and celestial," so that "order would be destroyed." For were men placed at once in the highest degree of the ministry, without passing through its lower degrees in the preparatory putting off of what is unsuitable, and the gradual acquisition of suitable qualifications, there would be rule in high station from the self-intelligence of proprium, instead of the intelligence of wisdom. In short, the development of ministerial capacity in degrees of ministerial function and character, should be representative of the translation of the ark from Gibeah, through Gath, to Zion; or of "the progressions of the church with man from its ultimates to its inmost principle." For "those progressions are effected by divine truth;" and the ministers of the church are the ministers of the truth; hence there must be the same gradual progressions in the formation of the ministers of truth that there are in the advances of men in the reformation and regeneration which it effects in them, so that the rising of ministers from the lowest through the middle to the highest grade of the ministry, may itself represent the advances which the man of the church makes "from the natural principle to the spiritual, and through this to the celestial, and this continually from the Lord by his divine truth." Or, as the priesthood represents the Lord in his work of saving men in the three heavens, this regular ascent of ministers through the three discrete degrees of the priesthood should invariably be observed, that it may represent "a similar progression" of the man of the church in the "goods of the three heavens," or man's "ascent through them in their order." Thus the priesthood in just order is proved to consist of priests of three discrete degrees, by this "law of external order" in the Word, which requires its development in *successive*, that is, *discrete, ascending order.*

In confirmation of the above, and as affording one of the most remarkable authorities for the trine, let it here be observed, that Swedenborg, in illustrating the progress of the Lord towards union with the father, in which he passed through two states, called states of exinanition and of glorification, and the progress of every man, who from natural becomes spiritual, by passing through the two states of reformation and regeneration, shows the indispensable necessity of previously going through the first, as a preparatory stage, before the second can be well and truly entered. "These two states," he says, "are represented by various circumstances and effects in the universe; and the reason is, because they are according to divine order, and divine order fills all and every thing in the universe, even to the most minute particulars." Thus he teaches that "divine order," which "is nothing else but a perpetual commandment of God," requires that a man in becoming spiritual, must necessarily first pass through the natural plane, that is, rise by a discrete degree; or, in becoming regenerate, must necessarily first be reformed, which implies the renunciation of evils as sins by life according to the truths of doctrine from the Word; by this a man becomes regenerate, that is, comes into the good of truth as the central and controlling principle of his soul. Thus from natural a man becomes spiritual by ascending in the order of discrete degrees, as the Lord did in uniting humanity with divinity within him. This progression in successive ascending order, Swedenborg goes on to exemplify by several of the "various circumstances and effects in the universe," which "are according to divine order," that "fills all and every thing in the universe, even to the most minute particulars." After citing the states of infancy and childhood in man's progressions to manhood—also the state of a prince, or the son of a king, or of a duke, before he becomes himself a king or a duke—also the state of a citizen before he becomes a magistrate—the state of a subject of government before he is an officer of the government to which he owes allegiance, he proceeds to the following most express specifications: "likewise of *every student who is preparing for the ministry, before he becomes a priest; and of every priest before he becomes a pastor, and of every pastor before he is a primate;* also of every virgin before she becomes a wife, and of every maid-servant before she becomes a mistress; of every soldier before he is made an officer; and of every servant before he becomes a master." He then goes on to illustrate the same circumstances and effects cited from the animal and vegetable kingdoms—only one of which citations we will quote and italicise for the purpose of comparison with the instance above underscored. "In like manner *in the case of caterpillars, the first state is represented by their creeping, and feeding on the leaves of trees, and the second by their casting their skins and becoming butterflies.*" In this last instance there is the state of the egg,—which the parent moth has deposited on the leaf that is to become the pabulum of the future being,—before it is hatched into the worm, and the state of the worm before it becomes a nymph, and the state of the nymph before it becomes a butterfly. Thus, in the full development of the insect, there is a trine of discrete degrees, namely the worm, the nymph, and the butterfly. And let it be well observed that this is the progression that Swedenborg expressly specifies· as that which is according to the divine order, that fills all things in the universe even to the most minute particulars, in developing the priesthood. First there is the state of the student as preparatory to the priesthood; then there is in the priesthood, firstly, the *priest*, secondly, the *pastor*, and thirdly, the *primate*—the first preparatory to the second, and the second preparatory to the third. Thus there is a trine of degrees in *successive* ascending order, which are just as discrete as the worm is discrete from the nymph, or the nymph from the butterfly. Can any thing be more express, conclusive, and irrefutable than this? Is it not an unanswerable authority from the writings of Swedenborg that there should be A *trine* of DISCRETE *degrees* in the new-church ministry, whenever it is developed and formed according to "the divine order which fills the universe" and is "a perpetual commandment of God"?

We do not suppose that Swedenborg intended to teach that the ministers in the trinal order of the new church are to be called by the names of *priest, pastor* and *primate.* He merely cited that form of the trinal order as it existed in the leading denominations of the christian church of his day. He cited a particular case to illustrate the general law of order; and, therefore, he teaches by this nothing but the general law in its application to the New Jerusalem. And he *certainly does teach* that the "divine order which fills all and every thing in the universe, even to the most minute particulars," when it flows into the various ecclesiastical organizations of the New Jerusalem, must develope in successive order *a* trine of discrete degrees in their ecclesiastical officers. The form of this trine, the names of its officers, the nature of their powers, the extent of their jurisdictions, or the kind of their distinguishing characteristics, may be various, according to the circumstances, times, and states of the church, or the genius, wants, and destinies of its members. But in all cases, there must be *a* trine of some sort. And thus we conclusively prove, from the Word, as explained by Swedenborg, that, in the ministry or priesthood of the New Jerusalem, there must be, in just order, a trine of discrete degrees; the lower of which must be as subordinate to the higher, as a prince is to a king, a common citizen to a magistrate, a maid-servant to a mistress, a clerk to a merchant, a soldier to an officer, and a servant to a master. For this is the just subordination of the natural to the spiritual man, or the spiritual·to the celestial man, or the celestial man to the Lord.

But candor and fairness require that we should present and notice the plausible objection which is wont to be made to the authorities here advanced. It is objected that the priesthood of Aaron, which represented the Lord as the Great High Priest, was wholly abolished by the coming of the Lord, who in his humanity is the sole head of his church. In respect to the specific priesthood of Aaron himself, contradistinguished from the priesthood of his sons and the priesthood

of the Levites, this is granted. And hence there is not to be in the
universal christian church one individual man as a *pontifex maximus*.
The function of the high priest was to enter into the holy of holies
once a year, on the day of solemn expiation, to make atonement for
the sins of the *whole* people. This confessedly is the function of
the Lord alone in the christian church ; and therefore there is no high
priest needed to represent the Lord in this church. For this represented the Lord's assuming humanity in ultimates, so that,—after his
resurrection and full glorification by union with the divine good of
the divine love, in order that, by ascending far above all heavens, he
might " fill *all* things,"—he became actually present in the whole
church as a soul in its body ; and, therefore, he is the sole head of his
church. Neither is there needed now revelation or prophecy by the
urim and thummim, according to Exodus, xxviii. 30; for since the
coming of the Lord and his actual presence in the ultimates of order
by his divine humanity, there is a shining forth of divine truth from
himself in ultimates, which illuminates and illustrates the men of the
church by the light of truth in their own minds—the light that shines
from good, into which the Lord immediately flows. But there are
needed in the christian church, priests to represent the Lord as the
sons of Aaron ; and such in the Lord's time were his twelve apostles.
There are also needed ministers to represent the Lord as the Levites ;
and such in the Lord's personal presence in the world, were his seventy
disciples.

Paul declares, " We have a great high priest that is passed into the
heavens, Jesus the son of God"—" called of God an high priest after
the order of Melchisedec"—"and not called after the order of Aaron"—
springing " out of Judah, of which tribe Moses spake nothing concerning priesthood"—having " an unchangeable priesthood"—" the
apostle and high priest of our profession"—" counted worthy of more
glory than Moses"—so that " we have not a high priest which cannot
be touched with a feeling of our infirmities"—" we have an high
priest, who is set on the right hand of the Majesty in the heavens; a
minister of the sanctuary, and of the true tabernacle which the Lord
pitched, and not man." But Paul also declares that " the priesthood
was *changed*," not abolished. The " high priest of our profession" is
of another tribe—of Judah and not of Levi. But " if he were on
earth, *he should not be a priest*, seeing that there *are* priests that offer
gifts according to the law, who *serve unto the example and shadow of
heavenly things*." Still, then,—although we have only one high priest
in heaven,—there is a priesthood in the church on earth—a christian
priesthood, which although it is not the *same* as the levitical priesthood, must have the same representative character and be in the same
heavenly order. For the tribe of Judah had a trine, as well as the
tribe of Levi, in the encampments of the children of Israel around
the ark in its journeyings to the land of Canaan. (Numbers, ii.)

If, then, the priesthood of Aaron, and even that of the sons of Aaron,
are both abolished in the christian church, there is still the priesthood
of the Levites, which is the representative of the natural heaven, or
which represents the laws of heavenly order in ultimates. And in

this plane itself there is a trine—Merari, Gershon, and Kohath—the
gate of the court, the brazen laver, and the brazen altar—the porter
of the gate, the priest of purification, and the priest of sacrifice.
Hence, in the priesthood of the christian church, there must be a trine
of priests, even if it is only the priesthood of the natural degree.
There must be a grade of priests, whose specific province it is to
make disciples; another, whose specific province it is to *baptize all
nations;* and a third with the province of *teaching them the Lord's
commandments.* This follows from the perpetual correspondence of
the church on earth. It corresponds to the *three* heavens. For "the
heavens stand upon the church which is with mankind, as *man* doth
upon his *feet.*" (Ap. Ex. 413.) Hence there must be the same order
in the church on earth, that there is in the foot of the human body.
But in the foot, there is the trine of *foot, sole* and *heel.* And, as we
have before shown, there is, in the anatomy of the foot, a double trine
of bones. Consequently, in the church on earth, which is the feet
of heaven as a man, there must be a trine both of its members and
its ministers. There must be a priest to represent and correspond to
the celestial heaven; another to represent and correspond to the
spiritual heaven; and still another to represent and correspond to the
natural heaven. For, as we have already shown, if these three
degrees were not in the natural plane, in simultaneous order on earth,
the priestly offices and officers could not subsist in the three heavens,
and their influences perpetually flow from thence in successive order.

And that the priests of the christian priesthood should be in the
order of discrete degrees, just as the priests of the levitical priesthood
were, appears from the discreteness of their sacraments. For Swedenborg teaches that the two christian sacraments are as two gates,
between which there is a plane to be passed over. (U. T. 721.) By
the first is introduction into the church through truth and the life of
it; and by the second is introduction into heaven through good and
the life of it. Hence the supper is as discrete from baptism, as good
is discrete from truth; and baptism is as subordinate to the supper, as
truth is subordinate to good. Again, Swedenborg compares the two
sacraments to "a double temple, one of which is below and the other
above. In the lower the gospel of the Lord's new advent is preached,
and also regeneration and consequent salvation by him: from this
temple, near the altar, is an ascent to the upper temple, where the
holy supper is celebrated; and from thence is a passage into heaven,
where the worshipers are received by the Lord." (Ibid. 669.) Hence
the priest who administers baptism, should be as discrete from, and
subordinate to, the priest who administers the supper, as the first story
of a house is discrete from, and subordinate to, its second story. He
also compares them expressly to "the tabernacle, wherein, behind the
entrance, the table appeared on which the show-bread was placed in
order—also the golden altar for incense, and the candlestick in the
midst with its branches lighted, so that all those objects are rendered
visible; and at length, for those who suffer themselves to be enlightened, the veil is opened to the holy of holies, where, instead of the
ark which contained the decalogue, the Word is deposited, over which

is the mercy-seat with the golden cherubim. *These things are representations of those two sacraments with their uses.*" (Ibid.) This is
conclusive, in showing, that not only the levitical priesthood, but also
that of the sons of Aaron, thus the discrete arrangements of the holy
place, as well as those of the court of the tabernacle, are representations of the christian sacraments, and, of course, of the christian
priests who minister them. Hence baptism and the supper are as
discrete as two temples, and the one is as subordinate to the other as
the lower temple is subordinate to the higher, or as the church is subordinate to heaven, or as the natural heaven is subordinate to the
spiritual heaven. They are just as discrete, too, as the arrangements of the holy place, and as subordinate as the sons of Aaron
were to their father, all of whom ministered in the worship of the
holy place of the tabernacle. Can any thing, then, be more clearly
or conclusively shown, than that there should be at least two grades
of christian priests, one to stand at the first gate and representatively
introduce people into the church; and another to stand at the second
gate, and representatively introduce people into heaven? Farther,
that these priests are of degrees just as discrete and subordinate as
their functions? But we have proved that there should be a *trine* of
priests in the priesthood of every church, when in just order. Hence,
in the priesthood of the christian church, there must be three degrees
of priests, as discretely distinguished from one another as two gates
with a plane between them, or two temples, one above another, or as
the distinct arrangements of the tabernacle; and as subordinate, the
lower to the higher, as the Levites were to Aaron and his sons.

Again, it is objected that representatives are wholly done away in
the abrogation of the jewish ritual, and therefore *such* a representative priesthood as the jewish, can in no respect remain in the christian
dispensation. This objection we have answered at great length in
another part of the present report. But we will, in fairness, present
here one of the strongest authorities from Swedenborg's writings for
its support, and very briefly repeat the argument from other parts of
his writings in its explanation.

In Daniel, iii. 15, 16, the Lord says, " I will give you pastors according to my heart, and they shall feed you with knowledge and intelligence : and it shall come to pass when ye shall be multiplied, and
bear fruit in the land, in those days they shall no more say, the ark of
the covenant of Jehovah, neither shall it come up upon the heart,
nor shall they make mention thereof, neither shall they desire it,
neither shall it be repaired any more." And in explaining this passage, Swedenborg writes—"These things are said concerning the
advent of the Lord, and concerning the abolition of the representative rites of the jewish church which should then take place. That
the interior things of the church should be manifested, which
were veiled over by the representative external rites, and that they
should then become interior or spiritual men, is signified by pastors
being given according to the heart of the Lord, who shall feed them
with knowledge and intelligence. By pastors are understood those
who *teach good* and *lead* thereto by truths, [christian *priests*, as we

have shown.] The multiplication of truth and fructification of good, [two distinct functions,] is signified by, then it shall come to pass, when ye shall be multiplied and bear fruit in the land in those days. That then conjunction with the Lord will be by the interior things of the Word, and not by things exterior which ONLY *signified* and *represented* things interior, [those exterior things, however, as we have fully shown, not being wholly done away as the externals of the Word and of worship—a representative ritual being still there, but not conjunction by it alone as formerly,] is signified by; they shall no more say, the ark of the covenant of Jehovah—the ark of the covenant of Jehovah there denoting the externals of worship *which were then to be abolished*, [not all .externals of worship,] the same as by the daily or continual sacrifice which was to cease, as mentioned by Daniel, viii. 13; xi. 31; xii. 11. That there was to be no longer external worship, [that is, external worship without any corresponding internal principle in it,] but internal, [that is, a worship in which "its internal is in an appropriate external, A. C. 4288,] is signified by, it shall not come into the heart, neither shall they make mention thereof, neither shall they desire it, neither shall it be repaired any more." (Ap. Ex. 700.)

In this passage we observe that Swedenborg says, as it were absolutely, representative rites were so to be abolished "that there was *no longer to be external worship*, but internal." A stronger authority for the entire abolition of all external worship cannot be adduced. And it is just such isolated sentences as this, which superficial receivers of our doctrines take, to support the position, that, "in the true church, when it is fully developed, there will be *no external worship whatever*": for Swedenborg says, in just so many words, "there was no longer to be external worship, but internal." But that he did not intend to teach that there was to be no external worship whatever—thus no external church—no priesthood—no ritual worship whatever, in the christian church, is most manifest from even this passage of his writings itself, and, as we think, is very expressly taught by other passages which we have brought forward. For the Lord, by his Word, teaches here, that he would give the christian church pastors, who were to be christian priests, that were to feed the members of that church with knowledge and intelligence. Hence there was to be an external church amongst christians, with its external worship, and of course an external priesthood to minister in that worship. And this external worship of even the New Jerusalem was represented to John in the Revelations by the ark of the covenant which he saw in the temple of God that was opened in heaven. (Rev. xi. 19.) Therefore Swedenborg adds—" Hence also it may appear, that the ark of the covenant seen by John in the temple of God, which is the vision now treated of, was an appearing of the divine truth, whereby is effected the conjunction of the new heaven and the new church with the Lord, and that *this was so seen in order that the Word in the letter might be every where like to itself*, [thus the same in the New Jerusalem that it was in the Old Jerusalem,] *consisting of such things as were* EXTERNALS OF WORSHIP *and* REPRESENTED *things*

internal." Thus there are to be, in the christian church, externals of
worship from the letter of the Word, which are to represent the internal
things of this church, although the *mere, pure,* or *sole* representatives—
" the representative *external* rites " " of the jewish church," have been
wholly abrogated in it. These, as we have shown, were idolatrous
superadditions to the true or internal representative rites of the ancient
church, which, as involucra, being peeled off, have left true representatives still to remain in the christian dispensation. Some of these true
representatives as existing still in the jewish ritual, we have shown
were not abolished in the christian church. We have also shown,
from Swedenborg, that the internals of the ancient and christian
churches were precisely the same; and that the christian church had
also " a similar ritual "—the sacraments, " alike representative of the
Lord," being substituted in it for the sacrifices of the ancient church.
We have also shown among the true representatives of the ancient
church, which were not abolished in the abrogation of the jewish
ritual, " priestly offices, and whatever pertained to them "; and it is
manifest that there must be priestly officers to minister in the christian
sacraments, which are " only representative and significative rites."
(Ap. Ex. 475.) Wherefore, it is clear, according to Swedenborg,
that there must be in the christian church a strictly representative
priesthood. And that the order of this priesthood and the order of
its priestly functions are the same as those of the levitical priesthood,
which were represented by the arrangements of the court of the
tabernacle, is fully evident from what we have just now shown. It
is evident from the fact, that the christian sacraments of baptism and
the holy supper were instituted instead of the washings and the
sacrifices of the jewish church, which were performed at the brazen
laver and the brazen altar of the court. Wherefore, although the
jewish ritual of the court and its tabernacle were abolished, still there
is " a similar ritual," with sacraments " alike *representative* of the
Lord," in the christian church—requiring, of course, priests alike
representative of the Lord for the ministration of those sacraments;
and, consequently, requiring, in just order, just such an arrangement
as existed in those things of the court of the jewish tabernacle, which
represented the internal order of heaven and the christian church.
And thus we prove, conclusively, from the Word of the Old Testament, that, as there was a trine of discrete degrees in even the *court*
of the tabernacle in the jewish church, so *there must be a* TRINE OF
DISCRETE DEGREES *in the ministry of the new church.*

The above authorities for a ministerial trine, are a specimen of very
many that might be drawn from the Word of the Old Testament. In
the Word of the New Testament, which is distinctively the Christian
Scripture, there are also many more authorities than we can even
think of quoting here. One or two, from the Book of Revelations,
have been advanced above. And for a very full quotation of them,
we here refer to the able argument of Mr. Cabell in the preceding
pages. To that argument we shall leave entirely the citation of
authorities from the Acts and Epistles of the Apostles, as well as

from the ecclesiastical history of the first three centuries of the church which the Lord established through them. We do not think that we are confined exclusively to those parts of the Word which have a spiritual sense, or that we ought not to go to the Acts and Epistles of the Apostles, in determining what was the external order of the ministry of the first christian church which the Lord established; because, not only does Swedenborg say, in general, that "the writings of the apostles are very good books of the church," as confirmatory of the doctrine of charity and faith which the Lord taught in the Gospels, (Let. to Dr. Beyer;) but he also says, more particularly, "the periodical changes which succeeded in the christian church, are described in the Word of both the Old and New Testaments; in particular, *its rise or morning is described in the Evangelists*, IN THE ACTS, AND THE WRITINGS OF THE APOSTLES; its progression towards midday, in the ecclesiastical history of the first three centuries; its declension, or evening, in the history of the following ages; and its vastation and final consummation, or night, in the Apocalypse." (Con. of Cor. XI.) From this it would seem to be right and proper for us to go, not only to the Acts and Epistles of the Apostles, but also to the ecclesiastical history of the first three centuries of the christian era, for the true external order of the Lord's first christian church. This Mr. Cabell has done for us. He has our thanks for doing that part of our task so well; and the church at large will see how needless he has made any attempts of ours to perform it here. But, a few authorities from the New Testament may be cursorily presented as specimens of the rest. ·

5. On opening the New Testament, the first thing we see is the Lord's genealogy. This we know is the spiritual pedigree of the Lord as the Word. In other words, here is a correspondential and representative statement of the spiritual productions of faith and love that are derived from the Lord in his divine spiritual and celestial genesis. These productions are recorded by the expression of various names significant of their qualities. And what is remarkably pertinent to the subject before us, is the singular fact that there is in the expression of these names a *trine* of *trines*. For they are a series of trines, which may be reduced to *three* classes : the first of which is celestial, the second spiritual, and the third natural—all of which are most holy, because they are a *trine* of *fourteens,* that is of *sevens* multiplied by *two*. (Matt. i. 2 to 6, 7 to 12, 12 to 16, and 17.) Therefore, the divine order, which pervades the universe, filling all things therein even to the most minute particulars, determines all to arrangements in trinal order. Thus, in the spiritual and celestial generations of the Word of God, the divine truth, as it begets images and likenesses of the divine good "in the heavens above, in the earth beneath, and in the waters under the earth," invariably produces a series of trines. Consequently, in the Lord's fulfilling every jot and tittle of the Scriptures, and in the record of such fulfilment by the Evangelists who have written his Gospel, there are every where types and proofs of the trinal arrangement of discrete and subordinate degrees as the just order of *all* things in heaven and in the church. Wherefore, the

true order of a christian priesthood is a trine of discrete and subordinate degrees.

6. When the Magi came from the East to see Him who was to be born King of the Jews in Bethlehem of Judah, and to worship Him, as Immanuel, the Saviour of his people from their sins—"And when they were come into the house—they saw the young child with Mary his mother, and fell down, and worshiped him: and when they had opened their treasures, they presented unto him gifts—*gold*, and *frankincense*, and *myrrh*." (Matt. ii. 11.) "Gold signifies celestial love; frankincense spiritual love; myrrh those loves in the natural principle." (A. C. 4262.) "All worship of Jehovah God, must be from the love of good by truths. Worship from *the good of love alone*, is not worship; neither is that worship which is *from truths alone*, without the good of love. *There must be both :* for the good of love is the essential principle of worship. But good *exists* and is *formed* by truths. Hence all worship must be by truths grounded in good." (Ap. Ex. 696.) "The worship of God consists essentially in a life of *uses*" (A. C. 7884)—truths done, and so made goods in ultimate form. Thus "that is worshiped which is loved, and love worships." (A. C. 10.414.) Yet "the worship of the Lord is either from faith or from love. . . . But by merely *believing* and by merely *loving*, the Lord is not worshiped, but by *living* according to his precepts." (A. C. 10.645.) Hence in true worship there are these three—*loving, believing*, and *living;* and worship must be constituted *one* thing, by these three flowing in successive and simultaneous order. The gifts of the Magi represented christian worship. They were *gold, frankincense*, and *myrrh*—"the good of love, the good of faith, and the things which are of each in externals." (A. C. 9293.) Wherefore, in true christian worship there is a trine of discrete degrees. And as there must be "priests appointed to administer those things that relate to this worship," (H. D. 319,) which are to be "superior and inferior governors, amongst whom there is subordination," (H. D. 313;) that is, a priesthood arranged in the order of the worship which they administer; therefore, there must be in the christian church ministers of three discrete degrees.

7. John was the forerunner of the Lord. He, like Elias, represented the Word in its letter. And they who were baptized by him denoted the external church as it is formed by life according to truths from the letter of the Word. "Then went out to him, *Jerusalem*, and all *Judea*, and all the *region round about Jordan*, and were baptized of him in Jordan confessing their sins." (Matt. iii. 5, 6.) "All the tracts or countries, with the cities in them, in the land of Canaan, were representative, as in the spiritual world, with respect to regions there, and the cities of those regions. In every region, and also in every city whatever, in the spiritual world, they who are in the good of love dwell to the east and west, . . . ; and they who are in the light of truth dwell to the south and the north. . . . . . . But in the land of Canaan, and in the cities thereof, the *places* themselves represented, and not *persons*." (Ap. Ex. 700.) Hence Jerusalem, Judea, and the region about Jordan, are put for the persons—all

those who made up the church represented by John the Baptist. Hence, in this church, there are those who are in the truth of doctrine from the letter of the Word, those who are in the internal acknowledgment of that truth unto the putting away their evils as sins, and those who are in a corresponding ultimate life. Thus there is a trine in the church. And from this we conclude, as above, that there must be a trine in the ministry who represent the trine of the church in administering its worship.

8. The Lord's temptations were typical of his reformation of man, and of his formation of the church in him for his regeneration. Hence, as those temptations were *three-fold*, (Matt. iv. 3–10,) we conclude that, in the church and its ministries, there must be a trine.

9. Matthew, v. 2–11. There were *nine* blessings—a trine of trines. One of the celestial, another of the spiritual, and a third of the natural church.

10. Matthew, vii. 7. The Lord enjoins it on his disciples, to *ask, seek, knock*—a trine.

11. Matthew, ix. 35. "And Jesus went about all the cities and villages, *teaching* in their synagogues, and *preaching* the gospel of the kingdom, and *healing* every sickness and every disease among the people." The Lord was the first priest and minister of his church. This text displays his ministry. And proves that in his ministry there was a trine of distinct functions—which, for its proper representation now in the visible body of the church should have a trine of distinct functionaries.

12. The Lord ordained twelve to be with him. (Matt. x. 1; Mark, iii. 14, and vi. 7; Luke, vi. 13, and ix. 1.) He also appointed seventy, to go two and two before him into those cities and places whither he himself was to come. (Luke, x. 1.) Thus there was in the Lord's time, a trine in the christian ministry—himself, the twelve, and the seventy. That there was due subordination in this trine, is self-evident as to the two higher degrees; also as to the lowest in respect to the highest; and is presumable as to the lowest in respect to the second; from Luke, xxii. 26, 27, where there is evident indication that there was among the Lord's disciples the relation of "him that doth serve" to "him that is chief;" or the relation of "the younger" to "the greatest among them," that is, "the eldest"—for age might, in some cases, have determined precedence. And that there was precedence among the twelve, appears from John, xiii. 23—"Now there was leaning on Jesus's bosom, one of his disciples whom Jesus loved." And *through* this disciple, Simon Peter, and the rest, interrogated the Lord, and received from him information, as to who it was that should betray him. We are aware that some *professed* teachers of truth as taught by Swedenborg, even in the new church, maintain that there was the most perfect equality, and no sort of precedence or subordination, amongst the twelve. They also teach, we know, that Peter represents *all* that appertains to the ministry of the new church, because of his representation of natural truth, the first principle of the church, which principle was represented by the twelve in their apostleship. But this is a fallacy of the old christian church, which Swedenborg notices as

such, and is not a truth of the new christian church as taught by him. The fallacy springs out of the apparent truth that faith is the first principle of the church, having precedence of charity because it appears first in time; and therefore that Peter, the type of faith, has precedence amongst the other apostles,—if there is any,—and the office of the whole christian ministry is fully and perfectly represented in him alone. But we believe that James and John represented the Lord in the christian ministry as well as Peter—we believe that all three represented him, and that until "these three were together," there could not be a "full formation" of his representation. And in this representation of the Lord by *three*, which signifies *all*,—consequently amongst the whole twelve,—we believe that John, as the *celestial* principle of the Lord in the natural degree, took precedence of all the rest. For *he* represented the Lord as Samson,—divinity in humanity, the divine spirit in the letter of the Word, where it is in its greatest fulness, sanctity and power, or the divine love in ultimate good or use, thus the *strongest* of all men,—slaying the Philistines. And we believe that this precedence of John is proved by this text which we have quoted from the twelfth chapter and the twenty-third verse of the gospel according to him, because Swedenborg says so, thus :— "For this reason, Peter, by whom was represented the faith of the church, is said to be the first of the apostles, *when yet John was the first*, inasmuch as by John was represented the good of charity. *That John and not Peter was the first of the apostles*, is evident from this circumstance, that John lay at the breast of the Lord; and that he and not Peter followed the Lord. See John xxi. 20, 21, 22." (Ap. Ex. 229.) Therefore, we say this clearly indicates precedence of one and subordination of others. The same seems to be indicated by Mark, xv. 40—where mention is made of "James, the less." And that certain of the twelve had offices to perform distinctly from the rest, is evident from John, xiii. 29—which shows that "Judas had the bag," with the offices of purveyor of the feast and almoner of the poor: and from Mark, xiv. 13—where the Lord sends forth *two* of his disciples to make ready the passover; or xi. 1-7—where he sends forth two to bring a colt for him to ride into Jerusalem. And, more-over, that there were distinct ceremonial duties assigned to the ministers of this trine, is clear from John, iv. 2—"Jesus himself baptized not, but his disciples:" and Matt. xxvi. 26; Luke, xxii. 19; 1 Cor. xi. 23—Jesus administered the supper, and commanded his twelve to administer it after him. The deacons, or evangelists, ordained by the apostles as ministers of a lower grade, (Acts, vi. 5, 6; viii. 38,) baptized; while Paul, an apostle, (1 Cor. i. 14, 16,) indicates that he rarely performed that ceremony. It is clear, then, that the Word of the New Testament, by these acts of the Lord, teaches the order of a trine of ministers in the ministry of the christian church, among whom there is to be the just subordination of younger to elder, lower to higher, less intelligent to more intelligent, less wise to more wise, and of lower functionaries to higher functionaries. And the higher functionaries may perform the functions of the lower degrees; but they are supposed to descend, for the time being, into the lower planes:

32

for the higher heavens flow into the lower, and the angels of the higher heavens 'may occasionally descend into the Jower to perform uses there. But the lower functionaries may not perform the functions of the higher degrees: for the lower heavens do not flow into the higher, and the angels of the lower cannot ascend into the higher heavens to perform uses there.

13. The same doctrine is taught by all those passages which assign a trine of functions to the christian ministry, or indicate a trine of degrees in the church, or the regenerative process by which the church is formed in man. For example: Matt. x. 1—where the Lord gives to the twelve power over unclean spirits—power to cast them out—power to heal sickness and disease; x. 9—tells them to provide neither *gold, silver*, nor *brass*, in their purses; xi. 5—where the Lord indicates to John's disciples the functions of his own ministry in a double trine; xi. 7-9—where he characterizes John, as a reed shaken—a man in soft raiment—a prophet; xi. 19—where he speaks of what he himself was called, a glutton, a wine-bibber, a friend of publicans and sinners; xii. 50—where he distinguishes the members of the complex church by brother—sister—mother; xiii. 15—where, in characterizing the consummated church, he speaks of the heart as gross—the ears as dull—the eyes as closed, or of seeing with eyes—hearing with ears—understanding with heart; xxi. 9—where there is a trine of glorification. Hosanna to the son of David—Blessed is he that cometh in the name of the Lord—Hosanna in the highest; xxi. 12—where the Lord, in purging the temple, cast out all that sold and bought—overthrew tables of money-changers—threw down the seats of them that sold doves; xxi. 39—where, in the wicked husbandman's treatment of the householder's son, they caught him—cast him out of the vineyard—slew him; xxiv. 7—where the Lord, in predicting the consummation of the church, describes its complex vastations by, famines—pestilences—earthquakes; Mark ii. 11—where he commands the sick of the palsy to arise—take up his bed—go his way; iv. 20—where a double trine is indicated, in such as hear the Word—receive it—bring forth fruit, some thirty—some sixty—some an hundred fold; iv. 28—where the process of regeneration is pictured by, first the blade—then the ear—at last the full corn in the ear. So we might go on in filling pages with citations of passages from all the Books of the New Testament, which prove the trine to be the true order.

14. In a former report, we showed that the priesthood should represent the Lord as three persons, because he appeared to Abraham as three men. (Gen. xviii. 2.) For we argued—" Thus the *trine* in the Lord is represented. Therefore the *trine* in the Lord should be represented to the church by the priesthood, as three distinct men, or as so many discrete grades of its functionaries." To this it is replied, that the Lord appeared to John as one man. Therefore the Lord should be represented to the New Jerusalem by the priesthood as one man, or by priests in only one grade. We rejoin, that the Lord appeared to John as one man, *in* whom was a *trine* of distinct constituent parts, so that the three grades of the priesthood were just as

much indicated to John as to Abraham, who also saw and addressed the three men as one. (Gen. xvliii. 3, 22, 23.) See A. C. 2149— "Hereby is signified the essential divinity, the divine humanity, and the holy proceeding ; . . . . for it is known to every one, that there is a trinity, and *this trinity is one*. . . . . . Wherefore it is said, in verse 3, ' *my Lord* . . . . . pass not *thou*, I pray '; . . . . . and afterwards '*He* said,' '*Jehovah* said,' '*I* conceal,' '*I* do,' &c. &c." The doctrine, then, is, that there are to be priests as three men, but a priesthood as one man. Or a trine of priests constitutes one priesthood. Or three men in the priesthood, represent the trinity in the Lord, and the priesthood as a complex man, like the universal heaven, represents the unity in the Lord. And this doctrine, we think, is taught by Matthew, xvii. 1–8. The Lord takes Peter, James, and John his brother, up into a high mountain apart, where he is transfigured before them. Moses and Elias appear talking with him. Peter proposes to make *three* tabernacles—one for the Lord, another for Moses, and a third for Elias. At last the disciples come into their natural state and see "no man, save Jesus only." Here Peter, James, and John, represent faith, charity, and good works— the trine of internals which the priesthood represents in the Lord, and from him in the christian church. The trine of Moses, Jesus, and Elias, represented the Word, or divine truth flowing from divine good in the three discrete planes of the Word, in the three heavens, and in the "three degrees into which his church on earth is distinguished." The three tabernacles denote holy worship in those degrees of heaven and the church. Here, then, was a three-fold representation of the Lord's work of saving men in the three discrete degrees of his divine operation, that is, of the triple order of his priestly offices. By the Word all things are made in God's spiritual creation, which is the reformation and regeneration of men. This is the Lord's priesthood. In both the internal and external of this priesthood there is a trine of discrete degrees—the first represented by Moses, Jesus and Elias, the second by Peter, James and John. And these in the celestial, spiritual and natural degrees of worship, are represented by the three tabernacles. And that these in the complex form appear as one man, is denoted by its being said, the disciples, " lifting up their eyes, saw no one except Jesus alone ;" or, as Luke has it, " when the voice was past Jesus was found alone." For in him is the whole Word, and in him, as the complex of father, son and holy spirit, " dwells all the fulness of the godhead *bodily*."

15. The Lord was the first member of his church, and was its first teacher and pastor, as well as its sole high priest. Ordination to the ministry is such a representative ultimate as determines into the subject of it the influx of the holy spirit. All ordination is from *love* as the supreme principle of the Lord, of heaven, and of the church. The ordination of love, that is, the arrangement into order which the influx of love produces, is expressed in the Word by the voice of the father coming from heaven. Now that there is a trine of discrete degrees in the christian priesthood, is proved by the fact, that the Lord was thrice thus ordained of the father. First, in Matt. iii. 13–17,

the Lord is baptized by John—the heavens are opened unto him, and he sees the spirit of God descending like a dove and 'lighting upon him—and a voice from heaven declares, "This is my beloved son, in whom I am well pleased." There were three regions of the holy land in general, Judea, Samaria, and Galilee, which denoted the celestial, spiritual and natural degrees of the church. That this first ordination was into the natural degree of the ministry, is proved by the fact that it took place in Jordan, the confine and entrance of the holy land, and by the further fact that Jesus first began to preach in Galilee. (Matt. iv. 17.) Second, Matt. xvii. 5, while the Lord was transfigured on the mount, a bright cloud overshadowed the disciples and a voice out of the cloud said, "This is my beloved son, in whom I am well pleased, hear ye him." This voice, addressed to Peter, James, and John, who represented all in the church that are in the good of faith, the good of charity, and the life of both, was an ordination of the Lord as a minister of the church, distinct from the first. And that it was an ordination into the spiritual as a discrete degree of the ministry, is evident from its having taken place on a mountain of Galilee, which was the lower confine of Samaria, and was preparatory to his passage through this intermediate region on his way to Jerusalem in Judea. Third, in John, vii. 39, it is said, "the holy ghost was not yet, because that Jesus was not yet glorified." In ch. xvi. 7, the Lord says to his disciples, "If I depart I will send the comforter unto you." But in ch. xii. 28, "Father, glorify thy name. Then came there a voice from heaven, saying, I have both glorified it, and will glorify it again." The father's name was the humanity which Jehovah assumed. This the father glorified twice; first by making it divine truth in the world, and second, by making it divine good after it left the world. By this second glorification the father gave his spirit without measure to the humanity. And a voice from heaven, declaring this in the hearing of the people that stood by, was the Lord's third ordination from his father. Now it must be observed that this ordination is recorded by John only ; and this fact alone indicates that it was an ordination into the celestial degree. But it took place in Judea, at Bethany, where Lazarus was raised,—a new church of a celestial genius was raised up amongst the Gentiles. It took place just as Jesus was about to go up to Jerusalem as the king of Israel, the king of the daughter of Zion. It was preceded by the anointing of him by Mary, which was the consecration for his burial, that is, for his resurrection, or the union of his humanity with his divinity. In short, it was the glorification of his humanity by making it the divine good itself, which was the humanity's inauguration into the great high priesthood, by which, as Paul expresses it, Christ entered once for all into the holy of holies, beyond the veil of his flesh, and became our intercessor with the Divinity for ever, a priest after the order of Melchisedec, "an high priest over the house of God," "a minister of the sanctuary, and of the true tabernacle which the Lord pitched, and not man." Thus it is evident that this third ordination of the Lord, was the father's ordination of him into the divine celestial degree of his priesthood. And thus we have, in this example of the

Lord's priesthood, not only the proof that a trine of discrete degrees is the true order, but also that there should be three distinct inaugurations or ordinations into those degrees. The Lord, also, thrice ordained his apostles. First, when he sent them forth to preach, with power to exorcise spirits, cast out devils, and heal diseases. Second, when he breathed on them, and said, "Receive ye the holy ghost." Third, when he caused the holy ghost to descend in cloven tongues of fire upon them at pentecost. Wherefore, there is a trine of discrete degrees in the christian ministry, and there should be a distinct ordination for each degree.

16. As the feast of the passover approached, when the son of man was to be betrayed to be crucified, it is written—"Then assembled together, the *chief priests*, and the *scribes*, and the *elders*, unto the palace of the *high priest*." (Matt. xxvi. 3.) This shows the priestly order of the jewish church in the Lord's time. And here is a trine. the high priest being the presiding or head officer of the highest grade. So far as this was an influx of the universal divine order. which fills all things even to the most minute particulars, it is a proof that the trine is the true order for any ministry. In a parallel passage of Mark, (xiv. 53,) it is said, "And they led Jesus away to the *high priest:* and with him were assembled all the *chief priests* and the *elders* and the *scribes*." Here the elders are the middle, and the scribes the lowest degree; which was probably the real order. In Mark, xv., 1, the chief priests consult with the elders and scribes, and the whole council. The high priest is not here mentioned, being doubtless included among the high priests, or "the whole council," the complex of the three, being named instead of the high priest who represented it; and they carry Jesus away to Pilate, the civil magistrate. In Luke, xxii. 52, we have chief priests, captains of the temple, and elders. In John it is the band, and the captain, and the officers of the Jews, who took Jesus and led him away to Annas, the father-in-law of Caiaphas the high priest. In all cases, there is a trine; and so the trine is shown to be the true order.

17. In the Lord's final commissioning of the eleven disciples, in Galilee, after his resurrection, (Matt. xxvii. 16–20,) we have the doctrine of the trine variously taught. The Lord's command to them is—

1. Make disciples of all nations.

2. Baptize them into the name of the father, and of the son, and of the holy ghost.

3. Teach them to observe all things whatsoever I have commanded you.

Here is a trine of apostolic functions, corresponding to the trine in the church as indicated in Mark, iv. 20—

1, Such as hear the Word—2, Such as receive it—3, Such as bring forth fruit. Or, in another place,

1, Those who are the blade—2, Those who are the ear—3, Those who are the full corn in the ear.

This trine of functions in the apostolic office, indicates that, in just order, there should be a trine of apostles. Hence we believe that there was. The seven deacons ordained by the twelve, according to Acts, vi. 1-8, were appointed to the discharge of apostolic duties, which, without their appointment, would have been discharged by the twelve themselves. Hence they were apostles of a lower degree— evangelists, preachers of the gospel, and the doers of " wonders and miracles among the people." Thus there were two grades of apostles in the beginning of the apostolic ministrations; and, in the process of time, Paul assures us, (Eph. iv. 11,) that Christ gave his church *apostles, prophets*, and *evangelists*, together with *pastors* and *teachers*. Hence we think there were three degrees of apostles, making a trine in the highest grade of the ministry of the first christian church. The trine of that ministry in general was—*apostles, pastors*, and *teachers*, or *apostles, prophets*, and *teachers*. (1 Cor. xii. 28.) The prophet was a preacher of the more hidden wisdom of God, which required spiritual discernment. Hence he was the minister of the spiritual degree. The teacher instructed novitiates in the elements of divine knowledge; and hence was the minister of the natural degree, who built up the church as the body of Christ *from the foundation*, by teaching truth from the *letter* of the Word. The teacher in the lowest apostolic grade, like Judas, "had the bag," "to buy the things needed in the feasts" of the church— thus he was a spiritual purveyor for the higher grades; and, as the instructor of the ignorant, who, being in externals, are the ultimate of the three degrees into which the Lord's church is distinguished, (Ap. Rev. 744,) is in a spiritual sense an almoner to the poor. But as "the letter killeth, while the spirit giveth life," it was the more especial duty of the prophet to expound the letter, so as to extract the spirit from it. He taught the *good* that was *in* the *truth ;* and by this fed the members of the body as the sheep of the Lord's fold and pasture. Hence the prophet was a pastor of the flock, the feeding of which with suitable spiritual food was emphatically "the *work* of the *ministry*." The apostle, as standing in the highest ministerial grade—although the duties of both the teacher and the prophet, or pastor, would be included in his functions, so that he might call himself, as Paul does, a teacher and a preacher, as well as an apostle (1 Tim. ii. 7; 2 Tim. i. 11)—yet the apostle *par excellence* would have for his especial and distinguishing province, " the *perfecting* of the *saints :*" for this clearly would be the duty of a master workman under the Lord: this would emphatically be the function of the *minister of love*. Thus the three might be distinguished in respect to their intellectual functions as *science—intelligence—wisdom ;* or as to their moral functions, as *life—wisdom—love*. Hence it was that the apostles alone ordained : for, as we have shown, it is *love* alone that ordains, or arranges all inferior things in order, and governs them in subordination. Hence the apostles, as specifically the officers of love, or wisdom in the highest degree, were the sole ordainers in the church. And for the same reason, the highest grade of ministers in any church should alone ordain. The general trine, then, in the priesthood of the apostolic church, was—*apostles, pastors*, and *teachers*, whom the Lord gave " for the perfecting of the saints, for the work of the ministry," and " for the edifying of the body of Christ." (Eph. iv. 12.)

This trine of functions in the christian ministry, is also indicated by the trine within the trine of the apostolic functions as above stated. It is observable in the second term of the divine command to the eleven disciples—2. Baptize in the name of the *father*, and of the *son*, and of the *holy ghost*. Baptism in the *name* of these *three*, is purification from evils in the three discrete planes of the mind and of the church. Of course it denotes, as the consequent of this, the implantation of goods in a like order. It therefore denotes the Lord's work of the reformation and regeneration of mankind in its three discrete degrees. Consequently it denotes the victory of the Lord as the "Lamb of God, who taketh away the sins of the world," in overcoming those who fight with him, so as to make them his *"called, and chosen,* and *faithful."* It denotes his work of saving men in those "three degrees" into which his "church is distinguished," so as "to have them with him in heaven—some in the ultimate heaven, some in the second, and some in the third, every one according to reception." (Ap. Ex. 744.) But this work is the Lord's priestly office, in which the christian priesthood is appointed to represent him upon earth. Therefore, it proves that the true order of the christian priesthood is a trine of discrete degrees; because it denotes such a trinal order in the functions of that priesthood, and the same order should prevail among the priests of a priesthood that obtains in its functions.

We should not fail to observe in this portion of the Word of the New Testament, that the Lord adds—(Matt. xxviii. 20)—"and lo, I am with you alway, even unto the end of the world"—the consummation of the church. The bearing of this on our present subject is important. In instituting the jewish church, the Lord by Moses consecrated Aaron as the high priest of that dispensation; so that then the Lord was represented as the head of his church by an individual man. But in the institution of the christian church, the Lord himself became a man in ultimates, and as such was the actual, and not the mere representative, visible head of this church on earth. Hence he could then no longer be represented by any other individual man, in that capacity. He himself became the "apostle and great high priest of the christian profession." And now, when he leaves the world, or has left it by resurrection from the sepulchre, and, appearing to his disciples again in Galilee, there commissions them as the representative of himself in his future work on earth, he does not appoint any one apostle to represent him in the high priesthood, as Aaron had done; but he here commissions *eleven*, and afterwards *twelve*, to represent him in his church as a complex man, and so as his visible humanity or body still on earth—which the church established by the apostles would be until it wholly ceased to be the true christian church, which was the consummation of the age. Therefore, in commissioning them, he says—"Lo, I am with you even unto the consummation of the age." Thus, as "the husband is the *head* of the wife," even so "Christ" became "the *head* of the church," "the saviour of the *body*." (Eph. v. 23.) Therefore, being actually present in the church as a soul in its body, there is no longer needed now a high priest, a *pontifex maximus*, to *represent* him to the christian

church. He is now represented by the *whole* church as his body; for
the body is the only *true* representative of its soul. And he is represented by those who represent his body, by his twelve disciples, whom
he calls to himself as a soul calls a body to itself in the womb,—a
complex representative of his whole church,—and whom he sends
forth from himself as the germinal complex representative of all the
goods and truths which flow from him and form the church in mankind. And as he could not by these *form* to himself a body of human
beings like himself and arranged in the order of his humanity in
heaven and on earth by their ministrations in the first christian dispensation, (see Brief Con. of Cor. XXXVI.-XLIV.) he has now again
commissioned them (U. T. 791) for a repetition of that work in the
spiritual world, in the formation of such a body for himself in the new
heaven above and the new church which is now to be thereby established
below. As the father had sent him, so sends he them—as good sends
forth truth, or flame sends forth light. But as they, when first sent,
were not yet regenerated men in the higher degrees, and could not
possibly be, he sent them, as the father sent him, representatively.
He, in his speaking and acting according to true representatives, had
made them disciples, and he commands them to go and make disciples
of all nations. For their sakes he had purified himself, that they
might drink of his cup and be baptized with the baptism with which
he was baptized, and he commands them to baptize all nations in his
three-fold name. He was taught of God, and all things that the father
made known to him had he made know to them, and now he enjoins
it on them to teach all nations to observe the commands which they
had received from him. All this was divine action in and by representatives. Thus he appointed them as his priests on earth, to continue his work of reforming and regenerating men in three degrees,
by them as his ambassadorial representatives, and through them as a
complex man—a body of which he was to be the soul—a germ which
was to expand into a larger body, and a church, which was to be
formed, from him through them, a *maximus homo* or grand collective
image and likeness of himself—in which he was to dwell until the
consummation of the age, until spiritual disease and death should make
the body no longer correspondent to, and thus *truly representative* of
the soul, and therefore the soul would have to leave it, and make to
itself a new body. Thus, in the christian church, the highest ministers
are but apostles of the Great High Priest as the actual and sole head
of his church on earth. The head of the church as a visible body of,
the Lord on earth, like the head of his universal heaven, consists now
of *all* who are in its inmost principles—" the *called* "—all who are in
the third of "the three degrees" into which "the Lord's church is
distinguished," and these are now represented by the ministers of the
third degree as a complex man, and not by any individual man. These
are, relatively to inferior ministers as christian elders and scribes, only
chief priests—no one of whom can sustain the relation to the other
ministers and members of the church of THE *high* priest; so that any
Christian can say I am of Paul, or I of Apollos; for Jesus Christ, the
divine humanity of Jehovah God, is now alone the high priest of the

church on earth, and all other priests, as his apostles, are but "ministers by whom" members of the christian faith are set out as plants,
and watered, in the garden of God—into which he flows, and giveth
increase, as a soul into its body. For, says Swedenborg, the chief
teacher of the new and true christian church, "it is a truth acknowledged in all christian countries, that the church constitutes the body
of Christ, and that Christ is the life of that body." (U. T. 608.) And,
says the apostle to the early Christians, "ye are the body of Christ
and members in particular," (1 Cor. xii. 27;) and Christ "is the *head*
over all things to the church, which is his body," (Eph. i. 22, 23:)
and, having placed in this body "apostles, prophets, and teachers,"
(1 Cor. xii. 28,) among all Christians as other members, so that apostles as well as the rest "are one body in Christ, and *every one* members one of another," (Rom. xii. 5,) "therefore, let no man glory in
men: for all things are yours: whether Paul, or Apollos, or Cephas;
or the world, or life, or death; or things present, or things to come;
all are yours: and ye are Christ's; and Christ is God's." (1 Cor. iii.
21, 22, 23.) The whole christian church as a body, including ministers and people in three degrees, are one in Christ, as he and the father
are one. (John, xvi. 20, 21.) There is "one fold and one shepherd."
The Lord is "the good shepherd"—is "the door"; his minister is
"the porter that openeth" the door, and giveth entrance to the
sheep. "And when he putteth forth his own sheep, he goeth before
them, and *the sheep follow* HIM." (John, x. 2, 3, 4, 9, 11, 16.) The
Lord alone is the bridegroom, or husband, and so the head of his
church; the minister of any and every degree holds that relation to
him which John did—"the friend of the bridegroom, which standeth
and heareth him, rejoicing greatly because of the bridegroom's voice."
(John, iii. 29.) The highest ecclesiastical officer of the church is still
no more than the disciple and apostle of the Lord, and the medium of
illustration and instruction in the highest degree from him to the
people.

Wherefore, our conclusion is, that, in the christian dispensation, the
true representative of the Lord in his priestly office on earth, is a *complex* man—that, in his work of reforming and regenerating mankind,
his highest and truest representative is the whole church as his body—
that he chose twelve disciples and commissioned them as his apostles,
and so his ministers of the highest grade, because all he did on earth
was representative, and all he said was significative, and *twelve* such
general ministers were the proper representative of his *whole* church,
through which, as a heart and lungs, he imparts spiritual life and
health to all mankind as his own more common body. Thus he sends
his twelve, his whole church, endued with power from on high, to
make disciples of, to baptize, and to teach, *all nations*. But in this
church as a body, of which he himself is head, and which "is distinguished, like heaven, into three degrees," he places a christian
priesthood, as heart and lungs, or other members, and that this priesthood, too, "is distinguished, like heaven, into *three degrees*." So that
in the christian church, there may be apostles, pastors, and teachers,
who shall hold the same relation to this church, which the chief

priests, the elders, and the scribes, did to the jewish church. And as "there are three things which fully constitute and form every universal essential principle, namely, the good of love, the truth from that good, and the consequent good of life," which, in both heaven and in the church, are as discrete " as the pulse of heart, the respiration of the lungs, and the action of the body ;" and as "three like principles are in every thing that exists; and when the three exist together, there is a full formation;" therefore we conclude, that there *must be* together in the christian priesthood, so as to constitute it *one* thing, *three discrete grades* of ministers, for its "*full formation*," and so for its "*just order*."

———

Having thus drawn sufficient authorities for a trinal order of the new-church ministry from the Word of the Old and New Testaments, we shall now offer a few, more specifically, from the writings of Swedenborg. Some of them we shall barely quote, reserving as much of our space as we can for extended comment on the last.

18. "In every thing divine there is a first, a middle, and a last; and the first passes through the middle to the last, and thereby exists and subsists: hence the last is the BASIS. The first also, is in the middle, and by means of the middle in the last; and thus the last is the CONTINENT. And because the last is the continent and the basis, it is also the FIRMAMENT. . . . These three may be called end, cause, and effect. . . . Consequently, *in every complete thing, there is a trinity*." . . . . From this ground it is that by the number THREE, in the Word, according to its spiritual sense, is signified what is complete and perfect, and also the all or whole together." (U. T. 210, 211.) This is complete authority for teaching in the new church, that the priesthood as "a complete thing" *must* have "a trinity." And as it must be constituted *one* thing by a trine of degrees, therefore we hold, that the ecclesiastical organ of the church as a whole, or as a general body, should not consist of ministers of the highest, or of any one grade alone, but of all three grades together.

19. "The science of geometry teaches that *nothing can be complete or perfect, except it be a trine, or a compound of three;* for a geometrical line is nothing, unless it becomes an area, nor is an area any thing, unless it becomes a solid. Wherefore, the one must be multiplied into the other, in order to give them existence; and in the third they co-exist. And as it is in this instance, so it is likewise in the case of all and every created thing; they have their limit and termination in a third. Hence *three* in the Word signifies what is complete and perfect. Hence charity, faith and works, one without another, or any two of them without the third, are nothing. (U. T. 387.) "The Lord, charity and faith constitute a one, like life, will and understanding. (U. T. 363.) Hence, as "all priests" are among "the representatives which exist even at this day," (A. C. 3670,) representing the Lord in his priestly offices even now, therefore the ministers of the christian church, as christian priests, should be in three discrete or successive degrees, constituting one priesthood. For

"*nothing* can be complete or perfect except it be a trine, or a compound of three."

" Every one receives life from God according to his form." (U. T. 366.) The form of every one is the state resulting from the arrangement of constituent parts. If this arrangement is perfect, the form is perfect; if it is imperfect, the form is imperfect. The same is true of order. For " order is the quality of the disposition, determination and activity of the parts, substances, or entities which constitute the form of a thing, and whereon its state depends." (U. T. 52.) Therefore, that life may flow from God into any thing truly and effectively, such thing must have its constituent parts arranged in the form of true order. And only so far as it is brought into this order, can the Lord be present in it. For " where order is, there the Lord is present ; and where the Lord is present, there is *life*." (A. C. 5703.) Now " divine truth is the order itself of the Lord's universal kingdom," while " divine good is the very essential principle of [this] order," (A. C. 1728 ;) and this "order, when it is represented in form, appears as a man," (A. C. 4839 ;) which " order consists in celestial things bearing rule over spiritual, and by spiritual over natural, and lastly by natural over corporeal," (A. C. 911 ;) so that when the constituent parts, substances or entities of a thing are in the form of that true order in which the Lord is present with his life, and its will and understanding, there will be such an arrangement and subordination of them as to cause every " inferior thing to be subservient to a superior," (A. C. 5305)—" the natural man to serve the rational, and this the spiritual, and the spiritual the celestial, and the celestial the Lord." (A. C. 2781.) Thus in every form of true order, there is an arrangement of its constituent parts in a trine of discrete degrees, in which the inferior parts are subordinate to superior. In other words, *three* principles, [like " the good of love, the truth from that good, and the consequent good of life,"] are in every thing that exists; and when the three exist together, there is a *full formation* "—a perfect form, a just order. (Ap. Ex. 435.) Hence, as " every one receives life from God according to his form," or every thing " receives influx according to the form of the contexture of its parts," (U. T. 366,) therefore the christian priesthood, which represents the Lord in the church on earth, to represent him—with his charity and faith, or his life, will and understanding—truly, must be in such a form of order as arranges its priests in three discrete and subordinate degrees, as the celestial, spiritual and natural principles, or " the pulse of the heart, the respiration of the lungs, and the action of the body," in man. And as the Lord's " influx is differently received by one stone, mineral and metal, and by an other ;" that is, perfectly in a perfect form, but imperfectly in an imperfect form ; so that some variegate the influx of light " with most beautiful colors—some transmit the light without variegation, and some of them confuse and suffocate it in themselves ;" in like manner must the Lord's influx be differently received by the priesthood of the church according to its form—perfectly if its form be perfect, but imperfectly if its form be imperfect. Hence we argue, most conclusively, that the priesthood of the new church, to receive and transmit ordinately and efficiently, the Lord's influences of good, truth, and the life of both, must be in the just or perfect order of a trine of discrete degrees. For .without this the new church cannot so correspond to, and represent, the Lord in the three heavens, as to " convince by the Word," and so win unto him, " the *called*, the *chosen*, and the *faithful* " here on earth. And our strong argument against the order of a *one* or a *no*-graded ministry is, that this is an imperfect form, is such an amorphous arrangement of priests in a priesthood, that they cannot " transmit the [Lord's] light without .variegation,"—without darkening · by their proprium,—but must " confuse and suffocate it in themselves." It is the same thing in the ministry, that faith *alone* is in the church. This order took its ·rise in the solifidian church. It is the true correspondent form of a solifidian priesthood. Hence, it is *that* " man " who has divided " the Lord, charity and faith," so that he is no longer " a form *receptive*, but a form *destructive*, of them." (U. T. 367.) And hence we solemnly believe, that it is no small sin thus to destroy the order of the trine in the christian priesthood.

20. " Some time ago a sheet of paper was seen to come down from heaven to a certain society in the spiritual world, where there were two prelates of the church, with inferior canons and presbyters." (U. T. 389.) This shows that a trine of ministers—prelates, canons and presbyters—in the church, is the order of a society of the spiritual world. Therefore, it ought, by correspondence, to be the order of the natural world. That these prelates were false teachers, who had perverted the internals of the church, and destroyed by dividing them, is no argument against the *trine* as the *order* in their ministry. That was true order, which had flowed from heaven into their church in its purity and integrity, and which had not yet been perverted by them. The assumption of arbitrary power, supremacy and government by the highest grade was a corruption of the purity of the pristine christian trinal order. The trinal order itself was not yet destroyed, because the solifidian principle had not yet come out to the external forms. In the catholic superstition, charity and good works were not yet wholly separated from faith. To effect a more thorough division of the Reformers from the Catholics, this dogma of salvation by faith alone was invented and magnified into the whole of religion—was made the Palladium of the christian temple. So far as this principle of· religion flowed out and produced what was correspondent to, and representative of, itself in the external forms of the church and its ministry, the form of trinal order in the ministry, which represents and · corresponds to charity, faith and good works together in the church, was destroyed, and the form of parity amongst ministers of one grade prevailed ; because this represents and corresponds to the notion of salvation by only one of the principles in the trine of the christian church, separated from the other two, namely, truth and the faith of it. For when faith so took the precedence of charity and good works, as virtually to exclude them from the *means* of salvation, then the *preaching* of the *truth*, and this too *natural* truth from the literal sense of the Word, became the *sole* province of the christian

ministry. For then *Peter*, the type of *faith*, became representative of all that appertains to the ministry of the church; and the christian ministry, having no other correspondence than that of natural truth, or truth in the understanding, teaching, *thus* leading to good, became alone representative of the Lord as the truth of the Word in its literal sense. And as Peter—the type of faith as the first principle of the church—*alone* represented *all* that pertains to the ministry of the church, so that the preaching or teaching of truth in the natural degree of the Word was the *only* duty appertaining to the christian ministry, therefore there could justly be but one order of priests in the church—but one ordination into its priesthood, and not the slightest distinguishment of higher and lower, not the slightest subordination of inferior to superior, but the most perfect parity amongst its ministers. Thus the notion of salvation by faith alone produced, in certain reformed churches, as its correspondent representative in their external worship, the destruction of the trinal ministerial order which had obtained in the primitive christian church. This notion prevailed to a great extent in the catholic church too : but it did not come out so fully into the life. It was rather a corruption of internal principles than of external forms, and hence was represented in that church by the separation of the sacred elements in the eucharist—and the taking of the wine by the priest alone, while the bread was given to the people. This denoted that faith was separated from charity in the church, while the simply good in it still held to good works. But in the reformed churches the principle of faith alone descended so as to affect the life of the people; hence it altered the external forms of the church and destroyed the trinal order of the ministry in the most distinctive antinomian sects. The armenian sects of the reformed church, like the Catholics, had solifidianism more on the inside, hence the trinal order of the ministry was retained by them. ·Such probably was the character of this society in the spiritual world here noticed by Swedenborg. Faith alone had not yet come out so fully as to destroy the trinal ministerial order. But the tendency to destroy this order, which there is in the principle of faith alone, is indicated by one of the prelates tearing the mitre from his head, throwing it down on the table, and the monster with the feet of a bear, the body of a leopard and the mouth of a lion, taking it from the table, spreading it out wide, placing it on his seven heads, and sinking down with it out of sight beneath the earth. For this is submerging and profaning the dignity and power of the priestly office in the mass of the laity of a draconic church. "Presumptuous are they, self-willed, they are not afraid to speak evil of dignities." (2 Pet. ii. 10.) "Likewise also these filthy dreamers defile the flesh, despise dominion, and speak evil of dignities." (Jude 8.)

21. "Who loves a *prelate*, a *minister* of the church, or any *canonical person*, except for his learning, integrity of life, and zeal for the salvation of souls?" (U. T. 418.) This passage of Swedenborg's writings is thought by some to afford authority for the order of a trine in the ministry.

22. We suppose that the order of a trine in the ministry rests on

the grand and universal law, that there are in the Lord, and in every
man from his birth, three infinite and uncreate, or three finite and
created, degrees of altitude. For the priesthood is·a complex man
that represents the Lord. And, to represent him, it must have in it
three discrete degrees. And it must also have three continuous
degrees, because "there are degrees of both kinds in the greatest and
least of all created things." (D. L. & W. 222.) It is needless to take
up space with quotations from the writings of Swedenborg on this
subject. We will merely refer to the work on Influx, 16, and to D.
L. &!W., Part III., nn. 173–236. See also A. C. 3691, 9825, 5114,
10.181 ; Sac. Scrip. 6 ; H. & H. 33–39 ; U. T. 33, 75, &c. &c. &c.

23. We believe it must be conceded, that Swedenborg has no where
professedly taught what should be the true external or formal order
of the priesthood, or ministry, of the New Jerusalem. He has not
published a work expressly upon the order of the ministry. Neither
has he written upon what should be the true external order amongst
the officers of civil government. The precise external order of the
church too, has not been laid down by him. He has written a work
on conjugial love, and declared the laws of marriage with much precision : but even in this work, he has not prescribed any of the laws
of external order for the administrators or the administration of the
marriage ceremony. It was no part of· his functions to teach ceremonials for the new church ; and quite as little to lay down the mere
externals of either priestly or regal order. He had to teach the
general and universal principles of the faith, and to illustrate this
teaching by known truths or established facts in all the domains of
science, intelligence and wisdom. Hence he has not prescribed any
formularies of worship, for the New Jerusalem. Because, according
to his own doctrine, this is to be a universal church ; and, as such,
may have every variety of external form, either of worship or of
government, which is compatible with the harmonious union of all
its parts ·in charity. And it is manifest that he could not teach any
precise external form of order or arrangement for the priesthood of
the church ; because, from her universal nature, she must necessarily
have varieties in all priestly forms that pertain to the administration
of either her external worship or her ecclesiastical government. All
he could have been expected to do, was, to teach the universals of
these things. And having in fact taught the universals of the priesthood, for instance, now, according to his own showing, "whosoever
is acquainted with universals, may afterwards comprehend singulars,
since the latter are contained in the former, just as parts are in the
whole." (U. T. 661.) Hence, he has merely taught that there
should be priests in the church, assigning the reasons why there
should, and detailing their general functions. He has also taught
the same in respect to the officers of civil government. But he has
no more taught precisely the true formal order of the priesthood,
than he has taught that of the civil magistracy. He has, however,
taught those universal principles of all affairs, divine and human,
which will infallibly lead us to the discernment of what is true
external order in both ecclesiastical and civil government, if we will

faithfully follow his guides. He has, with singular precision, and in the most lucid manner, taught us the fundamental laws of all external order. He has shown us that all things in the natural world exist by influx from the Lord God through the spiritual world—that all things in the natural world correspond to, and represent, similar things in the Divine Being and in the spiritual world through which they are thus created and sustained from' him—that, by correspondence, precisely the same arrangements of things in order take place in the natural world which obtain in the orderly arrangements of similar things in the spiritual world; and he has most distinctly portrayed to us what the orderly arrangements of the spiritual world are. He has not only revealed to us that there is a heaven and a hell, but he has given us a specific revelation of the *facts* which exist in them, and of the *principles* by which those facts are determined. And he has moreover shown us how these facts and principles are the forming and determining causes of all the natural things which exist on earth. And not only so; but, when he is teaching us the general principles which apply to the formation and regulation of natural things—when he is teaching us, for instance, concerning the Lord's operations in redeeming and saving mankind, that great end of all his work, and that mighty purpose, of which his material creation, with all its laws and orders, is but an outward means and shadowing type—or when he is teaching us concerning the constituent being and nature of the Great Creator himself, whose images and likenesses in lower forms, all natural things are made—he brings in to illustrate the applications of his general principles whatever is known to be true in the existence and order of the natural things which flow from and correspond to them. Thus, in displaying the Lord's grand work 'of glorifying his humanity, by which he was inaugurated into his great priestly offices of redeeming and saving mankind, and in which he brought humanity into that state of utter humiliation before the Divinity which is the essence of all true worship, Swedenborg illustrates this work by those various circumstances and effects which divine order, flowing into the most particular and singular things of the universe, produces; and in this illustration he specifies the arrangement which divine order effects in the priesthood. Thus he teaches, by necessary implication, what is the general order of the priesthood, in illustrating the general principles of those divine things in the Lord which the priesthood is appointed on earth to represent. The only way, therefore, in which we are to expect that Swedenborg has taught the true external order of the new-church priesthood is, the declaration and illustration of the universal or general principles—in the Lord, in the heavens, in the church as his kingdom on earth, or in the natural world as the theatre in which his operations are represented—which, descending into and forming the priesthood as a cause forms its effect, do in fact produce in it its true external order. All then, we have to do, in finding authorities for the true external order of our ministry in the writings of Swedenborg, is honestly to inquire, and' faithfully to display, the *universals* which apply to this subject. For when these are known, then we cannot

help discerning what *must* be the external order of the priesthood
that represents them. Now whither shall we go to find these universals, if not to "the work, entitled TRUE CHRISTIAN RELIGION,"
where may be "seen in the light and acknowledged, *divine truths
revealed by the* LORD"?

The fact that there should be an external or formal priesthood in
the church on earth is clearly proved by Swedenborg in H. D.
311–319 and A. C. 10.789–10.799. "There are two things appertaining to men which ought to be in order"—things of heaven or
ecclesiastical things, and things of the world or civil things. Order
cannot be maintained in the world without governors—of course, in
both of the *two* things needing to be in order amongst men. Hence
"it is expedient that there be governors to keep associations of men
in order" as well in ecclesiastical as in civil affairs. For both "ought
to be in order"; and order cannot be secured in "the things which
are of heaven,"⁺ any more than in "those which are of the world,"
without both governments and governors, of higher and lower degrees,
amongst whom there must be subordination. Hence there are governments and governors, in both ecclesiastical and civil affairs, in the
heavens as well as on the earths. "There are in the heavens, as on
the earths, distinctions of dignity and pre-eminence, with abundance
of the richest treasures; for there are governments and forms of
government, and consequently a variety of *ranks* and *orders*, of greater
and lesser power and authority." (C. L. 7.) And that there are *ecclesiastical* as well as civil distinctions of ranks, orders, dignities, powers
and authorities in the societies of the heavens, may be seen in the
same work, 266—"We have let ourselves down from heaven by the
Lord's command, to speak with you respecting the blessed lot of those,
who are desirous to have dominion from the love of uses. We are
worshipers of the Lord. I am prince of a society; my companion is
chief priest (summus sacerdos) of the same." The priest says, ".The
dignities which we enjoy, we indeed sought after and solicited, but for
no other end than that we might be enabled more fully to perform
uses, and to extend them more widely. We are also encompassed
with *honor,*" &c. Here there is a chief or "*highest*" priest in one
of the societies of heaven. Of course, there must have been inferior
and lowest priests there. This does not indeed prove that *all* the
societies of heaven have chief priests too. For the forms of government vary in the different societies according to their various ministries
in the grand man. But it proves that there are higher and lower ecclesiastical functionaries of some sort in all the heavens. For there are
goods and truths of subordinate degrees, and the angels must be
arranged in the heavenly societies in the same order as the goods and
truths in which they are principled. Hence the most wise must be
in the centre and the least wise in the circumference. And, hence,
because all of a society are in similar good, but not in similar wisdom,
"there are governments in heaven; for order must be observed, and
all things of order are to be kept inviolable." (H. & H. 213.) "In
the spiritual kingdom of the Lord, there are various forms of government, differing in different societies, and their variety is according to

the ministries in which the societies are engaged : their ministries also are similar to the functions of all the things in man, to which they correspond." (Ibid. 217.)   Hence, as there are superior and inferior functions in man, so there must be superior and inferior functionaries of government in the heavens, the lower subordinate to the higher as their functions are.   They who are in love and wisdom more than others, being central to the rest, are in higher governing stations, in "magnificent palaces," and in "glory and honor" above the rest. (Ibid. 218.) ·And as this is the order of heaven, as·to ecclesiastical government, much more must it be the order of the church on earth.   Hence there must be ecclesiastical governors "to keep associations of men in order."   "These governors must be skilled in the law, full of wisdom and of the fear of God.   It is expedient also that there should be order amongst the governors, lest any one, through lust or inadvertence, should allow evils against order, and thereby destroy it ; and this may be best effected by an appointment of governors of different degrees, higher and lower, amongst whom there shall be subordination.   Governors in things ecclesiastic, or in the things of heaven appertaining to man, are called priests, and their office the priesthood."   "They are to *teach* men the way to heaven, and likewise to *lead* them."   They are not to "claim to themselves *any power* over the *souls* of men"; but they "ought to have *dignity* and *honor* on account of the sanctity of their *office* "—not merely the honor which is due to their personal virtues.   For "no honor of any employment is in the person, but is adjoined to him according to the *dignity* of the *thing which he administers,* and what is adjoined is separate from the person, and also is disjoined with the employment."   Hence, as there are higher and lower uses and functions in the ministry of the church, and higher and lower administrations in its ecclesiastical government, there must be higher and lower priestly administrators of them, with higher and lower dignities adjoined to them, proportioned to the eminence of the uses they perform, or of the functions they discharge.   So that priests ought not *only* to teach the people and lead by truths to good of life ; but they should also "administer those things which pertain to the divine law and worship ;" and should be clothed with sufficient official power and authority to separate from the church any one "who makes disturbance" in it ; "for this also is agreeable to the *order,* for the sake of which the priesthood is established."   Thus order requires that there should be an appointment of *ecclesiastical "governors of different degrees, higher* and *lower, amongst whom there shall be subordination";* or, as Swedenborg elsewhere says, "ministers small and great ;" to regulate ecclesiastical things amongst men, so that "order may be observed, and all things of order be kept inviolable" in the church on earth as well as in heaven.   For "the security of a large as well as a small society depends on order." (C. L. 283.)   "A society is like one man—those who enter into it compose, as it were, one body, and are distinguished from each other like the members in one body." (U. T. 412.)   So that no society of the church, small or large, in its least or largest form, can be secure without that orderly arrangement of higher, intermediate, and extreme

33

parts, with all their subordinations and co-ordinations, which exists in the human body. For " in tracing up effects to their causes, it is very plain to discern that on order depends the consistence of all things; and that there are manifold orders, both general and particular; and one which is most universal of all, and on which the general and particular depend in a continual series, and that this most universal one enters into all the rest as the essence into its forms—to which circumstance alone it is owing that they form a one. It is this oneness which is the cause of the conservation of the whole, which without it must needs drop asunder, and not only relapse into its first chaotic state, but even become nothing. What, let me ask, would be the case with man, unless all and every single part of his body were arranged in a most distinct and orderly manner, having a general dependence upon one heart and lungs? What would the whole be but a heap of confusion? for how else could the stomach, the liver and the pancreas, the mesentery and mesocolon, the kidneys and the intestines, perform each their respective offices? It is by the order reigning in and amongst these several organs, that they appear to man all and each of them as a one. Without distinct order, again, in man's mind or spirit, and without a general dependence on the will and the understanding, what would it be but a confused and undigested chaos? Without such order, how could a man think and will, any more than his portrait or his statue which ornaments his house? What, again, would man be without a most orderly arranged influx from heaven, and the reception thereof? and what would this influx be without that most universal one, the influx from God, on which the government of the whole and of all its parts depends, and unless all things had their being, lived and moved in him and from him? . . . . What is an empire or kingdom without order, but a troop of robbers, several of whom collected together would slay their thousands, and at last a few of this band would slay the rest? What would become of a city, or even a house without order? and what would become of kingdom, city, or house, unless there were in each some supreme head and director? And what is order without distinction; and what is distinction without proofs; and what are proofs of distinction without signs or tokens, by which its qualities may be known and ascertained? for without the knowledge of qualities, order is not known to be order. The signs, or distinguishing marks, in empires and in kingdoms, are titles of rank and powers of administration annexed to them, whence come subordinations, and hence the co-ordination of all into one body. In this manner the king exercises his royal authority according to order; it being thus distributed amongst a variety of persons, in consequence of which the kingdom is a kingdom. The case is similar in many other things: as, for instance, in an army of soldiers; which would not be efficient unless the men were arranged in an orderly manner, and formed into divisions, and these into battalions, and these again into companies, with subordinate leaders appointed to the command of each body, and one supreme commander over all. But where would be the efficacy of these arrangements and divisions, without signs, which, in armies, are called standards, to point

out to every soldier his proper station? By these means all act in
the field of battle as one man: whereas, were those means of order
wanting, they would rush headlong against an enemy, open-mouthed,
like so many dogs, with tumultuous sounds and empty fury, till they
were all cut off by their opponents—not so much in consequence of
superior courage, as of better discipline; for what can a disunited
mob do against a well disciplined and united army?" (U. T. 679, 680.)
" God is order, by reason that he is substance itself and form itself."
(n. 53.)   All things " were so arranged as to conjoin themselves with
the common order of the universe, so that each particular order
should subsist in the universal order, and thus altogether constitute
one whole.   Man is created according to his proper order, and likewise every particular part according to its order—as the head and the
body according to their respective orders; the heart, the lungs, the
liver, the pancreas, the stomach, according to their orders; every
organ of motion, which is called a muscle, according to its order; and
every organ of sense, as the eye, the ear, the tongue, according to its
order; nay, there is not the smallest artery or fibril in the body which
is not created according to its order: and yet these innumerable parts
are connected with the general order, and so inserted in it, that
altogether they constitute a one" (n. 54): and this general order,
" when it is represented in form, appears as a man." (A. C. 4839.)—
Would it not be strange if the priesthood of the New Jerusalem were
an exception to this universal law—if it were not formed according
to an order proper to itself—if its priests were not arranged " in a
most distinct and orderly manner," having a general dependence upon
superior and supreme functionaries as the members of the body have
upon one heart and lungs—and if its order had not its distinctions,
proofs, signs or tokens of official rank, power and administration,
whereby there might be suitable subordinations, and hence the co-
ordination of all into one body? How could the ministry of the
New Jerusalem as a general or universal church, without such an
order as exists in the human form, be so connected with the general
order of that form, as to be inserted in it, and together with all its
other component parts help to constitute it a one? In short, without
such orderly arrangement, how could the complex clergy of the new
church act as one man in defending her faith against the combined
assaults of its wily, powerful and well-appointed adversaries? Suppose that all the ministers of the New Jerusalem, throughout our
common country, or throughout the whole christian world, were
required to act against the catholic clergy, for instance, in defending
the principles of our faith against their combined assault upon them;
and suppose the catholic priesthood were arranged in the order of the
human form as above described by Swedenborg; what would a one-
graded or a no-graded ministry of the new church be but a vast clerical mob, affording, alas, but a too melancholy exemplification of the
utter inefficiency of badly arranged, undisciplined and disunited troops,
in their combats with a well arranged, strictly disciplined and firmly
united army!
   " As to what concerns the order, according to which God has esta-

blished his church, it is this, that he should be all and all; both generally and particularly, therein; and that the laws of order should be
practised by every man towards his neighbor. The laws of this order
are as many and various as the truths contained in the Word—the
laws which relate to God forming the head of the church, those
relating to a man's neighbor forming the body, and ceremonial laws
forming the dress." (n. 55.) The ceremonies of religion, the representative rituals of worship, the priestly administration of the functions of that worship, must all exist in their proper order as an external and visible church, for a covering and defence of those interior
things which are involved in its spiritual body and its divine head;
for unless these formations of an external and visible church, as a
dress, contained and preserved those internals in their order, " it
would be as if the body were stripped naked, and exposed to the
summer's heat, and the winter's cold: or as if a temple should be
bared of its walls and roof, so as to expose the altar, the pulpit, and
other holy parts within to the violence of every storm and tempest."
Hence there should be priests in an orderly priesthood; and it is the
part of true charity in the body of the church to provide them.
Since " the church is more a neighbor than a man's country; for he
who provides for the church, provides for the *souls* and *eternal* life
of the men who inhabit the country: and the church is provided for
when man is led to good; and he who does this from a principle of
charity, loves his neighbor, for he wishes and wills heaven and happiness of life to eternity as the portion of another. *Good* may be
insinuated into another by every one in the country, but not *truth*
except by *those who are teaching ministers;* if others insinuate truths,
it gives birth to heresies, and the church is disturbed and rent asunder."
(A. C. 6822.)   Thus there must be *teaching ministers,* there must be
priests, to keep the church from being disturbed and rent asunder;
because this " is agreeable to order, for the sake of which the priesthood is established." (H. D. 318.)   The New Jerusalem cannot be
established on earth except so far as the falsities of the old and consummated christian church are extirpated; " for what is new cannot
gain admission where falsities have been implanted, unless those falsities are first rooted out; and this must first take place among the
clergy, and by their means among the laity," (n. 784.)   Hence there
must be a clergy in the New Jerusalem on earth.   For the church can
be established on earth only by the influx of the holy spirit of its
Divine Head.   And " the divine principle called the holy spirit passes
through the angelic heaven into the world, thus through the angels
to men;" and " thence it passes through men to men, and, *in the
church, especially through the* OLERGY *to the* LAITY." (Can. Ch. III., iv.)
And the clergy are the special mediums of that divine virtue and
operation of the holy spirit which consists in illustration, perception,
disposition and instruction, (nn. 146 and 155.)   Wherefore, Swedenborg expressly teaches, that there must be priests and a priesthood in
the New Jerusalem.   And it is hard to conceive how he could have
taught more directly that there should be in this priesthood *an order*
corresponding to that in the Lord, in the heavens, in the church, in

universal nature, and in *man* as the form of all these in their universal, particular and singular existences. Consequently, it is perfectly clear, that the true external or formal order of the priesthood is involved in the universal order of those existences, "just as parts are in the whole."

What then is this universal order as displayed in the True Christian Religion by "the divine truths revealed by the Lord in the work"? This is the whole and the sole question which we have now to determine in finding authorities for the true order of our ministry. And we confidently assert that such order can never be rightly determined except so far as the divine truths thus revealed "are seen in the light and *acknowledged*."

Now let the reader, divesting himself of all passion, prejudice, party feeling and preconceived opinion, look up to the Lord with a sincere desire to know the truth for its own sake, and opening the True Christian Religion, peruse the following numbers—24, 32, 33, 34, 42, 75, 76, 195, 210–214, 370, 395, 603, 608, 609, 618, 677–687, 712, 713, 777. If these numbers are carefully and studiously read in connection with others in other works therein referred to, we are sure it must be seen and acknowledged, that the universal principle of all order, in the Lord, in his Word, in heaven, in the church, in man both as to his soul and his body, and in universal nature, is *a* TRINE *of* DISCRETE DEGREES. This is that *universal* of all order, which must enter into every particular and singular thing that exists, so that it may be "connected with the general order of all things, and so inserted in it, that altogether they may constitute a one." And without this form of order in any one particular or singular thing, it is utterly impossible for it to be inserted in the Lord, or heaven, or the church, or man in any of his complex forms, so as to be a constituent part in true order, while it is the eternal law of every perfect form in heaven above, and in the earth beneath, and in the waters under the earth, that the whole and its parts shall be reciprocally exact images and likenesses, the one of the other. (H. & H. 62.) As then the priesthood is a representative of the Lord, is a component of heaven and the church, must be in the same order as the representatives of heaven in the letter of the Word, is composed of individual men, must therefore be a man in complex form, and thus must have within itself an image and likeness of the universal order which pervades all of them, hence it follows, without the possibility of right contradiction, that the true external or formal order of a new church priesthood is A TRINE OF DISCRETE DEGREES.

We have not the time nor the space to show this by displaying here any one of the above named exemplifications of this universal law. Mr. Powell has shown it in respect to the heavens. And we think his argument for a trine of discrete degrees in the external or formal ministry of the new church, from the trinal order of the heavens, is perfectly conclusive and altogether unanswerable. Mr. Cabell, too, has very ably proved the same from the trinal order of the Word. Therefore, referring the reader to their parts of our

report, we now go to the last authority for this order which we have
to present.

24. We now come, at last, to that much noted passage from number 17 of the Coronis to the True Christian Religion, which is so
direct, express and positive a proof of the trinal order in the minis-
try, that the opponents of this order have been exceedingly worried
in explaining it away, or weakening its force. Mr. Powell has given
it at length in english, (*supra*, p. 399,) and it is useless for us to iterate
that quotation of it here.   We think it is a matter of much importance that we should see and comment on it in the original language.

In a note to page xiv. of our Appendix, the Rev. Mr. Noble says,
"the latin of the last clause is, 'Similiter in ecclesia, primas infulatus, antistites parochi, et flamines sub illis.' "   On what authority he
makes this assertion, we do not know. Has he seen the original
manuscript of Swedenborg, and discovered that Primus in the edition
of the Coronis printed at London in 1780 is a typographical error?
If not, we must think that it is assuming too much to suppose so. We
have that edition now before us, and give to the church at large this
reprint of the whole of number 17. · It is a fac simile of the original
print as to capitaling and punctuation.

17. Notum est, quod ut aliquid perfectum sit, erit TRINUM in justo
ordine, unum sub altero, & communicatio intercedens, & quod hoc
Trinum faciat unum; non aliter a Columna, super qua Coronamentum,
sub hoc teres subtensio, and sub hac stylobata. Tale Trinum est
Homo, supremum ejus est caput, medium ejus est Corpus, & infimum
ejus sunt Pedes & Plantæ. Omne Regnum in hoc æmulatur Hominem,
ibi erit Rex ut Caput, Præterea Tribuni & Officiarii ut Corpus, ac
Rustici cum servis ut Pedes & Plantæ: similiter in Ecclesia, Primus
infulatus, Antistites parochi, & flamines sub illis. Ipse Mundus nec
subsistit nisi tria consequentia in ordine sint, quæ sunt Mane, Meridies
& Vespera; ut & quotannis Ver, Aestas & Autumnus, Ver ut fiat
seminatio, Aestas ut Germinatio, ac Autumnus ut fructificatio; Nox
autem & Hiems, non conferunt ad stabilimentum Mundi. Nunc quia
omne perfectum erit Trinum, ut sit unum contineatur cohærens; ideo
uterque Mundus tam Spiritualis quam Naturalis, ex tribus Ath-
mosphæris seu Elementis consistit & subsistit, quaruum Prima proxime
ambit Solem, et vocatur Aura, Altera sub hac & vocatur Aether, ac
Tertia sub illis, & vocatur Aer; tres hæ Athmospheræ in Mundo
Naturali sunt naturales, in sé passivæ, quia ex Sole qui est purus ignis
procedunt, at tres illis correspondentes in Mundo, Spirituali sunt
Spirituales, in se activae, quia ex Sole, qui est purus Amor procedunt;
Angeli coelorum in regionibus trium harum Athmosphaerarum habi-
tant; Angeli supremi Coeli in Aura Cœlesti quae proxime ambit
Solem, ubi Dominus, Angeli medii Coeli in Aethere spirituali, sub
illis, & Angeli infimi Coeli in Aere spirituali naturali, sub duobus
illis: ita constabiliti sunt omnes Coeli, a Primo ad ultimum hoc,
quod hodie a Domino conditur. Ex his animadverti potest, unde est
quod per Tria in Verbo significatur Completum, videatur APOCALYPSIS
REVELATA, n: 505. 875.

In carefully reading this over, the first thing we observe is, *erit*

TRINUM, ibi *erit* Rex, in the future tense; and *faciat* unum, in the subjunctive mood. We should not notice this peculiarity,—if such it may be thought,—if the Rev. Mr. Wilks had not founded upon it what seems to us a most fallacious argument. He argues—Swedenborg uses the future tense merely to denote *what is*, not what *must be*. There *is* a trine in just order—there *is* a capital to a column—there *is* a king in a kingdom, and there *is* a Primus infulatus in the church as it now exists. This is *all* that Swedenborg intends to teach. Therefore, he "did not mean to teach the necessity of such an external order in the new-church ministry." He does indeed say there *is* a *trine* in the governments and churches of the present day; but he cannot mean, by saying this, to teach that there *must* be in the ministry of the new church, a trine of discrete officers, the lower subordinate to the higher; for, "as it can be satisfactorily shown, from the Word and the writings of Emanuel Swedenborg, that the order of the ministry instituted by the Lord for the christian church, admits of no distinction of superior and inferior degrees among the clergy; that all who teach the Word are on the same plane, being representatives of natural truth; and that no one should acknowledge any other above him than the Lord alone, he being the teacher, the father, and the master of all whom he calls to be the ministers of his Word; therefore, to teach the necessity of a trine of discrete officers in the ministry of the new church, the lower subordinate to the higher, would be to teach a doctrine which is most emphatically contrary to the Divine Word, and which, consequently, cannot be true. Wherefore, although Swedenborg does indeed teach that the Lord, in establishing the new heaven and the new earth, that is, a new church on earth, introduces this trinal order into them, yet in this abstract illustration of that order, he teaches no such thing as that a *trine* of ministers of discrete grades *must* exist in the new church on earth; but, on the contrary, teaches that "there should be *but one order* of priests in the new church, and but one ordination into the priesthood."

What we believe Swedenborg *did* mean to teach in this passage, we shall state presently. We say now, we believe this passage *does not* imply what Mr. Wilks imagines it does, namely, that there ought to be a sovereign *pontiff* in the new church, or that there ought to be a new-church *high-priest* for this *nation*. And we are sorry that he has felt obliged to resort to so perfunctory a criticism as the above, to clear Swedenborg's skirts of such a false doctrine. Nothing can be clearer to our mind than that Swedenborg did not use the specification of Primus infulatus, Antistites parochi, et flamines sub illis, because that *is* the order of the roman-catholic church, or to denote the roman pontiff by the first term. Nor do we believe that he intended to teach what *will* be the trine in the new church. Nor even what *must* be the officers, or the kind of functionaries, that will be required to make the trine of ministers in the new church when her ministry is in just order. All that Swedenborg intends to teach is, that there *must* be *a trine* in the priesthood. We have shown that it was no part of Swedenborg's function to teach formularies for the new church; not to lay down the external order for her ministry.

We do not believe, therefore, that he *has* done it *here*. We no more believe that he has taught what should be the external *ecclesiastical* order of the new church, in this passage of the Coronis, than we believe he has taught in it what should invariably be the external *civil* order of all those countries which embrace her faith.

But Swedenborg says, *erit* Trinum, and *erit* Rex. Well, what should he say, according to the latin idiom, to express obligation or necessity? We confidently assert that he does not use the future tense here to express merely what is. Had he intended this, he would have used the present tense, as he does in some of the other sentences. For mark, he says—Tale Trinum *est* Homo. Man *is* a trine, for he already exists, as to his physical frame, in divine order. So, speaking of a column, in architecture, which is part of a temple supposed to be built, and to which he in imagination points, he says, super qua *est* coronamentum. But when speaking of a kingdom or a church in the abstract, the idea of the mind is of their production and consistence according to the laws of their appropriate order. Hence it does not do to say, of either of these that it *is* a trine; for the mind does not yet regard it as existing; but that it *should be* a trine to be in the order appropriate to it. Swedenborg is stating a certain law, by which the Lord reduces the heavens and hells to order, so that they may stand under his auspices and in obedience to him to eternity. This law is the arrangement of all things by discrete degrees in trinal order. And now he is illustrating this law by *things known*. His argument is—What observing and philosophical minds *know* of the order in which things actually exist in this world, shows that the Lord, when he founds a new heaven and a new church, and puts them in order, so that they may stand under his auspices and in obedience to him to eternity, *must needs* arrange them in trines of discrete and subordinate degrees; for this is that *just* order, by which "the most perfect ordination of all things in the heavens and of all things in the hells" may be effected. For "*it is known*, that, to have any thing perfect, it should be a *trine*, [or three distinct parts,] in just order, [that is,] one *under* another, [not side by side and continuous in the same plane,] and interceding communication, [without any thing like intervals between them,] and that this trine [should not be so distinct as to be three separate things, but] should make *one*" [thing.] Thus he states the principle of philosophy in its abstract form;—in which form the principle is expressed as a *requisition*, as a thing that *should* be;—and then he proceeds to exemplify it by some of the most obvious and best known facts. Pointing in imagination to a temple, he says—"Just like a column, upon which is a capital, under this a long round shaft, and beneath this a pedestal." According to true architectural order, you see that there must be these *three* distinct parts in a column—one under another and communication between them. If there were but one part, as a continuous shaft, it would be like a beam of the builder, placed to prop up the superincumbent parts temporarily; and not a regular column in architecture, put permanently where it stands, according to the just order of the architectural art. And if there were any transposition of the parts; or if there were interstices between them, so that the three did not make one coherent thing, you see that the true principles of architecture would be outraged. · "*Such* a trine is man. His head is his supreme part, his body is his intermediate part, and his lowest part is his feet and the soles of his feet." If his head were severed from his body, or his feet from both in their connection—thus if *these three discrete* *parts* did not flow into one another in coherent and subordinate unity, it is perfectly manifest that he would not be a man. Now "every kingdom resembles man in this respect." For " in it [order requires that there should be, and therefore] there must be a king as the head, besides magistrates and officers as the body, and husbandmen with servants as the feet and·soles of the feet." Just as if he had said, if there were not a king, it would not be a kingdom; and if there were not these ·discrete and subordinate parts so under him in his administration, as that the functions of royalty might be extended from the king as the head to husbandmen with servants as the feet and soles, there could not be an orderly kingly government in the nation. Therefore, in order that there *may* be such a governmental *unity*, there *must* be such a *trine*. He then specifies the church, as affording another instance; and goes on to show the *necessity* for this order by observing that the world itself could not *subsist* without it. At last, assuming his general postulate as an established law, namely, that every perfect thing *should* be a *trine* that it *may* contain a coherent unity, or *may* be a *one* made up of *cohering parts*, he takes his stand on this to explain certain universal facts in the creation of both the spiritual and natural worlds—as that they severally consist of and subsist in *three* atmospheres, which are natural and passive in the natural world, but spiritual and active in the spiritual world— that in these atmospheres of·the spiritual world angels of *three* heavens have their abode;· and, in *consequence* of their being *so* arranged in discrete and subordinate *trinal* order, that all the heavens have been firmly bound together from the first to this last which is now founded by the Lord.

Now, if this be the drift of Swedenborg's argument, who is right, Mr. Wilks, or Mr. Hindmarsh, in the rendering of *erit?* Does not the future tense of the latin language, as well as of ours, imply obligation and necessity, as well as futurity? Does it·not mean *shall* as well as *will?* is not that which is *future* in time and space *certain* in spirit, which is above time, and without space? And is there not a moral and spiritual *certainty*, that all things which are·in just order, *will* exist in a trine of degrees : and thus is there not a moral and spiritual *necessity*, imperatively *requiring* all things so to exist, that they *may* be *perfect* things? If so, it is impossible that Sweden‑ borg could have taught more expressly that there *must* be such a trine in the priesthood of the New Jerusalem, in order that *that* MAY *be a perfect* thing, so as to stand *under* the Lord, and in *obedience* to his divine influences, to eternity. Finally, then, let any one compare these two sentences :

Notum est, quod ut aliquid perfectum sit, *erit* Trinum in justo ordine, unum sub altero, &c., et quod hoc Trinum *faciat* unum. (*Cor. ad. V. C. R. p.* 14, *n.* 17.)

Non *erit* tibi dii alii coram faciebus meis. (*Ar. Coel. Tafel's Lat. Ed. Vol. XI. p.* 213.)

And we are sure that he must see the meaning of Swedenborg in the first sentence to be—It is known that, to make any thing perfect, there *must* (*shall*) be a trine in just order, having one thing *under* another, and the lower subordinate to the higher, so that this trine *may* make a one. And that, if Swedenborg had intended merely to say there *is* a trine in every perfect thing, he would have used the present, instead of the future, tense; thus—Tale Trinum *est* Homo.

But let Mr. Wilks go further back to the premises of Swedenborg's argument in the, passage in which this sentence is found. Let him read numbers 14, 15 and 16 of the Coronis, in connection with number 17. And will he not there find that Swedenborg is explaining those passages of the Word in which Jehovah predicts that he will create a new heaven and a new earth which is to be the new church called the New Jerusalem; and that, in this explanation, he is showing that the Lord, when he actually founds that new heaven and that new church, does in fact introduce into them, both in general and in every the most minute particular, a trine of discrete degrees? Well, if the new heaven and the new church are, as Swedenborg says in n. 15, to have this trinal order induced in them because they "appear before the Lord as one man;" and "*similiter* in Ecclesia, *erit* Primus infulatus, Antistites parochi, et flamines sub illis," would-be to teach "what is emphatically contrary to the Divine Word," if by this he is supposed "to teach the necessity of a trine of discrete officers in the *ministry* of the new church, the lower subordinate to the higher"—is it not equally clear, that it is just as contrary to the Divine Word to teach the necessity of a trine of discrete *offices, functions, uses,* or *persons to perform them,* in *heaven* or the *church itself?* Nay, is it not just as contrary to the Divine Word to teach that there are *three discrete heavens,* and *three discrete introductions* into them, instead of *one order* of angels, and *one ordination* of angels into *the heqven?* Certainly it does seem to us that Mr. Wilks, in *proving* that Swedenborg, if he were to teach in Coronis 17, that there must be *a trine* of discrete officers in the ministry of the new church—not as there is a trine in the romish hierarchy, but—as there is a trine of *head, body* and *feet* in man, would teach what is "*most emphatically* contrary to the Divine Word," *proves far, far* TOO MUCH!!! For he proves, with equal clearness, that Swedenborg, in teaching that there is a similar trine in heaven or the church itself, has alike taught *what is* CONTRARY *to the* DIVINE WORD!!!

In the next place, we will make an observation or two upon the phrase—flamines *sub illis.* What does Swedenborg refer to? Does he by *sub illis* mean simply Antistites parochi, or *both* Primus infulatus *and* Antistites parochi? We should not ask this question, if the Rev. William Mason, too, had not founded upon this sentence a fallacious conclusion. [See Ap., p. xxix.—"in violation of the professedly adopted pattern of the three degrees in the Coronis, each of which administers both sacraments (which pattern is also violated by the first (centralist) degree not officiating *under the* SECOND *in the* SAME PLACE *of worship, as curates officiate under parish priests*".)] For thus Mr. Mason argues. Swedenborg by *sub illis* means under the ministers of the *second* grade in the trine alone. Therefore ministers of the first grade are nothing more than assistants of parish priests in the same place of worship. And hence he stigmatizes our subordination of ministers of the first grade to those of the two higher grades *in general*,—as the lowest grade of officers are in general subordination to their superiors in all the ultimate provinces of an army,—as a *violation* of the pattern of the three degrees here in the Coronis. It becomes important, therefore, that we should inquire what Swedenborg alludes to by *sub illis*. Now it seems to us that he does not allude to *Antistites parochi* alone. And we reason from analogy with other trines which he specifies in subsequent parts of the paragraph. Thus he says—Angeli supremi Coeli in Aura Cœlesti quae proxime ambit Solem, ubi Dominus; Angeli medii Coeli in Aethere spirituali, *sub illis*, et Angeli infimi Coeli in Aere spirituali naturali, *sub duobus illis*. He had previously said, more pointedly, though more generically, ex tribus Athmosphaeris seu Elementis consistit et subsistit, quaruum *Prima* proxime ambit Solem, et vocatur 'Aura, *Altera* sub *hac*, [i. e. *Prima*,] et vocatur Aether, ac *Tertia* sub *illis*, [i. e. *duobus*, viz. *Prima* et *Altera*,] et vocatur Aer. As then air is under both ether and aura; and as the angels of the natural heaven are under both the angels of the spiritual and the celestial heavens, so that in the lowest heaven there must be *celestial*-natural as well as *spiritual*-natural angels ; hence we conclude—that *flamines* are *sub duobus illis*, that is, under both the *Primus* and the *Antistites*. Hence, when Swedenborg says, *flamines sub illis* in their trine, he means the same as *Aer sub illis* in the trine, *Aura, Aether, et Aer*. And thus we further conclude, that the ministers of the first degree in the new-church ministry should stand and act in a plane as discretely below that of ministers in the second grade, as air is discretely below ether ; and should be subordinate to ministers of the second grade as things in air are subordinate to things in ether ; that is, as *truth*, and the ministers of truth, are subordinate to *good*, and its ministers. Hence, as baptism is reformation by truth, and the supper is regeneration by good, the province of the minister who administers the one is just as discrete from, and subordinate to, the province of the minister who administers the other, as truth and reformation are discrete from, and subordinate to, good and regeneration. Are, then, truth and good, or reformation and regeneration, *continuous* or *discrete* things ? If they are continuous, then the minister of the first grade is to be distinguished from the minister of the second by only a *continuous degree* : but if they are discrete, then the one is to be distinguished from the other by a *discrete degree*. The latter is our conclusion, because they are to be distinguished as air is from ether and aura ; or as the angels of the natural heaven are from those of the spiritual and celestial heavens— which are confessedly distinguished and subordinated by *discrete*, and not merely by *continuous*, degrees. Wherefore, the Central Convention, in her application of the trinal order of Coronis 17, to her ministry, is not obnoxious to the awful charge of having *violated the divine precept*, " what God hath joined together, let not man put asunder;" nor to that hardly less serious charge of her own son, of having made " a *palpable perversion*," or ". a *bungling imitation*," of " the order mentioned by Swedenborg in the Coronis." The imitation is indeed not complete, inasmuch as any thing properly like the third grade has not yet been developed ; but it is as near an approximation to the true order as the early fœtal state of the new church in this country would allow.

We are now to extend and particularize some remarks which we made on this notable passage from the Coronis in a previous part of the present report, when we were considering the views of the General Convention upon this subject. In showing the present state of the question of a ministerial trine in that general body of our church in this country, we had to review a report on this subject, which was made to it in 1843. Some of the observations of that report we approve. We generally concur in this criticism upon Swedenborg's language in the sentence before us.

The words in the original are, " *Primus infulatus, Antistites Parochi, et flamines sub illis.*" To a person tolerably versed in the latin language, a slight examination is enough to show that the above version is not a proper translation of these words. *Infulatus*, may very well be rendered *mitred ;* but *Primus* does not mean prelate, but literally *first*. So, too, *priest* is altogether too wide in its signification to be a proper translation of *Antistes ;* and though *Parochus* is allied to the greek word from which our term *parish* is derived, yet it meant a minister who was over a large district, and who had under him many subordinate priests to assist in dispensing the ministrations of the church. Again, the *flamen* was a priest among the ancient Romans, who exercised a very important and strictly defined duty in his own right; and it cannot properly be translated by *curate*, which means one who discharges certain functions in the church as the substitute of another. It thus appears, that though our version conveys to the reader some general idea concerning three grades in the ministry, yet it is wholly inadequate as a translation of Swedenborg's words.

In examining Swedenborg's language here used, your committee were struck with another consideration, which is, that these terms are not the usual language of ecclesiastical and theological writers in any age or any portion of the christian church. Indeed, they were confirmed in this view by the opinions of some of the ablest theologians and philologists in this country. *Primus* is not an ecclesiastical term; and *infulatus* is very rarely used, and then in a kind of a poetical sense. *Antistes* is not a proper technical term, for an order of the ministry, though it is sometimes used as such in a kind of figurative sense; there being two words in the latin language, *episcopus* and *prœsul*, which are used in different countries to designate the second order of the priesthood. *Parochus* was used for the same purpose in the earlier centuries of the christian church, but it has become obsolete, unless it is perhaps occasionally employed by the Catholics. *Flamen* is a purely heathen term, and has not been used in the christian church, except occasionally by way of figure or analogy.

From these remarks it is manifest, that Swedenborg, in thus laying down the three grades of the ministry, not only has not employed the technical epithets of any ecclesiastical hierarchy whatever, but has avoided using the terms which are common with theological writers. His language is certainly remarkable. If he had merely wished to show, in a general way, that there must be three orders in the ministry, he would most naturally and most probably have employed the three terms of some known great division of the christian church; the lutheran, or the english episcopal, for example. But these he has evidently shunned, and seemingly purposely so; otherwise it seems difficult to account for his employing, to designate the highest grade of the ministry, a term which is not known to theology, and for his resorting, for the lowest grade, to the hierarchy of pagan Rome. These facts seem to show, that he selected his terms with care; and that it was not his intention to perpetuate any of the known forms of church order.

There is another consideration which ought to be taken in connection with this view of Swedenborg's choice of terms in this case; and this is, that some of these terms, as *Primus* and *Antistes* for example, are words of extremely general import, and can in no way be regarded as prescribing names by which the grades in the ministry are to be called, but as expressing in the most general way the nature of the office and its duties. A similar view must be taken of the other terms, *Parochus* and *Flamen ;* since it cannot be supposed that by employing the former, Swedenborg meant to revive a title used in the christian church in the fourth and fifth centuries, nor by using the latter, to renew one of the names in the priesthood of pagan Rome; but, to indicate, by the use of both of these terms, a description of duties similar to that which was embraced in the original meaning and use of the words. It would thus appear, and it will more strongly appear when we come to a correct translation of his language, that it was not his intention to give the names by which the different grades in the ministry should be called, but to use such words as would convey a general idea of the nature of the office and duties of each grade.

These in part were our sentiments before we read that report. They are much more fully so since we have enjoyed the privilege of inspecting and studying the whole of number 17 of the Coronis in the original latin. From this inspection we are fully convinced that Swedenborg "selected his terms with care;" that they *are* terms of "extremely *general* import;" that he chose them for this very reason; that, therefore, in using them, he had no intention whatever of employing "the technical epithets of any ecclesiastical hierarchy whatever, but avoided using the terms which are common with theological writers;" and that it was most certainly "not his intention to perpetuate any of the known forms of church order." Hence we conclude, that the Rev. Wm. Mason has no ground whatever here for maintaining, that the minister of the first grade should *only* be the curate of the parish priest, with the *sole* duty of assisting him in the same place of worship; and that it is a violation of the order here laid down, to give to the first grade of ministers a province of their own, on a plane discretely below, but still subordinate to, and so *under* the plane on which the ministers of the second grade stand and act. We also conclude, that the Rev. Thos. Wilks has still less ground—has not even the *shadow* of a basis—for maintaining, or *imagining that we who are in favor of the trine maintain,* that Swedenborg here authorizes the order of a pontiff, or any thing *precisely* like the trinal arrangements of the romish hierarchy.

We do not, however, coincide with the report in thinking that Swedenborg chose these terms for the purpose of expressly teaching

what should be *the* order of the new-church ministry. We have no
idea that he *intended* by these *terms* to express what should be the
specific "nature of the office and duties of each grade" in the trinal
arrangement of ministers which was to obtain in the New Jerusalem.
For this, as we have shown above, was no part of his function. He
has here taught the *universals* of new-church ministerial order, and
no more. And hence, the labored effort of the report to deduce the
precise trinal order of the new church and her ministry *from the
interpretation of his language*, is, in our view, extremely wide of the
mark. We *do* believe that "he merely wished to show, *in a general
way*, that there must be three orders in the ministry;" and that he
very *carefully* chose terms "of *extremely general* import," for this
very reason.

But here comes up the question, which the report very justly deems
a highly important one—"How, then, is his language to be interpreted?" As we have before intimated, we do not think that it is to
be interpreted by the aid of etymology and the lexicon solely. But
we ought to interpret the meaning of the sentence in question by the
general drift of the passage in which it is found and by what Swedenborg says specifically in other parts of his writings on the same subject.
And as to the lexicographical meaning of the terms used, we think they
are of far too general a nature to sustain that very precise discrimination of the distinct offices and officers in the trine, as well as of the
duties of the three grades in the ministry, and of the relations of these
grades to one another, which the report has founded on them. Let us
first look and see what is the general drift of Swedenborg's argument
in the whole passage of which the sentence in question is a part; and
then consider the etymological import of the terms used in reference
to that drift.

We have shown the general drift of Swedenborg's argument in
numbers 14—17 of the Coronis, just above. But we may again remark
here, that he is showing the truth of the general position, that the
Lord induces order in both the new heaven and the new hell, as well
as the new church on earth, when he establishes them in the final
consummation of all previous dispensations of good and truth. Hence
he is treating of order in the new heaven and the new church in the
abstract; and, therefore, in taking exemplifications of this order from
either civil or ecclesiastical affairs on the earth, he must needs use
abstract exemplifications of the church and kingdom. It would not
therefore do, for him to take examples from churches in the concrete,
or to specify the trine as it actually existed in the churches of his day.
Hence *we* think "he would most naturally and most probably" *not*
"have employed the three terms of some known great division of the
christian church—the lutheran, or the english episcopal, for instance;"
lest, he *might* be supposed to teach that *such* should be the *precise*
form of the trine in the new church, and thus it might be concluded
that it *was* "his *intention to perpetuate*" some one "of the known
forms of church order." We have seen that he states his law of trinal
order as a formula of philosophic knowledge, thus in the form of an
abstract scientific *requisition*, as that which *should* be in the order of

a *perfect* thing. Then he illustrates his theorem by the specification of certain things that *are* in the divine order of creation—as in man, who is God's workmanship, and in a work of that "architectonic art which is in its perfection in the heavens." But, when he comes to the case of "every kingdom," he speaks of a thing which "*emulates* man;" and in which, therefore, that it *may* be like man, he says there *should* be such and such parts. And then he places the church in precisely the same category by next saying, *similiter* in Ecclesia. *This*, too, that it *may* be a *one*, *should* be a *trine;* and that its trine may be in just order, it should have a highest, an intermediate, and a lowest part, and the intermediate so under the highest, and the lowest so under both, that the highest, passing through the intermediate in successive order, and both the highest and the intermediate subsiding in the lowest in simultaneous order, *may*, as *three*, make a *one*, like man. Thus—Omne Regnum in *hoc* æmulatur Hominem, *ibi erit* Rex *ut Caput*, Praeterea Tribuni & Officiarii *ut Corpus*, ac Rustici cum servis *ut Pedes* et *Plantae: similiter* in Ecclesia, Primus infulatus, Antistites parochi, et flamines sub illis. Now what is this more than saying, that, in a kingdom or a church in the abstract, either of them, *to be like a man*, SHOULD or MUST have a part in it *as the head*, another part in it *as·the body*, and still another part *as the feet* and *soles?* Therefore, in the just order of the kingdom or the church, there should be a *trine* of *discrete* parts, the one so under another, with such communication between them, that the *three* MAY ·make a *coherent unity*. Philosophy teaches this—common sense teaches it. *It is well known*, that; in *every* thing which has any claims to being a *perfect* thing, such an order as this prevails. Consequently, it must be manifest, that, when the Lord founded the new heaven and the new church, and introduced order into them, that they might stand under his auspices, and in obedience to him, to eternity, he would introduce just such an order as this, and no·other. This, we take it, is the general drift of Swedenborg's argument. But, if this is his drift, then it is clear to our minds, that he could not have introduced the sentences in question for the purpose of teaching what should be the precise civil or ecclesiastical order in the new church on earth ; but merely to give generic illustrations, from known truths in the natural degree, of the grand order which he was teaching us that the Lord induces upon the new heaven and the new church, when he establishes them, that they may stand under his auspices and in obedience to him as a body does to its soul.

Now let us look attentively at the sentences that refer both to the kingdom and the church, and see how they float in the current of this argument. And first, as to the kingdom—

Omne Regnum in hoc aemulatur Hominem, ibi erit Rex ut Caput, Praeterea Tribuni et Officiarii ut Corpus, ac Rustici cum servis ut Pedes et Plantae.

Does Swedenborg here intend to teach what is to be, or what should be, the precise order of civil government in those nations which embrace the faith of the New Jerusalem? Does he by this mean to intimate that the regal is the only truly orderly civil government for

the new church? Or has he carefully selected the terms of this
sentence so as to teach, by the import of them amongst those who
spoke the latin language in its purity, what should or must be the
precise form of the trine in a new-church kingdom—to teach the
nature of the office and duties of each civil grade, or of the relation of
the three civil grades to each other? There have been in our connection,
we believe, those who have held the affirmative of at least the second
of these questions. But to all of them we answer, most unhesitatingly,
No! And the following are the grounds on which we hold this
negative.

Firstly, Swedenborg is not here teaching in general of civil government. Therefore he could not have introduced this specification of
every kingdom, to show what should be the precise order of civil
government in the new church. He is teaching the universal principle of all order in the heavenly, the ecclesiastical, and the civil
planes. And he is illustrating what must be the order in *general* of
the two higher planes, by what is well known to be the order in *general*
of the civil plane. Therefore, in specifying the order of *every* kingdom,
he uses terms to signify, in the most general manner, those distinct
parts of a kingdom which are most manifestly in it the orderly constituents of the human form, in which both heaven and the church
appear before the Lord, and by the subordinate arrangements of which
he keeps them *under*, and *in obedience* to, himself to eternity. Thus
he uses the term *Rex* to signify the part in a kingdom which is *ut
Caput* in man; not thereby to teach that the head of a kingdom is
nothing but the king, or that the head of the kingdom is *but one man;*
but because the king is the representative or type of *all those persons*
in a kingdom, which hold the same relation to the rest that the head
of man does to the rest of his body. So he uses the terms *Tribuni et
Officiarii,** to signify the part of a kingdom that is *ut Corpus* in man;
not thereby to teach—what is the precise nature of the offices and the
duties of officers of the second grade in a kingly government, or what
is the precise nature of the relation which these officers should hold to
the king on the one hand, or to husbandmen and their servants on the
other—by the etymological or the lexicographical import of the word
Tribunus as used by the Romans, or by the nature of the office of a
tribune of the people in the roman government; but in *general* to
represent *all those persons,* or classes of persons, in a kingdom, who
are intermediate between all those represented by the king and the

---

* This word is rendered *officers,* as if it denotes the official attendants upon magistrates, or those who discharge magisterial functions in a derived or subordinate capacity.
But is not the proper latin word for this *officiales ;* and does not Swedenborg, by
officiarii, mean the performers of useful offices to the community in general, so that
this word denotes here these who are engaged in those "various pursuits, businesses and
services" which he says are meant by "offices" in "The Doctrine of Charity," n. 69?
Officia were acts of friendly service done to other people. *Officium* was a kindness
done from good will. And *officiarius,* therefore, would be the doer of good services to
the community, as all men are who act honestly and faithfully in those occupations
which are good uses. We therefore think a more proper rendering of *Tribuni et Officiarii* would be *magistrates and business men.*

tillers of the soil, who, like the *earth* they cultivate, are the basis of all other uses, or occupations, as of manufactures, commerce, art and science, which form the *good offices* to humanity in general; and hence are *significatively* and *representatively* called by Swedenborg the *feet* and the *soles* of the feet. Hence it is perfectly plain that Swedenborg did not use these terms to teach the specific external order of civil government in the church. It is most evident that *he was not thinking of that at all.* He was merely illustrating the general law of trinal order as it exists in the human form by the *types* of that order as it *should* exist in a kingdom. And the terms to express these types were the most generic which he could find. He speaks of the king simply as denoting that in the kingdom which is *as* the *head* in a human body, or as the celestial heaven in the universal heaven, or as that which *corresponds to* the celestial heaven in the universal church on earth. He speaks of the *king* in reference to that complex part of the kingdom, just as he would have mentioned his *throne* to denote all that pertained to his kingly *government throughout* the *realm.* And so of the other terms which he uses. And we confidently say, that he did not intend to teach by this specific illustration of his general law of order, what was to be the precise civil order of the New Jerusalem on earth; because we are sure, that, if he had intended to teach this, he would not have expressed his doctrine in such *general* terms as to have led us to conclude that the *feudal* type was to be the only true form of civil order for the new church on earth! We are sure that he could not have intended to teach us that the true form of a new-church civil government is a sort of *no-body*—a regal *head*, with official *breasts* and *shoulders*, clapped immediately upon two *ankles* and *feet*. In short, we do not believe he would have presented, as a perfect form of the civil trine, —a *king, magistrates* and *officers*, with *agriculturalists* and *laborers*, under them—to the entire exclusion of all the *middle classes* which modern civilization has upreared out of the civil chaos of the *dark* ages and *feudal* times! And we are sure that it is much more reasonable to argue from this sentence for the propriety of a *russian serfdom* in the New Jerusalem, than to argue from the sentence that follows it for a *pontifical hierarchy.*

Secondly, Interpreting Swedenborg's language here by other passages from his writings in which civil governments are alluded to, we conclude that he did not intend to teach, either that a regal government is the only truly orderly one, or that the head of a kingdom is the king alone. In U. T. 55, he says, " Who does not see that there is neither *empire, kingdom, dukedom, commonwealth, state,* nor *private family*, but what is established by laws which constitute the order, and thereby the form, of its government? The laws of justice in all of them have the first place, political laws the second, and economical laws the third; which, on comparison with the human frame, will answer respectively to these several parts; the laws of justice to the head, political laws to the body, and economical laws to the dress: wherefore, the latter, like garments, may be changed at pleasure." Here Swedenborg cites an empire, a dukedom, a commonwealth, or

34

republic, (*Respublica*,) and a state or city, (*Civitas*,) as orderly governments, as well as a kingdom; and alludes to the principle of trinal order in them in its resemblance to that of the human form. The *real* head " in all of them," consists of the laws of justice, and *all* the executors of these laws in a complex form constitute the *apparent* head. ' Hence the emperor, king, duke, president, or mayor, is not *alone* even the apparent head of a civil polity, much less the real head. He is only the leading, principal, or most general functionary of the apparent head. Hence Swedenborg expressly says, " the king is as the head in a rank of servants." " By magistrates are meant those who have supreme authority in, and civil jurisdiction over, kingdoms, commonwealths," &c. (Doct. of Char. 87.) The king is the officer of most extended jurisdiction. (U. T. 412.) And the *chief* magistrate " *where such a form of government prevails*, is called king." (H. D. 314.) These passages show that other forms of government than the regal, are orderly, and may be the proper forms of civil government on earth; and that the chief magistrate in any form of government is only called head in a relative sense. And that there may be various forms of government on earth is clear from the fact that " there are various forms of government," in heaven, " differing in different societies," and being various " according to the ministries in which the societies are engaged," which ministries, also, " are similar to the functions of all things in man—to which they correspond." (H. & H. 213, 217.) Thus forms of civil government may be as various in the different nations which embrace the faith of the New Jerusalem as " the functions of all things in man" are various. And hence it cannot be that Swedenborg intended to teach, by the sentence which we are here considering, that the regal form of government is the only truly orderly one for the new church; or that the king is the head of the kingdom as an individual. (See H. D., 320–325.)

These observations on the first sentence before us, enable us to see more clearly the true import of the second—

Similiter in Ecclesia, Primus infulatus, Antistites parochi, et flamines sub illis.

For Swedenborg no more intended to teach by *this* what should be precisely and invariably the only true *ecclesiastical* order of the new church, than he did by *that* what should be precisely and invariably her only true *civil* order. He is speaking of the church in the abstract, just as he had before spoken of " every kingdom" and " man " in the abstract. And hence, when he said, *similiter in Ecclesia, Primus infulatus, &c.*, he no more intended to teach that the head of the visible body of the church should be one person, than he intended to teach that the head of a kingdom should be one man; and he no more intended to teach that *the church* should consist of *the clergy alone*, or of a hierarchy,—as some may think these words in strictness imply,—than he intended to teach that a kingdom should consist of a king, magistrates and officers, with husbandmen and servants alone. He says generally and universally that *in* the church—not as *composing it solely*—there should be a trine of priestly officers. The trine here mentioned is, indeed, an *ecclesiastical* trine in the technical sense of the term, for it is a trine of ecclesiastics alone. But Swedenborg mentions these ecclesiastical functionaries as generic types of all those members of the church as a man before the Lord, which are " distinguished, like heaven, into *three degrees*." (Ap. Rev. 744.) He mentions the *Primus infulatus* as the type of *all* those who, in the church as a complex human form, are *ut caput* in man, just as he mentions the *Rex* in the same reference to the king-.dom. So of the *Antistites parochi* and the *flamines*. The former of these are mentioned as the type of all those who are *ut corpus*, and the latter as the type of all those who are *ut pedes et plantae*, in man. Hence, Swedenborg did not intend to teach, that, in the whole new church of any nation, or of the world, there should be any *one man* who should hold the relation to all the rest of the church which the head does to the rest of the body in man; or that the church should consist of ecclesiastics alone. He no more intended to · teach this latter than he intended to teach that all in a kingdom, besides the king, with magistrates and officers, should be *only* rustics and servants. Therefore, there is no ground here for the order of a new-church pontiff—no call for a new-church pontifex maximus. There should indeed be, in every organized body of the church, an ecclesiastical chief magistracy, filled by an officer who *represents* the common weal or the general good. But the ecclesiastical chief magistrate, is, like the king, in a kingdom, only the head of a rank of servants. He is only the representative, for the time being, of the whole body of some general church, as the chief magistrate of a republic is a repre-sentative of the whole body of the people. And as there may be various forms of government in the churches as well as in the nations of earth, we may have this representative head in an occasionally . elected president of a general convention of the brotherhood of churches, as well as in a prelate or head bishop appointed for life. Or there is no reason why the visible head of. the new and true christian church may not be a *complex* man, representative of the whole church, as the visible head of the first christian church was after the Lord's ascension. As to the whole body of the church in any other sense of the term—in any sense of the church as a universal human form of societies in the Lord's aspect—we think we shall show presently that Swedenborg does not speak of any man as the head of the church in the way that the king is the head of the kingdom. In · this sense, the Lord, in his divine humanity, is alone the head of the church—thus the sole ·head of the church is God. And, therefore, he could not have intended by the term *Primus infulatus*, to have implied that the visible head of the new church, in any of her more general forms, should be one person.

By *in the church*, then, is here to be understood a generic expres-sion, a sort of *indefinite article*, which refers to no one church in par-ticular, but which involves, in what is said of it, that which is true of all churches·in particular. It is like saying *in the army*, when the general principles of military tactics are treated of. Hence, as, if Swedenborg had said, *in the army* there must be a major general, besides brigadiers and colonels, and captains under them, we should

not have inferred that he intended to teach that an army should consist of these officers alone; so when he says, *in Ecclesia*, Primus
infulatus, Antistites parochi, et flamines sub illis, we do not understand him to teach that the church consists of these ecclesiastics
solely. Thus to say *in the church*, is like saying *in the family*, when
we wish to express what is true in relation to all families. Or it is
like saying *in man*, when what is universally applicable to all men is
to be stated. Therefore, it cannot be, that Swedenborg here teaches
expressly any thing in relation to what *will* be the precise external or
formal order of the priesthood or ministry of the New Jerusalem:
and we do not bring forward this sentence as an authority for that.
We say he teaches, in Coronis, 14–17, the trine as a *universal* principle
of order in the new heaven and the new church. Therefore, if he
had said nothing about the church as a mere ecclesiastical polity, this
would have been our authority for a trine in the new-church ministry,
because it is involved as a particular in that universal of order. But he
expressly cites the church in the abstract as a thing which *it is
known* must, to be perfect, be in trinal order. Therefore, as Swedenborg
expressly says there must be in the church in the abstract a trine of
priestly officers, we conclude there must be in the New Jerusalem, as
a church in the concrete, a similar trine, in order that she may be
perfect. Thus we do not say that Swedenborg has by this sentence,
expressly taught that there will or must be precisely such a trine
as the terms here used import particularly; but as he here says, there
must be in *every* church a trine of ecclesiastical officers *such as* he
names, therefore, *by implication* we conclude that there *must* be *some
such* trine of ecclesiastical officers in the New Jerusalem. But what
the precise form of such trine is to be in any particular part of this
universal church, must depend upon the *genius* of that part, or upon
the peculiar nature of its distinctive ministry in the common man.
    Thus we conclude, that there is not in this sentence of n. 17 of
Coronis, any authority for a particular form of the trine of ministers
which will or must be invariably and solely that of the new church;
because we do not believe that Swedenborg ever intended to teach
this—because the external forms of ecclesiastical government and order
are to be various in the societies of the new church on earth, as they
are in the societies of heaven, and therefore any one precise and particular form of the ministerial trine would not be applicable, and could
not be prescribed, to all the societies of this church—and because the
terms here used by Swedenborg are too general to express any specific
form of the ministerial trine. All he teaches is, that there must be
a trine of some sort, which may assume various forms in different
churches, and be variously determined by their peculiarities of genius
and character.
    These remarks enable us now to proceed to the lexicographical
interpretation of Swedenborg's language in the sentence before us,
under the guidance of a general principle which will be likely to lead
us to satisfactory results. As, therefore, Swedenborg was illustrating
a sort of universal theorem by the specification of a generic fact considered abstractly, he would " probably and naturally " use terms, in

speaking of it, of the most general import; and, if he did not find any sufficiently general in the language in which he was writing, he would invent them. This is evidently the case with *Primus infulatus*. It is most manifest that he chose this term purposely to express in the most abstract form possible, and without any reference whatever to the highest ecclesiastical functionaries of any of the denominations of the prevalent christian church, a chief ecclesiastical magistrate, who should hold the same relative position in ecclesiastical organizations that a king, or other chief civil magistrate, should in civil organizations. Like an algebraic formula, it was to express the rule for *every* church. Therefore we believe that Swedenborg uses *Primus*, an adjective expressive of *degree* in the *highest*;—(for it is an adjective in the superlative degree—*prae, prior, primus*)—and *infulatus*, another adjective, expressive of *function*. He uses adjectives because they are abstract terms. And he gives either of them a substantive form, merely to express the highest degree of function in the church abstractly considered. Master of the language which he was using, as Swedenborg was, we are *sure* that he did not employ *Primus* instead of *Primas* without mature thought and deliberate design. And we hold that *Primus infulatus*, as he uses the expression, is precisely equivalent to Cicero's *Primus civitatis*—*Primus infulatus* being in the church, just the same, relatively, as *Rex ut Primus civitatis*, is in the state. It would not have done for Swedenborg to say *Primus ecclesiæ;* because he wanted to signify the highest functionary of the *priesthood*, and *ecclesia* implies more than that. It was needful, therefore, that he should use a word appropriate to the priestly function in general, and he very properly chose the word that implies the general badge of that function. *Infulatus* being an adjective, is made to agree in the nominative case with *Primus* used substantively, instead of being governed by it,—as it would have been, if it were another substantive,—in the genitive case, as *civitatis* is. Cicero also has *Primus ex omnibus*, also *Primus de privatis*—Virgil *Primus ante omnes*—to denote the chief person. Terence says, *Quia sum apud te primus.* Ovid says, *his mihi primus erit.* Quintilian—*Primus post eos.* Lucretius—*Primi virorum.* All these show that Swedenborg was justified in using substantively the superlative adjective *Primus* to signify, in an abstract sense, the highest or chief functionary in the church. Therefore, because he has used this *adjective*, and not any *substantive* that is in fact a term of technical ecclesiastical usage in the prevalent christian church, we conclusively argue, that he did not intend, either to perpetuate any of the known forms of church order, or expressly to teach what would or should be the precise order, in the New Jerusalem : but purposely intended to express the thing in its most general and abstract form, merely to illustrate and confirm the general proposition which he was discussing.

And the same reasoning enables us to comprehend fully the term *infulatus*, in his use of it. The *infula* was a badge of the priesthood, not only in use among the Romans, but among all the ancient nations. It was a crystal of the *debris* of representatives, which the flood of time had washed down from the primeval granite hills and mountains of the ancient and most ancient churches. It was the same in ancient ecclesiastical affairs that the *corona* was in civil matters. This was originally a chaplet of leaves or flowers worn on the head, so as to lie over that part of the skull, where anatomists find what they call for this reason the *coronal* suture. A certain kind of crown, used in modern times, is called a *coronet*, for the same reason. The *infula* was an ecclesiastical *corona* or *coronet*, made of *wool* or *woollen* threads or ribbons. It was not exclusively the badge of the highest order of priests. It was alike the ensign of the priestly office in all the grades. And it was also the designation of a sacred victim's consecration to the altar. Moreover, the prisoners of a conquered army were decked with it when led in those triumphal processions by which the ancients designed to ascribe their success to the favoring auspices of the gods. In like manner a ship, brought in in triumph—*velata infulis ramisque oleae*—according to Livy. *Hostes inermes cum infulis sese porta foras proripiunt*, says Caesar. *Infulae in destinatam morti victimam conferebantur*, says Florus. Cicero has—*Praesto mihi fuerunt sacerdotes Cereris cum infulis et verbenis.* And, according to some, *flamines* is a word derived from *filum*, *filo*, the thread, of which the head dress of the priests so called was made, and on account of which they were first called *filamines*, and afterwards *flamines*. Others derive the term from *flameo*, because the head dress of the priests called *flamines* was of a *flame* color, like the lightning of Jove. In either case the name was derived from that which those priests wore on their heads instead of the woollen *fillets* of more ancient times. Thus the *infula* was the badge of the priesthood or priestly office in general; so that *infulatus* meant a priest in general; and to make this word denote a high priest, or a priest of the highest grade, it was joined to a substantive denoting such a priest. Thus we have *infulatus mysta*, denoting an hierophant, or a priest of sacred mysteries, whose high office was denoted by the sacred diadem, or head-band, which he wore. He was one that was learned himself, or instructed others, in the sacred mysteries of religion, which was invariably the *prelatic* office of the ancient priesthood. But Swedenborg joins this word, not to a substantive denoting a priest, but to an adjective simply denoting grade in the highest degree. What other inference can we make, then, than that he simply intended thus to express the idea of priestly function in its highest grade?

But we go further, and suppose that Swedenborg *carefully* chose the word *infulatus*, to signify the *priestly thing*, that is, the *spiritual quality* of the priest, that was to designate him for the highest priestly function in the church. The *infula* was a sacred *fillet* of *wool*, used as a priestly *crown*. Now we know that the crown is the representative of wisdom. The crown or fillet of *wool* therefore is the emblem of *superior* wisdom—the wisdom of love. Consequently, by the use of the term *Primus infulatus*, Swedenborg meant to teach, in its most abstract form, the important truth, that in the church, those who representatively are the head, and are to exert a governing ecclesiastical function over the general body, should be not, in *particular*, that *one* person, but, in *general*, *all* those who are most distinguished for their *wisdom*, the *laurelled* teachers of the church, who are *ut caput in ecclesia*, because they can and will govern the body from *love*. For no one person but the Lord, *can* sustain that relation to the whole body of his church, which is implied in a term expressive of chief or supreme governor of the church from love. The only other human representative of the Lord as such a governor on earth *can* alone, and therefore *must*, be the *complex* of *all* who are in the wisdom of love from him. And, therefore, in no possible case, can there be any *one man* who can sustain the relation of visible head to the whole body of the Lord's church on earth. For the sake of order and just government in ecclesiastical affairs, there may and should be a presiding general officer; but he is only *ut caput* to other *officers*, who are, for the sake of use and efficiency, subordinate to him. And this alone is Swedenborg's doctrine here. So that the *Primus infulatus* being only a *capital* ecclesiastical *officer*, cannot be supposed to be *ut caput* to the church as the Lord's body. *This* relation to the church, *no other one man can* sustain but God in his humanity. This is our firm and solemn conviction, in a prayerful study of this passage before the Lord.

Well, then, what is the conclusion? *Most certainly* that Swedenborg did *not* intend to teach, that, in the new church, in any of its larger or more congregate forms, *any one man* is to hold that relation to a complex body of societies or associations that a pastor does to a single society, or a husband to a wife. And equally clear is it, that he did not intend to teach that the new church in its most general form as a visible body would have, or should have, or *could* have, *any one man* as a *pontifex maximus*. As this is the main point of our argument, we will dwell upon it here, before we proceed to say a very few words about the other terms used by Swedenborg in this sentence.

Above, we have endeavored to interpret Swedenborg's language, by following it, with our mind's eye, in the general current of his argument in the whole passage wherein it is found. Let us now interpret it by what Swedenborg says specifically in other parts of his writings on the same subject.

First, Does Swedenborg mean to teach that any one man is to be regarded and respected as the visible head of the whole church, in the same way that the king is as the visible head of the whole kingdom? This must follow from Swedenborg's language in the two sentences which we have quoted, if it is taken in its strict literal import, and if we suppose him to intend to teach what is to be the specific external order of the New Jerusalem. For he says, immediately after the sentence which speaks of the king as the head of the kingdom—SIMILITER *in ecclesia, Primus infulatus*. Therefore, in strict interpretation, the first priest of the church, holds the same relation to the church that the king does to the kingdom, that is, *ut caput* in man. And, consequently, the first priest of the whole church must be regarded as the head of the church, just as the king is of the kingdom. But, if Swedenborg had intended to teach this here, would he not, in speaking of the church and kingdom together, in other parts of his writings, invariably so regard and speak of them himself? But does he? Let us see. In D. L. & W. 24, we find the following—"Every man, although he is ignorant of it, thinks of a collective body of men as of a single man; wherefore, also, he immediately perceives what is meant when it is said that the king is the head, and his subjects the body. . . . . The case is the same with the spiritual body as with the civil body: *the spiritual body is the church*—ITS HEAD is GOD-MAN." . . . . "One God is the head, and the church is the body, which acts from the control of the head, and not from itself, as is also the case in man." . . . "There is only one king in a kingdom: for more than one would distract, whereas one may preserve it in unity. *The case would be similar in the church*, dispersed over the whole world, which is called a communion, because *like one body it is under one head.* It is well known, that the head governs and controls the body under it. . . . The body cannot act at all but from the understanding and will in the head; nor *can the man of the church act at all but from God.*" This is one of several passages which might be quoted, if we had the space. But this one is enough to show that in a passage, in which the subject is precisely similar to the one before us—in which a parallel between the church and kingdom is drawn—Swedenborg speaks of God-man as being the head of the church as the king is the head of a kingdom. He could not have meant, therefore, that the *Primus infulatus* is to be regarded as the head of the whole church as the king is the head of a kingdom. The Lord alone is to be so regarded.

Second, does Swedenborg mean to teach that any one man is to be regarded as a pontiff in the new church, or that there is to be a *pontifex maximus* for the whole new church? One can hardly think so after reading the following:—"They who strain the literal sense, suppose that the words—'and I will give unto thee the keys of the kingdom of heaven'—were spoken of Peter, and that he had this great power given him; when yet it was well known that Peter was a very plain, simple man, and that he in no case exercised such a power, and that to exercise it is contrary to what is divine: nevertheless, under the impulse of a wild and infernal love of self and of the world, in consequence whereof they would arrogate to themselves the highest power on earth and in heaven and make themselves gods, some explain this according to the letter, and are vehement in defence of such explanation." (Pref. to Gen. xxii.) "Those who prevailed over the rest in dignity and authority assembled together and in an obscure chamber concluded that both a divine and human principle should be attributed to the Lord, principally on the account, that otherwise the papal chair would not subsist; for if they had acknowledged the Lord to be one with the father, as he himself saith, it would have been impossible that any vicar of his should be acknowledged on earth." But if this were acknowledged, "they hereby could have dominion in heaven and in earth, because they knew from the Word, that to the Lord was given all power in the heavens and in the earths, which could not be attributed to any vicar, if the human principle was also acknowledged to be divine; for they knew that no one was allowed to make himself equal to God, and that the divine principle had the above power of itself, but not the human, unless it was given to it, as also afterwards to Peter." (A. C. 4738.) The power here supposed to be given to Peter alone, was that of the head of the church; for "the head governs and controls the body under it," and to have power over the souls of men so as to be able to admit them into, or shut them out of, heaven, is to be the head of the church as Christ is. This is to regard a man as sovereign pontiff; and it cannot for an instant be imagined; that Swedenborg, in the sentence before us, intended to teach; that any one man was to be regarded by the whole new church even *representatively* in *this* light.—No one man can be the head of the visible body of the church on any other principle than that he is the Lord's *vicar* on earth—representing him to the church, or in his office of the church's high priest, as the king represents him to the kingdom. Does Swedenborg's doctrine that there must be *in Ecclesia Primus infulatus*, teach this? and is this sustained by his teachings in other parts of his writings? In A. C. 4818, where he is giving examples of evils of life derived from false doctrinal tenets, he says—"with those who believe, from the evil of self-love and the love of the world, *that* ANY ONE *shall be the Lord's vicar on earth*, and that he hath the power of opening and shutting heaven, thus of bearing rule over the minds and consciences of men, and confirm *this false tenet* from the sense of the letter of the Word," &c. Here he expressly denounces the idea of any one man's being the vicar or representative of the Lord as the head of the church, as a *false* tenet. Could he, therefore, have possibly meant to inculcate such an idea in any part of Coronis, 17? Again, in Ap. Rev. 802, he says it is a "*divine truth*" that "the pope's vicarship is an *invention* and *fiction, which ought to be rejected*"! Could *any thing like* it, then, be taught in an appendix to that work in which "divine truths are revealed by the Lord"? These passages are surely enough to give a most decided negative to the two questions last propounded. Well, then, as, in true order, the whole and the parts must be reciprocally images and likenesses of one another, (H. & H. 62,) and as the whole church on earth cannot have *any one man* holding the relation to it which the head does to the body, so in the church in any of its parts, or in any of its lesser forms, *no one man* can hold the *ut caput* relation to that. Consequently, neither a convention, conference, or consociation of associations, nor an association of societies, nor a single society should have *any one man* holding to it the relation of a *pastor* as the *head* of a *body*, in the sense that a husband is the head of a wife, and Christ is the head of the church. Hence we hold that, in even the smallest society of the church, the pastor *alone* is not as the *head ;* but that *he together with all the communicants*, both male and female, must be regarded as *ut caput* to others, who shall hold the two lower and subordinate relations of *ut corpus* and *ut pedes*.—But may there not be a *pontifex maximus* in the new church? We suppose there may be in the greatly qualified sense of a presiding or chief ecclesiastical officer, as the head of other such officers—as may be seen in the note at the bottom of page 106 of this report. But certainly not in the sense of a *pontiff*, to whom the *whole* church is, to bow. And we refer to the words of Swedenborg, quoted in that note, for proof of this position. For he expressly says, "Christ our Saviour is the ONLY *pontifex maximus*—the states of the kingdom are his *vicarius*—the senators are the *vicarius* for the states. That the pope of Rome called himself *pontifex maximus*, is of pride, because he has taken and assumed to himself all the power of Christ our Saviour, and placed himself on his throne, making the people believe that he is Christ on earth." Wherefore we conclude, that, as Swedenborg here expressly says, "Christ our Saviour is the *only pontifex maximus*," and that the states general are his vicar, with senators as the vicar of this vicar, so that, in all cases, the representative of the Lord as the head of his church is a *complex* and not an *individual* man, therefore, when he says, *in Ecclesia erit Primus infulatus*, he by no means intends to teach that *any one man* should be *ut caput in Ecclesia*, in any of her larger or smaller forms; and, of course, that no one man should hold the office of *pontifex maximus*, or be regarded as *pontiff*, in the New Jerusalem on earth.*

Antistites parochi—What do these terms imply? They are rendered parish priests. But we cannot think that Swedenborg employed them in so technical a sense as to signify any such particular officers of the prevailing christian church. He is not teaching what should be the precise external order of the new church. He is illustrating a universal principle of orderly arrangement in the new heaven, the new hell, and the new church, by what is known to be true of the church abstractly considered. Therefore he designedly uses terms of the most general import to denote the functions and functionaries that are subordinate in the second degree to those of the highest degree of all churches. · Consequently, he could not have intended to specify the functionaries of the lutheran or any other particular church, as those who *shall* or *will* be officers of the second degree in the trine of the new-church ministry. He selects such words as will "convey a *general* idea of the *nature* of the *office* and *duty* of," officers of the second grade in general. Therefore, he purposely selects his words from ancient usage, instead of taking "the technical terms of any known body of the christian church"; and even of *those* words, he takes those that have the most *general* import. *Antistes* was a latin word not exclusively used in reference to the ecclesiastical order. It was used to signify the master of any art—the man who, by his ori-

---

* Swedenborg, in the continuation of the Last Judgment, n. 59, speaking of Pope Sextus V., says—"It rarely happens that any one, who had been pope in this world, acts as pontiff in the spiritual world. Nevertheless, he, who was pope of Rome twenty years ago, was appointed to this office, by reason of the belief he had entertained in his heart, that the Word was more holy than is generally imagined, and that the Lord ought to be worshiped. But after having exercised the papal function for some years, *he resigned it of his own accord*, and betook himself to the Reformed Christians, among whom he still abides, and enjoys a blessed life." Is not this indirect proof that the office of a pontiff is not in true order? Therefore, *erit Primus infulatus*, does not imply that there must be a pontiff in the new church.

ginal inventions and masterly executions, not only stood before and
above all other men in it, but who was, as it were, the creator or
father of his art: as such he was called *antistes artis*. It was also
used to signify one who stood at the head of his profession. Thus a
lawyer of great eminence was called *juris antistes*. It was a general
term for the ministers of religion. Hence Cicero has—*Antistites cere-
moniarum et sacrorum*, who were to exercise *auctorem et magistratum
publicæ religionis*. It was used to denote the priests who presided
over and directed the performance of religious rites in the temples of
divine worship, in contradistinction to those who were the preachers
or expounders of the principles of religion. Thus Gallius says—
*Alii antistites Deorum immortalium, alii interpretes religionem requi-
rendi*. It was a term especially applied to the priestesses of the
temple of Ceres. The word being a common noun, was applied to
both male and female priests. But Cicero preferred giving to the
word a femine termination when it signified the priestesses of Ceres,
and called them *antistitæ*. The fact that this term was applied to the
priests of *Ceres*, the deity who provided men with the fruits of the
earth for their bodily support and pleasure, is pertinent. Thus *antistes*
was a term used to signify a priest of a higher order—one who stood
above or before others in rank, function or excellence. Hence it
signified a high priest of religion. It is plain, then, that Swedenborg
uses it to signify a priest of the higher order; and uses the term
parochus, to denote the peculiar *function* of the priest of this degree.
Parochus, as anciently used, had no ecclesiastical import whatever.
Its strict meaning was, a public purveyor—one who, under the roman
government, furnished entertainment to foreign ambassadors at the
public expense. An entertainment, or repast, so given was called
parocha. The meaning of *parochus* was gradually extended to one
who more generally provided necessaries for those who travelled at the
public expense. And as such an officer became, in process of time,
what we should now call a government *contractor* for a defined district of country, the word, that at first only denoted the contractor,
came at length to signify his district; and hence the derivation of our
word *parish*. For the early theologians of the christian era, called a
minister,—who had the care of souls, and acted in the office of providing for their spiritual support on their heavenward journey, in a
certain district of country,—*parochus*. But it is presumable that
Swedenborg employs the term, not in its early christian, but in its
ancient roman, usage: and in that usage it denoted a provider, at the
public expense, of necessaries for those who travelled. Hence, also,
parochius was used to signify public provision and largess. The latin
word is, in fact, nothing more than an adoption from the greek. In
the greek language, πάροχος derived from a word signifying to *place
near* and to *present*, signified both one who sat beside another in a
chariot, and also one who furnished necessaries. *In view of both of
these senses*, we suppose that Swedenborg carefully and designedly
chose the word, and joined it to *Antistites*, to denote, in general,
priests of a secondary order, and their distinctive function. For as
the πάροχος drove the chariot for his superior officer, sitting beside

him, so ministers of the second grade in the church, should give doctrinal instructions in religion, in due subordination to ministers of the 'highest grade.' Ministers of the highest grade teach and govern the church from love, or the wisdom of love. Ministers of the second grade should teach the church from the intelligence of wisdom. And thus the one should be subordinate to the other as intelligence is subordinate to wisdom. This should not be any thing like the subordination of arbitrary government or of imperious sway; but the willing, free, and spontaneous deference which we pay to those who, in our own perception and by common consent, are in superior love of souls and of heavenly use, and are, consequently, in eminent station above us; And as the *κοροχος* furnished supplies to those who travelled at the public expense, so the ministers of the second degree in the church should provide spiritual food for those who are travelling to Canaan at the expense of the King of Kings. In Swedenborg's use of the terms, then, *Antistites parochi* signify ministers of the second degree in the church, whose especial function it is to furnish spiritual necessaries to the people.

Parochi is here a noun governed in the genitive case by *Antistites*, and is precisely equivalent, in grammatical construction, to *Primus civitatis.* If this word had been an adjective, it would have been put in the nominative, plural, masculine, to agree with *Antistites* as *infulatus* does with *Primus.* But it is a noun used adjectively, that is, it is the name of a functionary used to denote his function abstractly. And the term *Antistites* is used to denote those who *excel* in that' function—stand before, above, or ahead of, others in it. Wherefore, *Antistites parochi*, who should be *ut corpus in Ecclesia*, are, in general, priests of a second discrete grade in the priesthood, whose especial function it is to *feed the flock* as *good shepherds of the sheep.* Therefore, ministers of the second grade are *pastors;* that is, those who excel in spiritual intelligence; and, from superior intelligence, instruct the people in those spiritual truths that pertain to their eternal good, and by wise example, as well as wise counsel, go before them and lead them in "the way everlasting"—in wisdom's ways, which are pleasantness, and in her paths of peace. "By viaticum, (provisions for the journey,) is signified support from truth and good." (A. C. 5490.) "Spiritual food is science, intelligence and wisdom; for from these things spirits and angels live and also are nourished." (A. C. 4792.) The provider of spiritual food for the journey of life, which is advancement in regeneration, is one who, by instructions, helps to store up truths adjoined to good in the interiors of the natural mind, there to be preserved together for the use of the subsequent life, especially for use in temptations during man's regeneration. (A. C. 5342.) "It is known in the church, that to feed signifies to instruct; pasture signifies instruction; and a pastor, or shepherd, signifies an instructor." (Ap. Ex. 482.) "To find pasture denotes to be taught, illustrated and nourished in divine truths." (Ap. Rev. 914.) And "a shepherd of the flock is one who exercises the good of charity. He who leads and teaches is called *shepherd;* they who are lead and taught are called the *flock.* He who does not lead to the good of charity, and does not teach the good of charity, is not a true shepherd; and he who is not led to good, and does not learn what is good, is not of the flock." (A. C. 343.)

Flamen is a pure latin word. Its derivation we have already stated. It had none but an ecclesiastical acceptation with the Latins. The Romans used it as a generic name for a certain order of priests. *Flamines, quod in licio capite velato erant semper, ac caput cinctum habebant filo, Flamines, dicti,* says Varro. There were other derivations of the term; but they all took their rise from the head dress, which, in winter, was made of yarn, and, in summer, of thread, and of a red or flame color. Hence, whether the term was derived from *filo, pileo,* or *flammo—flamines* became a generic priestly appellative. Hence, also, *flaminium* denoted the priesthood, and *flaminio abire* meant to resign its functions. The Romans were eminently and deeply a religious people. Or, perhaps, it would be more proper to say, they were in the highest degree a *superstitious* people. Of them, it might truly be said, they had "god's many;" and in all things they acknowledged them. From them they sought inspiration in their poems and epic literature. They invoked their auspices on going to battle, and hung up in their temples the trophies of victorious war, in devout acknowledgment of their favoring smiles. In short, nothing was projected, and nothing done, without imploring their blessing, or deprecating their wrath. Hence, they not only erected temples for their public worship, but they consecrated to them their halls of legislation, their courts of justice, their political meeting-houses, their places of business and their private dwellings. They adored personifications of human virtues and vices, deified their heroes and remarkable benefactors, and acknowledged presiding deities in all the hidden powers of nature. Emerging from the relics of ancient times, they had around them, in dim and obscure twilight, the many-shaped and variegated shadows of perverted representatives. Hence, in their chief magistrate were combined the regal and priestly offices. Romulus, the founder of their city and first king, was also their high priest. He acknowledged the gods of the Latians, and respected their religious rites. He was too much occupied with the warlike cares necessarily attendant on the founding of a state in those times, to pay much or sufficient attention to the institutes of religion. But he succeeded in finishing his regal work, and, leaving to his successor a fuller discharge of the duties of his priestly office, received in death " an apotheosis and rites divine." Numa Pompilius, the second king of Rome, was a man of peace, and therefore of religion. Secure in the possession of civil power, he applied himself to the thorough regulation of ecclesiastical affairs. He wrote eight books, in which he treated fully of the various kinds of religious rites and ceremonies. And he it was who first instituted the priesthood of the *flamines*. As we have seen, these were strictly *priests,* who officiated in making sacrifices to the gods, in contradistinction to those who were teachers of religious principles, and makers of ecclesiastical laws or judges in sacred causes. These latter were called *pontifices*. Besides these, there were what were called *sacerdotes*. The functions of the *sacerdos* were of a mixed nature. He might be the priest of several and various gods. The *pontifices* were the priests of all the gods in general; and were united in a college, with a *pontifex maximus* at their head, and the *sacerdotes* and *flamines* in subordination to them. Each *flamen* was the priest of a particular deity, who presided over, directed and performed the sacred rites appropriate to the temple of that god, and by no means had any thing to do with those of any other. His wife was a priestess, and officiated in the performance of certain sacred rites, like himself. Under these there were both male and female officials, called *flaminii* and *flaminiae*. Of these priests, Numa, originally, appointed three, and called them after the gods to whom they severally sacrificed. The chief deities of Rome then were, Jupiter, Mars and Quirinus, the divine appellation of Romulus. From these three deities the priests appointed by Numa were called, *Flamen Dialis, Flamen Martialis,* and *Flamen Quirinalis.* The first named was the highest in dignity and authority. In process of time, there were twelve more added to these three, making in all fifteen. These were priests of inferior deities, named after the gods whose worship they superintended, and taking rank according to the honor in which their deities were respectively held by the people. The lowest of the twelve was the *Flamen Pomonalis,* because the goddess Pomona, was the fostering divinity of the less valued fruits. Between the first three and the subsequent twelve flamines, there was a remarkable distinction. The former were appointed from the patricians and were called *flamines majores;* the latter were appointed from the plebeians, and were called *flamines minores.* The *flamines minores* were elected by the people in their primary meetings, but were inaugurated into the priestly office by the chief priest, being taken by the hand, and led up to him, for that purpose, by the patricians. The *flamines majores,* although not members of the pontifical college, were allowed to sit as judges in that college, together with the *pontifices,* whenever there was any cause to be tried concerning matters within their special jurisdiction. Besides these fifteen superior *flamines,* there were thirty others of a still lower grade—one for each of the thirty *curiae,* into which the three tribes of the city of Rome had been divided by Romulus. In each of these *curiae,* Romulus himself had appointed a chief or head man, called *curio,* who was at the same time the priest of the city district under his control. For, as we have seen, the Romans had religious rites performed in all of their meetings—in the hall of legislation, the court of justice, and the place of political meeting—in the senate, the forum, and the curia. These *Curiones* were the representatives of the king in his pontifical character in these lowest districts of his government. Numa perpetuated them, giving precise formularies for the regulation of their sacred rites in his Institutes of Religion. And the reason assigned for his creation of the higher *flamines,* and especially the *Flamen Dialis,* is thus stated by Livy :—Tum Sacerdotibus creandis animum adjecit, quanquam ipse plurima sacra obibat, ea maxime quae nunc ad Dialem Flaminem pertinent. Sed quia in civitate bellicosa plures Romuli quam Numae similes Reges putabat fore, iturosque ipsos ad bella: ne

sacra regiae vicis desererentur, *Flaminem Jovi* assiduum Sacerdotem
creavit, insignique eum Veste et Curuli regia sella adornavit : huic *duos*
Flamines adjecit, *Marti* unum, alterum *Quirino.* The *curia* was both
a ward of the city, and a council chamber, in which the citizens of
that ward met for political purposes. The meeting of the citizens was
called *comitium*, which term also was applied to the place of meeting.
And the houses in which they were held were also sacred edifices or
temples on account of the sacred rites which were performed in them.
In after times, these *Curiones* were special priests, chosen *a populo*
Comitiis Curialis;—each priest by the votes of his own ward,—inaugurated or consecrated by the *Pontifex Maximus*, and called *Curiales*
Flamines, because they performed sacrificial rites in these wards of
the city, or arranged and directed the religious ceremonies of the
curiae. Each *flamen* had the charge of religious rites in his own
ward, uncontrolled by the other flamines in his duties, and uncon-
trolling them in theirs. But they were all under the supervision and
direction of a president, called *Curio Maximus*, who was elected
omnium Curiarum suffragiis. Besides these, there were less regular
sacred functionaries, such as augurs, diviners, soothsayers, oracular
priests, &c. Thus there were, in ancient Rome, three orders of regular
priests—*Pontifices, Sacerdotes, Flamines*—with the *Pontifex Maxi-*
mus or *Rex sacrorum* at their head. And there were also three
degrees of the flamines—*Flamines Majores, Flamines Minores, et*
Curiales Flamines—with the *Flamen Dialis* at their head. Or there
were *Flamen Dialis vel Primus*, praeterea *Flamines Majores et*
Minores, et Curiales Flamines sub illis; affording a very remarkable
illustration and verification of what Swedenborg teaches, that the
divine order, which fills all and every thing in the universe, even to
the most minute particulars, tends to produce every where, and at
all times, an arrangement of all things in trinal order.

Now there can be very little doubt that Swedenborg, by *Flamines*
sub illis, meant priests of the lowest or most inferior order, like these
Curiales Flamines in the roman polity. They might, therefore, be
called *curates*, because priests of the *curia*, but not because they were
to be curates *under* parish priests in the *same* places of worship; for
this *flamen* was himself the presiding minister of religion in his own
place of worship, with *flaminii* under him. Nor have we the least
idea that Swedenborg purposely chose this term to teach that the
lowest grade in the trine of the new-church ministry should be the
pastor of a society. He merely intended to signify priests of the
lowest degree, which should be *ut pedes et plantae in ecclesia.* And
in view of this, it is not a little remarkable, that he should have
written *Primus* and *Antistites* with a capital first letter, but *flamines*
without. All, then, that Swedenborg here teaches is, that there must
be in *every* priesthood a lowest grade of priests, standing and acting
on a plane as discretely below the planes of two higher grades as air
is discretely below ether and aura, and being *sub illis*, or subordinate
to the priests in those two higher grades, as the *Curiales Flamines* were
subordinate to the *Flamines Minores et Flamines Majores.* What
may be the particular nature of each grade—what the special func-

tions of each, or what the relative jurisdiction, power and authority of the three, is certainly not taught by Swedenborg in this sentence, and is to be wholly determined by the state and genius of the particular parts of the general or universal church, and by the nature, degree, or extent of the priestly offices which are to be filled or the priestly uses which are to be performed. Hence, in one form of the new-church trine, the pastor of a society may be the minister of the lowest grade; in another, the lowest minister may be the curate of a parish priest. In one, the minister of the lowest grade may be the assistant of the minister of the second grade in the same place of worship; in another, the minister of the lowest grade may stand and act on a discretely lower plane of his own. And the reason is, because there may be a trine of discrete degrees in each plane, as well as a trine of discrete planes. The most perfect order requires both. But, in the incipiency of a church, both may not yet be fully developed.

Flamines sub illis, then, is a general formula to denote a lowest grade of priests or ministers in every church. Of the precise nature of the functions of ministers of this grade it teaches nothing. *Sub illis* merely denotes subordination in general. It denotes, relatively to higher ministers in the ecclesiastical trine, *pedal* subordination. And what this is in the ministerial functions of the church, we must infer from the functional character of the other two grades. If, then, the priest of the highest grade is distinctively the minister of *wisdom;* and the priest of the middle grade is distinctively the minister of *intelligence;* then the priest of this lowest or pedal grade must be distinctively the minister of *knowledge:* for priestly wisdom and intelligence stand upon the knowledges of spiritual truth as upon their feet, the soles of which are those natural sciences by which spiritual truth is illustrated in the natural mind. We take this to be the true import of this much mooted authority from Swedenborg for a trine in the new-church ministry. And we shall make it the basis of the particular order which we design to recommend for our church in this country.

We might here argue, that Swedenborg did not intend to designate the precise offices and officers of the trine in the new church by his occasionally mentioning such a trine in the course of his writings, because he does not uniformly use the same terms. Thus we have—

Primus infulatus	*Antistites parochi*	*flamines*
Primate	*Pastor*	*Priest*
Primate	*Minister*	*Canonical Person*
Prelates	*Inferior Canons*	*Presbyters*

Summus Sacerdos, (C. L. 266,) &c.

Is it not evident, from the bare inspection of this list, that nothing can be more inconclusive, than a deduction, from the terms used by Swedenborg in denoting a trine of the priesthood, of what should be precisely the kind of external or formal trine in the new church? In showing the futility of baptism without its uses, Swedenborg says, (U. T. 673,) "Baptism, therefore, if it be without its uses and fruits, contributes no more towards salvation than the *triple cap* on the *pope's* head, and the *sign* of the *cross* on his shoes, contribute towards his pontifical super-eminence; nor than a *cardinal's purple robe*, to his dignity; nor than a *bishop's lawn sleeves*, to the discharge of his ministry." Here we have the trine—pope, cardinals, and bishops under them. And there is the trine of official badges—the triple cap, the purple robe, and the lawn sleeves. Now, because Swedenborg mentions these in connection with baptism, and for the illustration of its true order, are we to infer that he means to teach that the trine in the new-church ministry, and the badges of their discretely official functions, should be precisely these which are mentioned here? We presume that no one will say so. Yet it seems to us no more reasonable to suppose that Swedenborg any more intended to teach this by either of the verbal triads which we have given in the above list. We conclude, then, that nothing more is to be inferred from Swedenborg's language in each and all of these cases, than that there must be in the new-church ministry, to make that a perfect thing, or a full formation, a trine of priests, one under another, with interceding communication, and all together forming one coherent priesthood, as the head, body and extremities form one man. And we repeat, that, as to the precise nature of the gradation amongst these priests, or the precise relation of their distinct duties, functions, jurisdictions, authorities or powers, to one another, all this must be determined by the state of the general church, by the character of its distinct parts, and by the more or less perfect development of the external order that is truly representative of, or correspondent to, its internal principles. As an expression of such a trine in its most abstract and most generally applicable form, Swedenborg uses the formula—*In Ecclesia, Primus infulatus, Antistites parochi, et flamines sub illis*. And to render this properly into english, we must use the terms of a formula equally generic and abstract. In want of a better, we propose the following—*In the church, there must be a wise head officer, intelligent pastors, and subordinate teachers*.

In concluding this topic of authorities for the trine, we have one application to make. The priesthood of the new church is a strictly representative one. It is to represent the Lord in the three degrees of his work of saving mankind. This work is all uses in the complex. The Lord's priestly offices are priestly uses. Of these uses, it is conceded that there is a trine. As priestly functions they may be indicated by the trine in baptism—1, Introduction into the church and insertion amongst Christians in the spiritual world—2, Acknowledgment of the Lord as the Redeemer, which implies such a reformation by truth in the life of his precepts as gives the *quality* of that *truth*, and so the *name* of Christ—3, The being regenerated by him, which implies such an implantation of good as effects a radical change of the will, bringing it under the impulses of love to God and charity to the neighbor, instead of love to self and love to the world, and so giving the *name* of Jesus, in the *quality* of the *good* which that most sacred name denotes. According to the universal law, these three uses of baptism cohere in one. Thus, as there is a trine of uses in baptism, so there is a trine of uses in the ministry of the new church. For the three uses of baptism are as man's ascent by reformation and

35

regeneration in the order of the three heavens, which order of ascent the priesthood represents. Now these three uses are first, as science (or knowledge) and obedience; second, as intelligence and wisdom; third, as wisdom and love. There is, then, this double trine to denote what is essential and formal in the uses, the ministries and the ministers of the priesthood, namely, obedience, wisdom, love, and knowledge, intelligence, wisdom. What, then, should be the trine of uses in our priesthood? The report of the English General Conference has answered the question. The Rev. William Mason has favored us with his views. These differ from those set forth in the report of Conference. May there not be various trines of ministerial uses, and all be right? Well, what other view have you to present? The following. We think that all priestly uses are subject to this most general trinal demarcation—

I. The use of *representing the Lord* in and to the whole church.

II. The use of *representing the church* in worship, and of *serving the church* in the administration of whatever pertains to the divine law.

III. The use of *disseminating those knowledges of truth* by which alone there can be conjunction of man with God for the salvation of souls.

If 'there is any conceivable use that a minister of the church can perform in the discharge of priestly functions, which is not embraced in the above trine of general uses, we shall feel happy to have it pointed out. The first embraces, we believe, all the functions of the ministry in general, but particularly those of a minister of the highest grade—in ordaining other ministers, consecrating places of holy divine worship, and in giving whatever benediction or blessing, or in performing whatever general priestly function, that pertains to the administering on earth of the things belonging to the priesthood of the Lord, that is, to the work of his love, in the highest degree. The second embraces all the functions of the *pastoral* office, generally in all the grades, but particularly in the second. The third embraces all the functions of the *ministerial* office, generally in all the grades, but particularly in the first.

The duties of a christian priest, in particular, may be seen to be three-fold, thus :—

I. To teach the people, and lead them by truth to good.

II. In their name, and on their behalf, to present before the Lord their offerings of prayer, praise and thanksgiving, which are spiritual oblations.

III. To administer the sacraments, which are the christian purificatory and sacrificial rites, instituted instead of the jewish washings and sacrifices.

And all the authorities for the trinal order which have here been presented, are rays of light and evidence converging to this focus—there must be in the priesthood of the New Jerusalem an essential trine, as representatives of *Love, Wisdom,* and *Use;* and a formal trine, as representatives of *Wisdom, Intelligence* and *Science.* This is the doctrine of the ministerial trine in the abstract. What it may be in the concrete, we shall now proceed to show in the following and last head of this report.

IX. AS TO WHAT MAY BE A PROPER FORM OF THE TRINE IN THE NEW CHURCH AND HER MINISTRY IN THE UNITED STATES.

We confess, we have little hope that any thing which may be offered under this head will be available in practice. Not because we have any doubt of the truth of the order here advanced, or any misgiving as to its being the best to establish and extend our heavenly faith, but because we imagine it is so contrary to preconceived opinion or pre-established usage, that the church cannot be readily brought to its adoption. Still we feel it our duty to submit to the consideration, not only of our own convention, but of the church more at large, the conclusions on this subject to which our minds have come, after a long and prayerful study of what, under Divine Providence, might be the most effectual means of establishing our church, of widening her borders, of securing her integrity, and thus of advancing our holy cause on earth. And we do trust, that hints here thrown out, may prove seeds sown, to produce a harvest of use in the future.

The first thoughts that come up to the mind in contemplating the subject before us, are the questions, What is primarily and chiefly to be done in effecting the Lord's end in establishing the church on earth? What is that end? What are the means of effecting it? What is to be done, and how are we to do it, so far as the priesthood, or ministry, as the Lord's instrument, is concerned? All will agree that these are most momentous questions, which deserve the profoundest attention and the wisest answers that we can give them or get for them. We shall, of course, look for light where alone we have any reason to expect we can find it clearly true and rightly guiding. We purpose merely to throw out hints, founded on the following teachings of Swedenborg, and on the conclusions to which we have come in this report.

1. It is conceded on all hands that there is a trine of ministerial uses. We believe that there should be a trine of ministers to perform them. We also believe that the trine of ministers should correspond to, and be determined by, the uses they are to perform. We know "the use of every thing is *pre-existent*"; but we also know that it "ought to be *foreseen* and *provided for*." (Spirit. Diary, 3574.) "By uses are meant goods; and hence, by doing uses, is meant to do goods; and by doing uses or goods, is meant to serve others and to minister to them." (D. P. 215.) "There are two things which constitute a church—good of life and truth of doctrine; the marriage of these is the church." (U. T. 510.) Consequently, the church has two chief ministries, the ministry of good, and the ministry of truth: the former laical, the latter clerical—the one, insinuation of good into another, the other, insinuation of truth—the one, the province of every man in the community, the other, the especial province of "teaching ministers." (A. C. 6822.) "The good of charity from the Lord, and the truth of faith with man as from him, when conjoined, make the church." (C. L. 126.) "Charity is an affection of being serviceable to others without having respect to any recom-

pense"; and "the neighbor, towards whom charity is to be exercised, is *all* in the universe, but still *each* with discrimination." (A. C.
2417.) "The church is more a neighbor than a man's country; for
he, who provides for the church, provides for the souls and eternal
life of the men who inhabit the country; and the church is provided
for when man is led to good. . . . Good may be insinuated into
another by every one in the country, but not truth, except by those
who are teaching ministers; if others insinuate truth, it gives birth to
heresies, and the church is disturbed and rent asunder. . . Every
one ought *first to acquire truth to himself from the doctrine of the
church*, and afterwards from the Word of the Lord, and· this truth
must be the object of his faith." (A. C. 6822.) The Lord's end in
creating mankind is a heaven of human beings. (D. P. 323.) The
church on earth is established as a means of attaining this end, by
consociating mankind with heaven, and conjoining them, through
heaven, with the Lord. (A. C. 637.) "The Lord's kingdom is
nothing but a kingdom of uses." (A. C. 5395.) "The kingdom of
the Lord is the same with the church, only with this difference; that
the kingdom of the Lord on earth is called the church." (A. C. 8900.)
So that "the church is the Lord's kingdom in the earths." (Ap. Ex.
630.) The way to attain the Lord's end in the creation of mankind
is, therefore, to establish and extend the church, which, being charity
in form, does the Lord's work by her works of charity; "for the
divine principle, when it descends to the natural principle appertaining to man, fixes its descent in such 'things as works of charity,
with discrimination as to genera and species." (A. C. 2417.) Consequently, as to attain the Lord's end is to do his work, the only way
to attain his end is to establish his church, and extend her works of
charity. Now the church, consisting in charity, or "in performing
uses," (A. C. 8253,) is established and extended by the ministry of
truth; for "a life of charity is a life of use" and "the life of charity
is in continual birth, and growth, and receiving of increase, and this
by means ·of truth. Therefore, the more truth is inseminated, so
much the more the life of charity is perfected. Consequently, the
state of charity in man, is according to the *quality* and *quantity* of
truth." (A. C. 2189.) Of course, a chief means of effecting the
Lord's end, as above set forth, is a true and orderly "teaching
ministry": for this is the only proper means of insinuating truth, by
which the life of charity, that constitutes the church, has birth and
growth; and this ministry must be true and orderly, because on this
depends the *quality* and *quantity* of truth insinuated, according to
which the *state* of charity is in man. Hence, as the first ingredient
in "the common good that exists from the goods of use performed by
individuals," is "what is divine among the people," therefore the
first among the "ministries, functions, offices and various employments, or the goods which individuals perform, and from which the
community exists," are "priestly offices, and the duties annexed to
them;" for "they who belong to the ministry, provide for the
existence of things divine." (Doct. of Char. VI. 62–70.) Hence
"the priesthood is the first order of the church," (Ap. Ex. 229;)

for its ministries are of the highest order, and its ministers perform
the highest uses. They are the medium of that illustration and
instruction which the influx of the Lord's holy spirit effects. (U. T.
146.) The holy spirit passes "especially through the clergy to the
laity." (Can. ch. iv.) And the falsities of the old faith are first to
be extirpated from the minds of the clergy, and by their means from
the minds of the laity, (U. T. 784,) before the truths of the new faith
can be inseminated for the establishment and extension of the church.
As, then, ministerial uses are the highest in kind and first in order,
and, although they may be "pre-existent," yet "ought to be *foreseen*
and *provided for*"; it is clearly the very first duty of "Eve, the
mother of all living"—of the church, as the mother, to provide
priests for priestly ministries. This is the first work of her charity.
The second is, to provide for their maintenance in the discharge of
their functions. And the provision of priestly functionaries implies
the determining of their true form of order from their true use: for
"use is as it were the soul, because its form is, as it were, the body,"
(D. L. & W. 310;) and hence, in bringing the ministry into its true
external order, there is, as it were, a provision of a body, in and by
which ministerial use, as a soul, may be developed in its true form
and efficiency. If, then, these things be true, it is the first and paramount duty of every general church in this country, to provide a
true and orderly ministry—to provide for its efficient support, and,
that it may act efficiently in performing its appropriate uses, to form
and establish it in its true external order. And that a ministry may
be formed and established, the true principles of its external order
must be determined and set forth. Thus do we magnify the necessity
and importance of what ought to be presented under this head of our
report.

2. But a ministry must be first produced, before it can be established
and sustained in true external order—must be created, before it can
be formed. The Lord's end in creating mankind is their eternal happiness. They are created to be happy for ever in heaven. And this
end cannot be effected without *their conjunction with the God who
made them.* For this purpose the church is established on earth. For
this purpose, as we have seen, the holy sacrament of baptism, and
the most holy sacrament of the supper, as mere representative and
significative rites, were instituted. (Ap. Ex. 475.) And for this purpose the priesthood is chiefly required and established. What, then,
is the especial thing which the priesthood is to be the instrument of
effecting in promoting this purpose? Perhaps the following extracts
from the writings of Swedenborg will fully instruct us on this point.
"The sons of Jacob being born in Padan Aram, represented that the
man of the church *must be born anew, or regenerated, by the* KNOW-
LEDGES *of good and truth;* for Padan Aram signifies those knowledges,
and nativity represented the new birth by faith and charity—thus
first by the *knowledges* thereof." (A. C. 6025.) "For the knowledge
of a thing must needs precede the perception of it." (A. C. 5649.)
"No one can be purified from filthy loves unless he be principled in
truth. It is by virtue of truth that he knows what is pure and impure,

and what is holy and profane. Before this is known, there are no mediums on which and by which heavenly love can operate, which continually flows in from the Lord, and *which cannot be received except in truths.* Wherefore, *by the knowledges of truth man is reformed and regenerated;* and reformation and regeneration *cannot be effected before man is initiated into truths.*" (A. C. 2046.) " The Lord's external man, or human essence, was joined to the divine essence by degrees, according to the multiplication and fructification of knowledges. *It is not possible for any one, as man, to be joined to Jehovah, or the Lord,* EXCEPT BY KNOWLEDGES : for *by knowledges man becomes man.* This was the case with the Lord, inasmuch as he was born like another man.*" (A. C. 1616.) . In view of these teachings, there surely need be no doubt in answering the question, What is to be first done in establishing the church ? Does it not follow, from the above, that the first thing is the procuring the knowledges of truth, and employing the best means for their dissemination ? And if, as has been shown, " the priesthood is the first order of the church," the provision of " what is divine among the people " is charity's first duty, and " they who belong to the ministry, provide for the existence of things divine," is it not the very first duty of the general church to provide those who may " belong to the ministry " ? And if the Lord's end of conjoining mankind with himself for their eternal happiness—if the reformation and regeneration of mankind for this purpose—if the purification of them from filthy loves—*cannot possibly be effected except by knowledges of truth,* and if the best means of providing and disseminating these is the provision of those who may belong to the ministry—is it not, most clearly, the first and paramount duty of charity to provide men of suitable *learning,* and for this to provide the requisite *education ?* For how else can the *knowledges* of truth be procured; and, when procured, how can they be conveyed to others for their conjunction with the Lord except by ministers, both *versed in them,* and APT *to teach them* to other men ? Certainly our duty is clear enough. And a voice from on high does now most emphatically say, " This is the way, walk ye in it!" Wherefore, in our efforts to establish and extend the New Jerusalem, we greatly err, if the first thing we do is to provide for the mere performance of external worship in public, by building a temple, or hiring a room, and appointing a sayer of prayers, and singer of psalms, and reader of sermons. For the very first thing is to provide the means of *education*—especially the education of those who may " belong to the ministry," and by the acquisition of the requisite learning themselves, be able to " provide for the existence of things divine" among the people. When ministers are thus provided by the Lord;—for the Lord cannot or does not provide them in any other way ; " because the love of the Lord is to perform uses to the community, and to each society in the community, and *he performs these* BY MEANS OF MEN *who are principled in love to him* " (Ap. Rev. 353;)—*then,* and *not till then,* are places of worship to be provided for them to preach in, and is provision to be made for their support in leading worship and teaching truth in temples. Thus the first thing in order is the production of a priesthood by suitable education and training.

3. This leads us to see the use of the trine for the gradual development of the priesthood in the ascending order of the ark's translation from Gibeah of Judah, through Obed-edom, to Zion, of which we have treated at length under our head of authorities. For we are led to see the need of gradual preparation for the ministry by the state of a student before he becomes a priest, and of the preparatory state of a priest before he becomes a pastor. This results from the need of education, not only for the ministers, but also for the people. For there is another reason why, education should thus precede provision for public worship in temples, namely, the *foundation* of the house should be laid, and *well* laid, *in the minds of the people*, before the *superstructure* is put upon it. The great use of worship in temples, is the conjunction of the souls of men, through heaven, with the Lord. This cannot be effected, we have seen, without the knowledges of truth. Hence the need of a priesthood to acquire such knowledges by learning, and to communicate them by preaching. But these are knowledges of *spiritual* truth, which cannot be received by the people, if they be not first instructed in the knowledges of *natural* truth. For *natural* truth is the *foundation* of spiritual truth in the mind. And the knowledges of natural truth must first be acquired by prior *education*, before there is any plane in the minds of the people for the reception of the instructions of a spiritual teacher from the pulpit. And is not the *want* of such a prior education, the true reason why the preachers of the spiritual sense of the Word from our new-church pulpits have had such little success hitherto, in either gathering large flocks around them, or in properly feeding the few and scattering sheep of whom they have been made the pastors? Without suitable education in the knowledge of natural things amongst the people, the preacher of spiritual truth is not able to illustrate things as they exist in the spiritual world, and so in the spiritual sense of the Word, by the knowledge of those natural things which correspond to them in the natural world. And there is no other way of making the unknown things of the other world comprehensible by men while they reside in this. " For the invisible things of God, are clearly seen from the creation of the world, being understood by the things that are made." (Rom. i. 20.) Hence, if people do not know the things that are made, the invisible things of God, which are spiritual and celestial truths in his Word, cannot be understood. Hence Swedenborg says, " The illustration of things unknown, [by which he means the spiritual sense of the Word,] and such as transcend the apprehension, tends rather to render them obscure than to throw light upon them; *besides that such things ought to be established as a* SUPERSTRUCTURE *on the* IDEAS OF NATURAL TRUTHS, *whereby they are to be apprehended; and these also are at this day wanting*." [A. C. 3596.) Can any thing be clearer? Would that the instructions from our new-church pulpits were half as clear as this! Is it not perfectly clear that *the ideas of natural truths* must first be laid by previous education in the minds of worshiping assemblies as a foundation for the superstructure of those knowledges of spiritual truth from the internal sense of the Word, without which it is impossible for man-

kind to be conjoined with God and so eternally happy ?* Therefore it is clear that there should be in the priesthood a grade of priests to teach spiritual truth in the natural degree, who must stand and act on a plane as discretely below that of the spiritual pastor as the natural heaven is discretely below the spiritual heaven. And is it not equally clear, that not only the true sense of the Word, but also the true order of heaven, which is the true order of the church, cannot "be apprehended" without the ideas of natural truths having been laid as a foundation in the minds of the people by suitable education? Then, may not *this* be the true reason why so much needs to be said, and why it is now so hard for people generally to receive what is so truly said, about *the trine in the ministry*? Certain are we, that, if professing members of the new church generally were better informed in natural science, or were to apply their knowledge of natural things to the elucidation of the subject, not half of what has been written would be needed to convince every one of them that there *must* be a trine in the new-church ministry; and that so much labor is needed on our part to make this subject perfectly clear and universally convincing, must be imputed to *the sin of ignorance* which lies at their door!

Well, to attain the Lord's end in creating man, there must be the knowledges of truth. The church must provide them, and must provide the ministers of truth for their dissemination amongst mankind. That ministers may be the efficient servants of mankind in this function, they must be themselves well and thoroughly learned. That the people may be able to receive the knowledges of spiritual truths from their ministers, they also must be previously educated, so as to have those ideas of natural truths whereby alone spiritual truths can be apprehended. Therefore, it is the first and most imperative duty of the church to provide education for her children. This is a pre-existent use which she must "*foresee* and *provide for.*" And for this purpose she must provide a ministry. For *in Ecclesia, erit flamines, ut pedes et plantae* in man. And as natural knowledges are the foundation for the knowledges of spiritual truth, just as science is the foundation of intelligence and wisdom, so there must be priests as

---

* All the objections to this view arise out of old-church prejudice. In the old christian church, which is now consummated by the extinction of all genuine charity and the consequent want of all true faith—in which the understanding is bound in chains of adamant to the absurd dogmas of an irrational faith—and in which almost the whole of religion consists in the excitements of enthusiastic spirits, determined by glowing appeals to the passions or feelings of the natural man, the need of an educated ministry, and of an educated people, cannot be so easily felt. But even amongst the enthusiastic sects of the day, the absurd idea that the Holy Spirit magnifies his power by inspiring ignorance in the clergy and unbridled *passion* in the people, is becoming exploded; and we see them very generally raising the standard of theological attainment in their ministers, by institutions of learning for their better training, and of scientific attainment in their congregations, by popular lectures on the most needed branches of natural knowledge. This is remarkably the case with the Methodists, who, perhaps, more than all others, founded their sect upon enthusiastic religious excitement in its origin. But that any members of the New Jerusalem, over whose temple is now written "*Nunc licet*," should not see and feel the need of a well educated new-church clergy and laity, is astonishing indeed!

teachers of spiritual truth in the natural degree, *ut pedes*, with teachers of the sciences of natural truth, *ut plantae*, to prepare a plane in the minds of children and other people for the reception of the knowledges of spiritual truth, or for the illustration of those truths in their minds by the *pastoral* instructions of the pulpit—thus to serve as feet and soles to higher ministers *ut corpus et caput* in man. Thus does the principle, that the trine of the ministry should correspond to, and be determined by, the uses they are to perform, show us that there should be a priest of a first or lowest degree; and that the province of this priest should be, instruction in truth from the letter of the Word, and in all those natural sciences which are not only germain to the Word in the letter, such as the geography, natural history, and biography of its letter, but such sciences as afford those ideas of natural truths which are needed as a foundation for the apprehension of those spiritual truths which are to be built up as a mental superstructure upon them. Such a priest we suppose to be representatively a clerical foot in the priesthood. Below him, there should still be the state of a student, who is preparing for the ministry before he becomes a priest. He should be well versed in all the knowledge which natural education affords, before he begins the study of theology. And then, in our opinion, he should study from three to seven years, according to genius and capacity, but in all cases, at least three years, under an intelligent and settled pastor of the church, before he enters the ministry. This is indispensable to secure proper qualification for the ministry before entering it. During all the years of this probationary state except the last, the student for the ministry should be employed as the teacher of the children of the society. This teaching of children by the student, is a needed preparative to the teaching of adult persons by the minister. To show this might be well; but we have neither time nor space here: it must be taken for granted, and it is sufficiently obvious for that. The student will not only be directed in his studies by the pastor, but will also learn the exercise of pastoral duties by his example—as the student of medicine, under a talented and skilful practitioner, learns from him the *practice*, as well as the *theory*, by his example or clinical instructions. And this, in our opinion, is a most essential preparation for the pastoral office. None can so well know the use of such a preparation as those of us whose great inefficiency in the pastoral office can be clearly traced in our own minds to our not having enjoyed the privilege of so needed a probationary training. During the last year of the student's probationary state, he may be a licensed preacher under the pastor. In this capacity he may assist the pastor by reading prayers for him, and reading his sermons in case of his sickness or absence. During this year the licentiate may also perform the duties of the priest of the first grade in teaching natural science and truth from the letter of the Word to the society. He will himself begin to write sermons under the supervision and correction of the pastor. And thus he will be prepared to enter by ordination into the priesthood at the end of his probationary stage. How the province of the minister of the first grade should be distinct or discrete from that of the minister of the second grade, will be shown presently. Thus much has been stated here to show how provision for *education* in the church will be made in providing ministers of the first grade, and in preparing students for the ministry. It is sufficiently manifest, how this grade of the new-church priesthood may be made the basis for its two higher grades, in laying the *foundation* in the church itself, for them, as higher workmen, to rear the superstructure of spiritual illustration and instruction upon. It is clear, how the minister of the first grade may be as the foot, and the student for the ministry as the sole of the foot, in the priesthood, just as the letter of the Word, and the natural science which illustrates spiritual truth, are as the foot and soles to the church or heaven in man.

4. Now we discern what is to be *first* done, and *how* we are to do it, so far as the priesthood or ministry is concerned, in effecting the Lord's end in establishing the church on earth. The first thing is to establish a new-church seminary or university, for the general education of new-church children, in the higher branches of learning, and for the provision of students for the ministry in particular, and thus for teachers of new-church schools in societies. This, we believe, is the only effectual way to provide those knowledges of truth that are needed to conjoin mankind with the Lord for their salvation, as well as to provide the most effectual means of disseminating those knowledges. We know it is commonly said, the Lord will provide ministers for his church. This is true. But *how* does he provide them? We have just shown that his love performs all such uses to the community, and to each society in it, "*by means of men* who are principled in love to him." Now men who are principled in love to the Lord constitute his visible church—are in fact his *visible body*, by which he performs uses to the community, especially that highest use by which he provides those "who belong to the ministry," and in that capacity "provide for the existence of things divine," or provide "what is divine among the people." And as no one individual member of the church can or ought to perform this use, which is so common to all—as no one society of the church can or ought to do it—as, probably, no one of the present general conventions can properly perform this use—let all the receivers of our doctrines in the United States come together in convention for this purpose. It is a universal use, in the performance of which all should join, and which should receive the concentrate energies of the whole church for its best performance. And this, therefore, is one ground for the constitution of a most general body of the new church in the United States.

5. But suppose ministers have been furnished in the Lord's providence; and suppose the question to be, What is the first thing to be done in arranging and subordinating them as a priesthood for the firmest establishment and the widest extension of the church on earth? What would you do then? In answering this question, we may say, briefly, that we would first establish a *general* ministry, to preach this "everlasting gospel" to the gentiles, or honest men and sincere lovers of truth, wherever they may be found, *out* of the first or old christian church. Our law of action in this case, we have stated in a previous part of this report. It is not less full than simple and direct—*Follow*

the Lord's example, and do what we believe he would, were he now on earth. In determining action under this law, we observe what the Lord did, in his first advent, when he established the first christian church through his apostles; and we note what he did, in his second advent, when, to prepare the way for the establishment of the second christian church, to be called the New Jerusalem, in the natural world, he called the same apostles together and commissioned them afresh to preach the gospel in the spiritual world. For we reason, that *the best way* to establish and extend the church on earth—which we have shown is the most direct and primary means of attaining his end in the creation of mankind—*is the Lord's way.* In the establishment of the new and true christian church, he himself has revealed divine truths in the form of a universal theology for the use of that church in the work entitled " True Christian Religion :" so that the dissemination of that theology, and its reception in the understandings, the wills, and the lives of men, is the direct and most efficient means of the new and true christian church's establishment. Now the following has been revealed to us (U. T. 791)—"After this work [The True Christian Religion] was finished, the Lord called together his twelve disciples, who followed him in the world, and the next day he sent them throughout the whole SPIRITUAL WORLD, to preach the GOSPEL, that the LORD JESUS CHRIST reigneth, whose kingdom shall endure for ever and ever according to the prophecy in Daniel, (vii. 13, 14); and in the Revelation (xi. 15); and that they are blessed who are called to the marriage supper of the Lamb (Rev. xix. 9). This was done on the 19th day of June, in the year 1770. This is understood by these words of the Lord. 'He shall send his angels, and they shall gather together his elect from one end of heaven to the other' (Matt. xxiv. 31)." In a previous number of the same work (108) Swedenborg says—"I shall here add this extraordinary information : Some months ago the Lord called together his twelve apostles, and sent them forth throughout the whole spiritual world, *as he had formerly done throughout the whole natural world*, with a commission to preach *this gospel;* and immediately *every apostle had his particular district assigned him;* and they are each of them fulfilling their charge with the utmost zeal and industry." And still previously to that, in number 4, where he states that the infancy of the christian church " was in the days of the apostles, when they preached throughout the world repentance, and faith in the Lord God the Saviour;" and then adds, " It is here worth remarking, as a memorable circumstance, that not many months ago the Lord called together his twelve disciples, now angels, and sent them throughout the spiritual world, with a commission to preach there the gospel anew, since the church which he had established by their labors, is at this day brought to such a state of consummation that scarcely any remains of it are left."* See in this connection, Brief Continuation of the

---

* We believe it is somewhere stated, that Swedenborg was ten or twelve years in digesting the True Christian Religion and that it was completed in his own mind, and in, perhaps, rough drafts of its general contents, before he began to transcribe it for the press. Hence he could state what took place upon the finishing of the work, as having happened some months before, as he here does, in the beginning of the printed book.

Coronis, XXXVI—XLIV.—We here see that the Lord in his second
advent, repeated in the spiritual world, what, in his first advent, he had
done in the natural world. Thus he re-declares the ministerial order of
the first christian church to be the true order of the church on earth.
And by the natural and proper correspondence of this act of his in the
spiritual world, the true order of the new church on earth now is, for
the whole body of the receivers of the doctrines contained and set
forth in "The True Christian Religion," in any sufficient province of
a general church, to commission in his name, and by his authority,
twelve apostles, as the representatives of him in that whole church,
and, as the highest grade of its priesthood, to proclaim "this gospel"
throughout its province. And on this authority, on the authority of
the Lord's example, in both his first and second advent, we now recommend this order to the general church. Of which order, we shall say
more presently.

6. Now we are to see that the new church is to be established
amongst the gentiles, as at the time of the Lord's first advent; and
therefore there must be new-church apostles to the gentiles. Swedenborg says, "A new church will be raised up in some region of
the earth, *whilst the present church abides in its external worship, as
the Jews do in theirs*—in whose worship it is well known there is
nothing of charity and faith, that is, nothing of a church." (A. C. 1850.)
This we judge to be perfectly conclusive against the doctrine of those
in our connection, who hold that the New Jerusalem is not to be an
external church distinct from the first christian church; but is to come
forward as a new doctrine and life of charity amongst the various
denominations of that church. For if this were so, how could the
new church be raised up in some other region of the earth whilst the
present church abides in its external worship as the Jews do in theirs?
And how *can* a new doctrine and life of charity, come forward in an
old church, "in whose worship it is well known there is nothing of
charity and faith"? The doctrine and life of the first christian church
could not thus come forward in the jewish church; what good reason
is there to believe that the doctrine and life of the second christian
church will come forward in the first, contrary to the general law?
Is it any more practicable now than formerly, to put new wine in
old bottles without their bursting and spilling? Is it any more possible spiritually than naturally to put *new* life, not only into an *old*
body but into a *dead* one? But although the new christian church
may not come forward in the old, and will be established amongst
nations, or gentiles, out of it; yet it may take its beginning in and
from the first christian, as the first christian did from the jewish,
church. And this it must do, because the first christian church has
the Word, by which alone the church can be established any where.[*]
Hence the internal sense of the Word is revealed by Swedenborg, and
his works, containing that revelation, are sent to the universities in
christendom, from whence he assures us will come ministers for the

---

[*] " The church cannot exist but where there is a just understanding of the Word;
and the state and nature of the church is always to be determined by the manner in
which the Word is understood by those who belong to the church." (S. S. 79.)

new church, because the new heaven, from which the new church
is to descend, has no influence over the old clergy. And Christians
are to be made for the new heaven now as they were formerly—by
the preaching of the apostles in the spiritual world, and by the preaching of ministers holding their office in the natural world. (See Brief
Con. of Cor. XXXVI—XLIV, as before cited.) Therefore, *new-church
apostles must be provided in universities of general learning, and sent
to preach "* THIS GOSPEL*" to the* GENTILES. And as such institutions in
the christian world, are under the bigoted control of some one or
other of the religious denominations of the old christian church, it is
the especial duty of Newchurchmen, particularly in these United
States, to unite, as one collective man, in instituting a university of
their own, in which the sciences shall be taught on distinctively new-
church principles, and be learned in the seven-fold light of the New
Jerusalem. Such is our firm and solemn conviction! And, therefore,
we hold it to be the duty of every Newchurchman, who is "principled
in love to the Lord," to become the member of a general church, so
that a general *body* of the Lord, as its divine *soul*, may be formed,
whereby *he* can perform this first and highest use, "to the community and to every society in it," providing, "*by means of men*," those
who may now act as his apostles on earth, for the dissemination of
these new knowledges of truth that he has given for the higher and
vastly more felicitous conjunction of men with him in this his last,
best and for ever enduring dispensation of mercy and grace to mankind. It is the paramount duty of every Newchurchman to provide
first for such a general education by the establishment, endowment
and support of *such a new-church university* as can and will provide
thus for the dissemination amongst all good gentiles of that hid
treasure—those most precious, priceless pearls of heavenly wisdom—
which is given to him, as talents, to trade with in purchasing *souls*
for his Divine Lord and Master! And wo to him if he hides his
talents in a napkin! Yes, *general* preachers of new-church truth to
the *gentiles* must now be provided. For again Swedenborg says—
"When the church is consummated and perishes, then the Lord
always raises up a new church elsewhere, yet seldom if ever from the
men of the former church, but *from the gentiles*, who were *before in
ignorance*." (A. C. 2909.) See A. C. 2986, where it is expressly
said, "the case will be the same with this church which is called
christian." And again he says most expressly, "By the New and
Holy Jerusalem is signified *the new church* of the Lord, which *is about
to* SUCCEED *to the christian church existing at this day*." (A. C. 8988.)
In A. C. 9407, explaining the signification of Rev. xxi., 19, 20, he
has these words—"speaking of the Holy Jerusalem coming down out
of heaven, by which is meant *a new church amongst the nations*, after
that *the church at this day, which is in our european orb, is vastated*."
Still further—"A new church is always established amongst the
nations which are out of the [former] church: which is the case
when the old church has closed heaven to itself, as was said above.
Hence it is that the church was translated from the Jews to the gentiles; and also that *the church at this day is now transferring to the*

gentiles." In Isaiah, ix. 1, 2; xi. 10; xlii. 6, 7; lv. 4, 5; lx. 3, 4, 5; Luke, ii. 30, 31, 32—" the subject treated of is concerning the Lord, that the gentiles were to come to him; and they come to him when they acknowledged him for their God. · And what is wonderful, the gentiles adore one only God under a human form. Wherefore, when they hear of the Lord, they receive and acknowledge him. *Neither* CAN *a new church be established amongst* OTHERS. Matt. xxi. 42, 43; Luke, xiii. 29, 30." (A. C. 9256.) See, in this connection, U. T. 761, for the words—" Since all light departs at midnight, and the Lord is the true light, (John, i. 4; viii. 12; xii. 35, 36, 46,) therefore he said to his disciples, when he ascended into heaven, 'Lo! I am with you always, even unto the consummation of the age,' (Matt. xxviii. 20:) and *then he departed from them to a new church.*" Can any thing be clearer from this, than that the Lord, in the consummation of the old christian church, has left its clergy, as the successors of the apostles, as well as its laity; and therefore, in proclaiming his gospel anew in the spiritual world, he could not take any of the clergy of the old church who now go into that world from this, but had to take his original apostles, "now angels," to do this work for him? Well, if he cannot employ the old church clergy in the spiritual world, to preach the gospel anew there, is it at all presumable that he can employ the old-church clergy to preach this gospel anew in the natural world? And, therefore, is it not perfectly clear, that new-church apostles must be provided by him, in the way we have stated, and thus a totally new priesthood be formed by him for the establishment and extension of his new church amongst the gentiles of the present day. How, then, it is possible for any intelligent receivers of our doctrines in the present day, with all this express testimony of Swedenborg to the contrary, before them, still to hold, that the New Jerusalem is coming forward as a universal church in the various denominations of the first christian church—that the ministers of those denominations will receive the doctrines of the new church and preach them to their congregations, so that we need not provide distinctive new-church ministers for the establishment of any external church distinctive or separate from that of the old church—that the christian sacraments are still valid in the former church, so that there need be no distinctive sign of baptism for the New Jerusalem—and thus, in fact, that the New Jerusalem that is to come down from God out of the *new heaven,* is not to be a *new earth* instead *of the former earth,* which, with the old heaven, is to pass away like a rolled up scroll—how any intelligent Newchurchmen can still hold to all this, and *practise according to their tenet,* is to us utterly inconceivable! When the doctrines of the New Jerusalem were first promulgated, and the first receivers of her doctrines, in the dim twilight of her early morning, were in a state of transition from the old church to the new, it is easy to imagine that they should entertain such ideas as these. But now, when longer experience of the true quality of the old christian church has come to the aid of deeper insight into Swedenborg's true doctrine on this subject, must we not think that those who still hold to such notions are *not* intelligent

Newchurchmen; but, while they are standing beneath the shade of their old tree, our church is infested, tempted, or sorely tried by them as Oldchurchmen, who have been too hastily allowed to assume the livery of the New Jerusalem? But, in view of what we have here advanced from Swedenborg, our ardent prayer to the Lord is, that he may open the eyes of all who are principled in any degree of love to him, so that they may see, and, seeing, *do* their duty—to provide, in his name, strictly, truly, and *distinctively new-church apostles to the* GENTILES. To enable them to see that neither their *sole* nor their *primary* duty is done, when they have prepared a place for *themselves* to worship him in public, and a teacher, or pastor, to point out to *them*, and lead *them*, in the way of life eternal: but that the far higher, nobler, and more imperative duty devolves on them, to *reflect* and *transmit* the light which shines on them, "to give it freely, as they have freely received it," so that it may be "a light to' lighten the gentiles," and so that now, as in the Lord's first advent, "the people who sit in darkness, may see great light; and to them who sit in the region and shadow of death, light may spring up"!

Some have concluded, from one or two of the passages above quoted, that the new church is not to exist at all, in an external or visible form, in any of the present christian lands. But may not Swedenborg allude to *state* rather than to *place*, when he speaks of "s' me other region of the earth;" may he not allude to gentile *minds* in what are only ostensibly christian *lands*? The first christian church was established amongst gentiles, that is, those out of the jewish church, in all lands, and even in Palestine. May not the second christian church, in like manner, be now established amongst those who are gentiles in all lands, and in nominally christian lands with the rest, because they never have yet come into the first christian church? For the vast body of mankind have never yet been converted to christianity. Besides, the Jews are either now or about to become gentiles—such of them, certainly, as hold their jewish principles loosely—as the people of the adamic church were gentiles in Noah's time, and the people of the noahtic church were gentiles in the times of Abraham. And are there not real gentiles, those who are in simple good, without regard to the peculiar doctrines of the consummated christian church, as mere professors of its religion, amongst all of its denominations, who will flock to the rational instructions of true new-church preachers, as "doves to their windows"? We think so: and we think that Swedenborg expressly alludes to such as about to receive the doctrines of the New Jerusalem on earth, as they receive those doctrines by instruction in the world of spirits, and go into the composition of the new heaven. Hence we find him using such expressions as these—"Our churches at this day are almost all of this character, [such as make faith essential and reject charity,] except that which is in *christian gentilism*, where it is permitted to adore saints and idols." (A. C. 3447.) He here alludes to Catholics, who, being in simple good, have not separated good works from faith and charity; and, therefore, as he expressly says, in other parts of his writings, more readily receive the doctrine of the Lord in the other

world, and go into the natural degree of the new heaven, than any of
the confirmed solifidians. In A. C. 3667, also, he has these words—
" Hence it is evident, that neither did the house of Jacob acknowledge
Jehovah, but yet was willing to acknowledge him, in case he proved
a benefactor ; *as is exactly the case at this day in* GENTILE CHRISTEN-
DOM." Besides, other parallel passages of his writings express uncer-
tainty on this point—indicate that he did not know, and therefore
would hardly positively teach, that the new church would not exist
at all in nominally christian lands ; or would only say *conjecturally*
that it was to be raised up in some other nation. Thus he says,
(A. C. 3898,) " The church at this day is vastated to such a degree,
that is, is so void of faith and love, that, *although men know* and
understand, still they do not ACKNOWLEDGE and *still less* BELIEVE, (see
3398, 3399,) *except the few who are in the life of good,* and are called
the elect, who *now may be instructed,* and *amongst whom a new church
is about to be established.* But *where* these are, *the Lord alone knows.*
There will be few within the church, [that is, the former christian
church.] The new churches established in former times, were established amongst the gentiles." " The christian church, such as it is
in itself, or its true nature, *is now commencing,* the former church
being christian in name only ; but not in essence and reality." (U. T.
668.) " The christian church was *founded* by the Lord during his
abode in the world, and is now *beginning to be built up* by him."
(Ibid. 674.) These passages show, with sufficient clearness, that Swedenborg does not intend to teach positively that the new church is not
to exist in christian lands, but that it is not to come forward in the
old christian church. On the contrary, he intimates that it is to be established amongst " *all in all nations* who fear him and work righteousness, and therefore are accepted with God," (Acts, x. 35)—thus is
to be established amongst " the few who are in the good of life," and
so are God's " elect," even in christian lands, *where* " they are now to
be instructed," and so the new church " is about to be established "
amongst them. But we hope the reader will study the passage from
A. C. 3898, in connection with those cited within it, namely, A. C.
3398, 3399. It is important that he should do this : for it will not
only convince him of the futility of attempting to teach the doctrines
of the new church to the various denominations of the vastated one,
because, although he may make them " know and understand " the
spiritual truths which those doctrines convey, yet he cannot get them
to *acknowledge* and *believe* them ; but it will also show him the *danger*
of *profanation* which he subjects *them* to, by such a course. And it
does seem to us that nothing *can* be more conclusive against our
attempts to insinuate new-church truths into the old-church denominations, than the simple fact, that the Lord did not, and *in his mercy
could not,* reveal those truths for the New Jerusalem, until *the old
christian church had become totally vastated,* and so was in a state
*necessarily to reject those truths whenever and wherever presented to
her !*[*] Do ministers of the old church, who come into our connec-

---

[*] " The interior things of the church are not revealed until the time that the church
is vastated, because then they are no longer believed—thus neither can they be profaned." (A. C. 6595, 3398.)

tion, and essay to preach our doctrines to the church which they
have left, on the principle that they are to be mediums of bringing the
denominations of the old faith into the new faith; or, refusing to take
the distinctive badge of the New Jerusalem, essay to resuscitate the
dead body—of men who are so void of faith and love as not to be able
to acknowledge, much less believe, the truths of the new faith, lest
they might profane them—by infusing into it the new charity as a principle of universal good; *think of* THIS? Like Paul of old, they may
be willing to be even themselves accursed, if so be they might save
some of their kinsmen after the flesh; but when they see how mercifully the Lord has provided, that "hearing they should hear and not
understand, and seeing they should see and not perceive; because the
heart of this people is waxed gross, and their ears are dull of
hearing, and their eyes have they closed; lest they should see with
their eyes, and hear with their ears, and understand with their hearts
and should be converted and he should heal them" (Acts, xxviii. 26,
27; comp. with Isaiah, vi. 9; Matt. xiii. 14; &c.;) such ministers
will surely then learn, that now, as of old, "the salvation of God *is
sent unto the gentiles*, and that *they* [*only*] *will hear it.*" For our parts
we are now, and long have been, fully convinced, that the only ground
for new-church operations in our country is " gentile christendom,"
which we suppose to embrace all those sincere lovers and honest
seekers of truth who have not been confirmed in old-church doctrines,
and *so* are good gentiles *out* of the old church. And to such,
wherever they may be, it is our most incumbent duty to *send* the
glad tidings of great joy, which, even in this our day, are revealed,
"to give light to them that sit in darkness, and in the shadow of
death," as well as "to guide *our* feet into the way of peace." In
short, it is the chief duty of the new church in our country,—if she
would most effectually co-operate with the Lord in attaining his end
of a heaven of human beings,—to provide a *general* ministry, to be
sent as new-church apostles to the gentiles.

· 7. Thus the highest grade of the new-church priesthood must now,
for the first time, be formed. For the *use* to which it corresponds,
and from which it should be determined, is now to be developed. We
believe the time for this use is approaching: we are not sure that it
has arrived. We regard all that has transpired from the last judgment
till now, as in the *analytic* process of the formation of the new and
true christian church, similar to that which transpired, in the formation of the first christian church, from the Lord's baptism till his resurrection,[*] when he commissioned the eleven and afterwards ordained
the twelve at pentecost. We may be deceived by appearances; and
we certainly do not pretend to any thing like prophecy; but there
is a deep *feeling* within us; and the signs of the times seem to indicate, that the period is nigh at hand for the beginning of the *synthetic*
process of the new church's formation. A chief object of the histo-

---

[*] This formative period is thus indicated in Acts, i. 21, 22—" Wherefore, of these
men which have companied with us, all the time that the Lord Jesus went in and out
among us, *beginning from the baptism of John unto that same day that he was taken
up from us*, must one be ordained to be a witness with us of his resurrection."

rical sketch of the trine, which we have given in this report, has
been to show, that what is properly the highest grade of the christian
ministry has never yet been discretely formed in our church. By
referring to page 129, the reader will see why we think the designation of ordaining ministers in this country, was not the proper
formation of, the highest discrete grade in our ministry. And the
history of the trine in England, which we have given, will show
clearly enough, we presume, that strictly but two grades of the ministerial trine have as yet been formed in that country. We believe
that the highest grade of our ministry must be made distinct from its
two lower grades by a discretely superior degree of use. It must be
made distinct by a discrete extension of province, jurisdiction, or
official function. Now in what we have called the analytic formation of the new church in this country, a beginning has been made
in forming a minister of the lowest grade first. A few receivers have
assembled together for public worship ; and being unable to sustain a
settled pastor, have appointed a reader to lead the worship and read
sermons. Schoolmasters, lawyers, or other men of literary avocations
and some leisure, have been chosen for this office, because they could
give a portion of their time to writing sermons, while they made a
support for their families by some secular calling. They have been
ordained indeed *as ministers with full powers*; but this merely formal
and external ordination, did not make them such : for it did not and
could not give them the requisite talents, nor place them in the true
province of such ministers, nor enable them to discharge the proper
functions of that province. Next, men, properly educated for the
ministerial office, and set apart and supported in an exclusive devotion
to the duties of the ministry in connection with a particular society
or church, were provided. This we believe was the institution of the
pastoral office as truly the second grade of the ministry. And as the
highest minister now is only the pastor of a particular society with
ordaining powers—but one function of the highest grade—attached,
there yet remains to be created a minister who shall be as discretely
above the pastor, as a general society is discretely above a particular
society. And he must be a minister so constantly engaged in the
discharge of general functions in a general church, that he cannot
remain located as the mere pastor of any particular church.
     The following is the groundwork for the position, generally stated
above, on which we build in the writings of our church. . "There
must needs be a general thing in order that there may be any particular thing ; and what is particular can in no wise exist and subsist
without what is general—indeed it subsists in what is general; and
every thing particular is circumstanced according to the quality, and
according to the state, of what is general." (A. C. 4325.) "Prince
denotes what is primary—also what is general or common: for *what
is primary is also common*, inasmuch as it rules in the rest of the
principles: for particulars have relation to primaries as to things
common, that they may make one, and lest contradiction should
appear." (A. C. 5082.) "There must needs be a general sphere in
order that there may be particular spheres, *which cannot exist but in*

a general one; for all particulars relate to generals, which direct particulars, and, at length, *reduce them into that order in which generals are;* otherwise they must of necessity be expelled from the general sphere." (Diary, 210.) On these fundamental principles of our church, so clearly expressed, we found the order of the Central Convention. According to this order, the general church, composed of receivers of our doctrines in a large province of country, is first constituted and organized; and then particular churches are formed and organized within it. ' The order opposite to this is, to constitute and perfect a particular society in some city, town, or much smaller district of country, and then form and govern the whole church through and by this. The latter is the analytic, the former is the synthetic, process of formation. Or the latter is the fœtal formation before birth and the growth to manhood after birth, while the former is the forming work of a man acting in his own right. If an army is to be raised by analysis, the smaller divisions are first enlisted, then the inferior officers are appointed to command these. These united in the next larger divisions have superior officers then appointed. And at last, when these larger divisions are united in one army, the general is appointed to command the whole. ' But when an army is to be raised by synthesis, the general is first appointed, and the men who enlist do so with the common principle of confidence in his skill, bravery, and every fitness to command them victoriously. If a regiment, battalion or company is to be raised, the men know the colonel, the major, or the captain they are to serve under, and enlist to fight under him. So of the smaller divisions of companies. In the other process, men enlist to fight under any body and every body ; and are more influenced in their enlistment by regard to the *bounty* than to the *glory.* Thus, in synthesis, the unity and efficiency of the army solely depend upon the generals: for "what is primary is also common," and "every thing particular is circumstanced according to the quality, and according to the state, of what is general." Hence the character of an army depends wholly upon the quality of its general officers. For if these are skilful and brave men, cowards and inefficient men will not enlist under them: or if they do, most certainly, in the organization and discipline of the army under the general sphere and influence of its general officers, "they must of necessity be expelled from the general sphere," or become brave and efficient men, by being "reduced into that order in which the generals are." And precisely so, we maintain, it is and must be in the church. We can no more make a general church by aggregating particular churches in its formation, than the earth could have been created by first creating its particular parts and then hooping them together as staves in a barrel. Love creates, arranges and governs all things. ' The head of the church as a visible body consists of *all* those who are principled in love to the Lord. The general officers of the church are the representatives of these, and are, comparatively, the electric points, which draw off, conduct, and convey, the 'Lord's influences through them. The "church in general is constituted by a company of men who are principled in good and truth." (A. C. 6113.). "When a man is in this good and truth, the kingdom of the Lord is then in him—consequently, he is a church, and, together with those who are in like disposition, constitutes the church in general." (A. C. 5826.) "The church in general consists of several individuals." (A. C. 2851.) Or "the church in general is constituted of those who are churches in particular, howsoever remote they are from each other as to place of abode." (A. C. 6637.) But all these are collected in the Lord's aspect so as to form one man. (U. T. 412.) Therefore, in the general church, we must have the arrangement and order of the human frame. (See Doct. of Charity, 74—78.) Thus the church must be formed, and established, and made to grow up to adult stature, as the human body is. Hence, as the human body is formed and perfected through general organs, so we must have general officers in the church, who shall be as discretely superior to pastors of particular societies, as a general church is discretely superior to a particular church. We must have apostles in the new and true christian church, as there were in the first christian church. And the unity, efficiency and whole character of our church, in all its smaller subdivisions, will depend upon the *quality* of these apostles, just as the whole character of an army depends on the quality of its general officers. And *without them we can have no more* UNITY *in our church in this country than we have hitherto had.* Without them *we cannot possibly have one, united, harmonious* and *efficient* MAXIMUS HOMO. The process of forming a general church by the mere aggregation of particular societies, and the formation and government of *all* by *one* VERY PARTICULAR *society*, has bred division, dissension, and unharmonious counteraction of distinct and independent parts. And nothing but the *natural persuasions* of a sort of spiritual brick machine, which makes distinct particles cohere by external pressure, can at all avail to produce those semblances of *external* order and arrangement, which should alone result from the internal force of attraction of cohesion in the crystalline formations of spiritual affinities. Let us go up to the mountain top of clear intellectual discernment, above the clouds of all personal consideration, and, standing there, let us ask ourselves, What ought we to have expected would now be the character of our general church in this country, from the quality of those men who were put prominently forward *to go through the motions* of *its general officers* in its beginning? Were they men of superior spiritual *love*, and appointed to the highest grade for that reason? Were they men of superior *wisdom*, and for that reason appointed? Were they men of superior *learning*, with the *modest diffidence in themselves* and *their own attainments* which true learning always generates in the human soul, and therefore best fitted *intellectually* to command and *morally* to control inferior clerical officers in subordinate provinces of the church? Were they men of *ripened years*, laden with the autumnal fruits of spiritual experience, and endued with that insight into *spiritual human nature* which alone can give prudence, judgment and *tact* in rightly influencing general bodies of men, so as, imperceptibly to others and unfelt by themselves, to draw, like human magnets, the grains of precious ore from the common sand, and arrange them in the general sphère of true order? Far be it from us to ask these questions with any invidious feeling! In the sight of heaven and of Heaven's King, we desire to look on the past only for the sake of right action in the future. And now, for the great end of our heavenly church's true, lasting, and most widely extended establishment in our beloved country, are we not bound, by every the highest and best affection of our souls, to provide, appoint, and support, such *general officers* of our church, as shall give to her, her proper character—her true unity, her right formation, her due subordination in true order, and an efficiency commensurate with the immortal interests of mankind? Then we must have *general* learning. There must be *general* effort to provide it. Thus there must be the function of a *general* body of the church, and *a* GENERAL *body of the church* for the discharge of that function, before particular churches " can exist and subsist." In vain shall we essay to impart the needed knowledges of truth to societies in particular before we have a general institution of new-church learning. For it is just as impossible for us to have either particular or general ecclesiastical officers of the right *quality* in our church, without such an institution, as it is to have such officers in our army or navy, without a military academy or a naval school. And if the children of this world were not wiser in their generation than the children of light, the american arms, recently, would have been no more efficient against the enemies of our country, than our ecclesiastical organizations and efforts have been efficient against the enemies of our church. There have not, then, been officers of the highest grade—not simply of mere *official* station or rank, but of spiritual, mental, or educational *quality*—in our church in this country. Such a grade is yet to be opened in our priesthood. We do not say the time for its development has come. But we do say the time is full come to "*foresee* and *provide for*" this discretely higher priestly *use*. We do say that *general* officers, as the third grade in our priesthood, are now to be provided and sustained by the *whole church* as the *Lord's body on earth*, acting, as one man, from him as her soul. And we do say that they should possess all that *quality* and *state* which are requisite "to direct particulars, and at length to reduce them into that order in which generals" *should be* in the New Jerusalem.

8. But now we are to display the grounds of arranging the various parts of the church, and subordinating the distinct grades of the ministry, in trinal order. We will here present some detached passages from Swedenborg to show the principles of this subordination and arrangement, and then proceed to state it in form. First, as to the functional grades and subordination of the ministry. According to our law of action, above laid down, we adopt the ministerial arrangement of the apostolic church, which was the christian church, as established by the Lord through his apostles, in its infancy; and would have, in our ministry, the trine of *apostles, pastors*, and *teachers*. These ministers should be discrete and subordinate as are their offices and uses. And the uses and offices are discrete and subordinate according to the extent of their sphere and the scope of their jurisdiction. Uses are good services rendered to the commu-

nity from the affections of charity or disinterested good will. The neighbor to whom this charity is to be exercised is all with discrimination: and this discrimination is according to the extent of the good which is to be consulted for. Thus a society of several individuals is more a man's neighbor than any one individual; and the society is more the neighbor in the degree that it is larger and more comprehensive. In general, uses are discreted and subordinated as the heavens, because the heavens are the discrete generic grades of goods in successive ascending or descending order. They are like the three atmospheres—air, ether, and aura: they are in fact the three atmospheres of the spiritual world corresponding to the three atmospheres of the natural world. Now the law of the discrete gradation of the three atmospheres is, that the highest is the most universal and pervading. Thus aura flows into and forms ether, and through ether forms air—through air, water; and through ether, air and water forms all other material substances, and pervades them all when formed. So with the uses of the ministry, the highest is the most universal and pervading. So also with the offices or functions of the ministry. And so with the ministers who fill those offices or discharge those functions. The highest minister, is the one who has the largest field of labor, the greatest extent of service, the widest scope of jurisdiction, or the most unbounded sphere of use. Now, as to the trinal functions of the new-church ministry, the following short passage of Swedenborg's writings, sufficiently, though very succinctly, displays them. Explaining Rev. xix. 7, "And his wife hath made herself ready," he says, this "signifies that they who are to be of the Lord's church, which is the New Jerusalem, will be *collected, initiated* and *instructed*." (Ap. Rev. 813.) Here is most evidently the proof of a trine in the new-church ministry, at the same time that it is the indication of the precise nature of its three-fold functions. To *collect* is evidently the function of the highest officer, because it is bringing together from the most extended sphere of official operation. To *initiate* is evidently the function of the lowest officer; because it is insinuating elementary principles, or introducing, as it were at a door, which is the least extended sphere of official operation. And to *instruct*, is, without question, the function of a pastor, who holds the grade intermediate between the highest and the lowest. It is, then, the function of an apostle to collect, or gather into the fold. It is the function of the teacher to initiate those that are gathered into the elementary principles of religion. And it is the function of a pastor to feed the collected and initiated flock;* that is, to instruct them in its higher principles.

---

* "Flock signifies both good and the church, that is, *those who are in* GOOD *and of the church ;* for the two are so conjoined that one cannot be separated from the other : for he who is in the good of faith is the church, and he who is the church is in the good of faith." (A. C. 6788.) This shows distinctly the special province of the pastor: that is, to feed or instruct those who are in the *good* of faith. But men must be led to good by truth. Good is received in the will, truth in the understanding. The understanding is an outer court to the will. So those whose understandings only are instructed in the *truths* of faith are the external of the church, are standing, as it were, in an outer court or portico of the church. The church itself, as the house of God, is the will, and the

To see the due subordination of these ministers, we have only to recall what was said under another head. "The general principle is that to which singular things are to be subservient." (A. C. 5305.) Or, "it is grounded in order that an inferior thing should be subservient to a superior." Thus an officer in a singular, particular, or inferior sphere of use, should be subordinate to one in a general or superior sphere. Their subordination will be, too, according to the extent of their province, or scope of official action. But this is according to the trinal arrangement of the church; which we are to notice presently. We need only here repeat what was stated in another place, that their subordination is according to the form of government in the other life, and such is the government in the other life, that good spirits are subordinate to angelic spirits, and angelic spirits to angels, so as to constitute an angelic society," (A. C. 1752.) Good spirits are as goods or uses in the natural heaven; angelic spirits are as goods or uses in the spiritual heaven; and angels are as goods or uses in the celestial heaven. Thus the subordination is that of natural uses to spiritual uses, and of spiritual uses to celestial uses. Or it is as the subordination of science to intelligence, and of intelligence to wisdom: This takes from the subordination for which we contend, all idea of pride, pomp, and imperiousness. It is the free and willing subordination of inferior to superior service. There is to be no desire, or thought, of either eminence or super-eminence in any external thing. The common end is the common good. And he is to be deemed highest by others, without his thinking of it himself, who has the greatest ability, from superior intelligence or superior wisdom, to promote that good in the greatest degree. The only super-eminence is, that of highest and most extended usefulness amongst those who *all* mutually desire to serve each other. He who serves few and less, spontaneously subordinates himself to him who serves many and more. And superior honor is awarded to superior intelligence or wisdom, because it is superior intelligence and super-eminent wisdom which qualify for higher degrees and wider scopes of service. In this we suppose our form of ecclesiastical government to differ from the *episcopal* and *papal.* As our trine is to be representative of the Lord's work of saving men in the three heavens, therefore, comparatively, the ministers of this trine are to be subordinate to one another as the angels of the heavens are; and we have seen that "the angels who are in the first heaven are subordinate to the angels who are in the second heaven; and these to the angels of the third: but *this subordination is not like that of rule and*

good of faith which is therein received. Initiation into the church, therefore, is the instruction of the understanding in the *truths* of faith; and this is the province of the minister of the first grade; who stands, as it were, in the gate-way of the church as a sheepfold. Within the fold stands the pastor, and feeds the flock. by so instructing their minds from without that the Good Shepherd can flow into their will from within, and *there* "satisfy the hungry soul with *good*"—the *good* of faith. Thus it is clear that the first and second grades of the ministry are to be discreted as understanding and will; or as the *truth* of faith and the *good* of it. And the apostle is to be discreted from the pastor, as the *good* of *love*, which is the *use* that love effects, is discrete from the *good* of *faith*, which is the *use* that obedience to divine command effects.

authority, [as is the subordination of the episcopacy and papacy which prevail in the old christian church,] but it is like the subordination of things external to internal things in man" (A. C. 1802)—which is as the subordination of the lungs to the heart, of muscular action to the will, of the organs of sense to the understanding, of speech to thought, of thought to affection, and of affection to love—all of the actions and reactions of which, as we well know, are spontaneous and reciprocal, having nothing like arbitrary rule or constraining authority.*

* We have said that the highest grade of the priesthood are the ministers of *love.* And in another place we said that all men, in general, are distinguishable into three discrete degrees—men of *will*—men of *understanding*—men of *obedience.* We also asserted that men of strong wills are those that command in armies or navies, and become emperors, kings and other chief magistrates in civil governments. The inference from this in some minds was, that we held that men of strong wills should be priests of the highest grade in the church. But this was a wrong inference. For we hold that super-eminent *love* in a true priest of the church is a very different thing from predominating love and its strong will in officers of civil government. We were merely illustrating the doctrine of the trine in general, and proving that there should be a trine of discrete degrees in the priesthood, by the very manifest fact that there is a trine of discrete degrees among men in general; from which fact we argued, that there must be a trine of priests, who should be as discrete as will, understanding and obedient action. We did not intend to imply that the will or love of the highest order of priests should be precisely that which distinguishes the head men of arbitrary governments. For the Lord's king-dom is not of this world; and we are to render unto Cæsar the *things which are Cæsar's;* but unto God the *things which are God's.* Now ministers of the church are all from the Lord's *spiritual* kingdom, which is the kingdom of *truth.* Therefore the love of ministers must be *intellectual* love. But this is not *ruling* love. *That* is always *voluntary.* Hence the highest grade of ministers must not *needs* be men of strong *will*—this is rather a disqualification for the ministry. And hence there need be no fear of a spirit of arbitrary domination in a priest of the highest order, if he be of the true sort, or of the right genius. Priestly love is *love of truth.* The highest degree of this constitutes a priest of the highest order. It makes him a man of superior *wisdom;* and in this there is always modesty, diffidence of itself, and least of all a desire to rule other men. Love as strong will in the unregenerate natural man, is lust of dominion and desire of great wealth. These do not necessarily enter into priestly love. They may; but then they pervert a priest's representative character and vastate the church, as they did in ancient, and have done in modern, Babylon. But the love of rule is essen-tial to an eminent military or naval officer. It is essential to an emperor. It must characterize in some degree masters in the government of servants. And it is always the predominating trait in men of strong wills. Hence it has become an adage, that such men are born to command, while men of weaker wills are said to be born to obey. Their sway is government of the *will,* and therefore belongs to the *celestial* kingdom. The sway of the minister of the church is the government of the *understanding,* and therefore belongs to the *spiritual* kingdom. It is the sway of superior wisdom, which is truth made good in the highest degree. Ministers of *love,* therefore, in our accepta-tion of the term, are those whose natural wills—whose natural desires for rule or wealth —are *most subdued* by the chastisements of spiritual truth. So that, in this sense, he who is most abased is the most exalted. These are the men that we think should hold the highest rank in our ministry, as the apostles to the gentiles, and the peacemakers of love in the church. Their dominion is to be that of the love of truth made good. And as our apostles are to be chosen by the votes of the general church, electing them on account of their superior love of truth, their superior learning, their superior wisdom, their greater age and their greater experience, it will be the church's own fault, if they should turn out spiritual tyrants, and lord it over God's heritage.—See, in connection with this note, our former report, p. 37 of Journal No. VIII.

˙ 9. Having thus displayed ˙the grounds of subordinating the distinct grades of our ministry in trinal order, let us now show the grounds of arranging the various parts of the church. ˙This, also, to be in just order, must be a trinal arrangement. We˙ suppose that the three grades in the church on earth are to be discriminated according to social arrangements in the spiritual world; for the one correspond to ˙ the other. "Heaven is distinguished into several common or general societies, and into lesser societies subordinate thereto; but still they are one by good." (A. C. 4837.) ˙On this ground we deem the order ˙ of the apostolic church right; and think it is our proper model. The order of. the apostolic church was not one universal church in visible form,.with one person as a visible head, and made one by external conformity to prescribed rules of ritual observance and forms of ecclesiastical government. It was not with them *the* church, but the *churches*. John addressed the *seven churches* of Asia. ˙Thus the apostolic order was a brotherhood, complex; or collective man of churches, with each its angel, and not *a* universal church, with a Peter as God's vicegerent òn earth. So we, in our new-church ˙order in these United States, embracing as they do such a vast extent of territory, would have "*several general* societies" or churches with "*particular* societies [or churches] subordinate thereto."* We would have the general church; not a mere convention of delegates from particular societies meeting occasiotally in some point of space, but a general society composed of receivers and livers' of the new-church doctrines, "ʳhowsoever they may be separated as to place of abode," and embrac⸗ ing lesser societies within it, as what *is* general embraces what ˙is particular. But, in the heavens, there are some angels who do not live in societies, but "who live solitary, as it˙were, in separate houses and families." (H. & H. 50.)˙ And the inhabitants of the third earth in the starry heaven, "do not live in societies,˙but in houses˙apart by themselves; and are joined in societies, when they meet for worship." {A. C. 10.513 to 10.518.) In the heavens, then, there is the trinal arrangement of general societies, particular societies, and families. On this ground, we would have a corresponding trinal arrangement for our church. The Lord preached in cities and villages. At that time˙ ˙ cities were streets of houses surrounded by walls and other fortifications; and villages were composed of scattered houses outside of the walls. The distinction now may be, town ánd country; oʳ those who live. in cities, in the various occupations of art, science, manufactures ˙ or commerce, and those who live in the country, on farms or plantations, in the various pursuits of agriculture, horticulture, or grazing. On this distinction, we would found our arrangement of the church in ˙ general. There would be families·in the country, particular societies in cities oʳ large villages, and general societies in certain districts of country, comprising both of the former. In the country, families

---

* The subordination of a particular church to the general church need no more inter· fere with its true and proper independence of imperious sway and arbitrary control in the general government, or jts general officers, than the subordination of· the state to the general government in our country, interferes with its integrity as an independent sovereignty in all those affairs that pertain ·to its own local government. ˙

would unite in meetings for worship, statedly or occasionally, as circumstances would permit. But every family would have family worship on the Lord's Day in its own house, if there were no other families in sufficiently near proximity to join with it; and one exercise of such a family's sunday worship would be, the teaching the younger children by the parents or the older children. Families in their country meetings should be the special province of the teacher, who might teach a new-church school in the week days and preach on Sunday; particular societies in cities and villages, should be the special province of the pastors, having a teacher of the societies' new-church school, as a student preparing for the ministry, under him; and general societies in districts should be the special province of the apostle. But the teacher might also assist the pastor in a larger society, and pastors and teachers, who were not particularly engaged in either of their special provinces, might both assist the apostle in his district. Indeed the apostle should always be attended by one or more of the ministers of the lower grades, who, by accompanying and assisting him in his apostolic duties, would be in the way of finding particular and singular fields of their own special action. Such would be our trinal arrangement of the church in general.

10. But, lastly, we would have a trinal arrangement for each particular society. And here, in laying down the grounds for this arrangement, we will state some principles of universal application to all social arrangements. It is now revealed to us from heaven, that there are the following six universal laws, by which all distinct heavenly societies are arranged so as to consist in enduring unity and harmony :—1, That every unity in the form of the heavens exists according to the heavenly harmony of several consociated.[*] 2, That love is spiritual conjunction, whence comes heavenly harmony. 3, That there must be a universal bond, to the intent that singular things may be kept joined together one with another. 4, That the universal bond must flow in into the singular bonds, and constitute them. 5, That the universal bond is the Lord—thus love from him, and love to him. 6, That the singular bonds are thence derived, and that they are of mutual love, or charity towards the neighbor. (A. C. 9613.) The first law imperatively calls for the trine. The second makes *love* the basis of social conjunction and harmony ; and by this term is meant a common end and all ruling purpose of useful service to all others in general and to one another in particular. If this principle of love be wanting in a society, it cannot possibly be a true, united and harmonious church. The third law calls for a universal bond to bind distinct and variant parts in harmonious unity. Now "bonds, in the spiritual sense, are nothing else but the affections which are of the love; for these are what lead man, and what restrain him." (A. C. 9096.) Without the strong affection of some common love, or end of use, no society of men in this world, differing as all men do in distinctive particularities of character, can, therefore, "be kept joined together one with another." Hence blind and unyielding self-will,

---

[*] "A one, in all cases, is composed not of *same* principles, but of *various* principles in form, which constitute a one according to the form." (A. C. 4149.)

which impels men to have their own peculiar way, or to force their
own distinctive opinions on others, or their own peculiar measures
through general or particular associations of men, is constantly dis-
turbing, rending, or paralysing societies of the church, as well as all
other societies.   The fourth law requires that the strong affection of
some common love should flow into and constitute the singular affections of each individual member of the society, restraining, at the
same time, the particular and singular affections of selfish and worldly
loves.   This is the reason that a heavily impending common danger
makes men forget, for a time, their individual disputes, and unite in
warding off the common peril.   Thus the fear of death, in shipwreck,
will make a mutinous crew, for the time being, subordinate to him
who is truly the captain of the ship.   The fifth law makes the
universal bond the Lord, that is, a supreme regard to the universal
good.   This is the only adequate corrective to individual and particular
self-will.   The sixth law requires that this supreme regard to the
universal good, shall so reign in each and every member of a society,
that all will in fact strive honestly to promote the true and lasting
good of one another.   It will bring into practical operation the apostolic injunction—" Let no man seek his own ; but every man another's
wealth." (1 Cor. x. 24.)   And it will cause all " in honor to prefer
one another." (Rom. x. 12.)   If these laws can be made to rule in our
churches, general and particular, then we shall have little difficulty in
coming into true order.   For just so far as these laws *do* rule, self-love
and self-intelligence, those grand disturbers of all human associations,
will be put and kept effectually down.   Then the ministry will come
into its trinal order without let or hindrance from the lust of pre-
eminence and rule on one hand, and from the fear of usurpation or the
resistance of imperious sway on the other.   And then will particular
societies of the church come readily into the trinal arrangements of
universal order, unobstructed by the petty jealousies of greater wealth,
superior worth, higher intelligence, or more refinement, which are the
curse of envious, vulgar minds, or by the haughty pretensions and
vainglorious conceits of people of the opposite sort.   And it is much
to be apprehended, that self-love, and love of the world, in these or
some other of their hideous forms, of aspiring pride and vain conceit,
may far too much prevail in preventing the unity which " exists
according to the heavenly harmony of several consociated " in the
nominal societies of the new, not less than in those of the real societies
of the old, christian church.   Let, then, these six laws of heavenly association be graven deep on the fleshly tablets of our hearts, and from
thence transcribed, in living characters of social order, on all the
scrolls of our external arrangements.   Let *Love, Universal Love*, be our
Grand Master of Ceremonies !   <
   We have seen that the arrangement of the tabernacle was the type
of heavenly order.   The true church is heaven upon earth.   By the
laws which we have just stated, all heaven is one unanimous body of
the Lord.   The church on earth should represent and correspond to
heaven in this.   For " the church is the *image* of heaven, because it
is the Lord's kingdom in the earths." (A. C. 4337.)   Now the whole

heaven is arranged generally and particularly in trinal order. Therefore, so should it be with the whole church, and every particular society of it. Hence every particular society of the church should be arranged in trinal order : for " what is unanimous is composed of so many images of itself." (A. C. 4625.) Therefore, we would recommend, that every particular society be arranged in the general trinal order of the tabernacle, that is, have those who represent the part within the veil, those who represent the part without the veil, and those who represent the court. And as the christian sacraments are alike representative, we would determine the arrangement by them. Or we would recommend the following trine :—I. The internal of the church—II. The external of the church—III. The congregation. " They who are led from good to truths are they who constitute the *internal church;* but they who are in the course of being introduced to good by truths are they who constitute the *external church.*"* (A. C. 7992.) The Lord's supper is the most holy sacrament, and representatively the holy of holies to the christian church. Let the internal of the church consist of those who are habitual partakers of the Lord's supper. Baptism is the holy sacrament, and represents the holy place. Let the external of the church consist of those adult members of the society who have been baptized into the faith of the New Jerusalem, but have not yet become regular communicants. And let the congregation, as the court of the tabernacle, consist of such receivers of the doctrines of the new church as contribute to the support of public worship, but are not yet baptized or communing members of the church. This external *representative* trinal arrangement affords all the uses of external order, without judgment of the internal states of men, which are and can be known only to the Lord. And any arrangement in external order, which is an external *correspondent* of the *essential* trine of those who are really the *celestial*, the *spiritual*, and the *natural* men of the church, is utterly impracticable in this natural world. Because, in the first place, these degrees are not *discretely* opened in the natural world, but only *continuously* in the natural plane ; (see S. S. 66 and D. L. & W. 256 ;) and, in the next place, if they were opened discretely, no man on earth has the insight requisite to discern and discriminate who are in this degree or who in that.

The internal of the church also might be discreted into a trine. I. The minister or pastor—II. Three or seven elders as his advisers and assistants—III. The communicants. The pastor should have the superintendence of all things relating to the administration of the divine law and worship. The elders should provide means for the

---

* " The external church is with those who are in natural lumen, and live a moral life from the obedience of faith, although not from internal affection." (Ap. Ex. 163.) " They are of the external church, who do good to the neighbor and worship the Lord merely from the obedience of faith ; but they are of the internal church who do good to the neighbor and worship the Lord from love. . . . They who are of the external church, are clearly in its externals, but obscurely in its internals ; whereas they who are of the internal church, are clearly in internals, and obscurely in externals." (A. C. 8762.)

administration of the holy supper and other sacraments; should counsel and aid the minister in the discharge of his duties; and, either in person or by substitute, should lead the public worship of the society in his absence. The communicants, together with the minister and the elders, should form a unity in all deliberation and action upon the society's highest spiritual concerns: and, in the absence or want of a pastor, should, with the elders, perform the function of an ordinary church committee for the whole society. This they might do as a body, when their number was small, or by a sub-committee together with the elders, when large. The internal of the church, as the trinal unity thus described, should be as the head to the rest of the society. And to it, in this capacity, should pertain the entire control of the pulpit, with the appointment of the times and places of the holy supper, and other festivals of the church. The internal and external of the church together as a one, should have the entire control of the place of worship for all religious purposes; should determine the admission of persons into the church by baptism; should direct and secure the religious instruction of children; should decide upon the fitness or suitableness of persons who were baptized in infancy or childhood, to become members of the society as they arrive at adult years; and should have the nomination of suitable persons as candidates for the pastorship of the society. The internal and external of the church, together with the congregation, as a one, should have the determination and management of all the society's secular concerns. This unity, as a common body, should conspire, contribute, and co-operate in the performance of all those common uses which societies are usually constituted to perform for the establishment and extension of the church on earth. The members of the society of whom both the internal and external of the church consist, should subside in this congregational unity as a common plane whilst engaged in the performance of its appropriate uses. And the society, as composed thus of a church and congregation, might, if its members thought proper, and agreed for this purpose, perform all the uses, and secure to its members all the benefits, of an ordinary benevolent society,—which certainly seem uses of new-church charity in the natural plane,—in which capacity it should, as the sphere of its uses extended, provide for its widows, orphans and destitute, through the agency of the elders of the church as its almoners. It should also have charge of and control any school for the education of the children of its members which it might think proper to establish. It should have the choice of the teacher or teachers needful for such a school; and should control it through a committee, or other organ, to be chosen from its members by its own vote. It should have the election of the pastor, the candidate or candidates for that office having been nominated by the church. It should, by trustees, to be chosen from its members for the purpose, or in any corporate capacity which it might think proper to receive from the civil government, hold property needful for the performance of its uses, and engage in such transactions with the surrounding community as the efficient performance of those uses might require. And for all these purposes it should be organized by the appointment of such officers as might be needed.

Such, we suppose, might be a useful arrangement of a particular society of the church in trinal order. By the congregation the church, properly so called, would have a useful intermediate between itself and common society. Here, as in an ante-chamber, those who were approaching the church, might stand on a useful plane of probation before entering it. And through this medium the church could spread an accommodated sphere of its distinctive principles for the good of the civil community. Of course, every society of the church is to be in the most entire freedom to come into that order which to its own rational perceptions and convictions seems best. We fully believe that the order and arrangement of different societies may and should vary according to their genius and the respective administrations which they may have to perform in the body of common society. And nothing like authoritative prescription has been intended by what is offered under this head of our report. Far be it from us even to desire, much less to strive for, unity from conformity in externals. We have wished and designed to do no more than throw out *hints* of what *might* be *useful*, and therefore proper and advisable to such, as might freely and rationally deem them so in their own cases. We have also designed these suggestions as a sort of practical illustration of the general principle of the trine, which it has been the object of this report to set forth in clear light.

11. Perhaps it will be expected of us to say something, in this immediate connection, about the question, What is the true relation of a pastor to a society of the church? A good deal has been said, in our historical sketch of the trine in this country, respecting the theory of a *conjugial* pastoral relation. And as we have been implicated somewhat as to that theory, which is so signally condemned in the report on the trine that the English General Conference sent to this country, we may at least be allowed to express our sentiments on this subject here. It might be enough for us simply to say, that we do not now, and never did, regard the relation of a pastor to his society as any *thing like* a conjugial one. We have always thought it is a relation of *charity*. "A priest," says Swedenborg, "who teaches truths from the Word, and by these leads his flock to good of life and so to heaven, such a priest, since he provides for the welfare of the souls of those who belong to his church, is pre-eminently *in the exercise of charity*." (U. T. 422.) And the priesthood is the servant of the church, that is, of the good and truth which constitute the church; and therefore is to be regarded and loved as a servant, not as a husband, by any associated bodies of such persons as are principled in those goods and truths. In short, we believe the true relation of the priesthood cannot be better expressed than it is in these words of Swedenborg:—"The priesthood is not to be loved in a superior degree, and the church subordinately, but the good and truth of the church should be loved, and the priesthood on their account, *since the priesthood is designed to act as a* SERVANT *to such good and truth*, and *should be respected in proportion to the service*

which it yields." (U. T. 415.) This is a perfectly clear and common-sense view of the matter, and places the priesthood in so true and good a position, that no sensible man can hesitate for a moment to yield to it what is here asked for it. Priests hold to the community precisely the same relation in kind which any useful civil functionary does; he is the *servant* of the community, and he is to be *respected* according to the service which he renders. But it may be well for us to give, as succinctly as we can, an idea of what we think should be the true nature of the ministerial function in a society of the new church.

The Word should be regarded as the sole medium of truth. The ministry is merely a medium of illustration and instruction from the Word. And it should be the duty of a minister or pastor of a society to teach truths from the Word of God according to the doctrines of the New Jerusalem as set forth in the theological writings of that servant of the Lord, and instrument of his second advent, Emanuel Swedenborg. He should faithfully endeavor to illustrate the rational mind of the society, so that its members might see, in the light of their own minds, what is true, and, acting in freedom according to their own reason, reduce the truth so seen to practice. Thus it should be the duty of the minister of a particular church, to act as a spiritual pastor, in leading the society, as a spiritual flock, by the truth of a rational faith, to the good of a spiritual life. Hence, in all his teachings, he should expect the society to assent to his propositions because they are true and right, and not because he proposes them. He should on no occasion seek to exercise any other authority than that of his own Divine Master—*The Truth Itself*. Thus he should not endeavor to exert a mere persuasive influence. And the society should not be bound to receive his teachings any farther than its members themselves see them to be true in the light of the Word, which is the light of the Lord's own divine countenance. For the Lord alone is the bridegroom and husband of his church. Such is our view of the true relation of a pastor to a society, and of the function which he should discharge in its connection. And we have no hesitation in saying, that we believe that the connection of a pastor with any particular society should be determined by *their choice*. The Lord could not gather the children of Jerusalem as a hen gathereth her chickens under her wings, because "they *would* not." This shows that the Lord himself being a minister to his church is grounded in the *choice* of his church's *will*. And the same principle must apply to the minister who is his representative in the church. Members of the church in a particular society should choose him because they believe him best qualified to teach and lead them to heaven. And the basis of his connection with them should be *mutual confidence*: for this is the correspondent of that *charity* which constitutes the church in men. When either party ceases to feel this, the connection between them should be freely, and of their own accord, dissolved. Hence, should a pastor, however talented and worthy he might be, cease to be congenial to any society, his connection with it should be dissolved, without any episcopal or apostolic interference whatever, by a vote of its members in a meeting properly called for the purpose: *provided*, that no such action of the society should be made to injure his reputation or usefulness with other societies of the church which might need or desire his services. And the pastor of a society, like any other member of it, should be free to withdraw from its connection, whenever a sense of duty to his Divine Master, or to the church at large, might incline or constrain him to sunder such connection *without violence to the bonds of charity*. This provision against official injury in the one case, and this guard against the rupture of the bonds of charity in the other, would require that the parties in this social relation should wish to be guided by the dispassionate counsel of those intelligent, wise, and elder persons, who, our church teaches us, (A. C. 6766,) have, by "more advanced age," and by having "the interiors of their understanding illustrated," acquired the "ability," which "comes by successive degrees," "to settle disputes or disagreements within the church." And the apostles of the general church, being men of advanced years and superior wisdom, should be called on to advise with and counsel societies and their pastors in any difficulties which might unhappily arise between them. It should be one of their functions to act as umpires in the arbitration of those difficulties. They should be the peacemakers of love. But they should have nothing like an arbitrary or constraining authority in the matter. They should have no right to assign a pastor to a society, nor authoritatively to remove him. They might recommend pastors to societies which had none. Their extensive acquaintance with the peculiar characteristics of the societies in their districts, as well as with the peculiar qualifications of those who might be holding the pastoral office, or might be candidates for it, would peculiarly fit them for the beneficial performance of this service to societies. But they should have no power of *setting* teachers or pastors *over* societies. This would be allowable in a mere natural church; but not in a spiritual or celestial one. And herein we would have our government of the church differ from civil and military government. The subordination of pastors to apostles, or particular societies to the general society, should be free and spontaneous; and there should be no sort of coercive authority. If *this* were needed, *the church*, as charity and its mutual confidence, would cease to exist, and the visible existence of a religious association of members of the new church under such a bondage of *external constraint*, would be a worse evil than its dissolution. Let it never be forgotten, that the new church does not *begin* to exist, where there is no genuine charity and no true faith. And the church that is constituted by these principles, must and will have the same subordination of inferior to superior parts as exists in the heavens; "but *this* subordination *is not like that of rule and authority*, but it is like the subordination of things external to internal things in man." (A. C. 1802.)

12. We will now close this head of our report with some cursory observations upon what should be the trinal order of our ministry. These, too, are thrown out as only hints of what *may* be, and not at all in the way of authoritative prescription of what *must* be.

All of our external order is founded upon the human economy. Our form of ecclesiastical government is wholly determined by this type. And once for all—for first and for last—we here present this type from Swedenborg's posthumous Tract on Charity, 74–78. He is illustrating the position that "*all offices and employments, in their regard to the good of the community, constitute a form which corresponds to the human form,*" and says—"The same thing exists in the human body, where all the parts are goods of use in the most perfect form, and, being in the most perfect form, are perceived as one; when yet they all are various, and all the things in each variety are in their own series and order. . . . The common things in the body are the heart and the lungs. Their actions inflow into all the parts of the body, organs, viscera and members. The common things in the mind are the will and the intellect. *The common things in the body respect the individual things as their parts, from which they subsist; and the parts respect things common, from which they exist.* All things there are formed from use, in use, and to use. All are forms of use. Such is the form of government in the animal body, that each particular derives its appointed task from what is general, while it is provided that what is general confers subsistence on each particular part. The heart gives blood to all the parts of the entire body, and each part, according to its need, takes what is proper to itself; and each one gives out from itself what is peculiar to itself. A form and motion which is wonderful. That the body contains a form of heavenly use, is confirmed by the fact, that each heavenly society is as a man, and indeed appears as a man. Its uses constitute that man; because the form of a heavenly society corresponds to the form of the animal body in regard to uses. *In the least things, and in the greatest, the heavenly form is a man.* Hence the universal heaven is a man, every society is a man, each angel is a man. The reason is, that the Lord, from whom is heaven, is a man. That man is a form of heaven."

We hardly need repeat that on this grand doctrine, thus so simply yet sublimely taught, all our argument for external order in our church, and for its kind, entirely rests. The passage above quoted was our main authority for the trine from the writings of Swedenborg. But it did not appear under our head of authorities, that it might serve for a climax and crown of our argument in this place. See how direct and conclusive it is. In general, the human form is the external embodiment of all uses. "All things there are formed from use, to use, and in use. All are *forms* of *use.*" Hence priestly uses, when they come into their proper form, must come into the human form. Therefore, the priesthood, which must correspond to its uses, must be in form a man. But in man there is a *trine* of head, body and feet. Therefore, *there must be a similar trine in the priesthood.*—But, again, let us argue more particularly. "In the least things and the greatest the heavenly form is a man. The universal heaven, every society, and each angel, is a man. The reason is, the Lord is a man." Hence every thing that bears his image and likeness is in the human form, the form of heaven. Hence the church, individually and collectively,

37

in the whole and in all its parts, is a man, or in the form of the
human body, wherein all the parts are the goods of use in the most
perfect form. Consequently, the priesthood, which is a part of the
church, whose functions are goods of use of the highest kind and in
the supreme degree, should be in the most perfect form—a man. But
"man is a trine: his supreme part is the head, his middle part the
body, and his lowest part the feet and soles of the feet." For "it is a
well-known truth, that, in order to give perfection to any thing,
there must be a trine in just order, one under another; and that there
must be communication between the members of the trine; and that
such a trine constitutes one thing." (Coronis, 17.) Therefore, there
must be in the priesthood of any and of every church, consequently
in the priesthood of the new church, such a trine as there is in man—
a supreme part as the head, an intermediate part as the body, and a
lowest part as the feet and the soles of the feet. So in regard to ecclesiastical government. The government of heaven is that of the human
body, because all the distinct and several parts of heaven correspond
to the uses of the distinct and several parts of the human body. But
the church is heaven as the Lord's kingdom upon earth. Therefore
the general government of the human body should be the general
government of the church upon earth, because it is the government of
the Lord's kingdom in heaven.

When, then, we come to the question, What should be the trinal
order of our ministry in these United States? we simply turn to the type
of all our order, and find a ready and satisfactory answer. It is well
known that, in the body, what is general is first formed, and in this and
through it are successively formed all the particular and singular parts.
There are certain general fluids, with containing membranous sacs, in
which the human fœtus itself floats, and from or through which its soul
takes to itself its incipient formations. And let us not fail to observe
even in these the trinal order. Then the heart and brain are first developed in the fœtal state, and through these as the most general organs
of physical and mental life all the other parts are formed. A most
beautiful illustration of this law is afforded by the ossification of the
cranium. First there is a lymph, then a jelly, then a gristle, with
suitable limiting, discriminating and containing membranes; in this
there are gradually formed certain general divisions for the occipital,
parietal, frontal and other parts of the skull; and in these are gradually
formed several centres of ossification, from which points the bony
matter radiates, until the several circumferences blend in one coherent
bony mass, only marked by the sutures which bound the general territorial divisions above mentioned. Now upon this law of the human
economy, we found the order of several general churches, which are
to exist first in the general form, for the gradual formation in them of
particular societies or churches. And as subsistence is perpetual
creation, the parts are to be sustained, defended, and governed by the
general church, from and in which they exist and subsist. In like
manner general officers are first to be formed, or developed, in and
from the general church, to represent it, to go forth from it, to be supported by it, and to exercise its power and authority in collecting all

who are to be initiated into its elementary principles, and instructed
or built up fully, according to the forms and order of its interior life—
thus to develope and form all the particular and singular parts of its
human form.   Thus the common things in the body respect the individual things as their parts from which they subsist. And reciprocally,
the parts should regard things common from which they exist.   And
hence every individual receiver of the doctrines throughout our
country should belong to, and act for, some general body, which he
should regard as more his neighbor, to whom the services of charity
are to be rendered, than any less general, or more particular, society
to which he may belong. And to the support of that, according to its
needs, he should devote the due proportion of his means. Charity
indeed *begins* at home. But charity works at home to acquire the
means of performing use abroad. ·And now, as there must be what
is general, that what is particular may·be formed, exist and subsist
within it; and· hence, as there must be *general* education before
there can be the particular tuition of particular societies, it is the
most imperative duty of new-church charity, in every individual
receiver of our doctrines throughout our whole country, to contribute all that he can, or all that wise prudence makes it proper for
him to give, towards the founding and supporting of a general
institution of new-church learning in these United States. And if
every individual *felt* this strongly enough to do the utmost he could,
not three years would elapse before such an institution—though in a
small way, as an acorn—*would be in successful operation in this
country,* located in some geographical centre of our land; and, like a
heart and lungs, pulsating and respiring with heaven, would be
sending the vital streams and motions of the Lord's creative and formative energies throughout a gradually more and more efficient visible
body of our heavenly church.   For, in a new-church university—the
university of a church that is founded primarily on charity, and only
secondarily on piety—there should be the educative and.formative
processes of *all good uses in general.*   In short, a new-church university should not be a mere academy for scientific or literary attainments, nor a mere theological seminary, but also a sort of new-church
polytechnic school. And this would require, as foremost amongst
good natural uses, a printing press—a new-church university press—
for. printing the writings of the church, and disseminating them, in·
vital streams, by arterial action, throughout the whole land. Here
too, would be a *general* depository of all the books of the church.
This too should be, the centre of the church's *general* government as
to the " administration of what pertains to the divine law and worship." This central seat of government should be as near a geographical centre of the country as convenient or practicable. There
should be land enough and the requisite buildings for all the purposes
of such an institution. The president of the general church should be
the president of its university. The general branches of ecclesiastical
affairs should have heads of departments under him. Here should be
the general consistory of the church. Here general conventions and
councils should meet. From hence - apostles might be sent forth.

Here should the periodical literature have its chief centre—not excluding other centres. Here, in short, should be all that pertains to the centre of general government of the church as a sort of spiritual District of Columbia and Washington City. This would no more impair or interfere with the freedom of particular churches, than the government at Washington impairs or interferes with the freedom of the particular states. And the officers of general ecclesiastical government here, as well as the consistory, and the ecclesiastical congress, should represent, and be sustained by pecuniary contributions from, all the members of the new-church throughout the United States, just as similar civil functionaries do and are at Washington. This order we now propose and recommend for the New Jerusalem in the United States. It may not be immediately practicable just now, but we hold it up to the church as a use, which her charity should now foresee, and provide for now. And we solemnly aver that our only end in this recommendation is *the* USE! As heaven and the Lord are our witnesses, we ask not, we want not, any sort of high station or central power for ourselves! We are too sensible of our utter unfitness for the right discharge of such high functions ever to endanger that holy cause which we have so much at heart by giving to the visible body of our beloved church "the falling sickness" through our mal-administration of them! Let not, then, this bugbear be raised up to fright our church from her propriety. Let all, as we do, look to the use; and, for the sake of that, make every personal and pecuniary sacrifice in their power. In this, we here publicly pledge ourselves not to be one whit behind the foremost, according to our slender means. And now, for the sake, and in the sacred name, of *the high, the paramount use*, we most affectionately appeal to *all* of our common faith in this our common country, to come up to the help of the Lord—whose "love is now desiring to serve our community, and every society in it, by *means of men* who are principled in love to him"—to come up to the help of the Lord in founding, endowing and adequately supporting a new-church seminary in the United States of America! If the hints we throw out as to the way are not true and good—or if the way we recommend is not the best—let the best be found out! Let the whole church in convention deliberate on the best way—find it—point it out—and then let *the whole church as one man* run and struggle in it for the goal—the most thorough and effectual co-operation with the Lord in attaining his end of the salvation of souls. "Who does not remember and love that person, who, from the zeal of love to his country, fights against her enemies, and by the loss of his own life rescues his fellow-citizens from the yoke of slavery? And who does not remember and love that person, who, seeing his fellow-citizens in extreme want, and reduced by famine to the brink of death, moved with compassion, brings forth all his silver and gold from his house, and freely distributes it among them?" (U. T. 710.) And who shall not remember and love those of us, who, from the zeal of love for our church and the Lord's kingdom; fight against the enemies of men's souls, and, to provide against the now all-raging "famine in the land, not a famine of bread, nor a thirst for water, but of hearing the words of the Lord," (Amos, viii. 11,) by every sort of self-sacrifice, " lay down our lives for the brethren"?

In a country so extended as the United States, we have already said, we think there should be three general churches. In fact, there is just as good reason for seven, or twelve, as for three. In the very long process of time, there may, indeed, be as many general churches in this country, as there are states in this union. But, then, there might be trines of these general churches, to form more general unities, as each particular has a trine like the general thing which contains it. These, acting distinctly, should co-operate as one in each of the more general governments, which we have proposed. At present, the three would be made one more general government in sustaining the most general or common uses at the university. They would be a trine making a one in the consistory and the ecclesiastical senate there. (See note at the bottom of page 106 supra.) The members of our church in all of them would make one in the ecclesiastical house of representatives there. But each general church should have a convention of its own, that should meet on the nineteenth day of June in every year, at first to commission and send forth twelve apostles; and afterwards to supply the places of any of the twelve who may be removed by death or otherwise, as well as to consult for the performance of general uses in the general province of each general church. Its whole province should be divided into twelve geographical districts. To each district one apostle should be assigned, to travel constantly through it, preaching in its cities and villages: stopping in a city or a village as long as the good of the general church there seemed to require. Each apostle should be supported according to his station by contributions to a general fund from each and every member of-the church throughout the district. For the receiving and disbursing of this fund, each general church, by its conventional or other general organization, should have suitable general and particular officers. In the discharge of his apostolic function thus, the apostle would collect the good gentiles, of whom we have spoken, into particular societies of the church; whose first duty should be to establish a new-church school for the education of their children in and upon the principles of the new faith. The teacher of this school should be a minister of the first grade, who should, at the same time, lead the worship of the society on Sunday, and initiate its members into the *truths* of faith, besides being the society's lecturer on the natural sciences. Thus the society would be gradually formed into a church by the reformation of the understanding through those truths. And as baptism is the sign of this introduction into the church, this "washing of water by the Word," the minister of the first grade should be the administrator of the holy sacrament of baptism. Thus the external church would be first laid as a plane for the development of the internal church that is latent within it; as the organs of the mind in the brain are first formed for the subsequent development of the mental faculties. " They who are in the external church are in the good of life according to the truths of doctrine ; and they who are in the internal church, are in the truths of doctrine according to which the life is formed." (Ap. Ex. 392.). Here is a clear distinction of the two discrete grades of teaching and of teachers in the church. The minister of the first grade is the teacher of the external church, while the minister of the second grade is the teacher of the internal church. The one is specifically the *teacher*, the other is specifically the *pastor*. The one *initiates* into the *truths* of faith, the other *instructs* in the *goods* of faith. The one represents the *reformation* of the *understanding* by *truth*, the other represents the *regeneration* of the *will* by *good*. The one directs the *obedience* of the life in external conformity to *truth*, as the *good* of *truth*, the other unfolds the *truth* of *good*. These are discrete planes, having communication between them by distinct grades. The former is a first gate, opening to a plane, that has to be passed in coming to the latter as a second gate. In opening the first gate and leading an incipient society over its plane, we suppose the minister of the first grade to act. In this he may still act as the assistant of a minister of the second grade, when the society has advanced to the second gate; or he may then become himself a minister of the second grade, by rising from the plane where the truths of faith are insinuated for the reformation of the understanding, and being ordained the pastor of a particular church for the implantation of the *goods* of faith in the reformation of the will. The *teacher*, or minister of the first grade, should be ordained by the imposition of the hands of *one* apostle; the *pastor*, by the imposition of the hands of *two* apostles; and in both cases in the name, by the authority, and with the consent, of the *whole general church*, expressed through its general representatives. As the supper is the sign of the reformation of the will, which is the progressive regeneration of man by good, and his gradual introduction into heaven, the pastor should be the administrator of the most holy sacrament of the Lord's supper. And, as we have before suggested, each pastor should have under him one or more students for the ministry, who should now be the teacher or teachers of the society's school, lecturer or lecturers to the society itself, on those natural sciences which pertain to the illustration of spiritual truth, and the assistant or assistants of the pastor in his duties. These should invariably be graduates of the university, having a diploma from the president, bearing, on the face of it, his certificate, that the graduate who has received it has evinced to his teachers a natural genius for the clerical office. He may have studied theology in general at the university; but he is now to study it in particular, with a view to such an application of its general principles to the states of particular men, as will give *tact* in the discharge of specific pastoral duties. Whenever the student has passed his probation under his pastor, and has acted under his license to preach for one year, he should be ordained into the first degree of the priesthood, and, as a *teacher*, become the assistant and attendant of an apostle in his ministrations throughout the *country* of his district. If the apostle has several of these attendant teachers, he may, while he himself is engaged in collecting societies in cities or villages, depute such of them as have been for a considerable time with him as missionaries to the country, where they may visit the isolated families of the church and become the ministers of religion to them in their isolated condition.* The apostle, too, should visit all such families and collect them into country associations for worship, and into combinations for the common education of their children in the principles of their faith. When a sufficient number of new-church families in a country neighborhood could be found to unite in supporting a school, a school-house should be built by their combined efforts, having a ground-floor for school purposes, and a second story for a temple of common worship in that new-church neighborhood. As the teacher of this school, and the leader of this worship, any one of the apostolic *teachers* might be chosen by the families of the neighborhood. And then the *teacher* would become settled in this neighborhood, and supported by it, as a *teacher* of natural science to it, and as a priest of the first grade in our priesthood. As such he would administer the sacrament of baptism. But the most holy sacrament of the supper should be administered to these country associations by the apostle of this district—unless the members of them should be sufficiently numerous, and their residences sufficiently contiguous in space, to form societies of the church, in which case their *teachers* should be ordained as their *pastors.*†

* We were led to this suggestion by a conversation which we not long ago held with an intelligent member of our church, who had resided as a schoolmaster in one of the counties on the western shore of Maryland. He observed that the Episcopalians; who were the persons of leading influence in that county, had been somewhat excited in the discussion of the propriety of their having in their church a class of ministers lower than the deacons—a sort of clerico-laico-ministers, who should go into, and perform religious ministrations in, the remote bounds of country parishes. As it was, the country parishes being of large extent, the families in the remote circumference of the parish could not easily attend, and in fact rarely attended, worship in the parish church. They would stay at home on Sundays, leaving their children to run wild on those days. But the Methodists, by their itinerating clergy, came to their houses, preached to assembled families in some one of the largest, or preached in their school houses, and by this means were carrying away the scattered sheep from the episcopal folds. To counteract the Methodists in this, the Episcopalians were casting about for ways and means as above mentioned. And reflection upon the facts thus related, led us to see what we thought to be a discrete distinction between town and country; and to suppose that the latter should be made, in the way we have above suggested, the appropriate province of the priest of the lowest grade in our priesthood. In the greater complex perfection, to which our church will doubtless attain in the long process of time, each of the grades of our priesthood will itself be discreted into a trine of degrees; and then, in the three degrees of the lowest grade, a much more ample provision will be made for the various circumstances and wants of a country church.

† Mr. Cabell, from Acts, viii. 14–17, suggests the propriety of the new church's retaining the rite of confirmation from the episcopal church. But is not the holy supper, in strict propriety, the new-church rite of confirmation? When baptism, as the first gate, is opened to the infant, or child, the plane, between that and the supper, as the second gate, is that course of instruction and reformation by truth which brings him up to the ability to subscribe the doctrines of faith in the right of his own rational volition; and then he is in the state to enter into the good of truth, which is relatively the gate of heaven. We would object to the introduction of any rite in our church which had not a more clear and express authority of Swedenborg for it. And as he has not even indicated such a rite as occurring on the plane between the two gates of baptism and the supper, we incline to the opinion that it is inexpedient for us to place the episcopal rite of confirmation there. Swedenborg says that infants and children, who die before they

As the apostles are distinctively the ministers of *love*, and to love belongs all consecration, we incline to the opinion-that not only should they alone ordain other ministers, and consecrate holy places of public worship, but that *they alone should consecrate marriages in the new church ;* and that, as *baptism.* is the representative sign of the first grade, and the *supper* is the representative sign of the second, so *marriage* might be the distinctive representative sign of the third grade of our priesthood.   We know it may be said that the supper is the -most holy rite of the. *church's* representative worship: but *marriage* is a representative of the Lord's conjunction with his church in *heaven,* where neither baptism nor the supper exists as an external rite.   And as marriage is in fact the most holy representative every where, because it represents the union of divinity and humanity in the Lord, and of good and truth every where and in every thing throughout his kingdom in the heavens and on the earths, we have ever believed that it should be a sacrament of the church, performed in the adytum of her temple, and, as we now think, consecrated by her priest of the highest order.   One of the most distinguishing features of the new church is the great exaltation which she gives to marriage.   And this making of the marriage ceremony a most holy representative of the church on earth, seems to us altogether consonant with her spirit.   Is it possible to magnify its sacredness and its importance too much in the eyes of her members ? The acknowledgment of the Lord in marriage, which the parties would thus make in contracting its covenant, would tend, not only to draw down into their married life the holiest divine and heavenly influences, but especially to cause them to found their external union on the principles of their religion, so that conjugial love might in fact become in them the foundation and fountain of all other loves.   Surely, as conjugial love and the state of the church invariably correspond in human minds, the ceremony of marriage should ever be regarded as a most sacred representative sign of that correspondence.   And as Swedenborg says " a sacrament.is nothing else but a binding," (A. C. 3046,) why should not *marriage,* which binds two souls in the bonds of that true conjugial love which descends from the Lord out of heaven and forms the church in human souls, be regarded as a *sacrament* of the *church ?* And if such a.sacrament,—as it is·the most holy representative of the Lord's conjunction as a husband with the church as his bride and wife,—why should it not be administered by the Lord's

have arrived at an age suitable to take the most holy sacrament of the supper, are introduced into heaven by baptism. And hence we think that any mere act of priestly confirmation, which is not at the same time a holy representative institution of the Lord in his church, is needless. The additional communication or translation of the holy spirit, which ·was effected by the laying of the hands of the apostles on the converts baptized by Philip the deacon, can now be effected by the holy representatives of the Lord's supper. And, on this apostolic precedent, we would found the order above laid down— for our apostles to administer the supper to those incipient societies, whose members, baptized by the *teachers,* are sufficiently advanced, by their initiatory teachings, to receive an appropriate sign of their rational confirmation in the essential principles of the new faith. We also found this order on the precedent of the seventy's being sent before the Lord to places whither he himself would subsequently come. (Luke, x. 1.)

highest and most especial representative in the priesthood? We think it should. And therefore we think that marriage should be consecrated by the Lord's apostle alone. The betrothing before marriage might be witnessed and consecrated by the priests of the two lower grades in their respective provinces, as it is by the priests in heaven; but the marriage itself should be consecrated by the priest of the highest grade, and its rite be invariably performed as a ceremony of worship in the most holy place of the temple of divine worship; and if, invariably on the Lord's day, accompanied by instructions from the pulpit as to the holy nature and uses of marriage, so much the better. The consecration of marriage being the sole and an especial function of the apostle, this would be one of the uses which he could perform for isolated families of the church scattered throughout his district in common with the members of the church in cities. There can be no reason for that *haste* in the marriage ceremonies of the new church, which seem so urgent in civil contracts that go by that name. They should be looked forward to for even years, by those who would not have the consummation of marriage unduly precipitated in any case or in any way. Hence the coming of an apostle into any part of his district could be prudently anticipated by any who might be intending to enter into the state of wedlock there. The sacrament of marriage, being performed as a holy religious ceremony in the temple of worship, should be kept distinct from the wedding festivity, with its joyous hilarity, which should be enjoyed at another time and place. And such a sacrament being performed as a religious ceremony by the apostle, would, by the association of ideas, cause a sort of renewal of the marriage covenant throughout the earthly career of the married pair, every time the apostle paid his periodical visits to the part of his district in which it was originally contracted. That visit might be the occasion of a kind of anniversary celebration of all the married pairs in that neighborhood. And how the holy influences of marriage, with constant renewals of its holy vows and blessed joys, would descend from heaven in the felicitous successions of happy married lives on earth, in the carrying out of such an order as we here propose, can be more easily conceived than described. Therefore, we would at least suggest that the consecration of marriage should be the distinguishing function of an apostle throughout his district. This will give him something to do in the cities and villages as well as in the country of his district; and will make his occasional preaching to the societies of the church there always necessary, as well as his apostolic preaching to their general communities. And if the districts are too large for one apostle to discharge his duties throughout their whole extent, let as many apostles be appointed in one district as may be necessary; or let the general churches be multiplied, and the districts of them be more circumscribed. But perhaps this might lead to a trine of apostles, as each grade of the ministry, like each of the three heavens, may itself be distinguished into three degrees. In this case, there might be apostles for large cities, apostles for the smaller cities and larger villages, and country apostles. And as the population of the country became more and more dense, or the geographical extent of the district was greater, there might be more and more apostles of each of these grades appointed. But all this would flow in order from the law, that "all things," in the general church, as in the human body, "are formed from use, in-use, and to use."

In process of time, as the population of our country became more dense, and the numbers of members in the general churches greatly increased, each of these general churches might have a new-church. college and sub-polytechnic, subordinate to the university. And it is impossible to foresee. or foretell what special arrangements or organizations might be necessary-for the development of more particular or singular uses in the subordinate parts of the most general church. We only know that the universal law must apply—that the whole and the parts must be reciprocally images of one another, and hence that the order of the human form must obtain in every part as it does in the whole. Yet as all the parts have special functions to perform for, the good of the whole; hence, as there is perpetual variety in the parts harmonizing in general unity; and thus, as each part will have a form appropriate to the special use which it administers for the universal good; we may conclude, that each less general division of the church may assume somewhat different modes of arrangement and forms of organization, while they all agree in essential constituent principles—among which is most manifestly the trine. Undoubtedly, all must have the trinal arrangement, to be in just order; but this arrangement may come into many and great varieties of form. The most general form of apostles, pastors and teachers, founded as it is upon the Lord's example in first establishing his church, is supposed to be the true order of our church in her beginning. What varieties, in the. impletion of the general form, may arise to change, alter, or modify this trine, as our church rises into adult perfection, it is neither our purpose, nor in our power, to foreshadow. We ardently desire that the long mooted question of the trine may be now settled in such a way as to meet with general concurrence, for the firmer establishment and wider extension of our church now in our day and generation. If we *begin* rightly under the Lord's auspices, we are sure that he will enable our posterity to take care of themselves. And if we begin *as He did*, we are sure that we shall begin *rightly*. We say, then, let each general convention, which in fact has apostolic men in its bosom, meet in June of some year. Let the bounds of the convention be divided into twelve districts. To each district let an apostle be assigned, if there are so many as twelve men suitable for apostles to be found. If not, assign to one or more of the most prominent districts one or more apostles according to the number found. While the districts are themselves unable to support each its own apostle, all should be supported by a common conventional fund, to which every member of the convention should contribute. This fund, as we have said, should be collected, received, held and disbursed by the appropriate officers of the convention. The apostles themselves, while travelling and preaching throughout their districts, might be the medium of receiving and transmitting the contributions for their own support. By the general mode.of contribution which we have suggested, the superabundance of one able district might 'be made to supply the wants of another less able one. And the apostles should labor most assiduously in those parts of their districts which most needed their services, or in which those services were likely to prove most efficient for the general cause, without any reference whatever to their ratio of pecuniary contribution. The apostle should constantly look to the common good, of which he is the special representative; and therefore should labor in that particular place, and as long in any particular place, as the common good required, for the sake of the common good. And, for this reason, he should be sustained by a common fund—on the principle of the human economy, "that each part derives its appointed task from the general government, while it is provided that the general government confers subsistence on each particular part."

We think that apostles should invariably be commissioned by the general convention, and ordained in the name and with the authority of the general church, on the nineteenth day of June in each year.[*] We have so fully shown, in another part of this report, why we think ordaining power is vested in the *whole* church as the Lord's

[*] A young friend of ours, while ploughing in a cornfield in one of the counties of Kentucky, was bitten in the great toe of his right foot by a copper-head snake. The bite of that snake is most venomous. Our friend was for a long time disabled by the severe inflammation and swelling of the bitten part; but he eventually got over it, and the part seemed to be restored to its wonted soundness. Yet, regularly, every year, at the same time in June when the incident first happened, the bitten toe would inflame, swell up, and give our friend the most painful reminiscence of his first affliction. Why should this be so? Is it not because forms received in the body, and generally in the natural degree, determine periodic influxes from those spirits in the spiritual world which at all times correspond to them and originally produced them? And if so, is not this a cogent argument for the forms of baptism and the holy supper in determining specific influxes from the spiritual world into those who at first and habitually receive them? Is it not an argument for religious festivals and anniversary celebrations in general? Is it not a most cogent argument for the anniversary celebrations of those natural events which correspond to high and important principles in the spiritual world? Is not this a good and a strong reason why the grand national event of the declaration of our country's independence should be annually celebrated as a great civil festival throughout all time? And a still better and stronger reason why the infinitely more momentous and important event of our blessed Lord's incarnation should be ceaselessly celebrated as a religious festival of our church? We certainly think so. And, for the same reason, because the Lord commissioned his apostles to preach his gospel afresh in the spiritual world "on the 19th day of June, in the year 1770," (U. T. 791,) would we, as a perpetual anniversary celebration of that event, have conventional meetings of our general church in that month, so that every kind of initiative action might be taken on that day for the propagation of the same gospel here on earth. And, therefore, whenever an apostle was to be sent forth, we would have it invariably done on that day; because we believe that then a more potent periodic functional influx could be determined from the spiritual world than at any other time. On this same principle, we think it is a good custom to observe the anniversaries both of our baptism and of our marriage. For, although the religious rites are not to be repeated, there may be such festal or other celebrations of them as may admit of our incessant renewal of their sacred vows or engagements. Would not this be one of the most effectual ways of meliorating, if not of obviating, the alas! too common janglings and miseries of married life on earth? It is customary to celebrate the birth day of a child. But would it not be better to celebrate the day of his baptism, as a constantly recurring sign of his rebirth?

body on earth, that nothing more need be said on this point here. Nor need we repeat that ordaining power should be exercised by the whole church from the Lord through those ministers alone who represent him in the highest degree. But when these ministers of the highest degree are to be appointed, we would adopt the mode of Acts, i. 21-26. We think that double the number of the apostles to be appointed should be chosen by all the members of the general church. That is, two candidates for the apostleship should be nominated for each apostle that was to be appointed. These candidates should be nominated by the general convention. The same convention which divides the whole province of the general church into districts, should nominate two candidates for the apostleship in each district. These nominations as a general ticket should be voted for by all the members of the general church in their primary assemblies, as the president of the United States is now elected by the whole people; or if it were deemed more proper, the two candidates of each district might be voted for in that district alone. The members of the church in general, or in each district, might, by a certain common-sense perception, choose and vote for other candidates than those nominated by the general convention, if this should be generally deemed the more proper mode of nomination. But the candidates should be designated in some way by the whole church. And when these candidates were so elected, they should be present in general convention on the 19th of June ensuing their election. Then and there lots should be cast, with solemn prayer to the Lord, according to Acts, i. 21-26, on one of every two candidates so elected; and that one of the two upon which the lot fell, should then be solemnly ordained an apostle by the general convention, in the name, and by the authority, of the Lord in the general church, and sent to preach the gospel to the gentiles throughout his special district. And in case of his death or removal, his place should be supplied in the same way. He should be ordained by the imposition of hands and the solemn invocation of the Lord's holy spirit. The ceremony of ordination should be performed at first by three of the head officers of the convention for the time being; but afterwards by three apostles. No apostles should be ordained by a less number than *three*, because this is a full and perfect number, and is needed properly to represent the communication of priestly powers in their fulness, and in their highest degree. The apostle, so commissioned, should preach to general communities throughout his district, and collect scattered members of the church into societies for their initiation into the truths of the new faith by teachers, and their instruction in the goods of that faith by pastors. He should have no sort of arbitrary authority or government in any part of the church whatever. A minister of love, and man of high intelligence, he should and would receive, every where, the respect and deference due to his station as such. In the societies formed by him he would be regarded as a father, and they, looking to him as such, would receive from his age, experience and wisdom a paternal ecclesiastical control. By his moral suasion he could enact the peacemaker, as we have before stated, in those societies where unhappy difficulties may have arisen. And if, in any part of his district, dissatisfaction with him, or opposition to his ministries, should arise, they would certainly not spring out of any thing wrong in this trinal order and its just subordinations which we here recommend, but from one of these two sources—either the appointment of an unsuitable person for so high a ministry by the general church, or the inevitable reactions of unregenerate natural men upon the pure spiritual principles which he was instrumental in bringing to bear upon them. As far as the true church, or as far as the true receivers of her doctrines and the genuine manifesters of her faith, are concerned, there can never be any serious objection to the Lord's apostolic order, or any difficulty in the way of their subordination in love to those who, by their fruits, shall show themselves to be trees of his right hand's planting—apostles really chosen and truly sent by Him. We, therefore, feel more rational confidence in recommending to the adoption of our church in this country now, the trinal order of the first christian church in its infancy, and therefore in the state of its ecclesiastical innocency—the order of apostles, pastors and teachers. We believe the vastly great and important uses of the firmer establishment and wider extension of our heavenly church in this beloved country of ours, imperatively demand, for their effectual development, such a trine of priestly functionaries. And as we, in our inmost souls, believe, that this is the order of heaven and the whole spiritual world, and that the natural world cannot be made to correspond to heaven for the descent of the true church from thence to earth without its adoption in the external church's arrangements, we do most affectionately intreat our whole visible church in this country now to consider this matter with prayerful hearts and dispassionate minds, so that, under the divine auspices of our Common Lord and Master, all may now come, with enlightened eyes, to see this to be the true order, and harmoniously, because freely and rationally; to arrange themselves in it as a body under him as their Great Head.

Such is the trinal order which, in the abstract, we think *should* be that of our new-church ministry in this country. But we have no idea that this or any other abstract general order should be hastily introduced. The church, like nature, is abhorrent to all sudden changes. Therefore, should this be generally deemed the true order, we have no idea that it ought to be introduced by any sudden or violent rupturing of previous usages. It ought to be looked to as an architectural plan of a structure which is to stand where other buildings now do, and which can only be reared when those other buildings have been previously, carefully, and cautiously removed. We ourselves very much doubt whether the human instruments of such an order as this here proposed have yet in the Lord's providence been provided. But as the internal of man must first be regenerated, and through this his external; so must the general *mind* of the church be first well made up in respect to this general order, before any attempts are made to carry it out in external arrangements. Let us first see and know what just order is, and what it requires, and then let us set to work in providing the instruments requisite to carry it into effect. All we could ask, and all we should expect, therefore, is, that the general church should consider this order; and, if it deems it just and right, should now simply declare it to be true, and propose it for future adoption. Yet, if judged and declared to be true, preparatory measures, also, should now be set on foot to lead the way for a gradual, safe, and lastingly effective adoption of it hereafter. And first among such preparatory measures, we rank such a provision for general education as we have recommended. For this and other most general uses, we think a bona fide general body of the whole church in our whole country should be constituted. And for the constitution of such a body, in what we have in this report shown to be the right way, and for the support of such a body when so constituted, we here declare, and give our solemn pledge. We are now, and have ever been, the advocates of union, and not of division, in the church; and if we have taken part in the divisions which the erroneous and arbitrary proceedings of our general conventions have made necessary for the church's good, it has only been to seek and promote a general union of our whole church on a truer, wider, deeper, and more lasting basis.

X. CONCLUDING REMARKS.

More than fifteen months have elapsed since this report was commenced. Little did we imagine then that we should now inflict upon the church such a *book* as this! About fifty pages in manuscript were completed with Mr. Powell's co-operation and concurrence, with the view of submitting them as our report to the seventh annual meeting of our convention in October, 1847. But learning that two of the members of our council would not concur with us in this report, had not attempted to perform their tasks in the division of our labor in getting it out, and were actually engaged (at least one of them) in elaborating one of a contrary tenor, we concluded to withhold ours, and avoid any thing like further collisions in our conventional meetings. On this account we neither presented our report, nor attended the seventh annual meeting: and had not that meeting required us to furnish our report for publication with its journal, it would have been thrown aside, and the church, most probably, would never have heard from us again on this or any other subject. But feeling it our duty to go on, in compliance with that requisition, we sent our manuscript to the printer, and took up our pen again to add a few pages more to what we had already written, when the difficulty occurred with the publishing committee of our convention which is mentioned in the note on page 21 of the report as here published. Our report being excluded from the Journal and printed in the Newchurchman-Extra alone, we altered entirely our original plan, and determined to give a more extended history of the new church in this country, as well as to introduce other topics, and much more matter, than was at first intended. Being a member of a standing committee "for preparing a history of the causes which have led to the establishment of the Central Convention," and being, as we believe, the only person now living who, from his own knowledge and documents in his possession, could give such a history truly, we felt it our duty to incorporate that matter in this report, where it might incidentally and very well come. This required a pretty voluminous appendix of documents, and much discursiveness in the body of the report. We also enlarged greatly on the subject of representatives, introduced one or two other heads which would not have appeared at all, and expanded much that would have appeared in a condensed form, if the report had been published with the Journal. But, in a repeated review of the work as it has advanced, we have felt deeply impressed with a conviction, that the change of plan has been ordered by Divine Providence for the greater use: and, therefore, we do not now regret, or feel at all hurt at, the difficulty, above alluded to, which occasioned this change. We have, in consequence, been favored with the able, instructive and convincing papers of Messrs. Cabell and Powell. And we do hope, and trust, that enough has now been advanced, to enable any and all to make up their minds and come to a definitive settlement of this long agitated question in our church. At any rates, we feel that we have done our duty, and, with the pleasing inward consciousness of this, can now retire from all conspicuous station in the general church, as we shall most certainly avoid any thing like further controversy in it.

To complete our plan, there yet remains a *Postscriptum*, that was to contain three reviews. But our work has swelled to such a size,— having, in fact, already exceeded greatly the boundaries at first marked out for it,—that this cannot now be given. Such an extended historical sketch of the rise, progress and present state of the Western Convention as we intended to have given, together with the documents necessary to illustrate it, would itself have required a good deal of space. We must let this go entirely by. The reviews of Mr. Wilks's report and Mr. Mason's letter, we should much like to let go by too. But, considering how much both of these, but especially the former, have been vaunted in our borders, we fear that our failure to notice them would be misconstrued. And, as extended reviews of them are now out of the question, we will take leave to conclude our report with a few brief and cursory remarks upon those kindred productions.

THE REV. THOMAS WILKS'S REPORT.

"Reasons and Principles," prefixed to Volume I. of the Journals of the Central Convention, display in clear light the origin of that body. It is not necessary to repeat here any thing that is there said. But it must be obvious, from the stand which the Central Convention took in relation to the General Convention, that the movers in it must have been solicitous not to be found in any false position. The subject of the trine in the ministry had not only agitated the general church in this country for years, but had particularly provoked the opposition of some who took part at first in the Middle Convention, and who left it when our constitution adopted that principle. The question of a ministerial trine seemed, indeed, to have been very

generally settled at that time; but the fact that the trinal principle
was strongly opposed in the forming of our constitution, shows that it
was still an open question in some minds, and that it was not likely
our body should have come into existence without the ministers who
engaged in it having had their minds drawn to, and their opinions
made up, on this subject. We are not aware that there was a single
minister among us who was in any degree opposed to the trine; and
we do know that both of the ordaining ministers would have avoided
any of the responsibility of setting on foot a co-ordinate general body
of the new church in these middle states, if Article XVII. of the
Constitution had not been inserted. They both regarded the trine as
an essential principle of all order, and a trine in the ministry as a
fundamental principle of the church, without which it could not
exist in its order or subsist in its integrity. And if the article of the
constitution which acknowledges this order had not been inserted,
they would then have withdrawn from the body, as they would have
done at any subsequent period, whenever it should have been called
in question. Why Mr. Doughty's article in the original draft of the
constitution defining the trine in our ministry was expunged, has
been stated in the beginning of this report. But that was thrown up
to us in reproach in a communication from some members of the
New York society to the sixth annual meeting of our convention in
1846. The ecclesiastical council or committee of our convention
had failed to do their duty in determining from the Word and our
church's writings what should be the special form of the trine in our
ministry, and were deemed now, since the decease of Mr. Doughty,
to be incompetent to this task, so that these five lay members of the
New York society feel themselves in duty bound to essay the performance of their task for them. They actually prescribe to the convention a precise determination of "the grades in the ministry,"
which would have restored the old and exploded order of the mere
licentiate as a minister of the first grade; and they ask ordination into
the new-church ministry, with almost its entire powers at once, for
an old-church minister, who had been a reader of our writings or
receiver of our doctrines for only some two years. Thus these leading
members of the New York society, in 1846, not only acknowledge
the trinal order, and reproach us for having expunged Mr. Doughty's
translation of the General Convention's determination of it into his
draft of our constitution, but they as laymen actually prescribe a precise determination of it for our body, on the ground that it has not
"an experienced ecclesiastical board, that will impart confidence, and
whose *decisions* may be regarded with *authority*." It was exactly to
avoid any *such authoritative decisions* of the question, that Mr.
Doughty's insertion of the General Convention's decision of it had,
on our motion, been expunged. We wanted the authorities of the
Word and of Swedenborg's writings for our order whenever it should
be adopted; and we were quite as much opposed to this prescription
of it by a *resolution* of the New York society without these authorities, as we were to the General Convention's prescription of it without
them. We had moved the expunging of Mr. Doughty's determination

of the trine, and had caused the insertion of an article of our constitution making it the duty of our ecclesiastical council to determine it
from the Word and the writings of Swedenborg, merely for the purpose of enabling *him* to give us those authorities on which he and
others had founded that determination in the General Convention
itself. We thought that all who opposed the trine in our connection
did so because they imagined it was not taught in the writings of our
church, nor in the Word, but was authoritatively prescribed by our
conventions; and we imagined that all they as honest men needed to
make them freely and rationally adopt the trinal order, was to have
the light of the Word and the new church reflected to their minds
truly. We did not imagine that they were men whose old-church
prejudices had so encircled their heads with its mists, that the clearest
new-church light would appear hazy to them, and make new-church
truths look like frightful spectres instead of substantial and beautiful
heavenly realities. We felt sure that they would as readily embrace
the trinal order when they saw what the new church does indeed
teach concerning it, as we would have certainly rejected it, if our
views of it had remained like theirs; for we too had been among
them in opposition to it, while we were ignorant of its true nature,
and were unenlightened by true new-church light on the subject.
But ill health, or other causes, and at length his death, prevented Mr.
Doughty's giving us his authorities. The other members of the
council would not act, notwithstanding they were pressed by the
weightiest importunities. They assigned to us the task of a scribe,
but they gave us nothing to write. At the same time, they reproached
us for not doing the whole work—from even the attempting of which
we shrunk with instinctive diffidence of our competency, and with
appalling dread of its responsibilities. Still our convention was hampered in all of its ecclesiastical action by the want of the determination of its ministerial trine. We felt that we had no right to exercise
the ordaining powers of a general church before this order was determined; and we felt greatly reluctant to exercise the powers of another
general body, although the right to exercise them was still accorded
to us by it, while we remained in so conspicuous an attitude of opposition to its leaders. Thus the matter stood, when application was
made for the ordination of Mr. Powell, into the second degree, by
the Danby society, through Dr. Beers. The exigency was so clear in
his case, that he was ordained under the authority of the whole
church in the United States. When Mr. Benade came into our
church, the New York society were for having him ordained into our
ministry at once, without his acting on the preparatory plane of a
licentiate and student of our ministry. This order had been established
in our convention on the authority of Universal Theology, number
106. And it is easy to see, that self-willed reaction upon this order,
as it was advocated by Mr. Burnham, then minister of the New York
society, in the Fifth Annual Meeting, of 1845, (see Journal, No.
VII., p. 29,) lies at the root of the opposition to it which is manifested
in the communication from the five members of that society to the
Sixth Annual Meeting mentioned above. Yet the New York society

38

observes the order of the licentiateship as a preparatory plane in Mr.
Wilks's case, having asked and received a license for him, under which
he preached for them one year.   But in 1846, they ask his ordination
into our ministry at once, with all of its powers except that of ordaining other ministers, on the ground of "his age, experience and acquirements," as well as his "being moreover an ordained minister of the
old church," having "*eminently* fitted him for a *full measure* of usefulness in the [new] church." And as it was known that objection had
been made, and probably would. again be made, to the ordination of
ministers by our convention before its trinal ecclesiastical order was
determined, hence "decisive action on the subject of *defining the
provinces of the* THREE DEGREES OF THE MINISTRY," was pressed upon
us, "from an imperative sense of the. urgency and necessity of the
convention's now assuming a decided form." This led to the hasty
report on the subject of the trine, with the presentation of a temporary
platform of laws of trinal ministerial order for our convention, to
meet the exigencies of the Philadelphia and New York societies in
the cases of Messrs. Benade and Wilks, which were made to the sixth
annual meeting. (See Journal No. VIII. pp. 28–44.)   For the constitution of our convention (Art. XX.) required that the ecclesiastical
council should determine such order from the Word and the writings,
and that laws on the subject should be made only by the body in
general meeting assembled.   And until some such determination was
made by the council, and some such laws were passed by the body,
we could not constitutionally ordain Mr. Wilks into the first, or Mr.
Benade into the second, grade of our ministry.   In this we were
prompted by a strong desire to comply with the wishes, and supply
the wants, of those societies.   In only the night between two sessions
of the general meeting, we hastily collected our thoughts, offered
such authorities as occurred on the spur of the moment, and perpe-
trated those crude suggestions to the convention, which have drawn
down upon our heads such wide-spread condemnations, and brought
forth this twelve months' gestation of the Rev. Thomas Wilks in
formal review and lengthened answer of them.   Sweltering all night
long in one of the hottest of a hot June nights to afford to our convention good reasons for such a "defining the provinces of the *three
degrees* in the *ministry*" as would answer the demands and meet the
wishes of the New York society, little did we dream that we should
be accused, by a leading member of that society, in one short year
afterwards, of having "adopted the views of the Eastern Convention,
as respects the trine in the ministry of the new church,"—of having
"changed our opinions, and of advocating their views." And quite
as little were we prepared to see, in the official communication of the
New York society to the seventh annual meeting, in 1847, the following—"There is no doubt, but *our society stands more decidedly on
the ground originally assumed by the Central Convention*, than at *any
former period*, as will be *amply evinced by the report which the Rev.
Thos. Wilks will read before you ! ! !*—in the conclusions of which
our society *generally* concurs, the *tendency of our opinions, for a long
time, having been* TOWARDS THAT POINT.   For the sake of. peace,

however, the society, notwithstanding it has regarded *the adoption of a temporary order for the ministry* AS UNCONSTITUTIONAL, yet, concluded to await the action of the convention of 1847, before *asking of its minister* the ordinances of the church : [would that have been *constitutional ?* or would it have been constitutional for its minister to have granted its request?] we therefore trust that Mr. Wilks will return to us clothed with *full* powers." We here for the first time learn, that the ground originally assumed by the Central Convention was, that " there should be *but one order* of priests in the new church," and " but one ordination into the priesthood;" because " to teach the necessity of a *trine* of discrete officers in the ministry of the new church, the lower subordinate to the higher, would be to teach a doctrine which is most emphatically contrary to the divine Word, and which, consequently, cannot be true:" and this notwithstanding the *constitution* of the Central Convention declares, " As ' it is well known, that, in order to give perfection to any thing, there must be a trine in just order,' therefore this convention recognizes the principle of a *trine* in the *ministry*"—not merely in the *minister!* How can we account for this inconsistency in the New York society? Why did not that society perceive a little more clearly this ground *originally* assumed by the Central Convention, when the constitution of that body was drafted and presented by its most worthy and able minister, Mr. Doughty—whose " age, experience, and acquirements" did indeed "eminently fit *him* for a full measure of usefulness in the church": and why did not that society *state* it a *little* more clearly, when they reproached us for having had expunged from his draft the very determination of the trine, which *he* as *their minister* had mainly helped to bring about in the Eastern Convention? Can there be any question that this society did not see this "ground originally assumed"—nor *begin* to see it—till they were peculiarly enlightened by their new minister, the Rev. Thos. Wilks, who, in consequence of " his age, *experience,* and *acquirements,*" and his " being moreover an *ordained minister* in the *old church,*" having " eminently fitted him for a full measure of usefulness in the [new] church," was enabled, not only to know a great deal more about the constitution of the Central Convention than those who framed it, but also to see far more clearly what are the true teachings of Swedenborg in respect to the trine in the ministry than Jones, Howarth, Noble, Weeks, and such like old plodders who had blindly and lazily gone over those writings before him! Certainly, as enlightened by him, the " opinions" of the New York society seem to have undergone a *very remarkable change,* however strong "their tendency " may have been " for a long time *towards that point.*" And, as they shoved their boat from our shore, they, deceived by a very ordinary fallacy, thought we were moving off from them, instead of perceiving that they were moving off from us!

Unfortunately, there were other grounds of difference between us and the New York society, which were likely to obscure their view of the trinal order as presented by us. . One chief object in establishing the Central Convention was to print and publish the theological writings of Swedenborg by a general body of the church on the ground of pious devotion to the eternal interests of mankind. It was held

that these works ought to be given to mankind at as little as possible
over the cost of their production; and that it was essentially wrong
to tax men with a per centage on each and every copy of those works
sold throughout our whole country for the *gain* or *support* of *individuals* engaged in producing them on the plane of ordinary business
transactions. Of course, action on our principle would run against
the individual interests of booksellers in our connection : but we supposed that those booksellers would no more complain of us in this,
than they, as the printers of ordinary newspapers, would have complained of us, if we had given our money, our time, our talents, or
our labor, to the gratuitous printing and publishing of works containing the true political principles of our country's welfare. These
things are done on the ground of patriotic devotion to our country ;
and we did not see why they might not with equal or more propriety
be done on the ground of pious devotion to our church. On the same
ground, we would have had a periodical owned by our convention,
sustained by the voluntary contributions of its members, edited by its
organ, and supplied with matter by the gratuitous pens of the lovers
of truth for its own sake. We were opposed in principle to the *form*
of *a fifty cent* or *one dollar per page* CONSIDERATION for literary contributions to a *new-church periodical !* If there is any thing which a
man should *freely give*, without the least *appearance* of *any* return, or
recompense of reward, it seems to us it should be that *light* which
we have *so freely* and *so abundantly received !* Now it happened
that the New York society differed widely with us on this "ground
originally assumed by the Central Convention." They thwarted the
operations of our acting committee in the publication of certain works
of Swedenborg because our publication of them would interfere with
the individual interests of certain booksellers who were engaged in
publishing them. They differed from our acting committee in regard
to what works should be published ; and because they could not have
their own way in that, employed one of their own members, a book-
seller, to publish them *on the principles of the Eastern Convention*,
at the very time they were accusing us of having gone over to the
principles of that body on the subject of the trine in the ministry !
Nay, in the seventh annual meeting of our convention, they help to
make it the " duty of the acting committee to take into immediate
consideration the publication of a periodical under the auspices of this
convention, not as a party organ, but upon the most free and liberal
basis, as a new-church theological, scientific and literary journal, open
for the discussion of all subjects of importance and interest to the
general church," directing the appointment of the editor by the acting
committee, and subscribing for twenty-five copies of the work in the
name of the convention—and then go right home and *join with members of the Eastern Convention* in getting up just such a periodical,
to be controlled in part by the New York society through its minister
and publisher, on the opposite ground of catering for individual
interests—on the principle that " a *workman* is worthy of his *hire* "!
The same persons who do this, did, in the sixth annual meeting, take
a member of the New York society to task for moving, in that meet-

ing, the publication of the sermon which appears printed as Appendix V. to Journal No. VIII.! And if any one will read that sermon, he will see, more distinctly than we have time now to show him, what were those other grounds of difference between us and the New York society, which were likely to prompt this formal review and labored demolition of our, former report, upon which it is now our painful duty to make some remarks.

Our first remark, in reading the " Report of the Rev. Mr. Wilks on the Trine in the Ministry," is, to use a figure of speech of an able coadjutor of his, that it affords very striking evidence of there being many fragments of *the old egg shell* still clinging to his head.   Nay, we cannot help thinking that some parts of this report are very much like the peeping of an ecclesiastical chicken when the old egg shell is only just broken.

We next remark, that Mr. Wilks is rather bold in so soon coming forward in the judgment and settlement of difficult questions in our church.   He begins by observing that he, as a member of our council, had accepted a part in the division of our labors for finding in the Word and the writings of our church, authorities for the trine in our ministry, which, as a principle, the constitution of our convention had recognized : but, as a member of that council, he felt it his imperative duty, to go beyond that constitution, "to ascertain what the Word and the writings of Swedenborg teach concerning the external order of the ministry " in general.   The result of *one year's* investigation of all of Swedenborg's very voluminous works, and of the whole Word, besides a faithful discharge of his pastoral duties to the New York society, is, essentially different views of the subject from those which we have now shown were entertained by all the leading minds of our church both in England and in this country from its beginning up to his time.   Now we could not have had the least objection to Mr. Wilks's original investigation of this subject ; and we would have thanked him for all the *new* light which he could have thrown upon it *in our council*.   His *lights* would have made the *shades* of our picture more conspicuous.   He indeed might have helped us, as his brethren in the church, to have seen and renounced our errors.   But to say nothing at all to us on the subject, to give us not even the least hint that he was not co-operating with us in the work of which he had voluntarily taken a part, to go on and elaborate *in secret* a formal answer to our former hasty and weak effort, and then to bring up his huge " peace-maker " and explode it in our convention without the least intimation to us, as chairman of the council, of his intention to do so, was any thing but a kind and properly respectful regard to the *station* which we so reluctantly, however incompetently, held! This, however, is of very little consequence.   Mr. Wilks was bound to make an original investigation of this subject. The principle of a trine is one which so widely and deeply underlays the whole theological system of the new church as taught from the Lord by Swedenborg, that every man who takes the awfully responsible stand before the world of an official expounder of her doctrines, should have previously so thoroughly investigated the repositories of that system as to have obtained a clear insight into, and have fully made up his mind on, a subject so radical as this. Therefore Mr. Wilks was indeed bound " to ascertain what the Word and the writings of Swedenborg teach concerning the external order of the ministry." But he ought to have done this *before he sought to come into that ministry himself*. Above all, he ought to have been well satisfied in his own mind on this subject *before he publicly and solemnly signed the constitution of the Central Convention in the presence of its sixth annual meeting*. For, by that solemn act, he gave us to understand, that he recognized the principle of the trine as the constitution did: and without this, we, as an ordaining minister of our church, would not have involved ourselves in the responsibility of introducing him into any grade of her ministry. Objections to those forms of the trine which had been determined by the Eastern Convention were indeed rife among the members of our body. There were honest differences of opinion as to whether there should be a trine of *discrete* or *continuous* degrees in our ministry. But that there should be *a* trine of some sort in the *ministry* of our church, was a point conceded on all hands by those who framed the constitution of the Central Convention and signed it after its formal adoption in the first annual meeting. And we cannot conceive how any intelligent member of our church—much less one of her teaching ministers—could, in good conscience, have signed that instrument, without having come rationally to the same conviction, unless his object had been traitorously to subvert it afterwards. To say the least, therefore, Mr. Wilks's very proper original investigations of this subject were ill timed.

But we hesitate not to say they were insufficient. *One year*, if he could have given all the time to a concentrate investigation of all the voluminous writings of Swedenborg, and the whole Word too, was not sufficient to enable him, who had so recently come out of the ministry of the old christian church, and one of the most perverted sects of it, to acquire that clearness and distinctness of vision in the whole field of new-church theology, needed in the settlement of such a question as this. Mr. Wilks ought to have known—probably did know—that this subject had agitated our church for many years, and had been deeply investigated by her ablest men; and he ought to have been more cautious how he *so soon* arrayed himself against *them* in our connection. It was sorry work in him to shoot such small game as he aimed at in this report of his to the Central Convention. And it would have been well if he had stretched the horizon of his view across the Atlantic, and looked up to the eagles who have soared so high and so admirably in our church's firmament there! Perhaps this thought did not occur to him; or his innate modesty would have checked his coming, so soon after his admission into our ministry, as a Daniel to judgment, upon its knottiest points, and against its wisest men! As it is, we cannot divest ourselves of the idea, that, if he faithfully investigates the Word and the writings of Emanuel Swedenborg for *ten years*, instead of *one*, he is doomed to experience the mortifying conviction, that he has too hastily propounded to our church the decision of a deep subject on very superficial grounds.

And if he is a sincere lover, and an honest seeker, of truth for its own sake, we are sure that the day is not very far distant, when he will be brought to see, that the conclusions of this report of his are not less unsound, than the investigations upon which they rest are superficial.

These most general and very cursory remarks on Mr. Wilks's report, were all we thought of making; but some one seems to whisper, that these will be regarded as ill natured, if you do not proceed to give a more particular notation of what seem to you its weak points. Well, Mr. Wilks first expounds the constitution of the Central Convention, in order to show, that the temporary platform, which we had hastily erected, in express conformity with that constitution, for the very purpose of ordaining him into our ministry, was unconstitutional. Those who framed that constitution, regarded our convention as a *general church, embracing societies within it* as the human body embraces its organs and members within it. But Mr. Wilks makes this body consist of " simply individual receivers, forming a self-constituted body, as independent of, and unconnected with, the societies, as the societies are in relation to each other." The fact is, that he is in the too common fallacy of confounding the annual or general meeting with the convention; which are two very distinct things, as may be seen by comparing Articles I. VI. VII. of the Const. and XXI. of Dec. Prin. with Articles VIII.—XV. of the Const. But it is conceded that neither the Central Convention itself, nor the annual meeting in its name, has any right whatever to exercise *control* or *dominion* over the members of the new church in their individual or collective capacity—nor to *coerce* them in any way whatever. Hence Mr. Wilks argues that "the law which establishes a trine of discrete or distinct offices in the external order of the ministry, and thereby makes pastors subordinate to a superior ruling priest, must necessarily invest that superior with *power* or *dominion* over *pastors* AND *their societies*, [does not follow at all;] otherwise *pastors* could not be subordinate to *him*. Consequently, by the establishment of such a law, this convention, notwithstanding its constitution, most positively declares that it neither has, nor could have, nor should have, any right whatever to exercise control or dominion over the members of the new church, in their individual or collective capacity, yet *most arbitrarily* exercises dominion over them, so far even as to *deprive* the *societies* of the *power* of *self-government*, and *makes them* AND *their pastors* subordinate to the *rule* of another, whom it places over *them*, as *their* superior, in ecclesiastical authority and power. It is, therefore, most obvious that the institution of such a law by this body, even temporarily, *is a palpable violation of its constitution*, and should, for this reason, *be immediately repealed*. If it be necessary to establish such an order in the church, it must be done, not by this convention, *whose constitution denies it the power in any instance whatever, to legislate for the church*, but by a body of men delegated by the societies, and fully authorized by them." This is a first-rate specimen of Mr. Wilks's argument—of both its nature and its force. It shows how *able* he is in *proving too much*. In another place, we have displayed his masterly skill in convicting even Swedenborg of·teaching what is *contrary* to the *Divine Word!* And here he proves, to our fullest conviction, that *he and the New York society do not* BELIEVE *what he says to be* TRUE. It is "*most obvious*" that all this is argumentative bluster for a certain effect. .For if Mr. Wilks had believed that the temporary platform on which he himself was ordained in·our convention was *unconstitutional*, why did he not tell us so at the time of its erection? Why did he receive ordination on it? Or, if he did not then see it in that light, why did he not resign the office so soon as he discovered that his ordination into it was *null* in consequence of the unconstitutionality of the laws under which it was made? Nay, how could he, and the New York society, both consent to ask and receive, from the very annual meeting to which this redoubtable report was read, his ordination into the second degree, upon this very platform, which he deems "a *palpable violation* of its constitution," that "should, for this very reason, be *immediately* repealed"? There is but one answer to this question. Either Mr. Wilks and· his society *did not believe* that this platform was a.palpable violation of our constitution that ought to be immediately repealed; or they both yielded to the foul temptation of receiving unjust powers unconstitutionally bestowed! They may take which horn of this dilemma they choose. Charity impels us to take the former; and to conclude that they did not believe a word of what is here said—that they wanted Mr. Wilks to return to them "with full powers", and blustered just so much, and in just such a way, as was likely to attain that end. Most certainly we shall wash our hands of any more ordinations into our ministry under such equivocal circumstances!

Now the simple truth of the matter is, that the fourth article of our constitution disclaims any right whatever in our convention, either as a general church, existing at all times in space, or a general meeting of its members in their "personal capacities," (See Art. XII.) once a year, to exercise the powers or authorities of an *ecclesiastical council.* That is, no measure of our convention was to have any binding force upon individual or other members of the church, *because ·it was a measure of our convention.* No individual member of our body, no society within its bosom, was at any time to be at all bound to believe a thing, or do it, *because* an annual or other general meeting *decreed it.* All our general church was to do, was to *recommend*—by wise counsel and intelligent deliberation to ascertain and show—what *the Lord and the church teach* upon any given subject; and then every individual or other member of the church was to be bound to believe or do what was so taught on "no other authority than its own intrinsic truth," of which "every one was to judge for himself in the light of God's Word and the writings of his church." Thus our convention's hands were not so tied by its own constitution that it could do nothing as a general church in the way of rightly governing the parts that composed it by *the statutes of heaven* which respect "the administration of the divine law and worship." All that it bound itself to do, was, not to exercise any thing like an arbitrary, or compulsory, or coercive, authority of its own in regard to those matters. It acknow-

ledged solely the authority of the Lord in his Word and the teachings'
of his church. It acknowledged as such a teaching the principle of
a trine in the ministry. It acknowledged the grades of that trine as
they had already been established by the general church in the United
States at the time of its constitution.·(See Art. XIX.) It made it the
duty of its ministers "to determine the trine in the ministry as taught
in the Word, and from thence in the writings of Swedenborg, and to
make such *rules* and *regulations with respect to their own government*,
and the proper discharge of the ministerial functions, as *they may
think necessary*." It further made it their "province to determine
the qualifications required for admission into the ministerial office; to
prescribe the mode and manner of ordination; and, *the convention concurring, to admit suitable persons into the same*." It, however, provided, "that nothing which the ministers of this convention in their
official capacity might determine, should be a law binding on this
body, until the body should·adopt it in general meeting assembled."
Now suppose that the Lord does in fact teach that the ministry of the
new church, to be a perfect one, should have a trine of superior and
inferior ministers, among whom there is a subordination of the lower
to the higher as what is external is subordinate to what is internal in
man—suppose the ministers of the Central Convention, called upon,
by two of its societies, to admit ministers into the ministerial office
for them, do report to its annual meeting some of those passages from
the Word and from the writings of Swedenborg in which they believe
that the Lord does in fact teach this doctrine; but not being able, for
want of time, to bring forward all of the passages which are supposed
to bear on this doctrine, and yet, being pressed by the exigencies of
said societies to make such a determination of the trine as will allow
the immediate admission of their ministers into our ministry under
our constitutional provisions, propound a platform of laws of order
respecting the grades of the ministry, their *own* government, and the
proper discharge of the ministerial functions, for the time being—and
suppose that the annual meeting to whom these· laws are propounded,
does adopt them with only one dissenting voice—can it be said, with
any show of truth, propriety, or sound judgment, that this is a *palpable violation* of the *constitution* which, *for this very reason*, should be
immediately repealed! The ordination of Mr. Benade, or Mr. Wilks,
was his admission into the ministerial office, not merely in connection
with the Philadelphia or the New York society, but in connection
with the general church in the United States. They were thereby
admitted into the ministry as a general body. And how could such a
body receive and sustain them without general laws of ecclesiastical
order? And how could such general laws, made as rules and regulations for the government of the *ministry* itself, be construed into
arbitrary dominion over the whole church? Were not the New York
society and Mr. Wilks both bound by the Lord's doctrine in the Word,
and from the Word in the writings of his church? And could the
Central Convention's acknowledgment of that doctrine and declaration of it as its law, be construed into the exercise of arbitrary dominion over him and that society? If the New York society perceived

that these laws were against the teachings of the Lord by his Word and the writings of his church, all it had to do was to withdraw from the Central Convention on that ground. The Central Convention had not the least power to *coerce* it in this matter in any way whatever. We are informed that its minister could have very easily procured ordination in another quarter; and indeed subjected himself to a charge of breach of promise by accepting ordination where he did. So that the New York society was under no sort of constraint in this matter. The only question was, then, in respect to the doctrine of the trine as it was involved in the platform of laws so propounded. If the Lord does not teach this doctrine—if our ecclesiastical council was mistaken in its view—if the annual meeting was unduly influenced or persuaded to adopt the laws propounded to it against its own rational conviction of what is true in the light of God's Word and the teaching of his church—and if this can be shown by Mr. Wilks or the New York society, then indeed is the platform on which he and Mr. Benade were ordained into the first and second degrees, and Mr. Powell into the third degree, of our ministry, most unconstitutional and most worthy of being instantly repealed. But to argue that it is unconstitutional and to be repealed, merely because the Central Convention has bound itself by the fourth article of its constitution not "*to legislate for the church* in any instance whatever," is astonishingly weak. For the Central Convention did not obligate itself, by its constitution, or in any other way, to prevent the ministers of the general church in the United States who joined it, from exercising the power which they possessed prior to their becoming its members, or from making such laws for their own government as they might think proper, provided their laws did not in any way bind the convention without its own adoption. The sole reason assigned by Swedenborg for superior and inferior officers in ecclesiastical affairs, amongst whom there is subordination, is order amongst the governors. The Central Convention, by its fundamental law, assigns the *duty* to its ministers of making such rules and regulations for their own government, and the proper discharge of the ministerial functions as they may think necessary; and gives them power to determine the trine in the ministry as the basis on which those rules and regulations shall rest *for their own government*. And when this is done, shall it be said that these rules and regulations, as laws adopted by the body in general meeting assembled, are enacted in legislation *for the whole church*, so as "to deprive its *societies* of the *power* of *self-government?*" Where is the science of optics—where the optical instrument—which will enable any one to see in the temporary platform on which Messrs. Benade, Wilks and Powell were ordained into the three grades of our ministry, the *most arbitrary exercise of dominion* over the Philadelphia and New York societies, so far even as to deprive *them* of the *power* of self-government, and make *them and their pastors* subordinate to the *rule* of another"! What was there *any way like* to control, dominion, or a right to *coerce* those societies in the laws of that platform? Was it not made to *accommodate* those societies in the utmost concession to their wants and their wishes!

And how was the New York society *constrained*, in the least degree, "to await the action of the convention of 1847, before asking of its minister the ordinances of the church," by any *authority* which the Central Convention had assumed over it in the platform on which we had ordained that minister at its request—nay at its *demand?* If there was any constraint in this matter, it was a constraining of the ministers of our convention to act against their convictions in pre- mature and hasty compliance with the wishes of those societies. If the New York society believed that its minister, the Rev. Thos. Wilks, had the Lord's authority to administer to it the ordinances of his church, and all it, *in right*, had to do, was *to ask him* to administer them to it, and if it thought our ecclesiastical council had not the Lord's authority for the doctrine of the trine which they taught, why should it come to the ministers of the Central Convention to admit him into the ministerial office? To say they did it "for the sake of peace," is fudge. What power had the ministers of the Central Con- vention to make "the law which establishes a trine of discrete or distinct offices in the external order of the ministry"? If that law is not made by the Lord through Swedenborg, it is no law at all—has no binding force whatever upon the New York or any other society; and that society knows it so well, that they would never have thought of coming to us to ordain Mr. Wilks under it, on the supposition that our convention had made it. Our ministers had the power given them by the constitution of the Central Convention, which the New York society had a chief hand in making as its own and our funda- mental law, to determine from the Word and the writings what the trine should be. They determined it according to the platform in question. The authority for that determination was the doctrine of the Word and the writings which they quoted. The laws, therefore, if truly founded on that doctrine, were those of the Word and of the church's writings: so that all that is arbitrary in them must be ascribed to that quarter. The platform that contains them was not enacted by the ministers in any violation of Article XX. of the constitution. It was merely propounded by them to the annual meeting of the con- vention. The New York society, fully represented in that meeting, *freely adopted that platform as* ITS LAWS. And then we ordained its minister under those laws. Is it not absurd in the highest degree, then, for that society and its minister afterwards to turn round and accuse the Central Convention of "*most arbitrarily* exercising domi- nion over them, *so far even as to deprive the society of the power of self-government*, and making it and its minister subordinate to the *rule* of another" by simply acting under laws which they and he had adopted without the least dissent in an annual general meeting of that body? That society, or its minister, surely will not presume to say that our convention had even attempted to exercise any thing like arbitrary dominion or rule over them between the period of his ordination and the rendering of this his report! We answer, then, that the platform in question was *not* a violation of any part of the constitution of our convention. But if it were such a violation, then is the Rev. Thomas Wilks's ordination under its laws *null* and *void*.

We hesitate not thus officially to pronounce it so. And if he really thinks that platform "a palpable violation of our constitution," we call upon him, as an honest man, to resign the office which he holds, in testimony of the truth of his convictions.

Mr. Cabell has fully answered the position that we are not allowed to draw our argument in *confirmation* of the external order of our ministry from the Lord's example in. founding the first christian church as set forth in the Acts and Epistles of his Apostles.

We think we have quite as fully answered the argument that the christian ministry is "altogether different in its character from the jewish priesthood," because the representative ritual of the jewish church was wholly and for ever abrogated in the christian dispensation.

Mr. Cabell has also most signally convicted Mr. Wilks of a partial quotation of Swedenborg's explanation of Matt. xxiii. 8–12, to prove a perfect equality of the christian ministry as established by the Lord in his first advent. And we perhaps vainly imagine that we have shown against him that, "according to Swedenborg," there should be christian *priests* as well as *preachers*, and that the christian ministers *have* something more to do than merely to teach truth and lead to good thereby. And other leading and prominent points of his report have been so fully answered elsewhere, that we will now only run over it and remark upon a few sentences of it as they here and there strike us most forcibly.

"Peter was representative of *natural* truth derived from good, for he was representatively *the* rock on which the Lord said *he would build his church.*" This, to our minds, is a very striking instance of a complete non sequitur. Perhaps Mr. Wilks can tell us what is the distinction between *natural good* and *good of the natural principle.* If he can, then, *perhaps*, he can see that there is a difference between *natural truth* and *truth of the natural principle.* The Word in its letter is *divine truth* of the *natural principle;* and, therefore, is *divine* truth in its fulness and its power. Is not "*natural* truth" a very different thing from this? "Truths from the good of love to the Lord," or "doctrine from those truths," "were represented by Peter." Was Peter, in representing those, the "representative of *natural* truth derived from good"? Are not "truths from the good of love to the Lord" *spiritual* truths of the highest order? Is not *that* truth which Peter confessed, and on which the Lord builds his church, of all others the *most spiritual?*

"Further, Peter, we are informed, represented all those who, being in truth from good, teach in the church, and thus, by teaching, lead to good—*the only duty*, which, according to Swedenborg, appertains to the christian ministry. Consequently, Peter was representative of *all* that appertains to the ministry of the new church, in his representation of natural truth, the first principle of the church; *the same principle being represented by the twelve in their apostleship.* It is therefore manifestly evident, that the christian ministry *can have no other* CORRESPONDENCE *than that of natural truth, or truth in the understanding, teaching, thus* leading to good; the ministry being thus representative of the Lórd as to *the truth of the Word in its literal sense.*" This is a pretty striking instance of *vox, et preterea nihil*—*assertion*, and *nothing but* assertion. If Swedenborg teaches any thing, it is that the twelve apostles represented *all* the *truths* AND GOODS of the church in the complex. We will not insult our readers. by citing the parts of Swedenborg's writings where he teaches this. We need not say again that James and John represented the new-church ministry as well as Peter. Nor that "*according to Sweden-borg*" John had precedence of Peter. Nor that christian ministers are called in the Word *priests* because they teach *good*, as well as *prophets* because they teach *truth*. Nor that christian ministers represent *doctrine from* the Word which is its *spiritual sense*—that those who teach from the letter of the Word only, without the lamp of doctrine previously drawn from the Word by those who are in illus-tration from the Lord, grope in darkness, see phantasies, and confirm heresies. If Mr. Wilks will turn to U. T. 508, he will see a revela-tion of the character and quality of the new church and her priest-hood by the representative emblem of a temple: and we would par-ticularly call his attention to the signification of what was seen in , that temple—especially " within, on the south side, verging towards the west," where "was a pulpit, on which, towards the right, lay the Word *open*, encompassed with *a sphere of light*, whose *brightness surrounded and illuminated the whole pulpit:*" while " in the midst of the temple was a sacred place, with a veil to cover it," having within "a cherub of gold with a sword in his hand that turned every way." Perhaps Mr. Wilks will find in that revelation reason to change his opinion, that Peter, in his representation of *natural* truth— of the Lord as to the truth of the Word in its *literal* sense—was representative of *all* that appertains to the ministry of the new church!

We cannot express our astonishment at the consummate assurance of this assertion—" Now it is evident that in the christian ministry, instituted by the Lord, revealed in the Word, and explained in the writings of the church, there is nothing *which in the least indicates!!!* that there should be in the church three distinct classes of priests, the lower subordinate to the higher; nor that *in the least implies* that there should be *any* distinction of rank or order among the clergy: but, on the contrary, *all that is said upon the subject*, ALTOGETHER DISCOUNTENANCES EVERY THING LIKE *such distinction*, and most evi-dently shows, that, among christian ministers, there should be *perfect equality.*" If there is any thing more astonishing than this assertion, it is the quotation of the Lord's words to prove it. We suppose the reader has Mr. Wilks's report opened at page 48 before him, and has read the first two-fifths of that page: and we ask, Does he not see a most strange perversion of the Lord's very words?—" He that *is greatest* among you," turned right upside down to mean *no one is* greatest! Does not the greatest *serve* in *ruling?* The greatest rules as the younger when the intellectually strong man rules from love and its innocence. And the *younger* has the *most* power, because he has the power of innocence, the power of love. And we have

advanced at least one passage of Swedenborg's writings, in which he
pretty strongly countenances the idea, that John, who reclined on
the Lord's bosom, and followed him when Peter did not, was, on
these accounts, greater than Peter, and therefore not on a perfect
equality with him.　　There is, also, very considerable *probability*, that
Judas, who had the bag, was *somewhat* inferior to Peter, James, and
John.　　Yet we suppose we shall have to admit, under the irresistible
conviction wrought in our mind by Mr. Wilks's *able* report on the
trine in the ministry, that to say that John was the Lord's *beloved*
disciple, *perhaps*, does not *in the least imply* that there was *any* distinction of *representative* rank or order between him and Judas!

We have borne as well as we could Mr. Wilks's utter demolition
of our feeble argument from Gen. xviii. and from A. C. 3670 for a
trine of priests, still to be representative of the Lord in his priestly
offices of redeeming and saving mankind, as well as perpetually
blessing them.　　What force there may be in the rejoinders of this
report, remains to be seen.

Our argument for grades of superior and inferior priests from H. D.
313-319, is assailed on page 53.　　After quoting our argument, Mr.
Wilks observes, "Such is the language of the report; but the doctrine
here taught *is not the doctrine taught by Swedenborg*."　　Indeed!!
Yes, Mr. Wilks knows better than we do on this subject.　　"*Nothing
is said* in H. D. concerning superior and inferior *governors* in the
church, amongst whom there is subordination, *nor concerning order
amongst ecclesiastical governors*, lest any one, from caprice or inadvertence, should permit evils which are against order, and thereby
destroy it."　　Swedenborg, in "what is said in H. D. concerning
governments and governors" "is speaking of order, *not in the church*,
but *in the world*."　　"There are," indeed, "*two things* which *ought*
to be in order *amongst men*, viz. *the things which are* of *heaven*, AND
the things which are of *the world*," that is, "ecclesiastical things"
and "civil things."　　And "*governors* over *those things amongst men
which relate to heaven*, or over *ecclesiastical* matters, are called priests,
and their office is called the priesthood."　　But mark—pray do not
fail to mark, by any means—that Swedenborg only says *they* are
called priests, and *their office* is *called* the priesthood.　　He does not
say they *are* priests or that their office *is* the priesthood.　　He says this
only in accommodation to the usual mode of speaking in the church
of his day.　　He did not mean that they *were* to be called priests, or
their office the priesthood.　　For there are no priests in heaven—there
are only *preachers* there—and therefore christian ministers should not
be called priests, but preachers on earth; and their *only* duty is to
preach and teach *natural* truth from the letter of the Word.　　Therefore, Swedenborg says what he does not mean, in saying "*Governors*
in ecclesiastical matters amongst men are *called* priests and their office
the priesthood."　　Consequently, in "what is said in H. D. concerning
governments and *governors*" he "is speaking of order, *not* in the
church, but in the *world*."　　*This* is as *Mr. Wilks* READS Swedenborg!
Well we suppose his confident assertion in these premises settles this
question for ever.　　All we can do is to bend our heads and say, the

Gamaliels at whose feet we sat, all read Swedenborg differently; as our readers may now see by consulting the reports on the trine, which we have given, of Noble, Howarth, Smithson and Weeks. In short, all of the most distinguished men of our church, both in England and in this country, whom we have consulted on this point—and we can assure our readers that they have not been *few*—have uniformly understood Swedenborg to speak in H. D. of *both* ecclesiastical and civil governors, and to apply to the former as much as to the latter, what he says in number 313. Now we do not presume to set up *our* reading of Swedenborg as of any consequence against that of the Rev. Thomas Wilks; we merely say *we have adopted* that of the above mentioned leaders in our church *in preference to his.* Of course, all the members of our church, who, like us, are not able to form an opinion for themselves from Swedenborg's own words, will know " which of the two to choose."

But "it is unnecessary to make further comment, as the meaning of the language of the illumined teacher *cannot be misunderstood.*" Indeed! Then why has Mr. Wilks misunderstood it?

His garbled quotation of H. D. 314, to show that priests should have *no sort* of ecclesiastical *government* in the church, we have already noticed; and can only now remark, that it deserves the severest animadversion.

Mr. Wilks comes at length to Coronis 17, in which it is said, "*Similiter in Ecclesia, primus infulatus, antistites parochi, et flamines sub illis.*" And as we have so fully answered what he says on this famous sentence in another part of our report, we need make no more remarks upon it here. We will merely quote these words of his :— " Here, then, Swedenborg is speaking of the trine which *now exists* in civil and ecclesiastical governments; *such a trine being the natural and necessary consequence of such forms of government :*"—and ask, is this the doctrine of Swedenborg in Coronis 17? "His language, certainly, by no means implies that governments cannot properly exist without *such* external forms." What external forms? Regal? Granted. But does it imply that any governments can properly exist without such a *trine* as there is in man? " It simply means, that where a kingdom exists, that kingdom will naturally assume such a form. In like manner in the church, under *its present form,* [this is a very material interpolation, which the words of Swedenborg do not at all justify,] there will naturally be in it such a trine as that mentioned by him : for he says, that, in *every order* and in *every thing,* there will be *a trine,* and that *nothing* CAN *exist without it.*" This Swedenborg does, indeed, in substance, say. He undoubtedly teaches this. And the only thing that surprises us is, that Mr. Wilks should state and admit this, and yet *conclude* that the new-church ministry *may* exist without it.

Mr. Wilks's first reason, that Swedenborg, by this number of Coronis, did not intend to teach there should be a trine in the new-church ministry, like the head, body and feet in man, because such an order is utterly impracticable at the present day, has no force whatever in our minds. " The external order" which he supposes to be implied by the terms of Swedenborg's language, is not, we believe, taught by him.   We have no idea that by a *primus infulatus* he meant "a high priest at the head of a nation." We agree with Mr. Wilks that "the end 'of order is use, and that only can be divine order which is not only practicable, but which is best fitted for the church, in its present state, to perform the uses for which it is established, and by which it can most efficiently perform the greatest amount of good in the world." And precisely on this ground do we argue that there *must* be in the ministry of the new church *Primus infulatus, Antistites parochi, et flamines sub illis*—not only because this trinal order is now practicable, but because it is now and at all times essential and indispensable to the existence and subsistence of our church in her true order and efficiency.   For all her uses, and especially her priestly uses, are in form a man; in whom there is a trine of head, body, and feet with soles.   And it is impossible for "the church, in its present state," or in any future state, "to perform the uses for which it is established, and by which it can *efficiently* perform the greatest amount of good in the world," unless her ministry has priests of a discrete grade, *as a head*, for the performance of *head ecclesiastical uses;* and another discrete grade of priests under these, *as a body*, for the performance of *corporal ecclesiastical uses;* and still another discrete grade of priests under these, as *feet and soles of the feet*, for the performance of *pedal ecclesiastical uses:* because "in every order, and in every thing, there will be a trine, and *nothing* can *exist without it.*"   The only question is, *Is there* A TRINE OF PRIESTLY USES NOW *to be performed in our church*? If there is, then there are *capital* priestly uses which need to be performed *now*. And for the performance of these in each particular church we must have a *capital* ecclesiastical officer. And such an officer is just as practicable now, as the uses which he is to perform are now practicable. To say that the order which calls for a pontiff as a head officer for the whole new church in any nation, or throughout the world, is not practicable now, is most true. For no order is practicable in the new church but *true* order, and this order is not true. The *uses* of such a *head* for the whole new church are utterly impracticable to any one mere man; they can be performed by God-man alone. And therefore the order which calls for such a head is now and at all times utterly impracticable. But this is a very different thing from concluding that it is impracticable to have, in the *ministry* which *represents* the Lord to the church, those priests who represent his head, with others under them to represent his body, and others still under these to represent his feet. And as the dignity and honor are in the office, not in the man who fills it, there is nothing impracticable in regard to finding a man for the office, if the office itself is not impracticable. Let us, then, look at the *use;* and provide the man for its performance: and when there is a man who, in the Lord's providence, by our instrumentality, does in fact perform this *representative* use, let us respect him for the sake of the use, and not the use for the sake of him. If we are careful to avoid man-worship in *this* way; we shall not find it long, or very, impracticable to worship the Lord in *that* way.

Mr. Wilks reasons—"Secondly; if the trine mentioned in the Coronis were essential to the order of the priesthood, it would, doubtless, like every other doctrine of the church, be plainly taught in the writings of the church, and not merely in a cursory manner be alluded to, or simply mentioned in illustration of the fact that in all things there is a trine, whilst in no one instance, either before or after, in all the writings, is one word said upon the subject." We answer that it was impossible for Swedenborg to have taught more plainly that "*the trine is essential* to the order of the priesthood," than by teaching that "in *all things* there *is* a trine," and "that *nothing can* exist without it :" for this is in *general* to say that *no priesthood can exist* without it : but when he says *in particular*, in that immediate connection—*Similiter in Ecclesia, erit Primus infulatus, Antistites parochi, et flamines sub illis*—he expressly, positively and most plainly teaches the particular truth, that *every* priesthood, to be in just order, must be just such a trine as man. And if he had uttered this particular truth in every possible variation of phrase, and in every page of all his other writings, he could not have taught it more plainly. And as to the rest, we further answer, if it were essential to the order of the priesthood, "that there should be *but one order* of priests," and "but one ordination into the priesthood," it would, doubtless, like every other doctrine of the church, be *plainly taught* in the writings of the church; and not merely in a *most cursory* manner *run over* without *ever mentioning it once*—without *ever alluding to it at all*, and without, *in a single instance*, mentioning it in illustration of the fact that in *all* things there is a *trine !* In short, when Mr. Wilks can produce a single passage of Swedenborg's writings in which it is in any way stated that, to give perfection to the priesthood, there should be *but one order of priests*, amongst whom there is *the most perfect equality*, with *but one inauguration* into the *single plane* of ministerial *labor* and *use*, and that *such a one is man;* we will admit that he has made out his case by something else than mere ratiocination, which proves the true order of the priesthood by reasoning from those passages of Swedenborg's writings which *have no material relevancy whatever to the subject !*

It is most obvious to our minds that Mr. Wilks came to the investigation of this subject in the Word and the writings of Swedenborg with *a preconceived opinion*. His object was, not simply to learn what Swedenborg does indeed teach respecting a *trine* in the ministry ; but, with a mind made up, that there is but one order of priests and a perfect parity between them, he has looked through the Word and Swedenborg's writings only for battering-rams to demolish our former report. Hence he does not see a trine even in those passages which do really teach it. Thus he quotes U. T. 55, which teaches a trine most conclusively to us, and sees in it only an argument against a trine in the ministry. These are his observations on that passage :—"Here we are taught that the *ceremonies of the church*, that is, the externals of worship, and the external order of the church, are its dress, which

39

may be changed as the internal state of the church may demand. Many such changes have, during the past, taken place in these externals, corresponding with the differences in the internal state of the church; and *as the internal state of the new church is to be essentially different from that of the jewish and papal churches, the external form also of the new church should differ as widely from theirs.*" Swedenborg says, " in the order according to which the church is established by God," " the laws which relate to God will make its head, the laws which relate to the neighbor will make its body, and the ceremonies will make the dress"—the last being necessary to hold the others together in their order so as to preserve them from dissolution.   Here we see the doctrine of a trine in the order of the church quite plainly taught, although in a more general way than in Coronis 17.   Here the church has a head, a body, and a dress.   The feet and soles of the feet are not mentioned; and what is *extraneous to the body of the church itself* is mentioned as the third term of its trine. And it is most obvious that Swedenborg is not teaching any thing here specifically concerning the priesthood.   It is evident that he does not allude at all to the priestly offices or functionaries of the priesthood in the mention of *ceremonies* as the *dress* of the church.   For "the priesthood is the *first order of the church*" itself, (Ap. Ex. 229,) and not merely a garment that is put on to its body.   Yet Mr. Wilks seizes hold of so much of this passage as will countenance his idea, that the priestly offices of the jewish church were wholly abrogated in the christian church on account of that change in the external order of this church which was necessary to correspond with its internal state, which he assumes is " essentially different from that of the jewish and papal churches "; and he concludes from it, that the external order of the christian priesthood must, in true correspondence with its internal state, differ so totally from that of the jewish priesthood, as to have only one order of priests instead of three.   We trust this argument has been completely confuted in another place.   Here we will only remark, that the *ceremonies* of the *church,* and the *constitution* of its *priesthood,* are two very different things.   And cannot Mr. Wilks see, that the establishment of a priesthood is not a ceremony of the church?   Therefore, that a change in *ceremonies* does not imply a change of *priesthood?*   Priesthoods are indeed changed, but not in the same church.   The ceremonies of the same church may constantly change, like a man's dress.   But the priesthood of a church remains while the church itself exists, because it is an essential part of the church's very constitution—being the internal of its visible body, as the laity is its external. (Ap. Rev. 567.)   When an old church ends, and a new one begins, then there is a change of priesthood.   But, as we have shown, the priesthood in all cases represents the Lord, and must exist in trinal order, because this is essential to its full formation.

Mr. Wilks's third reason, why Swedenborg did not intend to teach, in Coronis 17, that the trine is the true order for the new-church ministry is, "that his writings every where show that the perfection of the external order of a government, be it civil or ecclesiastical, is in exact ratio to the internal corruption of that government; and

purely for the reason that internal evils necessarily demand external
restraints to keep men in order, otherwise the human race would
perish." When we first read this position as it is stated here, we
were filled with unmingled surprize. And this surprize was only
equalled by the astonishment which we afterwards felt at hearing
this part of Mr. Wilks's report generally and loudly extolled for its
wonderful acuteness! We knew, indeed, that strong and arbitrary
civil governments had sprung up in providential reaction upon the
grasping and domineering lusts of selfish and worldly loves. But that
this was applicable as a universal law to the external order of a
church, or to ecclesiastical government; and that Swedenborg's
" writings *every where*" showed this; was what it had never entered
into our heads to conceive! Even in regard to civil governments,
we do not understand him to teach that their external order is *more
perfect* in the exact ratio to their internal corruption. For all history
proves, that internal corruption has enervated governments and
destroyed nations. Perhaps no government of ancient or modern
times was more perfect than that of the Roman Empire : but was not
that destroyed by its internal corruption? Was it not destroyed by
excess of love of dominion and love of wealth from the love of self—
manifested in luxury and vice? So of ancient Babylon—of Greece,
and Macedon, and Persia, and the myriads of other nations which
have risen like fire balls high in the zenith of earth's atmosphere,
glared in fearful portent, and sunk at last extinguished in eternal night!
Besides, the perfection of government consists in its thorough adaptation to effect and secure the general good. This is effected and secured
by general obedience to just laws. While men are selfish and worldly,
such general obedience can be secured only by the restraints and
coercions of the arbitrary sway of the love of dominion from the love
of self; and for mankind in this state such government may be the
most perfect. But "there are two sorts of dominion, one of love
towards the neighbor and the other of self-love; and the dominion of
love to the neighbor prevails amongst those who live separated into
houses, families and nations, but the dominion of the love of self
amongst those who dwell together in society." Government from the
dominion of love to the neighbor is like that of a father in his family—
in which there is the most perfect subordination and obedience to
those laws of order by which the general good of the whole house,
family or nation is secured. Nothing can be more full and therefore
perfect than are the subordination and the obedience which spring
spontaneous from love and without any sort of external constraint.
The utmost restraint and coercion of the external force of arbitrary
civil government cannot produce a superior if an equal subordination
and obedience to the laws which secure the common weal. Therefore the external order of the government of the dominion of the love
of the neighbor, is certainly as perfect, if not more so, than that of the
dominion of the love of self. And, therefore, it is not true that the
perfection of the external order of a government is in exact ratio to
the internal corruption of that government. For, "although the dominion of self-love is such in societies, there is, nevertheless, given a

dominion of love towards the neighbor, in kingdoms also, with those who are wise by virtue of faith and love to God; for these love the neighbor." (A. C. 10.814.) And the external order of a government in kingdoms also, whose internal is wisdom "by virtue of faith and love to God," will certainly be as perfect, if not more so, than the external order of a government in a kingdom whose internal is the most of all corrupt. The fact is, there is no power but in truth. Evil may assume the form of truth; but this is permitted in the divine economy for its correction. Hence, as we have abundantly shown elsewhere, the externals of churches have always been "the laws of order in the external form" *representing* "the laws of order in the internal form"; and hence the external order of all governments, however corrupt, that is, however selfish and worldly mankind may have been under them, have been the mimicry of truth; and they could have no power to restrain or correct evil any farther than they were forms of truth: because there is no power whatever in the falsity of evil to correct it. What is false only confirms what is evil. Truth only can restrain and correct it. Now the whole question is narrowed down to this simple point, has truth more power when it is the truth of evil than when it is the truth of good? Surely the *same* form of government, as a kingdom, for instance, is not more perfect, in the exact ratio to its internal corruption, than it would be if its internal were the wisdom and virtue of faith and love to God! The great fallacy of Mr. Wilks is, that the government of *external force* is more perfect than the government of *internal force*—thus, that the government of hell is more perfect than the government of heaven; for "the dominion of love towards the neighbor differs as much from the dominion of self-love as heaven differs from hell." (A. C. 10.814.) One fact proves that the Lord's government in heaven is more perfect than the strongest governments of hell, namely; that a single naked arm stretched out in the world of spirits causes all who see it to tremble. (A. C. 878.) Farther, the infernal hosts who "supposed that they had all power to do what they pleased" . . . "were thrust down to their infernal abodes by a little child, at whose presence they began so to totter and tremble that they could not help expressing their anguish by cries," (A. C. 1271;) and "one angel can put to flight myriads of evil spirits," (A. C. 1398:) and hence "it is the province of angels to rule infernal spirits." The external order of the government of the Lord in the heavens is not the less perfect, or the less strong and effective, because his government is free, and finds in the angels a most willing and unconstrained obedience. And the perfection of the external order of a government of hell, be it civil or ecclesiastical, is certainly *not* in the exact ratio to the internal corruption of that government. And if it be not so in the spiritual world, it cannot be so in the natural world. Therefore, Mr. Wilks's third reason, is just no reason at all, why Swedenborg means not to teach in Coronis 17, that there should be a trine in the new-church ministry like head, body and feet in man.

Mr. Cabell has so closely followed Mr. Wilks in this part of his argument, and has so ably exposed its fallacies, that it seems unnecessary for us to comment on his position that "the perfection of the external order was in proportion to the internal departure of the men of the church from the order of heaven." We admit, that there is great plausibility and apparent force in what Mr. Wilks advances to maintain this position. He displays the power of the serpent, which was "more subtle than any beast of the field which the Lord God had made." The power of the sensual principle ·lies in the *appearances* of *truth* in the ultimate plane of the mind. The dragon, which is a winged serpent, has now great power in the old christian church by reasonings from the appearances of truth in the letter of the Word. And the sect of the old church from which Mr. Wilks has come out, is, perhaps, more remarkable than any other for the exercise of that power which lies in the dragon's tail. He has brought with him into our church the great power of reasoning from the fallacies of sense. Now it does indeed *appear*, that the more external the church became, the more perfect was its external order. And as the church became external by the closing of its internal or spiritual principles and the opening or sole activity of its external or natural principles, that is, of selfish and worldly loves; hence it does indeed appear that the external order of the church became more perfect in the ratio of its internal corruption. In other words, the external order of the church in its celestial and spiritual states is more *simple;* but as it becomes more natural, its external order is more *complex.* This is the appearance. Hence the ritual of the jewish church is far more complicate and onerous than that of the christian church, which is relatively much more simple and easily to be observed. But this is only an *apparent* truth : because the forms of external order are more *manifest* than the forms of internal order. And as the church becomes more external, the perfection of its external order is more *seen :* while, as the church becomes more internal, the perfection of its external order is less obvious, because, in that ratio, it puts off mere external forms, and comes into internal ones, which are less conspicuous. For instance, it would seem that the laws concerning divorce and adultery were more complicate and severe in the jewish than the christian church; but in reality the laws of marriage are far more strict for the Christian than for the Jew, because more internal—"He that *looketh* on a woman to lust after her *hath committed adultery* with her *already* in his *heart.*" The truth is, then, that the forms of order in an internal church are not less perfect ; they are only less obvious. They are in fact *more perfect* in the degree that they become internal: because internal forms are more perfect than external ones. And, therefore, the *real* truth is, that the external order of a church is *more perfect* in the exact ratio of its *internal purity.* Consequently, the reverse of this, namely, that the external order of a church is more perfect in the exact ratio of its internal corruption, is a fallacy of sense.

Swedenborg very clearly and expressly teaches that forms are more perfect the more internal they are. Thus the forms of the brain are the most perfect of any in the human body. And as human society, in all of its existences, from first to last, or from highest to lowest, is in the most perfect form just so far as it is in the forms of the human body, therefore government will be in its most perfect external order, when its forms are those of the human brain. Consequently, the external order of the spiritual church must be more perfect than that of the natural church ; the external order of the celestial church still more perfect than that of the spiritual church; and the external forms of angelic society surpassingly more perfect than any external order of the church on earth in its utmost perfection. For "the forms of heaven are still more wonderful [than those of the human brain;] and such as cannot in any wise be comprehended, not even by the angels. *In such a form are the angelic societies* in the heavens, and into such a form the thoughts of the angels flow, and almost in an instant to a considerable distance, because *according to a form infinitely perfect.*" (A. C. 6607.) The reason of this is thus stated in D. L. & W. 204—" It *appears* as if *prior* things were *less* perfect than posterior things, or simple than compound things." Here, then, we have the ground of the fallacy, that the form of government is more perfect the more external the church or nation becomes. " It *appears* as if *prior* things were *less* perfect than posterior things; nevertheless prior things, from which compounds are formed, *are the more perfect.*" This is the *real* truth. "For prior or simple things are more naked and less covered with substances and matters void of life, and are as it were more divine; wherefore, they are nearer to the spiritual sun, where the Lord is: for perfection itself is in the Lord, and thence in the sun, which is the first proceeding of his divine love and divine wisdom, and thence in those things which proximately succeed, and so in order to the lowest, *which, according to their distance, are more imperfect.*" This, we should think, is clear enough in showing us the real truth of the matter. And in the light of this tuition we can plainly see that, in the descent of the church from the most ancient, or celestial, to the catholic hierarchy, which Mr. Wilks displays, the perfection of the external order must really have decreased according to its distance from the Lord, and the spiritual sun in which he is. In him is " perfection itself;" and the church must become more perfect, in both its external and its internal order, in the exact ratio of its approximation to him. See, in this connection, D. P. 6; and also C. L. 329—where these words occur : " Every thing divided is more and more multiple, and not more and more simple ; because what is continually divided approaches nearer and nearer to what is infinite, in which are all things infinitely."* Thus, as the complicate external order of the jewish church is put off, and the apparently more simple external order of the christian church is put on, there is really a more perfect external order assumed in the latter case, because it is more multiple, and nearer to the external order of Him who is " perfection itself."

" In the english protestant church, the inferior clergy, in many respects, *act altogether independently of the authority of the bishops:*

---

* Does not this principle explain truly the increased potencies of homœopathic triturations and dilutions ? And in this view how beautifully just is Dr. Hering's maxim, (either his own, or quoted by him,) " Die milde macht ist grosse " !

hence the case of the Rev. J. Clowes, who in that church preached
for so many years the doctrines taught by Emanuel Swedenborg—one
out of many cases of independence of thought and act, which are
almost daily occurrences among the english clergy." Is this really
so? Or has Mr. Wilks made another of his assertions without sufficient grounds for it in fact? The independence of *thought* in the
english clergy is, we believe, very great: so great that very many of
them are supposed to be Arians, Socinians, Deists and even Atheists.
But the inferior clergy are not at all independent in *official act*. Mr.
Clowes was arraigned before his bishop for preaching the doctrines of
the new church; and, it is thought, was tolerated only because Bishop
Porteus was himself tinctured with the same heresies. The fact is,
however, that the english protestant church is a civil establishment;
and not much notice is taken of its minister's private sentiments, provided he helps to sustain the establishment, pleases the people for
whom he officiates, and enjoys the patronage of the titled and great.

As to " the order of the church of Scotland," &c., we leave Mr.
Wilks in Mr. Cabell's able hands; and will only say a single word
about his fourth reason, why " Swedenborg, in the above passage of
the Coronis, does not teach the necessity of the external order therein
mentioned to the ministry of the new church," namely, because " to
suppose this is to suppose that he there teaches a doctrine which is
contrary to the Word of God, and the opposite of that in his own
writings, which is explanatory of the Word." The plain english of
this is, that Swedenborg, in illustrating his universal law, that " in
every thing there *is* a trine, and *nothing can exist* without it," has
used the example of a priestly order which is founded on what is
contrary to the Word of God and to the tenor of his own writings
in explanation of it. And all we have to say in answer is—*Let any
body believe it, who can!*

But Mr. Wilks, with most remarkable complacency, proceeds to
state, " We have already, we trust, *satisfactorily shown,* [to whom?—
not at all to us!] from the Word and the writings of Emanuel Swedenborg, that the order of ministry instituted by the Lord for the
christian church, admits of no distinction of superior and inferior
degrees among the clergy; that all who teach the Word are on the
same plane, being representatives of natural truth, and that no one
should acknowledge any other above him, than the Lord alone, he
only being the teacher, the father, and the master of all whom he
calls to be the ministers of his Word." On this we merely endorse—
*False—directly in the teeth of what both the Word and Swedenborg
teach:* as any one will see, who consults Swedenborg's explanations
of the part of the Word which Mr. Wilks quotes to prove it. But Mr.
Wilks says, " *Farther proof upon this point would be needless* "! We
answer—Yes, a *little* more is *desired;* a good deal more is *needed!*

But does not Mr. Wilks hold to a trine in our ministry in any
sense? Oh yes! He holds to a trine in *the* minister. Listen to him.
" Consequently such a trine [as *primus infulatus, antistites parochi
et flamines sub illis*] must necessarily exist in *every one* who rightly
teaches the truths of the new church; otherwise he cannot properly

perform the duties of his office-; for without the power to will what is good, the understanding to see truth and to judge how properly to instruct those whom he is appointed to lead, and the natural ability rightly to perform the uses of his calling, he cannot be a pastor, who will feed the spiritual flock with knowledge and understanding from the Word." As we read this, we were very forcibly reminded of one of Swedenborg's memorable relations, in which the spirits surrounding a conclave of celebrated ecclesiastics are heard, as some of the speakers deliver their sentiments, to exclaim, "How wise! how wise!! how wise!!!"

"Such pastors the Lord has promised to provide for his new church, *each one* of whom, like Peter, *representative of those who are called to preach*, [and not of the Lord in any degree of his priesthood!] WILL HAVE THIS TRINE IN HIMSELF, and who, consequently, *in his office** as a teacher of truth, will represent the Lord as far as it is necessary he should be represented by the Christian ministry." This, to our mind, is next to the most obnoxious form of a representation of the Lord by *one man*. It is, we confess, not so bad as a pontiff for a visible head of the whole church. But it is a younger brother of that impracticability. For *where* shall we find the *one man* who *has* in himself the church's perfect unity constituted by the full trine of its parts and principles? Will Mr. Wilks permit us to ask him, Has the Lord provided "*such pastors*" now? It seems to us almost as impracticable to find men whose *personal* and *official* qualifications shall *fit each* and *every one* of them to "represent the Lord *as far* as it is necessary *he should be* represented by the Christian ministry," as it would be to find in the United States any one "man in whom the church could be united, to whom to bow as its pontiff." But perhaps we may write over against the signature to the "Report on the Trine in the Ministry," which makes Appendix V. to Journal No. IX. of the Central Convention—*Ecce Signum!*

To show that the christian ministry should represent the Lord as one individual man to the new church, Mr. Wilks quotes the following relation:—"There appeared a tabernacle, as to its outward form, plain and simple. And the angels who were with me said, 'Behold, the tabernacle of Abraham, such as it was when the three angels came to him and announced the future birth of Isaac; it appears indeed simple to the eye, but, nevertheless, according to the influx of light from heaven, it becomes more and more magnificent!' And they were permitted to open the heaven which is the abode of angels who excel in wisdom, and then, by virtue of the influx of light from thence, the tabernacle appeared as a temple, resembling that at Jerusalem; and in looking into it, I saw that the stone in the floor under which the Word was deposited, was set with precious stones, from which there issued forth the bright rays, as of lightning, that shone

---

* Swedenborg says a *priest* "*represents* the *Lord* as to his work of salvation;" and "by *his office*" represents "*the work* of salvation itself." Thus the *officer* represents the *Lord* himself, and the *office* his *work* itself. But Mr. Wilks makes the pastor "in *his office* of teacher of *truth*," represent the Lord. Is not this a lamentable perversion or misapprehension of Swedenborg's doctrine?

upon the walls, and caused beautiful variegations of colors on certain cherubic-forms that were sculptured on them. As I was admiring these things, the angels said, 'Thou shalt yet see something more wonderful.' And it was permitted them to open the third heaven, which is the abode of the celestial angels, who excel in love; and then, by virtue of the influx of flaming light from thence, the whole temple disappeared, and in its stead was seen the Lord alone, standing on the foundation stone, which was the Word, in the same form as that in which he appeared to John, Rev. i." (Ap. Rev. 926.) Thus far Mr. Wilks quotes; but it is added, "But inasmuch as the interiors of the minds of the angels were then filled with holiness, occasioning in them a strong propensity to fall prostrate upon their faces, suddenly the passage of light from the third heaven was closed by the Lord, and that from the second heaven opened again, in consequence of which the former appearance of the temple returned, and also of the tabernacle; but this was in the midst of the temple. Hereby," &c. This latter part of the relation shows that the Lord could not be permanently seen in his representative form as *one* man by even the angels of heaven; how, then, can he be so seen by the members of his church on earth in her incipient, natural and imperfect state? Yet in this relation, Mr. Wilks thinks "it is obvious that, agreeably to the divine revelations, and the appearance of the Lord to his new church, as representatively seen by John, and Emanuel Swedenborg, the ministry of this church represent him, not as three, but as one man, in whom is the trine, and should, according to the instructions of the Word, and the order of heaven, consist simply of one order of priests, whose duty it is to teach truths, and thereby lead to heaven, in perfect freedom, those who are willing to be led and governed by the Word." *Such* is Mr. Wilks's *authority*, from the Word and the writings of Swedenborg, for but one order of priests in the new-church ministry! And upon this authority he asserts that "the Central Convention *has power to establish no other* than *such* an order of priesthood; and therefore should not *presume* to do so." Well, we have only this simple remark to make—If the authority for a trine in Coronis 17, is *slim*, this authority for one order of priests is much *slimmer!*

"The wisdom of the angels consists solely in this, that what they think, they see and comprehend." (Doct. of F. 4.) "They who are in illumination from the Lord have a spiritual idea that the thing which they are hearing or reading, is true or not true." (Ibid. 5.) And Mr. Powell, with singular acuteness and truth of observation, has told us that we are first to see that the thing which we are now discussing is true before we attempt to confirm it. Swedenborg, in Coronis 17, where he speaks expressly of the church, says directly there should be such a trine as man, that is a head, body and feet—a *Primus*, an *Antistes*, and a *flamen*. Thus he says there should be three priests, that should hold the same relation to one another that the head, the body and the feet do in man. Now, Mr. Wilks—True or not true? You say—Not true! Swedenborg does not mean to say that it *must* be so, nor that it *will* be so, in the new church: he only means to say it *is* so in the catholic church. He means to say, and "it is obvious" from what he here says, "that agreeably to the divine revelations and the appearance of the Lord to his new church, as representatively seen by John and himself, the ministry of this church should, according to the instructions of the Word, and the order of heaven," which in this part of the Coronis he is expressly setting forth and illustrating, "*consist simply of one order of priests.*" Do *you see* that Swedenborg teaches this in Coronis 17, or any sentence of it? Can you, by any sort of intellectual *rack*, so *torture* his words, in that number, as to *make* them say *any thing like it*? Well, if you do, then you are entitled to *confirm* this truth, that in the church there should be only one order of priests, by reasoning from Ap. Rev. 926, where Swedenborg is not treating of the priesthood, nor specifically of the ecclesiastical order or government of the church; and, therefore, cannot be supposed to be teaching any thing upon the subject of order in the new-church ministry. In Coronis, Sect. V. of Lemma I., you will observe that Swedenborg is treating expressly of the order which the Lord induces upon the new heaven and the new church, so that they may stand under his auspices, and in obedience to him, to eternity. And, in this connection, he says there must be a trine in every thing, and that nothing can exist without it, according to your own admission. So that it is most reasonable to conclude, that his specification of the church in juxtaposition with "*every* kingdom" might include "every church," and therefore the case of the new church, *about which he is expressly treating.* So that we may say, and see, that he is here expressly teaching that there must be in the new church a trine, and that this church cannot exist without it. But as he specifies only priests, we must infer that he teaches there must be a trine in the priesthood, and that the priesthood cannot exist without it. All this follows, on his own principle, that particulars may be known from the universals which contain them. But no sort of ingenuity can, by any possibility, make Ap. Rev. 926 treat of the ministerial order in the new church. And there is not a line, or one word of a line, which says that in the church there is, will, shall, must, can, would, or should be "but one order of priests in the new church." Swedenborg no more says this, in Ap. Rev. 926, where he is not treating of the ecclesiastical order of the new church at all, than he says it in Coronis 17, where he is treating of that order expressly. In the sacred name of Truth, then, we solemnly call upon you to say—How *can* you see *this* to be true any more in Ap. Rev. 926, than in Coronis 17?

Reader! is it not now most obvious to your mind, that the Rev. Thos. Wilks had made up his mind previously, that it is true there is but one order of priests in the christian ministry, and with this preconceived idea has seen in the Word and the writings of Swedenborg only those things which confirm it, while he has not seen or looked over those that did not confirm it? Is it not clear to your mind that, with this idea in his mind, he has looked at Coronis 17 and Gen. xviii. and tried to explain them so as to make even *them* confirm his preconceived notion, instead of meekly learning from them what they do truly and originally "teach concerning the external order of the ministry"? But suppose Mr. Wilks had at first assumed the affirmative .instead of the negative of the question which we propounded to him. Suppose that he, when reading Coronis 17, saw it to be true that there is and must be in both the new church and her ministry just such a trine as there is in man ; so that there should be *persons* in the church and in her ministry as the head; and other *persons* in the church and ministry *under* those, as the body ; and still other *persons*, under both these and those, as the feet and soles of the feet ; would he not then see every where in the Word and the writings something to confirm this truth? Suppose him to go to Ap. Rev. 744—which see on p. 473 of this report—would he not find the truth that there is a trine of discrete degrees of persons in the church confirmed by that? Suppose him to go to Gen. xviii.—would he not *now* see in the incident of Jehovah's appearing to Abraham as *three men* "confirmation strong as proof of Holy Writ" that there should be *three* orders of priests instead of *one* in the new-church ministry? Would he not now see that when John saw the Lord as the Son of Man in Rev. i. the trine of the priesthood was still presented to view as it is "in man" by Swedenborg in Coronis 17?—"such a trine is man." And would not this memorable relation which he quotes from Ap. Rev. 926 present to him now a very different aspect? All we can say is, it is passing strange that Mr. Wilks should not see the *three* degrees represented here, viz. :

I. The simple tent—natural degree.
II. Temple-like that at Jerusalem—spiritual degree.
III. The Lord standing alone—celestial degree.

For which, in the complex priesthood as one man, there should be—

I. The natural priest—to represent the tent.
II. The spiritual priest—to represent the temple.
III. The celestial priest—to represent the Lord alone.

The tent, the temple, and the Lord alone, represent *worship* in its three discrete degrees, just as Elias, Moses and the Lord, or Peter, James and John, and the three tabernacles to be made for them, did on the mount of transfiguration.

Now, reader! if you will do the same; that is, assume it to be true, that there is and must be such a trine in every church and every priesthood; then, wherever you look, with this affirmation in your mind, you will every where see confirmations of it in both the Word of God and the writings of Swedenborg. Be assured that your experience in this respect will be like ours. But, if you assume the negative of this principle, as Mr. Wilks has done, then you cannot find confirmations of it any where. Be assured that your experience in this respect will be like his. Sir Isaac Newton, observing an apple fall from its parent tree to the ground, reasoned that it so fell because the earth *attracted* it. From this postulate, as golden or silver stuff, he spun and wove the theory that has fully explained all the phenomena of planetary movements in the whole starry heavens, as well as in our particular mundane and solar spheres. It is concluded that these motions are all produced by mutual attraction, because Newton's theory of gravitation fully explains them. If, then, we assume it to be true, from Coronis 17, that there is such a trine of discrete degrees of persons in both the church and its priesthood as corresponds to head, body and feet in man, and the whole Word and all of Swedenborg's writings do not contain a single passage contradicting this in words, but, on the contrary, may be made to confirm it as Rev. 744 and Gen. xviii. do, then, reader! we ask you to conclude with us that *this is a truth*, taught both by the Word and Swedenborg under the Lord's special illumination : so that "the Central Convention, agreeably to its constitution, *has power* to establish *no other than* such an order of priesthood ; and therefore *should not presume to do so* "!

We now dismiss the Rev. Thomas Wilks's report with this most general and concluding remark—in our estimation, it is the most plausible and subtle, yet fallacious and unsound, argument upon the subject of which it treats that our new-church literature has ever produced.

THE REV. WILLIAM MASON'S LETTER.

We purpose to say a very few words on this topic. We have animadverted pretty much upon all of the contents of Mr. Mason's letter in the body of our report. We should not have noticed it at all, if it had not been sent to us by Mr. Mason in his official capacity of president of the General Conference. This fact gave to his assertions the weight of that most respectable body's authority. To say that his official censure wounded us to the *heart*, is true, but not strong enough to express the anguish which it gave us. We had respected Mr. Mason highly, and loved him greatly. We were looking up to him as a spiritual Mentor, whose words of monition and of counsel were to distil that "wisdom which is from above, which is first pure, then peaceable, gentle and easy to be intreated, full of mercy and good fruits, without partiality and without hypocrisy." And when this letter came, full of objurgation, with its petulant, irascible and jarring tone of rebuke, and with the startling enunciation of the most questionable propositions of new-church theology, it was far from the least source of our pain, that a man who had stood so high, should now sink so low, in our estimation! Can it be possible, we said to ourselves, as we read his letter over and over, that this is the same Mr. Mason who wrote the former letter to our convention, whose works we have read with so much admiration, and whose instructions we have received with so much profit! Can it be possible that these are his views—especially in regard to marriage! Surely these are not the views which generally prevail in England on this most peculiar and most prominent new-church sanctity! If so, how greatly have we been mistaken in our profound reverence for the high intelligence of our church in England!

On page xxvii of our Appendix, the reader will find the letter of Mr. Mason, on which we now proceed to make one or two brief remarks. In regard to Mr. Mason's construction of Coronis 17, we imagine it will now be seen that we do not differ very widely from him. Nor do we dissent from his position that uses are prior to the mediums of use, and that priestly uses must determine the external order of the priesthood. But we differ from him as to the time and way of instituting external representative order in the hew church. We also differ from him in respect to what the three uses which are implied by the three offices of the priesthood are; and therefore differ in respect to the three officers which those uses, when foreseen and provided for by the church, will bring into determinate existence. And we think we can now pretty confidently say, there is nothing in this difference of opinion which justifies Mr. Mason's severe charge against us, of having indicated " a somewhat superstitious state of mind," " which appears to have led to a *forced construction* and *misapplication* of passages in the writings of Swedenborg, cited in the Journal in support of the *superstitious conclusions* sought to be established thereby, and which have grown out of the *unwarranted* construction of Coronis 17, in attempting to carry that construction into practice." We could say a good deal about the first paragraph, or that marked " L", of the letter,—especially about the Lord's actual presence in the good and the truth of the laity instead of his representative presence in the *offices* of the priesthood which are still holy representatives,—and also about the " *unquestionably unauthorized* and *practically injurious* (!) sundering of the two sacraments, in *violation* of the *professedly adopted* pattern of the three degrees in the Coronis," &c. &c.,—but our space is so completely exhausted that we are utterly prevented.

There are but two things upon which we wish to remark in the letter now before us. First, Mr. Mason's petulant defence of his hymn book from the rather sweeping " condemnatory judgment " of it by the report of our acting committee. It is proper for us to say here, that we had no hand in writing that report, and did not like what was said in it respecting the Conference Hymn Book. The condemnation of that book *is* far too sweeping, and savors too much of the prejudice against it which has been engendered in another general body of our church in this country. We have ever thought it, in general, an excellent hymn book—as good a one as we ought to have expected in the incipiency of our external church. We have always used it ourselves; and tried to introduce it wherever we have officiated. But we cannot disguise the fact, that there *is* a prejudice in this country against it—that there is, in fact, a difficulty in using it on account of the *metrical* composition of very many of the hymns not allowing them to be easily sung in public worship. This· is in fact the complaint made by those who lead our singing here in Baltimore. *We believe* that this arises out of *fastidious* and *unreasonable* prejudice. But it is a fact—so stubborn that it cannot be helped, nor *forced* out of the way. We want in this country that for our church which we want in our nation—spiritual songs which shall so embody the affections of the doctrinal truths of our church as to excite those affections in our public worshipers, just as appropriate national songs excite the affections of patriotism in our citizens. We want *truly poetic illustrations* of the Universal Theology of the New Heaven and the New Church. Cannot these be produced—will they not be produced? Not, we admit, till the heavenly and pure affections of the divine truths revealed by the Lord in that work are

by regeneration formed and made to glow with the *melting* heat of
the Sun of Righteousness, so as to flow forth in true poetic liquidity !
Perhaps the truths of the New Jerusalem are now only stored in the
scientific mind of the visible church on earth, as lumps of precious
ore in crucibles or furnaces, and cannot flow as liquid fire into
moulding forms of true poetic thought, until the coals from off the
altar are fanned by the breath of heaven into sufficiently fervent heat.
We *do* expect that the time will come, when poetry, as well as
music, painting and sculpture, will lay her master-work as an offering
on the altar of the Living God!   The first fruits and the ingathering
of the year of all true science and of all good art must, sooner or
later, be consecrate to the holy divine worship of the Lord!   And
we only know that our hearts now yearn with insatiable longing for
such songs of Zion, sung by sweet choral voices, as will excite in our
worshiping assemblies the pure affections of our heavenly truths,
comparatively as the songs of virgins and young girls from the houses
of heavenly societies "so affect and move the hearts of the hearers
by their sweetness, that they perceive sensibly a blessed serenity
instilled into their joys, which at the same time exalts and renews
them." (C. L. 19.)   Can not our brethren in England help us to such
songs?   May we not stretch out our hands to them in supplication
for the performance of this sweet, good use?   We were, in fact, just
about to write to Mr. Mason, and others of our english brethren, for
their aid in this, when his letter came as an extinguisher upon our
lamp.   We want a hymn book with hymns composed so as to express,
in smooth and simple versification, the appropriate affections of the
truths taught in the Universal Theology; arranged, therefore, under
heads similar to those of the chapters of that work; and poetically
illustrative of the truths taught in those chapters and their subdivisions.   We also want each hymn set to appropriate music; so
that the same hymn shall always be sung to the same tune, which, if
sweetly harmonious and properly expressive of the sentiment of the
hymn, will, by the ever continuous association of holy thoughts and
affections, be more and more infilled with a sphere of holy divine
worship the longer it is sung by ourselves, and our children, and our
children's children, to the remotest generation.   What Englishman
ever tires of hearing or singing his most sublime national anthem—
God save the king?   What American ever tires of hearing or singing
his almost equally sublime national air?   Old Hundred has never
become too old—never grown superannuated—in the old christian
church.   And may we not look for a few new-church hymns which
will bear to be embalmed in the best religious affections of our souls,
and be as perpetually and tirelessly sung in our public worship?   Our
plan may be chimerical, our aspirations vain; but *this* is what the
writer of the report of our acting committee had in view when he
asked for hymns which would "give the spiritual affections for the
heavenly truths of the New Jerusalem in *pure poetic* garb and
expression"; or for "such hymns, for our use in worship, as shall
truly and *beautifully express* deep spiritual affection for the holy
verities of our church."   We are sorry that he mentioned the

"English Conference Hymn Book." He need not have done so. The mention of that book was not wholly pertinent. And we acknowledge that what he said was justly obnoxious to the displeasure of our english brethren, and especially of Mr. Mason, who was a sort of father to that compilation. His notice of it was certainly *not courteous.* And our whole convention is bound to make the *amende honorable.* But we *know* that the offence thus given was most unintentional on the part of the writer of that report. We can assure Mr. Mason that he is the last man in our country who would give intentional offence to our brethren in England—whom no one respects more highly than he does—or to any body else. And we are satisfied that he meant to say no more in condemnation of the book of which he spoke, than we have since found that Mr. Mason himself has said of it. If the reader will turn to our Appendix, page lxxix, he will find, as Document No. LXII., a "Report of English Hymn Book Committee," made to the Seventeenth General Conference, in 1824, by Mr. Mason, as secretary of that committee. This committee had been appointed by a former conference to get out a hymn book for the use of the new church, and, having completed their task, they report the "Preface" of the original edition in explanation of the plan of the work. In the course of the preface so reported, we find this sentence—"Those [hymns] which have been introduced from other sources [than new-church writers,] will all be found to breathe, in *beautiful* and *energetic language,* the *spirit* of the 'New Jerusalem.'" Now why should this be stated, if it were not desirable in England, as well as in this country, that hymns for new-church worship should "give the spiritual affections for the heavenly truths of the New Jerusalem in *pure poetic garb* and *expression*"? Hence, although "the uses of piety" are certainly to take precedence of "the powers of poetry," yet "it must needs be that the uses of piety and the language of the hymns" *ought* "*always* to be made to exist together in *equal* perfection"; and if this is not done, the hymns are in so far *defective.* Now, as the English Conference Hymn Book proves, in our attempts to use it in this country, to be in fact thus defective in *literary* adaptation to the uses of piety, there is certainly good reason why we should wish, and seek for, greater literary and poetic excellence than that book affords us. And that this was still confessedly a desideratum with even some of our english brethren at the time when their Conference Hymn Book was first published, will appear in the following quotation from its preface:—"The committee are aware that some individuals will necessarily find compositions inserted which they will think might as well have been omitted, while the same compositions will, to persons of a different taste, appear quite indispensable. This variety of taste and judgment the committee have, as far as their abilities go, endeavored to suit; but *so far are they from conceiving that their best endeavors have been completely successful,* that they would rejoice to see *the church grow in interior qualities and* LITERARY ACQUIREMENTS, *so as to render a new and improved hymn-book necessary to the improved condition of the church. An event so* DESIRABLE *cannot happen* TOO SOON, for any

well-wisher to the 'New Jerusalem.'" This is a clear admission, not
only that *good taste in composition* ought to be regarded in the preparation of hymns for the new church, but that the committee who compiled the Conference Hymn Book did in fact pay their utmost regard
to it. It is also conceded that said book might not be suited to the best
taste in England: ought, then, Mr. Mason to find so much fault with our
complaints against it in this country, if it is not in fact suited to ours?
And as he admits that the church may grow in literary acquirements,
as well as interior qualities, "so as to render a *new* and *improved*
hymn-book *necessary* to the improved condition of the church," ought
he now to feel so much hurt at our wishing and striving to get just
such a one instead of that with which he was chiefly instrumental in
furnishing us nearly *twenty-five years ago?* At any rates, it was not
our intention to speak any more disparagingly of his book than he
himself has here done. And by the "pure poetic garb," or more
"perfect poetical productions by an 'influx from the Lord' which we
are seeking after," we mean nothing more than the greater "literary
acquirements," which Mr. Mason himself admits our church may
grow in, as she "grows in interior qualities." Nevertheless we do
not want what is usually understood by *fine writing*, in the composition of new-church hymns. The chief element of sublimity, *simplicity* of diction, is most wanted. But a portion of our hymns, to be
suited to the use of large promiscuous audiences, where many common
minds are congregated, should have something of the ballad style, if
its simplicity can be made to correspond to pure devotional feeling.
The precise thing that is wanted, however, like all the productions of
true genius, can be better felt and appreciated after it is furnished for
our use, than we can say what it ought to be before it is produced.

We have now, secondly, to say a few words about Mr. Mason's
views of marriage as *not a sacrament* of the new church. This part
of his letter pained our spiritual man far more than the scourging of
its other parts lacerated our natural feelings. These are his words—
"a state of mind which has led to *the elevation of a* HUMAN INSTITU-
TION of a *ceremonial* in *celebration* of marriage (which is *not a sacrament* because *it does not open heaven*) above the *divine institution* of
baptism, (by apportioning baptizing but not marrying to the lowest
degree,) regardless of the fact that *only the two sacraments* are INSTI-
TUTIONS OF THE CHURCH, and that *marriage is not an institution of the
church,* but *of the* WHOLE HUMAN RACE"!!! Well, that is certainly
putting marriage *low enough!* Is it not making it nothing more,
essentially, than *concubinage?* If *marriage* be nothing more than the
union of man and woman from the *general love of the sex,* which is a
natural love, and not from *pure conjugial love,* which is of all other
loves the most heavenly, pure and clean—the most spiritual, celestial
and divine—then Mr. Mason is right in calling it an institution of the
whole human race. But never, since we came into the new church,
have we been so shocked as by this proposition! The loveliest feature
of the New Jerusalem, as she first beamed in all her virgin beauty on
our ravished eyes, was the transcendently high estimation in which she
placed the marriage covenant! And nothing could shock us more

than this detrusion of it by this so celebrated preacher of her doctrines and advocate of her faith.

In recently looking over the old english new-church periodicals, we have been struck with some things in "A Few Hints towards framing a rational and useful external mode of worship for the New-Jerusalem Church, accommodated to the present state of Man," communicated to the editors of the New-Jerusalem Magazine published in London in 1790. What peculiarly struck us was his section concerning "The *Consecration* of Marriage." This is put after the two sacraments of baptism and the supper, and is to "be performed in the manner of a simple *love repast* in the *interior* apartment" of the place of worship. "The bride should be seated on the right side of the minister, and the bridegroom on the left, and their friends as witnesses round the table. The minister takes their hands, joins them, blesses them, &c., holding a discourse on marriage, while a small frugal repast of bread and wine is distributed amongst the company. Prayers, music and singing also form a part of the ceremony. If instead of a fixed partition* between the two apartments, there is a loose partition, which can be occasionally removed, on marriage solemnities, both the apartments, thrown into one, may be illuminated with lustres and lamps. At the celebration of a marriage, printed covenants should likewise be used, signed by the parties, &c. For in marriage the most perfect freedom in all respects should exist on both sides, and the reciprocal duties clearly pointed out." Further on we find—"It would also be a recommendable institution in the church, if every single person was once a year to celebrate his baptismal covenant, and then, as it were, renew it: also every married pair their marriage covenant, and as it were renew it." We have not quoted this, because we think it indicates what should be the true form of a marriage ceremony in the new church. To say nothing of its defects in other respects, we think it is defective in not allowing the celebration of the nuptials with that "*festivity*" which Swedenborg calls for in C. L. 309. We, however, do think that it is right in making the *consecration* of marriage by the priest a strictly religious ceremony, to be performed in the adytum of the temple of holy worship; and we think the celebration of the wedding festivities should be an entirely distinct thing, to be observed around the family altar, in the hilarity of extraordinary convivialities and feastings. But it is principally remarkable as making marriage, in opposition to Mr. Mason's view, a holy sacrament of the church, instead of a mere insti-

---

* "In my idea of the external form of a church for the new doctrine," says Mr. Nordenskjöld, "I represent to myself two apartments, one within the other: the exterior dedicated to *preaching* and *baptism*, the interior for the administration of the *holy supper* and the *consecration of marriages.* [Awful profanation, thus "to separate what God hath joined together"!] Thus in the exterior part will be performed those ceremonies which belong to the implantation of truth; but in the interior such as regard the implantation of good, or rather the *marriage of* GOODNESS *and* TRUTH.

"The exterior apartment I represent to myself as calculated for a place of meeting for conversation, with an aisle in the middle, seats on each side, and a rostrum or elevated platform at the upper end, on which is placed a chair, where the moderator or minister is to sit with a table before him."

40

tution of general society. As such an institution Mr. Nordenskjöld considers *burial of the dead:* "for as to burials or interments," says he,, "they belong properly to the office of the civil magistrate ; or, if performed by the minister, he ought not to be considered as officiating in the character of a clergyman, but of a magistrate. *Let the. dead bury their dead.*" And just so we regard Mr. Mason as saying—"Let the dead *marry* their dead : " or if the marriage ceremony is performed by the minister,—as it belongs properly to the office of the civil magistrate, being "not an institution *of the church,* but of the whole human race,"—he ought not to be considered as officiating in the character of a clergyman, but of a magistrate. Mr. Nordenskjöld thinks "external worship consists in these four ceremonies, baptism, the Lord's supper, consecration of marriages, and preaching." We should hardly think the latter is strictly a *ceremony* of the church : but we do think with him that marriage *is* a sacrament—a consecrated thing—in the church, as well as the supper and baptism. It is rather remarkable, too, that the same person, in presenting a form for "an Ecclesiasticum Consistorium" for the new church, offers the following :

"III. In order to form regularly such a consistory, you may here see the analysis or anatomy of the New Church, or the *Marriage* of the Lord and Church called the New Jerusalem.

THE LORD.		THE CHURCH.	
Jesus Christ.	The Word.	The Doctrine.	Life.
That Jesus Christ is the Saviour and Redeemer.	The Natural Sense,	Of Repentance.	Baptism.
That his Humanity is Divine.	The Spiritual Sense.	Of Reformation,	The Holy Supper.
That he is the only God of Heaven and of Earth.	The Celestial Sense	Of Regeneration.	Matrimony.
The Man.	The Eagle.	The Calf.	The Lion."

It is remarkable, in this analysis, that marriage is in the celestial degree of the last trine. Of which it is said—" In the three last, viz. Baptism, the Lord's Supper, and Matrimony, *the power* and *strength of the whole church* are *concentrated.* The *protection* and *security* of the *whole church lie* in *these three,* for which reason they also *must be guarded with all possible care.*" Hence, in the consistory, "One, who is properly the bishop of the church, studies and guards the *three essentials* belonging to the LIFE of the new church, namely, *Baptism,* the *Holy Supper,* and *Marriages.*"

Now whatever may be thought of Mr. Nordenskjöld's views in general respecting an external worship and a consistory for the new church, we are satisfied that his view of the subject before us is more sound than that of the Rev. William Mason. He unquestionably puts marriage in its right place. It is relatively the celestial sacrament of the new church. Hence we think it is the appropriate rite of the priest of the highest grade in our priesthood—the minister of

love. And so we have placed it in the order that we have recommended for our church in this country. But we almost tremble at
the bare thought of the awful condemnation that awaits us, on all
hands, for the still greater "indication of a superstitious state of
mind" leading to a far more "forced construction and misapplication
of passages in the writings of Swedenborg in support of *such* a superstitious conclusion" as this! We have only one sense of security—
the utter insignificancy of our present position in the church here,
which will make it as little worth while to notice any thing we may
say on this or any other subject, as to even think of "attempting to
carry" the constructions of this report "into practice."

But still we cannot think that marriage is any less a divine institution, or any less a holy sacrament of the church, than baptism or
the holy supper. Our Blessed Lord himself says, "He who made
them at the beginning made them a male and a female, and said, For
this cause shall a man leave father and mother, and shall cleave to
his wife; and they two shall be one flesh. Wherefore, they are no
more two, but one flesh. What therefore *God hath joined together*,
let no man put asunder." Is not this a divine institution of marriage?
Where is there a more direct divine institution of baptism, or the
holy supper—baptism, certainly? Is not the ceremony of marriage
as much a part of the Word of God, as either of the other two sacraments? The law of the decalogue makes what were previously
natural laws, or "institutions of the whole human race," laws of God
or spiritual laws also. Do not the enactments of the Lord in both
the jewish and christian dispensations respecting marriage, divorce
and adultery, make marriage, as an institution of the whole human
race, or a natural law, a law of God also, and so a sacramental institution of the church? But marriage cannot be a sacrament "because
it does not open heaven"! Is this Swedenborg's criterion? *He says*,
in A. C. 3046, "a sacrament is nothing else but a *binding.*" And it
is in reference to "the servant placing his hand under the thigh of
Abraham, his lord, and adjuring him upon this Word," (Gen. xxiv. 9,)
that Swedenborg says this—which passage of the Word denotes "a
binding of the natural man, as to power, to *the good of conjugial
love;*" and is an adjuration signifying "a sacrament—a binding, and
indeed the *most holy*, because by Jehovah God of heaven and God of
earth." Is not, therefore, the "binding of the natural man, as to
power, to the good of conjugial love,"—the very end and object of
that "ratification of the conjugial covenant in the presence of witnesses" which constitutes marriage a religious ceremony according to
C. L. 308,—a "most holy" sacrament? So we regard it on this as
the authority of the Word of God. And as conjugial love descends
from the Lord out of heaven, and corresponds to the marriage of the
Lord and the church—as it descends from the marriage of good and
truth—as it is spiritual in it's nature in proportion as the church has
place in man—as it is the foundation in man of all loves celestial and
spiritual—as it has place with the angels of heaven, and its uses are
more excellent than the other uses of creation, because it fills heaven
with happy and immortal souls, so that in its essence it is pure and holy,
nay, essential purity and holiness—who can doubt that marriage on

earth, as the ultimate and representative of all this, *must* open heaven
to all who are parties to its covenant on true religious grounds! . Our
memory does not now serve us to cite the passage, but we feel confident that Swedenborg does somewhere, in substance, say, that the
angels ascend from chaste marriages on earth with peculiarly felicitous
perceptions of all their heavenly delights. And is it to be believed,
that baptism and the supper as "only representative rites" do conjoin
the angels of heaven with men on earth, and yet marriage, as such a
rite, can have no such conjunctive power? We are sure that marriage, as a rite representative of the union of the Lord and his church,
does open heaven in the human soul on earth; and therefore is, for
this reason also, to be esteemed a sacrament of the church.

That marriage is a divine institution of the church, and not merely
" the human institution of a ceremonial in *celebration*" of an obligation
natural to the "whole human race," is manifest from its being a thing
which is to be *consecrated* by a priest. See on this subject what we have
so repeatedly quoted before from C. L. 308. "As the ecclesiastical
order on the earth minister those things which appertain to the Lord's
priestly character, that is, *to his love*, and thus also to those which
appertain to benediction, it is expedient that *marriages* be *consecrated*
by his *ministers*." In C. L. 21, also, it is said, "it is expedient that a
, priest be present and minister at the marriage ceremony on earth," and
that "even in the heavens a priest ministers in whatever relates to
betrothings, or marriage-contracts, and hears, receives, confirms and
consecrates the consent of the parties:" for "consent is the essential
of marriage; and all succeeding ceremonies are its formalities." If,
then, the essential of marriage is to be consecrated by a priest in
heaven, and the marriage-ceremony is to be consecrated by a priest
on earth, is it not unquestionably true that this marriage ceremony is
a sacrament of the church, and marriage itself an institution of the
church?

That marriage is a higher and holier sacrament or ceremony than
both baptism and the supper, is because it is a higher representative
of what the supper represents, namely, the union of good and truth
in the Lord's glorification and man's regeneration, which is the same
thing as the marriage union of the Lord and the church. We say a
higher representative, because it is a representative in heaven, while
the supper is a representative only on earth. Baptism is a gate
which introduces to the church; and the supper is another gate
which introduces to heaven. But "marriages *in heaven* represent
the marriage of the Lord with the church." "This representation
lasts no longer than the day" of the marriage ceremony. (C. L. 21.)
So that marriage is a representative ceremony in heaven; at which a
priest is not needed "by reason of the representation of the Lord
himself and the church" there. But a priest should be present and
minister at the marriage ceremony on earth, because the ecclesiastical
order are appointed here to "minister those things which appertain
to the Lord's priestly character, that is, to his love, and its benedic-
tions." (C. L. 308.) Consequently, the marriage ceremony is a
heavenly representative on earth—of course higher than any earthly
representative whatever—in which that priest should minister who is

most especially the representative of the Lord's priestly character, the one who especially represents him as to *love*, thus the priest of the highest order.

Such are some of the grounds on which we differ from Mr. Mason in his view of marriage. And we believe all the most intelligent members of our church in this country will be found to side far more with us than with him in this matter. At all events, we feel very confident that marriage cannot be too highly elevated any where, but especially in the New Jerusalem, that comes down from God out of heaven. And sure are we, that regarding it ourselves, and teaching our children to regard it, as a most holy sacrament of our faith—as a holy covenant entered into before the Lord God Almighty himself!— we shall do the most that we can to found our holy church upon its only true and lasting basis—the Rock of Ages!

We have now done. We cannot review our work. The sight appals us. We too well know how heavily laden it is with defects; and, not bearing to look upon its deformities, we would much more gladly consign it to the darkness and silence of oblivion, than now usher it to the searching light of such a day as this. But this may not be. Though it be a deformed one, we dare not strangle our offspring at its birth! It was begun at the mandate of imperative duty. We sought the Lord's auspices in its beginning. We have incessantly prayed that it might be continued under his providential guidance and governance. And it is now most devoutly ended in Him. May his blessing be upon it! May his church throw her mantle of charity over it! Mercifully pardoned by him, and considerately borne with by her, may it do its feeble work of use, and then go down soon to merited forgetfulness. The Central Convention, to which this report was to have been made at first, is now virtually defunct. The most wise and intelligent of those who took part in constituting that body have gone into the spiritual world, or otherwise left it. To judge from its recent proceedings, those who are now leading it, or controlling its measures, do not see the principles on which it was originally founded, or are not able to carry them out. Any how, those principles are in fact abandoned. So that we do not see how we can remain much longer in its connection. And we have not the least idea that what is set forth in this report can receive from it even kind consideration, much less any thing like adoption. Therefore, although we apprehend that the views herein set forth will be deemed by many too high for practical application in the present state of our church, yet trusting, in the divine providence of our Heavenly Father, that they may be of use in some not far distant time, this report is now most respectfully submitted to the candid judgment of all sincere seekers and lovers of truth, receivers of our heavenly doctrines, in these United States,

By their servant in the Lord,

R. DE CHARMS.

Baltimore, Nov. 10, 1848.

A FEW OMITTED NOTES.

Owing to the fact that this report was printed in Philadelphia, while the writer of it was residing in Baltimore, and therefore the proof sheets had to be sent to and fro between the two cities, a good many mistakes have been suffered to go uncorrected. And in the hurry of transmitting copy, one or two bottom notes were omitted, which are inserted here.

On page 70, line 10 from the bottom, there should have been an asterisk at the word "number," referring to this note—

* In a letter from Mr. Francis Bailey, directed to "John Young, Esq., Westmoreland," and dated "Philad., April 10, 1792," there is the following paragraph: "I know it will give you pleasure, when I tell you that, on Sunday was a week, the doctrine of the New Jerusalem Church was publicly preached in Baltimore court house by Mr. Wilmer, formerly an episcopal clergyman of Harford County. Mr. Bayard writes, 'there were *twenty-five* of the brethren, and that the house was much crowded.'"

Again, a note was omitted at the bottom of page 76 also. With an asterisk at the word "Paris," in the 22d line from the top, there should have been the following—

* The Rev. Mr. Clowes, in a letter to the Rev. Mr. Hargrove, dated "Manchester, Dec. 29th, 1802," says—"By a letter received lately from Paris, I find that your friend Mr. Mather is at present settled in that city, where there is a small society of readers, amounting to ten or twelve, who meet every week at his house."

Page 161: "This Mr. Silas Ensign probably received a license to preach and baptize from the church at Philadelphia, as did Mr. Adam Klingle and Mr. John Lister, who are not mentioned, as having been licensed, on its Book of Records." After our report was finished, we incidentally laid our hands on a package of documents which had been misplaced. Among others was a loose half sheet of paper, on which were written the minutes of "a meeting of the minister and vestry of the New Jerusalem Church of Philadelphia." As these minutes throw light upon the above sentence, as well as set forth the official concurrence of the minister and vestry of the Philadelphia church in Mr. Holley's ordination, we transcribe them here—

October 22d, 1822.

At a meeting of the minister and vestry of the New Jerusalem Church of Philadelphia—present, Rev. M. M. Carll, J. W. Condy, D. Thunn, W. Schlatter, D. Lammot, J. Parr, and S. Hemple—the Rev. Mr. Carll presented a letter from the Rev. J. Hargrove of Baltimore, containing a communication from John Campbell, Sen., Robert Campbell, Wm. McKee, and A. Russell, on behalf of the church at Abingdon in Virginia, requesting the assent of this church to the ordination of Mr. Nathaniel Holley as a priest and teaching minister of the New Jerusalem.

Whereupon, *Resolved*, That the minister and vestry of the New Jerusalem Church of Philadelphia do approve and assent to the ordination of Mr. Nathaniel Holley as a priest and teaching minister of the Lord's Church of the New Jerusalem, with power, under the authority and at the request of the church of Abingdon in Virginia, and in the manner, and under such restrictions as they may prescribe, to ordain other priests and ministers of the New Jerusalem; with power also to conduct public worship, to celebrate the sacrament of the Lord's supper, marriages, baptisms and funerals, and generally to perform all holy rites and divine ordinances in the church.

The Rev. M. M. Carll submitted to the consideration of the vestry the propriety of granting a license to Mr. Andrew Klingle, whereupon it was

Resolved, That Mr. Andrew Klingle be licensed to preach and teach the doctrines of the New Jerusalem as contained in the theological writings of E Swedenborg, to administer the sacrament of baptism, and to officiate at funerals, agreeably to the order heretofore prescribed in such cases.

Rev. Mr Carll also submitted the propriety of granting a license to Mr Seddons, of Frankford, and Mr. John Lister, now of Hulmeville; whereupon it was
Resolved, That a license be issued to each of them according to the order heretofore prescribed.

On motion, it was *Resolved*, That the Rev. Mr. Carll be authorized to issue from time to time, as he shall think proper, a certificate of ordination on parchment, with the seal of the church, to such priests and teaching ministers as have already been ordained under the authority of this church.

Adjourned.

These, having been minutes of the Vestry and not of the Church, were not entered on the Church's Book of Records; and therefore we could not state positively, what is here seen to be true, that not only Messrs. Klingle and Lister, but also Mr. Seddons, of Frankford, were licensed by the Philadelphia church. Among the documents above mentioned, there are also the blank forms of license for Messrs. Klingle and Lister; and it is remarkable, that the form for Mr. Klingle's license has this clause—"Do hereby grant unto the said Andrew Klingle, for the term of   years from the date hereof, License and Authority to teach the said Doctrines, to celebrate public worship, *the sacrament of the Lord's supper*, baptisms and funerals . . ." It will be recollected that Mr. Klingle asked for ordination into the ministry; that his application was made to Mr. Carll, and by him laid before the church; and that the meeting of the church, to which it was submitted, referred it to the vestry. By this blank form—evidently drawn up by an officer of the vestry—it will be seen that it was contemplated to give to Mr. Klingle a license similar to that given to Mr. Samuel Worcester. But the vestry concluded to give him a license with more limited powers; which, from this time, became the general rule.

Page 163: The Rev. M. B. Roche's "new-church brethren in Philadelphia . . . tacitly concurred in his ordination." Among the misplaced documents above mentioned was the following, which indicates that a formal letter of recommendation to the church in Baltimore was given to Mr. Roche by the church in Philadelphia. There is, however, no documentary evidence of the fact that such a recommendatory letter was given or authorized by the Philadelphia church in any of its stated or special meetings; and, in the absence of such evidence, it does not do to assume that his ordination had the *official* concurrence of the church in Philadelphia:—

To the New Jerusalem Church of Philadelphia:

BRETHREN—Having, by divine mercy, been enabled to receive the heavenly doctrines of the Lord's New Church, and wishing to devote my future life to promote the truths now revealed by the Lord's Second Advent, I offer myself as a candidate for the sacred ministry, and desire your recommendatory letter to the Church in Baltimore.

Yours, in New-Church Love,

M. B. ROCHE.

Philadelphia, June 2d, 1823.

Page 168: "It had ceased to exercise any longer the functions of an ordaining minister." The last minister, in whose ordination the Philadelphia church took part, was the Rev. Isaac C. Worrell. Application for his ordination was made by the Free Will Baptists, of Frankford, who had come into the new church in a body under the lead of their minister, the Rev. Mr. Boyle. The application was made to the Rev. Messrs. Carll and Roche conjointly; but appears to have been submitted by Mr. Carll to the church of which he was the minister; for, in his case, the church, and not he, possessed the ordaining power. As we have seen, it was different in Mr. Roche's case; for ordaining power was given to him, and not to his church; so that there was no need of his submitting it to the church of which he was pastor. The following is the original application for Mr. Worrell's ordination, in the form of a recommendation to that effect, which we have found in the archives of the Philadelphia church:—

Frankford, July the 4th, 1823–67.

The Free Will Baptists of the New Jerusalem Church do certify that our brother Isaac C. Worrell is a regular Member in our connection, and in good standing with us; and we believe that he is called to disseminate the Heavenly Doctrines of the Lord's New Church, he feeling it his duty to be ordained according to the order of the same: we do, therefore, recommend him to our Brethren, the Rev. M. M. Carll and the Rev. M. B. Roche, of the New Jerusalem Church in Philadelphia, for the above mentioned purpose.

Thomas Rorer,	*Richard D. Evans,*	*Thomas Jones,*
Samuel Swope,	*Thomas Rowland,*	*Robert Glenn,*
Isaac Clayton,	*William Andrews,*	*John Baird,*
Joseph Hallowell,	*William Birch,*	*Thomas Shoemaker.*

This document has the following endorsement:—

"*Submitted to the N. J. Church of Philada.,* 31 *Aug.,* 1823–67.

D. LAMMOT, *Sec. of Vestry.*"

———

N. B. The Postscriptum was to have come between this and the Appendix. The three Reviews in this were to have been numbered as Documents for History Nos. XLV. XLVI. and XLVII.; so that the first document of the Appendix,—which, to facilitate the publication of our work, was printed some time ago, with numeral folios,—is No. XLVIII. This statement is made here to account for the hiatus of the three above numbers in the series of our documents.

APPENDIX

REPORT ON THE TRINE,

CONTAINING

FURTHER DOCUMENTS FOR HISTORY.

No. XLVIII.

INQUIRY RESPECTING THE OFFICE OF MINISTERS IN THE NEW CHURCH.

By way of Answer to the Question, " By whom can the Sacraments be lawfully and properly administered ?"

BY THE REV. S. NOBLE.

In order to see the question respecting the administration of the sacraments by the proper persons in its true light, it is necessary to be previously satisfied upon these three points: *First*, Whether a peculiar order of persons to act as ministers or priests is to be maintained in the New Church;—*Second*, What are the functions belonging to them ; —*Third*, How they are to be appointed.

1. As to the first question,—Whether a peculiar order of persons, to act as priests or ministers, is to be maintained in the New Church. Upon this, there cannot be any doubt; the herald of the New Church, Emanuel Swedenborg, having expressly declared the affirmative, in the work on the New Jerusalem and its Heavenly Doctrine. He there says, (n. 311) " There are amongst men two classes of affairs which ought to be conducted according to the laws of order; namely, that which relates to the things of heaven, and that which concerns the things of the world. The former are called ecclesiastical, and the latter civil affairs." He says also, (n. 312) that " It is impossible that order can be maintained in the world without governors;" that " there must also be order amongst the governors themselves; lest any of them, from caprice, or ignorance, should sanction evils which are contrary to order, and thereby destroy it. This is guarded against by the appointment of superior and inferior rulers, amongst whom there is sub-ordination" (n. 313), and that " governors appointed over those things amongst men which relate to heaven, or ecclesiastical affairs, are called priests, and their office is called the priesthood." (n. 314.)

Here we have the most direct assertion, that the administration of ecclesiastical matters, belongs, according to order, to priests or ministers. It is also indicated that there should be ministers of different degrees ; for by the " superior and inferior rulers," here spoken of as necessary, are meant governors of both classes, both ecclesiastical and civil. And we find in the Coronis, (n. 17,) and elsewhere, that according to the views of order recommended by E. Swedenborg, the number of degrees in the ministry should be three.

2. With regard to the *functions* belonging to ministers, E. Swedenborg states, in the chapter of the Heavenly Doctrine already referred to, that they are " to teach men the way to heaven, and likewise to lead them therein" (n. 315); and that, " they are appointed to *administer those things which belong to the divine law and worship.*" (n 319) This, of course, includes the administration of the ordinances of Baptism and the Lord's Supper; nor is any intimation to be found either here or elsewhere, throughout the whole of the writings of the enlightened author, that these functions can lawfully be discharged by any others.

What Swedenborg thus delivers as the doctrine, upon this subject, of the New Church, is founded, like all the doctrines of the New Church, upon the statements of the Holy Word.

The Lord Jesus Christ, when about to leave the world, gives the command, " Go ye and teach all nations, baptizing them in the name of the Father and the Son and the Holy Ghost; teaching them to observe all things whatsoever I have commanded you " (Matt. xxviii. 19, 20.) This command, as we find from ver. 16, was delivered to " the eleven disciples" or apostles, who were the first Ministers of the Christian Dispensation. In cases of necessity, as when a child was not expected to live, and no minister was to be had, it certainly was the practice, from early times, to allow the baptism to be performed by others; but that the duty is properly part of the ministerial office, and not to be undertaken by others without such necessity, appears clear from this passage.

In regard to the administration of the Lord's Supper, the testimony of Scripture is not so direct; but it necessarily follows, that if the administration of the ordinance which is introductory into the church, belongs properly to ministers, that of the ordinance which is introductory into heaven is not less peculiarly their province. Indeed, this may probably be intended to be intimated in the Lord's words at the institution of his supper, " Do this in remembrance of me :" this injunction was addressed to the twelve apostles; and while the words, " Take, eat; this is my body," &c. are addressed to them as *receivers* of the Lord's Supper, the words " Do this in remembrance of me," appear to be addressed to them as the future ministers of the Christian church, and to all who should succeed them in that capacity; if so, they contain a command to the ministers, and to the ministers only, to *administer* the ordinance of the Lord's Supper.

Thus we find that the Word of God, as far as it speaks at all upon the subject, supports and sanctions the Heavenly Doctrine of the New Jerusalem, as delivered by E. Swedenborg, in regard to the functions of ministers. " They are appointed to administer those things which belong to the divine law and worship," which especially include the ordinances of Baptism and the Lord's Supper; and no sanction whatever can be drawn from the inspired pages for the administration of those holy rites by any other persons.

If reasoning by analogy, from the practice in previous dispensations, is admissible on this subject, the case, with regard at least to the Lord's Supper, will appear in fuller light still. Swedenborg declares, that baptism was appointed in lieu of circumcision, and of the washings used in the Jewish Church, and that the Lord's Supper was instituted in lieu of the sacrifices. But, in the Jewish Church. the performance of sacrifice belonged solely to the priests of that dispensation; the inference is direct, that the corresponding ordinance of the Christian Church belongs solely to the ministers of the Christian dispensation. With respect to circumcision, nothing can be concluded with certainty, from the only place where it is mentioned in the Levitical law (Lev. xii. 3), as to the persons who performed it. Certainly, however, it was either administered by the priests altogether, or not at all; as it was not allowable for others, under that dispensation, to perform the priestly functions. But it is certain, that baptism was first administered, after the Christian dispensation had commenced, by the apostles and other ministers, who were the priests of that dispensation; and it cannot be proved from any of the books commonly included in the New Testament that it was ever performed by others.

3. With respect to the third question, How ministers are to be appointed.—Swedenborg has not given any instructions in a direct form; but he has plainly intimated that,

according to his views of divine order, a solemn inauguration, or a devotional service, accompanied with imposition of hands, is the proper method. To cite only one passage out of several to the same effect, he says in the Conj. Love (n. 396). "The reason why communications of the mind are effected by the sense of touch, is, because the hands are the ultimate principles of man, and his first principles are together in the ultimate, whereby all things of the body and all things of the mind are kept together in inseparable connexion. Hence it is that Jesus touched infants (Matt. xvii. 6 Mark x. 13, 16), and that he healed the sick by the touch, and that they were healed who touched him; hence also it is that inaugurations into the priesthood are at this day effected by the laying on of hands." C. L. 396.

That he understands that the imposition of hands should be accompanied with prayer, is plain from what he says respecting the order to be observed in the dedication of places of worship; that, after all things are prepared, it is to be "sanctified by prayer. that God would make it the abode of his presence," &c.—(*Tr. Chr. Rel.* n. 126.) If prayer is requisite at the dedication of a building to the service of the Lord, it assuredly is no less necessary at the ordination of the minister who is to perform that service.

That such was the order of proceedings at the ordination of priests or ministers from ancient times, is stated generally by Swedenborg, and is evident from the Word of the Old Testament. In the *Word* of the New Testament there is not, indeed, any express command upon the subject; but what, under the Christian dispensation, was understood to be the requirement of order, is plain from the practice of the apostles. The appointment of the first deacons, though their peculiar duties were not altogether ecclesiastical, was, by the choice of the people and ordination from the apostles. We learn from Acts vi. 3—6. that, at the desire of the apostles, the people chose "seven men of honest report, full of the Holy Ghost, and of wisdom, whom they set before the apostles; and, *when they had prayed, they laid their hands on them.*" And Paul says to Timothy, (1 Tim. iv. 14.) who had been appointed chief minister at Ephesus, "Neglect not the gift that is in thee, which was given thee by prophecy, with the laying on of the hands of the presbytery;" the *presbytery* were the other ministers. So he says again (2 Tim. i. 6), "I put thee in remembrance that thou stir up the gift of God which is in thee by the putting on of my hands." Strictly in agreement with this, is the statement of Swedenborg, speaking of illustration and instruction as the peculiar graces of ministers, that "their ordination to the ministry conveys those graces" (T. C. R. 146); meaning, of course, with those who worthily assume the office. We see, then, that the order of inauguration into the ministry from ancient times, and as practised in the primitive Christian Church, and recognised by Swedenborg as the right order still, is, by prayer and the imposition of hands.

What then is the result of the whole? That the administration of the sacraments properly belongs solely to the ministry; and that admission into the ministry can only be lawfully performed by the religious solemnity which is of divine origin.

It is plain, then, that the Conference can have no power, by any act of theirs, to confer *directly* the right of administering these ordinances. The Conference is a mixed body, partly civil and partly ecclesiastical; consequently, it cannot itself administer ecclesiastical functions. All that it can lawfully do in the appointment of persons to perform ecclesiastical functions, is what the primitive Christians did in the case of deacons, as stated in the passage above cited from the Acts—to present to the ministers, for ordination by them. such persons as they (the Conference) deem suitable characters. And did the Conference consist altogether of ministers alone, they still could not appoint persons to officiate in holy things by a mere vote or resolution; to give effect to such vote, the solemnity of ordination must be duly performed. For the Conference to undertake to *dispense* with the requirements of divine order upon the subject, would be to assume a papal power indeed. They might as well undertake to dispense with the observance of the ten commandments. And any acts which might take place under such dispensation, would be in themselves null and void, being contrary to the prior obligations of the laws of God.

SOME REMARKS ON THE SAME SUBJECT.

BY THE REV. D. HOWARTH.

Whatever may be the final decision of the Conference upon the long agitated question of arranging the ministry, &c., it may be useful, in the mean time, to state in what manner the Committee appointed by the last General Conference entered upon the performance of their duty, and to mention, also, some of the ideas suggested, and conclusions arrived at, while thus engaged. Their labors were begun upon the understanding, that the object of the various Conferences, under whose view the subject has been brought, was, *first*, to constitute the Ministry of the New Church into a trine or threefold order, answering to the three degrees of life in man, the three heavens &c.; *second*, to extend and facilitate the means of having the Sacraments administered to the various Societies, according to their respective wants, and to inquire whether it be allowable, upon the principles of order, for unordained persons to administer either or both of them.

In attending to the first part of this object, namely, *to constitute the Ministry into a trine*, they were led to examine what is contained in the Word of God, and in the writings of Emanuel Swedenborg, as to the order of the priesthood in the representative Judaic dispensation; for although that Church and Ministry was merely external, yet its outward rites and official distinctions were the exact emblems of the orders which ought to prevail in a truly spiritual church. What the three orders in that priesthood represented, is declared, in very explicit terms, by the enlightened Swedenborg. " There are (says he) three things which succeed in order; there is the celestial principle, which is the good of love to the Lord; there is the spiritual principle, which is the good of charity towards the neighbor; and there is the natural principle thence derived, which is the good of faith; inasmuch as these three things are what succeed in order. There are also three heavens, and in them goods in that order. The work of the salvation of those who are in celestial good, is represented by the priesthood of *Aaron:* but the work of the salvation of those who are in spiritual good, is represented by the priesthood of the *Sons* of Aaron; and the work of the salvation of those who are thence in natural good, is represented by the priesthood of the *Levites*." (A. C. 10,017.) This passage sufficiently evinces, that the Jewish priesthood consisted of three orders or degrees, and, also, that they were, both nominally and actually, distinct: peculiar duties were accordingly appointed to each; one class or degree being prohibited from interfering with the duties of another, under penalty of death, as appears from Numb. chaps. iv., viii., xviii., and elsewhere.

The Committee, therefore, thought, that if the Ministry of the New Church is to be formed into a trine, answering to that of the three heavens, the three degrees in man, and their representative – the priesthood amongst the Jews, it should be a trine, not in name *only*, but also in *reality*, consisting of a distinction in *ecclesiastical privileges*, since it cannot, with propriety, be affirmed, that any difference of titles and *civil* privileges can constitute an ecclesiastical trine. Could the peculiar duties of each order in the representative priesthood, and their exact relations to the duties of the Christian Ministry, be accurately ascertained, the analogy would assist in forming a right judgment concerning a threefold order in the Christian church; and although information on this subject may not be to the full extent of our wishes, it is, notwithstanding, worthy of some attention.

The representative Church of the Jews was distinguished by the rite of circumcision, various washings, burnt offerings and sacrifices, meat offerings and drink offerings, all of which are comprehended in, and were succeeded by, the rites of baptism and the holy supper in the Christian church. (See T. C. R. 670, 674, 675; A. C. 2165- 3830, 10,143.) Whence it is manifest that by baptism and the holy supper, the same things are signified as were represented by the whole of the rites, sacrifices, and oblations amongst the Jews. If, therefore, their priests, of divine appointment, performed those things, it follows, by parity of reasoning, that the administration of the corresponding rites—baptism and the holy supper—is the proper duty of the Ministry in the Christian church. Whether the priests, after their formation into three orders, were the operators in the act of circumcision, is not declared with sufficient clearness in the Holy Word, to furnish the means of a satisfactory decision; but that the washings and sprinklings were done by them, and under their direction, may be concluded from Levit. vi. xiii. xiv. xv. xvi., &c.; and that they were appointed to do the work of sacrifices and offerings, and, indeed, all things of public worship, is abundantly evident. Their duties are also summarily stated by Emanuel Swedenborg, in the following words; "Inasmuch as the priesthood was representative of the Lord, as to all the work of salvation derived from the Divine Love, therefore, also, all divine worship was of the office of the priest, which worship, at that time, chiefly consisted in offering burnt-offerings, sacrifices, and meat-offerings, and in arranging the bread upon the table of faces, in kindling the lamps every day, and in burning incense; consequently, in expiating the people, and in remitting sins; moreover, also, in explaining the law divine, and in teaching, on which occasion they were, at the same time, prophets: that Aaron, with his sons, performed all these things, is manifest from the institution of the priesthood of Moses" (A. C. 9809.) "They who officiated in holy things, were called priests, and were of the seed of Aaron, and Levites." (6148.) "Holy things, denoting the gifts which they brought to Jehovah or the Lord, that they might be expiated from sins, which [gifts] were burnt-offerings, sacrifices, and meat-offerings." (9937.) "Because priests presided over worship, and likewise taught, therefore by their ministry was signified worship and evangelization." (9925). These passages establish the fact, on unquestionable authority, that the performance of the various rites of worship in the representative Church, belonged, of divine appointment, to the priesthood, and therefore, on the principle of analogy, divine order requires, in the Christian Dispensation, that the corresponding rites—baptism and the holy supper—be also performed by the ministry.

With regard, then, to a *trine* of duties, if the above conclusion is just, baptism and the holy supper are *two* acts or duties peculiar to the ministry, to which may be added a *third*—that of ordaining or inaugurating others into the office. These three functions, therefore, whether exactly answering to the relative duties of the three orders of priests in the representative Church, or not, would, at least, mark a real distinction between three orders in the New Church; whilst, at the same time, preaching and expounding the Word would be common to the whole. This plan or some other, amounting to a real as well as a nominal difference, must, it is presumed, be adopted, or otherwise the idea of a trine, as a principle upon which to arrange the Ministry, must be abandoned. What were the particular duties of the first order of priests—the Levites, more especially after the building of the temple, it is not very easy to ascertain; but it appears from Numb. iv. and other places, that they were of a lower kind than those of Aaron and his sons; which may also be inferred from the following remark of Emanuel Swedenborg: "The Levites were given to Aaron and his sons, that they might perform the ministry of the priesthood *under them*." (A. C. 10,017.) If the administration of baptism can justly be considered a lower duty, when compared with that of the holy supper, it clearly follows that, so far at least, it answers to the lower duties of the Levites, compared with those of Aaron and his sons, and therefore might properly distinguish the first order in our Ministry.

The holy supper, it has been already shown, involves the same things as the sacrificial duties of Aaron and his sons, and therefore might correspondently belong only to the second and third orders; and as Aaron, in his *peculiar work*, was the highest representative of the Lord in that priesthood, so he who performs the solemn act of ordination—conferring ministerial functions upon others, sending them forth on their sacred missions, after the example of his Divine Master, stands pre-eminently, as it were, in the Lord's place; and therefore such a duty is proper only to the highest order of the Ministry. The propriety of thus dividing the two sacraments, by appointing the first order of the Ministry to perform the one and not the other, may perhaps be questioned; yet it appears this was done in the days of the apostles; for the deacons, whom they ordained, preached and baptised, as may be seen in the Acts of the Apostles; but there is no account of their administering the holy supper. That the two sacraments are indeed quite distinct, is sufficiently clear from the writings of Emanuel Swedenborg. "Baptism (says he) is an introduction into the church, and the holy supper is an introduction into leaven. These two sacraments are, as it were, two gates leading to eternal life; by baptism, which is the first gate, every Christian is initiated and introduced into those truths and doctrines which the Church teacheth out of the Word concerning a future life, all which are so many means whereby he may be prepared for, and led to heaven; the other gate is the holy supper, through which every one who hath suffered himself to be prepared and led by the Lord, is introduced and admitted into heaven. After passing through the first gate, he cometh to a plain, over which he is to run his course, and at the end of which is the other gate, where is the goal and the prize, towards which his course was directed." (T. C. R. 729.) Again; "those two sacraments may be compared with a double temple, one of which is below, and the other above; in the lower whereof is preached the gospel concerning the new advent of the Lord, and also concerning regeneration and salvation by him in consequence thereof; from this temple, about the altar, is an ascent to the upper temple, wherein the holy supper is celebrated; and from thence is a passage into heaven, where the worshipers are received by the Lord. They may also be compared with the tabernacle, in the inside whereof appeareth the table on which the show bread is placed in order, and likewise the golden altar for incense, and the candlestick in the midst with lighted tapers, which, by their light, render all other things visible; and at length, for those who suffer themselves to be enlightened, the veil is opened to the holy of holies." (T. C. R. 669.) The plain inference from these extracts, is, that the two sacraments are as obviously distinct as the life of man upon earth, and his life in heaven, or as the two stories of a house, or as the two parts of the tabernacle, which latter, in particular, inasmuch as they represented two heavens, are therefore clearly indicative of a *discrete degree*, and if so, the dividing the sacraments, as above suggested, is in perfect agreement with order. And if the proposed arrangement would at all facilitate the more frequent administration of baptism in those Societies who experience the want of it, such a circumstance is an additional recommendation to its adoption, grounded in utility and expediency. Both sacraments, it is true, should be duly attended to wherever practicable, but the holy supper may be more or less frequent according to circumstances, and the communicants can generally be present, without much inconvenience, at such times and places as may be appointed, even should the place be several miles distant from their abode; but with respect to baptism, the case is otherwise; the taking an infant a similar distance is far more inconvenient, and attended also with considerable risk of injuring its tender frame; neither can baptism so properly be subject to any stated periods, for children are being born at various and almost all periods of time; and their baptism, on account of its spiritual uses, should not be protracted, but take place as soon after birth as may be, consistently with safety and real prudence. To show the necessity and uses of baptism, and the expediency of its early administration, the following observations of Emanuel Swedenborg will suffice :—" Baptism signifies initiation into the Church, thus it signifies regeneration; not that by baptism any one is regenerated, but that it is a sign thereof which *should be remembered*." (A. C. 4255.) "They who are of the Church are distinguished from all others in the universal orb of earth by baptism." (10,238.) "As soon as infants are baptised, they are placed under the tuition of angels, by whom they are kept in a state of receiving faith in the Lord; and as they grow up, and become capable of thinking and acting for themselves, the tutor angels leave them, and they draw into association with themselves such spirits as make one with their life and faith; hence it is evident, that baptism is an insertion amongst Christians, even in the spiritual world." (T. C. R. 677.) "In the spiritual world all things are most distinctly arranged, both in common and in every part, or in general and in every particular, and on this distinct arrangement the preservation of the universe dependeth; this distinct arrangement, however, would be impracticable, unless every one, after his birth, be distinguished by some sign whereby it may be known to what religious community he belongeth; for without the Christian sign, which is baptism, some Mahometan, or some idolatrous spirit, might apply himself to new-born Christian infants, and instil into them an inclination in favor of their religion, and thereby distract their minds, and alienate them from Christianity, which would be to distort and destroy spiritual order." (T. C. R. 678.) In these passages, the importance of facilitating, as far as possible, the administration of baptism whenever infants can be brought, is clearly set forth, and also the indispensable duty devolving upon parents to bring their children to be baptised as soon after birth as conveniently practicable. The same remarks do not, however, apply to the holy supper, because, as above said, this may be subject to stated periods, longer or shorter according to circumstances, without any violation of the divine command; all that is required of the Members of the New Jerusalem, in reference to this sacrament, is, that they cultivate the proper desire, seek the opportunity, and actually become communicants as often as opportunities occur. And if such be the duty of parents with respect to baptism, and of the Members of the New Church generally, in regard to the holy supper, it follows of consequence, that the administration of the sacraments in every Society, according to its wants, is a most desirable object.

But it should always be borne in mind, that every good desire is connected with and subordinate to the *love of order;* when, therefore, the thought is engaged upon the *desirableness* of any good things, the most *orderly means* of obtaining it should not be forgotten; consequently the final subject of inquiry, namely, whether it be allowable, consistently with order, that unordained persons should administer either or both the sacraments, is now to be considered. And let it be remembered, this is not an inquiry about individual excellence,—it is not asking whether this or that man is worthy and good enough to perform those duties, but it is purely a question of order, and should, therefore, be viewed abstractedly from persons. The Lord is order itself, and by his divine truth arranges all things into order; wherefore, whatever is consistent with truth is also consistent with order; consequently, what the divine truth teaches relative to the present subject of inquiry ought to be consulted, as essential to a just decision. The only instance to be found in the Word of God, of specific instructions respecting the appointment of Ministers, is in the case of the Levitical priesthood; all the orders of which were solemnly and formally inaugurated, though not all in the same manner, into their respective offices, as recorded in Exod. xxix. and xl., and Numbers viii. And all the people, not thus inaugurated, were prohibited from taking any part in the peculiar duties of the priesthood. Many particulars indeed of this ceremony necessarily ceased when the Lord, at his coming, abolished generally mere representative worship; but that circumstance is no reason for supposing that *all forms* of inauguration should therefore be altogether discontinued; for if such an inference were to be drawn, it might, also, with the same propriety be said, that, because the Lord abolished the *Jewish sabbath.* *therefore* Christians need not keep *any sabbath whatever.* Admitting these to be parallel cases, the language of Emanuel Swedenborg, relating to the latter, is amply sufficient to remove all doubt respecting the former. The command, "Thou shalt remember the sabbath day, to keep it holy," is one of those laws which, "*at this day,* ought *altogether to be observed and done.*" (A. C. 9349.) And he farther says, "the Lord, when he was in the world, and united his human [principle] to the divine itself, abrogated the sabbath as to representative worship, or as to the worship which prevailed amongst the Israelitish people, and *made the sabbath day a day of instruction in the doctrine of faith and love.*" (A. C. 10,360.) Since, therefore, the abrogation of the Jewish mode of keeping the sabbath, gives not the least sanction to Christians for *discontinuing every mode* of keeping the sabbath holy, so neither does the abrogation of the *Jewish form* of ordination give any sanction for discontinuing *every form* of ordination. And as, when *one mode* of keeping the sabbath was abrogated, the Lord himself instituted *another* mode of keeping it, suited to the Christian Dispensation, so, when *one kind* of ordination is abrogated, *another kind,* suited to a truly spiritual church, is proper to be instituted, and thus, amidst all changes, and all abuses, the *thing itself* be preserved. That the Lord did also himself institute ordination for the Christian church, is evident from Mark iii. 13, 14, 15. "And he goeth up into a mountain, and calleth unto whom he would : and they came unto him. And he ordained twelve, that they should be with him, and that he might send them forth to preach, and to have power to heal sickness and to cast out devils." See also chap. vi. 7; Luke x. 1; Matt. xxviii. 19, 20. And the remarkable circumstance of the Lord *repeating* this act in the spiritual world, at the commencement of the New Jerusalem Dispensation, must surely be regarded as an additional proof that ordination, or a special commission to perform the functions of the ministry, should be recognised in the New Church as an appointment of divine order. The circumstance alluded to is stated by Emanuel Swedenborg, as follows: "The Lord called together his twelve apostles, and sent them forth throughout the whole spiritual world, as he had formerly done throughout the whole natural world, with a commission to preach this gospel, [that the divine trinity is in the Lord,] and immediately every apostle had his particular district assigned him." (T. C. R. 108.)   Whether the primitive ministry under the Christian Dispensation bore any analogy to the Levitical priesthood as to a threefold order, we are not directly informed; but it deserves to be noted that the great "Lord of the harvest" was himself, externally as well as internally, the ordainer—the sender forth of his laborers, and that the persons ordained by him were two classes—the *twelve* and the *seventy*.   It will also be admitted, that the Lord conferred upon his disciples the privilege of ordaining others, when he said to them, "As the Father hath sent me, even so send I you; and saying this, he breathed on [them]. and saith unto them, receive ye the Holy Spirit," (John xx. 21, 22;) which words, doubtless, related to their external duties, as well as to internal states, and, therefore, the apostles afterwards exercised this privilege accordingly. (Acts vi. 6.)

On the whole then it appears, that not only the divine truth of the Old Testament. but likewise that of the New, manifestly indicates, as far as the subject is therein spoken of, that there are certain duties peculiar to the ministry, and also that some form of inauguration, into that office as an *ultimate of divine order*, is absolutely requisite. before any person can be considered fully and duly authorised to discharge those duties, particularly the administration of the two sacraments, Baptism and the Holy Supper, which, as Emanuel Swedenborg declares, are "the most holy [solemnities] of worship." (T. C. R. 667.)   Every member of the New Church will acknowledge that the love of order should descend even to ultimates, for it was evidently upon this principle that the Lord instituted, as ultimate rites, the two sacraments; and it is constantly maintained in the doctrines of the New Church that order in ultimate things is essentially necessary to the preservation of interior things.   If, therefore, the above conclusion respecting ordination be just, namely, that it is absolutely requisite as an ultimate of divine order, every one who loves order, both internally and externally, will desire, not only that the sacraments be administered to every society, but also, that such administration be performed consistently with divine order *in ultimates* as well as in first principles.   At present, it is true, the ordained ministers of the New Church are few in number, and it may therefore be doubtful whether they could supply the wants of all the societies in regard to the sacraments; but this cannot be determined until those wants are made known.   Let the societies, therefore. make known their wants. and if they concur in the above view of order, let them manifest their love of it, by endeavoring to enter into an arrangement with the Missionary Societies, or in some other way, to be visited by such ordained persons as can be provided; and let the ministers on their part endeavor to lay aside all needless diffidence—all apparent reluctance, and, no doubt, such reciprocity of action would have the happy effect of bringing themselves and the societies together, for the purpose of the administration and mutual participation of the sacraments, much more frequently than has heretofore taken place

---

No. XLIX.

REPORTS OF COMMITTEES

Appointed to consider the Question, Whether it is in accordance with the laws of divine order to admit persons by some solemn service, to administer the Sacrament of Baptism only, and not that of the Holy Supper?

I.

REPORT OF THE COMMITTEE IN MANCHESTER.

The Committee, in bringing their labors to a close, consider it to be their duty to put the General Conference in possession of the substance of their views and the information they have received.

At the commencement of their duties, the Committee thought it advisable to send circulars, in addition to those forwarded by the Secretary of Conference, to the various Societies of the New Church north of the Trent, in the hope, that this course would prove an additional excitement to their early attention to the subject.   As the result of this two-fold application, answers were received from about twenty Societies,* and are herewith forwarded for your inspection.

From the language of the greater portion of the letters, it would appear that the question has been considered, not as Conference intended, separately from the arranging or ordering of the Ministry, but as connected with and forming part thereof.   And so various and so diverse are the views, that it is difficult to collect from the whole anything decisive and satisfactory.   However, a negative to the question appears to preponderate.

The Committee have bestowed upon the subject no inconsiderable share of attention : they have deliberated upon the different and opposite sentiments contained in the letters, not only in respect to the propounded question, but also relative in general to the ministry, and the external order and government of the Church : they have reflected upon the unsettled state of thought and feeling which seems to actuate the members of the Church ; and after having done so, they are unanimously of opinion that the time to legislate upon this subject, with real and permanent advantage to the Church, has not yet arrived ; they would, therefore, respectfully recommend the Conference to relinquish it for the present.

With regard to the question itself, in the abstract, the Committee are of opinion that the plan it involves might be adopted in perfect accordance with Divine order.

The principal objection against it, found in the letters, and, indeed, the only one that appears to require particular consideration, is that founded on the supposed impropriety and disorder of dividing, as it is called, the Sacraments ; and it is intimated, in two or three of the letters, that to do this is to " put asunder what God hath joined together."

This objection has a rather formidable aspect, and if well founded, is sufficient to silence and overthrow every attempt at the plan contemplated, and to set it for ever at rest.

The Lord's words, thus employed, and which seem to convey apparently so astounding an objection, were evidently used by Him in reference to the heavenly marriage of goodness and truth ; for these principles the Lord joins together, and requires that they be not put asunder.   Now, if Baptism and the Holy Supper are, and mean such heavenly marriage, and the proposed plan puts them asunder, then the objection is valid ; but if they are not, and do not mean, such marriage, then, of course, the objection is inadmissible and powerless.   That they are not, and do not mean this marriage, is clear from the fact, that the Holy Supper is *itself alone* the heavenly marriage, the essential constituents being signified by the bread and wine.   With this marriage Baptism has no other connexion than as a means of introduction ; that is, as a gate and way leading to a house.   He who administers Baptism is as a servant stationed at the outer gate, who receives a traveller, and guides him along the way to the door of the house ; and he who administers the Holy Supper, is as another servant who opens the door, admits the traveller within the house, and introduces him to the marriage chamber.

If, indeed, Baptism and the Holy Supper are and mean the two essentials of the heavenly marriage, it follows, inasmuch as these essentials must always be together, that both should be administered at the same time ; consequently, every time a communicant partakes of the supper, he must also be baptized, which, with some, would be about twelve times a year.   Infants are baptized and derive benefit thereby, but no one can participate in the heavenly marriage, signified by the Holy Supper, before he arrives at adult age.   From these and many similar considerations it is obvious, that the two sacraments, in the sense implied in the objection, are not joined together ; but, on the contrary, are actually distinct and divided, like the two general states with man, the first of which is that of truth leading to good—looking towards heaven and desiring marriage ; and the second is when he is regenerated or in *good*, in *heaven*, and in marriage.

---

* The Letters received by the London Committee were afterwards forwarded to Manchester, and in a subsequent communication, the Committee observed that the perusal of them did not render it necessary for any alteration to be made in their report.

Baptism and the Holy Supper are, according to Emanuel Swedenborg, two representatives, which the Lord was pleased to retain in the Christian Church, and involve all that was meant in the whole ritual worship of the Jews; this being the case, the office of administrator must also be representative. But the sacraments represent two distinct states of things; a state as *to means* and a state as *to end;* wherefore, the *representative character* of the administrator must of necessity change in the performance of these two distinct rites, so much so, that no one can administer both sacraments in the same representative character. If, then, the representative character of the administrator does and must change, it surely follows, according to the same order, that the person of the administrator may be changed also; since Baptism represents state *as to means*, from which it is not possible for man instantaneously to pass into the state *as to end*, meant by the Holy Supper, nor consistently with his freedom can the Lord introduce him into this state.

Agreeably, therefore, with this law of order, a regulation might be adopted, appointing certain persons to administer that rite which represents a state as to means; and, at the same time, restrict them from administering that which represents a state as to end.

From the above remarks, you will perceive, that the Committee here, viewing the matter abstractedly, are decidedly in favor of an affirmative answer to this question; but as a measure of expediency, viewed in connection with the apparent state of the Church, they are no less decisive in saying, the time is not yet.

DAVID HOWARTH, Chairman.
SAMUEL E. COTTAM, Secretary.

II.

REPORT OF THE LONDON COMMITTEE.

The Committee appointed as above-mentioned confess that they have been somewhat indisposed to enter upon the duty thus assigned them, because nearly the same individuals had, in the previous year, constituted a Committee appointed by the Twenty-fourth General Conference for maturing a Plan which had been proposed to, and, as to its general features, approved by, that Conference, having for its object the providing for the wants of the Societies not having Ordained Ministers in regard to the administration of the Sacraments. That Plan was finally rejected by the last Conference, and instead of it, a Committee composed of nearly the same members was appointed in London, and another at Manchester, to consider the question recited above. The Committee in London, therefore, having before labored upon a plan which proceeded upon the supposition, that any measure founded upon an affirmative answer to the question now proposed would be insufficient to meet the wants of the Church, cannot be supposed to look with great interest to the solution of that question. Nevertheless, being required by the Conference to give an opinion upon this abstract point, they will endeavor to do so, according to the best light which they have been able to obtain.

The question proposed is, "Whether it is in accordance with the laws of Divine Order, to admit persons, by some solemn service, to administer the Sacrament of Baptism only, and not that of the Holy Supper." To assist their judgment in coming to the consideration of this question, the Committee have carefully examined the answers from various Societies and individuals to the Circular issued by the Secretary, requesting opinions upon the subject; and also to a Circular issued by the Manchester Committee to the Societies in the northern part of the Kingdom. The communications which have thus come before them amount in number to about twenty-six. They regret to observe, that the object of the question does not, in general, appear to have been well understood, and that comparatively few of the letters throw any direct light upon the subject. Most, also, mix the question with other topics; and most treat it more upon the ground of *expediency at the present time* than of *principle*. Several seem to suppose, that the conclusion, that it is lawful to ordain persons to the administration of the Sacrament of Baptism, without giving them authority to administer the Lord's supper, would be an exclusion of many Societies from the Lord's supper entirely; which, certainly, the Conference never could contemplate. A few of the letters enter into the question of the propriety of there being any distinction whatever of order or degree in the ministry, and urge arguments against it. And one or two propound the opinion, hitherto quite unheard of in the New Church, that every society is competent, not only to determine whom they will accept to be their minister,—a right which, in the New Church, has never been disputed,—but actually to confer upon the object of their choice the ministerial character, and *ordain* him to the office. In a very few instances (happily—and the circumstance should be mentioned for the honor of the church—they are very few indeed) a warmth is displayed, and an intolerance of feeling towards the sentiments of others is manifested, which are most deeply to be regretted. Why should this be? The Conference has never yet shown a disposition to press any measure upon the Church, or upon individual Societies, contrary to the feelings of Societies; and most unquestionable it is, that, whether right or wrong in judgment, the Ministers and Members of the New Church in Conference assembled have always proved that they were actuated by none but the best of motives,—a sincere desire to do, according to the best of their judgment, what is most conducive to the general good of the Church. To insinuate the contrary, is sadly to violate that charity which should ever reign in the bosom of the member of the New Church. Whenever we feel disposed to urge our own opinions in an intolerant spirit, we should do well to remember, that we thus evince that our own views are very much combined with our own self hood,—an alliance which should induce us, not to confide in, but to distrust, their truth. Such an affair as the ordering of the Ministry in the New Church, and the providing for the orderly administration of the sacraments, can only profitably, and with the prospect of a happy result, be discussed in a spirit which may bring down upon the discussion the divine blessing; and that is the spirit which assumes that all who offer an opinion on the subject have as sincere a good intention as ourselves; and that every one who has the same means of forming a right judgment, from his acquaintance with the Holy Word and with the Writings of its New-Church Expositor—which are open to all,—has the same right to have his opinion carefully and respectfully considered. In this spirit the Committee have endeavored to approach the consideration of the matters before them; and if they shall not have been enabled to offer much that may conduce to their satisfactory adjustment, they trust, at least, that they shall not have done any thing that can promote disunion.

As the letters received embrace, as just observed, so wide a field, it appears proper, in this Report, to include something more than a simple answer to the question proposed by the last Conference, and to touch a little upon the topics introduced in the various communications respecting the institution of a Ministry and its constitution in general.

I. Here, then, in the first place, the Committee beg leave to recite the preliminary observations which were prefixed to the plan drawn up by the previous Committee appointed by the Twenty-fourth General Conference. Those observations contain the most general principles respecting the institution of the Ministry which are contained in the writings of the New-Church Herald. The validity of the arguments and proofs has never yet been directly called in question, nor does it appear to this Committee how it can be called in question, without denying the authority of the source from which they are taken. And if they are admitted to establish the true principles of the Institution of a New-Church Ministry as far as they go, they will completely remove several of the mistakes adverted to above, as contained in the letters which have come before the Committee. The observations are as follows:

That there is to be an institution of Ministers, as a distinct order of persons for the performance of ecclesiastical functions in the New Church, and that "they are appointed to administer those things which belong to the divine law and worship," are truths acknowledged by all the receivers of the heavenly doctrines, being in those doctrines explicitly declared. (See *New Jerusalem and its Heavenly Doctrine*, n. 311, 314, 315, 319.)

The chief of "the things belonging to the divine law and worship" which persons invested with the ecclesiastical character are to administer, are—the leading of the congregation in public worship—the edifying of them by preaching—the sacraments of Baptism and the Lord's Supper—the Consecration of Marriages—the Consecration of Places of Worship—and the Ordination of Ministers. Of these, the regular performance of the first four is necessary to the distinct existence of every society, congregation or church.

It belongs to the Lord alone to appoint Ministers in his Church; and all who duly fulfil the sacred function are considered to derive their authority from him. Nevertheless, for the prevention of disorder, confusion, and the dissemination of heretical opinions, no person can lawfully exercise the duties of the ministry, from a persuasion that he has received a divine call to that office, till the validity of his claim is recognised by the judgment of the Church. The grounds upon which the Church is to act in judging of such cases, are—the qualifications which the person manifests for the office, particularly in regard to aptness to teach and irreproachableness of life; and, the bias or impression on his mind, inclining him to the work.

These things are preliminary or preparatory to a person's taking upon him, or being admitted to, the ministerial or ecclesiastical character; but order requires that he should be fully invested therewith by a solemn form of inauguration or ordination. Not only is the recognition of his call to the office hereby solemnly certified before the world, but there can be no doubt that, where the will of the Lord truly concurs with the admission of the party into the ministry, a divine influence from Him is present in the ceremony, more fully investing the person ordained with the graces requisite for the right performance of his duties. Thus the writings of the New Church not only state, "that the divine virtue and operation which is signified by the mission of the Holy Spirit, consists, with the clergy in particular, in illustration and instruction," but also that "their ordination to the ministry conveys those graces."* Of course, the meaning is, *to those who worthily engage in the work*; just as heavenly blessings are communicated to all who worthily approach the Lord's table; though with those who approach unworthily, or without sincerity, the effect is different.

That a solemn inauguration or ordination is necessary, according to the doctrines of the New Church, to the rightly engaging in the office of the ministry, is evident from the passage just cited, speaking of the divine influence which attends it. The same may be conclusively inferred from what is stated in the writings of the New Church respecting the religious solemnization of another divine institution—that of marriage. It is said, *Conj. L.*, n. 306, "There are solemnities which are mere formalities, and *there are solemnities which are at the same time essentials*. Among these are nuptials [or the rites of marriage.] That these belong to the class of essentials which are to be manifested with solemnity and celebrated in form, is confirmed by these reasons: 1. That the nuptials form the end of the former state entered into by the betrothing, which was principally a state of the spirit, and the beginning of the subsequent state to be entered into by the marriage, which is a state of the spirit and body together, &c. 2. That the nuptials are an introduction and entrance into a new state, &c. 3. That the nuptials are an entrance to the entire separation of the love of the sex from conjugial love, &c. 4. It appears as if the nuptials only formed the interval between those two states, and thus that they are only matters of form, which may be omitted; nevertheless there is also in them this essential, that the new state beforementioned is then to be entered into by covenant, and the consent is to be declared in the presence of witnesses, and to be consecrated by a minister." Here it is affirmed that *there are formalities which are at the same time essentials*; and that the solemnization of nuptials is *among* these: consequently, there are *others*. And it seems impossible to conceive that the religious solemnization of the nuptials can be more essential to the due establishment of a marriage, than is a solemn form of inauguration or ordination to the due conferring of the ecclesiastical character. All the reasons, likewise, which are given for the necessity for the religious solemnization of nuptials, will equally apply, *mutatis mutandis*, to the religious initiation into the ministry. A little below, in the same work (n. 308,) is this statement: "As the ecclesiastical order *administers on earth the things belonging to the priesthood appertaining to the Lord*, that is, the things belonging to his love, and thus *those relating to benediction or blessing*, it is needful that marriages should be consecrated by his ministers." It can hardly be imagined to be less needful, that those who are initiated into the ecclesiastical order should be consecrated by the Lord's minis-

* Tr Ch Rel. 146   The Latin is,—*innuguratio in ministerium illas secum portat;*—literally—' inauguration into the ministry carries with it those [graces."]

ters previously exercising that function, and should receive, through them, *the benedic-tion of the Lord*, the administering of which is here declared to be a part of their office. Nor can these conclusions be invalidated, merely because the herald of the Lord's second advent has not said so in so many words. The only reason why he has not, appears to be, because he has never expressly and directly treated of the subject: had he written a work upon the ministerial office, as he has on marriage, it seems almost unquestion-able that it would have contained statements to the above effect.

As the writings of the New Church recognise the necessity of a solemn inauguration or ordination to a due admission into the " ecclesiastical order," without stating, in a direct form, how such ordination should be performed, it is to be concluded that the enlightened Scribe approved of the mode which has prevailed in the Christian Church from the beginning, and which is an adaptation of the form practised from ancient times, and which originally was of divine institution. This is, by prayer and the imposition of hands. Accordingly, this is frequently spoken of in the Author's writings, and its appropriate signification explained. He does not indeed say, in so many words, that it is to be continued in the New Church ; but as he does plainly recognize the necessity of a solemn religious ceremony, and mentions no other than this, it seems reasonable to conclude that he expected this to be continued. Admitting, also, what seems unques-tionable, that some solemnity is to be used, it would be difficult to devise any that is more affecting, significant, and impressive. Every other, likewise, must necessarily be altogether of human invention, and may thus be supposed to include more of man's pro-prium, and to be necessarily less orderly and appropriate.

Since, then, there is to be an " Ecclesiastical Order" in the New Church, and they who enter into it are to be solemnly inaugurated or ordained it appears pre-eminently necessary that the representative sacraments of Baptism and the Lord's Supper, and especially the latter, should only be administered by a person who truly belongs to the Ecclesiastical Order, by having entered it in this solemn and orderly way. The divinely ceremonial and representative character of both sacraments seems to require this; and, with regard to the Holy Supper, its pre-eminent holiness. In regard to preaching, though this involves more exercise of the intellectual powers, yet such an idea of sanctity does not attach to it. Both in the primitive Christian and in the Jewish Church, well-instructed persons, though not priests, were allowed to exhort the brethren : nor is it possible to judge of a person's fitness for regularly filling the office of a teaching minis-ter, unless he have previously had opportunity of making trial of his gifts. But this does not apply to the administration of the sacraments, which appears exclusively to belong to the ecclesiastical order.

Here end the observations of the former Committee. They seem to comprise all that it is needful to state respecting the necessity for what the enlightened Swedenborg calls an " Ecclesiastical Order," in general, and the functions that belong to the office ; one of which, and not the least important, unquestionably is, the admission of others into the ministry by a solemn inauguration or ordination. To suppose that a society or con-gregation can itself duly ordain its minister, is to suppose that influx can flow from the external into the internal, and, indeed, that the external can produce the internal, and the expanse the centre ; which, as they are things obviously impossible, are also declared in the writings of the New Church to be contrary to divine order.

II. It being then certain that, in the New Church also, there is to be an Ecclesiasti-cal Order, " to administer those things which belong to the divine law and worship,' thus " the things belonging to the priesthood appertaining to the Lord," " and thus those relating to benediction or blessing," it may be inquired, in the second place, whether all the ministers of the Church should be of the same degree, and empowered to exercise the same functions, or whether there should, in this respect, be a distinction. A few of the letters which have come before the Committee go into the examination of this ques-tion, and attempt to decide it in favor of the first alternative, or that there should be but one order only.

That a true Church may exist, admitting no distinction of order or of function among its ministers, or whose Ecclesiastical Order should be founded on the principle of simple oneness, the Committee readily acknowledge. Nor. it is supposed, will any deny, how-ever persuaded they may be of the propriety of this arrangement, that a Church may have a subordination of degrees among its ministers, and yet be a true and pure church. But if either mode of arranging the Ministry be allowable, which is the preferable? Which is the higher and more perfect order? The Committee can have no hesitation in stating it to be their conviction. that that order of arrangement is the preferable. because in itself the more perfect, which adopts a distinction of degrees. And this appears to them so clear, if the authority of the Lord's servant Emanuel Swedenborg is to be allowed to be of weight, that it cannot be gainsaid, without incurring difficulties which no ingenuity can palliate. This, they think, is obvious, from the ablest and most elaborate of the letters which maintain the contrary opinion, in which the writers themselves appear to the Committee to *feel* that the opinion of Swedenborg is against them.

The most unequivocal passage on the subject in the writings of our Author is that which has often been adduced, in the App. to Tr. Chr Rel n. 17; where he declared that "in order that ANYTHING may be perfect, it is necessary that there be a Trine in proper order, one under another, with a communication between them, and that this Trine constitute a One; much like a column, at the top of which is the capital, under this the shaft, and under this the base. Such a trine is man, whose supreme part is the head, whose middle part is the body, and whose lowest is the feet and soles. In this respect, every kingdom emulates a man; therein must be the king as the head, various officers and functionaries as the body, and peasants and servants as the feet and soles; so also, in the Church, the mitred primate, the parish ministers, and the priests under them."* Wh t he here states, also, will appear still stronger, if compared with what he had advanced in the two preceding paragraphs. In them he says (n. 15) that " The Lord Jehovah, when he founds a new heaven and a new church, induces on them such an order, as that they may stand under his auspices, and in obedience to himself, to eternity :" and that (n. 16) " The arrangement of all things in the heavens, and of all things in the hells, is most perfect; for every heaven, which is founded by the Lord after the consummation of a church, is made threefold, there being a supreme, a middle, and a lowest.—These three heavens form three expanses, one over another, between which there is a communication by the divine influx from the Lord out of the sun of the spiritual world. In the deep beneath them are also three expanses, into which the hells are divided ; between which likewise there is a communication by influx through the heavens from the Lord.—From this arrangement (he adds) induced on both, it results, that they both stand under the Lord's auspices, and in obedience to him, to eternity." If such are the results of the threefold arrangements of heaven and hell, we may at least infer that a corresponding order in the Church must have a tendency to contribute to its permanence, and to its standing more fully under the auspices of the Lord. Since, also, as we are elsewhere assured, in all the three heavens there are preaching and priests, it is unquestionable that there are actually ministers of three degrees in heaven; if, then, the influx from heaven be allowed an uninterrupted descent into ultimates, it can hardly be doubted that it would effect the arrangement into three degrees of the ministry in the Church. It could only fail to do so through the resistance of its recipients.

If we go to the plenarily inspired Scriptures of the New Testament, we there find clearly that the Lord instituted two classes of ministers, in subordination to himself, at that time ; for if " he chose twelve, whom he named apostles" (Luke vi. 13), he likewise " appointed other seventy also" (ch. x. 1). And it has been justly observed, that while the Lord was in the world, he performed the functions of a minister himself; and thus the Trine is complete. But why, except arbitrarily, and without reason, are the plenarily inspired Scriptures of the Old Testament to be cast aside in this inquiry ? Notwithstanding the objections which have been made against drawing any conclusion on this subject from the priesthood of the Jewish Church, it is more easy to reject this evidence in the mass, than to show, by any valid proof, that that priesthood, as to its threefold order, is not, together with its purely spiritual signification. a representation of what a Christian Ministry ought to be, " in order that it may be perfect." We may wish to

---

* The Latin of the last clause is, "Similiter in ecclesia, primas infulatus, antistites parochi, et flamines sub illis " The word *flamines* has been rendered "curates;" but it is a general word signifying *priests*. By the three terms the author doubtless means the same distinctions as he expresses, in the passage quoted below, from T. C R n 106, by the terms " primate" (*primas*), " pastor" (*pastor*), and " priest" (*sacerdos*).

exclude, if it were possible, with some classes of the dissenters in the Old Church, all
representatives from the Church and from the world; but this never will be possible, so
long as the influx from heaven into the world takes place according to correspondences.
Where there are correspondences, there will be representatives; and the ministry or
priesthood under the Christian dispensations remains as truly representative as it was
under the Jewish. So says Emanuel Swedenborg. In illustrating the truth, that, under
the representative dispensations, it made no difference whether a representative person
was a bad or a good man, he has these observations : " 'he same may appear from *the
representatives which exist even at this day*. For all kings. be they who or what they
may. represent the Lord by virtue of the regal office appertaining to them : so likewise
do all priests, be they who or what they may. by virtue of the sacerdotal office; for the
regal office itself, and the priestly office itself, is holy, whatever be the quality of him
who administers it." (Arc. Cœl. 3670.) If then, ministers or priests still represent the
Lord as to his divine priesthood, just as. according to what has been seen above, they
" administer on earth the things belonging to the priesthood appertaining to the Lord,"
it seems preferable that there should be the same distinctions of degree among them now
as, when accuracy of representation was more important. was made indispensable. Nor
will it hence follow that the priesthood should be hereditary and confined to the same
family. What is thereby represented, in application to a Christian ministry, is provided
for, when they derive their ordination from each other, and are grounded in, and teach,
kindred principles of life and doctrine.

Some persons seem to disapprove of there being more degrees than one in the Ministry, because this resembles Episcopacy. which, in their estimation, involves all that is
hateful, and is only to be mentioned as a term of execration. But surely it is not for
members of the New Church to take up the prejudices of certain classes of dissenters in
the Old Church, who assuredly do not retain among them anything more of a true church
than exists in that form of the Old Church which they have forsaken, and who, in withdrawing from the establishment on such frivolous grounds, have evinced how entirely
they make the whole of the Church to consist in faith alone, to the utter rejection of
charity. And however, like other things intrinsically good, the episcopal constitution of
the Church may have been corrupted and abused, it will not be easy to show that some
arrangement of the ministry, so far partaking of the same order as to admit a variety of
degrees, is wrong in itself, and the necessary parent of such corruptions and abuses.
The Scriptures themselves have been grossly corrupted and abused by the false doctrines
pretended to be built upon them : yet the New Church, in rejecting the corruptions and
falsifications, does not think of rejecting the Scriptures also. The sacraments have been
grossly corrupted and abused by the false notions connected with them. and the superstitious use of them; but the New Church, in rejecting the false notions and superstitions,
does not reject the sacraments themselves. And if the kind of ecclesiastical order which
admits of more than one degree in the ministry, has, under the name of episcopacy,
been made the subject of various abuses it does not follow that, in rejecting and guarding against the abuses, the New Church is to reject that species of order itself.

It is now generally admitted by candid men, that nothing conclusive can be drawn
from the Apostolic writings, either for or against this species of order : yet though the
precise species of ecclesiastical order called the episcopal may not be obviously acknowledged in them, they afford the plainest proofs of there existing at that time various
functions in the ministry, discharged by various persons. But no fact in ecclesiastical
history is more certain than this,—that if not introduced immediately by the apostles,
such an arrangement of the ministry was established throughout the Christian Church
very soon afterwards. Now we have the authority of Emanuel Swedenborg for asserting, that the Christian Church existed as a true and pure Church till the Council of Nice,
in the year 325 : surely then it cannot be concluded, that a species of order in regard to
the ministry, which was established in the Christian Church as soon as ever it had
arrived at any degree of maturity, and which prevailed exclusively for more than two
hundred years while the Church was yet in its purity. is in itself disorderly, and such as
ought not to be tolerated in a pure and enlightened Church. And when it is considered,
further, that the same general principle of ordering the ministry, though gradually mixed
with many abuses, continued to be the only one acted on for twelve hundred years

more ;—that it was not till what is called the Reformation, in the sixteenth century, that the principle of admitting but one class of ministers was any where established; and that of all the Reformers, this was broached and adopted by Calvin and his followers only, who, as is well known, more than all the other Reformers, aimed at establishing, in every thing, the contrary of all that he found previously existing, and acted most purely from a spirit of opposition :—when these facts are borne in mind, it will be difficult to infer, that the principle which admits but one order in the ministry must be right, and that which admits more must be wrong.   The former is properly to be called the Cal- vinistic constitution of the ministry ; the latter is the constitution of the ministry which prevailed in the Christian Church when in its state of purity: and the New Church, which regards Calvin (with the exception, perhaps, of Socinus) as the greatest heresiarch of modern times,—as the man who, of all theological leaders, had the least light in interpreting the doctrines of Scripture combined with the greatest ingenuity in perverting them.—will hardly believe that this same man, in regard to the proper constitution of the ministry, possessed the only true light which has ever shone upon the world.

It appears then clear to the Committee, that the most perfect arrangement of the minis- try is that which admits a distinction of degrees, and that the number of degrees is properly three ;—that this is agreeable to the testimony of Scripture and to the doctrines and truths of the New Church as contained in the writings of Emanuel Swedenborg ;— also, to the practice of the first Christian Church when in its state of purity—which, while admitting a variety of functionaries in its ministry, has generally acknowledged that there are but three really distinct degrees.   It appears also to the Committee, from a careful examination of the letters which have come before them, that no really valid argument can be urged to the contrary, and that they who object to it are actuated more by a vague dread of abuses, which are by no means necessarily connected with the system itself, than by any certain principle founded either in Scripture or in reason

III. At length, then, in the third place, the Committee proceed to offer such ideas as have occurred to them, after consulting the communications, on the question referred by the last Conference for their consideration, viz. " Whether it is in accordance with the laws of Divine Order to admit persons, by some solemn service, to administer the sacra- ment of Baptism only, and not that of the Holy Supper "

The Committee approached the consideration of this question with a sense of awe, fearful of concluding anything, without very clear light, affecting so holy a sub ect as the sacraments.   After, however, carefully weighing the sentiments expressed in the various letters, they were of opinion, that, while a numerical majority is against it, the weight of argument decidedly preponderates in its favor.   They were much surprised to find the Lord's words, " What God hath joined together, let not man put asunder," cited in several of the letters, as a conclusive argument for the negative ; when it appears so obvious that that divine saying can have nothing to do with the subject.   The marriage of goodness and truth is thereby spiritually signified ; which also is represented in the Holy Supper : but Baptism represents the state which precedes such marriage, when man is principled in truth, and is looking towards good. but has not yet attained the happy union.   Baptism and the Holy Supper are no more *joined together*, than is a state which *precedes* and a state which *follows ;* which, by that very order, never can exist *together*.   A man can no more be at once in the state represented by Baptism and in that represented by the Holy Supper, than he can at once be in the avenue leading to a palace, and in the palace itself.   In the order of his regeneration man cannot but be, for a considerable period, in the state which corresponds to baptism, before he can be in that which corresponds to the Holy Supper.   To this it appears quite analogous, that a minister, on being first introduced into the Ecclesiastical Order, may be admitted to administer the ordinance of Baptism some time before he is admitted to administer that of the Lord's Supper.

The only other argument which the Committee have met with against the lawfulness of such a measure, is, that the Lord appointed the same persons to administer both the sacraments ; and as he did not appoint different individuals to administer them severally, it would not be in accordance with the laws of divine order to admit persons to administer baptism alone.   This might be a valid argument, if it were proposed, that they who are admitted to baptize should never be admissible to enter on the full functions of the ministry, or that the ministers who can dispense the Lord's Supper should never baptize : but no such separation as this being intended, the reasoning is not conclusive ; and what force it retains is completely taken away by the following affirmative argument.

It is remarked in several of the letters, that the apostles themselves were admitted to baptize long before they were authorized to administer the other sacrament; for they baptized while the Lord was with them in the world (see John iv. 2), but did not administer the Holy Supper till after his resurrection and ascension. To this it may perhaps be objected, that this only arose out of peculiar and accidental circumstances, such as cannot occur again—the Holy Supper being not capable of being instituted, nor, consequently, of being administered, till the Lord's glorification was on the eve of its entire completion. Yet, perhaps, these circumstances, instead of forming a just ground of objection, are rather confirmatory of the sentiment against which they may be thought to militate. For it is certain that all things connected with the Lord's proceedings while in the world took place according to the most perfect divine order ; and, if so, it may be inferred. not only that they who *receive* baptism and the Holy Supper should undergo the former before they are admitted to the latter, but also, that they who *administer* them should be limited. for some time, to the administering of the initiatory sacrament before they proceed to that of the Holy Supper. It *appears* as if the apostles were thus for a time restricted through merely accidental circumstances : but it is most certain that there could be nothing truly accidental in the case ; and if so, the apparently accidental circumstance becomes an indication of what is the true course of divine order.

The wide distinction which Swedenborg makes between the two sacraments as to their nature and uses, and the things to which he compares them (*True Christian Religion*, n. 721), are also mentioned, in one of the letters, as a ground for concluding, that no law of divine order would be violated by admitting persons to administer baptism only. In the passage referred to, the Author writes thus : " These two sacraments are as it were two gates leading to eternal life. By baptism. which is the first gate, every Christian is initiated and introduced into the doctrines which the church teaches from the Word respecting eternal life, all which are so many means to prepare him, and conduct him to heaven. The other gate is the Holy Supper, through which every one who has suffered himself to be prepared and led by the Lord is introduced and admitted into heaven. There are no other universal gates than these. The intent and uses of these two sacraments may, in this respect, be compared with the case of a prince who is born to the government of a kingdom : he is first introduced into the knowledge of the principles of government, and is then crowned and admitted to the government itself. They may be compared also with the case of a son, the heir of a great estate, who is first instructed in such matters as relate to the right management of his wealth and possessions, and, afterwards, comes into the actual management and possession. They may be compared, too, with the case of a house, which is first to be built and afterwards to be inhabited ; and also with a man's education from his infancy till he comes to years of discretion, and with his rational and spiritual life afterwards : one period must needs precede that the other may be obtained ; for it is not possible to attain the latter but by means of the former. These instances may serve to illustrate how Baptism and the Holy Supper are like two gates through which man is introduced to eternal life ; and that after passing through the first gate he comes to a plain, over which he is to run a race, and that the second gate is the goal, where the prize is placed, towards which he directs his course; for the palm is not given till the race is run, nor the prize adjudged till the contest is decided." This passage certainly cannot be considered as affording ground for a positive conclusion : yet since the sacraments and their uses are shown to be so very different, it may be inferred that there may be no necessity that, in all instances, they should be administered by the same persons ; and that a person may for some time be confined to perform the one before he is admitted to dispense the other.

As is remarked in another of the letters, " Baptism being a symbol of purification, and a sign of introduction into the church ; and the Holy Supper a symbol of the conjunction of goodness and truth, and consequent conjunction with the Lord, and a sign of introduction into heaven ; and as repentance with respect to time precedes. and is a preparatory step to conjunction ;—the administration of baptism may be a step and degree

2

in the ministry, preparatory to the administration of the other and more sacred ordinance of the Holy Supper."

IV. In conformity with this last remark, the Committee would add, in the fourth place, that if it is allowable, in agreement with the laws of divine order, that persons should be admitted, in a solemn manner, to administer the ordinance of baptism, without being at the same time empowered to administer that of the Holy Supper, it appears to this Committee, that this would constitute a preparatory and introductory degree of the Ministry, and that. If established, no candidate for the ministerial office should afterwards be admitted into that office without passing through this initiatory stage, and tarrying for sometime therein. It will not follow, that every one thus admitted should afterwards proceed to the other functions of the ministry—this will depend upon his general qualifications and ability to devote himself to the work—but only, that every one who enters the ministry at all should commence with this step. As, also, baptism is the proper introduction into the church, and the state represented by it is to be experienced by every member of the church, so, if the power of administering baptism is to be, in any case, separately conferred, analogy seems to dictate, that it is by entering into this ecclesiastical function, and passing through the exercise of it, that introduction should be given to the ministry itself.

If we are to judge by the dictates of reason, and by analogy with other cases, respecting what is agreeable to divine order in regard to an introductory station in the Ministry, the Committee think that we must conclude in its favor. No one enters on the exercise, for himself, of any art, trade, or profession, without having been initiated into the practice of it as an apprentice, pupil, or clerk; in which subordinate station he exercises, for a time, the inferior branches of the business, till he is equal to the whole, and capable of pursuing it without any limitation by another. Swedenborg uses this very illustration, and introduces for the purpose this very case of introduction into the Ministry, and, successively, into all the three degrees, which, as we have seen, there is reason to believe that he thought necessary to its institution in the most perfect order. Having stated the proposition, "That the Lord's progress towards union (with the Father) was his state of Exinanition, and that the union itself is his state of Glorification" (*True Christian Religion*, n. 104), he shows that man also goes through two corresponding states as from being natural he becomes spiritual: to which he subjoins a paragraph of illustrations (n. 106), from which the following is an extract: " Those two states are represented by various circumstances and effects in the universe; and the reason is, because they are according to divine order, and divine order fills all and every thing in the universe, even to the most minute particulars   The first state is represented in the life of every man by his state of infancy and childhood till he grows up to riper years of youth and manhood, which is his state of humiliation and obedience under his parents, and of instruction by masters and teachers; but the other state is represented by the state of the same person when he becomes his own master, or when he has no one's will and understanding to consult but his own; in which state he has absolute rule in his own house   Thus the first state is also represented by the state of a prince or king's son before he becomes a king; also by the state of every citizen before he is advanced to the office of a magistrate, and of every subject before he holds any post in the government; likewise, *of every student who is preparing for the ministry before he becomes a priest, and of every priest before he becomes a pastor, and of every pastor before he becomes a primate.*" By a pastor the author here evidently means, a minister who has the care of a congregation, and is competent to perform for them all the ministerial duties: by a *priest*, then, who is not a pastor, he must mean one who is in an initiatory degree, competent to perform some of the ministerial functions required in a congregation, but not the whole.—capable, perhaps, of assisting a pastor, or of taking charge of a congregation which is without a pastor for a time. The Author does not indeed here say, that divine order requires that there should be all these classes of ministers: but he does say, that the relation of the member of the Ecclesiastical Order whom he calls a priest to him whom he calls a pastor, and his being a priest some time before he is a pastor, are among the results which the divine order that fills the universe produces And perhaps it may be concluded, that he would not have mentioned all the three classes, unless he considered the existence of them all as agreeable to the most perfect order ; to which, indeed, as has been seen, he elsewhere speaks of them as being necessary.

Nor would the formation of an initiatory class in the Ministry, if made a necessary step to the full entrance into the office, be without considerable use. Applications for the consent of Conference to the ordination of a candidate are sometimes made, where, either because it is thought that a longer probation of the party is required, or for other reasons, the Conference feels it to be its duty to demur : commonly with much unintended offence to the candidate and his friends. But, in the generality of cases, there would be no objection to the admission of such applicants into an initiatory and probationary degree. Many, also, would be glad to enter into such a degree, who, from unsuitableness of situation in life, or a consciousness of deficiency in some desirable qualifications, do not think of coming forward as candidates for admission into the full pastoral office.

On the whole, the Committee give it as their opinion, from a very careful investigation of the entire subject, that it is fully agreeable to the laws of divine order that there should be an initiatory degree of the Ecclesiastical Order. They also are of opinion, that the reasons in favor of the sentiment—that it is agreeable to those laws that the distinguishing feature of such initiatory degree should be, the power to administer the first of the sacraments but not the second,—are stronger than those on the other side.

It is somewhat remarkable, that the distinctions which, according to these views, would be made between the three degrees of the Ministry, are precisely the same as the chief distinctions in the three degrees of the Ministry of the Established Church in this country and in most other nations of Christendom ; in which, the ministers of the lowest degree have the power of administering baptism but not the holy supper, those of the second degree have power to administer the holy supper, and perform all the functions required in a congregation, but not to ordain other ministers, this belonging to the third order alone. But if this coincidence should recommend the view to some, it will proportionably depreciate it with others. It shows, however, that such a view cannot be condemned on the ground of novelty.

In concluding this Report, the Committee beg to state, that, while giving a qualified affirmative answer to the abstract Question which was submitted to their consideration, they are of opinion that it will not be advisable to act upon it in the present state of the Church. At present, it is evident, there is, in some quarters, a strong feeling against such a measure ; and the Committee conceive that, in a matter relating only to the ceremonials of the Church, the Conference would not be justified in acting in a way that might offend or alienate any of their brethren. By thus setting an example of moderation and forbearance, it may be hoped that the Conference will remain united in bonds of love with those who hold different opinions on these matters, and that nothing like dissent or separation from the general body of the Church will ever be resorted to by any. Should the persuasion finally prevail, that the Ministry should be constituted, upon the plan introduced by Calvin, without any difference of degree, the members of this Committee are prepared to acquiesce, being satisfied that a true Church might still exist under that constitution. But they must nevertheless be of opinion, that the most perfect order of the Ministry is that which is arranged in three degrees ; that, with its Ministry so arranged, the Church would be in a form into which the heavenly influx could flow more interiorly and copiously than would be possible under a lower and more external species of constitution ; and that the final prevalence of the Calvinistic plan could only be, because it was most in correspondence with the present low and external state of the human mind, out of which, even the profession of the heavenly doctrines of the New Church does not raise men at once. But while the Committee conceive that, if the Calvinistic mode of constituting the Ministry should finally prevail, it can only be from such a cause, they trust in the Lord that this will not be the case ; that the apparent bias towards it at present existing arises out of the present political situation of the country ; that the clouds which have thence, in some degree, overcast the vision even of some of the members of the New Church, will have but a temporary prevalence ; and that the clear light of heaven will again ere long burst forth, and will lead the Church to do what is most agreeable to genuine order, and what will most tend to keep her under the Lord's auspices, and in unreserved obedience to him, for evermore.

SAMUEL NOBLE, Chairman.
JOHN NEWBERRY, Secretary.

No. L.

SUPPLEMENT

To the " Inquiry respecting the Office of Ministers in the New Church," —" read in Conference by the Rev. S. Noble, and printed in the Appendix to the Minutes of the Twenty-third General Conference, held in the year 1830."

DEAR BRETHREN,—I should not, so long afterwards, have thought of adding a Supplement to the " Inquiry" mentioned above, had I not something of far greater importance to lay before you, and, through you, before the Church at large, than any thoughts of my own.

I call what I am about to offer, a Supplement to the " Inquiry" read by me in the Conference of 1830, and printed by its order, because I have no right to add a Supplement to any but my own individual productions : I shall, however, have occasion to refer also to Reports upon the subject of the Ministry since published by authority of the Conference.

The object of the " Inquiry" above-named was to show, *first*, That there is to be a peculiar order of persons to act as priests or ministers in the New Church : *secondly*, That to them it properly appertains to administer those things which belong to the divine law and worship, especially the sacraments of Baptism and the Lord's Supper; and, *thirdly*, That the orderly way of admitting persons into the ministry, is, by a solemn inauguration, or a devotional service, accompanied by imposition of hands, to be performed by ministers who had themselves been admitted in a similar manner. These points were established by testimonies of Scripture and of the New Church writings. The conclusion deduced from these premises, in reference to questions then agitated in the Church, was, That the Conference can have no power, by any act of theirs, to confer, *directly*, the right of administering the sacraments. It was observed (I still believe most truly) that " all that the Conference can lawfully do in the appointment of persons to perform ecclesiastical functions, is what the primitive Christians did in the case of deacons, as stated in Acts, vi. 3—6,—to present to the ministers, for ordination by them, such persons as they (the Conference) deem suitable characters." It was also remarked, that " For the Conference to undertake to *dispense* with the requirements of Divine order upon the subject, would be to assume a papal power indeed. They might as well undertake to dispense with the observance of the ten commandments."

It could not well be supposed, that in this last observation it was meant to be affirmed that any rule of external order can be of the same rank as the laws of internal order, or that anything relating to ceremonies can be of the same importance as what relates to moral and spiritual life : but what was intended was this : That every law of Divine order, whether relating to little matters or to great, to externals or to internals, is equally incapable of being abrogated by any human authority. " Whosoever shall break one of the least of these commandments shall be called least in the kingdom of heaven." " He that is faithful in that which is least is faithful also in much ; and he that is unjust in the least is unjust also in much." As, however, though *examples* are not wanting, there is not, in the New Testament, any *direct precept* respecting the ordination of ministers, nor any *direct* instructions regarding it in the printed works of the Lord's servant

Emanuel Swedenborg, some still were of opinion, that ordination by prayer and imposition of hands performed by other ministers, or even any ordination whatever, is not
required by any law of divine order at all. On this account, in the Preliminary Observations of the Committee appointed by the Conference of 1831, and recited in the Report
of a Committee appointed by the Conference of 1832 (printed in the Appendix to the
Minutes of the last Conference—1833), it was shown, that if Swedenborg does not *direct*,
he *supposes* ordination as essentially necessary, when he affirms, that it actually " conveys," or " carries with it," the specific graces of the Holy Spirit belonging to the ministerial function. It was also shown, that he declares a religious service, and consecration
by a minister, to be "essential" to the due solemnization of nuptials; whence it was
argued, that it cannot be less necessary to an orderly initiation into the ministry; and
that the only reason why Swedenborg has not said so in so many words, appears to be,
because he has never expressly and directly treated on the subject.

Now it certainly is not a little remarkable (as it is obviously providential) that all that
was thus advanced respecting the doctrine of Swedenborg, both in regard to ordination
in general and the proper mode of it, is now found to be fully substantiated by a document from his pen, the existence of which was unknown to the above-named Committees,
and to myself individually.

I have lately had occasion to examine a volume of the manuscripts of our enlightened
Author in the possession of the Rev. Mr. Sibly. Among others, it contains the heads of
a work entitled " Canons of the New Church," which appears intended to form part of
a body of doctrine much like the True Christian Religion. It contains a Division " On
the Holy Spirit;" in turning over the leaves of which, in a casual manner, my eye was
caught by the passage which I shall presently recite; having, with Mr. Sibly's permission, copied it for the purpose.

This Division of the work is divided into several chapters, each containing various
distinctly numbered propositions. The third and fourth chapters are headed thus:

" Ch. III. That the Divine Principle called the Holy Spirit, proceeding from God by
his Humanity, passes through the Angelic Heaven into the world, thus through the angels
to men."

" Ch. IV. That thence it passes by (or through) men to men, and in the Church, especially by (or through) the Clergy to the Laity."

This chapter contains nine propositions, the first six of which are of a general character, and the three last, being the passage to which I specifically wish to call attention,
relates to the ordination of ministers, and the communication of the Holy Spirit, through
their ministry, to the people, in these words:

" 7. That every clergyman [or minister], since he is to teach from the Word the
doctrine concerning the Lord, and concerning redemption and salvation by Him, is to be
inaugurated [or ordained] by the [supplicated] promise of the Holy Spirit, and by a representation of the transfer [or communication] thereof; but that this is received by the
clergyman [or minister] according to his faith of life.

" 8. That the Divine Principle which is understood by the Holy Spirit proceeds from
the Lord by the Clergy to the Laity, by preaching, according to the reception of the
doctrine of truth thence.

" 9. And also by the sacrament of the Holy Supper, according to the repentance
exercised before receiving it."

In the first of the above propositions, we have, in a very few words, a clear statement
of the great truths respecting the necessity of the ordination of ministers and the proper
mode of it, just as they are advanced in my " Inquiry" (Minutes for 1830), and in the
Reports of the Committees (Minutes for 1833). The necessity of ordination is declared
by the divinely illuminated writer when he says, " Every clergyman [or minister] is to
be [or *must* be] inaugurated [or ordained] " That the mode of it is to be by prayer
and the imposition of hands performed by ministers previously ordained, is declared,
when he says, that it is to be done " *by the [supplicated] promise of the Holy Spirit,
and by a representation of the transfer [or communication] thereof.*"

In the same proposition, also, the manner in which the gifts of the Holy Spirit proper
to the ministerial office are " conveyed" by the ordination, is authoritatively stated, in a
manner precisely equivalent to the explanation offered in my Inquiry and in the Commit-

fees' Reports. In those documents it was observed, that when the Author says, that those graces are conveyed by the ordination, he of course means, to those who receive it worthily, and that otherwise the effect is different: so, at the close of the above proposition, the Author says, that the "[supplicated] promise," with "the representative transfer," of the Holy Spirit, "is received by the clergyman [or minister] according to his faith of life."

What the divinely instructed Herald of the New Church regarded as the laws of Divine Order with respect to the initiation into the ministry and the proper mode of it, is now rendered indubitable: and all that was advanced upon these subjects in the Inquiry and the Reports, is thus found to be established by his unequivocal authority.

Trusting, Dear Brethren, that you will deem the above, on account of the testimony of our venerated Author which it brings to light, of sufficient importance to, be printed with the Minutes,

I am, your co-adjutor and servant to my power, in your labors for the establishment of the Lord's New Church,

SAMUEL NOBLE.

Subjoined is a copy of the original Latin of the titles of the first three chapters of the work above mentioned respecting the Holy Spirit, and of the whole of the fourth chapter.

DE SPIRITU SANCTO.

CAP. I. *Quod Spiritus Sanctus sit Divinum quod procedit a Deo Uno, Infinito, Omnipotente, Omnisciente, et Omnipræsente, per Humanum Ipsius in mundo assumptum.*

CAP. II. *Quod Spiritus Sanctus, qui a Deo Uno per Humanum Ipsius procedit, in Essentia sua sit idem Deus, sed quod apparenter ad subjecta, quæ in spatiis sunt, sit Divinum Procedens.*

CAP. III. *Quod Divinum quod vocatur Spiritus Sanctus, procedens a Deo per Humanum Ipsius, transeat per Cælum Angelicum in mundum, ita per angelos ad homines.*

CAP IV. *Quod inde per homines ad homines, et in Ecclesia imprimis per clericos ad laicos.*

1. Quod nemo possit accipere Spiritum Sanctum nisi a Domino Jesu Christo, quia ille a Deo Patre per Ipsum procedit. Per Spiritum Sanctum intelligitur Divinum Procedens.

2. Quod nemo possit Spiritum Sanctum, hoc est Divinum Verum et Bonum, accipere, nisi qui Dominum immediate adit, et simul in dilectione est.

3. Quod Spiritus Sanctus, hoc est Divinum Procedens, nunquam fiat hominis, sed quod constanter sit Domini apud illum.

4. Quod ideo Sanctum, quod intelligitur per Spiritum Sanctum, non inhæreat, et quod nec manet, nisi quamdiu homo, qui illud accipit, et in Dominum credit, et simul in doctrina veri ex Verbo est, et in vita secundum illam.

5. Quod Sanctum quod intelligitur per Spiritum Sanctum, non transferatur ab homine in hominem. sed a Domino per hominem in hominem.

6. Quod Deus Pater non mittat Spiritum Sanctum, hoc est, Divinum suum, per Dominum in hominem, sed quod Dominus mittat illum a Deo Patre.

7. Quod Clericus, quia ex Verbo docturus est doctrinam de Domino, deque Redemptione et Salvatione ab Ipso, inaugurandus sit per sponsionem Spiritus Sancti, et per representationem translationis ejus; sed quod a Clerico recipiatur secundum fidem vitæ ejus.

8. Quod Divinum quod intelligitur per Spiritum Sanctum, a Domino per Clericum procedat ad laicum, per prædicationes secundum receptionem doctrinæ veritatis inde.

9. Et per sacramentum Sanctæ Cœnæ, secundum pœnitentiam ante illud.

To complete the sense, in English, of Prop. 7, it will be observed, that the word "[supplicated]" is prefixed to the word "promise," because it is evident that no man can *give* the Holy Spirit, he can only *supplicate the Lord to give it* , which, therefore, must be the author's meaning. although, on account of the brevity with which he has expressed himself, this is left to be inferred. But whether the necessity for the explanatory word in English be admitted, or not, is of little consequence. None will deny that ordinations, if performed at all, should be accompanied with prayer for the gift of the Holy Spirit to the person ordained: the only point that might admit a question was, whether there should also be " a representation of the transfer thereof:" and this is unequivocally declared. None, also, it is supposed, will contend, that the imposition of the hands of the ordaining minister upon the head of the person ordained is not the representation alluded to.

No. LI.

ORIGIN OF THE NEW-CHURCH MINISTRY.

On page 15 of our " Report on the Trine" there occur these sentences: " It is a matter of new-church history that such a clergy had in fact been formed;" and " The persons who called the first general conference were the same who had previously formed the first ministry of the new church." In proof of these assertions we here give an account of the first formation of a ministry by the new-church society of London, by which the first general conference was called. Although this paper has no manifest bearing upon the history of a *trine* in our ministry, it undoubtedly possesses much interest in its bearings upon the general history of our church, and therefore may very properly be inserted here as a " Document for History." As here given, it is taken from " The New Church Advocate," Vol. II., p. 172.

It may be necessary to describe the mode adopted by the New Church to commence that institution, without deriving it from any authority heretofore recognized in the Christian world. As the New Jerusalem Church is altogether a New Church, distinct from the Old, of which it is written in the Revelation, chap. xx. 5, " *Behold I make all things New;*" it was conceived, that this declaration applies not only to the doctrines of the Church, but also to its institutions and ordinances of every kind, and among the rest to that of the Ordination of Ministers, whose authority to teach, and preach, and administer the sacraments, must be derived from the Lord alone *in his own Church,* and not from any Priesthood of a fallen, consummated, and finished Church This was precisely the situation of the primitive Christian Church, which derived no authority by succession from the regular Priesthood of the Jewish Church, but commenced its ordination *within itself,* from the immediate presence and authority of the Lord. Besides, how inconsistent would it have been, if not plainly impossible, to derive authority from the Old Church *to oppose its own doctrines,* and thus to undermine and subvert it from the very foundations! A kingdom. a city, a house, or a church, thus constituted, thus divided against itself, could not possibly stand. (Matt. xii. 25.)

Among the male members present at the first Ordination, sixteen in number, besides the two, who by experience had been found qualified to officiate as Priests or Ministers of the New Church, no one entertained the 'most distant idea, that he had, in his *individual capacity,* the smallest right or authority to send forth laborers into the Lord's vineyard: and hence it was plain to them, that the ordination could not commence in such a way, or by such individual authority. It was therefore suggested, that twelve persons should be selected from all the male members present, to represent the whole body of the Church; that those twelve should be chosen by lot; that when so chosen, they should all place their right hands upon the head of the person to be ordained : and that one of these should be requested by the rest to read and perform the ceremony : this proposal was acceded to, and adopted, for the following among other reasons :

First, Because no individual person either in the Old Church or in the New, could be acknowledged by the Society as possessing in himself the smallest title to authority or pre-eminence over others, in a case of such vital importance to the interests of the Church at large.

Secondly, Because the future prosperity and well-being of the Church required, that no time should be lost in forming an Institution, which should hereafter become an orderly and well-regulated safeguard for the protection, due administration, and succession of the sanctities of the Ministerial function.

Thirdly, Because when the Apostles of the Lord found themselves in a somewhat similar situation, in consequence of the defection of one of their number, they, judging themselves incapable of determining who was most fit for the vacant office, from which Judas by transgression fell, had recourse to the drawing of lots, " That the Lord who knoweth the hearts of all men, might show which of the two persons (Barsabas or Matthias), proposed to fill up the place of Judas, he had chosen." (Acts i. 24.)

Fourthly, Because again on another occasion the drawing of lots was adopted as a decision of the Divine Providence, when there did not appear to be sufficient ground for the determination of human judgment. See the treatise on *Influx*, or on the *Intercourse between the Soul and Body*, n. 19, first edition, in quarto ; from which the following extract is taken : " Do not suppose, that this lot came to hand by mere chance ; but know, that it is by Divine direction, that so you, who could not discover the truth because of the confusion of your minds, might have it thus presented to you in the way of your own choosing."

Such being the situation of the Church, and such the reasons for proceeding in the way described, we shall here annex an extract from the Minute book of the Society, in which the first ordination took place. It is as follows :—

"ORDINATION OF MINISTERS IN THE NEW CHURCH.

" *Sunday, June* 1, 1788.

" At a full meeting of the members of the New Church this day, in Great East Cheap, after the morning service, it was unanimously agreed to ordain JAMES HINDMARSH and SAMUEL SMITH, as Ministers and Priests in the New Church, in the manner following ; viz.—Twelve men to be chosen by lot out of the Society, as representatives of the New Church at large, and these to lay their right hands on the person ordained, agreeable to the form of Ordination.

" The following persons drew lots for that purpose.

" 1. Robert Hindmarsh	" 9. Samuel Bucknell
2. Thomas Wright	10. John Swaine
3. Thomas Willdon	11. Daniel Richardson
4. John Willdon	12. George Robinson
5. John Rainsford Needham	13. John Augustus Tulk
6. Manoah Sibly	14. Isaac Brand
7 Alexander Wilderspin	15. Isaac Hawkins
8. Richard Thompson	16. John Sudbury.

" And the lots fell on the twelve first mentioned, who appointed ROBERT HINDMARSH to read the service."

A remarkable circumstance occurred on the occasion, and at the time of this ordination, which we shall relate in Mr. ROBERT HINDMARSH'S own words. " Being (says he) Secretary to the Society, when it was determined that twelve men should be selected by lot from the body of the Church, to lay their hands on the heads of the persons to be ordained, it was my office to prepare the tickets. I accordingly made sixteen tickets, answering to the number of male persons present, members of the church, and marked twelve of them with a cross. Being desirous, for my own private satisfaction, to ascertain which of the twelve to be selected by lot it might please the Lord to appoint to read or perform the ceremony, I wrote, unknown to the rest of the society, upon one of the twelve tickets, thus marked with a cross, the word ORDAIN ; I then put the sixteen tickets into a receiver, when a prayer went up from my heart, that the Lord would show whom he had chosen for the office of Ordination. The members being properly arranged, I went round to them all; and each one took a ticket out of the receiver, leaving me the last ticket, on which was written, as before stated, the word ORDAIN. Still the other members of the Society were not aware of what I had done; and when the twelve were separated from the rest, after consulting together a few moments, they unanimously requested that I would read and perform the ceremony of Ordination Whereupon JAMES HINDMARSH was first ordained, and immediately afterwards SAMUEL SMITH." The reader, keeping these observations in view, will now see the reason why, in the following list of Ordained Ministers, the name of ROBERT HINDMARSH stands at the head of them; and why it is stated, that he was himself *Ordained by the Divine Auspices of the Lord.* How could we otherwise describe an appointment, which had the evident sanction both of God and man?

LIST OF ORDINATIONS OF MINISTERS.—*Those marked thus * have departed this life*

No.	Names of Persons Ordained	Of what Place.	Where Ordained.	When Ordained.		By whom Ordained.
1	Robert Hindmarsh*	London	London	June 1,	1787	By the Divine Auspices of the Lord.
2	James Hindmarsh*	London	London	June 1,	1788	Robert Hindmarsh.
3	Samuel Smith*	London	London	June 1,	1788	Robert Hindmarsh.
4	Joseph Wright*	Keighley, York	London	April 7,	1790	James Hindmarsh.
5	Manoah Sibly*		London	April 7,	1790	James Hindmarsh.
6	Francis Leicester*	London	London	Sept.	1790	James Hindmarsh.
7	Robert Jackson*	Jamaica	London	Sept.	1790	James Hindmarsh.
8	Joseph Proud*	Birmingham	London	May 3,	1791	James Hindmarsh.
9	Robert Brant*	Birmingham	London	May 3,	1791	James Hindmarsh.
10	William Faraday*	Birmingham		June	1797	Joseph Proud.
11	George Nicholson*	Hull	London	Dec 25,	1804	Joseph Proud & Manoah Sibly.
12	William Pownall*	Bristol	London	Dec 13,	1804	Manoah Sibly.
13	James Hodgson*	London		Mar 31,	1805	Manoah Sibly.
14	Isaac Hawkins*	Wivelscombe	London	April 13,	1806	Manoah Sibly.
15	William Ellis*	Newcastle-on-Tyne			1806	James Hodson.*
16	Richard Jones*	Manchester		June	1808	Manoah Sibly & Joseph Proud.
17	Thomas Furlong Churchill*		Brightlingsea	Aug. 16,	1812	Manoah Sibly & Joseph Proud.
18	Arthur Munson*	Brightlingsea	London	Aug. 15,	1813	Manoah Sibly & Joseph Proud.
19	Joseph Enoch	Keighley, York.	London	Sept. 19,	1815	Manoah Sibly & Joseph Proud.
20	Thomas Vaughan	London	London	Oct. 29,	1815	Manoah Sibly & Joseph Proud.
21	Thomas Goyder*	London	London	July 13,	1817	Manoah Sibly & Joseph Proud.
22	Edward Madeley*	London		Aug. 13,	1818	Manoah Sibly & T. F. Churchill.
23	James Bradley*	Derby		Aug. 16,	1818	Joseph Proud.
24	James Noble*	Newcastle-on-Tyne		Aug. 16,	1818	Joseph Proud.
25	Samuel Noble*	London		May 21,	1820	Manoah Sibly & T. F. Churchill.
26	James Robinson*	Derby		May 10,	1822	Manoah Sibly & R. Hindmarsh.
27	John Pownall*	Bristol		Nov 3,	1823	Richard Jones & R. Hindmarsh.
28	David George Goyder*	Derby		Nov 3,	1823	Thomas Furlong Churchill.
29	Thomas Pilkington*	Haslingden		Mar. 2,	1824	Richard Jones & R. Hindmarsh.
30	David Howarth	Manchester		Aug. 9,	1824	Richard Jones & Manoah Sibly.
31	Edward Madeley, Jun.	Birmingham	Birmingham	Aug. 12,	1835	Joseph Proud.
32	Jonathan Gilbert*	Leeds	Derby	May 8,	1835	Manoah Sibly.
33	William Mason	Derby	Derby	July 14,	1835	Robert Hindmarsh.
34	William Bruce	Edinburgh	Edinburgh	Aug. 14,	1835	Samuel Noble.
35	Elias De la Roche Rendell	Newcastle-on-Tyne	Manchester	Sept. 19,	1839	Samuel Noble.
36	John Wickham Barnes	Bath	Manchester	July 21,	1840	Samuel Noble.
37	Jonathan Bayley	Accrington	Manchester	Aug. 13,	1842	R. Hindmarsh; S. Noble, D. Howarth
38	John Henry Smithson	Manchester	Bath	Aug. 19,	1832	Samuel Noble & D. Howarth.
39	Thomas Chalklen	Liverpool		Oct. 30,	1836	David Howarth.
40	Woodville Woodman	Brightlingsea		Oct. 3,	1837	David Howarth.
41	John Cull	Leeds	Birmingham	Sept. 17,	1837	Samuel Noble.
42	Richard Storry	Heywood	Heywood	Aug 12,	1838	Manoah Sibly.
43	Thomas Clarke Shaw	London	Brightlingsea	Nov 30,	1840	David Howarth.
44	Joseph Francis Wynn	London	Brightlingsea	Nov 25,	1842	Manoah Sibly.
	David Thomas Dyke	Sudbury	Norwich	Aug 18,	1844	Thomas Goyder.

This document shows that a ministry of the new and true christian church, called the New Jerusalem, which is now coming forward on earth, was first formed, in the city of London, June 1, 1788; and it very minutely and satisfactorily displays the reason for asserting that this ministry then sprung from " the divine auspices of the Lord."

No. LII.

REV. WILLIAM MASON'S LETTER TO THE CENTRAL CONVENTION.

The English General Conference has, for some years past, appointed members of its body, especially leading ministers, to address, in its name, the three conventions of the new church in America. The task of addressing the General Convention has been assigned to the president of the conference—that, doubtless, being deemed the oldest, largest and most respectable body of the church in this country. But that the addresses sent to the Western and Central Conventions might have the fuller sanction and credit of the General Conference, the writers of those addresses were directed, previously to transmitting them to this country, to submit them to the president of the conference, for the time being, that they might bear his countersignature as the seal of the conference in his approval. Such was the case in respect to the communication made by the Thirty-Ninth General Conference through the Rev. Woodville Woodman, to the Central Convention, and laid before this body in its seventh annual meeting. Of that conference the Rev. William Mason was president. To him, therefore, Mr. Woodman's communication to our convention was sent. But Mr. Mason, having seen something to disapprove in the Journal of the Central Convention in its sixth annual meeting,—not received by the General Conference, when Mr. Woodman was appointed to address our body,—and seeming to infer that the conference would not have directed such an address as Mr. Woodman's, if it had seen our Journal previously, does not sign it in his capacity of president of the conference without taking certain marked and severe exceptions to the Journal's contents. It is, in fact, thus subscribed: " Signed by me, WILLIAM MASON, as President of the Thirty-ninth Conference, on the 11th March, 1847, but with the qualification set forth in the accompanying letter of the same date." This subscription, or endorsement, the publishers of Journal No. IX. have, in our opinion, very improperly omitted from Mr. Woodman's letter as printed in Appendix III. pp. 28, 29. For they have *mutilated* a document of the General Conference, in cutting off the *official endorsement* of its presiding officer. By this endorsement the conference was made responsible for the act of its servant, the president: and it could only be erased by the express vote or order of that body itself; and not even by that, in strict propriety, after the document had been sent and received in its name. Hence, although the conference tacitly disapproved of the act of its president, by not acting on his letter to us, or publishing it in connection with its minutes, it has, nevertheless, suffered his endorsement to remain attached to Mr. Woodman's communication to us, as printed in the appendix to its last Minutes. (See Min. 40th Gen. Con., Ap. p. 88.) How could the General Conference have done otherwise? It could not mutilate its own document, as we have done for it. It could not, *in truth*, have published a communication as sent to our convention *without the endorsement of its president*, when that communication, as in fact received and read in the annual meeting of our body, *bears it in most distinguishable black and white upon its face.* And we cannot ' see how the Central Convention could any more *in truth* publish the same document without the same official endorsement. But the Central Convention did not, by any vote which appears in the journal of its proceedings, direct that this endorsement should be omitted; and as we cannot see any even implied authority for altering *this* communication in number 62 of our last annual meeting's proceedings, we must think that our publishing committee, in making this omission of an official signature, have assumed a most unwarrantable, and exercised a most reprehensible, responsibility. As to Mr. Mason's *letter*, to which he refers in this official subscription of the General Conference's address to us, that is a very different matter. In leaving that out, the publishing committee exercised a wise discretion. And the Fortieth General Conference, in expressly forbidding its publication in connection with its Minutes, evinced an equally commendable spirit of true new-church charity. But the *truth* of history, and not less the *good* or *use* of history, especially the *private* history of the new church, for which we are now engaged in furnishing materials, demands that this letter of William Mason, as president of the General Conference, should be published. And here it is.

Melbourne, near Derby, 11th March, 1847

To the President of the Central Convention of the New Church in the United States of America.

DEAR SIR—The Conference had not received the Journal of the Central Convention when the accompanying address, prepared by the Rev. Woodville Woodman, was ordered to be sent. After perusing the Journal, and hearing the sentiments of various members of the Church concerning it, I am able to say, that I have not found any one who approves of its contents. For my own part, I shall propose the subjoined resolutions thereon (God willing) to the next Conference. It may be, that from a regard to a pacific policy, these resolutions may not pass; but I feel assured, that they will not be rejected owing to any disagreement with their *import.*

Resolutions to be proposed to their Conference of 1847. '

I. That this Conference, having reference to minute 49 of the Journal No. VIII of the Central Convention, not received at the last Conference, is of opinion, that when Swedenborg argues in the *Coronis* to the True Christian Religion, no. 17, for the existence of a trine in all things of nature, and all things of man, and specifies as an instance the trine of bishops, parish priests, and curates *under them,* as a trine that *must be* in the church, he did not mean to be understood, by citing such instance, that the New Church, of which he was the harbinger, should artificially construct any kind of trine of orders or degrees of ministers in *imitation* of the trine then existing in the Lutheran Church, inasmuch as, if the fact he was contending for (namely, that a trine is essential to all existence and cannot be excluded) was yet in the case of the New Church, *to be artificially contrived before it could exist,* in that church, and to be contrived not at the prompting of use, but at the dictate of ingenious speculative theories concerning order, the argument of Swedenborg, so far as regards the trine in the Church, as a spontaneous, and unavoidable existence (supposing a church to exist at all) would be invalid, seeing that it would depend upon the *contingency* of the New Church constructing, or not constructing, such an imitative trine, whether his argument should be, so far, externally confirmed or nullified. But it appears to this Conference, that Swedenborg's proposition, that "there *must* be a trine in just order," required that he should mean by his reference (to the Church) to be understood, that wherever, and whenever, a church is established, *it cannot be otherwise* than that there will be found in it, in actual operation, a trine of *uses,* which providentially have created for themselves corresponding social organs or mediums of use, in whom they have become functions of use, and that this trine of *uses* is implied by the *titles* of the offices of bishops, parish priests, and curates *under them.* It is clear that he could not have mentioned those offices in a merely personal sense, or in a local sense, having a reference merely to the externals appertaining to them; but that he must have referred to them in a philosophical sense, as personal representatives of abstract uses, or as terms implying specific uses. (How uses are prior to mediums of use, and how uses produce, and adapt mediums for themselves, see A. C. 4223.) Accordingly it appears, that the three uses implied by these three offices are, *first*. the use of appointing ministers and superintending their ministry; *secondly*, the use of officiating in the administration of the Word and sacraments; and, *thirdly*, the use of so officiating subordinately in the same church or place of worship. The proof that such a trine of uses exists. and must exist, in every church that has ministers belonging to it, will appear, on reflection, to be self-evident. Thus in the English New Church already it will be found, that the *first* use, in respect to appointing ministers exists and is discharged *conjointly* by the assembled Church (not as divisible into clergy and laity, but as the personal representatives of the *good and the true* which constitute the Church *in which the Lord is present*, or Conference and the ordaining ministers, while the other portion of the *first* use,—that of superintending the ministers, exists and is discharged *conjointly* by the Conference and the societies to which they respectively minister, that is, by the good and the true in the members of societies in which the Lord is present); that the *second* use exists and is discharged by the stated minister; and the third use exists and is discharged by the friend or novitiate preacher (excepting the administration of the sacraments) who occasionally officiates for him, under the appointment of himself and the society. Whether these uses can best be carried out in one way or another, must depend on actual circumstances. It *may* be the case, that, when the New Church becomes as extensive as was the Lutheran when Swedenborg wrote, then these uses may best be carried out by officers *externally* analogous to those of bishops, parish priests, and curates *under them;* but it does not appear wise to externally imitate these officers of the Church by a merely artificial contrivance not suggested as the best mode of effecting ministerial uses; but to follow out *the dictates of use* simply, for this is to follow the Lord. "When man regards uses as an end, he regards the Lord as an end; for the Lord arranges things for uses, and arranges uses themselves." (A. C. 5949.)

II. That this Conference must dissent from the sweeping condemnation, published in page 22 of the Journal of the Central Convention, upon the Conference Hymn Book; and cannot but express its conviction, that as the hymns were prepared expressly to promote the uses of piety, rather than to display the powers of poetry, so those persons in the country who regard such uses have, by universal admission, extensively realized them. It must needs be, that the uses of piety and the language of the hymns cannot always be made to exist together in equal perfection, and it is clear, that it is much better that the uses of piety should be regarded in the first place, and the poetry of the language in the second. than *vice versa*. The Conference is not unaware that, to some extent, hymns are found in its collection which could easily be replaced by others better every way, if it were convenient to undertake the task of improvement at present; but the Conference is also convinced that, as a whole, no volume of hymns more happily combining truth, poetry, and practical piety, has ever yet existed, or does exist; and, therefore, it is not accurate to say, that "but FEW (of the whole 600 hymns that is) *give the spiritual affections for the heavenly truths of the New Jerusalem in pure poetic garb and expression.*" What the authors of the condemnatory judgment may mean by "pure poetic garb," it is probable they could not easily define; but if it means language unobjectionable to a right critical judgment, and suitable to the purpose in view, this Conference must dissent altogether from the judgment given, both as being *inaccurate* and *uncourteous*. As to seeking after perfect poetical productions by an "influx from the Lord," rendering writers of hymns in some remarkable manner and degree poetical—a consummation which the Central Convention hopes for—it appears to this Conference to indicate a somewhat superstitious state of mind,—a state of mind indicated also in other remarks in the same page; and, indeed, those who have read the Journal alluded to in England, have greatly lamented the manifestation of such a state of mind. as observable in several places between pages 29 and 44;—a state of mind painfully at variance with the professions of a primary regard to use, contained in the last address from the Central Convention, and also in preceding addresses; a state of mind which has led to an unquestionably unauthorized and practically injurious sundering of the two sacraments, in violation of the professedly adopted pattern of the three degrees in the Coronis, each of which administers both sacraments (which pattern is also violated by the first (centralist) degree not officiating *under the second in the same place of worship*, as curates officiate under parish priests); and what is worse, in opposition to the precept, " what God hath joined together, let not man put asunder ;"—a state of mind which has led to the elevation of the human institution of a ceremonial in celebration of marriage (which is not a sacrament because it does not open heaven) above the divine institution of baptism (by apportioning baptizing but not marrying to the lowest degree) regardless of the fact that only the two sacraments are institutions *of the Church*, and that marriage is not an institution *of the Church*, but of the whole human race ;—a state of mind which appears to have led to a forced construction and misapplication of passages in the writings of Swedenborg, cited in the Journal in support of the superstitious conclusions sought to be established thereby, and which have grown out of the unwarranted construction of *Coronis* 17, in attempting to carry that construction into practice.

I am, dear sir,

Yours faithfully in the cause of truth,

(signed)   WILLIAM MASON,

President of the 39th Conference.

P. S. I think it is right to mention, that I have sent copies of this communication to the General and Western Conventions, in order that the sentiments generally entertained in this country by members of the New Church may not be unknown throughout the United States.   W M.

No. LIII.

AN ADDRESS

To George Washington, Esq., President of the United States, from the Members of the New Church at Baltimore.

SIR,

While the nations of the earth and the people of United America especially, have, in their various denominations, paid the tribute of respectful deference to the illustrious president thereof; permit, sir, a society, however small in number, yet sincere, they trust, in their attachment, to offer up, in the dawn of their institution, that mark of dutiful esteem, which well becometh new associations, to the Chief Magistrate of America.

We presume not, sir, to enter into a reiterated panegyric of matchless virtues or exalted character : but judging of causes by effects, we are led to believe, that you were a chosen vessel for great and salutary purposes, and that both in your actions and in your conduct, you justly stand one of the first disinterested and exemplary men upon earth; neither in this address can we, were it expected, enter into a detail of the profession of our faith; but we are free to declare, that we feel ourselves among the number of those who have occasion to rejoice, that the word literally is spiritually fulfilling; that a new and glorious dispensation, or fresh manifestation of divine love, hath commenced in our land; when as there is but One Lord so his name is becoming one throughout the earth; and that the powers of light, or truth and righteousness, are in an eminent degree, universally prevailing, and even triumphing over darkness; when all corruptions in church and state shall be corrected to the gospel state of divine love and wisdom, and the love of God and man be the only ground of action throughout christendom.

Oh! sir, could we, without being charged with adulation, pour out the fulness of our souls, to the enlightened conduct of him, who stands chief amongst the foremost of men, what a volume of Truth might we deservedly offer to the name of WASHINGTON, on the ALTAR OF LIBERTY, uncircumscribed.

Allow us, by the first opportunity, to present to your Excellency, among other tracts, the Compendium of the New Church, signified by the New Jerusalem in the Revelations, as the readiest mean to furnish you with a just idea of the heavenly doctrines.

That the Lord Jesus, whom alone we acknowledge as "the true God and Eternal Life," will preserve you long to reign in the hearts of the people, and finally to shine as a gem of the brightest lustre, a star of the first magnitude, in the unfading mansions above, is the fervent aspiration of your faithful fellow-citizens and affectionate brethren.

Baltimore, 22d *Jan.*, 1793.

GENERAL WASHINGTON'S REPLY.

To the Members of the New Church at Baltimore.

GENTLEMEN,

IT has been my pride to merit the approbation of my fellow-citizens, by a faithful and honest discharge of the duties annexed to those stations, in which they have been pleased to place me; and the dearest rewards of my services have been those testimonies of esteem and confidence with which they have honored me. But to the manifest interposition of an over ruling Providence, and to the patriotic exertions of United America, are to be attributed those events, which have given us a respectable rank among the nations of the earth.

We have abundant reason to rejoice, that in this land the light of truth and reason has triumphed over the power of bigotry and superstition; and that every person may here worship God according to the dictates of his own heart In this enlightened age, and in this land of equal liberty, it is our boast that a man's religious tenets will not forfeit the protection of the laws, nor deprive him of the right of attaining and holding the highest offices that are known in the United States.

Your prayers for my present and future felicity, are received with gratitude; and I sincerely wish, gentlemen, that you may, in your social and individual capacities, taste those blessings which a gracious God bestows upon the righteous.

GEO. WASHINGTON.

No. LIV.

VALEDICTORY ADDRESS TO THE PEOPLE CALLED METHODISTS.

To the Rev. John Harper, Resident Minister, and the Members of the Episcopal Church in Baltimore.

RESPECTED AND DEAR BRETHREN,

As a very important change has taken place in our sentiments, respecting an article of the christian religion, which, in our view, is one of the most essential, and which, if erroneous, of consequence, must have its influence upon *all other doctrines* which flow from it, or are connected with it; and as we already feel that this change will subject us, in future, to considerable embarrassment, or, what is far worse, *unfaithfulness* in our public ministration and services; we have, therefore, after the most solemn and serious consideration of the subject and its consequences, both with respect to the welfare of the church to whom, *until now*, we have been connected, as well as that of our own souls, come to this 'conclusion :—That it is best for us peaceably and quietly to withdraw ourselves, and resign our membership in the Methodist Episcopal Church; that we may more consistently enjoy our present religious sentiments in a state of perfect freedom, and act accordingly.

Upon a retrospect of our general conduct amongst you for near thirty years past, we trust none of you can find just cause to suspect our sincerity, when we declare to you that no base considerations of any kind have influenced us; but that we do in our hearts believe, that it is *now* required of us, to take this unexpected and unpopular step —a step not unattended, on our part, with much regret.

The protracted and pleasing intercourse of christian fellowship which has heretofore happily subsisted between us;—the many personal and endearing attachments which we have formed amongst you;—the conspicuous and sacred stations which we have so long held in the church—joined to the high esteem we still entertain for you;—all conspire to render this step that we have now taken, one of the most painful and self-denying acts of our past lives—an act which nothing less than a solemn sense of duty (and of otherwise offending God) could have prompted us unto. We do not wish to enter into any controversy with any person or persons upon earth, respecting our sentiments; for, " *where contention is, there is every evil work :*" yet we conceive it may be but consistent with our present duty, calmly and meekly to mention, that the leading article in which *we* differ from *you*, is, the *doctrine of the Trinity ;* concerning which, we beg leave to say, that we think this doctrine, *as generally apprehended*, to be neither consistent with, nor reconcilable to, *scripture* or *reason*, to wit, that the TRINITY, in the GODHEAD, consists of *three distinct* DIVINE PERSONS, each of whom, *separately*, and *by himself*, is very and eternal GOD.

On the contrary, we believe, that the LORD JESUS CHRIST, in whom dwells all the fulness of the GODHEAD—who is the "*everlasting Father*" as well as the *Son*,—who hath declared that *He* and the *Father* are *One*,—and that he that seeth *Him* seeth the *Father*,—is the TRUE AND ONLY GOD of heaven and earth; and that in *Him* is a divine Trinity of Father, Son, and Holy Ghost; that the *Divinity* within him is the *Father :* the *Humanity* is the *Son :* and the *divine proceeding thence* is the *Holy Ghost ;* constituting ONE adorable and glorious object of christian worship.

We have not adopted this belief in a hasty precipitate manner, nor yet because we have found it in certain *human writings ;* but because we find it to be a doctrine contained in the word of GOD, from the whole of which we learn, that GOD is *one* in *essence* and in *person*.

That this doctrine has a direct influence upon other doctrines derived therefrom, is plain to see; yet we conceive it needless, and by you it might be deemed impertinent, if, in this place, we were to adduce proofs and arguments in support of our sentiments, especially as *our request is*, that this address should be read to the society; but we shall not be backward to state them at large, when called upon, or when it may appear necessary for us so to do.

Could we have thought it possible to have enjoyed our present sentiments amongst you, *in a latitude suitable to our stations*, we should not thus withdraw ourselves; but as we have no doubt, such indulgence would, *on your part*, be deemed wholly inadmissible, we have no other alternative left us to preserve a consistent character and a good conscience.

Our wish and desire is, notwithstanding, to live in as much peace and friendship with you all, as on our part it will be possible.

ADAM FONERDON,
JOHN HARGROVE.

Baltimore, 5th June, 1798.

No. LV.

SOME TRANSACTIONS IN THE FIRST NEW JERUSALEM SOCIETY OF CINCINNATI.

EXTRACTS FROM THE RECORDS.

These extracts are taken from the Records in a course of years. They most generally have dates, which are given. But occasionally there are no dates; simply the number of the meeting from the first is indicated by figures between parentheses. All the meetings are so marked. So that some have both this indication and a date, and others have it alone.

(34)

Sept. 9, 1822.—66.

This day a meeting of the society was held at the meeting house in Cincinnati. Present—Adam Hurdus, John W. Silsbee, Oliver Smith, Marcus Smith, Silas Smith, Josiah Smith, Wright Smith, Dudley Andrews, John Coombs, Thomas Reddish, Thomas F. Smith, Marston Allen, Ephraim Carter, Oliver Lovell, Jacob Resor, Thomas Carter, A. M. Bolton, Nathan Sampson, Elisha Wood, John Ramsdale, Isaac Burton, Theodore B. Barrett, Charles Sonntag, Samuel Badger, Benjamin Lamphier, Calvin Sampson, Daniel Roe.

A. M. Bolton, D. Roe, Josiah Smith, Oliver Lovell, Marston Allen, Ephraim Carter, and Adam Hurdus, were appointed a committee to report amendments to the By-Laws, or Rules for the government of this society, to a meeting, in this house, next Friday evening, at 7 o'clock, P. M. Adjourned to the 13th Sept., 1822.

EPHRAIM CARTER, *Chairman.*

Attest, DAN'L ROE, *Clk.*

(35)

13th Sept., 1822.

This day a meeting of the society was held pursuant to adjournment. Marston Allen was appointed to fill the chair. After the meeting was called to order, the committee appointed at the last meeting to report amendments to the By-Laws or Rules, reported as follows:—

Repealed Monday, 2th August, 1824—page 6.

The committee appointed on the 9th instant, Sept., 1822, to report amendments to the By-Laws or Rules of the First New Jerusalem Society, report the following, as what may be useful:

1st. In whom is the right to ordain ministers considered to exist?

Answer. In a majority of the male members of this society for the time being

2d. What shall be considered a suitable form of ordination?

Answer. A vote of the majority of the male members who may be present at granting a right to teach the doctrines of the New Jerusalem, and to administer the ordinances thereby maintained.

3d. What evidence shall be given to a brother that he is ordained by this society?

Answer. A certificate signed by the trustees and clerk of the society.

4th. Is a teacher or minister entitled in the society, or as a member of the church, to any authority or right, not possessed by every other member of the society, except what his certificate expresses?

Answer. Not any; and said certificate shall express on its face that the privileges granted are only to remain during the pleasure of the society from which it issued.

5th. How are we to construe the rule respecting offenders?

Answer. Not literally, but according to the spiritual, sense ; and only as between brethren ; and with no reference to trial or expulsion.

Signed,　　　　　　　　　　　　　　　DANIEL ROE,

MARSTON ALLEN,

O. LOVELL,

JOSIAH SMITH,

A. M. BOLTON.

Whereupon, the said report being read, the several sections or parts thereof were taken into consideration, and finally adopted by a vote unanimous, excepting one ; and are now a part of the rules of the society.

DANIEL ROE, *Clk.*

(37)

Monday, May 5th, 1823.

At a meeting of the members of the First New Jerusalem Society, this day held at their usual place of public worship, John Scudder, Marston Allen, and Daniel Roe were appointed a committee to report, to the next stated meeting of this society for business, such regulations, respecting the mode of administering the ordinances of baptism and the Lord's supper as may appear best to comport with the Sacred Scriptures and the writings which are illustrative of the doctrines therein contained.

It was further determined by a vote of the society, that, in future, Brothers Hurdus, Roe and Lovell shall occupy the pulpit at regular and successive periods—fixed on by themselves, and then to be uniformly adhered to, health and business permitting.

(38)

Monday, 19*th May,* 1823.—66.

The society met at the meeting house to hear and act upon the report of the committee, appointed on the 5th inst., to confer and report relative to the ordinances of baptism and the Lord's supper. Brother Aquilla M. Bolton was chairman. The meeting being called to order, the committee reported as follows :

The committee appointed, on the 5th inst., to take into consideration the propriety of altering the manner of administering the ordinances of baptism and the Lord's supper, having had the same under examination, beg leave to report : That, in their opinion, all forms and ceremonies which at present attach to the use of these ordinances, which are repulsive in their operation, and which are not supported by the precepts of the Word, nor by the example of the apostles in the first christian church, should be abolished ; and that, in lieu thereof, there should be adopted such forms as are essential to these administrations, and adapted to the present liberal and charitable doctrines of the Lord's New Church. Your committee therefore recommend the following rules, to be adopted as permanent *guides* in this matter ; and that the same be recorded as part of the rules by which this society professes to govern itself.

1st. Whenever any person is to be baptized, the same shall be made known to that minister, who, for the time being, is in the habit of administering that ordinance. at least one day prior to the Sabbath on which he or she may be baptized ; so that suitable preparation may be made for a discourse upon baptism to the candidate and the congregation immediately preceding its administration. That, at the close of the discourse, the minister about to baptize the applicant shall give a general invitation to all who may desire baptism ; and, if any come forward, he shall, without further ceremony, baptize by the sprinkling of water on the forehead, saying. "I baptize thee in the name of the *Lord Jesus* ;" and, after the ceremony has closed, the minister shall retire to the pulpit, and cause a suitable hymn to be sung, and the congregation shall be dismissed in the usual way.

If a candidate for baptism should prefer immersion, he shall signify it to the minister. and a suitable time and place shall be appointed ; and, after public notice to the congregation, it shall be administered in that way.

Repealed 24th August, 1824.

3

2d. When the day for administering the Lord's supper shall arrive, the bread and wine being previously provided by the trustees, shall be set as usual: and, previous to its being taken by the people, a discourse, explanatory of the design of this ordinance, shall be delivered, in which the minister shall be careful to inform the audience that none but such as have been baptized, both by water baptism, and, in some degree, by the holy spirit and by fire, are invited to partake; and, after having clearly informed the congregation that the supper is about to be administered, and that, as it will be offered to all who choose to remain, (but that it will not be expected of all who remain to partake,) and observing that such as feel no desire to remain are at liberty to withdraw; two brethren, previously appointed for that purpose, and who shall receive the bread and the wine from the hand of the minister who is in the habit of baptizing for the time being, shall take the same down the alley, and present the same, without remark, to each person successively—the bread to be presented first in order, and immediately followed by the wine. When the ceremony is closed, the minister who delivered the discourse shall cause a suitable hymn to be sung, and the congregation shall be dismissed in the usual way.

The public discourses preceding the administration of the ordinances, may be delivered by the several ministers of the congregation alternately. or as they may agree.

Whereupon, the said report, having been read publicly and discussed, was, by a vote unanimous, excepting one voice, adopted and ordered to be recorded as part of the rules for the government of this society.

DANIEL ROE, Clerk.

(46)

Brought up to wit :

That so much of the by-laws as relates to the ordinances of the society which were, on the 13th Sept., 1822, and the 19th of May, 1823, and have since been in force, be, and they are hereby repealed ; and that the society in future observe the former rules and ceremonies.

Attest,   JOHN SCUDDER, <i>Secretary</i>.

The committee, appointed 17th August, 1824, having taken into consideration the by-laws as they then stood on the records of this society, and wishing that universal love and harmony may be a constituent principle in the New Church wherever brought forward—we, therefore, wishing to harmonize in charity with the rest of our brethren, do recommend, that so much of our by-laws as orders the administering of the sacraments of baptism and the holy supper contrary to established custom in the New Church, be repealed ; also, so much of the by-laws as relates to ordaining ministers in this society, be repealed ; and to substitute in its place a law for choosing of leaders or teachers, according to usage in the New Church.

Signed,   ADAM HURDUS,
                                                 O. LOVELL,
                                                 DANIEL ROE.

(74)

April 19th, 1829

New Jerusalem Society in special session. Calvin Washburn in the chair.

Resolved, That a committee of five persons be appointed to settle any difficulty that may exist in this society.

(75)

April 27th, 1829.

First New Jerusalem Society assembled by adjournment. Brother Calvin Washburn in the chair. The committee appointed to inquire into the cause of differences of opinion existing in the society with respect to the standing of the several ministers and teachers beg leave to report :

That, after carefully examining the records of the society, we are of opinion, that the proceedings with respect to the appointment of ministers and teachers have been orderly. The by-laws adopted February 4th, 1828, provide that a majority of the qualified voters of the society shall have power to elect their ministers and teachers, and to dismiss them at pleasure. An amendment to the by-laws, made August 4th, 1828, provides that the ministers and teachers of the society shall be elected annually on the first Monday in May each year. Immediately after the appointment of the by-laws, in February, 1828, the society proceeded to elect Brother A. Hurdus a minister, and Brother O. Lovell a minister ; who, of course, hold their offices until the first Monday in May next, unless vacated by resignation or removal, neither of which has taken place. At a meeting held on the 30th September, 1828, it was "*Resolved*, That this society request Brother Alexander Kinmont to deliver an address in this house as often as he thinks proper, provided the house is not otherwise engaged;" and, on the 5th of April, 1829, it was "*Resolved*, That the clerk be requested to invite Alexander Kinmont to lecture in the New Jerusalem Temple on Sundays in the afternoon." As there was no appointment of either minister or teacher in these resolutions, but barely a request to lecture when the temple was otherwise unoccupied, they cannot (we think) be considered a violation of the by-laws of this society, which provides that the ministers and teachers shall be elected on the first Monday in May annually.

At a meeting held on the 2d of February. 1829, it was "*Resolved*, That a committee be appointed to confer with Dr. Edwin A. Atlee upon the subject of removing him to Cincinnati as minister of the First New Jerusalem Society of Cincinnati; and that they be instructed to take such measures as they may deem proper to bring about the event without delay." . On the 22d of February, this committee reported, that they had circulated a paper for Dr. Atlee's support,

*   *   *   *   *   *   *

A communication of the result of this labor and calculation has been made to Dr. Atlee, and he has, in consequence, sent for his family. "*Resolved*, That the report of the committee be accepted."

It does not appear from these proceedings that Dr. Atlee has as yet received any appointment from the society, although, from what has been done, we think the society has laid itself under obligation to elect him a minister at the annual meeting in May.

The committee are of opinion, that much difficulty would be avoided by clearly defining the duties and functions of the several orders of ministers. The General Convention has recognized three orders, which may be denominated licentiates or teachers—ordained ministers or pastors—and ordaining ministers or primates. In the True Christian Religion, No. 106, one author designates three orders by the terms, priest, pastor and primate. We have in our society one ordaining minister and two licentiates; and, as it is not improbable that others may be added to the list, we would respectfully recommend to the society to appoint a committee for the purpose of defining the duties and functions of each, which committee might report at the annual meeting in May. It must be obvious to every one, that no society, civil or ecclesiastical, can exist without a head and subordinate officers. To appoint three ministers in one society, without assigning to them different ranks, would be analogous to the hierarchy of heaven, as believed and taught by the old church, wherein they say there are three divine persons equal in power and glory. Of this trinity, our author says, no other possible conception can be formed in the minds of men than as of a trierarchy, or as of a government of three kings in one kingdom, or of three generals over one army, or of three masters in one house, each of whom hath equal power ; the certain consequence of which must be ruin and destruction. (U. T. 171.)

We cannot close this report without expressing our earnest desire that harmony and good feeling among the members of this society may be established upon a permanent basis. In order to accomplish so desirable an end, each member should recollect, that, as all cannot see exactly alike, it is necessary to exercise a spirit of christian meekness and forbearance. Where there is a difference of taste, there will be a difference of appetite for spiritual food. Some will prefer one preacher, some another. Christian charity would certainly teach that all should be accommodated, as far as practicable. Let us, therefore, mutually assist each other in attaining these objects; and the bonds of brotherly love will thereby be strengthened. We occupy a very important point in this western country : and if a proper unanimity and zeal in the cause of the church were prevalent among us, we might, by divine assistance, be instrumental in doing much good in extending our exertions to the surrounding country. But if matters of little or no consequence are suffered to divide us, we shall be instrumental in retarding instead of promoting the cause of truth.

Signed,   O. LOVELL,   LUMAN WATSON,   M. G. WILLIAMS.
                    WRIGHT SMITH,   JACOB RESOR,

(77)

Resolved, That a committee of five persons be appointed for the purpose of defining the duties and functions of the several orders of ministers, and that they be requested to report at the next regular meeting in May next. Committee—Messrs. Kinmont, Watson, Muscroft, O. Lovell and W. Smith.

(84)

The Minority of the First New Jerusalem Society of Cincinnati to their Brethren the Majority.

DEAR BRETHREN,—You will permit us the liberty of addressing you in the spirit of friendly and open communication ; as we believe it necessary, in order that no uncharitable misunderstandings in the present crisis may arise among us and thereby destroy the blessings of union and zealous co-operation in the advancement of the Lord's New Church.

You will have heard it rumored among you that some few of us (and we are indeed few) have intended to establish another society of the new church in this city, in opposition to that which is already on foot; and it is for the purpose of correcting this misapprehension of our intentions and motives that we are now compelled to address you

We have no wish or intention to establish a society other than is now existing, of which we are anxious to continue, to the best of our abilities, faithful and active members ; and we trust our brethren will always hail and honor us as such. And neither do we blame or accuse you of any wrong ; or, if we do, we are fully sensible we are actuated by a most improper spirit, which we pray the Lord to enable us to resist and overcome. But we feel it a very great spiritual deprivation, that we have not been permitted to enjoy the instructions of our beloved and aged pastor, the Rev. Adam Hurdus, as heretofore ; and, at the same time, we think it ungenerous to ask him, now in the vale of years, to instruct us at any other time of day than when his bodily strength is most fitted for the duty; and it is on this account that we are compelled by our spiritual necessities,—and we will add, also, by our *spiritual appetites*,—to assemble ourselves on Sunday mornings for social worship in a place separate from yours, although united with you, we trust, in the spirit of a pure and elevated devotion.

It will give us extreme pain if our brethren shall ascribe this act of ours to any other than a right motive ; or think that we are not a part of them, because appropriate food from a different table, or prepared after a different manner—the manner of preparation being that which is most agreeable to our peculiar tastes, and, in some measure, necessary to the preservation of our spiritual health. And we are also far from saying our taste is right and yours is wrong. Nay, we even fear that our own taste of evil requires that kind of instruction and spiritual nourishment which our inclinations also prefer. Regard us not, therefore, as in any way separated from you, for we feel we shall love you the better, and the more, for being thus associated. And if you find hereafter that you can accommodate us with the use of the temple at such time of day as will suit the bodily infirmities of our pastor, we shall most thankfully accept of the indulgence. But we request of you, at the same time, not to abandon your own views of usefulness or your own spiritual and necessary gratifications, on account of what you may consider as accommodation to us, for, in all cases of this sort, it becometh the minority to bear the inconveniences which either one party or the other must submit to. In the mean while, we shall be most happy to meet with our brethren in the evening at the temple, whoever may occupy the pulpit; and, in whatever object or pursuit co-operation is required, we trust our activities and diligence shall never be wanting to our friends, fellow-laborers, and brethren in the new vineyard of the Lord's spiritual church.

Signed,

A. KINMONT,
GEO. MUSCROFT,   } Committee in behalf
J. A. AUSTIN,   of the Minority.

(86)

ANSWER.

The Majority of the First New Jerusalem Society of Cincinnati, to their Brethren the Minority.

DEARLY BELOVED BRETHREN,—Your communication has been received, and deliberated on: and the spirit of conciliatory charity which it breathes throughout duly appreciated. Convicted that our strength consists in harmony, and that the prosperity of the Lord's New Church can only be promoted by the united exertions of its members, we are disposed to approve of the measures that you have taken, and, whatever may have been the fears of any of our brethren, we are satisfied that you are actuated by correct motives, and rejoice in the assurance that you are disposed to unite with us in all measures calculated to advance the cause of the church.

We cordially approve of your assembling in the manner you contemplate, until such arrangements can be made as shall be satisfactory to all. Meantime we hope that our respected and beloved Brother Hurdus will continue his pastoral duties; and that, in the administering of the sacrament of the Lord's supper, we shall all feel it our duty to participate.

Although it appears to us that Brother Atlee is best qualified to address a popular audience, yet we are far from underrating the services of Brother Hurdus; on the contrary, we consider him as eminently qualified to instruct those who have passed the outer courts of the temple, and are directing their views to those spiritual things which lie within the veil.

As it is not unlikely that Brother Atlee may sometimes be absent from the city for the purpose of preaching in the country, it will give us great pleasure, on such occasions, if Brothers Hurdus and Kinmont would occupy the pulpit at the temple; and as, by a late resolution of the society, Brother Atlee will in future preach at 11 o'clock. A. M., and at 3 o'clock, P. M., we hope that one or other of the above named brethren will feel disposed to fill the vacancy in the evening.

O. LOVELL,
C. CHESEBROUGH,   } Committee in behalf
L. WATSON,   of the Majority.

(88)

Resolved, That three orders of ministers be recognized in this society; and that they shall be known by the name of pastor, minister and teacher.

On motion, *Resolved,* That it shall be the duty of the pastor to ordain ministers agreeable to the rules of the General Convention—to perform the ordinances of baptism and the holy supper—to celebrate nuptials, when called upon—to preach or instruct from the pulpit when his pastoral office shall seem to require it; and generally to superintend the spiritual interests of the society; and to administer consolation to the distressed and afflicted, leading men to the good of life by the inculcation of truths from the Word, either publicly or privately, as he shall see fit opportunity and occasion.

Secondly, *Resolved,* That it shall belong to the minister, or the next in order, to administer the ordinances of baptism and the holy supper, when the office of pastor may be vacated by resignation or otherwise, or the pastor unable to attend to those duties; to celebrate nuptials, when called on and when legally qualified—to preach or instruct from the pulpit regularly, some portion of each Sunday—to visit the sick—and to perform such other active duties as a faithful minister and spiritual instructor shall judge appropriate and suitable to his function.

Thirdly, *Resolved*, That it shall belong to the teacher, or the third in order, when requested by the society, and duly authorised by the pastor, also to instruct from the pulpit, by written discourses or otherwise.

(94)

On motion, *Resolved*, That we go into an election of pastor, minister' and teacher. When, on counting the ballot, the following brethren were found to be duly elected :

Rev. Adam Hurdus, *Pastor.*
"   E. A. Atlee, *Minister.*
"   A. Kinmont, *Teacher.*

(102)

On motion made by Brother Chesebrough, it was *Resolved*, That a committee of six be appointed to inquire into the causes of the differences existing between the members. ministers and teachers; and to endeavor, if possible, to prescribe a remedy, and report at the next meeting.

(105)

The Rev. Adam Hurdus was duly elected pastor.

On motion, *Resolved*, That we omit going into the election of minister.   Carried.

On motion, *Resolved*, That we now go into the election of two teachers.   When Brother E. A. Atlee and Brother A. Kinmont were duly elected.

On motion. *Resolved*, That the committees which made report this evening be continued, with the exception of Brother White, who declined serving, and whose place was supplied by Brother Chesebrough, whose duty was assigned to fix the time when the ministers and teachers were to perform their services in the church.

On motion, *Resolved*, That we adjourn.

JAMES A. AUSTIN, *Clerk.*

(123)

On motion, it was *Resolved*, That the committee of ways and means. appointed at the last meeting, be authorised, provided they deem it expedient, to open a correspondence with Mr. Kinmont and Mr. De Charms, and ascertain on what terms and conditions each can be procured to serve the society as minister.

To the Committee, Messrs. Watson, Silsbee, &c., on the subject of the ministry.

BRETHREN—That you may be the more fully in possession of my sentiments on the subject of a ministry, on which you consulted me to day, I deem it proper that I should state them to you in writing, that you may lay them before the society.

I have never felt it a burthensome, but, on the contrary, a delightful duty, to explain to my brethren, as myself one of the many, the doctrines of the new church.   I have never looked upon myself as a clergyman, and I do not relish either the name or the function; but while Mr. Hurdus would be able to attend to the ordinances of the church, I also am willing to explain the doctrines as a teacher, *without fee or reward*, as I consider myself called upon to do, since the Lord graciously enables me to supply my temporal wants by temporal labors during the six days of the week.

If, however, it be the wish of the society, as I understand from you that it was, that they should have a minister after the model and the fashion at this day prevalent among the different sects in the christian world, who is exclusively to make preaching and its collateral duties his business and profession, and from thence to draw his principal or entire pecuniary support ; such a function I decline, as I am by no means satisfied in m ' own mind that it is after the model of a perfect and orderly church, however convenient or even necessary it may be in the present stage of human society, and the but very partially liberated state of the human mind.

Yours truly,

A. KINMONT.

The committee beg leave to report, that in the performance of their duties relating to a minister, they have called on Brother Kinmont, to ascertain whether he would be willing to accept the office of minister on any terms. His reply was, that he would not— believing that the interest of the present state of the society required that he *should not*. If this society, therefore, can unite on Richard De Charms as minister, then, in order to bring the subject before them, this committee guarantee to the society the sum of three hundred dollars as a remuneration, for his services for one year, should Richard De Charms accept it.

The committee will not be prepared to report in regard to the erection of a new temple until the point is first settled about a minister.

Signed on behalf of the committee.

OLIVER LOVELL, *President.*

CHARLES SONNTAG, *Secretary.*

Cincinnati, February 11th, 1833.

The foregoing document displays, in a manner that no verbal explanation could show, what were the difficulties that *any* minister of the church would have to encounter, who might go from a distance to Cincinnati to officiate for the society there while Messrs. Hurdus and Kinmont were ministers in connection with it. All know the hard fate of Dr. Atlee. That of Mr. De Charms was not less hard—though it was not quite so easy to prostrate him. His greatest sin, perhaps, was his stubbornly standing bolt upright, when he ought to have been lying flat—in not allowing himself to have been killed off as easily as he should have been! It may be his duty to give, in another place, a more extended historical sketch of the church in the West during his ministry there. This has been his intention; but he may not do it. If he should, he will want the foregoing document for reference elsewhere. He will only state further here, that, when his pastoral connection with the First Cincinnati Society was dissolved, said society very unkindly seemed to impugn his motives, or principles of action, in the course which he had felt obliged to take in sundering that connection. That society, in reporting the fact to the Sixth Annual Meeting of the Western Convention, say—"At a special meeting of the society, held July 3d, 1837, brother R. De Charms, through the trustees, tendered his resignation as pastor of the society—a movement sudden and unexpected to many; *causing fears, anxieties* and *doubts, as to the* TRUTH *of a* PRINCIPLE *which could actuate the measure.*" All the troubles which Mr. De Charms had experienced in the West put together, did not give him so much interior pain as this imputation on the *truth* of the *principle* by which he had been actuated, cast *publicly* and *officially* upon him by the society, whose spiritual interests he had so faithfully, under the Lord, endeavored to serve for four years! Truth, integrity, honor, every personal virtue, forbad his officiating for that society in any clerical capacity while that stigma remained not washed out. And he never could, and never did, preach in the pulpit of the First Cincinnati Society, even when the Western Convention was holding its sessions in its temple, until the imputation contained in the above report, was disavowed by an official act of the society which made it. In the autumn of 1842, he was called from Philadelphia to Cincinnati to officiate at the marriage ceremony of the Rev. N. C. Burnham. The First Society, through the Rev. M. M. Carll, at that time its pastor, tendered to him its pulpit, and invited him to preach in it. He declined, for the reason stated above. Whereupon, the society sent to him, by the hand of Mr. Carll, the following:

Cincinnati, Nov. 8, 1842.

Rev. M. M. Carll, Pastor of the First New Jerusalem Society in Cincinnati.

SIR—Below I send you a preamble and resolutions from the minutes of the proceedings of our meeting last evening, as directed by said meeting.

At a quarterly meeting of the First New Jerusalem Society in Cincinnati, held at the temple, Nov. 7th, 1842,

On motion of Brother Jas. S. Glascoe, the following preamble and resolution was adopted:

Whereas this society has learned, with regret, that the Rev. R. De Charms has misconstrued the meaning of an act of this society, passed July 3d, 1837, in meeting, in their report to the next Western Convention, respecting his resignation as pastor; therefore,

Resolved, That this society, individually and collectively, in passing the resolution referred to, *did not* intend to censure Mr. De Charms or impugn his motives.

On motion, *Resolved*, That the clerk be directed to place in the hands of the Rev. M. M. Carll, a copy of the above preamble and resolution.

A true copy,

CHAS. S. CHEEVER, *Clerk.*

On receiving the above, Mr. De Charms preached according to invitation. He had no personal wish to, but charity constrained him. The above resolution says "motives." But the writer of that preamble and resolution was not remarkable, either for great accuracy of thought, or for much precision in the use of words. He meant *principles;* for these, as they move men to action, are their motives. It is remarkable, however, that he was the writer of the report of the First Society to the Western Convention, which cast the imputation on Mr. De Charms of having acted from a *false principle* in having suddenly and unexpectedly dissolved his pastoral connection with it. The same person also wrote the letter to Dr. Atlee, then in Michigan, giving the account of the "blow up" in his society, by which Mr. De Charms was thrown sky-high; and assigned as the *principle* of Mr. De Charms's action,—the truth of which was called in question in the report,—his having regarded his pastoral relation with the First Society a *conjugial* one ; so that, when said society wished Messrs. Hurdus and Kinmont to preach again in its temple, and actually invited the former to administer the sacrament of the Lord's holy supper to it, in his brief absence at the Eastern Convention, only two weeks after it had been administered in the Western Convention, he, as a pastor, abandoned his flock, because "his heart was troubled to the *core*, and lamented that there had been *adultery committed with his wife during his absence"!* Thus it was believed, and told *throughout the whole United States*,—even echoed from Boston,—that Mr. De Charms, in dissolving his pastoral connection with the First New Jerusalem Society of Cincinnati, had acted on the principle, that such relation was a conjugial one, and had been grossly violated by the society. And there was direct allusion to *this* in the society's report to the Western Convention. In 1842, developments had been made which satisfied the First Society in Cincinnati that their imputation upon Mr. De Charms of his having acted from a false principle were unfounded; so that it could pass in good faith the above resolution: but there can be no question that that society, or some of its leading members, did intend to impute to him that bad principle of action in 1837, when its report to the Western Convention was made. Cannot, then, any one see, that the imputation of that report would be in Mr. De Charms's mind a serious matter? Is it not clear, from what is here stated, that he was compelled to vindicate himself from so foul a charge thus offi-cially made to a general body of the church? And can any one now con-demn him for having been the innocent instrument of agitating this matter again, although it has led to such searching exposures, and such signal con-futations of the errors of others? Well, his vindication has required the publication now of the foregoing extracts from the Records of the First Cincinnati Society; for it was impossible, without the display of the pro-ceedings therein detailed, to show the state of that society for some time before his connection with it, to explain the nature of his difficulties in that connection, and thus to make manifest the true grounds of his action in then dissolving his pastoral relation. And to make this fully manifest now, it is only necessary to state, that, in his view, the First Society were endeavor-ing to bring about again that connection of Messrs. Hurdus and Kinmont with it, which he had expressly stipulated against on becoming its pastor, and which he then saw, and which the whole church may and should now see, had produced such irreconcilable divisions and difficulties in the case of other ministers in former years. He regarded the transaction during his absence, as an entering wedge to such a final result, and therefore he felt it his duty to act against it.

This matter is introduced here, because it is intimately connected with that subject of church order and government which has been supposed, on all hands, to be involved in the question of trinal order in the ministry—the history of which in this country we are now endeavoring to sketch. The order of the trine has been opposed in this country because it was supposed to involve necessarily the peculiar notions of order and government of our eastern brethren. Hence, in advocating the trine, as a principle of true new-church order, we have to disentangle it from those notions, which have flowed into or enveloped it in the minds of such as are opposing it, as well as from the organic changes which our eastern brethren have produced in the general body of our church in this country. In fact, as the conjugial theory has pervaded the actual application of the trinal principle to the ministerial arrangement and the ecclesiastical government of the new church of our country, it has been necessary to notice that theory in this history of the trine. And the writer of this historical sketch has been obliged to bring into view *his* difficulties in the West, and to explain them here, be-cause certain persons have *very industriously talked in secret of those diffi-culties to his disparagement, as a fractious, unruly and disorganizing spirit,* who deserves to be *rebuked* by the whole church! Let the whole church now judge righteous judgment.

No. LVI.

MR. DANIEL ROE'S LETTER,

Or a Communication from the Cincinnati Society to the Seventh Gene-ral Convention in 1824.

Cincinnati, May 21st, 1824—68.

DEAR BRETHREN—As the Lord's New Church is beginning to obtain a considerable extension in the world, and very much of the peace and happiness of its members depends on its external relations and duties (in which alone it can exist in ultimates), we feel ourselves bound, because of our peculiarity of sentiments, to call your attention to a subject of vital importance as connected with so desirable an end. We trust that a candid and fair discussion of any point not *settled* by the plain mandate of the Lord, either in the Word, or in those writings by which he has graciously illustrated it, will be regarded by you as a proper subject to be laid before the Convention for its deliberation. The subject we have alluded to is that of *ordination*. If it stood simply a question as to the form, we should not, perhaps, be so tenacious of our views on the subject as to ask you to consider it, although we totally deny its claim to a higher origin than the Romish Church, and all benefit resulting from its use. But as this form has somehow perhaps necessarily been transmitted from the Church which has been *abolished*, and has obtained some degree of sanction from custom in the "New Jerusalem," it becomes necessary, *if the Church would rid itself of the evils resulting from the use of the form*, to show, that the form itself is an assumption not warranted by the Word of God. As it would be impossible to show that the form is not warranted by the Word, without bringing *all* the Word into the argument, and showing that each *part* was without relation to it, it will, we conceive, be sufficient, until the contrary appears, to deny that it receives sanction from that source. It may, however, be contended, that the form is apostolic. This we deny. We have examined the Acts of the Apostles with considerable care, and find only three places where the laying on of hands is spoken of. Chapter vi. first part speaks of it as used *by* the Apostles on seven men of honest report, *full of the Holy Ghost* and wisdom, who were appointed to see that the widows were not neglected in the daily ministration. But of the Apostles it is said, (as a reason no doubt why they could not attend to this ministration,) that they would give themselves continually to prayer and the ministry of the Word. So that it clearly appears this was not an ordination of ministers to preach. In the eighth chapter, about the seventeenth verse, there is also an account of the Apostles laying their hands on those that only had been baptised in the name of the Lord Jesus, and with this laying on of hands it is said they received the Holy Ghost. But there is no inference to be drawn from this passage any more than from the sixth verse of the nineteenth chapter, where they are spoken of, on whom Paul laid his hands, and who received, at the same time, the Holy Ghost and spake with tongues. This receiving the Holy Ghost and speaking with tongues appears to have been common amongst all the first believers and followers of the Lord, and was no doubt intended to constitute a part of that great system of miracles necessary for the establishment of the Church amongst that external people, and cannot, we think, be applied as proofs of the correctness of the present form of ordination, without wresting the Scriptures, as St. Peter said many did the writings of Paul, as well as other Scriptures, to their own destruction. In truth, the word *ordained*, as applied to an apostle, preacher or minister of the Word, *as an act* of man, is not to be found in the Old or New Testament. and is, we conceive, as totally inapplicable to a minister as the title reverend, which belongs to the Lord only. To be an ordained minister in the acknowledged form, the person must have the hands of some other person or persons laid on his head, who have had the hands of some other person or persons laid on their heads. To show any validity in this, would require it to be traced to the person or persons, whose heads were first so consecrated by the command of God, with the right of appointing his successor with equal powers for ever. This, we believe has been claimed by the Pope only. But who does not see that if such right has had any being, it must have ceased with the Church that preceded, or else you must make that which is *created* to depend upon that which is destroyed. Whereas, the Lord hath declared by his own mouth in relation to all things predicated of that Church as to truth, that "not one stone shall remain upon another that shall not be thrown down." It is not therefore a truth that God communicates the power of the ministry by laying on of hands; but that as at the time of his first appearing "at mid-day a light shall shine around about them above the splendor of the sun and (spiritually) they shall hear a voice" by which as in the case of St. Paul they shall be instructed in their duty, and like him without consulting with flesh and blood shall obey the heavenly calling. Indeed there is no account of any Preacher or Apostle in that day who pretended to derive authority from any other but the Lord himself. The only one I can refer to where it does not appear expressly to be by his oral command is the case of Apollo, Acts 18th, v. 24; and he, though *found* preaching and teaching from the Scriptures, that Jesus was the Christ, received the sanction of the Apostles, who without inquiry as to his authority wrote letters to the believers elsewhere recommending him.

We need not however be surprised that the love of rule should have showed itself in after ages of the Church. For it is one of the strongest principles of our nature and even manifested itself amongst the Apostles. John on a certain occasion said unto the Lord, Master, we saw one casting out devils in thy name, and *we forbad him*, because he followeth not with us And Jesus said unto him, *forbid not*, for he that is not against us, is for us. And it ought to be noted well that this was part of a conversation in which there was a reasoning among them *which of them should be the greatest*. And in which the Lord showed that receiving a little child in his name would be receiving him, and that the least among them all should be *great* but *not greatest*. We have thus far by a negative mode of reasoning endeavored to show that the *form* of ordination now in use is not predicated on the Scriptures. It remains to show the evil which has resulted and is still likely to result from its continuance. And first, if this *form* be acknowledged to have *authority* from the Lord when at the same time it is apparent that it is not so, there will always be found those in the Church who will feel it their duty to *resist* what appears to be an assumption in one *brother* to rule over another. And resistance will necessarily produce strife and division or a repulsive sphere which never ought to be found in children of the same family and which cannot exist without *evil*. Thus we find in all past ages of the Christian Church since the Reformation, that amongst the Protestants every new sect which has sprung up has been compelled from the denial of their doctrines by their predecessors and from their consequent refusal of ordination to set up for themselves an authority and which they have each as fallaciously attempted to exercise over succeeding sects—So that each in its turn has occasionally denied to the other all authority in the Ministry. The Church of Rome has in conformity with their opinion bastardized the children of Marriages solemnized by Protestants, and Protestants in their turn as if the laws of the country had aided them have in their degree invalidated what has been done by each other, until the Lord in his divine mercy has been pleased to expose the fallacy of such pretensions, through the multiplication of them. And it has become again an admitted truth that although "the princes of the gentiles exercise dominion over one another," amongst the worshippers of the Lord it shall be otherwise. For the Lord is again heard to say by his Word revived in his second advent, "It shall not be so among you, for ye are all brethren." We have barely hinted at some of the evils that have grown out of the acknowledgement of this assumed authority. But as it is a single item in the great scheme of *Antichrist* by which the Christian Church has been destroyed it would be impossible to enlarge the subject to its utmost without embracing the whole Romish hierarchy. We have only therefore said enough to call your attention to a serious investigation of the subject, and do not entertain a doubt that by an unprejudiced use of the light you have received (which as well as ours is "a morning with clouds" and "a day of darkness" in comparison of that which is rising upon the world), you will become to others of your own time and to generations that shall succeed you, a reflecting and refracting medium of a day in which "the light of the moon shall be as a light of the sun, and the light of the sun seven-fold as the light of seven days."

We will close our remarks on this subject by stating what has been adopted by our Society as a *Rule* sufficient in our opinion to meet the *case*. If a brother believes himself in duty bound to preach because he considers himself possessed of qualifications for use in that capacity, the society being apprized of this, request him to make the attempt. If he displays sufficient promise of use according to their judgment he receives their sanction and is entitled to be respected accordingly. And if he were to remain continually located among us, we should think nothing further necessary had not the laws of the state made it necessary he should be ordained before he can be allowed to solemnize marriages. But as the laws make this requirement and as his qualifications and character cannot be known abroad where he may sometime conceive it to be his duty to preach—it is thought proper to adopt a plan to meet both these contingencies. Wherefore the Society hold a formal election. If the applicant is elected by a majority he receives a certificate from the officers of the Society. *And thus he is ordained.*

We wish to have it distinctly understood that we are not tenacious of the *form* provided that each Society is left to choose its own, and that difference of form shall not produce a sphere of separation. For viewing it as a *mere form* without authority in any who use it to condemn or so far *disapprove* as to say, that another is not equally entitled to respect it, becomes no longer important But as consequences have already grown out of an adherence to it which have rather tended to obstruct than to promote that mutual love and esteem which is the *best fruits* of the *tree of life* which mortals can enjoy, it becomes a matter of serious import to remove " this merchant, this *great man of the earth,*" this remnant of that great Babylon the smoke of whose burning was seen by John, and over whom, "the merchants of the earth shall weep and mourn, *for no man buyeth her merchandize any more,*" or to convince of their error by authoritative evidence those who apprehend it to be of such a character. The Lord himself hath said " I judge no man." Neither do we presume to do it. He came not into the world to condemn the world. We therefore consider ourselves precluded from condemning any. But as brethren, as those who feel an affectionate regard for your peace and happiness in time and eternity, and with regard to those who we are sure feel an equal regard for us and for all men, we have thought it our duty to lay this matter before you as worthy your prayerful and elaborate attention. And that you may so advise with us and with others as shall advance the good of all, we pray the Lord to afford you the light and love of truth.

We are happy to be enabled to say that our Society is living in the greatest peace and harmony—that real brotherly love continues, and every returning Sabbath affords new proof of the affectionate regard felt by the most attentive audience for the truths of the New Dispensation. The actual addition to our Society is much greater than the numbers who have subscribed our by-laws would indicate, although they are considerable. One thing however worthy of note and which is most cheering to the lovers of good, is, that the seed is generally received into good ground, and brings forth in some thirty, and some sixty, and some an hundred fold.

The immense distance from hence to the seat of the Convention, and the consequent time consumed and the expenses attending it has alone prevented our sending a delegate. We highly approve an annual consultation and interchange of thought and affection relative to advancing the Church; but in this instance, have to ask your attention to the foregoing, as an humble attempt to supply the place of a Messenger.

> From your affectionate brethren,
> On behalf of the First New Jerusalem Society, Cincinnati.
> (Signed,)   DANIEL ROE,
>   *Corresponding Secretary.*

No. LVII.

Rev. Holland Weeks's Report on the Trine.

Your committee to whom the communication from "The First New Jerusalem Society of Cincinnati" was referred, beg leave to report.

The subject to which their communication alludes, " is that of ordination." They consider themselves to have adopted " a peculiarity of sentiment," " of vital importance." As to the form of ordination by imposition of hands, they say, they " totally deny its claim to a higher origin than the Romish church." They affirm, that " the form itself is an assumption not warranted by the Word of God ;" and " deny" the fact of its being " apostolic." To several passages, which they consider as unappropriate, in the Acts of the Apostles, they appeal; as if this would evince that none can be adduced, appropriate and decisive.

We consent to have the peculiarity of their sentiment tried by the apostles' writings. " Hast thou appealed unto Cæsar? unto Cæsar shalt thou go." That the form itself is not apostolic, is evidently a mistake, the apostles' writings themselves being the test; for Paul, referring to the induction of Timothy into the ministry, says to him, ". Neglect not the gift that is in thee, which was given thee by prophecy, *with the laying on of the hands of the presbytery.*" I Tim. iv. 14. Again, he says to him, "*Lay h·nds suddenly on no man.*" I Tim. v. 22. These passages our brethren of Cincinnati must, we think, have overlooked; or they could not have expressed, and repeated, assertions directly in the face of them.

As regards the form, an appeal may here be made, by your committee, to the apostle of the new dispensation. "I have often wondered," he says, "that the angels have such knowledge from the mere action of the body by the hands; but nevertheless it has occasionally been made manifest by lively experience; and it has been told me that this is the reason why inaugurations into the ministry are performed by imposition of hands, and why by touching with the hand is signified to communicate." See the Wisdom of Angels concerning the Divine Love and the Divine Wisdom, n. 220.# From this, it appears that the form of ordination has its origin in the order of influx and correspondence; that in this form the order of influx from the Lord through heaven is in its fulness; and that this evinces the incorrectness of the assertion, that the form itself has no higher origin than the Romish church.

Our Cincinnati friends deny the substance as well as the form; they not only discard imposition of hands, but ordination also. They say, "In truth, the word *ordained,* as applied to an apostle, preacher, or minister of the Word, *as an act of man,* is not to be found in the Old or New Testament; and is, we conceive, as totally inapplicable to a minister, as the title *reverend,* which belongs to the Lord only."

Not to insist, in reply, that, by parity of reason, the terms *good,* and *true,* and *life,* and *light,* and even *man,* as well as reverend, should not be applied to ministers, because in the highest sense they belong to the Lord only;—as respects the word *ordained,* your committee have quoted Titus, i. 5, in which Paul says to one of his clergy, "For this cause I left thee in Crete, that thou shouldst set in order the things that are wanting, and *ordain* elders in every city, as I have appointed thee." Also, Acts xiv. 23, "And when they had *ordained* them elders in every church, and prayed, with fasting. they commended them to the Lord, on whom they believed." Likewise in the Old Testament, speaking of Jeroboam, whose conduct was a counterfeit of the genuine, it is said, "He *ordained* him priests, for the high places." II Chron. xi, 15. These instances are sufficient to show that passages are not wanting, either in the Old Testament or New, in which the word *ordained, as an act of man,* is applied to such as either were, or professed to be, ministers of the Lord.

Our brethren of Cincinnati infer the invalidity of ordinations from the claims of the pope, and from the corruptions of the papal church. "The Lord," they tell us, "hath declared with his own mouth, in relation to all things predicted of that church, *as to truth,* that ·not one stone shall remain upon another that shall not be thrown down.' By inference," they say, "it is not therefore true that God communicates the power of the ministry by laying on of hands." Now is not this the kind of argument which proves too much! for what were the stones which were thrown down but divine truths? Are they not admitted to have been such by this strange argument? By what means have they been thrown down, except by their adulteration and falsification? Has this made them cease to be truths? Are they not truths still in themselves considered? Our Lord liveth, as divine good and divine truth; and is "made dead," not in himself, but in those by whom he is rejected. Does it follow, because divine truths have been thrown to the ground by the old church, that they are to be rejected by every succeeding generation world without end? and is it of course a fact that they were never divine truths? Is it not the manifest duty of the new church to gather them up, and arrange them in the beautiful order of the Lord's new temple? In this way, what had been converted by a false church into spiritual traffic, "shall be holiness to the Lord," and "her merchandise shall be for them that dwell before the Lord, to eat sufficiently, and for durable clothing." Isa xxiii. 18. Otherwise, we are to acknowledge nothing as good and true, except what Babylon has not adulterated and falsified; the sacred scriptures are still, and for ever, to go into perdition; no christian verity is any more to be received, because the Babylonians and the dragonists have cast every truth to the ground;

See also Conjugial Love, n. 306, near the end.

it was to be the case that there should not be one stone remaining upon another. Is this a safe and true mode of reasoning? We are sure it is not. But is it not just as safe and correct in its application to *every* truth, as it can be in its application to apostolic ordination? It is not seen why this mode of reasoning would not remove at once from the New Jerusalem her twelve gates and her twelve foundations!

Our Cincinnati brethren object to the form of ordination in present use, because, as they say, in direct opposition to several passages already cited, "it is not warranted by the Word of God." Yet they themselves devise a form for which they do not even pretend that they have a divine warrant.

They say, moreover, "It remains to show the evil which has resulted, and is still likely to result from its continuance. And first," they affirm, "if this form be acknowledged to have authority from the Lord, when, at the same time, it is apparent it is not so; there will always be found those in the Church who will feel it their duty to *resist* what appears to be an assumption in one brother to rule over another." Is not this again the species of argument which proves too much? For what good rules, or rulers, would not be exploded by reasoning from the evils which have resulted from their abuses? And in what conceivable case might not resistance be justified as duty? for where in the universe has there been a state of order which has not been abused and resisted? Let insubordination find a basis in this sort of argument, and the order and authority even of the divine government cannot be supported. The Lord's kingdom, upon this principle, has no constituted authorities, and no insignia of divine appointment, by which the ministers of the Word can be distinguished. If his empire is not without laws, it is without executives; the sheep of his pasture have no shepherds, by prescribed rules; their being no divine authority for any such thing. it is a mere assumption of Romish origin. Yet our mistaken brethren contrive a substitute for the present form of ordination, to be more than equivalent, allowedly not of divine authority—which of course can be nothing but an assumption; and equally evil, and even worse in its tendency, because every brother who sets himself up in this way " to rule over another." will be looked upon as assuming, and as running before he is sent, which will not fail to excite resistance to a much greater degree. Besides, the question may justly, and will certainly occur, how " the form" in present use can " be *acknowledged* to have authority from the Lord, and at the same time it is apparent it is not so ·"

But, not to add any further remarks upon these peculiarities of sentiment, your committee desire the indulgence of stating the true ground of ordination. It is very clear to our minds that there should be some kind of government in religious, as well as in civil society; of course, that there must be laws, regulations, and constituted authorities : otherwise, who can see how the subsistence of order and harmony can be promoted? Speaking of ecclesiastical and civil government, Swedenborg says, " There are two things which ought to be in order amongst men, viz. the things which are of heaven and the things which are of the world : the things which are of heaven are called ecclesiastical, those which are of the world are called civil." H. D. n. 311. After thus telling what is understood in the New Jerusalem by ecclesiastical and civil government, he says, " Order cannot be maintained in the world without governors; who are to observe all things which are done according to order, and which are done contrary to order; and who are to reward those who live according to order, and to punish those who live contrary to order. If this is not done, the human race must perish : for the will to command others, and to possess the goods of others, is hereditarily connate with every one ; whence proceed enmities, envyings, hatreds, revenges, deceits, cruelties, and many other evils; wherefore, unless men were kept under restraint,—by laws, and by rewards suited to their loves, which are honors and gains for those who do good things , and by punishments contrary to those loves, which are the loss of honors, of possessions, and of life, for those who do evil things,—the human race would perish." Ibid. n. 312 ·. There must therefore be governors, to keep the assemblages of men in order, who should be persons skilled in the laws, and men who fear God. *There must also be order amongst the governors ;* lest any one, from caprice or inadvertence, should permit evils which are against order, and thereby destroy it; which is guarded against when there are *superior and inferior governors* amongst whom there is subordination.'' Ibid. n. 313. These observations are applied to the order of government which is called civil ; but it should be well considered, that, between the civil and the ecclesiastical, there is an analogy. and the relation of correspondences. Hence it is, as Swedenborg says, that "from and according to the states of the church, all the civil states of kingdoms, in respect to justice and judgment, have their existence, their vigor, and their life." Coronis, n. 2. Nor is it less requisite in the ecclesiastical than in the civil government, that there should be *order amongst governors, superior and inferior,* amongst whom there is *subordination,* to guard against evils; and therefore, that they should have their distinctive insignia by ordination.

Swedenborg tells us that "governors over those things amongst men which relate to heaven, or over ecclesiastical matters, are called priests, and their office is called the priesthood." H. D. n. 314. He affirms that "the sanctity of their office is derived from the Lord;" that "they ought to teach the people, and to lead them by means of truths to the good of life ;" and that "they are appointed to administer those things which relate to the divine law and worship" lb. nn. 317, 318. Whence it is deducible, that the office itself is not an assumption; and that the only case in which the fearful epithet will apply, is when an unqualified person usurps it without ordination.

But, to come more directly to the object of our present inquiry, it will be proper to ascertain what our apostle means, in this case, by *order.* The term he abundantly uses in all his writings and particularly in his instructions concerning ecclesiastical and civil government. He says, (Coronis, n. 17,) "It is well known, that, in order to give perfection to any thing, there must be a TRINE in just order, one under another, and communication between them ; and that such a trine constitutes one thing ; not unlike a pillar, the top of which is the chapiter, under this the longthened shaft, and under this again the pedestal. Such a trine is man; his supreme part being the head, his middle part the body, and his lowest part the feet. Every kingdom in this respect emulates a man: in it there must be a king as the head,* also magistrates and officers as the body, and yeomanry with servants as the feet and soles of the feet. In like manner in the church, there must be a mitred prelate, parish priests, and curates under them. Nor does the world itself subsist without three things following each other in order. Every perfect thing must be a trine, in order to be a one regularly coherent." Now does not this evidently show that the christian ministry, to be "in just order," must be a trine ? Is not the servant of the Lord here speaking of the church, and of the priesthood, in just order? Is he not showing what order is ? Does he not mention the church, and the three classes of her clergy, as an example of the order which he is endeavoring to illustrate ? Would he bring that which is out of order, and contrary to order, as an example of order ? Does he not lead us, if we are willing, to see that. as the divine order is a trine, so all and singular things in just order are a trine ? and that, as there is a trine in the Word, a trine in the heavens, a trine in the very atmospheres, a trine in the church, and a trine in every man of the church; in short, as there is a trine in all things which are in just order, so there is a trine in the christian ministry ? And does he not, moreover, say expressly, that "in the church there must be a mitred prelate, parish priests and curates under them ?" But is it reasonable to suppose the subsistence of this trine in the priesthood can be perpetuated, and regularly transmitted to faithful men, without ordination? To what but an orderly transmission of the sacerdotal office, with the form of inauguration, does Paul refer where he says to Timothy, "Lay hands suddenly on no man"—"the same commit thou to faithful men, who shall be able to teach others also"? To guard against assumptions and distracting innovations, what other method has ever been authorized by the Word ? Its abuses amongst the papal and protestant heresiarchs, is no just argument against the thing itself.

In the Arcana Cœlestia, n. 10,017, speaking of the priesthood, the servant of the Lord says, "There are three things which succeed in order ; there is the celestial principle, which is the good of love to the Lord ; there is the spiritual principle, which is the good of charity to the neighbor ; and there is the natural principle thence derived, which is the good of faith; inasmuch as those three things are what succeed in order, there are also three heavens, and in them goods in that order; the work of the salvation of those

---

* "Where such a form of government prevails," as Swedenborg says. Heavenly Doctrines, n 314.

who are in celestial good, is represented by the priesthood of Aaron; but the work of the salvation of those who are in spiritual good. is represented by the priesthood of the sons of Aaron; and the work of the salvation of those who are thence in natural good, is represented by the priesthood of the Levites; and since those things which succeed in order proceed from the good of love to the Lord, which is represented by Aaron and his priesthood, therefore it is said of the Levites, that they should be *given* to Aaron; and that the Levites *were* given to Aaron and his sons, that they might perform the ministry of the priesthood under them. See Numbers iii, 1 to the end." This teaches the sacred verity of a trine in the priesthood, in heavenly order, with the reason for it, in the spiritual sense of the word. Indeed the nature of the case renders it necessary that there should be in the christian ministry, an outer court, the holy place and the sanctum sanctorum; that those who sustain the sacred office, may not be placed in a grade above their capacity and fidelity; that they may have every possible motive to make full proof of their ministry; that they may be in the best situation to be useful; that the several departments may operate as checks upon each other; and that "they who have used the office of a deacon well, may purchase to themselves," as Paul says, "*a good degree*, and great boldness in the faith which is in Christ Jesus." 1 Tim. iii. 13.*

That this order, with its insignia, should be observed by the New Jerusalem, and guarded against every abuse and intrusion, is deducible from the following passage of what Swedenborg denominates "The Divine Truths *revealed by the Lord*, in the work entitled *True Christian Religion*," nn. 679, 680. It is here said that, "in tracing up effects to their causes, it is very plain to discern that the consistence of all things dependeth on order; and that the kinds of order are manifold, general and particular; and that there is one which is most universal of all, and on which the general and particular ones depend in a continued series; and that this most universal one entereth into all the rest, as an essence into its forms, thereby forming one connected whole, which otherwise could not possibly exist. It is this unity which causeth the preservation of the whole; and, in case this was wanting, all things must needs fall to pieces, and be dissolved, relapsing, not only into their first chaotic state, but even into nothingness. What, let me ask, would be the case with man, unless all and every part of his body was arranged in a most distinct and orderly manner, having a general dependence on one heart and the lungs? On any other supposition, must not the whole machine of the human body be a heap of confusion? for how else could the stomach, the liver, the pancreas, the mesentery, the mesocolon, the kidneys, and the intestines, perform each their particular offices? It is by virtue of the order ruling in and amongst the several parts of the body, that all and every thing contained therein appear, in a collected view, as one. Without distinct order, again, preserved in man's mind, or spirit, and unless all the parts thereof had a general dependence on the will and the understanding, what could it be but something confused, and undigested, in such a state of incoherence, that man would have no more power to think and will than the picture and statue have, which ornament his house? What. again, would man be without a most orderly arranged influx from heaven, and the reception thereof? and what would this influx be without that most universal one, on which the government of the whole, and of all its parts. dependeth; that is, the influx from God; and unless all things did exist, live, and move in him and from him?

"The above reasoning may be illustrated by numberless cases, adapted to the comprehension of the natural man; as, for instance, what is an empire or kingdom without order? but a troop of robbers, several of whom collected together would slay their thousands, till at last, only a few would be left to survive the slaughtered multitude. So, again, what is a state without order, or a house without order? and what is a kingdom, state, or house, unless their be in each some supreme head or director? Besides, what is order without distinction, or what is distinction without its badges. and what are the badges of distinction without signs or tokens, whereby qualities may be

---

* In the True Christian Religion. Swedenborg mentions "the state of every student who is preparing for the ministry, before he becometh a priest, and of every priest before he becometh a pastor, and of every pastor before he is a primate." n. 106. He says, "the reason of which is because they are according to divine order; and divine order filleth all and every thing in the universe, even to the most minute particulars." n. 106.

known and ascertained? for, without the knowledge of qualities, order is not known to be order. Signs or signatures, in empires and in kingdoms, are dignified titles, and powers of administration annexed to them; whence come subordinations, whereby all things are kept together in orderly arrangement, as in unity : and in this manner, a king exerciseth his royal power according to order, distributed amongst a variety of persons, by virtue whereof a kingdom is a kingdom. The case is similar with respect to various other things; as, for instance, with respect to an army of soldiers; which could be of no efficacy, unless the men were arranged in an orderly manner, and divided into battalions, and each battalion into companies, and each company into troops, with inferior officers appointed to the command of each, and one supreme commander to bear rule over all. These arrangements and divisions, again, would be of no efficacy without signs,—which, in the case of armies, are called standards,—to point out to every soldier his proper station. By these means, all act in the field of battle as one man, or in unity; whereas, were those means of order wanting, they would rush head-long against an enemy, like so many dogs with open mouths, barking and howling with vain fury, till they were all cut off by their opponents—not so much in consequence of superior courage, as of better discipline, and more orderly arrangement; for what can a disorderly, disunited mob do against a well disciplined and well united army?"

" These instances," our Swedenborg says, " may serve to illustrate the first use of baptism, as a sign, in the spiritual world, that the person baptized is of a christian community." And are they not equally applicable to the order of the christian ministry? Do they not equally illustrate the use of ordination, as a sign that the person ordained is a minister of the new dispensation—a prelate, a priest, or a curate, according to the degree of the trine in the priesthood designated by his ordination?

All which is respectfully submitted.

No. LVIII.

HON. JOHN YOUNG'S LETTER

To the Rev. John Hargrove on the Same Subject.

RESPECTED AND DEAR BROTHER,

The several societies of the New Jerusalem Church in the United States, were requested by the last convention at New York, to send in by their delegates or otherwise, to the next general convention, their sentiments upon the mode of Ecclesiastical Government to be adopted. Although the society in this place be small in number, we trust that all of us entertain a lively attachment for the heavenly doctrines of the new church and her prosperity. In compliance, therefore, with the desire of the former convention, who were aware that some more definite order and mode of ecclesiastical government than does at present exist, ought to be adopted, I have now the honor of submitting my sentiments to you and the ensuing convention, which the circumstances mentioned in a former letter to you, prevent me from attending in person.

It appears from the journal of the convention in 1824, that a " communication from the society in Cincinnati " on the important subject in question was referred to a committee, whose report was laid before the convention of the last year, and that a second committee was appointed for the purpose of adapting it for publication with the journal. This latter committee being unable to agree in the opinion that it was advisable to publish the report, it appears they did nothing in the way of preparing it for the press. This disagreement is the more to be regretted on account of the several societies having been invited to express their sentiments on the mode of Ecclesiastical Government. The printing of the report itself or the substance of it, must therefore have been intended as a preparative measure to excite the serious consideration of the several societies, and members of that church which is emphatically declared the crown of all preceding

4

churches. It may be hoped then that the present convention will throw aside the fear of man, which casteth a snare, and direct the publication of the report entire, and without either adaptation or qualification to suit the particular views of any person or persons. Should the reasons contained in it be not fully supported by the Sacred Word and the authority of the Lord's herald and messenger, an opportunity will be afforded hereafter of discussing those reasons and for proposing a system of government on better principles. In the mean while ought not every possible light be afforded to enable a future convention to conclude upon the best system with that union and harmony which should characterize their proceedings in all cases, and particularly in one of such momentous concern to the progress, the peace and prosperity of the church?

When we take into view that no society, great or small, can subsist without order, and that this cannot be maintained without some fundamental principles, and corresponding regulations, the duty or rather necessity of establishing the best possible state of order that the present imperfect condition of human nature will admit of, is incontrovertible. It ought also to be admitted that the nearer this order can be brought to approximate that which prevails among the societies of heaven founded on the divine wisdom which is revealed to them in greater purity than to men on earth, so much the better will the order become. But it may be supposed that the opinions (to say nothing of the prejudices arising from habit) being so various, respecting ecclesiastical regimen, and that no precise or positive direction being laid down in the Bible concerning it, each society is at liberty to adopt such modes as may be considered most expedient by a majority of its members. So far as respects matters of a temporary and fleeting nature, this may be right, although even as to them a due degree of prudence, resulting from spiritual principles, in the management of them, for the purpose of attaining the great objects of which they are best the means, is a requisite. In those, however, which are spiritual and relate to the church, which in all essentials, whether of doctrine, life, or worship, is, or rather ought to be catholic, embracing one Lord, one faith and one baptism, as the origin and means of regeneration, the case is different. Its members renounce all party names, such as Lutherans, Calvinists, Baptists, &c., but no more than they, can they be known and distinguished without government, which, in those things which concern heaven, is termed ecclesiastic. It is equally clear that there can be no government without suitable laws to regulate the community who are the subjects of it, because but for these every thing would be influenced by the arbitrary caprice of a majority or by a kind of despotic power. Such extremes, of which history furnishes many examples, are equally to be avoided. The illustrious herald of the New Church expressly declares that order, whether in civil or ecclesiastical affairs, cannot be preserved in the world without governors, to observe whatever is according to order and whatever is contrary thereto. This may be best effected, he adds, by an appointment of governors of *different degrees*, some of higher others of lower authority, who shall be governed themselves by the *laws of subordination*. In addition to the just reasoning in favor of a trine in the ministry, contained in the report, I beg leave to refer you, and the other members of the convention, to the Universal Theology, n. 106, alluding to the state of every student who is preparing for the ministry, before he becometh a priest, and of every priest before he becometh a pastor, and of every pastor before he is a primate. The reason given for this subordination is, " because these three degrees are according to divine order, and divine order filleth all and every thing in the universe even to the most minute particular." Ibid. It may be alleged that the time for introducing order and particularly that of the trine has not yet arrived. But in answer to this, it may be observed that procrastination may increase the difficulty of establishing order as the church shall increase in numbers. Disorders may intervene. Some persons *assuming* clerical functions, may declare independence, draw particular societies within the sphere of their influence and gradually acquire an authority inconsistent with that unity in the new church which ought to distinguish it from all other denominations of professing christians. The leaders of the old being mostly either disaffected or opposed to the new, will lay hold of every advantage that may spring from dissentions or differences among its societies or the individuals composing them unregulated by "Heaven's first law." By a reference to the proceedings of former conventions, it will appear that hitherto there has been no precise order in the ministry. This may have been unavoidable. But I can assert from experience that the want of it has been the cause of exciting in several quarters strong prejudices against the heavenly doctrines. A very intelligent friend has observed that there is a wide distinction between what *is* and what *should be*. The present state of the church is not the rule. The only safe rule is what she ought to be. If we make a rule of what she is, or of what she *will be*, we make her state, whatever it is, the standard of just order; and consequently foreclose the idea of her ever being in "a more mature state," unless we admit that the standard of just order is liable to an endless series of changes, and that whatever the state of the church is, it is right. We cannot but be aware, Reverend Sir, of the effects of early education and habit in all cases, but especially in religious matters. The present members of the new church have been collected from the old, and some of them have imbibed more or less of the old leaven respecting public worship, order and discipline. But when rules are laid down or are clearly deducible from the Holy Scriptures, sanctioned by the apostles and recognized by that undoubted servant of the Lord, Emanuel Swedenborg, who has expressly declared that the divine truths revealed by the Lord in the work entitled *True Christian Religion*, are seen in the light and acknowledged—ought any genuine new church man to hesitate after such authorities?

It afforded me pleasure to observe that you, Reverend Sir, acknowledged in one of your letters to me the principle of a trine in the ministerial office, but you intimated that we ought to do nothing before the time, the church being in a state of infancy, and your apprehension of abuses. In answer, permit me to quote the language of one of my correspondents in reference to those difficulties, "As the twig is bent, the tree's inclined". "Thus speaketh the Lord of hosts saying, this people say, the time has not come, the time that the Lord's house should be built." See Haggai, i., 2 to 11. Although this prophecy had an immediate relation to the first advent of our Lord and the devastation of the church at that period, it may be justly applied to the like estate of the church now at his second coming in power and great glory. As to the abuses of good things, they do not prove that good things are not good things. What judges can *we* be of *the times* unless it be by ultimates? How can we promote the intimates of order unless it be by ultimates? Are not the ultimates the recipient vessels of the intimates? If, then, we would have the intimates in successive and simultaneous order, let us have the ultimates in which alone they can exist and find rest in their basis. To discard the basis of order, is in effect to discard all the higher principles of the superstructure. Take away the pedestal and heaven falls! There is no doubt a time for every thing, of which examples are given by the wise writer of that maxim, but they relate more to the things under the sun of this world which are for a season, than to those which are eternal and founded on the principles of Love and Wisdom. and are unchangeable. The latter and not the former, except in due order and subordination, should be our principal study, the primum mobile of our conduct. Is there not a danger of not only incompetent but unworthy persons intruding themselves into the ministerial office without suitable guards? And would not its prosperity be thereby impeded? We may rest assured indeed that the gates of hell cannot prevail against the *Lord's Own Church;* but this grand truth ought not to prevent us from using our best efforts for the prevention of disorders, tending to cause her heavenly goods and truths to be evil spoken of by her adversaries and enemies."

I am fully persuaded that the principle of a trine in discrete order is fully sanctioned by the Holy Word, confirmed by the illustrious messenger of the Lord, and agreeable to a rational analysis. If so, it cannot but be adopted sooner or later. It has been recognized by our brethren in England, and, as I have been informed, the only difficulty which has occurred in adopting the whole of the three distinct degrees, has been owing to personal and delicate motives which cannot last long. The ordination of ministers has hitherto depended on no stable principles. Let us use our best endeavors to bring about the best possible order in humble dependence on our heavenly father, who has promised his blessing on them. As obstacles or difficulties, there can be no grounds for apathy and indolence. The whole of our present life is a state of warfare and probation. Should we faint and hang down our hands when engaged in the best of causes whilst the Almighty is our commander and his angels our guardians in the combat? Obstacles are not reasons. Can there be any reason opposed to just order? However incipient our states may be, either as individuals or as a church, in the process of regeneration, ought not we to make order the object of our undeviating efforts? What difficulties can be rationally placed in competition with this object? Can we give way to them without a dereliction of order as the end of our pursuits? To give way to imaginary difficulties in the way of obtaining it, would be following the example of the heartless Jews as recorded in Numbers xiii. 27 to 33, which you will be pleased to have read in the convention. *This* passage applies, as respects the difficulties in the way of coming into a state of order, both as to the church in her smallest and her largest form. Let us look at the effect of such discouraging considerations in the following chapter. " All the congregation lifted up their voice and cried, and the people wept *that night*. And all the children murmured against Moses and against Aaron, and the whole congregation said unto them, Would God we had died in the land of Egypt, or, Would God we had died in this wilderness! And wherefore hath the Lord brought us unto this land to fall by the sword, that our wives and our children should be a prey?" Were it not better for us to return into Egypt? Numb. xiv. 4 to 6. This shows us what will be the tendency and natural, yes natural consequences of making difficulties and of setting them as Anakim in the way of our coming into a state of just order. It leads to a perpetual disruption, to a lamentable longing for the leeks and garlick of Egypt, and to have a captain of *our own choice*, not to be conducted unto the good land of milk and honey, but *down* to the land of Ham. How much better is it to say with Joshua and Caleb, " The land which we passed through to search it is an exceeding good land. If the Lord delight in us, then he will bring us into this land and give it us; a land which floweth with milk and honey. Only rebel not ye against the Lord, neither fear ye the people of the land; for they are bread for us; their defence has departed from them and the Lord is with us; fear them not," verses 7, 8 and 9. Through the mercy of the Lord such are *our* views in relation to the grand object of just order. By no " evil reports" do we feel disheartened. On the contrary, we are stimulated to greater exertions, for we feel the delight of use, in subordination to the best of causes; and as there is more occasion for use, so there is a better opportunity for delightful operations. Our order is a regular trine of discrete degrees, and a just correspondence from the highest to the lowest. The Kingdom of God must indeed be first established in our own minds. *External Order* (as an effect from a cause) will flow from internal order, the Lord's kingdom within us. With natural men, however, (I mean spiritual-natural, which we always are in this world,) every act of worship must be based and fixed in ultimates. Hence we all perceive the duty of external worship, of celebrating the sacraments, and of becoming in all respects a *visible church*. I hope the preceding sentiments will be favorably received by you and the convention. My zeal for the peace and prosperity of the new church increases with my age. It will serve as an apology for any unintentional errors I may have committed. At the convention in 1822, you may recollect of my having taken an active part in its proceedings. It is to be feared that one of the best means then recommended for promoting the success of the best of causes, in our own hearts, as well as in leading others to unite and co-operate with us, has been too much overlooked or neglected. But let me ask what will public worship itself, (by some thought of little moment,) or a mere acknowledgment of heavenly truths, avail without frequent reading and meditation on the Word of God, and daily family and private devotion. They would degenerate into mere formality and solifidianism.

Wishing you and our Brethren a happy meeting,

I remain yours and theirs affectionately,

⸲ No. LIX.

CORRESPONDENCE BETWEEN THE REV. C. J. DOUGHTY AND THE REV. T. WORCESTER.

I.

New York, April 28th, 1840.

DEAR BROTHER—In forwarding you a copy of the accompanying address, I feel a disposition to say a single word in explanation.

I do not consider the approbation I have expressed in the certificate which bears my name, with that of others, as compromitting me in regard to previous views and opinions. I have long felt, and more especially, since the course pursued by the society here, under the direct influence and control of the Massachusetts Association, have I felt the full force and effect of many of the truths contained in it.   In fact, I may say, that my own case enables me to bear living testimony, that the practical results of our late course are as are there stated.

I have signed the address, or rather expressed my approbation of it, under a solemn and sincere conviction of its truth; and I now repeat that conviction, in the hope that you and others of my friends in the east will regard the part I have taken in its true light.   It will not, on my part, break any of those charitable relations which have hitherto existed between us; and I shall regret exceedingly if it does so on the part of others.

Truly yours,
C. J. DOUGHTY.

This letter was sent in company with copies of "Reasons and Principles," which Mr. Doughty forwarded to Messrs. Samuel and Thomas Worcester. It expresses his reasons for endorsing that pamphlet, which would not have been published without his approval.   His reference to his own case, as affording living testimony of the truths contained in that pamphlet, is most significant.   Something on this subject may be seen in Newchurchman, Vol. II., p. 685.   Still it was not Mr. Doughty's intention to break abruptly away from the General Convention.   He still wished to be in charity with that body and all its members.   Hence he attended its meeting which was held in Philadelphia just after the first meeting of the Middle Convention was held there, and his presence gave occasion to Letters III. IV. and V. below.

II.

Boston, May 4th, 1840.

DEAR BROTHER—I have just received yours of the 28th ult., together with two copies of an address, for all of which please accept my thanks.

In your letter you remark, when speaking of the address, "I have long felt, and more especially, since the course pursued by the society here, under the direct influence and control of the Massachusetts Association, have I felt the full force and effect of many of the truths contained in it."

Now I have to beg of you the favor to explain this matter, for I do not know what it means.   And to show you how much in the dark I am, I will just say that I did not know that I had done any thing in relation to affairs in New York, which did not meet your approbation.   And I supposed that my brother could say the same with regard to what he had done.

You express the hope that what you have done will not break the charitable relations which have existed between us hitherto.   I hope so too; but I do not know what to expect as well as you do, for I do not understand so well what you have done, and do not know what course you intend to pursue   You have taken a new position, and I must wait for you to let me know how I am to treat you.

In the meantime, I remain yours truly,
THOMAS WORCESTER.

III.

New York, July 13th, 1840.

DEAR BROTHER—You may remember I asked you in Philadelphia (at the Convention,) if it did not require the sanction of three ordaining ministers for the ordination of Messrs.

Barrett & Dike. I understood you to say in reply, that some alteration had been made in the rule, and that the report presented to the Convention in their case was sufficient.

My object in making the inquiry then was to give validity to the report, if necessary, by the addition of my signature. I do not remember whether I stated this to you or not; because your answer, for the time, satisfied my doubt. .

On my return home, however, the subject again invited my attention; and I yesterday took occasion to look into the journals. I find there has been an alteration in the rule; but it does not strike me that it meets the case; and I should like to have your understanding of the matter.

As the rule stood previous to 1839, all applications for ordination were to be made to the ordaining ministers in convention assembled, and if granted, their decision was to be made known to the convention previous to ordination.

As the rule now stands, all applications for ordination into the first degree are to be made to the ordaining ministers, any *three* of whom may grant the same. And applications for ordination into the other degrees stand as before.

The report in the case of Messrs. Barrett & Dike was signed by Mr. Roche and yourself only. This was the reason of my original inquiry, and is now my reason for asking further explanation.

Yours,

C. J. DOUGHTY.

IV.

Boston, July 17th, 1840.

DEAR SIR—Yours of the 13th inst. is just received. You know that when we adopted the rules of order, we abolished the use of the word *license* and still retained the old rule, that all applications for ordination should be made to the ordaining ministers in convention assembled. This made it impossible for us severally to introduce into the first degree, and indeed impossible for any one to be introduced in any way in the interim between two sessions. This result was not anticipated by any one.

At the next session I stated this difficulty to the convention; and they in consequence adopted the rule of 1839 to which you refer. On account of this origin of it I have always understood it to apply to the intervals between the sessions and not to the time of the sessions. During session I supposed that application must be made according to the old rule. I do not wonder, however, that you understood it differently.

As to the proceedings in relation to Messrs. B. & D., sometime before the convention, it was doubtful whether they would attend, and Dr. Beers, of his own accord, sent me a written approbation and request that I should ordain them here, if I thought proper. And thinking that it might appear best to do so, I concluded to obtain the approbation of another one of the ordaining ministers; and not feeling free to apply to you after you had signed that pamphlet, I applied to Mr. Roche and obtained his approbation; so that I had authority to ordain them without any further action of the convention.

But I afterwards thought it would be best for them to attend the convention; and then no other course occurred to me but that of giving up all that had been done according to the rule which I understood as applying only to interims, and of laying the application of the candidates before the ordaining ministers in convention assembled, according to the former rule. This I therefore did at their meeting the day before convention. The committee of ordaining ministers decided that the request ought to be granted, and the next day reported the same to the convention.

When, therefore, you spoke to me about having *three* names, I replied that I did not think it necessary—I replied so, because I did not think that we were acting under the rule that requires *three*, but does not require us to report to the convention, and does not require the convention to act upon the subject; but that we were acting under the former rule, which has nothing to do with the number *three*—but requires the committee to report their decision to the convention, and then requires the convention to act upon it.

Whether I understood the rules rightly and took the right course in the case, I cannot say; but that other people understood things in the same way is evident, because the convention *received the report and acted upon it* ; which it would not have been proper for them to do if we were acting under a rule which did not apply to the case.

I hope I have given my views in such a way that you can understand them, and written them so that you can read them.   The thermometer is somewhere above ninety, and I cannot do any thing very well.

Yours truly,
Thomas Worcester.

V.

New York, July 23d, 1840.

I do not know whether Mr. Worcester expects me to reply to his of the 17th inst. or not.   Still I feel, under the circumstances of the case, that a reply is necessary.   And I hope he will give me credit for sincerity, when I say, that it is with unfeigned regret that I feel it to be so.

My letter to him of the 13th inst. was not prompted by any wish or desire to produce embarrassment.   And I think he will perceive in the fact, that I was willing, in Phila-delphia, to relieve both the convention and the committee from embarrassment, that I could not possibly have had any sinister motive.

In my mind, the subject now assumes an unfavorable aspect, and I shall be glad if Mr. Worcester can change my views of it.   I can excuse, on his part, the wish not to have *my* co-operation in the matter; but I do not feel the same readiness to excuse an open violation of the rules of order, where order is so strongly insisted on.   If I do wrong in the suggestion, my apology must be found in my entire conviction of its truth.   If you did not feel free to apply to me *before* the convention, I take for granted you did not feel free to apply to me *at* the convention.   Is or is not this a just conclusion?

You say you consider the present rule as applying only *ad interim* ; and that you look to the old rule when the convention is in session.   Might you not as well, under the rule existing previous to 1839, have looked to the former rule *ad interim*, and have left the then existing rule where you found it.   This would have placed you merely where, by your construction, you now stand, viz: having an *existing* rule for *one case*, and an *old* or *abrogated* rule for *another*.   Then you would have applied an *existing* rule to the case of application made at the convention, and an old or *abrogated* rule to the case of applications made *between the sessions*.   *Now*, you apply an existing rule to applications made *between the sessions*, and an old or abrogated rule to applications made at the sessions.   If it was meant to retain the *old* rule and add the *new* one, as an amendment, the *old* one would have appeared in the rules of order, *modified* by the *new*.   This however is not the case; the rule has been *changed* and not *modified*.   You will be satisfied of this by a reference to the resolutions by which these alterations were made.   The present Sec. 3, Art. iv., Chap. I, is a *new* section ; and the present Sec. 4 (then Sec. 3) was modified so as to leave the present Sec. 3 entire and independent.   There is in fact, therefore, no *old* rule to refer to, the whole having been changed so as to make the applications for ordination into the first degree, a *new rule, in toto* ; and to make the provisions of the *old* rule apply to the second and third degrees *only*.   (See No. 96, et seq. Con. Jour. 1839.)

From these facts, I think it is evident that the construction you have adopted is not warranted.   There is a marked distinction designedly made in the rules between appli-cations for ordination into the *first* and into the *other degrees* of the ministry.   In the latter case, the decision of the ordaining ministers is to be made known to the convention for their approbation, previous to ordination.   Not so in the former.   And I infer that the ordaining ministers who signed the report in the case of Messrs. Barrett and Dike, enter-tained the same opinion.   For they do not ask the *concurrence* of the convention in the act granting ordination ; but merely express the *desire* that the convention should fix *the time when, the place where*, and *the person by whom* the service of ordination shall, in these cases, be performed.   The *concurrence* therefore of the convention, in the report of the ordaining ministers, granting the requests of Messrs. Barrett and Dike, and their *agree-ment* that they be ordained into the first degree of the new-church ministry, was mere *gratis dictum* ; and the request that they should fix the *time* and *place*, and designate the *person* to perform the service, was mere courtesy shown them, to which, under the circumstances, there could be no objection.

You conclude by saying, " that whether you understood the rules rightly, and took the right course in the case, you cannot say, but that other people understood things in the same way is evident, because the convention *received the report and acted upon it*, which it would not have been proper for them to do, if we were acting under a rule which did not apply to the case."

With me, this is a very inconclusive argument. We all know how things are done in the convention, where there is no particular interest or feeling excited. I take for granted the convention did not *think* about it. They trusted to the correctness of the ordaining ministers, and passed the resolution of concurrence as a matter of course. If they did not, and if, from a full understanding of the case, they undertook to legislate under an *old* and *abrogated* rule, they stand, where the ordaining ministers stand, open to the charge of having, in an essential particular, violated their own rules of order.

For my own part, I can see but one way in this matter. To follow the rule which is in existence so long as it exists, and if it is found inconvenient, to change it.

Yours truly,
C. J. DOUGHTY.

We refrain from any remarks upon this correspondence. It speaks so fully for itself, and is so strikingly expressive of the spirit of the transaction, that any remarks of ours are wholly unnecessary. We cannot, however, but commend to the close attention of the reader, the last two paragraphs of No. V. He will see a remarkable confession, of one who ought to know, how the General Convention has sometimes acted under the lead of the ordaining ministers. The president did as he liked. "The convention did not *think* about it"! But the convention must be held responsible; and is obnoxious to the charge of "having, in an essential particular, violated its own rules of order." And all to punish Mr. Doughty for having "*signed* that pamphlet." Of how much sorer punishment must he be deemed worthy, who *wrote* it! Notwithstanding, both were done "under a solemn and sincere conviction of its truth." That, indeed, is the rub. Surely no one can fail to see, from this document, what would be the quality of a government of the whole new church in this country, were its chief power vested in one man! And it is certainly clear enough "what flimsy bonds are laws of order on paper, when they come athwart arbitrary or ambitious men in effecting their purposes!'"

No. LX.

DOCUMENTS RESPECTING THE REV. SAMUEL WORCE-STER'S DIFFICULTIES WITH THE BRIDGEWATER SOCIETY.

Bridgewater, November 14th, 1835.

MRS. —— —— ——,

MY DEAR SISTER—You must be well aware that your proposed marriage to Mr. ——, is calculated to excite great surprise among your friends, and some doubts in respect to its being conformable to the principles of the church. For this reason, it has seemed to be your duty to converse with your new-church friends, and give them all the good reasons that you suppose you see, for this engagement. It has been painful for me to learn that the whole affair has been matured secretly, and that you have not made your motives and reasons known, even since you have been published.

That I might have an opportunity of free and full conversation with you on this subject, Mrs. —— requested you to call on me. But the term of your publishment has almost expired, without my having any means of understanding the meaning of this strange affair.

If it were an engagement of a common character, no explanation would be necessary ; and even now I do not *demand* it. I only suggest that it seems to me proper for you to give it, and that it will make you better and happier to give it. A true marriage is the most holy of all relations ; and all things concerning it, should be performed in the most holy manner of which we are capable. How is it possible that you can be married so separately and distinctly from the church, that none of them understand the meaning of what you are doing ? I still hope for a friendly explanation before you are married.

Your affectionate pastor,

SAMUEL WORCESTER.

Bridgewater, November 16th, 1835.

RESPECTED SIR—It would be useless for me to attempt to describe my feelings, on the perusal of your letter, received Saturday evening. I can only say that it is with the greatest astonishment, that I find myself called upon to give my reasons for a contemplated alteration of my domestic affairs, and that I am lost in wonder, in trying to discover from whence this authority proceeds. I find it not in the bondage of the old church, much less in the freedom of the new. When, by your request, Mrs. —— invited me to her house, I gave her my reasons for not being able to go that week, but intended to go as soon as possible, and looked forward to the time with pleasure, not in the least expecting to be censured for my conduct, much less that any one would go so far in judging of my internals, as to intimate that I was not actuated by good motives, in forming the connection I was about to form. It pains me to heart, when I think from whence came these insinuations ; but I hope, by acting in that freedom which the new church guaranties to all those that endeavor to do the good which its truths teach, and depending upon Divine Providence for protection, that I shall be enabled, not only to ask forgiveness for my own transgressions, but to exercise charity for those that accuse me of acting disorderly. Hoping that nothing further will transpire, to debar me from that freedom in which I have thus far acted, or weaken the confidence I have heretofore placed in you as my teacher, I conclude by subscribing myself

Your affectionate sister in the church,

—— —. ——.

Bridgewater, November 20th, 1835.

To

MR. —— ——.
MRS. —— —. ——.

MY DEAR FRIENDS—I think it my duty to decline uniting you in marriage. As this decision must become known to others, and the grounds of it may not be rightly understood, I think it my duty to state them; and I request that you will give the following reasons for my conduct, to all who remark upon it. I shall do the same.

1. The difference of your ages is fourteen years : and this is, at least, as much as seventeen years would be, if the man were the elder. I do not regard this as a merely natural objection. Our minds as well as our bodies change with age. They are perpetually coming into new states : and the difference of states produced in so many years is very great. In order that a true marriage may take place between two minds, they must be in corresponding states, and it seems to me not probable, and scarcely possible, that such agreement in states of life can now exist, or can be produced, between two whose ages are so different. It is the will of the Lord, and must be the constant effort of his Providence, to bring together those who can be true partners : and it does not seem to me rational to suppose that he would produce such partners with so great a difference of ages. In most cases, this difference prevents the possibility of persons being united ; and this indicates that it is contrary to the order of Divine Providence that persons should be united whose ages are so different. And besides all this, the fact

that this great difference of ages *is on the wrong side*, has great weight in my mind. Seventeen years on the other side, would be a much less objection.

2. The second reason relates merely to your condition in respect to family and property. Your domestic and pecuniary circumstances seem not to be such as Swedenborg mentions as reasons for second marriages. They would seem to be unfavorable even to a first marriage, and must be still farther from furnishing a ground for second marriage. I do not press this objection as a very strong one, but I think we ought to regard such external circumstances as of the Divine Providence, and thus teaching us our duty.

3. The third reason relates to Mrs. ————'s opinions and feelings respecting her former marriage. I had been told that she had expressed her belief that Mr. ———— was her true partner; and this I stated to both of you. She denied ever having said this, or any thing implying it; but she did not tell me whether this had or had not been her belief. There are several persons who have heard her converse in a manner which they *understood* to imply fully and distinctly, that she believed the marriage between Mr. ———— and herself to be genuine: but some of them do not remember any particular expression which would *prove* that such was her meaning. Still there is some evidence, which I know not how to reject, that she has used explicit language implying this belief. You will see, therefore, that this objection is not removed, although the painful conflicting testimony respecting it renders it impossible for me to decide what weight should be given to it.

4. The fourth reason respects your views and feelings concerning me and others. You assume that neither your pastor, nor your new-church friends generally, have a right to call in question the propriety of any thing you may think proper to do respecting marriage. You take it as very wrong in me and them to express any doubt that you are doing right; and the feelings which you manifested on this subject, seem to me very unfriendly. Mrs. ————'s letter to me, and the conversation of both of you, plainly imply that you deny my official relation to you, and the duty which this imposes on me, of teaching you what is right, and admonishing you against what is wrong, in respect to marriage. You were careful to let me know, that in paying attention to what I have said on this subject, you were showing indulgence, and favor and courtesy, rather than performing your duty to your pastor. You also signified that for me to question the propriety of your conduct, was claiming authority over you which does not belong to my office. All this seems to render it difficult and improper for me to marry you. So unfriendly a state of mind as yours appears to be, is opposite to true marriage; and your objecting to my performing towards you the proper duties of a pastor, would reduce me to a mere civil officer in marrying you. If I acted merely as a civil officer, I would marry you; but as a priest, I must sanction marriages under spiritual law as well as civil. I cannot sanction your marriage as your pastor, while you deny my right to treat you respecting it as your pastor.

You will see, from this statement, that I consider a priest as under the same obligations to regard both the civil law and the truths of the Church, when uniting persons in marriage, that a civil magistrate is, to regard the civil law. The truths of the Church guard most strictly against disorder among those who know them best.

And now, my friends, let me say, that my declining to marry you, makes no difference in my desire that you may be blessed with every blessing of the Lord. It appearing to me that you do wrong in this case, makes me not the less desirous to teach and lead you to do right in all other cases. I have not said, nor do I say, nor mean to imply, that you are actuated in this case by evil motives. Judging as well as I can, the proposed connection is not conformable to spiritual truths; and my judgment must regulate my conduct, while I concede to you the liberty of following your own. In every relation and duty in which you may ever suppose that I can be useful to you, call on me freely, and you will find me your affectionate friend and pastor,

SAMUEL WORCESTER.

SIR—Feeling it my duty to become united with the Church in this place, and expecting that it would be more agreeable to them to receive some communication from you on the subject, has induced me to write this, requesting a dismission from your church, together with such recommendation as you (or, if more proper, your church) may think I am entitled to receive.

Yours, &c.

——— —. ———.

The Lady now married.

To the Rev. Samuel Worcester, Pastor of the N. J. Church, S. Bridgewater.

Bridgewater, Jan. 7th, 1837.

MRS. ——— —. ———,

Your letter of the 4th inst., requesting a dismission from this church, and a recommendation to the church in North Bridgewater, has been referred to our committee. This reply will contain nothing but what they and myself are unanimously agreed in adopting as the proper answer.

We do not think it necessary to call a meeting of the church to act on the subject, because we suppose there is no reason to doubt that our own views coincide with those of nearly all the members of the church.

You cannot have forgotten that we thought there was reason to fear that you were guilty of a false statement in respect to what you had said of your relation to your first husband. Nor can you have forgotten that the church, by their committee, urgently requested you to adopt certain measures for enabling us to judge fairly concerning what you had said; and that you refused to comply with this request.

Your conduct in relation to this subject left very unfavorable impressions on our minds. Our fears that you had been guilty of falsehood, were strengthened, and we have good reason for believing that such was the effect upon the minds of many others. It is, therefore, our duty to say, that it will be necessary for you to comply with our request, and remove these grounds of suspicion that you were guilty of falsehood, before we can recommend you to any church. If you have considered the subject wisely, you must have been aware that you were not considered as in good standing in this church, after refusing to perform the duty which they recommended, and which they told you was necessary for removing the unfavorable impressions which existed against you. We have waited in hope that you would become sensible of your wrong, and correct it; and now we can only request again, that you will do all that is in your power to remove our painful fears.

We do not think it proper for this church to separate you, and dismiss you from their care, unless they should have conclusive evidence of great and continued sin, without repentance. If they have proof that you wholly separate yourself from them, they may by a vote acknowledge that you are separated.

If you should doubt whether our decision would be sustained by the church, you are at liberty to appeal; and if you inform me that you wish to appeal to the whole church, the committee will call a meeting, and give you notice, that you may attend and produce all the evidence of your innocence that you desire. We believe that you have been told that we ought to call you innocent, till you have been proved to be guilty; but it is wholly impossible to regard you as innocent while you refuse to meet the evidence that is against you. We therefore desire you to change your resolution, and we will show you all the tenderness and charity of affectionate brethren.

SAMUEL WORCESTER, *Pastor.*

To the Rev. Samuel Worcester, and the Members of the First Society of the New Jerusalem in Bridgewater,

The undersigned, being of the opinion that the good of the society would be better promoted by a separation between the present pastor and the society, and being very confident that his usefulness as teacher to them is nearly if not entirely destroyed, respectfully request that a separation may take place, and that it may be effected in as quiet and peaceable a manner as possible.

Signed, Holmes Sprague, Edwin Keith, Joel Shedd, Asa P. Keith,
Virgil Ames, Ephm. H Sprague, Horace Ames, Asa Copeland, Jr.
Jos. A. Hyde, Bela Mitchell, Geo. W. Bates,

Bridgewater, Aug. 9th, 1830.

Bridgewater, Nov. 17th, 1839.

To Messrs. H. Sprague, J. H. Hyde, and H. Ames, Committee,

The answer which I gave last evening to your communication from the legal society, would, I think, be in a more suitable form, if reduced to writing. It ought to be recorded; and it must be related to many, and I cannot expect that errors will be avoided, unless I give the whole answer in a written form.

You may, therefore, expect me to send you a communication, to be presented to the legal society, containing a full and explicit answer to their message.

Your obedient servant,

SAMUEL WORCESTER.

Bridgewater, Nov. 18th, 1839.

To Samuel Alden, M. D., Moderator of the Meeting of the Legal Society of the New Church, to be holden, by adjournment, Nov. 23d, 1839,

DEAR SIR—A committee, consisting of Messrs. Holmes Sprague, Horace Ames, and Joseph A. Hyde, called on me, on the evening of the 16th inst., and stated that they were directed to inform me, that it was the wish of the society that the connection existing between me and the society should be dissolved.

I hereby express to the society my entire concurrence in the wish which has thus been communicated. And as the connection between me and the society was never sanctioned by any authority above us, nothing but our mutual consent is necessary to dissolve it. It is therefore dissolved. In expressing my willingness that this connection should be dissolved, I wish to be distinctly understood as referring to the legal society as a body, and not in the slightest degree to any of the individuals who compose it. I am not willing to do any thing to produce separation between me and these persons; but I wish to do all that I can to produce a state of genuine spiritual consociation with them. Any causes of alienation, existing between me and any of them, I wish to have investigated, judged and removed in an orderly manner.

The connection which has existed between the legal society and the church and its pastor, has never seemed to me an orderly connection; but I have always desired and endeavored to produce a state, in which the church alone would be the legal society; and I am now quite convinced that this object ought to have been accomplished before I consented to any connection with this people. No such object ought to have been permitted to remain, to be effected by my ministry.

The existence of this connection placed the members of the legal society and myself in a relation that has been unfavorable to my being a good medium to them, and to their receiving my instructions in a useful manner. So far as I have exercised the proper freedom of my office, it has seemed to them an assumption of authority, and an infringement on their rights.

The society will see from this statement, why I rejoice in having the former connection dissolved; and I wish it also to be inferred, that I think it very desirable to have the connection between the legal society and the church dissolved in an amicable manner.

With great respect for yourself and all the friends of this religious institution, I am, dear sir, your sincere friend,

SAMUEL WORCESTER.

Bridgewater, Nov. 29th, 1839.

Rev. Samuel Worcester,

DEAR SIR—In compliance with a resolve of the First Society of the New Jerusalem in Bridgewater, we herewith transmit to you the accompanying preamble and resolutions adopted by them on the 23d inst.

You will observe that the dissolution desired by them and concurred in by yourself in your communication of the 18th inst., has been finally acted on by the society, and that the connection between yourself and them is therefore at an end.

The undersigned, in behalf of the society, join with you sincerely in the desire, that any causes of alienation existing between yourself and individuals of the society may be investigated, judged and removed; and as repeated attempts to remove such causes of alienation have been made by individuals of the society without success, we leave it to you to adopt such a course in regard to them as will, in your opinion, produce the result which all are so desirous to effect.

The expression in your communication to the society that "you wish it also to be inferred, that you think it very desirable to have the connection between the legal society and the church dissolved in an amicable manner," seems to the society to have been altogether uncalled for at the present time, and they are at a loss to understand the kind of dissolution it was your intention to recommend. The members of the society have always understood it to be your desire, and many of them have concurred with you in the belief, that there should be no other legal society than the church itself, and that this could be effected in no other orderly manner than by having all the members of the legal society connect themselves with the church. This would effect a still closer connection between the church and legal society, and is a state to which many of the society have always looked forward, and still hope to see attained.

In conclusion, permit us to say, that, in our opinion, the good of the whole society would be greatly promoted by a separation between yourself and the church. Should this separation take place, we sincerely believe that the legal society and the church would not longer remain distinct bodies, but would soon be merged in one.

With a sincere desire that the best results may ensue from the dissolution which has taken place, and for your future welfare in whatever relation you may stand towards us,

We remain your friends,

H. AMES, } Committee of the First So-
H. SPRAGUE, } ciety of the New Jeru-
J. A. HYDE, } salem in Bridgewater.

To Mr. Joseph A. Hyde, Clerk of the First New Jerusalem Society in Bridgewater,

SIR—Circumstances having arisen that make it no longer proper for me to hold the office of leader of the society, I hereby, through you, respectfully tender to the society my resignation of that office. Yours, &c.

THOS. CUSHMAN.

Bridgewater, Nov. 28th, 1839.

Bridgewater, Nov. 30.

Mr. R. Copeland, Secretary of the Church,

DEAR SIR—At the last meeting of the First Society of the New Jerusalem in Bridgewater, the connection between the society and the Rev. Samuel Worcester (as you are aware) was dissolved. Since that time, the leader of the society has resigned his office. It has, therefore, devolved upon the committee of the society, who were chosen " to make such arrangements with regard to public worship in future as may seem most useful until some permanent arrangement is made" to provide, in some way, for the service to-morrow.

Learning that the church were to hold a meeting this afternoon, the committee of the society respectfully request that you would lay this communication before the church, and ask them to appoint some one of their number to lead in the service to-morrow, or until some more permanent arrangement is made.

Very respectfully yours,

H. SPRAGUE, in behalf of the Com.

Bridgewater, Nov. 30th, 1839.

Mr. Holmes Sprague,

SIR—The communication sent to me this day, has been laid before the church, upon which the following action has been had :

Whereas we have received a communication from the legal society requesting us to appoint one of our number to lead in their worship to-morrow; therefore,

Resolved, That, under the present circumstances, we cannot comply with their request.

A true copy of the records,

RALPH COPELAND, *Secretary.*

Bridgewater, Dec. 2d, 1839.

Rev. Thos. Worcester,

DEAR SIR—You will recollect that some time in August last, two of the undersigned committee called on you, at Boston, and held a conversation in regard to the difficulties in the new-church society in this place, and that you suggested the propriety of calling a legal meeting of the society to consult as to the orderly course to be pursued under the circumstances.

Since that time, as you will see by the accompanying documents, a meeting of the legal society has been called, and a dissolution taken place, by mutual consent, between the pastor of the church and the legal society.

During the past week, the leader of the society, a member of the church, has resigned that office, and a request to the church to appoint some one of their number to lead in the service until some further arrangement could be made, has been refused A copy of our request to the church, and their reply to the same, are also sent herewith.

Under these circumstances, the undersigned, a committee of the legal society, respectfully request your advice and direction, as to what course they should pursue, in order that the meetings of the society for worship may be conducted in an orderly manner.

It is our wish, should it be consistent with your views, that you would appoint some one to lead in our worship for the present, and that you would afford us such counsel and aid as may seem to you most useful for us. If not incompatible with your other engagements, it would give us great pleasure to have you visit us during the coming week, that we may have an opportunity of communicating with you more freely than we can by letter, and that you may be better able to appreciate our wants.

We remain, &c., very respectfully yours,

H. SPRAGUE,
H. AMES,
J. A. HYDE,
EDWIN KEITH,
NAHUM WASHBURN.

P. S. Please to address Mr. Holmes Sprague in reply to this as soon as convenient.

Messrs. Sprague, Ames, Hyde, Washburn and Keith,

DEAR BRETHREN—Yours of the 2d inst. I received this morning. It seems to me exceedingly important for us all, that we should do what is right in this case, and that we should abstain from every thing that is wrong; that is, I regard the case as a very important one, as it concerns the peace of the church in your neighborhood. I have, therefore, concluded that it would not be well for me to act upon my present individual impressions with regard to what is right; but that it would be better to wait awhile and take advice. I therefore propose to lay the subject before the ministers of our association at their next meeting, which will be in about a month. I did at first think of calling a special meeting at an earlier time ; but, upon further reflection, it seemed better to wait until the regular meeting, and I hope that this course will not be disagreeable to you.

For the same reasons, it seems to me best that I should not visit you at present, unless it should seem necessary for the sake of obtaining more information.

In the beginning of your letter you refer to something that I said to two members of your committee as to calling a meeting of the legal society. The question under consideration was, as to what course the " *eleven*" ought to pursue, seeing that my brother had refused to meet them altogether.

Now I presume that the two members will recollect that I proposed several things as good and orderly; for example, that every one of the "*eleven*" should go to my brother, and endeavor to settle his own difficulty; also, that the "*eleven*" should join the church, and act as church members, and so have the privileges of members.

I presume, too, that they will recollect that the calling of a legal meeting was suggested as a thing proper to do in case that other things failed. And, I presume, that they do not recollect that I said or implied that I thought that they had already done all this preliminary work, and that it was then time to call the legal meeting.

It would not be strange, if the conversation should leave different impressions upon our minds, on account of our different ways of appreciating the things which were said.

And now, my dear brethren, let us humble ourselves, and pray and labor for the peace of Jerusalem; for our church is not the New Jerusalem any further than it is a city compact together and a quiet habitation.

I am very truly, yours,

THOMAS WORCESTER.

Boston, Dec. 8th, 1839

Bridgewater, 12 Dec., 1839.

Rev. Thos. Worcester,

DEAR SIR—Yours of the 8th inst., was duly received. We had been somewhat impatient to hear from you last week, and were careful that our communication should be left at Mr. Clapp's store on the 3d inst., to be sent to you immediately; but it seems, from yours, that it did not reach you until the morning of the 8th.

Whilst we all agree with you fully as to the importance of a deliberate decision in our case, we should have been gratified to have received from you ere this, some advice as to the manner of conducting our meetings for worship until the subject should be brought before the ministers of the association. And we feel now extremely desirous that you should point out to us, the proper course to pursue in our meetings for worship. The society have met at their house as usual, since they were separated from the pastor of the church, and one of our number has been induced, with great reluctance on his part, to officiate as leader, in the daily expectation of receiving from you some direction in this matter. We regret that you have not thought it best to come to us and learn more fully from *us* our present state, and many particulars in regard to our situation, which cannot be communicated to you by letter, and still hope that you will visit us.

The two members of the committee who held the conversation with you, on the 9th August last, at your house, recollect distinctly, that after informing you that an informal meeting of eleven individuals had been holden, and that a committee of three, appointed by them, had waited upon your brother, requesting him to meet "the eleven" in friendly conference with a view to the adjustment of difficulties, and that your brother said to the committee, that he did not distinctly see the relation in which he stood towards them, that it was *then* his impression that it would not be orderly for him to meet them—he thought there was some connection between him and them, yet he could not grant their request, but would meet each of them individually, and invited such a meeting—"after they had related these things to you, they recollect that you proposed to them a compliance with the rule in the 18th chapter of Matthew—it was replied, that such a course had been pursued by some of "the eleven" and that the result had been far from satisfactory:—you then objected to the meeting of "the eleven," and said it had the appearance of "*faction*," and immediately made a remark, which proved that you intended nothing hard or unkind by that expression:—it was then, and immediately in this connection, that you said you thought it would have been better to have called a legal meeting of the society, and that you thought your brother would then feel obligated to take some notice of their proceedings They recollect a suggestion of yours, in some part of the conversation, that it would have been well if they had drawn near to your brother and helped him discharge the duties of his office, but they *do not* recollect that you proposed that "the eleven" should join the church and act as church members, and so have the privileges of members"—nor can they suppose that it was your intention that they should imply this from what you did say, or to recommend to them to connect themselves with the pastor, entertaining such views of his character and conduct as they then expressed to you.

It may seem to you that we have been somewhat minute in detailing the conversation referred to, as impressed upon the minds of those of us who took part in it, but it seems to us of some importance that their recollection of it should be known to you—and there were some parts of it so strongly marked, that they think and feel that they cannot be mistaken.

Permit us again to remind you of our immediate want of your advice in regard to our meetings for worship, and to assure you that we are, with much esteem,

Yours, truly.

Bridgewater, Dec. 14th, 1839.

To Holmes Sprague, Esq., and others, Committee,

GENTLEMEN—In my communication to the legal society, Nov. 28th, I said that I thought it very desirable that the connection between the legal society and the church should be dissolved. Your reply shows that the legal society were displeased with this remark. You will remember what that reply was, and it is not now at hand for reference.

The construction which you gave to my remark, does not give my meaning; and I regret that I was not more careful to define my wishes. One of the passages of my letter tells what kind of connection between me and the legal society, I was willing to have dissolved; and then it states what I was unwilling to have dissolved. Then I state that I have always desired and endeavored to produce a state in which the church alone should be the legal society. I wished this state produced by having those who desire to be Newchurchmen, join the church, and having others withdraw their names from the legal society. The legal society would then be the *external*, and the church the *internal*, of ONE MAN.

But the connection between the church and the legal society which has existed, has been different. It has been a connection between the church as one man and the legal society as another man; a part of the members of the church being of each man, but a majority of the members of the legal society being distinct from the church. This is the kind of connection which I wished to have dissolved. I did not wish such a kind of separation as the late measures of the legal society have produced. I desired only such a *separation* as there should be between the internal and the external of one mind; and I desired such a *connection* as there should be between the internal and the external of one mind.

Be so kind as to make this statement known to the legal society, and oblige

Your obedient servant,

SAMUEL WORCESTER.

Boston, Dec. 16th, 1839.

Dear Sir,

I am requested by Mr. Worcester to communicate to you that he has received your letter, but is unable at present to attend to the subject of it. He is suffering, as you may probably have learned, from the effects of an accident which befel him last Wednesday. He was riding with Mr. J. L. Smith, in Roxbury, when the chaise was upset, causing, besides other slight injuries to both, a dislocation in Mr. W.'s left foot. Although the injury was a severe and painful one, and such as was feared might require a long confinement, yet every thing has taken the most favorable course; he suffers but little pain, and we hope he will be able to resume his duties sooner than was at first expected. Nothing else new here of importance.

Very respectfully yours,

LUTHER CLARK.

Mr. Holmes Sprague.

Bridgewater, Dec. 26th, 1839.

Rev. Samuel Worcester,

SIR—Yours of the 14th was duly received, and will be laid before the society at their adjourned meeting, which will take place on the 4th of January next. You speak of your former communication as having been dated the 28th of November, we find, by reference to that communication, that it is dated the 18th.

Yours, truly, for the committee, HOLMES SPRAGUE.

Bridgewater, Dec 28th, 1839.

To Holmes Sprague, Esq.

SIR—I received your note of this date; and thank you for noticing the error in my last. I find that my copy of the letter referred to is dated the 18th November. Be so good as to correct the error in my last note, and oblige

Your obedient servant, SAMUEL WORCESTER.

Bridgewater, January 6th, 1840.

Rev. Thomas Worcester,

DEAR SIR—We duly received Mr. Clark's favor of 16th ult., informing us of the accident which had prevented you from acknowledging in person the receipt of our last, and we were glad to learn from him, that you were suffering but little pain from the injury, and that the prospect was, that you would soon be able to resume your duties. Since writing you last, the enclosed correspondence has passed between your brother and ourselves. We also annex a copy of the written request of the "*eleven*" which was handed your brother on the 10th of August last, and a copy of the same to the clerk of the church at the same time; no reply was made to this request, and no notice taken of it, that we are informed of, although your brother informed one of us that he had furnished you with a copy. We remain, with sincere esteem,

HOLMES SPRAGUE, *for Committee.*

To Messrs. H. Sprague, H. Ames, J. A. Hyde, N. Washburn, E. Keith,

DEAR BRETHREN—I hasten to reply to your communications, dated the 2d and 13th December and the 6th January. I say *hasten*, for though it is several days since the meeting of the association, this is the first hour in which I have been able to do any thing upon the subject.

In the first place, allow me to say, that I very much regret that any one has been led to suppose that I regarded it as the best thing that you could do, to call a meeting of the legal society. And I now wish you to understand that what I said in conversation about calling such a meeting, was said out of respect to your rights as members of the legal society; and not as expressing my opinion of what you ought, under present circumstances, to do as Newchurchmen. And, besides, while speaking of a meeting of the legal society, I had no idea of its undertaking to do any thing else, but to devise means of reconciliation and the settlement of difficulties; for I did not know that the "*eleven*" had already sent a request to the church that a separation might take place between it and its pastor. Consequently I spake as if no such thing had been done or thought of; and as if your only object had been a reconciliation. But a meeting has taken place; the connection between the legal society and the pastor of the church has been dissolved; the legal society has taken possession of the meeting house; the church with the pastor have left it; the legal society has appointed a committee to make arrangements for public worship; and this committee now "request my advice and direction as to what course they should pursue, in order that the meetings of the society for worship may be conducted in an orderly manner."

After a good deal of reflection upon the subject, and consulting others upon it, I must say that I do not see how your worship can be orderly, or how you can be in such states of mind as to receive the blessings of worship, while you hold meetings separate from the church. For when we go forward to worship, the influx of him into whose presence we go, is an influx of forgiveness, reconciliation and peace. It endeavors to make us forgive, unite with, and live in peace with one another. It says unto us, "If thou bring thy gift to the altar and there rememberest that thy brother hath aught against thee, leave there thy gift before the altar, and go be reconciled to thy brother, and then come and offer thy gift." It says to us, "and when ye stand praying, forgive, if ye have aught against any, that your Father also, who is in heaven, may forgive you your

5

trespasses; but, if you do not forgive, neither will your Father, who is in heaven, forgive your trespasses." It says to us, "if thy brother shall trespass against thee, go and tell him his fault between thee and him alone; if he shall hear thee, thou hast gained thy brother. But if he will not hear, take with thee one or two more, that in the mouth of two or three witnesses every word may be established. And if he shall neglect to hear them, tell it unto the church, and if he neglect to hear the church, let him be unto thee as an heathen man and a publican." And when we ask how often shall we forgive—whether until seven times? the influx of the Lord answers us, "I say not unto thee until seven times, but until seventy times seven." Such are the things which are continually proceeding from the Divine Humanity. Of such things the Divine Humanity is full. And such things must we receive, if we would receive him. In going to him, there is no evading, or getting round these things, any more than there would be such a thing as evading or getting round the heat and light if we were approaching the natural sun. We may indeed close our eyes, and harden our hearts, so as not to see or feel the things which come from him; and we may then imagine that we are near him, because we can call him by name and not feel a sphere of judgment and condemnation; but we are not really near him—we are not near him in spirit and in truth—nor does he then meet with us and bless us. And if it is necessary for you all to unite together in order that your worship may be orderly and that you may receive the divine blessing, the question arises as to how you are to be united together; and to this I think the answer is plain—you must come together on church grounds, you must be united on church principles—that is, by the principles contained in the passages of scripture which we have been reading. These are the Lord's means of bringing men together and keeping them together. When you come together by the application of these principles, you come together in his name, and lo, he is in the midst of you. I am not telling you any thing new. You have long known all these things, and I have no doubt that you have in some degree practised according to them. But the difficulties still continue, and that shows that you have not fully conformed to these principles: for the Word of the Lord is all powerful, and it will prosper if we believe it and do it.

I understand from you that your difficulties are principally in relation to the pastor of the church—that you complain of him on many accounts, and that you think that you cannot join the church while he continues to be the pastor of it. Now, it appears to me, that the Lord would have you go directly to the pastor and make your complaints to him between you and him alone;—that you should go under the influence of love to him—in hope that you may gain your brother. If he will not hear you, then take one or two more, that in the mouth of two or three witnesses every word may be established. And if he shall neglect to hear them, tell it to the church. It appears to me that you should take and pursue this course, in full confidence that it is the one which the Lord points out; that it is the one which his spirit endeavors to cause you to pursue, and that it is the one which he will bless.

The idea may arise, that this course is not a proper one for you, because you are not in form members of the church. But I think that this makes no difference; for these are divine laws, and you are bound to observe them whether you are members of the church or not; and all those who are true members of the church will be glad to have you observe them, and will rejoice to meet you upon that ground.

With the best wishes for your welfare, I am truly yours,

Boston, 15 *January,* 1840.   THOMAS WORCESTER.

Bridgewater, 3d Feb., 1840.

Rev. Thomas Worcester,

DEAR SIR—At a legal meeting of the First Society of the New Jerusalem, in Bridgewater, holden on the 1st inst., it was voted unanimously, that the committee of the society be instructed to invite the associated societies of the New Jerusalem in Massachusetts, to hold their next meeting in their meeting house at Bridgewater, and that a communication be addressed by the committee to the Rev. Thomas Worcester, the presiding minister of the association, informing him of the same. The undersigned, in behalf of the committee above referred to, takes pleasure in acquainting you with the wish of the society as expressed above. I remain, with much esteem, yours truly,

Bridgewater, Feb. 29th, 1840.

Mr. Ralph Copeland, Secretary of the N. J. Church in Bridgewater,

DEAR SIR—At a meeting of the legal society of the New Jerusalem, holden on the 1st inst., it was voted, unanimously, that the use of their meeting house be offered for the next meeting of the Massachusetts Association of the New Jerusalem, which, we learn, is to be in this place in April next. The committee of the legal society are authorized to communicate the above. And it gives the committee pleasure to offer to the church the use of the meeting house, for the meeting of the association, and hope it will be acceptable to them. By order of the committee, yours truly,

HOLMES SPRAGUE.

The above was handed to Mr. Copeland, March 1st, 1840, by Dr. Samuel Alden.

Bridgewater, March 7th, 1840.

Mr. Holmes Sprague,

DEAR SIR—At a meeting of the church, held March 8th, your communication of February 29th, was read. Whereupon the following preamble and resolutions were adopted :—

Whereas, The committee of the legal society which now holds the meeting house in which this church formerly worshiped, have offered said meeting house for the use of the association at their meeting in April next ; therefore,

Resolved, That this church will return and occupy said meeting house whenever the legal society shall have complied with the advice of the presiding minister of the Association, so far as to give the church full control of all things concerning the worship in said meeting house.

Resolved, That a copy of the above preamble and resolutions be sent by the clerk to Holmes Sprague, Esq., chairman of the committee of the legal society.

A true copy of record. RALPH COPELAND, *Secretary.*

Bridgewater, 23d March, 1840.

Rev. Thos. Worcester,

DEAR SIR—On the 3d inst., we communicated to you a vote of the legal society of the N. J., offering the use of their meeting-house to the association for their next meeting, which we learned would be in this place.

We have not been advised by you of the receipt of our communication, but learned from another source, that you had received it, and that you considered the course taken by us, in making the communication to you, an improper one.

We have since made a similar communication to the church, supposing this course would meet your approbation. We enclose copies of this and of their reply to the same.

Yours truly, for the Committee, H. SPRAGUE.

Holmes Sprague, Esq.

DEAR SIR—I received, in its due season, a communication from you, enclosing a vote of the legal society in Bridgewater, inviting the association to meet in your meeting house.

But, as the church in Bridgewater had invited the association, and had engaged to provide a place for the meeting, it seemed proper to communicate your invitation to them ; and this I accordingly did, with the hope that it would be acceptable to them. It is with much regret that I now inform you that they do not think it proper for them to accept your offer. Will you please give my thanks to the legal society for the good will which they have shown in giving this invitation, and believe me to remain,

Very truly yours, THOMAS WORCESTER.

Boston, 23d March, 1840.

Holmes Sprague, Esq., for the Com. of the Leg. Soc. of the N. J. in Bridgewater,

DEAR SIR—I have just received yours of the 23d inst., enclosing a copy of a correspondence between the legal society and the church in Bridgewater. I am very glad that you have been led to offer the meeting-house to the church. You say that you have learned that I regarded your course in offering the meeting-house to me as "an improper one." This is not quite correct; for I have constantly regarded your offer to me as a good act, and therefore a proper one; but I did not regard it as quite so good, as it would have been, if the offer had been made directly to the church in Bridgewater, and therefore not quite so proper. But I did not think of calling it improper.

My delay in replying to your former communication was occasioned by an unwillingness to return such an answer, and in hope of being able to give a different one. I ought to feel thankful, and I do feel thankful, for every good thing you do; and I pray that the Lord will increase your disposition, and bless your endeavors.

I am very truly yours,   THOMAS WORCESTER.

Boston, March 26, 1840.

Bridgewater, 3d April, 1840.

Mr. John Prentice, Leader of N. J. Society, Providence, R. I.

DEAR SIR—Since the separation of the legal society of the N. J. in this place from the pastor of the church, (of which you are informed,) the society made application to the church to appoint one of their members to lead in the worship of the society at their meeting-house. This request was refused by the church. Since that time, one of our number, (not a church member,) has led in our worship, with a good deal of reluctance on his part, and it is our purpose, in addressing you at this time, and through you the church of which you are leader, to request that Mr. Waldo Ames, who is now with us, may be deputed by your society to lead in our worship, until some more permanent arrangement is made by the society here in regard to worship. Hoping to see yourself or some one else of your society the coming week, we remain yours very truly,

Pawtucket, April 7th, 1840.

Mr. Holmes Sprague, Leader of the N. J. Society, Bridgewater, Mass.

DEAR SIR—Yours to Mr. Prentice, our leader, of the 3d inst., was duly received, and laid before the society on sabbath day last. I am directed to say that the society think they have no authority to depute Mr. Ames. But the society will seek advice, and if an orderly way can be pointed out, whereby we can assist you, it will be done most cheerfully. I am, dear sir, yours truly,   J. F. STREET, *Sec. Prov. N. J. Soc.*

Bridgewater, April 12th, 1840.

Rev. Thos. Worcester,

DEAR SIR—The legal society of the N. J. held a meeting yesterday, at which they voted, unanimously, to invite Mr. Waldo Ames, (a member of the Providence N. J. Society who now resides in Bridgewater, as you are aware, and is, and has been for a long time, a member of the legal society in this place,) to lead in their worship on the Sabbath, until the members are ready to unite upon some more permanent plan for meetings. The society requests us to inform you of this, that they may learn from you if it meets your approbation. An early reply will much oblige, yours very truly,

Boston, Dec. 5, 1840.

Rev. Thomas Worcester,

DEAR SIR—Enclosed you will find a petition for organization of a church in Bridgewater. I was requested by the petitioners to see you personally while in the city, but not having time, I wish you to inform me, by mail, of your decision in regard to it, and also the time most convenient for you to organize them, if you decide so to do. You will see that the time was fixed on the 12th of last month, but I was requested to consult with you in regard to it, and to propose Wednesday, the 9th inst., if agreeable to you.

I am, &c., yours truly,   JOS. A. HYDE.

Boston, Dec. 8th, 1840.

Mr. J. A. Hyde,

DEAR SIR—Yesterday, in the afternoon, I received a note from you containing an application to me, as presiding minister of the Massachusetts Association of the N. J., requesting me to meet with eighteen receivers of the heavenly doctrines and form them into a society. The rules of convention require of me, in such cases, to visit the applicants and to become acquainted with their condition. This I propose to do to morrow, and I shall then be glad to meet with all of the eighteen, or as many of them as can attend in the forenoon, afternoon, or evening, at such a place as you may agree upon I shall go to Bridgewater to-day for that purpose, and may be found at my brother's.

I am very truly yours, THOMAS WORCESTER.

To Mr. Jos. A. Hyde and the seventeen others who have applied to me that I should form them into a Society according to the Rules of Order,

DEAR BRETHREN AND SISTERS—On the 7th inst. I received your application to me, as presiding minister of the Massachusetts Association of the New Jerusalem, that I should visit you, and form you into a society according to the Rules of the General Convention. Those rules require of me, that in such cases I should, in the first place, visit the applicants and become acquainted with their condition. You have probably been informed that I made an effort to do this on the 8th inst., and you have probably been informed of the reason why I did not succeed at that time, and also that with the concurrence of two of your number I have proposed to meet with you on the evening of the 23d inst.

In the mean time it seems to me that it may be well for me to propose some things for your consideration. In proposing to be formed into a society, and thus received into the church in a formal manner, you propose to come into a state of union and brotherhood with those who are already in the church. It consequently follows, that if you have any difficulties with any who are already in the church, a part, and an essential part of the work of coming into it consists in settling, or endeavoring to settle, those difficulties. If the fault is on the part of those who are in, they should see it, confess it, and put it away; and if the fault is on the part of those who are coming in, they should see it, confess it, and put it away; so that those who are in, and those who are coming in, should meet and come together as brethren. Now it is well known that there are serious difficulties between you, or some of you, and the Bridgewater Society, or some of them, difficulties which have caused much trouble among yourselves, much grief among all the friends of the Church, and much scandal among its enemies. This is a lamentable state of things. It is lamented by all that there is of the church in all of us, and shall I be saying too much, if I say that all there is of the church in all of us, will be disposed to labor to put it away? Let us, therefore, not be discouraged by the greatness of the evil, or the long continuance of it, but let us co-operate with the influences of the Lord, of heaven and the church, in endeavoring to remove it. I am willing to do whatever I can for this purpose; and as you have applied to me to form you into a society according to the rules of convention, and as those rules require of me that I should in such cases visit the applicants and become acquainted with their condition, I am willing to visit you, that I may become acquainted with your condition as to all things which appertain to your being formed into a society—and among other things your condition as to the difficulties above alluded to. And if the difficulties are not previously removed, it will be necessary for me to see those between whom they exist, face to face, and thus to learn whether the fault is in those who are now members of the church, or in those who desire to become members. I am sensible that this is a great undertaking, and I have no disposition to engage in it alone. I therefore propose to select from the several societies composing the Massachusetts Association, excepting the Bridgewater Society, a number of intelligent, judicious and impartial men to aid me in the examination and decision.

Now I want you to understand that I do not propose this mode because I desire to take any part in this preparatory labor, for the truth is far otherwise. And if you can propose any mode that is better than this, or if you can settle the difficulties, or any part of them, among yourselves, so that I may have nothing or but little to do with respect to them, it will be altogether agreeable to me. And if for this purpose you should think it best to have my visit postponed, I hope you will give me notice.

Dear brethren and sisters I am very truly yours, THOMAS WORCESTER.

Dec. 15.

Mr. Joseph A. Hyde,

DEAR SIR—At the meeting of the association this day, a standing committee of laymen was chosen, a part of whose duty it is to meet in consultation with the committee of ministers. It consists of two persons from the Boston society and one from each of the other societies. The names are, C. Reed, Wilkins, Green, Hobart, Harris, and Bisbee. They were chosen by ballot, and without reference to any particular case, but for general purposes. There is to be a meeting of this committee together with the ministers on the 20th inst., when I intend to lay before them the application of the eighteen persons in Bridgewater wishing to be formed into a society. After consulting with them, I may have something further to communicate. I am very truly yours,

Boston, Jan. 7th, 1841.   THOMAS WORCESTER.

To Mr. Joseph A. Hyde, for the eighteen persons who have requested to be formed into a society,

DEAR BRETHREN AND SISTERS—According to the notice which I communicated to you immediately after the association, a meeting of the committee was held on the 20th inst., and I consulted them on the subject of your application. It so happened that none of the ministers except myself were present. The committee felt the need of having more information before they could express an opinion; they therefore drew up the enclosed statement of their views on the general subject, together with inquiries concerning your views.   I am very truly yours,

Boston, Jan. 21st, 1841.   THOMAS WORCESTER.

Whereas, an application has been made to Mr. Worcester, as presiding minister of the Massachusetts Association, by Joseph A. Hyde and seventeen others, receivers of the heavenly doctrines in Bridgewater, to institute them into a society, agreeably to the Rules of Order of the General Convention. And whereas, certain difficulties are understood to exist between some or all of said receivers and the pastor of the Bridgewater society, and perhaps the society itself. And whereas, Mr. Worcester has laid the subject before the committee of laymen of the association for advice ; and the said committee having considered the subject, have come to the conclusion that nothing but what are clearly essential things should be required as preliminary to the institution of said proposed society; however desirable it may be for the growth and prosperity of the church, that other difficulties of less vital importance should be adjusted as soon as practicable. The committee consider the great essential principle to be this :— That the receivers proposing to be formed into a society should regard themselves as in a state of charity with the ministers of the church and with the societies already instituted, and as disposed to perform, as a society, their duties towards them, and to co-operate with them in the uses of the church ; just as an individual applicant to join a society is understood to regard himself as in a state of charity with the members of the same, and as disposed to perform the duties of a brother in relation to them. This principle the committee do not regard as any thing new, but as virtually involved and acknowledged in the application already made, when taken in connection with the Rules of Order, (Ch. 2, Art. 1.) Thus, at the close of the service, after pronouncing the new society to be regularly instituted, the presiding minister is required to " recommend them to the fellowship of all other societies of the church." Now by applying for institution, application is also made by implication, for a recommendation to the fellowship of the churches ; which certainly must imply a willingness and desire to be in a state of charity with them.

But nevertheless, in consequence of the difficulties above referred to, it seems advisable to the committee, that the applicants should be inquired of, if they view the subject in this light, and assent to the above principle.

Rev. T. Worcester,

DEAR SIR—Above I send you a copy of the conclusion, at which the committee unanimously arrived yesterday, in regard to the Bridgewater application.

Very respectfully and truly yours,

Boston, 21st *Jan.,* 1841.   CALEB REED, *Chairman.*

Bridgewater, 25th Jan., 1841.

Rev. Thos. Worcester,

DEAR SIR—Yours of the 21st inst., with enclosure, came duly to hand, and most of the eighteen applicants have been made acquainted with its contents. If, by enclosing the report of the committee, you intended to make the inquiry of us whether we assent to the principle referred to by them, and understand it to have been involved in, and acknowledged by the application for organization, we say at once, that we so understand it, and only regret that such an inquiry should have been thought necessary by the committee, from any representation made to them. Please inform us of your decision on our application. Yours, very truly, for the eighteen applicants, J. A. HYDE.

To Mr. Joseph A. Hyde, for the eighteen applicants,

DEAR BRETHREN AND SISTERS—Your answer, through Mr. Hyde, to the inquiry of the committee of the association has been received.

The committee considered it necessary to make that inquiry, for the reason stated in their communication. And now the same reason makes it necessary for me to send a copy of their inquiry and of your answer to the pastor and society of the New Jerusalem in Bridgewater. And, upon receiving their answer, I shall probably have something further to communicate to you—but perhaps not till after another meeting of the committee.

At the close of your answer, you say, "Please inform us of your decision upon our application." Perhaps you are not sufficiently sensible, that in affairs which concern many persons, it is important to move slowly—so that, when a thing is done, it may be well done. I do not intend that there shall be, on my part, any unnecessary delay in coming to a decision, or in communicating it to you after I have come to it.

I am very truly yours,

Boston, Jan. 27th, 1841. THOMAS WORCESTER.

To Mr. J. A. Hyde, for the eighteen applicants,

DEAR BRETHREN AND SISTERS—We had a meeting on Wednesday forenoon and afternoon, and again on Thursday, in relation to your affairs, and then we adjourned to meet again on the 10th of March.

In our conversations I was frequently asked by members of the committee what accusations you bring against the pastor of the Bridgewater society. In reply, I stated some general things—such as a want of confidence in his veracity, &c. This was not satisfactory to them, and they asked for particulars. These, although I have heard an abundance of them, I did not feel willing to give on the strength of my memory.

Now I think that it may aid us in our deliberations when we come together again, if you will state your charges against him in writing. From what I have said, you will see that I want particular, not general, charges. I am very truly yours,

Boston, Feb. 26th, 1841. THOMAS WORCESTER.

Bridgewater, 9th March, 1841.

Rev. Thos. Worcester,

DEAR SIR—Yours of 26th ult. came duly to hand. The applicants have carefully considered your suggestion, "that it may aid the committee in their deliberations, if they state charges against the pastor of the Bridgewater society in writing." It does not seem to the applicants to be incumbent upon them, in their present position, to prefer charges against any one; and they hope the committee will appreciate their views in declining to do so at this time. Yours, &c., for the eighteen applicants, J. A. HYDE.

To Mr. Joseph A. Hyde, and seventeen other applicants,

DEAR BRETHREN AND SISTERS—I received yours of the 9th inst., declining to prefer any charges against the pastor of the Bridgewater society.

On the 10th and 11th we had a meeting of the committee of ministers and the committee of laymen. Without coming to any conclusion as to what course to pursue, they adjourned, with the understanding, that they would come together again whenever I should have any thing to lay before them. Now I want to have you understand distinctly the position in which I am placed ; and for this purpose I propose to make a brief statement of the case, leaving out every thing which I do not esteem absolutely necessary.

You apply to me as an officer of the General Convention to form you into a society. As an officer of convention, I am bound to consult the good of the whole-church. And, as there is already one society in Bridgewater, and as, at first view, it would seem better that you should join that society, than that you should be formed into a separate one, therefore, a regard to the general good requires me to take notice of this fact. It requires of me to ask for reasons and explanations ; and, if these are satisfactory, then the apparent objection is removed.

Now I have heard your reasons, and they consist merely of accusations against the pastor of the Bridgewater society. Your accusations are numerous and varied. The case is one of great magnitude, and the person accused is my natural brother. This circumstance might have, and, at any rate, it would be supposed to have, an influence upon my feelings and judgment. I have therefore called in the assistance of the committee of ministers and the committee of laymen of the Massachusetts Association.

But I cannot lay the case before them, so that they can advise and assist me in my duty, unless you will give them also your reasons for wishing to be formed into a society, in other words, your reasons for not joining the present society—or, in other words, your accusations against the pastor of that society. Without a knowledge of these things, their advice and assistance could be of no use to me, and if you cannot furnish them with it, I shall be obliged to decide the question alone, unless some other mode of proceeding is pointed out, with which I am not now acquainted.

I make this statement so that you may see my situation, and thus be led to make some suggestions or advances that will aid me in the performance of my duty.

I am very truly yours,

Boston, March 13th, 1841.   THOMAS WORCESTER.

Bridgewater, 16th March, 1841.

Rev. Thos. Worcester,

DEAR SIR—Yours of 13th inst. was handed us on the morning of the 14th. We have carefully considered, and have endeavored fairly to appreciate, your views in regard to the position in which you are placed, by our application to you to organize us into a society, and we regret that after repeated consultations with the committees of the association, you have been unable to come to a decision with regard to it. We are aware that your position is a very important and responsible one, and we think that ours also is deserving of some consideration.

It is now a long time since we made application to you to organize us into a society in accordance with the rules of convention—in accordance with those rules you visited us, and afterwards laid our application before the committee of laymen for consultation, and advice. Their report embracing what they considered to be essential for us to assent to was communicated to us, and we assented to it most fully. It seems to us that this fact has been overlooked by you, as no mention is made of it in your recent communications ; but you now call upon us for accusations against your brother. Are we to infer from this that a want of confidence in the pastor of the Bridgewater society and an unwillingness to approve of his conduct, is a sufficient ground for withholding from us the rights and privileges of a new-church organization ? You say that unless we make accusations against your brother, you shall be obliged to decide on our application alone. We wish you to understand that we have no further suggestions, or advances to make—and shall consider it a favor to receive your decision without further delay. Yours, &c.   [Signed by 16—two of the 18 being absent.]

To Joseph A. Hyde and Seventeen other Applicants,

DEAR BRETHREN AND SISTERS—Yours, with date of the 16th, and post mark of the 19th, came to hand this morning—the 20th. When you applied to me for institution, I regarded it as of Divine Providence, and I did not intend to fail or be discouraged, nor of my own accord, to give up the case, till something should be done for the peace of

Jerusalem. Therefore, although the burden has been heavy and the labor difficult, still it was not without some regret that I read the following passage in your letter : "We wish you to understand that we have no further 'suggestions' or advances to make, and we shall consider it a favor to receive your decision without further delay." As it seems necessary for me to come to a decision *now*, I must decide the case as it *now stands*, and I must say that *under present circumstances*, it does not seem to me to be my duty to form you into a society.

For the reasons of this decision I must refer to my former communications, in which I have pointed out things, which I thought you ought to do, and which I suppose you have not done. But still perhaps I ought to take some notice of the question contained in the following passage of your letter, lest my silence should be taken for assent.

"You now call upon us for accusations against your brother——are we to infer from this, that a want of confidence in the pastor of the Bridgewater society and an unwillingness to approve of his conduct, is a sufficient ground for withholding from us the rights and privileges of new-church organization?" In reply I say, that I do not insist, and that I never have insisted, that you should have confidence in him, or that you should approve his conduct, but merely that you should treat him according to the laws of true christian charity.

Please to accept my best wishes for your welfare, both spiritual and natural ; and believe me to be,   Very truly yours,

Boston, March 20th, 1841.   THOMAS WORCESTER.

                                Boston, 23d March, 1841.

Mr. Joseph A. Hyde, (to himself and others,)

DEAR SIR—You have already been informed by Mr. Worcester, that the meeting of the ministers and committee separated without coming to any agreement. The chief difficulty was in regard to the mode of proceeding. We have seen the correspondence which has since taken place between you and Mr. Worcester, and which appears to have terminated without effecting any thing. Under these circumstances we have conferred together, and consulted with one or two other friends ; and we take the liberty of suggesting the propriety of your making application for institution, to the next General Convention. We suppose that the natural course might be, for the convention to appoint some other Ordaining Minister, and perhaps a committee of assistance, to investigate and act in the case ; and we should entertain strong hopes that it might be brought to a satisfactory result. Should this be the case, we conceive that a most important end would be obtained. This course is not without precedent; as you will see by the Journal of Convention for 1838, published in the 11th volume N. J. Magazine, p. 384; and we regard it as not only proper in itself, but as perfectly safe and judicious, and as most likely to preserve you in connection with the receivers and societies for whom we suppose you feel most sympathy, and who. we are sure, reciprocate the feeling.

       Very truly and respectfully yours,

         CALEB REED, JNO. H. WILKINS, BENJ. HOBART.

                             Bridgewater, 1st April, 1841.

Caleb Reed, Esq.

DEAR SIR—Your very kind favor of 23d ult., signed also by Messrs. Wilkins and Hobart, was duly received. We feel greatly obliged to you for your suggestion in regard to our application, to the next Convention, for institution as a society, as well as for the very kind manner in which other suggestions are made.

We are as yet undetermined what course to pursue, there are a great number of receivers in this place and vicinity, who are waiting our movements, and who feel extremely desirous to connect themselves with us, whenever we are in a situation to receive them. The delay and discouragement which has thus far attended all our efforts for organization, makes us unwilling to place ourselves in a position where there is no surety of a different result. We shall at all times however be grateful for advice and assistance from our friends.

       We remain very truly yours,

         JOSEPH A. HYDE, and others.

Bridgewater, 2d May, 1841.

Rev. C J. Doughty,

You have probably been informed that the legal society of the new church in this place dissolved their connexion with the Rev. Samuel Worcester a long time since. Since that separation, eighteen of the society have made application to the presiding minister of the Massachusetts Association, for institution as a society, but their petition has been rejected. I have been requested by the applicants for organization, and others who meet with us, to write you to visit us, as soon as your own convenience will permit, that you may become acquainted with our condition, and thus be enabled to advise us as to the course most proper for us to pursue in regard to further efforts for institution as a society. We shall expect a sermon from you while with us—and are desirous that you should give us as long a visit as will consist with your other duties.

There are many particulars in regard to our present position, which we cannot well communicate by letter, and therefore prefer to reserve them until an opportunity presents of making you acquainted with them by a personal interview. HOLMES SPRAGUE.

To Mr. Caleb Reed—or either of the Delegates of the Boston Society of the New Jerusalem, to the Twenty-third General Convention of the New Jerusalem to be holden in the city of New York on the 3d of June next,

DEAR SIR—I have been requested to address to you the following communication in behalf of eighteen receivers of the New-Church Doctrines, residing in the town of Bridgewater, Mass. Sometime in the fall of 1839, the connexion existing between the legal society of the New Jerusalem in this town and the Rev. Samuel Worcester was dissolved by mutual consent. Since that time an application has been made by us to the Rev. Thomas Worcester, presiding minister of the Massachusetts Association, for institution as a society—this application having been laid before a committee of the association, was rejected. We now desire through you to present our situation to the consideration of the General Convention, that they may adopt such a course in regard to us, as our circumstances may seem to require.

Should the Convention take the subject into consideration it is our earnest desire that the action may be prompt, and whatever it may be, that it be communicated to us as soon as determined.   JOSEPH A. HYDE, for self and 17 others.

Bridgewater, May 31st, 1841.

June 6th, 1841.

Mr. J. A. Hyde,

DEAR SIR—, You may wish to know what was done in respect to your communication to the convention. A committee, consisting of Dr. Beers, Mr. Pettee, Mr. Sewall of Bath, Mr. Wilkins and Mr. Hunt of N. York, was appointed to investigate the matter, and do what they find to be proper. Dr. Beers is so feeble that I think he cannot attend. The committee will fill vacancies, and probably Mr. Roche will be the ordaining minister. Yours,   S. WORCESTER.

Mr. Joseph A. Hyde,

DEAR SIR—As secretary of the Twenty-third General Convention, it becomes my duty to communicate to you, and through you to the 18 receivers at Bridgewater, the following documents, and extracts from the journal of that body.

Respectfully and truly yours,   T. B. HAYWARD, Sec. Con.

(*Extract from Journal.*)

New York, Thursday, June 3d, 1841.

" A communication from 18 receivers in Bridgewater, Mass., was presented, read, and referred to a special committee to report to-morrow morning." (For this communication see just above.)

" New York, Friday, June 4th, 1841.

" The Committee to which was referred the communication from receivers in Bridgewater, presented a report, which was accepted, and approved; and the committee therein proposed, was raised." The following is a copy of this report.

"The Committee to whom was referred the communication from 18 receivers in Bridgewater, Mass., report, That from the correspondence of the presiding minister of the Massachusetts Association and the receivers at Bridgewater, which your committee have heard read, it appears that the application for institution, was not refused, but delayed because the presiding minister was not satisfied of the propriety of immediate institution. They therefore recommend the appointment by convention, of a committee, consisting of one ordaining minister, one pastor, and three laymen, with the full power to act in the case, according to the Rules of Order for the institution of societies; and that the Secretary of the Convention be requested to notify the receivers at Bridgewater of the appointment of this committee. (Signed) M. B. ROCHE, *Chairman.*"

A committee was appointed to nominate the committee proposed in this report; and the following is from the journal of the *afternoon session* of the same day.

The committee to nominate a committee to act in the Bridgewater case presented a report, nominating the following persons as said committee : viz., Rev. Lewis Beers, ordaining minister, Rev. Joseph Pettee, pastor, and Messrs. John H. Wilkins of Boston, Wm. D. Sewall of Bath, and Samuel Hunt, of N. York, laymen. Also, the following resolution, offered in said report, was adopted :

Resolved, That the ordaining minister of the above committee, be clothed with authority to appoint a substitute, if he be himself unable to attend to the duties of the committee, and that any other vacancy, which may occur in the committee from resignation or any other cause, be filled by the acting ordaining minister of the committee.

 A true copy,   Attest,   T. B. HAYWARD, *Sec. of Con.*
June 8th, 1841.

             Bridgewater, 5th Aug., 1841.

To the General Convention of Societies of the New Church in the United States,

We have learned from your secretary. under date 8th June last, that a committee of five were appointed to act on our application to the convention at their last session.

Our communication to the convention expressed our "*earnest desire*" that the action of the convention should be "*prompt.*"

Two months have elapsed since the appointment of this committee, and we have not learned from the chairman or either of the committee (a majority of whom some of us have seen personally) that any movement has been made, or any action had, or proposed, by them in regard to us. Under these circumstances, and in view of *all* the facts in the case, we wish to relieve the convention from any further duty or responsibility in the matter, and hereby withdraw our application.

  Very respectfully,   Jos. A. HYDE, for self and 17 others.

No. LXI.

ANSWER TO THE COMMUNICATION OF J. F. STREET, ESQ., TO THE SIXTH ANNUAL MEETING OF THE CENTRAL CONVENTION.

           Baltimore, August 10, 1846.

DEAR BRETHREN—Your communication to the Sixth Annual Meeting of the Central Convention, through our much esteemed brother Mr. J. F. Street, was received and laid before that meeting. It was made my duty to respond to it. I am directed to refer you, in answer to your inquiries, to the preamble and resolutions of our convention, which were adopted at its meeting of the 15th of June, 1844, and which you may find in Journal No. VI. p. 9, nn. 76 and 77.   You will read these numbers in connection with nn. 72 and 73 of the same journal.   From the principles laid down and established there, you will learn that, in the opinion of our body, you cannot remain members of the Central Convention, if you join a society for the purpose of becoming members of the Eastern Convention also.   But you may remain in external connection with such a society for the purpose of public worship, or other merely *local* uses, provided such external connection does not in any way make you members of that society so far as it is a part of the Eastern Convention.   This resolution was introduced in express reference to the case of Mr. Cushing Allen, of Bath, Maine, and it is founded on the custom in your part of the country, of making a distinction between *the church* and *the civil society*.   In some of the New England states the civil law requires every man to contribute for the support of public worship, but leaves every one free to choose the religious society to which he will pay his tax.   In consequence of this, there are some who contribute to the support of religion in certain religious societies, the faith of which they do not themselves receive.   This latter produces an external connection with a religious society for the purpose of public worship, but constitutes no union with the brethren of the peculiar faith as a church in a smaller form, and the particular component of some general church.   Such a connection you might form with the new-church society in Pawtucket, if the majority would admit you on that ground.   But if your joining that society makes you thereby in *any way* members and supporters of the Eastern Convention, you cannot, in strict propriety, join it without previously sending in your resignation of your membership of the Central Convention : for "this body is in all respects co-ordinate, and in no respects sub-ordinate to any general body of the New Jerusalem in the United States;" and "the *same persons*, in *any form of organization, cannot*, in just order, *be members*, or *help to constitute organs*, of *two co-ordinate bodies at the same time*."

This order is founded upon the heavenly law that angels are most distinctly arranged into societies according to the genera and species of good.   On this law the order of the human body is founded; because the human body is created and sustained by influx from the Lord through the heavens.   Hence the component parts of the human body are most distinctly arranged, so that on this distinct arrangement the preservation of the whole body depends, just as the preservation of the whole universe depends on the distinct arrangement of all in the spiritual world according to their religions.   (See T. C. R., 678.)   Thus in the body you find a fleshy membrane, which lines the cavities of the chest and the abdomen, and gives to each viscus a distinct covering of its own, by which it is most thoroughly distinguished from the rest, at the same time that it is connected with them by this as a common covering.   In this way the heart and the lungs, though lying and acting reciprocally in the same chamber, are kept most distinct, the one by its pericardium, and the other by its pleura, which are fleshy coverings from the same common membrane : and the death of the body would most inevitably occur, if these partition walls were broken through.   So if the diaphragm, which separates the abdomen from the thorax, were ruptured, the whole body would be inevitably destroyed.   And the same catastrophe would ensue upon the cutting of the peritoneal membrane in the distinctions which it makes between the parts of the abdomen.

On this same law are founded the distinctions which are observable in the animal kingdom ; for all animals are but the correspondents and types of human affections as they exist in the spiritual world.   Hence it is that animals of distinct kinds are segregated, and "birds of a feather flock together."   And to violate this distinction, would be to destroy the animal kingdom.   Hence human attempts to confound it are foreclosed by barrenness, as in the mule.

Now what is true of the spiritual world, and of the human body and the natural world by derivation thence, must be true of all the collective bodies of men.   Hence there may and must be distinct general bodies of the church.   And the whole church is not to be made one by confounding these distinctions, in a promiscuous mixture of their masses, but by harmonizing their distinct organizations in co-operations from the common ends of charity as the performance of uses.   Hence Swedenborg says "the church of the Lord in the earth cannot be otherwise than various and diverse" (A. C. 3451) ; but "there would be but one church, if all were regarded from charity, although they might differ as to opinions of faith and rituals of worship." (A. C. 1286.) And "the life of charity consists in the performing of uses" (A. C. 8253.) See also L. J. 73, where Swedenborg, speaking of the state of the church hereafter, says "it will be similar as to external appearance, but dissimilar as to internal; in regard to the external appearance, *there will be* DISTINCT CHURCHES *as before,*" &c. Compare with H. and H. 7, where are these words: "there are also several churches, and yet each is called a church, and likewise is a church, so far as the good of faith and of love rules in it: the Lord also, in such case, from variety makes unity—thus from several churches makes one church." "Supposing this to be the case, all would be governed as one man by the Lord, for all *would be as members and organs of one body,* which, *although they are not of similar forms* nor of *similar* functions, have nevertheless relation to one heart, on which they all depend, both in general and in particular, be their respective forms ever so various." (A. C. 2385.) In this last passage Swedenborg is speaking of the ancient church which extended itself over several kingdoms of Asia. And you here see that several general churches make one universal church as the members and organs make one body. So that there must be as much distinction between the general churches as there is between the members and organs of a body; and destruction will ensue from the confounding of this distinction as surely in the one case as in the other. Supposing then that the Central and Eastern Conventions are co-ordinate members and organs of the whole new church in this country, these two bodies must be, and be kept, as distinct as any two co-ordinate members and organs of the human body; and the individual members of the one can no more be members of the other, than the muscular fibres of a man's right arm can help to compose the muscles of his left. And, in our view, the only reason why an attempt has been made to induce those who are members of the Central Convention as individuals to become members of the Eastern Convention also as societies, is because thereby the one would be absorbed in the other as an inferior and subordinate in a superior and supreme body. Look, we pray you, at the example which is furnished here in Baltimore. A large majority of the members of the first or old society here are members of the Central Convention as individuals, while they claim to be members of the Eastern Convention as a society. And what is the consequence? *They as individuals do nothing towards aiding the Central Convention in performing its uses,* stand aloof from its organizations, do not report themselves to it, but on the contrary report themselves to the Eastern Convention, and contribute funds to that body to do the very same uses which they have morally bound themselves to do in the Central Convention by signing its constitution. They moreover enter into correspondence with what is misnamed the Pennsylvania Association, which was established most manifestly to root out the Central Convention from these middle states, and to give plausible coloring to the assertion that there is no need of the Central Convention even here in what is claimed to be its especial province. Look, too, in Bridgewater. Was not the freedom of the second society there vindicated and secured by the action of the Central Convention? But how are we repaid! Do the members of our body there sustain our distinctive organization, and conspire with us in the performance of our uses? Do they do the same for *our* freedom which we did for theirs? Will they do this by having joined with the society of the Eastern Convention in their vicinity and reporting themselves to that body, while they make no report of themselves to us, and *do not the least thing* in the way of co-operation in our uses? Do they not in fact act on the ground that "there is *no need* of the Central Convention"? And if you and all other members of our general body were to act on the same ground, would not our general body become defunct by the total loss of its *distinctive* form, through absorption into the Eastern Convention as the only true general body of our church in the United States?

Well, then, brethren, if these things are so, what *can* we, what *should* we, advise you to do in your case? Should we, in a mistaken notion of charity, advise you to take that course which will lead you from spiritual communion with us, and involve you in the sphere of another general body, which not only stands on the same plane with ours, but is secretly hostile to it? Let us suppose a case. Were you living in this country at the time when the colonies were declared rebels by the mother country, and you were *Whigs*, could you join with *Tories,*—however honest, and worthy, and conscientious they might be as men,—in forming a society for local purposes, when this connection would amount to your separation from the cause of the colonies in their struggle for independence, and throw the weight of your influence in the scale of the mother country, which was striving to retain her authority over them on the ground that there was no need of their existence as an independent nation? And do not imagine that there is no parallelism in the two cases; for by reference to p. 426, of the Journal of the Twenty-fourth Convention, [N. J. Mag. for July, 1842,] you will find it proclaimed, that we, " being led by spirits who delight in such things, have raised the standard of *revolt*"—which is the next thing to stigmatizing the leading and other members of the Central Convention with the brand of *rebellion!* Now, brethren, while you admit that there *is* need of the Central Convention, while you see and acknowledge the manifest good effects produced by it, since its commencement, on the so-called General Convention, and while you hail for it on the principle that there *should* be more than one convention of the new church in this vast country, shall we advise you to take a course which we believe will lead you out of our general body so as to help on its destruction. If there has been good produced by the existence of the Central Convention, should not that good continue to be produced by its continued existence? For will the effect continue when the cause ceases? If the so-called General Convention has needed a check, will it not continue to need checks? What security can there be that it will not manifest again the errors into which it once run, when all restraints upon the old spirit that is still latent in it have been removed. Be sure that the Central Convention has taken its rise in the good providence of the Lord for good in all coming time, and that you cannot abandon it now, without being recreant to the best interests of the New Jerusalem in this country. We cannot therefore advise you to join a society which will connect you with the Eastern Convention. We do not see why your " brothers *cannot* join the General Convention unless you all as a society join with them "—unless they have purposely designed, by this order of their constitution as a society, to draw you persuasively away from our body, on the ground " that there is no need of the Central Convention." We see the same spirit of persuasive influence operating in Bridgewater and Baltimore as well as in the Pennsylvania, Illinois and Indiana Associations; and to advise you to throw yourselves into the stream of that influence, would be to advise our own destruction; and thus to sanction, if not to commit, conventional suicide. This we cannot do. But, on the contrary, we do most warmly and strenuously advise you to join with the three in Bridgewater who have reported themselves to our Convention this year, and form a society *in the Central Convention, for effective co-operation in doing its uses.* This we believe to be the duty of every member of our body in New England, and all there, who conspire with us in affection and thought, will, we trust, emulate, in this respect, the example of the Washington Society this year, and of the Lancaster Society last. Indeed, there can be no question that all of the members of our body, wherever they may be located, who hold to the distinctive principles of our convention, are bound in solemn duty to associate with one another, in the nearest practicable proximity, for combined effort in carrying those principles out. And all who do not do this ought to be able to satisfy us, as well as themselves, that they are not thereby subjecting those principles to the danger of defeat by virtual abandonment.

In fine, brethren, if the Central Convention is indeed a distinct general body of our church in this country, and if there is any use in its continuing such, it ought, in every right and efficient way, to be sustained. If it is not, it ought to be abandoned. Choose ye between these two, and act accordingly in your present case. For our part, believing fully and firmly that our convention ought to be sustained, and by no means be given up, we strongly advise, and affectionately entreat, you, to unite with us in the way herein proposed, so that, to use a very expressive phrase of common society, we may advance the cause we have at heart, by " a long pull, a strong pull, and a *pull* ALL TOGETHER" !

In behalf of the Sixth Annual Meeting of the Central Convention, I am, brethren, very truly and affectionately your servant in the Lord,

R. DE CHARMS.

To Messrs. J. F. Street and others, members of the Central Convention, in and around Pawtucket, R. I.

No. LXII.

REPORT OF ENGLISH HYMN-BOOK COMMITTEE.

To the General Conference of the Ministers and other Members of the New Church signified by the New Jerusalem in the Revelation.

The Committee appointed by the Fifteenth General Conference, to prepare a Hymn-Book for the use of the New Church, feel great satisfaction in reporting, that they have closed their labors; and they humbly trust, that their best endeavors to accomplish the important object confided to them, will meet, in some degree, with the approbation of the Church.

As the preface to the Hymn-Book briefly explains the Plan adopted by the Committee, they will beg permission to quote it in their Report.

"PREFACE.

" The Collection of Hymns here presented to the public, has been framed in pursuance of Resolutions of the General Conference of the Ministers and other Members of the New Church signified by the New Jerusalem in the Revelation, held at Manchester in 1822—66, and of the General Conference held at London in 1823—67. The preparation of the work, which is intended for general use in that Church, was confided to a Committee; who, in laying the result of their labors before the Public, deem it necessary, in a few words, to put the reader in possession of a view of the plan which they have adopted.

" It appeared to them, in agreement with the sentiments expressed at the Conference, that a General Hymn-Book ought to be adapted, not only for public devotion, but also for private meditation and instruction; that it should form a useful and agreeable companion on every day of the week as well as on the sabbath, and at home as well as in the public assemblies of the Church. With this intention, a *small* number of Hymns have been admitted, which, perhaps, will seldom or never be used in public, but which, it is hoped, will frequently cheer and delight the serious hour of retirement.

" It has also been endeavored to introduce Hymns on all the principal subjects of doctrine and practice; so that the book might form not only a complete Manual of Devotion, but also, in a small compass, a Body of Divinity. The great utility of this to that numerous class of sincere worshippers of the Lord, whose means do not admit of their purchasing many books, must readily be seen: and at the same time that the Work is thus adapted to improve those who have already joined themselves to the New Church in the knowledge of her doctrines, as well as in affection for them, and for the life to which they lead, it may also form a pleasing medium of introducing her pure truths to others.

" In the selection of the Hymns, the sole principle regarded by the Committee has been USEFULNESS. It will be seen, that great assistance has been derived from the valuable works of the two most extensive authors of Hymns on the subjects of the New Dispensation—the Rev. J. Proud, and the Rev. M. Sibly. A very considerable number of the Hymns in this collection, many of them quite new, are also the composition of other Members of the New Church in this country and in America. Those which have been introduced from other sources, will all be found to breathe, in beautiful and energetic language, the spirit of the ' New Jerusalem.' Such of them as did not, originally, fully express her doctrinal sentiments, have been carefully corrected, and, where necessary, in great part re-written: and it is hoped, now that they have been studded with the gems of heavenly truth, and freed from all tarnish of error, that they will be found greatly to adorn the Collection, and give reason to rejoice, that ' things new and old ' have thus been dedicated to the service of the Lord. The doctrines of the New Church afford us the pleasing assurance, that many excellent persons now adore and serve the Lord Jesus Christ in the ' new heaven,' in the language of genuine truth, who had not the opportunity of perfectly learning that language while on earth: of this happy number, doubtless, are the authors of many of the Hymns in the Collections of various denominations of Christians; whose compositions often exhibit light drawn from the Word itself, and far superior to any which they could have derived from the doctrines of their respective churches: it is quite agreeable then, to right order, that the productions of such persons should, like themselves, be purified, and consecrated to the worship of the one true God of heaven and earth.

"The *arrangement* of the Hymns, it will be perceived, has been carefully made, to afford facility for reference. In the large section under the title of REGENERATE LIFE, the reader will observe, that the Hymns are disposed in a progressive order, commencing with the earliest state of the heavenly life, and rising to the highest; so that a little acquaintance with that Section will render reference as easy, as if the *specific* heads had been collected in the table of contents.

"The Committee, and all who have been engaged in preparing this Hymn-Book, trusting that their endeavors have been actuated by a 'single eye' to the benefit of the Lord's true church, humbly hope that a divine blessing has accompanied the progress, and will crown the conclusion, of their labors; by causing the Work to be affectionately received by their brethren, and rendering it both acceptable and edifying to all tastes and classes,—to the simple and the well-educated, to the devotional and the intellectual."

Considering the great convenience in finding a Hymn suitable to any subject, which is afforded by the insertion of a short title at top; and also, how much the effect of a Hymn containing a paraphrase of, or allusions to, any portion or portions of Scripture, is assisted, when the reader is aware of this while reading it; the Committee have herein deviated from the recommendation of Mr. Hindmarsh (as expressed in a letter to them*) but have taken care to compress these notices into so small a compass as to make very little difference in the size of the book. It is proper here to observe, that the Committee received from Mr. Hindmarsh very extensive and efficient assistance, both with respect to the selection, from the mass of materials, of the Hymns to be finally adopted, and to their general revision and preparation for the press.

It may appear to some members of Conference as requiring explanation, that the Committee should have made up the number of Hymns to the full extent allowed by the Conference, namely 600: On this point they have therefore to observe, that they were not desirous of having any particular number, but desired to regulate the number by the advantage or necessity of inserting any particular composition or subject. After the subjects had been completed, as far as the Committee could discern the want of any particular Hymns, and after a large number of the least eligible of the materials had been withdrawn, there remained above 1000 to select from, and from these the final selection was carefully and scrupulously made. On counting these over, it was found that they exceeded 600 by a very small number, and it therefore only remained for the Committee to reduce the number to the assigned limit by withdrawing such as could best be spared. The number printed is therefore very near to that which the Work would have consisted of, had the Conference fixed no *limit* to the number. The Committee are aware that some individuals will necessarily find compositions inserted which they will think might as well have been omitted, while the same compositions will, to persons of a different taste, appear quite indispensable. This variety of taste and judgment the Committee have, as far as their abilities go, endeavored to suit; but so far are they from conceiving that their best endeavors have been completely successful, that they would rejoice to see the church grow in interior qualities and literary acquirements, so as to render a new and improved Hymn-Book necessary to the improved condition of the church. An event so desirable cannot happen too soon, for any well-wisher to the "New Jerusalem."

*   *   *   *   *   *   *   *   *   *

Signed on behalf of the Committee,

WILLIAM MASON, *Secretary.*

London, 5th of August, 1824.

\# The recommendation here alluded to was, "that *one general head*, be given, for a certain series of Hymns, and another *general head* for another series, without a second explanatory head, or any reference to chapters and verses in the Word, in a separate line or lines."

Lightning Source UK Ltd.
Milton Keynes UK
UKHW022217191118
332602UK00012B/1119/P